DATE DUE

PUBLIC PAPERS OF THE PRESIDENTS
OF THE
UNITED STATES

Published by the
Office of the Federal Register
National Archives and Records Administration

For sale by the
Superintendent of Documents
U.S. Government Printing Office
Washington, DC 20402

Foreword

In my Inaugural Address, I stated that America stood at a moment rich with promise, with new ground to be broken and new action to be taken. And we have succeeded. The first six months of this Administration was a time of growth and stability. Our economy remained strong; in June 1989 we concluded 78 consecutive months of economic expansion. Real per capita income, output, and business fixed investment were at record levels, and unemployment fell to levels not seen in sixteen years.

We moved to build a better America by emphasizing fundamental values. We worked to reinvigorate our competitiveness, conserve and protect our environment, promote educational excellence, increase ethical standards in government, strengthen law enforcement to fight the scourge of drugs and crime, and restore confidence in our savings and loan industry.

Abroad, we began to witness developments in Eastern Europe and other parts of the world that indicated change in the East-West relationship that has predominated since the end of World War II. In the face of these developments, the United States reaffirmed its leadership role in the pursuit of democratic values, arms control, and a strong Western alliance. We dealt with these challenges in a positive and constructive manner. During this period, I traveled to Canada; to Japan, the People's Republic of China, and the Republic of Korea; and to Western Europe for a highly successful NATO Summit.

As we look back on the first six months of this Administration, we see a new breeze blowing. We move forward on this breeze, showing the world that the United States will continue to build a better nation at home and to lead in the articulation and demonstration of democratic principles.

George Bush

Preface

This book contains the papers and speeches of the 41st President of the United States that were issued by the Office of the Press Secretary during the period January 20–June 30, 1989. The material has been compiled and published by the Office of the Federal Register, National Archives and Records Administration.

The material is presented in chronological order, and the dates shown in the headings are the dates of the documents or events. In instances when the release date differs from the date of the document itself, that fact is shown in the textnote. Every effort has been made to ensure accuracy: Remarks are checked against a tape recording, and signed documents are checked against the original. Textnotes, footnotes, and cross references have been provided by the editors for purposes of identification or clarity. Speeches were delivered in Washington, DC, unless indicated. The times noted are local times. All materials that are printed full-text in the book have been indexed in the subject and name indexes, and listed in the document categories list.

The Public Papers series was begun in 1957 in response to a recommendation of the National Historical Publications Commission. An extensive compilation of messages and papers of the Presidents covering the period 1789 to 1897 was assembled by James D. Richardson and published under congressional authority between 1896 and 1899. Since then, various private compilations have been issued, but there was no uniform publication comparable to the Congressional Record or the United States Supreme Court Reports. Many Presidential papers could be found only in the form of mimeographed White House releases or as reported in the press. The Commission therefore recommended the establishment of an official series in which Presidential writings, addresses, and remarks of a public nature could be made available.

The Commission's recommendation was incorporated in regulations of the Administrative Committee of the Federal Register, issued under section 6 of the Federal Register Act (44 U.S.C. 1506), which may be found in title 1, part 10, of the Code of Federal Regulations.

A companion publication to the Public Papers series, the Weekly Compilation of Presidential Documents, was begun in 1965 to provide a broader range of Presidential materials on a more timely basis to meet the needs of the contemporary reader. Beginning with the administration of Jimmy Carter, the Public Papers series expanded its coverage to include all material as printed in the Weekly Compilation. That coverage provides a listing of the President's daily schedule and meetings, when announced, and other items of general interest issued by the Office of the Press Secretary. Also included are lists of the President's nominations submitted to the Senate, materials released by the Office of the Press Secretary that are not printed full-text in the book, acts approved by the President, and proclamations and Executive orders. This information appears in the appendixes at the end of the book.

Volumes covering the administrations of Presidents Hoover, Truman, Eisenhower, Kennedy, Johnson, Nixon, Ford, Carter, and Reagan are also available.

The Chief Editor of this book was William King Banks, assisted by E.B. Swidal, Karen Howard Ashlin, and Bill Rozday.

White House liaison was provided by Marlin Fitzwater, Assistant to the President and Press Secretary. The frontispiece and photographs used in the portfolio were supplied by the White House Photo Office.

Martha L. Girard
Director of the Federal Register

Don W. Wilson
Archivist of the United States

Contents

Cabinet

Secretary of State	James Addison Baker III
Secretary of the Treasury	Nicholas F. Brady
Secretary of Defense	Richard B. Cheney
Attorney General	Richard L. Thornburgh
Secretary of the Interior	Manuel Lujan, Jr.
Secretary of Agriculture	Clayton Yeutter
Secretary of Commerce	Robert Adam Mosbacher
Secretary of Labor	Elizabeth Hanford Dole
Secretary of Health and Human Services	Louis W. Sullivan
Secretary of Housing and Urban Development	Jack Kemp
Secretary of Transportation	Samuel Knox Skinner
Secretary of Energy	James D. Watkins
Secretary of Education	Lauro F. Cavazos
Secretary of Veterans Affairs	Edward J. Derwinski
Director of the Office of Management and Budget	Richard G. Darman
United States Trade Representative	Carla Anderson Hills

Administration of George Bush

1989

Inaugural Address
January 20, 1989

Mr. Chief Justice, Mr. President, Vice President Quayle, Senator Mitchell, Speaker Wright, Senator Dole, Congressman Michel, and fellow citizens, neighbors, and friends:

There is a man here who has earned a lasting place in our hearts and in our history. President Reagan, on behalf of our nation, I thank you for the wonderful things that you have done for America.

I've just repeated word for word the oath taken by George Washington 200 years ago, and the Bible on which I placed my hand is the Bible on which he placed his. It is right that the memory of Washington be with us today not only because this is our bicentennial inauguration but because Washington remains the Father of our Country. And he would, I think, be gladdened by this day; for today is the concrete expression of a stunning fact: our continuity, these 200 years, since our government began.

We meet on democracy's front porch. A good place to talk as neighbors and as friends. For this is a day when our nation is made whole, when our differences, for a moment, are suspended. And my first act as President is a prayer. I ask you to bow your heads.

Heavenly Father, we bow our heads and thank You for Your love. Accept our thanks for the peace that yields this day and the shared faith that makes its continuance likely. Make us strong to do Your work, willing to heed and hear Your will, and write on our hearts these words: "Use power to help people." For we are given power not to advance our own purposes, nor to make a great show in the world, nor a name. There is but one just use of power, and it is to serve people. Help us remember, Lord. Amen.

I come before you and assume the Presidency at a moment rich with promise. We live in a peaceful, prosperous time, but we can make it better. For a new breeze is blowing, and a world refreshed by freedom seems reborn. For in man's heart, if not in fact, the day of the dictator is over. The totalitarian era is passing, its old ideas blown away like leaves from an ancient, lifeless tree. A new breeze is blowing, and a nation refreshed by freedom stands ready to push on. There is new ground to be broken and new action to be taken. There are times when the future seems thick as a fog; you sit and wait, hoping the mists will lift and reveal the right path. But this is a time when the future seems a door you can walk right through into a room called tomorrow.

Great nations of the world are moving toward democracy through the door to freedom. Men and women of the world move toward free markets through the door to prosperity. The people of the world agitate for free expression and free thought through the door to the moral and intellectual satisfactions that only liberty allows.

We know what works: Freedom works. We know what's right: Freedom is right. We know how to secure a more just and prosperous life for man on Earth: through free markets, free speech, free elections, and the exercise of free will unhampered by the state.

For the first time in this century, for the first time in perhaps all history, man does not have to invent a system by which to live. We don't have to talk late into the night about which form of government is better. We don't have to wrest justice from the kings. We only have to summon it from within ourselves. We must act on what we know. I take as my guide the hope of a saint: In crucial things, unity; in important things, diversity; in all things, generosity.

America today is a proud, free nation, decent and civil, a place we cannot help but love. We know in our hearts, not loudly and proudly but as a simple fact, that this country has meaning beyond what we see, and that our strength is a force for good. But have we changed as a nation even in our time? Are we enthralled with material things, less appreciative of the nobility of work and sacrifice?

My friends, we are not the sum of our possessions. They are not the measure of our lives. In our hearts we know what matters. We cannot hope only to leave our children a bigger car, a bigger bank account. We must hope to give them a sense of what it means to be a loyal friend; a loving parent; a citizen who leaves his home, his neighborhood, and town better than he found it. And what do we want the men and women who work with us to say when we're no longer there? That we were more driven to succeed than anyone around us? Or that we stopped to ask if a sick child had gotten better and stayed a moment there to trade a word of friendship?

No President, no government can teach us to remember what is best in what we are. But if the man you have chosen to lead this government can help make a difference; if he can celebrate the quieter, deeper successes that are made not of gold and silk but of better hearts and finer souls; if he can do these things, then he must.

America is never wholly herself unless she is engaged in high moral principle. We as a people have such a purpose today. It is to make kinder the face of the Nation and gentler the face of the world. My friends, we have work to do. There are the homeless, lost and roaming. There are the children who have nothing, no love and no normalcy. There are those who cannot free themselves of enslavement to whatever addiction—drugs, welfare, the demoralization that rules the slums. There is crime to be conquered, the rough crime of the streets. There are young women to be helped who are about to become mothers of children they can't care for and might not love. They need our care, our guidance, and our education, though we bless them for choosing life.

The old solution, the old way, was to think that public money alone could end these problems. But we have learned that that is not so. And in any case, our funds are low. We have a deficit to bring down. We have more will than wallet, but will is what we need. We will make the hard choices, looking at what we have and perhaps allocating it differently, making our decisions based on honest need and prudent safety. And then we will do the wisest thing of all. We will turn to the only resource we have that in times of need always grows: the goodness and the courage of the American people.

And I am speaking of a new engagement in the lives of others, a new activism, hands-on and involved, that gets the job done. We must bring in the generations, harnessing the unused talent of the elderly and the unfocused energy of the young. For not only leadership is passed from generation to generation but so is stewardship. And the generation born after the Second World War has come of age.

I have spoken of a Thousand Points of Light, of all the community organizations that are spread like stars throughout the Nation, doing good. We will work hand in hand, encouraging, sometimes leading, sometimes being led, rewarding. We will work on this in the White House, in the Cabinet agencies. I will go to the people and the programs that are the brighter points of light, and I'll ask every member of my government to become involved. The old ideas are new again because they're not old, they are timeless: duty, sacrifice, commitment, and a patriotism that finds its expression in taking part and pitching in.

We need a new engagement, too, between the Executive and the Congress. The challenges before us will be thrashed out with the House and the Senate. And we must bring the Federal budget into balance. And we must ensure that America stands before the world united, strong, at peace, and fiscally sound. But of course things may be difficult. We need to compromise; we've had dissension. We need harmony; we've had a chorus of discordant voices.

For Congress, too, has changed in our time. There has grown a certain divisiveness. We have seen the hard looks and heard the statements in which not each other's ideas are challenged but each other's motives. And our great parties have too often been far apart and untrusting of each other. It's been this way since Vietnam. That war cleaves us still. But, friends, that war began in earnest a quarter of a century ago, and surely the statute of limitation has been reached. This is a fact: The final lesson of Vietnam is that no great nation can long afford to be sundered by a memory. A new breeze is blowing, and the old bipartisanship must be made new again.

To my friends, and, yes, I do mean friends—in the loyal opposition and, yes, I mean loyal—I put out my hand. I am putting out my hand to you, Mr. Speaker. I am putting out my hand to you, Mr. Majority Leader. For this is the thing: This is the age of the offered hand. And we can't turn back clocks, and I don't want to. But when our fathers were young, Mr. Speaker, our differences ended at the water's edge. And we don't wish to turn back time, but when our mothers were young, Mr. Majority Leader, the Congress and the Executive were capable of working together to produce a budget on which this nation could live. Let us negotiate soon and hard. But in the end, let us produce. The American people await action. They didn't send us here to bicker. They ask us to rise above the merely partisan. "In crucial things, unity"—and this, my friends, is crucial.

To the world, too, we offer new engagement and a renewed vow: We will stay strong to protect the peace. The offered hand is a reluctant fist; once made—strong, and can be used with great effect. There are today Americans who are held against their will in foreign lands and Americans who are unaccounted for. Assistance can be shown here and will be long remembered. Good will begets good will. Good faith can be a spiral that endlessly moves on.

Great nations like great men must keep their word. When America says something, America means it, whether a treaty or an agreement or a vow made on marble steps. We will always try to speak clearly, for candor is a compliment; but subtlety, too, is good and has its place. While keeping our alliances and friendships around the world strong, ever strong, we will continue the new closeness with the Soviet Union, consistent both with our security and with progress. One might say that our new relationship in part reflects the triumph of hope and strength over experience. But hope is good, and so is strength and vigilance.

Here today are tens of thousands of our citizens who feel the understandable satisfaction of those who have taken part in democracy and seen their hopes fulfilled. But my thoughts have been turning the past few days to those who would be watching at home, to an older fellow who will throw a salute by himself when the flag goes by and the woman who will tell her sons the words of the battle hymns. I don't mean this to be sentimental. I mean that on days like this we remember that we are all part of a continuum, inescapably connected by the ties that bind.

Our children are watching in schools throughout our great land. And to them I say, Thank you for watching democracy's big day. For democracy belongs to us all, and freedom is like a beautiful kite that can go higher and higher with the breeze. And to all I say, No matter what your circumstances or where you are, you are part of this day, you are part of the life of our great nation.

A President is neither prince nor pope, and I don't seek a window on men's souls. In fact, I yearn for a greater tolerance, and easygoingness about each other's attitudes and way of life.

There are few clear areas in which we as a society must rise up united and express our intolerance. The most obvious now is drugs. And when that first cocaine was smuggled in on a ship, it may as well have been a deadly bacteria, so much has it hurt the body, the soul of our country. And there is much to be done and to be said, but take my word for it: This scourge will stop!

And so, there is much to do. And tomorrow the work begins. And I do not mistrust the future. I do not fear what is ahead. For our problems are large, but our heart is larger. Our challenges are great, but our will is greater. And if our flaws are endless, God's love is truly boundless.

Some see leadership as high drama and the sound of trumpets calling, and sometimes it is that. But I see history as a book with many pages, and each day we fill a page with acts of hopefulness and meaning. The new breeze blows, a page turns, the story unfolds. And so, today a chapter begins, a small and stately story of unity, diversity, and generosity—shared, and written, together.

Thank you. God bless you. And God bless the United States of America.

Note: The President spoke at 12:05 p.m. at the West Front of the Capitol. Prior to his address, the oath of office was administered by Chief Justice William H. Rehnquist. The address was broadcast live on radio and television.

Remarks to White House Visitors
January 21, 1989

The President. Good morning, everybody. [*Applause*] Thank you. Thank you all very much. Let me just say that I know some of you have been up all night long. And so, what we want to do is not delay this but take whoever is first. And I gather that's been sorted out by whoever got first in line into the——

Visitors. No!

The President. Not quite?

Visitors. No!

The President. Okay, so there's some injustice out there. [*Laughter*]

Visitor. We love you, George! I love you!

The President. No, but this is the people's house, and it just seemed appropriate on this first day that we welcome as many as we can. I have a little hiatus in the middle because I do have to go over to this building. I'm sure most of you recognize that as the West Wing, and then the office you see in the corner is the President's Oval Office. And I have to go sign one or two things and at least start to work over there, and then I will come back. Barbara will be here—some of our kids inside. But we just wanted to wish you well and welcome you to the people's house.

Thank you all very, very much. Thank you. We'll scoot on in.

Note: The President spoke at 8:05 a.m. at the Executive Entrance of the White House.

Question-and-Answer Session With Reporters
January 21, 1989

The President. Good morning, Helen [Helen Thomas, United Press International].

First Day as President

Q. How are you? How does it feel to be President?

The President. It feels just fine—setting in now, after the glamour and excitement of the inauguration. It's a great joy to have my mother here, the leader of our family, a great joy to have our ten kids over there last night. One got sick, so I had the duty at about 6 a.m. this morning. Ellie LeBlond—pumped a half a Tylenol into her, and she's looking good. Ate two pancakes—what you'd call a rapid recovery.

Q. Which one was ill, sir?

The President. Ellie, Doro's daughter, the Thousand Points of Light kid that ran across in the commercial. No, but it's so exciting over there and just a joy to have the family all there. They'll start leaving. We have a luncheon today with 240.

Mrs. Bush. Oh, really?

The President. Yes, 240—family.

Mrs. Bush. Oh, my Lord!

Q. Are you responsible for all that? Are you responsible for 240?

Mrs. Bush. No. [*Laughter*]

Q. What are your thoughts, Mrs. Bush?

Mrs. Bush. What did you say?

Q. What are your thoughts about today?

Mrs. Bush. Oh, I think it's the most exciting day of my life so far. It's just been wonderful. Everything has been perfect. Everything is so beautifully arranged.

The President. This is the one that told me not to brag about myself and to bend my knees when I volleyed. Right here, you're looking at her. [*Laughter*]

American Hostages

Q. Mr. President, you seem to be holding out an olive branch to Iran or the Shi'ites in terms of Terry Anderson and the hostages. Were you hinting a movement there, or a change of policy, or——

The President. No, Helen, I don't think it's a change of policy, but I wanted to be sure I mentioned in that speech my absolute determination not to forget either category: POW–MIA or these hostages. And I wanted that right in there. It was one of the few specific points in an otherwise thematic speech. And in terms of your question, I hope it was heard around the world. You know, we keep hearing rumors that countries want to have improved relations with the United States. I wanted to make clear to them that good will begets good will. I also know enough about the situation to think, in fairness, that because of the nature of the hostage-holding you can't finger any one country for holding Americans hostage against their will. But people have, in the past, facilitated the release of our citizens, and I'd love to see that happen again. And I won't forget it. Having said that, we're not going to escalate the currency of holding Americans hostage. We're not going to have people feel that we are going to make concessions in order to free those precious lives. We simply can't.

Q. You talk about a fist, sir.

The President. Yes. That is a broad term to indicate that the United States will stay strong, and occasionally Presidents are called upon to use force in one situation or another around the world. And this President will be no different. It wasn't in the context of the people held against their will necessarily.

Relations With Congress

Q. Do you plan any official business today, Mr. President?

The President. There just is—no, today——

Q. Like the ethics order, for instance.

The President. ——I haven't talked to John Sununu. We had one or two formal things we were going to do, I think.

Mr. Sununu. Yes, but ethics is not today.

The President. Ethics won't be today. We're going to talk to the leadership early next week—the bipartisan leadership of the Congress—on how we proceed on the budget. We're contemplating how we best make clear to the Hill my determination to do one of the things I talked about yesterday and try to reach for bipartisanship in foreign affairs. And so, we're thinking of a meeting that will say to those who have shown the most interest in that in Congress, Look, we're ready. The President has unique responsibilities under the Constitution for foreign policy and for the national security. But we want, through consultation, to have the Congress in as much as possible on the takeoff. We've got to figure out how we do that.

There was a very good letter sent to me before I was elected President by David Boren and Senator Danforth—Senator Boren and Senator Danforth. I'm sure that has been released. There's been some editorial comment on it, and that caught my imagination. And I wrote him back and said, "Okay, let's talk about it." We can't do it one way. The President has certain unique responsibilities, and I intend to carry those out. But we can, I think, do a better job of having the Congress understand initiatives that we might take. Certainly, in some difficult areas I need their advice. I welcome it, but I'd love to think we could go back to the Vandenberg days, partisanship stopping at the water's edge. But I'm not naive. I know they're very difficult.

One thing, however, having said all those sweet and nice things, I am concerned, as a lot of Congressmen are, as a lot of Senators are, about the erosion of Presidential power, and I have been. And so, I want to talk with reasonable Members in the Senate and the House, Democrat and Republican. Some have told me they share that concern. And I say, what do we do about it? How do we work with you people in consultation not only to avoid the erosion of power but to reestablish in the Presidency the firm hand that I think the Constitution gave the President?

Q. Well, the Constitution also lets Congress declare war.

The President. Well, that's right.

Q. And Vietnam was the part of the not keeping Congress really informed as they made these moves. So, don't you think that what you're really saying is, you want something different from the Reagan administration.

The President. I'm saying I've just spelled out what I want for the Bush administration.

Inaugural Address

Q. Sir, there was criticism of your speech that there wasn't any meat in it, that it set a tone, but that you didn't have any specific initiatives. What do you say to that?

The President. I haven't heard too much criticism about that. I've been very pleased with the wonderful—well, put it this way—very overly, perhaps, generous response, at least from the Members of the Hill. But I say, stay tuned. February 9th we'll have something a little different, if that's the date that's settled on.

Q. Is that the State of the Union?

The President. Yes. That'll be up there with the Congress.

Communications With Foreign Leaders

Q. Mr. President, often, a President on his first day makes some kind of communications with foreign leaders. Have you spoken or sent notes to any of the allies or to Mr. Gorbachev, or has he tried to contact you?

The President. Well, he has contacted me through a nice, very generous letter, pledging to work for world peace, something of that nature. And clearly I will respond not only to that communication from Mr. Gorbachev but to expressions of good will from all around the world. It's been very heartwarming, and I want to be sure we do get these responses out.

President Reagan's Farewell Note

Q. What did the President's note say?

The President. Grab it out of the drawer there, Tim. Tim, could you get the note from the President there?

Mr. Fitzwater. Wait. Wait. Let's restore the lights here. The stills are okay.

The President. Am I violating any rules here, Marlin?

Q. They're your rules, sir. They're your rules.

The President. Oh, I set the rules. Okay, but we've established one thing, haven't we: that this is not a "photo op."

Q. That's right.

Q. Whatever you say, sir.

The President. No, that was—Marlin, help me.

Mr. Fitzwater. That's right. We've talked earlier and said you'd have a chance for a discussion here and questions and——

Q. We don't care what you call it, just so you answer the questions.

The President. No, no. I care what I call it because I don't want to demean your profession further by making you raise your voice, Helen. I love it when it's tranquil and peaceful like this.

Q. We do, too.

The President. I know you do.

Q. I know about Presidential power.

The President. Let me see if I can—[*laughter*]. And I know about UPI [United Press International]—[*laughter*]—let's see whether I dare read you this:

"Dear George"—this is from President Reagan—"You'll have moments when you want to use this particular stationery. Well, go to it. George, I treasure the memories we share and wish you all the very best. You'll be in my prayers. God bless you and Barbara. I'll miss our Thursday lunches. Ron"

The heading on the paper is "Don't let the turkeys get you down." So, nobody here should take personal to this at all. I mean, this is a broad, ecumenical statement: "Do not let the turkeys get you down."

Q. That's not written.

The President. Don't know who he's speaking about there. And it shows a bunch of turkeys trying to get an elephant down.

And it says "Boynton" on the bottom.

First Day as President

Q. How does it feel, sir, to be in the Oval Office the first day?

The President. It's wonderful. I can't wait to get to work—I mean, serious work. And we're going to do some here today with the Chief of Staff—go over some. But it really feels wonderful, and I know how to begin. And we're going to start right in Monday, and then we'll have a good, full schedule on Tuesday. And I couldn't wait to come over here this morning. I did because we had some people, you know, come through the White House just to symbolically open the door of the people's house. I must say that was kind of interesting, the expressions. I was saying to myself, Now, what does it take for somebody to stay awake all night to come into the White House? What kind of people are they? Well, they were all different kinds of people: a lot of kids, a lot of young people, some older, some with their children, a couple of families. Three had been to one of these balls—black ties—and just pitched—you know, like we used to do when we were little, maybe—slept out there. But the common thread was that they felt they were lucky to be there, which amazed me, in a sense, because I thought we were so lucky to have people that would care that much.

Q. Do you feel the same way, sir?

The President. A lot of people—I do. I do. All right.

Q. Have you gotten lost?

The President. What?

Q. Have you gotten lost?

The President. I got lost in the White House yesterday evening when we came in, trying to find a couple of kids' rooms, yes.

Q. Thank you.

The President. Thank you all.

Q. And there was one for every room?

The President. Ten children. I mean—five kids and ten spouses and ten grandchildren, and then Paula, who has lived with us for 29 years.

Q. It's a nice hotel, isn't it?

The President. It's unbelievable, Helen. It's unbelievable.

Note: The exchange began at 9:09 a.m. in the Oval Office at the White House. John H. Sununu was Chief of Staff to the President. In his remarks, the President referred to Timothy McBride, Assistant to the President, and Marlin Fitzwater, Assistant to the President and Press Secretary.

Remarks to Campaign Staff Members and Political Supporters
January 21, 1989

Thank you, Governor Sununu. And let me say at the outset—I'm sure you all know John Sununu, but I am very grateful that he has agreed to—having just left the Governorship of his State—to be our Chief of Staff. And I know he'll do a superb job over there. In fact, he already put me to work this morning signing things. The Republic is still in reasonably good shape, I think, but I signed a bunch of stuff and—[*laughter*]—looked official in there.

And it is a wonderful feeling. We have a tremendous—Barbara's not here. And I called her on the phone a minute ago, and I said, "Bar, are you coming over to the State Department—going to the State Department?" She said, "We have 240 family members coming here at 12 o'clock, and you'd better be back." [*Laughter*] So, she's not here, but we have one representative: the singing and dancing star the other day at Bar's, Noelle Bush from Miami. You get over there. I don't want to be upstaged. [*Laughter*]

But look, I will be very informal because I look around the room and see just so many people from here, from Puerto Rico, from out in the Pacific and all 50 States; people that have made it possible for me to take on this new responsibility. And people say to you—we had a press group over at the White House. I took my mother over there to the Oval Office, and then we took some questions from the press. And they asked a very appropriate question that seems very obvious: But has it all sunk in yet? And I guess the answer is: When you spend the first night in the White House and then when you go to work in that Oval Office, it does sink in, but it sinks in in a wonderful way.

I opened the top drawer of my desk now—a beautiful, historical Presidential desk—and here was a really lovely, warm note from my predecessor, which I think demonstrates more than the continuity. It says a lot because it said a lot about our own personal friendship, and it said a lot to me—though he, the modest, now former President, would never say it—but a lot of how I got the chance to be in this job. And so, it was emotional, and yet it had a very nice steady feeling to it: that the Presidency goes on. I heard, when he got to California, that President Reagan said he left me a note over where the underwear goes—[*laughter*]—or wherever that top right hand drawer, but I haven't found it yet. I'll have to keep looking. [*Laughter*]

But I wanted to come over and thank the movers and shakers of the Team 100—Larry Bathgate of the National Committee, and Mel and Joe and Wally Ganzie—Mel Sembler and Joe Zappala, Wally Ganzie—who these three I single out with some trepidation in this room because there are various other stages along the way to the White House. Each and every one of you came out and did disproportionately more than his or her share. Bobby Holt is here, who has blossomed forth from being not only one of the classic arm-twisters and—[*laughter*]—persistent fundraisers, but now his new horizons are frightening in that he was kind of running parades and running all kinds of marvelous events—[*laughter*]—to save the Republic. And I'm very grateful to him. I don't know that Penne Korth is here, but she was our peripatetic—I've just learned what that means—[*laughter*]—everywhere, never lets up, always around co-chairman. And she did an outstanding job as well.

But to each and every one of you, really, I am very, very grateful to you. A serious note—I said some of it yesterday, perhaps with less specificity than I will when I address the Joint Session of the Congress in early February. And what I wanted to say is: Yes, the problems are big out there. There's no question of it. And I did single out the Federal budget deficit yesterday. I talked about the new relationship with the Soviet Union. But let me just say a word on each.

I'm convinced that if we approach it properly with the Congress, without rancor, that we can get it done. I know it's not going to be easy, and I know they're not going to accept even some of the fundamental premises upon which I was elected. I'm sure of that. But I also know that with Governor Sununu at my side coming out of the political process, and with me in a sense a creature of Congress as well, that we're going to try. And I think maybe we can make the headway that the American people are really properly demanding in terms of addressing ourselves to this one fundamental remaining problem.

I put the trade deficit in a different category because I think if we get demonstrable progress on the Federal budget deficit that will send a psychological signal to world markets that will help us enormously in terms of the expense of interest, for example, on the Federal debt. So, we're going to start, and we're going to reach out. And on Tuesday of next week, we're going to have our first meeting with the bipartisan leadership—House and Senate, Democrats and Republicans—to start addressing this. We're not expecting miracles, but I want them to know we are going to try. I'm going to try to do that which I said, in that speech on the west front of the Capitol, I wanted to do.

And then the second point—we're standing in this spectacular building which George Shultz so ably led and that now will be led by my friend of such long standing, Jim Baker. And somebody—there was an editorial in the Times the other day that said the Vice President—or the President-elect has been dealt a good hand on foreign affairs. I think that's true. We've got some tough problems in our own hemisphere. We're got some problems we're watching very carefully in Africa. We've got problems in the subcontinent in terms of nuclear proliferation.

So, you've plenty of problems to go around. But because of the reestablished credibility of the United States, because our word is seen as good, because our determination is not doubted, I think I have been dealt a very good hand. And I salute, obviously, President Reagan and men with whom I worked, women of ability in the trade areas or in the defense areas or wherever is it, because I think I come in with a stronger hand now, and I think the horizon is bright. I'd talk to kids in the campaign, and I'd tell them, listen, if I were in your shoes, I'd be optimistic that I might grow up in a land less afraid of nuclear holocaust, less worried about regional conflagration, more optimistic about human rights worldwide.

So, the agenda, though fraught with some problems, is one that I look forward to tackling. We already had a first meeting—Governor Sununu and Brent Scowcroft and me—this morning. We met first with the Director of the Central Intelligence and one of our regular briefers, and then Bob Gates, the new Deputy over there, joined us. And you begin to get the sense where we should start, what areas we should tackle first, and again going right back with the Congress, trying to do a better job in letting them understand.

The President has a unique responsibility. I am concerned about the erosion of Presidential power, particularly in the field of national defense and foreign policy. But I want to work with Congress. They want in on the takeoff—fine. I've got to make the decision. I have constitutional responsibility, and they have theirs—largely in the purse strings and whatever—and responsibilities there. But again, we're going to approach it with openness, with firmness, but with a spirit that, look, we really should try to return to the Vandenberg days of partisanship stopping at the water's edge.

So, this challenge, this one of foreign affairs and working so Noelle back here can grow up in a world much more peaceful, so the kids don't have to worry quite as much about the tensions that perhaps their mom and dad had to do, is a good one. And we're ready for it, and we're putting together a first-class team.

Lastly—again, thank you—but lastly, this morning Barbara and I, having attended I think it was 14 events last night—[*laughter*]—there's somebody behind the scene. You say, who's responsible for this? [*Laughter*] I looked around and can't find anybody. The only body that's come close to taking credit is Bobby Holt, and he even jumped sideways on me there a time or two at the end of the 12th event the other night. But so, we got home last night—I say "home"—we did, climbed into bed. And I—nervous guy, you know, tension and work—my system working on the 6 o'clock call. So, they got the coffee. And I looked out the window of the White House, and here were people all over the darn place. [*Laughter*] They'd spent the night there, literally, in the cold, some of them later coming through the receiving line with their blankets. And some of them had been there for 12 hours, staying out there. Some of them got there—I know one—I said, "What time did you get there?" And he said, "4 o'clock." He's near the end of the line, so I don't know whether that means you had to be there before 4 o'clock, but a lot of them literally had spent all night long there. And they came to the White House, and they were thanking us for giving them this fantastic opportunity to spend all night—[*laughter*]—outside when it got colder than the devil. But there is something wonderful about that. It made a tremendous impression on both Barbara and me. I should have known it because we see the lines along here all the time—probably out there right now if the place is still open for the tours. But it said something wonderful about the stability, the continuity, and the greatness of the United States.

Thank you. Thank you all.

Note: The President spoke at 11:12 a.m. in the Diplomatic Reception Room at the State Department. In his remarks, he referred to John H. Sununu, Chief of Staff to the President; Laurence E. Bathgate, finance chairman of the Republican National Committee; Wally Ganzie, Mel Sembler, and Joe Zappala, members of the State Election Committee; Bobby Holt and Penne Percy

Korth, cochairmen of the American Bicentennial Inauguration Committee; Brent Scowcroft, Assistant to the President for National Security Affairs; and Robert Gates, Deputy Assistant to the President for National Security Affairs.

Letter to Congressional Leaders on Deficit Reduction Efforts
January 21, 1989

Dear ________:

Yesterday, in my Inaugural Address, I suggested that together we should begin the process of working to achieve a deficit reduction plan—and that we should do so soon. I had previously stated that I would lead such an effort on behalf of the Executive branch and that I would begin the process promptly upon taking office.

In accord with that commitment and our discussions, I extend to you today an invitation to join me in a meeting at the White House on Tuesday, January 24. At that meeting, I would hope we could discuss how best to proceed toward deficit reduction. I would also like to take the opportunity to follow up on suggestions made by you and your colleagues on ways we can move towards effective bipartisan support for our foreign policy.

In addition, I would like to confirm my request, which you indicated could be honored, for the opportunity to address a joint session of the Congress on Thursday, February 9.

Again, let me say how much I look forward to our working together on these critical issues. I am sure the American people expect that concerns of such national import should be tackled in a spirit of bipartisan cooperation, and am hopeful that we may prove worthy of the confidence they have placed in us.

Sincerely,

GEORGE BUSH

Note: Identical letters were sent to Jim Wright, Speaker of the House of Representatives; George J. Mitchell, majority leader of the Senate; Robert Dole, minority leader of the Senate; Thomas S. Foley, majority leader of the House of Representatives; and Robert H. Michel, minority leader of the House of Representatives.

Remarks and an Informal Exchange With Reporters During a Walk With Family Members
January 21, 1989

The President. This is going to be the scene of a lot of real action. Marlin, do you think this would be an appropriate time to mention the first exhibition match?

Q. Yes.

The President. It has nothing to do with betting. This is a very important announcement: that this spring sometime a match that was rained out last year is going to be played here. And the players are Pam Shriver and Chris Evert versus Marvin Bush and Neil Bush. These women, confident of their own ability, have suggested that the Bush boys will not get over two games a set. And yesterday Chris Evert renewed the bet, renewed the challenge.

I am absolutely confident that the Bush boys will get over two games a set. [*Laughter*] And reliable tennis authorities, like Jeff Austin, the brother of Tracy Austin, thinks that those two Bush boys have a reasonable chance to beat Chris Evert and Pam Shriver. And there's going to be a tremendous match right here on this court as soon as spring is here. And it's going——

Q. What's the——

The President. Did you get all that down? It is 6–2, 6–2, and it's Evert and Shriver versus Bush and Bush. [*Laughter*] That's true. They are dead serious.

Q. What's the prize?

The President. Well, we don't bet on the White House grounds. I don't know what's going on on the off-the-record kind of a thing. I'll tell you there's going to be a lot of hostility on this one, a lot of—building. The pressure's mounting.

Q. Where are you going to put the horseshoe pit?

The President. We're looking for the horseshoe place right now.

Note: The President spoke at 11:40 a.m. on the South Lawn of the White House. In his opening remarks, he referred to Marlin Fitzwater, Assistant to the President and Press Secretary. A tape was not available for verification of the content of these remarks.

Remarks at the Swearing-in Ceremony for Members of the White House Staff
January 23, 1989

Well, that official act having been completed, we all now are about to embark on a really great adventure. And I've often said that I see responsibilities in life as missions defined, and so I want to just say a few words, first welcoming all of you to what I know will be a superb White House staff. And we have a tremendous opportunity to make life better for people in this country, better in so many ways. And I think we can, by hard work, make this a safer and a more secure country.

The long hours and hard work that's associated with the White House staff are well-known. But these long hours can result in a country with more opportunity for all. And we've got to tackle, as you know—some of you actively involved in this already—the budget deficit and ensure an economy that is sound and stable. We can do a lot through the wonder of the White House to exhort, to use government resources widely, to make the educational system second to none.

As I mentioned in the Inaugural Address, many of you here will be involved in what I mentioned, which was the antinarcotics effort. And I said in the Inaugural Address we've got to get rid of the scourge, and some of you will be involved in all of that. We've got to challenge all elements of government and the private sector in the environment, to do better in protecting our land and water so these kids back here will grow up in a happy, sound—I'm glad they're somebody else's kids, I'll tell you. [*Laughter*] You ought to have been around here the last 48 hours; it's been fantastic. [*Laughter*]

But the mission is great. But it really has to be accomplished in the finest tradition of our nation: pride, honesty—spirit of idealism when it comes to public service, knowing that our actions must always be of the highest integrity. It's not really very complicated. It's a question of knowing right from wrong, avoiding conflicts of interest, bending over backwards to see that there's not even a perception of conflict of interest.

And so, I know that we'll all set a high standard in that regard. We've got to try. I am very proud of all of you. I think we have a wonderful team, and I'm confident that when our time is over in this marvelous place, I'll be just as proud of you. I'm delighted to see the families here today, and I would simply ask for your understanding because your spouses, husbands and wives, are embarking on an ordeal that is known to be a time-consuming killer in a lot of ways. The lights burn brightly well after dark around this place. And I just hope you'll be understanding because the system works that way. Work is really never done. And I thank you all for sharing your spouses with us.

I want you to know that all of you are important also as part of a team. Those who work in the White House make the personal commitment, and with that comes this sense of personal sacrifice. And I know that you all will be struggling at times with the give-and-take that goes hand in hand with assignments like this.

Barbara understands this. She set a good example, it seems to me, in a lot of volunteer action, and I hope that all of us in the White House and outside will do our part in terms of encouraging the volunteer sector, the Thousand Points of Light that I plan to keep on talking about. Government itself can't do it all.

So, I really came over with the Vice President to thank you all, to encourage your understanding, those here and to all of you here standing up here with me. I'm very, very proud to have you on our team. And now I understand there is going to be a little chance to browse through the room and wander down there and have a cup of coffee. But let's go to work!

Thank you all, and God bless you.

Note: The President spoke at 8:20 a.m. in the East Room at the White House. Prior to his remarks, Vice President Quayle swore in the members of the White House staff.

Remarks to Participants in the March for Life Rally
January 23, 1989

Good afternoon, ladies and gentlemen. This is George Bush in the Oval Office. And before you begin your march today, on this first Monday of my Presidency, I wanted to take just a few brief moments to restate my firm support of our cause and to share with you my deep personal concern about our American tragedy of abortion on demand.

We are concerned about abortion because it deals with the lives of two human beings, mother and child. I know there are people of good will who disagree, but after years of sober and serious reflection on the issue, this is what I think. I think the Supreme Court's decision in *Roe* versus *Wade* was wrong and should be overturned. I think America needs a human life amendment. And I think when it comes to abortion there's a better way: the way of adoption, the way of life.

I know that this morning several of your leaders had a meeting in the White House with Vice President Quayle. I know, too, that you and hundreds of thousands with you across the country have raised a voice of moral gravity about abortion, a voice of principle, a voice of faith, a full voice that properly asserts and affirms the basic dignity of human life. I'm confident that more and more Americans every year—every day—are hearing your message and taking it to heart.

And, ladies and gentlemen—and, yes, young people as well—I promise you that the President hears you now and stands with you in a cause that must be won. God bless you all, and God bless life.

Note: The President spoke at 12:05 p.m. from the Oval Office at the White House via a loudspeaker hookup with the rally site. Participants had gathered on the Ellipse for a march to the Supreme Court on the 16th anniversary of the Court's decision of "Roe v. Wade," which legalized abortion.

Interview With Gerald Boyd of the New York Times and Katherine Lewis of the Houston Post
January 25, 1989

Abortion

Q. We just had a few things we wanted to get your views on.

Q. What has Sullivan [Secretary of Health and Human Services-designate] told you about his views on *Roe* versus *Wade*? Can you straighten that out?

The President. Exactly what you heard him say when he was announced. He has supported my position 100 percent.

Q. Even privately on *Roe* versus *Wade*?

The President. One hundred percent. The only thing he said, and that's what he said.

Q. So, you don't envision dropping him under any circumstances?

The President. None. And I've not heard anyone suggesting that he will not be confirmed. I haven't heard one single person suggest that.

Q. If *Roe* versus *Wade* is overturned, as you support, how concerned would you be about women being allowed to have abortions in cases of rape, incest, and——

The President. We'll have to wait and see what the decision is on *Roe* versus *Wade*. Obviously you have to comply with the law, and what the law is is defined by the courts.

Savings and Loan Crisis

Q. What about this new Brady [Secretary of the Treasury-designate] option we're hearing about on S&L's—the idea of charging for insurance for depositors?

The President. That's one option. It hasn't come to me as a formal recommendation. And so, I'm not going to say what I'm going to do, but that is one option.

Q. Would that not be a tax?

The President. I will answer the question with a question. Is it a tax when the person pays the fee to go to Yosemite Park?

Q. Well, on that point——

The President. Using the park—there will be a lively debate on this, but I would simply leave that rhetorical question out as one way of answering your question.

Q. Well, Governor Sununu [Chief of Staff to the President] is——

The President. I don't want to signal that this is what we're going to do. I'm not trying to suggest that.

Q. But it sounds like you're receptive to the idea, though?

The President. I'm receptive to any idea that will solve this problem. I'm not receptive to a tax increase.

Tax Increases

Q. Governor Sununu said over the weekend—he was talking about whether your no-tax pledge increase is a 1-year increase or is it throughout your term. Can you sort of clarify your thinking on that?

The President. I'm not thinking beyond anything other than to say I will not raise taxes, and I've got to stay with that approach. And again, we're going to, you know, just send a proposal up there that solves this budget problem without raising taxes. And the fundamental reason for that is, I want to keep the economy going. I want to keep the recovery—not recovery, but the growth going in this economy. I do not want to kill off investment or employment opportunity. And the higher the taxes, the more you do that. So, I really feel strong on that particular point, and I haven't thought beyond 1 year, Jerry, or anything of that nature.

Q. So, no timeframe.

War on Drugs

Q. You mentioned in your Inaugural Address that you wanted to eliminate the scourge of drugs. How can you do that? I mean, what do you have in mind when President Reagan was unable to eliminate drugs?

The President. I think the elimination of drugs is going to stem from vigorous change in the society's approach to narcotics. It's going to be successful only if our education is successful. The answer to the problem of drugs lies more on solving the demand side of the equation than it does on the supply side, than it does on interdiction or sealing the borders or something of that nature. And so, it is going to have to be a major educational effort, and the private sector and the schools are all going to have to be involved in this.

Q. More money on that?

The President. I don't know what resources are going to be available yet. I would like to think that we can funnel more money into it, but I also have this overriding problem of the deficit to contend with. So, the question is, we cannot permit the measure of concern on any issue—drugs or education or environment—to be determined simply by how much Federal money goes after the problem. We can't do it. We have got to use this office to encourage all elements in our society to participate in the fight against drugs, in the fight to improve education, or working to make the environment better. Because we're dealing with scarce resources in terms of Federal money. And the law has constraints on all of us in that regard.

Human Rights Summit Meeting

Q. Secretary [of State-designate] Baker said in the confirmation hearing that he was concerned about going ahead with the Moscow summit on human rights in 1991. Are you concerned about that?

The President. Well, I think that we need to look for performance. And there will be time in which to see performance in that regard. And I think the Soviets know that we feel this way after the Secretary's testimony. And I think that Mr. Gorbachev knows of my commitment to human rights because I had several meetings with him. And I'd say that there has been definite improvement in some ways there. But let's see what develops as we move towards that conference date.

Interest Rates and Inflation

Q. What are your views on Mr. Greenspan's [Chairman of the Board of Governors of the Federal Reserve System] comments on inflation from yesterday?

The President. I haven't read them yet, and I want to be sure to read them. I must say I'm encouraged that the markets, at least recently, have been saying that things are reasonably stable and certainly not there's no signals out there in the markets that this economy is in real trouble. I haven't talked to Alan lately, but I don't want to see us move so strongly against fear of inflation that we impede growth. We have to keep expanding opportunities for the working men and women of this country. I just saw this little summary of what Greenspan said.

Mr. Fitzwater. I think his comments were a lot closer to our position than was reported, too.

Q. That's what I was told.

The President. That's why I don't want to get into commenting on his——

Visit to China

Q. Are we going to China?

The President. Stay tuned.

Q. Sounds like yes.

The President. We may have it. We may have something on that—you know, yea or nay—before the close of business today. But I just don't know yet.

President's Agenda

Q. There's talk that you're hitting the ground walking.

The President. Where'd you get "we"? Are you going?

Q. Yes, she's going.

The President. Oh, great. Oh, that's right, you don't go off till——

Q. November.

The President. Oh, November.

Q. There's a lot of talk that you're hitting the ground walking rather than running, that you're taking—or that you're starting slow. Are you concerned about that?

The President. In what sense starting slow? In sense of—talking about——

Mr. Fitzwater. You missed the 7 a.m. starts at the South Ground races.

Q. No, but you're not moving ahead on the budget. You're not moving ahead on any agenda.

The President. Moving ahead on the budget—I mean, we're spending a lot of time on it. I know we've got some meetings—meeting with budget team, 10 a.m. Can't do anything about that for 15 minutes. But you mean in terms of sending up legislation or——

Q. Yes, and that there's no sort of an active agenda that you're pursuing from day one and that you're putting things off, you're studying things, you're waiting.

The President. Well, I've been a President since January 20th, and I think it's a little early to make conclusions one way or another on all that.

Environmental Issues

Q. The environmentalists say they're going to be making a litmus test out of ANWR [Arctic National Wildlife Refuge]. Is there any chance you're going to reconsider the Interior seat?

The President. I'm in favor of prudent development there. I remember the pipeline. I remember the arguments against it. And I also know the effect it did not have on the caribou. You may remember that. Phrases that lived on from campaign history about caribou bumping up against the pipeline. [*Laughter*]

Mr. Fitzwater. We've got to stop.

Mr. President. No—so, I mean, I think I'm determined to be an environmentalist. I am one, and I'm concerned that we not do irreparable damage to the environment. On the other hand, I remember some of the same arguments being made against the Alaska pipeline. And we have some national security interests at stake here, and I'm one who believes we can find the balance between environmental interests and national security interests that dictate prudent development of our domestic oil and gas resources.

President's Style

Q. A lot's been made about how you're doing things differently—you have a different way of doing business. Was it important to you to particularly demonstrate that in this first week in office?

The President. Not to do it differently, but it's important to me to do it my way. And that's what we're trying to do, and what I will do. I have to do that. Like the old advice from Jackman—you remember the guy that came out—character. He says, "And then I had some advice: Be yourself." That proved to be the worst advice—[*laughter*]—I could possibly have. And I'm going to be myself—do it that way.

Note: The interview began at 9:38 a.m. in the Oval Office at the White House. Marlin Fitzwater was Assistant to the President and Press Secretary.

Remarks on Signing the Executive Order Establishing the President's Commission on Federal Ethics Law Reform
January 25, 1989

Well, I want to—especially at the opening of these brief remarks—thank Judge Wilkey and Judge Bell, former Attorney General, for joining me today and for agreeing to take on this critical task.

Our National Government depends for its success on the excellence and the integrity of those who serve the public. And in choosing officials from my administration, I have sought out individuals of unquestioned competence and the highest integrity. But along with these high standards of selection, we need an unambiguous code—a code of conduct—to ensure that those who serve the public trust avoid any actual or apparent conflict between their personal and public interests.

As we've seen in the recent debates about ethics legislation, current Federal ethics rules do not adequately serve to eliminate abuse of public office for private gain. And the current framework is fragmented; it's confusing; and most important, does not incorporate sufficient safeguards to protect the public interest in honest and fair government. It's the difficulty of these issues that leads me to create the President's Commission on Federal Ethics Law Reform.

Judge Wilkey, thank you, sir, for taking

on the arduous responsibilities of Chairman. And Judge Bell, thank you for agreeing to be the Vice Chairman. You both come to this task with extensive experience in public service and a deep interest and understanding of these interests in, and understanding of, ethics matters. And I'm asking you and other members of the Commission to take a fresh look at the ethical standards that apply to all three branches of the Federal Government and to give me your recommendations by March 9th, if you can. I know this does not give you a lot of time, but I'm eager to move forward with reform, and I'm confident that you can get this job done.

Before I issue this Executive order, let me leave you with four key principles to guide you as you take up your efforts. One, ethical standards for public servants must be exacting enough to ensure that the officials act with the utmost integrity and live up to the public's confidence in them. Two, standards must be fair. They must be objective and consistent with common sense. Three, the standards must be equitable all across the three branches of the Federal Government. And the fourth one—we cannot afford to have unreasonably restrictive requirements that discourage able citizens from entering public service.

The task of reforming and revitalizing Federal ethical standards is really of the highest importance to me and to the American people. And I'll await your recommendations with great interest.

And now I'll sign this Executive order.

Note: The President spoke at 2:36 p.m. in the Roosevelt Room at the White House. The Executive order is listed in Appendix E at the end of this volume.

Nomination of Donald J. Atwood To Be Deputy Secretary of Defense
January 25, 1989

The President today announced his intention to nominate Donald J. Atwood to be Deputy Secretary of Defense. He would succeed William H. Taft IV.

Mr. Atwood has been vice chairman of the board of General Motors, 1987 to the present, and a member of the finance committee and the executive and administration committees. He was appointed president of Delco Electronics Corp. in 1988. He has served as executive vice president of General Motors and a member of the corporation's board of directors since January 1, 1984, and president of GM Hughes Electronics Corp., since 1985. Mr. Atwood was vice president and group executive in charge of the worldwide truck and bus group, 1981–1984.

Mr. Atwood attended the Massachusetts Institute of Technology. He served in the U.S. Army, 1943–1946. He was born May 25, 1924, in Haverhill, MA.

Nomination of W. Henson Moore To Be Deputy Secretary of Energy
January 25, 1989

The President today announced his intention to nominate W. Henson Moore to be Deputy Secretary of Energy. He would succeed Joseph F. Salgado.

Mr. Moore has served as a Member of the U.S. House of Representatives from the Sixth Congressional District in Louisiana, 1975–1987. He has served on the Energy and Commerce Committee, Ways and Means Committee, and the Budget Committee and has worked extensively in both energy and tax policy. Mr. Moore has also been a partner with the law firm of Sutherland, Asbill, and Brennan, an Atlanta/Washington-based firm since January 1987. He was also a Republican candidate for U.S. Senate in 1986. Between 1987 and 1988, he also served as one of three American commissioners of the Panama Canal Consultative Committee created by the Panama Canal Treaty.

Mr. Moore graduated from Louisiana State University (B.A., 1961; M.A., 1973) and Louisiana State University Law School (J.D., 1965). He served in the U.S. Army, 1965–1967. He was born October 4, 1939, in Lake Charles, LA. He is married to the former Carolyn Ann Cherry of Franklin, LA, and has three children.

Nomination of Susan S. Engeleiter To Be Administrator of the Small Business Administration

January 25, 1989

The President today announced his intention to nominate Susan S. Engeleiter to be Administrator of the Small Business Administration. She would succeed James Abdnor.

Mrs. Engeleiter has served as the senate minority leader in the Wisconsin State Senate since 1984, and served as assistant minority leader, 1982–1984. She was first elected to the State senate from the 33d district of Wisconsin in 1980. She also was a candidate for the United States Senate, 1987–1988.

Mrs. Engeleiter received a bachelor of science degree from the University of Wisconsin and a juris doctorate degree from the University of Wisconsin Law School. She was born March 18, 1952, in Milwaukee, WI. She is married and has two children.

Nomination of William M. Diefenderfer III To Be Deputy Director of the Office of Management and Budget

January 25, 1989

The President today announced his intention to nominate William M. Diefenderfer III to be Deputy Director of the Office of Management and Budget. He would succeed John F. Cogan.

Mr. Diefenderfer is currently a partner in the law firm of Wunder & Diefenderfer in Washington, DC. Prior to this he served as chief of staff and counsel to the chairman of the Senate Finance Committee, 1985–1986. From 1983 to 1984, he was a partner with the law firm of McNair, Glenn, Konduros, Corley, Singletary, Porter & Dibble in Washington, DC. He was chief counsel of the Senate Committee on Commerce, Science, and Transportation, 1979–1983, and administrative assistant/legal counsel for Congressman Bruce Caputo, 1977–1979. He was Assistant Director for the Domestic Council at the White House, 1976–1977.

Mr. Diefenderfer graduated from Dickinson College (B.A., 1967); Duquesne University School of Law (J.D., 1973); and Kings College, University of London (L.L.M., 1974). He served in the U.S. Army, 1970–1972. He was born May 3, 1945. He is married, has two children, and resides in Great Falls, VA.

Nomination of Paul D. Coverdell To Be Director of the Peace Corps
January 25, 1989

The President today announced his intention to nominate Paul D. Coverdell to be Director of the Peace Corps. He would succeed Loret M. Ruppe.

Mr. Coverdell is currently president and chief executive officer of Coverdell & Co., Inc., in Atlanta, GA. He has served in the Georgia State Senate since 1970; as senate minority leader since 1974; and chairman of the Fulton County senate delegation, 1974–1984. He was chairman of the Georgia Republican Party, 1985–1987, and was president and a member of the board of directors of the Urban Study Institute of Georgia and the Georgia Health Foundation.

Mr. Coverdell received a bachelor of arts degree from the University of Missouri. He served as a captain in the U.S. Army. He is married to the former Nancy Nally of Atlanta, GA.

Nomination of Constance Berry Newman To Be Director of the Office of Personnel Management
January 25, 1989

The President today announced his intention to nominate Constance Berry Newman to be Director of the Office of Personnel Management. She would succeed Constance Horner.

Ms. Newman has been a codirector for outreach programs in President Bush's transition office. Prior to this she was deputy director of national voter coalitions for the Bush-Quayle '88 campaign. She has also served as Assistant Secretary of Housing and Urban Development, Director of VISTA, Commissioner of the Consumer Product Safety Commission, and president of the Newman & Hermanson Co., a consulting firm.

Ms. Newman received an A.B. degree from Bates College and a bachelor of science degree from the University of Minnesota Law School.

Nomination of Bruce S. Gelb To Be Director of the United States Information Agency
January 25, 1989

The President today announced his intention to nominate Bruce S. Gelb to be Director of the United States Information Agency. He would succeed Charles Z. Wick.

Mr. Gelb is currently vice chairman of the board of directors of Bristol-Myers Co. Mr. Gelb became president of Bristol-Myers consumer products group in 1981 and was named executive vice president in charge of both Bristol-Myers consumer products and health care groups in 1984. He is a member of the Public Sector Committee of the USIA, and vice president and a board member of the Proprietary Association.

Mr. Gelb graduated from Yale University (B.A., 1950) and Harvard University (M.B.A., 1953). He is married and has four children.

Nomination of Fred M. Zeder II To Be President of the Overseas Private Investment Corporation
January 25, 1989

The President today announced his intention to nominate Fred M. Zeder II to be President of the Overseas Private Investment Corporation, U.S. International Development Cooperation Agency. He would succeed Craig A. Nalen.

From 1987 to 1988, Mr. Zeder was senior adviser for President Bush's transition office. He served on the committee on special projects and surrogate speakers panel for the Bush-Quayle '88 campaign and on the finance committee of the George Bush for President campaign. Prior to this he was President Reagan's personal representative for Micronesian status negotiations serving with the rank of Ambassador, 1982–1987. He has also served as Director of Territorial Affairs at the Department of the Interior, 1975–1977.

Mr. Zeder attended the University of Michigan and the University of California at Los Angeles. He served in the U.S. Army Air Force, 1941–1946, and Air Force Reserve, 1946–1950. He is married, has 5 children and 10 grandchildren.

Remarks to Members of the Senior Executive Service
January 26, 1989

Mr. Vice President, thank you for that very warm welcome. Mr. Vice President and members of the Cabinet and designees and ladies and gentlemen: Let me first recognize especially the recipients of the Presidential Distinguished Rank Award who are with us here today. And it's great to be here with all of you, the men and women whom I regard as certainly among America's finest. You're the first group that I am addressing as President outside the White House, and you're one of the most important groups I will ever speak to.

And you know, I wanted to be fully briefed before I came, so I asked one of my staff, "When does open season begin?" [*Laughter*] And he says, "For you, sir, it begins as soon as the honeymoon ends." [*Laughter*]

We're all wise in the ways of Washington, especially you who've served this country with such distinction. And we know there are ups and downs. But I must say, there is a nice feeling around today in the country. I think people, when a new President comes in, do root for him regardless of partisan politics. That comes up tomorrow. But for today, why, I think there's a good mood out there, and I thank you for that welcome to me and to the members of my Cabinet and designees and others that are here with us on this platform. Pundits agree, regardless of party, that of all the candidates I had the best Form 171. [*Laughter*] But really, what we do have in common is that each of us is here to serve the American people. Each of us is here because of a belief in public service as the highest and noblest calling. And each one of us, on our first day, took a solemn oath: We pledged to defend the Constitution of the United States. And that is exactly what we shall do.

And our mandate comes from the people, because as Abraham Lincoln said: "No man is good enough to govern another man without that other's consent." And so, now that the people have spoken, I'm coming to you as President and offering my hand in partnership. I'm asking you to join me as full members of our team. I promise to lead and to listen, and I promise to serve beside you as we work together to carry out the will of the American people.

Our principles are clear: that government service is a noble calling and a public trust. I learned that from my mom and dad at an early age, and I expect that that's where many of you learned it—there or in school. There is no higher honor than to serve free men and women, no greater privilege than to labor in government beneath the Great Seal of the United States and the American flag. And that's why this administration is dedicated to ethics in government and the need for honorable men and women to serve in positions of trust.

Yesterday I appointed a bipartisan commission, headed by Judge Wilkey and former Attorney General Griffin Bell, to develop ethics reform proposals which will include all branches of the Federal Government. The guiding principle will be simply to know right from wrong, to act in accordance with what is right, and to avoid even the appearance of what is wrong. Our duty is to serve, and my strong conviction is that we must do it only for the right reasons, as you do: out of a sense of service and love of country. Government should be an opportunity for public service, not private gain. And I want to make sure that public service is valued and respected, because I want to encourage America's young to pursue careers in government. There is nothing more fulfilling than to serve your country and your fellow citizens and to do it well. And that's what our system of self-government depends on.

And I've not known a finer group of people than those that I have worked with in government. You're men and women of knowledge, ability, and integrity. And I saw that in the CIA. I saw that when I was in China. I saw it at the United Nations. And for the last 8 years, I saw that in every department and agency of the United States Government. And I saw that commitment to excellence in the Federal workers I came to know and respect in Washington, all across America, and, indeed, around the world. You work hard; you sacrifice. You deserve to be recognized, rewarded, and certainly appreciated. I pledge to try to make Federal jobs more challenging, more satisfying, and more fulfilling. I'm dedicated to making the system work and making it work better.

Starting 8 years ago, I led a task force to remove unnecessary regulation of the private sector, to free up the energies of the American people. But I think we also need to continue to remove unnecessary and counterproductive regulation of Federal workers and senior executives. I believe that there is tremendous pent-up energy in the Federal Government, a powerful force for good that needs to be released. And I want to be the President to do that, to release the Federal manager from bureaucratic bondage so that together we can, as I said on the steps of the Capitol, use power to serve people.

I think Connie Horner has done an outstanding job at OPM, at the Office of Personnel Management. And I'm delighted that my new Director of OPM will be Connie Newman. She is an outstanding executive. I have great confidence in her, and I think she's learned a few things on her way up since 1962—that's the year she began in Federal service as a clerk-typist at the Department of the Interior. And just as the award winners here today represent the best and the brightest, I think in choosing Connie I found one of the best and brightest, as well.

Now, as the Cabinet Secretaries staff their agencies—particularly the senior positions—they'll be looking for ability, for people committed to fulfilling the mandate we received from the American people and to doing it with excellence. And if we find that the best choice for an appointment is a career government executive, I am for that, and I hope that my selection of Tom Pickering to be our Ambassador at the United Nations is underlining that point.

I have a conservative vision of government. I ran and was elected on those terms. And I see no strain or tension between those values and the values of a professional civil service whose highest principle is one of patriotism, whose foremost commitment is to excellence, whose experience and expertise is in itself a national resource to be used and respected. I urge all my appointees to build a spirit of teamwork between the political and career officials. And each of you has a special role to play here. You've reached the top of your profession, and you're skilled managers, knowledgeable in your fields, respected by your colleagues. And I'm asking you to join with our political appointees not only in setting an example of cooperation but, again, one of excellence as well.

To those who work outside Washington, I would send a special message. At times it may be frustrating when it seems that the head office is thousands of miles away and the message is not getting through. But if I may, I'm going to issue a verbal Executive order: We're going to listen, because the heart of our government is not here in Washington, it's in every county office, every town, every city across this land. Wherever the people of America are, that's where the heart of our government is. And since, in any organization, so many of the best ideas come from the bottom up, I hope the people in this room will listen, listen closely, to the people who work for you. The civil servants on the front lines know what works because they're right there. Whether they're working with disadvantaged children, promoting American exports, or managing our public lands, they are in touch with the American people.

And there's much we need to accomplish for America. There is a mandate to fulfill, and there are problems to solve. We have work to do in promoting education, protecting the environment, and certainly in fighting crime. We have work to do in our cities and on our farms, and we have a war on drugs to win. We must provide for the common defense, strive for a lasting peace, and we must keep our economy growing so it can keep producing jobs and opportunity. Above all, we have a compact with the American people. They pay for excellent government, and they deserve to receive it. And together we can assure that that is done.

And there's one more thing we need to do. The Government is here to serve, but it cannot replace individual service. And shouldn't all of us who are public servants also set an example of service as private citizens? So, I want to ask all of you, and all the appointees in this administration, to do what so many of you already do: to reach out and lend a hand. Ours should be a nation characterized by conspicuous compassion, generosity that is overflowing and abundant. And you can help make this happen outside of your workplace, in your communities and your neighborhoods, in any of the unlimited opportunities for voluntary service and charity where your help is so greatly needed.

Well, I'm honored to be with you, to work with you, you here in Washington, your colleagues in the Federal service around the nation. They're some of the most unsung heroes in America. The United States is the greatest nation in the world because we fulfill that mission of greatness one person at a time, as individuals dedicated to serving our country.

And as we embark on this great new chapter in our nation's history, I want to tell you—came over here to tell you—that I am proud of you and very glad that we will be working to write this chapter together. Thank you all, and God bless you in your important work. Thank you very, very much.

Note: The President spoke at 2:10 p.m. at DAR Constitution Hall.

The President's News Conference
January 27, 1989

The President. Harmony and peace in here. [*Laughter*] First, I sound worse than I feel. Let me——

Q. What's wrong with you?

The President. Slight cold. But it's been a full week since the inauguration. I just wanted to stop by under our new policy, give you an update.

I've been talking this week about ethics and the emphasis is not, believe me, a fad or some passing fancy. We're going to be hearing more about it—I think a lot more. In broader terms, I'm trying to set high standards for government service: duty, honor, personal sacrifice for the common good. And I want to assemble a government that the people of this nation can be proud of. That's our goal; that's our mission. We did appoint this week, as you know, a new commission on ethics. We've got two able Chairmen, Vice Chairmen: Judge Wilkey and [Attorney] General Griffin Bell. That commission started a fresh, constructive dialog with Congress on both sides of the aisle. I'm pleased with the way those initial meetings have gone. So, we're ready to roll.

I think it's been officially announced that we're going to—certainly to Tokyo, then on to China, and I'm looking forward to it very much. And then, also, we'll be stopping for a relatively brief stop in Korea on the way back from China. We've had other invitations. That's about all we can do. And in a nostalgic basis, needless to say, Barbara and I are looking forward in a very personal way to going back to Beijing.

Now, with no further ado, I'll be glad to take some questions.

Terry [Terence Hunt, Associated Press]?

Federal Pay Raise

Q. Mr. President, you said before you became President that you supported Ronald Reagan's decision on a 50-percent pay raise for Members of Congress and that you'd have something more to say about it once you'd get to the Oval Office. Most of the polls show that a vast majority of Americans oppose that pay raise.

The President. Yes.

Q. Now you're President, what's your view on that pay increase?

The President. Well, I did say I supported it, and I do support it. A raise is overdue. There's no question about that. There are some good things in this. The reform of the honorarium, payments for these speeches, I think, is very, very good. I think it's good government. It's a complicated formulation. There are some elements that bother people, including me. But the President did consider all this carefully. He went forward with the Commission's [Quadrennial Commission on Executive, Legislative, and Judicial Salaries] recommendation, and because of the way it works on Congress—and the ball is clearly in their court—it leaves us with either the Commission recommendation or nothing. And so, seeing the problems as I do, I still feel that I should not go about undoing the Reagan decision.

Yes, Helen [Helen Thomas, United Press International]?

Savings and Loan Crisis

Q. Mr. President, your trial balloon on the S&L's taxing savings and checking accounts has fallen like a lead balloon. Are you dropping that plan? Do you have any other plans?

The President. First place, I think it's a little absurd to be commenting on a facet, a possible facet, of solving a problem when it hasn't even come to me. You're talking about speculating on something that hasn't even reached the desk of the President even as an option—say nothing of its being a proposal.

Q. Well, it certainly has come from your people.

The President. Well, as an option, not as a proposal. And I think you're right. There seems to be some controversy around it. But that doesn't mean that any thinking along those lines should cease. But I'm going to reserve comment until I actually have it presented to me. And I expect this is the first of many such things that's going to happen of this nature. I will say this: that the savings and loans deposits are backed by the full faith and credit of the Government. And they are sound; they are good—dollar good. And I just want to assure the American people of that, and nothing is going to change in that regard. But in terms of this one idea, let them float around. It doesn't bother me for a lot of ideas to be considered and debated.

Q. The reaction is very negative—the public reaction, congressional reaction. Will that enter into your decision?

The President. Anything I do on savings and loans or when we get into this budget deficit reduction program—look, I don't expect it's all going to be sweetness and harmony and light. The minute we get those proposals up there on February 9th, I expect we're going to have other firestorms swirling around. But I have not made decisions on this one. I'll wait until I get all the facts, call them as I see them, and hope that we can convince the American people that that's the way to go.

Relations With Congress

Q. Mr. President, you've set a tone of high-mindedness and propriety this week with your emphasis on ethics, also of bipartisanship in your discussions with Congress. Beyond those matters of process and tone, sir, what would you like the country and the world to say is the message of your first week in office as to what your administration is about?

The President. Reaching out to the Congress. I really am serious about this trying to get more of a bipartisan foreign policy, for example. And though we haven't addressed that specifically in terms of issues, I have addressed it in broad terms to the Members of Congress with whom I've met here and with whom I met over in the Residence. And so, I'd like to signal an era of real openness with Congress.

Look, I know we're going to have conflicts, Brit [Brit Hume, ABC News]. And I know we're going to run up against each other. But I want to start with that approach. And we're in a broad review—as you've heard from my various nominees as they appear before the Senate—on specific areas of foreign policy. A message would be taking steps to make clear to the congressional leadership that that's what I want to do. The other one, as I mentioned, is trying to set a tone, in terms of conflict of interest, that I hope will serve us in good stead.

Visit to China

Q. What signal do you think it may send the world, sir, that you're making your first visit to China—after, of course, the ceremonial trip to Tokyo—while Soviet leader Gorbachev, having asked for early talks, is still waiting for a response?

The President. Well, I don't know what signal it sends in that regard. But let me just remind you that I'm the one who does not believe in "playing the Soviet card" or "playing the China card." We have a strong bilateral relationship with the People's Republic of China. I have a personal acquaintance with the leaders with whom I will be meeting there, including Deng Xiaoping [Chairman of China's Central Military Commission], and being that close—it just seemed like an appropriate visit, but not to signal a playing of the card to go one up on Mr. Gorbachev. There's nothing of that nature in this visit. That is a strong, important strategic and commercial and cultural relationship that we have with the Chinese—the largest number of people in the world, in that country. And so, the visit stands on its own and does not have any signaling that should be detrimental to anybody else's interest.

Going right across here. How do we get in the back here, Marlin?

Soviet-U.S. Relations

Q. Mr. President, your national security adviser, Brent Scowcroft, said last week on television that the Cold War was not over and that he felt that Mr. Gorbachev was trying to make trouble for the Western alliance. What is your view, sir?

The President. Well, I'm not sure that's an exact—I should let the General defend himself. But I've expressed my view not only in the campaign context but in several times afterward, and also to Mr. Gorbachev. And our administration position, in which General Scowcroft is in total agreement—indeed, he'll be one of the leaders in this reassessment—is: Let's take our time now. Let's take a look at where we stand on our strategic arms talks; on conventional force talks; on chemical, biological weapons talks; on some of our bilateral policy problems with the Soviet Union; formulate the policy and then get out front—here's the U.S. position.

And I don't think the Soviets see that as foot-dragging. I'm confident they don't. Indeed, I made that clear to General Secretary Gorbachev just this week in a rather long talk with him. So, I want to try to avoid words like "Cold War" if I can because that has an implication. If someone says Cold War to me, that doesn't properly give credit to the advances that have taken place in this relationship. So, I wouldn't use that term. But if it's used in the context of do we still have problems; are there still uncertainties; are we still unsure in our predictions on Soviet intentions? I'd have to say, yes, we should be cautious.

Yes, Lesley [Lesley Stahl, CBS News]?

Tax Increases

Q. Mr. President, there seems to be some question about just how long your no-tax pledge applies. Is that a 1-year pledge, a 2-year pledge, a 4-year pledge?

The President. I'd like it to be a 4-year pledge.

Q. Is it a 4-year pledge? Are you——

The President. I'd like it to be a 4-year pledge, yes.

U.S. Contact With the PLO

Q. Mr. President, Yasser Arafat [Chairman of the Palestine Liberation Organization] has been over in Europe meeting with Foreign Ministers of Spain, France and Greece. Marlin has said, and so has Mr. Scowcroft, that it's too early for Arafat to meet with Secretary of State-designate Jim Baker. On what level would it be appropriate for Arafat to meet with an American official? An Assistant Secretary of State, for example?

The President. As we changed the policy on the Middle East on dealing with—I mean, as the change came about in the policy on communicating with the PLO, it was based on their acceptance of three principles. As long as they stay hooked and stay committed to those three principles, we will have, when appropriate, meetings with the PLO.

I haven't given any thought at all to when a meeting with the Chairman—Arafat with an American official—is appropriate. And I would wait to see how we go forward. The point in talking to them is to try to facilitate peace in the Middle East. And it seems to me that if there's some logical step that requires high-level sign-off by various participants over there, then, and then only, would it be proper to elevate the meetings to that level. You crawl before you walk. We're just starting to talk to them because they have, dramatically I'd say, agreed to the principles that are part of our policy.

U.S. Foreign Policy Initiatives

Q. Let me ask you if I can in that regard: You said in a wire service interview the other day that you needed to have some foreign policy initiative early in your administration. It seems the Soviet relationship is going on the back burner while you discuss the nuclear force structure, for example. In what area are you going to try to move forward? Central America? The Mideast? Where?

The President. All of them. But we've got to have a little time. We're not going to let this Soviet thing put us in the mode of foot-draggers. We're going to be out front. There's no reason to suggest that all we have to do is react to a speech by the General Secretary. I want to take the offense in moving this relationship forward and taking steps that are in the interest of freedom around the world, whether it's in Eastern Europe or in strengthening our alliance.

But there's plenty of troublespots—one of them, as you mentioned I think, Central America. But we need to complete the reviews. But I can't tell you, John [John Cochran, NBC News], where you will see the first major initiative—whether it's going to be the Middle East, whether it's going to be Central America. We've got problems, of course, that afflict the whole continent and other continents in this Third World debt problem, and then, of course, the Soviet Union.

But, no, I don't want to play defense, and I don't want to look like we're foot-dragging, just waiting around to, you know, let others set the agenda, but prudence is the order of the day. And when you're gunning for something as important as a bilaterally supported policy in Central America, it does take a little time. I've only been here less than a week.

Yes, Owen [Owen Ullmann, Knight-Ridder]?

Minimum Wage

Q. As you know, the minimum wage has been frozen for even longer than congressional pay raises. Since you support a large increase in pay for the most affluent 1 percent of the country, would you favor pushing for an increase in the minimum wage, which would benefit the lowest income groups of the country, as part of your promise in your Inaugural Address to reach out to all the people?

The President. I've always said that my position on minimum wage is that I would want it linked to a training wage, to a differential of sorts, so that you don't throw people out of work by raising the minimum wage. And I'm not one who has felt that the minimum wage is the key to economic prosperity for people on the lowest end of the economic spectrum. But as I indicated, a certain flexibility on that question—and again I'll wait for Elizabeth Dole—takes office next couple of days—to come in with her recommendation.

Saul [Saul Friedman, Newsday]?

Followup Questions

Q. If I could just follow: Do you——

The President. Now, let me ask you to stop the proceedings. Don't take it out of their time. What would be the fair and noble way to handle followup questions as we do these things? Would it be good to have them or not have them?

Q. Handle them. Handle them, yes.

Q. There should be one followup.

Q. One followup.

The President. But then if we do it, everybody else doesn't get a chance to ask a question, and I'm about to pull the ripcord on this thing. [*Laughter*] No, seriously, how do we—I want some——

Q. Stay longer. [*Laughter*]

Q. If you make the statement and just leave and not have anyone follow it up, it just hangs out there.

The President. Yes.

Q. Suppose you don't answer the question?

The President. You mean my first answer is less than precise? [*Laughter*]

Q. Yes—[*laughter*]—on occasion. [*Laughter*]

The President. On occasion. No, but I'm asking. I'd like to get—because here we are, all these——

Q. One followup.

Q. Make a deal: one followup.

Q. You'll just have to be more precise.

The President. ——women and men who have a Leubsdorf area there—untested on the question. [*Laughter*]

Q. And the standee!

Q. Spread it out.

The President. And the standees have gotten no time at all, so——

Q. When, in fact, it's a true followup.

The President. Instead of yet another question, you mean?

Q. Yes.

Q. Right, right.

Q. A real followup.

Q. Exactly, you decide. If you think somebody's playing games with you, say, I'm sorry.

The President. Say I've already answered that? Then what happens? [*Laughter*]

Saul?

Q. Wait a minute. Where's my followup?

Q. You're finished. [*Laughter*]

The President. You didn't have a follow——

Q. The first row gets to follow up? That wouldn't be fair.

The President. All right. I've already answered that one.

Yes, Saul? [*Laughter*]

Q. I yield to Owen first.

Federal Pay Raise and the Minimum Wage

Q. Are you concerned from the standpoint of perception you're supporting a pay raise for a high-income group and not pushing on an equal basis for a lower income group to give the public the perception that you're lobbying for a wealthy sector of the country?

The President. No, I'm not concerned about that perception, but I am troubled by certain aspects of the proposal, as I think I've indicated—the pay raise proposal. But we're down to the crunch here: recommendations up there on the Hill. It's yea or nay. I mean it's one way or another. But I don't think that would be fair at all.

I think the main thing in terms of the question you raise: Jobs—how do we continue to create jobs, keep it going? And I've given you one ingredient that I think has to be a part of any consideration of the minimum wage. But as I've indicated, I'm flexible on how that should be accomplished.

I'm not sure that one can make a connection between the minimum wage and more employment. If you raise the minimum wage without this differential, I think you will reduce employment. So, I think the main thing in the area you're talking about is: How do we increase economic opportunity? And maybe there is a way to do it, but I don't think it would be fair to say when you take a pay raise that affects a tiny fraction—judges and Congressmen—that that has a broad economic impact on the country. I've expressed some concern about it, but for other reasons.

Strategic Defense Initiative

Q. Do you agree with Senator Tower's [Secretary of Defense-designate] testimony in which he doesn't seem to believe that the SDI program, as envisioned by President Reagan, is likely? And if you do agree with it, can you expand on that, please?

The President. No, I think I should wait and see a little more what John Tower means. My position has not changed on SDI.

Q. Which is? I mean, John Tower has said that he doesn't believe that a large-scale SDI to protect the population, as envisioned by Reagan——

The President. I'd better——

Q. ——is likely.

The President. Saul, before I comment on Tower's testimony, I'd better read it. If he's talking about a shield so impenetrable that that eliminates the need for any kind of other defense, I probably would agree with that, certainly short-run. But I'd better cover by waiting until I see what he said.

The standees, two standees?

Afghanistan

Q. Thank you. The first action taken by your Secretary of State was to order the boarding up of the Embassy in Kabul. Does that indicate that this administration, this country, then, has no influence with the rebels and you are now fearful of chaos and massacres there? And to what extent did you discuss this with Gorbachev the other day?

The President. Did not discuss it with him the other day. And what it indicates is a prudent policy to protect a handful of American life. And it's a step that other countries have taken. In Afghanistan, certainly, I think we'd all agree there is uncertainty about what follows. I'm convinced the Soviets will continue their withdrawal, and well they should. But it is simply a prudent way in which to protect life, I think. We've had meeting after meeting with Afghan rebels, and there's no question in their mind how we feel about, say, a Soviet presence in that country. But I think there's a lot of uncertainty. And there's enough uncertainty that a Secretary of State was taking prudent action in this regard.

Q. What role do you see for the United States after the Soviets withdraw in that country?

The President. Catalytic role for helping bring about stability hopefully in a government where the people have a lot of say. And it won't be easy.

Yes, Tom [Tom DeFrank, Newsweek]?

Federal Pay Raise

Q. Mr. President, I'd like to try the pay raise one last time. As you just said, it's not just for Members of Congress and not just for Federal judges. It's for a lot of senior officials of the Government, political appointees. You also have told some reporters in recent days that you're concerned about the long-term pension implications of all these larger salaries. Wouldn't you be happier with a pay raise that's a little bit less rich than 50 percent?

The President. I don't have that option to get into that now. I have, I think, expressed myself in the past on separating out some of these categories, but regrettably you're never dealing with just the way I would like it to be. And so, I'll just leave it that—my earlier statement.

First Days as President

Q. Sir, this is a thematic question. You've had a week on the job. Has it been easier or tougher than you expected? Any surprises? And did you find the note in your underwear drawer? [*Laughter*]

The President. No note in the underwear, and it's been a good, easy week. And I expect it will change dramatically in the days ahead. But my view is to—if it weren't for the cold—smile and enjoy it while you can, because I can already sense, you know, looking forward to a little more confrontation out there.

Q. Have there been any surprises, sir?

The President. None particularly, no. And I think one of the reasons is that I've been around here in a different role for 8 years and then in and out on other jobs. But there's still the wonder of it all. I mean, it still feels different, but not surprises.

Q. A followup, sir?

The President. You already had a followup. Nice try. [*Laughter*]

Rita [Rita Beamish, Associated Press]?

Drug Control Policy Director Bennett

Q. Mr. President, there seems to be some brouhaha about the fact that Bill Bennett's not an actual member of the Cabinet, as are the USTR [U.S. Trade Representative] and the OMB [Office of Management and Budget] Director. In light of the fact that you emphasized drugs as an overriding consideration in your campaign and also that public opinion polls show consistently this is among the top priorities of the public, why isn't he in the Cabinet? And do you foresee that you might change your mind on that?

The President. No. The reason he isn't in the Cabinet is that I tried to reduce down the numbers of full Cabinet members. And I think Bill Bennett's time is best spent not worrying about agricultural subsidies, when we have a meeting on agriculture, but concentrating on drugs. To the degree there's symbolism that this means I think it's less important, I'd like to knock that down hard. And I have to do that in substantive ways: sitting at his side as we meet with his peers at Cabinet level, making clear to them that I will be insisting on cooperation as he asks for the support of the Defense Secretary for military assets on interdiction, as he asks for the support of the Education Secretary on certain educational initiatives.

But the Cabinet rank is there, giving him the standing that I think the job not only requires but demands. And I think the idea of not sitting through Cabinet meetings that have nothing to do with that subject should be a rationale for having Cabinet level, but not being in all those meetings.

I'm glad he mentioned this because I think there's been some feeling, well, that means I'm less interested in drugs. That's not right. I'm very interested in the economic statistics, but our chief of economic advisers [Michael J. Boskin] is not a Cabinet member, as he's been designated by previous Presidents. Our Chief of Staff, in whom I have full confidence, is not a Cabinet member, but I think we have a very strong Chief of Staff setup.

Over here, way up in the window—innovative standing.

Monetary Policy

Q. You just touched on the issue of Third World debt. There are many experts who are saying that if there's any danger for the U.S. economy it's in how greatly leveraged it is, both in terms of corporate indebtedness and Third World debt. And they say that the S&L crisis, for example, is simply a subsumed feature of this. Do you see this as a real problem that you're going to address aggressively, and what kind of steps would you take to overcome the high proportionality of debt to equity that exists in the U.S. economy now?

The President. The question of corporate debt—on that one, the role of the White House and the role of the Federal Government ought to be to do its level best to keep a strong economy. And I don't believe that it's the government role to assign levels beyond which a corporation can't borrow. In terms of Third World debt, we do have a responsibility, and a lot of that's going to be working with the private banks and others. And again, we'll have some recommendations; we have to have them pretty soon on that question.

I'm not sure I got to the substance of your question—separating out these two things.

Q. Try another one.

Q. ——reported differences that you have with Alan Greenspan's [Federal Reserve Chairman] testimony in Congress earlier this week with regard to interest rates and monetary policy.

The President. I'll be honest with you. I don't think I'm far apart from Chairman Greenspan at all—far apart. There may be some differences. Because of plant capacity, utilization, he is more concerned about inflationary pressures than I am right now. Seems to me, there's an area of difference, but basically and generally speaking, I think we're fairly close together.

Government Ethics

Q. Mr. President, by spending your first week dwelling as you have on ethics, aren't you voicing an implicit criticism of the Reagan administration's ethical record?

The President. No.

Q. Why else was it necessary to declare National Ethics Week, so to speak?

The President. Because I feel strongly about it.

Q. Can I follow on that line, sir?

The President. No, she's in first, and then you. Need to cool off on that one. [*Laughter*]

Savings and Loan Crisis

Q. Mr. President, given your strong anti-tax ban in the campaign, why are you allowing Mr. Brady [Secretary of the Treasury-designate] to consider as an option for the S&L's a tax increase?

The President. I'm not. He has thrown out a lot of different possibilities in discussions we've had. We have people that are experts on what a tax is. I would refer you to Richard Darman, who is the head of the OMB. And he's the guy that defined that very well up there with the duck test on the Hill and——

Q. So, you're not thinking of a tax?

The President. Well, I'm just saying I'm not prepared to say what I think on it right now till I hear from it, because the more I discuss it, the more you all go out and say this is something that I'm considering when I'm not. It hasn't come to me yet. But I've been around for a long time, and I don't remember hearing people talk about the fee that went into covering the FDIC [Federal Deposit Insurance Corporation] or FSLIC [Federal Savings and Loan Insurance Corporation] as a tax. I don't remember people writing that before. But—not trying to get into the fight anymore right now. I'll be back.

Government Ethics

Q. You've mentioned ethics in a number of ways, and you've talked about the value of service this year. The last 2 days we've picked up the headlines in the papers, and they've read President Reagan has a $5 million book deal. He's got a $50,000 a speech deal. With all respect for the office and the former President, do you think it's appropriate to cash in on the Presidency?

The President. I don't know whether I'd call it cashing in. I expect every President has written his memoirs and received money for it. Indeed, I read that a former President—was it Grant? Grant got half a million bucks. That's when half a million really meant something. [*Laughter*] I mean, you know, so I think there is plenty of tradition that goes with Presidents' writing memoirs and being paid for it.

Q. But you've also talked about perceptions. Is there a perception problem here?

The President. No, because I think there has been a long history of that, and I don't think it's ever been challenged as inappropriate.

Secretary-Designate Sullivan

Q. Mr. President, would you try to clear up the continuing controversy over the reported disagreements on abortion between your nominee for Health and Human Services and yourself? Are you in sync?

The President. Yes.

Q. Is he in sync with you? Does it matter? Do you have to be absolutely in sync as long as once in office he would support your position?

The President. Well, I think that last point is the important point, but also, we are in sync. And so, I have a person who has stood in front of you all when I nominated him and said that, and I have no reason to think anything differently.

Tax Increases

Q. Mr. President, a few moments ago you talked about—on your no-new-taxes pledge—the idea that you'd like it to be a 4-year pledge, and that does appear to be a softening of language from the campaign. I wonder, has anybody—Mr. Darman or any of your advisers—told you to change your mind about the duration of that pledge—revenues needed and so on?

The President. No, that hasn't changed my mind—anything in the last few days of talking like that.

Abortion

Q. Mr. President, we've heard a lot about your position on abortion this week because of Mr. Sullivan. Are you planning any initiatives from the White House related to abortion? Or are you going to wait and see what the Supreme Court does, number one? And number two, as a person who's always, from what we know, had the financial and emotional resources to know that you could raise your children comfortably, do you feel any awkwardness about telling other people, whose situations you don't know, how they should run their lives?

The President. Not when it comes to the question of life. I do feel an awkwardness in terms of having been able to take care of my kids when they were sick or raise them properly or something like that. I feel a certain privilege. I was very fortunate in that regard, and I know a lot of people aren't. But on this issue, I think we're talking here of principle. And I sure would like to put the emphasis on adoption, and that means a broader acceptance of that principle.

Q. Are you going to have any White House initiatives, or are you going to wait for the Supreme Court?

The President. I think probably wait, but I have been pledged, as you know, to an amendment. But I'd like to see the Supreme Court decision as soon as possible.

One, two, three.

Iran-U.S. Relations

Q. Mr. President, a Teheran radio report this morning seems to indicate that they are rejecting your statement of a week ago today that good will would beget good will. While you didn't specifically mention Iran by name in your speech, what would your message to them be on relations, and what would your message be to them about helping get the hostages out?

The President. Well, I would make a broad appeal, transcending Iran, to anybody that can be helpful to get the hostages out. I haven't seen the wire copy, but if there is such a story by them, maybe they're saying, Well look, we're not holding your hostages. And I'd have to say, Well, from our intelligence, our information, that's probably correct—probably correct. In terms of the future—there was a period of time when we had excellent relations with Iran, and I don't want to think that the status quo has to go on forever. But I do think that the renunciation of terror in any form and a facilitating to the degree they can the release of the hostages would be a couple of good steps they could take.

Q. A followup, Mr. President—follow up on that?

The President. No, you don't get to follow his question. [*Laughter*] Ann [Ann McFeatters, Scripps-Howard] and then here. We've got to get these ground rules—sure.

Affirmative Action

Q. Mr. President, you've spoken frequently about reaching out to blacks, that you want that to be an important goal of your administration. This week the Supreme Court issued a decision that may kill many of the minority set-aside programs that have been so helpful to blacks across this country. Does that concern you? Are you worried about these programs?

The President. It didn't kill all set-asides, and it didn't kill off affirmative action. I have been committed to affirmative action. I want to see a reinvigorated Office of Minority Business in Commerce. I want to see our SBA [Small Business Administration] program go forward vigorously. And so, I would say that decision spoke to one set of facts—in Richmond, I believe it was—but I will not read into that a mandate to me to stop trying on equal employment and on affirmative action generally.

Capital Gains Taxes

Q. You said during the campaign, Mr. President, that you would roll back taxes on capital gains if elected. Now that you've begun to look at the budget numbers, is that going to be a promise you can keep when you make your submission to Congress, or is that no longer affordable?

The President. I hope it's affordable; it gains you revenue. And we've got a big argument with some people about that. They don't want to go back and look at what happened in 1978. It gains revenue. Now, I know we've got all kinds of bureaucracies around here that doesn't agree with that, but that was discussed in the campaign. I'm convinced it will bring in additional revenue and, in the process, create additional jobs for men and women. So, I would like to see it a fundamental part of whatever we do.

Now, if your question is: Can I get it done?—that's something else again. But I want to see it done. There was an issue in our campaign where there was a clear difference. That was when there was a clear difference. The opposition was saying: My opponent is proposing something that'll cost the taxpayer $30 billion. And I'm saying: It'll create jobs. And indeed, I've seen estimates by intelligent people thinking it'll bring in revenues in excess of $4 billion. And so, I'm going to keep pushing that, because I know it's right, and I ran on it.

Federal Pay Raise

Q. Mr. President, once more on the pay raise. You've portrayed yourself as a latecomer on the issue who has no real power to affect it. But in point of fact, I believe that you do have the power, if you want to, to limit the pay raises that would otherwise automatically go to your own staff. Will you do that, number one? And number two, do you think both Houses of Congress ought to vote on this?

Q. Sununu already——

The President. Well, I think in the best of all worlds—[*laughter*]—wait until I get——

Mr. Fitzwater. It's a trick question, sir. [*Laughter*]

The President. He's a fairminded guy. [*Laughter*] No, I think our Chief of Staff has tried to hold the line in increases in hiring people. And I think you're all aware of that. And I think he's done a very good job on it. I don't know how the law affects the staff in terms of automatic increases, but there's a nice little problem that if you do go forward with automatic increases, or any money that has to be appropriated some way. So, we'll have to talk about what we'll do.

What was the other part of it?

Q. Do you think both Houses of Congress ought to vote on this issue?

The President. In a perfect world, in a world where you're starting over, yes, I'd have to say I do. But that isn't the proposal that's up there, and it's all or nothing. And in my view, I've told you where I come down on that.

We've got time for a couple of more, because it's 3857.89, 58.80—this thing is buzzing away up here.

Yes, go back——

Hostages in the Middle East

Q. Mr. President, a few minutes ago on the answer concerning the hostages, you indicated that Iran was probably not holding the hostages. Did you mean to say that we believe that Iran exercises no control over the people who are holding the hostages?

The President. No, I mean to say they are not holding the hostages. Do they have any control? I think you can get varying degrees of intelligence on that, various assessments as to how much control they have over Hizballah [radical Shi'ite terrorist group] or these families or whoever it is. And also, you've got different groups involved in the holding of these hostages. But, no, I'm glad to get a chance to clarify it because, unless the information I have is wrong, Iran itself, the government, is not actually holding these people. And if they were, I would just reiterate my view that the way to improve relations is to let them go, give these people their freedom. They didn't do anything wrong.

Q. And a followup, Mr. President. Do we believe that Iran can exercise influence to gain the hostages' release?

The President. I think they can have influence.

Defense Spending

Q. You inherited a budget from President Reagan that calls for something like a 2-percent real increase in defense spending. In the campaign, you seemed to think that maybe zero real growth in defense spending would be adequate. With deficit pressures, do you think there's some room for reduction in the Reagan defense budget to fund some of the other programs, like the S&L problem that you've got to worry about?

The President. We're wrestling with that problem right now. I'm committed to a strong defense. I did say certain things in the campaign that fit into our flexible freeze concept. And so, I will have to address that with some detail on February

9th, and I will. We've got time for just a couple of more.

War on Drugs

Q. Mr. President, just the other day that education was the main way of dealing with drugs.

The President. Yes.

Q. Isn't that a backing away from your commitment on drugs? Certainly there are other things than education to deal with the problem.

The President. Absolutely. And I was surprised when I read that some interpreted what I said as suggesting that interdiction is not important, or cooperation with foreign governments in terms of eradication at the source is not important. They are very important. My point is: We are not going to solve the problem of drug use in this country through interdiction alone, through cutting off the supply alone. And a larger component of this solution lies in education, and in that whole demand side of the equation: law enforcement at home—these things.

Last one here. This is a followup?

Q. It is a followup. But, Mr. President, how much money are you going to spend on drugs? If it's a major problem that you say it is, certainly education is just one very small part of it, isn't it?

The President. It's not a small part; it's a tremendous part. And the Federal Government can spend some on it, and the private sector has got to spend enormous amounts. The media has done a good job in terms of pro bono advertising, and that's got to be enormously stepped up. So, look, it has got to be a tremendous increase not only on the money but the emphasis on the educational side. I do want to find a way to step up the total funding on antinarcotics.

And I want to go back to what I said on Bill Bennett, because this question of Cabinet rank and whether that shows less an interest in narcotics troubles me. You will see me side by side with Bill Bennett, on putting the proper emphasis from the Oval Office on my determination to do everything in the Government's power, Federal Government's power, to eliminate this scourge.

Last one.

President's Agenda

Q. Mr. President, you and your aides have talked about the need for a fast start, and you've talked all week about ethics and about bipartisanship. And yet the week has been marked by unexpected controversies over Dr. Sullivan's views on abortion and then the S&L issue, which is sort of a self-inflicted wound. Are you finding it harder to control the agenda here than you thought you would?

The President. No, no. I'm just getting a preview of coming attractions, and it's been lovely. [*Laughter*] And it's going to change, and I know it. But, no, I think it's been a wonderfully harmonious week, and these are just little ripples on the surface of an otherwise calm pond.

Q. You're not concerned that if you just talk about things that—I mean, everyone approves of ethics, just about, and everyone approves of bipartisanship. Isn't there a danger of people saying that there's not much meat behind the words?

The President. There's a danger of that, yes, but people realize that we've been here 4 days of this week, or 5—this is the fifth day in office after the weekend. And they understand that in things like the foreign policy area that it's prudent to have a review. They understand that we've got to get our people in place. And so, there's some danger I guess, Carl [Carl Leubsdorf, Dallas Morning News], but I wouldn't say an overwhelming danger. I mean, we just go forward. If we just sat around and did nothing except be pleasant to people on the Hill or something, why I expect that would grow a little old for you all.

But we're going to—[*laughter*]—I think we set a certain tone and certain outreach and then go forward. As soon as these specific proposals start up there, whether it's on education or antinarcotics or on foreign policy or on some bilateral foreign visitor coming in, there will be plenty of time for controversy and plenty of time for lively debate on substance. But I would simply say that'll follow, and follow pretty soon.

Thank you all very much.

Note: The President's first news conference began at 11:02 a.m. in the Briefing Room at the White House. Marlin Fitzwater was Assistant to the President and Press Secretary.

Remarks at the Swearing-in Ceremony for James A. Baker III as Secretary of State
January 27, 1989

The President. Well, if I could ask the Secretary of State and Mrs. Baker and Chief Justice to come forward, we'll get on with the program here.

[*At this point, Secretary of State Baker was sworn in.*]

Mr. Vice President, distinguished Members of the United States Senate and House, Mr. Speaker—Mr. Chief Justice, thank you, sir, for doing the honors today.

This is a very special occasion for me because, as you all know, Jim and I have been friends for a long time, going back perhaps more years than either of us would care to admit—long, really, before our public lives began. And we've served in government together, campaigned together, traveled a long way through some rough and tumble times. And it's well known that the new Secretary of State is my friend. I have great confidence in him. And judging from how he sailed through the confirmation process—thank you, gentlemen—the United States Senate shares that confidence.

And as Secretary of State, he will be my principal foreign policy adviser. As I pledged in my Inaugural Address a week ago, my Presidency will usher in the age of the offered hand, and that applies certainly to foreign policy. I've also spoken of a new engagement. Nowhere is the need for a new engagement greater than in foreign policy.

The postwar generation has come of age, and today we live in a distinctly different world than that which we were born into: a world that demands new strategies and new solutions. And today we see a process of change in the Soviet Union and Eastern Europe, in the Middle East. A changing situation creates new possibilities as well as dangers. In southern Africa and in Indochina, there is diplomatic progress. And in Central and South America, totalitarian forces still threaten to undermine the will of the people. We must keep democracy on the march. And we're faced with change and the potential for change all over the world. And it's up to us to guarantee that the United States remains an engaged power for positive change.

In another era, the Secretary of State's role was largely confined to matters of war and peace. Today's world is much more complex than that—more dangerous, too. Today's Secretary of State must be prepared to work with our allies to solve such global threats as the international narcotics trade, terrorism, the degradation of the world's environment, and the economic distress of developing countries. And that's why I chose James Baker. He's savvy; he's sensitive; he's tough—a rare combination, indeed. And so, Jim, you've got a big job ahead of you, leading; coming up with bold, new initiatives; helping all of us fulfill the President's special role in foreign policy. We will also try to restore bipartisanship to foreign policy. It will be a bipartisanship based on trust, open communication, and consistency of action.

This is a time for America to reach out and take the lead, not merely react. And this is a time for America to move forward confidently and cautiously, not retreat. As the freest and the fairest and the most powerful democracy on the face of the Earth, we must continue to shine as a beacon of liberty, beacon of justice, for all the people of the world.

And those of you who are here today—Jim Baker's family, closest friends—know something that many other people will soon learn for themselves: Jim Baker will be a great Secretary of State.

Jim, congratulations! The floor is yours.

Secretary Baker. Mr. President, Barbara,

Mr. Vice President, Mr. Speaker, Mr. Chief Justice, distinguished Members of the Congress, my friends—most of whom are relatives—[*laughter*]—I am truly honored and privileged to stand before you today. Many of you have come a long distance to be here, and as you mentioned, Mr. President, you and I have come a long distance together. I hope to continue to merit your confidence. I know I will continue to enjoy our friendship. One other thing: I hope that in foreign policy we're going to make a better team than we oftentimes did on the tennis courts in Texas. [*Laughter*]

Ladies and gentlemen, the taking of an oath is always a solemn moment. Yet I cannot help but think that there will be even more solemn moments to follow, because it's been my experience for 8 years here now in Washington that after the swearing-in, sooner or later, comes the swearing at. [*Laughter*]

Mr. President, through your choice and the Senate's consent, I will occupy an office that dates from the infancy of our Republic. Over the last few weeks, I've learned a lot about the job. I find the more I learn about it the more humble I become. Yet mixed with that humility is a pride—not in myself but in our great country.

One of his statutory duties of the Secretary of State is to be the custodian of the Great Seal of the United States. We're all pretty familiar with the great eagle holding the olive branches—but also holding the arrows. There's a reverse side to that seal, however, that interests me. And on it is an unfinished pyramid. And on the bottom, a Latin inscription which means, "A new order of the ages." It's dated 1776. To me this expresses our forefathers' conviction that our country offers something new. Our Constitution, our democracy is a new order of human activity. And the unfinished pyramid is a symbol of strength, and it's a symbol of continuity.

America rests on the broadest possible base which, of course, is the contribution of every American. But the work of America—to perfect our society, to strengthen and extend freedom—is really never finished. So, as I stand here today, very grateful to you, Mr. President, I recognize that we are entering a new era of international relations. One that's filled with more than its share of promise, but perhaps more than its share of perils as well. I also recognize that our country is ever new in our capacity to meet the challenge and to advance the cause of freedom.

I enter this office secure in the knowledge that under your leadership, Mr. President, and with the support of the Congress and the support of the American people we can continue successfully what we began two centuries ago.

Thank you very, very much.

Note: The President spoke at 5:02 p.m. in the East Room at the White House.

Remarks at the Swearing-in Ceremony for Elizabeth H. Dole as Secretary of Labor

January 30, 1989

The President. Well, first, my respects to the former Secretaries of Labor who are here. Secretary Usery I know is here and Secretary McLaughlin, Secretary Brock, and I hope I'm not missing others—maybe they're there. So, I bid welcome to all of you, certainly to our new Secretary Elizabeth Dole and her mother and others that are here with us today—certainly to her husband, Bob Dole, who is with us up here. And, Reverend, thank you, sir, for those lovely, lovely words of prayer. Actually, I've been planning to come over to the Labor Department since last year to play it safe. I figured if I won the election I want to be here for Elizabeth's swearing-in, and if I lost the election I'd come by to fill out an unemployment form. [*Laughter*]

But I've come here to introduce the new Secretary of Labor, something that I did back in 1985, when Bill Brock took his office, which he did so well. And then last year, I was a guest of Ann McLaughlin here in the building. So, I have some familiarity with your work. I'd be remiss if I—as I look around this crowd—if I didn't single out Lane Kirkland and say how pleased I am that he's here to welcome our new Secretary, too. You've heard of Elizabeth Dole. [*Laughter*] She obviously will be my top adviser on labor issues per se. And I will also call upon her advice as counsel, as a key policy adviser on my economic team, because, indeed, the economic side of the labor issue is tremendously important.

To the people of this Department: You do touch the lives of virtually every American. And if at times you feel like you're taken for granted, let me just say whether you're the newest clerk-typist who just started or whether, like Jim Taylor—[*laughter*]. Now, where is Jim? Is he here? There he is, right there. You've got to see this guy. He's been here since the days of Secretary Frances Perkins—[*laughter*]—and it looks like he's still running about 10 miles a day, too. [*Laughter*]

Mr. Taylor. It's my second wind.

The President. That's good. But there's something about Jim's being here and new people, as well, to show the continuity of this Department. But let me just say sometimes, I expect, you wonder if people care. I want you to know that this President does not take you for granted and never will. And when people need you, you have been there. And what you do in the Labor Department is a good example of the many different ways in which government serves the American people. From enforcing child labor laws to protecting retirement pension rights, from job training to workers compensation, you look out for the working people of America.

And I want this administration to be about working people. Part of that will come from excellence and responsiveness in government. Part of that will be holding the line on taxes so working people, like you and the people you serve, can keep more of the money that you earn. Part of it will be a new voluntarism: people helping people. And I know a great many of you on your own time do work for your churches and in your communities and for charities. And I want to thank you, and I want to encourage everybody to be involved in this kind of work. From long talks with Elizabeth Dole, I know of her commitment to this whole concept of American helping American.

I believe in government service. I believe that it plays a vital role. But it must complement individual service. And nothing can replace personal commitment, both in our jobs and in our private lives. Many people look to you, the people in government, to do all things and solve all problems. Well, I think as a people we need to renew our sense of commitment, to take greater responsibility not only for ourselves but for one another. John Kennedy challenged us to ask ourselves what we could do for our country. And let us also each day ask: What can I do for another person? How can I make someone else's load a little lighter? How can I help to go a little farther? How can I be a friend to someone lonely or a comfort to someone in pain? Each of us can make this a kinder and gentler nation just by the way we treat one another each day.

I believe in government that is excellent and people who are compassionate. I think of the mine safety experts from this Department who after the Mexican earthquake were able, with their special skills to find people—still alive—who had been trapped under the rubble. But I also think of the secretary who after a day at the office takes that time to volunteer and help a child in the neighborhood learn how to read.

Now, the position of Secretary of Labor is a very important one, and our outgoing Secretary, Ann McLaughlin, certainly left big shoes to fill. All of you have been doing an excellent job in so many ways, and there's a lot to feel good about on the labor front. The economy is growing, producing jobs and opportunity. Those of you handling unemployment claims can see those rolls going down, and I want to keep it that way with sound economic policies.

But there are important tasks that lie ahead, and I don't think that the working people could hope to have a greater champion than Elizabeth Dole. She is smart. She is effective. She cares deeply about people.

You know, earlier in her career she worked as a lawyer. Her first case—not exactly profound, nor did it reach the Supreme Court—[*laughter*]—was to defend a fellow accused of annoying animals in the zoo. [*Laughter*] He was charged with, among other things, patting a lion. [*Laughter*] Elizabeth won the case—[*laughter*]—arguing that "without the lion in court as a witness there was no way to tell whether or not he was annoyed by that." [*Laughter*]

Secretary Dole. How did you find out about that?

The President. So, you can see that early on she made a career out of standing up for the little fellow against the lion. [*Laughter*] And at the Federal Trade Commission, and again at the White House, she showed real leadership and effectiveness. And in her 4½ years in the Cabinet, she distinguished herself. She was our longest serving Secretary in the Department of Transportation and certainly one of the best. And she took the lead on transportation safety, and she made a valuable contribution to her country—to our country. And I know that she will do a great job over here working with all of you.

America faces important challenges as we prepare the work force for tomorrow. There will be jobs in abundance, but we'll have to make sure that our workers have the skills that they need to fill those jobs with excellence. We have a new generation of workers, a new generation of families, who are finding new ways of balancing the responsibilities of the workplace and the home. And there are new competitive forces in the world economy that demand a commitment to excellence from every American worker so we can continue to lead America into the next century.

I can think of no one better qualified to head the Department of Labor during this exciting challenge than Elizabeth Dole. And, Elizabeth, it will be a great pleasure to have you in my Cabinet. And now, we're going to watch you take the oath of office one more time. Congratulations!

[*At this point, Secretary Dole was sworn in.*]

Secretary Dole. Thank you very much, ladies and gentlemen. What a joy to see you all here today. Mr. President, thank you for your gracious remarks, for your expression of confidence, and for the opportunity to serve the most valuable resource this country has: its people—the American work force.

And as Secretary McLaughlin and Secretary Brock, Secretary Usery—all who made such enormous and positive contributions to our nation—to Lane Kirkland and other leaders of labor who are here today; to our Members of Congress, who have been kind enough to take time to join us; to my minister, Edward Bauman; my Harvard law classmate, Chief Judge Judith Rogers; and to each of you—my family; my husband, of course; my friends; my coworkers and colleagues—I just thank you—a heartfelt thanks for joining me in an occasion that, of course, is very special to me today.

Like you, Mr. President, I have built my life on the ideal of public service. And this opportunity represents to me much more than a job or a career choice; rather, it's a personal commitment akin to a special calling. The mission of the Department of Labor is well-known and very clear: to foster, promote, and to develop the welfare of working men and women. How we define and fulfill that mission will help determine America's place in the 21st century. The policies, programs, and regulatory responsibilities of this Department are front and center in assuring the continued growth of the American economy and a vital increase in our productivity and the ability of the United States to compete effectively on a global basis.

Demographic projections indicate that our work force will grow at a much slower pace than in the past. In a tight labor market, for American businesses to compete successfully abroad, they must first compete successfully for workers at home. This is good news for U.S. working men and women. It means that issues once defined as social problems will be dealt with more out of economic necessity. In tighter labor markets, employers cannot afford to discriminate. They can't afford to put workers at health and safety risk. In tighter labor markets, they cannot afford to ignore workers' obligations to family. Employers who do will simply lose out to employers who don't. Just a week ago, in my confirmation hearing, I stressed that the goal of the Department of Labor must be to coordinate a strategy of growth-plus; that's continued economic growth plus policies to help those for whom the jobs of the future are now out of reach because of the skills gap or because of family pressures or due to a lack of supportive policies.

With the talents of the outstanding civil servants of this Department, I believe that we can get the job done in five broad areas: first, ensuring that American workers are the world's best trained and most highly skilled, placing special emphasis on the disadvantaged; second, developing policies that make work and family complementary; third, establishing sound and comprehensive pension and retirement policies; fourth, seeing to it that the American workplace is as safe, as healthy, and as secure as we can possibly make it; and fifth, encouraging management and labor to continue to move beyond confrontation and conflict, to work together on behalf of interests held in common.

Ladies and gentlemen, we have a chance to fulfill a dream: that every person in America who wants a good job can have a good job if they have the proper skills. We don't have unlimited funds, which means we must make those funds we do have work for us. But it won't be enough to be efficient if we're not effective. If we think big, if we select the right goals, if we target our initiative, if we work smart—in short, if we redouble our efforts without duplicating our efforts—we can assure that all of our people get their foot on the first rung of that economic ladder. And what could be more effective in the war on drugs, alcoholism, crime, and poverty, than a good job?

The ideal of independence has always been one of the cornerstones of the American experience. And today we're here to celebrate the independence, the strength, the self-reliance, and the sense of purpose that only meaningful work can provide.

What a joy it was for me this morning to hear a Job Corps graduate and Department of Labor employee, Lois Best, introduce the President of the United States. And to lay my hand and take my oath on a Bible held by Tony Bond, President of the Potomac Job Corps class. And I just might add, Tony, that that Bible is one of my most cherished possessions. It belonged to my grandmother who lived to within 2 weeks of her 100th birthday. Imagine that 2 more weeks, she would have been 100 years old. And she was a beautiful woman of great faith. To have so many students from Potomac and Chesapeake Job Corps Centers with us today brings an extra measure of excitement to Job Corps' 25th anniversary. With over 100 centers nationwide, this partnership of business, labor, and government has touched the lives of well over a million young men and women and made them part of a great American success story.

It's time to add new chapters to that success story. Two-thirds of the work force of the year 2000 is already on the job. Those trying to balance work and family deserve our support. Those who are older and who wish to work, but face barriers to reentry, we must enlist. Those who've been dislocated as jobs change, we must retrain. Our challenge will be to reach more of our people, whether young, old, disadvantaged, dual-career, or disabled, to give them the skills and the support they need so they can seize their share of prosperity and help to create more of it.

Yes, we have within our reach the fulfillment of a long-awaited dream: that every American who wants a good job can have a good job. But this is not a visionary idea; it's a practical challenge, a challenge for each of us in this Department. Our government's strength lies in the quality of those who do their jobs outside the headlines and without great fanfare. As John Gardner has said: "Democracy is measured not by its leaders doing extraordinary things but by its citizens doing ordinary things extraordinarily well." I was told, and I'm convinced, that Department of Labor employees are a strong team of men and women dedicated to doing their job extraordinarily well.

With their help, Mr. President, and by working with a vital new generation of young people like these Job Corps members, by working with the Congress, with labor, with schools, private enterprise and community groups, by coordinating carefully with other Federal departments and State and local government, by working together as people of indomitable purpose and collective will, we can build a culture of high expectations, and we can surely help fulfill those expectations. I'm confident that we can advance from the promise of full employment to the promise of fulfilling employment for every working man and woman in this great nation. And I believe there can be no higher calling as we approach the 21st century.

Thank you, each of you, for being here today, and God bless you all. Thank you.

Note: The President spoke at 10:12 a.m. in the Great Hall at the Department of Labor. In his remarks, he referred to Edward Bauman, pastor of Foundry United Methodist Church; Lane Kirkland, president of the American Federation of Labor-Congress of Industrial Organizations (AFL–CIO); and James F. Taylor, who had been an employee of the Department of Labor since 1941.

Remarks to the Crew of the U.S.S. *America* and Naval Shipyard Employees in Norfolk, Virginia

January 31, 1989

Admiral Dunleavy, thank you very much, sir, for that welcome to *America,* and thank all of you for that response. Admiral Trost, and to our Secretary of the Navy, and all involved in this wonderful day, I say thank you. I want to single out to Members of Congress who are here, many members of the Armed Services Committee, and others who've been strong backers—have a strong military for this country, and I'm delighted to see them here. I'm pleased to be on one of the greatest ships in the world, with a crew that knows the meaning of the words, "my ship, my country," the crew of the *America.*

You know, as an old carrier pilot, today is a very special day for me—the Admiral touching on that. I can't help thinking of the carrier I once sailed on, the U.S.S. *San Jacinto,* namesake of which is right next door here. Carriers weren't as big in those days. Technology was very different: narrow deck; slower planes; strictly visual contact with the LSO, the landing signal officer; no electronics. But some things stayed the same. And Admiral Dunleavy touched on it; and I've, as Vice President, had a chance to visit the fleet. And you can't help but sense that same spirit of camaraderie, devotion to duty, patriotism, service to country. We knew then, in those days, just as you know now, how much we owed to the men and women in the bases, in the shipyards. And from the day of the Revolutionary-era sloops to the most modern supercarriers, none have written a prouder chapter in the history of the United States Navy than the Norfolk Naval Base. All over the world, those who love the sea and the ships that sail on it know that Norfolk, or Hampton Roads, if you will, stands for excellence—a national treasure. And let me just say to all assembled: We are going to keep it that way!

My visit today is the final stop on what you might call an inaugural trip. For the past several days I've been visiting with the men and women who are my colleagues in service to our nation, from senior appointments in the administration to rank-and-file civil servants. Most are outstanding; most do a superb job. But still you might say, with no disrespect to others, that I've saved for last those whose service demands the most. And I mean you, the men and women who keep our ships and guard our shores, the men and women who serve with the Armed Forces of the United States.

In the months ahead, I'll be taking a great deal of time to talk about service, not service that is compelled but service that is given freely and openly, the service of the strong heart and the questing soul. I will speak about those who give their time and love to their communities, to help those who cannot fully help themselves. Long ago it was written that the quality of mercy is not strained, and I will speak of those who dedicate a portion of their lives to mercy for humanity. And I'll speak about you, in a way that every American knows and every man, woman and child in our land salutes. You stand here today setting an example for our nation's standard of service.

And let me start right now by recognizing one of your own, your Sailor of the Year, Aviation Ordinanceman 1st Class Joseph Robinson. Joseph was awarded this honor for two reasons. First, for his contributions to the running of this ship, but Joseph has also been recognized for his contributions to his community, where he helped establish a Neighborhood Watch—called it a watch program and devoted over 100 hours to its success. Now, Joseph is right here, and if you'll come forward, sir, I'd be proud to shake your hand and present you with a letter of commendation. Congratulations!

What a wonderful example for us all. All of you keep the peace on the frontiers of freedom around the world. And in every corner of the globe, millions recognize you, and the flag you carry is their symbol of hope. And, yes, wherever you go, you take America and all it represents with you; and you do it with a pride and dedication that few have ever matched. I know some say that it's just a job. But when a sailor must put to sea for 6 months or more at a time and come home to find that a child who could barely crawl, can walk and say a few words, that's more than a job—that is service and, more importantly, sacrifice. When a soldier spends long hours on cold night's sentry duty at the DMZ or at Checkpoint Charlie in Berlin, he's not just filling a job, but he's answering the call of service. And the mechanic who inspects the plane's engine or ship's power plant one last time and makes double and triple sure that every screw, every hose, every weld is as it should be, that mechanic is dedicating himself or herself not simply to a job but to a concept of service to country that is the highest in the world. Around the world, others have seen and know what your dedication to service means.

You remember, maybe, last year the Soviet Union's top military man at the time, Marshal Akhromeyev, visited the United States. He spent a day on a carrier, not unlike yours, as it went through exercises in these waters. And he visited installations across our nation. And he saw much of the amazing weaponry and machinery in our arsenal, and when he finally came to visit the White House, he let it be known that he was impressed. And what most impressed him was not our miraculous technology or incredible firepower but the enlisted men and women that he had met on these tours. He couldn't believe that we gave our enlisted men and women jobs that only officers would be permitted to handle in his own military. He couldn't believe the obvious dedication of America's enlisted men and women to their jobs, their knowledge of the machinery they handled and their readiness and ability to answer questions. In short, he couldn't believe your dedication to service.

I know you've heard it from your parents. Those of you who are married have heard it from your husbands or wives and from your children; but it goes from everyone across the country. Let me just say that we are all very, very proud of you and of the job you're doing. In the years ahead, I want to make sure that those who build our ships, planes, and weapons live up to the standards of service and dedication and duty that this crew and this base has set.

I've been inside a submerged submarine while depth charges were going off all around it. And I know what it's like to hear the vessel strain and shake and pray to God that the people in charge of buying and building cared as much about the vessel as you do. And I believe that the overwhelming majority of procurement officers and defense contractors do care that much. And I am determined to make sure that every single one of them does. My message to them will be just this simple: Don't think it's just anyone out there. Think it's your son or daughter and remember that their lives depend on the things you make. And if you're not ready to care that much and work that hard, you are not ready to do business with the United States Government.

Let me give you an example: cost overruns. Overruns didn't start just yesterday. The first dry dock ever built for our Navy is still operating, I'm told, not far from here, in this yard. And it was finished more than a century and a half ago. And the actual final cost was three times the original estimate. But even if overruns are not new, they are still wrong and hurt the national security, particularly when budgets are tight. We want tighter controls and higher standards in weapons procurement, and we will get tighter controls and higher standards in weapons procurement. You deserve the very best equipment and weapons. You are getting them most of the time now, and we're determined that you will get them all of the time.

And one other thing: I am determined to expand the national consensus that is necessary for proper support for our nation's defense. I'll do this because the first bulwark of our national defense is our national will. And if our will is ruptured, our ship of state cannot sail, or at least sail safely. I firmly believe that the vital first step to broadening our national consensus on defense is to wring the last drop of waste and mismanagement out of the way we buy our weapons. And that's what we intend to do. It's what you might call my bond to you. When a family sends a son or husband to sea or to boot camp or to flight school to defend our nation, they are making a sacrifice, and it is a great and noble sacrifice. Think of all the good all those sacrifices added up to together and what they have meant around the world in the last few years.

When the record of our time is finally written, I hope it will be the story of the final triumph of peace and freedom throughout the globe, the story of the sunrise in the day of mankind's age-old aspirations. And on that day, "Who were the heroes?"—generations to come will ask. "Who drove the chariots of fire across the sky? Who brought the day to the Earth?" And the answer will be you. During the next 4 years, I will not be just your Commander in Chief but your friend. And together we will work to spin the gossamer thread of human dreams into a sturdy fabric of peace that will last for generations to come.

Thank you for your incredible service to this, the greatest, freest, and most wonderful country on the face of the Earth. God bless you all.

Note: The President spoke at 11:01 a.m. on the deck of the U.S.S. "America." He was introduced by Adm. Richard Dunleavy, Commander of Naval Air Forces, Atlantic Fleet. In his opening remarks, the President referred to Adm. Carlisle A.H. Trost, Chief of Naval Operations, and Secretary of the Navy William L. Ball III.

Message on the Observance of National Afro-American (Black) History Month, February 1989

February 1, 1989

Since 1976, the month of February has been designated National Black History Month, a time for all Americans to celebrate the rich heritage of Afro-Americans and their contributions to our nation.

Despite first slavery and then segregation, Afro-Americans have overcome seemingly insurmountable odds to be at the cutting edge of change and progress in American society. From the winning of Independence—when Crispus Attucks gave his life in the Boston Massacre and Benjamin Banneker helped draw the plans for our nation's capital—to the present day, Black Americans have played a vital role in the development of the United States. One thinks of Dr. Daniel Hale Williams performing the first successful heart surgery and of George Washington Carver revolutionizing southern agriculture with his countless innovations.

There have been so many more. This month gives us all a chance to reflect on how much Afro-Americans have contributed, a chance to learn from the past in order to look confidently toward a new century, with a commitment to lasting harmony between the races and a bright future for Americans of every background.

Barbara joins me in commending all of you for your observance of Black History Month 1989, and in sending you our best wishes.

GEORGE BUSH

Nomination of Kenneth Winston Starr To Be Solicitor General of the United States
February 1, 1989

The President today announced his intention to nominate Kenneth Winston Starr to be Solicitor General of the United States, Department of Justice. He would succeed Charles Fried.

Since 1983 Judge Starr has been a judge of the U.S. Court of Appeals for the District of Columbia. Prior to this he was Counselor to the Attorney General at the Department of Justice, 1981–1983. He was an associate partner with Gibson, Dunn & Crutcher in Washington, DC, 1977–1981, and a law clerk to Chief Justice Warren E. Burger of the U.S. Supreme Court in Washington, DC, 1975–1977. From 1974 to 1975, Judge Starr was an associate with Gibson, Dunn & Crutcher in Los Angeles, CA.

Judge Starr graduated from George Washington University (B.A., 1968), Brown University (M.A., 1969), and Duke University (J.D., 1973). He was born July 21, 1946, in Vernon, TX. He is married and has two children.

Continuation of John W. Vessey, Jr., as Special Presidential Emissary to Hanoi for POW/MIA Affairs
February 1, 1989

The President has asked General John W. Vessey, Jr., USA, Ret., to continue in his role as Special Presidential Emissary to Hanoi for POW/MIA Affairs. General Vessey has served in this capacity since being named to the position by President Reagan in February 1987.

Beginning with his initial visit to Hanoi in August 1987, General Vessey's efforts have resulted in substantial progress in resolving this pressing humanitarian issue and ending the uncertainty for the families of our missing in Southeast Asia. The President is pleased that General Vessey has agreed to continue to serve his country in this position of great importance to all of us.

Remarks at the Annual National Prayer Breakfast
February 2, 1989

My special thanks to Bob Stump and Doug Coe, to our honored guests throughout this country and from our foreign lands, and it is a pleasure for Barbara and me to be here once again.

There is no greater peace than that which comes from prayer and no greater fellowship than to join in prayer with others. And coming to the prayer breakfast is, for us at least, like coming home. The

Lord works in mysterious ways. There is nothing mysterious, however, about His priorities. I'm the one with the laryngitis, and Sandy Patti is the one that lifted our spirits with that magnificent voice, clear as the finest crystal. We're grateful to her. And the Lord works in very mysterious ways, but I wonder why it is that under the protocol sense of things I always have to follow my friend Al Simpson. [*Laughter*]

Let us all thank the Lord for having granted us this day, making it possible for us to spend this time together. Billy Graham, my dear friend, tells me that when he was a boy living on a farm in North Carolina one of his jobs was milking cows. And one day he was sent out to milk one of their cows named Brindle, a cow he'd never milked before. And he was told that it was a gentle cow, that it would be very cooperative. When he sat down on the stool to milk the cow, she switched her tail, slapped him in the face, nearly put his eye out, a few minutes later kicked the bucket all the way across the barn, and then tried to kick him. And at that point, he began to wonder if the person who described this kind and gentle cow had ever sat down next to her in the barn. [*Laughter*] And I've thought of that story in the light of my request for America to become a kinder and gentler nation. It's one thing to request it, and it's another thing to see it actually happen. And maybe a lot of folks out there, cynics, are thinking, well, if you people in Washington will stop trying to milk us, we'll stop kicking. [*Laughter*]

But we're facing some serious opportunities and some great opportunities in our country—tough problems and great opportunities. And I believe that a wonderful resource in dealing with them is prayer—not just prayer for what we want but prayer for what is in the heart of God for us individually and as a nation. And shouldn't we also remember, with all that we have to be grateful for, to pause each day to offer a prayer of thanksgiving. All of us should not attempt to fulfill the responsibilities we now have without prayer and a strong faith in God. Abraham Lincoln said: "I've been driven many times to my knees by the overwhelming conviction that I have nowhere else to go." Surely he was not the first President, certainly not the last, to realize that.

It's not just Presidents. I heard about a little boy whose elderly grandmother came to live with them for the winter. And the first day the little boy played hard inside the house, and he wanted to turn the heat down. But grandmother insisted on keeping it high. And when he opened the windows, she closed them. And for several days it went on like this, up and down, back and forth, with the little boy too hot and the grandmother too cold. After about a week, the little boy knelt beside his bed one night and prayed, "Lord, bless mother and daddy, and make it hot for grandmother." [*Laughter*]

Well, I suppose there may be some people in Washington, around the country, who have already begun to pray, "Make it hot for George." [*Laughter*] Those prayers will be answered over time. Be patient. [*Laughter*] But I can also tell you from my heart that I freely acknowledge my need to hear and to heed the voice of Almighty God. I began my Inaugural Address with a prayer out of a deep sense of need and desire of God's wisdom in the decisions we face. And if we're to walk together toward a more caring, more generous America, let us all share in paving the way with prayer.

Thank you all, and God bless you.

Note: The President spoke at 9:18 a.m. in the International Crystal Ballroom at the Washington Hilton Hotel. In his remarks, he referred to Representative Bob Stump; Doug Coe, an associate of the National Prayer Breakfast Movement; gospel singer Sandy Patti; Senator Alan K. Simpson; and evangelist Billy Graham.

Remarks Following Discussions With Prime Minister Noboru Takeshita of Japan
February 2, 1989

The President. Mr. Prime Minister, ladies and gentlemen, let me begin by expressing once again on behalf of the American people the condolences on the passing of Emperor Showa, a most gentle man of great learning. And I look forward to calling on the new Emperor when I visit Japan later this month.

It has been a pleasure and honor for Barbara and me to welcome you, Mr. Prime Minister, Mr. Takeshita, to the White House. You are one of our first official visitors, and this reflects the importance I place on the relations between our two countries, the strength of our nations' ties, and the promise that our relationship holds for the future of the world.

Two weeks ago, here in Washington, the United States conducted a ritual that spoke of both continuity and change. For the 41st time in 200 years, the United States swore in a new President. And in the transition from one President to the next, we Americans reaffirmed the strength of our democracy and our commitment to values on which it was built. Japan and the world can count on the United States to continue to work for peace, democracy, freedom, and justice around the world. The scope of America's vision is global, and we will continue to shoulder the obligations that belong to a global power.

Continuity will also be the mark of relations between the United States and Japan. On occasion, we may have differences, but these are the differences of friends. And in the last 40 years, our two nations have been truly close friends. The peace and prosperity we both enjoy today are among the fruits of that friendship. Simply put, we respect one another. We need one another, and we will continue to work together for the good of our peoples and of all humanity.

During this visit, the Prime Minister and I worked on the continuing business of the friendship between our countries. We confirmed that the treaty of mutual security and cooperation is the foundation of our relationship. I noted the importance of allies assuming greater responsibilities in the cause of peace. The Prime Minister and I agreed that these responsibilities take many forms. In this regard, I applaud Japan's pledge to make further significant increases in Overseas Development Assistance programs.

At the same time, we believe that the most powerful engine for economic development and growth—in fact, the only engine that works—is the entrepreneur, large and small. And entrepreneurship is a product not of massive aid packages but of free and open economies that do not carry crushing burdens of taxation and regulation and that maintain the rule of law, including contract and property law.

Along these lines, we agreed on the importance of supporting democracy and sustained growth and reform in the Philippines. Toward this end, we pledge to make every effort to launch the Multilateral Assistance Initiative for the Philippines this year.

The Prime Minister and I reviewed the progress our nations have achieved in bringing our economies into better balance and in further opening our markets to each other's goods and services. We also recognize the need for continued policy efforts in these areas. The Prime Minister reaffirmed Japan's determination to promote strong domestic growth and structural adjustments. And I told him that I am determined to reduce our budget deficit.

In the area of multilateral cooperation, we agreed that we would continue to coordinate policies through established settings, especially the economic summit. We will look forward to the next summit meeting, which will be held in Paris. We also agreed on the importance for continued global prosperity of a successful Uruguay round. And we agreed on the importance of frequent consultation at all levels on economic issues.

All in all, our talks were positive and

forthright, befitting close allies. The Prime Minister and I first met some time ago, and this week's meetings have helped us become even better acquainted. We've laid the groundwork for close cooperation, as we deal with the issues and the opportunities of the last decade of the 20th century.

We're glad you came our way, sir.

The Prime Minister. Thank you, Mr. President, for your heartwarming remarks. Mr. President, I wish to convey on behalf of the Japanese people my deepest appreciation to the Government and people of the United States for their expression of sympathy and condolences on the demise of Emperor Showa. The people of Japan are also deeply touched that you and Mrs. Bush will attend the funeral ceremony.

Mr. President, looking back upon the 43 years since the end of the war, I am reminded anew of the friendship and cooperation the American people have consistently extended to us through the years. Mr. President, I am truly grateful that you have so graciously invited us to Washington at this busy time, so soon after your inauguration.

I appreciate the remarks you have just made on the thoughts we shared in our first meeting. Our first meeting was truly promising in opening the perspective into our future. I believe it marked a new start for U.S.-Japan cooperation, which will serve to help ensure peace and prosperity for the world, as we move towards the 21st century. Fortunately, the basis of our cooperative relationship is firm and sound. The Japan-U.S. security arrangement upon which this relationship rests has never been better. The successful solutions we have been able to achieve regarding bilateral economic issues have demonstrated the resilience of our relationship. Thus, through a dialog, issues between our two countries can be resolved.

In sustaining noninflationary growth of the international economy and in reducing external imbalances in our economies, the President and I shared the view that macroeconomic policy coordination is of crucial importance. I stated to the President that the Japanese economy will continue to grow through strong domestic demand, that imports are expected to continue to increase, and that structure adjustment efforts will be further enhanced. The President stated that he will make determined efforts to reduce the budget deficit.

The world faces a number of challenges, but is rich with promises. In your words: The new breeze is blowing. Mr. President, you and I share the conviction that now is the time for Japan and the United States to further strengthen policy coordination and to joint endeavors in order to create a better world. We will consult closely on our policies toward the Soviet Union, which offers new challenges and opportunities for East-West relations. We will work together to ensure peace and prosperity in Asia, the Middle East, Central and South America, and other parts of the world. We will work together to strengthen the free trading system and agree to cooperate closely for the progress of the Uruguay round negotiations.

No nation can substitute the United States as the leader of the democracies around the world. I look to you, Mr. President, for wise and firm leadership, and you will have my full support. For my part, I will continue to pursue my diplomatic goal of Japan contributing more to the world.

Japan and the United States have a number of common tasks ahead. Together we must take those initiatives to solve the many problems facing our world. Our meeting today confirmed that if our two peoples work together, hand in hand, there is nothing we cannot achieve.

Thank you very much.

Note: The President spoke at 1:30 p.m. at the South Portico of the White House. The Prime Minister spoke in Japanese, and his remarks were translated by an interpreter. Earlier, the President and the Prime Minister met in the Oval Office and then attended a luncheon in the Residence.

Nomination of Richard R. Burt for the Rank of Ambassador While Serving as United States Negotiator for Strategic Nuclear Arms
February 2, 1989

The President today announced his intention to nominate Richard R. Burt for the rank of Ambassador during his tenure of service as United States Negotiator for Strategic Nuclear Arms. He would succeed Stephen R. Hanmer. Since 1985 Mr. Burt has been Ambassador to the Federal Republic of Germany. Prior to this he was Assistant Secretary of State for European and Canadian Affairs, 1983–1985. He was Director of the Bureau of Politico-Military Affairs at the Department of State, 1981–1982. From 1977 to 1980, he served as a correspondent for the New York Times in Washington, DC. He was also assistant director at the International Institute for Strategic Studies in London, England, 1975–1977.

Mr. Burt graduated from Cornell University (B.A., 1969) and Fletcher School of Law and Diplomacy (M.A., 1972). He was born February 3, 1947, in Sewell, Chile. He is married and has one child.

Nomination of Ivan Selin To Be an Under Secretary of State
February 2, 1989

The President today announced his intention to nominate Ivan Selin to be Under Secretary of State for Management. He would succeed Ronald I. Spiers.

Dr. Selin is the founder and chairman of the board for American Management Systems, Inc., a computer systems, services, and consulting firm. From 1986 to 1988, Dr. Selin was a member of the advisory board on the U.S.S.R. and Eastern Europe at the National Academy of Sciences. Prior to this he was a member of the board on telecommunications and computer applications at the National Academy of Sciences, 1985–1988.

Dr. Selin graduated from Yale University (B.E., 1957; M.S., 1958; Ph.D., 1960). In 1962 he also received a degree from the Université de Paris.

Nomination of Edith E. Holiday To Be General Counsel of the Department of the Treasury
February 2, 1989

The President today announced his intention to nominate Edith E. Holiday to be General Counsel for the Department of the Treasury. She would succeed Mark Sullivan III.

Since 1988 Ms. Holiday has been an Assistant Secretary (Public Affairs and Public Liaison) of the Department of the Treasury and Counselor to the Secretary. Prior to this she was chief counsel and national financial and operations director for the Bush-Quayle '88 Presidential campaign and served as director of operations for George Bush for President. She was also special counsel for the Fund for America's Future and Executive Director for the Quadrennial Commission on Executive, Legislative, and Judicial Salaries, 1984–1985. Ms. Holiday practiced law with the firm of Dow, Lohnes & Albertson, 1983–1984 and with the firm of Reed, Smith, Shaw & McClay, 1977–1983. She also served as legislative director for then-U.S. Senator Nicholas F. Brady.

Ms. Holiday graduated from the University of Florida (B.S., 1974; J.D., 1977). She was born February 14, 1952, in Middletown, OH. She is married to Terrence B. Adamson and currently resides in Atlanta, GA.

Nomination of Richard Thomas McCormack To Be an Under Secretary of State

February 2, 1989

The President today announced his intention to nominate Richard Thomas McCormack to be Under Secretary of State for Economic and Agricultural Affairs. He would succeed Allen Wallis.

Since 1985 Ambassador McCormack has been the Permanent Representative of the United States to the Organization of American States. Prior to this he was Assistant Secretary of State for Economic and Business Affairs, 1983–1985. He has also served as a Consultant on International Economics at the Department of State, 1981–1982.

Ambassador McCormack graduated from Georgetown University (M.A., 1963) and the University of Fribourg in Switzerland (Ph.D., 1971). He was born March 6, 1941, in Bradford, PA. He is married and has two children.

Nomination of Robert Michael Kimmitt To Be an Under Secretary of State

February 2, 1989

The President today announced his intention to nominate Robert Michael Kimmitt to be Under Secretary of State for Political Affairs. He would succeed Michael Hayden Armacost.

Since October 1987 Mr. Kimmitt has been a partner with the law firm of Sidley & Austin in Washington, DC. Prior to this he was General Counsel for the Department of the Treasury, 1985–1987. He was Executive Secretary and General Counsel of the National Security Council at the White House, 1983–1985, and a member of the National Security Council, 1978–1983. In March 1988 Mr. Kimmitt was appointed by President Reagan to a 6-year term as a United States member of the Panel of Arbitrators of the International Centre for the Settlement of Investment Disputes.

Mr. Kimmitt graduated from West Point in 1969. He served in the 173d Airborne Brigade in Vietnam, earning three Bronze Stars, the Purple Heart, the Air Medal, and the Vietnamese Cross of Gallantry. He is currently a lieutenant colonel in the Army Reserve. Mr. Kimmitt was born December 19, 1947. He is married, has five children, and resides in Arlington, VA.

Nomination of Reginald Bartholomew To Be an Under Secretary of State

February 2, 1989

The President today announced his intention to nominate Reginald Bartholomew to be Under Secretary of State for Coordinating Security Assistance Programs. He would succeed Edward J. Derwinski.

Since 1986 Ambassador Bartholomew has been the United States Ambassador to Spain. Prior to this he served as the United States Ambassador to Lebanon. He was Director of the Bureau of Politico-Military Affairs at the Department of State in 1977 and was detailed to the National Security Council at the White House, 1977–1979. From 1974 to 1977, he served as Deputy Director of Policy Planning Staff at the Department of State.

Ambassador Bartholomew graduated from Dartmouth College (B.A., 1958) and the University of Chicago (M.A., 1960). He was born February 17, 1936, in Portland, ME. He is married and has four children.

Nomination of Morris Berthold Abram To Be United States Representative to the European Office of the United Nations
February 2, 1989

The President today announced his intention to nominate Morris Berthold Abram to be the Representative of the United States of America to the European Office of the United Nations, with the rank of Ambassador. He would succeed Joseph Carlton Petrone.

Since 1970 Mr. Abram has been a partner in the firm of Paul, Weiss, Rifkind, Wharton & Garrison in New York City. Mr. Abram has been the chairman of the National Conference on Soviet Jewry, 1983 to present. From 1984 to 1986, he was Vice Chairman of the Commission on Civil Rights. He served as a member of the President's Commission for Study of Ethics in Medicine and Biomedicine and Behavioral Research, 1979–1983, and Chairman of the Moreland Act Commission on Nursing Homes and Residential Facilities, 1975–1976. From 1968 to 1970, Mr. Abram was president of Brandeis University in Waltham, MA.

Mr. Abram graduated from the University of Georgia (A.B., 1938), the University of Chicago (J.D., 1940), Oxford University (Rhodes Scholar) (B.A., 1948; M.A., 1953), and Davidson College (LL.D., 1972). He was born June 19, 1918. He is married and has five children.

Remarks on the Savings and Loan Crisis
February 3, 1989

The President. While we have the quick exposure here, let me just thank you all, Mr. Speaker, Leader Mitchell, Dole, Bob Michel, for coming down here. This is a listening session. We've got a big problem in this savings and loan. There are no easy answers and no worrying about the blame—plenty to go around. I want to see the problem solved. We've had a lot of consultation up on the Hill, and good consultation. And Treasury will come, I think, to meet me tomorrow to present their views, but they're not being presented here with this stacked deck. We need ideas, and if we're overlooking something, we want to know what it is.

But I think we all agree that it's time to get on with the problem. And so, what I wanted to do this morning is simply ask your advice and listen. And whatever we come up with will not be popular. And I expect then whatever you come up with will not be popular, but we've got to get on and get the problem solved. And I appreciate your coming down here early to discuss this today, and then I'll be meeting, as I say, some more today. And then tomorrow I think we have more final recommendations. I'll go out with it publicly probably early next week—I think that's the plan—and see where we go from there.

But, Speaker, if you can talk, you're entitled a rebuttal. [*Laughter*]

Speaker Wright. I'm not sure, Mr. President, that any rebuttal is necessary. We're here to listen, and we're here to join with you in trying to find some creative solution to a very serious problem.

Majority Leader Mitchell. I think the Speaker has expressed it for all of us, Mr. President. We want to work with you. This is a serious problem for the country; it's not just for us. We've got to do the best we can to come up with the fairest, most efficient way to solve it.

The President. Before we break up here to start on our consultations, let me say—and I think I speak for everybody here—that the safety of those deposits is guaranteed, will continue to be guaranteed, and that there should be no feeling around the country that some solution will do anything to diminish the credit of the United States being behind the deposits in the FSLIC [Federal Savings and Loan Insurance Corporation], FDIC [Federal Deposit Insurance Corporation], whatever it is. And I thought I'd just take this occasion to make that statement. Thank you all very much, and now let's all go to work.

Note: The President spoke at 8:04 a.m. in the Cabinet Room at the White House, prior to a meeting with congressional leaders. In his opening remarks, the President referred to Jim Wright, Speaker of the House of Representatives; George J. Mitchell and Robert Dole, majority and minority leaders of the Senate, respectively; and Robert H. Michel, ranking minority member of the House of Representatives.

Remarks at the Swearing-in Ceremony for Robert A. Mosbacher as Secretary of Commerce
February 3, 1989

The President. Thank you for that warm welcome. This is a very special occasion for me because, as most—I'd say please be seated, but—[*laughter*]—I don't think that would go over too well back there. What a wonderful, wonderful turnout for our new Secretary. But this is a special occasion, Bob Mosbacher and I have been friends for a quarter of a century—more. And I trust his advice; I respect what he's accomplished in business. And I know he will be a very valuable member of our economic team.

It's also an honor for me to participate in this swearing-in in a hall that's named after another dear friend of mine: Mac Baldrige. He was a tremendous Secretary of Commerce, and I know he would have been so pleased to see that this Department, which meant so much to him, will be in such capable hands.

When what was then called the Department of Commerce and Labor, established back in 1903—Congressman Charles Cochran described what he believed were the ideal qualifications for the Secretary. He said: "Above everything, he should be a man of affairs, acquainted with the vast subject with which he must deal, vigilant, enterprising, resourceful, and possessed of the sagacity which distinguishes the American man of business from all others."

Well, ladies and gentlemen, those of you who know anything about Bob Mosbacher know that he fits that description to a tee. And he's a savvy international businessman, an entrepreneur who built his own extraordinarily successful business and kept it on solid footing even during tough economic times. He also is known as a world-class sailor—won international and national championships. And to use a sailing analogy, he will now take the helm at Commerce and help chart America's economic course into a new era of prosperity.

It's Bob's mission to foster, promote, and develop the foreign and domestic commerce of the United States, a mission that's easily stated, but not so easily executed. As Secretary, he will promote American exports aggressively, continue our support of R&D, research and development, operate an export control program balanced between safeguarding security and encouraging exports, responsibly manage our vast national fisheries resources, and play an important role in this administration's efforts to clean up the oceans and America's coastlines. I know that preserving and protecting the environment is a special concern of Secretary Mosbacher's. Bob will work with business to create innovative programs and achieve scientific breakthroughs in manufacturing, transportation, communications, and other areas to guarantee that the United States maintains its leadership role in the world marketplace.

Both Bob and I are committed to making America more competitive than ever before. Our businesses can compete with anyone, anywhere in the world, if we're given a fair chance. Our commitment to free and fair trade will enable us to ensure that our trading partners respect our right to compete in their marketplace, while they compete fairly in ours.

Bob has a big job ahead of him. But whether it's trade or tourism or NOAA or the Bureau of Standards, Minority Business Development, the Census—any of the important areas of this Department—I know that he has a great team behind him, willing to give 100 percent. And one of the reasons I wanted to come here to the Department is to express my confidence in those of you who have worked as careers for the Federal Government.

The growth of commerce, both nationally and internationally, is the key to guaranteeing that America's most productive and prosperous days are still ahead. As a fellow Texan said recently: "Bob Mosbacher is the right man to do the job that has to be done." So, I came over here to wish him well—wish all of you well.

Mr. Secretary, congratulations, good luck, and God bless you!

And now Secretary [of State] Baker will do the honors.

[*At this point, Secretary Mosbacher was sworn in.*]

Secretary Mosbacher. Mr. President, Secretary Baker, if I may digress for a second: two wonderful, wonderful Americans who this country is so proud of and so lucky to have, friends of over 30 years. Thank you, sir—and, of course, my family and, of course, all of us who are going to work together, fellow employees of the Department of Commerce. I look forward with great enthusiasm to addressing the challenges and opportunities the American people have in several vital, important walks of our national life.

Mr. President, on behalf of this Department of Commerce, we accept our mission. Of course, it's a mission—and a major objective of ours at this Department is to promote our economic growth and competitiveness. We must ensure that trade is a two-way street for American business by expanding overseas markets for top U.S. goods and services while ensuring fair competition through effective enforcement of our trade laws.

Another vitally important mission is to improve the beauty and quality of our oceans, shorelines, and estuaries. Our fine people in the National Oceanic and Atmospheric Administration—NOAA, as it's known to all of you and now many of us—are already working vigorously at cleaning up our oceans. But of course, even though they're working on this, more work can and must be done because we have been blessed with an abundance of beautiful natural resources, including our oceans, estuaries, our beaches, our shoreline; and we must do all in our power to preserve and protect these precious assets.

Third, as an old sailor, I know how vitally important it is to keep our weather forecasts accurate and our warnings early. You know, Mr. President, there are a lot of people in this country who view Willard Scott as our weatherman. [*Laughter*] But we in this Department know that NOAA is the bureau that serves as the provider of the meteorological data to the Nation's weathermen, and so, we are really your weathermen.

We must also enforce our national capability to develop the best in modern technology. We must pursue policies that will speed commercialization of technology. Our new technology administration will be in the forefront of this effort. Our colleagues in economic affairs must continue their diligent efforts to measure efficiently and accurately the successes and failings of our diverse economy. In the same vein, we must ensure an accurate and fair census in 1990.

A challenge? Sure, and a tough one. But to do anything less than to strive to succeed as never before would not be right.

Finally, let me say, Mr. President, you have given us—and to me and to all of us here—a special assignment that is near and dear to your heart. We know this. Specifically, we're going to strengthen the Minority Business Development Agency so that all Americans will have the fullest opportunity to participate and enjoy the great American dream. It's important, and it must happen.

I'm humbled by the challenges that lie before us and confident that together we will offer our hands to help achieve our President's goals. As Reverend Parker said: "If we work together, all is possible."

Again, my thanks to you, sir, to the family I love, and to all of you. Together we can do the job. God bless you.

Note: The President spoke at 10:40 a.m. in the Malcolm Baldrige Great Hall at the Department of Commerce. Reverend Diana Parker delivered the invocation.

Remarks at a White House Luncheon for Business Leaders
February 3, 1989

The President. Ladies and gentlemen, thank you very, very much for being with us today. Before I make some remarks, I just want to introduce you to some of the people with whom I'm working here in the White House, with whom a lot of you will be interacting one way or another.

I know you know our Secretary of Labor over here, Liddy Dole. Roger Porter is going to be doing a lot in our domestic policy. Over at this table is Bonnie Newman, who has got a major management responsibility in the White House. And Andy Card is the Deputy to the Chief of Staff. And Boyden Gray many of you have worked with in regulatory relief. He's the General Counsel to the President and is heading a lot of the issues as it relates to ethics. Steve Studdert over here and Dave Demarest are in our outreach and our communications end of things. General Scowcroft most of you know—I don't want to date him, but most of you know him from previous incarnations—[*laughter*]—is the national security adviser. Richard Breeden over here worked very closely with me in the past on regulatory matters. He's now wrestling with the savings and loan problem. So, if he looks discomforted, why, it wasn't the food. [*Laughter*] Gregg Petersmeyer at this table, here from Colorado, back in the White House after quite a few years absence, but he is handling this concept of voluntarism, national service. I can't see over here who we—oh, Marlin Fitzwater is our Press Secretary, and with him, Joe Hagin, fresh from Ohio, who is handling the scheduling. Michael Boskin is head of our Council of Economic Advisers. And Bobbie Kilberg, sitting over here, is part of our major outreach to the different communities. And Jim Cicconi is the Staff Secretary that keeps everything moving inside the White House. And of course, on my left here is John Sununu, our Chief of Staff.

And if I missed somebody, it's the glare. [*Laughter*] It's not that I don't know the names of the people with whom I work. [*Laughter*] But listen, I wanted to thank you all for being here. It's great to see so many old friends. Having made my living in the hydrocarbon business—that's a polite name for what's left of the oil business—[*laughter*]—I do have some appreciation of what some of you all face in business.

And today we're in the midst of a long

peacetime economic recovery. Productivity is up; real family income is up. A higher percentage—you know this litany—percentage of the work force at work than any time in history and a lot of job creation, better than Europe and Japan. So, I am very proud of what the business sector has accomplished. And we are the most prosperous and most generous and most productive Nation. But I would say that we've still got a long, long way to go, and we've got some big problems out there. But if we need a reminder of who we are, you can look around this room and see the creativity of business and see how you have added tremendously to the GNP of our country.

Lately we've been talking a lot publicly—the last couple of weeks—about ethics. And I need your help in establishing and then achieving the highest possible standards and then performance in the field of ethics. It isn't just government. I think we need to set the best possible example in corporate America, in the workplace itself, and then, certainly, in government service. We've got to do better in terms of eliminating conflicts of interest for those who serve. And we need to assemble a government that the people can be proud of: a government, to a large extent, already comprised, I'd say, of honorable men and women who share conviction that a public office is, indeed, a public trust.

So, my emphasis on ethical public service is not some fad or passing fancy. It's something that I would like to see our administration institutionalize as best we can. Having said that, I am concerned about the excesses. And I'm talking to some right here in this room. I don't think we ever want to make it so it's impossible for men and women who have accomplished something to come and serve because of perception—it might throw a conflict of interest out there. And so, as we try to achieve our standards now and as we try to codify these standards, I hope we can do it without discouraging men and women from coming to Washington to serve.

Last week, I appointed a bipartisan commission headed by former judge and now our Ambassador Malcolm Wilkey. Cochairman of that is Griffin Bell, who is favorably known to everybody in this room, a former great Attorney General of this country—to develop ethics reform proposals that are going to address all the branches of the Federal Government. And again, we welcome from the business community the advice and counsel on this effort.

Some of you have sent Boyden Gray, my General Counsel, your own codes of ethics and worked with him in this regard, and that's been very helpful to us. It's because some businesses are way out front on setting standards that I think will have good relevance for the Federal Government. We have to simultaneously assure that our public servants have the highest possible ethical standards at the same time we ensure that we don't create this bureaucratic quagmire that keep honorable men and women from serving. And this one, as I just mentioned, is not easy. It is a delicate balance.

The American people know that we're facing some very tough choices in the weeks and months ahead. I still feel that they want us to hold the line on taxes and that they want us to keep this economic engine going. They realize that that's mainly a function of the private sector. But we in government have a responsibility to see that we don't enact things that inadvertently slow down the economic engine of this country. I've got to have as a prime goal seeing the creation of more jobs, more growth. And so, next week we're going to have to come forward with some tough decisions when I send a budget message up there to the Congress a week from yesterday.

We want to keep this deficit heading downward. And I've heard from a lot of you here the importance of having what we send up there credible so that world markets will understand that this is for real. And if the world markets understand that it's for real—it doesn't have to happen overnight—then I think we're going to see a very salutary effect on interest rates. So, we want to keep the deficit heading downward. And I'm pledged, obviously, to that goal.

There's another thing about the people of this country. Americans have long been committed to helping people at home and abroad in achieving literacy, housing, and safety—a commitment that stems from our innate sense of fairplay as a people, innate sense of justice, if you will. So, there's more than altruism involved. And when I talk about a kinder and gentler nation, I realize that you cannot legislate kindness. The President can't sign an Executive order and decree that we have a gentle nation.

But the Presidency does provide an incomparable opportunity to set a tone, to lead a movement. And so, I wanted to ask all of you to do that which so many of you are already doing: Involve yourselves in this vast cooperative movement, unparalleled in magnitude, certainly unparalleled in its nobility of purpose. And I'm talking about the concept of voluntarism, the concept of national service. It's going to be a movement whose leadership extends from the South Lawn of the White House to the grassroots of America. But really, it's the other way around because it's the communities and it's neighbors that really have the line action on this concept—a movement that respects the dignity of the individual and that is steeped in the values that have made this country great for more than 200 years. And it is this spirit that de Tocqueville found when he looked at this country of neighbor helping neighbor that has made us decent and generous, more so, I'd say, than any other country. And if we can revitalize the embers of that spirit, we will be this kinder and gentler place to live.

And that's where many of you, as I say, have already starred. As I look around this room—and I'm not going to start singling out the examples that are represented here of your commitment to literacy or fighting drugs or whatever it is—and you can do it far better, far more effectively than the Federal Government in Washington, DC. The essence of our government, of course, a democracy of and for and by the people.

To be successful, our movement on national service has got to be exactly the same thing. And the challenges are great. Government, as I say, cannot do everything, certainly can't do it alone without the will of the people. It really can't do anything.

But we've opened here now an Office of National Service. Gregg Petersmeyer, under the Chief of Staff, has the lead on that. It will be in the White House. It will help lead the community and national service programs. We will not only build on what was known as the private sector initiatives, which President Reagan began and which many of you in this room were actively involved in, but, actively, I'll be seeking your leadership and involvement on specific initiatives; one, the Yes to America Foundation, Youth Entering Service, which I talked about last fall and which I'm determined to implement this winter.

I don't want the Federal Government getting in the way, incidentally, of the tens of thousands of volunteer programs that work effectively. I simply want to encourage more voluntarism. You know, each of us is shaped in life by little events or things that he or she encountered. And I remember 8 years ago—or maybe 10 now, campaigning in John Sununu's State, and being told of the Meals on Wheels program in Salem, New Hampshire—that the volunteer aspect of that program had been eroded out by Federal legislation and that the regulations were drawn in such a way that the neighbors that had been helping older neighbors no longer were free to participate and volunteer. So, I certainly think we have to avoid that kind of crowding out on the part of the regulators, on the part of my administration, or on the part of the United States Congress.

During the past several months, you've heard me speak of a Thousand Points of Light. That's given the cartoonists a wide array of new material—[*laughter*]—the best one being a Thousand Pints of Lite keg—[*laughter*]. But other people are beginning to understand what I perhaps very inarticulately talked about. I've been using that phrase as shorthand for the fact that we're a nation of communities, thousands of business and professional and religious and ethnic communities and in this diversity is our key to success, it's our strength.

The community, next to the family, is the most important unit of our nation. And I've got to remember that as we kind of come up with urban policies—or Liddy and I work together on child care, or whatever else it is—a community has got to be more than just the bricks or mortar. Our community, our town, our neighborhood: It's where we live, where we work, where the kids play, and it's where we invite friends over. And so, we've got to keep these communities strong by whatever kinds of policies we spell out in our administration.

I'm committed to dramatically increasing, and a lot of this is simply exhortation, community participation in order to pragmatically address the difficult problems that are challenging our country. We need to build this community spirit in every community, large and small. And we need to tap America for its very best in terms of dedication and the leadership.

You all have been more active than most, I know, in community service and so I again want to say thank you. You have my heartfelt respect. We need your work. We need your experience. And to those of you who are still looking for ways to help, I just would urge you to come on in, the water's fine. We need you to help us face this challenge. It's not just your money, individually and corporate, it's time and, again, it's exhortation on the part of the leaders of the business community. So, I would welcome your help on all of that.

Let me just end by a quick update. I know it's of interest to people here, the visit yesterday with the Japanese Prime Minister went well. Prime Minister Takeshita was our first official formal foreign visitor to come here to this country. And during our discussions yesterday we simply reaffirmed our responsibilities in the cause of world peace. We also reviewed the progress that our nations have achieved in bringing the economies into better balance and in further opening our markets to each other's goods and services. We, in this country, carry a disproportionate responsibility for the defense requirements of free countries. Japan, given its economic standing today, is willing to accept much more in the way of responsibility for helping in the whole development aid side of things.

So, we had a good chance to discuss that. We did not go into every trade problem that faces our country. Both of us are realistic men, the Japanese Prime Minister and me, and we realize we're going to have some confrontation at times or certainly some differences of opinion. But I'm going to do my level best, working with our good new trade team, to be sure that we are treated fairly, that we have access, that we are not operating under standards that favor one side to the detriment of the other.

But the visit went well, and I think Prime Minister Takeshita wants very much to have that cooperative relationship. And we don't want to take these things for granted. It's not the reason I'm going to Japan for the funeral to pay my respects on behalf of the American people to the Emperor, but it has something to do with it that's broader. I should be doing that—looking to the present and to the future. But I just wanted to assure you that the visit yesterday had gone reasonably well.

In the meantime, we still are under study in terms of our relationship with the Soviets. I know everyone here is very much interested in that relationship. I am confident that General Secretary Gorbachev knows that our review is not a foot-dragging operation. I don't want to miss an opportunity, but I don't want to do something that's imprudent either. And so, with our Secretary of State, ably backed up and assisted by my National Security Adviser, we are undertaking a policy review with the Soviet Union. There will be no great shocks. There will be no turning our back on the potential for progress. But there will be taking the proper amount of time so that when we do go forward, whether it's on conventional arms control, or strategic arms, or whatever else it is—the economic front, regional problems, human rights—we're going to be marching together in this administration.

And the Soviets, I think, now understand that there's no foot-dragging. But I wanted you to know that I understand the importance of this relationship and that I am determined to see us move forward. I want to see us get out in front if we possibly can, but I don't think that we have to be just restless because General Secretary Gorbachev made a very interesting set of proposals at the United Nations a few months—now a month or so ago. So, we're going to look at the whole array of these issues. In the meantime, we're taking a look at the hemisphere.

Some of you have read about trying to work with the Congress. I'm very serious about it, and the product of the Congress in some ways—I realize that maybe we can wait until February 9th, which is only 6 days away, before we go after each other on things. But we're realists, and we know there is going to be differences on what I send up. But I think most people that understand the Congress certainly would give them credit, and I do, for a willingness at this juncture to talk.

We had a very interesting, and I'd say productive, meeting with the leaders of key committees—Ways and Means and Finance and Banking and Banking—and then the leaders today and this question of facing this savings and loan problem. And they're not going to agree with everything I propose next week, but we've had a chance to consult and to listen to them, and I'm determined to try that, carry that forward. And I think it will be good for domestic policy, and I'm absolutely convinced that it is vital for foreign policy because we've been sending confusing signals around the world of two major branches of government that can't ever quite get together on something important. I'm not naive. I know we're going to have differences, but I just wanted you to know I think that approach is certainly worth a try. And so, that's about where we stand.

I'm delighted you all are here. Again, I ask for your help, and lest you be unpersuaded by what I've said, I would now like to be one who has been—invite one to come in here who has been dubbed by no less an authority than Time Magazine as the Silver Fox because—[*laughter*]—she's worked for so many of you in education that I want her to come in and say thank you if she's here. Barbara, enter. I've got all your education crowd around.

Mrs. Bush. Thank you.

The President. I've been making a pitch for voluntarism.

Mrs. Bush. I heard you.

The President. And they're going to do it.

Mrs. Bush. I heard you. I heard him. I heard what he said. And what I really came in to say was use me. I'm willing to come. If you'll do what he asks, I'll come and help in any way I can—literacy, the homeless—anything. You call, and I'll come. Thank you very much.

Note: The President spoke at 1:03 p.m. in the East Room at the White House.

Remarks Congratulating the Super Bowl Champion San Francisco 49'ers

February 3, 1989

The President. Welcome. Please be seated. Jack—that's our Cabinet star, Jack Kemp. Did you all get a chance to see him? Good.

Well, Eddie DeBartolo and Coach Walsh and the staff and all the players here from the 49'ers, let me just say first congratulations to all of you and welcome to the White House. This victory last month of the 49'ers as indisputably the world's champion sets you up as that in every sense of the word. And with this, your third Super Bowl title in 8 years, you rewrote the record books and raised the game of football to a new level of excellence. In devising your game plan, Bill Walsh proved once again why he's considered one of the greatest coaches ever, and in leading your team 97 yards in the final 3 minutes, Joe, you once again showed your grace under pressure. I guess we all wonder why did it take so long—[*laughter*]—but nevertheless the country saw it.

And, Jerry Rice, what can I say that hasn't already been said? I've heard there is a new TV series coming out based on your Super Bowl performance—Miami Rice. [*Laughter*] Available in every city in the country except one—[*laughter*]—Cincinnati, that is. [*Laughter*] And Joe and Jerry handled the aerial attack, but when your team needed the tough yardage on the ground you turned to Roger Craig. And in his years as a 49'er, Roger has given a whole new meaning to the words "gold rush," and when he runs the football, the chances are he is headed for paydirt.

It wouldn't be fair to mention the offensive stars without also giving great credit to the defense. And during the first half, when the offense was having a tough time, the defense kept you in that ballgame with their cool, smart, hard-hitting football.

And speaking of tough times, in all of the hoopla surrounding the Super Bowl victory, most people have forgotten the adversity that you overcame just to get there. But you never gave up, you pulled together as a team, you came back step by step, game by game, and you eliminated mistakes, never stopped striving for excellence. And there is a lesson in that for—I think for all of us, but maybe particularly for the student body presidents and athletes that are here in the audience with us today.

And that's why I wanted you to share in this ceremony. To the young people here and across the country, I'd like to remind you that what you achieve in your life depends a lot on what you achieve in school during the next few years. And if I could offer one piece of advice, it would be this: Strive for excellence in all things and don't accept mediocrity. Being satisfied with mediocrity might be the easy way, but striving for excellence is the only way up.

Some of you have already achieved excellence in football and perhaps in other sports as well. And I can tell you and the 49 players, I'm sure—49'ers—will agree, I am sure, that being good in sports is not enough to achieve excellence. You just have to be educated for excellence. The main ingredient in each person's success is individual initiative. It always has been, and it always will be. So I would say, if you're willing to work hard and make sacrifices, you can accomplish just about anything you set your mind to. And that's what the American dream is all about.

And, again, to all the 49'ers, and to you, Coach Walsh, and to all the 49'ers—my congratulations to you! And thanks for setting a superb example for our country. Thank you and God bless all of you.

Mr. DeBartolo. Mr. President, it's a great honor being here. And there's a few presentations that Coach Walsh and the players want to make. I want to just make one announcement that we did find out that your ring size is 11 and a half. And we're going to give you the first ring that comes out of production because we want you to be an honorary member of our team. And we're with you a thousand percent in everything you do. And God bless you and all that you do and thank you, sir.

The President. Thank you.

Mr. Montana. Thank you. Mr. President, first let me congratulate you also on your victory. And secondly, I also would like, on behalf of my teammates, say thank you for your hospitality here this afternoon. It means a lot to all of us. Not very often do I get to see many of these guys in ties. [*Laughter*] And thirdly, we'd like to present you with a little token of our appreciation, little autographed balls from the Super Bowl, and say best of luck to you. We wish you the best and thank you.

The President. Thank you, that's great. Thank you very much.

Mr. Rice. Mr. President, we're glad to be here. We'd like to thank you for bringing us out into your wonderful home. [*Laughter*] You know, I looked forward to this day and I just hope that we get an opportunity to come back next year and stand right here before you. And on behalf of the San Francisco 49'ers, I'd like to present you with this ball and——

The President. Thank you so much—the real thing. [*Laughter*]

Mr. Rice. That's the real thing from the Super Bowl.

The President. Thank you very much. Thank you so much. Good luck to you.

Mr. Walsh. Mr. President, we have also—we know you're a runner, so we have a running suit. I'm not sure we suggest running the streets of Washington, DC, in this suit. [*Laughter*] In fact, we're somewhat concerned we're sort of—a little bit of overkill here. Remember, the Redskin fans are all around us. [*Laughter*] But we do feel so proud to be part of this, to have won a world's championship, but also, to be in your presence because we think you're going to do the greatest job we've seen in many, many years as President of the United States. Thank you very much.

Note: The President spoke at 3:05 p.m. in the East Room at the White House. Edward J. DeBartolo was the owner of the San Francisco 49'ers.

White House Statement on Secretary of Health and Human Services-Designate Louis W. Sullivan
February 4, 1989

Louis W. Sullivan, M.D., Secretary-designate of Health and Human Services, has requested the executive committee of the board of the Morehouse School of Medicine to grant him an unpaid leave of absence as a professor of medicine. Such an action by the executive committee would suspend any salary payments by the school to Dr. Sullivan while he served as HHS Secretary.

Morehouse School of Medicine, like most academic institutions, affords its faculty a paid leave of absence based upon years of service. After 13 years of uninterrupted service, Dr. Sullivan had earned, and was granted, a paid sabbatical leave of absence.

Dr. Sullivan made the following statement in connection with his request to the Committee to forego the paid leave: "President Bush has called on all of those in his Cabinet, and indeed throughout the Federal Government, to set the very highest ethical standards and to avoid even the appearance of potential conflicts of interest. I agree emphatically with the President, that it is crucial to establish the highest ethical tone, and it will be my intention to uphold those same high principles at HHS if I am confirmed as Secretary. Accordingly, I have requested the executive committee of the board of the medical school to grant an unpaid leave of absence during the time I may serve as HHS Secretary. In this way, I intend to preclude even the remotest possibility of any appearance that my actions as Secretary might be influenced due to any outside income. I look forward to many productive years of service at HHS. And I believe that an unpaid leave of absence from Morehouse Medical School will help establish a firm groundwork for such service to begin."

Remarks at the Swearing-in Ceremony for Carla A. Hills as United States Trade Representative
February 6, 1989

The President. Well, it is a great pleasure for me to be here for the swearing-in of our friend, Carla Hills, as U.S. Trade Representative. This is a position of great importance to our country. And with the emergence of a truly global economy, trade issues have taken on a new prominence. And I think, as Lord Macaulay so rightly said, that "Free trade is one of the greatest blessings which a government can confer on a people."

I have great confidence in the ability, the wisdom, and the toughness of Carla Hills, which is why I chose her in the first place for this critically important post. This is her second Cabinet position, and she won universal respect for her service as Secretary at the Department of HUD, Housing and Urban Development. And I know that she'll win strong support in this important current role. She's a skilled negotiator with a strong international background and extensive experience in government. Trade issues involve listening to many voices within our nation while working with the full breadth of government and maintaining a clear sense of mission. As I said when I nominated her, I can think of no one better suited to be America's trade minister at home and abroad.

And Carla will have a very committed and talented group of people at USTR who work hard and bargain hard for the people of our country. I greatly respect, incidentally, the dedication and expertise of those with whom Carla will be working at USTR, and I'm glad that many of you are here with us today.

America, as the world's number one trading nation, has the largest stake in the continued expansion of world trade, which has been one of the key factors in our growing prosperity. In addition, our trade relationships are a vital factor in America's international alliances that help secure freedom and stability for so much of the world. We will apply firmness to help promote what is fair, but we will always remember that our major trading partners are not our enemies but, indeed, they are our allies.

We have a leading role to play in modernizing a trading system that has served the world well for over four decades. There's a new and dynamic international order in the economy that offers the chance for higher levels of prosperity for all nations which freely participate in this international economy. We want to do more to remove trade barriers; to address the issue of agriculture; and to bring the benefits of free trade to new areas, including services, investment, and the protection of intellectual property. The current Uruguay round of the GATT [General Agreement on Tariffs and Trade] talks holds many opportunities for progress in multilateral negotiations. There's also a new international impetus for trade expansion created by our U.S.-Canada free-trade agreement. This agreement can serve as a model, and it proves that freer trade between nations is the wave of the future.

Ladies and gentlemen, the goal of this administration's trade policy, simply put, is to open markets, not close them; to fight protectionism, not to give in to it. We don't want an America that is closed to the world. What we want is a world that is open to America. We're going to work to promote American exports and to see to it that in dealing with the United States other nations play by the rules. As Carla said during her own confirmation hearings, we will open foreign markets with a crowbar where necessary, but with a handshake whenever possible.

And, Carla, it is now my pleasure to witness you take the oath of office. And we're very fortunate that Judge Scalia, one of our Supreme Court Justices, is here with us today.

[*At this point, Ambassador Hills was sworn in.*]

Ambassador Hills. Mr. President, Justice Scalia, Members of Congress, distinguished guests, and dear friends, I thank you one and all for being here. And I especially want to thank the members of my wonderful family for their enormous support, and I confess that I am absolutely thrilled that they're all with me today.

I am honored, and I look forward to serving as the United States Trade Representative. And to all of you I pledge to devote all of my energies to carrying out the trade policy goals that you, Mr. President, have just outlined. We will seek to open markets, not close them; and we will fight protectionism, not give in to it. You can be certain—absolutely certain, Mr. President—that those are the goals of the Office of U.S. Trade Representative. We seek free trade not just for a more prosperous America, we seek it as a part of our great quest for a freer, fairer, and more prosperous world. Rather we seek to have our foreign markets opened to the entire community of nations, rich and poor, and from that unfettered commercial exchange comes healthy world growth and increased prosperity for all people. As a nation, we seek open trade because that goal is as morally correct as it is economically beneficial.

During the past week, I have had the opportunity to meet with and work with the extraordinarily talented and dedicated women and men at the U.S. Trade Representative's office; and, Mr. President, with this group of splendid professionals, we can meet the challenge that you have given us. Our office will work closely with other Federal agencies and with Congress. And I know that you, Mr. President, share my gratitude for the commitments that Members of both the House and the Senate have made to work alongside of our trade negotiators. And we all have gained immeasurably in drawing upon the experience and the commitment of the private sector. Together we can build an expanding multilateral trade system based upon equitable, clear, and enforceable rules. We can strengthen our bilateral relationships, and we can uphold our trade laws. In short, we can do great things together.

Now, last month, Mr. President, you called your Cabinet together to receive your very clear marching orders. Your first commandment was: Think big. Well, the Office of the United States Trade Representative is small, but its talent and dedication is enormous, and your commandment is our motto. And in that spirit, Mr. President, we offer you a token of our wholehearted commitment to your goals and our great affection. And so, if I could just give you—[*laughter*]——

[*At this point, Ambassador Hills gave the President a sweatshirt that read: Think Big.*]

The President. I have a funny feeling, having worked with Carla and knowing her ability, that that handshake, backed up by a lot of conviction, is going to get the job done for the most part. But I was thinking the other day, when we had the Prime Minister of Japan here and he met Carla—perhaps not for the first time, but the first time officially with her new role about to unfold as USTR—and maybe I was dreaming something, but I thought I saw him looking her over very carefully. [*Laughter*] And I just have a funny feeling that that combination of the handshake and the crowbar is going to be tremendously successful. [*Laughter*]

Ambassador Hills. Thank you very much. Thank you all for being here.

Note: The President spoke at 1:45 p.m. in the Indian Treaty Room of the Old Executive Office Building.

Remarks at the Swearing-in Ceremony for Samuel K. Skinner as Secretary of Transportation

February 6, 1989

The President. Well, Barbara and I are delighted to be here. And, Governor Thompson, delighted to see you, sir. But I'm here today to welcome into our Cabinet a man who I believe is destined to go down in history as one of the truly outstanding Secretaries of Transportation: Sam Skinner. He does indeed have big shoes to fill. And I see one of his predecessors sitting over here, Jim Burnley, who did an outstanding job.

And he comes here having made a name for himself as a miracle worker of sorts in transportation. Several years ago, Governor Thompson put him in charge of the Regional Transportation Authority of Northeastern Illinois. And at that time, the RTA, as it is known, was plagued with financial troubles and declining levels of service. And some said that Sam was inheriting an impossible job. But he rolled up his sleeves and set to work, and in short order, he put the RTA on a sound financial footing for the first time in years.

His expertise in transportation doesn't stop there. He's an instrument-rated pilot who has flown in and out of Chicago's O'Hare Airport, one of the busiest in the Nation—[*laughter*]—more times than he can count. And here he is. [*Laughter*] But when it comes to air travel, he'll bring a pilot's perspective to the highest levels of our government, and that means a perspective that puts safety first, above all other considerations.

You'd think all this would be enough, but I haven't quite finished his qualifications for the job. Besides overseeing the Federal

Government's role in maintaining and improving our nation's transportation system, the networks, the Secretary of Transportation has another critical duty: He commands the Coast Guard. And the Coast Guard serves on the front lines of our war on drugs. And I can't think of anyone in America who has Sam Skinner's background in transportation and has been a distinguished U.S. Attorney, prosecuting a number of major cases—outstanding combination.

And, yes, he is the ideal man for a job that will, in the years ahead, present extraordinary challenges. I'm sure that I don't need to remind anyone in this audience of the high priority my administration places and intends to place on the war on drugs. I pledged in my Inaugural Address that this scourge will stop, and I really mean that. I'm determined to see that happen. Sam will be working closely with Bill Bennett [Director of National Drug Control Policy], and I know that they're going to make a great team.

And let me mention another area in which Sam will face challenges; that's aviation. The U.S. is the safest place in the world to fly, and it is getting safer. And that safety record is your record. This Department carries a great deal of the responsibility for the safety of the skies, and carries it with ability and certainly justifiable pride. And I know that you join with me in saying that we won't rest until every possible step has been taken to make air travel in America as safe as it possibly can be.

By the way, in one area critical to safe skies, Sam is hitting the ground running. Next week he will head a delegation to the ICAO, Montreal, the special session of the Council of the International Civil Aviation Organization. He has my mandate to do all he can at that meeting to hasten the day when the international community puts an end to terrorism in the sky.

Aviation is not, of course, the only area in which Secretary Skinner and you will work together for a better America. I look forward to his leadership in the other areas: highways and bridges and urban mass transit, intercity rail, and maritime transportation. And I think once you get to know him you'll see why I say that I can't think of anyone I'd rather have in charge than Sam Skinner.

And having said so much about him, let me now say a few words to our new Secretary about how I feel about you all. It would be hard, Sam, to find a more dedicated group of people in the entire Government than the men and women in the Department of Transportation. And thanks in part to their effort, America's transportation is the best system in the world. And they represent a long and proud tradition of reaching back to the very founding of our Republic, for roads, shipping, and protecting our coasts from smugglers have been concerns of our government from the very beginning.

Somebody said of Sam that he's a visionary who thinks big. Well, I expect that you'll find that your new colleagues are visionaries who think big as well. And I know you're as proud to serve with them as I am.

And so, as they say in the railroad business, welcome aboard. It's great to have you on the team. And so, now let's get on with the swearing-in. Congratulations!

[*At this point, Secretary Skinner was sworn in.*]

Governor Thompson. Following the brilliant career in Federal law enforcement of which the President so eloquently spoke, Sam Skinner has served the people of Illinois for the past 12 years with rare fidelity, integrity, and honor. He made things move, and he got things done. And it is with the high hopes born of that experience that we in Illinois now proudly give him to the Nation. Ladies and gentlemen, the Secretary of Transportation.

Secretary Skinner. Thank you, Mr. President, for your kind words and for making me part of your team. I want to personally acknowledge all my friends here, especially Barbara Bush, my good friend for many years; my family, my mother and my brother; the Governor; my good friend Judge Flaum; and all of you. I wouldn't be here if it weren't for your efforts, and I know it.

Mr. President, the Department of Transportation's team is, in fact, made up of many members. Each one plays an important role. I have asked some of these outstanding members of that team to join us, from each of our units, and I would like to introduce them to you now. They're on the left. And maybe to break a little protocol here, they can—which I think I'm allowed to do, at least at my swearing-in ceremony—I'm going to ask them to stand forward a little bit. Maybe, Mr. President, you could shake their hands.

Muriel Clarke. Muriel is the financial specialist for the Urban Mass Transportation Administration's New York regional office. She has won many awards for her performance in government and has been involved in voluntary community efforts for over 40 years.

Frank J. Mammano, a 29-year veteran in the Federal Highway Administration, has been a leader in the development of Pathfinder, a cooperative effort by the Federal Highway Administration, the California Department of Transportation, and General Motors that applies advanced technology to solve metropolitan area congestion problems.

Romell Cooks of the National Highway Traffic Safety Administration has energized a network of health professionals to act as allies with government in the safety belt usage and anti-drunk driving campaigns.

Barbara Schroeder, one of the two female wage-grade employees at the Saint Lawrence Seaway Development Corporation—in a nontraditional job as a labor-line handler and as a single parent with three daughters, she gives freely of her time to numerous volunteer efforts.

Donald Simonds of the FAA, is a full-performance-level air traffic controller and has been actively involved in the recruitment of minority candidates for that critical job.

Anthony A. Schiavone, Superintendent of the James River Reserve Fleet at the Maritime Administration, maintains custody of approximately 125 oceangoing merchant-type vessels that are on ready reserve for national defense purposes.

Susan Hedgepeth, Chief of the Exemption Branch in the Office of Hazardous Materials Transportation, develops special requirements for the transportation of hazardous materials.

Sondra F. Talbert of the Federal Railroad Administration, moved into the Department's Upward Mobility Training Program in 1975 and is the first female inspector at the Interstate Commerce Commission in the Federal Railroad Administration.

United States Coast Guard Petty Officer Kelly M. Mogk, was recently awarded the Coast Guard Air Medal for heroic achievement in aerial flight while serving as a helicopter rescue swimmer on January 2, 1989.

Let's give these outstanding employees a round of applause. [*Applause*]

Mr. President, these individuals' achievements reflect the spirit of this Department. They are our unsung heroes, the dedicated public servants who serve the American traveler, the pilot, the truck driver, the boater, and the commuter.

The Department's team faces many challenges. We must be in the forefront in the fight against terrorism. We must do everything we can to stop the flow of drugs into this country. We must keep our aviation system both safe and competitive. And we must maintain our significant and important presence in the maritime industry. We must also continue to build and maintain our infrastructure. And I want to acknowledge—as I look on the next step—are Congressman Martin, are Congressman Mineta, Congressman Coughlin. We must work with Congress, and I will work with Congress to develop a visionary and comprehensive transportation policy for the 21st century, a policy that recognizes the transportation system is the essential lifeblood of our economy and also for our defense.

These goals cannot be achieved without the energy and commitment of thousands of team players like those you have met today. I know already from my brief introduction to this Department that this team is ready, willing, and able to do this important job. The American people have selected you as their President, and you have asked me to be your wing man. I am humbled by your offer. I accept, and I am ready to roll up my sleeves and get the job done.

Thank you very much.

Note: The President spoke at 2:42 p.m. in the Federal Aviation Administration auditorium. Secretary Skinner was sworn in by U.S. District Judge Joel M. Flaum.

The President's News Conference
February 6, 1989

The President. Well, for the more than half a century, the U.S. has operated a deposit insurance program that provides direct government protection to the savings of our citizens. This program has enabled tens of millions of Americans to save with confidence. In all the time since creation of the deposit insurance, savers have not lost one dollar of insured deposits, and I am determined that they never will.

Deposit insurance has always been intended to be self-funded. And this means that the banks, the savings and loans, and credit unions that are insured pay a small amount of their assets each year into a fund that's used to protect depositors. In every case, these funds are spent to protect the depositors, not the institutions that fail.

For the last 20 years, conditions in our financial markets have grown steadily more complex, and a portion of the savings and loan industry has encountered steadily growing problems. These financial difficulties have led to a continuous erosion of the strength of the Federal Savings and Loan Insurance Corporation, FSLIC. Economic conditions have played a major role in this situation. However, unconscionable risktaking, fraud, and outright criminality have also been factors. Because of the accumulation of losses at hundreds of these thrift institutions, additional resources must be devoted to cleaning up this problem. We intend to restore our entire deposit insurance system to complete health.

While the issues are complex and the difficulties manifold, we will make the hard choices, not run from them. We will see that the guarantee to depositors is forever honored. And we will see to it that the system is reformed comprehensively so that the situation is not repeated again. To do this, I am today announcing a comprehensive and wide-ranging set of proposals. The Secretary of the Treasury, Nicholas Brady, will describe these proposals to you in detail in a few minutes. However, I think it's important to summarize some of the major points. The proposals include four major elements.

First, currently insolvent savings institutions will be placed under the joint management of the FDIC [Federal Deposit Insurance Corporation] and FSLIC pursuant to existing law. This will enable us to control future risktaking and to begin reducing ongoing losses.

Second, the regulatory mechanism will be substantially overhauled to enable it to more effectively limit risktaking. The FDIC would become the insurance agency for both banks and thrifts under this system, although there's no commingling of funds. The insurer will have the authority to set minimum standards for capital and accounting. Uniform disclosure standards will also be implemented. The chartering agency for thrifts would come under the general oversight of the Secretary of the Treasury.

Third, we will create a financing corporation to issue $50 billion in bonds to finance the cost of resolving failed institutions, which will supplement approximately $40 billion that has already been spent. All of the principal of these bonds and a portion of the interest on them will be paid from industry sources. However, the balance would be paid from on-budget outlays of general revenues. Hopefully, some of these revenues will be recovered in the future through sale of assets and recovery of funds from the wrongdoers.

Fourth, we plan to increase the budget of the Justice Department by approximately $50 million to enable it to create a nationwide program to seek out and punish those that have committed wrongdoing in the management of these failed institutions. These funds will result in almost doubling the personnel devoted to the apprehension and prosecution of individuals committing fraud in our financial markets.

As you can see, these proposals are based upon several overriding principles. First, I will not support any new fee on depositors. Second, we should preserve the overall Federal budget structure and not allow the misdeeds and the wrongdoings of savings and loan executives and the inadequacy of their regulation to significantly alter our overall budget priorities. And third, I have concluded that this proposal, if promptly enacted, will enable our system to prevent any repetition of this situation. And fourth, I have decided to attack this problem head-on with every available resource of our government because it is a national problem. I have directed that the combined resources of our Federal agencies be brought together in a team effort to resolve the problem. And fifth, I believe that banks and thrifts should pay the real cost of providing the deposit insurance protection. The price the FDIC charges banks for their insurance has not been increased since 1935. We propose to increase the bank insurance premium by less than 7 cents per $100 of insurance protection that they receive. Every penny collected would be used to strengthen the FDIC so that the taxpayers will not be called on to rescue it a few years from now.

And I make you a solemn pledge that we will make every effort to recover assets diverted from these institutions and to place behind bars those who have caused losses through criminal behavior. Let those who would take advantage of the public trust and put at risk the savings of American families anticipate that we will seek them out, pursue them, and demand the most severe penalties.

In closing, I want to just say a word to the small savers of America. Across this great land, families and individuals work and save, and we hope to encourage even greater rates of savings to promote a brighter future for our children. Your government has stood behind the safety of insured deposits before, it does today, and it will do so at all times in the future. Every insured deposit will be backed by the full faith and credit of the United States of America, which means that it will be absolutely protected.

For the future, we will seek to achieve a safe, sound, and profitable banking system. However, integrity and prudence must share an equal position with competition in our financial markets. Clean markets are an absolute prerequisite to a free economy and to the public confidence that is its most important ingredient.

I've determined to face this problem squarely and to ask for your support in putting it behind us. I have ordered that the resources of the executive branch be brought to bear on cleaning up this problem. I have personally met with the leadership of Congress on this issue. My administration will work cooperatively with Congress as the legislation that we will submit in a few days' time is considered. I call on the Congress to join me in a determined effort to resolve this threat to the American financial system permanently, and to do so without the delay.

I welcome the leaders that are with me here on this platform. I think their support says a lot about the efficacy of our proposal. And now I propose to take just a few questions. On the technical aspects, I will defer to these people, and then I'll be glad to turn this over to Secretary Brady. I believe we start with Helen [Helen Thomas, United Press International] and then Terry [Terence Hunt, Associated Press], and then get going——

Q. Mr. President, are you guaranteeing that the extra costs—premiums, increases, and so forth—will not be passed on to the depositors and taxpayers? And also, what is your responsibility in this debacle—I mean, the Reagan-Bush zeal for deregulation of business and banking?

The President. On the first place, we're not guaranteeing that. I would hope that wouldn't happen, but there is no guarantee what the institutions will do. Secondly, there is enough to be said for everybody in this together trying to solve this problem, so I can't equate any personal—not inclined to go into any personal blame, simply to say that we've got to solve this problem, and we're on the path to doing that.

Federal Pay Raise

Q. Mr. President, the House votes tomorrow on that controversial pay raise plan, and the Senate has already voted against it. Would you sign a bill that vetoes the pay raise not only for the Members of Congress but also for Federal judges and other high officials in the Government?

The President. I've said I support it.

Savings and Loan Crisis

Q. Mr. President, there is a feeling that part of this problem is attributable to deregulation of the financial industry. In retrospect, do you think that deregulation might have gone too far in the last 10 years or so? And in the future, is your marching order to your administration to be a little more careful in regulating this particular industry?

The President. Jerry [Gerald Boyd, New York Times], I don't know the answer. I'd be most interested to know what our experts here feel about how much of the problem could be attributed to deregulation. I just don't know the answer to your question, so I can't reply.

Government Ethics

Q. Mr. President, you have placed considerable stress in these early days of your Presidency on ethics and propriety, yet in recent days there has been controversy on Capitol Hill concerning the propriety of some of Tower's [Secretary of Defense-designate] alleged behavior; questions raised over the weekend about the financial investments on the private funds of the man in charge of ethics, your counsel, Boyden Gray; and other questions involving members of the administration, or members-to-be of the administration. And I wonder, sir, what's happened here? Is it too harsh behavior on our part, too lax behavior on your part? What?

The President. I don't think anything has happened. I learned long ago in public life not to make judgments based on allegations. But having said that, I want to have my administration aspire to the highest possible ethical standards. And we have appointed a commission to go out there now and try to detail what these standards should be. And we are in a new era on these matters. Matters that might have been approved and looked at one way may have a different perception today.

And so, what I want to do is finalize our standards and then urge everybody in all branches of government to aspire to those standards. But I do think, Brit [Brit Hume, ABC News], that it's fair that we not reach judgment on Senate hearings before the Senate hearings are concluded because it's very hard to filter out fact from fiction, spurious allegations from fact. And I am not about to make a judgment based on a sensationalized newspaper story. I'm simply not going to do that. That wouldn't be fair, and I'm not sure how ethical it would be. So, let's wait and see this—you're referring to the Tower matter up there. That matter has been looked at by the FBI. The committee now has that. They have the responsibility to make determinations, and I'll be very interested to see what they say. But I am not going to jump to conclusions based on stories that may or may not have any validity at all.

Secretary of Defense-Designate Tower

Q. Mr. President, even if, as your spokesman says you do, you continue to back Senator Tower for the position, there are those you've heard who say that the best thing he could do for you is to step aside because even if confirmed he then would become damaged goods, weaker in administering a very, very tough job on your behalf. How do you respond to that suggestion?

The President. Well, I think people would not want a person to step aside—[*inaudible*]—rumor, particularly if the rumor is baseless. And the process is taking a little longer than I would like. And yet I think the Senate has got to do what they're doing: looking at these allegations very carefully. But you know, as I said here at this same podium a while back, the American people are basically fair. And if these allegations prove to be allegations without fact behind them, I think the people are going to say: Wait a minute! What went on here? How come it was all this? We read this one day, and then kind of a puff of smoke the next. And so, I don't think—in your substantive question, though—that if the Senate committee gives its endorsement to the Senator, particularly after all of these allegations, that there is any danger at all of damage to his credibility or his ability to do the job.

Q. Mr. President, there are new and substantive allegations that Senator Tower lost control over the highly classified security documents and computer disks that were used in Geneva under his watch. If those allegations prove to be founded, would you then withdraw his nomination?

The President. I would not answer hypothetical questions of that nature. You're telling me something that I haven't heard before. And we did have access to FBI reports. So, if this matter is now before the Congress, let them investigate it. But I can't go into a hypothesis. All I would be doing would be adding to, I think, speculation that is not helpful at this juncture.

Q. But, sir, will you pursue these allegations in the executive branch? Are you going to track what the FBI is looking into? Are you going to personally surveil these kinds of allegations yourself?

The President. Every rumor and every innuendo? No, but if there's some substantive allegation of this nature, of course, it would concern me.

Savings and Loan Crisis

Q. Mr. President, back to S&L's if we might. Millions of—[*laughter*]—millions of Americans save alternatively. That is they save in mutual funds, stocks, and that kind of thing. As I read it, you've now outlined a plan that places a lot of the S&L bailout on the backs of the general Treasury. How fair is that?

The President. We've got a major problem, and something has to be done. And this is the fairest system that the best minds in this administration can come up with. And so, I again would ask you to ask the specifics of the Treasury burden to the Chairman of the Federal Reserve [Alan Greenspan] or the Secretary of the Treasury [Nicholas F. Brady]. Ask how they see that. But look, as I've said, there is no easy answer to this. All I want to do is make a sound proposal, work to put it into effect, and have that proposal such that the country won't have to face this problem again.

Q. Mr. President, you said you dropped the deposit fee idea, but this plan you've given us has an increase in premiums that may be paid by consumers, as well as a large amount of taxpayers' funds. Isn't that the same thing: Consumers and taxpayers are still going to have to pay the price for this?

The President. Well, as I indicated earlier on, there is no guarantee of passing this on to the consumer, nor is there a guarantee it won't be passed on. But this arrangement has been there for 50 years, and you might argue whether it's been passed on or not. I just don't know. I haven't seen the flow-through in the industry, but nothing is without pain when you come to solve a problem of this magnitude.

Q. Mr. President, you've talked to several Members of Congress in various receptions and dinners and personal conversations over the past couple of weeks, and in many of them, you have discussed your plan for this problem. What is your feeling of the reception that it's going to get on Capitol Hill and of the selling job that awaits you to get it passed?

The President. We may have a big selling job, but I've been encouraged so far with the spirit epitomized by the Members of Congress, particularly at the joint leadership meeting the other day. We didn't go into every detail of this. These plans were still being formulated, and I wanted to get their views. I was encouraged by what Bill Seidman [FDIC Chairman] told me earlier on about what he felt the receptivity of the plan will be. But I don't think it's fair to the Congress to say that they have signaled to me that they are going to be enthusiastic on this plan, although I hope they are.

I'm going to take about three more and then turn this over to these gentlemen here, who are prepared to go into as much detail as you want.

Secretary of Defense-Designate Tower

Q. Mr. President, these allegations that surround Tower now, at least variations on the theme, surfaced early in the transition—allegations of womanizing and taking money from defense contractors, that sort of thing. Have you satisfied yourself that he is still the nominee you want? Can you give us at this time a full-hearted endorsement of Tower?

The President. Yes, I can, and I will right now because some of the very same allegations that were floated that long ago apparently have been looked at and examined by the best possible examiners—and I'm talking about the FBI—and found to be groundless. So, therefore, I'm not about to change my view. If somebody comes up with facts, I hope I'm not narrowminded enough that I wouldn't take a look. But I am not going to deal in the kinds of rumors that I've seen reported and then knocked down—and then reported and then knocked down.

One—two to go.

Central America

Q. There have been hints that Gorbachev may propose steps to diffuse the situation in Central America. I wonder if you see the possibility of superpower deals in Central America, and, if so, if you could suggest what would be acceptable for you?

The President. I don't know about a deal, but I can see a possibility of cooperation in Central America because I would like the Soviets to understand that we have very special interests in this hemisphere, particularly in Central America, and that our commitment to democracy and to freedom and free elections and these principles is unshakeable. And I don't think they really have substantive interests in this part of the world, certainly none that rival ours. So, I would like to think they would understand that. And there are so many areas where we could demonstrate a new spirit of cooperation, and this would clearly be one of them. So, I'd like to think that is the way that the matter would be approached by the Soviets.

Yes, followup?

Q. If I could follow up and ask you whether you'd be willing to include abandonment of aid to the *contras* as part of such an understanding?

The President. I wouldn't make a deal on that with the Soviets, nor would that come up. I don't believe we'd ever have a—I can't see a situation of that nature arising, knowing as I do what will be negotiated and discussed with the—so I think that's so hypothetical as to not even be a possibility of any kind.

Yes, Charles [Charles Bierbauer, Cable Network News]? And then I do have to run.

Savings and Loan Crisis

Q. Mr. President, we still don't know what the taxpayers' burden is in here out of this $40 billion. It says first from S&L funds and the shortfall from Treasury funds. How big is it; and have you, in going through your budget, had to knock out some things to pay for this?

The President. We've had to knock out a lot of things on the overall budget for a lot of different reasons. But I'd like to leave this for Dick [Richard G. Darman, Director of the Office of Management and Budget], for the questioning, to give the specific amounts. It is shared, as I've indicated, and he can give you the amounts that are involved.

Listen, thank you all very much, and now I'm going to turn this over to Secretary Brady. And then in order, I guess they'll refer to each of these others.

Q. Mr. President, one more word for the small——

Q. ——seats back here, Mr. President?

The President. What was that substantive question? [*Laughter*]

Q. In the back—we didn't see you get back in this area.

The President. We didn't get that far back, no. But if there's been an egregious offense to those in the back benches, I will take one parting question. And inasmuch as you raised it, fire away.

Government Ethics

Q. Thank you very much, sir. Back on the ethics issue, a couple of——

The President. Mindful that the last question always does get you in great trouble—[*laughter*]—go ahead.

Q. One of your perspective nominees and your Counsel have just recently changed their minds on matters that would have violated the ethics rules under the Reagan administration. Did you have difficulty in getting the word out that times would be tougher under your administration?

The President. No. I don't think so. For example, if you're referring to the Boyden Gray [Counsel to the President] matter, which I think you are, that matter was reviewed every single year by the Office of Government Ethics, and he was deemed in compliance every single year. But now we've got a new ballgame here. He's the General Counsel here in the White House, and I'm the President. And I've set out, rhetorically, the highest possible standards, and we're trying to back that up by findings from this Commission. And so, I do think that we've got to be very careful about perceptions of impropriety when it comes to conflict of interest—not rumors or innuendoes of one sort or another. I don't think I should deal in those things. But when it comes to perceived conflicts of interest, I'd like our people to bend over backwards.

And I think that's what has happened in both the question of Lou Sullivan [Secretary of Health and Human Services-designate]. All he did was ask: Am I entitled to continue these arrangements with this small university? And all Boyden did, in my view now, is to try to go a step beyond what the Government Ethics Office has said to avoid the perception of impropriety. So, I think it might be different now. I have to approach it differently as President. Not that you have lower standards. But I just think that, again, this whole question of perception—we've got to look at it very, very carefully.

But I want to be fair. I do not want to have the loudest charge, no matter how irresponsible, be that that sets the standards. We've got to achieve more objective standards. And that's why I'm putting a lot of faith in the—hope to put a lot of faith in the findings of Judge Wilkey and former Attorney General Griffin Bell. And they will be looking at all these matters in terms of reality, and then, to some degree I'm sure, in terms of perception. So, what might be legal and might be perfectly sound ethically might have to be altered, given this new approach because of perception. It's a delicate one.

I don't want to have the standards set in such an irresponsible way that good people just throw up their hands and say: Look, who needs that kind of grief, who needs it? Why should I have to give up all my whatever it is—a health plan from the XYZ company. And yet on the other hand, we're in a different time now. We're in a time when we've got to try to set these standards as high as possible. So, I think Dr. Sullivan did the right thing in asking what was proper. I think Boyden Gray did the correct thing every year in asking what was proper and reviewing his own personal holdings in a family company with the Ethics Office, but now taking another step because of perception in this case. So, we've got to work with these individuals to find the proper answer, and we've got to work with the Commission to try to codify these standards.

Q. Sir, by following, you said during the campaign very clearly that your staffers would not take outside income. I wonder why they need a legal opinion to understand that?

The President. They had a legal opinion saying it was perfectly proper from this family company, and so, now we're changing that and saying, Look, there is this different perception problem here in this new era, so let's bend over as far backwards as we possibly can, you know, to recognize that.

Thank you all very much.

Q. What about leveraged buy-outs, Mr. President?

The President. There's your LBO man right there.

Note: The President's second news conference began at 4:10 p.m. in Room 450 of the Old Executive Office Building.

Statement by Press Secretary Fitzwater on the Acquisition of Monsanto Electronic Materials Company by a West German Firm

February 7, 1989

The President today decided against intervening in the proposed acquisition of Monsanto Electronic Materials Company (MEMC) by Huels AG of West Germany. MEMC manufactures silicon wafers for use in making semiconductors.

The President based his decision on the results of the investigation by the Committee on Foreign Investment in the United States (CFIUS), chaired by Treasury Secretary Nicholas Brady. The CFIUS conducted a thorough investigation of various issues related to silicon wafers, including reliability of supply, technology transfer, and the relationship of the transaction to the semiconductor industry research consortium SEMATECH. CFIUS staff and policy-level officials also met with representatives of SEMATECH, of Monsanto, and of Huels.

The Huels-MEMC investigation was the first formal investigation by the CFIUS under section 5021 of the Omnibus Trade and Competitiveness Act of 1988. That provision, known as the Exon-Florio provision, authorizes the President to investigate and, if necessary, to suspend or prohibit a proposed foreign acquisition of a U.S. business engaged in U.S. interstate commerce. The criteria to suspend or prohibit are that the President must find:

- credible evidence to believe that the foreign investor might take actions that threaten to impair the national security, and
- that existing laws, other than the International Emergency Economic Powers Act and the Exon-Florio provision, are inadequate and inappropriate to deal with the national security threat.

Statement on Signing the Bill Rescinding Proposed Increases in Executive, Legislative, and Judicial Salaries

February 7, 1989

Today I am signing H.J. Res. 129, passed overwhelmingly by both the Senate and House of Representatives, which rescinds the proposed pay increase for Members of Congress, executive branch officials, and our Federal judges. I recognize this legislation has been a source of considerable public controversy with much concern about the process by which this pay increase was considered. I applaud the Members of Congress in both the House and the Senate for taking their recorded votes on this measure. The American people deserve to have had this issue openly discussed, debated, and voted upon.

I believe that some level of pay increase is in order, and I will be working with the House and Senate leadership to develop proposals to achieve that end. I would also like to express my special concern about the level of compensation for members of our Federal Judiciary.

GEORGE BUSH

The White House,
February 7, 1989.

Note: H.J. Res. 129, approved February 7, was assigned Public Law No. 101–1.

Remarks at the Swearing-in Ceremony for Manuel Lujan, Jr., as Secretary of the Interior

February 8, 1989

The President. It is a pleasure to be here today. Mr. Justice Scalia and distinguished Members of the United States Senate and House of Representatives, and all the distinguished guests here, thank you. I'm proud to be over here for the swearing-in of my friend Manuel Lujan as the 46th Secretary of the Interior. I've known Manuel from the days when we first came to Washington and served in the United States House of Representatives together. He's an extremely capable man, a very fair man—you'll find that out—and a man dedicated to his country. And I also have to mention what a great contribution his wife has made over these many years.

Manuel Lujan has long experience with the important issues that face this Department. He served with distinction as the ranking member of the House Committee on Interior and Insular Affairs, and he's demonstrated commitment to public service with some 20 years in the United States Congress. And through his work with his constituents and with those who came before his committee, he's been in very close touch with the people of our country, the people who are affected by the policies of the United States Government. And that quality of receptiveness, being a good listener, is so essential because government must serve the people. And that's what we are all here for.

Manuel knows how much I enjoy going fishing—got his priorities sorted out here—[*laughter*]—no favoritism. If I'm fishing in a national park, I don't expect special treatment upstream so the 12-pounders come my way. [*Laughter*] I want to fight for my rights like every other American.

But the Department of the Interior is our nation's principal conservation agency. And I think you know how deeply I care about issues of conservation and the wise management of our public land. Secretary Lujan has my total confidence.

Together we've laid out a 10-point agenda called Stewardship that speaks to the broad responsibilities of your Department. From environmental and resource issues to our commitment to the dignity and well-being of Native Americans in the territories, I know that this Department will continue to demonstrate leadership, sensitivity, and professionalism. I want to recognize the outstanding work done by all of you at the Department of the Interior, and certainly the men and women who are working for this Department all across our country. There's also a great contribution being made by volunteers who participate in the many programs to keep America beautiful and to make it possible for more Americans to use and enjoy the outdoors.

I believe, as you do, in clean air and clean water and the protection of American wildlife. I also want to see our nation's public lands preserved so that this generation and future generations can use and enjoy our natural bounty: the great outdoors. You know, I have to say, it's only in Washington that the agency that handles the great outdoors would be called the Department of the Interior. [*Laughter*] But whether it's managing wildlife and fisheries or our national parks or administering the lands that constitute a third of our nation, I want to be sure that our grandchildren will be able to enjoy that same natural abundance that we enjoy today.

One of my favorite Presidents was Teddy Roosevelt, and he said that "A grove of giant redwoods or sequoias should be kept just as we keep a great and beautiful cathedral." Well, I think we all agree with that, and I know that Manuel feels the same way. I think he's going to be a superb Secretary of the Interior. I know he's going to be a very valuable member of my Cabinet. So, it is my pleasure to see him now take the oath of office as Secretary of the Interior. Justice Scalia, would you do the honors please, sir?

[*At this point, Secretary Lujan was sworn in.*]

Secretary Lujan. Mr. President, Justice Scalia, Father Haddad, Members of Congress, Jean, my family and friends and fellow Interior employees, I'm deeply honored and, of course, humbled by the opportunity to serve you, Mr. President, and the American people as the 46th Secretary of Interior.

I wasn't going to say anything, but since you mentioned that you didn't want any special treatment on your fishing trips, you should have told us that before you went down to the Everglades National Park—[*laughter*]—and we made arrangements for you to catch that 13-pound bonefish. [*Laughter*] We won't do it again, I promise.

Mr. President, I grew up in New Mexico, where love of the land, if not inbred, is one of the earliest lessons of life. One thing that a native of any Western State also learns very early is that the Department of Interior has vast power over much of the land and its resources. Never did I dream back then that I would someday have the opportunities and the responsibilities for stewardship of such treasures.

And as you have stated, Mr. President, how well we carry out our stewardship responsibilities today will determine how well people will live in the future. You have emphasized, Mr. President, our goals for stewardship cannot be accomplished without teamwork between those of us in your administration and the career professionals. In meeting with my new Interior family, I have shared with them the commitment and the goals that you and I share for this Department. Each employee received this brochure which outlines the 10-point Stewardship program you and I agreed upon. As you can see, it's not chiseled in stone, but we are referring to it as the "Ten Commandments." [*Laughter*]

You should feel quite at home here, Mr. President, as I do, because within this audience are people who have devoted their careers and their lives to the environmental ethic represented in these 10 points. All of us share your love and your reverence for our great natural heritage. Your words have touched our hearts. Your vision of America has inspired our spirits. We will put both our heart and our spirit into the task before us. Thank you for this magnificent opportunity to serve you and this country. Thank you very much, Mr. President.

Note: The President spoke at 10:15 a.m. in the Department of the Interior auditorium. In his opening remarks, the Secretary referred to his wife, Jean; and to Reverend Norman Haddad, who delivered the invocation.

Remarks at the Swearing-in Ceremony for William K. Reilly as Administrator of the Environmental Protection Agency

February 8, 1989

The President. Well, I'm told that this is the first time that a President has visited the EPA. Well, not exactly the EPA, but all the stores underneath the EPA. [*Laughter*] And I think I should, at the outset of these brief remarks, just express my appreciation to the merchants and to the others who have this vibrant mall in their custody—[*laughter*]—thanking them for the opportunity to have this ceremony here so we could meet with as many of the EPA employees as possible.

I'm delighted to be here. And in my search for a new, first-rate EPA Administrator, one of my top priorities was to find someone with strong credentials as a leader in the environmental community, and that man is our new Administrator, William Reilly. He's got big shoes to fill, though. I know that, and I have great respect for those that have preceded him. Lee Thomas did an outstanding job here, and I want those who worked with him to know how strongly I feel about that. I want to salute the members of the diplomatic corps who were nice enough to be with us today. I think that puts appropriate emphasis on the fact that many of the problems that we face in the environment are global problems. And I'm delighted that they're with us here today—pleased to see Senator Chafee and other Members of the United States Senate and Members of the House with us as well.

I hope it is plain to everyone in this room and around the country that among my first items on my personal agenda is the protection of America's environment. I am pledged to improving the quality of life: for improving the quality of the air we breathe and the water we drink and the land that, as Father O'Reilly said, God has entrusted to us.

I have just come from the swearing-in of Manuel Lujan, our new Secretary of the Interior. EPA and Interior have got to work as partners, keeping our land and our air and our water clean—public land secure. And I'm sure all of you know by now Bill Reilly's incredible background in environmental protection: president of the Conservation Foundation, one of the Nation's outstanding environmental think tanks; president of World Wildlife Fund, U.S. And I'm pleased that my friend Russell Train is still talking to me, having moved in on that cozy arrangement that served the private sector so well.

Mr. Reilly began his career in this field as a senior staff member of the President's Council on Environmental Quality, the CEQ, in the early seventies and then as executive director of the Task Force on Land Use and Urban Growth. A leader in one of the other major environmental organizations has said of Bill that he has, and I'm quoting now, "without question the most personal knowledge of the substance of issues of any of the CEO's of any of the conservation organizations." And that gives you an idea of why we are very lucky to have him here and why I selected him.

I thought I'd tell you a story that will tell you something more about why I picked him. About a year and a half ago, he convened a forum on the wetlands crisis. He brought together 25 people who, as the Washington Post put it, would normally have difficulty agreeing even on a place for dinner. Environmentalists, developers, industrialists, State and Federal regulators all were there. And the result: Well, by the time he was through with them, which took more than a year, they put aside differences and called for no net loss of wetlands, and they agreed on 100 reforms to achieve that goal.

I spoke the other day about wanting to broaden the consensus for defense, but that's not the only consensus that I would like to broaden. I want to broaden the consensus for a clean environment, and I believe doing that requires finding ways to clean up the environment without stifling the economy. During the campaign I noted that environmental action has too often been marked by confrontation among competing interests. Well, the fact is that more often than not there is common ground if the parties will make an effort to find it. Our great common desire is a better life for all Americans. And I believe that economic growth and a clean environment are both part of what all Americans understand a better life to mean. I also believe that the American people are impatient for results. They won't accept excuses anymore. And they won't accept finger pointing. They want us to get all the sides together and find a way to achieve both their goals.

By the way, the other day I got a little lesson in how impatient the American people are. In the morning mail, this marvelous mail that comes in to the President of the United States, I found letters from seventh graders at a church school in California. I thought I'd share one with you. It was dated Inauguration Day, January 20th; and it said, and remember this was just on the day that I was taking office,"Dear Mr. President, Would you please do something about pollution. I'm not saying you're doing a bad job, but could you put a little more effort into it." [*Laughter*]

Well, with William Reilly at the helm here, we're going to put a hell of a lot more effort into it. And now, Bill, let's do the honors.

[*At this point, Administrator Reilly was sworn in.*]

Administrator Reilly. Mr. President, on behalf of all 15,000 of my closest and most valued new colleagues, welcome to EPA. And great thanks to all of you who worked so hard to make this event possible this morning. We had to reschedule the opening of Black History Month. I'm pleased to say that that has been rescheduled. We appreciate all the effort that has gone into accommodating this event in these halls. We chose the place that would accommodate the very largest number of the EPA staff, and this is the place. And we put nice blue bunting in front of the lingerie store—[*laughter*]—and Roy Rogers. And we're grateful, as the President said, to everybody who worked to make this come off so well.

Well, it's just great to have you here, Mr. President. Several Senators asked me during last week's confirmation hearings about EPA's access to the White House, and that, of course, is a very crucial question. But I would add just one reassurance to my answer: Mr. President, you will always have complete access to us here at EPA. [*Laughter*] So, feel free to drop by any time. [*Laughter*] Our door will always be wide open to you, won't it, my friends? It will also be wide open to you, my friends in the Congress—Senator Burdick, Senator Chafee, Senator Wilson, Senator Baucus.

We, as the President said, are beginning, I think, on a great note. We've had great cooperation through the confirmation period, and I appreciate that very much.

Well, it is clearly a very great honor to serve as Administrator of the Environmental Protection Agency. I thank you for your confidence in me, for nominating me, Mr. President. I thank you, Chairman Burdick, Senator Chafee, members of the Environment and Public Works Committee, for the great many courtesies that were extended to me over the past weeks in the course of the confirmation. I feel equally honored to be able to serve, to look forward to working with this very fine EPA staff. I wish all of them could be here today. I have got to say, I've been enormously impressed with the capabilities of the dozens or so of people who have come into contact with me in the course of the last several weeks. I can honestly say that EPA professionals began shoring me up and bailing me out a full month before my confirmation, and now is no time to stop. [*Laughter*] I will need all the help that I can get. I should say I owe a special debt of gratitude to those hard-working souls who assisted me in handling the written questions that followed our hearing on the Hill. We were pleased to be able to move the confirmation very fast. But in the course of doing that, we were given some 315 written questions, the answers to which were due 24 hours later, and many of you stayed up through the night. I was able to tap off the answers to 305 or so of these, of course, with no difficulty. [*Laughter*] But those last ten—I really did appreciate your help, and we met that deadline.

Well, for the staff here today, let me reassure you: You are not dreaming. This is the President of the United States. [*Laughter*] He is standing here at the headquarters, or as close as we could get him to it, of the Environmental Protection Agency. And he's not up for reelection for another 4 years. [*Laughter*] I think, as a matter of fact, he's probably smiling for all three of those reasons. [*Laughter*] The President is here for a very simple reason: He cares. He cares urgently about protecting the environment. He said so during his campaign, and his commitment came through to me in my very first meeting with him. And it has since been reinforced in countless ways, only one of which is the fact that he's here with us today.

This powerful statement, this important symbol of the President's interest in the environment, may not, in fact, make our jobs here any easier. If anything, I think our work will be judged by even higher expectations than ever before. But isn't it encouraging to have an environmentalist in the White House who comes here to signal his close and public commitment to the work of the Environmental Protection Agency? Mr. President, I know that you appreciate—as I do and as Russ Train was saying in his remarks before you arrived—that life is not easy on the front line of environmental protection. Probably no other Federal agency touches so many lives as EPA touches. Probably no other Federal agency faces so many complex and fiercely controversial decisions.

Looking out over this group, you can almost see the powder burns. I don't think it's simply that it's Ash Wednesday today. [*Laughter*] By the way, I don't know if there's any symbolism in this, but we are taking office on the very first day of Lent. [*Laughter*] So, to my friends and colleagues here at EPA, let me say simply this: Through the end of the century and on into the next, the quality of human life and of the environment will be very powerfully influenced by your energies, your imagination, and your dedication. The public demand for a safe, clean environment has probably never been firmer. And so, the demands that you face, that we face, have probably never been greater.

In the confirmation hearing, there were two themes that were sounded again and again from across the political spector [spectrum]: "The Environmental Protection Agency should be an advocate for the environment," the Senator said. "EPA should enforce the laws of the land," we heard. And so we shall.

I think, as I stand here, about the extraordinary sweep of the responsibilities we here at EPA exercise. I think of so many places in America that have touched me and my family in a very special way, as I was growing up with my parents and my sister, who I'm proud to say are here today, and later on with my wife and children and friends, many of whom are also here today, Lake Michigan, the Rio Grande and the Gulf of Mexico, Narragansett Bay, Cape Cod, and the Chesapeake—these we lived on or near.

And it's personally stirring for me to have some responsibility for them now, for them and for other resources of air, water, and land in a country where the real crown jewels are the wonders of nature. And now even the stratosphere is receiving our attention. And we're called upon to offer the ideas and experiences of the United States to other nations in a search for environmental policies that may be crucial to keeping this planet habitable. The cause of the environment is so vital and so personal that working in this vineyard is its own reward.

One of the hallmarks, I think, of this agency is that many of the people who work here are very powerfully motivated: motivated to help the environment. The idealism and the commitment to a better environment makes you EPA's employees very, very special, and it makes the prospect of working with you here for me a very, very happy one. So, I could not be more pleased or more proud to have the opportunity to work for the environment, to work for President Bush, and to work with you, my EPA colleagues. I think that we are going to do great things together.

Thank you very much.

Note: The President spoke at 10:43 a.m. at Waterside Mall. In his remarks, he referred to Lee M. Thomas and Russell Train, former Administrators of the Environmental Protection Agency. Rev. William H. O'Reilly delivered the invocation.

Statement on the Economic and Domestic Policy Councils

February 8, 1989

Today I am announcing that I will use the Economic Policy Council and the Domestic Policy Council to advise me in the formulation, coordination, and implementation of economic and domestic policy. Along with the National Security Council, the Economic Policy Council and the Domestic Policy Council will serve as the primary channels for advising the President on policy.

The close interrelationship between the U.S. and international economies illustrates the need to review economic policy issues in a comprehensive manner that best serves the national interest of the United States. The Economic Policy Council will serve as the primary channel for advising me on the formulation, coordination, and implementation of economic policy, both domestic and international.

The important social issues facing our nation require thoughtful and creative solutions. The Domestic Policy Council will serve as the primary channel for advising me on the formulation, coordination, and implementation of domestic and social policy.

My commitment to this Cabinet Council structure reflects my conviction that effective decisionmaking depends on the President receiving the best information available from his senior advisers. I believe that these policy councils will effectively coordinate advice from the various departments and agencies.

Remarks and a Question-and-Answer Session With Reporters Prior to a Meeting With William J. Bennett
February 8, 1989

The President. Let me say this. This is not what we call a normal photo op. It's somewhere in between a press conference and what we call a press availability. We'll try to define that for you later on. But the purpose of this meeting is to visit with our new czar, the antinarcotic czar who has come in here, I'm told, with a million ideas, which is typical of him and what I want him to do as we start spelling out how this administration is going to do what this country wants; and that is to fight against and win the fight against narcotics.

And Bill Bennett has a big assignment—a big one. And a lot of it is coordinative. The law is very unclear on how we use his imagination and ability to bring together all agencies of this government in this fight. So, that's what the meeting is about; that's what we're about to start on.

And I'd like to just take this opportunity to say that this isn't a question of whether the law spells out specifically how he does the job—can't get bothered with those details. He is shoulder-to-shoulder with the President as the top official charged with this responsibility. And we're going to figure out a way to live under the drug czar law—and to make it work. And so, we've got a big job ahead. But that's what this little meeting is all about.

Now I'd be glad to take a couple of questions. Then we've got to get on with that.

Secretary of Defense-Designate Tower

Q. Could you comment, Mr. President, on the controversy surrounding the Tower nomination?

The President. Which controversy?

Q. The fact that some of the committee members——

The President. Can you qualify that for me a little, because yesterday when I had a press conference, or last week when I had a press conference, they were asking me about some allegation on national security? And the question was phrased, "Would you be concerned if this hypothetical charge against Tower proved to be true?" And I said I don't like to deal in hypothesis, but subsequently, that charge has been looked into—found to be without validity. And that has happened to this man over and over and over again. And I have seen nothing, not one substantive fact, that makes me change my mind about John Tower's ability to be Secretary of Defense, and be a very good one. And so, I have to ask you, because there's always some other allegation. And to my knowledge, each one of them has been reviewed and shot down in flames. So, what's fair? What is fair in the American process? That's the question I would rhetorically ask in defense of my nominee.

Now, if somebody has some hard information, if somebody has something other than rumor and frenzied speculation, please get it to the FBI, or get it to the White House staff, or certainly get it to the committee in the Senate. But let us be fair enough that we do not deal in rumor after rumor.

Q. What about the question——

Q. What about Senator Nunn's comments today? He said he believes that Senator Tower may still have an alcohol problem and he fears it might impair his running the Department of Defense.

The President. And if he feels that way, they should do exactly what he is doing: look into it. But it ought not to be tried in public by people that don't have any evidence at all to support the fears that Senator Nunn appropriately expressed. If he's got those fears, I have no problems with his expressing them. And I know him to be a fair man, and I know that he will look into that and satisfy himself or not satisfy himself. But it doesn't help for me to speculate on something when there's no evidence that's been presented to me.

Q. What about these new allegations that surfaced yesterday afternoon that have now held up the investigation? Could you tell us anything about these, the seriousness of them?

The President. No, I think I know what

you're talking about. And the problem you get is that some allegations are laid to rest, and then in another form, they come back again, but without any foundation in fact that I know of. But look, the process has to be thorough. I'm not agitated about that, just as long as it's fair. But what I think has been a little unfair is that people are asked across the country to make up their minds without the evidence, without the facts. And so this, I will confess, troubles me some. And yet I'm not challenging the integrity of the people that are seized with properly doing the hearing work for the United States Senate. They've got to do their job.

Q. Sir, how do you explain the fact that Senator Nunn presumably has reviewed the same information that you have and he and some of the others have expressed reservations and say that this evidence presents enough of a question in their mind that they couldn't support Tower? And you're saying that having reviewed——

The President. But then my appeal would be: If you've made up your mind, let the process go forward; let's have the vote. Each Senator has a vote; there's 100 Senators. On this committee there are fewer, but they have an obligation to vote their conscience, to look at the facts and vote their conscience. Now, if your question is to me, have I seen any facts or has anything in the FBI report made me want to change my mind as one who would be concerned about insobriety or about failure to be ready for duty 24 hours a day, the answer is no, I have not. But if somebody else sees the evidence——

Q. But yet you've seen the same facts.

The President. Yes, and if somebody else has seen some evidence that they want to interpret differently, that's not only their right but their obligation. But I don't think it helps for us to sit here discussing allegations in any detail, where none of the American people have had access to the facts. And I have had access to the facts.

Q. Why do we have—there are so many allegations?

The President. I don't know. I'm troubled by that, and I just don't know the answer. So, my plea would be for prompt fulfillment of the responsibilities of the Senate committee, prompt action by the United States Senate, and then a broad appeal for fairplay. Put yourself in the position, each person, if you were charged with certain of these charges out there with no evidence to substantiate it so the American people could fairly make up their mind. Then let's err on the side of fairplay. That's all I'm saying.

Q. Apparently, you will not get a vote this week. They've recessed for the week. Is this going to hurt if it's going to be this delayed?

The President. It doesn't hurt my confidence.

Q. Do you object to the fact that the Senators have spoken out in public on this matter?

The President. I have no objection at all.

Q. Has the investigation gone too far? Personal standards and morality not appropriate?

The President. Well, what's gone too far is allegations that the Senators themselves would agree are totally unfounded to have been floated around for a long period of time and damaged the integrity and honor of a decent man. And that is not good. And I don't know what you do about it, but it's not good. And everyone here knows it's not fair. And so, I don't know what you do about it. But when there's a new allegation—look, the Senator has an obligation; the Justice Department has an obligation to follow up if it has any substance to it. And so, some of the allegations have been looked at and found nonsubstantive.

And I would urge you to go back and look at the transcript of the last press conference I had—that's the full-blown job we do over on the other side there—and there you will see that one questioner raised a question to me about some alleged security violation. I heard Senator Nunn today say that he had no evidence of any kind to substantiate such an allegation. And yet I think it's fair to say that because that very question was raised publicly—and maybe it was my fault in responding to it and everybody else's discussing it—there's been an allegation floating around Senator Tower that, in one way or another, he was less than prudent in terms of national security matters. And I don't think it's fair. I do not think that is fair.

So, how you do your business, and to go the extra mile to get the facts out there, you've got to sort that out. And how I conduct myself in even discussing this, I've got to sort it out a little more clearly because I may have contributed—even though I think I refused to answer this guy's question—by even taking it, to this frenzied air of speculation that does not help anybody. It doesn't help the national security of our country. It doesn't help Senator Tower. It doesn't help the standing of the United States Senate. It might not help the way this President is viewed because I do not want to be out there as less than fully supportive of my nominee. And that's where I stand. And thank you, and this——

Q. Are you mad?

The President. Not mad—I'm calm and contained. I don't get mad easy anymore.

Hey listen, we've got to get one drug question, please.

Q. Secretary Bennett, have you given up smoking?

Mr. Bennett. I won't comment on that allegation. [*Laughter*]

Q. Are you thinking about sending U.S. troops to Latin America?

The President. Is that a drug question? Nobody's discussed that with me. And you're talking about one who is very wary of committing U.S. troops overseas. But I said in the campaign, that there could be times, working cooperatively with leaders in the hemisphere, that American assistance would be sought and American assistance would be granted in wiping out insidious factories that send poison in to poison our kids. And it has happened in the past. You recall U.S. choppers were used in cooperation—I think it was either Bolivia or Peru—Bolivia, I think, and it was effective. So, you don't rule something out.

But I think in reply to your question—stems from some planning that supposedly is going on that we make some big strike somewhere. And I know nothing about that and would be very reluctant to prove some—until I've given it a lot of thought.

Thank you all very much.

Note: The President spoke at 2:25 p.m. in the Oval Office at the White House. William J. Bennett was National Drug Control Policy Director-designate.

Address on Administration Goals Before a Joint Session of Congress
February 9, 1989

Mr. Speaker, Mr. President, and distinguished Members of the House and Senate, honored guests, and fellow citizens: Less than 3 weeks ago, I joined you on the West Front of this very building and, looking over the monuments to our proud past, offered you my hand in filling the next page of American history with a story of extended prosperity and continued peace. And tonight I'm back to offer you my plans as well. The hand remains extended; the sleeves are rolled up; America is waiting; and now we must produce. Together, we can build a better America.

It is comforting to return to this historic Chamber. Here, 22 years ago, I first raised my hand to be sworn into public life. So, tonight I feel as if I'm returning home to friends. And I intend, in the months and years to come, to give you what friends deserve: frankness, respect, and my best judgment about ways to improve America's future. In return, I ask for an honest commitment to our common mission of progress. If we seize the opportunities on the road before us, there'll be praise enough for all. The people didn't send us here to bicker, and it's time to govern.

And many Presidents have come to this Chamber in times of great crisis: war and depression, loss of national spirit. And 8 years ago, I sat in that very chair as President Reagan spoke of punishing inflation and devastatingly high interest rates and people out of work—American confidence on the wane. And our challenge is different. We're fortunate—a much changed landscape lies before us tonight. So, I don't propose to reverse direction. We're headed the right way, but we cannot rest. We're a people whose energy and drive have fueled our rise to greatness. And we're a forward-looking nation—generous, yes, but ambitious, not for ourselves but for the world. Complacency is not in our character—not before, not now, not ever.

And so, tonight we must take a strong America and make it even better. We must address some very real problems. We must establish some very clear priorities. And we must make a very substantial cut in the Federal budget deficit. Some people find that agenda impossible, but I'm presenting to you tonight a realistic plan for tackling it. My plan has four broad features: attention to urgent priorities, investment in the future, an attack on the deficit, and no new taxes. This budget represents my best judgment of how we can address our priorities. There are many areas in which we would all like to spend more than I propose; I understand that. But we cannot until we get our fiscal house in order.

Next year alone, thanks to economic growth, without any change in the law, the Federal Government will take in over $80 billion more than it does this year. That's right—over $80 billion in new revenues, with no increases in taxes. And our job is to allocate those new resources wisely. We can afford to increase spending by a modest amount, but enough to invest in key priorities and still cut the deficit by almost 40 percent in 1 year. And that will allow us to meet the targets set forth in the Gramm-Rudman-Hollings law. But to do that, we must recognize that growth above inflation in Federal programs is not preordained, that not all spending initiatives were designed to be immortal.

I make this pledge tonight: My team and I are ready to work with the Congress, to form a special leadership group, to negotiate in good faith, to work day and night—if that's what it takes—to meet the budget targets and to produce a budget on time.

We cannot settle for business as usual. Government by continuing resolution, or government by crisis, will not do. And I ask the Congress tonight to approve several measures which will make budgeting more sensible. We could save time and improve efficiency by enacting 2-year budgets. Forty-three Governors have the line-item veto. Presidents should have it, too. And at the very least, when a President proposes to rescind Federal spending, the Congress should be required to vote on that proposal instead of killing it by inaction. And I ask the Congress to honor the public's wishes by passing a constitutional amendment to require a balanced budget. Such an amendment, once phased in, will discipline both the Congress and the executive branch.

Several principles describe the kind of America I hope to build with your help in the years ahead. We will not have the luxury of taking the easy, spendthrift approach to solving problems because higher spending and higher taxes put economic growth at risk. Economic growth provides jobs and hope. Economic growth enables us to pay for social programs. Economic growth enhances the security of the Nation, and low tax rates create economic growth.

I believe in giving Americans greater freedom and greater choice. And I will work for choice for American families, whether in the housing in which they live, the schools to which they send their children, or the child care they select for their young. You see, I believe that we have an obligation to those in need, but that government should not be the provider of first resort for things that the private sector can produce better. I believe in a society that is free from discrimination and bigotry of any kind. And I will work to knock down the barriers left by past discrimination and to build a more tolerant society that will stop such barriers from ever being built again.

I believe that family and faith represent the moral compass of the Nation. And I'll work to make them strong, for as Benjamin Franklin said: "If a sparrow cannot fall to the ground without His notice, can a great nation rise without His aid?" And I believe in giving people the power to make their own lives better through growth and opportunity. And together, let's put power in the hands of people.

Three weeks ago, we celebrated the bicentennial inaugural, the 200th anniversary of the first Presidency. And if you look back, one thing is so striking about the way the Founding Fathers looked at America. They didn't talk about themselves. They talked about posterity. They talked about the future. And we, too, must think in terms bigger than ourselves. We must take actions today that will ensure a better tomorrow. We must extend American leadership in technology, increase long-term investment, improve our educational system, and boost productivity. These are the keys to building a better future, and here are some of my recommendations:

I propose almost $2.2 billion for the National Science Foundation to promote basic research and keep us on track to double its budget by 1993.

I propose to make permanent the tax credit for research and development.

I've asked Vice President Quayle to chair a new Task Force on Competitiveness.

And I request funding for NASA [National Aeronautics and Space Administration] and a strong space program, an increase of almost $2.4 billion over the current fiscal year. We must have a manned space station; a vigorous, safe space shuttle program; and more commercial development in space. The space program should always go "full throttle up." And that's not just our ambition; it's our destiny.

I propose that we cut the maximum tax rate on capital gains to increase long-term investment. History on this is clear—this will increase revenues, help savings, and create new jobs. We won't be competitive if we leave whole sectors of America behind. This is the year we should finally enact urban enterprise zones and bring hope to the inner cities.

But the most important competitiveness program of all is one which improves education in America. When some of our students actually have trouble locating America on a map of the world, it is time for us to map a new approach to education. We must reward excellence and cut through bureaucracy. We must help schools that need help the most. We must give choice to parents, students, teachers, and principals; and we must hold all concerned accountable. In education, we cannot tolerate mediocrity. I want to cut that dropout rate and make America a more literate nation, because what it really comes down to is this: The longer our graduation lines are today, the shorter our unemployment lines will be tomorrow.

So, tonight I'm proposing the following initiatives: the beginning of a $500 million program to reward America's best schools, merit schools; the creation of special Presidential awards for the best teachers in every State, because excellence should be rewarded; the establishment of a new program of National Science Scholars, one each year for every Member of the House and Senate, to give this generation of students a special incentive to excel in science and mathematics; the expanded use of magnet schools, which give families and students greater choice; and a new program to encourage alternative certification, which will let talented people from all fields teach in our classrooms. I've said I'd like to be the "Education President." And tonight, I'd ask you to join me by becoming the "Education Congress."

Just last week, as I settled into this new office, I received a letter from a mother in Pennsylvania who had been struck by my message in the Inaugural Address. "Not 12 hours before," she wrote, "my husband and I received word that our son was addicted to cocaine. He had the world at his feet. Bright, gifted, personable—he could have done anything with his life. And now he has chosen cocaine." "And please," she wrote, "find a way to curb the supply of cocaine. Get tough with the pushers. Our son needs your help."

My friends, that voice crying out for help could be the voice of your own neighbor, your own friend, your own son. Over 23 million Americans used illegal drugs last year, at a staggering cost to our nation's well-being. Let this be recorded as the time when America rose up and said no to drugs. The scourge of drugs must be stopped. And I am asking tonight for an increase of almost a billion dollars in budget outlays to escalate the war against drugs. The war must be waged on all fronts. Our new drug czar, Bill Bennett, and I will be shoulder to shoulder in the executive branch leading the charge.

Some money will be used to expand treatment to the poor and to young mothers. This will offer the helping hand to the many innocent victims of drugs, like the thousands of babies born addicted or with AIDS because of the mother's addiction. Some will be used to cut the waiting time for treatment. Some money will be devoted to those urban schools where the emergency is now the worst. And much of it will be used to protect our borders, with help from the Coast Guard and the Customs Service, the Departments of State and Justice, and, yes, the U.S. military.

I mean to get tough on the drug criminals. And let me be clear: This President will back up those who put their lives on the line every single day—our local police officers. My budget asks for beefed-up prosecution, for a new attack on organized crime, and for enforcement of tough sentences—and for the worst kingpins, that means the death penalty. I also want to make sure that when a drug dealer is convicted there's a cell waiting for him. And he should not go free because prisons are too full. And so, let the word go out: If you're caught and convicted, you will do time.

But for all we do in law enforcement, in interdiction and treatment, we will never win this war on drugs unless we stop the demand for drugs. So, some of this increase will be used to educate the young about the dangers of drugs. We must involve the parents. We must involve the teachers. We must involve the communities. And, my friends, we must involve ourselves, each and every one of us in this concern.

One problem related to drug use demands our urgent attention and our continuing compassion, and that is the terrible tragedy of AIDS. I'm asking for $1.6 billion for education to prevent the disease and for research to find a cure.

If we're to protect our future, we need a new attitude about the environment. We must protect the air we breathe. I will send to you shortly legislation for a new, more effective Clean Air Act. It will include a plan to reduce by date certain the emissions which cause acid rain, because the time for study alone has passed, and the time for action is now. We must make use of clean coal. My budget contains full funding, on schedule, for the clean coal technology agreement that we've made with Canada. We've made that agreement with Canada, and we intend to honor that agreement. We must not neglect our parks. So, I'm asking to fund new acquisitions under the Land and Water Conservation Fund. We must protect our oceans. And I support new penalties against those who would dump medical waste and other trash into our oceans. The age of the needle on the beaches must end.

And in some cases, the gulfs and oceans off our shores hold the promise of oil and gas reserves which can make our nation more secure and less dependent on foreign oil. And when those with the most promise can be tapped safely, as with much of the Alaska National Wildlife Refuge, we should proceed. But we must use caution; we must respect the environment. And so, tonight I'm calling for the indefinite postponement of three lease sales which have raised troubling questions, two off the coast of California and one which could threaten the Everglades in Florida. Action on these three lease sales will await the conclusion of a special task force set up to measure the potential for environmental damage.

I'm directing the Attorney General and the Administrator of the Environmental Protection Agency to use every tool at their disposal to speed and toughen the enforcement of our laws against toxic-waste dumpers. I want faster cleanups and tougher enforcement of penalties against polluters.

In addition to caring for our future, we must care for those around us. A decent society shows compassion for the young, the elderly, the vulnerable, and the poor. Our first obligation is to the most vulnerable—infants, poor mothers, children living in poverty—and my proposed budget recognizes this. I ask for full funding of Medicaid, an increase of over $3 billion, and an expansion of the program to include coverage of pregnant women who are near the poverty line. I believe we should help working families cope with the burden of child care. Our help should be aimed at those who need it most: low-income families with young children. I support a new child care tax credit that will aim our efforts at exactly those families, without discriminating against mothers who choose to stay at home.

Now, I know there are competing proposals. But remember this: The overwhelming majority of all preschool child care is now provided by relatives and neighbors and churches and community groups. Families who choose these options should remain eligible for help. Parents should have choice. And for those children who are unwanted or abused or whose parents are deceased, we should encourage adoption. I propose to reenact the tax deduction for adoption expenses and to double it to $3,000. Let's make it easier for these kids to have parents who love them.

We have a moral contract with our senior citizens. And in this budget, Social Security is fully funded, including a full cost-of-living adjustment. We must honor our contract.

We must care about those in the shadow of life, and I, like many Americans, am deeply troubled by the plight of the homeless. The causes of homelessness are many; the history is long. But the moral imperative to act is clear. Thanks to the deep well of generosity in this great land, many organizations already contribute, but we in government cannot stand on the sidelines. In my budget, I ask for greater support for emergency food and shelter, for health services and measures to prevent substance abuse, and for clinics for the mentally ill. And I propose a new initiative involving the full range of government agencies. We must confront this national shame.

There's another issue that I've decided to mention here tonight. I've long believed that the people of Puerto Rico should have the right to determine their own political future. Personally, I strongly favor statehood. But I urge the Congress to take the necessary steps to allow the people to decide in a referendum.

Certain problems, the result of decades of unwise practices, threaten the health and security of our people. Left unattended, they will only get worse. But we can act now to put them behind us.

Earlier this week, I announced my support for a plan to restore the financial and moral integrity of our savings system. I ask Congress to enact our reform proposals within 45 days. We must not let this situation fester. We owe it to the savers in this country to solve this problem. Certainly, the savings of Americans must remain secure. Let me be clear: Insured depositors will continue to be fully protected, but any plan to refinance the system must be accompanied by major reform. Our proposals will prevent such a crisis from recurring. The best answer is to make sure that a mess like this will never happen again. The majority of thrifts in communities across the Nation have been honest. They've played a major role in helping families achieve the dream of home ownership. But make no mistake, those who are corrupt, those who break the law, must be kicked out of the business; and they should go to jail.

We face a massive task in cleaning up the waste left from decades of environmental neglect at America's nuclear weapons plants. Clearly, we must modernize these plants and operate them safely. That's not at issue; our national security depends on it. But beyond that, we must clean up the old mess that's been left behind. And I propose in this budget to more than double our current effort to do so. This will allow us to identify the exact nature of the various problems so we can clean them up, and clean them up we will.

We've been fortunate during these past 8 years. America is a stronger nation than it was in 1980. Morale in our Armed Forces has been restored; our resolve has been shown. Our readiness has been improved, and we are at peace. There can no longer be any doubt that peace has been made more secure through strength. And when America is stronger, the world is safer.

Most people don't realize that after the successful restoration of our strength, the Pentagon budget has actually been reduced in real terms for each of the last 4 years. We cannot tolerate continued real reduction in defense. In light of the compelling need to reduce the deficit, however, I support a 1-year freeze in the military budget, something I proposed last fall in my flexible freeze plan. And this freeze will apply for only 1 year, and after that, increases above inflation will be required. I will not sacrifice

American preparedness, and I will not compromise American strength.

I should be clear on the conditions attached to my recommendation for the coming year: The savings must be allocated to those priorities for investing in our future that I've spoken about tonight. This defense freeze must be a part of a comprehensive budget agreement which meets the targets spelled out in Gramm-Rudman-Hollings law without raising taxes and which incorporates reforms in the budget process.

I've directed the National Security Council to review our national security and defense policies and report back to me within 90 days to ensure that our capabilities and resources meet our commitments and strategies. I'm also charging the Department of Defense with the task of developing a plan to improve the defense procurement process and management of the Pentagon, one which will fully implement the Packard commission report. Many of these changes can only be made with the participation of the Congress, and so, I ask for your help. We need fewer regulations. We need less bureaucracy. We need multiyear procurement and 2-year budgeting. And frankly—and don't take this wrong—we need less congressional micromanagement of our nation's military policy. I detect a slight division on that question, but nevertheless—[*laughter*].

Securing a more peaceful world is perhaps the most important priority I'd like to address tonight. You know, we meet at a time of extraordinary hope. Never before in this century have our values of freedom, democracy, and economic opportunity been such a powerful and intellectual force around the globe. Never before has our leadership been so crucial, because while America has its eyes on the future, the world has its eyes on America.

And it's a time of great change in the world, and especially in the Soviet Union. Prudence and common sense dictate that we try to understand the full meaning of the change going on there, review our policies, and then proceed with caution. But I've personally assured General Secretary Gorbachev that at the conclusion of such a review we will be ready to move forward. We will not miss any opportunity to work for peace. The fundamental facts remain that the Soviets retain a very powerful military machine in the service of objectives which are still too often in conflict with ours. So, let us take the new openness seriously, but let's also be realistic. And let's always be strong.

There are some pressing issues we must address. I will vigorously pursue the Strategic Defense Initiative. The spread, and even use, of sophisticated weaponry threatens global security as never before. Chemical weapons must be banned from the face of the Earth, never to be used again. And look, this won't be easy. Verification—extraordinarily difficult, but civilization and human decency demand that we try. And the spread of nuclear weapons must be stopped. And I'll work to strengthen the hand of the International Atomic Energy Agency. Our diplomacy must work every day against the proliferation of nuclear weapons.

And around the globe, we must continue to be freedom's best friend. And we must stand firm for self-determination and democracy in Central America, including in Nicaragua. It is my strongly held conviction that when people are given the chance they inevitably will choose a free press, freedom of worship, and certifiably free and fair elections.

We must strengthen the alliance of the industrial democracies, as solid a force for peace as the world has ever known. And this is an alliance forged by the power of our ideals, not the pettiness of our differences. So, let's lift our sights to rise above fighting about beef hormones, to building a better future, to move from protectionism to progress.

I've asked the Secretary of State to visit Europe next week and to consult with our allies on the wide range of challenges and opportunities we face together, including East-West relations. And I look forward to meeting with our NATO partners in the near future.

And I, too, shall begin a trip shortly to the far reaches of the Pacific Basin, where the winds of democracy are creating new hope and the power of free markets is unleashing a new force. When I served as our representative in China 14 or 15 years ago, few would have predicted the scope of the changes we've witnessed since then. But in preparing for this trip, I was struck by something I came across from a Chinese writer. He was speaking of his country, decades ago, but his words speak to each of us in America tonight. "Today," he said, "we're afraid of the simple words like 'goodness' and 'mercy' and 'kindness.' " My friends, if we're to succeed as a nation, we must rediscover those words.

In just 3 days, we mark the birthday of Abraham Lincoln, the man who saved our Union and gave new meaning to the word "opportunity." Lincoln once said: "I hold that while man exists, it is his duty to improve not only his own condition but to assist in ameliorating that of mankind." It is this broader mission to which I call all Americans, because the definition of a successful life must include serving others.

And to the young people of America, who sometimes feel left out, I ask you tonight to give us the benefit of your talent and energy through a new program called YES, for Youth Entering Service to America.

To those men and women in business, remember the ultimate end of your work: to make a better product, to create better lives. I ask you to plan for the longer term and avoid that temptation of quick and easy paper profits.

To the brave men and women who wear the uniform of the United States of America, thank you. Your calling is a high one: to be the defenders of freedom and the guarantors of liberty. And I want you to know that this nation is grateful for your service.

To the farmers of America, we appreciate the bounty you provide. We will work with you to open foreign markets to American agricultural products.

And to the parents of America, I ask you to get involved in your child's schooling. Check on the homework, go to the school, meet the teachers, care about what is happening there. It's not only your child's future on the line, it's America's.

To kids in our cities, don't give up hope. Say no to drugs; stay in school. And, yes, "Keep hope alive."

To those 37 million Americans with some form of disability, you belong in the economic mainstream. We need your talents in America's work force. Disabled Americans must become full partners in America's opportunity society.

To the families of America watching tonight in your living rooms, hold fast to your dreams because ultimately America's future rests in your hands.

And to my friends in this Chamber, I ask your cooperation to keep America growing while cutting the deficit. That's only fair to those who now have no vote: the generations to come. Let them look back and say that we had the foresight to understand that a time of peace and prosperity is not the time to rest but a time to press forward, a time to invest in the future.

And let all Americans remember that no problem of human making is too great to be overcome by human ingenuity, human energy, and the untiring hope of the human spirit. I believe this. I would not have asked to be your President if I didn't. And tomorrow the debate on the plan I've put forward begins, and I ask the Congress to come forward with your own proposals. Let's not question each other's motives. Let's debate, let's negotiate; but let us solve the problem.

Recalling anniversaries may not be my specialty in speeches—[*laughter*]—but tonight is one of some note. On February 9th, 1941, just 48 years ago tonight, Sir Winston Churchill took to the airwaves during Britain's hour of peril. He'd received from President Roosevelt a hand-carried letter quoting Longfellow's famous poem: "Sail on, O Ship of State! Sail on, O Union, strong and great! Humanity with all its fears, With all the hopes of future years, Is hanging breathless on thy fate!" And Churchill responded on this night by radio broadcast to a nation at war, but he directed his words to Franklin Roosevelt. "We shall not fail or falter," he said. "We shall not weaken or tire. Give us the tools, and we will finish the job."

Tonight, almost half a century later, our peril may be less immediate, but the need for perseverance and clear-sighted fortitude is just as great. Now, as then, there are those who say it can't be done. There are voices who say that America's best days have passed, that we're bound by constraints, threatened by problems, surrounded by troubles which limit our ability to hope. Well, tonight I remain full of hope. We Americans have only begun on our mission of goodness and greatness. And to those timid souls, I repeat the plea: "Give us the tools, and we will do the job."

Thank you. God bless you, and God bless America.

Note: The President spoke at 9:07 p.m. in the House Chamber of the Capitol. The address was broadcast live on nationwide radio and television.

Message to the Congress Transmitting the Fiscal Year 1990 Budget
February 9, 1989

To the Congress of the United States:

I hereby transmit a supplement to the Message I am delivering to the Joint Session of the Congress tonight. It is titled "Building a Better America," and it contains further description of the plans and proposals mentioned in the Message. I urge the Congress to give favorable consideration to these proposals and renew my invitation to the congressional leadership to work together to assure that America is united, strong, at peace, and fiscally sound.

GEORGE BUSH

The White House,
February 9, 1989.

Remarks and a Question-and-Answer Session With Reporters Following a Luncheon With Prime Minister Brian Mulroney in Ottawa, Canada
February 10, 1989

The President. Let me just say on behalf of Mrs. Bush, our Secretary of State, and others, this has been a good visit. It is an important visit because it symbolizes the importance that we place on the relationship with Canada. We're each other's largest trading partners. We are friends. We share a long, peaceful border, and we have many common interests. And today we had an opportunity to discuss not just the bilateral relationship that is very, very strong and very good but we had a chance to talk about the East-West relationship. I had a chance to talk about the problems on trade; indeed, our trade ministers are talking right now, you might say. And so, I felt the visit was outstanding.

The Prime Minister and I reviewed the concerns that he has about acid rain; and I referred him to what I said last night to the American people: my determination to move on forward with setting limits, with legislation, and then moving to discussions with Canada, leading to an accord that I think will be beneficial to both countries. And so, that problem—and it has been a problem—is one that we are both determined to move forward towards solution. In terms of the trade agreement, we, of course, have saluted the courageous position taken by the Prime Minister of Canada. We have great respect for that in the United States; and we want to now do our part, part of the United States, to follow through with whatever implementation is required.

So, the mood was upbeat, the spirit good, and I am very glad that this was my first visit outside of the continental United States as President. And we will keep in touch, and each of us has pledged to see that this strong relationship becomes even stronger.

I think we both agreed we'd take a question or two at what we affectionately call a scrum. [*Laughter*] I've been looking for words to describe what we do at press occasions like this down across the border, and that's an appropriate word.

Acid Rain

Q. Mr. President, to what degree did you assure the Prime Minister of your feeling of confidence that the Congress will go along with you on your acid rain request last night?

The President. I think the Prime Minister is aware of the political divisions and political waves there in our country on this issue. But I assured him that the time for just pure study was over and that we've now approached the time for legislative action. And I pledged that in the campaign. And so, to the degree there is disparity, a lack of uniformity in the Congress, I think the Prime Minister sees it as my responsibility to try to move forward to do that which I said I wanted to do.

Agricultural and Environmental Issues

Q. ——concern that the Arctic blast that just swept across the continent following on last summer's drought has created some permanent damage in the agricultural regions on both sides of the border? I wonder if you discussed that at all and whether there could be a cooperative way of dealing with this and maybe at some point making a proposal to get some of the surplus Canadian water down into the drought-stricken regions of the U.S.?

The President. We did not discuss water diversion. We did not discuss the effects of the Arctic cold air. We did talk about the need for a global approach to environmental concerns.

Do you want to add something to that, Mr. Prime Minister?

The Prime Minister. No.

Q. Mr. President, were you——

The President. The gentleman right here, and then I'll be right over.

Acid Rain

Q. Do you have an estimate of how long it will take, assuming the Congress goes along with your legislative program, before you are ready to talk about a bilateral accord?

The President. No, but we're going to press forward with this right away. We have a brand new Administrator of EPA. We've got a legislative team to propose the legislation I talked about last night. And we've gotten some reasonable levels of funding. So, we're on the move. But we did not discuss an exact timeframe. I would be misrepresenting or understating things if I didn't say that the Prime Minister once again impressed on me the urgency of moving as fast as we can, but we didn't set a time.

Who had one back in here?

Q. Yes, sir, you were saying, Mr. President, that you weren't in a position yet to discuss a specific timetable and targets for reduction of acid rain.

The President. We will be discussing targets, and we will get agreement on that, I'm sure. But I have an obligation now to recommend to our Congress the setting of certain limits, so we will move forward with that much specific.

Q. Mr. President, what kind of reductions and what kind of timetable do you have in mind?

The President. I have in mind as fast as possible.

Q. Mr. Prime Minister, I wondered, sir, if you are satisfied with the steps that the President has outlined to deal with the acid rain question or whether you have asked for more here?

The Prime Minister. Well, I think that this represents quite substantial progress. You know, it wasn't so long ago that Canada was sort of going it alone in many ways in this area. The President's position puts a great impetus for action domestically in the United States, which is a condition precedent, and the President is signaling, as well, subsequent discussions that will lead to an acid rain accord to benefit both the United States and Canada. This, I think, is real progress. And while I suppose I'm like a lot of people who would like it done tomorrow in this area, I know it's not going to happen, but this represents a very measurable progress. And I view it as evidence of the commitments that the President gave during the campaign and has referred to since, including his speech to the Congress last night, which is, for a neighbor and friend troubled by this problem for some time, very encouraging.

Q. Presuming you and the President reach an agreement, could you begin to discuss an accord before the full U.S. program is in place on acid rain, or will it be necessary to wait until its legislation is through Congress?

The Prime Minister. The Americans will, of course, deal with their own problems domestically, free from any comment by me about what happens internally. But clearly, what the President is saying is that he has a two-pronged approach: one that will summon the legislative authority of the Congress of the United States to put in place those mechanisms that are required there; and secondly, an arrangement which will be negotiated with Canada to conclude an accord which will deal, hopefully, in a definitive manner with this.

Q. How soon can those negotiations——

Q. Would you prefer to undertake negotiations immediately with the United States instead of waiting for them first to pass laws?

The Prime Minister. First, it is necessary for the President to talk about this with legislators and that the Americans are prepared to pass their own laws for the purification of their atmosphere in this domain. In the second place, as the President has just indicated, we are on the way to advance, rapidly I hope, towards the conclusion of the negotiations for a bilateral accord about the international environment. Therefore, we are encouraged by the developments and the declarations of President Bush today.

U.S. Economy

Q. Back at home today, both consumer prices and bank prime rates went up. To the extent that that goes against your assumptions in the budget, how badly do you see that hurting your budget?

The President. You've got to wait to see how long interest rates stay different from that which we've projected. But I would not make assumptions based on one monthly release of figures on either the CPI [Consumer Price Index] or in this instance—I guess you're talking about the Producer Price Index—because we've found that they jump around some. And I am not overly concerned about inflation, at this point, in the United States. I don't like the figures; but I'm not concerned, long-run, about inflation in our country. We still have excess plant capacity. The economy is growing, and I think that's good.

I pointed out last night that we expect revenues in 1 year of $82 billion—I think is the figure—more just from growth. So, it is important we keep growing. Any President should be concerned if there are persistent signs of inflationary pressures to come. But I don't see the signs now that had me worried at all. So, I would hope that these figures would prove to be just a blip on an otherwise rather calm and hopeful radar screen.

Canadian Steel Exports

Q. Prime Minister, did you discuss the steel issue, and did you make any mention of keeping Canada out of the voluntary export program that the steel lobby in the United States wants?

The Prime Minister. There is a meeting going on now between Ms. Hills [U.S. Trade Representative] and Minister [of International Trade] John Crosbie in regard specifically to that. But as you know, Canada is a fair trader, and we should not in any way be impacted by that kind of proposition. We wouldn't deserve in any way to be included within its purview. And that would be the position that Mr. Crosbie will be explaining to Ms. Hills.

Une dernière question, a final question, Mr. President, and then——

The President. Dernière?

The Prime Minister. Une dernière question pour le Président?

The President. Mais oui. [*Laughter*] *C'est* fine *pour moi.* [Sure, this is fine for me.] It's colder than hell. Yes, sorry about that. [*Laughter*]

Acid Rain

Q. In 1995 or the year 2000—for a 50-percent cut in acid rain?

The President. Qu'est ce que c'est la ques-

tion? [What is the question?] *Je ne comprends pas.* [I don't understand.] [*Laughter*]

Q. Would you like 1995 or the year 2000 for a 50-percent cut in transporter emissions on acid rain?

The President. Too early to answer that.

Q. Will negotiations start this year, Mr. President?

The President. I hope so.

East-West Relations

Q. Were you on the same wavelengths on East-West relations in your discussions this morning?

The President. Certainement! [*Laughter*]

The Prime Minister. May I introduce my Quebec—[*laughter*].

The President. No, we were. And I have great respect for the Prime Minister's views. I have great respect for his understanding with his experience of the alliance and its importance. I value his judgment on what's happening inside the Soviet Union. And so, we had a long, I think productive, discussion about that. And I had an opportunity to explain to him that our review of our national security policies, our foreign policy objectives—it's a serious thing. It is not a foot-dragging operation. It is not trying to send a signal to Secretary Gorbachev that we want to move backwards. It is simply prudent. And I am absolutely convinced that the Soviets understand this; and I'm also convinced that the—I don't want to put words in his mouth—but the Prime Minister of Canada, a very important part of all of this, understands it as well.

The Prime Minister. Thank you very much.

Note: The President spoke at 3 p.m. in the Prime Minister's residence. Prior to the luncheon, the President met with the Prime Minister and U.S. and Canadian officials. Following the exchange, the President and Mrs. Bush went to Kennebunkport, ME, for a weekend stay.

Remarks to Members of the Business and Industry Association of New Hampshire in Manchester
February 13, 1989

Thank you, ladies and gentlemen. Thank you, Governor. Thank you for that welcome back. Judd, thank you for that warm introduction, and thank all of you for that welcome. I want to thank Bill Gingrich and others at BIA for arranging on relatively short notice this wonderful meeting. I want to pay my respects to our outstanding congressional delegation—our two Congressmen are here—and our senior Senator Warren Rudman, here with us today. But you're well represented in Washington with these four outstanding individuals. I'm very sorry if I'm late—a little trouble parking the 18-wheeler. [*Laughter*]

A few things have happened since I spoke to you 2 years ago at the BIA. For one thing, I got a new job. And so did Bonnie Newman. [*Laughter*] And I'm very pleased on both counts. It really is great to be back and see so many old friends.

Last week I made an address to the joint session of Congress, spelling out my policies and my priorities as America moves into a new decade—a whole new century 11 short years away. And I offered my hand to the Congress in a spirit of bipartisan cooperation and said, "Together we can build a better America."

And this week, I'm traveling to different parts of the country to talk as directly as possible to the American people. And it's no coincidence that this very first stop is here in New Hampshire. Actually, I thought we were heading south. But John Sununu, you know, the new Chief of Staff, had his way, and here we are. [*Laughter*] Some said I just wanted to come back and drink with the boys at the Alpine Club again right here. [*Laughter*] What a great evening that was, I'll tell you.

A year ago at about this time, I was here

in New Hampshire under different circumstances—literally a year ago. I had just been defeated in Iowa. I was up at 6:50 a.m. my first morning here, outside on a cold day—a little colder, as I remember, than today even—holding my coffee in one hand and shaking hands with some of the guys at the factory in another. And the columnists had begun to write my political obituary. Well, I knew things seemed worse than they actually were. And let me tell you why I say that. I knew we were strong here. Governor Sununu was at my side, Judd Gregg and, of course, his dad, Hugh. And I had so many people, including many in this room, who helped me assemble a statewide organization, A–1 in every single way. And you never can forget in American politics the importance of people being involved.

And I also had a message, a message that the people of New Hampshire, and then all America, understood: Sensible ideas work; we can do the job, and we can do it without new taxes. And the foundation that we built held firm; it never cracked or crumbled. And the steadfast support that I received gave me the chance to pick myself off of that canvas, and the rest, as they say, is history. And so today, now that I've returned to your State for the first time as the 41st President of the United States, let me repeat those four little words that I said on election night: "Thank you, New Hampshire."

But as Judd reminded us, the journey goes back longer than just a year ago today. It goes back to '79 and '80, when I first ran for President. In 1980 things were different in America. Our economy was stagnant. Inflation and interest rates were peaking at unprecedented highs for our country. Our workers were out of jobs. And America's respect around the world was on the decline.

And since then, under the leadership of a great President, America is once again proud and prosperous. And our economy is now in its 75th month of expansion—the longest period of uninterrupted economic growth during peacetime in our nation's history. And our people are back at work. In fact, the proportion of Americans with jobs is at a post-World War II high. And America is once again respected around the world as a resolute force for peace and freedom. And because we did strengthen this country, I am optimistic about our chances to enhance the peace worldwide. We're headed in the right direction, and I mean to keep us headed in the right direction. We've made tremendous progress, and I mean to build on that progress.

Last Thursday night, I presented to the Congress a realistic plan for dealing with the Federal budget. And my plan has four broad features: attention to urgent priorities, investment in the future, an attack on the deficit, and no new taxes. And this budget plan represents a commitment to meet our national priorities and at the same time keep faith with our promise to the American people on the tax front of no new taxes. There are some areas in which we would all like to spend more, but we cannot until we get our fiscal house in order and bring the Federal budget deficit down.

In the next fiscal year, under current law with no changes or new taxes, revenues will grow by over $80 billion—$80 billion more revenue to the Federal Government in 1 year under existing law. And that's an increase of nearly 8½ percent. And that should be enough to finance our priorities and bring the deficit down without taxes.

The Federal budget will not be balanced overnight, but our plan is a realistic one. And right here I'd like to salute Warren Rudman for his role in disciplining both the executive branch and the Congress by being a part of that historic Gramm-Rudman-Hollings bill. It's very important legislation. Yes, it requires tough choices. Mine is a budget plan that will work, but not with business as usual. It will require a partnership with the Congress. And as I said on Thursday night, my team and I are prepared to work with the Congress; to negotiate in good faith with the leadership; to work day and night, if that's what it takes, to meet budget targets; and to produce a budget on time.

I've spoken about priorities; let me just share with you briefly what those priorities are. First, let's make sure that America remains the greatest and the most productive nation on the face of the Earth. We should begin to invest now in ways that will make

America more competitive in the future. And that means continuing America's leadership in the knowledge business: more funds for basic research; a permanent tax credit for R&D, for research and development; a strengthened role for science and technology in our national policy deliberations.

When I was Vice President, I chaired a task force on regulatory relief, which was intended to help survey the wilderness of government regulation to determine which rules were hurting private productive activity and which were helping. And we did a lot of good early on. We got rid of some needless regulation, and still protecting the safety in the workplace and things of that important nature. But the work of this task force will continue, and its mission expanded, however. The Vice President, Dan Quayle, will head this new task force on competitiveness to explore a range of issues, from regulatory reform to training for the work force of the future.

I've also asked the Congress for its cooperation in passing what I believe is the most important competitiveness package of all: a package of bills to improve education in America. You know, Louis Pasteur once said: "Chance favors only the prepared mind." Our children deserve every break that we can give them because they do represent our future. And so, for America to be prepared for the future, our children must be educated for the future.

And part of our education effort must be in the area of drugs. Education is still our best means of prevention. And we will fight drugs on all fronts, not only education but treatment, interdiction, and law enforcement. But for those who are already hooked on drugs, we've got to expand treatment. For those who are dealing drugs, I want them to know how serious we are about stopping them. And I have asked for and will insist on tougher penalties. And, yes, that does include the death penalty for those drug kingpins. I believe it will inhibit the continued flow of drugs into this country. And I think the dealers who prey on our kids should know what's coming when they get caught. The kids of America will not become the broken debris of a failed war on drugs—period. We simply can't have that. And a drug-free America has to be the foundation of a healthy, stronger America.

We also must protect our environment: the air we breathe, the water we drink, the beautiful land we live on. And we do need a new attitude, a new commitment to preserving our planet.

We must protect those members of our society who are the most vulnerable: the infants; the pregnant women; children living in poverty; and, yes, the elderly. And we must protect the homeless. Greater support is needed for emergency food and shelter, for health service, and for clinics for the mentally ill. And I've asked for those funds to confront the problems of the homeless, recognizing that most of the work in this field, as in education, will be done at the local and the State and the neighborhood level. We must never let the Federal Government preempt and push aside the activities of our citizens at the family and neighborhood level. The Government, as I said the other night, cannot stand on the sidelines—not in the face of the national shame of the homeless or the depressed stage of our education.

What I also want to say is that government is not the only answer, though. Government has a role. Government's got to do its part, but it can't do everything. And without the will of the people, it really can't do anything. The essence of our government is that it is a democracy of, for, and by the people. To be successful in the years ahead, our mission must also be of, for, and by the people. And really, that's why I've come here today: to look back one final time and to let you know I know why I'm here and how I got here. I don't think there's ever anything wrong in life for saying, "Thank you very much."

And that's exactly what I wanted to do when I came here today: say thank you; but more importantly, now that I am the 41st President of the United States, to look ahead, to thank you for what you can do in the future, and encourage you to give it your all. Join me with a spirit that I know is the spirit of not only this BIA but also the people of New Hampshire, generally, and together we will keep America moving forward, always forward, on a journey that leads to a better America of absolutely limitless opportunities. Thank you all, and God bless you. And it's so nice to be here. Thank you very much.

Note: The President spoke at 9:31 a.m. in the Armory at the Center of New Hampshire Holiday Inn. In his remarks, he referred to Gov. Judd Gregg; William Gingrich, chairman of the Business and Industry Association of New Hampshire; Representatives Charles Douglas and Robert C. Smith; Bonnie Newman, Assistant to the President for Management and Administration; and Hugh Gregg, former Governor of New Hampshire. Following his remarks, the President returned to Washington, DC.

Remarks to Representatives of the Boy Scouts of America
February 13, 1989

Well, I'm just delighted to see all of you here, and to my friend of longstanding, Harold Hook, delighted he's here. Mr. Graves—Earl, Mr. Love—Ben, Boy Scouts and Scouters, and to you three guys who presented these honors to me in a report to me, I'm very grateful to you.

First, I want to thank you for having me now be the honorary president of the Boy Scouts. And I want to thank you for that annual report. But even more, I want to thank you for the good turns—as you call them—the good turns that you do, as your own motto says. Boy Scouts are helping, as Mr. Graves said, the homeless and disabled and the elderly and, in short, the most vulnerable in our society. And to those that have been left behind, you guys are saying, "Hey, we're going to help you catch up." And to those who have given up on themselves, you say as Scouts and Scouters, "We've not given up on you." And you made a difference, helping to combat drug abuse, child abuse, hunger, illiteracy—working with the homeless, unemployment.

You believe in America's greatest treasure—its ability to care. And for nearly a century now, the Boy Scouts have cared about our children. And you've helped them, enriched them, and helped our children enrich mankind. And so, I want to come by and say: Keep up the good work! I think if we do this enough and if I make the point how strongly I feel about what you do, I think the country will understand very clearly what I mean when I talk about One Thousand Points of Light, because I think of the Scouts, and I think of what you all do to help others. And it's clear, bright light, bright and shining, and you're an inspiration to all of us. And I'm grateful that you came here, and I'm proud to have my gold card here that I promise I'll keep right there in that desk in the Oval Office to remind me of the good work that the Scouts do for everybody.

Thank you very much.

Note: The President spoke at 2 p.m. in the Roosevelt Room at the White House. In his opening remarks, he referred to Harold S. Hook, Earl G. Graves, and Ben H. Love, president, commissioner, and chief executive, respectively, of the Boy Scouts of America. Boy Scout representatives presented the President with a certificate naming him the honorary president of the Boy Scouts, a gold lifetime membership card, and a copy of the Boy Scout Handbook.

Remarks at the Swearing-in Ceremony for Jack F. Kemp as Secretary of Housing and Urban Development
February 13, 1989

The President. I'd say be seated, but I don't want to win the Smart Aleck of the Year Award. [*Laughter*] Thank you very much. I open with a question: Jack, now that you're going to be in charge of Federal housing, does that make you my landlord? [*Laughter*]

It's a pleasure, it's a real pleasure for me to be here for the swearing-in of Jack Kemp as Secretary of Housing and Urban Development. I've known Jack a long time—Joanne, too. And I've seen him in action, and I think he's going to be a great HUD Secretary. For Joanne, she's an important part of everything he does. And I think of the Thousand Points of Light that I'll keep talking about. No one is more engaged in helping others than Joanne Kemp—doing a great job out there. They'll be a wonderful team.

You know, Jack served nine terms in the House. He was an all-pro Congressman—[*laughter*]—voted by his colleagues three terms as chairman of the House Republican Conference. And Jack's record is an impressive one: more completed passes than any other Member of Congress. [*Laughter*] I count the tax rate reductions of '81 and '86 as being touchdown passes, a couple of his ideas that got across the goal line, incidentally. And the tax cuts did more than put points on the board: They helped produce the longest peacetime expansion ever recorded.

Both Jack and I are dedicated to making America, to the fullest extent possible, an opportunity society. And that means an economy that's thriving and creating jobs; cities that are filled with enterprise and offer residents a good life and a good living; neighborhoods that are vibrant and safe, with affordable houses going up, old ones being restored. It means giving people—working people, poor people, all our citizens—control over their own lives. And it means a commitment to civil rights and economic opportunity for every American. The chance for a greater America lies before us, and we're going to seize that chance.

To all the fine people here at HUD, I want to say that I greatly respect you and the work that you do. You face tough problems every day, and you do it with a tremendous sense of commitment. I think you're a great team, and I think in Jack Kemp you'll have a great quarterback. I also want to pay my respects to Sam Pierce, his predecessor, a faithful, loyal member of the President's Cabinet, who did an outstanding job here. And, Jack, I know you can fill those big shoes.

Jack's a man of ideas, and I've made clear that I want him to apply his creativity and energy to the area of housing and urban policy, which are among the most important and challenging issues in America today. These problems require a compassionate strategy, and that's the reason that I thought of Jack immediately and asked him to take this job. While still in Congress, he developed some innovative ideas, many of which won support from Members on both sides of the aisle.

Our plan is to use enterprise zones to bring jobs, investment, and opportunity to depressed areas. And I believe that, given a chance, economic freedom can bring a revival to the inner city; and it can create jobs and housing and dignity for every citizen. I want to use urban homesteading to enable public housing residents to gain a stake in their own communities and in their own futures. And I want to work toward giving tenants in Federal housing the right to manage and buy their own homes and apartments. Where whole neighborhoods have been blighted and boarded up, sometimes by misguided policies—I want to change those policies and empower residents to rebuild their neighborhoods, with the public and private sectors working together. And I think you know how strongly I feel, but let me say it again: I am committed to equal housing opportunity for all our citizens and to the strong enforcement of the laws against discrimination.

And I want to see us finally end the tragedy of homelessness. I do favor full funding for this McKinney Act. We've got to care for those who for various reasons are unable to care for themselves, and we must identify and remove the obstacles that prevent people from being able to acquire housing.

So, these are our goals. And for these ideas I have clicked off here today—Jack Kemp has been out front for those very principles for a long, long time. A lot of the most innovative thinking on the inner city has come from him. Throughout his political career, he reached out to work with talented people of every race and background, and he's made his commitment to inclusion something visible, something important in everything he has done. And I want him to continue working to open the doors wider, with more opportunity for everyone.

And so, before we go to work, there's one important thing to do, and that is the official swearing-in of the new Secretary of Housing and Urban Development, Jack Kemp.

Thank you all very much.

[*At this point, Secretary Kemp was sworn in.*]

Secretary Kemp. Thank you for that standing ovation. [*Laughter*] Thank you, Mr. President, not only for being here today but for the inspiring mission and exciting goals you've laid out for the Department of Housing and Urban Development. I particularly like the part, Mr. President, about a kinder, gentler quarterback in Jack Kemp. That's going to—[*laughter*].

Thank you, Justice O'Connor. What an honor it is to have Sandra Day O'Connor here to do me the high honor of swearing me in as the new Secretary of HUD. Special thanks to my good friend, the Reverend Keith Butler, of Detroit, who's come down to deliver his moving invocation. To my friend, the NFL [National Football League] Hall of Famer, former Oakland Raider, enemy—[*laughter*]—and dear friend now, leader of the NFL Players Union—I was the former president of the American Football League Players Union, and he is the executive director of the NFLPA [National Football League Players Association], Gene Upshaw—very honored for him to be here, leading us in the Pledge of Allegiance.

I want to take a moment to introduce each and every one of you to my precious family and my inspiration. First, my wife, Joanne. [*Applause*] Our daughter—you don't need to applaud for every one of them, but I have a—[*laughter*]. Our daughter, Judith, who worked in the Reagan-Bush White House—stand up, Judith. Our daughter, Jennifer, who's a public school teacher. Her fiance, Scott Andrews. They're getting married in May, which we're all excited about. Our son, Jimmy, who just recently signed a football—notice I said a football—scholarship to Wake Forest, and we're very proud of Jimmy. [*Laughter*] Our oldest son, Jeffrey, and his wife, Stacy, could not be here today. They're in Seattle, and he's preparing for his ninth season as an NFL quarterback. Joanne Kemp is the only wife and mother of an NFL quarterback in history, so—[*laughter*].

President Bush, as I said, it's a particular honor to have you with us today and to have other members of your team. I'm very pleased that Secretary of Treasury [designate] Brady is here, Secretary of Transportation Skinner, Secretary of Labor Elizabeth Dole, Secretary of Health and Human Services [designate] Lou Sullivan. I'm honored that Chairman [of the House Committee on Banking, Finance and Urban Affairs] Gonzalez is with us today to give evidence of bipartisan support for HUD. I want to thank each and every one of them for coming—family and friends from all over the country.

President Bush spoke eloquently about HUD's special mission. We operate in a market that contains the most visible symbol of the American dream: home ownership. Our mission, I believe, is to inject oxygen and seed corn and new life and new hope into those distressed inner cities. Mr. President, you talked about free enterprise zones, which include dramatic, some would say radical, tax incentives for entrepreneurship and the creation of new jobs in those areas. You talked about the need to empower the poor with home ownership and equity through initiatives like tenant management and urban homesteading, an idea which Kimi Gray [president of the Kenilworth/Parkside Resident Management Corp.] has helped make work in the District of Columbia and I believe can be a model for other cities, and most importantly, for other people.

You talked, Mr. President, of helping recapture the American dream for first-time homebuyers, young families just starting out. And you asked us at HUD to lead an all-out public and private effort to help end the appalling tragedy of homelessness, which really is a reflection of the tragedy of hopelessness for which housing is just only part of the solution. And we at HUD will carry more than our share of the load in helping end this tragedy.

This is a compassionate society, and we'll be compassionate at HUD. In a Judeo-Christian society, the ultimate compassion, however, is not measured by how many people are on welfare or government assistance. As the philosopher Maimonides said in the 12th century, "the noblest charity is to prevent people from having to take charity in the first place."

We here at HUD know that there are other challenges facing us: the need to build better public and private partnerships to promote economic development and entrepreneurship; the need to ensure that we expand the number of eligible families receiving housing assistance and housing opportunities; the need to change the red lines around distressed areas of our cities into green lines, where there can be success and jobs and entrepreneurial opportunity.

We want to work with local officials to reduce the barriers to growth and that opportunity not only in the days and months ahead but in the years ahead. And of course, Mr. President, you have challenged us here at HUD with the obligation—indeed, I consider it an opportunity—to fully, effectively, and vigorously implement the civil rights laws with regard to the new Fair Housing Act; and I pledge my best efforts in that regard.

I want to, for just a moment, speak about a more personal challenge facing you and me—each and every one of us as public servants and keepers of the public trust. You said, Mr. President, when you recognized the fine people and dedicated public servants who work here at HUD and the rest of the Federal Government, that government service is a noble calling and a public trust. Indeed, it is. You said that you learned from your parents, your mother and your father, that there is no higher honor than to serve free men and free women, that there is no greater privilege than to labor in government beneath the Great Seal of the United States and the American flag. Well, I agree. Not only do I agree but I applaud your recognition, Mr. President, of the dedicated public servants in the Federal Government of the United States of America.

With that in mind, let me set out two touchstones for our work here at HUD. First, we need to adhere to the very highest standards of integrity, ethics, and the law. President Bush, you've made this standard the watchword of your administration. And I want to help you and help you at HUD make this an agency in which it is enthusiastically and vigorously upheld. Second, to my colleagues at the Housing and Urban Development agency, we all must keep our minds, our work, and our hearts focused on those we are meant to serve: not just the homebuilder but the homebuyer, not only public housing authorities but the public housing resident, not just mayors and city managers but the poor and those who live temporarily on the streets or in shelters.

We need to keep them foremost in our minds and our hearts because our job is to give them what Dr. King called a stake in the American dream: a helping hand, the equality of opportunity to build a better future for themselves and their children. No one has to lose in this equation. America is not a zero-sum game of static conditions on this Earth in which one gains at another's expense, or someone's job must come at another's loss, or someone must profit while others must lose. I don't see America that way. I don't believe in the perpetuity of poverty.

So, I'm excited about the challenge ahead. I'm thrilled and honored to have the opportunity to help implement George Bush's agenda for the nineties here at HUD, an agenda of compassion and opportunity, of hope and the promise of a better and brighter future for America in housing, economic development, in home ownership, and in jobs.

Today is special—special for me—and special not only because President Bush is here at HUD but also because it's the day after the 180th anniversary of the birthday of Abraham Lincoln. So, I want to close with one of my favorite quotes from Abraham Lincoln. One day in New England, Mr. Lincoln addressed some shoemakers who happened to be on strike. He told them he didn't believe in laws that prevented men from getting rich. He said it would only do more harm than good. Mr. Lincoln went on to say he did not propose any war on capital, but that he wanted to allow the humblest man an equal opportunity to get rich with everyone else. He went on to say, when one starts poor, as most people do in the race of life, in a free society it is such that that person knows that he can better his condition, that he knows that there's no fixed condition of labor for his whole life.

Well, ladies and gentlemen, that's our mission. That's our mission here at HUD and in America: to give every American man, woman, and child, regardless of their race or creed or their economic or their social condition, the opportunity to be what God meant them to be. And I believe we can make this system work. Indeed, I believe we have the moral and profound obligation to make it work. We can make it work together. We have the tools. And as you said, Mr. President, we know what works. Now we need to put it to work in our cities. We can't leave people behind. Mr. Lincoln said: "America cannot exist half slave, half free." In the 19th century, today, the next century, we can't have this country half or three-quarters prosperous and some folks left behind. The Good Shepherd would not have it be that way.

So, HUD is open for business. Let's get moving. God bless you here at HUD, and God bless America. Thank you very, very much.

[*At this point, the band began playing.*]

Now, one second, one second. Ladies and gentlemen, band leader, thank you. [*Laughter*] Well, that was gentle and kind and—[*laughter*]. It would not be a Kemp event—not that this is—[*laughter*]—but it wouldn't be Kemp at an event if we didn't do something a little bit different and special. And having Gene Upshaw here is symbolic of my many years in pro football and my friendship with him. And I asked a special guest to come here. I know you're excited about seeing Gene. But I asked a young man who is probably one of the great heroes of this town to bring a football on your behalf to the President from the Washington Redskins. Join with me in greeting Joe Gibbs, the coach of the Washington Redskins. [*Applause*]

Note: The President spoke at 4:18 p.m. in the cafeteria at the Department of Housing and Urban Development.

Letter to Congressional Leaders Transmitting the Report on International Agreements
February 14, 1989

Dear Mr. Speaker: (Dear Mr. Chairman:)

Pursuant to Section 708 of Public Law 95–426 (1 U.S.C. 112b(b)), I transmit herewith a report prepared by the Department of State concerning international agreements.

Sincerely,

GEORGE BUSH

Note: Identical letters were sent to Jim Wright, Speaker of the House of Representatives, and Claiborne Pell, chairman of the Senate Foreign Relations Committee.

Nomination of Roy M. Goodman To Be a Member of the Board of Directors of the Overseas Private Investment Corporation
February 14, 1989

The President today announced his intention to nominate Roy M. Goodman of New York to be a member of the Board of Directors of the Overseas Private Investment Corporation, U.S. International Development Cooperation Agency, for a term expiring December 17, 1991.

Mr. Goodman currently serves as a member of the New York State Senate, representing the 26th district in Manhattan. He chairs the New York Senate's committee on investigations, taxation, and government operations, and the legislative commission on public-private cooperation. State Senator Goodman is also a member of the senate's standing committees on rules, finance, education, cities, transportation, and crime and correction. He is vice chairman of the senate special committee on the culture industry and holds the post of assistant majority leader.

Mr. Goodman graduated from Harvard College (A.B., 1951) and Harvard Graduate School of Business Administration (M.A., 1953). He was born March 5, 1930, in New York City. He is married, has three children, and resides in Manhattan, NY.

Remarks to the South Carolina State Legislature in Columbia
February 15, 1989

Thank you, members of the legislature, for that really friendly South Carolina welcome. And thank you, particularly, Governor Campbell, my friend; Lieutenant Governor; Mr. Speaker; Members of the Congress that are with us here today, Senator Thurmond, Floyd Spence—and maybe I'm missing some. If so, I apologize. And ladies and gentlemen, thank all of you. It's a great honor to be addressing this joint session of the general assembly, and I really mean that. This is a chamber rich in history and tradition, and I'm grateful for the privilege of joining you in the hall today.

There's something wonderful about how the United States comes together. And driving in on that great big, long car and having the school kids and others out there really demonstrating their respect for the institution of the Presidency is something that was special to me. And I think of it as something that South Carolinians understand very, very well, indeed. I was just saying this to the Lieutenant Governor.

One very concrete way that I plan to express my appreciation is by not going on too long. [*Laughter*] If I exceed my limit and we start to press up against lunchtime, I expect that the spirit of the late Speaker Blatt will rise up, and in this chamber will echo with the words: "It's cornbread and buttermilk time."

Now, I speak to you today with great respect and in accordance with the plan of our Founding Fathers designed two centuries ago: as a President of the United States addressing the freely elected government of a sovereign State. And I speak to you in the spirit of bipartisanship. I've got to; you've got us outnumbered. [*Laughter*] And I realize that some of you people favor the Tigers and others favor the Gamecocks and, of course, some favor one or another set of Bulldogs; but as President, I must remain neutral. I stand with the people. [*Laughter*] And this morning, in that same spirit of neutrality, Lee Atwater [chairman of the Republican National Committee], as far as I'm concerned, will be thought of simply as one native son of South Carolina who happens to be a rhythm and blues guitarist. God save the Republic! But I don't have to be neutral now in recognizing and thanking for appearing and congratulating the Division I–AA national football champions, the Furman Paladines. I just met them downstairs; and we are all, nationwide, very proud of that team and what it's accomplished.

A President can't stand here without noting that the great State of South Carolina has one of the oldest histories in our Republic, spanning nearly five centuries. But with all of South Carolina's great sense of tradition, this has also in recent years been the site of dynamic economic growth that has so greatly improved the lives of the people of this State. And I believe that South Carolina is proof that an abiding respect for traditional American values is not a hindrance to success in a modern economy but, in fact, it is essential to it. And I want to keep the economy expanding so that it reaches every person in South Carolina and in the Nation.

And there are a number of very sound provisions South Carolina uses in this whole budget process which I think our nation as a whole would benefit from now. I think it is long overdue for the Federal Government to catch up with South Carolina by giving the Chief Executive a line-item veto and by adding a balanced budget amendment to the Constitution of the United States. These are essential elements, disciplining the executive branch as well as the legislative branch for controlling government spending. You have them; you use them; they work. And they help protect the pocketbooks of the working people, men and women, of South Carolina. I believe that the rest of the American people deserve the same at the Federal level, and they deserve a budget process that they can point to with pride. And I will work for the budget reforms that we need.

Your Governor, Carroll Campbell, has been an innovative leader who has set an example that is being acknowledged around the country. He and you, working together, have made South Carolina a model of what can be accomplished with sound policies and wise leadership. I particularly want to recognize and applaud your Governor's plan for promoting even greater economic growth by modernizing your tax code and by cutting the State capital gains tax.

Our experience at the national level is clear: Reducing the capital gains rate has resulted in more revenue to the Federal Government, not less. And it spurs investment; and investment means more jobs. And jobs mean more opportunity. And opportunity is the foundation of American progress. And a lower capital gains rate helps our international competitiveness—all of our biggest trading partners, including Japan and West Germany, tax capital gains modestly if at all. Even as you're taking up this issue in South Carolina, my proposal at the Federal level is to cut the capital gains rate down to 15 percent for investments held for 3 years or more.

Now, as you know, last week I proposed a budget plan for the Federal Government. You may have heard about it. It's getting some attention. And I'm pleased to say no one has said that it's DOA. If anyone does, I'll interpret that as: "Defining Opportunity for Americans." [*Laughter*]

But when it comes to the Washington budget process, so much of the rhetoric is, as you know, a bit extravagant. Once in the heat of budget politics, a former member of this chamber, Goat Leamond, stepped back from the fray to utter the now-immortal words: "When in doubt, run in circles, scream and shout." Washington all over again. [*Laughter*]

But in Washington, with all the shouting that sometimes occurs, the words don't mean the same things that most people think that they mean. When they talk about budget cuts in Washington, that usually doesn't mean that spending is going down. And this is the key point. It seems to be the obvious meaning, but it's not. It usually means that spending is going up, but at a slower pace. Senator Rudman of New Hampshire said this week: "Washington is the only town where a man making $20,000 can go in and ask his boss for a raise of $10,000, and then when the boss gives him instead a $5,000 raise, the story comes out: 'Man's Salary Cut by $5,000.'" [*Laughter*]

On the revenue side, I've taken a pledge to the American people, and I'm going to keep it: No new taxes! You see, I believe that is what the people of this State and the people of America voted for as a whole. And the bottom line in the Federal budget is that it's not my money, it's not the Congress' money, it's the American peoples' money.

And one group in Washington, Citizens for a Sound Economy, commissioned the Roper organization to conduct a poll on taxes, spending, and the budget deficit. And three out of four Americans surveyed said that the way they want us to reduce the deficit is by holding down spending, controlling the growth of spending. Only 5 percent in this national survey wanted to do it by raising taxes.

My budget is based on a flexible freeze with no tax increases. This budget recognizes that there are three ways government must serve the people: first, by not taking any more of their hard-earned money than is absolutely necessary; secondly, by creating the environment that permits economic growth, new jobs, and greater opportunity; and finally, by doing the very best to help people with the money that is spent by government, caring for those in need, protecting what we hold in common, and serving the people with efficiency and, yes, compassion.

Even in times when reducing the deficit means tough choices, we must still set priorities. And my budget is a realistic plan that does more for education, more for the environment, and more for the space program. And it makes a larger investment in scientific research to help keep America competitive into the next century. It spends more on the Head Start program to help make America strong into the next generation. And there is another $1 billion in outlays to fight drugs, because we cannot let this menace rob our children of their future. And we propose a new child care initiative, targeted at low-income families and designed to give real choice to families. The family unit is vital to the economic fabric of our society. And government must not discourage parental choice and family involvement. And in this budget, we also restore and double the tax deduction for adopting special-needs children. And we commit a billion dollars to deal with the problems of the homeless. And we don't touch Social Security—that's off-limits.

And we keep our defenses strong. Defending America is one task which is an absolute responsibility for the Federal Government. And this budget enables our national defense to keep up with inflation. It's gone down, net terms, for 4 out of the last 4 years. When our young men and women make a commitment to join our Armed Services, they have the right to know that we will give them the tools to defend themselves and to defend America.

This budget helps assure a sound economy not by raising taxes but by cutting the Federal deficit by more than $75 billion. That will not only meet the Gramm-Rudman-Hollings targets but it does even better than that. This budget will bring the deficit as a percentage of gross national product to its lowest level since the 1970's.

Now, already some people have asked me how is it possible to do all this without raising taxes. The answer is straightforward, and it needs to be emphasized again and again: Because of economic growth—and you've seen this here in South Carolina—because of economic growth, tax revenues are going up with no new taxes. Our projections show that without raising taxes, the Federal Government will get an additional $80 billion to spend. The Congressional Budget Office, using their own set of economic assumptions, predicts—not my estimate, but theirs—that Federal tax revenues will increase next year by even more, by $86 billion. I think our number is closer, but whether you use the Congress' number or the OMB number, that's enough money to reduce the deficit down to the levels required by Gramm-Rudman-Hollings and to spend more money on priority programs.

But to do this does require that choices be made, which is what this budget does. And I'm prepared to work with the Congress to make those hard choices. We weren't sent to Washington—any of us up there—to sit on our hands, either to pass the cost of indecision on to working Americans by raising their taxes or to fail to reduce the deficit, which will cause the cuts to be done automatically under the law. And that's why we must make choices that keep the economy growing, preserve our national defense, and allow government adequately and compassionately to perform the services which it should do. And if we do, we can get the job done—but not with business as usual.

One of the great United States Senators, John C. Calhoun, once said: "The very essence of a free government consists in considering offices as public trusts, bestowed for the good of the country, and not for the benefit of an individual or a party." And it's in that spirit that I will seek to work with the United States Congress, not as members of competing political parties but as cooperating public servants.

And the members of this legislature, all of you, have a vital role to play. You're closer to the people—you really are—than those of us in Washington. You not only serve your constituents, you're their neighbors. And you speak with the authority of people who know that government firsthand. And as we form the Federal budget and reduce this deficit, I want your voices to be heard. We need your leadership. And working together, we can make a great difference for all America.

You know, I've visited South Carolina enough times to learn that the State flower is the yellow jasmine. And I've been told that it was selected not just for its fragrance but for its resilience. And the budget debate is important, but even more important is the knowledge that America is strong and she is great and, yes, she is resilient. And we're thriving as a nation, thriving in the world—we're the envy of the world. And we're providing for our people—got to do better. As Americans, we don't seek a world without challenges, but rather a chance to overcome the challenges that are before us and to leave this nation that we love a little better for our having passed this way. I'm glad that you and I are passing this way together.

Thank you, members of this assembly, and God bless each and every one of you. And God bless the United States of America. Thank you.

Note: The President spoke at 11:25 a.m. in the house chamber of the State capitol. He was introduced by Gov. Carroll A. Campbell. In his opening remarks, the President referred to Lt. Gov. Nick Theodore, Speaker of the House of Representatives Robert J. Sheenen, and Representative Floyd Spence. Prior to the remarks, he met with the Furman University football team and was given a team jacket and football by coach Jimmy Satterfield. Following his remarks, the President attended a luncheon at the Governor's Mansion and then returned to Washington, DC.

Nomination of Richard J. Kerr To Be Deputy Director of Central Intelligence

February 15, 1989

The President today announced his intention to nominate Richard J. Kerr to be Deputy Director of Central Intelligence. He would succeed Robert M. Gates.

Mr. Kerr joined the Central Intelligence Agency in 1960 and has served in several capacities, most recently serving as Deputy Director of Intelligence. Prior to this he served as Deputy Director for Administration. In 1982 he was Associate Deputy Director for Intelligence. From 1976 to 1982, Mr. Kerr was Deputy Director, then Director of offices responsible for regional and political analysis worldwide. He has also served as the Directorate of Intelligence's representative in Honolulu.

Mr. Kerr graduated from the University of Oregon, receiving a bachelor of arts degree. He is married and has four children.

Appointment of Francis S.M. Hodsoll as Executive Associate Director and Chief Financial Officer of the Office of Management and Budget

February 15, 1989

The President today announced the appointment of Francis S.M. Hodsoll as Executive Associate Director of the Office of Management and Budget and Chief Financial Officer. Mr. Hodsoll will have responsibility for OMB management functions. His responsibilities will also include advising the Director of OMB on procurement policy and privatization, as well as selected issues associated with OMB's division of national security and international affairs. It is the President and the Director's intention, working closely with Congress, Federal departments and agencies, to strengthen the management of Federal agencies, building on the initiatives of the Reagan administration in this area.

Mr. Hodsoll is currently Chairman of the National Endowment for the Arts, where he has served since November 1981. He was previously Deputy Assistant to President Reagan and Deputy to White House Chief of Staff James A. Baker III. Mr. Hodsoll has held senior positions in a variety of Federal agencies, including the State Department, the Department of Commerce, and the Environmental Protection Agency. He is an attorney and former managing director of a British trading company in the Philippines.

Mr. Hodsoll has degrees from Yale, Cambridge, and Stanford Law School. He is married to the former Margaret McEwen, has two children, and resides in Arlington, VA. He was born May 1, 1938.

Remarks at the Swearing-in Ceremony for Clayton Yeutter as Secretary of Agriculture

February 16, 1989

The President. Thank you, Peter, and all the members of the Cabinet, the Members of the United States Congress here, distinguished Ambassadors, and others. I've come over here today for the swearing-in of our Secretary. Clayton Yeutter is about to make an enduring commitment to this Department. And I should acknowledge the fact that I think five of his predecessors are here today, Democrats and Republicans, which I think gives him an extraordinarily good send-off.

There's a difference, you know, between involvement and commitment. You all know it. Remember the old farmer making eggs and bacon. The chicken is involved, but the pig is committed. [*Laughter*] And it's a particular pleasure here today because yesterday marked the 100th anniversary of Cabinet status for this Department. As the distinguished former Secretaries that are joining us today know, the Agency has met many difficult challenges over the past century, and this really is just a beginning. There are many more challenges that this Department will encounter over the next hundred years. And who better to lead the Department at this time than Clayton Yeutter.

Somebody reminded me Yeutter rhymes with fighter. And that's what he is—tough as nails, knowledgeable. And that's why I picked him. And I know he's going to fight hard for farming, for fair trade, and for all the other important responsibilities of this Department. And I know that everyone here is familiar with his outstanding tenure as United States Trade Representative. The list of things he's accomplished just in the past year is truly, truly impressive: bringing down barriers to American beef and citrus in Japan, ushering a comprehensive trade bill through Congress, concluding the free trade agreement with Canada and moving that through the Congress, and pressing forward on the Uruguay round of multilateral trade negotiations. And now he's putting down the trade portfolio and taking up the agricultural portfolio. But, as all of you know, that's hardly a change.

Agriculture is one of the most difficult areas in our trade talks, and agriculture is an area to which we attach an extraordinarily high priority in international discussions. I'm confident that our partners in the Uruguay round of talks will see Clayton's appointment as just what it is: a signal that this administration has an extremely strong sense of purpose and determination in these crucial negotiations. He's going to be working closely with our USTR, with our Trade Representative Carla Hills, who I spotted a minute ago; but where is she? Maybe I didn't spot her. Right, here she is—with Carla to make sure our objectives in agriculture are achieved.

And I said in the campaign and let me repeat: As President, I want to work to level the playing field. We've got to knock down barriers, and we will relentlessly pursue negotiations to end subsidies that distort markets and that restrict trade. Fair, free, and open world markets—that's what we want; that's what we're working for; and in the end, that's what we are determined to get.

Trade may be a hot issue right now; but the Department, as you all know better than any, has many other critical responsibilities: our nation's farm and soil conservation programs, forestry, nutrition, rural diversification and rural development, the environment. You're involved in all of these important questions. And you perform your work in all these areas with energy and dedication. The "Ag" Department has a long, proud history, and each of you helps to continue that tradition.

And I know you'll find that Clayton Yeutter is your kind of guy: dynamic, always has been. When he graduated from the University of Nebraska, he was named the Outstanding Animal Husbandry Graduate in the Nation. And later, he finished first in his class in law school and then took a Ph.D. in agricultural economics. And I've heard that he's said it isn't all that far from the farm he grew up on to a Ph.D. or trade ambassador. On the farm, he said, he developed physical stamina and learned self-discipline, and those have come in handy ever since. And there's one other thing about Clayton that I'm very happy about. Many kids want to grow up to be President; not Clayton. [*Laughter*] When he was a boy, he wanted to be Secretary of Agriculture. And here he is, and that's a lucky break for America.

Now the oath of office.

[*At this point, Secretary Yeutter was sworn in.*]

Secretary Yeutter. Thank you very much, ladies and gentlemen. It's really a marvelous privilege and pleasure and opportunity for me to be here this morning. And as I look out over this audience, I see a multitude of longtime friends, and I'm so pleased and gratified that all of you were willing to take time out of your hectic and demanding schedules to be here and share this occasion with us.

I'm not going to make any profound policy pronouncements this morning. I'm not sure that I could make them in any case, but I'm not even going to try. I'd like to basically concentrate in my very short time with you on some comments about people.

First of all, on behalf of everyone here, Mr. President, we want to thank you for coming over to participate in this ceremony. We know how much it carves time out of your schedule to do so, and it's a tremendous personal gesture on your part to do that. It's an honor not only for those of us in the Cabinet who are experiencing this privilege but it's an honor for the folks in all the Departments, including USDA this morning, who have an opportunity to see you up close, first hand, as a part of this ceremony. So, thank you for coming.

And although you've all heard lots of great things about President Bush during the campaign and through the inaugural period, I want to just embellish those, if I may, for just a few seconds by saying that—confirming and ratifying, if I may—that without question this is one of the best prepared Presidents that we've ever had in the history of the United States, one of the most substantive Presidents we've ever had in the history of the United States. Both those attributes and characteristics are going to serve us all well, indeed, in the coming years. But more importantly, George and Barbara Bush are two of the finest human beings on the face of this Earth, and that's why it's a distinct pleasure for all of us to be a part of this government.

Then I want to say a word about Justice O'Connor, and if she'll forgive me for telling this anecdote one more time, I'm going to do so. First of all, it's a great privilege for me to have her swear me in again for the second time now. She did the honors 3½ years ago, when I was sworn in as U.S. Trade Representative, and she very graciously consented to come here this morning and do them again. Dick Lyng was just saying in the waiting room that she also did the honors for him when he became Secretary. So, I think you're an honorary member of this Department by now, Justice O'Connor.

But I wanted to share an anecdote with you which reflects the nature of this fine and distinguished lady. Back in 1972, I was involved in the Presidential campaign and was working on the agricultural campaign nationwide; and I paid a visit to Phoenix, Arizona, where the Arizona chairman of the Presidential campaign was a leading businessman in that city. The cochairman that year happened to be a lady whose name was Sandra O'Connor. And I met with those two folks during the day, as we were getting organized in the campaign. And at one particular point during the day, I said to the gentleman who was campaign chairman, "Where in the world did you get Sandra O'Connor? She is just fantastic." And he said, "You're absolutely right. She is fantastic." This was 1972, remember. And he went on to say at that time, he said, "Someday she's going to become the first woman on the U.S. Supreme Court." That was a remarkably prescient comment, as you know, because a decade or so later she became, deservedly, the first woman on the U.S. Supreme Court.

Then I want to say a word about my wife, Jeanne. She doesn't know that this is coming. [*Laughter*] But I think everyone here of my generation would appreciate the fact that 30 years ago, or thereabouts, when we were coming out of college ready to go to work, it was still a man's world. And in some respects, it's still a man's world today. But that's changing very rapidly. I think it's important for all of us as we share and enjoy all of these fine honors—being named Cabinet members and doing fascinating things around the world—a little humility is sometimes in store. And I think it's important for some of us to recognize that we have spouses who, but for that generation gap of 30 years ago, might be standing in front of this microphone accepting honors as appointments as members of the Cabinet just as easily and deservedly as we. And Jeanne fits that category.

And a word about Kim, since she's up here, too. You can tell by what she had to say in the invocation that she has her head screwed on right, at least we hope so. This is a little parental pride coming out there. And I mention this for a particular reason. Kim has just finished a double masters degree program, getting a masters in business and a masters in international relations. And although she doesn't speak Japanese as well as Ambassador Matsunaga does yet, she's working hard at it. That's the way that we have to educate at least some of our children if we're going to be competitive, Mr. President, in the world in which we find ourselves going into the next century. And we hope Kim is prepared for that.

And finally a word to Peter Myers, who is also sharing the area here with us this morning, because Peter has so graciously handled this ceremony and so graciously handled the transition from one administration to another.

Then moving very rapidly out to the distinguished guests here. We don't have time to introduce them all or comment on them all, but I want to say how appreciative I am of my fellow members of the Cabinet coming over to join in the ceremony this morning—a good number of Ambassadors who are here and a substantial number of Members of Congress, even though they probably ought to be out in their home districts right now. I'm glad that they're here joining in on the ceremony, and I'm honored to have them here.

I'm not going to introduce them all, but I want to pay special attention to just three who are here. Congressman Tom Foley—Tom, don't stand up. You're comfortable; stay there. But a particular mention to Tom, because as all of you know, he's the distinguished majority leader of the House and former chairman of the House Agriculture Committee, a longtime great friend. And I know he postponed a trip back home for a day just to be here this morning. So, Congressman Foley, it's especially nice to have you here.

And I want to say the same for Congressman—sorry—Senator Jesse Helms, who's been a Senator for a long time, likewise, distinguished chairman of the Senate Agriculture Committee. Our relationships go back many, many years; and, Senator Helms, it's great to have you here.

And then, finally, Bob Dole. Senator Dole has been Mr. Agriculture in the Midwest, distinguished Senate career, Presidential candidate, and a great friend for a long period of time.

And then, finally, mention of the former Secretaries of Agriculture who are here. I will not have you all stand up either; but for those of you who are out here, you'll have a chance, hopefully, to say hello to them as we have the reception in a few minutes. But with us here this morning are Jack Knebel, Bob Bergland, Jack Block, Dick Lyng, and Cliff Hardin. I want to make special note of Dick Lyng, my predecessor, because I worked for Dick when I first came back here in 1970. And a special note of Cliff Hardin, because Cliff was my mentor, Mr. President, way back in my days as a young faculty member at the University of Nebraska, when he was chancellor at that time. And it was Cliff who brought me here to Washington, DC, in 1970, when he was Secretary of Agriculture here.

And just one final closing comment, Mr. President. I first came here almost 20 years ago in the South Building, which is over thataway, in my first position as Administrator of what was then the Consumer and Marketing Service. And I had some of the same misgivings about the Federal bureaucracy then that most people do when they come to Washington. And you've heard all those stories also, Mr. President. They come up when we discuss things like increases in salaries back here in Washington, DC, because a lot of folks think those are undeserved. I happen to think they are deserved, and I learned that by experience. I was a bit wary and skeptical, Mr. President, about whether you can move the bureaucracy back here in Washington. And when I came, I took over an agency, Mr. President, that had about 16,000 employees, and I think there were about 2 of us in that 16,000 who were political appointees at the professional level. And I thought, oh, my God, you know, how are a couple of people going to change a 16,000-person bureaucracy? And I wasn't sure it could be done. But as Cliff Hardin and Dick Lyng will remember, it could be done because we made some major changes in those years in a very successful way.

What I discovered, Mr. President, was that folk here at USDA at least—I won't speak for the rest of the Government—but folks here at USDA will listen if you have something worthwhile to say. They listened to me back in 1970, and they've been listening to a lot of folks who have given them leadership since then. And I discovered that they'll not only listen, Mr. President, but they'll respond. They are responsive to leadership. That's true of most human beings in this world, as a matter of fact, and we have to remember that that's the way to achieve progress in this country.

So, in closing, Mr. President, my commitment to you, my commitment to the folks from USDA who are here this morning, and my commitment to the folks out in farm country who are watching this program, is a very simple one: I promise you that we will put together a team at the top echelon of USDA that will be strong, competent, and energetic. And I promise you that we will provide leadership. You may not always agree with the leadership that we provide, but we're going to lead. And I hope that you'll be with us as we attempt to do that and as we work with you, Mr. President, over the next few years.

Thank you all for coming very much, and please join in the reception in just a few minutes. Thank you. Godspeed.

Note: The President spoke at 10:10 a.m. on the patio at the Department of Agriculture. He was introduced by Deputy Secretary of Agriculture Peter C. Myers. Kim Yeutter delivered the invocation.

Remarks on Afghanistan and a Question-and-Answer Session With Reporters
February 16, 1989

The President. Let me just say, I am going to hand you all, or Marlin will provide it later on, a statement on Afghanistan. I'll just give you a little summary of it at the outset here.

We support the Afghan efforts to fashion a stable, broadly based government, responsive to the needs of the Afghan people. Throughout the long, dark years of Afghanistan's occupation, the international community has been steadfast in its support of the Afghan cause, and this certainly has been true for the United States. Our commitment, the commitment of the United States to the people there, will remain; and it will remain firm, both through our bilateral humanitarian aid program and through the United Nations efforts to remove the mines and resettle the refugees and help reconstruct the war-torn economy.

So, we would call upon the Soviet Union to refrain from other forms of interference in Afghan affairs. The Soviet Union has nothing to fear from the establishment of an independent, nonaligned Afghanistan. And they do bear a certain special responsibility for healing the wounds of this war. And I would hope that the Soviet Union would generously support international efforts to rebuild Afghanistan.

And there will be a fuller statement on this later on.

Q. Were you hoping also that the rebels would not conduct a bloodbath once they get in the ascendant and really take power?

The President. Yes.

Q. I mean, it's a two-way street, isn't it? In victory, magnanimity. Is there any sense that you would like to convey that to the rebels, or do you think it's just a one-way street for the Soviets?

The President. Well, I don't think a bloodbath is in anyone's interest. And I think if we had a catalytic role, I would hope it would be, along with others, working towards reconciliation and towards a peaceful resolution now to all the problems. There's been enough of a bloodbath there. And so, I think you raise a good point, Helen [Helen Thomas, United Press International]. And, yes, I feel strongly that the time for recrimination is over, the time for bloodbaths is over. And I would like to see the various factions get together and come up with recommendations that would lead to a peaceful Afghanistan with no more bloodbaths.

Q. Mr. President, the Soviet Union is calling for an immediate cease-fire in Afghanistan and an embargo on arms shipments. Would you go along with that idea?

The President. Here's one of the complicating factors on that call. There is some concern about what we call stockpiling; and it would not be fair to have tremendous amounts of lethal supplies left behind and then cut off support for resistance and—thus, leaving an unacceptable imbalance. And so, before one could do anything other than appeal for peaceful resolution, which I've done, one needs to know the real facts on this question, this troublesome question of stockpiling.

Q. So, does that mean that you will continue to aid the rebels?

The President. That means we will do what we need to do to see that there is a peaceful resolution to this question, that one side does not dominate militarily, and we will be encouraging reconciliation.

Nicaragua

Q. Mr. President, what is your reaction, sir, to the action by the Central American countries yesterday that appears to undermine the standing of the *contras*, to say the least, and leave them in a very vulnerable position? And was your administration, as has been reported, caught off-guard on that?

The President. Let me say, Brit [Brit Hume, ABC News], on that one, that there's some positive elements of what's taking place there. There are also some troublesome elements. Positive because the Nicaraguans appear to be taking steps in accord with the Esquipulas agreements; they're talking about national reconciliation and full freedoms, including complete freedom of the press and free and fair elections and an end to subversion. To the degree that rhetoric goes forward and is enacted, that's good. But there's 90 days now in which to finalize arrangements. And what's troubling to me is that claims like this have been made at one time, only to see those claims repudiated—promises made, promises broken. And so, I think we have to be wary of supporting any positive elements like commitments to democracy and yet say, Wait a minute, let's be sure that we not leave the resistance standing alone, leave them twisting out there without fulfillment of the commitment to democracy on the part of the Sandinistas.

So, in terms of being caught off-guard, we are in the midst of a review of our whole policy there. If you ask me would I have predicted that the five Presidents would have worked out agreement in this detail at this time, I'd have to tell you that, having talked to President Azcona, having our Secretary of State deal with two foreign ministers just recently, I think within the last 10 days, that I wouldn't have said that they'd do exactly what they did do. But as I say, there's some positive elements to it, and there's some troublesome elements.

Q. How does that note of caution, sir, translate into policy and action on your part?

The President. You mean from the future? Work here in the next 90 days with the leaders to see that there's not just some fluffy promises out there but that there's some teeth in the promise of democratization. And that is what has to be done. And so, we are going to keep our resolve to have the people of Nicaragua have what these other countries have there: democracy. And we're talking about freedom of the press, freedom of elections, freedom of worship. And it's fine to spell these things out in generalities, but now let's get down to how we proceed. What does a free and fair election mean? I want to see some certification of the election process. But we've got time now, little bit of time now, in which to make very clear that our resolve, our commitment to democracy is still there.

Q. Mr. President, how do you intend to stand by your commitment to the resistance? And might that mean a request for additional nonlethal aid, at the end of which——

The President. It could mean that. It could mean that. But again, I think we've got to work with this process now the best we can. But I don't think anybody would want to suggest that we would leave people with no humanitarian aid. I can't imagine anyone taking that view.

Q. Will you intend to ask Congress to approve of that aid?

The President. Well, we have some time on that, too. But I obviously want to know what the status quo is at the time. But I have every intention of seeing that these people receive humanitarian support, but how that comes about, we'll just have to wait and see.

Appointments and Nominations

Q. Mr. President, have you been dismayed at all at the slow pace of filling jobs in the State Department and, of course, in the Defense Department, elsewhere in your government? Has it slowed you down at all?

The President. I worry a little about it, but not dismayed. The ground rules have changed. I was talking yesterday to one of our appointees who I will leave—the way you like to put it—who asked to remain anonymous. And he told me that to fill out the forms required 36 hours, and the forms are different in different departments. I hope that this new Ethics Committee that we've got will take a look at this and try to see if we can't do better. The ground rules have changed from 8 years ago.

And there's one other substantive point here. I don't worry about it as much as I would have if I were President 8 years ago, when we came in on the wake of an administration that I was opposed to and everything. I've come in as President to build on the record of an administration of which not only I was a part of but whose objectives I strongly support. And so, the people that are running the various departments now are people who generally are good people and share my objectives for this country. So, it's not like you're having to worry that your departments are going to be coming out with a lot of last-minute rules and regulations that will be an anathema to everything you believe in.

So, that's a substantive point. The nature of the clearance process is a substantive point. But back to your question, I do worry about it. I am concerned about it. And I'd like to see if we can't speed the system up in some way. We're getting good people to nominate. There used to be a real quick turnaround on what they call a name check, but now, under the new procedures, that takes a lot longer. So, there's some frustrations. I don't want to mislead you, but for the reasons that I gave you, I don't think it's hurting the Government. I think our Cabinet appointments—I want to get them done as soon as possible, all of them.

Government Ethics

Q. Sir, could we take up a question you said a couple days ago: Why is it that the ethics questions get so complex in practice and yet were so simple in your campaign language? Why is it that straightforward questions of accepting outside income now require a legal opinion?

The President. Well, give me an example of what you mean "straightforward" about outside income. Maybe I can answer it by rhetorical question. Take the case of Lou Sullivan [Secretary of Health and Human Services-designate], who had earned a pension from a medical school, working not for exorbitant sums, as the president of a black medical college. And it is now suggested that—if he accepts money from a pension that he earned—that he is doing something illegal. We have other questions of that nature. Some people who are interested in being in the Government find that they have to give up medical benefits that they earned from a major company, lest it be seen that they are beholden to that major company. So, I've set the goal to have high standards, but in doing that, all kinds of cases of this nature are coming out. And I don't think that in those two cases I've given you, if the status quo remained, that that should disqualify somebody. In Lou Sullivan's case, though—and he can't afford it—he bends over backwards to avoid the perception that some people in politics and in the media lay on him for accepting benefits from a medical school that he worked his life for.

Q. But Baker was——

The President. So, these are different, these are different questions.

Q. Could we ask, however—the perception is out there. The perception is apparent. It's why——

The President. Apparent to what?

Q. Apparent to anyone looking at the situation that acceptance of money in any form is acceptance of money. The question is not whether or not Mr. Sullivan deserved the money. The question is whether or not he could accept it when you had said no members of your Cabinet would accept outside income.

The President. Earned income—I didn't say outside income. If a person has some trust fund that pays—blind trust that distributes funds to him, I've never said that. See, I think there are some perception problems that maybe I need to help clear up, and this gives me an opportunity here today to do it. All I say is: I want high ethical standards, but I don't want to have it so it goes so far, bends over so far backwards, that a person that knows something about a subject matter is disqualified from serving, or a person that has some means is disqualified from serving, or a man that worked his heart out building a black medical college is made to feel that there's some perception of immorality if he keeps a pension that he's earned. I worry that I may have created something that's—certainly I know it needs clarification, and our commission will help do that. And secondly, I hope I haven't created something that just carries things too far. For one day a guy gets a ruling from the Ethics Office that a way of treating with one's asset is acceptable. It's given a stamp of approval. And then because of what you properly call perceptions, a person has to change the ground rules.

Q. But you're not thinking it was wrong for Baker to——

The President. No, I said I think he made the right decision. But what I think is wrong to do is to go back in retrospect and have him twisting in the wind out there because we use a 90/90 hindsight on the poor guy when he's gone far beyond what he might have done, and who—everybody that knows Jim Baker knows that he is highly ethical. But to suggest there's a perception here that is looked at differently today, now, than used to be when he asked for a ruling from the Government Office of Ethics, that he's done something wrong, I do reject that, Helen.

Mr. Fitzwater. We're going to take a couple of more questions, if you have any other subjects.

Interest Rates and the Budget

Q. Are you concerned that the Fed is increasing interest rates at this point? And how much time do you think you have to cut a deal with Congress on budget negotiations?

The President. The best thing to do—you coupled them just right because if we can get a—well, I don't think the American people see that, so let me expand a little bit. The best thing to do about interest rates is to get a budget agreement. And in my view, once that's there, particularly if it's along the lines that I have suggested to the Congress, I can almost guarantee you the pressure is going to come off on the interest rates. So, that's the way to solve the problem of concern about higher interest rates. The interest rates will be lower if we can promptly get a budget agreement.

So, do I worry about it? I don't see the inflationary pressures as so bad or enough to warrant a substantially higher interest rate. I don't see that. I've looked at the economic numbers. And people, I think, like to try always—whoever's President—drive a wedge between the President and the Chairman of the Fed. It's one of the best fights in town. You all love it. All politicians love it. All bankers like it. All editorialists for the Wall Street Journal love it. But I want to avoid that because we aren't far apart. And I will keep in touch in my own way. Our top people here will with the Chairman of the Fed, for whom we all have great respect. And maybe we'll get into a fight down the road. But I don't think it's at hand, and I don't think Greenspan and I are far apart. And I think he would also confirm that.

NATO Unity

Q. Mr. President, West Germany wants to postpone the modernization of the shorter range missiles. Obviously, this is not the American position. They want also to open negotiations with the Soviets on that. How do you respond to that? If you don't agree with that, are you concerned by the unity of NATO?

The President. I would respond to it this way: The Secretary of State is talking to all the NATO leaders; he'll be back in town over this weekend. I will sit down here in this chair and talk to him about what he has found. In the meantime, I am inclined to feel that we are far closer to West Germany than the public perceptions might be. And I have been in touch with Helmut Kohl [Chancellor, Federal Republic of Germany], and there have been opportunities for him to express to me inordinate concerns on this question. And other German leaders have been here recently, and the Secretary of State's been there. So, I would use this opportunity to shoot down the concept that there are major divisions between ourselves and the Federal Republic on this question.

But I'm not worried about NATO unity. You always worry that you have your act totally together, and that's one of the reasons I wanted these early consultations. And then, I think now, as a result of our Secretary of State's wonderful trip over there—and I say wonderful because he's touched a lot of bases and the cables are most encouraging along the lines of NATO unity—that having said that, that the mood is pretty good. I don't worry too much about divisions in NATO, and I do then feel that we will be in a position with a united NATO to move forward in consultation with the Soviet Union. That's the next step, and we have certain leadership responsibilities that all of us here are prepared to accept in that regard.

Q. One last question——

The President. Ann [Ann McDaniel, Newsweek], and then Brit. And then I'll quit.

Iran Arms and Contra Aid Controversy

Q. It appears that the Oliver North trial will go forward next week now. Are you aware of secrets so damaging to our national security that might come out in that trial that would be so damaging that you would ask the Attorney General to halt the prosecution?

The President. I think the Attorney General knows everything I know, and I think he's handled it very well.

Q. Are you concerned about the trial going forward? Do you think national security can be——

The President. Not under the existing agreements.

Q. Do you think the trial——

The President. I think Dick Thornburgh took a very difficult question and balanced interests and has worked out an agreement that hopefully is workable. But we'll see, because there are legitimate national security interests that he is obliged to protect. And he understands this, but he also understands that the judicial system should be operative and the trial should go forward. And I think we'll just say that all parties have worked towards that end, and it looks like agreement has been reached.

Yes, last one—Brit?

President's Budget Proposal

Q. Some congressional Democrats are now saying, sir, that you have outlined and gotten some considerable credit for a lot of spending increases while leaving open the question of where cuts would be made, particularly in an area where a kind of net freeze is being asked for. And they are saying that you really have been vague and have left it to them to do the dirty work. How do you react to that?

The President. Slowly—[*laughter*]—and very carefully. I don't think that is the informed opinion of the key leaders in Congress today. And the reason I say that is I think that Dick Darman [Chairman, Office of Management and Budget] and Nick Brady [Secretary of the Treasury] and our Chief of Staff, John Sununu, have all done a good job in not only presenting broad parameters to the Congress but have gone into a considerable amount of detail with them. And I would readily say, yes, there's a lot of negotiation that needs to be done to get all the T's crossed and every I dotted. But I don't think, Brit, that that's a commonly held view of the leadership. But if I said it was the commonly held view of the Democratic leadership—I know it's not of the Republican—then we will redouble our efforts to be sure they understand that there's no validity to that.

But having said that, yes, there's a lot more detail that has to be hammered out and ironed out, and we will work with them to satisfy their interest and to find out what they want to do. It's a two-way street. And so, I'm going to start working here, getting together meetings with the leaders down the road fairly soon, and we'll have a chance to explore that. If some feel that way, it would be a good opportunity to discuss it. So, it's going better than I thought it would, and I'm pleased generally with the reception.

I said ahead of time that I didn't expect everybody would jump up and down and say this was the greatest thing since sliced bread. But for the most part, I think it's fair to point out there has been a responsible look given this budget. The Republicans have generally been enthusiastic, some reservations on the part of some. The Democrats, though not endorsing it quite as much, have seen some positive direction and some positive objectives in that budget. And so, I've been pleased with the reception to that, and I've been pleased with the reception of the savings and loan.

Both of these two were major—I won't say hurdles—but major things that we had to accomplish, and I think we have. We've got a good proposal out there on the savings and loan, and we've got a sound budget proposal that is not meeting with everybody's acceptance and—or put it this way, with anybody saying what we've suggested is perfect. But there's enough solid food for thought there for the executive branch to be in a very sound position when we go into an open negotiation that we want.

And it gets right back to the overall economy. It's important that we go forward and go forward soon. And so much of the economy today is on perception as opposed to reality. This recovery is real; business is good. The insured deposits of depositors in savings and loan and banks are solid—dollar good, strong. But there are some perceptions out there that can best be turned around by a quick, or relatively quick, resolution of the budget question. It's the firm projecting down of the deficit that will result in lower interest rates which will guarantee continuation of this, the longest expansion in our history, and continue expansion at lower rates of interest.

So, I'm not euphorically optimistic. I'm certainly not pessimistic. And I think we're off to a pretty good start. And I credit not just the Republican leaders on the Hill but the spirit that the Democratic leaders have demonstrated. And I've been very pleased with it. And I've had an opportunity to tell them that.

Gun Control

Q. Mr. President, even though there's been a cutoff, there is something called guns that is so rampant in this country——

The President. Helen, it's been a great pleasure. The last question——

Q. Why won't you answer the question, because this is one of the most clearly——

Mr. Fitzwater. Thank you.

The President. What was your question?

Q. The question is: Are you going to exert any leadership in trying to forestall these——

The President. Do you know that there are laws on the book outlining the import of AK–47's—automatic——

Q. No, I didn't.

The President. Well, see, there's a fact. So, where does that lead you? You already had laws that prohibit the import of fully automated AK–47's. That law is on the books. So, are we talking about law enforcement? Are we talking about——

Q. We're talking about semiautomatic AK–47's, sir. We're talking about semiautomatic guns.

The President. What do you mean by semi?

Q. I mean no cocking, pull the trigger, the gun fires each time I pull the trigger.

The President. Look, if you're suggesting that every pistol that can do that or every rifle should be banned, I would strongly oppose that. I would strongly go after the criminals who use these guns. But I'm not about to suggest that a semi-automated hunting rifle be banned. Absolutely not. Am I opposed to AK–47's, fully automated? Am I in favor of supporting the law that says they shouldn't come in here? Yes. But Helen, with all her experience, didn't even know it was there. Nor did I until I looked it up. [*Laughter*]

Q. I don't know how you—when did you find out? I don't know how you can read the paper every day—13 deaths on Valentine's Day.

The President. Exactly, which concerns me enormously.

Q. What will you do——

The President. When you let a guy out of jail to commit a crime like this, it's outrageous. Two of these people were people that already had—have—help.

Q. So, you think it's okay for people to have guns?

The President. To have guns? Yes, I do. Do I think it's all right for people to have fully automatic AK–47's? No, I think the law should be——

Q. Sir, the issue is the—in Stockton, that was a semiauto. That was not a fully automatic weapon.

The President. Well, but I've answered your question on that question. I'm not about to propose a ban on service .45's or something like that.

Q. On semiautomatics—right?

The President. No, I'm not about to do that. And I think the answer is the criminal. Do more with the criminal. Look, the States have a lot of laws on these things. Let them enforce them. It's hard, very hard, to do. But that's my position, and I'm not going to change it.

Q. Is there nothing you can do about the murder capital of the United States? As the number one resident?

The President. Well, we need the help of

all the press to do something about it.

Q. When did you find out that they were banned? Today? [*Laughter*]

The President. Slightly before you did, put it that way—slightly before you did.

Note: The exchange began at 2:24 p.m. in the Oval Office at the White House. Marlin Fitzwater was the President's Press Secretary. In his remarks the President referred to Patrick Purdy who, armed with a semiautomatic AK–47, shot and killed six schoolchildren on a playground in Stockton, CA, on January 17.

Statement on the Soviet Withdrawal From Afghanistan
February 16, 1989

Today marks the start of a new chapter in the history of Afghanistan. For the first time in over 9 years, Soviet forces no longer occupy that country. This development marks an extraordinary triumph of spirit and will by the Afghan people, and we salute them for it.

Much remains to be done, however. For the Afghan people, the struggle for self-determination goes on. We support Afghan efforts to fashion a stable, broadly based government, responsive to the needs of the Afghan people. We call upon Afghan resistance leaders to work together towards this end. As long as the resistance struggle for self-determination continues, so too will America's support.

Throughout the long, dark years of Afghanistan's occupation, the international community has been steadfast in its support of the Afghan cause. This is also true for the United States. U.S. support for the Afghan people and the subsequent Soviet military withdrawal from Afghanistan constitute a powerful example of what we Americans can accomplish when Executive and Congress, Republican and Democrat, stand together. The Government and people of Pakistan also can take particular satisfaction from this event; their courage and solidarity contributed significantly to the Afghan struggle.

Now, more than ever, the Afghan people deserve the continuing help of the international community as they begin the difficult process of reclaiming their country, resettling their people, and restoring their livelihood. The commitment of the United States to the Afghan people will remain firm, both through our bilateral humanitarian aid program and through United Nations efforts to remove mines, resettle refugees, and reconstruct Afghanistan's war-torn economy. We call upon other nations to contribute all they can and hope that the United Nations and the resistance can come to mutually acceptable arrangements for the nationwide distribution of needed food supplies.

The Soviet Union has now fulfilled its obligation to withdraw from Afghanistan. We welcome that decision. We call upon the Soviet Union to refrain from other forms of interference in Afghan affairs. The Soviet Union has nothing to fear from the establishment of an independent, nonaligned Afghanistan. At the same time, the U.S.S.R. bears special responsibility for healing the wounds of this war, and we call upon it to support generously international efforts to rebuild Afghanistan.

Nomination of Elaine L. Chao To Be Deputy Secretary of Transportation
February 17, 1989

The President today announced his intention to nominate Elaine L. Chao to be Deputy Secretary of Transportation. She would succeed Mary Ann Dawson.

Since 1988 Ms. Chao has been Chairman of the Federal Maritime Commission in Washington, DC. Prior to this she was Deputy Administrator of the Maritime Administration at the Department of Transportation, 1986–1988. She has also served as vice president of syndications for BankAmerica Capital Markets Group in San Francisco, CA, 1984–1986. Ms. Chao was a White House fellow in the Office of Policy Development at the White House, 1983–1984. From 1979 to 1983, she was senior lending officer, European banking division for Citibank, N.A., in New York City.

Ms. Chao graduated from Mount Holyoke College (A.B., 1975) and Harvard University Graduate School of Business Administration (M.B.A., 1979). Ms. Chao currently resides in Washington, DC.

Remarks to Students at Washington University in St. Louis, Missouri
February 17, 1989

Thank you, Chancellor Danforth; Chairman Liberman; our distinguished Governor, John Ashcroft; and Senator Bond; Congressman Buechner here; and to your student body president, Cynthia Homan; and other student leaders that have given me this warm reception. I really am pleased to be here, and I've looked forward to sharing this occasion with you.

Mark Twain once wrote: "In Boston, they ask, How much does he know? In Philadelphia, Who were his parents? In New York, How much is he worth?" [*Laughter*] But Mark Twain was a Missourian. He would agree with me that you couldn't put a pricetag on this morning. Believe me, I'm delighted to be here, back in St. Louis and back at this university of excellence; the home of the State of Missouri; the home of ragtime and aerospace, agriculture; the State whose native sons include Omar Bradley and Harry Truman and that master linguist, Yogi Berra—[*laughter*]—the State—oh, I love to quote Yogi. Do you remember when he said: "Let's pair 'em off in three's"?—[*laughter*]—and, nevertheless, this State whose citizens embody the best of America and know that the heart of America is good, working, serving others, hoping and dreaming.

For 136 years your excellent university has played a part in that effort. Your community has built a pioneering effort in science and math. Your teaching, research, and soaring admission applications tell a story summed up best by two words: academic excellence. But there's another side of it, another side of the story that Washington University has to tell, a story from which all America can learn. It's a story about investing in America's future, how as students and faculty, administrators and alumni, you have shown that service and voluntarism can enrich education and enrich America. You work with the Special Olympics. Sunday's Special Olympics is but one chapter in that wonderful story. And around the Nation, other chapters are being written every day. And we're writing another chapter—trying to—in Washington, by opening in the White House the Office of National Service, which will lead my administration's community and national service programs. And our goal is simple: more Americans helping others by effectively serving their communities and the Nation. And these symbols, these signs around this room, I think, sum up what I talk about when I talk about a Thousand Points of Light: It is neighbor helping neighbor. It is kid helping kid. It is friends holding out their hand to other friends.

From now on, in America any definition of a successful life must include serving others—in a child care center, the corporate boardroom, in the Rotary or Little League or a tutoring program or a church or a synagogue. Our new initiative will reflect that spirit, once called America's genius for great and generous deeds. And I take special pride in our YES, our YES program, Youth Entering Service, which I proposed last fall to encourage American youth to give of themselves to help others in need. And I'm convinced that we can help alleviate many national problems by substantially increasing the involvement of young Americans in voluntary service. And the establishment of the YES Foundation will help lead that effort. Together, we can show that what matters in the end are not possessions. What matters is engaging in high moral principle of serving one another. And that's the story of America that we can write through voluntary service.

Eight days ago, in a joint session of Congress, I proposed a budget to complement voluntary efforts to help serve the gentler impulses of mankind. I listed four national objectives: to bring the deficit down, to invest in America's future, to find solutions to an urgent set of national priorities, and no new taxes. And our budget curbs the growth of Federal spending while providing for the most vulnerable among us. It is responsive and responsible, and it will ensure a strong and stable economy. Our budget balances social concern with fiscal sanity and leaves power in the hands of the people. It shows that we can have a government with a heart as well as a head.

And when it comes to reducing the deficit, some people say it can't be done without neglecting our urgent social needs. It can be done, but it can't be done with business as usual. Next year alone, thanks to economic growth—it's essential we keep the economic growth going in this country—but thanks to economic growth next year alone, Federal tax revenues under existing law will rise by more than $80 billion—more than $80 billion in new revenues under existing law in 1 year alone. And our job is to allocate these new resources wisely: to reduce the Federal deficit by more than 40 percent, with no new taxes, and yet investing in key priorities.

Budget consultations with the Congress, as some of you may have read, are already underway; and we are making progress. And yesterday I called the five congressional leaders and invited them to come to the White House for another round of budget talks next Tuesday morning. I am committed to working closely with my friends on the Hill to help them meet the target date set by Gramm-Rudman-Hollings for an April 15th budget resolution. And together, we've got to make the process work.

There are certain priorities that demand attention. And, yes, we can afford to increase spending—modestly, selectively, but only after tough choices are made. And we must spend enough to protect our national security, and that is a chief responsibility of every President of the United States. And certainly we must not fall back on the tax-and-spend policies of the past. But programs that can work must be protected and, in some cases, funding increased. Our budget is fair to recipients, fair to taxpayers, and fairminded in its strategy. It embodies two qualities which are always in season: the common sense that Justice Learned Hand termed "the eventual supremacy of reason" and America's capacity to care.

Most Americans believe that in the America of the 1990's our challenges must be met in several ways—by government, by thousand upon thousands of other institutions, and by the people themselves working together—or they won't be met at all. The Government's contribution is critical, but by itself is insufficient to solve all of our national problems. And yet most Americans believe that our efforts must reach beyond government to care about our communities and to assist our neighbors. I called it, in a speech earlier on, a Thousand Points of Light; and some of the columnists have had fun with that, interpreting it as a Thousand Pints of Lite. I'm surprised you didn't get that one here in Missouri. But I think people are beginning to understand what I mean by a Thousand Points of Light. And if they'd look at these signs and talk to some of you responsible for them, I think they'd understand it without contradiction. I believe that government can be an important catalyst in that process of helping individuals, helping our communities, helping our nation.

And our budget does more, for instance, for environment, more for the space program, invests almost $2.2 billion for the National Science Foundation—a lot of that going to universities to help basic research.

It increases funding for the Head Start Program and allocates $1 billion more in additional outlays to stop the deadly scourge of drugs. We have got to fight the drug fight on two fronts—supply and demand—to reclaim the lives of addicts who want help, educate young people about the dangers of drugs, and then enforce our laws. All this is what I mean when I speak of investing in the future.

To minority Americans, this budget says: Education means opportunity, and bigotry will not be tolerated anywhere in the United States of America. To the homeless, this budget targets $1 billion, saying: Our nation must leave no one out. To the elderly, this budget vows: Your dignity and concerns will be respected. And to the Nation's youth, the budget says: The promise of tomorrow lies in the children of today.

Consider this: We've proposed a new child care initiative. It's not going to take care of everybody. It's targeted at low-income families. We've restored and doubled the tax deduction for adopting special-needs children. We want those kids in families of love. And even more, we've made education the Gateway Arch of the Bush administration. For our pursuit of excellence is central to the future of America; and if excellence breeds achievement, then excellence must be rewarded in grade school, in high school, and in the colleges and universities of America.

Last Thursday, I asked Congress to begin a $500 million program to reward America's best schools, merit schools, and to establish a special Presidential award for the best teachers in every State. I urged expanded use of what are known as magnet schools, giving families and students a choice in education. And I proposed a new program to encourage what we call alternative certification. It is wrong if one of you guys who graduate from this school of excellence, one of you wants to go and give of yourselves to teach in some urban area in a public school—it is wrong to have this excellence go to waste because of some hidebound restrictions having to do with too many certifications that keep idealistic young people for [from] teaching. I want to change that and have alternative certification.

We must bring more of our best minds back to the teaching profession. And through a new program of National Science Scholars, we can inspire their students, also giving America's youth a special incentive to excel in science and mathematics. In short, I wish to achieve nationally what this university has done historically: to make excellence in learning a national way of life. Education can ennoble the American story. It's the best way to invest in our future and to make this better, more selfless, and a more tolerant world.

And, yes, in some areas, I've got to confess, I wish we did have more money to spend—key areas like drugs and education. I will candidly admit that the Federal Government could use more resources to bring to bear on these problems. But we've had to set priorities; we've had to make the tough choices. And I believe we have set the right priorities in this budget. Ours isn't the total answer, but in this budget, we've made a good beginning. And now I've asked the Congressmen to come—the leaders to come—meet with me and, in a spirit of bipartisanship, get on with the Nation's business of getting a quick and early resolution to this budget crisis. And now we have work to do. There are many problems that must be solved in America today, and I remain confident that our nation can solve them. But America must go far beyond the Federal budget to achieve its goals. We've got to forge strong partnerships between all levels of government and voluntary organizations and business corporations and individuals, to lend a hand and mend a wound and help the less fortunate.

Next week, Barbara and I are going to embark on a long journey. We're going to be trying to pursue peace and friendship, a journey that's going to take us across the Pacific to Japan and China and to Korea. And we go to attend the funeral of the late Emperor and to consult with the leaders of many of America's allies and friends there in Tokyo, who will be attending those ceremonies. And my visit to China is a bit of a sentimental journey to a country where I served as America's equivalent then of Ambassador 14 or 15 years ago. And several days ago, preparing for our trip, I came across these words of an old Chinese proverb: "One generation plants the seed; another gets the shade." Think of the investments that we make in our future as America's seeds. And we can lift hearts; we can change lives. And we can shape the 1990's, just one decade before a whole new century.

It's a tall order, but it has been the American story for over 200 years. And let's write it together. And let me say in conclusion, just being here, just seeing these symbols of voluntarism, make me absolutely convinced that if we take this spirit evident in this gym here today and then multiply it by those thousands we can do the job. Let's write the next chapter together. Thank you all for this wonderful welcome, and God bless you all. Thank you very much.

Note: The President spoke at 10:33 a.m. in the university field house. Following his remarks, the President returned to Washington, DC.

Nomination of Sidney Linn Williams To Be a Deputy United States Trade Representative

February 17, 1989

The President today announced his intention to nominate Sidney Linn Williams to be a Deputy United States Trade Representative, with the rank of Ambassador. He would succeed Alan F. Holmer.

Since 1985 Mr. Williams has been a partner with the law firm of Gibson Dunn & Crutcher in Tokyo, Japan, and Washington, DC. Prior to this he was vice president and general counsel for Sears World Trade, 1984–1985, and vice president and general counsel for Overseas Private Investment Corporation, 1981–1984. Mr. Williams practiced law with a Washington, DC, law firm from 1975 to 1981.

Mr. Williams graduated from Princeton College (B.A., 1968), Harvard Law School (J.D., 1971), and Cambridge University, Fulbright Scholarship (1972–1974). He is married, has two children, and resides in Yokohama, Japan, and McLean, VA.

Letter to Congressional Committee Chairmen Transmitting the Report on Appropriations for Strategic Weapons

February 17, 1989

Dear Mr. Chairman:

The provisions of the fiscal year 1989 Defense Authorization and Appropriations Acts require that I submit to the Committees on Armed Services and Appropriations of the Senate and House of Representatives a report on the "anticipated obligations for the remainder of the fiscal year 1989 for the Small ICBM, the MX Rail Garrison program, and other ICBM Modernization programs; and the purposes those obligations are intended to accomplish." Until April 3, 1989, I anticipate obligating no more than $250 million of the $600 million appropriated for the fiscal year 1989 MX Rail Garrison program.

Between now and April 3, we will be reviewing various ICBM modernization options in the context of my recently announced national security strategy review. The modernization of our land-based strategic forces has raised a number of issues that will necessitate consultations with you and other members of Congress before any final proposals are made on this critically important matter.

Sincerely,

GEORGE BUSH

Note: Identical letters were sent to Sam Nunn and Les Aspin, chairmen of the Senate and House of Representatives Committee on Armed Services, respectively, and Robert C. Byrd and Jamie L. Whitten, chairmen of the Senate and House of Representatives Committee on Appropriations, respectively.

Nomination of Rufus Hawkins Yerxa To Be a Deputy United States Trade Representative
February 17, 1989

The President today announced his intention to nominate Rufus Hawkins Yerxa to be Deputy United States Trade Representative, with the rank of Ambassador. He would succeed Michael A. Samuels.

Mr. Yerxa is the assistant chief counsel of the Committee on Ways and Means, U.S. House of Representatives, and has been the staff director of the Subcommittee on Trade, since 1984. Mr. Yerxa joined the Committee as a professional staff member in 1981. From 1977 to 1981, he was a legal adviser for the U.S. International Trade Commission.

Mr. Yerxa received his undergraduate degree from the University of Washington, his law degree from the University of Puget Sound, and a master's degree in international law from Cambridge University in England.

Statement by Press Secretary Fitzwater Concerning Secretary Baker's Report to the President on Meetings With NATO Allies
February 18, 1989

The President today, at Camp David, received a report by telephone from Secretary of State James A. Baker III on the Secretary's recent trip to NATO capitals. The President will receive a personal report from Secretary Baker at Camp David on Sunday.

President Bush asked Secretary Baker to undertake this mission in order to emphasize that the North Atlantic alliance is central to our foreign and security interests. European leaders, in turn, told the Secretary that their countries are firmly committed to the alliance as the key to the continent's past and future security.

The President reviewed at length with the Secretary a variety of issues that had been discussed with the allies, including the generally shared view that East-West relations are now clearly proceeding on the basis of the West's agenda. The President expressed his conviction that NATO unity is strong and his confidence that the allies will move together in addressing the major questions of international stability. In particular, the President noted that he looks forward to meeting with his allied counterparts at an early date to further advance the Western strategy to promote world peace and security. At the close of the Secretary's report, the President expressed appreciation to him for undertaking this very important but arduous trip and complimented him on his effective demonstration to our allies of the high value we place on a closer, cooperative relationship.

The President's News Conference
February 21, 1989

Representative Bill Grant of Florida

The President. With me is Congressman Bill Grant, from the second district of Florida, and his wife; new chairman of the Republican Party in the State of Florida, my old friend, Van Poole; and our chairman of the national committee, Lee Atwater. And I just wanted to bring Congressman Grant in here to say how pleased I am that he is switching over to become a Republican. Florida is on the move. The Nation, I think, benefits from this. And Bill can answer any questions. He has a short statement, but this is good news for our party not only in Florida; not only in the South but nationally. And I welcome him to the party.

The way it will work is: I've asked him to say a few words, and then I'm going to step back in and take a couple of questions and then turn it over to Bill for follow-on. And Lee Atwater will be with him.

Congressman Grant, welcome.

Representative Grant. Thank you, Mr. President.

The President. I'm pleased you're here under these circumstances, too.

Representative Grant. Thank you very much. Well, I'm here this morning to announce that I intend to reregister as a Republican in my hometown of Madison, Florida, this afternoon. After a period of prolonged and careful deliberation, I've determined that I can better represent the values and the priorities of north Floridians in the State of Florida as a Republican.

Please understand, I've been a Democrat all of my adult life. And I want the people who've sent me to the Congress to understand that my actions are not going to change me as a person. It will not change my heritage. This action is not going to change my values nor will it change the way that I vote. I'm registering as a Republican because I can best serve the people of Florida's second congressional district in a working partnership with this President, with this administration, and with this Republican Party. I've been assured by President Bush that he will work closely and cooperatively with me to ensure that the force of his administration is brought to bear to improve the lives of the people that I represent.

I'm reregistering as a Republican because I share this party's commitment for inclusion for all of the American people. I'm reregistering as a Republican because I share the values for which the party stands. Those values include a commitment to a strong national defense, where we're assured that our friends love us and our enemies fear us; a commitment to fair and equal opportunity for all of the citizens of our land; and an unswerving commitment to fighting the crime and drug abuse that plague our society. I believe that these values are shared by the people that I represent, and I am convinced that I can best serve them as a Republican. And I'm proud to make this announcement today. Thank you.

The President. Now, I'll be glad to take a couple of questions. As you know, we're leaving on this trip tomorrow, and there may be some on that, which I doubt. [*Laughter*]

Salman Rushdie's "The Satanic Verses"

Q. Mr. President, what's your reaction to Iran's death threat against the British author Salman Rushdie? And do you think that the British allies—or that the Western allies should impose economic sanctions against Iran in retaliation?

The President. Well, I strongly support the EC–12 declaration in response to the Iranian threats against Rushdie. However offensive that book may be, inciting murder and offering rewards for its perpetration are deeply offensive to the norm of civilized behavior. And our position on terrorism is well known. In the light of Iran's incitement, should any action be taken against American interests, the Government of Iran can expect to be held accountable. And so, that is my view on it, and I think the EC–12 did the right thing.

Q. How about the economic sanctions

part of it?

The President. They will be discussing that, I'm sure, but I don't know where we go from there. As you know, we have certain economic sanctions. I know I'll be talking to [French] President Mitterrand, and I expect this subject will come up, and maybe others. I'm not sure exactly of the bilaterals we're having, but it'll be a matter—

Helen [Helen Thomas, United Press International], and then we'll start moving around, trying to get to the back of the room.

Q. Yes.

U.S. Foreign Policy

Q. Basically, in a way, a question about your trip: There is a widespread perception that you don't have a foreign policy, that you have permitted the Russians to move into the vacuum in the Middle East—you were surprised on Central America—that your go-slow attitude really says: Let the Russians grab the ball.

The President. Well, I've never heard such outrageous hypothesis. [*Laughter*] The fact that the Soviets—you fail to point out that the Soviets moved out of Afghanistan; some good things happening. I don't worry about a trip by Mr. Shevardnadze to the Middle East. I have no worry about that.

Q. That was pre-Bush.

The President. No, it happened just this week, and they're out of there. I don't worry about that. And we have a foreign policy. We are reviewing appropriately East-West relations, the way we look at South America. But this doesn't trouble me one bit. We've established and are following on with certain principles that are out there. And I think that [Secretary of State] Jim Baker, when he came back, made very clear that the NATO alliance still looks to the United States. I'll have an opportunity to discuss a lot of things as we go on this particular trip. So, I simply don't agree with that. I really hadn't ever heard such a negative approach to foreign policy.

Q. Well, what is your Middle East policy?

The President. Middle East policy is to encourage discussions between King Hussein and the Israelis and to build on the progress that has been made already. I've already said that I think it was very useful—the changes that the PLO [Palestine Liberation Organization] advocated. Now we want to see that there's some follow-on there.

So, the policy is set. I campaigned on what the policy is, and I think it's quite clear. The question is what specific steps we take next. And I don't want to be rushing out because Mr. Shevardnadze went to the Middle East. I'd like for the first step we take of that nature, to be a prudent step. So, the principles are there, and I think we're—you know, we've got to now flesh that out and figure out what we do specifically.

Secretary of Defense-Designate Tower

Q. Mr. President, the FBI's final, or presumably final, report on Senator Tower is now in. You are reported to have read some of it. The Senate Committee has it. I would like to know what you got from it, and also whether you have any reason to believe that the Senate will go forward—any reason from private conversations with members of the Armed Services Committee—will go forward with a favorable vote on this nomination?

The President. What I got from it—and I reviewed some of the parts that related to some of the allegations against Tower—what I got from it was that there has been a very unfair treatment of this man by rumor and innuendo, over and over again rumors surfacing with no facts to back them up. And I saw this as a reaffirmation of what I felt all along, and that is that John Tower is qualified to be Secretary of Defense. He will be a good Secretary of Defense, although the report didn't answer that. But the allegations against him that have been hanging over this simply have been gunned down in terms of fact. And so, that's positive. And I had had a little preview—so, when I held my thumbs up, I was glad to get that report, and I hope that the Senate will move forthrightly on this nomination. And I don't know, Brit [Brit Hume, ABC News], where it stands. I had some of the leaders down this morning, but the only one I got to talk to on this was Bob Dole. And I'd like to see it go forward, obviously.

Q. If I might follow up——

The President. I've never wavered in my support for John Tower.

Q. If I could follow up, sir: There is a report in the Wall Street Journal this morning that Senator Tower promoted a Federal judgeship for the son of a man with whom he had done business to his own personal benefit. And I was wondering if that was news to you, sir, or did it trouble you in any way?

The President. I never heard such a report. And you know, one thing after another, and you're telling me something I don't know anything about.

State Representative David Duke

Q. Mr. President, does this announcement by Congressman Grant this morning overcome the embarrassment to the party of the election Saturday of David Duke, a former member of the Ku Klux Klan? You came out for his opponent in the election; so did former President Reagan. What does the party do next about David Duke?

The President. Well, I'll leave that to Lee; but I strongly support what our National Chairman, Lee Atwater, has said in this matter. And maybe there was some feeling in Metairie, Louisiana, that the President of the United States involving himself in a State legislative election was improper or overkill. I've read that, and I can't deny that. But what I can affirm is: I did what I did because of principle, and Lee has done what he's done because of principle. And this man—his record is one of racism and bigotry—and I'm sorry, I just felt I had to speak out. But whether it helped or hurt, I don't know.

Strategic Defense Initiative

Q. Mr. President, you said during your speech to the Joint Session of Congress that your support to the Strategic Defense Initiative was unqualified; but the Office of Management and Budget Director, Richard Darman, when he briefed on your budget, said that it was conditional on the outcome of this 90-day review that's coming up. Is it or is it not conditional, and would you rule out curtailing the program to an accidental launch protection?

The President. I'm not ruling anything in or out. I have stated my support for the principle of SDI. I have not favored what some would call premature deployment, but, on the other hand, I will be very interested in seeing what this overall review comes up with. And I'm not going to close any doors or open any in regards to this or any other systems. We're going to have to make some tough choices on defense; I'm aware of that. And so, let's wait and see what the review produces.

Secretary of Defense-Designate Tower

Q. Mr. President, back on John Tower, if we could. You said that the process has been unfair. And I'd like to ask you specifically about Sam Nunn, who some people say will now run defense policy because John Tower has been so weakened and damaged by this drip, drip, drip of allegations.

The President. I think Sam Nunn would be the first to deny that. I think he's been fair and have so stated before.

Q. So, who's been unfair?

The President. The rumors. And he's not been promulgating a lot of endless rumors that prove to have no basis in fact—none. So, but the idea that he will run defense policy—I think he'd be the first to say that's not true. He will be a key player in it, and I hope that he'll be able to support Senator Tower.

Q. Is Senator Tower damaged in his ability to speak out for the Pentagon now that he's had such a lengthy process?

The President. No. Anybody that's been through this ordeal will be stronger, not weaker.

Q. But Senator Nunn is concerned about these reports of Senator Tower's drinking problems. The FBI report acknowledges that the Senator apparently did have a drinking problem in the 1970's. Do you think he's overly concerned? And why are you so convinced that this won't present a problem?

The President. Because I know Senator Tower. I've talked to a lot of people that have worked with Senator Tower. I've seen the report on Senator Tower. And I see nothing in there that would make me, if I were a Senator, vote against Senator Tower. Now, Senator Nunn, he's got to reach his own conclusions, and I think he's been fair. And I think he is approaching it in a very professional manner, but I hope he reaches the same conclusion that I've reached.

Urban Violence

Q. Mr. President, Washington, DC, and other big cities have been besieged with violence lately. Do you see any role at all that the Federal Government can play to help in that area?

The President. Well, I hope so. But certainly in Washington we have a responsibility. It's a Federal city, and a lot of the funds obviously come from the Federal Government. But there isn't any easy answer to that. And yet I campaigned strongly on enforcing existing law, on being tough on criminals, on more prison space; and I think that those things all will be caught up in our new antidrug effort that I'm looking to Bill Bennett [National Drug Control Policy Director] to lead. And so, it's a complicated problem, where everybody in the country has a stake in it. Everybody should be trying to do something about it. And, yes, I think the Federal Government has a role in that.

Q. If I may follow: Is there any Federal money for it? Is this something that you really do not have the resources to attack on the Federal level?

The President. Yes, there will be Federal money, and I wish we had more.

Q. Mr. President——

The President. How far do we go to be democratic here? No, that's too far. Here. [*Laughter*]

The Middle East

Q. Mr. President, you've said in answer to Helen's question that you wanted your first step in the Middle East to be prudent. What do you mean by a prudent step? What do you have in mind?

The President. What I have in mind is: I don't want to just send somebody charging off on a mission to counter Mr. Shevardnadze's trip to see Mubarak and others. Let's do something that's going to hopefully have results. And I'm not saying we have to know that a trip by the Secretary or instructions to an ambassador are going to result in a settled policy. Everything's settled in the Middle East, but I don't want to be stampeded by the fact that the Soviet Foreign Minister takes a trip to the Middle East. So, in my view, that's a good thing.

Q. What role do you think Mr. Shevardnadze and the Soviets could and should be playing?

The President. I think it should be a limited role, and I think that's what it's going to be. And that's exactly the way it should be, and I think the people in the Middle East feel that way. But the fact that he goes there really shouldn't be bad.

West Germany and the NATO Alliance

Q. Mr. President, if the West Germans refuse to modernize short-range weapons, will that hurt the alliance in the long run and perhaps result in the denuclearization of Europe?

The President. Too hypothetical a question, Gerry [Gerry Watson, Chicago Sun-Times] for me to answer.

Q. Mr. President, I'll ask you a Japan question.

The President. Shoot.

Foreign Investment in the U.S.

Q. With the summit starting tomorrow, how do you reassure those Americans who are afraid of Japanese economic power, who think they are buying and are owning too much of the United States economy?

The President. I tell them that the Japanese are the third largest holder of investment in the United States, behind the U.K. and the Netherlands. I tell them that it is important if we believe in open markets that people be allowed to invest here, just as I'd like to see more openness for American investors in other countries. I tell them that we have to do a better job in knocking down barriers to American products in the various markets. I tell them, don't get so concerned over foreign ownership that you undermine the securities markets in this country. We have horrendous deficits, and foreign capital joins domestic capital in financing those deficits. I also tell them I have a responsibility as President in terms of our technology, in terms of our national security, and I intend to exercise that responsibility.

Secretary of Defense-Designate Tower

Q. Yes, Mr. President, I think what concerns some people about Senator Tower is the fact that he has admitted that he had a drinking problem in the seventies, and he hasn't really had any kind of treatment program or been enrolled in any kind of treatment program. What do you say to people about the potential of a relapse?

The President. I say that there is no evidence of any kind of the disease alcoholism. None, none whatsoever. And that would be something that your question is addressed to. And I'd say that I looked at the reports with this in mind, and I didn't listen to rumors; I didn't listen to mindless allegations. I was fair enough to look at the facts. And I've known Senator Tower and known him professionally and known him as a friend, and I do not think that these charges—that are tried and then shot down and then tried again and then shot down again—have helped the process. And so, I am not about to make a judgment on some rumor or some innuendo. And we've looked at the facts, and I think the report speaks to the fact that a lot of the charges—most—well, I'd say all of these charges that we've read about have been rumor, and a lot of it vicious rumor. And, so, I am convinced that he is not only capable of doing this job but will do it in an outstanding way.

Q. Mr. President——

Q. Can I follow up on that?

The President. How many more we got?

Mr. Fitzwater. One more.

Q. Mr. President——

Q. Question.

The President. Who is that voice I hear in the back? [*Laughter*] Could it be Sarah McClendon? [*Laughter*]

Q. In the back——

Q. Yes, sir.

The President. Sorry, it's a democracy.

Gun Control

Q. Mr. President, I want to ask you about gun control. All over the country——

The President. Oh. [*Laughter*]

Q. ——the parents and the people—now don't leave me, don't leave me. [*Laughter*]

The President. Sarah.

Q. All over the country, the parents now are going to city hall about this. Cleveland has just had a vote. Polls are being taken. Mothers are up in arms about this. Something is going to have to be done about stopping guns. And you say you're for them.

The President. For what?

Q. You said the other day that you were not going to be for the ban on gun control.

The President. I'd like to find some way to do something about these automated weapons. I'd like to see some way to enforce the laws that are already on the books about automated AK–47's coming into this country. And I'd like to find a way to be supportive of the police who are out there on the line all the time. And maybe there is some answer to it, but I also want to be the President that protects the rights of people to have arms. And that——

Q. So, you don't want——

The President. ——so you don't go so far that the legitimate rights on some legislation are impinged on——

Q. Sir, that's what we said last year, but now——

The President. But, Sarah, look at the laws on gun control and you'll find where some of the most stringent gun control laws exist, that weapons are procured there and weapons are used there. So, you're not going to get me to do anything other than to say, Look, I'm very concerned about this. I'd like to find a way to do something about this; and we're going to take a hard look to see what we can do about it, if anything, that would be helpful. But whenever there is a crime involving a firearm, there are various groups—some of them quite persuasive in their logic—that think you can ban certain kinds of guns. And I am not in that mode; I am in the mode of being deeply concerned and would like to be a part of finding a national answer to this problem.

Now we've got time for one more, right in the middle. You two fight about it.

Salman Rushdie's "The Satanic Verses"

Q. Speaking of rights, I want to ask you if it disturbs you at all that American booksellers were intimidated into taking Mr. Rushdie's book off the shelves and if you've given any thought to some sort of Federal protection to help them defend the——

The President. The answer is yes. And

Federal protection would be to enforce the laws that exist against people doing violence. And of course, I'm concerned about that. Who wouldn't be?

Owen [Owen Ullman, Knight-Ridder Newspapers] gets to follow up, and then I'm leaving.

Q. Follow up on that.

The President. I know there's an overwhelming—Owen has got the last question, and I got the last word. [*Laughter*] Just a second—sorry.

Q. You've been asked about Iran. My followup will be on the budget.

The President. Get out of there. [*Laughter*] You may ruin it for everybody, because what we're going to do then is stay with one question. I'm thinking very hard about this, and I know that there's—no?

Q. No.

The President. Go ahead. [*Laughter*]

Q. Do you plan to take any unilateral action toward Iran because of these death threats? Since Karen [Karen Hoestler, Baltimore Sun] mentioned American booksellers have had to already—as a precaution they claim—to remove books from their shelves, there is an American connection. And you've also been slow to speak out about that.

The President. Our Secretary of State spoke out on my behalf the other day. We're speaking out here today. My view is that we are an open society. None of us like everything that's written, but certainly people should have protection of the law if they decide to go ahead and sell a book of this nature. That's the answer I'd give to it.

And as to the Iran factor, I've just laid down how I feel in terms of this case: the Imam [Ayatollah Khomeini] exhorting people to go out and commit murder.

Q. Where's Sununu?

Q. Mr. President, about the budget——

Q. Mr. President, Alan Greenspan [Federal Reserve Board Chairman] has just testified on the Hill that he's going to tighten credit. President Bush, Alan Greenspan has just testified on the Hill that he's going to tighten credit.

The President. I've got to go. Thank you all.

Chief of Staff to the President

Q. Where's Sununu?

The President. Has an important meeting with an important element of the Washington press, Jerry [Gerald Boyd, New York Times].

Note: The President's third news conference began at 10:31 a.m. in the Briefing Room at the White House. Marlin Fitzwater was the President's Press Secretary.

Appointment of G. Philip Hughes as Executive Secretary of the National Security Council

February 21, 1989

The President today announced the appointment of G. Philip Hughes as Executive Secretary of the National Security Council.

Prior to assuming his current duties, Mr. Hughes served as the first Assistant Secretary of Commerce for Export Enforcement, where he was primarily responsible for directing enforcement of the provisions of the Export Administration Act. Prior to joining the Commerce Department, Mr. Hughes served as Deputy Assistant Secretary for Political-Military Affairs at the Department of State from 1986, with responsibility for policy problems involving strategic trade and technology transfer. Mr. Hughes began his tenure in the Reagan administration, serving as Vice President George Bush's Deputy Assistant for National Security Affairs from February 1981 to September 1985, when he joined the National Security Council staff as Director for Latin American Affairs. Mr. Hughes served previously as Assistant Director for Intelligence Policy in the Office of the Secretary of Defense from 1979 to 1981, as research fellow in defense policy studies at the Brookings Institution from 1978 to 1979, and as assistant analyst in the national security and international affairs division of the Congressional Budget Office from 1975 to 1977.

Mr. Hughes received a B.A. in political science from the University of Dayton in Ohio; a M.A. in law and diplomacy from the Fletcher School of Law and Diplomacy, Tufts University; and a masters of public administration degree from the Kennedy School of Government, Harvard University. He is married to the former Victoria Knipper, and they reside in Falls Church, VA.

Appointment of William L. Roper as Deputy Assistant to the President for Domestic Policy and Director of the White House Office of Policy Development

February 21, 1989

The President today announced the appointment of William L. Roper to be Deputy Assistant to the President for Domestic Policy and Director of the White House Office of Policy Development.

Since 1986 Dr. Roper has served as Administrator of the Health Care Financing Administration, Department of Health and Human Services (HHS). In this position, he has directed all Federal health care financing programs under Medicare and Medicaid. Prior to HHS, Dr. Roper served at the White House, where he was Special Assistant to the President for Health Policy from 1983 to 1986. From 1977 to 1983, Dr. Roper was health officer of the Jefferson County Department of Health in Birmingham, AL, serving also from 1981 as assistant State health officer. Between 1979 and 1983, he served in several positions on the faculty of the University of Alabama at Birmingham in the school of public health, department of pediatrics, and the graduate program in hospital and health administration. On leave from his Alabama health position, he was a White House fellow in the White House Office of Policy Development from 1982 to 1983, with responsibility for health policy.

Dr. Roper was born July 6, 1948, in Birmingham, AL. He received an associate of arts degree from Florida College in 1968; a bachelor of science degree from the University of Alabama in 1970, where he was elected to Phi Beta Kappa; a doctor of medicine degree from the University of Alabama School of Medicine in 1974, where he was president of his class all 4 years; and his M.P.H. from that institution's school of public health in 1981. He is board certified in pediatrics and in preventive medicine and is licensed to practice medicine in Alabama. Dr. Roper resides in Arlington, VA, with his wife Maryann Roper, a pediatric oncologist.

Appointment of Shirley Moore Green as Special Assistant to the President for Presidential Messages and Correspondence

February 21, 1989

The President today announced the appointment of Shirley Moore Green to be Special Assistant to the President for Presidential Messages and Correspondence.

Since July 1987 Mrs. Green has been Deputy Associate Administrator for Communications at the National Aeronautics and Space Administration. Prior to this she was Director of Public Affairs for NASA. From 1981 to 1985, Mrs. Green held the position of Deputy Press Secretary to Vice President George Bush. In that capacity, she was responsible for planning and coordinating media activities for the Vice President on domestic policy, including the Task Forces on Regulatory Relief and Drug Interdiction. She also accompanied Vice President Bush to 62 foreign countries. Mrs. Green served previously as a member of the George Bush for President campaign staff in 1979–80, as public affairs director for the Texas Federation of Republican Women from 1969 to 1973, on the staff of Congressman Bob Price in 1967, and on the headquarters staff of the Texas Republican Party from 1965 to 1967. She was a local campaign chairman for numerous Republican candidates in Texas, including President Gerald Ford in 1976 and James A. Baker in 1978.

Mrs. Green received a bachelor of business administration degree from the University of Texas in 1956. She is a member of the American Newswomen's Association, Women in Communications, and Executive Women in Government. Mrs. Green was born December 21, 1933. She has two daughters and resides in Washington, DC.

Message to the Congress Transmitting the Switzerland-United States Social Security Agreement
February 21, 1989

To the Congress of the United States:

Pursuant to Section 233(e)(1) of the Social Security Act, as amended by the Social Security Amendments of 1977 (P.L. 95–216, 42 U.S.C. 433(e)(1)), I transmit herewith the Supplementary Agreement Amending the Agreement between the United States of America and the Swiss Confederation on Social Security ("Supplementary Agreement"), which consists of two separate instruments—a principal agreement and an administrative agreement. The Supplementary Agreement was signed at Bern on June 1, 1988.

The U.S.-Switzerland agreement is similar in objective to the social security agreements in force in Belgium, Canada, France, the Federal Republic of Germany, Italy, Norway, Spain, Sweden, and the United Kingdom. Such bilateral agreements provide for limited coordination between the United States and foreign social security systems to overcome the problems of gaps in protection and of dual coverage and taxation for workers who move from one country to the other. The present Supplementary Agreement would amend the original agreement with Switzerland to update and simplify several of its provisions in view of changes in U.S. and Swiss law and to simplify the method of computing U.S. benefit amounts.

I also transmit for the information of the Congress a comprehensive report prepared by the Department of Health and Human Services, which explains the provisions of the Supplementary Agreement and the effect on social security financing as required by the same provision of the Social Security Act. I note that the Department of State and the Department of Health and Human Services have recommended the Supplementary Agreement and related documents to me.

I commend the U.S.-Switzerland Supplementary Social Security Agreement and related documents.

GEORGE BUSH

The White House,
February 21, 1989.

Nomination of John D. Negroponte To Be United States Ambassador to Mexico

February 21, 1989

The President today announced his intention to nominate John D. Negroponte to be Ambassador Extraordinary and Plenipotentiary of the United States of America to Mexico. He would succeed Charles J. Pilliod, Jr.

Ambassador Negroponte has most recently served as Deputy Assistant to the President for National Security Affairs at the White House, 1987–1989. Prior to this he was Assistant Secretary of State for Oceans and Environmental and Scientific Affairs, 1985–1987. From 1981 to 1985, he was United States Ambassador to Honduras; Deputy Assistant Secretary of State for East Asian and Pacific Affairs, 1980–1981; and Deputy Assistant Secretary of State for Oceans and Fisheries Affairs, 1977–1979. Ambassador Negroponte was consul general in Thessaloniki, Greece, 1975–1977, and counselor for political affairs in Quito, Ecuador, 1973–1975. From 1970 to 1973, he was a staff member for the National Security Council, and served as a member of the U.S. delegation to the Paris peace talks on Vietnam, 1968–1969. In 1960 he entered the Foreign Service, serving in Hong Kong and Vietnam.

Ambassador Negroponte graduated from Yale University (B.A., 1960). He was born July 21, 1939, in London, England. He is married, has two children, and resides in Washington, DC.

Written Responses to Questions Submitted by the Kyodo News Service of Japan

February 16, 1989

Japan's International Role

Q. What kind of role will the Bush administration expect Japan to play in the global economic and Western national security spheres?

The President. First of all, a word about the global role of the United States during my administration. Japan and the world can count on America to continue to work for peace, democracy, freedom, and justice around the world. The scope of America's vision is global, and we will continue to shoulder the obligations that belong to a global power.

At the same time, of course, it is important that our allies assume greater responsibility in the cause of global peace and prosperity. It is not for me to prescribe Japan's role in the world. The decision is up to the Government and people of Japan. During Prime Minister Takeshita's recent visit to Washington, he and I agreed that there are many ways Japan can contribute to global peace and prosperity. Our defense cooperation is one of those ways; another is foreign economic assistance.

I welcome Japan's pledge to make further significant increases in overseas development assistance programs. Along these lines, Prime Minister Takeshita and I agreed on the importance of supporting democracy and sustained economic growth and reform in the Philippines. Toward this end, we pledged to make every effort to launch the Multilateral Assistance Initiative for the Philippines this year. I also welcome Japan's decision to take part in peacekeeping operations and your generous offers of financial support for the relief and resettlement in Afghanistan and southern Africa. Those are also ways to contribute.

The United States and Japan, the world's two largest economies, have special responsibilities to sustain free trade. Prime Minister Takeshita reaffirmed in Washington Japan's determination to promote strong domestic growth and structural adjustments. In the area of multilateral cooperation and global economic growth, we agreed that we would continue to coordinate policies through established fora, especially the economic summit. We look forward to the next summit meeting, which will be held in Paris. We also agreed on the importance of a successful Uruguay round [multilateral trade negotiations]. And we agreed on the importance of frequent consultation at all levels on economic issues.

Japan-U.S. Relations

Q. How do you envision U.S.-Japan relations under your administration? Some of your advisers have recommended forming a "new partnership" with Japan. What are your feelings about this recommendation?

The President. We have used the word "partnership" to describe our relationship for a number of years now, and during the course of the Reagan administration, we gave new meaning to that term. Our partnership is bilateral, regional, and global. We consult frequently and cooperate closely on virtually every issue of importance. This is not a "new partnership" but a continuing one that has developed over 40 years of cooperation. I am confident it will continue to develop and acquire new meaning, but rather than a "new partnership," it will be a continually "renewed partnership."

Japan's Defense Role

Q. Defense Secretary-designate Tower said Japan should extend its sealane defense beyond the present 1,000-mile limit. Do you support this view? Would you ask Japan to beef up its defense? If so, how much of its GNP should Japan allocate for defense spending?

The President. We are fully satisfied with the mutually agreed division of defense roles and missions in our security arrangements, under which Japan has primary responsibility for defending its territory, seas and skies, and sea lines of communication. We are also encouraged by Japan's continued and steady progress in improving its defense capability within the framework of those roles and missions, recognizing there is still room for greater improvement, especially in the area of sustainability. Further, we appreciate Japan's increasing contribution to the cost of maintaining U.S. forces in Japan. Rather than engage in a sterile exercise of measuring security in arbitrary terms such as GNP, the United States and Japan are putting our efforts toward a much more productive and important purpose: that of working together to attain defense capabilities which will ensure our mutual security.

Japan-U.S. Trade

Q. Would you support a U.S.-Japan free trade agreement modeled after the U.S.-Canada free trade agreement? The U.S. deficit with Japan has been on the rise again in recent months. Do you favor the yen's further appreciation against the dollar?

The President. The U.S. and Japanese Governments agree on the need to pursue multilateral and bilateral efforts to create a more open international trading system. We will stress the multilateral approach.

We are always open to new ideas. But in our view, the key now is to work hard for the success of the Uruguay round. At the recent G–7 meeting, the financial authorities of the major countries agreed the global economic situation and outlook remain positive and that no changes in their commitment to cooperation on exchange rate policies were needed.

During our recent meeting, Prime Minister Takeshita and I noted progress that both the United States and Japan have made toward reducing external imbalances, but we also agreed that further policy efforts are needed. The Prime Minister assured me that Japan remained determined to encourage strong domestic growth and structural reform. And I reaffirmed our strong determination to reduce our budget deficit.

Soviet-U.S. Relations

Q. A reduction of conventional arms is said to be the top priority of the Bush administration in the U.S.-Soviet arms negotiations. What is your response to President Gorbachev's announcement to cut 500,000 Soviet troops? Do you foresee a U.S.-Soviet summit by next summer?

The President. It is true that a major priority of my administration is in the area of conventional arms control. Thus we welcome and look forward to the Negotiations on Conventional Armed Forces in Europe (CFE). We, along with our NATO allies, will seek in CFE to enhance stability and security at a lower level of forces. To that end, NATO will seek the elimination of the Warsaw Pact's substantial superiority in Europe. Accordingly, we welcome the announcement of Soviet force reductions as a positive step in the right direction and look forward to the full implementation of the force cuts described by Chairman Gorbachev. Even with these reductions, however, the Warsaw Pact has far to go to correct the conventional forces imbalance in Europe.

Regarding a summit, both sides, of course, want to be well-prepared before engaging in a summit. We are in the process of reviewing elements of our policy toward the Soviet Union and consulting closely with our allies and friends to ensure that we have a sound foundation for long-term progress in East-West relations. Secretary of State Baker and Foreign Minister Shevardnadze will have several opportunities in the months ahead to begin addressing the many issues between our countries. Thus, while I am confident a summit will take place sometime in the future, it is too early to discuss a specific date.

Note: The questions and answers were released by the Office of the Press Secretary on February 22.

Remarks to Armed Forces Personnel at Elmendorf Air Force Base in Anchorage, Alaska

February 22, 1989

Thank you very much, Governor Steve Cowper and Senator Murkowski; my friend, Congressman Don Young; and Lieutenant General McInerney; and all the citizens of Alaska; all the men and women of the Armed Forces in Alaska. Thank you for this wonderful turnout.

As I climbed off the airplane, I was thinking of the Inaugural Address of President William Henry Harrison. I believe it was he who spoke for 3½ hours, or close to it, caught pneumonia, and died some 30 days later. [*Laughter*] I will be brief. [*Laughter*] But I am pleased to have this opportunity, however brief, to speak here at Elmendorf to the members of our Armed Forces, their families, and to the people of this great State.

I also want to wish a belated but nevertheless happy birthday to Alaska, this great land. What you have accomplished in your 30 years of statehood is something all Alaskans can be proud of. I thank all of you again for this very warm greeting here at Elmendorf. Elmendorf has long served as the departure point for Presidents en route to the Far East. And I want it to serve as an arrival point for a President to come fishing in this great State. But as I make my first journey to Asia as President of the United States, I'm especially pleased to draw on this fantastic support and your obvious good wishes. My only regret is that I will not have an opportunity, at least on this trip, to see Alaska in all its glory. After all, there's nothing quite like the "Fur Rondy."

I know that it's been a bitter winter, even by Alaskan standards. As one Alaskan put it, "It's not too bad at 45 below, but 60 below takes it out of a fellow." [*Laughter*] I'll take his word for it. But from what I've heard, any battle between Alaskans and the elements is no contest. The cold is no match for the vibrant sense of community that all Alaskans share. We often think of frontier values, you know, as being summed up in the phrase "rugged individualism." Now, I'm sure Alaskans possess plenty of both. But the real frontier creed, as all of you know, is the community, and that is the key. And whether it's the Alaskan Native or the families whose forebears came here generations ago or the last-arriving newcomer from the lower 48, you stand ready to welcome all into the family of Alaskans. Adverse conditions bring out the best in Alaskans. When the temperature drops, you close ranks, pull together, pitch in; and that's the American spirit at its very best, and it's an inspiration to us all.

In the minds of most Americans, Alaska is our last frontier—vast, untamed, with plenty of room for opportunity and optimism. And at the same time, Alaska is a vital source of energy for the Nation as a whole. Alaska's abundant resources—in all their diversity—are, indeed, a sacred trust. But I am convinced that our natural resources can be developed without spoiling our environment. The plan to open the coastal plain of the Arctic National Wildlife Refuge meets these twin objectives. And I know, as a businessman formerly and now as President of the United States, that we can and must develop our energy resources for the sake of economic development and particularly for the sake of the national security of the United States. There is too much dependence on foreign oil as it is. And as a sportsman, though, with a love and respect for our country's unparalleled natural beauty, I could never support development that failed to provide adequate safeguards for land and wildlife.

And Alaska, so rich in resources, also serves as the gateway to Asia. Let me speak for a moment about this trip I'm about to embark on, our trip to the Far East. I'm here on my way to Japan for the funeral of the late Emperor. It was here, as General McInerney reminded us, here at Elmendorf in Hangar 5, that he became the first Emperor of Japan's long history to set foot outside his homeland 18 years ago.

Alaskans understand that America is as much a Pacific nation as it is an Atlantic one and that the Pacific region is of great and growing importance in international affairs. The timing of my trip is dictated by the passing of the Japanese Emperor, to whom I and other heads of government will pay our final respects. It is, as well, a measure of our respect for a valued ally and a fellow democracy that I make this trip.

In China, then, I hope to build on the friendly and stable and enduring relationship that now exists. This will be my fifth trip back since Barbara and I left there in 1975 and her sixth trip back to China since we left, that long ago. And there's something more than symbolism. That relationship is fundamental in any foreign policy equation of the United States. We don't want to take our friends for granted—be they Japan, be they China, be they Korea—as we wrestle with the problems that face our new Secretary of State [James A. Baker III] and General Scowcroft [Assistant to the President for National Security Affairs], who's here with me today, and this President. We wrestle with the troubled areas of the Middle East, the East-West relations—what's going to happen in Europe, how do we handle matters south of the Rio Grande? These are important policy decisions we'll be facing, important areas. But we don't ever want to neglect our friends.

And, yes, things in the Pacific seem to be going reasonably well. But we are a Pacific power, and this visit will demonstrate that we tend to stay a Pacific power. In Korea, I'll meet leaders of a nation that is rapidly joining the ranks of the world's first-tier economies, and one where democratic institutions are gaining strength each day. And at each stop, I aim to strengthen key relationships with our friends and partners in the Pacific regions.

And finally, a word to the airmen and their families who serve here at Elmendorf, the soldiers and their families who are here today from Fort Rich. As I look around this crowd—I'm probably leaving some people out—but let me put it this way to all the members of the Armed Services: Your service and sacrifice deserve special notice. And from this President who proudly served in the Armed Forces for several years—many, many years ago, I will admit—I know that your duty is demanding. But I also know that the reward is great—the respect and the gratitude of your country.

And make no mistake about the importance of your task. Alaska's strategic position, at the point where the Far East and the Western Hemisphere and the Arctic meet, is proof enough that the missions you perform here are vital to our national security. You're the forward edge, the cutting edge, if you will, of our national defense. And we rely on you to keep the watch and to hold the line. And your dedication and your vigilance and your sense of duty help our nation remain safe and secure. As your Commander in Chief, I salute you. And rest assured that I will do everything in my power to see that the United States continues to prosper, continues to remain strong, continues to remain free and at peace. Thank you all, each and every one, and God bless you.

Note: The President spoke at 9:47 a.m. in Hangar 5 at the base. In his remarks, he referred to Lt. Gen. Thomas G. McInerney, Commander of the Alaska Air Command. Following his remarks, the President and Mrs. Bush traveled to Tokyo, Japan.

Nomination of John E. Robson To Be Deputy Secretary of the Treasury

February 22, 1989

The President today announced his intention to nominate John E. Robson to be Deputy Secretary of the Treasury. He would succeed M. Peter McPherson.

Since 1986 Mr. Robson has been dean and professor of management, school of business administration, at Emory University in Atlanta, GA. Prior to this he was a member of the U.S. Aviation Safety Commission, 1987–1988. He was president and chief executive officer for G.D. Searle & Co., 1984–1985; executive vice president and chief operating officer, 1983–1984; and executive vice president, 1977–1982. He also served as chairman of the U.S. Civil Aeronautics Board in Washington, DC, 1975–1977. From 1970 to 1975, Mr. Robson was a partner and member of the executive committee for the law firm of Sibley and Austin in Chicago, IL, and Washington, DC.

Mr. Robson received his B.A. degree from Yale University and his J.D. degree from Harvard University Law School. He served in the U.S. Army, 1955–1957. Mr. Robson is married and has two children.

Nomination of Robert R. Glauber To Be an Under Secretary of the Treasury

February 22, 1989

The President today announced his intention to nominate Robert R. Glauber to be an Under Secretary of the Treasury. He would succeed George D. Gould.

Dr. Glauber is currently a consultant to the Department of the Treasury in Washington, DC. Prior to this he was chairman of the advanced management program and a member of the finance department at Harvard Business School. Dr. Glauber joined the Harvard faculty in 1964 and became a full professor in 1973. He has also served as a visiting professor at Stanford University's Graduate School of Business. Dr. Glauber also served as Executive Director of President Reagan's Task Force on Market Mechanisms (1987–1988).

Dr. Glauber received a bachelor of arts degree from Harvard College and his doctorate in finance from Harvard Business School. He was born March 22, 1939, in New York City. He is married, has two children, and resides in Arlington, VA.

The President's News Conference in Tokyo
February 24, 1989

The President. I've got to get a ruling on whether this is a—this is not a photo op. This is what we call a press availability, and I'll be glad to take two or three questions—not many because we're late. But let me make a little comment, if I might, Helen [Helen Thomas, United Press International]. And then I'll be glad to take questions. This has been a very moving day in a lot of ways, and I simply want to thank our Japanese hosts, who managed this complicated logistics and put on a marvelous pageant in honor of the late Emperor, beautifully staged and beautifully carried off, on schedule, working against the elements, but nevertheless with a dignity and a ceremony that was appropriate. And I have great respect for what they did and the way in which they did it, and I am proud to have represented the United States of America here today.

Now, Helen.

Secretary of Defense-Designate Tower

Q. Well, on the question of Senator Tower, it looks like he's going down the drain. Are you going to continue to back him, or do you think he ought to pull out?

The President. I'm going to strongly continue to back Senator Tower, and I do not believe he is going down the drain. Nobody has challenged his ability and knowledge to be a good Secretary of Defense, and I'm hoping that the debate that will follow next week will clear up any questions that the Members at large may have. And so, I wish the committee vote had been different, but I have not considered any options. I stand strongly with John Tower. I know of nobody else whose knowledge in defense matters can equal his, whose knowledge of how the Hill works can equal his? So, he is my choice, my only choice, and I am standing with him.

Q. Do you still think Sam Nunn [chairman of the Senate Armed Services Committee] was fair?

Q. Why would the end result in the Senate be any different than the result in committee?

The President. Because I think they're going to have a lively public debate in the Senate.

Q. What plan do you have, sir, for trying to bring that debate around to your side?

The President. Well, I think the Republican leaders—Bob Dole is already contemplating what to do on the Senate floor, but he knows, because I've talked to him, that when I get back—and I will be back before the vote—he knows that I will do whatever I can to talk to individual Members and have them know how strongly I feel about it and hopefully persuade some who have looked at evidence so far and may have a different opinion. So, there's no animosity; it's simply a question of fighting for something I believe in.

Q. Is this purely politics in your opinion, and is Sam Nunn responsible for this personally?

The President. I wouldn't say that.

Q. Do you still think he's been fair?

Q. Is it party line? I mean, is it partisan? Is it politics?

The President. Well, is it party line when all Democrats voted one way and all Republicans voted another? I suppose without acrimony it could be said that that was a party line vote. But do I suggest that there's no chance to pick up Democrats next week? No, I don't. I believe that I can do that, and I believe that the Senators that are for it——

Q. You haven't got them yet.

Q. Is the honeymoon over, Mr. President?

The President. No, the honeymoon's still going fine, and I'm not going to get total agreement on every issue. I hope I can get agreement on this question. But I've never expected—nobody's suggested they were going to do it just my way. But this one's important; it's important to our country. And I want somebody in that Defense Department that has Tower's expertise and who knows the defense mechanism as well as he does, and he's the only one that comes to mind.

Q. Mr. President, why would there be

such a difference—interpretation between——

Q. ——Senators to break with Sam Nunn?

The President. I don't know. Go ask the people that voted. I'm halfway around the world.

Q. Don't you risk an even more damaging defeat by taking it to the Senate——

The President. I don't look at it as defeat or victory. I look at doing what's right, supporting somebody I believe in and looking at the facts. And that's exactly what I'm doing.

Q. Do you still think Senator Nunn has been fair?

The President. I am not going to challenge Senator Nunn's motives at all. I never have, and I've never expressed anything other than my strong support on the merits after reviewing the information for Senator Tower. And that's the way I'm going to continue to do this.

Q. Have you talked to Tower at all?

The President. Since I've been over here?

Q. Since the vote.

Q. Well, since all of this has happened today.

The President. I talked to him the day before we left, but I haven't talked to him since then.

Q. Senator Nunn says that——

The President. I've got time for one or two more, and then I've got to go clean up and warm up and go to the next reception and keep working this diplomacy that I thought you all would be interested in.

Q. How much of a problem——

Q. Senator Nunn says that Tower——

The President. Wait just one minute, I'll just be right over there. Can't see, but I'll be there.

Q. How much of a problem has the delay in getting Senator Tower or somebody to run the Defense Department created for your review of foreign policy and your conduct of foreign policy?

The President. Well, the review is going forward. I would like to have the Secretary of Defense in place. There's no question that the Department needs a new leader. But it isn't interfering with our challenge to the Department to participate in these reviews. In fact, we've ordered a certain number of reviews—they're going to be started. But I'm not going to mislead you. I want my Secretary of Defense in place to further these reviews, to enhance the studies that are going forward, and to have our input on these studies, to input the person that I select to be Secretary. In the meantime, I'll have to credit Will Taft, who I told the other day, I said, "Will, you are doing a very good job, and it isn't easy." But he is doing—yes, Lesley [Lesley Stahl, CBS News], and then please, I must go forward.

Let me get down here so I can hear this.

Q. Thank you. Senator Dole said that this vote was a real kick in the teeth to you while you're off representing the United States abroad. Do you see it that way?

The President. I see it as the Senate expressing themselves. And inasmuch as I want this man confirmed, I can't say it's a pat on the back. But on the other hand, I have no acrimony about it. I'm convinced that when the Senate gets into full debate on this that reason and logic are going to prevail. And so, I can't say I'm happy with what the committee did because I would like to have seen the same kind of approval given John Tower's nomination that was given to [Secretary of Health and Human Services] Lou Sullivan. It was widely reported that Dr. Sullivan was in serious trouble—I've seen that over and over again. And he gets universal approval, one abstention—very good, and I thank the Senate for that.

Now I hope that they give this due deliberation in the full Senate and they do what's right. In this instance, I think approving my nominee is right. But I have no acrimony, and I'm not going to be drawn into name calling or a political accusation here. I'm not going to do that. I've got to work with the Senate on a lot of issues. But I want them to know how strongly I feel. And I feel it's not a personal win or lose; it's what's right: who best to run the Defense Department. And that's what's at stake.

Q. Aren't you whistling in the dark?

The President. And I'm going to win this battle.

Q. Mr. President, so much of this seems to depend on different interpretations of that FBI report.

The President. It does.

Q. Obviously that'll be a factor in the

Senate debate. If you see it as being in your favor and your side's favor in this, is there anything you can do to make that public, sir?

The President. Well, I'd like it to be as public as possible, the debate, because I think then there will be plenty of Senators that will want to defend Senator Tower against these allegations which I feel have been—and I'll use the expression again—"gunned down." Now, clearly some have looked at the evidence, and I'm sure in their opinion they differ with me on that. But that's what a good, lively debate can do on the floor. And Senator Tower is entitled to that kind of debate on the issues—not on hearsay. Nobody will be able to sustain an objection based simply on hearsay or on some rumor. So, that's why I look forward to a fair, open debate. And let the Senators who've made up their minds in opposition to what I'm advocating spell out for their constituents and for the country why they feel as they do. And I expect others will stand up and take a different side. That's what our process is all about. So, I don't fear it; I welcome it. I welcome it.

Q. If that report is still secret, though, sir, how are people to know who is right about it?

The President. Well, it's not secret from the Senators, and how much they refer to it, I don't know. We'll have to look into that when I get back, Brit [Brit Hume, ABC News]. I don't know what the ground rules are on how much people can refer to those reports. But the more open it is, the better I like it. Now, whether what precedents are set, I'd have to think very carefully about that. But we're not worried about this debate.

President's Physical Condition

Q. Are you tired?

The President. I thought I'd be more tired. No, I feel like a spring colt, ready to charge.

Q. Ask us.

The President. No, now come on! [*Laughter*]

Note: The President's fourth news conference began at 6:30 p.m. in the U.S. Ambassador's residence.

Written Responses to Questions Submitted by Xinhua News Agency of China

February 16, 1989

International Relations

Q. What is the general assessment on the current world situation? Since there exists a wide disagreement on whether the process of détente is irreversible, I would like to know your views on this question.

The President. I am cautiously optimistic. The one constant in today's world is change. For the most part, the direction of change is positive from the standpoint of America's values and interests. Around the globe, I see increased respect for and interest in democratic values of openness, human dignity, pluralism, democracy, individual initiative, and entrepreneurship. I see a worldwide trend toward greater recognition of the need for cooperative solutions to worldwide concerns, such as peaceful resolution of conflicts, environmental issues, and ensuring global economic growth. Balance has been restored in the international system by a Western policy of strength and realism.

Important differences based on fundamental values and interests continue to guide the policies of nations, both toward their own citizens and toward other members of the international community. Being fundamental, these differences must not be minimized, nor do they lend themselves to easy resolution. In addition, our world still is a tumultuous, dangerous place. Just as we appear to be making headway in reducing the threat of nuclear war through the arms reduction process, we must grapple with the proliferating dangers to civilized society from terrorism, the use and spread of chemical and biological weapons, together with sophisticated delivery systems, ballistic missiles, and international drug trafficking.

Yet I would argue that the world is significantly less turbulent and less dangerous today than it would otherwise be, thanks to the farsighted statesmen in recent decades. China's leaders were some of the first to contribute to this effort, and as chief of the U.S. Liaison Office in Beijing in the 1970's, I was privileged to have been part of this historic process. Today we find ever-broader acceptance of the proposition that in our increasingly interrelated world, national security cannot be achieved through military means alone. Moreover, through their own experience, more and more nations are realizing that the freeing of market forces and human creativity is the true basis for sustained prosperity and national success.

Nothing in this world is irreversible from a political, military, economic, or social perspective. That is why America's foreign policy is grounded on values that abide and a realistic determination to safeguard our interests and those of our allies and friends. Finally, I would say that any man with 11 grandchildren is a cautious optimist by definition. He has a big stake in the future.

Arms Control

Q. With regard to disarmament, in which area do you think breakthrough will be most feasible, the nuclear, conventional, or biochemical? And it is widely reported here that your administration might slow down the SDI program. If that is the case, doesn't it mean the U.S.-Soviet talks on concluding a START agreement will be accelerated? What is the prospect of an early START agreement?

The President. The United States is committed to progress in all aspects of arms control—nuclear, conventional, and chemical. Our goals include a strategic arms agreement which will enhance strategic stability and security; conventional arms reductions in Europe which will result in stability at lower levels of conventional forces; and a comprehensive, truly global and effectively verifiable chemical weapons ban. One cannot predict which arms control negotiations will meet with the earliest success, but I hope for significant progress in all fields. My administration is reviewing the current status of negotiations in each of these areas even as I visit your country.

Chemical weapons have been much in the news recently. Unfortunately, over the past decade, the world has witnessed an accelerated erosion of respect for international norms against the use of chemical weapons. The United States seeks to reverse this trend. Our first objective is the negotiation of a comprehensive, truly global, and effectively verifiable CW ban. In this connection, I am proud to have presented to the Geneva Conference on Disarmament (CD), in 1984, a U.S. draft treaty to ban chemical weapons, which remains the basis of the CD negotiations for such a ban. The United States is also working to stem the proliferation of CW and to restore respect for and strengthen the norms against illegal CW use. The Paris conference on chemical weapons use, held in January, was a helpful step in this regard.

In the conventional area, new negotiations on conventional armed forces in Europe will begin in Vienna in March. At present, the Warsaw Pact has a more than 2-to-1 advantage in tanks and artillery over NATO. While I welcome the recently announced Soviet conventional reductions as a step in the right direction, even with these cuts, Warsaw Pact forces will still retain substantial conventional superiority over NATO. Redressing this military imbalance in forces will be a prime objective of NATO at the upcoming talks.

In the START talks, U.S. and Soviet negotiations have made solid progress, including the development of the outline of an effective verification regime, an absolute necessity for a successful START agreement. While the strategic arms reduction process will be a major focus of my administration's review of U.S. arms control positions, the United States is committed to working toward a START agreement which will improve strategic stability and reduce the risk of war.

As to the Strategic Defense Initiative, it is an important program which is designed to contribute to stability. We will continue our research in this area to help us understand how and when we might move in the direction of a greater reliance on defenses.

Korean Peninsula

Q. As the two parts of Korea are prepared to hold high-level talks, the protracted tensions on the peninsula seem somewhat relaxed. So, do you think the time is coming for the United States to respond positively to the DPRK's demand for the withdrawal of U.S. troops from South Korea?

The President. I am encouraged by regional trends affecting Korea, particularly China's positive role in seeking reduced tensions on the peninsula. While the atmosphere has improved somewhat, hard realities remain. North Korea has a very large standing army stationed well forward. It would be far too optimistic at this time to suggest that tensions have been reduced to the point where the deterrence provided by U.S. forces in Korea is no longer needed. At the request of the Republic of Korea, our forces are in Korea to deter aggression from the North. They will remain as long as the Government and the people of South Korea want us to remain and as long as we believe it is in the interest of peace to keep them there.

Regional Conflicts

Q. Thanks to the efforts made by the parties concerned, some hot spots in the world are cooling off. As a result, the world public opinion is focusing its attention on the Middle East and Central America, where the United States has remarkable influence. Do you intend to make some readjustment to the U.S. policies toward these two regions and more actively make use of your influence to help promote early and just solutions to the problems there?

The President. The United States continues to seek a just solution to conflicts in Central America, based on democracy, respect for human rights, and security. In El Salvador, the popularly elected government of President Duarte has worked, with our support, to institutionalize democracy, despite an organized military assault by Communist forces. There has been considerable success in curbing human rights abuses from the far right and within the military. We will continue to support the Government of El Salvador in its efforts.

In Nicaragua, the Sandinistas still seek to consolidate their totalitarian control and regional hegemony. The press and church remain harassed. Political opponents are jailed. And the economy continues in a downward spiral while the Sandinistas maintain by far the largest army in Central America. A just peace can come to Nicaragua only when the Sandinistas negotiate in good faith with the democratic resistance and the civic opposition and cease to threaten the neighboring Central America democracies.

In Central America, the United States Government continues to support the Esquipulas II agreement in all of its provisions, which include provisions calling for democratic freedom of the press; labor rights; freedom for opposition groups to organize, hold meetings, demonstrations, etc. We believe that all the commitments, including those to democracy, must be complied with if there is to be lasting peace in the region. In verifying compliance with all the principles of Esquipulas II, there also needs to be an enforcement mechanism to promote adherence to its provisions, particularly concerning democracy and cessation of support for subversive groups in the region. In this regard, economic aid to Nicaragua should be conditioned on actual performance, not just on words but deeds.

The Arab-Israeli conflict is among the most difficult of regional conflicts. The United States has long been committed to a just settlement of this dispute based on the principles embodied in UNSC Resolutions 242 and 338. Our commitment to a negotiated settlement will not waver; we will continue to work closely with the parties to forge a common basis that will facilitate negotiations among them and a durable settlement.

There are also a number of difficult and dangerous problems in the Middle East. We must find a way to deal with the missile proliferation, chemical and biological weapons, the conventional arms race, as well as other conflicts, such as Lebanon and the Gulf. These are problems in which the international community can play a leading role.

Free and Fair Trade

Q. Your country is still playing a leading role in the fields of economy and technology, but the challenges from Japan and Western Europe are getting serious. How do you evaluate the challenges, and what would you do to handle them during your tenure?

The President. The Japanese and European economies are indeed growing strongly, as are the newly industrialized economies which follow free market practices. We regard this growth as a highly positive development. It has been a priority of our foreign policy since World War II to encourage the economic development of friendly countries. We take some justified satisfaction, I think, in the current success of free and open world trading and financial systems. The vigorous competition in world markets has been, and will continue to be, a driving force for the improvement of world living standards. By keeping world markets open, we will reward those entrepreneurs and managers and workers who can adapt most quickly to changing markets. I have every confidence in American business and American labor. They will handle the challenges, and we expect to continue to be the world's leading economy.

China-U.S. Relations

Q. What do you think should be and could be done to make the current Sino-U.S. relationship, which is healthy, even better and more solid?

The President. First let me say that I certainly agree that the current state of our relationship is healthy. Both countries have come so far since my stay in China 13 years ago. We now cooperate in many areas—political, economic, scientific, cultural, educational, and military. U.S.-China trade is booming, and U.S. companies are making a strong and growing contribution in China. Thousands of Chinese and American students and professors are involved in educational exchanges with some of the finest institutes and universities in both our countries. American tourists are visiting China by the hundreds of thousands. And perhaps most importantly, our two governments maintain a serious and cooperative dialog on a wide range of bilateral and international issues, finding that we have many interests in common.

To improve relations further and make them more solid, I think we should build on what we have already accomplished. We need to keep up the dialog between our two governments on political issues of mutual concern: global peace, regional conflicts in Asia and elsewhere, arms control, how to combat the scourges of terrorism and drugs, and the multiple threats to the global environment. We see eye-to-eye on many of these. We also need to encourage more people-to-people contacts, which have grown so dramatically in the last decade. These promote understanding and trust.

We should also seek to expand our economic relationship. The opportunities for trade and investment between our countries are enormous. We have to find ways of taking advantage of them. To do this will require efforts on both sides. Continued steps by China to make its trade practices compatible with those of its major trading partners and remove barriers to trade and investment are important if China is to expand commerce and attract capital for its modernization. For example, improvements in intellectual property protection, a less regulated trading system, and more effective legal protections for investors could have a very favorable effect. The United States, for its part, must keep its markets open to Chinese exports and continue to give China access to advanced technology needed for modernization.

Science and technology cooperation should also expand. We have developed a unique relationship in this field. Cooperation involves some of our best scientists and most advanced technical facilities and covers a wide range of important endeavors in such fields as fusion energy, public health, and the environment. Both countries have a lot to gain from these joint activities.

Cultural and educational exchanges in other fields should grow as well. A good example of successful bilateral cooperation in education is the Management Training Center at Dalian. Since the U.S. and the

Chinese Governments established the center in 1980, with the help of U.S. corporations and universities, it has produced over 2,300 graduates trained in modern business and management practices. The Dalian center has become a model for other management centers in China. It can also serve as a model for bilateral cooperation in other fields.

In addition to the positive developments in our political and economic relations, I think it is especially noteworthy that friendly cooperation is also taking place between our defense forces. We are looking forward to continuing and expanding these activities in the future.

The United States recognizes that Taiwan is an important issue for the Chinese Government and people. We are pleased to see that the growing opportunities for trade and travel between both sides of the Taiwan Strait have contributed to a climate of relaxed tensions, and hope these trends will continue. The United States is committed to abide by the three communiques of 1972, 1979, and 1982, which provide a firm basis for the further development of our relations.

One final point on building relations for the future: When differences arise between us, as they inevitably will, we need to continue to approach them in a constructive spirit. If we do, I think we will build a strong foundation for bilateral ties and see expanding cooperation in new fields that will benefit both our peoples.

Note: The questions and answers were released by the Office of the Press Secretary on February 25.

Written Responses to Questions Submitted by the Yonhap News Agency of the Republic of Korea

February 16, 1989

South Korean Foreign Relations

Q. Would you tell me your views on South Korean efforts to increase economic cooperation and political relations with Socialist countries?

The President. I support these efforts. President Roh's opening to the Soviet Union, Eastern Europe, and China is aimed at fostering world peace and understanding. Today almost every country recognizes South Korea's great economic importance. I am sure more countries in time will move from economic ties to full political and diplomatic ties with the Republic of Korea.

Conference on Korean Reunification

Q. In his address before the U.N. General Assembly in October last year, President Roh proposed a six-party conference, calling for South and North Korea, the United States, Japan, China, and the Soviet Union to discuss a peaceful reunification of the divided Korean Peninsula. What is the U.S. position on the proposal?

The President. President Roh's six-party conference idea is an imaginative, forward-looking proposal. It is another example of the Republic of Korea Government's new approach of reconciliation and accommodation in dealing with peninsular political and security problems. Obviously, such a conference would require careful preparation and a cooperative attitude by all participants.

North Korea-U.S. Relations

Q. While seeking improved relations with China and the Soviet Union, the South Korean Government has asked the United States to open its doors to the isolationist North Korea, hoping that exchanges between Washington and Pyongyang will contribute to reduction of tension on the Korean Peninsula. Have you seen any fruits of progress in U.S. efforts to help North Korea to get rid of its isolationist policy?

The President. We have long supported North-South dialog as the key to peace and reunification of the peninsula. President Roh's initiatives to that purpose in July 1988 and in his October speech at the United

Nations were most welcome. In the spirit of these measures, the United States announced last October 31 some new steps to encourage private academic, cultural, and other nongovernmental exchange with North Korea. We also authorized the export of humanitarian goods to North Korea and again authorized substantive exchanges between our diplomats in neutral settings. Since then, the United States and North Korea have had substantive contacts in Beijing on December 6 and January 24. There has been greater academic exchange between the United States and North Korea as well. Several American universities plan to host North Korean scholars this year. I do not know how far these academic and diplomatic contacts will go, but they are useful first steps.

U.S. Forces in South Korea

Q. Radical Korean students with anti-American sentiment are demanding the withdrawal of U.S. troops from South Korea. At the same time, I know that there are some American experts on northeast Asian affairs who speak of a symbolic or gradual reduction of the troops. Do you envision any possibility of the troop withdrawal in the near future in light of the security situation on the Korean Peninsula?

The President. There are no plans to reduce U.S. forces in Korea. Our soldiers, sailors, airmen, and marines are there at the request of the Republic of Korea to deter aggression from the North, and their presence contributes to the peace and stability of northeast Asia. They will remain in the Republic of Korea as long as the Government and the people of South Korea want us to remain and as long as we believe it is in the interest of peace to keep them there. Our two governments periodically review the appropriate strength and composition of U.S. forces stationed in Korea under our mutual defense treaty obligations.

South Korea-U.S. Trade

Q. The United States has continued to ask South Korea to open its markets fully for more U.S. exports. The Korean people have an understanding of U.S. efforts to reduce its large trade deficits, but they think that current U.S. pressure is excessive. I would like to hear your views on trade friction existing between the two countries.

The President. Korea has enjoyed very open access to the American market, especially in cars, consumer electronics, and machinery. This has been crucial to Korea's achievement of the world's highest economic growth rate during the last 3 years. We seek access to all world markets. A free market enhances a country's standard of living. Consumers benefit from lower prices and a wider variety of goods and services. The United States and Korea have prospered together on the strength of a free world trading system. I believe it is in Korea's self-interest to work to preserve this system. Therefore, I do not see U.S. market-opening efforts in Korea or elsewhere as excessive.

President's Trip to China

Q. Your visit to Beijing will be followed by the visit by Soviet leader Mikhail Gorbachev, which is expected in April or May, for the first Sino-Soviet summit talks in three decades. Do you have any special reasons for your decision to go to China after attending the funeral of the late Japanese Emperor? Do your discussions with Chinese leaders include the problem of the Korean Peninsula?

The President. Having represented my country in China, I have fond memories and close ties there. Barbara and I are looking forward in a very personal way to going back to Beijing. We also have important matters to discuss with the Chinese leaders. I am sure our talks will touch on issues affecting the Korean Peninsula.

Note: The questions and answers were released by the Office of the Press Secretary on February 25.

The President's News Conference in Tokyo
February 25, 1989

The President. I have had an extremely useful set of meetings with leaders familiar with the problems and prospects of the major geographic areas of the world. And as all of you are aware, international affairs have entered an extraordinarily interesting period, a period of fluidity in which several regional problems—Afghanistan, Cambodia, Angola, the Middle East, to name just a few—have renewed prospect for resolution. Many of the parameters of these complex regional problems are in flux. And therefore, it is important to converse with the men and women who are the most influential leaders on the scene.

I enjoyed meeting with the European leaders. During my lunch with President Mitterrand and in discussions with President Cossiga of Italy, with the King of the Belgians, with President Soares of Portugal, King Juan Carlos of Spain, the President of the Federal Republic of Germany, Prime Minister Özal of Turkey, I emphasized that our relationship with Europe and the North Atlantic alliance remains central to our foreign policy and our security interests. And they all assured me that their countries shared this strong commitment to the alliance and considered it the key to their past and their future security.

The meetings with the Presidents of Egypt and Israel and with the King of Jordan form part of a larger effort to bring peace to the Middle East. And I made clear the continuing readiness of the United States to facilitate this effort in a manner that's consistent with the security of Israel and the security of our Arab friends in the region as well. We discussed what new opportunities may exist for our diplomacy, the importance of moving forward to take advantage of the positive elements in the current situation.

The meeting with Prime Minister Bhutto of Pakistan, an important new leader, addressed a number of important issues, including our common interest in promoting Afghan self-determination in the aftermath now of the Soviet troop withdrawal. The emergence of democracy in Pakistan is something that we Americans all salute. Consistent with this development, we also discussed what might be done to promote greater prosperity and security in south Asia and particularly between Pakistan and India.

With the President of India we talked about the good nature of our relationship and the opportunities for improving the climate of peace in the region. He expressed to me his interest in the talks that their Prime Minister has had with the Prime Minister of Pakistan.

In my discussion with Prime Minister Chatichai of Thailand, with Lee Kuan Yew of Singapore, and President Corazon Aquino of the Philippines, we had a chance to talk about the latest developments in the area, with particular emphasis on Kampuchea, on Cambodia. What remains clear from these discussions is the absolute requirement that we maintain ASEAN [Association of South East Asian Nations] unity and support for a political settlement in Cambodia featuring an interim government led by Prince Sihanouk, with whom I'll be meeting, I believe, in China—I believe that's set. The goals as ever are twofold: full and permanent Vietnamese withdrawal from Cambodia and the permanent prevention of a return to power by the Khmer Rouge.

I also met with President Mobutu of Zaire. We discussed important economic issues and the new prospects for peace and self-determination in Angola and Namibia. I'll shortly be discussing the problems and opportunities of development with the President of Brazil, President Sarney, and the President of Nigeria—I'll be meeting with him in just a few minutes.

Throughout all of our discussions on a variety of issues, I found a shared sense of satisfaction that East-West relations—they all were interested in this—that East-West relations are now clearly proceeding on the basis of an agenda favorable to the United States, its allies, and its friends. And as a result of my discussions, I feel more confident than ever that we and our allies will move together to promote global peace, prosperity, and security. And in all these sessions, though highly concentrated, have been very useful to me overall and have provided me with an opportunity to exchange views with many of the most important world leaders.

And then, I should add, Barbara and I and Secretary Baker had an opportunity to pay our respects just now to the new Emperor and to express to him our pleasure at being here. It was right and proper that the United States be represented in this way and to give, in a personal sense, our condolences to him, to the Empress, and to his family.

Now I'd be glad to take some questions.

Secretary of Defense-Designate Tower

Q. Mr. President, back home, the burning issue clearly is the nomination of John Tower. I understand you're going to be doing some personal lobbying when you return. With whom are you going to meet? What could you possibly tell them that they haven't heard already? And isn't this too little, too late?

The President. No, it's not too little, too late. The matter will be decided on the Senate floor. I think everybody knows I am committed to John Tower. There is no fallback; there is no option. And I'll be talking to whomever has any kind of an open mind on this question. I'll do it personally, and I'll do it as forcefully as I can. And I will encourage people to look at the facts. I heard some comment yesterday about, well, there were these perceptions out there. That's not enough. That's not a fair enough or a high enough standard when it comes to the confirmation of an important nominee of this nature. So, I have made some calls. And I will be talking to whoever, as I say, remains openminded. We'll just work our way across here.

Q. Mr. President, on the FBI report, did you think that Mr. Tower does not have a current drinking problem? Is there any way of getting that out into the public? Are you talking about a sanitized version that you would release to the public, or maybe an unsanitized version? There's this problem of confidentiality.

The President. Well, that is the problem. And people that were asked to give interviews were assured that that testimony or that witnessing or whatever you want to call it would be confidential. And so, that presents a real problem. It doesn't present a problem for individual Senators to go take a look at the report. But in terms of your question, I had hoped there was some way of sanitizing or something, and maybe there still will be. But I was reminded that confidentiality is vital here and that the people who have been interviewed have been guaranteed such confidentiality. And I think in the long run the process is best served by that. But in short run, I would like to see every Senator personally take a look and not make up his or her mind on perception, but to do it on reality. And that, I think, is only fair.

Q. Mr. President, another subject.

The President. Hooray!

Interest Rates and Inflation

Q. I thought you might enjoy it, but we'll see. The Federal Reserve has increased the discount rate again. I'm wondering if you still feel that you and Mr. Greenspan [Federal Reserve Board Chairman] are not that far apart on how to solve our economic problems and if you think this move is going to begin to hurt your effort to reduce the deficit.

The President. Well, obviously higher interest rates are not helpful in deficit reduction. But what I would say is, this argues even more forcefully than I've been able to argue that we need to get an agreement on the budget. The sooner we get an agreement with the Senate and have the country have a budget agreement, you will see an amelioration or a lightening up on these interest rates. So, that is the only positive thing. It sends a strong signal. Let's get on with solving the problem of how we're going to bring the deficit down.

I don't think Greenspan and I are far apart. I talked to him—what was it, just the day, I think, before we left, we talked about this. He was more concerned about, I think—although I haven't talked to him personally on this part—with the last CPI figures. But I don't think you can make a judgment on one month. I've gone back and looked over the ups and downs on the CPI. But look, if he's right on inflation, his concerns—if they're a little more than mine, we should be alert to that. But I gave you my reasons on why I am not overly concerned about inflation, and I haven't changed my mind on that.

Q. The markets think we should raise the rate even more. Would you support that?

The President. I don't know that the markets think that at all.

Secretary of Defense-Designate Tower

Q. Mr. President, back on Tower. It seems to come down, really, sir, to a contest between you and your clout on this issue and that of Senator Nunn [chairman of the Armed Services Committee]. Obviously, you can't be happy with Senator Nunn's vote or his statement yesterday. And I was wondering if there comes a time, sir, when you think you might have to come out and criticize him, indeed, perhaps attacking the record for which you must feel is an unfair approach to your nomination.

The President. I don't see any point in making this personal. I have enough respect for Senator Nunn to know that he is not pursuing a frivolous course in this matter at all. And I know everyone would like to see a great confrontation and love to hold my coat and maybe hold his as we get into a big brawl, but there's no need for that. I want to talk on the merits here and encourage Senators, all of them, to take a look at the facts, not at the rumor, not at the innuendo; and therefore, there's no point getting into a fight. We're going to have to work together on a lot of other issues.

This one is important to me. And there is no pulling back as far as I'm concerned. And I have made up my mind firmly, and I'm going to fight it right through to the end. But I'm not going to then jump off and start hurling charges against any Member of the United States Senate with whom I will work constructively in the future. But I would simply ask that everybody review the evidence, and I expect Senator Nunn feels he's done that. And now I would appeal to every other Senator to do just that.

Q. Doesn't that create the possibility that Members of the Senate will see that it is not possible to attack your nominee and, indeed, you indirectly and pay no price for it?

The President. No, I don't think it raises that at all. This is just the beginning.

Q. What do you think the prospects are of winning this battle, and hasn't it really thrown a cloud over your Asian trip? They say this is the second time you've been shot down over the Pacific. [*Laughter*]

The President. An interesting analogy. [*Laughter*] I think people that are serious students of foreign policy and are interested in foreign policy objectives are not going to view this trip in the context of the flap over the John Tower nomination. I think there's much more serious points in foreign policy to be made, and if it's beclouded by some political battle back home right now, so be it. But what we're doing is laying the groundwork for the security interests of the United States, for the mutual interests of a lot of our bilateral relationship. What we've done is reemphasize the importance we place on the Japanese relationship. We're going to have, I'm sure, fruitful discussions in China. So, I think what we're talking about here—this turmoil over Tower and the nominating process there—will give way, whatever the result, to the importance of this mission and the talks we've had.

Q. Do you have a head count? Do you have any possibility of winning?

The President. Well, I wouldn't be in a fight that I felt we were going to lose.

Interest Rates and Inflation

Q. Mr. President, you've said that what's happened to the interest rate sends a strong signal that we need to go down and address the deficit problem. How much danger is there, sir, that the tightening of credit will choke off economic growth and throw the economy into recession?

The President. Well, I think that Chairman Greenspan would be very wary of an interest-rate policy that would choke off growth. He is not antigrowth in order to kill inflation. That is not the Greenspan position. So, I am not worried about that. But I can't say I'm happy about the rise in interest rates. But I don't want to overstate his position, on the other hand.

Human Rights

Q. Yes, Mr. President, the U.S. has been very firm with the Soviet Union in recent years on human rights issues. Do you intend to be equally firm with the Chinese? And are you taking a list to them of dissidents? And whose cases are you interested in?

The President. I think our position is so well known to the Chinese—indeed, they have had an opening, a *glasnost*, if you will, that I wouldn't have thought possible, and—you know, if you set the clock back to when I was Ambassador there—whether there's any specific list, I'm not familiar with that right now. I'll be briefed on the approaches we'll take as we fly to China. But I think both the Soviet Union and China know of our commitment to human rights. And it is beholden on any American President to reiterate our commitment to human rights.

Secretary of Defense-Designate Tower

Q. Mr. President, you seem quite committed then to Senator Tower in your support. But some other White House staffers seem a little bit less strong in their support. Last night, for instance, Secretary Baker gave an interview, and he said he supposed that you would go to a full floor fight. Are some of your aides suggesting to you it's time to pull the plug, that the political costs are too great to continue this?

The President. No, and obviously Secretary Baker is not. And he can speak for himself, which he does very eloquently. And so, I think you ought to be careful about interpretations. And if you would put a name next to some of my staffers who are feeling this, I would like to kick some serious—[*laughter*]—hide on this question because I am committed. And I saw some stories out there that staffers are known to feel this and that. And I'm calmer now, Ann [Ann Compton, ABC News], than you remember from the campaign, and I'm going to remain that way. It's a whole new feeling inside. But I must confess to a certain irritation when I see comments like that that I think have no validity. Obviously, some that print them think they have validity, but let me at them. Let me at the staffers that say that. They will be history; they will be looking for another line of work. But I can't ever find them.

Q. Let me just follow up by asking: Do you have any members of your staff—advise to you not to continue the fight for John Tower?

The President. Not one single member of my staff has said that. And maybe that's because they know how strongly I feel, but I don't think so. I think they all agree. I mean, I know all our top-level people agree that this is a fight that is important to wage, and it's one that I perceive it to be on the merits, on principle, not on rumor, not on innuendo. We cannot have a matter of this seriousness decided because, well, there used to be the perception of this or that. That isn't good enough now. It isn't fair enough. And so, I don't know of any staffers that feel that way. And yet I'm sure you have your sources, but please tell me who they are.

Q. Does that mean if Tower said, Enough, I'm worn out, that you would indulge him on——

The President. He's not going to do that. And I don't go into such far-fetched hypothesis.

Jerry [Gerald Boyd, New York Times]?

Emperor Hirohito's Funeral

Q. Mr. President, I'm just curious whether you, as a World War II veteran who was shot down not all that far from here, felt any sense of unease yesterday appearing before the coffin and bowing before the Emperor and the new Emperor?

The President. No, I didn't. And I can't say that in the quiet of the ceremony that my mind didn't go back to the wonder of it all, because I vividly remember my wartime experience. And I vividly remember the personal friends that were in our squadron that are no longer alive as a result of combat, a result of action. But my mind didn't dwell on that at all. And what I really thought, if there was any connection to that, is isn't it miraculous what's happened since the war. And I remember the stories, in reading as preparation for this visit—the visit of MacArthur and the former Emperor here. That was historic, and that set a whole new direction. And MacArthur's decision at that time proved to be correct in terms of Japan's move towards democracy.

And so, I honestly can tell you that I did not dwell on that and didn't feel any sense other than my mind thinking of personal relationships and things of that nature, but nothing to do about whether it was right to be here. I was certain from the day that I committed to come here that this was correct for the United States. And perhaps having been in combat in World War II, maybe the decision was more correct; maybe it was more profound to be here. It leaves out my experience.

I'm representing the United States of America. And we're talking about a friend, and we're talking about an ally. We're talking about a nation with whom we have constructive relationships. Sure, we got some problems, but that was all overriding—and respect for the Emperor. And remember back in World War II, if you'd have predicted that I would be here, because of the hard feeling and the symbolic nature of the problem back then of the former Emperor's standing, I would have said, "No way." But here we are, and time moves on; and there is a very good lesson for civilized countries in all of this.

Middle East

Q. Mr. President, you referred in your opening statement to your talks with Middle East leaders and new opportunity as a positive element in the region. Can you elaborate on that and perhaps tell us when you conclude your review when you're going to take some——

The President. In which area are you talking about?

Q. In the Middle East?

The President. In the Middle East? Sure. You mean, what I see as positive in there? Well, I think the whole acceptance by Arafat of the conditions for talks is positive, and I think that is seen as a very positive signal in the Arab world. And I think that there's a recognition in the part of Israel that with the Intifada and the difficulties on the West Bank that something needs to be done. And I think there's a readiness on the part of other Arab States to get serious about negotiation and discussion. And I think Egypt's new standing in the area is a very important ingredient that could lead to where they could be more of a catalyst for peace. So, all of these are ingredients that I think offer opportunity. And I think everybody understands that before we just go rushing out to do something for the sake of doing something that we take a step that is prudent.

I've been in this job for 1 month, and this problem has been there for year after year after year. But when I talk about the underlying potential for peace, I think that's widely accepted now. There's still some very tough elements. You've got some radical elements in what I would say the far left of the PLO. You have a couple of countries that have not been overly constructive towards the peace movement. But that's overridden, it seems to me, by these elements that I've just described.

Interest Rates and Inflation

Q. Mr. President, you keep on saying that you and Mr. Greenspan aren't that far apart on inflation, but he keeps on nudging up interest rates. Do you think it would be advisable if the two of you got together and sat down and hashed this out?

The President. Well, we have gotten together; we haven't hashed it out in total agreement. He hasn't done it exactly my way, nor am I about to change what I've said. Ask him; I don't think we're far apart at all. We've got a little difference of interpretation at this point as to how you read the indicators on inflation, and that's the only difference we've got. We share the common objectives of needing to get the deficit down. And I still maintain we are not far apart. And I think where we have total agreement is—regardless of what the Fed has done and regardless if I would have done that or not had I been the independent Chairman of the Fed—we have total agreement that we need to get the budget deficit down and that that itself would be the best way to lighten up on these interest rates. So, the areas of agreement far outweigh the nuances of difference, in my view.

President's Health

Q. How do you feel?

The President. Feel all right. I've done my exercise every day. I didn't go running, but they had a bike over there, and I've been pedaling on that thing, which is very important. It really makes a difference in how I feel. I'm looking forward to the next stop on this trip. And I know that there's been a preoccupation. You've got editors, and you've got interest at home. But I'm telling you we've laid some good groundwork here. I think the Secretary of State feels that way. I think General Scowcroft, [Assistant to the President for National Security Affairs] feels that way. And that'll help us as we move along. It'll help our country as we move along now and go down the road. So, I'm encouraged so far, these talks we've had. And I'll get back and get into the fray on this other matter that seems to be overriding.

This better be the last because we have another meeting in 4 minutes.

China-U.S. Relations

Q. You said you wouldn't believe the opening that has occurred in China when you were the U.S. Envoy there. How does it feel to be back as President of the United States?

The President. Well, I don't know. But I'm looking forward to it. This will be my fifth visit back since leaving China and Barbara's sixth. And I am told that the Chinese leaders are looking forward to this return visit. I'm excited about it, and I think that the relationship with China is strong. We obviously have differences with them, and they'll have something to say about that, I'm sure. I know I will marvel at the changes. I did on the last visit, and people have told me that just in the last 2 years there's been even more change. There is an openness in China today that I never would have predicted 15 years ago, and I can't wait to have the discussions with these top leaders because this relationship is very important. And we spend a lot of time when we're back home properly worrying about and being concerned about NATO and East-West relations, in the sense of U.S. versus Soviet; but we must never neglect our friends in the Pacific.

And this visit will be a way to talk about common objectives and hammer out the difference—working on the differences that we may have on trade or whatever else it is. But we've passed the day on the U.S.-China relationship where anyone talks about "playing a card." That was a term that was highly offensive to the Chinese, and properly so. And our relationship, the China-U.S. relationship, stands on its own in terms of cultural exchange and trade and on common strategic interests and on the way we view most of the world—not all of it, because we have some big differences with them on some areas. But what I want to do is to strengthen that and to build on those common perceptions and to make them understand that we will never take for granted this relationship and that we will never do anything in dealing with the Soviets that would inure to the detriment of our Asian friends, be they Chinese, be they ASEAN, be they Japanese. And that's an important point to make because we're going to have some very interesting work to be done with the Soviet Union. But I think the Chinese understand that, but I will make the point that we're not going to move forward in a way that would denigrate their interests or diminish the bilateral relationship between China and the United States, that it stands on its own. So, we've passed the days of "playing a card" and where only discussion with China had to do with the strategic equation—Moscow, the United States, Beijing. And it's past that now. We want to find ways to build.

So, we talk to Deng Xiaoping about this and Zhao Ziyang and Li Peng, President Yang, and then I can talk to you later on about what we might have accomplished or what big problems remain out there. The relationship is strong, and I'd like to strengthen it.

Soviet-China Relations

Q. Are you pleased to see them drawing closer to the Soviets themselves?

The President. I have no problem with this. I said this to Mr. Gorbachev before I became President. And this visit next spring is a good thing, and it's nothing detrimental to the interests of the United States in that regard. And even if there was—I mean, we should try to go about it in my view. But there isn't. So, if the question gets into this equation: Do you worry that the Soviets and the Chinese will get back to a Khrushchev era, almost unanimity on everything? No, I don't. There's a fierce independence in China today, and they've moved out early on in terms of market incentive and in terms of—oh, lots of things: privatization, no more communes in their agriculture, for example. And these are dramatic changes, and they haven't fully felt the effect of these changes. Now, they have some economic problems that go with fast economic change. Inflation is concerning them, and how you handle rapid growth is concerning them, but they're moving in this market-oriented way that we think is a very good thing.

And so, I'm not concerned, John [John Cochran, NBC News], about their going back to a relationship that was almost two against one automatically. It's not that kind of a thing anymore. And I don't think that's a concern we have.

Well, thank you all very much.

Note: The President's fifth news conference began at 10:30 a.m. in the U.S. Ambassador's residence. In his remarks, he referred to Deng Xiaoping, Chairman of the Central Military Commission; Zhao Ziyang, General Secretary of the Chinese Communist Party; Li Peng, Premier of the State Council; and Yang Shangkun, President of China. Following his remarks, President Bush traveled to Beijing, China.

Toast at the Welcoming Banquet in Beijing

February 25, 1989

Well, President Yang and Premier Li, distinguished guests, Barbara and I are delighted to be returning once again to China. I first came here in 1974 and departed at the end of 1975. And since then, including this visit, I have been back five times, and Barbara six times. And each time we come, we are fascinated by the dynamic change and growth, all of which takes place against an extraordinary, unchanging backdrop of a great culture several thousand years old.

There's a Chinese proverb that says: "One generation plants a tree; the next sits in its shade." And there's a timeless wisdom in that. But thanks to your courageous reforms—and I don't minimize the difficulties—the Chinese people are planting great and sturdy trees, some of which are bearing fruit right now for this generation.

Today the people of China have more opportunities to express themselves and to make important decisions in their personal and professional lives. And your new and farsighted economic program is already improving the lives of the people, as it will for generations to come. The expansion of your international relationships is also creating new possibilities for peace, prosperity, and world leadership, and the United States welcomes the enlarged role that China has taken in the world.

When I first arrived in Beijing in 1974, it was a period when our two countries were just beginning to renew contact after almost a quarter of a century of estrangement. And it wasn't easy. There were great differences between us. But in the principles of the historic Shanghai communique, signed 17 years ago this coming Monday, we found a common basis for moving beyond those differences to find our shared interests. So, together, we helped to plant a tree, and we should keep planting trees.

We value the new relationship our two countries have established with each other. Our friendship is continuing to develop, and that's good, for a relationship must be strong enough to tackle the areas of disagreement as well as those of common interest. And it must be based on respect for the individual as well as the integrity of the states. We remain firmly committed to the principles set forth in those three joint communiques that form the basis of our relationship. And based on the bedrock principle that there is but one China, we have found ways to address Taiwan constructively without rancor. We Americans have a long, historical friendship with Chinese people everywhere. In the last few years, we've seen an encouraging expansion of family contacts and travel and indirect trade and other forms of peaceful interchange across the Taiwan Strait, reflecting the interests of the Chinese people themselves. And this trend, this new environment, is consistent with America's present and longstanding interest in a peaceful resolution of the differences by the Chinese themselves.

The United States and the People's Republic of China have also found common interest in a growing economic relationship. When I came here in 1974, our two-way trade totaled about $900 million, and now it is some $14 billion. And for this we must credit the reforms China embarked upon 10 years ago under Chairman Deng Xiaoping's farsighted leadership.

And we've seen greater exchanges in education as well, with tens of thousands of Chinese students now studying in the United States, just as thousands of U.S. scholars have studied and taught in the farthest corners of China.

And we've developed an active program of military cooperation that is forging ties of friendship between our defense establishments, even as we've found a diplomatic unity in our shared opposition to policies of international aggression and domination. Our two countries, as nuclear powers, as permanent members of the United Nations Security Council, have a special responsibility for preserving world peace. We owe it to mankind to work together for peace and international stability.

The United States has pressed forward with the Soviet Union in the arms reduction process, achieving under the INF treaty an agreement to eliminate U.S. and Soviet intermediate-range nuclear missiles, on our insistence, from Asia as well as Europe. We are mindful of the danger posed to other countries by the proliferation of deadly weapon technologies, including chemical weapons, particularly in the regions of the world that are marked by conflict.

The prospect of improved relations between China and the Soviet Union inspires hope for new progress in the search for self-determination and peace for the Cambodian people and stability for Korea.

There can be little doubt that even as the people of our two countries are watching this meeting, the world as a whole is watching the larger movement of our two great nations as we build even firmer bonds across the vast ocean that joins us.

Barbara and I have had the great good fortune to travel around your vast and beautiful land as guests of the Chinese people. We went from the high plateau of Tibet to the great city of Chengdu, where we visited the home of your Tang poet Dufu and where we later personally opened the first American Consulate in the western part of the People's Republic of China. And we then had the unforgettable experience of traveling by boat through the hauntingly beautiful and historic Yangtze, the Gorges, where we relished the history of the Three Kingdoms and could almost hear the poet Li Bo's description of "the monkeys who screamed from the two sides without stopping." And then on to Wuhan and the first bridge to span the Yangtze, and finally Guilin and the beautiful Li River, where we saw the mountains and waters of your paintings and poetry.

Barbara and I are grateful for the friendship and kindness that we have been shown over the years by the Chinese people. And the expanding relationship between your country and ours has been a source of satisfaction to us as well. Let us continue then to work together, to plant trees together, so that the next generation, ours and yours, can sit together in the shade.

So, please, let me ask all of you to join me and Barbara in a toast: To the health of President Yang; to the health of Premier Li; to the health of Chairman Deng and General Secretary Zhao; to Barbara's and my dear close friends here tonight; and to Sino-American friendship: *Ganbei.* [Cheers.]

Note: The President spoke at 8:15 p.m. in the Western Hall of the Great Hall of the People.

Remarks at Chongmenwen Christian Church in Beijing
February 26, 1989

Pastor Kan and Pastor Shi and Pastor Yin, thank you, and thank this congregation for your generosity. You have met Barbara, but I want you to meet the Secretary of State of the United States. He and Barbara and I are members of the same church in Houston, Texas, in the United States. Jim Baker here, our Secretary of State.

It is a special pleasure for Barbara and me to return to this special place of worship. We have so many fond memories of our time in Beijing and the warmth of its citizens and the hospitality shown to us; the enduring friendships we made; and, yes, the place in history that those days represented. Perhaps our most quiet and personal memory is about this church. The building is different, but the church itself is the same; the spirit is the same. Our family has always felt that church is the place to seek guidance and seek strength and peace. And when you are away from home, you realize how much that means. This church, in a sense, was our home away from home. It's a little different, though. Today we came up with 20 motorcars in a motorcade, and I used to come to church on my bicycle, my Flying Pigeon. [*Laughter*] But it doesn't matter how you come to church; the important thing is that the feeling is the same, the feeling of being in the spirit of Jesus Christ. And, yes, our daughter, Dorothy, now the mother of two children, was baptized in this church; and that gives us a special feeling of identity and warmth.

Today the relationship between China and the United States is good. We are launching satellites together. The students of both countries study at each other's great universities. And Chinese and Americans enjoy the cultural treasures of both nations. We compete against each other on the athletic field and in the economic arena, but we compete as friends.

Much is different since Barbara and I journeyed to Beijing so many years ago, but some things have not changed, for example, what this church has represented over the years: that sense of community, family, and faith that binds us together as friends and neighbors. And in this accelerating world, that bond is a precious bond. Sometimes our problems can seem bigger than life itself, intractable and fearsome. But I am convinced that with each other, with our faith in God, we can meet any challenge, and we will.

Thank you for welcoming us back, and God bless each and every one of you. And now Barbara and I would like to make a small presentation to this church that means so much to us. This is a bigger Bible—[*laughter*]—but it comes to you with our heartfelt thanks and our love.

Note: The President spoke at 8:30 a.m. during morning prayer services. In his opening remarks, he referred to the Reverends Kan Xueqing, Shi Zesheng, and Yin Jiceng.

Remarks to American Embassy Employees in Beijing
February 26, 1989

Well, I want to thank Secretary [of State] Baker for that warm introduction and, on his behalf and mine and Barbara's and all those traveling with us, express our gratitude to each and every one of you in the Embassy. I'm proud to be greeted by the marines, proud to have been greeted before them by several of our Chinese friends, coworkers that worked with Barbara and me right in this very house.

You know, there's something about seeing familiar, friendly faces when you walk in a place that does make you feel at home, and then to see all of you. I don't know who the admin officer is here, who runs the administrative end of things, and those of you poor, suffering souls who work with him or her—[*laughter*]—but I will simply say—it is a her. I can't see her, but they tell me it is a she. [*Laughter*] Please stand up. Oh, she is standing up. Sorry. [*Laughter*] But let me thank you from the bottom of my heart because I know something about surviving a visit from a President. We had one when I was out here, before this was an embassy. [*Laughter*] And I was sure glad to see him go. [*Laughter*] And if that wasn't enough, we survived two from Henry Kissinger. Try that one on for size. [*Laughter*] You think we're bad, now, listen! [*Laughter*]

But to the Chinese employees here and to the families and to all——

[*At this point, the President was interrupted by a crying baby.*]

Oh, it's not that bad, kid. Wait a minute; it's going to get—[*laughter*]. To all of you here, really, I did want to say my special thanks. You serve a long way from home. This relationship, as I told Chairman Deng Xiaoping and others, is vital. It is absolutely essential to the foreign policy interest of the United States and, I'd say, in our own security interests as well. And so, you're doing a wonderful job for our country, and we are extraordinarily grateful to each and every one of you. And sometimes when you're halfway around the world, you expect nobody really gives much of a damn, but I do. And I care about it because I've been a part of an Embassy once, and when you've done that you know how people pull together. I have respect for the Foreign Service. I have respect for those in the military who serve abroad. And I have respect for those in the other departments that make up a great Embassy like this. And I might say, I have great respect for this Ambassador and for what he's done in building on this extraordinarily important relationship. And so, Barbara and I give our thanks to Betty and to Winston.

We're running behind schedule, and so, we've got to go off for yet another meeting. I was looking forward to this one, though, and I apologize. And part of the reason we're late is I had to stop at the International Club. I had to see those guys that I played tennis with because I read in the paper a terrible thing. Mr. Wong—modest man that he is, and some of you may know him—the tennis guy up here at the club, reported erroneously that he beat me regularly in tennis. [*Laughter*] And this was in the New York Times. [*Laughter*] And I had to stop off and talk to him about that story, and so, I apologize for being late.

But let me end by saying Barbara and I are thrilled to be back here. We've had a wonderful visit. And it is more than the symbolism; it is important that we make clear to our Chinese friends that we value this relationship, that we're going to work to strengthen it. And once again, that's where all of you come in.

So, thank you, and God bless each and every one of you for what you're doing for the greatest, the freest, and the best country on the face of the Earth: the United States of America. Thank you all.

Note: The President spoke at 1:55 p.m. at the U.S. Ambassador's residence. In his remarks, he referred to Administrative Officer Dorothy Sampas, Ambassador Winston Lord, and Mrs. Betty Lord.

Interview With Chinese Television Journalists in Beijing

February 26, 1989

China-U.S. Relations

Q. Mr. President, I'm sure millions of Chinese people are watching this program now. I wonder if you would like to say a few words to them first.

The President. Well, I do have an opening statement, but first let me thank you for this unique opportunity. It's a great honor for me to be the first American President to speak to the Chinese people in a live broadcast. And I feel as if I were talking to old friends who, while out of sight, have never, never been out of heart and mind.

Fourteen years ago, Barbara and I came to your beautiful land when I was, as you said, Chief of the United States Liaison Office. And for us, returning to Beijing is a homecoming. Our work here was a source of great personal satisfaction, a happy, challenging time in our lives. And we actually went to church here; indeed, our daughter was baptized in our faith here. And we rode bicycles down the *hutongs* [narrow streets] of Beijing and came to have a general feeling of affection for the Chinese people. And we knew then that the relationship that we would establish between our two nations would be a special one indeed.

And we were right. Today the bridges that started with the Shanghai communique years ago—today that relationship has joined our peoples together in friendship and respect. And our two countries continue to weave an increasingly rich fabric of relations through our expanding trade and cultural and scientific exchange. American students study at many of your finest universities, and we welcome thousands of Chinese students and researchers to educational institutions in the United States. The understanding and friendship that these students have developed will only help to improve and deepen relations between our two countries in the years ahead.

I've spoken to the American people about a new breeze blowing in the world today. And there's a worldwide movement toward greater freedom: freedom of human creativity and freedom of economic opportunity. And we've all begun to feel the winds of change sweep us toward an exciting and challenging new century. These winds—new, sometimes gentle, sometimes strong and powerful. China was one of the first nations to feel this new breeze, and like a tree in a winter wind, you've learned to bend and adapt to new ways and new ideas and reform.

Many challenges lie before our two nations. And together, we must find political solutions to regional conflicts. We must foster global growth. And together, in order to make life better for future generations, we must seek solutions to worldwide concerns, such as our planet's environment, the threat to all people from international terror, the use and spread of chemical and biological weapons, and international drug trafficking. I know your leaders share with me a determination to solve these and other problems, and as President of the United States, I look forward to continuing to work closely with them as I have done in the past.

The Americans and Chinese share many things, but perhaps none is more important than our strong sense of family. Just a few weeks ago, Barbara and I were blessed by a new grandchild. And when I think of her and I think of the beautiful children of China, my commitment to peace is renewed and reaffirmed.

I am confident that when future generations of Chinese and Americans look back upon this time they'll say that the winds of change blew favorably upon our lands. Thank you for your friendship, your hospitality, and the many warm memories of this wonderful country that Barbara and I take with us as we return tomorrow to the United States. Thank you all.

Q. Mr. President, you've been in office for just a month, and many people are probably surprised that you've decided to come to China so soon. Why now?

The President. Now because, you see, I view the relationship between China and the United States as highly significant, as one of the very most important relationships that we have. And so, it has a lot to do with bilateralism, with our trade and our cultural exchanges and what I said here about the children. But it's more than that. It really has, because of China's importance and ours, a lot to do with world peace. And so, before much time went by, I wanted to reaffirm the importance that the United States places on this bilateral relationship, and I wanted to pledge to the Chinese leaders—and I've met the top four leaders in the last day and a half—that this relationship will grow and it will prosper. And we have economic problems, and China has some. But together we're going to solve them, and we're going to move forward.

Q. Well, this is your second day in China.

How do you assess your time here? What specifically have you achieved on this trip?

The President. Well, really it's been a period to—just in that short period of time—to visit with the Chinese leadership and Chairman Deng Xiaoping and others—Zhao Ziyang and Li Peng, Chairman Yang—all of these men giving a lot of their time to explain the reforms in China, the new directions that China is taking in world affairs. We had an interesting exchange on the forthcoming visit of General Secretary Gorbachev coming here. And it is important that they understand what I'm thinking in terms of the Middle East or the subcontinent or our relations with the Soviet Union on arms control, and it's important I understand theirs. So, it hasn't been a visit that has three points on an agenda. It's a visit with a much broader perspective and a reaffirmation of a relationship that's strong.

Q. Mr. President, you know perhaps as well as anyone about the development of relations between your country and China. How would you say that relationship contributes to world peace and development?

The President. Well, I think it contributes a lot, because in the first place, we in the United States have a disproportionate responsibility for discussions on strategic weapons, for example, and we want to go forward with the Soviet Union, in this instance, on negotiations. But we don't want to do that in a way that would jeopardize the interests of any other country. And so, in that one area, we can have discussions with the Chinese, just as our Secretary of State, Jim Baker, had with the European leaders.

Another area is the economy. And we have some economic problems at home, and I wanted to assure the Chinese leaders that I am going to do my level best to get our deficit down. The Chinese people might say, Well, what in the world does that have to do with me living in Beijing or down in Shanghai or out further in the countryside? Well, the economies of the world are interlocked in a way. And if I can do my job properly, that might mean lower interest rates. And what does that mean to the average man on the street in China? That might mean that eventually his goods come to him at a lower price. So, I just come back to the fact that the visit is a chance to explore in depth the complicated international relationships and to build on this bilateral relationship.

China-U.S. Trade

Q. Well, it's said there's vast potential in strengthening both the economic and technological cooperation between China and the United States. How do we best tap that potential, and how do we overcome problems such as the restrictions on the transfer of technology?

The President. Well, in the first place, I had an opportunity just a minute ago—I was almost late for your program because I was talking to Zhao Ziyang, a very impressive leader, about the economy and about reforms. We congratulate the Chinese leaders in the steps they've taken towards economic reform.

Now, in terms of something technical like technological exchange, I made clear to the Chinese leaders, particularly in a conversation with Li Peng, that we are prepared to go the extra mile in terms of investment, in terms of business, exports and imports. You know, when I was here in China 15 years ago, total trade was $800 million. And now, depending on how one accounts for it, we would say we would use a figure of $14 billion. So, we're going to move forward. We will advance technology to China as much as we possibly can under what is known as the COCOM [Coordinating Committee for Multilateral Export Security Controls] arrangement. There are some highly sensitive, highly sophisticated military technologies that I'm not even sure China is interested in, but that we are prohibited from exporting under the law. Having said that, we have exported some highly sophisticated technology to China, and as President, I want to continue to do that. And that will benefit the life of the average Chinese citizen.

We're in an information society in many ways in the United States, and clearly that is going to come to China—computer knowledge and education techniques that are coming to the average Chinese kid from computers. And we've been blessed by advanced technology, and now we want to share it as much as we can.

Q. Well, you know there are reforms in China right now——

The President. I know it.

Q. ——and the Chinese Government is trying to attract more foreign investment. So, does your administration have or plan to have any specific measures to encourage American businesses to invest in China?

The President. Well, we had a chance to talk about that here today with the Chinese leaders, and I did point out to them that there are certain things that we'd like to see China move forward on that would enhance further investment here. I'd like to see an investment treaty between the two countries of some sort—an agreement, not a treaty but a bilateral agreement on trade. We—like we do not just with China but many other countries—talk about copyright and patent protection, and yet I find on this visit that China is moving forward with a new patent code and now drafting copyright legislation, which would be very helpful.

So, there are some artificial barriers. And the good thing about a visit like this is we can sit and talk to the leaders in a dispassionate way. And where they disagree with me, they will tell me, and where I disagree with them, I'm obliged to tell them. And that's what a good frank relationship can do.

But I told them that I must work to get the budget deficit in the United States now, because that does have an adverse impact on international interest rates. So, there are things that we can do, and there were things that I've asked China to do in terms of facilitating business. Sometimes I think your country is as bad as mine is on red tape. And to get the best flow of investment, China needs to do better on red tape, and so do we. It's a two-way street.

Q. Well, I've got more questions——

The President. Go ahead.

Q. ——but the time is up.

The President. Oh, dear.

Q. And I'm afraid you have another important activity right after this, so we have to end this interview right now.

Thank you very much, Mr. President. It's been a pleasure to have you here.

The President. Well, this has been a unique opportunity. And let me just conclude my part of your broadcast by again saying as President of the United States, the growing relationship between China and the United States is vital to my country. It is important to my country. And I hope it will benefit the people in China. I am confident that it will, and I know it will benefit world peace as well.

Q. Thank you very much, Mr. President.

The President. Thank you, ma'am.

Note: The interview began at 6:02 p.m. at the CCTV Studios. In his remarks, the President referred to Zhao Ziyang, General Secretary of the Chinese Communist Party; Deng Xiaoping, Chairman of the Central Military Commission; Li Peng, Premier of the State Council, and Yang Shangkun, President of China. Following his remarks, the President traveled to Seoul, Republic of Korea.

Statement by Press Secretary Fitzwater on the President's Trip to China

February 27, 1989

The President and Mrs. Bush were delighted by the warm reception in China. The entire range of Chinese leadership met with the President, showing their respect for him personally and for the United States. The luncheon hosted by Chairman Deng Xiaoping and the President's live appearance on Chinese national television were both quite unusual and underscored the Chinese appreciation for the trip.

The President feels the visit was successful in several ways. Both countries underscored their desire to move forward on bilateral issues, noting our bilateral trade level up from $10–14 billion, more Chinese students in the United States, a developing military relationship, and a large and growing science and technology relationship. The President expects both countries to move forward in all of these areas.

There are problems on both sides, of course. They are concerned about Taiwan and what they consider to be excessive United States export controls. In addition, we hope for more progress in human rights.

The President felt the talks on international issues went very well, especially the discussions on Cambodia. Both China and the United States agreed the liberalization of China's investment regulations is desirable, and the Chinese are pursuing this approach. The Chinese said they had completed a patent law and are working on a new copyright law, both of which are necessary to protect intellectual property rights.

The President and Mrs. Bush also shared a personal excitement about the private aspects of the trip. They were especially moved by the Sunday morning church service, the warmth of the Chinese people, and the many changes that have been made in Chinese society in recent years.

Remarks Following a Meeting With President Roh Tae Woo in Seoul

February 27, 1989

Well, President Roh and I had very useful, wide-ranging discussions. We reviewed the political situation in this part of the world. I told him about my China visit, and we had a chance to review our relations with the Soviet Union as well. We are both pleased by trends toward relaxations of tension in this part of the world. President Roh's *nordpolitik*—reaching out to China, the Soviets, and Eastern Europe—and his initiatives toward North Korea contributed importantly to these trends.

The U.S. fully supports Korea's creative diplomacy. Despite such positive policies, some hard realities remain. Among these is that North Korea maintains the world's fifth largest military force, a force deployed just 25 miles north of here. And the United States remains committed to the security and freedom of the Republic of Korea. And I had an opportunity to make that point very clearly to President Roh. Perhaps some of the confidence-building measures that we've proposed, measures that have worked well in Europe, will also be applied to the Korean Peninsula.

Besides the diplomatic and security issues, we discussed ways to strengthen the free world economic system. We had a frank discussion of economic problems—Korea being a very important trading partner with the United States. Korea has benefited from U.S. open markets, and I think we both agree we need to move as quickly as possible to fully open markets. We must expect fair access to the markets here. And I believe that President Roh understands that.

But all and all, the trip has been too short. The hospitality has been wonderful. And inasmuch as I do not want to make the Assembly mad—the elected leaders in the various parties that represent Korea's democracy—we should go.

But thank you, Mr. President, very much for an unforgettable visit.

Note: President Bush spoke at 2:49 p.m. at the Blue House, the official residence of President Roh.

Remarks to the National Assembly in Seoul
February 27, 1989

Thank you, Mr. Speaker. Thank you, and I hold out my hand to you, to the Government of Korea, and to the people of Korea. Mr. Speaker and Members of the National Assembly of the Republic of Korea and distinguished guests, I am honored by your invitation to address this body today. I stand in your Assembly as Presidents Eisenhower, Johnson, and Reagan have stood before me. And I reaffirm, as they did, America's support, friendship, and respect for the Republic of Korea and its people.

As a former Member of a body like this, of the House of Representatives of the United States, I take particular pleasure in coming back to this legislative chamber, where the freely elected representatives of Korea's own democratic success story meet to debate and implement the will of the Korean people. I know there must be times when this body, just like the United States Congress, is full of noise and contention and emotion. But that is the sound of democracy at work, and we wouldn't have it any other way. As the great statesman Winston Churchill once said: "Democracy is the worst form of government except for all others."

This is my first major address on foreign soil since becoming the 41st President of the United States of America. And my visit here today reflects the importance that I place on the relations between our two countries, the strength of our nations' ties, and the promise that our relationship holds for the future of the world. My inauguration as President a month ago represented a tradition in the United States that speaks of both continuity and change. Continuity and change will also be the guideposts of relations between the United States and Korea in the years ahead. Where change is needed or inevitable, let us be a positive force for change. Where continuity is our mandate, let us go forward, resolute in our commitment to freedom and democracy. Throughout, let our close economic and strategic relationship remain as it is: a pillar of peace in East Asia.

I first came to the Asian Pacific region during World War II, more than 45 years ago. I was a teenager, 19 years old. I was flying torpedo bombers in the United States Navy. It was then, for the first time in my life, that I truly appreciated the value of freedom and the price that we pay to keep it. Believe me, I have never forgotten.

In the early years following World War II, the future of Korea and of all Asia was very much in doubt. It was a time of great struggle between Korea's hope for freedom, Korea's hope for prosperity, and the twin menaces of war and invasion. On a June morning in 1950, the Communist army of the North smashed into the Republic of Korea, intent on destroying your nation. And without hesitation or delay, American and U.N. forces rushed to your aid. And together, Americans and Koreans fought side by side for your right to determine your own future. And I do remember the devastation of your country. Your cities lay in rubble. Your factories were in shambles. Millions of your people wandered the streets homeless and hungry. And in 1951, in the midst of the war, General Douglas MacArthur addressed a joint session of our Congress. And he spoke of Korea, saying, "The magnificence of the courage and fortitude of the Korean people defies description." And as he spoke those words, our Congress interrupted him with applause, sustained applause, for you and your people.

And after the war, you overcame every imaginable hardship. History will long record your story: how in less than a generation you stepped into the light of liberty and economic opportunity. You can be proud of the miracle that you've achieved. And we are proud to be associated with you.

Today Korea is a rising nation; a vibrant, dynamic nation; a nation riding the crest of the wave of the future. And never before has the pride and the progress of your nation been more evident than last summer when this magnificent city played host to the 24th Olympic games. Nearly 10,000 athletes from 160 nations were here. Another 3 billion people watched on television. And what they saw from the moment Sohn Kee Chung carried the torch into your Olympic Stadium until the last embers of the Olympic flame were extinguished at the closing ceremonies was an incredibly spectacular sports festival. You played host to the world, and what a truly gracious host you were. Congratulations!

The past several years have witnessed the emergence of the entire Asian-Pacific region. My trip—beginning in Japan, stopping in China, and concluding here in Korea—stands as testimony to the reality and what it means to the future of the world. Today Asia is one of the most dynamic areas on Earth—economically, politically, diplomatically. The Republic of Korea stands at the fore. You're a world-class economic power. Your commitment to democracy is demonstrated daily right here in this chamber. And your bold diplomacy, your *nordpolitik* [South Korean contact with Socialist States], is reshaping relations in and beyond the Asia-Pacific region.

In my meetings with Prime Minister Takeshita of Japan, China's Deng Xiaoping and the three other top leaders, and with you and your leaders, I've discussed challenging bilateral, global, and regional issues. And our discussions have been marked at all times by a spirit of friendship and cooperation.

I've come here today as the leader of a faithful friend and a dependable ally. And I'm here today to ensure that we continue to work together in all things. Our most important mission together is to maintain the freedom and democracy that you fought so hard to win. As President, I am committed to maintaining American forces in Korea, and I'm committed to support our Mutual Defense Treaty. There are no plans to reduce U.S. forces in Korea. Our soldiers and airmen are there at the request of the Republic of Korea to deter aggression from the North, and their presence contributes to the peace and stability of northeast Asia. And they will remain in the Republic of Korea as long as they are needed and as long as we believe it is in the interest of peace to keep them there.

In the years ahead, we must work together as equal partners to meet the evolving security needs of the Korean Peninsula. Peace through strength is a policy that has served the security interests of our two nations well. And we must complement deterrence with an active diplomacy in search of dialog with our adversaries, including North Korea. The American people share your goal of peaceful unification on terms acceptable to the Korean people. It's for that reason that we actively support the peaceful initiatives of President Roh to build bridges to the North. And I will work closely with the President to coordinate our efforts to draw the North toward practical, peaceful, and productive dialog to ensure that our policies are complementary and mutually reinforcing.

I've spoken of the need for vigilance, strength, and diplomacy to deter aggression and preserve peace. There's another source of strength, and it is well-represented in this Assembly. The development of democratic political institutions is the surest means to build the national consensus that is the foundation of true security.

Just as we must work together to achieve better security within a democratic framework, we must also work together to achieve greater economic prosperity within the system of free and open international trade. The progress of the Korean economy is an inspiration for developing countries throughout the world. By unleashing the energies and creativity of your talented people, you've led Korea into an era of unprecedented opportunity and prosperity. Korea has become an industrial power, a major trading power, and a first-class competitor. You are fulfilling the prophecy of the Indian poet Tagore who wrote: "Korea, once a bright light of the golden age of Asia, if it is relit, it will be the light of the East." Korea has achieved great prosperity through participation in the international trading system that has made the nations of free Asia the envy of the world. And all Koreans can take pride in what you, as a people, have achieved.

And yet we also cannot overlook that your economic success has created concern in the management of our bilateral economic relations. For the American people and for the Korean people, as well, reducing our bilateral trade imbalance will be both a challenge and an opportunity. The challenge will be to resist the calls for protectionism; the opportunity will be to expand the prosperity of both our countries. And we both, you and I, have a lot at stake. You are our seventh largest trading partner, larger than many of our traditional European trading partners, and our trade is growing. The United States is both Korea's largest market and second largest source of imports. And we're also a leading source of the investment and technology that you will need to fuel further economic growth and development.

Korea's economy has benefited greatly from the free flow of trade. And yet today, in many countries, there is a call for greater protectionism. And I'm asking you to join the United States in rejecting these shortsighted pleas. Protectionism is fool's gold. Protectionism may seem to be the easy way out but is really the quickest way down. And nothing will stop the engine of Korea's economic growth faster than new barriers to international trade.

We've made progress in this area. American exports to Korea are up. Korean tariffs are down, and its nontariff barriers are down, too. And the service sector is opening. And let me be candid. I want you to have this direct from me. If we are to keep our bilateral relationship growing even stronger, much more needs to be done. And I am confident that our two nations working together can accomplish the tasks still before us.

As one of the world's major trading powers, the Republic of Korea sets an example for other nations who are watching what you do. As an emerging economic leader, you inevitably shoulder important responsibilities to ensure the continued strength and stability of the global marketplace. You, the representatives of the Korean people, will face the challenge to improve living standards, to continue to open domestic markets, and to adopt appropriate international financial and exchange rate policies that reflect your standing as a prosperous and powerful trading nation. The United States shares similar responsibilities for the well-being of the world economy. Our two peoples should, at all times, bear in mind that our trading system is truly an international joint venture and that we share a special responsibility for its continued success.

My friends—and we are truly friends—I began today by talking about my inauguration as the new President of the United States of America just a few short weeks ago. The tradition of passing the torch of leadership from one American President to another is a time when we celebrate the strength of our democracy and a time when we renew our commitment to the values on which it is built. Today I am renewing my commitment to you, as the leader of one sovereign state to the elected legislative body of another. I am renewing my commitment to you to work together for the good of our peoples and of all humanity.

And as I reflect over the last 40 years of Asian history, the trend is remarkably positive. At the end of the Second World War, Asia lay in ruins. Through the 1950's and the 1960's, the forces of radical revolution at times appeared to be the wave of the future. And now, in the 1980's, human aspirations for basic political and economic freedoms have become almost universal. And as we gather here in your National Assembly, these aspirations are no longer a far-off dream for your great country, for Korea. Instead, through your devotion and hard work, they've become a reality, and we celebrate your triumph. In the years ahead, the United States will stand with you against the forces of oppression and for the forces of peace, prosperity, independence, and democracy.

And so, on behalf of my wife, Barbara; of our Secretary of State, Jim Baker, who is with me here today; and others, our leaders in our government, I came to observe, I came to reaffirm. And from the bottom of my heart, I thank you for the warmth and the hospitality you have bestowed upon all of us. Thank you, and God bless you all.

Note: The President spoke at 4:01 p.m. in the National Assembly Hall. In his opening remarks, he referred to Kim Jaison, Speaker of the National Assembly. Following his remarks, the President returned to Washington, DC.

Remarks Upon Returning From a Trip to the Far East
February 27, 1989

Let me just say that it's great to be back home again at the conclusion of a productive and rewarding trip to Japan, China, and Korea, a trip which underscored that America is and will remain a Pacific power.

There were important symbols. I'll never forget that solemn moment when we paid our nation's respect to the late Emperor of Japan, and the warm and genuine handshakes between old friends in Beijing's Great Hall of the People, the opportunity for the freely elected leader of a 200-year-old nation to address the freely elected legislature of a blossoming democracy, Korea.

But we laid out an important substantive course: thoughtful and candid conversations with world leaders, over 20 of them, leaders from Asia—China, Japan, Korea, Thailand, Singapore, India, Pakistan, and the Philippines—and our allies from Europe—France, Belgium, Italy, Portugal, Turkey, Germany, and Spain—and leaders from the Middle East—Egypt, Israel, and Jordan—and the Presidents of Brazil, Nigeria, and Zaire. And so, I return tonight pleased with the progress made toward lasting and mutually beneficial relationships with our allies and friends. Of course, differences remain. Work is yet to be done: opening foreign markets to U.S. competition, continuing to encourage the growth of democracy and human rights, and strengthening of our alliances. But common ground was found.

In Japan, we have our most important Asian ally and one of our largest trading partners. Our discussions there emphasized the responsibilities we share in the field of defense. But we also spoke of ways in which the world's strongest and most innovative economies can cooperate more closely to fuel growth not only at home but also in the developing world.

In China, I talked with the leaders that I'd known nearly 15 years ago, when I served as Chief of the U.S. Liaison Office. And it is clear from my trip that China approaches its thaw with the Soviets with caution and realism. We agreed that the Soviets must be judged not by their rhetoric but by their actions, such as whether the Soviet Union actually draws down its military forces along China's border and persists in encouraging Vietnam to completely withdraw from Cambodia. We also agreed that after Cambodia has achieved a genuine end to Vietnam's occupation, free elections should be held under a coalition government led by Prince Sihanouk, with whom I met in Beijing. The United States remains committed to a result that precludes a return to power by the Khmer Rouge. And the Chinese leaders appreciate our concern and are willing to work toward a peaceful coalition.

On the final leg of my journey I went to Korea, where I saw both democracy and economic liberty work in a country whose security is assured by our joint efforts in vigilance. Thirty years ago such progress was unimaginable, and it stands as a testament to the Korean people and our commitment to them.

From these 4 days of intensive discussions, I return with one especially vivid impression: The world looks to America for leadership not just because we're militarily strong, not just because we have the world's largest economy, but because the ideas we have championed are now dominant. Freedom and democracy, openness, and the prosperity that derives from individual initiatives in the free marketplace—these ideas, once thought to be strictly American, have now become the goals of mankind all over Asia.

The success of our nation's foreign policy is the responsibility of the President, with the counsel and support of the Congress. And this important trip has only underscored for me what can be achieved through a strong and bipartisan working relationship between the White House and Congress. I'm anxious to sit down with congressional leadership to brief them on details of these critical visits, and together we must ensure that this initial success is only a first step down a long path of peace and understanding with our friends and allies. If common ground can be found halfway around the world in the shadow of Mt. Fuji, the historic Great Hall of the People, or the garden of Korea's Blue House, surely it can be found at home among men and women of common purpose. We must respect each other and join together as one in pursuing a foreign policy that ensures the security of our country, its economic opportunity, and freedom and individual rights around the world.

It's great to be home. God bless the United States of America. Thank you all very much.

Note: The President spoke at 6:34 p.m. on the tarmac of Andrews Air Force Base in Camp Springs, MD.

Statement on the United Nations Human Rights Commission Report on Cuba

February 27, 1989

I wish to express my support for the U.N. Human Rights Commission's report on human rights in Cuba. We find the report full, balanced, and objective. Consideration of Cuba marks a watershed in the U.N. treatment of human rights abuses. For too long, the U.N. has focused on small countries which lack extensive support within the organization. Many of those countries today are either functioning democracies or have taken significant steps on the road toward full democracy. Meanwhile, longstanding violators of human rights have enjoyed immunity from scrutiny and have even fostered human rights investigations into other countries.

For more than 30 years, the people of Cuba have languished under a regime which has distinguished itself as one of the most repressive in the world. Last year the international community won an important victory when the U.N. Human Rights Commission decided to conduct a full investigation into the situation in Cuba. The report which was released in Geneva is based on firsthand testimony about persistent violations of human rights in that country and is the culmination of that investigation.

The United States firmly believes that this report should begin a long-term effort to bring about true and lasting changes in the Cuban Government's performance on human rights. In the year since the U.N. Human Rights Commission decided to investigate Cuba, there have been slight and superficial improvements. But much more needs to be done before the Cuban people can truly be said to enjoy the rights guaranteed them by the Universal Declaration of Human Rights. I call upon other members of the Commission and all countries that value freedom to maintain pressure on the Cuban Government by continuing U.N. monitoring of the human rights situation in Cuba. The people of Cuba and oppressed people everywhere look to the U.N. as their last best hope. We must not disappoint them.

Remarks and a Question-and-Answer Session With Reporters Following a Cabinet Meeting
February 28, 1989

Bookstore Bombings

The President. I have a brief statement. But lest there be any confusion about this occasion, this is what we called a modified press availability, unlike a photo op in which I do not take questions and will not take questions. So, this is a change, and I've explained this and asked the indulgence of our Cabinet, with whom we've just had an opportunity to brief and to talk about the trip that Secretary Baker and I and others are just back from. So, we've had a full meeting. But let me just read a statement relevant to current events here.

A press building in New York City and two bookstores in Berkeley have been targets today of bomb attacks. And while the details surrounding these incidents and the motives of those who carried them out are still unclear, I think that it is important to take this occasion to state where the U.S. Government and, I'm convinced, the American people stand on violence and on our rights. This country was founded on the principles of free speech and religious tolerance. And we fought throughout our history to protect these principles. And I want to make unequivocally clear that the United States will not tolerate any assault on these rights of American citizens. Should it appear that any Federal laws have been violated in these bombing attacks, I've asked Dick Thornburgh, our able Attorney General here, to use all of the resources of the FBI and all other appropriate resources of this government to identify and bring to justice those responsible.

We don't yet know if the bombings are related to the book "The Satanic Verses." But let me be clear: Anyone undertaking acts of intimidation or violence aimed at the author, the publishers, or the distributors of "The Satanic Verses" will be prosecuted to the maximum extent of the law. And, yes, some of the Muslim faith can interpret that book as highly offensive, and I can be sensitive to that, but we cannot and will not condone violence and lawlessness in this country. And I think our citizens need to know how strongly I feel about that.

I'll be glad to take a couple of questions before we have to go on to other——

Human Rights

Q. Mr. President, the Chinese Foreign Ministry has been suggesting that the incident involving Mr. Fang could have been avoided if the guest list for your dinner had been presented to them in advance. As a matter of policy, do you believe when you invite dissidents from countries to a social event that you should clear in advance with the host Government?

The President. No, and I think they understand that. They may have a point, that it might have been avoided; but that's not the whole question when it comes to the United States commitment to human rights.

Secretary of Defense-Designate Tower

Q. Mr. President, do you have any reason to believe that you will get the five votes or more necessary to get the Tower nomination through?

The President. I'm working hard at it, and I hope so, and all of us are. I am committed. I'm committed on two grounds, and I've just told my Cabinet this. One of them has to do with who best to run the Pentagon, and I haven't heard one single voice challenge this man's knowledge and his ability. And I've known John Tower a long time—longer than many that are criticizing him out there in various walks of life. And so, who best to do the job that I want done and that the country needs done.

And then the second one is America's innate sense of fairplay. There's a certain fairness, and I don't believe anybody should be pilloried on the basis of unfounded rumor. And so, if somebody has a specific objection, fine, they have every right in the world to state it. But I don't think it is fair to permit perception to be the guideline. And therefore, I will continue to fight for this man that I believe in.

Q. Have you picked up any Democratic Senators?

The President. Who knows?

Note: The President spoke at 2:40 p.m. in the Cabinet Room at the White House.

Nomination of Jack Callihan Parnell To Be Deputy Secretary of Agriculture

February 28, 1989

The President today announced his intention to nominate Jack Callihan Parnell to be Deputy Secretary of Agriculture. He would succeed Peter C. Myers.

Since 1987 Mr. Parnell has been director of the California Department of Food and Agriculture. Prior to this he was director of the California Department of Fish and Game, 1984–1987. From 1966 to 1983, he was a pedigree livestock auctioneer. He was also owner and publisher of the California Cattleman's Magazine, 1966–1972, and field editor for Pacific Stockman and Stockman Weekly, 1964–1966. Mr. Parnell has also managed and operated diversified agricultural operations.

Mr. Parnell attended Healds Business College in San Francisco, CA, and Sacramento City College. He was born May 7, 1935, in Leavenworth, WA. He is married, has three children, and resides in Auburn, CA.

Nomination of Constance Horner To Be Under Secretary of Health and Human Services

February 28, 1989

The President today announced his intention to nominate Constance Horner to be Under Secretary of Health and Human Services. She would succeed Donald M. Newman.

Since 1985 Mrs. Horner has been Director of the Office of Personnel Management in Washington, DC. Prior to this, she was Associate Director for Economics and Government in the Office of Management and Budget, 1983–1985; Director of VISTA and Acting Associate Director of ACTION, 1982–1983; and Deputy Assistant Director for Policy, Planning, and Evaluation of ACTION, 1981–1982. Mrs. Horner was a member of the Department of Education transition team in the Office of the President-Elect, 1980–1981. She currently serves as a Commissioner on White House fellowships and on the President's Commission on Executive Exchange.

Mrs. Horner graduated from the University of Pennsylvania (B.A., 1964) and the University of Chicago (M.A., 1967). She is married, has two children, and resides in Washington, DC.

Nomination of Mary Sheila Gall To Be an Assistant Secretary of Health and Human Services
February 28, 1989

The President today announced his intention to nominate Mary Sheila Gall to be an Assistant Secretary of Health and Human Services (Human Development Services). She would succeed Sydney J. Olson.

Since 1987 Miss Gall has been Chair of the President's Task Force on Adoption, and Counselor to the Director of the United States Office of Personnel Management, 1986–present. Prior to this she was Deputy Domestic Policy Adviser in the Office of the Vice President, 1981–1986. She was a senior legislative analyst at the House Republican Study Committee, 1980–1981; a member of the Reagan-Bush Presidential campaign and transition team, 1980–1981; and director of research for the George Bush for President campaign, 1979–1980. From 1971 to 1979, Miss Gall served in various legislative positions on the staffs of several Members of the Senate and House of Representatives.

Miss Gall graduated from Rosary Hill College in Buffalo, NY. She has two children and resides in Arlington, VA.

Appointment of Debra Rae Anderson as Deputy Assistant to the President and Director of the Office of Intergovernmental Affairs
February 28, 1989

The President today announced his intention to appoint Debra Rae Anderson as Deputy Assistant to the President and Director of the Office of Intergovernmental Affairs.

Since January 1977 Miss Anderson has been a State representative in the South Dakota House of Representatives. In that capacity, she has served as speaker of the house, assistant majority whip, and chairman of the health and welfare committee. Miss Anderson was also named Legislator of the Year in 1987 by the National Republican Legislators' Association. She also served as executive director of the George Bush for President campaign in South Dakota.

Miss Anderson graduated from Augustana College (B.A., 1971). She was born June 13, 1949, in Watertown, SD.

Message to the Congress Transmitting the Annual Reports on Highway and Motor Vehicle Safety
February 28, 1989

To the Congress of the United States:

The Highway Safety Act and the National Traffic and Motor Vehicle Safety Act, both enacted in 1966, initiated a national effort to reduce traffic deaths and injuries and require annual reports on the administration of the Acts. This is the 21st year that these reports have been prepared.

The report on motor vehicle safety includes the annual reporting requirement in Title I of the Motor Vehicle Information and Cost Savings Act of 1972 (bumper standards).

In the Highway Safety Acts of 1973, 1976, and 1978, the Congress expressed its special interest in certain aspects of traffic safety that are addressed in the volume on highway safety.

The national outrage against drunk drivers, combined with growing safety belt use and voluntary cooperation we have received from all sectors of American life, have brought about even more improvements in traffic safety.

In addition, despite large increases in the number of drivers and vehicles, the Federal standards and programs for motor vehicle and highway safety instituted since 1966 have contributed to a significant reduction in the fatality rate per 100 million miles of travel. The rate decreased from 5.5 in the mid-60's to the 1987 level of 2.4, the lowest in our history.

The important progress we have made is, of course, no consolation to the relatives and friends of those 46,386 people who, despite the safety advances and greater public awareness, lost their lives in 1987. But it is indicative of the positive trend established toward making our roads safer.

The loss of approximately 127 lives per day on our Nation's highways is still too high. Also, with the increasing motor vehicle travel, we are faced with the threat of an even higher number of traffic fatalities. Therefore, there is a continuing need for effective motor vehicle and highway safety programs.

We will continue to pursue highway and motor vehicle safety programs that are most effective in reducing deaths and injuries. We are convinced that significant progress in traffic safety can be achieved through the combined efforts of government, industry, and the public.

GEORGE BUSH

The White House,
February 28, 1989.

Nomination of Douglas P. Mulholland To Be an Assistant Secretary of State

February 28, 1989

The President today announced his intention to nominate Douglas P. Mulholland to be an Assistant Secretary of State (Intelligence and Research). He would succeed Morton I. Abramowitz.

Since 1988 Mr. Mulholland has served as an analyst for domestic policy and research for the George Bush for President Committee. Between 1956 and 1979, he was employed by the Central Intelligence Agency serving in various capacities, including Special Assistant to the Secretary of the Treasury for National Security, 1982–1987; Inspector at the Office of the Inspector General, 1979–1982; and Director of the Office of Current Operations, 1978–1979.

Mr. Mulholland graduated from Michigan State University (B.A., 1955; M.A., 1956). He is married and resides in Rockville, MD.

Nomination of Calvin G. Franklin To Be Director of the Federal Emergency Management Agency

February 28, 1989

The President today announced his intention to nominate Calvin G. Franklin to be Director of the Federal Emergency Management Agency. He would succeed Julius W. Becton, Jr.

Since 1981 General Franklin has served as Commanding General of the District of Columbia National Guard. Prior to this appointment, he was the marketing manager, advanced systems and special programs, of the electronics division of the General Dynamics Corp. His military career began in 1948, when he enlisted as a private in the California Army National Guard.

General Franklin received a bachelor of arts degree from National University and his master's from United States International University. He is married, has three children, and resides in Camp Springs, MD.

Nomination of James O. Mason To Be an Assistant Secretary of Health and Human Services

February 28, 1989

The President today announced his intention to nominate James O. Mason to be an Assistant Secretary of Health and Human Services (Health). He would succeed Robert E. Windom.

Since 1983 Dr. Mason has been the Director of the Centers for Disease Control (CDC) in Atlanta, GA, and administrator of the Agency for Toxic Substances and Disease Registry, 1983 to present. He was executive director of the Utah Department of Health, 1979–1983, and associate professor and chairman of the division of community medicine of the University of Utah, 1978–1979. He was also deputy director of health of the Utah Division of Health, 1976–1978.

Dr. Mason received his undergraduate and medical degrees from the University of Utah and his master's and doctoral degrees in public health from Harvard University.

Nomination of Herman Jay Cohen To Be an Assistant Secretary of State

February 28, 1989

The President today announced his intention to nominate Herman Jay Cohen to be an Assistant Secretary of State (African Affairs). He would succeed Chester A. Crocker.

From 1987 to 1989, Mr. Cohen was the Senior Director for African Affairs on the National Security Council at the White House. Mr. Cohen has also held other senior management positions at the Department of State, including Deputy Assistant Secretary for Personnel, 1984–1986, and Deputy Assistant Secretary for Intelligence and Research, 1980–1984. Since 1955 Mr. Cohen has served as a Foreign Service officer at the Department of State.

Mr. Cohen graduated from the City College of New York (B.A., 1953). He was born February 10, 1932, in New York City. Mr. Cohen is married, has two children, and resides in Washington, DC.

Nomination of John H. Kelly To Be an Assistant Secretary of State

February 28, 1989

The President today announced his intention to nominate John H. Kelly to be an Assistant Secretary of State (Near East and South Asian Affairs). He would succeed Richard W. Murphy.

Since 1988 Ambassador Kelly has been the principal deputy director of the policy planning staff at the Department of State.

Prior to this he was the United States Ambassador to Lebanon, 1986–1988. Ambassador Kelly has held several positions at the Department of State since 1964, including Principal Deputy Assistant Secretary of State for European and Canadian Affairs, 1983–1985, and Senior Deputy Assistant Secretary for Public Affairs, 1982–1983.

Ambassador Kelly was born in Atlanta, GA, in 1939. He graduated in 1961 from Emory University with a degree in history. He is married, has one son, and resides in Washington, DC.

Nomination of Richard L. Armitage To Be an Assistant Secretary of State

February 28, 1989

The President today announced his intention to nominate Richard L. Armitage to be an Assistant Secretary of State (East Asian and Pacific Affairs). He would succeed Gaston Joseph Sigur, Jr.

Since 1983 Mr. Armitage has been Assistant Secretary of Defense for International Security Affairs in Washington, DC. Prior to this he was Deputy Assistant Secretary of Defense, International Security Affairs for East Asia and Pacific Affairs, 1981–1983. In 1979 he established a Washington-based consulting firm specializing in Asian affairs. He also served as administrative assistant to Senator Robert Dole, 1978–1979.

Mr. Armitage graduated from the U.S. Naval Academy in 1967. He served in the U.S. Navy from 1967 to 1973. He is married, has seven children, and resides in Vienna, VA.

Nomination of John R. Bolton To Be an Assistant Secretary of State

February 28, 1989

The President today announced his intention to nominate John R. Bolton to be an Assistant Secretary of State (International Organization Affairs). He would succeed Richard Salisbury Williamson.

Since 1988 Mr. Bolton has been Assistant Attorney General of the Civil Division at the Department of Justice. Prior to this, he was Assistant Attorney General in the Office of Legislative Affairs at the Department of Justice, 1985–1988. He was a partner with Covington & Burling, 1983–1985, and executive director of the Committee on Resolutions for the Republican National Committee, 1983–1984. He was Assistant Administrator for Program and Policy Coordination, 1982–1983, and General Counsel, 1981–1982, at the Agency for International Development.

Mr. Bolton graduated from Yale College (B.A. 1970) and Yale Law School (J.D., 1974). He currently resides in Bethesda, MD.

Nomination of Bernard William Aronson To Be an Assistant Secretary of State

February 28, 1989

The President today announced his intention to nominate Bernard William Aronson to be an Assistant Secretary of State (Inter-American Affairs). He would succeed Elliott

Abrams.

Mr. Aronson is founder and director of the Policy Project, a consulting firm headquartered in Washington, DC. Prior to this he was director of policy for the Democratic National Committee, 1981–1983, and director of the Democratic National Strategy Council. From 1977 to 1981, he was Special Assistant and Speechwriter to the Vice President at the White House. Mr. Aronson has also been assistant to the president of the United Mine Workers of America International Union, 1973–1977.

Mr. Aronson graduated from the University of Chicago (B.A., 1967). He has served in the U.S. Army Reserves. He was born May 16, 1946. Mr. Aronson is married, and resides in Takoma Park, MD.

Nomination of Jewel S. Lafontant To Be United States Coordinator for Refugee Affairs

February 28, 1989

The President today announced his intention to nominate Jewel S. Lafontant to be United States Coordinator for Refugee Affairs and Ambassador at Large while serving in this position. She would succeed Jonathan Moore.

Mrs. Lafontant has been a senior partner with the corporate and labor law firm of Vedder, Price, Kaufman & Kammholz in Chicago, IL. From 1973 to 1975, she was Deputy Solicitor General of the United States. Mrs. Lafontant has also served as United States Representative to the United Nations, 1972.

Mrs. Lafontant graduated from Oberlin College (B.A., 1943) and received a doctor of law degree from the University of Chicago in 1946. She has one child and resides in Chicago, IL.

Statement by Press Secretary Fitzwater on the Review of Management Practices at the Department of Defense

March 1, 1989

The President has directed the Department of Defense to undertake a review of management practices throughout the Department. Together with this defense management review, the President has requested a plan which will accomplish full implementation of the Packard commission recommendations and realize substantial improvements in the acquisition process and in defense management overall.

The agenda for the management review closely parallels that of the original Packard commission. The focus now is to identify specific actions to address problems already clearly identified. These actions include both those which can be taken internally in the Department of Defense and subsequent actions the Congress could take to contribute to the more effective operation and management of the Department of Defense.

Examples of problems to be addressed include:

- People and Organization: Identifying ways to improve the capabilities of military and civilian acquisition personnel, spelling out the appropriate role for the Under Secretary of Defense for Acquisition, strengthening the notion of individual accountability, and streamlining the acquisition management chain for major programs;
- Improved Planning Processes: Reviewing the role of the Under Secretary of De-

fense for Policy in defense planning and in policy implementation and developing means to better link national security strategy and objectives to the overall defense program;

• Practices and Procedures: Identifying improvements in the process of defining military needs and their links to national strategy, developing options for overseeing new program starts, identifying ways to better use commercial-style acquisition practices, finding means to reduce cost through improved production efficiency, and finding means to enhance stability in defense programs;

• Government-Industry Relations: Developing strategies to encourage contractors to cut costs; improving government oversight through increased coordination, sharing of information, and clearer delineation of responsibilities; and identifying opportunities for improved implementation of standards of conduct for government acquisition personnel.

The plan resulting from this review is to be presented to the President by May 10, 1989.

Remarks to Members of the Small Business Legislative Council
March 1, 1989

Thank you all for that welcome, and thank you all for being here. And to Secretary [of Commerce] Mosbacher and other dignitaries here and all of you, I am grateful for this opportunity.

Before beginning to talk a little bit about the area that brings us together—business climate, business community, emphasis small business, entrepreneurship—I want to comment on an issue of particular currency in Washington. Three guesses. [*Laughter*]

No, the debate over John Tower's nomination as Defense Secretary should clearly be based on principle and on policy, and it ought not to be based on rumor and innuendo. And no one denies that Senator Tower is well-qualified, hardnosed, tough, experienced. No one denies that he knows the Pentagon well, and he knows the Congress. Those are the facts.

And Americans, whatever their policies—and I'll bet all of you agree with this—and whatever their politics, are committed to the concept of fairplay and are committed to decency. And all I am asking in the name of fairplay is that the man be judged on the facts, not on misperceptions. And this is a tough town—a lot of rumors out there. Public service is not made easier by claims that cannot be substantiated. It's made tougher.

Proceedings are starting in the Senate, as they should, and I've made my call. I've looked at the record. I've known this man since 1959, and my support is unequivocal. And John Tower is, in my view, the best man for this job. And so, my pitch, my appeal to the Senators, has been: Look, do what you've got to do, but remember fairplay; remember decency and honor; and then remember also historically the concept of advise and consent where reasonable doubt is given historically to the President of the United States who, after all, is responsible for the executive branch of this government.

So, that matter—I wanted to just speak to you on it. I know it's a matter that obviously concerns everyone because it's dominating the news.

But now, back here, you've heard from Gregg Petersmeyer [Deputy Assistant to the President and the Director of the Office of National Service], I know, Richard Breeden [Assistant to the President for Issues Analysis] and Secretary Mosbacher; and these are three key members of my team here in Washington—able members. And now that you have a feeling for their ideas and their priorities, let me ask and encourage you to work with them. Tell them what you're thinking. They know how to work with the private sector, and they're looking for ways to make this a responsive government, a government by and for the people. And all three of these men have been highly successful in the private sector.

While I was in Asia, this recent trip, I had a chance to think seriously about what sets our trading partners apart from us, and I realized that we may have erected a barrier to our own success and deprived ourselves of vital long-term investment that our competitors have always enjoyed.

In a few minutes, I'm going to have a suggestion for those who argue in favor of protectionist intervention. You know, there are some who say that Asia could become the economic center of the world. Some even suggest that America's power is on the wane. And, well, for them I have news: The 21st century can well be the next American century if we understand the challenges before us and move together to meet them.

More than ever, the world is connected, interdependent, changing rapidly. Barbara and I lived in China 14 years ago for a year and a half, and I've been back there—this is the fifth time since leaving China. And some of you have been there. But every time you go, you feel it, you feel the movement, and you feel the change. And that's just one part of this highly complex, highly interconnected world. More than any point in our human history, societies and economies rely upon one another. So, competitiveness, which is on everybody's minds these days, takes on a challenging new angle; and it means more than just market share and earned income. And it's more than a zero-sum, winner-take-all game.

Since 1980 the world trade volume is up nearly 40 percent, and almost a fifth of our industrial production is now in exports. Goods and services circle the globe overnight. [Secretary of the Treasury] Nick Brady told me just a while ago over in the Oval Office that clearing in the world markets every night is a trillion dollars' worth of securities—a trillion dollars one single evening. Instant transfers of funds around the world—capital, as I say, changes hands in seconds. In a world like that, all nations stand to benefit from the growth of their trading partners, and as long as markets are free and open.

So, I have two key priorities: to promote economic growth through low tax rates and to encourage the kind of free trade that makes all nations better off. General Brent Scowcroft [Assistant to President for National Security Affairs] is here with me, and he was on this trip with me. And at every stop, we made the point to some weary interlocutors, I might add, of the need for keeping these markets open. The goal of competitiveness is not simply to disadvantage the competition, it's to better deploy the advantages that we have and to create new ones.

And that's why the work that you all do is so important. American small business has always been our most creative source of innovation and economic growth. And you, we, have created 19 million new jobs in this country since the recovery began. Relative to population, that's more than twice the number of jobs created in Japan. And in the U.S. private sector, small businesses are responsible for two out of three jobs created—two out of three. Businesses like yours make America work. By creating jobs, you create opportunity, and while I'm President, government won't interfere with that.

We've got to do more in the field where Richard Breeden spent several years of his life trying to simplify the regulatory process. I'm going to try hard. We will assure you that you have the freedom you need to do what you do best. And I am still determined—I have not changed my mind on this next one—to hold the line on taxes, because if the experience of the last 8 years has proven anything, that lower taxes do mean a stronger economy.

Competitiveness demands two things: flexibility in the marketplace, and the right kind of investment at home. So, we want to give the employers and employees the flexibility to work out their own solutions on issues like parental leave and health insurance. And we intend to promote the kind of investment that will allow every American to share in prosperity and help to create more of it. And that's the idea behind a new proposal of mine. I believe that with the proper incentives, small businesses can help lead America's urban renewal. And so, to the entrepreneur, I say this: Start your business in an inner city where the need for jobs is greatest, and we will cut your Federal tax rates. We will create these enterprise zones, which I think would be the best antidote to poverty in the inner city. After all, you'll be saving the Government money by reducing the need for items like welfare and subsidized housing. And you'll help us bring urban enterprise zones to life in cities all across this country.

You know, decisions made and actions taken at the local level very often better serve the interests of those involved. What I'm talking about here is a fundamental American freedom: the freedom to choose, make up your own mind. And that's the driving principle behind the proposal I've made on child care. We want to establish a new, refundable children's tax credit for low-income parents and make the existing child care tax credit refundable as well. We mean to avoid burdensome Federal standards and regulation that would limit family, limit church, and limit community-based care. We will examine the liability insurance barriers for businesses interested in providing child care options. We've got to do something about this liability menace, you might say, which has gotten out of hand. And we need some advice from you on how to accomplish this. We've got some good ideas on proposals that can well be made. We'd like to put solutions and dollars in the hands of parents. We intend to promote choice. And this one is very important with me. As I look at urban America and I look at the complexity of society today, it's right back to the basics: strengthen the family, strengthen the community, strengthen the churches and other groups that are out there trying to help.

You know, flexibility can also promote risk-taking. It's always been the basis for real achievements in business. And so, we need to find new ways to encourage men and women to take risks. We need entrepreneurs who will invest their time, talents, and resources to build the businesses, unlock new markets, unleash new technologies, create new jobs. People who bring to the marketplace competitive products and quality services that are second to none in the world—they need to be encouraged. You know what the challenges are.

Last year a large survey of CEO's suggested that while American business leaders are inherently optimistic, they're aware that we have new and important work to do. Ninety percent of them said that American business is still too short-term oriented.

And, along with many here—I better not start telling you my war stories about business or you'll tell me yours, and we'll be here all night. [*Laughter*] But I have helped build a business from scratch. I happen to think that's a good criterion for being President of the United States, as a matter of fact. And I know that it can be extraordinarily tough. And I understand the pressures, I think, from having been there in a tiny little business many years ago—the pressures that you face. So, you don't need a lecture on the importance of savings and long-term investment. You need government that enables you to do what's good for business and good for America. And often, that means kind of getting out of the way.

Competitiveness demands the right kind of investment, yes. For a long time now, I've been saying that we must have a competitive capital gains tax rate. If we're to retain the American edge, we must give entrepreneurs and small businesspeople the incentive to keep dreaming and keep taking risks and keep creating good jobs for America. I see a capital gains rate cut as an important way to free up American businesses without distorting world markets. The economies of the Pacific rim—the "Four Dragons" of Hong Kong, Singapore, Taiwan, and South Korea—all exempt long-term capital gains from tax—total exemption. Japan also had no tax on capital gains during its meteoric rise to economic power.

And so, I call on anyone who talks about protectionism to consider this: By taxing capital gains, we impede our own progress, and we turn the playing field into an uphill climb. Restoring the capital gains differential would be a powerful incentive for businesses to invest, to innovate, to grow, and to create jobs. The Treasury estimates that the cut that I have proposed will add $4.8 billion a year to the revenue side of the ledger. So, let those out there charge me of taxes that are favoring the rich. I know that in proposing a capital gains differential, I am favoring innovation and risk-taking, and in the process, I am favoring jobs. And that's what it's all about. I'm committed to government policies that will allow business to invest with an eye toward the long term to assure our competitive future.

In my budget, I've proposed a 13-percent increase for science and technology programs in 1990. And we intend to stay on track in our effort to double the National Science Foundation budget by 1993; to develop engineering and scientific computing research centers; and to build the right links between university, government, and these industry labs. We're recommending a permanent extension of that R&E—research and experimentation tax credit, to keep us at the forefront of technological innovation, especially when it comes to basic research. And we want to encourage more domestic research by multinationals by stabilizing the R&E expense allocation rules. The uncertainty brought on by expiring temporary rules has gone on for two decades—hard to plan when you don't know what the rules of the ballgame are. Businesses should be able to make long-term research plans in a stable climate. And because of the tremendous taxing power of the Government, creating that climate is something government can, should and will do.

We're determined to bring down this budget deficit with my pledge on no new taxes. And we've proposed a major budget reform to put our fiscal policy on a sound footing once and for all. We need to do away with this wonderland concept of current services budgeting—a land of expanding baselines, where programs are assumed immortal, and cuts are actually increases. Federal policy should not start out with the presumption that the Government spending should go up and up and up.

Senator Rudman—I was riding with him the other day, and he described the Washington wonderland very well. He said, "Washington is the only city where I've ever seen—for a fellow who's making $20,000, goes to his boss, asks for a $10,000 raise. The boss says, 'No, you can have a $5,000 raise.' And the story says, Man Gets $5,000 Cut." [*Laughter*] And that's the way you look at it now in terms of these programs. But the most important investment that we can make to assure this competitive future is in training and education. Jobs are becoming more demanding. You all know that. The competition is getting tougher. Labor markets are getting tighter. So, we'll need to do more to develop a highly skilled, highly motivated, highly educated work force.

You know, when I was in the oil business, we invested heavily—my little company—in what was then a new technology—offshore drilling. That was back in the mid-fifties—brand new technologies coming out. And early on—I'll never forget it—we had three drilling rigs. And a hurricane came up in the Gulf of Mexico, and it just wiped out a brand-new—in those days $6 million, today I think the same thing would cost about $80 million—piece of drilling equipment. It was gone. I've never looked for something so hard that my eyeballs actually ached. [*Laughter*] And they really did. And we went out, and this piece of equipment was totally vanished, not a trace of it, one-third of our assets. And I knew that whenever you consider an investment you rightly tend to focus on the risks that are involved. But technology moved forward, and now the risks are much less. Where training and education are concerned, the biggest risk is not to get involved.

American public education needs more of our support. All of us—teachers, parents, administrators, local officials and, yes, private industry—all of us have a responsibility to ensure that our educational system is second to none. We should look to the vitality of our system and work to build strength through diversity. Successful schools happen everywhere, from rural communities to inner city neighborhoods. And they're shaped by people with high expectations, from both the public and private sector, who work within the schools to bring about the needed improvements. And this way of looking at it means that we are all accountable for the quality of our schools.

We need to strengthen incentives to do better, and we have a mandate to do just exactly that. I want to expand Head Start, reward schools that improve, recognize outstanding teachers right here in the White House. We're going to establish a National Science Scholars Program. We're going to work to free our schools—we've got to, all of us—from the pestilence of drugs. And we're going to be looking to you for help and guidance because good schools are good for business. Many of you are already involved with your own local schools, doing important work for the future of your communities and your country. But my pitch: More can be done. More must be done. And I know you'll be there when your community, your State, your country really needs you.

To compete successfully abroad, many of you will find yourselves competing for workers at home. I know managers who are seriously starting to worry about shortages of talented people. And there is a larger, untapped source of talent in this country. Such people are to be found and fostered among the young and the underskilled, who need training; the older and more experienced, who need retraining; the disadvantaged, whose lives can be turned to advantage; disabled workers, who ask only for a chance to prove their ability; dual career families, who need options. Opportunity doesn't necessarily knock on the door. It may be leaning against the wall or standing on the street corner, needing only to be seen for what it is. And in this, we need your leadership. The very heart of our ability to compete may depend on how well we enlist those who have, until now, been on the outskirts of economic growth. They will be needed.

Together, we can build businesses that outwit, outmaneuver, outproduce, and outperform the competition. We can achieve the kind of competitive advantage that comes from collective will. And we can make sure that the words "Made in the United States of America" simply mean the best that there is.

So, thank you very much for coming here today. I hope this will be the first of several visits that we have right here in the White House with this group, a group that I deem very, very important to the future of the United States of America. Thank you all, and God bless you, and thanks for coming.

Note: The President spoke at 2:41 p.m. in the East Room at the White House.

Letter to the Speaker of the House of Representatives and the Chairman of the Senate Foreign Relations Committee Reporting on the Cyprus Conflict
March 1, 1989

Dear Mr. Speaker: (Dear Mr. Chairman:)

In accordance with Public Law 95–384, I am submitting to you this bimonthly report on progress toward a negotiated settlement of the Cyprus question.

At this early point in my Administration, let me first reconfirm that the United States has a fundamental interest in assisting the people of Cyprus in the search for a lasting and just settlement. Over the years, American governments have come to appreciate that such a settlement can come only through a process of negotiation that expresses the desires and aspirations of the Cypriot people.

At the same time, there is a legitimate role for outside parties to play in supporting this negotiation process. Under my Administration, we will continue high-level attention to Cyprus. To assure day-to-day senior officer involvement with the issues and provide a point of contact with the Congress, the Department of State created the post of Special Cyprus Coordinator in 1981 and has assigned this responsibility continuously to a policy-level officer since that time.

To provide a basic framework for negotiations between the two communities, the best and most viable approach has been and continues to be the effort led by the Secretary General of the United Nations, Javier Perez de Cuellar. The United Nations has been involved with the Cyprus question for 24 years because the international community has recognized that the United Nations is uniquely placed to deal with the issue. The current Secretary General, Javier Perez de Cuellar, has considerable personal experience with the Cyprus question and a mandate from the U.N. membership to use his good offices to work for a solution. We share this high regard for his patience and abilities, have given him unwavering support, and will continue to do so.

We will take every advantage of opportunities to make constructive contributions to the Secretary General and to the parties. We believe it is important that the parties give full participation to the negotiating process and that the atmosphere between them be improved through contacts and confidence-building measures to help bring the two communities together. We also support efforts to achieve a workable plan for reducing military tensions.

We will continue to develop our longstanding relationships of confidence and respect with both parties to the dispute. The previous Administration also consulted frequently with allies and friends, particularly such interested parties as Greece, Turkey, and the United Kingdom. We plan to pursue such consultations and discussions vigorously.

With specific reference to the most recent 60-day period since the last report on Cyprus, Secretary General Perez de Cuellar continues his efforts to help the Cypriot parties reach a solution to the conflict. As agreed at the November 22–23 New York meetings hosted by the Secretary General, the two sides initiated a second round of talks in Nicosia on December 19 with the assistance of the Secretary General's Special Representative, Oscar Camilion. Discussions in Nicosia are continuing and will be followed by another meeting in April with the Secretary General to review progress.

In his latest report to the Security Council on U.N. operations in Cyprus (for the period June 1 through November 30), a copy of which is attached, the Secretary General observed that the talks that began last August mark "the first time in the past quarter of a century that the leaders of the two communities have committed themselves to such a personal and sustained effort to achieve an overall settlement and to endeavor to do this by a specific target date." He continued that a "good working relationship" had developed between the two leaders. The Secretary General also suggested that the two sides should begin exploring "a wide range of options for each of the issues that must be resolved."

Both sides responded to the Secretary General's suggestion with proposals. There are constructive elements in the ideas presented by both parties, and we hope that they will continue to examine new and/or expanded options in a spirit of constructive compromise.

I note that military deconfrontation is the subject of one of the papers presented by the Turkish Cypriot community and that both sides have indicated agreement in principle with the concept.

The Secretary General expressed concern that the "troops of both sides continue to be in dangerous proximity to each other" in Nicosia. Such proximity was the immediate cause of the death of a Turkish Cypriot soldier on December 12, 1988, and a Greek Cypriot National Guardsman on July 31, 1988, both killed by gunfire from the opposite side of the buffer zone. The United Nations is now working with the two parties to achieve some adjustments of military positions in Nicosia to ease this situation. We strongly support this effort as we have supported past efforts to reduce tensions and prevent further serious incidents.

The Secretary General's previous report also commented on the dangers of demonstrations close to the buffer zone. In his most recent report, he states that, in response to the expression of U.N. concerns about these events, the Government of Cyprus has given assurances that "it will in future do whatever is necessary to ensure respect for the status quo in the buffer zone."

As we enter 1989, peoples worldwide are reaching out for the wisdom to forge new understanding with old foes. Experience has given the people of Cyprus an intimate appreciation of the cost of bitterness and enmity. They are now engaged in a difficult negotiation that is the only route to reconciliation and peace. They merit America's continued support and have our most sincere wishes of success in their endeavor.

Sincerely,

GEORGE BUSH

Note: Identical letters were sent to Jim Wright, Speaker of the House of Representatives, and Claiborne Pell, chairman of the Senate Foreign Relations Committee.

Message to the Congress Transmitting a Report on the Establishment of the National Space Council

February 1, 1989

To the Congress of the United States:

I hereby transmit my report outlining the composition and functions of the National Space Council to be established by Executive order.

1. Composition. The National Space Council will be composed of the following members:

1. The Vice President
2. Secretary of State
3. Secretary of Defense
4. Secretary of Commerce
5. Secretary of Transportation
6. Director of the Office of Management and Budget
7. Chief of Staff to the President
8. Assistant to the President for National Security Affairs
9. Director of Central Intelligence
10. Administrator of the National Aeronautics and Space Administration

The Chairman of the Joint Chiefs of Staff, Assistant to the President for Science and Technology, heads of other Executive Departments and agencies, and other senior officials in the Executive Office of the President shall participate in meetings of the Council as appropriate.

The Council will be chaired by the Vice President. The Council will meet subject to the call of the Vice President.

The Vice President may authorize the Executive Secretary of the Council to establish such Council Working Groups, composed of senior designees of the above members and chaired by the Executive Secretary, or another official, as may be appropriate.

2. Functions. The National Space Council will oversee the implementation of the objectives of the President's national space policy and be the principal forum for coordination of U.S. national space policy and related issues. The Space Council will also review and recommend modifications of national space policy to the President where deemed necessary or appropriate. The Council will address major space and space-related policy issues in the two governmental sectors (civil and national security), as well as those policy issues involving the third, nongovernmental sector (commercial) that are affected by Government actions.

The Council will provide a means to foster close coordination, cooperation, and technology and information exchange among the sectors to avoid unnecessary duplication and to advance our national security, scientific, technological, economic, and foreign policy interests through the exploration and use of space.

GEORGE BUSH

The White House,
March 1, 1989.

Appointment of Mark Albrecht as Director of the National Space Council
March 1, 1989

The President today announced his intention to appoint Dr. Mark Albrecht as the Director of the staff of the National Space Council, which is to be created by Executive order.

Since 1982 Dr. Albrecht has been national security adviser to United States Senator Peter Wilson (R-CA), a member of the Senate Armed Services Committee. Prior to this he was with Science Applications, Inc., serving in various capacities, including deputy program manager of a major research effort on national command authority crisis management, 1981–1982, and senior policy analyst, 1980–1981. He was a senior research analyst for the Director of Central Intelligence in Washington, DC, 1978–1980. Dr. Albrecht was a member of the Rand Graduate Institute for Public Policy Analysis at the Rand Corp., 1972–1978, earning a Ph.D. in public policy analysis, 1978.

Dr. Albrecht graduated from the University of California at Los Angeles (B.A., 1971; M.A., 1972). He is married, has three children, and resides in Falls Church, VA.

Nomination of William Pelham Barr To Be an Assistant Attorney General
March 2, 1989

The President today announced his intention to nominate William Pelham Barr to be an Assistant Attorney General (Office of Legal Counsel). He would succeed Douglas W. Kmiec.

Since 1985 Mr. Barr has been a partner with the law firm of Shaw, Pittman, Potts & Trowbridge in Washington, DC, and an associate, 1983–1985. Prior to this he was Deputy Assistant Director for Legal Policy in the Office of Policy Development at the White House, 1982–1983. He was an associate with Shaw, Pittman, Potts & Trowbridge, 1978–1982; and a law clerk to the Honorable Malcolm Richard Wilkey, U.S. circuit judge, 1977–1978. From 1973 to 1977, Mr. Barr was a member of the Central Intelligence Agency in Washington, DC.

Mr. Barr graduated from Columbia University (B.A., 1971; M.A., 1973) and George Washington University National Law Center (J.D., 1977). He was born May 23, 1950, in New York City. He is married and has three children.

Remarks at a Reception for Participants in the National Endowment for the Humanities Teacher-Scholar Program
March 2, 1989

Almost everybody here is a teacher. I was coming through the line, and who was it from Tennessee spoke to me? Right there. [*Laughter*] And we started comparing notes, and she says, "Well, I'm a country music fan." And I said, "So am I. Guess who's staying with us in the White House?" And I said, "Crystal Gayle." And she said, "I don't believe it." So, I'm going to ask Crystal to stand up, and if any of the rest of you—[*applause*].

So, that is the last of our formal introductions. And I just wanted to say that I'm flattered to be in the company of the most accomplished members of a most important profession. And I know Barbara is, too. And without you, our links to the past and our vision for the future—all that we are, all that we've accomplished, all that we would be—would lay dormant in the minds of our kids. And I thank you for your dedication.

As you know, I've just come back from a long trip with Barbara to the Far East—Japan and China and Korea. And let me tell you, as fascinating as it is to travel, it's nice to be back in the States. And I think you'll like Baltimore; it's wonderful here. [*Laughter*] I'm a little jetlagged still. We're recovering.

But it was a vital trip, and it has laid the future for our future relations with our friends and our allies. In Japan, as all of you know, I saw a nation that has risen in 40 years from a postwar destruction to becoming a leading economic power. And I think it was right that the President of the United States pay our respects to the present and to the future by going there to the funeral of the late Emperor. In the Republic of Korea, I saw an industrial power just beginning to explore the measure of its future greatness. It's exciting what's happening there. And in China, where Barbara and I lived 14 years ago for a year and a half or so—just let me say that there have been spectacular changes in China since I represented our country there in Beijing, amazing.

In each of these countries, education has been an important ingredient for economic success. And our educational system has an equally critical role to play in ensuring the intellectual creativity, the economic opportunity, and the basic freedoms of our next generation. American teachers have a big job, and, I'd say, even a bigger responsibility. To educate the children of such a vast, diverse nation as ours requires men and women of talent and dedication to our children and the teaching profession both.

You in this room exemplify the kind of teachers that we need nationally, our very best. And as I read about the many subjects that you'll be studying next fall, I had two feelings: one, respect, and the other, delight that I'd already graduated—[*laughter*]—Shakespeare, Chinese literature, Hispanic literature, the Harlem renaissance, American Indian culture. And I realize that together you encompass the diversity of America. And that diversity gives our nation and our educational system a vibrance of spirit—

[*At this point, the President was interrupted by a crying baby.*]

That kid's making me feel at home. [*Laughter*] You should have seen it when we had our 10 grandchildren playing around this place the day we came in here. But anyway, that vibrance has produced men and women with inquisitive minds, dogged determination, and big dreams. And I'm sure you recall that I made a pledge during the campaign to become the education President, to try hard in this field. And I'm pleased to see Larry Cavazos here, our distinguished Secretary of Education, from whom I expect to learn a lot, but certainly who shares our commitment to educational excellence. And it's a pledge that I made that I intend to keep by working with you and thousands like you in classrooms from Connecticut to California.

You and I know that education is our most enduring legacy. You and I know that education is nothing less than the very heart of our civilization. And that's why I am bound and determined to use this office as a bully pulpit for progress in our schools. I'll make a renewed push for a shift in some of our priorities to concentrate resources on those who need help the most.

This nation grew into greatness because early Americans understood the value of education. In the one-room schoolhouse and the land-grant college—these were the crowning achievements of the pioneers. No less important were the urban pioneers who schooled the children of the ghettos. The challenge that faced our ancestors was not an easy one: to build a national public educational system from scratch. But they did it with blood, sweat, tears, and, always, joy. They were dedicated individuals whose traditions have come full circle in each of you here today.

With the dawn of a new century only 11 short years away, we're faced with a new challenge: to revitalize and restore the system our forebears bequeathed to us, to ensure that American education is second to none. And I've made a number of proposals to work toward this goal. Among them is my request to reward those schools whose students show measurable progress in educational achievement while maintaining a safe and drug-free environment. I've also asked for an annual fund of $100 million in new appropriations to help create magnet schools to broaden the educational choice of parents and students. And yet another one of our proposals is to allot a special $60 million fund over 4 years to develop endowments of historically black colleges and universities through a matching grant program. And during the coming weeks, I'll transmit comprehensive legislation to the Congress detailing our proposals and asking for cooperation in strengthening American education.

Today I want to single out one other aspect of my educational program, and that is rewarding the brightest and the most motivated teachers. Teachers don't choose their professions certainly because of financial reward. That has got to be the classic understatement of the day. [*Laughter*] But you know it, and I know it, and the Nation knows it. And there are too many other ways to make a living, and some might say even a better living. But teachers enjoy the immense satisfaction of raising the sights of the next generation. And their work makes our horizons longer and certainly our futures brighter. I consider one proposal to be critically important: the President's Award for Excellence in Education. This award combines the recognition of your profession and the respect of your colleagues with financial reward, an idea whose time has come.

With this in mind, I've proposed $7.6 million to be spent as $5,000 cash awards to top teachers in every State. Eligible teachers will be selected from all subjects and every grade level. I hope that this teacher's award program keeps all levels of our educational system focused on the need to show good teachers that we appreciate their dedication. I realize in something as large as our own national school system across this country that this may not seem tremendous. But I do think it's a good beginning to recognize and pay our respects in this manner to excellence.

Of course—and you know this and I certainly know it—public funds are tight at all levels of government. And as we develop new ways to reward and keep good teachers, we must also look to combine the resources of the public and private sectors. And this is precisely what the NEH-Reader's Digest Teacher-Scholar Program accomplishes. And I salute those people with vision who have created and are implementing this program.

I'm very grateful to our friend, Lynne Cheney, who's here, of NEH, and for all they've done. And I want to thank George Grune, to ask him to convey my gratitude and admirations to those who had the foresight to contribute to this effort. In making this grant, you've planted the seeds of literacy, and the learning curve as well, that will benefit our country for generations to come. And if it's of any collateral interest, you've sure made the First Lady, Barbara Bush, very, very happy because she is specializing in trying to help everybody in this room in raising our awareness as to how it would be very good if we could become a literate nation, battling against the functional illiteracy that is too widespread today.

But together, these two organizations have rewarded you with the most precious gift that can be bestowed on the teachers: time—time away from the report cards, library fines, hall passes; time to learn, to master a subject; time to write, hopefully publish; time to meditate, and just plain time to think. And so many will benefit. What you'll learn and accomplish and pass on to our children will ripple across the years like a stone across a still pond. And in perusing the list of your projects, my eye settled on one in particular, a project proposed by Barbara Whittaker, of Traverse City, Michigan, entitled, "The Origin of the American Dream and Its Development in Literature." I am sure Barbara will reveal deep insights into the American novel, but there's a larger point. I believe we can trace the origin of the American dream to a very ordinary place: It can be found between the hours of 8 a.m. and 3 p.m. in every classroom, in every city, and in every town in America.

And so, for all that you do, you have my highest respect, my gratitude, and in this instance, my sincerest congratulations. Thank you all for coming to the White House. God bless you all. Thank you.

Note: The President spoke at 3:10 p.m. in the East Room at the White House. In his remarks, he referred to Lynne V. Cheney, Chairman of the National Endowment for the Humanities, and George Grune, chief executive officer of the Reader's Digest.

Remarks on Drug Trafficking Prior to a Luncheon With Administration Officials
March 3, 1989

Let me just say this: We are gathered here, and we're going in to lunch in a minute. Thus, I will refer any questions to my able Press Secretary Marlin Fitzwater.

But the purpose of this luncheon is to really talk with the top people in our government interested in narcotics—Bill Bennett, who has gone beautifully through the hearings; Attorney General; Secretary of State; General Counsel; and national security adviser—about drugs and then give a proper send-off to Dick Thornburgh, who will be doing in South America that which he did in Europe: going, emphasizing the importance we place on the international fight against drugs, coming back, and reporting to me. And obviously, at my side will be our new drug czar—by then, hopefully, in office—Bill Bennett. And we will be formulating our drug plan, and the findings of the Attorney General will be cranked into it. And it's Colombia, Bolivia, and Peru. We go not in anger, but we go to ask for their total cooperation and support. And I'm confident that this mission of the Attorney General will be fruitful. But it will show dramatically, I think, the feeling of the American people transcends politics—the American people's determination to cooperate in a way that will reduce the flow of drugs into this country, and to help them with their problems. You know, Dick, that's a part of this. I mean, these countries that thought this was the rich consumers in the north, the only ones that had the problem, have realized that it is decimating their own economies and their own stability.

So, it's an important trip, and then when he gets back—with Bill Bennett—we'll be talking about not only the international implications but how that will fit into the overall drug plan. So, bon voyage, and have a good trip. And my respects to the Presidents you'll be meeting with and the various ministers you'll be seeing.

Note: The President spoke at 12:12 p.m. in the Oval Office at the White House. In his remarks, he referred to William J. Bennett, Director-designate of National Drug Control Policy; Attorney General Richard L. Thornburgh; Secretary of State James A. Baker III; C. Boyden Gray, Counsel to the President; and Brent Scowcroft, Assistant to the President for National Security Affairs.

Remarks to the Winners of the Westinghouse Science Talent Search
March 3, 1989

Thank you, Mr. Marous, and all of what you at Westinghouse do for this outstanding concept. Doctor Press—last time I saw Frank Press—maybe it wasn't the last time, but he'd just received an honorary degree at a graduation ceremony where there were 50,000 people present, at Ohio State University—well-deserved honor, that he well deserved, as a matter of fact, for prestige he's given to science in this country. And when he salutes a group like this, why, it makes a big impression on me as well.

I want to thank you all, Dr. Seaborg, whose reputation is well-known to everybody here, and John as well, for explaining some of the exhibits to me. [*Laughter*] I had done a lot in the field of the viability of MVM Parvo Virus. [*Laughter*] And then at night I like to curl up with a book on mapping mutants. [*Laughter*] And every once in a while, when I have some spare time, Barbara and I read aloud about the behavior of the inhibitions of sialidases. [*Laughter*] So, we have a lot in common with these researchers here. [*Laughter*] But I'll tell you, I'm glad there's no quiz. [*Laughter*]

And I am so impressed, and I expect everybody here has had a chance to look at these studies. And I'll tell you, it just reaffirms your basic faith in the young people of this country and, I'd say also, in the academic process. Yesterday we saluted some teachers over at the White House, and boy, I wish I'd seen this before I'd been over there to pay my respects to the teachers who help these young minds.

But really, what all of you have accomplished is really something to be proud of. Not only is it a great achievement but you really earned these honors. Thomas Edison said that genius is 1 percent inspiration and 99 percent perspiration. Well, each of you, with your academic diligence and your intellect and a lot of hard work, have won the oldest and largest national high school competition in the entire country. And past winners of the Westinghouse Talent Search have distinguished themselves in every field of science and mathematics. And your predecessors have received every major honor and award in their fields, including the Nobel Prize and the National Medal of Science. And what you've done is important for America. Scientific and technological advancement have always been at the very heart of our nation's pioneer spirit, pushing the boundaries of our knowledge, creating economic opportunity, and certainly increasing our standard of living and making this a healthier and safer world in which to live.

It is scientific advancements that made us aware of the damage to our Earth's protective ozone layer and the need to reduce CFC's [chlorofluorocarbons] that deplete our precious upper atmospheric resources. As a result of these advances, the United States and other nations have led the way, through the Montreal protocol, toward reductions of CFC's. And that protocol will reduce CFC's to 50 percent of 1986 levels by the year 1998. But recent studies indicate that this 50-percent reduction may not be enough. And I thought some of you interested in that field might like to know that I today asked Bill Reilly, our new EPA Administrator, to join with other nations this weekend as he goes abroad in supporting the call for the elimination of CFC's by the year 2000, provided, you know, that safe substitutes are available. And of course, such a phaseout must be guided by the scientific, economic, and technological assessments under the protocol.

As a nation, we have no natural resource more precious than our intellectual resources. In fact, it's only thanks to human knowledge and ingenuity that crude oil became a valuable fuel and that fields of grain become methanol or that grains of sand become silicon chips. Scientific knowledge must be renewed and expanded in each generation. Many of the miracles that we take for granted in everyday life originated in defense and space research. This investment in new technologies and new plant and equipment helps expand our competitive edge as a nation, and thereby assuring future opportunities for America's next generation in science, engineering, and manufacturing. But for our country to maintain its technological and scientific excellence, no investment in machines or laboratories, as vital as that may be, will by itself be sufficient. There have to be the people who have the knowledge and the commitment, and that will be men and women like yourselves who will lead America into the next century.

You know, by one estimate, it takes 10,000 high school students expressing an interest in a science or engineering major to assure us of 20 men and women who will go on to receive doctorate degrees. And I hope that each student in this room gets a doctorate or pursues a career of one kind or another in science and technology and that some of you consider returning to the classroom as teachers to inspire a new generation of scientists for the future. The fruits of investing in science and scientists are evident. Human intelligence has explored the vastness of outer space and the inner frontiers of the particles of the atom. Diseases have been cured. Knowledge has been harnessed. And energy—I was going to say that energy has been created, but then I remembered the laws of thermodynamics. So, let's just call it a wash—[*laughter*]—and say that energy has neither been created nor destroyed. [*Laughter*] And please don't debate me on that, Glenn. [*Laughter*]

But we truly have seen the scientific knowledge developed in the United States vastly improve the lives of our citizens and of people around the world. And today international scientists and science students are coming here to America to do research, to study, to teach. And this is something that our country greatly benefits from. Yet, still, as a nation, let's face it, we've got to do better. We're not producing enough scientists and mathematicians and engineers. American universities confer only about 77,000 engineering degrees a year at the undergraduate level. And that's about the same number that Japan produces with a total population of only half our size.

Initiatives from Washington are important, but they're not enough. Students and parents and teachers will determine the direction our young people take and, ultimately, what direction, therefore, that our country takes. And there's only one goal that is worthy of us as Americans, and that is to be the very best in the world, to be number one. That's our history, but it is also, I believe, our destiny. Our national qualities of intellectual curiosity and innovation, our frontier spirit and our habit of problemsolving, all uniquely equip America for the great technological age that is dawning.

To help us move in that direction, the Federal budget I propose would, as Frank said, increase funding for—maybe he didn't cover this point—but for NASA [National Aeronautics and Space Administration] by 22 percent, would also advance us toward our goal of doubling the budget for the National Science Foundation by 1993. I also proposed full funding for the superconducting supercollider—and even though I'm from Texas, people seem to understand—[*laughter*]—and as an incentive for private industry, a permanent research and experimentation tax credit.

But one of the most important investments that I want us to make is in science education. So, I have proposed a National Science Scholars Program that would provide 570 scholarships a year. And these would be for up to $10,000 a year, for 4 years. And this program would be based on merit, and it would draw at least one young scientist from every congressional district—435 across the entire United States—providing local inspiration and national leadership for the study of science. And I think no one proves better than all of you just how much our students are capable of and how important it is to provide the encouragement and resources that you need. And when you couple this modest Federal effort with what Westinghouse and others are doing in this area across the country, we do have something significant and, I'd say, unique in our country.

So, I came over here to congratulate the sponsors, to congratulate the scientists who have given their blessing to this innovative program, and especially to congratulate all of you achievers. I think all of you are destined for great things. And if you've got any skeptics out in the audience, go next door and take a look, and you'll see exactly what I mean. Thank you, and God bless all of you.

Note: The President spoke at 2:20 p.m. at the National Academy of Sciences Building. In his opening remarks, he referred to John C. Morous, Jr., chairman and chief executive officer of Westinghouse Corp.; Frank Press, president of the National Academy of Sciences; and Glenn Theodore Seaborg, chemist and Nobel Prize winner.

Statement on the Labor Dispute Between Eastern Airlines and the International Association of Machinists and Aerospace Workers

March 3, 1989

The National Mediation Board has recommended that I appoint an emergency board before March 4, pursuant to section 10 of the Railway Labor Act, as amended, to investigate the dispute between Eastern Airlines and the International Association of Machinists and Aerospace Workers. I have decided not to accept this recommendation.

The National Mediation Board has for many months attempted unsuccessfully to bring the parties to an agreement, and I have no reason to believe that an additional investigation or the 60-day delay that would be entailed would produce such an agreement. In light of the well-publicized threats of a strike and related activities, the Department of Transportation will monitor the situation and will, in addition, take whatever steps are needed to protect the safety of the traveling public.

I urge responsible labor officials not to try to influence resolution of this dispute by disrupting the Nation's transportation systems through secondary boycotts against uninvolved parties. Such boycotts would unfairly burden millions of citizens, not only preventing necessary travel but also affecting shipment of consumer goods and the ability of many workers to earn a living. For these reasons, secondary boycotts are not permitted in any other sector of the economy.

Accordingly, if secondary boycotts threaten to disrupt essential transportation services, I will submit, and urge that Congress promptly enact, legislation making it unlawful to use secondary picketing and boycotts against neutral carriers. We cannot allow an isolated labor-management dispute to disrupt the Nation's entire transportation system.

Remarks at the Annual Conference of the Veterans of Foreign Wars

March 6, 1989

Well, thank you very much, Larry. I remember when Larry Rivers first took over. I was Vice President—came in to greet me. I wasn't sure he knew what he was getting into. But he's holding up real well—[*laughter*]—and doing a first-class job, and you're lucky to have this dynamic young man as your leader.

You know, it's a pleasure to be here. I also want to express my best wishes to a real institution of the VFW; you know who I'm talking about—Cooper Holt. I can't believe it, I can't believe that he's stepping down this year, after more than a quarter of a century of distinguished service as the executive director. But let me tell you something: Members of the VFW—others who stand for a strong defense, whoever they may be—Cooper has earned the gratitude of veterans everywhere for making the VFW his life-long cause, but also the way he has conducted himself in Washington and elsewhere in this high office. He has my respect and my friendship, and I don't know what it's going to be like without him around here, I'll tell you.

I want to pay my respects to General Al Gray, member of the Joint Chiefs of Staff, a Commandant of the Marine Corps, outstanding soldier—outstanding marine, I should say. Sorry, Al. [*Laughter*] Really know how to hurt a guy, but—[*laughter*]—an outstanding leader. And also, to my former colleague and dear friend, the veterans' friend, Congressman Sonny Montgomery, over here.

Before I begin—and I want to talk to you about two or three major issues—but before I begin, let me just say a word about an issue that is of particular importance, I'd say, to the people in this room. You know John Tower as a fellow veteran, and you know him as a lifelong public servant. And you also know him as a fighter. And he's fought for his country as a 17-year-old enlisted man in the United States Navy. And now he and I are fighting for what I think are some very important principles, principles that the American people understand, like fairness and truth, and principles like the prerogative of a President of the United States to assemble the most talented and qualified team to guide this nation forward.

And I have asked the Senate to vote on this nomination with those principles in mind, asked the Senate to put aside partisanship. I've asked them to use their own experience with John Tower as an expert on defense issues; as a former colleague; and as a tough, hardnosed negotiator to guide them as they move towards a vote on this nomination. It is very interesting that not one single United States Senator has challenged John Tower's knowledge on defense matters or his experience to do this job—not one single Senator.

And I stand by this man, I stand by him because he is uniquely qualified as the right man to take charge of the Pentagon. Enough of that now. [*Laughter*] I wanted to get it off my chest. I'm getting sick and tired of some of the rumors and the innuendoes that are used against this decent man. Back to the gentler and kinder message. [*Laughter*]

Look, it's always an honor to meet with fellow members of the VFW. The love of liberty is the birthright of all men, certainly all Americans, and that's why our nation owes a special debt of gratitude to its veterans, who freely and courageously took up the defense of freedom. I am especially pleased to welcome the Department of Veterans Affairs to a place in the Cabinet, and it's a cause, I might add, that you were in the lead on. And it's a sign of America's commitment to her veterans, of the importance we place in repaying in some way the sacrifice that veterans have made in answering their country's call. And in my view, it is important that the first Secretary is someone who is close to the President, who has the President's full confidence on a personal basis, and Ed Derwinski, my former colleague in Congress and my friend of longstanding, fits that description to a tee. He will be an outstanding Secretary.

Some facts: Today there are six times as many veterans alive as there were when the VA was created in 1930. Ed already has come to see me to discuss some of the challenges facing us in these programs. With the pressure the country is under—and let's make no mistake about it, the pressures are great—to solve our massive Federal deficit, we may not be able to do everything we'd like to do in the way of adding resources, but I can tell you that Ed is your strong advocate. And like me, he understands the needs, including the crying need for strong health care for the veterans. He already is an advocate for that.

I want to speak this morning about a matter of the utmost importance to the VFW—keeping America strong—today and then, just 11 years from now, into the 21st century. Opinion is nearly unanimous that today is a time of transition in world affairs. That means our powers of observation and analysis, our ability to sort out change and continuity, will be put to the test. And when it comes to predicting the future, Winston Churchill's rule is the best. It is: "I always avoid prophesying beforehand because it's much better policy to prophesy after the event has already taken place." You've got to think about that one for a while, and maybe I'm the guy to do that. Last year I told the American Legion about Pearl Harbor being on September 7th. [*Laughter*] Just think, if Franklin Roosevelt had listened to me, think what we could have spared the Nation. [*Laughter*]

You know, maybe you've read and maybe you haven't that we are in the midst of a series of systematic strategic reviews, and I've asked the members of my national security team to look hard at the international landscape and to look forward to assess the combination of security threats, technological change, and political and economic developments that will shape our security horizon well into the next century. And I am convinced that this important review, this important exercise, will have lasting benefits to our national security. In my address to Congress last month, I set a 90-day deadline for this important work. And I won't rush the final results. The insights we will gain into the problems we will face in the decades ahead are worth waiting for. And the other day I went over to the Pentagon and met with certain members of the Joint Chiefs and those running that building, and I must tell you, I'm very pleased these reviews are going forward.

But today I want to speak about the foundations of an adequate national defense program, about the world we live in, and the challenges and opportunities we'll encounter, and about the approach I'll take on issues integral to our own national security.

First, the foundations: A month ago, I presented to the Congress a sound defense spending plan that makes sense, strategically and fiscally. As a sign that my administration is serious about the deficit, I called for a freeze in defense spending in 1990, adjusted only for inflation. And I'm well aware that our national strength rests ultimately on the health and vigor of the American economy. And we need a strong defense, and we need a strong economy. And I mean to preserve both, but our crucial military modernization plans and the diverse defense commitments that we must keep cannot be achieved without additional defense funding. And that's why the budget plan follows the freeze for 1990 with real increases—albeit they're small—with real increases: 1 percent in 1991 and 1992, and a 2-percent increase for 1993. And my aim is to put defense spending on a modest, manageable growth path, one that we can afford and then one that will allow us to modernize and maintain forces that are formidable, flexible, and ready.

But in the defense debate, what we can and can't afford isn't just a matter of economics. It's a matter of vital national security. And I say we can't afford to continue the downward trend in defense spending. 1989—now listen carefully to this—1989 will be the fourth straight year that budget authority for defense has declined in real terms. And we've worked hard to rebuild America's strength, and it's paid off. Today America is strong; its voice is heard. Its forces are ready, and the values we stand for are more secure.

Secondly, we can't afford to mistake a more stable international environment as proof that we can spend less on national defense. The secret to our success can be summed up in a single word: strength. And let's sustain the military strength that helped turn the world situation around.

And finally, we can afford adequate defenses. The defense budget that I'm calling for in 1990 represents 5.5 percent of our annual gross national product. And that's a far smaller share of our national wealth than the United States spent on defense at any point throughout the 1950's or the 1960's—periods of rapid and sustained economic growth though they were. The bottom line is not a question of cost or a question of resources: It's simply a question of will. And you have my word, as long as I am President: America will stand fast on the front line in defense of freedom.

Today around the world, a number of longstanding regional conflicts are closer now to resolution than ever before. The stirrings of freedom and the advance of democratic rule are evident and undeniable. In the economic sphere, the free market is increasingly seen as an engine of growth and development unmatched by any other system. And freedom is on the march. But there are still forces arrayed against it, regimes whose interests and systems are at odds with our own and with those of our allies. And then there's the spread of chemical and biological weapons, along with the means to deliver them. It's likely to make the flashpoints that always exist more dangerous than ever before.

And the key issue of change within the Soviet Union—there are still far more questions than answers. There is no doubt that the changes taking place are significant and far-reaching, but it is equally true that the ultimate outcome of the events unfolding in the U.S.S.R. remains certain [uncertain]. My view is this: We should press for progress that contributes to a more stable relationship between the United States and the Soviet Union, but we must combine our readiness to build better relations with a resolve to maintain defenses adequate to secure our interests.

America and her allies must recognize that even in light of the military cuts proposed by President Gorbachev the Soviet Union remains the most formidable military power facing the free world. We must be ready to cope with change and favorable opportunities and ready in any event to defend our interests and ideals. And what this means in terms of our national security should be clear. We need to maintain and modernize our forces, nuclear and conventional. For America and its allies, a survivable nuclear force will remain the ultimate deterrent of aggression.

We need to make a concerted effort to turn our technological strengths into a source of advantage to our national security. And that includes, in my view, vigorous pursuit of the Strategic Defense Initiative.

And we need to make an active effort in arms control, to strive for increased stability at lower levels of armaments. But I will strongly oppose legislative attempts to withdraw U.S. troops from Europe unilaterally. Imprudent unilateral reductions are not the path to peace and security and freedom.

And I've been listening to General Gray. We need to keep our forces ready and well-trained. The dedicated men and women who serve our country deserve no less.

We need to reform our procurement process to deliver a dollar's worth of defense for every dollar we spend. And the way to do that is to begin to follow through on the sensible reforms suggested in the Packard commission report and the findings of the defense management review now underway. I'll look carefully at those management review findings and then move to implement them.

And we need to maintain the alliance of like-minded nations in Europe and Asia that have helped us keep peace in the postwar era. As strong as we are—and we are strong—as strong as we are, the United States of America in this complex world cannot go it alone. Keep our alliances strong.

Before I close, I want to focus for a moment on a threat no less real than the adversaries you have battled. And I'm speaking about not a military threat; I'm speaking about the insidious threat to our society and our values: drug abuse. The notion that America is a nation at peace is only partly true as long as the violence and destructive power of drugs assault our communities.

As I talk, our Attorney General is holding a series of talks with three South American Presidents and their attorney generals or their ministers, seeking their full participation in this war and offering our full cooperation. My able drug czar, Bill Bennett—some of you know him, able man—he will be confirmed as my hard-hitting point man to be at my side in the White House to keep the focus on winning this unconditional war; and I mean to mobilize all our resources, wage this war on all fronts. We're going to combat drug abuse with education, treatment, enforcement and, yes, interdiction and, yes, with our nation's armed services. When that prudently can be done and when that's what it takes, we are going to have to go all-out. We need to break the deadly grip of drugs and prevent the drug scourge from taking hold.

And the VFW can help. Many of you have already started. Many of your posts are actively involved. You've got 2.3 million members, 750,000 auxiliary members, 10,000 chapters nationwide. The VFW is, and always will be, a respected member of communities across our country; and today I call on you to form a community of action. "For America, whatever it takes"—that's the motto of the VFW. And you've fought for your nation once, and your nation needs you again. And today I want to enlist you in the antidrug campaign. Meet with other leaders in your community—church, clergy, law enforcement officers—tell them the VFW volunteers are ready to help. And go to the schools and put the full weight of this magnificent organization behind the antidrug education effort that provides our kids with the reasons and willpower that they need to resist drugs. Speak to your State and local elected officials. Urge them to make the passage of strong antidrug legislation a priority.

I am reaching out to you, so I want to extend my help as well. Bill Bennett stands ready to meet with the VFW leadership to share ideas that can help you map a strategy. VFW has proven many times over its dedication to the health and well-being of our nation, proven it over and over and over again. And the 50 young people that you've honored here today, with whom I had a chance to meet very briefly a minute ago, underscore the VFW's interest in our nation's youth and in our future. I know that we can count on the veterans of America all across this country to help us wage and win the war on drugs. Your country needs you once again.

Veterans share a special bond. We've seen the face of war; we know its terrible costs. Americans never willingly choose conflict. But we know, as well, that we must be ready and willing to respond when our interests and our ideals come under threat.

Let me be very clear. I prefer the diplomatic approach. Nations can and should explore every avenue toward working out their differences without resorting to force or military intimidation, but I'm also a realist. I know that there is no substitute for a nation's ability to defend its ideals and interests. And too often we hear that we face a stark choice in coping with conflict. We can pursue a diplomatic situation, or we can seek a resolution through military means. One, we're told, is incompatible with the other.

Well, this doesn't square with real-world experience. Diplomacy and military capability are complementary; they're not contradictory. Creative diplomacy can help us avert conflict. Negotiations stand the greatest chance of success when they proceed from a position of strength. The fundamental lesson of this decade is simply this: Strength secures the peace. America will continue to be a force for peace and stability in the world provided we stay strong.

Let me close with a word to these young people, who you appropriately are honoring here today. If I were in your shoes, I'd be an optimist. I'd be an optimist about world peace, changes in the Soviet Union. As I said earlier in this talk, nobody is talking about the Socialist model or the Communist model as to a way to solve their problems. But never forget that, when a President of the United States goes to the negotiating table, the way to enhance our values, the way to enhance the principles that everybody in this room holds dear, is to be dealing from a position of a strong America. We have the ideals. Keep America strong! Thank you all, and God bless you. And good luck to you guys.

Note: The President spoke at 11:08 a.m. in the Sheraton Ballroom at the Sheraton Washington Hotel. In his remarks, he referred to Larry W. Rivers and Cooper T. Holt, national commander in chief and executive director of the Veterans of Foreign Wars, respectively; Gen. Alfred M. Gray, Commandant of the Marine Corps; Representative G.V. (Sonny) Montgomery, chairman of the Veterans' Affairs Committee; and Edward J. Derwinski, Secretary-designate of the Department of Veterans Affairs.

Message on the Observance of St. Patrick's Day, 1989
March 6, 1989

It is a pleasure to send greetings to everyone celebrating this St. Patrick's Day.

The feast of the Apostle of Ireland occupies a special place on our calendar because it is a fitting time to celebrate the vibrant heritage of millions of Irish Americans, as well as the many contributions they have made to our country. Among the first of immigrant groups, the Irish overcame poverty and prejudice to become productive members of the American workforce and an influential voice in United States politics.

Today, our Nation continues to be inspired by the deep faith, strong family life, and hard work of Irish Americans. Their legendary sense of humor and resolve are an example to us all.

Barbara joins me in commending all of you on keeping alive the joyous spirit of St. Patrick's Day. May God bless you.

GEORGE BUSH

Nomination of Anthony Joseph Principi To Be Deputy Secretary of Veterans Affairs
March 6, 1989

The President today announced his intention to nominate Anthony Joseph Principi to be Deputy Secretary of Veterans Affairs at the Veterans Administration. This is a new position.

Mr. Principi has been Republican chief counsel and staff director of the Senate Committee on Veterans' Affairs, 1984–1988. He was majority chief counsel and staff director for Senator Alan K. Simpson, 1984–1986, and Deputy Administrator for Congressional, Intergovernmental, and Public Affairs for the Veterans Administration, 1983–1984. Mr. Principi entered the United States Navy in 1967 and has served as senior staff counsel and professor of military law for the U.S. Pacific Fleet in San Diego, CA, 1978–1980, and chief defense attorney for the Naval Legal Service Office, 1975–1978.

Mr. Principi graduated from the United States Naval Academy (B.S., 1967), and Seton Hall University School of Law (J.D., 1975). He resides in Rancho Sante Fe, CA.

Nomination of Gerald L. Olson To Be an Assistant Secretary of Health and Human Services
March 6, 1989

The President today announced his intention to nominate Gerald L. Olson to be an Assistant Secretary of Health and Human Services (Legislative Affairs). He would succeed Mary T. Goedde.

Since 1978 Mr. Olson has been vice president for government relations for the Pillsbury Co., in Minneapolis, MN. Prior to this he was executive director for government and community relations at the Cummins Engine Co., 1975–1978. He was vice president and division manager for Irwin Management Company, 1971–1975, and assistant to the chairman of Cummins Engine Co., 1969–1971. Mr. Olson was special assistant and presidential campaign director for Governor Nelson A. Rockefeller, 1967–1969, and campaign manager and legislative liaison for Governor Harold LeVander, 1966–1967.

Mr. Olson graduated from Mankato State University (B.S., 1958). He was born December 3, 1933, in Sioux Falls, SD, and resides in Deephaven, MN.

Announcement of the Continuation of Roberts T. Jones as an Assistant Secretary of Labor
March 6, 1989

The President today announced that Roberts T. Jones will continue to serve as an Assistant Secretary of Labor (Employment and Training).

Mr. Jones currently serves as Assistant Secretary of Labor at the Department of Labor, 1987 to present. He was Deputy Assistant Secretary of Labor, 1985–1987, and Senior Administrator for Job Training Programs, 1972–1985. From 1968 to 1972, he served as administrative assistant for Congressman Marvin L. Esch and Congressman Charles E. Wiggins.

Mr. Jones graduated from the University

of Redlands with a bachelors degree in psychology, 1962. He was born April 24, 1940. He is married, has three children, and resides in Alexandria, VA.

The President's News Conference
March 7, 1989

The President. Well, as you know, we got canceled out of Lancaster, Pennsylvania, and Wilmington today. And so, I thought it might be an opportune moment to stay indoors, take a few questions. The Lancaster trip has been rescheduled for the 22d of March; and I look forward to going there, talking to the people, and really discussing that community participation in drugs.

I want to take this opportunity to restate my belief that free collective bargaining is the best means of resolving the dispute between Eastern Airlines and its unions. I continue to feel it would be inappropriate for the Government to intervene and to impose a solution. This dispute has gone on for more than 17 months, and it's time for the parties involved to get down to serious business and reach an agreement. The action-forcing event, in this case, is the strike. And that is the tool at the disposal of labor, and they're properly going forward with that. Management and the labor now have to find a settlement.

But let me just say that I hope my position on secondary boycotts is well-known. Thankfully, these boycotts have not yet materialized, and I hope they don't. Temporary restraining orders have been in effect yesterday and today in the New York and Philadelphia areas. But even when those restraining orders lapse, I remind all parties that secondary boycotts are not in the public interest. And I will send legislation to Congress to forbid them if that is necessary. It is not fair to say to a commuter on a train coming in from Long Island that you're going to be caught up and victimized by a strike affecting an airline—simply isn't fair, in my view.

Secretary [of Transportation] Skinner has been monitoring the situation from the very beginning—my view on top of it. The Department of Transportation and the FAA have taken every precaution to ensure airline safety during this period. And I understand that the pilots are talking about a work slowdown beginning today. Certainly, I must recognize their special concerns for safety during this period, but I also would urge them not to make the innocent traveling public a pawn in this dispute.

So, that's my view on the airline strike. And I hope that it is settled in the traditional way—management, labor sitting down and working out an agreement.

Wait a minute! We've got to go to—protocol has—sorry about that.

Administration Accomplishments

Q. Mr. President, your struggle to win the confirmation of Senator Tower and the seeming lack of direction has caused a lot of criticism that your administration is in drift, there is malaise. What is your response and what are you going to do about it?

The President. My response is that it's not adrift, and there isn't malaise. And I talked to a fellow from Lubbock, Texas, the other day, which is the best phone call I've made; and he said, "All the people in Lubbock think things are going just great." And so—and he is a very objective spokesman, a guy that—[*laughter*].

Q. Do you really think you're doing fine when nobody knows where——

The President. I think we're on track.

Q. ——and nobody knows where your administration is going——

The President. Well, let me help you with where I think it's going. First place, in a very brief period of time, we addressed ourselves to a serious national problem: the problem of the S&L bailout. That is still moving forward; it takes a little time. I've challenged the Congress to act. Secondly, we came up in a very short period of time with great amount of detail, far more than the two previous administrations, regarding the budget—sound proposals. The number one problem facing this country, in my view, is getting this Federal budget deficit down. Not only did we address it but we addressed it in considerable detail, and talks are going on right now to try to solve that problem.

I've taken a substantive foreign policy trip that took me not only to 3 countries, but where I met with, I think, some 19 representatives of 19 countries and talked about their objectives and mine for foreign policy. Our Secretary of State [James A. Baker III] has not only touched base with all the NATO leaders but has had a productive meeting with Mr. Shevardnadze [Soviet Foreign Minister]. The defense reviews and the other foreign policy reviews are underway. And I will not be stampeded by some talk that we have not come up with bold new foreign policy proposals in 45 days—not going to be.

So, I think plenty of substantive things are going on. And then I have made clear—you saw my statement on the CFC's [chlorofluorocarbons] on the environment. Our environmental man is over there, Bill Reilly [Environmental Protection Agency Administrator], a very able administrator, attending a conference that will then lead, in my view, to unilateral proposals by the United States, not in terms just of CFC's but other global environmental matters. We are confident of the confirmation of Bill Bennett, and he is charged with a 6-month's mandate to do something—map out the drug program. And he will be very serious about going forward on that.

I appointed early on an ethics commission which has been meeting and will be coming out with, I think, sound proposals. And so, we'll start moving forward legislatively there. I spelled out in my speech an education agenda, and that will be followed—the speech—very shortly with legislative initiatives. We're moving forward with our volunteer approach—the organization to pursue national service—under Gregg Petersmeyer [Deputy Assistant to the President and Director of the Office of National Service] here in the White House. Our Secretary of HUD [Jack F. Kemp] has taken some fact-finding trips and made some good comments, speeches, about our objectives in terms of the homeless.

So, I would have to urge—and everyone here is familiar with my position on child care. That's going to take legislation, but I think the Congress clearly knows where we want to go there. So, I would simply resist the clamor that nothing seems to be bubbling around, that nothing is happening. A lot is happening. Not all of it good, but a lot is happening.

Human Rights

Q. Mr. President, you mentioned your Asian trip. Now, one of the issues that arose there was kind of a disagreement or a dispute with China over a dissident attending your dinner. And it seemed that you failed to raise human rights in your meetings with Chinese leaders. Is this going to be your preference for conveying harmony rather than confrontation over human rights?

The President. No, it was raised. When Marlin spoke to you—the beginning of the trip there in China—and said it hadn't been raised, he was right. It hadn't been raised publicly in the meetings that I'd had up to that moment. I believe Deng Xiaoping was the one—where he spoke, but it was raised by me personally.

But you know, there's two schools of how you do the human rights agenda. I think that President Reagan was correct when he raised the human rights agenda with the Soviets privately rather than beating his breasts and doing it publicly. And I think the results have been rather penetrating—still a long way to go with the Soviets. But I have not only raised them, but the very invitation to that dissident, that they thoroughly disapproved of, shows our public commitment to it. And there was a reference to it in a speech. So, it all depends how you, how—in our toasts—so it all depends, you know, what approach you take. But I think quiet discussion is a good approach to try to effect the human rights objectives that I feel very strongly about.

Q. On that regard, on human rights, will it always be the first thing you mention with the Soviets, as it was under President Reagan?

The President. I don't recall it always

being the first thing. Because the last meeting I attended with him and Mr. Gorbachev, it was raised, but it wasn't the first thing. But it will be high on our agenda—I confidently expect that Jim Baker will continue to raise it. And, yes, it will be an agenda item.

Eastern Airlines Strike

Q. Mr. President, on the air strike, your opposition on Capitol Hill, many of the Democrats up there, wanted you to intervene in the strike. Should you have to go to Congress for emergency legislation to deal with secondary boycotts, it is likely they are going to say, "No, no, we want you to intervene first." If the Eastern pilots succeed and the machinists succeed in imposing secondary boycotts, you seem to be on a collision course there. Will your policy hold firm?

The President. It will hold firm. The Secretary [Samuel K. Skinner] is testifying, I think, at this very moment about the kind of legislation you're talking about and some wanting to compel the President to convene this Board. So, there are two schools of thought. I still feel that the best answer is a head-on-head, man-to-man negotiation between the union and the airline. And I think that is better and more lasting, incidentally—the agreement that would stem from that—more lasting than an imposed government settlement which could cause the airline to totally shut down. So, I think there could be some, you know, confrontation. But I will stick with my view; and if, indeed, innocent parties are threatened through the secondary boycott mechanism, I will move promptly with the Congress. And I don't want to buy into a lot of hypothesis here, but you would have an outcry from the American people on the basis of—that I mentioned about that commuter. It is not fair to, you know, have innocent people victimized by a struggle between Eastern Airlines and the machinists' union. So, there may be a closely fought contest, and I know there are some widely differing views on this.

Q. If that should happen, sir, you must recognize that there'd be great pressure on you to at least stop it for 60 days. Are you intent on not doing that?

The President. I'm intent on staying with what I've outlined is our administration's policy. And it is the correct policy. And I think it's the best way to have a solution to this question.

We'll go right across here and then start—go ahead.

Secretary of Defense-Designate Tower

Q. Mr. President, back to Helen's [Helen Thomas, United Press International] question, this sort of sense that's developing that—let's say the John Tower fight is sapping you of your ability to get on with other issues. How long are you willing to fight this fight, let the debate go on? Are you ready to now call for them to have a vote, say, today or tomorrow, just to get this behind you, one way or the other?

The President. No, no, because Lesley [Lesley Stahl, CBS News], first place, there's two major principles: fairplay and, secondly, the right of the President to have—historical right—to have who he wants in his administration. And I've heard a lot of judgments on Tower based on reports—hearing people reading the same report and coming out with different judgments. I want him. I believe he is the best man for the job. There are a lot of historical precedents behind my desire to have him and, you might say, right to have him, barring any very clear reason not to; and therefore, I will stay with it. And secondly, it's the Senate that controls when they vote or not. And I will leave that to Bob Dole and George Mitchell, both of whom I think are conducting themselves very well.

There's a followup. Yes?

Q. May I ask you a question about the chain-of-command question? Because the Senator admits to excessive drinking, which would disqualify him for a job in the so-called chain of command, does this not disturb you at all that that's the qualification for a job?

The President. No, I think he'll measure up to that qualification. Indeed, he has said he'd never touch another drop of liquor, and you'll have 25,000 people in the Pentagon making sure that's true. So, what I mean, here's a, I'd say, a fail-safe guarantee. Doesn't bother me. And I——

Q. The past?

The President. No, I think when you look at the record and look at the testimony as I have—and I haven't had one single Senator, not one, served with him over the years, say, I have seen him, my firsthand evidence is, this man is ineligible because of his consumption of spirits—not one. And isn't that a little bit unusual? So, I go right back to the President's right to have his choice. Let's keep it on a nonpartisan basis. I would just urge that both Senator Nunn and George Mitchell have told me, "Wait a minute, this isn't a partisan fight." And I would simply ask that they keep reiterating that to those Senators who may not have made up their minds with finality and let's go to a vote. But I'm not going to pull back on this.

And, Lesley, it isn't iron-willed stubbornness. There's a question of fundamental principle here. And I've spelled out my call for fairplay, and I'm going to keep reiterating it. So, let the Senate work its will; it's not going to hurt. And this concept that you can never work in the future because people disagree with you in the Senate—I simply don't accept that.

Q. Mr. President, you have said that the FBI report guns down the accusations against Senator Tower. And yet you have also said that there can be no release in practical terms because of the confidentiality of people interviewed. Had you given consideration, given the problem with the nomination, to asking those interviewed to waive the right of confidentiality so that the public doesn't have to take your word for it as to the degree to which this report exonerates the Senator or the opponent?

The President. Or the word of the opponents? Yes, we have thought about that. And I'm not sure where our Counsel's office stands on it. But I'll tell you that the precedent is troubling. When you take testimony and then—and certainly you can't go ahead and release—I mean, I just could not do that. And I think it's very damaging in the future. So, I'm saying I have read it; this is my view. And it's inhibiting because it does confine the debate on the floor. But I really worry about the precedent. So, I have not been pushing for sanitization and then release, or for selective release, or for—I hadn't thought about this concept of going to somebody and say, "Would you release us from confidentiality?" I think that would chill future proceedings.

Let's go back in the back. We're not—right in the middle back there.

Department of Defense Review

Q. Mr. President, you mentioned yesterday in the speech to the VFW that this 90-day deadline that you had imposed on yourself for the strategic review might slip because you said that the results wouldn't be rushed. Is there going to be a new deadline? And is the fact that you don't have a sitting Defense Secretary contributing to that?

The President. I hope there's not going to be any slippage. I want that; I want the budget review. I want the management review completed by then. And look, not having a Defense Secretary in place—no question that it's an inhibiting factor. But I went over to the bureau the other day, I mean the Defense Department, in a trip that was interpreted for one purpose; and what I went over, really, for was another purpose. And the purpose I went over there for was—please, understand we've got to keep these reviews going forward. And I am very grateful to those people, some of whom won't be there in a new administration, all of whom—or most of whom had served in the past administration, for seriously addressing themselves to these various reviews. I hope we can make the target. The minute the target is made and the review comes, then we have a lot of decisionmaking. But I don't want to be foot-dragging. And therefore, I'm going to try to keep the heat on without slippage there.

Eastern Airlines Strike

Q. The head of Eastern Airlines, Frank Lorenzo, is from Houston, Texas. Is he a friend of yours? Did he give money to your campaign? And one of his vice presidents is on your staff as head of congressional relations. Is he giving you advice?

The President. He has recused himself, as I understand it, from the Eastern Airlines; and he's not giving me advice. I know Frank Lorenzo, and in all probability he gave money to the Bush-Quayle campaign.

Now, followup?

Q. Does that influence you in any way?

The President. No, it does not influence me in any way.

War on Drugs and Gun Control

Q. Mr. President, the theme of the week is drugs this week, and you mentioned again this morning your commitment to ridding the country of drugs. But your designate for drug czar, William Bennett, has said that as part of the way that he would like to help end drug violence would be to consider a ban on semiautomatic weapons, which is opposed to your own viewpoint. And we're getting more and more evidence from doctors and police that there's gunfire in the streets and wounds that they haven't seen since the Vietnam war because of these weapons. What do you say to people whose families have been maimed by these kind of weapons?

The President. I say the same thing I say to a person whose family has been maimed by a pistol or an explosive charge or whatever else it might be—fire. This is bad, and we have got to stop the scourge of drugs. And I talked to Bill Bennett about that, because I said, "Bill, what can be worked out with finality on AK-47's? What can be done and still, you know, do what's right by the legitimate sportsman?" I'd love to find an answer to that, Rita [Rita Beamish, Associated Press], because I do think that there has to be some assurance that these automated attack weapons are not used in the manner they're being used. And I told Bill—I said, "Look, don't worry about what you said up there." I said, "I can identify with what was behind your thinking on that very, very easily." I'd like to find some accommodation. The problem, as you know, is that automated AK-47's are banned and semiautomated are not. So, in they come, and then they get turned over to automated weapons through some filing down. It isn't as easy as it seems to those who are understandably crying out: Do something! Do something!

But I've tasked Bill. I've said, "Bill, work the problem. Find out. And I'm not so rigid that if you come to me with a sensible answer that takes care of the concerns I've felt over the years I'll take a hard look at it, and I'll work with you to that end."

Speaker of the House Jim Wright

Q. Mr. President, do you support the Republican Congressional Committee's decision to make Jim Wright its number-one target next year? And doesn't that conflict with your——

The President. Hey, listen, I've got enough fights on my hands now, Dave [David Montgomery, Fort Worth Star Telegram]. [*Laughter*] I'm not looking for any more. Let the Congress do its thing, and I'll just stay right where I am, plugging away on a matter of principle for a battle that's going on in the—I'll let you know if I want to take on any more.

Soviet-U.S. Relations

Q. Mr. President, on foreign policy, there is some confusion about how you feel about linking Soviet good behavior, particularly in Central America, to granting them technological transfers and economic credits. If Gorbachev helps you in Central America, specifically in Nicaragua, are you willing to help him economically?

The President. Look, the more cooperation we can get on regional objectives—in this instance, the democratization of Central America—the more help we can get towards that end by the Soviets with pulling back their large amount of military support, the better it would be between relations. So, there is linkage, but when it gets to the specifics of what I'll be willing to do—that will come under this whole policy review. But we are not going to back away from agenda items, including regional tensions. And when something good happens, give some credit. When Soviets come out of Afghanistan, which happened here not so long ago, give them credit for that. When you get lightening up a little bit on the question of Soviet Jews or something of that nature, give some credit. So, don't know exactly how to help you in terms of how much linkage there is, but there's clearly got to be some linkage.

Q. Sir, you've been getting cables back from Vienna from Secretary of State Baker, he's been meeting with Foreign Minister

Shevardnadze. Is Shevardnadze saying anything encouraging along this line?

The President. Well, I haven't seen the overnight cable from Baker reporting on that meeting, so I can't comment. I read some reports of what Shevardnadze said in terms of conventional forces, and it looks to me like he's moving towards the oft-stated public position of NATO in this regard, and that is good. Where it's not a question of numbers you take out, it's a question of the numbers that are left when you finish taking troops out. So, I think there's been some encouraging—but I have not yet seen the Baker report, and I haven't talked to him since his visit.

Aid to the Contras

Q. Mr. President, nonmilitary aid to the *contras* will run out at the end of the month. Do you plan to propose new aid to the *contras* and some package of carrots and sticks for the Sandinistas?

The President. Well, I hope there is some understanding on the Hill that these people must not be left without humanitarian aid. And we have already—through the Secretary of State before he left—pointed out that that was my inclination was to strongly support the appeal for humanitarian aid. We simply cannot, and I will not, leave the *contras* out there with no humanitarian aid at all—ability to stay alive at this juncture.

Q. But will the package include some promise of renewed military aid depending on the Sandinistas' behavior at this point?

The President. We are talking, as I think the Secretary said the other day, about how best to move the process of democratization forward. I had a very interesting talk with Mr. Cervezo [President of Guatemala] on that. And I am hopeful that before the 90-day period is up, you know, on the Presidents coming out, that we can get some very clear statements. But in terms of humanitarian aid, I don't think there will be much resistance to that at all.

Terrorist Raids in Israel

Q. Mr. President, on another regional question, Yasser Arafat [Palestine Liberation Organization chairman] has refused to criticize any of the raids within Israel that have been carried out. Is he backing down on his promise against terrorism?

The President. I hope not, and I'd like to see him forthrightly condemn any terror that might be perpetrated by the Palestinians. I stop short of saying he's condoning it or that he is furthering it. I'm not saying that. But I'd like to see him speak out. It would do wonders. It would be very good for future dialog.

Q. Well, is he jeopardizing the dialog as it sits now?

The President. To the degree terroristic acts are condoned, it doesn't help the dialog.

Administration Accomplishments

Q. There is a school of thought in Washington, Mr. President, that perception is often reality or becomes reality. The perception is that your administration is floundering, that the White House staff is inept. How do you deal with that? How do you turn that around?

The President. I ask for your forbearance and leadership in this regard, pointing out all the things that I spelled out in the beginning, comparing that with the terms of appointments. I've spared you the statistics on appointments, which I had prepared, because one of the hits is, you haven't sent up any names. You haven't done anything about names. And so, I would refer to my notes, Gerry [Gerald Boyd, New York Times], if that's all right. And I have lost my notes on this—no, here they are. And in terms of the Reagan-Bush administration, at this juncture, 55 names as of March 6th had been announced. On the Bush-Quayle administration, 67 had been announced. So, it's not bad. We're a little bit ahead in terms of announced names. Now, you've got some different problems here because one is nomination, the other is intent to nominate. And intent to nominate means there's still some more paperwork to be done. But in terms of who we want in place, we're moving along all right. I'd like to see it faster, of course.

But that's one of the allegations—disarray. First, I have great confidence in my staff. And every Chief of Staff goes through this drill, where he gets saluted for his brilliance, and a month later gets attacked for his something else. And I have total confidence in John Sununu; he knows the way this town works. He has the respect level that comes from being—there he is—[*laughter*]—the respect level that comes from being a Governor. And so, we're all used to this. Hey, this is light compared to what is was like about a year ago in my case. So, that's why I still feel relaxed.

But the point is, if you would just write down all those wonderful things I told you that are happening and get it out to that wide readership, it would be very helpful to me. And also, I refer you to the phone call in Lubbock. [*Laughter*] And that is: Never get too uptight about stuff that hadn't reached Lubbock yet. And be sure that there's some accomplishments going on——

Q. Is that your Peoria?

The President.——accomplishments going on that people can say, "Wait a minute, there's quite a bit happening here."

Q. If I could follow up: Is there a danger here, sir? Is there a potential danger if the perception lingers?

The President. You're in a better position to answer that than I am. However, you know, I come back to the Tower—I think people are fair. They are not making up their minds on perceptions, make them up on facts. And I am one who felt that way coming out of the campaign. That's why I go back to that. It was a very important thing to me—what happened out there about a year ago. And here I stand here. And so, I don't think the American people make up their minds on perceptions. I think they make up their minds on facts. Now, you can have various waves of approval or disapproval, but I think if we can just get our message out on the facts the way I've spelled them out here I think we'll do fine. But I've——

Federal Budget

Q. Mr. President, I'd like to ask you about one of the facts that you cited in your list. You said the budget that you sent to the Hill has more detail than any budgets of the last two administrations. I'm a little confused about that. What are you referring to, since yours did not list any of the domestic——

The President. More detail has been sent to the Hill at this time in our administration—let me clarify that—than at any time for either the Reagan administration in 1981 or the Carter administration in '77. They hadn't gone up with near this amount of detail to the Hill. And we have a document that we should pass out to you because it is quite important that this be understood.

One more.

Q. Mr. President, you've——

The President. Make it two. Two more—one, two. Sorry.

Administration Accomplishments

Q. Thank you, sir. You've heard the commentaries and read the articles about the—as have been described here—the foundering and the lack of ideas of the administration. I'm wondering what your reading is on the motivation for all of this at this point in the administration.

The President. The motivation for these groundless stories? [*Laughter*] Let me see what it would be.

Q. They're coming from Republicans and Democrats.

The President. Well, who are some of the sources? Help me, and then I can give you the motivation. Give me two Democratic sources and two Republicans that have said this, and then let me try to——

Q. Kennedy.

The President. Ted Kennedy? Enough said.

Q. You have David Gergen's commentary.

The President. And do you have him down as an objective journalist or a Republican?

Q. Maybe both.

Q. Republican.

The President. Republican? Well, I think he's wrong. [*Laughter*]

Q. But what do you think the motivation is, coming at this particular point——

The President. Look, I told you what I think. Go back and look at history; it kind of goes in cycles. But I'm not deterred at all. And I've seen them, and I've seen some of the things that are cited in the stories as evidence of this, and I just disagree with the facts. So, keep on doing your job; that's my answer.

Q. Well, sir, one more crack at the "hitting the ground crawling" concept here. [*Laughter*]

The President. I read that—I give—sorry about that. Go ahead.

Policy Reviews

Q. You made much, sir, during your campaign of how close you were to President Reagan 8 years, you were very much involved, and so on. What is the need then, sir, for these 90-day reviews that you keep referring to? Why do we need 3 months to review our strategic policy, our foreign policy?

The President. Because it is a prudent thing to do. You have new people in the administration. You have rapid change inside the Soviet Union; you have certain things going on inside the Soviet Union we're not particularly sure about. And it is prudent at the beginning of any new administration, with new people involved, to have strategic and management reviews in the Defense Department. It's prudent to take a hard, new look at some of the problems that plague us in terms of the Third World. It is prudent in terms of some of our domestic objectives, although they're quite a bit clearer, Ellen [Ellen Warren, Knight-Ridder Newspapers], it seems to me. And we just have a question now of getting legislation to match those objectives that I spelled out in that report to the Congress.

Q. Well, then, to follow up, sir: In terms of the prudent review, have you come up with any novel or remarkable new approaches to old problems?

The President. Well, the reviews aren't completed yet. Stay tuned. We might well do just that. Really surprise the socks off you.

U.S. Economy

Q. Can we have an economics question?

Q. One economic question?

The President. No, those are the ones that get you in trouble—[*laughter*]—those economic questions. I feel pretty good about the economy, though.

Howard University Student Protest

Q. How about an Atwater question?

The President. An Atwater question?

Q. Yes. You're going tomorrow to speak to the United Negro College Fund. Right now the students at Howard are protesting Atwater on the board of Howard. Do you think they have a legitimate grievance about Atwater's conduct during the campaign?

The President. No. No, and I think it's a good thing he's on the board. I think it's a good thing he's going to talk to these students. And I think that will work out just fine. He's doing a first-class job.

Secretary of Defense-Designate Tower

Q. Would you like to see John Tower defend himself before the actual Senate board?

The President. I would not presume to recommend to the Senate what it should do, but Bob Dole knows that he has my full confidence in the way he's handling this matter in the Senate.

Q. Even though it's almost unique, would you like to see it happen?

The President. I have told you my answer. I don't think the White House—I think we've got to be very careful here that we don't try to dictate procedures to the Senate. I have full confidence that the leader, if he decides to propose that with finality, will be doing what he thinks is best; and I will strongly support him.

Q. Have you found any other Democrats?

Q. See you in Lubbock.

The President. You didn't even ask for my source, which I would have traded you for some of yours.

Note: The President's sixth news conference began at 11:10 a.m. in the Briefing Room at the White House. Marlin Fitzwater was the President's Press Secretary.

Nomination of Thomas J. Collamore To Be an Assistant Secretary of Commerce
March 7, 1989

The President today announced his intention to nominate Thomas J. Collamore to be an Assistant Secretary of Commerce (Administration). He would succeed Katherine M. Bulow.

From 1987 to January 1989, Mr. Collamore was Assistant to the Vice President for Operations in the Office of the Vice President, where he also served as liaison to the transition offices of the President-elect and the Vice President-elect. From April 1985 to February 1987, Mr. Collamore was Deputy Assistant to the Vice President and Staff Secretary, where he created and managed a staffing system for all action items from the Vice President. Mr. Collamore served from December 1982 to April 1985 as Special Assistant to the Secretary of Commerce, where he served as the Secretary's adviser on Cabinet affairs and White House liaison. In 1982 Mr. Collamore was deputy director for operations for the Rome for Governor campaign in Connecticut. He served from 1981 to 1982 as a confidential assistant to the Secretary of Commerce. From June 1979 to March 1980, Mr. Collamore was a staff member for George Bush for President in Connecticut. And in 1978 he served as the personal aide to Lewis Rome, a candidate for Governor in Connecticut.

Mr. Collamore was born in Hartford, CT, and graduated magna cum laude with a bachelor of arts degree from Drew University in Madison, NJ, in 1981. He resides in Washington, DC.

Nomination of William Douglas Fritts, Jr., To Be an Assistant Secretary of Commerce
March 7, 1989

The President today announced his intention to nominate William Douglas Fritts, Jr., to be an Assistant Secretary of Commerce (Congressional Affairs). He would succeed Marc G. Stanley.

Since 1985 Mr. Fritts has been director of political affairs for the Health Insurance Association of America in Washington, DC. He was Senior Assistant to the Commissioner of the Social Security Administration, 1985, and Senior Adviser to the Secretary of Health and Human Services, 1984–1985. Mr. Fritts was manager of Federal Government relations for Philip Morris, Inc., 1982–1984. From 1981 to 1982, he was Special Assistant to the Deputy Assistant Secretary for Legislation at the Department of Health and Human Services. He was executive assistant and legislative director to Senator Robert Dole, 1979–1981, and assistant director of the Joint Republican Leadership Office and special assistant to House Minority Leader John Rhodes, 1977–1979.

Mr. Fritts graduated from the University of Vermont (B.A., 1974). He was born November 13, 1950, and resides in Arlington, VA.

Nomination of Deborah Wince-Smith To Be an Assistant Secretary of Commerce

March 7, 1989

The President today announced his intention to nominate Deborah Wince-Smith to be Assistant Secretary of Commerce (Technology Policy). She would succeed D. Bruce Merrifield.

Since 1984 Mrs. Wince-Smith has served as the Assistant Director for International Affairs and Global Competitiveness in the White House Office of Science and Technology Policy. Prior to this she served as program manager for international programs at the National Science Foundation.

Mrs. Wince-Smith graduated from Vassar College and received her master's degree from Cambridge University.

Nomination of J. Michael Farren To Be an Under Secretary of Commerce

March 7, 1989

The President today announced his intention to nominate J. Michael Farren to be Under Secretary of Commerce for International Trade. He would succeed W. Allen Moore.

Mr. Farren served as deputy director of President Bush's transition team from November 1988 to January 1989. He was counsel at the law firm of Wiggin & Dana in New Haven, CT, since September 1988. Mr. Farren previously served as Deputy Under Secretary of Commerce for International Trade from September 1985 to July 1988 and was responsible for management and policy development for the International Trade Administration. Prior to that Mr. Farren served as Counselor to the Secretary of Commerce from March 1985 to September 1985, advising the Secretary on policy development and Cabinet matters. From June 1983 to March 1985, he served as Director of the Office of Business Liaison at the Commerce Department, where he served as the Secretary's primary contact with the business community. He was director of White House liaison and executive assistant to the deputy chairman of the Republican National Committee from August 1981 to June 1983. Mr. Farren also served as vice president of the Greater Waterbury, Connecticut, Chamber of Commerce from December 1978 to August 1981. From March 1974 to November 1978, Mr. Farren was district representative and campaign director for U.S. Representative Ronald A. Sarasin.

Mr. Farren was born in Waterbury, CT, holds a juris doctor degree from the University of Connecticut School of Law, and is admitted to the practice of law in Connecticut and the District of Columbia. He holds a master's degree in public policy analysis from Trinity College and a bachelor of arts degree in political science from Fairfield University. Mr. Farren resides in Washington, DC.

Nomination of Susan Carol Schwab To Be an Assistant Secretary of Commerce
March 7, 1989

The President today announced his intention to nominate Susan Carol Schwab to be Assistant Secretary of Commerce and Director General of the United States and Foreign Commercial Service. She would succeed Lew W. Cramer.

Since 1986 Miss Schwab has been legislative director for Senator John C. Danforth in Washington, DC, and chief economist and legislative assistant, 1981–1986. She was a trade policy officer and international economist for the U.S. Embassy in Tokyo, Japan, 1980–1981, and an international economist and trade negotiator for the Office of the U.S. Trade Representative, 1977–1979.

Miss Schwab graduated from Williams College (B.A., 1976) and Stanford University (M.A., 1977). She was born March 23, 1955, in Washington, DC, and resides in Maryland.

Nomination of Thomas J. Duesterberg To Be an Assistant Secretary of Commerce
March 7, 1989

The President today announced his intention to nominate Thomas J. Duesterberg to be an Assistant Secretary of Commerce (International Economic Policy). He would succeed Louis F. Laun.

Mr. Duesterberg was director of operations of the transition for Vice President Dan Quayle. Prior to this he was administrative assistant for U.S. Senator Dan Quayle, 1983–1988, and legislative assistant, 1981–1983. He was senior research analyst for International Business Services, Inc., 1979–1981; associate instructor in the department of history at Stanford University, 1978–1979; and teaching assistant in the department of history at Indiana University, 1974–1978.

Mr. Duesterberg graduated from Princeton University (B.A., 1972) and Indiana University (M.A., 1974; Ph.D., 1979). He is married, has one child, and resides in Washington, DC.

Nomination of Richard Thomas Crowder To Be an Under Secretary of Agriculture
March 7, 1989

The President today announced his intention to nominate Richard Thomas Crowder to be Under Secretary of Agriculture for International Affairs and Commodity Programs. He would succeed Daniel G. Amstutz.

Since 1975 Dr. Crowder has been with the Pillsbury Co., serving in several capacities, including president of the Distron division for the Burger King Corp., 1987–1988; executive vice president and chief financial officer of the restaurant group, 1987–1988; senior vice president and corporate risk officer, 1987–1988; senior vice president for strategic planning, 1983–1987; and vice president and corporate economist, 1975–1983. Dr. Crowder was manager for economic analysis and operations research for Wilson & Co., 1971–1975, and manager for economic analysis, 1968–1971.

Dr. Crowder graduated from Virginia Tech (B.A., 1960; M.S., 1962) and Oklahoma State University (Ph.D., 1967). He served in the U.S. Army in Germany, 1962–1964.

Remarks to Members of the Woodrow Wilson International Center for Scholars
March 7, 1989

Well, thank you all very, very much; and Barbara and I are pleased, indeed, very pleased, to be here this evening. Yogi Berra, philosopher, said: "You can observe a lot by just watching." [*Laughter*] And I'm watching the Secretary of State [James A. Baker III] to see how in heaven's name he can stay awake—[*laughter*]—because it wasn't but a handful of days ago that he was covering 14 countries, or something of that nature, in Europe. A few days less than that, he and I embarked on a trip to Japan and China and then Korea. He's only back 3 days, and off he goes to Vienna. And so, I will be watching him, observing to see how he survives. But I am delighted to be introduced by him in this building. He'll be a great Secretary of State. And you watch, I made a good choice, a real good choice.

I want to thank Mr. Blitzer and Mr. Baroody, Dwayne Andreas, and all responsible for this lovely evening. Ever since I said I want to become the "Education President," I've had more than a few things to say about accountability in education. Well, Woodrow Wilson did once serve as president of Princeton University. And legend has it that one day a worried mother approached him and questioned him closely about what Princeton could do for her son. And he's said to have answered—historians may dispute this, but nevertheless, he's said to have answered—and here's the quote: "Madam, we guarantee satisfaction, or you will get your son back." [*Laughter*]

Well, I'm very glad to be back amongst the Wilson scholars, an honor to be here, celebrating the anniversary of this wonderful institution. The law establishing this national memorial to Woodrow Wilson called for a "living institution" to express his ideals and his concerns. And this one certainly does. In this alliance of scholars, now world-renowned for exploring some of the most vital issues that confront mankind, Woodrow Wilson's ideals find their highest and most effective expression.

The pursuit of knowledge and understanding that the center is committed to will be all the more crucial in coming years. We're going to depend more than ever on the counsel of learned men and women in a world that is changing rapidly, a world interconnected as never before in history. New ideas, new technologies, and the diplomatic and trading relationships that they spawn, are developing at literally an outstanding pace.

Barbara and I went back to China—my fifth visit and her sixth since we left there in the midseventies, 1975—astounding the change and the excitement in that place. And Jim—just filling me in briefly on a chat that he has had with the Foreign Minister of the Soviet Union, Mr. Shevardnadze. This is an exciting era in which we are living: new ideas, new technologies—very important to what's going on. And we weave a tapestry of shared concerns and relations worldwide. Threads are many—social, economic, environmental. Now world conscience—what the world conscience—has environmental questions out there, geopolitical, and really grows broader every day.

And much of what is occurring in the world presents us, I think, with remarkable opportunities. I said China is one. China really continues to experiment with free market capitalism—dramatic change. We're carefully, but optimistically, watching these internal changes in the Soviet Union that many in this room are interested in and, indeed, an area where many in this room have pioneered. And all over the world, opportunities are rising for new directions in foreign policy and trading arrangements, and new challenges are being issued to our competitive status in world markets.

During this recent trip to the Far East, I had many opportunities to observe and think about competitiveness. And there are many theories about the reasons for the industrial success that some of our Asian friends are enjoying today. But no one questions the importance of one factor: the highly skilled, highly motivated, and educated work forces in those countries. And out of the devastation of war, they had the courage to recognize how their future was tied to the quality of educations that their nations provided. And as this country prepares to—what are we, 11 years short of a new century?—to enter that century, we, too, must recognize how essential the education of the next generations has become to our economic future. Perhaps the highest praise that coming generations might bestow upon us is that we understood the changes that are occurring in the world and that we prepared them for the challenges we knew they would face.

And so, you who comprise the Wilson Center are devoted to the life of the mind. And I imagine you'll agree with me if I say that young minds will make or break the future of this and every other country. And I have two concerns about those young minds that I want to just share briefly this evening. The young people will have to be better educated than the previous generation. And to be so, they've got to be free of the scourge of drug abuse. You know, no matter what the problems we face, as I look at our country today, and really, indeed, internationally look around, this terrible scourge of drug abuse has got to be in the forefront. And it's fundamental, these things affect us all. Their solution is not a question of "whether," it's a question of "when." And so, I want to think—education, drug abuse—think of tonight as a celebration, but also a challenge. Consider what we've got to do.

Where the state of the schools is concerned, you've all heard the surveys. Last month's report from the National Science Foundation and the Department of Education over here put American seventh-graders—American seventh-graders—at the bottom of an international comparison of math and science skills. And who's to blame? Too late; that's not the issue. We all must be accountable for the quality of education in America. And to assure the competitive future of this nation and the overall standard of living enjoyed by its people will demand the best kind of collective effort. All of us must get involved.

I want to launch a crusade for excellence in American education. And, yes, we are living in a time of cramped resources; but we've got to do it. The crusade has to be driven largely by local energy and initiative, drawing on people from both the public and the private sectors, and determined to establish a culture of high expectations in our schools.

At the Federal level, I've made some proposals. I want to reward excellence and success by rewarding superior teachers, recognizing these Presidential merit scholars that make real progress in these merit schools. We will establish benchmarks for achievement and both commend and reward teachers and schools that succeed. I want to establish a National Science Scholars Program, to encourage students to succeed in science. It is incumbent upon us to restore the honor, indeed, the nobility, of good teaching in this country. And it won't escape the eyes of the young if we can show them how much we value learning in the way we value teachers.

And secondly, I want to put resources where they count, targeting Federal dollars to help those most in need, to places where support can really make a difference. We will also use funds in ways that build the right links between the university and government and industry, research labs to promote scientific education and basic research. And I intend to hold firm in our effort to double the National Science Foundation's budget by 1993.

And third, I want to promote choice and flexibility by devoting $100 million in new funding for magnet schools. These are the schools that increase choice, who expand opportunities for children, and generate healthy competition among the schools.

And lastly, I'm going to push for greater

accountability at all levels—among students, among teachers, administrators, and principals—to assure that students are actually receiving the highest quality education. For this is what excellence demands. It means setting high standards, standards that the rest of the world are going to look to. And it means constantly measuring yourself against those standards and not resting until you meet the standards. It means discipline—says, if we don't get it right the first time, we're going to try again and again until we do get it right.

But excellence in education will not be fully realized until we free our young people from that second problem I mentioned: the scourge of drugs, drugs that kill hopes and ambitions and kill kids. And to rid our schools and our streets of this scourge, I've proposed nearly a billion dollars in new outlays for antidrug programs. I've got to confess, I wish it were more. That's what we've proposed; it's a lot of money.

With the help of our new drug czar, Bill Bennett, I'm going to be implementing a comprehensive national drug control strategy. He has 6 months from the day he's confirmed to come up with a whole new plan. And our strategy will deal with both supply and demand, by educating and inspiring in our young an attitude of zero tolerance, reclaiming lives through more effective treatment, stopping drugs at their source, and enforcing tougher penalties.

You know, last week we did get some news on the drug front. In 1988, use of cocaine declined among high school seniors. In fact, student usage of almost every illegal drug, as well as alcohol, appears to be on the decline. So, in our schools the message is beginning to get out, but we have no reason to be complacent. The drug problem is much worse among high school dropouts. And international cultivation of the opium poppy and coca leaf increased sharply last year.

So, when I talk about a war on drugs, I mean more than a rhetorical war. I seek engagement on all fronts. And the Wilson Center is known as a vital point of contact between the thinkers and the doers of this country, and a number of scholars have shed new light on this drug problem. And I've heard great things about the conference that you all held on drug trafficking in the Americas last fall. And the proceedings of that conference provoked a great deal of thought. And for my part, the thoughts are haunting.

Sadly, the cores of many societies have been permeated by drug gangs and cartels and organized crime. Consider it economic; call it social; call it cultural; but consider it an international peril. And if we're to stop it, we've got to stop it together. And I encourage you in this great institution to continue searching for long-term solutions. In a city that's preoccupied by short-term policy issues, the Wilson Center encourages the longer view. And in a city preoccupied by politics, you draw support from all parties and all quarters, with funding from both the public and the private sectors.

And in this nation's efforts to educate its young and see them clear of the threat of drugs, you're in a position to help us make our battles winning ones. We need our young people to succeed. Our ability to empower them will reflect our character and our ideals as a nation. Woodrow Wilson put it this way: "The beauty of a democracy," he said, "is that you never can tell when a youngster is born what he's going to do, and that no matter how humbly he's born he has got a chance to master the minds and lead the imaginations of the whole country."

Well, I guess our challenge will be to give all young people the chance to fulfill their highest ambitions and their God-given potential. And I think it falls to us—and maybe more heavily on you all, interested in this marvelous center—to prove that Woodrow Wilson is right.

Thank you all. God bless you. Now the souffle, and then Senator Pat Moynihan. You've got it made. Thank you all very much.

Note: The President spoke at 9:10 p.m. in the Dining Room at the Department of State. In his opening remarks, he referred to Charles Blitzer, William J. Baroody, and Dwayne Andreas, Director, Chairman of the Board of Trustees, and Vice Chairman of the Board of Trustees, respectively.

Nomination of John Chatfield Tuck To Be Under Secretary of Energy
March 8, 1989

The President today announced his intention to nominate John Chatfield Tuck to be Under Secretary of Energy. He would succeed Donna R. Fitzpatrick.

Mr. Tuck has served in several capacities at the White House in Washington, DC, from 1986 to January 1989. He was Assistant to the President and Director of the Office of the Chief of Staff, July 1988 to January 1989. Prior to this he served as Deputy Assistant to the President and Executive Assistant to the Chief of Staff, April 1987 to July 1988. Mr. Tuck has also served as Deputy Assistant to the President for Legislative Affairs from October 1986 to April 1987 and Special Assistant to the President for Legislative Affairs, 1986. Mr. Tuck has also served as Assistant Secretary for the Majority of the United States Senate, 1981–1986. From 1977 to 1981, he served as the chief of Republican floor operations. Mr. Tuck has also assisted the Republican leadership of the House of Representatives in various positions from 1974 to 1977.

Mr. Tuck graduated from Georgetown University School of Foreign Service (B.S., 1967). From 1968 to 1973, he was on active duty in the U.S. Navy, serving on destroyers for 3 years and then at the Bureau of Naval Personnel for 2 years. He is currently a captain in the Naval Reserve and is assigned to the Deputy Chief of Naval Operations for Service Warfare. He was born May 28, 1945, in Dayton, OH. Mr. Tuck is married to the former Jane McDounogh of Garden City, NY. They have three children and reside in Arlington, VA.

Nomination of Donna R. Fitzpatrick To Be an Assistant Secretary of Energy
March 8, 1989

The President today announced his intention to nominate Donna R. Fitzpatrick to be an Assistant Secretary of Energy (Management and Administration). She would succeed Lawrence F. Davenport.

Since 1988 Miss Fitzpatrick has been Under Secretary of Energy in Washington, DC. Prior to this she was Assistant Secretary for Conservation and Renewable Energy, 1985–1988, and Principal Deputy Assistant Secretary for Conservation and Renewable Energy, 1984–1985. She was sole practitioner of law and consultant to the Secretary and Under Secretary of the Department of Energy, 1983–1984. She was also an associate attorney with O'Connor & Hannan, 1980–1983. In 1980 she served the office of the President-elect as a member of the transition team for the National Science Foundation. From 1976 to 1980, she was a legal assistant with O'Connor & Hannan.

Miss Fitzpatrick graduated from American University (B.A., 1972) and George Washington University (J.D., 1980). She is a native of Washington, DC, where she currently resides.

Nomination of David W. Mullins, Jr., To Be an Assistant Secretary of the Treasury
March 8, 1989

The President today announced his intention to nominate David W. Mullins, Jr., to be an Assistant Secretary of the Treasury. He would succeed Charles O. Sethness.

Dr. Mullins has been a professor of business administration at the Harvard University Graduate School of Business Administration. He has been faculty chairman of Harvard's corporate financial management program, an executive program for senior financial officers of major corporations. Dr. Mullins has also served as a consultant to a wide variety of firms and governmental agencies.

Dr. Mullins received a B.S. degree in administrative sciences from Yale University and a S.M. degree in finance from the Sloan School of Management at the Massachusetts Institute of Technology (MIT). He received his Ph.D. in finance and economics at MIT. Dr. Mullins was born April 28, 1946, in Memphis, TN.

Remarks at the Swearing-in Ceremony for James D. Watkins as Secretary of Energy
March 9, 1989

The President. Thank you very, very much. Of course, my thanks to the marines. I didn't get your name, but you're sure good on the "Star-Spangled Banner." [*Laughter*] And thank you for that wonderful rendition.

Chief Justice, and to the distinguished Members of the House and the Senate that are here today, to the members of my Cabinet who are here, and I think most of all today to the Watkins family, and to you who will be working with one of the outstanding Americans, the new Secretary, Jim Watkins, my greetings to all of you.

It is a pleasure to come over here for this swearing-in. And as I see it, the responsibilities before this Department have never been greater than today, and I have total confidence that Jim Watkins is the best man to meet the challenges ahead. For over four decades, he's demonstrated an unswerving commitment to our country and to the call of service. A graduate of Annapolis, he went on in his distinguished naval career to serve in such key posts as Commander of the Sixth Fleet, Commander in Chief of the Pacific Fleet, Vice Chief, and then later as Chief of Naval Operations. And most recently, the Admiral took on a difficult and important assignment as Chairman of the Nation's AIDS commission, performing brilliantly in that capacity, taking a piece of work that some were saying couldn't possibly succeed; but succeed he did. And throughout his long career, Jim has shown a mastery of complex organizations and issues, and he's demonstrated an outstanding concern for the people who have served under him. And you here at this Department are about to find that out.

To the 16,000 men and women of the Department, from Juneau to Georgia, and your 130,000 contract workers, I want to tell you how much I admire you. And I told Jim, who has already told me about his respect for you, that one of the reasons I wanted to come over here was to make that very clear to the men and women of this Department. I admire your professionalism, your loyalty, your tremendous technical expertise. And there's been talk in the past that perhaps this Department was not necessary, was redundant, or its responsibilities could be taken over by others. Let me say, you have important work to do; you're on the cutting edge now; and this Department is here to stay and will have the full support of this President.

You have broad responsibilities. The most pressing challenge that you face—I guess you might feel they're all pressing, and I think maybe I do, too—but the most pressing challenge is to manage the modernization of America's nuclear weapons production plants. This task is critical to maintaining in every way, perfecting our deterrent force which ensures our security and, thus, a safe and stable world. But we also have a major environmental challenge: We need to clean up the pollution that's been created at these plants. These problems developed over time, and they'll be fully solved only over time, but we'll waste no time in getting started on fixing these problems.

Admiral Watkins is well-qualified to take on these complex issues. He's an extremely capable manager, highly respected in this city and around the country, knowledgeable about nuclear energy, with considerable experience in the Navy's nuclear-powered submarine program, from bringing a new reactor plant on line to commanding a nuclear-powered submarine to managing nuclear programs right here in Washington, DC.

Jim and I have also spoken about our commitment to protecting the environment while assuring that our energy requirements and national security requirements are fully met. We need nuclear power, hydropower, oil, gas, coal to meet the total energy requirements of the United States. And we need to improve energy efficiency as well as develop competitive renewable technologies. No one or two sources would be sufficient alone, nor would they provide us with the flexibility that is necessary. For reasons of national security, we need to have domestic production in each area. And we will institute policies to promote that by restoring incentives and also through deregulation.

I want to see a recovery in the domestic oil and gas production. Our great economic expansion will not be complete until every area of our country is reaping its benefits. And I also want to see continued development of this clean-coal technology; a generation of safe nuclear energy; and also R&D, research and development, of alternative fuels and new technologies. And again, let me emphasize conservation methods as well. Energy is the most important basic ingredient in everything we produce, everything we consume, everything we import or export. For America's economy to be competitive, we need sound energy policies and competitive energy industries. And for our national security to be guaranteed, we need the strongest possible national energy policy.

The Energy Department has big challenges ahead. Issues of national security and competitiveness, environmental quality—they're all on the agenda. And so, I selected a big man to do a big job. So, Jim, we'd better get going—better swear you in and let you get to work. [*Laughter*] And thank all of you for the support I know you will give the newest Secretary of Energy.

Now on to the formalities here.

[*At this point, Secretary Watkins was sworn in.*]

Secretary Watkins. Mr. President; Mr. Chief Justice; Members of the Congress; my colleagues in the Cabinet; distinguished guests; my wife, Sheila; and family and friends. It's a great honor for me to appear before you today as your new Secretary of Energy. It's also a great personal honor to have been asked to serve in this capacity by a President who, by witness in the remarks we have just heard, has such an in-depth personal knowledge of this nation's energy needs and resources.

Mr. President, in your "Building A Better America," which was your budget message to the Congress only a few days ago, you affirmed the importance of energy security, safety, and environmental protection as co-equal national priority. As your Secretary of Energy, I pledge to support and promote those policies. And Mr. President, we are particularly edified today by your commitment to the Department of Energy as the viable Federal entity to do the energy job for the long haul.

Now, to all of you in the Department of Energy, I recently transmitted a memorandum to all hands outlining key policy areas that we will pursue in the very near term, giving you therein my philosophy of the importance of personal excellence and contribution to the Nation.

My Senate confirmation hearing statement and related followup questions and answers to the Congress have also been made available to you. These documents, along with my forthcoming 90-day message, will set policy direction for the Department, ones that I intend to take as Secretary. I want each of you to know what I'm doing so that you, in turn, can be important participants in the solution-finding process. There will be demands on you. But I, in turn, also will take personal interest in the well-being of our employees. For example, one of the first things that I will do here in headquarters is accelerate the opening of our child day-care center to help working parents. And Sheila has asked to join our parents committee as an added guiding force behind that project.

In addition, my long history of interest in education for America's youth will be put to work to bring our many and diverse activities across the Nation into a more visible and effective partnership with the private sector in order to inspire the very young to seek careers in mathematics, in science and engineering, so important to the Department of Energy and so many other facets of our society today, and giving particular emphasis in this regard to inspiring minorities to come into these fields. We simply have too few of them serving in these areas today, and we can do a lot more and inspire the Nation.

By so doing, we will do our part in helping to assure the President and the Nation that we can have a topnotch technical work force well into the 21st century. And as you can glean from my own biography and the program today, my training and experience began in the early days of the peaceful use of nuclear energy, where I learned the important principles of safe and reliable application of nuclear technology. But I also learned the importance of the human component, that is, individual responsibility for strict application of standards. Nuclear power demands no less than the best from all who control it.

This, then, is exactly what I ask of my Department: a commitment to excellence. So, I ask you to help me forge a workplace culture that rejects the mediocre and the substandard and create one that excites excellence in each employee. Our mission is an important one, but we'll only find success when each of us feels a personal ownership in mission control.

Among our special guests today, Mr. President, are people from all parts of this Department, from mailroom workers to our adopted Woodrow Wilson High School principal and students to security guards and secretaries, all of whom strive to excel in their daily work. Some of their contributions in the past may have gone unnoticed, but I can assure you that on my watch they will not.

The Department of Energy is one Department clearly involved in America's future, as the President so beautifully stated. We've been given a great and important job to do, and we are at a unique time in history to do it. And with your guidance, Mr. President, in full partnership with the Congress and industry, we will succeed.

In closing these brief remarks today, I first want to thank all of those responsible for preparing our cafeteria so beautifully for this very special ceremony. Second, I'd like to thank each one of you for coming today and taking the time to spend a few moments with us. And finally, I would like you to all rise and join me in paying tribute to our President, thanking him as he departs today for sharing a few of his precious moments with us on this very special occasion. [*Applause*]

Note: The President spoke at 10:13 a.m. in the cafeteria at the Department of Energy. In his opening remarks, he referred to the Marine Corps Band. Cynthia Gains, an employee of the Department, sang the national anthem at the ceremony.

Statement on the Negotiations on Arms Reduction and Security in Europe
March 9, 1989

Today marks the beginning of a process of great importance for the people of Europe, the United States, and Canada, and for all who share the hope of a safer and more secure Europe. In Vienna, the Nations who are members of the Conference on Security and Cooperation in Europe and the members of the North Atlantic alliance and Warsaw Pact will begin two negotiations whose goal is to reduce the threat of conventional weapons in Europe: one on conventional armed forces in Europe and another separate negotiation on further confidence-and-security building measures.

The negotiations on conventional forces in Europe offer a new opportunity to redress the imbalance in military forces which strongly favors the Warsaw Pact and which has been a source of tension since the end of World War II. The NATO allies aim to eliminate the capability for launching surprise attack and for initiating large-scale offensive actions.

The negotiations on confidence and security building measures will address the problem of mistrust in the military and security spheres and the risk of confrontation arising through miscalculation. Our aim is to lift the veil of secrecy from certain military activities and forces and thus contribute to a more stable Europe.

Although these two negotiations have different participants and aim at different kinds of accords, they share a common purpose. That purpose is to make Europe safer, to reduce the risk of war, and strengthen stability on the continent that has seen more bloodshed in this century than any other part of the world.

We and our NATO allies share a common commitment to democratic values, respect for each others' sovereignty, and support for a strong defense. NATO's approach to these negotiations, therefore, rests on two important principles: that maintaining strong and modern defenses is essential to our security and freedom, and that negotiated and effectively verifiable agreements can enhance our security and the prospects for lasting peace.

Of course these negotiations are part of a larger process, one which must address the causes as well as the symptoms of the current divisions in Europe. Progress in the military field alone is not enough to bring enduring peace. What is needed is genuine reconciliation and an end to the division of Europe. True security cannot exist without guarantee of human rights and basic freedoms for all people.

The negotiations on security in Europe offer new promise for the future. We embark on them with the hope that we can build a lasting framework for a more stable and secure future, but we are realistic about the difficulties ahead. With a renewed dedication to a constructive dialog, we can make progress. The commitment of the United States to this effort is unswerving.

Nomination of Michael Philip Skarzynski To Be an Assistant Secretary of Commerce
March 9, 1989

The President today announced his intention to nominate Michael Philip Skarzynski to be an Assistant Secretary of Commerce (Trade Development). He would succeed James P. Moore, Jr.

Since 1986 Mr. Skarzynski has been with Motorola, Inc., in Schaumburg, IL, serving as director of business development, 1988 to present, and director of marketing in the communications sector of the international group, 1986–1988. Prior to this, he was with G.D. Searle and Co., serving as director of finance of the consumer products group, 1985–1986; director of financial planning and analysis, 1984–1985; manager of corporate planning and development, 1982–1984; and corporate planner, 1980–1982. He was an associate with the Center for Strategic and International Studies, 1979–1980. He has also served as an economic consultant for economic consulting services of Clark, Gardner and Wolf International, 1978–1979.

Mr. Skarzynski received a bachelor of science of foreign service from Georgetown University and a master of management degree from Northwestern University.

Letter to the Speaker of the House of Representatives and the President of the Senate on Nuclear Cooperation With EURATOM
March 9, 1989

Dear Mr. Speaker: (Dear Mr. President:)

The United States has been engaged in nuclear cooperation with the European Community for many years. This cooperation was initiated under agreements concluded over 2 decades ago between the United States and the European Atomic Energy Community (EURATOM), which extend until December 31, 1995. Since the inception of this cooperation, the Community has adhered to all its obligations under those agreements.

The Nuclear Non-Proliferation Act of 1978 amended the Atomic Energy Act of 1954 to establish new nuclear export criteria, including a requirement that the United States has a right to consent to the reprocessing of fuel exported from the United States. Our present agreements for cooperation with EURATOM do not contain such a right. To avoid disrupting cooperation with EURATOM, a proviso was included in the law to enable continued cooperation until March 10, 1980, if EURATOM agreed to negotiations concerning our cooperation agreements, which it did.

The law also provides that nuclear cooperation with EURATOM can be extended on an annual basis after March 10, 1980, upon determination by the President that failure to cooperate would be seriously prejudicial to the achievement of U.S. non-proliferation objectives or otherwise jeopardize the common defense and security and after notification to the Congress. President Carter made such a determination 9 years ago and signed Executive Order No. 12193, permitting nuclear cooperation with EURATOM to continue until March 10, 1981. President Reagan made such determinations in 1981, 1982, 1983, 1984, 1985, 1986, 1987, and 1988, and signed Executive Orders Nos. 12295, 12351, 12409, 12463, 12506, 12554, 12587, and 12629 permitting nuclear cooperation to continue through March 10, 1989.

In addition to numerous informal contacts, the United States has engaged in 14 rounds of talks with EURATOM regarding the renegotiation of the U.S.-EURATOM agreements for cooperation. These were conducted in November 1978, September 1979, April 1980, January 1982, November 1983, March 1984, May, September, and November 1985, April and July 1986, September 1987, and September and November 1988. Further talks are anticipated this year.

I believe that it is essential that cooperation between the United States and the Community continue, and likewise, that we work closely with our allies to counter the threat of nuclear explosives proliferation. A disruption of nuclear cooperation would not only eliminate any chance of progress in our talks with EURATOM related to our agreements, it would also cause serious problems in our overall relationships. Accordingly, I have determined that failure to continue peaceful nuclear cooperation with EURATOM would be seriously prejudicial to the achievement of U.S. non-proliferation objectives and would jeopardize the common defense and security of the United States. I intend to sign an Executive order to extend the waiver of the application of the relevant export criterion of the Nuclear Non-Proliferation Act for an additional 12 months from March 10, 1989.

Sincerely,

GEORGE BUSH

Note: Identical letters were sent to Jim Wright, Speaker of the House of Representatives, and Dan Quayle, President of the Senate.

Remarks to Drug Enforcement Administration Officers in New York, New York

March 9, 1989

Thank you, Bob Stutman, and to Commissioner and, I guess, all our distinguished guests. Secretary Bennett—this is my man here on the left, the man that I have selected, and that the country, I think, overwhelmingly approves, to be the first drug czar in the history of this country. I'm glad he came up here with me today. And to all of the prosecutors, and especially each one of you out there on the cutting edge, on the front line, thank you for being here. And you have important work to do, and Bob gave you the time frame: short, but to me, very important. I have a chance to say hello to Ms. Hatcher—I wish the circumstances were different—but also to listen and learn when we finish here, listen to some of those who are out there every single day risking their lives.

In the empty streets of an island borough, the life of Everett Hatcher was ended with some four cowardly shots. And the echoes of those four shots were heard in Washington and, I'd say even more important, all across this country, where decent men and women share your sense of loss and share your sense of outrage. Here in New York, as in other cities across the country, the war is no metaphor. Before we could—I say "we," as a country—bury Everett Hatcher last week, another officer was gunned down, felled by a single shot fired pointblank beneath his bulletproof vest. And as we speak, those accused of ambushing Eddie Byrne, one of New York's finest, are standing trial in this city. And this week, the DEA group that helped handle security for Everett's funeral is in yet another New York courtroom, testifying about the attempted murder of Special Agent Bruce Traverse.

You know that my personal interest and the interest of the Nation goes beyond today's visit. As Vice President, I wrote to Bruce Traverse while he was in the hospital, and now, Bruce—all of us are glad that he's recovering so well. Last week, Matthew Byrne, the dad to Eddie Byrne, came down to the White House for dinner with Barbara and me, joining us for a private dinner there. He couldn't believe he was in the White House, and I couldn't believe I was, either. [*Laughter*] So, we had a nice private dinner. But it was important to me that he come. Earlier today, as I said, I had the pleasure to—privilege, put it that way, of visiting with Mary Jane, a woman of enormous dignity and strength—she and her two kids and husband's mother and sisters.

And so, it's been quite an education. And I understand, I think, the special and dangerous challenges that all New York drug enforcement officers face. This area leads the Nation in overall consumption, distribution, the importation of narcotics, run by a well-armed cross-section of drug traffickers as diverse as this city itself. Your role in this battle is very special. You put your life on the line every day. And if the legions of State and local patrolmen represent the infantrymen in this effort—and I salute them at every occasion—then you are something like the Special Forces, the Green Berets, if you will, of narcotics enforcement.

Like Everett Hatcher, many of you have worked undercover, in effect, operating, if you want to use the conventional war analogy, behind enemy lines. And I admire your courage. When I was a kid in World War II, I was behind enemy lines only briefly, sick and paddling in a little raft to get away from a Japanese-held island. But it was enough to know what it feels like—and I'll confess it—to be scared. And each of you probably has been there. You know the dry mouth and the moist palms and the ball of ice that grips your stomach.

And you know, it used to be unthinkable to shoot a cop. And no longer—Bob was telling me this upstairs—no longer. Today narcotics agents are sometimes the first ones shot, targeted by criminals armed with a staggering array of battlefield weaponry. The explosive, expensive lesson of the past year in New York is that the rules of the game have dramatically changed.

Well, we've got to deliver some news to the bad guys. The hunting season is over. The rules on our side have changed, too. And we still need more change in those rules. But they're changing fast, and it's about time.

The scales of justice are becoming more balanced because of the newly enacted Federal drug laws. New York policemen and all of you in this room deserve all the protection that tough laws can offer. I've asked Bill Bennett to look into what can be done to prevent these fully automatic assault weapons from falling into the hands of the criminals that you face. Drug dealers need to understand a simple fact: You shoot a cop, and you're going to be severely punished—fast. And if I had my way, I'd say with your life.

Drug traffickers used to know that. But it's been over 25 years since anyone has faced the death penalty in this State, and they may have gotten a little forgetful. But I want you to know that I have not changed my view. I strongly support the death penalty for the crimes we're talking about here today. And I want to have it as Federal law, and I want to see it swiftly and firmly, fairly enacted. The killing's got to stop.

I wish Senator D'Amato had come up with me today. He couldn't leave the Senate, and it was legitimate Senate business. He's been in the forefront, though, down there, of the drug question—a strong leader, a tough, no-nonsense fighter against drugs. And he has been very helpful to me in having me understand the problems that you face. I understand that this State is the home to an estimated 260,000 heroin addicts—half of all those in the United States. And in the city alone, another 600,000 people are believed dependent on crack or cocaine.

And not surprisingly, the seizures that you've made are correspondingly huge. DEA New York is responsible for 30 to 50 percent of all heroin seized by the DEA nationwide each year. And last year, you seized more than 10,000 kilograms of cocaine in or destined for New York, almost 20 percent of the entire DEA nationwide total. In January, you recovered nearly $20 million from a furniture store delivery van, said to be the largest cash seizure in the world. And these impressive figures are a credit to your talent and dedication and to the effective working relations you've forged with your Federal, State, and local counterparts.

And still, we in Washington understand that the importance of a case cannot be measured merely by the size of the seizures or the numbers of arrests. Statistics in the drug war become mind-numbing as well as mind-boggling. And wars aren't won by statistics. We know wars are won by winning battles, and in this war, battles are won by putting particular drug organizations out of business. It's done the old-fashioned way, one group at a time.

And you in New York have done just that. And the names are as familiar to you here as the battlefields of World War II are to my generation: United States versus Torres, Monsanto, LIDO, Based Balls—Bob was explaining this to me just a minute ago—the Flying Dragons, Lai King Man, Reiter-Jackson. These are more than buy-busts, more than just another news conference with powder on the table, no matter how impressive those conferences are. Each of these cases represents an entire organization put behind bars, out of business. And most importantly, each of these cases involved sophisticated, long-term investigations. And several were among the first cases in the entire country to make use of the new drug kingpin statutes. Nearly all involved task force cooperation and the pioneering use of forfeiture laws, in some cases to spectacular effect. The forfeitures from the Torres brothers, I'm told, may ultimately total $30 to $50 million.

And just as the death penalty for cop killers helps even the odds, stripping the enemy of their ill-gotten gains turns the tables in a dramatic and highly effective way. Perhaps you heard Woody Allen's wry observation: "Organized crime in America takes in over $40 billion a year and spends very little on office supplies." Philosopher, that he is.

Experts have estimated that today drugs alone count for $110 billion—an industry right here in our own country. We're hurting the drug kingpins where they live when we take their money, and we're going to get even better at taking it. We've got to be. Ladies and gentlemen, we do intend to prevail. The scourge will end. I will lead the fight. Bill Bennett, our nation's first drug czar—tenacious, unafraid—is going to be right there at my side.

And although we meet on a crucial battlefield of this war, you might say, it is a war that is being waged on many fronts. Last month I spoke to Congress about four areas: rehabilitation, education, interdiction, and enforcement. And in a time of budget constraints—and regrettably, we are living in such a time—I asked for an increase of $1 billion in budget outlays to fund these new efforts. And for you in Federal law enforcement, our proposal budgets a record $4.1 billion, fully 70 percent of the total. By 1995, we also intend to reduce present prison overcrowding by 50 percent.

And beyond enforcement, other monies will go to expanded treatment for the innocent and the poor, like the over 5,000 babies born in New York last year already addicted to drugs. Other new funds will go to cut the waiting time for the treatment programs, perhaps along the lines of the innovative oral methadone program at New York's Beth Israel Hospital, designed to get the addicts off the needles as well as heroin.

Mary Jane Hatcher spoke with eloquence last week about the responsibility mainstream America and so-called casual cocaine users must bear for the death of her husband. Well, $1.1 billion of our request will go for prevention and education, to let the casual users know the risk they take and the price they may have to pay and to tell our children that drugs are wrong.

While there may not be light at the end of the tunnel, there does seem to be some light coming in under the door. At the Apollo Theatre in Harlem one Wednesday last month, the amateur night performances were interrupted by spontaneous antidrug messages from the stage and then supportive chants from the crowd. And things like this don't happen because of government programs: They happen because attitudes are beginning to change, and they are changing because the American people are behind your efforts all the way.

Attitudes are beginning to change overseas as well. Your boss, the Attorney General [Richard L. Thornburgh], returns today from meetings with officials in Colombia, Bolivia, and Peru. And Bill and I will meet with him as soon as he gets back. I think we're having lunch tomorrow at the White House to be briefed on this trip. And I know that some of you have also served or will serve your own tours in South America, a tribute to our increased cooperation there.

When I first became Vice President 8 years ago, several South American Presidents told me: "It's your problem. You're the consumer. If it weren't for the rich gringos to the north, we wouldn't have the problem." But now they see that the narcotics have affected their own kids, their own society. Look at Colombia, where the Supreme Court Justices were mowed down like tenpins.

Obviously, the race is far from won. But there is power in us yet. And we in Washington will continue to understand, to learn—but certainly to support your work here. The Adamita trial, the Johnny Kon and Brooks Davis cases, the new seizure program in which whole apartment buildings are wrested back from the crack lords who control them—they're all important to this fight. But first and foremost, the killing must stop. And we must repeat it until we're hoarse, repeat it until we're heard, from the Apollo Theatre to the halls of Congress to anyone who doesn't seem to understand what it is you are up against out there on the street. The killing must stop!

And what happened on the streets of Staten Island last week was a horrible tragedy which means—you knew it all along—that you have an important task ahead. The cowards who murdered Everett Hatcher should be given no rest. But be careful out there. Remember the tearful salute of 9-year-old Zachary, and find these criminals. Bring them to justice. Nobody—nobody but nobody is going to beat the DEA.

May God bless you all, and thanks for what you're doing for the United States.

Note: The President spoke at 4:19 p.m. in the auditorium at the Drug Enforcement Administration. He was introduced by Robert Stutman, Special Agent in charge of the New York City field office. In his opening remarks, the President referred to New York City Police Commissioner Benjamin Ward and William J. Bennett, Director-designate of National Drug Control Policy.

Remarks at the United Negro College Fund Dinner in New York, New York
March 9, 1989

Thank you, Michael Jordan, for that introduction. Barbara and I are delighted to be with you, speaking before the olives, the celery, the raw carrots. [*Laughter*] But we've got to get back to Washington fast—[*laughter*]—the Senate is still in session, and our dog is pregnant. [*Laughter*]

I want to just add my voice of congratulations to Gus Hawkins and Larry Rawl and Paul Simon. You honor three good people. And I want to thank Hugh Cullman, who gives so much of himself to the United Negro College Fund, and, of course, salute Chris Edley, a friend of longstanding. You know, Paul Simon once wrote a song called simply, "Old Friends." And I'm delighted to see my old friends Bill and Vi Trent here with us tonight.

You know, as Michael said, my association with the UNCF got started there at Yale University in '48. And Bill Trent came up to New Haven and talked to a lot of young idealistic people about his vision for higher education, and he did a superb job. And so today, when he and Vi flew up with me on Air Force One, I had this great feeling of nostalgia. And his 79th birthday I think is tomorrow, but in any event, it's great to be with this old friend way down on the end of the line. Also with us on Air Force One was another executive director of the UNCF, Art Fletcher, who's here somewhere. But we had good representation. And you talk about the hard sell, they're still doing it. [*Laughter*]

Tonight, flanked by old friends and, in a real sense, family—because my brother, John, is active in this crusade, and I consider many of you here family—I am grateful for your company. During my student days at Yale, I first saw the fund invest in higher education and in America. And then, as now, it insisted that excellence become a way of life and a higher learning a bequest. And as an undergraduate, I came to grasp what Churchill talked about when he said, "Personally, I am always ready to learn, though I do not always enjoy being taught." [*Laughter*]

Well, for nearly half a century, this fund has taught so that America could learn, and the gentler impulses of mankind was high on the teaching agenda. And you have helped society's disadvantaged cast off despair and poverty. And through such friends as Bill Trent and now Chris and then Frederick D. Patterson—and, yes, he is still sorely missed—you have endorsed liberty, opportunity, and the dignity of work.

But most of all, you really have shown

how the conscience and education can fulfill the promise of America: to right wrong, to love freedom, to demand equality for all. And for that, I congratulate you. And yet I challenge you, too. Black and white, together—we know that America will not be a good place for any of us to live until it is a good place for all of us to live.

Most Americans, I'm convinced, believe that government can be an instrument of healing. There are times when government must step in where others fear to tread. My friends, I share those beliefs, and as President, I will act on them.

I'm delighted that my Secretary of Education, our distinguished Secretary of Education Larry Cavazos, is with us here tonight, sitting over here. For America, it seems to me, means pride—individually, culturally, racially. And America means, in the words of Dr. King, that "injustice anywhere is a threat to justice everywhere." And it does mean opportunity for those who need jobs and who dream of owning homes. And it means the hope that tomorrow will be brighter than today. How can we best inspire that hope and secure the promise of America? I do believe that the answer is in education. Education knows no barriers, accepts no limits. Education is a ladder; it embodies self-respect, not dependency. Education can give minorities a greater voice and then make sure that that voice is heard.

Since 1944, when Dr. Patterson founded the UNCF, your voice has resounded from colleges like Tuskegee and Morehouse and Spellman and Fisk. And I'm going to hurt a lot of feelings here tonight, because I was in a receiving line, and I was so impressed with the names that came flowing back as I met the presidents of these distinguished universities. Black colleges have ennobled such Americans as Leontyne Price, Frank Yerby, Azie Taylor Morton, and our next Secretary of Health and Human Services, my dear friend, Dr. Lou Sullivan, who is here with us tonight.

It is said that the woman who Time calls the Silver Fox—[*laughter*]—was responsible for Lou Sullivan's being appointed to this Cabinet, and I'll give her some credit. [*Laughter*] I want to gun down the rumor, though, that I appointed Lou Sullivan to be Secretary because when as president of Morehouse Medical School he was working my wife to death as a board member. And it's rumored I just wanted him to get out of there to let up on her—not true. [*Laughter*]

As you know, in September 1981, President Reagan signed that Executive Order 12320, committing the Federal Government to increase its support of historical black colleges and universities. And our goal was to identify and eliminate unfair barriers to participation in federally sponsored programs. And our means was to involve the private sector and to motivate the 27 Federal agencies which provide nearly all the Federal funding.

And did it work? Did it ever—in fiscal '81, historical black colleges received $545 million; fiscal year '87, $684. And moreover, research and development, which includes funds for nonscientific institutional development, comprised nearly half of all funding for historically black colleges. Our White House Science and Technology Advisory Committee fostered science, math, and engineering programs and curricula. And this comprehensive HBCU effort has attacked the four horsemen of the American night: illiteracy and inequality, indigence and fear. Great beginnings—crawling before we walk and then run. Great beginnings, and now let's build on them. And we have done much, but there remains so much more left to do.

My friends, 8 weeks ago I think it was, there in the White House complex, I met with the presidents of many of the colleges represented here tonight to probe exactly where we are going and how. And we discussed faculty development and merit scholarships, community college grants and institutional planning. And from that meeting, and others like it, came six new initiatives which will help do nationally what you have done historically: enrich education so that education can enrich our lives. And after listening to your presidents, I proposed that Congress fund $60 million over 4 years in endowment-matching grants. We put our money on the table. And now I want to challenge the private sector. It's a beginning. We need the help of the private sector; the time has come.

And secondly, if excellence breeds achievement, that excellence should be rewarded in grade schools, in high school, and at our colleges and university. And so, I want Congress to create a $500 million program to reward America's merit schools, the schools which improve the most.

And thirdly, I want it to create special Presidential awards for the best teachers in every State.

And next, I want to see the expanded use of magnet schools to give parents and students the freedom of choice.

And I've also proposed a new program to encourage alternative certification: to allow talented Americans from every field to teach in America's school classrooms. Consider that today, in many areas, a John Updike or an Alex Haley could not qualify to teach high school creative writing. There is something wrong, and we've got to change that system. My point is that when rules are so inflexible that creativity and talent and imagination aren't welcome in our schools it's time to change those rules.

And finally, through a new program of National Science Scholars, I seek to give America's youth a special incentive to excel in science and math. The National Science Foundation predicts a shortage of 400,000 scientists by the year 2000. Through excellence in education, we must and will reverse that trend. And I see the historical black colleges as an enormous resource to do just exactly that.

And yet I recognize that these proposals—all of this isn't enough; it never is. As Americans, we never are satisfied. We know that when a dream comes true it gives rise to even bigger and better dreams. And so, my appeal tonight is that we work to build a better America. I feel deeply in my heart about the United Negro College Fund. And I came up to tell you, at this highly successful dinner that Hugh and Chris and Michael and others here at this dais and all of you out there worked so hard on to make so successful, I want to help. I want the United States Government to help. And Barbara and I as individuals want to join you in this enormous power of the private sector to do all we can to help you achieve your goals and your ideals.

And thank you all, and God bless you.

Note: The President spoke at 7:51 p.m. in the Imperial Ballroom at the Sheraton Center Hotel. In his remarks, he referred to Michael H. Jordan, Hugh Cullman, Christopher S. Edley, William Trent, and Frederick D. Patterson, member of the board of directors, chairman of the board of directors, president and chief executive officer, first executive director, and founder of the United Negro College Fund, respectively. Representative Augustus F. Hawkins of California; Lawrence G. Rawl, chairman of Exxon Corp.; and entertainer Paul Simon were given the Frederick D. Patterson Distinguished Leadership Award. Following his remarks, the President returned to Washington, DC.

Statement on the Failure of the Senate To Approve the Nomination of John Tower as Secretary of Defense

March 9, 1989

John Tower has devoted his life to service of country. Whether in the U.S. Senate, at the arms control negotiating table, or in the privacy of his counsel to Presidents, he has always held the interests of this nation above all else. John Tower has been steadfast in his advocacy of a strong defense and consistent in support of the many principles for which he fought throughout his career. He is and will remain my friend.

I have read Senator Tower's statement regarding the decision of the Senate and find its dignity and lack of rancor to be typical of the man whose leadership, knowledge, and experience would have benefited the Department of Defense and the Nation.

Instead of the recompense of a grateful nation, John Tower's lot in the past weeks has been a cruel ordeal. For this, I am truly sorry for both him and his family.

The Senate has made its determination. I respect its role in doing so, but I disagree with the outcome. I am also concerned by the way in which perceptions based on groundless rumor seemed to be the basis on which at least some made up their minds in judging a man well-qualified to be my Secretary of Defense. Now, however, we owe it to the American people to come together and move forward.

Nomination of Wendell Lewis Willkie II To Be General Counsel of the Department of Commerce
March 9, 1989

The President today announced his intention to nominate Wendell Lewis Willkie II to be General Counsel of the Department of Commerce. He would succeed Robert H. Brumley II.

Mr. Willkie was counsel in the office of the President-elect, 1988–1989, and has served as special counsel to Bush-Quayle '88. He was General Counsel at the Department of Education, 1985–1988, and Chief of Staff and Counselor to the Secretary of the Department of Education, 1985. Mr. Willkie was Associate Counsel to the President at the White House, 1984–1985, and General Counsel for the National Endowment for the Humanities, 1982–1984. He was also an associate with the law firm of Simpson, Thacher & Bartlett in New York City, 1978–1982.

Mr. Willkie graduated from Harvard College (B.A., 1973); Oxford University, Rhodes Scholarship (B.A., 1975; M.A., 1983); and the University of Chicago (J.D., 1978). He was born October 29, 1951, in Indianapolis, IN. He is married and resides in Washington, DC.

Nomination of Michael Rucker Darby To Be an Under Secretary of Commerce
March 9, 1989

The President today announced his intention to nominate Michael Rucker Darby to be Under Secretary of Commerce for Economic Affairs. He would succeed Robert Ortner.

Since 1986 Mr. Darby has been Assistant Secretary for Economic Policy at the Department of the Treasury in Washington, DC. He was also a member of the National Commission on Superconductivity, 1988–1989. Prior to this he was at the University of California at Los Angeles, serving as professor, John E. Anderson Graduate School of Management, 1987 to present; professor of the department of economics, 1978–1987; associate professor, 1973–1978; and visiting assistant professor, 1972–1973. Mr. Darby has been vice president and director of Paragon Industries, Inc., 1964–1982.

Mr. Darby graduated from the Dartmouth College (A.B., 1967) and the University of Chicago (M.A., 1968; Ph.D., 1970).

Nomination of Dennis Edward Kloske To Be an Under Secretary of Commerce

March 9, 1989

The President today announced his intention to nominate Dennis Edward Kloske to be Under Secretary of Commerce for Export Administration. He would succeed Paul Freedenberg.

Since 1987 Mr. Kloske has been Deputy Under Secretary of Defense for Planning and Resources in Washington, DC, and serves concurrently as Special Adviser for Armaments to the Deputy Secretary of Defense. Prior to this he was detailed to the White House as Adviser to the Special Counselor to the President, 1987. From 1985 to 1987, Mr. Kloske served as Special Adviser for Armaments to the United States Ambassador to NATO and concurrently served as Special Adviser for NATO Armaments to the Deputy Secretary of Defense, 1986. From 1983 to 1985, he served as Special Assistant to the U.S. NATO Ambassador. Mr. Kloske has also served as director of strategic planning at the Georgetown Center for Strategic and International Studies.

Mr. Kloske graduated from Harvard College (B.A., 1976). From 1977 to 1979, he attended Oxford University as a Rhodes Scholar. In January 1989, he received the Medal for Distinguished Public Service, the highest civilian award in the Department of Defense. Mr. Kloske was born September 11, 1954, in Rome, Italy.

Nomination of Eric I. Garfinkel To Be an Assistant Secretary of Commerce

March 9, 1989

The President today announced his intention to nominate Eric I. Garfinkel to be an Assistant Secretary of Commerce (Import Administration). He would succeed Jan W. Mares.

Since 1988 Mr. Garfinkel has been a member of the transition team for the office of the President-elect. Prior to this he was Vice President and General Counsel of the Overseas Private Investment Corporation in Washington, DC, 1987–1988. He was a partner with the law firm of Anderson, Hibey, Nauheim, and Blair in Washington, DC, 1983–1987. Mr. Garfinkel has served as Deputy Assistant Director for Commerce and Trade in the Office of Policy Development at the White House, 1982–1983, and attorney-adviser in the Office of the U.S. Trade Representative, 1981–1982. He has also served as an associate with the law firm of deKieffer, Berg, Creskoff, 1980–1981.

Mr. Garfinkel graduated from the University of Maryland at College Park (B.A., 1976) and Emory University (J.D., 1979). He is married, has two children, and resides in Chevy Chase, MD.

Nomination of Michael Paul Galvin To Be an Assistant Secretary of Commerce

March 9, 1989

The President today announced his intention to nominate Michael Paul Galvin to be an Assistant Secretary of Commerce (Export Administration). He would succeed Michael

E. Zacharia.

Since 1978 Mr. Galvin has been a partner with the law firm of Winston & Strawn in Chicago, IL. He has served as president of the National Strategy Forum and has been involved in various civic and political activities.

Mr. Galvin graduated from Boston College (B.S., 1974) and Illinois Institute of Technology/Chicago-Kent College of Law (J.D., 1978). He was born July 8, 1952. He is married, has two children, and resides in Chicago, IL.

Nomination of Robert P. Davis To Be Solicitor of the Department of Labor

March 9, 1989

The President today announced his intention to nominate Robert P. Davis to be Solicitor of the Department of Labor. He would succeed George R. Salem.

Since 1985 he has been a partner with the law firm of Anderson, Hibey, Nauheim, and Blair. Mr. Davis served as Chief of Staff to Secretary of Transportation Elizabeth Hanford Dole, 1983–1985. He also served as a Special Assistant to the Deputy Attorney General at the Department of Justice, 1974–1980.

Mr. Davis graduated from Brown University (A.B., 1971), Boston University (M.A., 1972), and Georgetown University (J.D., 1980). He is married, has two children, and resides in Alexandria, VA.

Nomination of Dale Triber Tate To Be an Assistant Secretary of Labor

March 9, 1989

The President today announced his intention to nominate Dale Triber Tate to be an Assistant Secretary of Labor (Public and Intergovernmental Affairs). She would succeed Jerry D. Blakemore.

Since 1985 Mrs. Tate has served as deputy press secretary to Senate Majority/Minority Leader Robert Dole and has served as spokesperson for Senator Dole's Presidential campaign. Prior to this she was the chief economics reporter for Congressional Quarterly, 1979–1985, and was the congressional editor for the Oil & Gas Journal, 1975–1979.

Mrs. Tate received a bachelor of journalism degree from the University of Missouri (1969).

Nomination of Jennifer Lynn Dorn To Be an Assistant Secretary of Labor

March 9, 1989

The President today announced his intention to nominate Jennifer Lynn Dorn to be an Assistant Secretary of Labor (Policy). She would succeed Michael E. Baroody.

Since 1987 Mrs. Dorn has served as the director of strategic planning for the Martin

Marietta Corp. Prior to this she was an Associate Deputy Secretary at the Department of Transportation and served as Chief of Staff, 1985–1987. Mrs. Dorn was the Director at the Office of Commercial Space Transportation at the Department of Transportation, 1984–1985.

Mrs. Dorn received a B.A. from Oregon State University and an M.P.A. from the University of Connecticut. She is married and resides in Bethesda, MD.

Remarks at the Swearing-in Ceremony for Louis W. Sullivan as Secretary of Health and Human Services

March 10, 1989

The President. To Members of the United States Congress here, Senate and House; members of the President's Cabinet; to Judge Higginbotham, who'll be doing the honors here in a little bit; and old friend, Senator Ed Brooke, whom I'm so glad to see; distinguished dais guests; and of course, the Sullivan family, just let me say that Barbara and I are very pleased to be over here. I know the Sullivans, but I didn't know that Halstead Sullivan, outstanding student, president of his school, I believe, the University of Virginia, could sing. But you heard him not miss a note—unbelievable.

But, Lou, before beginning, I do want to make an announcement today. I think it's one that concerns people and everyone in this room. It's about a public health issue that I know this audience particularly can appreciate. Then a few words about our new Secretary. But this one relates to the health and well-being of our environment. I want to announce an important step that we're taking to address an environmental issue of great concern, and that is the transboundary movement of hazardous wastes.

During the past year, there have been many accounts of the risks to human health and the environment, too, posed by certain exports of hazardous waste, particularly to developing countries. And the U.S. has been a world leader in requiring the informed consent of receiving countries before allowing such exports of hazardous waste. And I intend to continue and to extend this leadership role by seeking new legislation that will give the United States Government authority to ban all exports of hazardous waste except where we have an agreement with the receiving country providing for the safe handling and management of those wastes. We're determined to work with other concerned governments to exercise wise stewardship over our environment, particularly where matters of health are concerned.

Now, on to the business at hand. The swearing-in of Dr. Louis Sullivan is a proud day for all involved: for this Department, whose dedicated workers are welcoming as their new leader a man of energy, enthusiasm, and intellect; for Dr. Sullivan's family—Ginger, Paul, Shanta, and Halstead—whose share in Lou's success has been beyond measure; and for all of us who know Lou, admire him, and consider him our friend. Dr. Sullivan has enjoyed a distinguished career as physician, scientist, scholar, teacher, administrator. But what sets Lou Sullivan apart is that something extra he brings to his work—a sense of mission.

As the first president of Morehouse—in this instance, Morehouse School of Medicine—Lou made it his goal not only to train a new generation of minority physicians but to instill in them this sense of service, a commitment to minister to communities in our inner cities and in rural America, where health care facilities are stretched thin and doctors are in short supply. In the past 7 years, Barbara and I have taken a special interest in the work being done by Dr. Sullivan at Morehouse. I knew that a man of his vision could contribute to our national well-being in much the same way he contributed to the health and well-being of so many people throughout his career in medicine.

Lou, the assignment that you are about to

undertake is among the most diverse and difficult public service has to offer. The Department of HHS is involved in a vast enterprise. You command a $400 billion budget and 114,000 employees. And in all, your responsibilities range from regulating food and drugs and conducting major medical research to providing support and care for the elderly, the disabled, and the disadvantaged. What this Department does affects the life of each and every American, and especially the lives of the least advantaged among us.

I know, Lou, that we spoke about the scope of the administrative challenges that you face here at HHS, but I'm not sure I mentioned to you that your budget ranks fourth in the world—behind the U.S., the Soviet Union, and Japan. Then comes HHS—[*laughter*]—do not declare your independence. [*Laughter*]

We look to you and the HHS team to meet a number of major challenges in the years ahead. We ask you to work to get better value for health care dollars, targeting effective services, finding ways to contain the escalating costs of medical care without compromising the quality of health service. Work to sustain programs like AFDC—Aid to Families with Dependent Children—and Head Start that help build the foundation for families and children to overcome disadvantages and difficult circumstances, to succeed and grow strong. Advance our understanding of the AIDS virus, and move us towards a cure. And to that end, I've directed HHS to pull together 23 separate AIDS projects now in progress into a more focused effort under the direction of the Public Health Service. I've called on Congress to provide $1.6 billion for the Public Health Service efforts in 1990. That's an increase of 24 percent over 1989. And finally, Lou, I know you'll take a position right on the front line, joining, I'd say, everybody in our Cabinet and certainly all here in the war on drugs. Too many lives have been imperiled or lost to drugs, too much human potential is being ground up and wasted. I've said it before, but this scourge must stop.

And I'll need you to train scientists, to conduct the right kind of research. I'll look to you to assess the data on drugs and tell us where and how to respond. And I'm counting on you to see that State organizations and hospitals, volunteer groups get the kind of technical assistance they need to help us win this battle. I'm asking you to work with me, with Bill Bennett, to find solid strategies for the prevention of drug abuse and effective treatment for those already caught in the trap.

And so, Mr. Secretary, I hope these and the many challenges that I have not named will be enough to keep you busy. Rest assured you'll have help. The staff over here is among the most talented and dedicated in the Federal service. And they understand the importance of the work that they do and the differences that HHS makes in the lives of the many millions of Americans served by this Department.

HHS is the Department that, more than any other at the Federal level, gives shape and form to the promise that America makes its people, the promise I've made to you: to fashion for ourselves, yes, a kinder and gentler nation and to take care of those in need, especially our children and the elderly, to steady those who seek only an opportunity to better themselves and their families.

So, it is noble work that you all are engaged in. And, Mr. Secretary, as you make this responsibility your own, you have our sincere best wishes, my complete confidence, and my full support.

And now on to the brief, but important, formal ceremony of swearing in Lou Sullivan as the next Secretary.

[*At this point, Secretary Sullivan was sworn in.*]

Secretary Sullivan. Mr. President, Mrs. Bush, friends and colleagues, let me thank all of you for being here. As you might imagine, this is a special moment for the Sullivan family. Mr. President, thank you for your friendship, your trust, and your confidence. Mrs. Bush, as a friend, for your work as a trustee of the Morehouse School of Medicine, for your efforts to advance literacy, for your help to those in need, thank you for reminding all of us of the importance of love, compassion, and care for our fellow man. I'm also grateful to Senators

Dole, Simpson, Mitchell, Bentsen, Packwood, Kennedy, and Hatch, Thurmond, and many others for their assistance in the Congress. Congressman Newt Gingrich and the entire Georgia delegation, I'm grateful for your support.

God has been good to Lou Sullivan for the past 55 years. And things have been particularly bright since I had the good sense to marry Ginger some 34 years ago. I've been blessed with a fine family. And for 21 years, I learned, practiced, and taught medicine and conducted research in some of the Nation's finest medical institutions. Then in July of 1975 I accepted the opportunity of a lifetime: to develop a medical school that would concentrate its energies on the education of those minorities who had been overlooked. It was a chance to see that young blacks, Hispanics, Native Americans, who might otherwise not have an opportunity, were given the same opportunities that I had received as a young man.

There's a special place for the Morehouse School of Medicine in the hearts of Lou and Ginger Sullivan. There's a special place in the hearts of the Sullivans for the people who worked so hard and unselfishly to make that school a reality, many of whom are here today and we count among our friends. When I was installed on July 1, 1981, as the first president of the medical school upon its gaining independence from Morehouse College, it never entered my mind that I would ever consider doing anything else. But one day a friend called. So, here I am, Mr. President. [*Laughter*]

There is no title, no award, no recognition which can compare to the trust of a friend. The honor of that call, Mr. President, will never be forgotten. You have given me the opportunity to serve—to serve you and our nation. You've given a challenge to me and to this Department, and I want you to know we will meet that challenge.

We will work to assure the ongoing solvency of programs like Social Security and Medicare. We will work hard to find ways to contain escalating medical costs without sacrificing our goal of quality health care for all. We will continue to look for ways to better serve our nation's poor and help them work their way out of poverty. Those programs like Aid to Families with Dependent Children and Head Start, which have been so beneficial to our disadvantaged citizens, will be sustained.

Mr. President, we are challenged to continue a strong biomedical research effort in our quest for a cure for AIDS, this disease which destroys our youth and saps our nation's vitality. We will continue our assault against cancer, heart disease, diabetes, arthritis, and the many other disorders afflicting our citizens.

The issue of drugs in our society is a problem that affects us all. It eats at the fiber of our families and at our very social structure. President Bush, today this Department joins with me in a commitment to work with you and with our drug adviser in doing all that we can to halt this terrible epidemic.

With your challenge, Mr. President, you've given us the opportunity to shape the future—to shape the future through the development of health promotion and preventive medicine strategies, to shape the future through the implementation of last year's welfare reform legislation. We will seek ways to strengthen family life in our country and to restore our sense of community, our shared sense of responsibility and commitment to each other.

We have been given the opportunity to stress the value of every life through the promotion of adoption and by focusing our efforts on the poor, the disadvantaged, and the neglected in our society. We have the opportunity to see that rural and inner-city health needs are not forgotten, that the poor of our nation are cared for properly and with dignity. The health of our minority citizens—black, Hispanic, Native American—and those others who have yet to fully realize the American dream is the concern of us all.

Mr. President, you've called for a kinder and gentler nation, a goal which I support with enthusiasm. As you have noted, there's no other department or agency of our government where that call can be more directly implemented than here in Health and Human Services. Health and Human Services is the hub of a vast wheel whose spokes radiate out to touch all Americans, from the onset of life through health and sickness, from the foods we eat to the medicines we take. Our children, our parents, our youth, our seniors—all are affected by the activities of this vast agency.

During my tenure, the offices of the Department will have a human face. The regulations promulgated will carry a gentle touch. Health and Human Services employees will be bound by the hallmark of service and take their pride in the health and assistance offered their fellow Americans.

Mr. President, you have delivered today a challenge; you have granted an opportunity. I'm grateful to you, sir. I accept your challenge. I cherish the opportunity. I will keep your trust. Thank you, Mr. President.

Note: The President spoke at 10:18 a.m. in the Great Hall at the Department of Health and Human Services. Halstead Sullivan sang the national anthem at the ceremony.

Remarks to Members of the National Conference of State Legislators

March 10, 1989

It's good to see all of you. Listen, nice welcome, thank you. To our Secretary, Secretary Dole, my greetings—delighted to see you here. And Andy Card and our—ripped off right out of the ranks of one of your States, the former speaker, Deb Anderson here, who I'm delighted to see in her official duties. And I'm pleased to be here. And I would like to thank the president and past officers for your gracious invitation—Sammy Nunez, Lee Daniels, Ted Strickland. I thank all of you.

The last time I spoke, we were in the middle of America, in the middle of summer, and in the midst of a tough campaign year. Fate has smiled since that July day in Indianapolis. Then we were all candidates, probably everybody in this room—maybe an overstatement. Today everyone in this room is a winner. And for those of you who are Republicans, you discerning devils—[*laughter*]—I've got to admit, there was a time when I thought I'd drag all of you down, but here we are. [*Laughter*] And for those of you who are Democrats, I'd like to claim credit, but I can't figure out how at all. But anyway, well done! And in all sincerity, I do want to congratulate every legislative leader in this room, Democrat and Republican alike, because you did win more than a political victory. The highest honor of all you won—opportunity to serve. And I feel that way, have always felt that way about public service. And certainly you do, or you wouldn't be here today.

The problems that confront our country as we near the end of this century often seem bigger than our individual ability to solve them—and they are big. And if we face these problems as only partisans—Democrats or Republicans—or parochial members of a region, or a faction, or an interest group, we've got real problems. But by working together as Americans, we can, I believe, lick any problem, no matter how big, how complex, or how deeply rooted it may be.

There are always naysayers who believe we're going to never clean up the environment or never shelter the homeless, never end that age-old affliction of mankind, poverty—poverty of knowledge and skills, of opportunity, and the poverty of hope. But the cynics never take into account one of the great success stories of our times. And I am talking about State government. In this decade, power flowed from Washington to Austin, to Atlanta, to Sacramento, and to every other State capital. And with it came new responsibilities. I'm talking, of course, of the concept of federalism. And history will remember that you met these broadened responsibilities with distinction.

I know that funds at all levels of State government are tight—all levels of Federal Government are tight. And I know that you're called on every day to make the hard choices, as I am. But by and large, you are meeting the challenge of a frugal age by devising creative new solutions to these age-old problems of care and concern for the very young, the very elderly, the disadvantaged, the dispossessed. So, whenever I see a problem that some say is insurmountable, I draw inspiration from what you are already doing in the States.

The resilience of the State governments in the eighties vindicates, in my view, the wisdom of the Founding Fathers and forever discredits those who would have Washington do it all. And let me assure you, I will preserve and protect a healthy balance, a sharing of power, between the States and Washington, because I fervently believe that federalism works.

And I remember meetings that I had with Governors at the time of the campaign, discussing the social issues. And I learned more from the briefings—this happened to be in a partisan context of a campaign—but I learned more from the briefing by the Governors than any of the people here in Washington to whom I had access because I was Vice President. And I thought about why it made such a difference and why I learned so much from them. And it was because they're on the cutting edge; they are out there working with you all to solve the problems, to figure out what works, to make the changes. And so, that may sound elementary to some, but I think you must know what I mean. Governors have to deal in what works, and they get that from you all, with the representation you give in your districts.

As you know, one policy area clearly designated to us here is national defense. And so, perhaps the appeal I'm going to make to you today will be all the more unprecedented. The time has come for me to enlist your energy and expertise in another national security crisis. And you know what it is, and I know what it is and the American people know what it is. And I'm talking, of course, about the threat of drug abuse to the health and the very future of our nation.

I wish that each and every one of you could have been with me yesterday in New York when I went to the DEA headquarters and I talked—with the widow of the latest victim of the drug criminals at my side—talked to the agents there. But the best part was the meeting afterward, talking in a very private setting to those agents who are undercover, couldn't be out there in public, but who told me, case by case, of the problems they face. And I don't want to get away from the text here too far, but the thing that really impressed me—and I expect some of you who have had leadership roles in your States could talk to this—is that the culture has changed. They say it used to be if you came in and identified yourself as a Fed or a police officer of any sort and drew a weapon on these people, they'd give up. And now they automatically shoot; they go to the barricades. And there's some reasons for that. They get the same penalty for killing a police officer as they get for being caught with a certain amount of narcotics.

We've got to do something about that. Crack, heroin, PCP—these drugs are a plague that leaves an aftermath of shattered minds and, you know, totally wasted potential. No State in the Union is immune to this plague. And drug crimes have claimed thousands of lives, and having seen some of the barricaded crack houses that have been knocked down by the battering rams of the police, it's everywhere. Los Angeles—I went out there one evening and took a look with Daryl Gates at what his officers face every day, and I'll tell you, it really drives it home.

As with every battle this country's ever fought, we are in it together as Americans. And as with a war, we've got to have a strategy, and ours is education, rehabilitation, law enforcement, and then doing better in interdiction. I'm encouraged to see so many State governments forming these intrastate drug task forces and interstate panels to share resources and intelligence. And I would appeal to every State to join these efforts. Every State should look for ways to toughen its drug laws.

The Federal Government, just like the States, is animated by a new get-tough attitude on drugs. And we've stiffened the Federal sentence for drug trafficking to a maximum of life. We've toughened penalties for dealers who use children to deal drugs or sell drugs to the kids. And if you commit a drug-related murder or kill a cop, the toughest sentence you can receive is now the toughest sentence there is, and that is the death penalty. And we've also increased our resources as we've stiffened the sentences.

Since 1981 the Federal antidrug budget has grown by nearly 370 percent. But more was needed, so I'm asking the Congress for $6 billion for our antidrug program in 1990. More than $4 billion will be spent to provide grants to the State and local law enforcement agencies to beef up the Federal enforcement, to enhance our prosecution, detention, and intelligence capabilities. And this includes sustaining the 150 million drug grant programs so that the Department of Justice can help State and local law enforcement agencies catch criminals and warn kids away from drugs.

Another shining example of Federal and State cooperation: the seizure and forfeiture of assets from drug dealers. State agencies that cooperate in drug cases will share the benefits from the sale of yachts, planes, and cars used in drug deals. Again, my experience yesterday—the head of the DEA showed me a table—$20 million of cash that they had gotten in—a part of it. I don't think all $20 million was on that table, but a lot of it was, in small bills, incidentally, twenties, tens, that kind of thing. They had taken this money in one—caught one truck loaded with $20 million, and nobody claimed it. Nobody even inquired about it. Obviously, they didn't want to get in too much trouble. [*Laughter*] But there was no undercover inquiry; that's just the cost of doing business. So, $20 million is down the tube, and go on about our business. Same as they dump their airplanes in the water off the Bahamas—the cost of business. Three Cessnas, and that's the cost of getting the stuff in here.

But even with these programs, the campaign against drug abuse will be hard-fought. It's a war, and it's going to last for years. And perhaps we should take inspiration from a nation at war almost 50 years ago. As Britain faced an adversary that tested the courage and character of its people, Winston Churchill vowed never to surrender. And in today's wars against the pushers, we must draw from these same deep wells of national purpose to summon the spirit of defiance.

Our single most important task is to keep the kids off of drugs and out of trouble, and toward this end I am proposing a $1.1 billion allocation for drug education and prevention—a 16 percent increase over 1989. Some $367 million of this is going to go to the drug-free schools and communities program to help keep the drugs out of our schools, campuses, and neighborhoods—an increase of $12 million here. The programs are many. You're going to be able to take the lead in this effort since more than 80 percent of the funds of the drug-free schools and communities will be allocated to the States and territories.

As you may have heard, we can already take heart from some good news from the classrooms. According to the 1988 national high school senior survey, the proportion of seniors using illicit drugs during the prior year fell from 42 percent in '87 to 39 percent—a modest drop, but at least a decrease. This compares with the peak year of '79, incidentally, when an astounding 54 percent of all American high school seniors used drugs.

Still, 39 percent is horrible. And we're going to spend money to get the job done, but we need to change something. We've got to have a national attitude of intolerance. Let me tell you, Presidents don't normally speak out in favor of intolerance, but the day must soon come when the Nation is utterly intolerant of this casual drug abuse. Back to yesterday, one of the undercover agents telling me about the white collar use—this guy was down somewhere on Wall Street, and it was just considered normal in the firm in which he was operating to—at the end of the day—to offer to the people doing the clerical work there some kind of line of cocaine if they would stay for an extra few hours. I mean we've got to change that whole toleration, that whole cultural identity that suggests that this is the fast lane or the easy way or that it's okay.

Over the next 4 years we're going to face a lot of common challenges. The environment—I do want to do something on that. With the help of the States, I'm convinced we can here. To our prosperity—we're going to ask your forbearance as we call for some tough measures to face down this Federal budget deficit. To our compassion—for those who have yet to participate fully in the American dream.

And the challenge of drug abuse is going to test our resolve and our mettle as a people. So, I just wanted to tell you and pledge to you, leader to leader, that I want to work with you in the State Governments in this struggle. Bill Bennett, our new drug czar, is charged with coming up with a national strategy, a national direction, in 6 months after he takes office. He'll be good. He'll be tough. He's got a difficult assignment because of the way government works—picture in your own State governments. It's not a very neat and easy way to draw the organization chart, because he has to not only get the attention of the Defense Department or the Attorney Generals without the protocol standing over them, he's got to get their attention and have us all marching in the same direction. So, what that means is the President is going to have to be shoulder-to-shoulder with Bill Bennett. And I'm prepared to spend the time and devote the energy necessary to give it that stature because it won't happen if it just bogs down in some kind of bureaucratic turf fights over who's going to do what on interdiction or education or crime-fighting or whatever it is.

So, I wanted to tell you we do want to work with the States. War tested America and her allies in the forties, and so our people are undergoing a test of national will today. To paraphrase Churchill again, we shall not flag or fail. We're going to keep going to win the fight against the scourge of drugs. And I'm confident; I believe it can be done because I sense a change in the country. I sense people; it's more than rhetoric now. I think it's into every community, every State, and certainly all through the Federal Government.

So, we're not going to give up on this one. We need your help; we need your leadership; we need your ideals. I wish that we had more funds to put in a program here or support of an initiative there. But I don't want to mislead you. We're dealing in a time of very constrained Federal resources. So, we've got to do a lot, working with you and working with the programs that I refer to as the Thousand Points of Light: the willingness of one citizen out there willing to help another.

And so, thank you for what you're doing. Thank you for coming here to the White House. I'm delighted to see each and every one of you. God bless you all. Thank you.

Note: The President spoke at 11:11 a.m. at a briefing in Room 450 of the Old Executive Office Building. In his opening remarks, he referred to Secretary of Labor Elizabeth H. Dole; Andrew Card, Assistant to the President and Deputy Chief of Staff; Debra Anderson, Assistant to the President and Director of Intergovernmental Affairs; Sammy Nunez, president of the Louisiana State Senate; Lee Daniels, minority leader of the Illinois State House of Representatives; and Theodore Strickland, president of the Colorado State Senate.

Nomination of Michael Hayden Armacost To Be United States Ambassador to Japan
March 10, 1989

The President today announced his intention to nominate Michael Hayden Armacost to be Ambassador Extraordinary and Plenipotentiary of the United States of America to Japan. He would succeed Michael Mansfield.

Since 1984 Ambassador Armacost has been Under Secretary for Political Affairs at the Department of State in Washington, DC. Prior to this he was Ambassador to the Philippines, 1982–1984. He has served as Principal Deputy Assistant Secretary of State for East Asian and Pacific Affairs, 1980–1981, and Deputy Assistant Secretary for Defense for International Security Affairs, 1978–1980. He has served as senior staff member for East Asia for the National Security Council at the White House, 1977–1978; a member of the policy planning staff at the Department of State, 1974–1976; Special Assistant to Ambassador Robert Stephen Ingersoll in Tokyo, Japan, 1972–1974; and a member of the policy planning staff at the Department of State, 1969–1972.

Ambassador Armacost graduated from Carleton College (B.A., 1958) and Columbia University (M.A., 1961; Ph.D., 1965). He was born April 15, 1937, in Cleveland, OH. He is married, has three children, and resides in Bethesda, MD.

Nomination of John Theodore Sanders To Be Under Secretary of Education

March 10, 1989

The President today announced his intention to nominate John Theodore Sanders to be Under Secretary of Education. He would succeed Linus D. Wright.

Since 1985 Mr. Sanders has been State superintendent of education in Springfield, IL. Prior to this he was State superintendent of public instruction in Carson City, NV, 1979–1985, and an adjunct professor in the College of Education of the University of Nevada at Reno, 1984–1985. He has also held several positions at the New Mexico Department of Education in Santa Fe, including assistant State superintendent for instruction, 1976–1979, assistant State superintendent for administration, 1975–1976, director of the Mutual Action Project, 1973–1975, and mathematics specialist, 1971–1973.

Mr. Sanders graduated from Wayland University (B.S., 1964), Washington State University (M.A., 1970), and the University of Nevada (Ph.D., 1987). He was born September 19, 1941, in Littlefield, TX. He is married, has four children, and resides in Springfield, IL.

Nomination of Nancy Mohr Kennedy To Be an Assistant Secretary of Education

March 10, 1989

The President today announced his intention to nominate Nancy Mohr Kennedy to be Assistant Secretary for Legislation at the Department of Education. She would succeed Frances M. Norris.

Since 1983 Ms. Kennedy was Special Assistant to the President for Legislative Affairs (Senate) at the White House in Washington, DC. Prior to this she was Administrative Assistant for the White House Office of Legislative Affairs, 1981–1983. She has also served in the congressional relations office for the transition of the President-elect, 1980–1981. Ms. Kennedy was Administrative Assistant to the Chairman of the Federal Elections Commission, 1979–1980, and Administrative Assistant for the Senate Republican Policy Committee, 1977–1979. She was Executive Assistant to the Assistant to the President for Legislative Affairs, 1969–1977, and deputy caseworker for the Republican leader of the Senate, Everett McKinley Dirksen.

Ms. Kennedy attended the University of Maryland at College Park. She is a native of Illinois and currently resides in Bethesda, MD.

Letter to the Speaker of the House of Representatives and the Chairman of the Senate Foreign Relations Committee Transmitting a Report on Arms Control Agreements Compliance
March 10, 1989

Dear Mr. Speaker: (Dear Mr. Chairman:)

I am pleased to transmit the enclosed report on the adherence of the United States to obligations undertaken in arms control agreements and on problems related to compliance by other nations with the provisions of bilateral and multilateral arms control agreements to which the United States is a party.

This report, updating last year's report, meets the requirements of Section 52 of the Arms Control and Disarmament Act, as amended by the Arms Control and Disarmament Amendments Act of 1987. It was prepared by the Director of the U.S. Arms Control and Disarmament Agency in coordination with the Secretary of State, the Secretary of Defense, the Secretary of Energy, the Chairman of the Joint Chiefs of Staff, and the Director of Central Intelligence.

In previous reports to the Congress, the United States has made clear its concerns about Soviet noncompliance. These concerns remain. The United States Government takes equally seriously its own commitments to arms control agreements and sets rigid standards and procedures for assuring that it meets its obligations. The United States has been and remains in compliance with all current treaty obligations and political commitments.

This report is unclassified and suitable for general release. However, a classified attachment, providing additional information not available in unclassified form, is being provided under separate cover.

Sincerely,

GEORGE BUSH

Note: Identical letters were sent to Jim Wright, Speaker of the House of Representatives, and Claiborne Pell, chairman of the Senate Foreign Relations Committee.

The President's News Conference
March 10, 1989

The President. Well, good afternoon. I am happy to be here this afternoon to present my nominee to be Secretary of Defense, Congressman Dick Cheney of Wyoming.

Dick is a widely respected man of principle, served his country with distinction for many years. I've known him as a Chief of Staff, government manager—all under President Ford, '75 and '76. I worked with him closely since he's been a part of the Republican leadership. In both the executive branch and in Congress, he's dealt with the problems of national defense. He struggled with the budget—some things every President has to do. And he's weighed the difficult national defense priorities that have come before the Congress. He's been a member of the Intelligence Committee for, I think, 5 years and—a leader in that area. I've heard his thinking on arms control, Central American policy, strategic defense posture, and on the difficult challenges that he knows he faces of reforming procurement process in the Pentagon.

He's a thoughtful man, a quiet man, a strong man—approaches public policy with vigor, determination, and diligence. And this afternoon, we discussed the defense needs of this nation and the heavy responsibilities that go with being Secretary of Defense. And Dick Cheney is a trusted friend and adviser, and I'm convinced that he's going to be a great leader of our nation's military forces.

And now I'd like to ask him to say a few words, and then he and I will be around to respond to a few questions. So, Dick, welcome aboard, and thank you for undertaking this very complicated and difficult assignment. You'll do great.

Representative Cheney. Well, thank you very much, Mr. President. Obviously, things have moved rather rapidly in the last 24 hours. I'm honored to be asked by the President to join his administration. I look forward very much to working with him; and especially also with Brent Scowcroft [Assistant to the President for National Security Affairs], who's an old friend of many years standing; and Jim Baker [Secretary of State], who's an old friend of many years standing, in the difficult assignment ahead. And I think the next 4 years hold significant challenge in terms of U.S. defense policy and foreign policy, and I am glad to be a part of the team and eager to get to work in terms of helping the President address some of those very important issues.

Q. Congressman, two questions. First, could you give us an update on your health, and also what can you tell us about the depth of the expertise you feel you have on defense?

Representative Cheney. Well, first of all, with respect to my health, I have, in the past, been a heart patient. Many of you know I underwent bypass surgery in August of last year. I was, after that surgery, back at work in about 3 weeks. I skied at Christmastime at Vail, if anybody's curious. Skiing was very good at Vail at Christmastime. And I talked just this afternoon with my cardiologist, who's followed my case for several years, to make certain he was aware of this and so that he would be in a position to say, as he has, as he did tell me just today, that there's absolutely no medical reason why I cannot undertake this assignment. I have no restrictions at this point in terms of my own activities.

With respect to my background in the defense area, it's a set of issues that I've been interested in for a long time—obviously had some exposure to them during the Ford years when I served as White House Chief of Staff and sat in on all the National Security Council meetings. I've had an active interest in it in the Congress and currently serve as the senior Republican on the Budget Subcommittee of the Intelligence Committee, which authorizes all of our intelligence programs and the activities of many defense agencies, such as the National Security Agency, Defense Intelligence Agency—all of the tactical intelligence programs across all the services in the Pentagon. So, obviously, there are areas that I need to know and I'll have to work hard on to master, but I feel that I do have a depth of understanding now in very specific areas that come within the general jurisdiction of the Defense Department and the national security in general.

Q. You said that Senator Tower was the best qualified for this job. Where does Congressman Cheney stand in this priority assessment?

The President. I said that on December whatever it was. And now we're in March whatever it is, and as of today, Dick Cheney is the best and the proper choice.

Senate Vote on the Tower Nomination

Q. Now, do you agree with the Vice President in his harsh indictment of the vote on Tower?

The President. I haven't read the harsh indictment. I expect he felt as strongly as many of the Senators, having served in the Senate. But look, that's history. We're moving forward with a new nominee. I told the Senators yesterday when they called—both Senator Mitchell and Senator Nunn—I think Marlin had the release on that—that I was going to work with the Congress. Dick Cheney and I have discussed that. He's confident he can work with the Congress, both Senate and House. And so, there's no point in my dwelling on what happened yesterday. I've got my own views about it. But we've got a big problem out here, and we need to work cooperatively in defense with the Senate and with the House. And we're going to do just that, as Dick Cheney has confirmed.

Secretary of Defense-Designate Cheney

Q. Mr. President, you said when you originally picked your Cabinet that you didn't want to pick anybody from the House or Senate because you didn't want to deplete the ranks of Republicans in Congress. Now you've picked Mr. Cheney. What happened to that rule?

The President. This is the exception that proves that rule. [*Laughter*]

Q. For Mr. Cheney. You've said many times that you've enjoyed your work in Congress. Why would you give up a post on the leadership ladder in the House? Are you frustrated because you think that the Republicans are going to be in a minority position ad infinitum, or why have you suddenly decided now to go into the executive branch?

Representative Cheney. Well, first of all, John [John Mashek, Boston Globe], I'm optimistic about the future of the Republican Party in Congress. I think we will become a majority within the next few years. Obviously, I've loved the House of Representatives. I've enjoyed it immensely. I thought that that's where I would spend the bulk of my political career. But when the President asks you to consider a proposition such as this one, you have to take it seriously. And when you look at the challenge that's involved, the importance that he assigns to the problems that have to be addressed in this area, and the basic attraction of taking on a difficult task after I agonized over it—and I did agonize; it was not an easy decision—I decided that I would, in fact, accept the post as Secretary of Defense.

Q. Mr. President, can you give us the timetable of how you reached the decision? When did you first start assembling a short list? How long was the short list? And you've taken so many people from the Ford administration, do you have any role for former President Ford? [*Laughter*]

The President. In inverse order, no. I talk to President Ford—get good advice from him. In terms of how long, I moved fast on this one. I was telling you the truth when I said I have not considered anybody else during the last days of the Senate debate. I wasn't about to shift gears or send a signal that wasn't true, that I was interested in anything other than the confirmation of John Tower. That's history; that's done. So, when it became clear yesterday that the votes weren't there yesterday, I began to think and talk to my top advisers here, get opinions from them. They reached out a little bit. And then I called Dick today, and he came over and visited with me about 1 p.m., I think it was. And I said I want to make a decision fast on this, because I know him well and have known him over the years well. And so, that's about the way it evolved.

He wants a followup. [*Laughter*]

Representative Cheney. If I may, John [John Cochran, NBC News], I was first contacted late yesterday afternoon by General Scowcroft and Governor Sununu. We had a discussion at that point that initiated my consideration of it, and I just discussed it with the President today.

Q. Mr. President, have you talked about this selection yet with Senator Nunn and Senator Mitchell? If so, can you describe their reaction a little bit? Did you get into kind of a commitment about the timing of confirmation hearings?

The President. Jerry [Gerald Boyd, New York Times], what we did on that was divide up here just recently the names to talk to, and I believe General Scowcroft talked to Senator Mitchell and to Senator Nunn. And I would let them characterize their reaction to it. And I've talked to the Speaker. The only one of the kind of hierarchy that we haven't reached is Bob Michel. And it's very important that he be notified, but I expect he will be by all of this. [*Laughter*] But nevertheless, we divided it up, and the reaction from the people that we've contacted—the understandable ones—has been very, very positive.

Q. Mr. President, about the hearing schedule——

The President. Oh, I don't know. John, did you talk about timing?

Mr. Sununu. I asked Senator Mitchell to evaluate how quickly it could be done, and we will talk again in the next day or two about what kind of schedule they can produce.

The President. Yes, and we've started the clearances. The name check has been completed—rapid-fire time—and Dick has undergone two thorough, full field checks. And he's had—has there been another one since those?

Representative Cheney. In '69 and '74.

Mr. Sununu. Preliminary check today.

The President. Yes, and the preliminary check today. So, I think that will go very well.

Senate Vote on the Tower Nomination

Q. Mr. President, can I ask more about the Quayle speech? He is out in Indianapolis this afternoon accusing Senate Democrats of using McCarthy-like tactics in the defeat of John Tower. With respect to your comments about putting the Tower nomination behind you, would you tell us if Mr. Quayle speaks for you?

The President. I haven't seen what he said, so I can't tell you whether he speaks for me. I speak for myself. He speaks for himself. But I explained why—that he feels strongly about it. I feel strongly about it, and I'm determined to move forward. And I think that this nomination will set that tone, and we'll see how we go from here.

Defense Budget

Q. Mr. President, one of the things that Senator Tower did in this period was work up a strategy which, apparently, you approved of, which was you would squeeze the defense budget down into the limits set by the Congress if the Congress would let you make some of the—or all of the choices. Is this strategy going to be passed along to Dick Cheney, and do you plan to pursue a similar strategy?

The President. I'm going to have to defer answering that because, though we talked about budget generally and making tough choices generally, we didn't go into that much detail yet. And I think he's entitled to giving me his views on it before we do.

Secretary of Defense-Designate Cheney

Q. Mr. President, have you asked the Congressman the obvious questions: Is there anything in his background that would be prohibitive or embarrassing or anything like that? How much detail have you gone into?

The President. Yes, and I'm satisfied on that.

Q. Mr. President——

Q. Mr. President, can you——

The President. Can't hear you, Sarah [Sarah McClendon, McClendon News Service]. Go ahead, please.

Q. Sorry. You've got me so flustered, I forgot my question. [*Laughter*]

The President. I'll come back. That's not fair.

Senate Vote on the Tower Nomination

Q. Mr. President, if we could go back to Mr. Quayle just for a second, I'm not sure that the American public really understands the difference between speaking for himself and speaking for you, since he is your Vice President. And he is out in Indianapolis, has used the words, "McCarthy-type tactics," and yet you're here wanting to have things go smoothly for the Congressman. I'm just wondering how you can square your desire to have peace with Congress and what your Vice President is saying in Indianapolis.

The President. Please don't ask me to comment on something I haven't read. That's what I'd say to that one.

Defense Policy

Q. A question for Congressman Cheney about defense policy: Does he have a view on the Strategic Defense Initiative? Does he believe America can erect a perfect defense or something more modest?

Representative Cheney. I have extensive views on defense policy, but I don't believe I'll share those today. It seems to me it's appropriate for me to discuss those matters before the Senate committee during the confirmation process and not in this forum.

Q. Star Wars? You support Star Wars? You always have, haven't you?

Senate Vote on the Tower Nomination

Q. Sir, there's been an incredible amount of analysis about what happened in the Tower nomination, as you're aware, and I think we've all heard your views about the Senate. But what I'm particularly interested in is whether you feel that your administration bears any responsibility whatsoever in the fact that Tower did not get confirmed?

The President. I have read that we made mistakes. I don't, I think. And if so, I would be glad to say so, but I don't know exactly. I can't think of a specific that we might have done differently in this circumstance. You have to remember, one of the allegations was I took too long to send it up. But what we were trying to do was the same thing that overtook events once it got to the Hill—gunning down groundless rumors.

So, you know, that's what took the time to begin with. Every time we'd get ready to go up with a nomination which I felt was a good one, there'd be some other allegation printed out there—not by the Senate, but just floating out there. And we'd have to say, what is this? Please send the investigators to Geneva to see if, indeed, the East Texas—not East Texas—[*laughter*]—the East German spy was true, you know. And then we'd find it wasn't true. And we'd be ready, and there'd be some other allegation. So maybe I made a mistake in not just going ahead. But what I wanted to do, and told our general counsel, is, look, I think we have an obligation to have the FBI look at these. I think that may—and I would have to bear full responsibility for that—maybe set a tone up there that then encouraged leaks, counterleaks, and investigation of rumor and innuendo.

So, I'd have to accept some responsibility for that, I think. And there may have been some other tactical things that went wrong; but please remember that when that nomination went up there, it was very well received generally and, indeed, Senator Nunn, I think, said on the floor that he was—you know, had been fully prepared to vote for it.

So, I don't know. But in that area I think there might—I may have made a mistake.

Q. Mr. President——

The President. She has a followup.

Q. Some of the things that have been analyzed have centered on the fact that it takes any new White House staff some time to get his act together and that this crisis came at one of the worst times it could have come for you in terms of having the same kind of weak and inexperienced staff that any President would have at this stage of the game. And we've all read things about some of the Senators weren't contacted and that you did not really go all out in terms of twisting arms and sort of appealed to fairness. Is there anything along this line that you think might have worked differently?

The President. I don't think I would do it differently to do over again, and I certainly am not going to fault my staff. I think this was historic in the—and I'm not—I don't think the time is appropriate to start trying to assess blame. I mean, I think there will be a lot of aftermaths in what happened. But we're going to go forward. And I, frankly, feel that I've given you a long list of things that make me feel the administration is moving forward appropriately. We're moving swiftly on this nomination. And I'm one who has a rather broad perspective of how things are in Washington, and tomorrow it'll be some other problem. And I will work with the Congress. And I think I will continue to keep this feeling that I can work with the Congress. And I'll keep fighting. And if we lose one, we'll be back and fight again. And I fought hard for John Tower because I believed in him. And I told you, I didn't think a lot of it was fair, but that's over, that's history. And now we are going to go forward. And I take Senator Mitchell and Senator Nunn at their word. They have given me their word, and that means a lot with me. And they want to move forward together, too.

We've got time for just a couple of more and then I've got to go.

Q. Mr. President, please—back here.

Strategic Defense Initiative

Q. Mr. President, to follow up on the strategic defense question, are you and Congressman Cheney of one mind on the matter of strategic defense, particularly deployment, or is there some distance between the two of you?

The President. Well, we're in general agreement. And I think as Dick gets over there and gets into the details, he's going to have to make up his, after he's confirmed, make up his mind on the—after the budget review is complete—as to exactly what can be done and how fast it can be done. There's no question of his support for SDI, nor mine. But we aren't there yet, Tom [Tom Raum, Associated Press], because we have to wait until the reviews that we talked about are finished before we, either of us, can definitively address levels of funding or where we might go on those things.

Secretary of Defense-Designate Cheney

Q. Mr. President, do you assume that this

nomination will receive clear sailing in the Senate?

The President. Yes, I do.

Q. Mr. President——

The President. I believe it will go very fast, and I believe that it will have smooth sailing. Why? Because of Dick Cheney, because of the merits, not because of anything that happened in the past—the merits. And we are going to try, incidentally, getting back to Mr. Duffy's [Michael Duffy, Time] question—I think it was or Jerry's—to accelerate the clearance process and get that moving. We've got to do that. It is very important. Too much time has been wasted here. And I believe we can do it. We may have to take FBI resources off of a series of other investigations for other appointments, but it's this important to the country. And so, we'll move very, very fast.

Q. Mr. President——

The President. Now, Marlin tells me that that was the last question, but out of respect for Sarah McClendon, who is persistent, but who—I will make a new announcement of press policy, Sarah. The squeaking wheel will not always get the grease in life, and the loudest voice won't always get recognized because it isn't fair to the others. And you all have been very cooperative with me on the policy on shouting over helicopter blades, and I hope it's been good for you. And I will continue to try, but I cannot identify people—I don't think it's fair to the others—who stand up and yell while others sit and raise their hands. But I don't mean to be pedantic about this or in some lecturing mode, but you and I have known each other a long time, and so this is the last time that I can succumb to the tendency to go to the loudest or most frantic wave. I can't do it, and it's not fair to calmer souls. But, Sarah, have you got a question? [*Laughter*]

Q. I want to know if——

The President. We've known each other so long, I can address her in this forthright manner. Yes?

Q. And thank you very much. And I wanted to ask your new man what he feels——

The President. Go ahead. [*Laughter*]

Representative Cheney. Never have I seen the press so well behaved as they are now. The President's got them——

Q. Give us some of your thinking about the troops out there that you'll have to command now. Do you think you're going to have a problem with recruiting and pay and benefits to keep these people going, or do you think that you'll have to cut back on the forces?

Representative Cheney. Sarah, those are very important questions, but they really are the kinds of things that I should not discuss until I have the opportunity to appear before the Committee and until I have the opportunity in many cases to discuss them at length with the President. Thank you all very much.

Note: The President's seventh news conference began at 4:06 p.m. in the Briefing Room at the White House. Marlin Fitzwater was the President's Press Secretary, and John H. Sununu was Chief of Staff to the President.

White House Statement on Secretary of Defense-Designate Richard B. Cheney

March 10, 1989

Secretary of Defense-designate Dick Cheney has served in the House since 1978 as the Representative from Wyoming, and has served in each succeeding Congress. In December 1988 he was unanimously elected House Republican Whip for the 101st Congress, the second-ranking leadership position. He is a member of the House Committee on Interior and Insular Affairs. He is also a member of the House Permanent Select Committee on Intelligence, serving as the ranking Republican on its Subcommittee on Program and Budget Authorization. He was ranking Republican in the 15-member House Select Committee to Investigate Covert Arms Deals with Iran.

Mr. Cheney began his public service in 1965, when he served as an intern in the Wyoming State legislature in Cheyenne. In 1966 he was selected by the National Center for Education in Politics to intern on the staff of Warren Knowles, then-Governor of Wisconsin. In 1968 the American Political Science Association selected him for its Joseph E. Davies Congressional Fellowship, which he served as an assistant to the late Congressman William A. Steiger (R-WI). In May 1969 Mr. Cheney began several years of Federal service under Presidents Nixon and Ford. From 1969 to 1970, he was Special Assistant to the Director of the Office of Economic Opportunity; from 1970 to 1971, he was Deputy Assistant to the President; and from 1971 to 1972, he was assistant director for operations of the Cost of Living Council. In March 1973 he left government service to become vice president of Bradley, Woods & Company, Inc., an investment advisory firm. In August 1974, when Gerald Ford assumed the Presidency, Mr. Cheney served on the Ford Transition Team, and beginning in September, as a Deputy Assistant to the President. In November 1975 he was named Assistant to the President and Chief of Staff.

Mr. Cheney was born in Lincoln, NE, on January 30, 1941. He attended Yale University in New Haven, CT, and Casper College in Casper, WY. In 1965 he earned a bachelor's degree from the University of Wyoming, and in 1966 earned a master's degree from the same university. He is married to the former Lynne Ann Vincent, and they have two daughters.

Nomination of Skirma Anna Kondratas To Be an Assistant Secretary of Housing and Urban Development

March 10, 1989

The President today announced his intention to nominate Skirma Anna Kondratas to be an Assistant Secretary of Housing and Urban Development (Community Planning and Development). She would succeed Jack R. Stokvis.

Since 1987 Ms. Kondratas has been Administrator of Food and Nutrition Service at the Department of Agriculture. She served as Director of the Office of Analysis and Evaluation, Food and Nutrition Service, at the Department of Agriculture, 1986–1987. Prior to this she was a policy analyst for the Heritage Foundation, 1984–1986. She has worked for the Republican National Committee as an economic analyst, 1981–1982, and deputy director of research, 1982–1984.

Ms. Kondratas graduated from Harvard University (B.A., 1965), Boston University (M.A., 1969), and George Mason University (M.B.A., 1981). She was also a Fulbright fellow in history at the University of Poznan, Poland, 1965–1966. She resides in Springfield, VA.

Remarks to Members of the National Association of Attorneys General

March 13, 1989

Well, I am just delighted to see this illustrious group here. I wanted you to meet Bill Reilly, who is our Administrator of the EPA and a man whose reputation many of you know about. And I've prepared just a few remarks that I want to make on a couple of subjects where this group has been out front. And when I finish, Bill will say a few words.

I would ask your forbearance. I just couldn't pull myself away from watching the *Discovery* take off, and it's now airborne and appears to be going well. So, I think that is always a rather tense moment; but the flight is underway.

I would say to Bob and everybody else that this association—as I look at your agenda, it's clear to me that this association and the White House are fighting the same battles and on the same agenda. Your reports on environmental protection and also on drug control strategies got you way out front on these two issues. And I think it's a good thing. And we are determined to have those as two prominent agenda items right here in the White House. Now, the approaches that you've taken reinforce my conviction that, together, where we have these shared concerns, we're going to find solutions, and we've got to find State and Federal roles that work. We're going to apply limited resources—and again, I wish they weren't as limited, particularly in these two areas—but we've got to apply the limited resources in a coordinated manner.

At the Federal level, I'm convinced that on many issues the time for study has passed—on these environmental issues—and I know that Bill agrees with me. So, we are proposing legislation to reauthorize the Clean Air Act. And I want to work with the Congress on a comprehensive acid rain program. And again, I think working with you all, we can do a lot on throwing the book at those who engaged in illegal ocean dumping. Bill is just back from a highly successful international conference that was opened by Margaret Thatcher in the U.K., and he can tell you perhaps a little about what went on there. But in these broad areas of global warming, we've got to do better, and we will.

Over the last decade, the States have taken on a key role, the lead, I might add, in many areas, in terms of protecting the environment. And I view that as good news. I believe that. I still believe strongly in federalism, and I think that's very, very important. So, I want to work with you on those environmental questions where we share responsibility. We need to step up that Superfund cleanup process and improve enforcement. We must assure compliance with the hazardous waste laws. And where enforcement of all the laws that protect our environment are concerned, I'd like you to think about the most serious cases, where you've got to move beyond civil penalties toward criminal enforcement, both as a sanction and as a deterrent.

In a few minutes, as I say, Bill will give a little more detail on our environmental agenda, and you will see in him what I have seen: that he is an expert here, an outstanding ally, and a fellow soldier in this struggle. He also understands the differences between the State responsibility and the Federal, but they need to work together.

So, let me just touch on the other subject that I mentioned up front before turning this over to him. We've got to see that the great cities—indeed, some of rural America—that they are no longer held hostage to the crack dealers. Our schools must not be locked in a state of siege. And you know, drugs are like chemical weapons that a society turns on itself. And they breed the most insidious forms of domestic terrorism. And they've got to be stopped, and we've got to vow that they will be stopped.

The budget that I sent up to the Congress a few weeks ago is a realistic, fiscally responsible plan that identifies key priorities requiring our immediate attention. One of these priorities is combating the scourge of drugs. And that's why I am asking for $1 billion in new outlays for the antidrug program. That's a 47-percent increase over 1988, for a total of $6 billion in budget authority for 1990. Most of that money, 70 percent of it, will beef up Federal enforcement; provide grants to State and local law enforcement agencies; build up our prosecution, detentions, and intelligence-gathering strength.

As chief legal officers, you know about enforcement, and you know how vital it is. And as my budget makes clear, I wanted to vote unprecedented resources to enforcement. But clearly, we've got to do more. This war won't be won by police work alone. Where there's demand, supply will always rise to meet it. And where there's no demand, supply is useless. And that's why I was glad to see your "Blueprint for Drug Control Strategies" broadens the goals of enforcement. You say that reducing demand must be the ideological cornerstone of any coherent drug enforcement policy. And you're right; enforcement strategies must look beyond effects to causes. Drug education, treatment, prevention provide our best hope for long-term solution, especially with our kids. And we need to tell them, of course, to say no; but we've also got to give them the wisdom to know why and the skills to know how to say no.

I want to ask you to continue looking closely at these drug enforcement programs. How can they help reduce demand? Less demand means more success on the war on drugs. And to the extent you can cut demand, you can make your jobs, my job, and those of everyone involved, a whole lot more rewarding. Our financial resources may be limited, but our resolve is unlimited. And with that limitless resolve, I know that we can inspire every child, teacher, and parent, every community group, religious institution, and tenant association, and every business and professional organization in this country. And then, united in common resolve, we will be truly invincible.

I've said before that we have more will than wallet, but the only limits on our will are the limits we place on ourselves. We can, we must, build a culture of zero tolerance. And then we'll send a message loud and clear to those who take drugs, and take our leniency for granted: The party is over.

And so, I will simply end by telling you about a visit I had to the DEA [Drug Enforcement Administration] up in New York. It was most interesting, and it was addressing all our agents. And I know many of you have worked with them, and like you, I was very much impressed by the caliber of the young men and women. You wonder what does it take to be a person that knows now that the culture has changed, that their lives are literally on the line.

After meeting with the big group, we went into a small meeting room and talked to the agents themselves, those that were undercover. And one of them explained it to me this way. It used to be if there was a drug bust people would say "police" or "DEA" or "FBI" or whatever it is, and the bad guys would stop what they were doing and, you know, submit to arrest. Now the culture has changed: The bad guys turn around and start shooting.

And so, it really drove home to me the need to support these enforcement officers with changes in the law and whatever else it's going to take. The penalty in some areas for killing a policeman is the same as being caught with *x* ounces of drugs on you. And so, how can there be any incentive if we don't have some differentiation? This is your business; you know this, but we would welcome recommendations to our Attorney General and to the White House on how best to effect the kind of changes that are going to be necessary in that aspect of the problem.

Now, back to the first agenda item: the environment. Bill has got a good way of building bridges between people. He's the first kind of certified environmentalist to be in this important post, and he's been called the Great Includer. You can figure that out when you listen to him. But he's devoted his career really to protecting our land, air, and water. He has my complete confidence. I expect when you've dealt with him for a while he'll have yours. I ask that you give him your full cooperation because, again, like the whole question of the second agenda item, this first one, the environment and the need to preserve it and to hand our kids something a little better than we found, is absolute priority.

So, with no further ado—and the only regret, that I won't have a chance to visit more informally with each and every one of you—thanks for coming. And let me introduce you to Bill Reilly, who I know will have your full support. Bill, all yours.

Note: The President spoke at 10:02 a.m. in the Roosevelt Room at the White House. In his remarks, he referred to Robert Abrams, president of the association.

Remarks Following the Swearing-in Ceremony for William J. Bennett as Director of National Drug Control Policy
March 13, 1989

The President. Mr. Vice President and members of the Cabinet—Justice Scalia, I believe, was here somewhere.

Justice Scalia. I'm here.

The President. There he is—present. But I cite that because he just did the honors over in the Oval Office for the swearing-in of Bill Bennett.

Honored guests and ladies and gentlemen, I'm delighted to be here. It's an honor for me to be here, with the Cabinet behind me, for this important occasion. There really is no greater test of America's greatness than its challenge on meeting this great challenge of drugs. And today I've come from the swearing-in, from Bill Bennett, the man who's going to lead this mission. We're going to need your help and the will and spirit of the American people to succeed.

Last month before a joint session of Congress, I said Bill Bennett and I will be shoulder-to-shoulder leading this charge, and here we are. And he has just been sworn in, and we are shoulder-to-shoulder, and the Cabinet will be shoulder-to-shoulder with him in this important effort. To free our nation from drugs is going to require teamwork and coordination between all levels of government, private enterprise, and then the voluntary organizations as well. It will mean building on your labors as activists, officials, public servants. For while you've done much, there remains so much more to be done. Most of all, it's going to require a sense of urgency to act now.

Drugs threaten what we are as a nation and as a family. And they chain the human soul, and they destroy the lives of our children. And so, Bill, I know that you share these beliefs. As Secretary of Education, Bill showed what worked, told us what didn't, broke a little china in the process—[*laughter*]—but challenged the establishment in a lot of ways; and that was a tremendous plus. And in the process he created a record of stunning achievement, and like you all, he's been a strong voice for excellence. And now you must work together.

Bill is the first Director of the National Drug Council Policy—you, soldiers of this crusade. And drug abuse assaults the mind and the spirit of America, leaving damaged lives and destroyed careers. So, we've got to mobilize our moral, spiritual, and economic resources to force a decline in drug trafficking and in drug abuse. We're going to seek to encourage the over 23 million Americans who last year used illegal drugs to get clean and stay clean.

And in that budget speech, I spoke about four critical areas: education, testing, interdiction, and enforcement. And I asked for an increase of $1 billion in budget outlays. In 1990 we're requesting $6 billion in new funding to fight this war. And some money will be used to expand treatment for the poor and to young mothers, and this will help many of the innocent victims of drugs, like the thousands of babies that are born addicted or with AIDS because of the mother's addiction. Some money will be used to cut the waiting time for treatment and to help prevention efforts in urban schools, where the emergency seems to be the greatest. And much of it will be used to protect our borders, helped by the Coast Guard and Customs Service and Departments of State and Justice and the U.S. military. To spread the word and thus stem demand, we're going to need more money for education and prevention. Our request totals $1.1 billion. And we need to educate, involve parents, teachers, and communities. And finally, to stop drug criminals, we will support unequivocally our drug enforcement officials: local, State, and Federal.

You know, we've talked a lot about zero tolerance. Well, it's not a catch word. It means, quite simply, if you do crime, you've got to do time. And our budget proposes $4.1 billion—the drug budget—fully 70 percent of the entire drug budget for law enforcement purposes. I want judges who strictly apply the law to convicted drug offenders, and then severe sentences for the dealers who hire kids to sell and carry these drugs. I want a new offensive against organized crime, and enhanced drug prosecution, detection, enhanced intelligence capabilities. We need increased prison sentences for drug-related crimes. And the death penalty—I believe in it firmly for drug kingpins who order and those who commit these drug-related murders.

Now let me speak very frankly about one other aspect of the fight on drug abuse. The effectiveness of the Federal Government's efforts to combat drugs has been hampered—sometimes severely—by inadequate cooperation and coordination among the many departments and agencies involved in this antidrug effort. There have been struggles over turf and budgets, and too often preoccupation with parochial interests.

Well, the soldiers in the drug battle have been risking their lives. Too often bureaucratic conflict here in Washington has hobbled our national effort. So, this has got to end. No war was ever won with two dozen generals acting independently. And I have chosen Bill Bennett to be the commanding general in the drug war. It is his responsibility, working with the departments and agencies headed by those you see here with me and others, to develop a strategy for this war. So, I charge him with putting all the parts of the Federal Government in harness, pulling together in a life-and-death struggle against a deadly enemy. I will not tolerate, and the country cannot afford, bureaucratic infighting that forces us to fight this battle with one arm tied behind our back.

And so, Bill has my total support. I call upon all of the parts of the Government to get behind him in charting our course toward victory. We must not waver in our resolve to overcome drug abuse. And we're going to need fortitude, patience, compassion, and certainly the support of all America. Without the people, we can't do anything, And with the people, we can do great things.

This morning, then, I ask all of you to work with Bill and with businesses, churches, families, and schools. Thank you very much for being here. And now the man of the moment, the man in whom I've placed great confidence and who I know will do a superb job: Bill Bennett.

Mr. Bennett. Ladies and gentlemen, members of the Cabinet who are so kind to be here this morning, thank you. And Mr. President, thanks especially to you for your kind words, for the trust you've placed in me, and for the firm commitment you've made to the work that I now begin.

No one who has fought this fight until now, no brave law enforcement officer, no teacher, no doctor need be told how hard and cruel America's drug problem has become. They know; we know. But those here and across the country who join me today in our just war against drugs may take some renewed confidence in our prospects for success because the President of the United States has placed this struggle at the top of his administration's agenda, at the top of our common national agenda where it needs to be.

The President has asked for total effort. He has asked for action on each and every front. He has asked for a sharp increase in funding to make that action possible. He has asked for an end to the petty bureaucratic bickering that has too often hampered Federal initiatives here in Washington. He has asked me to lead and to honor his mandate. Well, with your support, Mr. President, with your backing, much, indeed, can be done. I promise to give my all.

My office is already conducting an exhaustive review of our national fight against drugs on both supply and demand sides. Where past strategy has succeeded, we will see to it that it's continued. Where past strategy has failed, we will see that it's replaced or modified. And my Office will review the Federal drug budget. I plan no cut-rate, bargain basement initiative, but I also plan no bloated pork-barrel project, either. We will ask for what makes sense, no more, no less. And as you've instructed me, we will not play politics with drugs. That's one game the American people simply will not afford.

All this will mean change, substantial change in some cases. And change takes time and long, hard work, especially in Washington. We'll do it where necessary. We want to see waiting lines for drug treatment reduced and prison cells for drug pushers increased. We want to see the drug violence on the streets of our cities and the streets of our Nation's Capital stopped. And we want those overseas, too, to know that we mean business.

As the President has made abundantly clear, this administration wants to work with all the good citizens of America to win the war. There is good news, and we shouldn't ignore it. Drugs are no longer a thing of glamour. Our media and our culture now portray drugs accurately. They portray them for the death and ruin and despair that they are and that they bring. As the President sadly reminds us, 23 million Americans still use drugs regularly, but another 220 million Americans do not use drugs and never have.

We see the violence that drugs create. We see the damage drugs do to our economy, to our communities, and to our children. And the American people are made angry and determined, and that is a good thing. In neighborhood schools and churches across America there is a movement against drugs, and it's making a difference. Drug use is down among high school seniors. It is still too high, but it is going down. I believe that a persistent national commitment to this fight can and will bring it down further.

Many people have told me in recent weeks and months that my job will prove to be an impossible job. I think that's wrong; today I act on the assumption that that is wrong. I did not take this job to sit at stalemate. The people I'll be working with, including and especially the people seated behind me, and the people who lead our antidrug efforts here in Washington and across the country are men and women of great ability, dedication, and purpose. And best of all, the American people are with us. So, Mr. President, I have the best allies a man can have.

Mr. President, again I want to thank you for giving me the opportunity to make a difference on one of the critical issues of our time. And, ladies and gentlemen, members of the Cabinet, I thank you for your good wishes and for the help I know you'll give, because I'm going to ask you for it.

Now, ladies and gentlemen, I've been asked to invite you all to follow us to the Indian Treaty Room for a brief reception. Thank you all for coming. Thank you, Mr. President.

Note: The President spoke at 11:16 a.m. in Room 450 of the Old Executive Office Building.

Message to the Senate Transmitting the Yugoslavia-United States Consular Convention

March 13, 1989

To the Senate of the United States:

I am transmitting, for the Senate's advice and consent to ratification, the Consular Convention between the United States of America and the Socialist Federal Republic of Yugoslavia signed at Belgrade June 6, 1988. I am also transmitting, for the information of the Senate, the report of the Department of State with respect to the Convention.

The signing of this Convention is a significant step in the process of improving and broadening the relationship between the United States and Yugoslavia. Consular relations between the two countries are not the subject of a modern bilateral agreement. This Convention will establish firm obligations on such matters as the notification of consular officers of the arrest and detention of their citizens and permission for consular officers to visit their citizens who are under detention and to protect the rights and interests of their nationals and juridical persons.

The people of the United States and Yugoslavia enjoy a long tradition of friendship. I welcome the opportunity through this Consular Convention to improve further relations between our two countries. I urge the Senate to give the Convention its prompt and favorable consideration.

GEORGE BUSH

The White House,
March 13, 1989.

Statement by Press Secretary Fitzwater on the President's Meeting With Foreign Minister Moshe Arens of Israel

March 13, 1989

President Bush met with Israeli Foreign Minister Moshe Arens for approximately 30 minutes in the Oval Office. Also attending were Israeli Ambassador Moshe Arad, Policy Adviser to the Foreign Minister Sallai Meridor, Secretary of State Baker, National Security Adviser Scowcroft, and Chief of Staff Sununu.

The President emphasized the United States strong and enduring commitment to the security of Israel. The discussions focused on the intentions of both countries in moving the Middle East peace process forward. President Bush said the United States wants progress, new ideas, and looks forward to the visit by Prime Minister Shamir. President Bush emphasized that the United States does not want to miss an opportunity for peace in the Middle East and still believes in direct talks as the best path to peace.

Appointment of Burton Lee III as Physician to the President

March 13, 1989

The President today announced the appointment of Dr. Burton Lee III as Physician to the President.

Since July 1960 Dr. Lee has been with the Memorial Hospital for Allied Diseases at the Memorial Sloan-Kettering Cancer Center in New York, where he was the senior attending physician, fellow, and resident. In that capacity, he served on the combined leukemia-lymphoma service, the largest and oldest lymphoma service in the United States. In addition, Dr. Lee served as a member of the Presidential Commission on the Human Immunodeficiency Virus Epidemic from September 1987 to July 1988. Dr. Lee has been the principal or contributing author of 127 research publications to date.

Dr. Lee graduated from Yale University in 1952 and from Columbia University College of Physicians and Surgeons in 1956. He was born March 28, 1930, in New York, NY, and is married to the former Ann Kelly.

Appointment of Charles Nicholas Rostow as Special Assistant to the President for National Security Affairs

March 13, 1989

The President today announced the appointment of Charles Nicholas Rostow as Special Assistant to the President for National Security Affairs and Legal Adviser to the National Security Council at the White House.

Mr. Rostow held the same position during the last year of the Reagan administration, after having served as the National Security Council's Deputy Legal Adviser since March 1987. Prior to this he was Special Assistant to the Legal Adviser at the Department of State. Mr. Rostow also served as Counsel to the President's Special Review Board, providing legal counsel on all aspects of the Board's work and participating in the drafting of the Board's report. From October 1982 to July 1985, Mr. Rostow was associated with the firm of Shearman and Sterling in New York.

Mr. Rostow received his B.A., Ph.D., and J.D. degrees from Yale University. His published work is in the field of international law and diplomatic history. He is married to the former Ariana van der Heyden White.

Appointment of Karl D. Jackson as Special Assistant to the President for National Security Affairs

March 13, 1989

The President today announced the appointment of Karl D. Jackson as Special Assistant to the President for National Security Affairs and Senior Director for Asian Affairs.

Since 1986 Mr. Jackson was Deputy Assistant Secretary of Defense (East Asia and Pacific Affairs). Prior to this he was Deputy Director for Policy Planning, Office of the Assistant Secretary of Defense, 1983–1984, and assistant for the Philippines and Indochina in the Office of the Assistant Secretary of Defense, 1982–1983. Mr. Jackson has lived and conducted research in Indonesia, 1968–1969, and in Thailand, 1977–1978. He was editor of "Cambodia 1975–1978: Rendezvous with Death," "Political Power and Communication in Indonesia," "ASEAN Security and Economic Development," "ASEAN in Regional and Global Context," and "United States-Thailand Relations." As a professor of political science at the University of California at Berkeley, he has written on the politics, national security, and economic development of Southeast Asia. He is the author of "Traditional Authority, Islam and Rebellion."

Appointment of Robert D. Blackwill as Special Assistant to the President for National Security Affairs

March 13, 1989

The President today announced the appointment of Robert D. Blackwill as Special Assistant to the President for National Security Affairs and Senior Director for European and Soviet Affairs. He will succeed Nelson C. Ledsky.

A career Foreign Service officer, Mr. Blackwill served as Principal Deputy Assistant Secretary of State for Politico-Military Affairs, 1981–1982, and for European Affairs, 1982–1983. From 1983 to 1985, Mr. Blackwill was associate dean and faculty member at the Kennedy School of Government at Harvard University. He was the United States Ambassador and chief negotiator at the negotiations with the Warsaw Pact on mutual and balanced force reductions, 1985–1987. He then rejoined the faculty of the Kennedy School, 1987–1989. Mr. Blackwill's overseas assignments have included Kenya, the United Kingdom, and Israel. Mr. Blackwill is a member of the International Institute for Strategic Studies and the Council on Foreign Relations.

Mr. Blackwill is a graduate of Wichita State University. He is married to the former Anne Heiberg and has three children.

Appointment of William W. Working as Special Assistant to the President for National Security Affairs
March 13, 1989

The President today announced the appointment of William W. Working as Special Assistant to the President for National Security Affairs and Senior Director for Intelligence Programs at the White House.

In 21 years as a professional intelligence officer, Mr. Working has served in the Air Force, the Defense Intelligence Agency, and on the Intelligence Community Staff of the Director of Central Intelligence. He has also served as a staff member of the Senate Select Committee on Intelligence as the staff designee of Senator Jake Garn (R-UT). In 1987, he became the Director of the Program and Budget Office of the Intelligence Community Staff. Prior to this he worked with technical collection systems and operations.

Mr. Working graduated from the University of Tennessee and was commissioned in the Air Force in 1967. He is a lieutenant colonel in the Air Force Reserve. Mr. Working was born August 8, 1945, in Santa Monica, CA.

Appointment of David C. Miller, Jr., as Special Assistant to the President for National Security Affairs
March 13, 1989

The President announced the appointment of Ambassador David C. Miller, Jr., as Special Assistant to the President for National Security Affairs and Senior Director for International Programs and African Affairs. He would succeed Tyrus W. Cobb in International Programs and Ambassador Herman J. Cohen in African Affairs.

In 1988 President Reagan appointed Ambassador Miller to the Board of the African Development Foundation. He was Ambassador to Zimbabwe, 1984–1986, and Ambassador to Tanzania, 1981–1984. During his tenure in Zimbabwe, Ambassador Miller also served as the Director of the Southern African Working Group at the Department of State. He was a White House fellow and a Special Assistant to the Attorney General, 1968–1970.

Ambassador Miller was born in Cleveland, OH. He received his B.A. degree from Harvard University and a J.D. degree from the University of Michigan Law School. He is married to the former Mary Johnson Lake and has three children.

Appointment of Virginia A. Lampley as Special Assistant to the President for National Security Affairs
March 13, 1989

The President today announced the appointment of Virginia A. Lampley as Special Assistant to the President for National Security Affairs and Senior Director for

Legislative Affairs at the White House.

From 1983 to 1989, Ms. Lampley was a client executive with the Washington-based firm of DGA International, representing international corporations in the United States. Concurrently he served as a U.S. Air Force Reserve officer in the Directorate of International Security Assistance. Ms. Lampley served on active duty in the U.S. Air Force from 1974 to 1983. She spent 6 years in staff and management positions in Air Force Intelligence from squadron to Air Force headquarters level. From 1980 to 1983, she was assigned to Air Force legislative liaison and completed her active-duty military career as Air Force deputy director for the Senate liaison.

Ms. Lampley graduated from Miami University with a degree in political science and received her masters degree from Georgetown University in national security studies.

Appointment of Richard N. Haass as Special Assistant to the President for National Security Affairs

March 13, 1989

The President today announced the appointment of Dr. Richard N. Haass as Special Assistant to the President for National Security Affairs and Senior Director for Near East and South Asian Affairs.

Since 1985 Dr. Haass has been a lecturer in public policy at Harvard University's John F. Kennedy School of Government. Prior to this he was Deputy in the Bureau of European and Canadian Affairs (Policy) and Special Cyprus Coordinator, Department of State, 1982–1985; Director of the Office of Regional Security Affairs in the Bureau of Politico-Military Affairs, Department of State, 1981–1982; Special Assistant to the Deputy Under Secretary for Policy Review, Department of Defense, 1979–1980; research associate at the International Institute for Strategic Studies in London, 1977–1979.

Dr. Haass was born in Brooklyn, NY, on July 28, 1951. A Rhodes Scholar, Dr. Haass earned a bachelor's degree from Oberlin College, and he earned master and doctor of philosophy degrees from Oxford University. In addition to his doctoral thesis on U.S. foreign policy toward Southwest Asia between 1969 and 1976, Dr. Haass is the author of "Congressional Power: Implications for American Security Policy" (1979) and "Beyond the INF Treaty: Arms, Arms Control and the Atlantic Alliance" (1988). He is also coeditor of "Superpower Arms Control: Setting the Record Straight" (1987). Dr. Haass resides in Washington, DC.

Nomination of Kathleen M. Harrington To Be an Assistant Secretary of Labor

March 13, 1989

The President today announced his intention to nominate Kathleen M. Harrington to be Assistant Secretary of Labor (Congressional Affairs). She would succeed Francis J. Duggan.

Since 1988 Ms. Harrington has been Assistant Administrator for Public Affairs at the Federal Aviation Administration. Prior to this she was director of the office of Elizabeth Dole for the Robert Dole for President campaign, 1987–1988. She has also served as administrative assistant for Congresswoman Nancy Johnson, 1983–1987, and administrative assistant for Congressman Jim Dunn, 1981–1983.

Ms. Harrington graduated from Colgate University (B.A., 1972) and Catholic University of America (M.A., 1977).

Nomination of Roderick Allen DeArment To Be Deputy Secretary of Labor

March 13, 1989

The President today announced his intention to nominate Roderick Allen DeArment to be Deputy Secretary of Labor. He would succeed Dennis Eugene Whitfield.

Since 1986 Mr. DeArment has been a partner with the law firm of Covington and Burling in Washington, DC. Prior to this he was chief of staff for the Senate majority leader's office, 1985–1986. He has served in several capacities for the Senate Committee on Finance, including chief counsel and staff director, 1983–1984; deputy chief counsel, 1981–1984; and deputy chief minority counsel, 1979–1981. From 1973 to 1979, Mr. DeArment was an associate with the law firm of Covington and Burling.

Mr. DeArment graduated from Trinity College (B.A., 1970) and the University of Virginia School of Law (J.D., 1973). He was born March 3, 1948, in Fort Sill, OK. He is married, has two children, and resides in Great Falls, VA.

White House Statement on the Report of Presidential Emergency Board No. 218 Concerning a Railroad Labor Dispute

March 13, 1989

On March 8, 1989, the report of Emergency Board No. 218 was submitted to the White House. This Board, which was created on January 6, 1989, by Executive Order 12664, investigated a dispute between the Port Authority Trans-Hudson Corporation (PATH) and certain of its employees represented by the Brotherhood of Locomotive Engineers. The establishment and activities of the Board were governed by section 9A of the Railway Labor Act of 1926, as amended, 45 U.S.C. 159a. Its members were Robert J. Ables, Chairman; Herbert Fishgold; and Robert E. Peterson.

The same dispute was previously investigated by Emergency Board No. 216, and the task of Emergency Board No. 218 was to select the most reasonable final offer for settlement of the dispute proposed by the parties. The Board selected PATH's offer as the most reasonable. The main features of this offer are 5-percent annual wage increases over the 3-year term of the contract, the addition of Martin Luther King's birthday as a holiday, and increases in insurance coverage and meal allowances.

Statement on the Sudanese Civil War

March 13, 1989

Sunday, March 12, was the National Day of Concern for Sudan. It was organized by groups of Americans who are deeply distressed about the continuing human tragedy in Sudan. I want to add my support to this demonstration of concern for the Sudanese victims of war and starvation.

A month ago, Secretary of State Baker appealed to the warring parties to adopt a cease-fire, facilitate delivery of relief to those in need, and move the conflict to the negotiating table. The United States remains strongly committed to these goals.

All friends of Sudan, of which I am one, urge those responsible for the continuation of this war to agree to an early cease-fire, to place peace above military and political considerations, and to negotiate peace. I hope that the most recent political events in Sudan will enable the various donors to help those in that country who desperately require humanitarian assistance.

Remarks to Members of the Anti-Defamation League of B'nai B'rith

March 14, 1989

This is what they call a cameo appearance. [*Laughter*] I'm here very briefly before rushing off to the Hilton Hotel, but I just can't tell you how pleased I am to be with you. I told Abe Foxman here, "Why, we're practically going steady!" [*Laughter*] Because he was down here just last—was it Thursday of last week with the head of a lot of these most prominent organizations. And I'm delighted to be here with all of you today.

I don't want to speak too long because Bobbie Kilberg, I think, is next, and she'll kill me. [*Laughter*] But I might say she is doing an outstanding job—a friend of long-standing and now in an outreach capacity here, high level at the White House, and performing with the expertise that we have come to expect of her. I understand that Secretary [of Housing and Urban Development] Kemp is coming, or maybe—has he been, or coming over—and [Attorney General] Dick Thornburgh, I think, and our Chief of Staff [John H. Sununu]. So, you'll have a full program.

But I'm pleased to be here. I look at these briefing sessions as a two-way street. I hope that you'll have a chance to exchange views, get questions and answers with some—but in any event, an opinion at a forum for sharing of information and ideas. Certainly, the meeting that we had with Abe and those from the organization of presidents was that kind of meeting. And as I look around the room, I see many familiar faces and am delighted to be here.

For three quarters of a century, the Anti-Defamation League has played a central role in preserving and protecting that sacred right of religious freedom. And there is no single greater contribution that one organization can make to the Nation, and for that you've earned our gratitude, certainly my respect.

From the time the pilgrims landed at Plymouth Rock, the principle of religious freedom and the notion of America as a haven for those who seek to exercise that freedom has been deeply rooted in the American heritage. But the ADL knows well that, however well-established religious freedom may be, it can never be taken for granted. And our national conscience must take note whenever that freedom is violated, and all Americans then must rush in to the defense of that freedom. As one of our forefathers wrote nearly 200 years ago, the Government of the United States gives to bigotry no sanction, to persecution no assistance. May the children of the stock of Abraham sit in safety under his own vine and fig tree, and there should be none to make him afraid.

I know that the ADL recently issued its annual report, detailing rising incidents of anti-Semitism in 1988. And I want to come over here to tell you that we must condemn all attacks on the Jewish religion, the Jewish heritage—clearly, unequivocally, and without exception. This Nation must stand for tolerance, for pluralism, and a healthy respect for the rights of all minorities.

And I know many of you, and we've worked together in various common causes many times over the years, and I hope you know how deeply I cherish the principle of religious freedom. And I know how hard you've fought not only for your own beliefs but to protect the principle that recognizes the rights of all men and women to worship as they believe right. So, we must continue to work together as we have in the past to zealously protect these rights for all Americans. Rest assured that my administration will work to uphold this principle as the very cornerstone of our freedom. And sometimes they question the power of the President, and I understand that. But they should never question the President's willingness to use the bully pulpit of the White House, as Teddy Roosevelt called it, to speak out for what is just and right.

I've concentrated today here on just these brief remarks on antidiscrimination or other subjects of enormous concern. I wish you could have been there yesterday in the Oval Office to hear a representative of the Ethiopian Jews, a man who's living in Israel now, make this plea from the heart to continue the flow of the people there who are still not able to join their families in Israel. There's that subject.

We had a fascinating meeting with Mr. Arens yesterday where I reassured him of the United States commitment to Israel as a strategic ally and, of course, a lasting friend. And I think he understands that. I hope that when the Prime Minister of Israel [Yitzhak Shamir] comes here that we can move forward in some way toward the peace that everybody here really hopes that Israel and its neighbors will achieve. So, we're moving.

Thank you for letting me drop in in this cameo appearance. And keep up your commitment, keep up that commitment to fight against bigotry wherever it may surface. Thank you all very, very much.

Note: The President spoke at 9:50 a.m. at a briefing in Room 450 of the Old Executive Office Building. In his remarks, he referred to Abraham H. Foxman, national director of the league, Bobbie Kilberg, Deputy Assistant to the President for Public Liaison, and Israeli Foreign Minister Moshe Arens.

Remarks to the National Legislative Conference of the Independent Insurance Agents of America
March 14, 1989

Thank you all very, very much. Larry understands—[*laughter*]—but if I look a little frantic, our dog is expecting. [*Laughter*] And if you think I look frantic, you ought to see the Silver Fox! [*Laughter*] That's Barbara. No, but I'm delighted to be here; appreciate that warm welcome, complete with a few scattered Texas flags in the audience. And it is an honor to be before this group.

In this city, the currency of status is measured in titles, honorifics: Senator, Ambassador, Secretary. But in my book, this group holds one of the most impressive titles of all: entrepreneur. And I know that the hunger that you feel to own a firm of your own, start from scratch, build it, watch it grow. And I know the satisfaction of matching resources to needs and meeting deadlines and meeting payrolls.

A few years after World War II, when I got out of college, I moved out to west Texas; and a couple of years after that, the early fifties, started my own business. And it was a very small firm—not too small to teach me the facts of economic life. But we got started by risk-taking—got the business education by helping others make that company grow. And our company was a high-risk venture. There was new technology that was unproven, full of half-starts and failures in that—it was all called the offshore drilling business. And we took a gamble, and we invested in new technology. And then we eventually succeeded in pioneering a new way to find America's energy.

And it wasn't always easy, even in the

years that the company did reasonably well. And I recall our despair one time, and some of you in your business know what I'm talking about when you think of insurance. When one of those hurricanes swept through the Gulf of Mexico and one-third of our company's assets were invested in a brand-new drilling rig, with brand-new technology—a hurricane swept through the Gulf. And I went out with our drilling engineer and rented a little Piper, maybe it was a twin-engine plane, but anyway—in the aftermath of the hurricane and looked and looked and looked. And the rig had totally vanished. People had been taken off before the storm, but the rig was gone. One-third of the investment of our company totally disappeared. But from that and other such similar events, I learned some very important lessons. When that rig went down and people lost their jobs—when we rebuilt, there was the satisfaction of seeing people go back to work. And I saw the strain on the faces of the family breadwinners, but I also saw the joy.

So, Washington may not always appreciate the role of small business in creating jobs, but I do. And I think—you know, I used to get needled about the résumé to bring to be President of the United States. But like you, I think one of the most important things is the private sector: taking risks, competing, starting small businesses. And I hope I never forget the lessons that I learned as a small businessman.

I also appreciate this industry's role in society. Without insurance, the loss of spouse could mean the loss of a home. Without insurance, the loss of a parent could keep a child from attending college. We cannot offer protection against fate, but we can prevent the compounding of a tragedy so that a death or an illness doesn't leave a bitter legacy of poverty or despair for a whole family. You prevent that kind of double tragedy, and you add a little bit of comfort to the grieving and predictability for those who are victims of the unpredictable.

So, this is your service to society. It's as crucial a service as that of any social welfare agency. And you cannot continue to perform it if your industry is hamstrung by excessive regulation. And that's why we have worked to remove excessive regulations—the job's not done—to free the creative energies of small firms by ordering a review of more than 100 government regulations. The task force on regulatory relief, which I chaired as Vice President, saved the private sector more than 600 million man-hours of paperwork and billions of dollars in government compliance costs. And I want to work now to continue to work to free small businesses of the remaining excesses of regulation. My philosophy is this: that when it comes to necessary regulation of business, I'm committed to letting the States take the lead, not the Federal Government.

Reducing the regulatory burden is important, but we've got to take action on other fronts, as well, if we're going to do our part in keeping American small business strong. And that's why I've also proposed a cut in the capital gains tax rate. Most of our major trading partners do not tax long-term capital gains. They understand that a high capital gains tax unnecessarily hurts our competitive position by drying up the formation of capital, business, and jobs.

In 1978, when the Congress cut the maximum tax rate on capital gains, the result was an explosion of new companies and new revenues. The critics were still out there, back in '78, saying: "If you do this, you're going to lose revenues. If you do this, it's an advantage for the rich." Didn't work out that way. The Treasury estimates that the new cut that I am proposing will add $4.8 billion to the revenue side in fiscal year 1990 alone. So, let the critics carp. I am going to push for this idea that will stimulate jobs, risktaking, capital formation. And it's good for the economy, and it is not a special tax break for the rich.

Small businesses with less than 500 employees employ more than half of the U.S. workers. You understand this, but I don't believe many people in the United States understand it. So, any onerous new burden on small business will also throw workers out of their jobs. And it's for that reason that I oppose this kind of mounting movement towards mandated employee benefits.

In an area of tight budgets, there's always the temptation to drop the burden of social programs on the backs of the employers. But these policies, borne, I would say, of the best of intentions, can have unintended and counterproductive consequences. It's up to business and labor to negotiate their differences. And make no mistake, I support the right of labor to negotiate as an equal, but burdensome mandated benefits serve neither business nor labor. We've seen what happens in other countries, where mandated benefit programs create obstacles to productivity and growth and, thus, to new job creation. We cannot build a better America if we weigh down our own productive sector with mandated new burdens.

And let me address one other area that concerns your business and that, perhaps, you in this room are much more sensitive to than others. And I'm talking about tort reform. Of course, there are many litigants who deserve a jury's sympathy. We can start from that premise, but when local governments cannot install playgrounds, when businesses are bankrupted, when mothers struggle to find an obstetrician, when volunteer organizations—Boy Scouts and Girl Scouts and others—have to pull back for fear of excessive claims leveled against them, then it is time to consider limiting some of these outrageous settlements. Tort reform is critical to the health of businesses and volunteer organizations alike.

All of our policies are directed toward a single goal: building a better America. And to achieve this goal, my plan has four broad objectives: attention to urgent priorities, an attack on the deficit, hold the line on taxes—no new taxes—and an investment in the future. And without a strong private sector, our nation would be mired in the past, doomed to fail.

The entrepreneur is the man or the woman who is not only ready for change but who relishes the thought of it. And this thought leads me to speak to you in more general terms now about my Presidency, the challenges I hope to meet, the accomplishments that I hope we can make for our country.

I'm a man of this century. I fought in the century's greatest war and raised a family and built a business during the mid-century of America's greatness. But I want to be a President who is remembered for preparing our country for the next century. This is my entrepreneurial definition of leadership: to see the shape of things to come and to prepare for that 21st century world only 11 years away. By the year 2000, we will have experienced change as swift and fast as a torrent—change in the American family, in our work habits, change in technology, and change in the world economy, change in the rate of change itself. The makeup of our remarkable nation has been evolving constantly, but the qualities on which it was founded are timeless and true. And one of those constants is that we are an entrepreneurial people, at our best when we are challenged and when we boldly face the future.

And so, my agenda is this: to confront the emerging problems of the future today. A complacent society is doomed to comfortable decline, and we are not complacent. A dynamic society is one that keeps pace with the times. So, call it that if you will: a dynamic America. But recognize in the restless drive and vision of the American entrepreneur our best qualities as a nation.

A complacent nation would take comfort that America is free in a world at peace. But world events are moving too swiftly for us to relax in set ways and to cling to smug assumptions. The question we must answer is: Will American foreign policy be flexible enough to meet the emerging and potentially dramatic new world developments? And with this question in mind, I've asked all the appropriate agencies—State Department, Defense, other agencies—to reassess our foreign policy and defense strategy. And this comprehensive review will set the basis for our future actions and guide America into the next decade and toward the next century.

I see a couple of kids here. I believe they have a chance to grow up in a more peaceful world. I believe we have, with the changes in the Soviet Union, great challenge, but also great opportunity. But the answer is not to rush in. The answer is to take a prudent reevaluation and then move forward with the leadership that only the United States of America can provide the rest of the free world.

On economic policy, I've submitted to the Congress a budget that is fiscally responsible. This budget does four things: It substantially reduces the deficit; it includes no new taxes; it addresses key priorities; and it still provides for important investments which will help make us more competitive in the future. My speech to Congress, incidentally, was accompanied by 193 pages of specific recommendations for the budget. And looking back in the history books, if you will permit a comment about—it might sound a little bit prideful—we found that no other President in recent history has presented quite so much information to Congress at such an early date.

And I've also submitted a proposal to solve a festering problem that threatens our future prosperity: a plan to restore the integrity of our nation's savings and loan institutions. It's an enormous problem, and our plan has been well-received on both sides of the aisle on Capitol Hill. I've asked the Congress to take action within 45 days; challenged them, now that we've come up with the proposal, to move forward. This problem requires prompt and prudent action.

The changing nature of American society to more working parents is putting pressure on our most basic social institution. I'm talking about the family. How will we respond to this change? We simply cannot afford to create some massive new entitlement program, and that's why I am proposing a child-care plan that combines tax credits and private sector resources to offer parents a choice. I want to empower parents, not government, to seek the best and safest environment for their children. And the underpinning of my plan is the family—strength in the American family.

But many other areas of change. Homelessness affects a small proportion of Americans, but concerns us all. I drove here today—or when you look out the window of the White House and see the ragged, pathetic figures huddled over the steam grates of the Ellipse, I see an affront to the American dream, a national shame, if you will. And we must seek the root causes of and devise the most practical solutions for the homelessness.

The environment, once the concern of a farsighted few, is now a top priority of my administration at home and abroad. You know, this isn't a conservative or a liberal question—the question of the environment. I think of Teddy Roosevelt as one of the great conservationists, one of the great environmentalists. The time has come to lay aside partisan approach to these enormous environmental questions. We must devise a global approach to the problem of ozone depletion and global warming. We intend to make rapid progress on acid rain and see that a new clean air bill is produced. And we've already broken ground in joining with other nations to call for the elimination of the CFC's [chlorofluorocarbons] in adopting a tough new policy on the export of hazardous waste.

And there's drugs: The scourge of drug abuse will test our resolve and a mettle as a people. I'll bet you if I could talk to each one of you in a family setting that you'd tell me the things that concern you the most is the question of drugs—how it's affecting your schools, how it's affecting your own children or your grandchildren. And I'm concerned, as well. And I'm asking the Congress for $6 billion for our antidrug program in 1990 to beef up drug education, rehabilitation, law enforcement and, yes, interdiction.

And I'm also pleased that we have a strong, new drug czar. I'm a little confused as to why, in the United States—[*laughter*]—we want a strong, new leader, we call him a czar. [*Laughter*] But nevertheless, I'll defer to the Congress on this one. [*Laughter*] We've got a strong one. Call him a leader, call him a czar—Bill Bennett. And he's at my side, shoulder-to-shoulder to guide and coordinate this all-out effort against drugs. And it's not easy. When you look at the complexity of the Federal Government and the number of the agencies that are involved in this question of antinarcotics, it is a massive executive, coordinative job. And Bill Bennett will be superb as the first drug czar.

And finally, I want to single out one area which in so many ways is preeminently important to our nation. I am sure it is of particular importance to your family. We have got to protect and strengthen our schools. You and I know that education is our most enduring legacy. And you and I know that education is nothing less than the very heart and soul of our civilization. I want that control to remain with the families and the PTA and the local school boards and the States before the Federal Government when it comes to the control of our educational process, of our curriculum. And I will resist any effort to centralize all the answers for education here in Washington, DC.

But you know, education is this enduring legacy. And as we face a new decade and a new century, we also face a new challenge to revitalize and restore the system that our forebears bequeathed to us to ensure that American education is second to none. And I've made a number of proposals to work towards this goal, work with the States and the local to achieve that goal. Among them is my request to reward those schools whose students show measurable progress in educational achievement while maintaining a safe and drug-free environment. I've also asked for an annual fund of $100 million in new appropriations to help create magnet schools to broaden the educational choice of parents and students. And I've made many other proposals, including programs to strengthen the historically black colleges and universities, to reward our best teachers. And I appeal to you to get active in your schools, to share your knowledge, expertise, and resources where it is most needed.

I've laid out in broad terms, then, this agenda for building a better America. And, yes, it is ambitious; but it is no less ambitious, no less dynamic than the American people themselves. And as the business men and women, you can help me to fulfill this agenda, to meet the challenges that face our country. By working together, we can achieve absolutely anything. And so, the problems seem big at times out there, but believe me, never underestimate the ability of the American people if we together set our sights on achieving certain goals. I need your help.

I'm delighted to be here, and thank you for inviting me.

Note: The President spoke at 10:18 a.m. in the Presidential Ballroom at the Capital Hilton Hotel. In his opening remarks, he referred to Lawrence E. Hite, president of the Independent Insurance Agents of America.

Message to the Congress Transmitting the Annual Report of the United States Arms Control and Disarmament Agency
March 14, 1989

To the Congress of the United States:

I am pleased to transmit the 1988 Report of the United States Arms Control and Disarmament Agency. It reviews all aspects of last year's arms control policies, negotiating efforts, and the activities conducted in the process of meeting the statutory requirements of the Arms Control and Disarmament Act, as amended.

Of special interest are the sections on conventional arms control, the implementation of the INF Treaty, Nuclear Testing Talks, and the chemical weapons ban. The role of verification, a crucial element in any arms control agreement, is highlighted throughout the report.

The INF Treaty is a significant step in the quest for arms reductions. Reaching agreements with the Soviet Union on a START Treaty and a conventional arms control treaty are important objectives. We must also seek solutions to the serious problems of nuclear and chemical weapons proliferation.

While I endorse the broad approach to arms control taken in the past year, I am still reviewing specific details of the U.S. negotiating position. Statements of Administration views in the attached report, therefore, should be considered to be authoritative statements of past positions that may be subject to future modification following review.

I strongly believe that arms control should play a significant role in enhancing the security of the United States and its allies. The United States will continue to work toward effectively verifiable and stabilizing arms reductions.

GEORGE BUSH

The White House,
March 14, 1989.

Nomination of John B. Taylor To Be a Member of the Council of Economic Advisers
March 14, 1989

The President today announced his intention to nominate John B. Taylor to be a member of the Council of Economic Advisers. He would succeed Michael Mussa.

Since 1984 Dr. Taylor has been a professor of economics at Stanford University, and a professor of economics and public affairs at Princeton University, 1980–1984. He was a visiting professor of economics at Yale University, 1980. He has served in the department of economics at Columbia University as professor of economics, 1979–1980; associate professor of economics, 1977–1979; and assistant professor of economics, 1973–1977. Dr. Taylor previously served as a senior staff economist for the Council of Economic Advisers, 1976–1977.

Dr. Taylor graduated from Princeton University (A.B., 1968) and Stanford University (Ph.D., 1973). He was born December 8, 1946, in Yonkers, NY. He is married, has two children, and resides in Stanford, CA.

Remarks at the Swearing-in Ceremony for Edward J. Derwinski as Secretary of Veterans Affairs
March 15, 1989

Thank you all. Mr. Vice President and members of the President's Cabinet that are here; distinguished Members of the Senate and the House; and service Secretaries; and I see at least one member of the Joint Chiefs, General Vuono there, and distinguished guests over here, including Bill Mauldin: I'm just delighted to be here to salute Ed Derwinski, he with his family—Bonnie, Maureen, and Michael. I heard Maureen and Michael—I thought maybe President Reagan was back. [*Laughter*] But, no, this is the Derwinski clan.

And, Ed, I want to thank you for not wearing that gold and black checkered jacket with that tomato-red beret. [*Laughter*] I'm reliably informed that the White House camera crew would have gone on instant strike. We don't need another strike. [*Laughter*]

From where we're standing, most of the landmarks of this town are almost a stone's throw away. That's one of the beautiful things that Barbara and I have rediscovered, but discovered principally from living in the quarters above here. Just to the west of us Abraham Lincoln reposes majestically in his chair of stone. Straight ahead, Thomas Jefferson commands our respect, a bronze giant underneath a dome of marble. And the Washington Monument rises above the level of the surface of the Mall, much as our first President dominated his time. We glorify our greatest leaders, but we do not build these ivory temples to honor them alone. We honor the enduring principles for which they stood, and we honor the millions of men and women who have been ready throughout the history of our nation to defend those principles.

There've been four calls to arms in the living memory of most Americans or their parents. From the South Lawn of the White House, one can see a flaming sword, a tribute to the courage of the soldiers of the Army's 2d Division who fought so bravely in World War I. At the Iwo Jima Memorial just across the river, a fleeting moment of victory, first captured in an Associated Press photograph, is now cast for the ages in bronze. No one who lived through that war will ever forget that picture or what it meant to us. And we have yet to honor the veterans of the Korean war in such a way, although I'm glad to see that planning for a memorial is moving forward. But 3 weeks ago I saw a living monument to these brave Americans: the Republic of Korea itself, a newborn democracy aided by American sacrifice, protected by American strength. Just below the horizon, to our right, are the simple lines and chiseled names of the Vietnam Veterans Memorial, a somber salute to those who fell and to all who answered the call to duty. May we never cease to honor them, in name and deed.

And let us never forget those men and women in the Armed Forces who, even in peacetime, risk their lives in a hardship post or a dangerous assignment, whether it's standing on the deck of a carrier off the Persian Gulf or an antiterrorist unit waiting for a call that we hope never comes. The meaning of a monument, as Lincoln said of the battlefield at Gettysburg, is "far above our poor power to add or detract." These words are carved in stone in the Lincoln Memorial. But Lincoln himself acknowledged that speeches and statuary are inadequate repayment for those who made the ultimate sacrifice.

And our obligation is also for the living. If you go to the front entrance of the Veterans Affairs Department, you'll see another quote from Abraham Lincoln, cast in a plate of steel, calling on us "to care for him who shall have borne the battle and for his widow and his orphan." This is the mission of the new Department of Veterans Affairs, which today officially assumes the duties of the Veterans Administration.

I consider the new Department to have a vital mission. In fact, it is so vital that there's only one place for the veterans of America: in the Cabinet Room, at the table with the President of the United States of America. And as the first Secretary of this new Department, Ed Derwinski will set a precedent. He is uniquely suited for this role, having served with distinction in both the legislative and the executive branches of government.

My friendship with Ed goes back to my days as a freshman Congressman from Houston, Texas. Ed, a Congressman from Illinois then, was already a veteran of some tough congressional battles. And I know that for Ed the House of Representatives is still a second home with many, many friends. No former colleagues of Ed can ever forget his unfailing good humor and his concern for people. Nor will veterans forget his good work: Ed's handling of a heavy burden of casework, cutting redtape so that thousands of veterans could receive their pensions, medical benefits, deserved military honors.

At the State Department, Ed packed the achievement of a whole career into a few years. He worked with Congress; conducted special international negotiations with Canada, Iceland, the Pacific nations; acted as a senior official for refugee policy and programs; and prevented the diversion of the sensitive technology that belongs to the United States to unfriendly nations.

In short, Ed Derwinski has the skill of a seasoned legislator, the patience of a practiced administrator, the finesse of a diplomat, and the heart of a man who knows what it means to start his government career as a private in the United States Army. This is a unique combination of experience and skills. And make no mistake, this new job requires someone with Ed Derwinski's backgrounds and talents.

This new Department must manage its vast resources to meet vast needs. Almost one out of every three U.S. citizens is a potential VA beneficiary—count among them 27 million veterans and 53 million dependents and survivors. Ed will oversee a Department with almost a quarter of a million employees—the second largest civilian task force in the Government—administrating a budget of more than $29 billion. And the Department of VA provides compensation to service-disabled veterans; pensions for low-income, disabled veterans, and survivors; educational assistance; and vocational rehab. It guarantees the home loans for 12 million families and operates the fifth largest life insurance program in America. It also runs the Nation's largest medical system, with 172 hospitals and hundreds of outpatient clinics and nursing homes. But the best resource of the new Department is its people, men and women who live up to the highest ideal of public service every day. And they have my sincerest gratitude for a job well done.

It is only appropriate to note one other task assigned to the Veterans Affairs Department: to tend and care for 112 national cemeteries across America. There's no power, no glamour in such a job, but there is caring and respect for those who are gone and for those who grieve. In those gardens of stone sleep the heroes—men and women of every service, marine, soldier, sailor, airman—lost youth that can only be measured in centuries. A President could have no more poignant a reminder that he is charged with a great trust.

It is my duty as the Commander in Chief to see to it that our Armed Forces are so strong and our diplomacy so wise that we will never again need to erect another monument to the casualties of war. A free America in a world at peace—together we have achieved that goal; together we can preserve it. And if we do, then surely that peace will be the truest monument to our veterans.

Ed, congratulations! Thanks for all that you have already done, and we've got a big job ahead. And I look forward to working closely with you in the years to come. Thank you all, and God bless the United States of America.

Note: The President spoke at 1 p.m. on the South Lawn at the White House. In his opening remarks, he referred to Bill Mauldin, syndicated cartoonist and author.

Statement on Proposed Child-Care Legislation

March 15, 1989

Child care is one of the key issues facing the Nation. All of us—business, labor, nonprofit organizations, and governments at all levels—must play a role in helping families meet this important challenge. Our policy must have the family as its focus. We must put choices in the hands of parents and not in the hands of government. Increasing the range of child care options available to parents, particularly those who head families of modest means, will benefit the Nation's children, their parents, and the country as a whole.

Today I am transmitting to the Congress legislation to fulfill my commitment to child care. These legislative proposals will help us to invest in the future by investing in our children. When I presented my plan for "Building a Better America" on February 9, I urged that we help working families cope with the burden of child care. The legislative proposals I am forwarding to Congress today recognize that even at a time of fiscal restraint we can invest in priorities. These proposals implement ideas that I put forward to the American public during the campaign. These proposals were debated and contested, and the American people spoke.

My legislative proposals are based on four fundamental principles that must guide the Federal Government's role in child care:

First, parents are best able to make decisions about their children and should have the discretion to do so. Assistance should go directly to parents. They, not the government, should choose the child care they consider best for their children.

Second, Federal policy should not discriminate against families in which one parent works at home to care for their children.

Third, Federal policy should increase, not decrease, the range of choices available to parents. The Federal Government should not become involved in licensing decisions, and Federal financial support should not be made contingent upon State licensing decisions. Local governments are perfectly capable of addressing licensing issues. Churches play a vital role in making child care available. Neighbors and other family members can provide excellent care. Our policy should not discriminate against them.

Fourth, Federal support for child care should be targeted to the most in need—low and moderate income families—particularly those with young children, because they face the greatest difficulty in meeting the needs of their children. Our plan will benefit all low income working families with children, not just those who participate in government-sponsored child care.

These are the principles which underlie my proposals. These are the principles by which I will evaluate the congressional deliberations on my plan. I will be flexible in the details, but firm in my devotion to these principles.

The legislation submitted today will expand child-care assistance to low-income families by making a refundable tax credit available to families with children under age 4. The tax credit would equal 14 percent of earnings up to a maximum of $1,000 per child. The maximum credit would be phased out gradually, initially for families with incomes between $8,000 and $13,000, and by 1994 for incomes between $15,000 and $20,000. I propose to make the current dependent-care credit refundable so that low-income families with no income tax liability would still be eligible for assistance.

I am also proposing to expand the resources available to the Head Start Program by $250 million over the current level. This expansion would increase the range of child care choices available to poor families and meet my commitment to include more poor 4-year-olds in this program. In fiscal year 1990 these funds would extend the ladder of opportunity to as many as 95,000 more children who most need the assistance Head Start offers.

In addition, I have directed the Secretary of Labor to determine the extent to which market barriers or failures prevent employers from obtaining liability insurance necessary to provide child care on or near their employees' worksites.

At the center of my plan is parental choice. The future of this country is in the hands of its families. To the extent we can make their burden lighter and enable them to pursue the path they find best, we will be building a better America. I urge the Congress to act promptly on this legislation.

Note: A fact sheet entitled "Building a Better America: President Bush's Child-Care Proposal" was issued by the Office of the Press Secretary on March 15. In addition to covering the material found in this statement, the fact sheet also contained the following points:

"The [new child tax] credit would be provided in addition to the Earned Income Tax Credit (EITC) and would be available, as the EITC is, in advance as a payment in parents' paychecks.

"The current [dependent-care tax] credit would be an alternative to the new child credit. For each eligible child, parents could claim the one credit that best meets their needs and circumstances.

"The cost of the two [tax credit] proposals is estimated at $187 million for FY 1990, increasing to $2.5 billion by FY 1993."

Message to the Congress Transmitting Proposed Child-Care Legislation
March 15, 1989

To the Congress of the United States:

I am submitting the enclosed child care legislative proposals prepared by the Secretaries of the Treasury and Health and

Human Services for consideration by the Congress. I urge the Congress to act promptly on these important proposals.

The proposals, entitled the "Working Family Child Care Assistance Act of 1989" and the "Head Start Amendments of 1989," are a key part of my commitment to assist parents in making critical decisions about their children's care.

GEORGE BUSH

The White House,
March 15, 1989.

Nomination of James Roderick Lilley To Be United States Ambassador to China

March 15, 1989

The President today announced his intention to nominate James Roderick Lilley to be Ambassador Extraordinary and Plenipotentiary of the United States of America to the People's Republic of China. He would succeed Winston Lord.

During his government career, Ambassador Lilley has worked in Washington and in a number of American missions in East Asia, including the Philippines, Taiwan, Cambodia, Laos, Thailand, Hong Kong, and the People's Republic of China. In 1975 he was appointed national intelligence officer for China, the senior post in the intelligence community on Chinese affairs. In 1981 he served as political coordinator and senior East Asian specialist on the National Security Council. From 1984 to 1985, he was a consultant on international security affairs at the Department of Defense. He was Deputy Assistant Secretary for East Asian and Pacific Affairs in the Department of State, 1985–1986. In October 1986 he was appointed Ambassador to Korea and served there until January 1989. Ambassador Lilley has also served as an adjunct professor at Johns Hopkins School for Advanced International Studies for 3 years.

Ambassador Lilley graduated from Yale University (B.A., 1951) and George Washington University (M.A., 1972). He served in the U.S. Army, 1945–1946, and in the U.S. Air Force as a first lieutenant in the reserves. He also attended the National War College in 1972. Ambassador Lilley is married and has three children.

Nomination of Kay Coles James To Be an Assistant Secretary of Health and Human Services

March 15, 1989

The President today announced his intention to nominate Kay Coles James to be Assistant Secretary of Health and Human Services (Public Affairs). She would succeed Stephanie Lee-Miller.

Since 1985 Mrs. James has been director of public affairs for the National Right to Life Committee in Washington, DC, and has served as president of Black Americans for Life. Prior to this she was personnel director for Circuit City Stores, Inc., 1983–1985. She was director of community education and development for Housing Opportunities Made Equal, 1981–1983, and assistant to the housing coordinator, 1980–1981. From 1978 to 1979, she was conference coordinator for the State of Virginia Developmental Disabilities Protection and Advocacy Office. Mrs. James has served on the White House Commission on Children and the Task Force on the Black Family.

Mrs. James graduated from Hampton Institute (B.S., 1971). She was born June 1, 1949, in Portsmouth, VA. She is married to Charles E. James. They have three children and reside in Annandale, VA.

Remarks at the Electronic Industries Association's Government-Industry Dinner
March 15, 1989

Thank you for that warm welcome. I'm glad Pete was listening. I thought he thought I said a thousand pints of Lite— [*laughter*]—and that's why—[*applause*]. I'm delighted to be here, Chairman Little and President McCloskey. And I loved the invocation by Peter's brother. I want to greet the distinguished Members of Congress that are here tonight: I see Jerry Lewis over here and, of course, our distinguished majority leader, Tom Foley; Larry Welch, member of the Joint Chiefs; and, of course, one down from Pete, my colleague in the White House, our head of the National Security Council, Brent Scowcroft. And on my right, affectionately known as the Silver Fox.

I'm speaking before the olives, before the celery, and here's why: This is the most relaxed I've seen Barbara since our dog got pregnant. [*Laughter*] And we've got to go back to the White House. And I said to her, "Are you coming with me to Texas tomorrow morning?" She said, "No. What do you mean? Millie is expecting." So, you'll excuse us if we hit-and-run here. But I did want to say how pleased I am to be back with the members of the Electronic Industries Association, all you distinguished guests. Thank you, Pete, for the introduction.

Bishop Fulton Sheen once said: "The proud man counts his newspaper clippings; the humble man counts his blessings." Well, I am proud indeed to address this annual dinner. But let me confess: Tonight, flanked by colleagues and friends, and many of you all who I've known over the years, I am more grateful for my blessings.

And let me first congratulate the man with whom Bar and I just met, this year's EIA Medal of Honor recipient, Sid Topol. And I want also to say a word about this organization, the oldest and largest exploring the new horizons of America's technological future. Today, nearly 2 million Americans work in your industry. You're leading America's newest industrial revolution. You're helping us outwork and outperform the competitors around the world. And tonight we meet as neighbors and fellow businessmen, and our goal is a fairer, more productive, and ennobling life, not merely in our time but for the generations to come.

A more ennobling life can mean many things. It means education and opportunity. It means a nation of responsive citizens not only willing but eager to share, and it means the economic development which makes this sharing possible. For prosperity depends on growth, and growth depends on freedom. My friends, the freedom to dare, to risk, to defy the odds forms the heart of free enterprise, just as free enterprise is central to the American dream.

Freedom can give our kids a better land than we ourselves inherited. But to preserve it, we've got to protect it. And that's why I've proposed two major goals for objectives to build a better America: First, reduce that deficit; second, invest in America's future. And to round them out, address the problems of the present; the problems that cannot wait. And last, but not least: No new taxes!

And, yes, America faces immediate problems, problems like ocean dumping, the homeless, illiteracy. And, yes, I pledge to you we will address them now, not somewhere down the line. But as we do, let's move beyond the immediate. For today America is prosperous and at peace. And to be sure, there are enormous challenges, many opportunities presented by changes that are favorable to democracy, to liberty, to free markets, favorable to the principles this country has always stood for. And therefore, let's recognize that we stand at a special moment in our history. It's a moment not for complacency, not to sit back and reflect upon what's been, but to reflect on what might be. And it's an opportunity to look into the future and plan for it so that America's place and the well-being of her people are ensured for generations to come. We must remember the American tradition as we invest for the future of our own children.

My four objectives will allow America to honor that heritage and seize her moment. And together they will solidify economic freedom. They will expand that freedom. But above all, they will empower more people, more fully, to partake of the American dream. Reducing the deficit will free our children from interest debt which haunts their future. Investing in that future will prepare us as a people for a new century and its challenges. Focusing on urgent priorities will free government to marshal its resources. And no new taxes reflects that innately American quality, good old-fashioned common sense. These four objectives will build on the progress of the last 8 years. They will build a better America, and they will reaffirm our strengths, diffuse ticking time bombs, and reorient us as a nation. Above all, they form a new approach which looks to tomorrow, not just to today.

As President, I'm committed to this new approach. And that is why last month I proposed an agenda to cut the Federal deficit; help ensure our financial future; and thus enhance business' ability to plan, expand, and build. And I proposed to cut that deficit not by increasing the tax burden on the American people but by controlling spending and continuing economic growth so that as more people are working, revenues will rise as tax rates remain the same.

Next year alone, thanks to economic growth, Federal tax revenues will rise by more than $80 billion—more than $80 billion, even with no new taxes. And my plan will use that new revenue to slash the Federal deficit by more than 40 percent, in keeping with the Gramm-Rudman targets, bringing the deficit literally below the target.

And as you know, we've begun the budget process. The administration has acted. And now, in fairness, we are acting in a good bipartisan spirit on Capitol Hill to get action. Our task is to keep the economy going and growing. And only then can we create the investment that's so crucial to America to increase new jobs, to unlock new markets and, yes, to unleash new technologies. In a sense, this is typically American. For we're restless; we're never satisfied. We look to the next week and next year, not to the year 2000. Government's role challenges to harness that ambition by looking beyond a day.

Last year a large survey of CEO's revealed that, while American business leaders are inherently optimistic, they believe—in this poll by nine to one—that we're too short-term oriented. My plan speaks to the long-term and to a stable business climate. It says that to remain competitive we've got to look beyond the next quarterly statement. It says yes to America's standard of living and to her standing in the world.

For instance, let me address the investment that will result from cutting the maximum rate on capital gains. My plan supports reducing it to 15 percent on long-held assets. And moreover, it effectively eliminates the capital gains tax on people making less than $20,000. In 1978 this organization, following the leadership of my late departed friend, Bill Steiger, worked to reduce the capital gains tax. Well, today we've got to fight that battle all over again. We need the capital gains tax differential. Restoring the capital gains differential will lift revenues, help savings, and free American businesses without distorting world markets. Consider on the one hand, those competitors who tax capital gains punitively. By punishing risk takers, they stifle opportunity. Less opportunity means less capital to invest. Less capital, in turn, makes countries less competitive. It's a vicious cycle, a bit of a catch-22, and above all, an economic dead end.

On the other hand, keep in mind that some of the most successful economies of the Pacific rim—Hong Kong, Singapore, Republic of Korea—exempt capital gains from taxes. And our second biggest trading partner, Japan, scarcely taxed during her meteoric rise. As businessmen, you know this economic history. You know its lessons are clear. And like me, you hear a lot about competitiveness these days. Nothing can make America more competitive than restoring this differential. America's entrepreneurs should not have to run an uphill race against the rest of the world.

Tonight I challenge the Congress to join with me and level that playing field. I ask it to expand the marketplace and assist development. I urge it to increase competitiveness and link reward and risk. And the way you do that, once again, is by lowering the tax rate on capital gains.

My friends, the Treasury estimates that this cut in capital gains—restoring that differential—will add $4.8 billion to the revenue side of the ledger in fiscal year 1990. So, let us use it to expand economic freedom and help people help themselves. And let us build upon the over 19½ million new jobs created in this country since November of 1982—five times the number created in Japan.

Accordingly, my plan to build a better America recommends a permanent extension of the research and experimentation tax credit. It'll increase domestic research by multinationals and end the uncertainty of expiring temporary rules. And by adopting Federal enterprise zones, it'll help those untouched by the economic recovery. Enterprise zones are a pioneering initiative to create a number of federally targeted zones or areas in these economically distressed communities. By providing tax breaks in the relief from regulation, these zones foster a climate where businesses are founded and existing businesses expanded. Enterprise zones, like lowering the tax on capital gains, will invest in America's future.

And so will other investments. Investments, for instance, in education or the environment, in our children and in space. As a Texan, I know firsthand the role of space exploration. I know of your industry's involvement, your role in its success. My plans allocate an increase of $2.4 billion for the space program. This is as much an investment in our technological future as it is a reaffirmation of our national character. It supports affordable access to space through the National Aero-Space Plane Program and nine space shuttle flights by 1990. It funds space station *Freedom*, planned for operation in the mid-1990's. And I'll also elevate the status of the President's Science Adviser.

You cannot look into the next century without emphasizing the importance of science. All the unexplored frontiers are not in space. Many are found closer to home, as we seek to push back the frontiers of human knowledge. Toward that end, let us invest in the superconducting supercollider—a bold new experiment fusing science, technology, and education. And let us expand the work which will leverage America's technological prowess in such areas as microcomputers and automative electronics, bioprocessing, and then this high-definition TV. And because science is critical, as I have said, I intend to double the National Science Foundation budget. These investments are not some riverboat gamble in a distant future but a steadfast way to ensure the future.

And yet, my friends, remember that future is going to depend above all on our most precious resource—America's children. We've got to make sure that the kids are educated, the very definition of long-term investment in America's future. And that's why I want Congress to create a $500 million program to award merit schools. I intend to create special Presidential awards in every State. I urge expanded use of magnet schools, giving parents and students freedom of choice. And I propose a program to spur alternative certification, allowing talented Americans from every field, especially science and math, to teach in America's classrooms. It is simply a shame that the brightest among you men and women here tonight, coming out of science, wanting to give of yourselves to teach the kids, couldn't qualify because you didn't have the required number of formal education degrees. It is time we take a new look and permit those who want to give of themselves to teach in our public schools.

And you can't talk about a better America without worrying about the dangers of drugs. We propose the YES program, or

Youth Entering Service, to involve our kids in the communities. My friends, our children can make the 21st century a new American century. So, let's help them, guide them. And let us understand that we are one community—proud, united, and unafraid of the future.

A quote is attributed to Albert Einstein saying: "Everything that is really great and inspiring is created by individuals who labor in freedom." For more than 200 years, Americans have invested their labor, their talent, their compassion, and their vision to preserve freedom, to seize the moment and sustain our way of life. And I ask you, with America's tomorrow at stake, can we do anything less today?

God bless you all. Thank you very much for letting Barbara and me come to this outstanding dinner. We are very grateful to you. And God bless the United States of America. Thank you very much.

Note: The President spoke at 8:16 p.m. in the Grand Ballroom at the J.W. Marriott Hotel. He was introduced by Peter F. McCloskey, president of the association. Rev. Joseph M. McCloskey delivered the invocation. In his remarks, the President referred to William G. Little, chairman of the board of the association; Representative Jerry Lewis of California; and the late Representative William A. Steiger of Wisconsin.

Nomination of Rockwell Anthony Schnabel To Be an Under Secretary of Commerce

March 16, 1989

The President today announced his intention to nominate Rockwell Anthony Schnabel to be Under Secretary of Commerce for Travel and Tourism. He would succeed Charles E. Cobb, Jr.

Since 1985 Ambassador Schnabel has been the United States Ambassador to Finland. Prior to this he served as deputy chairman of the investment banking firm of Morgan, Olmstead, Kennedy & Gardner, Inc., in Los Angeles, CA, 1983–1985. In 1965 he joined Bateman Eichler, Hill Richards, Inc., serving in various senior management positions, including president of the firm's holding company. He has been very active in a number of civic, political, professional, and cultural organizations in Los Angeles, CA.

Ambassador Schnabel was born in 1936 in Amsterdam, The Netherlands, and attended Trinity College, 1952–1956. In 1957 he relocated to the United States and subsequently became a U.S. citizen and served in the U.S. Air National Guard Reserve, 1959–1965. Ambassador Schnabel is married and has three children.

Remarks at a Luncheon Hosted by the Forum Club in Houston, Texas

March 16, 1989

The President. Well, thank you all for that warm welcome back; and thank you, Dick, for the introduction, sir. I thank you and Dick Johnson for putting this little lunch together. I never saw such a wonderful crowd. They say that Texas is a state of mind, but it's still good to set both feet down on Texas earth and come back home to Houston. And I'm very pleased to be here.

This is my first trip back to the State since taking the oath of office some 55—56 days ago. My mind raced back as I was coming in on beautiful Air Force One to about 29 years ago, approximately—saw the medical center. And Barbara, I recall, was there awaiting the birth of our daughter, Dorothy. And now Barbara is not here—she is not expecting, but our dog is. [*Laughter*] And I think her priorities may be slightly askewed, but she doesn't. [*Laughter*]

But in any event, I am pleased to be back at this Forum Club, which has really contributed so much to the public debate on the important issues of the day. And I am delighted that Bob Mosbacher is with me, a past president of the Forum Club, now handling a difficult assignment there as Secretary of Commerce—not surprisingly for those who know him, and that's most of the people in this room—doing a superb job. And let me just say this: It's nice to have a person at Commerce who understands firsthand what it means to have built a business, to take risks; who understands that excessive regulation can be counterproductive in terms of job creation in this country. And also on a very personal side, it is very nice to have someone who you can kick your shoes off with and discuss the problems of the moment. So, I'm delighted that he is here with us today, and you should all be proud of the job he is doing. In addition to Dick O'Shields and Dick Johnson, I want to thank Judge Lindsay, Mayor Kathy Whitmire, and Lee Hogan for being here and welcoming me.

And I take great pride in what's happening here in Houston and, indeed, in our State. Houston has clearly turned the corner. I've looked at the statistics, and they're impressive: 280 new companies last month and nearly 90,000 new jobs in the area in the past 2 years. And the unemployment rate is almost half what it was just 2 years ago. And best of all, the new Houston is being built on a very broad economic base. And I've come here to Texas to tell you that we're hard at work in Washington; we are making progress. By the way, I came to Houston to share that news with you because they already heard it out in Lubbock. [*Laughter*]

We're working to drive down the deficit. We can, indeed, we must; but we can bring Federal spending under control and into balance with our resources. And under our budget, we'll have $80 billion in new revenue in 1990. You don't touch the tax structure, and you have $80 billion more in revenues to the Federal Government. We can stay on track to meet these Gramm-Rudman targets, and we can do it without raising the taxes on the working man and woman of this country. The key to building a better America is realistic—it's a realistic and workable budget, like the one we sent up to the Congress 5 weeks ago.

We're working now on a plan that will help developing nations cope with the burden of debt, a solution that promotes growth and stability in world markets. And frankly, it isn't just Latin America—take a look at Africa; take a look at Eastern Europe. Other countries have staggering debt problems; and we of the United States have to take the lead; and indeed, under the [Secretary of the Treasury] Brady ideas at the end of last week, we have stepped out to take the lead in trying to bring some solution to that very complex problem.

We're waging a war on drug abuse on every front—just gearing up now with our new drug czar in place—more effective education and awareness efforts to dry up the demand for illegal drugs, tougher law enforcement and interdiction to cut off suppliers and put the dealers behind bars where they belong. It's not going to be done just by the Federal Government. I might say parenthetically that I do want to find a solution to the so-called AK–47 assault weapon problem, one that protects the rights of the legitimate sportsman, but also protects the lives of our police officers who are laying their lives on the line for us every single day.

But as I say, this problem isn't a problem just for the Federal Government. I know that some may know the phrase, a Thousand Points of Light. In Washington, one wag called it a thousand pints of Lite, and I took umbrage with that. But I'm going to keep talking about a Thousand Points of Light because it is this volunteer spirit of American helping American that really has the most to do about solving this drug problem. And I salute Houston—with Houston Crackdown, a program that is such an effort of elected officials joining leaders in the community and education and labor and business and whatever to do something about this.

Another problem: We're working to establish a 6-month training wage as part of a package that raises the minimum wage from $3.35 to $4.25 an hour. And let me be clear and send this message to those Members of Congress that might be tuned in: $4.25 is my first and last offer. There will be no compromise on that figure. Anything higher will actually cost jobs by raising costs for many employers and will have an adverse affect on inflation and on productivity. A training wage does just the opposite. It provides the now-jobless, especially youth and minorities, a chance, a handhold on the economic ladder, a means of moving up.

And we're working on a serious problem that Texans are aware of—the threat to our financial system that's posed by insolvent savings and loans. Less than 3 weeks after taking office, we were faced with the enormity of this problem, and I announced a comprehensive set of proposals to take effective action on this problem. And we must clean up the S&L system so that the questionable practices and the outright illegalities that caused the current crisis will never happen again.

Nationwide, insolvent S&L's still in operation are incurring operating losses at a rate of about $300 million a month. That's almost $1 million during the course of this lunch. And if I speak too long, you can make that $2 million—during the course of this lunch. It's a very serious problem. Some of these savings and loan—the innocent victims—have changed economic times, but some, an outright violation of the norms of reasonable business behavior. Three weeks ago, I sent the Congress a bill that will enable us to take action to halt the dollar drain and move forward on stabilizing our savings and loan system. It is a sound and comprehensive plan. It has been well received. And I want to see that bill passed with its central provisions intact within the 45-day timeframe which I have challenged Congress to act upon—and there's no excuse for delay.

Once the legislation is enacted, we must turn our attention to careful and responsible handling of the assets of the failed S&L's. Let me be clear on a key point: Insured depositors, those across our great State and across this country whose deposits are insured, are not at risk. They are fully protected and will continue to be fully protected by Federal guarantees. Our solution must ensure the least possible disruption to local markets and, at the same time, keep costs to a minimum. And let me say clearly: We must see to it that those S&L officials guilty of criminal actions are pursued and punished for the losses that they've caused.

These are serious challenges, ticking time bombs that we need to defuse without delay, and we're trying to do just exactly that. These are by no means the only issues that demand leadership and prompt action. We're entering the 1990's, a horizon decade, threshold to a whole new century.

For people my age, and for people a good deal younger, the 21st century has been the place in our minds that we put all the fantastic ideas, all the discoveries and inventions we couldn't dream of experiencing in our own time. The 21st century was just another name for a future that seemed as distant as a voyage to the Moon. Here in Houston, we have a better sense of how we can cover that distance and transform a distant future into our destiny. The truth is the 21st century isn't far away at all. I graduated from school in the class of 1942. Our first graders today will be the class of 2000. The 21st century is here in our kids. The essential question today: What are we doing to prepare for the new world that begins 11 short years from now? And that's what my agenda is all about. Building a better America means laying the foundations today for the kind of future that we want.

Preparing for our future means investment in our economy and in our schools. It means safeguarding the environment against shortsighted actions that do long-term damage. It means finding ways to preserve and strengthen indispensable institutions like the family in the midst of social change. As I look at the fabric of society, and then look at the instability of family relationships, I see a real threat to our future. And so, a President, this President at least, should have everything he does be guided by how do we strengthen the American family? or put it in reverse: How do we keep from weakening the fabric of our society that is represented by the family?

Preparing our future means taking a long-range look at the international landscape to determine what policies and approaches will keep us free, prosperous, and at peace in the 21st century, as we are today. And speaking of freedom, it means formulating a multisource energy policy that, in the long run, will make us less dependent on the will of countries halfway around the world.

These aren't minor matters or unimportant issues. These are concerns that will determine what kind of world we live in and whether we as a people live up to our American ideals, and they're at the center of my agenda for the new American Century.

To prepare for the future, we've got to invest in our economy. We've got to create incentives for new investment and aggressive R&D programs that are catalysts to technological advance. And I have called for a permanent R&E—research and experimentation—tax credit to create that incentive and a 13-percent increase in federally funded science research. We've got to cut the capital gains tax—and I've asked the Congress to join with me on this—to spur the entrepreneurial activity that means new products, new industries, and new jobs. I've been hit in the political arena on this one, saying this is a tax cut for the rich—no such thing. It is opportunity and hope for those that want a job and don't have a job. And that's what this capital gains tax differential will do if we can get the Congress to promptly move forward.

Free enterprise is the engine of growth that can lead us into the next century. And it's up to the Government to maintain a climate that is hospitable to growth, competitiveness, productive investment, one that gives free enterprise as much free rein as possible. And by the way, that capital gains tax differential I talked about will bring in, in 1 year alone—estimate of the Department of the Treasury—will bring in, in 1 year alone, $4.8 billion more in new revenue if we go forward and enact what I am calling on the Congress to do.

To prepare for the future, we must protect our environment. Whether we're talking about the disposal of nuclear or other hazardous wastes or the discharge of CFC's [chlorofluorocarbons] into our atmosphere, the United States—on our own and more in concert with other nations—must make a clean environment a top priority. And what I've done so far is show that this isn't talk; we are taking action. And incidentally, maybe some of you saw it? This morning I talked to the astronauts, the *Discovery* group up there in outer space. And the need for us to all act on the environment was brought home to me again today when, in the Oval Office, I found myself talking to that spaceship and hearing from the crew that from their very special vantage point, looking down on planet Earth, the need was very clear to those five people that we must protect the global environment.

To prepare for the future, we must encourage and improve education. We must recognize and reward excellence in education: in our schools, our teachers, our students. My merit proposals for teachers, schools, and our nation's best young science scholars will reward the best and encourage others then to follow their example. Our National Science Scholarships alone will provide 570 top students up to $10,000 a year to attend the college of their choice.

And we can also strengthen our schools by introducing an element of competition into education. Magnet schools give parents and students the power to choose their schools, and that will serve as a powerful incentive for schools to improve their performance. This has been tested and tried, and it works. And that's why I've urged Congress to provide $100 million to help with the startup costs for new magnet schools.

Preparing for the future means confronting the changing nature of our society. What are we doing in the age of the single parent and the two-career household to help the family survive and prosper? I've called on Congress to adopt a set of child-care initiatives aimed at strengthening the American family, giving parents a choice. I don't want to regulate grandmothers. I don't want to regulate things from Washington so that church groups can't get together and provide day care service. I don't want the regulators to push the churches and the private groups out of the child-care business. We must preserve choice for the parents and diversity so that the kids can go and be in these child-care centers that their parents want them to be in. Our 1990 budget requests a 20-percent increase in the funding of the very successful Head Start program and institutes this child-care tax credit that I've referred to for low-income households to make balancing the responsibilities of work and family less difficult.

But let me just parenthetically mention a problem. I sent a bill to the Congress yesterday with choice intact; it's a beginning. It can fit into a very tough budget on the spending side, and I think the initial year proposal is, say, a quarter of a billion dollars. And the very day that that goes up there, the Congress—one of the committees over there on the Senate side comes out, or the House side—can't remember which—comes out with a budget ten times that much for the first year. And then they say, "What are we going to do about getting the deficit under control?" We've got to have some discipline in the Congress if we're going to meet the deficit needs and still start to provide the needs for the child care and other social causes that should really have a command on our resources.

To prepare for the future, we've got to map a national security strategy that ensures our freedom and gives due weight to each factor of change in the international scene. And that's the aim of this series of these defense and policy reviews that I've instructed my national security team to conduct. And some are saying, "You'd better hurry up. You don't want Mr. Gorbachev to capture the high ground with his speech at the United Nations, don't want him to mold public opinion further in Europe." Far more important is that we do a prudent review of our foreign policy, of our national security requirements, and then—in concert with our allies—move forward. We are prepared to lead this alliance, as the United States has in the past. But I am not going to be pushed into speedy action because Mr. Gorbachev gives a compelling speech at the United Nations, and I hope the Soviets understand that.

So, this is an American agenda for the long-term, and we aren't going to clean up the environment, turn our education system around, or create a more responsible business climate in one single day. But if we begin today and make steady progress, we will succeed. And in this kind of work, more is going on than meets the eye or makes the headlines.

The proof will come when we look back from the year 2000. And I'm confident we will be able to look back with pride on work we did to get ready for a new century provided we look forward today. We must enter the 21st century as a strong and trusted partner in the alliance of free nations and a frontline leader in the defense of freedom. We must enter the 21st century as a productive, energetic, and innovative member of the global economy, second to none in the technological competition that will determine economic leadership in the decades ahead. We must enter the 21st century as a nation whose people enjoy freedom, opportunity, and equality of life that fulfills the American promise: a society that draws its strength from the individual, the family, the community; and a government wise enough to respect those institutions as the cornerstone of our democratic system.

We've got work to do, work that won't wait, great work to ensure that the next century now on the horizon will be the American century. Thank you all very much. It's a great pleasure to be back, and I'll be glad to take a few questions. Thank you very much.

Decontrol of Natural Gas

Q. First off, of considerable interest is the topic of natural gas decontrol. Congress seems to be looking at this question again. And although it's been talked about much for several years, do you expect action this year, and will you actively work toward that goal?

The President. I am strongly for it; I've made this very clear to the Congress. There is a bill, I believe, being marked up on the House side right now. I think it has the best chance certainly in the last 20 years to get passed. And the administration will send no confusing signals on this one. I believe it is in our national security interest, as well as in the interest of freeing up markets that I've talked about here earlier on—so it will be priority. And I have a feeling that it is more apt to happen than any time since—well, certainly in the last 8 years that we've watched it and followed it and run into snags. But I'm for it; the administration is solid behind it. And the climate in Congress is much better today for this.

And some of it is environmental, and much of it is that people now realize we are becoming more and more dependent on foreign oil—it's getting close to 50 percent now. And most people, even if they don't come from an oil-producing State or a hydrocarbon-producing State, understand that that is not in the national interest of the United States. So, I'm optimistic about it.

U.S. Space Policy

Q. Mr. President, could you comment on your feelings about the future of NASA, particularly with respect to the space station and a manned mission to Mars by the end of this century.

The President. On the space station, I am strongly for it. We have taken the steps, budgetwise, to go forward on that. I have not reached a conclusion on whether the next major mission should be a manned mission to Mars. And so, I'd have to say it's not on hold, but we're asking the space council that has been reconstituted—or constituted now to come forward with its recommendations. The Vice President's chairing it. He'll be in Houston in about 2 weeks from now. So, no decision is made—what happens beyond the space station itself, and I will make that decision when I get their recommendations. And I would have to say this as a word of caution: Even though we've increased—or requested that NASA's budget be increased, there are constrained resources that I have to deal with as President, and so, I can't pledge instant commissioning of this follow-on mission to Mars.

Government Ethics

Q. Is the increased attention being given to the private lives of public officials and candidates a good thing or a bad thing for politics and government in this country?

The President. Well, I think there are excesses. I think there are intrusions into people's private lives that go beyond the public trust or go beyond one's ability to serve. And I don't like the excesses.

And I think you all here know how I feel about the recent proceedings regarding Senator Tower—didn't like that because I think it was unfair. I don't think it is fair to a man who has been in public life and has served his country with honor to be tried by perception and rumor. That is not the American way. And people say to me, "Well, didn't it drag your administration down to stand with Senator Tower?" The answer is no, and I'm very pleased the Senate committee moved this morning on our new nominee, Dick Cheney. But the answer is: I wasn't about to move away from John Tower. People are entitled to fairplay; they are entitled to have the rumor laid aside and people to make up decisions based on fact, not perception. And so, whether it damages me 5 percentage points or 10 doesn't matter.

I think it is proper to have full disclosure, particularly on financial conflicts of interest. We've just received a report from a nonpartisan ethics commission with Griffin Bell and Judge Malcolm Wilkey of Houston as a matter of fact—its Chairmen. There's some good recommendations in there. I want to have the highest possible ethical standards, but I think in some areas most people realize that we may have gone too far in terms of the intrusion on people's private lives.

U.S. Naval Power and World Peace

Q. Mr. President, we have time for one additional question. Would you discuss the future of the 600-ship U.S. Navy? Will we continue to rely on submarine-based nuclear defense?

The President. Well, submarine-based nuclear defense is and will continue to be a very important part of our deterrent. There's no question about that. There is nothing going on in the field of arms control thinking that would convince me to have anything other than to preserve our technology and our ability to deter war through preserving, strengthening that kind of defense.

In terms of the 600-ship navy—it's a goal.

I've been for it, will continue to be for it. But I have to defer now to this budget review and strategic review and administrative review that I've tasked the Defense Department to come up with. And it's serious business. They will report back soon, and then we'll have to make our budget choices. And so, I would have to defer answering how much more will be done on a 600-ship Navy within the next budget cycle. But as a goal, as an objective, I am for that. I believe naval power is a significant deterrent to aggression.

I might say this, inasmuch as that's the last question: We've got 11 grandchildren, and I expect, looking at the age lines on some of the men around here—notice that one—[*laughter*]—some of you may have some grandchildren. When you get to be President, one of the main concerns you have has got to be how do you feel about world peace. What can you do to strengthen it? Are you optimistic or pessimistic about the world moving away from confrontation towards more peaceful resolution of problems?

We're in the process of reviews, as I said, and I've met Mr. Gorbachev several times. I am convinced that I can say to our 11 grandchildren we have a real opportunity now to make this year 2000 and beyond, that I was talking about, more peaceful. The changes in the Soviet Union are profound. Gorbachev himself will tell you when you ask him about *perestroika*—he said it'll never go back to the way it was. Changes in China are profound. Barbara and I are just back from there. It will never go back to the days when the Soviet Union and China were in lockstep together. But we're facing a challenge in the United States—we've got to figure it out. We've got to measure Soviet intentions and then come forward with proposals that will enhance the peace for our kids and our grandkids.

But I wanted to leave you, my neighbors and friends, with this thought: There is reason to be optimistic because of the changes inside the Soviet Union and some of the changes that you're seeing surface now in Eastern Europe. And you saw the relief of regional tensions in Angola. Hopefully it will come to be brought to bear in Central America. So, I would say to you, my friends and neighbors, if we do it right, if we keep strong and are not naive in it, if we don't make drastic cuts in the security accounts of this country, I think all of us can look forward over that horizon to a much more peaceful world with the United States still in the forefront of what's right for democracy and freedom.

Thank you all very, very much.

Note: The President spoke at 12:30 p.m. at the George R. Brown Convention Center. He was introduced by Dick Johnson, president of the club. In his opening remarks, the President referred to Secretary of Commerce Robert A. Mosbacher; Dick O'Shields, chairman of the club; Jon Lindsay, Harris County judge; Kathryn J. Whitmire, mayor of Houston; and Lee Hogan, president of the Greater Houston Partnership. The President then traveled to Colorado Springs, CO.

Remarks at the Junior Achievement National Business Hall of Fame Dinner in Colorado Springs, Colorado
March 16, 1989

Thank you for that warm Colorado welcome. Thank you all. I am simply delighted to be here. A wonderful day—it started in the Oval Office about 8 a.m., when I talked to the astronauts up there in the space shuttle. And I listened to them very carefully as they shared with me their view from their special vantage point about the need of doing more for the world environment, and that meant obviously, more education—then to Houston, Texas, which for Secretary [of Commerce] Mosbacher and I was returning home. And I'm delighted that he's with me here today. It's wonderful to have a Secretary of Commerce who knows what it is to take risks, build, succeed, and work to help others. Bob Mosbacher is doing an outstanding job, and I'm delighted he's with me. And then on out here tonight for this very special occasion.

In Washington—you know the old saying: "If you want a friend, get a dog." [*Laughter*] And Junior Achievement has a different motto. They say: "If you want a friend, sign up Lod Cook." And what a job this guy's done.

And I, too, want to pay my respects to the six award winners, the six laureates honored tonight. And then when you look at that distinguished list, as Dinah and I were reviewing there in this program, you can't help but be impressed—the achievements that they've made and then what they're doing to help others achieve. And if it wouldn't be too subjective on my part, I would like to say how thrilled I am to see—perhaps he's the dean of the laureates. He's certainly one that the Bush family holds in great regard; we have him as a role model. And I'm talking about Mr. Erik Johnson, over here, from Dallas, Texas. And so, it's a special occasion for me to see him again.

I want to pay my respects to the great Governor of this State, Governor Romer, who is here with us tonight, and thank him for being with us. And to Congressman Joel Hefley who just arrived, but we're in his congressional district, and I want to thank him for being here as well.

And, Lod, thank you for the kind words in that introduction. I've been an admirer of Junior Achievement and all it's done to advance economic education for many years. And Lod has taken what is already a strong program and made it that much better. And going into that classroom to make the meaning of economics a little clearer is a tough assignment. I've heard about the volunteer who asked his class what the gross national product was—the boy who said "that's the most disgusting thing made in America." [*Laughter*] It's answers like that that make teaching a rewarding experience. [*Laughter*] But there's no doubt that Junior Achievement has a positive impact. In fact, based on what Lod's told me about the program, and others as well, I'm going to have to add a point or two to our GNP estimates as soon as I get back to Washington. [*Laughter*]

While all of you here tonight share in this success story, I want especially to commend Jim Hayes of Fortune. Jim, I know that you and a number of your staff have been actively involved in this Project Business—Junior Achievement's Project Business, taking your skills and talents into classrooms throughout New York City. The work you're doing with those junior high students is opening their eyes to a whole new world.

And Junior Achievement is a phenomenally successful enterprise by any measure. The numbers alone tell the story. You reach over a million children each year, from 4th through 12th grades, in more than a thousand communities across the country.

And I've spoken many times about the Thousand Points of Light, the dedicated and diverse volunteer organizations that contribute so much to American life. Those of you involved in Junior Achievement know exactly what I'm talking about. In fact, Lod tells me that a Thousand Points of Light doesn't begin to describe your efforts and that the 100,000 men and women involved in Junior Achievement is a supernova of volunteers. Let's agree that the volunteer ethic is the North Star. As long as that sense of service guides us, we'll be strong, a self-reliant people, as ready to help each other as we are to help ourselves.

Our young people especially can bring an energy and enthusiasm and ability to the volunteer effort. That's the idea behind our administration's new initiative that I call YES, Youth Entering Service, a new concept for the Federal Government's participation that encourages young people to help those less fortunate than they are themselves. And it's a good concept, and we've selected Gregg Petersmeyer of Colorado, now back in the White House, to run this program. And when we get going—it is, as Lod talked about, a public-private partnership—we're going to ask your help. It is important that young people have inculcated into them early in life a sense of service. And I believe the program will be good in helping those kids who haven't had an equal place at the starting line.

Tonight I want to talk to you just a little

about education, the issue at the heart of your mission. First, a word about the lesson in applied economics that are the hallmark of JA. In your creative hands, economics is anything but the dismal science, as some have called it. You give economics life, and you give our young people a real understanding of the stake that we all have in economic enterprise.

Like many in this room, I know what it means to have started a business and try to help build it. And I know the risk and the worries late at night, the responsibilities that you feel for the employees that are in it with you. And I don't need to tell all of you it's something you never forget. I also know the feeling that comes with some success: the pride; the exhilaration you feel when your business is on its feet and running; the feeling you get when you take an idea, something that exists only in your mind maybe, and turn it into something real, a common enterprise that meets the test of the marketplace, that carves out a little place in the larger economy. And all of you here today are helping people experience that same sense of accomplishment through their involvement with Junior Achievement. You're awakening the entrepreneurial spirit of a new generation.

All of you have heard me say that I intend to be the "Education President." And let me say now, I can't think of any issue that is larger or more far-ranging in its impact than the education of our young people. Think about the great issues of the day. Do we want to talk about America's place in the world? Then we'd better think about education. Do we want to talk about competitiveness and how we can improve it? Again, we'd better think about education. About productivity—how to keep it on the increase. Again, education. It's a matter of our horizons—our ability to see how we can meet and master the challenges we face, now and in the future. Planning for today—simply for tomorrow—is a guarantee for stopgap solutions. Education is long-range planning at its best. It's a solution for the next century, for problems we haven't even begun to recognize.

In 11 short years, we'll stand on the threshold of a new century. We know now that the world is in the midst of a technological revolution. We can see the pace of change always accelerating. And what will our world look like in the century ahead? Who will lead America a generation from now? Who will hold the top positions in government and in the private sector? Who will be the new pioneers in the fields of medicine, science, and engineering? And who will display the creative genius that will challenge, excite, and inspire us?

We don't know their names, but I can tell you where to find them: from 8 a.m. to 3 p.m., every day, in the schools all across this country. Look for that fifth-grader, who 40 years from now will find him or herself in the position that you're in today. Look for the 5-year-old, whose curiosity about everything is the first sign of a budding scientific mind. Look into the classrooms across this country today, where the spark of interest kindles a lifelong involvement in exploring, in expanding, and in advancing our knowledge. So, let's not make the mistake of underestimating education's importance on our national agenda. When it comes to our nation's future, education is the key. It is the best investment that we can make.

And now, we've all seen the studies—discouraging, some—that show American students trailing those of other nations in science and math skills. We all read the stories about the kid who can't even find America on a map. We all know the dropout rate, abysmally high. And it's high where it hurts—some of these minority communities across this country. We all know that the level of literacy is too low. We know that we must do more to open the door to advancement for our disadvantaged youth by helping them, providing them educational opportunities they deserve.

And the answer isn't to sit and wring our hands. We need to roll up our sleeves and take an active part in making our schools better. And that requires a totally cooperative effort involving all levels of government, the public and the private sector. I understand and I believe it's right that in our Federal system education is a shared responsibility. Federal policy must never, ever, crowd out local control—it's parents; it's local boards; it's PTA; it's State efforts. All have, themselves—all of them—important parts to play. All the primary responsibility rests with the States and the local school systems. The Federal Government can still serve as a catalyst for change—fresh thinking about how to build the best possible education system.

And so, I have built into my first budget a number of education initiatives that I believe can enhance the quality of our schools. Let me just mention four.

First we must recognize excellence, and we must reward it because excellence breeds excellence—reward it wherever it is found. And that's why I've proposed a $500 million dollar program, merit schools, it's called, and a Presidential Award for Excellence in Education for our best teachers. We must never forget the teachers who are out there on the cutting edge.

Secondly, we've got to strengthen scientific education. My budget includes an initiative called the National Science Scholarship Program. Each year, beginning in 1990, a total of 570 American high school seniors, at least one from every congressional district across this country, will receive up to $10,000 a year in scholarships to the college of their choice, renewable for 4 years.

And third, we need to remove the barriers that can keep talented teachers out of the classroom. Think of the knowledge assembled in this room this evening—the business acumen, the hands-on economic experience that you all possess. I was thinking of unleashing my Third World debt program here. Ron? Lod, I've got you down for a billion. [*Laughter*] Erik, half a billion. We can solve it right here. No, but seriously, think of the experience in this room.

Look at that honor roll. Measure it in terms of success and creativity and innovativeness, the hands-on economic experience that you possess. Junior Achievement makes it possible for you to pass that on to our schoolchildren. But what about people with similar schools of knowledge? Their entry into teaching as a profession is barred in our country by the excessive requirements of certification, requirements that many in this room, the brightest here, could not meet. And you could be a Ph.D., a tremendous success in business, and yet the layers of requirements for teaching in our public schools keeps you from volunteering, sabbatical year basis, for helping the young people of this country. Regulations make it impossible for schools to hire people with the capabilities that are represented in this room tonight. Teachers-by-training aren't the only ones who can teach. I'm not saying you don't need some education courses, but I urge the State and local school systems to take a look at their certification systems and make sure we open up our schools to those with a lifetime of experience outside the classroom, who are ready and willing to share what they know with our young people.

This was driven home to me when I moved to Odessa, Texas, in 1948. And I had done reasonably well at Yale—didn't bring my Phi Beta Kappa key along, but it's here—and went to volunteer to teach in a community college. Couldn't do it; didn't need that kind of help because I hadn't passed enough of the formal education requirements. We've got to change this. We're in changing times. "We've got to think anew," as Lincoln said.

And fourth, we must use competition to spur excellence in education. I support the use of magnet schools to introduce an element of choice into education. And I've requested $100 million to help with the start-up costs of new magnet schools. We all know the value—you all know it better than I—the value of competitiveness in the business world. Challenging schools to strive to match the best among them can push them all to new heights. Competition might just provide the quality schools that we are all looking for. And where it's been tried—parental choice—it has helped not only the kids but it has helped the schools that were achieving at the lower rates. It's a good idea; choice for parents works.

America—we're well positioned to remain productive and competitive in the world marketplace, but our strong suit is our abundant supply of the most inexhaustible resource on the planet: human ingenuity, and, of course, a system that gives that ingenuity free rein. We have the raw materials. We have the opportunity. What we need is a new sense of resolve, a commitment to shape our future by preparing today the children who will lead us into that 21st century.

Thank you all very much for what you are doing to lift the sights and give opportunity to the young people of the United States of America. Thank you, and God bless you all.

Note: The President spoke at 8:40 p.m. in the ballroom at the International Center. He was introduced by Lodwrick M. Cook, chairman and chief executive officer of ARCO and chairman of the National Business Leadership Conference. In his remarks, the President referred to entertainer Dinah Shore; Erik Johnson, founder of Texas Instruments; Charles G. Petersmeyer, Deputy Assistant to the President and Director of the Office of National Service; and James B. Hayes, publisher of Fortune magazine. The President stayed at the Broadmoor Hotel overnight and returned to the White House the following morning.

Nomination of Gilbert E. Carmichael To Be Administrator of the Federal Railroad Administration
March 16, 1989

The President today announced his intention to nominate Gilbert E. Carmichael to be Administrator of the Federal Railroad Administration, Department of Transportation. He would succeed John H. Riley.

Since 1961 Mr. Carmichael has been an automobile dealer for VW, Mazda, Chrysler, and Mercedes Benz and has been actively involved in real estate development. In 1973 he was appointed to the National Highway Safety Advisory Committee; and became Chairman of the Advisory Committee, 1974–1976. From 1976 to 1979, he was a Federal Commissioner for the National Transportation Policy Study Commission.

Mr. Carmichael graduated from Texas A&M University (B.S., 1950). He was also a fellow at the John F. Kennedy School of Government, Harvard University, 1976. He was born June 27, 1927, in Columbia, MS. He served in the U.S. Coast Guard, 1944–1945; 1951–1953. Mr. Carmichael is married, has one son, and resides in Meridian, MS.

The President's News Conference
March 17, 1989

The President. ——have my green tie when I climb off. How are you guys?

Japan-U.S. Jet Fighter

Q. Do you think you're going to approve the FSX?

The President. No decision on that yet.

Q. But do you think that it—is it a hard decision for you to make? Very complicated?

The President. Well, it's a good one to be sure you listen carefully to all sides of it, and that's what we were doing. We had a meeting on it just the other day, and I may have another one when we get back. Certainly I'll be talking about it over the weekend. Tom [Tom Baden, Newhouse Newspapers], it's—you know, you're torn several ways on it, but we'll make the right decision. No decision has been made.

Q. Have you generally decided to go ahead with the project?

The President. I just said I haven't made any decision at all, and I will, you know, wait until we have the benefit of all the Cabinet officers weighing in. The first meeting was very helpful. It went on a long time, and we'll have another one now. I've asked certain Cabinet members to get certain pieces of information.

Q. Some of your aides have suggested that the basic decision has been made and it's just a matter of you signing on——

The President. Well, help me with what aide has told you that, because I'd like to speak to him about it.

Q. So, you're still——

The President. Any aide told you that? Has he got a name to——

Q. We don't want to name any names.

The President. Is this a vicious assault on Marlin Fitzwater? [*Laughter*]

Q. Not on Saint Patrick's Day.

Mr. Fitzwater. I deny everything. [*Laughter*]

Q. Just so we know that no decision——

The President. I told you the answer. I make this decision. And so, some aide—if you would help me with that, he'd be looking for employment at the Associated Press, because he's not going to—[*laughter*]. I'm serious. I mean, I see all this stuff.

Terrorism

Q. Let me ask you a question. Have you decided that the Chilean grapes and fruit ought to now start coming in?

The President. I was told that we're going to lighten up on that, and I think that's fine.

Q. Do you think that restricting all those fruit imports was too severe?

The President. No, I think when the health of the American people might be threatened you've got to take prudent action. And I think HHS, working with others, have done a good job on this. It has caused some economic hardship, which I regret, but these are just some of the things you have to address yourself to.

Q. This wasn't an overreaction?

The President. Well, I don't think so. If one person had been adversely affected healthwise, maybe the charge would be the other way. So, I don't think so.

Q. What do you make of this grape scare? It's sort of one of those what's-this-world-coming-to questions.

The President. I know it; it worries you. Well, it ties into the whole concept of terrorism. When you try to effect change by action—you know, political change by action on the terrorist front—there is a similarity here, if the calling-in is accurate. You never know on a case like this. I mean, that's the trouble.

Q. On this same subject, apparently, Pan Am had been warned to watch for tape recorders that could be bombs.

The President. I haven't been briefed on that, so I'd be very careful about responding until I get the facts.

Gun Control

Q. Mr. President, do you have any reaction to the decision by Colt to ban sales of its own semiautomatic——

The President. Who?

Q. By Colt, the maker of the PR–15.

The President. I don't know whether they're totally banned or whether they're waiting to see what happens on this import decision. No, but I'm certainly not going to differ with that decision.

Q. There's a story today that actually the administration considered a ban on a number of about 25 other weapons along with what Secretary Brady——

The President. They've not discussed that with me.

Q. Do you think the temperature of the national debate over assault weapons has gotten too hot, or do you think——

The President. Yes, a little bit.

Q. How so?

The President. Just because it's gotten pretty hot. But we'll make our decisions from the administration in you know, a cool way, based on facts and not swayed one way or another by the temper of the debate. But I can understand when kids are shot down by a semiautomated weapon or automated—whichever it was—why, I can certainly understand the public outcry.

Q. Are you looking at a whole package of other things to do?

The President. Well, we'll let you know what we decide. We've got a brand new drug czar who has been in there about a week now, and so, we'll be sure to let you guys know when we make more decisions on this line. It's important.

American Hostages in Lebanon

Q. Sir, as you know, the hostage, Terry Anderson, started a fifth year of being held yesterday. Do you foresee any reformulation of our hostage policy?

The President. No.

Q. What are your thoughts about the plight of these people? President Reagan——

The President. I think it's terrible. It's with me every single waking hour. Very, very concerned about it. And any time anyone, particularly Americans, are held against their will, it is an enormous concern. But I'll stick with my answer in terms of reformulation of policy.

Q. Do you foresee any reissuing of the statement you made in your inaugural speech—"good will begets good will"—anything along those lines that you would say to those people?

The President. I think those people know how I feel, and I'd just leave it right there. I've really tried to make that very clear then, and I think it was.

Secretary of Defense-Designate Cheney

Q. Mr. President, have you been in contact with Mr. Cheney in recent days, since his——

The President. Dick Cheney? I talked to him 2 days ago, but I didn't talk to him since the committee acted. Very pleased the way it's going.

Q. I don't know—have your heard whether Cheney's——

Mr. Fitzwater. They were getting ready to, but they hadn't as of about an hour ago.

The President. I thought they were going to vote about 1 o'clock.

Q. Are you tempted to swear him in days—plan to get him on board?

The President. That's not a bad thought. He'll go to work right away, whether he's officially sworn in or not. What I've been doing with most of the Cabinet officers is going to the Cabinet Departments, and I think it does show an interest on the part of the President in those Departments. It might be a very important thing to do with Defense, given the delay that's taken place. But I'm very pleased about it, and I'm convinced he'll be a wonderful Secretary of Defense. I'm very happy with the public reaction, people that are in the decision-making process on the Hill and people he'll be working with at the Pentagon. It's been very well-received.

Inflation

Q. Mr. President, the Producer Price Index was up a full 1 percent this morning for February. That's the second month in a row it's been 1 percent, or more than 12 percent annual inflation so far, on wholesale prices. How do you view these figures? Do you still contend that inflation is not increasing substantially?

The President. My view is that you have to always be vigilant against inflation, always vigilant. As you know, there were other figures earlier this week that sent out a different message—plant capacity. And actually, these figures are based on mainly food and energy prices from a couple of months ago.

Having said that, I'd make two points: We can never relax in our concerns about inflation. And the best thing to do about it is to get the budget deficit down and to have speedy action along the lines of the budget proposals I've made. And I'll say this—I don't want it to come out that I think there's foot-dragging, because the meeting we had this week, Tom, with the leadership of the budget committees, appropriations committees, finance committees, was a very good meeting. And the leaders themselves are trying to be—on both Republican and Democrat—want to be cooperative. So, I can't fault the Congress at this point. But I do think that a signal of this kind, PPI, should not be overlooked and should be another clarion call for doing something about the deficit. We'll just keep saying that.

Q. Fed—[*inaudible*]—interest rates?

The President. I'm not about to fight with the Fed. I think there's a lot of indications that the economy is still in good shape, but that doesn't mean that we shouldn't be vigilant against inflation. But anytime there's an indication of this nature, I would say please, let's everybody—executive branch, congressional branch—go the extra mile on getting this deficit down. It's the best answer to it by far.

Gun Control

Q. Mr. President, can I go back to the gun issue one more time? There have been some news reports that charged that a decision by your administration this week to halt the imports represents for you a change in position on gun control. What's your reaction to that charge?

The President. It represents, certainly, a heightened concern on my part about AK-47's.

Q. But not a reversal——

The President. It's a pulse change.

Q. What's that?

The President. Pulse change—we're enforcing the law. Incidentally, it talks about the suitability of weapons for sporting purposes. And we're not changing the law by doing this or trying to have a different interpretation of the law.

Q. Some gun store owners say that they had no demand for this until the media hyped the issue, and that's why——

The President. Well, then they should address that to you, not to me. I'm not in the media.

Q. The police had a concern long before the media started talking about it.

The President. Absolutely, the police have been very concerned about this, and we've got to find an accommodation between the police and the sporting interest. In my view, there can be an accommodation. There must be an accommodation, but that's the way I look at it.

Aid to the Contras

Q. Mr. President, are you ready with a *contra* aid package?

The President. Not as of this minute. I think we'll be talking about that—I talked yesterday to Jim Baker [Secretary of State] and Brent Scowcroft [Assistant to the President for National Security Affairs] just before I left; we had an early meeting in the White House. And I've not talked to them since we've been gone, but I expect it will be awaiting me when I get back. I want to see something worked out where America speaks with one voice. It is not helpful to the foreign policy objectives to have divided voices: the Congress going in one direction and the Executive, who is responsible for foreign policy, going in another. So, we're trying to work all that out. And I think Jim Baker has been well received on the Hill from both Republicans and Democrats.

Q. I've got a really long question once we change this tape. [*Laughter*]

The President. How about a long answer while she's changing? [*Laughter*] Come on, a little hustle!

President's Personal Schedule

Q. While they're changing tapes, we were wondering whether you'll have a full weekend your first whole weekend in the White House?

The President. We're going to unleash all the athletic events. Horseshoes are ready, although the official opening of the pit—we now refer to it as the horseshoe pitching court—will take place probably 2 weeks from tomorrow in a very big gala opening with horseshoe pitchers from across the country coming, some of the very best. And that event will be, weather permitting, in a couple of weeks. I think the date is close to being set for Saturday, 2 weeks from tomorrow. But in the meantime, there'll be some preliminary pitching, which we would welcome participation from those who claim to have credentials in this sport right here. But then the tennis court, I'm going to hit today and tomorrow—tomorrow and the next day, I think. Might get the running going again—I felt pretty good yesterday. Although, I ran out of oxygen there, so I had to go down to less than the 2 miles—I like to run, but I'm going to do that. We've got great machines for that, too, incidentally—the Schwinn Aerodyne and the Pacer's latest running track, both of those are at the White House. So, I am excited. We have a lot of events going on.

Q. And you have the grandkids coming in next weekend?

The President. Next weekend—big event. That'll probably be at Camp David, though, Easter Sunday.

Q. How you been able to get in as much exercise as you had expected to?

The President. Yes, I can get it in. But I had that hiatus in there because of the lingering flu that I've never had before. So, I cut down on the running. A little overweight, but I really feel good. I was up early this morning, which was not early DC time, but went for a long walk out there. And wanted to tee it up on their golf course, it looked so good.

Q. Do you have the caged-in feeling——

The President. No.

Q. ——living in the White House that some of your predecessors complained about?

The President. Not yet. I don't think I will.

Q. ——living over the store, as President Reagan used to——

The President. No. It's wonderful—get to work quicker.

Visit to Cheyenne Mountain High School

Q. What did you and the kids talk about yesterday, running around the track? Conversation seemed to be——

The President. Well, one of them had just come back from China—a big, tall guy on my left. And he was asking me—I was very impressed with the guy; he kept hanging in there. I'm not sure he was their most athletic student because he was breathing even harder than I was. [*Laughter*] But he asked me which school would be the best to go to for foreign policy and things of that nature. He was talking about Lewis and Clark and Stanford. I said, Well, they're both fine schools, but I think the Fletcher School or Georgetown is also good in that regard. Another little guy, the guy on my right, heavyset kid—he's going to Baylor next year, and he started talking a little about Texas. And we got into a long discussion of different sports out there and what's popular in Colorado—lacrosse coming in now and soccer, mainly in the girls, but coming up in the men's side, too—hockey. It was wonderful. The baseball team was working out. So, it was mainly that kind of thing. But they were very nice, and they didn't seem to think I was disrupting their events.

President's Dog

Q. How many puppies are you going to have?

The President. If I had to bet—and we've done no sonograms—I would bet six.

Q. Are you going to keep any of them?

The President. Millie is one of eight—I don't think so. A tremendous demand out there, Tom, enormous demand for these puppies. And I'm particularly interested in the op-ed page in one of the great newspapers the other day, where they had two English spaniel breeders saying this was the most outrageous thing they'd ever seen—the attention to having these puppies there at the White House. And then, off-setting opinion, counterpoint, came by an 85-year-old woman who has written a book on English spaniels, who announced that this was one of the greatest things that had ever happened. So, it's causing a very lively debate, much like the AK–47 debate—[*laughter*]—a tremendous interest in this.

Q. So, you'll be happy when it's over.

The President. Yeah. It's changed my life. Seriously, you think I'm kidding about that. It's awful. Can I tell them what Barbara told me on the phone?

Mr. Fitzwater. Sure.

The President. She said, "Tonight, you're in the Lincoln bed, alone." I said, "Well, why?" She said, "Well, Millie had a very bad night last night, thrashing around, and you would be irritable." So, I'm being sent down the hall, which just suits the heck out of me.

Q. Well, who's in the doghouse? You or the dog?

The President. The dog refuses to go to the doghouse is the problem. There's a beautiful pen made for her to have this blessed event in. It's wonderful—little shelf built out so that the puppies can scurry under there and they don't get rolled on by the mother. I never thought we'd go through something like this again, after the 6 kids and 11 grandchildren. But it's a whole new thing.

Q. Is this worse?

The President. In a way, it is. In a way, it is. It's mainly because of Barbara's biding interest in it. She can't move without the dog being 2 feet away from her. But it's exciting, and we're real thrilled. Millie's mother gave birth on the Farish bed at night. He woke up, and he heard a little squeak, and there were three pups and more arriving—right on the bed. So, we're trying to avoid that. It's wonderful—[*laughter*]—great new dimension to our lives.

But, no, there's no—at least at this juncture—any confinement or all of that. I mean, you move and go out and do stuff, and the Secret Service are very—you know, they do their job, but they're very flexible in approach if you want to go someplace. You all have been most cooperative, for which I'm very grateful. Nobody's griping about it if we decide to do something on short notice.

Is that it? Painless. Does this get credit now—what is this? A photo-op? We're trying to count up the—a mini press conference?

President's Press Conferences

Q. I think this is the equivalent of the airport-Oval Office——

The President. What is it called?

Q. Plane-up.

The President. Plane-up?

Q. Yes. We came up with a new rule. These are unlimited.

The President. These are? [*Laughter*]

Q. We're used to the big East Room news conferences.

The President. I was talking to Marlin about that. I think we probably ought to do both. But I don't feel under any—I don't—put it this way, I don't think that my side of it is not getting out, and therefore, the thing is I need some other form of press. On the other hand, I don't want to deny everybody wearing the bright dress and the fancy necktie having the opportunity to get the question on TV—[*laughter*]—that kind of thing.

How do you all feel about it? Do you think there should be more of those—big, formal thing?

Q. We like it daytime.

The President. You like the day better?

Q. Absolutely!

The President. Wonder whether you could do a formal one in the daytime—more formal?

Q. Jimmy Carter used to do them at 4 p.m., in the afternoon, on a regular basis, saying he wanted—I think the evening ones are kind of fun if you've got something to announce or——

The President. I think there ought to be something to peg it to so it's not just some kind of an extravaganza. But we were just talking about that this morning, as a matter of fact.

Q. President Ford tried to have them out on the South Lawn and over in the Rose Garden, various different——

The President. Press conference on the South Lawn? How did that work? I don't remember that.

Q. It was early in his administration. They watered the grass that morning and all of us were knee-deep in mud.

The President. The press room, I think that's probably as good as you could do. I mean, most people have a little time to get there, and it always seems to be full.

Q. It doesn't become an extravaganza. That's probably part of the appeal.

The President. I don't know whether we get as good a coverage, but I would think so, except for the time. Prime time versus afternoon. I don't know.

But, no, we're going to have a good weekend if the weather holds. I hope you all do. I would have liked to have stuck around out here.

Easter Egg Roll

Q. —Easter Egg Roll? [*Laughter*]

Q. With puppies?

The President. I don't know what's happening on the Easter Egg Roll. It's being worked on, I know that. I went last year. It's kind of a push. It's a push.

Q. —families wait for hours.

The President. To get in there? Yes, well, I haven't seen the grassroots side of it. I just kind of walk down the center aisle.

Well, back to work. We've got to go.

Q. Have a good weekend, sir.

The President. We will.

Note: The President's eighth news conference took place aboard Air Force One en route to Washington, DC, from Colorado Springs, CO. Marlin Fitzwater was the President's Press Secretary.

Nomination of Kate Leader Moore To Be an Assistant Secretary of Transportation
March 17, 1989

The President today announced his intention to nominate Kate Leader Moore to be Assistant Secretary of Transportation (Budget and Programs). She would succeed Janet Hale.

Since January 1989 Miss Moore has been a policy consultant in the Office of Policy Development of the Executive Office of the President. Prior to this she was deputy director for planning in the office of policy development for the office of the President-elect, 1989, and deputy director of domestic policy for Bush-Quayle '88. Prior to this she was director of the Office of Policy, Planning, Research, and Budget for the National Endowment for the Arts, 1981–1988. She has also served as Special Assistant to the Chief of Staff at the White House, 1981; media coordinator for the Reagan-Bush Committee, 1980; and director of the advocate speakers program for the George Bush for President Committee, 1980. She was assistant product manager for Post Cereals for General Foods Corp., 1977–1980, and sales and promotion manager for Bellerophon Books, 1973–1975.

Miss Moore graduated from Yale College (B.A., 1973) and Stanford Graduate School of Business (M.B.A., 1977). She was born in Los Angeles, CA, and currently resides in Washington, DC.

Nomination of Galen Joseph Reser To Be an Assistant Secretary of Transportation
March 17, 1989

The President today announced his intention to nominate Galen Joseph Reser to be Assistant Secretary of Transportation (Governmental Affairs). He would succeed Edward R. Hamberger.

Since 1985 Mr. Reser has served as the director of the Office of the Illinois State Governor James R. Thompson in Washington, DC. Prior to this he held two positions in the Office of United States Senator Charles H. Percy of Illinois: director of legislation and projects, 1980–1984, and director of Illinois projects, 1979–1980.

Mr. Reser graduated from Bradley University School of Arts and Humanities (B.A., 1973). He currently resides in Alexandria, VA.

Nomination of Jeffrey Neil Shane To Be an Assistant Secretary of Transportation
March 17, 1989

The President today announced his intention to nominate Jeffrey Neil Shane to be Assistant Secretary of Transportation (Policy and International Affairs). He would succeed Gregory S. Dole.

Mr. Shane is currently a Deputy Assistant Secretary for Transportation Affairs at the State Department, serving in that capacity since 1985. Prior to this, he served at the Department of Transportation as a Deputy Assistant Secretary for Policy and International Affairs, 1983–1985, and Assistant

General Counsel for International Law, 1979–1983.

Mr. Shane graduated from Princeton University (A.B., 1962) and Columbia University School of Law (LL.B., 1965). He was born March 27, 1941, and currently resides in Washington, DC.

Nomination of David Philip Prosperi To Be an Assistant Secretary of Transportation

March 17, 1989

The President today announced his intention to nominate David Philip Prosperi to be Assistant Secretary of Transportation (Public Affairs). He would succeed Wendy Monson DeMocker.

Since 1988 Mr. Prosperi has been deputy press secretary in the office of the President-elect. Prior to this he was press secretary to Republican Vice Presidential nominee Senator Dan Quayle, 1988. He was assistant to the Secretary of the Interior and Director of Public Affairs, 1985–1988, and manager of government affairs for the Superior Oil Co. and Superior Farming Co., 1982–1984. Mr. Prosperi has served as Assistant Press Secretary to the President at the White House, 1981–1982, and press aide for the 1980 Reagan for President campaign, 1979–1981.

Mr. Prosperi graduated from the University of Illinois (B.S., 1975) and the George Washington University (M.B.A., 1983).

Nomination of Phillip D. Brady To Be General Counsel of the Department of Transportation

March 17, 1989

The President today announced his intention to nominate Phillip D. Brady to be General Counsel of the Department of Transportation. He would succeed B. Wayne Vance.

Since January 1989 Phillip Brady has been Deputy Assistant to the President and Director of Cabinet Affairs at the White House in Washington, DC. Prior to this Mr. Brady served at the White House as Deputy Counsel to the President, 1988–1989, and Deputy Assistant to the Vice President, 1985–1988. Mr. Brady has also served at the Department of Justice as Acting Assistant Attorney General for the Office of Legislative and Intergovernmental Affairs, 1984–1985; Associate Deputy Attorney General, 1983–1984; and Director for Congressional and Public Affairs, Immigration and Naturalization Service, 1982–1983. Other positions Mr. Brady has held include regional director, Region IX, ACTION, 1981–1982; legislative counsel for Representative Daniel E. Lungren, 1979–1981; deputy attorney general, California Department of Justice, 1978–1979; and an associate in the law firm of Spray, Gould and Bowers in Los Angeles, 1976–1978.

Mr. Brady graduated from the University of Notre Dame (B.A., cum laude, 1973) and Loyola University School of Law (J.D., cum laude, 1976). He was born May 20, 1951, in Pasadena, CA, and is married, has three children, and resides in Arlington, VA.

Nomination of Terence A. Todman To Be United States Ambassador to Argentina
March 17, 1989

The President today announced his intention to nominate Terence A. Todman to be Ambassador Extraordinary and Plenipotentiary of the United States of America to Argentina. He would succeed Theodore E. Gildred.

From 1983 to 1988, Ambassador Todman served as Ambassador to Denmark. Prior to this he was Ambassador to Spain, 1978–1983. He has served as Assistant Secretary of State for Inter-American Affairs, 1977–1978. He was also Ambassador to Costa Rica, 1974–1977; Ambassador to Guinea, 1972–1974; and Ambassador to the Republic of Chad, 1969–1972. He is a career member of the Senior Foreign Service.

Mr. Todman graduated from Inter-American University (B.A., 1951) and Syracuse University (M.P.A., 1952). He was born March 13, 1926, in St. Thomas, VI. Mr. Todman is married and has four children.

Accordance of the Personal Rank of Ambassador to C. Travis Marshall While Serving as Chairman of the United States Delegation to the International Telecommunication Union Conference
March 17, 1989

The President today accorded the personal rank of Ambassador to C. Travis Marshall, of Maryland, during the tenure of his service as chairman of the United States delegation to the 1989 Plenipotentiary Conference of the International Telecommunication Union.

Mr. Marshall is a 35-year veteran of the telecommunications industry. A 1948 graduate of the University of Notre Dame, he is presently senior vice president of Motorola, Inc. Prior to this he served in the U.S. Army from 1944 to 1946. From 1948 to 1951, he was with the Firestone Tire and Rubber Co., until he was again called to active military duty, serving from 1951 to 1952. He joined the Hallicrafters Co. as an assistant radio sales manager in 1952 and rose to the position of general sales manager by 1965. From 1965 to 1970, he was vice president of marketing for the E.F. Johnson Co. Mr. Marshall joined Motorola, Inc., in 1970, where his first position was as vice president and director of marketing operations for Motorola Communications and Electronics, Inc. In 1972 he was named director of government relations, and in 1974 was promoted to vice president and corporate director of government relations. In 1985 he was promoted to senior vice president and is presently serving in this same capacity.

Mr. Marshall was born January 31, 1926, in Apalachicola, FL. He is married, has three children, and resides in Bethesda, MD.

Nomination of James Buchanan Busey IV To Be Administrator of the Federal Aviation Administration

March 17, 1989

The President today announced his intention to nominate James Buchanan Busey IV to be Administrator of the Federal Aviation Administration, Department of Transportation. He would succeed T. Allan McArtor.

Since 1987 Admiral Busey has been Commander in Chief of Allied Forces in Southern Europe, and Commander in Chief of U.S. Naval Forces in Europe. Prior to this he was Vice Chief of Naval Operations, 1985–1987. He has served as Commander of the Naval Air Systems Command, 1983–1985, and Commander of the Light Attack Wing Pacific, 1982–1983. From 1980 to 1982, he was Deputy Chief for Resource Management at Headquarters of Naval Material Command. He was Auditor General of the Navy of the Office of the Under Secretary of the Navy, 1978–1980. He entered the U.S. Navy in 1952.

Admiral Busey received a B.S. and M.S. degree in management from the Naval Postgraduate School. He was born October 2, 1932, in Peoria, IL. He is married and has three children.

Nomination of Melvin Floyd Sembler To Be United States Ambassador to Australia

March 17, 1989

The President today announced his intention to nominate Melvin Floyd Sembler to be Ambassador Extraordinary and Plenipotentiary of the United States of America to Australia. He would succeed Laurence William Lane, Jr.

Mr. Sembler is currently one of the Nation's leading shopping center developers. In addition, he now sits on the executive committee of the International Council of Shopping Centers board of trustees and is serving as ICSC's international public service chairman. He also served as the president of the International Council of Shopping Centers from 1986 to 1987. In 1988 Mr. Sembler was a Presidential appointee to the White House Conference for a Drug Free America and was also a member of the Bush Coalition for a Drug Free America.

Mr. Sembler graduated from Northwestern University (B.S., 1952). He was born May 10, 1930, in St. Joseph, MS. Mr. Sembler is married and has three children.

Nomination of John Giffen Weinmann To Be United States Ambassador to Finland

March 17, 1989

The President today announced his intention to nominate John Giffen Weinmann to be Ambassador Extraordinary and Plenipotentiary of the United States of America to Finland. He would succeed Rockwell Anthony Schnabel.

Since 1988 Mr. Weinmann has been a member of the national finance committee for George Bush for President, and Louisiana State finance chairman for George Bush for President/Louisiana Victory '88. Mr. Weinmann has been president and director for Waverly Oil Corp., 1979 to the present. He was chairman of the board of Eason Oil Co., 1977, and director, 1961–1980. He has been involved in numerous professional and civic organizations.

Mr. Weinmann graduated from Tulane University (B.A., 1950; J.D., 1952). He was born August 29, 1928, in New Orleans, LA. He is married, has five children, and resides in New Orleans, LA.

Nomination of Jerry A. Moore, Jr., To Be United States Ambassador to Lesotho

March 17, 1989

The President today announced his intention to nominate Jerry A. Moore, Jr., to be Ambassador Extraordinary and Plenipotentiary of the United States of America to the Kingdom of Lesotho. He would succeed Robert M. Smalley.

Since 1946 Reverend Moore has been pastor of the Nineteenth Street Baptist Church in Washington, DC. He was chaplain for the DC Detention Facility, 1984–1988. He has been a councilman for the District of Columbia, 1969–1984; instructor for the Washington Baptist Seminary, 1964; and Baptist chaplain for Howard University, 1958. He has served on numerous business, government, and civic organizations and committees.

Reverend Moore received a B.A. degree from Morehouse College and B.D. and M.A. degrees from Howard University. He was born June 12, 1918, in Minden, LA.

Nomination of Joseph Zappala To Be United States Ambassador to Spain

March 17, 1989

The President today announced his intention to nominate Joseph Zappala to be Ambassador Extraordinary and Plenipotentiary of the United States of America to Spain. He would succeed Reginald Bartholomew.

Mr. Zappala is currently the chairman and chief executive officer of Joseph Zappala and Associates. He served as cochairman for the State of Florida on the George Bush for President National Steering Committee and National Finance Committee. He recently served as the national cochairman of finance for the American Bicentennial Presidential Inaugural. Mr. Zappala is the chairman of Home Town Investors, Inc., and owner and chairman of Tucson Greyhound Park in Tucson, AZ. He founded and was chairman of the board of the First National Bank of Seminole in Pinellas County, FL. In addition, he was cofounder and serves as president of Straight, Inc., a drug treatment and rehabilitation program for adolescents. Mr. Zappala serves on the board of the College of Veterinary Medicine at the University of Florida and on the board of the Police Athletic League. He is also the past chairman of the Pinellas Association for Retarded Children.

Mr. Zappala graduated from the New York Institute of Finance. He is married and has four daughters.

Nomination of Frederick Morris Bush To Be United States Ambassador to Luxembourg
March 17, 1989

The President today announced his intention to nominate Frederick Morris Bush to be Ambassador Extraordinary and Plenipotentiary of the United States of America to Luxembourg. He would succeed Jean Broward Shevlin Gerard.

Since 1979 Mr. Bush has been principal professional fundraiser for George Bush, serving as deputy finance chairman for the George Bush for President Committee; finance director of the Fund for America's Future; executive cochairman of the Presidential Trust and Victory '88 for the Republican National Committee; and senior adviser for the Team 100 Program for the Republican National Committee. He was president of the consulting firm of Bush and Co. in Washington, DC. He has served as Deputy Chief of Staff to the Vice President at the White House, 1982–1984, and Assistant Secretary of Commerce for Tourism, 1981. He was assistant for administration in the office of the Vice President-elect, 1980–1981, and national finance director for the George Bush for President Committee, 1979–1980.

Mr. Bush graduated from the University of Colorado (B.A., 1971) and American University (M.A., 1974). He is married, has four children, and resides in Chevy Chase, MD.

Statement on Meeting With Prime Minister Charles Haughey of Ireland
March 17, 1989

There are many excellent reasons for celebrating St. Patrick's Day. Traditionally this happy occasion provides a special opportunity to spotlight the Irish heritage in America and to affirm the ties of kinship and values which the American and Irish people share. On this St. Patrick's Day, 1989, we again pay tribute to the warm relationship between Ireland and America. We are honored to welcome to the White House the Prime Minister of Ireland, the Taoiseach, Mr. Charles Haughey, whose presence adds a special significance to our celebration.

St. Patrick's Day also provides a special opportunity to pay tribute to U.S.-Irish cooperation in the international arena in the cause of justice, peace, and progress, and to declare that working together to solve international problems encourages the development and maturation of our traditional bilateral relationship.

In the presence of the Taoiseach, I would also like to thank Ireland for its contribution to peacekeeping efforts around the world and to extend the appreciation and condolences of the American people to the families of the Irish soldiers who have given their lives in the cause of peace.

Today I express America's appreciation for Ireland's efforts to promote economic development, justice, security, and reconciliation in Northern Ireland. The U.S. supports the efforts of the Irish and British Governments to use the Anglo-Irish accord and the International Fund for Ireland to address the problems which have too long plagued Northern Ireland. We will continue to support efforts to promote fair employment and investment in Northern Ireland.

I call on the American people to support all those who seek justice and peaceful settlements to disputes in Northern Ireland. In the same spirit, I call on all Americans to reject those who seek to impose settlements anywhere through terror.

The comprehensive political, diplomatic, and economic ties between our two countries require recognition that U.S.-Irish relations are the responsibility of all Americans. Therefore, millions of Americans of many heritages and from all walks of life join in observing this fine day and in paying tribute to the friendship and cooperation between Ireland and America. Americans do not have to be Irish to treasure Ireland's contributions or to celebrate St. Patrick's Day.

Remarks at the Swearing-in Ceremony for Thomas R. Pickering as United States Representative to the United Nations
March 20, 1989

The President. We were reminiscing in the Oval Office with the Pickerings. And Barbara and I had visited them in four different posts: Jordan, Israel, Nigeria, and El Salvador. And in all likelihood, we will be visiting them in a fifth post. [*Laughter*]

But this is a proud day, I think, for the country, certainly for Tom and Tom's family, and for the Foreign Service. Ambassador Pickering, as we all know, is a skilled diplomat, a veteran of high-priority, tough assignments. He is one of only five FSO's that hold the rank of Career Ambassador. He's had extensive global experience, diplomatic experience that includes in a broad sense the Middle East, Central America, Africa. And now he's assuming a very important job.

I take the U.N. very seriously, and I'm pleased with the changes that have been taking place there. I salute, incidentally, his predecessor, my friend Dick Walters, who is with us today, for helping effect some of the changes, particularly on the financial side. I believe that the Secretary-General, an old friend of ours, Javier Perez de Cuellar, is doing a good job; and he deserves our support.

The U.N.'s Nobel Peace Prize for peacekeeping is a sign of new respect for the organization. And the U.N. is on the right track for reform. It is now certainly a more effective organization, and I expect under Tom's prodding that will continue—that reform momentum. Signs of greater political seriousness must continue. A case in point has been the approach to Cuba and human rights. As a result of the recent U.N. Commission on Human Rights meeting in Geneva, Cuba's human rights record will be in the spotlight. I'd like to have seen a continuation of that mission, but nevertheless, it has been spotlighted there. And I'm counting on Tom Pickering to make sure that the question of human rights in Cuba maintains an appropriately high profile and stays high on the United Nations agenda.

The U.N. can be a force for peace, a forum for resolving conflict. And as proof of this, consider its instrumental role in the Soviet withdrawal from Afghanistan, in the Iran-Iraq war—a very important role there. It's an important place in the international arena. There was a time when a lot of us got pessimistic about the U.N. role in peacekeeping—our interests mainly in the economic and social end. But I think both now are on the track towards significant improvement.

My point man there at the U.N., working with the Secretary and me, will be Tom Pickering, an able, articulate advocate for our administration's foreign policy. And so, it's a delight for me—and I seldom speak for the Secretary of State or the Vice President, but it's a delight for all of us, we three—to join his family and all of you in saluting Tom Pickering. And now, with no further ado, Jim, if you would do the honors, I will grab my toe mark here. [*Laughter*] Here we are. Here's your toe mark. [*Laughter*]

[*At this point, Ambassador Pickering was sworn in.*]

Ambassador Pickering. President and Mrs. Bush, Vice President Quayle, Secretary Baker, family and friends. Thank you very much, Mr. President, for your very kind words and your strong and ringing endorsement. And thank you both for being here with me this morning at this very important event in my life and in my hope to serve our country as well as possible.

Your faith and confidence in me and through me and the American Foreign Service is a special mark of honor for me and for all of us, many of whom are here with me today, who serve in the American Foreign Service. I think I share with Jim Lilley, who will soon be the next Ambassador in Beijing, a unique and historical distinction. We will be the first Ambassadors in American history to serve a President who knows just everything—more about our jobs than we do. [*Laughter*] That's a heavy load, but I will be on my toes in New York to try to do the best I possibly can in this endeavor. And I think it's symbolic that just a few minutes ago, Mr. President, a number of members of the Cabinet staff took all the dead wood out of this office. [*Laughter*]

Because this administration has already shown its interest, there is a new excitement in New York at the United Nations. As an institution under the able leadership of the Secretary-General, who was a companion and colleague of yours, it has made real progress over the last few years in peacemaking and in peacekeeping: in Afghanistan, in the Iran-Iraq war, and now in the Angola-Namibia settlement. It has supported free elections everywhere and the benefits of the market economies. It has helped with programs in the area of narcotics, in international terrorism, in human rights, and in national development. And it has begun building a program of far-reaching reforms.

This has been a result not only of our own policies but of changing views in the Soviet Union and elsewhere, and particularly the work of a number of my distinguished predecessors. And I want to mention particularly Dick Walters, who is here with us this morning. He has been a terrific predecessor, a great man to break in a new Ambassador, and—along with the very able staff of the mission in New York and the people who work on this subject at the State Department—has been an enormous help. Mr. Secretary, John Bolton, I look forward to working very closely with you in the days ahead on our policy at the United Nations.

It is a time for us to look ahead, cautiously but, I think, optimistically, in New York. U.N. reform can and should continue. Peacemaking in areas as remote, but as important, as Cambodia and the Western Sahara, and even in Cyprus, now show some sign of progress. Peacekeeping tasks are likely to continue to grow. Help in Central America will certainly be important in verifying a balanced agreement which includes the provisions for democratic processes in Nicaragua, dealing with global climate change with the environment, with human rights. And as you mentioned, Mr. President, especially for Cuba, where for the first time it is prominent in the world's agenda of human rights questions—will be high on my agenda, and I accept your instruction and will certainly proceed to continue to keep it there. Similarly, narcotics and terrorism, chemical weapons, and many other issues will be on our plate in New York.

Mr. Secretary and Mr. President, you are both here in this place sending a special signal, a special signal of support for me and our foreign policies in the U.N. I don't know how this will be received in New York, but I can assure you that for the first time in my history 110 percent of my family has taken this opportunity to attend a swearing-in. [*Laughter*]

I'm delighted as well to see so many friends here. But I do want to mention one special friend and supporter, without whom this day would not be possible. Alice has been part of a foreign service team with me for many years. She has done a fantastic amount of work around the world, much of it unsung. Indeed, I feel often I get the recognition and she gets the tough jobs. However that may be, I hope you will all consider with me that this is her day today as much as it is anyone else's. And I want to thank her from this platform for all that she has done; because she represents, as many others in the Foreign Service represent, the best in the way of loyalty and devotion to the ideals of the United States in unstinting service to our country. She very much took the oath with me, as she has six times before. And I'm delighted that she is here, and I hope that she will share in the recognition that's being accorded to me here today.

Thank you again, all of you, for being here. Tomorrow we leave for New York to take up a new assignment. I know I can say with safety that we will see all of you there from time to time—[*laughter*]—and I say with genuine sincerity that we look forward to seeing you there. Thank you again, very, very much.

The President. Barbara and I are going to ask Alice and Tom to come into the Oval Office, and it might be a nicer way to greet all of you that have come over to pay your respects to him. And so, if you don't mind kind of filing through, we'd like to welcome you there, and just a quick handshake and then you'll be summarily thrown out by—[*laughter*]—Joseph Reed, who knows how to do this because he's been at the U.N. for a long time.

Note: The President spoke at 10 a.m. in the Roosevelt Room at the White House. In his remarks, he referred to Vernon A. Walters, former U.S. Representative to the United Nations, and Joseph Reed, Chief of Protocol-designate at the Department of State and former Under Secretary-General of the United Nations. Secretary of State James A. Baker III administered the oath of office. In his remarks, the Ambassador referred to his wife, Alice Pickering, and to John Bolton, Assistant Secretary of State-designate for International Organizations.

Remarks and a Question-and-Answer Session With the State Legislators Working Group
March 20, 1989

The President. Well, let me just say in the beginning here I'm delighted to see all of you here—forerunner of things to come in the electoral process—because we do have to shift gears and look ahead to redistricting and to all the political process that you've participated in and in which you have been leaders. And so, we don't want to neglect anything that has to do with building our numbers. I'm glad to see Lee Atwater down there. And I can say that he and Jean—where's Jeanie Austin? Do I see her here? But in any event, they have done a fantastic job getting going at the Republican National Committee. And I'm glad to see Mary here, and of course Deb Anderson here, coming out of your elected ranks, here in the White House now. So, I hope that we'll have a sensitive White House: a White House sensitive to the political requirements out there from people that are seeking election. And one thing I wanted to urge was recruitment: getting good candidates in the State races, as well as those that are for Federal office. And I wanted to let you know that we want to assist in every way possible on that.

In terms of Washington, DC, I think things are off to a reasonably good start. I got here, and with the help of Governor Sununu down there and many others in this room, why, we addressed ourselves right up front with one of the—I guess the biggest problem, and that is how we feel the deficit should be brought down. And we're going to keep plugging away, working with the Congress. We have to do that, want to do that, will do that to get this problem solved. And it is one that there will be some give-and-take on it, but the ideas we've proposed are sensible. They are in keeping with the way I ran for office and the way many of you that ran this time ran for office. And I am convinced that we can get a good deal, project that budget deficit down with finality, and do it without doing what the American people don't want, and that is raising taxes. We've got to do it with holding the line on taxes, not raise them. And I believe that the proposals we made are very sensible in that regard.

But in any event, we're off and running

on that. Our Cabinet's in place. We're doing reasonably well in terms of our other agenda. I'm very pleased with the start that our drug czar is making—first testing waters, in a sense, because this is a new job. It's a coordinative job. But Bill is a good, strong leader, and he will certainly meet the deadline of coming up with a plan that is required under the law in 6 months. But it's going to be more than that, because in the meantime, we're—as you've seen—taking certain actions in the administration that I think are appropriate in this regard. We're moving forward with legislation on education that I'm pledged to go forward with. I think our environmental leader, Bill Reilly, is off to a good start—went to a conference in Europe, in England, and in a meeting with Margaret Thatcher, put the U.S. out front on the whole CFC [chlorofluorocarbons] question.

And so, we're moving. But we need your suggestions. We are going to be reaching out to you all. And I'm just delighted to see you here. And I'll be glad to take a question or two before we turn the agenda back. John, did I interrupt? Were you in the middle of something?

Mr. Sununu. No.

The President. But this is an important meeting for us. We want to keep you tuned in, and we want to ask your support and leadership out across the country.

Gubernatorial Elections

Q. Mr. President, I'm from Virginia. As you know, Virginia has a very important election this year for Governor, Lieutenant Governor, and attorney general. And I know that your high priority is to get back to Virginia and New Jersey this year, but I thought the members of the press might want to know how important you consider this. [*Laughter*]

The President. Nice slow ball. [*Laughter*] No, I do, and as you know, there are these two States that have the special timing here. And I've said all along—said it last year before I was elected—the importance that we place on Governors because we believe in the federalist system. Some of the soundest advice in the campaign came from the Governors and from State reps and leaders in the various State legislatures, because they're out on the delivering end. They're out on the cutting edge. And so, this Governor's race in Virginia—we have an opportunity to pick up a seat. In New Jersey we want to hold—Tom Kean leaving. So, we will put the proper emphasis from here. Lee Atwater's already begun working on setting our priorities and how much help we can give from the national [committee] on that. But I'm glad you raised it because it is key.

Women/Gun Control/War on Drugs

Q. Mr. President, two things: Number one, as a legislator who in the past has always had the NRA [National Rifle Association] backing, I want to applaud you for the action you've taken on the Federal level. As a State legislator, I think that's the only place that semiautomatic weapons can be dealt with, and I just want to tell you that I think that mainstream America is really with you on that action. And I hope that it will lead to something further. I don't know exactly what that should be.

The second point I want to make is that, although I think the bread-and-butter issues are really the women's issues just as much as men, I think many women experience poverty that men do not experience. I think also impressions are reality, perception is reality, as we know in politics. And giving lots of advice in the future with your other appointments—I've been very pleased with the appointments that you've made for women, for minorities. And I just want to encourage you to continue that if the Supreme Court or any openings there—that you would give, and I'm sure you will, enough consideration to other people of color, or a woman, for example. So, it's not just like the one woman on the Supreme Court—thank goodness that Mr. Reagan put Sandra Day O'Connor there—but that you, too, will continue your efforts to bring women and people of color into your administration.

The President. Well, we want to do that. We are doing it. I'd like to be further along. Recognizing that the subject might come up, we did a little homework in terms of an administration in which I proudly served. At this juncture they had—we had, I should say, because I was a part of it, something like 8 percent of the jobs for women—high-level jobs—and we're up at about 21. But we want to keep moving. I think we've done about 12 or 15 percent overall of the jobs, so we want to keep our sights set on doing the best possible job on appointments. And I think that is important, and I think—to the degree there is that visibility—I think it'll help in this recruitment that I asked you to engage in. I mean, I think the people see good signs here, and I think that they'll involve themselves—more apt to get into the electoral process. So, I think they are linked.

On the NRA, of which I'm a member—a proud member, I might add—I believe we can find accommodation between the legitimate interest of the sportsman and the interest of the police chiefs in protecting their people who put their lives on the line every single day. And Bill Bennett made this recommendation to me on these shipments coming in. That's well within the law. What we're doing is enforcing the law, determining the suitability for sporting purposes. That's the way the law reads. And so, I appreciate your support on that.

We haven't found the ideal answer. I know some of your State legislatures are working on this right now—California having moved out—and I'm interested that you have the NRA support, and I think you'll keep it, given the position you've stated, because the country needs to know that there is some answer to this. And I don't yet know what it is, and I was interested in your frankness saying you don't. And some of the legislators in California that voted for it or opposite the bill—they're not sure where it ought to go. But we're in very different times now, and I am convinced that reasonable men and women can work together to find an answer to the problem of these automated weapons. And I think we've already had some signs in the sporting community that there is support for what we've done, but we're going to keep working it.

I am very serious about this drug fight, and it's going to be fought on all different fronts. And we have got to give the police proper support when they lay their lives on the line for us. And so, we'll find some answer that is constitutionally sound and that also protects the lives, as best one can from Washington, of these officers. I'd like to tell you I think the solution can be found right here, and that'll solve it. But that's not true. It's going to be found in various ways out in the States, in my view. But we have a responsibility, and I appreciate the support for the action that we have taken.

Family Issues

Q. I was particularly pleased of your emphasis on family issues during the campaign. As I said to people, as a legislator working in the area of family and children's issues, that it is really encouraging because it is the first Presidential campaign that has really focused on family issues. While I don't think the Federal Government is the place to solve all those problems, I do think it's important for the Republican Party, and important for women in families in Pennsylvania, though, that those issues remain high priority to the administration and that direction, money is given to the States so that we can deal effectively with some of the issues that are particular, I think, to families today, with the breakdown in traditional family structure.

The President. Lois, I couldn't agree more. And we are not going to deemphasize the importance that I place on families. And indeed, one of the major tests right now is going to be the question of the approach one takes to child care. And we're talking about choice. We're talking about doing it in a way in which the family is emphasized and is strengthened. And so, there'll be this. There'll be other issues that come along. But I'm glad you raised it, and believe me, I have not diminished my interest in all of this. In fact, as you look at the problems facing society, so much of it gets back to the weakening of the family. So many of the problems are out there because of this new trend towards single-parent families and all of this. And it's a tragic thing in a way.

So, we are not going to depart from the traditional values. We're going to keep emphasizing them, and when it comes to Federal legislation, be sure that what we propose will strengthen, not weaken, the family group. And even things like education—as much choice as possible is a good thing there.

Yes? I've got time for just a couple of more, I've been told here.

Mrs. Bush's Literacy Efforts

Q. Yes. Mr. President, I wanted to tell you, first of all, I think those of us who are in the house and senate in the States who are Republican, first of all, would like to tell you that we think one of the biggest assets both the Republican Party and you have is Mrs. Bush.

The President. I agree with that.

Q. I'm particularly interested in her cause on literacy, and wonder if by any chance there has been any work done in any of the prisons? I have personally gone into our prisons and have found out that about 75 to 80 percent of our prisoners are functionally illiterate and, consequently, cannot be trained to do something. They can't even read the want-ad in order to get a job.

The President. I don't know that Barbara's done anything on that end of it. She's starting now a brand-new foundation that will help enormously in this whole private sector end. I know our Secretary of Education is very much interested in the education for the prison population. I don't know that Bar has gotten any of her volunteer work involved in that segment, but I expect she'd love to hear from you on it, because she is keeping up that interest.

Q. Mr. President, first of all, my daughter asked me to ask you if any of the puppies were left. [*Laughter*]

The President. The demand is intense, let me tell you. [*Laughter*]

Gasoline Taxes

Q. There's a good deal of concern in southern California, where there is high growth, rapid economic growth, but also concern on transportation. And it has been said that there's a possibility that the gasoline tax may be raised in order to help this budget reduction financing. Our concern, of course, is if this were to happen, what would happen then to the opportunity for California to go forward with gasoline tax increases in order to support our infrastructure needs, and would this be in conflict and perhaps cause us a problem?

The President. There are no plans for that, and I don't know where that is coming from. But the administration has no plans to raise the gasoline tax.

Ocean Dumping

Q. We appreciate your coming to the Jersey shore and just want to report that in this election year for our Governor in New Jersey the environment continues to be the number one issue. And certainly any support you can give us for a tough approach to polluters of our very precious ocean would be appreciated.

The President. We're going to continue. And as I say, I have great confidence that Bill Reilly, the new Administrator [Environmental Protection Agency], is going to be good in that sense, very good. And we're following up. I think we even have some legislation now in the mill that will be helpful on that ocean dumping. But I'll keep talking about it. I'll keep encouraging the States in this regard.

One more?

Republican Party Minority Participation

Q. There are many concerns in all of our States, but I think that we must get more Hispanics and blacks involved to run for office. And I think we have to put across to the people throughout the country that the Republican Party is the people's party.

The President. You make a good point, and I think that Lee Atwater, Mary, others here agree with you on that. And we've started moving out. How it gets into the recruitment business I would leave to our political people here. But that emphasis is important, and I agree with Lee that much progress can be made. And the issues that we're talking about—including inner-city fight on narcotics—we're on the proper side. These people are outraged by what's happening in their communities. They are concerned, Lois, about the disintegration of family in some of these areas.

And so, I hope it will mean that we can get our message out better by having quality candidates out there. So, we're going to keep trying. I've been pleased with the support so far, though I no longer live and die by the polls like I used to when you and I were working side by side in New Hampshire. But I've been pleased with the openmindedness, in the figures in terms of support for the President from groups where historically we haven't done well. That could change, but I want to keep doing it.

I think some of the reason for that is the beginning that the national committee has made. And so, we will try here, Deb Anderson, Bobbie Kilberg, and me, working with the Chief of Staff, to do what we can from this building to encourage that. But the field is open, there's an openmindedness in some of these areas—the blacks and Hispanics and other areas—that I think means that our ideas and our direction for the country makes a certain degree of sense. Now, I know we're up against formidable history in this regard. We've got to keep trying; we've got to keep reaching out. And I believe that we can do better—much, much better.

Listen, thank you all very much for your attention and for being here and for what you're doing. And I repeat: I do think it's important. Sam Rayburn talked about the critics of either him or the President at that time. He says, "Well, that fella's one of the severest critics." He says, "That guy's problem was he never ran for sheriff." [*Laughter*] And it was a very profound statement, I mean, because when you are in the arena and you do have to take your case to the people, why, you have a certain sensitivity to the government processes. And so, I think this group can do an awful lot. You all run for sheriff. Indeed, you've been elected—not sheriff, but something else. [*Laughter*]

So, thank you very, very much for being here today. And we appreciate the support, and we'll work hard to merit your continuing confidence. Thank you.

Note: The President spoke at 11:11 a.m. during a briefing in the Indian Treaty Room of the Old Executive Office Building. In his remarks, he referred to Lee Atwater, Jeanie Austin, and Mary Matalin, chairman, cochairman, and chief of staff of the Republican National Committee, respectively; Debra R. Anderson, Deputy Assistant to the President and Director of the Office of Intergovernmental Affairs; John H. Sununu, Chief of Staff to the President; William J. Bennett, Director of National Drug Control Policy; Lois Sherman Hagarty, State representative from Pennsylvania; and Bobbie Kilberg, Deputy Assistant to the President for Public Liaison.

Nomination of Julius L. Katz To Be a Deputy United States Trade Representative
March 20, 1989

The President today announced his intention to nominate Julius L. Katz to be a Deputy United States Trade Representative, with the rank of Ambassador. He would succeed Michael Brackett Smith.

Mr. Katz is a Deputy United States Trade Representative, serving with Sidney Linn Williams and Rufus Hawkins Yerxa. Since 1987, Mr. Katz has been chairman of the Government Research Corp., in Washington, DC. Prior to this he was vice president for the Consultants International Group, Inc., 1985–1987. He was with Donaldson, Lufkin and Jenrette Futures, Inc., formerly ACLI International Commodity Services, Inc., serving in several capacities, including chairman, 1982–1985; president and chief executive officer, 1981–1982; and senior vice president, 1980–1981. He has also served as Assistant Secretary of State for Economic and Business Affairs at the Department of State, 1976–1979; Senior Deputy Assistant Secretary of State, 1974–1976; and Deputy Assistant Secretary of State for International Resources and Food Policy, 1968–1974. From 1950 to 1968, he served in several positions at the Department of State, including Director of International Trade, Director of International Commodities, and Economic Adviser in the

Office of Eastern European Affairs.

Mr. Katz graduated from George Washington University, receiving a bachelor of arts degree.

Nomination of Jerry Ralph Curry To Be Administrator of the National Highway Traffic Safety Administration
March 20, 1989

The President today announced his intention to nominate Jerry Ralph Curry to be Administrator of the National Highway Traffic Safety Administration, Department of Transportation. He would succeed Diane K. Stead.

Before retiring, General Curry was deputy commanding general of V Corps in Frankfurt, West Germany. He has served as the commanding general of the U.S. Army Test and Evaluation Command in Aberdeen Proving Ground, MD, and commanding general of the U.S. Army Military District of Washington, DC. General Curry has also served as Deputy Assistant Secretary of Defense for Public Affairs.

General Curry received a bachelor's degree in education from the University of Nebraska at Omaha, a master's degree in international relations from Boston University, and a doctorate degree from Luther Rice Seminary. He is a graduate of both the U.S. Army War College and the Command and General Staff College. He is married, has four children, and resides in Virginia Beach, VA.

Remarks at the Swearing-in Ceremony for Richard B. Cheney as Secretary of Defense
March 21, 1989

The President. Mr. Vice President, members of the President's Cabinet, distinguished Members of Congress, the Joint Chiefs, I am very pleased to participate in the administration of the oath of office to our new Secretary of Defense, Dick Cheney.

This is a proud day for Dick's family: his wife, Lynne, who heads a vital effort of another sort—safeguarding our cultural heritage at the National Endowment for the Humanities—and their daughters, Elizabeth and Mary. I also want to welcome Dick's mom and dad, who are here from Wyoming, other family members as well, who came to join Dick on this very important day.

Let me outline some of the crucial responsibilities that Secretary Cheney is taking on in his new assignment: defense strategy and management, procurement reform, the day-to-day operations of our Armed Forces, and the long-range planning that will keep us free and secure into the next century. In a building where it can be a challenge getting from the A Ring to the E Ring without getting lost, the challenges that you'll face, Mr. Secretary, are truly enormous. Confession time: Dick told me that he's already gotten lost in the garage of this place—[*laughter*]—but things can only go up from there. [*Laughter*]

The challenges may be enormous, but so, Mr. Secretary, are the skills and talents that you bring to the job. Dick Cheney knows his way around Washington. He knows how things work on Capitol Hill and in the White House. And he'll draw on that wealth of experience to help make things work right here at the Pentagon. Dick and I worked together in the Ford administration on national security issues—he was the White House Chief of Staff and I was then

Director of Central Intelligence—and teamwork paid off then, and he was the best at it. And, Dick, you'll have help from the best Armed Forces in the world and a civilian staff equally dedicated to our national defense. I know they're ready to work with you and for you.

And I'm convinced the international scene today is defined by opportunity: a chance to advance America's interests and ideals, and to strengthen the forces of freedom now gaining a foothold in many places around the world. Dick shares my belief that the chief national security lesson of this decade is simply this: strength secures peace. That fact remains true, even in the present time of transition in world affairs.

Consider the key issue of change in the Soviet Union. I take a very positive view of the changes there, but there are still more questions than answers about the ultimate outcome of those changes. And until these questions are answered, we should continue our successful policy of flexibility, combined with strength and firm resolve. We must be ready to seize favorable opportunities to improve relations with the Soviet Union, but we must also remain ready and able in any event to secure our national interests. And let me say clearly, now is not the time for America and its allies to make unilateral reductions to relax our defense efforts.

Everyone here knows that we're facing tough choices on defense programs. We must move ahead with plans to modernize our strategic and conventional forces. We must continue to turn the nation's technological capabilities to our strategic advantage, in SDI and other programs. But our need to deal with the deficit means that we're working with limited resources. And, Dick, your task is to sort out those priorities—which programs should continue, which we can't afford in the current fiscal climate. I'm convinced these difficult choices can be made in a way that preserves our defense capabilities.

Close cooperation with the Congress is absolutely essential, and Dick's high standing on Capitol Hill will be an enormous plus. Procurement reform is a case in point. Our aim should be a more stable and streamlined acquisition system. But procurement reform can't be confined to the Pentagon alone. We will work with the Congress, our partners in the process, to move forward with the Packard commission reforms, to adopt a 2-year budget cycle, and to expand multiyear procurement for major weapons systems.

And stability begins with a commitment to maintain a steady, moderate, and affordable increase in defense spending, an increase we must have in order to maintain and continue to modernize our forces. Following the freeze for 1990, that means growth—1 percent—'91, '92, rising to 2 in '93, 2 percent. For too long, defense spending has ridden a roller coaster: unpredictable ups and downs, a recipe for waste and inefficiencies. Stable spending makes it possible to plan for the long term, and that's the basis of a more efficient and effective defense posture. And that long-term view is the one we must take, with the 21st century only 11 years away.

I'm convinced that in the years ahead the United States can take the lead in building a more peaceful international environment, in laying the foundations for a new American Century, where freedom and democracy will flourish. I am confident that Dick Cheney will play a pivotal part in keeping America strong and secure, free and at peace.

Secretary Cheney, congratulations. You have my complete confidence and my sincere best wishes as you undertake this extraordinarily important task for the greatest country on the face of the Earth.

[*At this point, Secretary Cheney was sworn in.*]

Secretary Cheney. Mr. President, distinguished guests, men and women of America's Armed Forces, ladies and gentlemen, it is a humbling experience to assume office as the Nation's 17th Secretary of Defense. Mr. President, I thank you for the confidence you've placed in me. I will do my best to justify your trust.

This transition comes at a time of significant change, change that may portend a more peaceful and prosperous world in the years ahead. Nations whose political and economic systems, like ours, are based on principles of freedom, democracy, individual liberty, and market economics are thriving. Those nations which derive their legitimacy from the authoritarian suppression of the human spirit are in retreat.

It's become clear in the last few years that freedom works. The Soviet Union is being forced to question its basic assumptions in light of its obvious failure to produce a prosperous economy at home or to enable it to compete abroad. Developing nations no longer look to the Soviets or their allies for a model upon which they can build successful economies. And in place of a hostile Soviet Union seeking to expand its empire by military means, we see an empire beset by difficulties, withdrawing from Afghanistan and talking about significant troop reductions in Eastern Europe.

In part, this change is attributable to more realistic leadership inside the Soviet Union. But it is also due in part to the success of the strategy of the United States and our allies. Containment has worked. Deterrence has held. Principle has paid off. Still, dangers abound. There are those who want to declare the Cold War ended. They perceive a significantly lessened threat and want to believe that we can reduce our level of vigilance accordingly. But I believe caution is in order. However real the reform rhetoric coming out of the Kremlin, Moscow's armaments compel caution on our part. To date, there's been no reduction in the strategic systems targeted against the United States. Until we see a significantly lessened military capability on the part of the Soviets, we cannot possibly justify major reductions in our own. We must guard against gambling our nation's security on what may be a temporary aberration in the behavior of our foremost adversary.

Mr. President, the military and civilian professionals of the Department of Defense stand ready to do everything possible to provide for the Nation's security with the resources the American people entrust to us. To that end, our strategy and policies must be carefully calibrated to an ever-changing international landscape. Our force is designed and equipped to meet the full range of likely contingencies, and our needed munitions acquired as efficiently as possible.

Today I would like to address myself to several key groups. To the men and women of America's Armed Forces: I am honored to serve with you in the defense of freedom. Every individual soldier, sailor, airman, and marine contributes to America's strength, and I pledge to do my utmost to provide you the quality, equipment, and support you must have to do the job we ask you to do for all of us. You, our uniformed men and women, are my number one priority. You and your families are the mind, body, and soul of America's military might.

To America's friends and allies around the world: I look forward to working with you in our common quest. Collective security is the only strategy for our democracies. We, therefore, must deepen our cooperation, especially to stretch scarce defense resources. And where we have differences, we must deal with them in recognition that cohesion is the most potent power and weapon of free nations.

To the United States Congress: Fresh as I am from your ranks, I appreciate your constitutional responsibility for America's defense. I pledge my full cooperation as, together, we wrestle with a shared challenge: too many claims on too few dollars. I've got to make the hard choices, and I seek your support so that these can be the right choices.

To America's defense industry: U.S. national security is vitally dependent on our defense industrial base. We must have top-notch firms willing to compete for defense contracts and able to fulfill those contracts with high-quality work efficiently delivered. Don Atwood and the rest of my staff are anxious to work with the defense industry to improve productivity, reduce costs, and advance new technologies. Defense acquisition is a partnership, and that spirit must guide our actions.

Finally, to the American people: The first obligation of the Federal Government is the defense of the Nation. You support that aim with your tax dollars and the sacrifices of your sons and daughters in uniform. We who are appointed to lead these defense preparations owe you, the American people, a high return on your investment and great care for the lives of your loved ones who serve. I accept that responsibility.

And with the support of my family and the President of the United States, and with many other dedicated Americans sharing the solemn stewardship, I am ready and eager to serve.

Note: The President spoke at 2:16 p.m. in the Center Courtyard of the Pentagon. In his remarks, the Secretary referred to Deputy Secretary of Defense-designate Donald Atwood.

Statement by Press Secretary Fitzwater on the Establishment of the Outer Continental Shelf Leasing and Development Task Force
March 21, 1989

The President announced today the establishment of the Outer Continental Shelf Leasing and Development Task Force.

In accordance with his address to the joint session of Congress on February 9, 1989, he has directed the establishment of the task force to examine in detail the concerns over adverse impacts of lease sales in three environmentally sensitive areas:

1. Lease sale 91 off the coast of northern California;
2. Lease sale 95 off the coast of southern California; and
3. Lease sale 116 off southern Florida, south of 26 degrees north latitude.

The President feels that oil and gas development of America's offshore areas is necessary to ensure a reliable supply of energy and provide for the Nation's economic and national security. He is committed to continued Outer Continental Shelf oil and gas development in an environmentally sound manner.

The task force will consist of the Secretary of the Interior, the Secretary of Energy, the Director of the Office of Management and Budget, the Administrator of the Environmental Protection Agency, and the Administrator of the National Oceanic and Atmospheric Administration, or their designees. The National Academy of Sciences will provide the task force with the necessary scientific and technical analysis. The Secretary of the Interior will serve as Chairman of the task force, which should report its findings to the President by January 1, 1990.

Nomination of Janice Obuchowski To Be an Assistant Secretary of Commerce
March 21, 1989

The President today announced his intention to nominate Janice Obuchowski to be Assistant Secretary of Commerce for Communications and Information. She would succeed Alfred C. Sikes.

Ms. Obuchowski is currently the executive director of international affairs for NYNEX. Prior to this she served in several capacities at the Federal Communications Commission, including Senior Adviser (International Affairs) to the Chairman of the FCC; chief of the FCC's International Policy Division of the Common Carrier Bureau, 1982–1983; and legal assistant to the chief of the Common Carrier Bureau, 1981–1982. Ms. Obuchowski was an associate with the law firm of Bergson, Borkland, Margolis and Adler, 1976–1980. From 1978 to 1980, she chaired the legislation committee of the American Bar Association's litigation section. Ms. Obuchowski is also an adjunct professor of international telecommunications law at Georgetown University Law Center.

Ms. Obuchowski graduated from Wellesley College (B.A., 1973) and Georgetown University Law Center (J.D., 1976). Ms. Obuchowski is married to Albert Halprin, and they reside in McLean, VA.

Nomination of Daphne Wood Murray To Be Director of the Institute of Museum Services

March 21, 1989

The President today announced his intention to nominate Daphne Wood Murray to be Director of the Institute of Museum Services, National Foundation on the Arts and the Humanities. She would succeed Lois Burke Shepard.

Since 1987 Ms. Murray has been director of development for the Houston Museum of Natural Science in Texas, and held various positions with the Contemporary Arts Museum in Houston, 1982 to present. From 1967 to 1987, she served in several capacities for the Museum of Fine Arts in Houston, including elective trustee, 1975–1986; secretary, 1982–1984; vice chairman, 1977–1980; vice president, 1975–1977; advisory trustee, 1969–1974; and Junior League representative, 1971.

Ms. Murray attended Finch College, 1959–1960; Villa Mercedes, University of Florence, Italy, 1958–1959; and the Master's School, 1958. She was born July 22, 1940, in Houston, TX, where she currently resides.

White House Fact Sheet on the President's Minimum-Wage Proposal

March 21, 1989

The President's Proposal

• A 27-percent increase in the minimum wage over 3 years to $4.25 for most workers.

• Maintaining the current $3.35 minimum for all new employees of a firm on the job for less than 6 months, regardless of age or previous employment.

• An increase in the small business exemption to include *all* firms, not just retail and service establishments, with gross sales under $500,000, up from the current $362,500.

• An increase in the tip credit from 40 percent to 50 percent.

Fundamental Principles Guiding the President's Proposal

• Provide higher earnings for long-term minimum-wage employees.

• Minimize the adverse economic impact of an across-the-board increase in the minimum wage.

• Maximize job opportunities for those who need it most, particularly young people, those with limited work experience or skills, and members of minority groups.

• Provide sensible exemptions to minimize the burden of the minimum wage on small businesses and on service firms, where tips are an important part of compensation.

Why Not Increase the Minimum Wage to $4.65?

• *To Save Jobs.* An increase in the minimum wage to $4.65 would cost 650,000 job opportunities.

• The President's proposal would save well over 400,000 of these job opportunities. The smaller increase, to $4.25, saves 200,000 job opportunities. The training wage saves up to an additional 170,000 job opportunities. The tip credit and small business changes save 54,000 job opportunities.

What Other Economic Effects Would Result From a $4.65 Minimum Wage?

- The 40-cent increase between $4.25 and $4.65 would mean a $0.6 billion *increase in the Federal deficit.*
- The 40-cent increase between $4.25 and $4.65 would *increase costs to the consumer* by $6.5 billion.
- Chairman Greenspan of the Federal Reserve has stated that raising the minimum wage would make the battle against inflation more difficult. A higher minimum wage could result in *higher interest rates.*
- A higher minimum wage would raise production costs, thus *reducing the competitiveness* of American manufacturers in international markets.
- A higher minimum wage would have an additional effect on employment costs, as many fringe benefits costs are tied to wages.

Why Have a 6-Month Training Wage?

- *To Save Jobs.* Under the President's proposal, the 6-month training wage could save 170,000 job opportunities.
- A 3-month training wage would save only half as many job opportunities.
- An increase in the minimum wage without an adequate training-wage provision means that many potential workers will have much greater difficulty getting their feet on the ladder of economic opportunity. Employers would be discouraged from creating new jobs at a higher wage for inexperienced workers.
- Those hurt the most without a training wage are the poor, many of whom are young, and minorities.

Why Not Have the Training Wage Apply Only to a Worker's First Job Instead of Each New Job?

- *To Save Jobs.* A new-hire training wage, such as the President proposed, could save *four times as many job opportunities* as would a first-job training wage: 170,000 vs. 40,000.
- New jobs require new skills. Someone who may have spent a few months on a different job may need time to learn new skills.

Why Not Limit the Training Wage to Teenagers?

- *To Save Jobs.* Many new workers, including people trying to escape from welfare, are in their twenties or older.
- The President's universal approach is administratively simpler and less likely to foster compliance problems.

Won't An Even Higher Minimum Wage Help Cure Poverty?

- The minimum-wage population and the poverty population are composed largely of different people. Sixty percent of those earning the minimum wage are young people. Sixty-six percent work part time. Seventy-two percent are single.
- Only 336,000 heads of households living in poverty earned the minimum wage. That is less than 2 percent of the working-age poverty population.
- The job opportunity losses from a universal $4.65 minimum wage may actually *increase poverty* by denying jobs to members of families living in poverty. Poor families would also be forced to pay the higher consumer and other costs associated with a higher minimum wage.

Won't a Higher Minimum Wage Increase Job Opportunities and Wages?

- Since 1982, with no increase in the minimum wage, the economy has added more than 19 million jobs. Yet the number of minimum-wage jobs has declined by 2.6 million, or 40 percent.
- In the last 7 years, 18.4 million jobs (an increase of 80 percent) paying more than $10 per hour have been added. Five million jobs paying between $5 and $10 have been added. The number of jobs paying less than $5 per hour has declined by 30 percent.
- With a constant minimum wage, the unemployment rate has been reduced to 5.1 percent, the lowest in 15 years.
- A higher minimum wage hurts small business the most. These firms are the key to future employment growth and opportunity for the economy.

Statement on the Death of John J. McCloy
March 21, 1989

Barbara and I extend our sincere condolences to the family and many friends of John J. McCloy. We share your loss. The American people join you in mourning the passing of one of the giants and true heroes of this country.

John J. McCloy helped shape American policy and perspectives during the past fifty years—in public service and in private life—as few others have. He was a trusted adviser of American Presidents from Franklin D. Roosevelt to Ronald Reagan. I shall miss the privilege of his counsel. But he also never flagged in pursuing the public good in the many private trusts he held. His energy and interests were boundless. So were his accomplishments.

Recalling his work as chairman of the Ford Foundation, of the Council of Foreign Relations, of the Salk foundation, of the Fund for Modern Courts in New York State, and of the American Council on Germany—to name but a few of his responsibilities—one cannot but stand in awe of this great man of humble origins. Not only his talents and experience, but also his dedication and sense of fair play, were rare indeed. We are poorer for his passing. But we as a country are so much richer for having had him with us for 93 years.

John J. McCloy was not only a prominent American, but also a citizen of the world. He served as President of the World Bank at a crucial time in that institution's history. In later years he became intensely involved with the United Nations Development Corporation.

He was also a pioneer in the field of arms control. In addition to being President Kennedy's chief disarmament adviser and negotiator, John J. McCloy served for a dozen years as Chairman of the General Advisory Committee on Disarmament Agency. His aim—which now is the long-established position of the West as well as part of the declared "new thinking" in the East—was to establish security at lower levels of armament.

But perhaps John J. McCloy's greatest mark was left by his service in Germany. I know he believed it was among the most important of his assignments. As the United States Military Governor and then High Commissioner from 1949 to 1953, John J. McCloy helped rebuild the economic structure of a nation in rubble, directly touching and assisting millions of Germans living in a country devastated by war. In perhaps his most lasting contribution, he helped establish the democratic tradition of the Federal Republic of Germany and the unbreakable bonds of friendship and solidarity between the German and American peoples.

As Chancellor Helmut Kohl has written of John J. McCloy: "He deserves much of the credit for the high quality of German-American relations which we today take for granted, but which at that time only a trusting friend of our people like John McCloy could see as an objective worth pursuing."

Friend of Germany, friend of Europe, friend of peace, America's friend to the world: John McCloy is a friend who will be missed.

Remarks to Students at Conestoga Valley High School in Lancaster, Pennsylvania
March 22, 1989

Chad, thank you, and Mr. Wirth, thank you, sir, for having us here. I'm sorry we had a little bad weather a week or two ago, and postponing this visit. Thinking back, regrettably quite a few years, to my own school days, I can imagine one thought that might have run through your mind: I hope he comes back—anything to get out of class.

[*Laughter*] So, I apologize for any inconvenience on the tests. But I want to thank the students; the parents; the teachers here; Mr. Wirth, your principal; and Chad Weaver, the student body president. Listening to him and his poise up here, I don't know how Senator Specter or Governor Casey or even I might feel. This guy might run against us someday. He sounds terrific—[*laughter*]—pretty tough.

I am particularly grateful to the Governor of the Commonwealth for being here with us and Senator Specter, a most respected leader in the United States Senate, for taking the time out to come here. Your own Congressman has a vote, an important vote, on our side of the aisle—his side—today that keeps determining the leadership there that keeps him. I think he planned to be with us if that vote hadn't taken place. But I do want to pay my respects to Bob Walker. And then my special introduction to you—one who you know well and who has been a symbol of propriety and leadership and enthusiasm for Pennsylvania—and that, of course, is your own ex-Governor and now the Attorney General of the United States, Dick Thornburgh. What a job he is doing! And the other—I'm not sure he's been here, but he's been almost every place else; I expect he's been to Lancaster. But Bill Bennett, a former Secretary of Education, is now the first drug czar. Why in the United States we use the word "czar" to establish a real leader, I don't know. But he's tough as the czars were, and he is going to help us whip the scourge of drugs. And here he is, Bill Bennett. [*Applause*]

You know, we often think of drug abuse as an urban, inner-city phenomenon. Millions of Americans think of their own communities, and they say it can't happen here. Well, the people of rural Pennsylvania know that's not true. And in the past couple of years, drug abuse has escalated here. And the good news is you're fighting back. Your community is too proud, your traditions here too deeply rooted for an invader to threaten your safety and well-being without a fight. And when drugs come here to the Conestoga Valley, that's proof that the drug epidemic is a national problem. Look, Lancaster is a strong community, a place where small town values is not a cliche. It's a way of life. And you know what matters: family and faith and being a good neighbor and a member of the community. The rising problem here simply shows how vulnerable every American city and town is to the menace of drug abuse. And recognizing this fact is the first step towards finding a solution. And Lancaster is on its way.

This morning you heard from Thomas Hipple and Peter True, two young men who for reasons of their own have made a commitment to help others understand the lasting damage that drugs can do and prevent their peers from making what can be a life-shattering choice. What Tom and Peter are doing takes tremendous courage and commitment. And I'm here to say that you're not alone in this—battling the drug problem. You have partners in your community and in others across the United States, and you have partners in the war on drugs in Washington, right there on Pennsylvania Avenue. And as I said in my Inaugural Address—and I will keep saying it because I feel driven by this commitment—I am committed to the ending of the scourge of drugs across the United States of America, and I need your help.

Our task is not just to deplore the drug problem but to take action against it. What the banners that I've seen here say to me is that this valley and the people of Lancaster are ready to take action to stop the drug scourge. And one of the most powerful weapons against drug use is education.

And of course, there's another side to the drug program. I'm going to be going down with Dick Thornburgh and Bill Bennett, down to Wilmington later on, on my way back to Washington. And there we'll be talking about interdiction, stopping drugs from coming in, and also enforcement, the law enforcement side that Dick Thornburgh has the responsibility for—our effort to stop the illegal drugs, shut down the trade. But this morning, I want to talk to you all on the means of prevention, on drying up the demand for illegal drugs.

Antidrug education and awareness can help provide the kids and the young adults with both the reasons and the willpower to resist the lure of drugs. And that's the aim of an antidrug education program called

DARE—D-A-R-E—Drug Abuse Resistance Education, and that's helping, as the people involved with DARE like to say, "drug-proof" our children. The program was pioneered, incidentally, by the Los Angeles Police Department and the L.A. public school system. I've been out there and witnessed the program in action, and DARE sends these police officers into the classroom to work with the kids, build their self-esteem, teach them that they can refuse when they're pressured to try drugs. And the DARE program is teaching youngsters something else: that the police and their schools are united in a common effort to stop drug abuse. In the 6 years since the program began in California, DARE has caught on nationwide. And this year, in 1,200 communities in 45 States, 3 million children will participate.

DARE is just one example of the kind of program that can provide our children both the reasons and the willpower to resist the lure of drugs. There is no one right answer when it comes to battling drug abuse. Each community will find what works best, and we'll learn from each other.

I'm told that right here in Lancaster you have a program called High-Risk Youth in the elementary schools and another called SCIP, the School Community Intervention Program, in place—that one's in the high schools and in the junior highs. And they aim at identifying young people whose circumstances and family situations make them most vulnerable to the lure of drugs. Targeting these youth for special attention is crucial, and with High-Risk Youth and SCIP, you're doing something to stop drug problems before they begin.

For my part, I'm going to see that drug education receives the funding it needs. Most of the funding, as you know, comes from local school boards and States. I think it's 7 percent of the funding is Federal. But our budget this year for 1990 calls for a full $1.1 billion for drug prevention and antidrug education activity. And even in these tight budget times, that's up 16 percent over 1989. I've urged Congress to provide $392 million for the Drug Free Schools and Communities program, funds that go to the States and institutions of higher education.

And then as I mentioned earlier with great pride, and I'll say it again, I have selected Bill Bennett to serve as the Director—this is his official title, I told you the nickname—the Director of the Office of National Drug Control Policy to map the strategy and oversee the antidrug campaign. And I'll tell you, I picked him because he's knowledgeable, he's tough, and he is determined and, most importantly though, he cares deeply about the young people of this country.

These initiatives are important, and they're going to have an impact. But there's a role for each of us in the war on drugs, and I hope you'll join me in asking what you can do to help, especially to advance the antidrug education and awareness. You know, we can all play a part in increasing awareness about the ravages of drug dependency. We must get the message across that drugs are not a form of entertainment or a helpless, harmless means of escape. Drugs are a poison, to users and to our communities. But a widespread awareness of the dangers of drug abuse depends on sending consistent signals, on sending a clear message that using drugs is not fashionable, is not fun, and above all else, it is not safe.

For too long—and this isn't the fault of the young people here—because for too long, our culture, our popular culture glorified drug use. I think that's changing now, and that's a real change for the better. Consider the anti-drug-abuse campaign on television. Not long ago, I was told a story about a little girl, 4 years old, who's getting the message. She got up from in front of the television to tell her parents something important. "Drugs," she said, "fry your brain like an egg." We've all seen that commercial the little girl was talking about. Whether you're 4 or 14 or 40, the message gets across. And let's carry that message, all of us. And I would say right here: I hope that the movie producers and the movie directors and those involved in the entertainment business will stop, will put an end to the glorification or its humorous treatment of narcotics.

And let's shed some of the perceptions about the drug problem that are comforting, but are completely incorrect. There's no room for saying, "Drug abuse doesn't affect me." Think about the costs of drug abuse: the lost time, the waste, the crime, the accidents that can be traced to the influence of drugs. Twenty-three million Americans used illegal drugs last year. Countless thousands died. And the fact is that none of us—none of us—is immune to the problems that drug abuse can cause. So, together, let's you and me send a message on drug abuse to the so-called casual user: Face up to the fact that your so-called recreational drug use contributes to the drug culture—to the crime, the death, and degradation associated with the drug trade.

The other day I was in New York, and I talked to a group of DEA agents, drug enforcement agents, who lay their lives on the line for us, as they try to interdict narcotics and stop it right there in the street. But there was a team that had worked in a white-collar business, in the brokerage business, of all things, down on Wall Street. They looked like they belonged on Wall Street—nice clean-cut guys, you know—a wonderful looking young man and a young woman. And they said that in that culture there, if people stayed over and worked overtime, their reward might be some cocaine to stay on a little later in the office. It isn't just the impoverished; it isn't just those who are fighting trauma in their lives. There's this whole concept that recreational drug use has been condoned, and we've got to stop it. We have got to make people understand, whatever walk of life you're in, that drug use is bad, it's death, it is degradation. And so, the fight is not going to be just in the ghettos, where the impoverished and the hopeless are; it's going to be all across the board.

To parents: Your children know more than you realize about drugs. Make it your business as a parent to know about drug abuse yourself. Educate yourselves. Don't hide from the reality of drug abuse in our communities and then hope for the best—hope that someone else will solve the problem. Your children depend on you to help separate the fact from the fiction, to help them make a choice and then stick with it, when it comes to resisting drugs.

To the kids: Let's send the message that drugs are dangerous; that you don't need drugs to feel good about yourself or to win approval from others; that your parents, the people in your schools and your community care. But most of all, you must understand that the decision against drugs is yours to make, no one else's. When it's time to draw the line against drugs, the final choice is yours.

I get a lot of mail. Some of it is very serious, some of it very disturbing, and some of it quite amusing. Get a lot of letters from school kids. I got one not long ago from a girl in California—fifth grader. She told me how she wanted to change the world—wonderfully idealistic—and that making the world a better place meant putting an end to drug abuse. And then she wrote, "I don't know if I can do it all by myself. I need your help." Well, she does, and she's going to get it. And, yes, I can help, and so can all of you. And that's the answer we owe our children. But there's something else that the little girl who wrote that letter needs to know. There is something that she can do, that all of us here can do, to bring ourselves one step closer to winning the war on drugs. We can take a stand and say, "We don't do drugs." And anytime anyone of us takes that stand, that is another battle won. As a community, we must work to make it as easy as possible for our children to make the choice against drugs. We can do it by creating an environment—a safe, secure space, if you will—where our kids can acquire a sense of self and self-confidence so secure that no amount of peer group pressure can push them into taking drugs.

I mentioned that I'm going to talk about enforcement later on today, but I don't want to leave here without saying to you the enforcement side of this equation is absolutely essential, whether it's in the corridors of this outstanding high achievement school or whether it's downtown Lancaster or wherever it is. The authorities must enforce the law, and we must make an example of those who are pushing drugs onto the lives of the others around here. You know, most Americans want to see their towns restored to a time when drugs came in from the prescriptions from the local doctor. But with your hard work and commitment, that day will come sooner. It must come.

So, my message to you today is: Don't do drugs. Keep fighting back. Fight for your community, for your children. The war on drugs will ultimately be won one day, one battle at a time—the battles each and every one of us wage to keep our families and communities free from drug abuse. We've learned a hard lesson. Unless we join together and fight, it can happen here. But if we do work as a team and as a community, it won't.

And so, let these banners be a battle cry—and that Conestoga Valley, in Lancaster, in communities like yours all over the country, we will join together, turn the tide, and bring the drug epidemic to an end with finality—over—history. Now, we need your help.

Thank you very much. Thank you all.

Note: The President spoke at 9:17 a.m. in the gymnasium. He was introduced by Chad Weaver, president of the student body. Prior to his remarks, the President met with participants in a drug rehabilitation program and their families.

Remarks at a Meeting With Amish and Mennonite Leaders in Lancaster, Pennsylvania
March 22, 1989

The President. Let me say in the beginning I appreciate you all taking time from your busy day. And one of the reasons I want to come here, accompanied by our Attorney General and former Secretary of Education, who has been charged with the whole program on fighting drugs, Bill Bennett, is to salute you, because as we look at a national drug problem, we find that in communities such as yours, because of your adherence to family values and faith, the problem appears to be close to nonexistent—hopefully nonexistent. And I have been over at the school talking there, and met with some kids where regrettably it isn't nonexistent. And I said in my comments there that these values of neighborhood and family and faith—somehow they come back to me, anyway, if we engage in this national crusade, to be fundamentally important.

So, I wanted to start by saying that, though this is an antinarcotics swing, this stop is to maybe hear from you all as to how your community manages to stave off the scourge of drugs. And anyway, that was one of the things. I don't know who wants to take the lead here, but we're very pleased to be with you.

Mennonite Leader. We thank you for coming here. First of all, we wish the Lord to bless our meeting here. And we are happy to have you here, but we are also somewhat saddened that it takes the drug issue and alcohol to bring you here.

My wife and I have eight children, two of which are married. And two are with a youth group. Three are going to school here. Our 18-year-old son was driving with a man one time, and he said, "Do you mind if I smoke pot?"

The President. Your kid was driving with—yes.

Mennonite Leader. In a pickup, he was driving along with the pickup—and "Do you mind if I smoke pot? Will you tell the boss?" He said, "I sure will."

So, it makes me almost quiver in my boots when I think that that youth could have been tempted to do that because he was exposed to it. And it's by the grace of God that we have what we have—what we have as values, that you were just talking about, handed down to us from our fathers. When they came to this country, it was the Indians and the bears that they feared for life. Now it's the highway with alcohol and the drug influence. When we drive down the road, we don't know what shape that man is that's coming towards us, and we are concerned.

What could we do as Christians to maintain that value? We do not want to uphold ourselves that we have something that we worked for and that we deserve, but it is by the grace of God that we have been given it through our parents and have withstood—took their stand to this day. And we would like to ask you what we could do as Christians to help to stop that flow from Lancaster County?

The President. Well, in terms of the interdiction of the flow, I would think that that would largely be the responsibility, to some degree, of local law enforcement, because I'm told that even in a marvelous rural community, some of the fields are used for illicit drops. And you know, they signal the plane, and the plane goes on. So, in that area, encouraging your local law enforcement people would be very important.

We realize that we have—the three of us and Senator Specter here and our Chief of Staff, John Sununu—a disproportionate responsibility in the interdiction. I say "we," the Federal Government, because we're talking about at the borders. And Dick Thornburgh is just back from meeting with various heads of government in Central America, where a lot of the crops, as you know, are grown.

But I guess what I'd say—and then I'd like to ask Bill Bennett, who, as you know, was formerly our Secretary of Education, to say a word—but I guess what I'd say is: keeping moral underpinnings with your community and then, hopefully, having others see that as an example. I don't want to argue with you because you're too good a host, but I think it is important I'm here because it gives us a chance to have a conversation like this and to understand a little better why it is—and you've already touched on it—faith—why it is that you all have been able to withstand the pressure when others have not.

Mennonite Leader. My concern is how can we maintain that? We have a preschool son, four-year-old. When he is 18 and the problem is exploding, so to speak——

The President. Exactly. Well, that's what our whole new—I don't want to say the word "crusade," that's a little like a cliche—but I view it as that in terms of both the demand and the supply side. You mentioned interdiction, and that's the supply. But the whole demand side—I have gotten to use the White House as a bully pulpit to argue and to encourage people all across the country on the demand side.

Mennonite Leader. We appreciate your concern.

The President. We met with some kids—we've got to do it.

But, Bill, now, you've fought this in the education role and now as our drug czar. Why don't you add some to that?

Mr. Bennett. Well, I just——

The President. That was a very good question you raised.

Mr. Bennett. ——wonder what your children say or your grandchildren say about this. Is it their sense that—as they report to you—that things are better, worse, or more temptation to do this out there, or less? What are the kinds of things that they report on this? As you see this threat—I think we all take it very seriously—but for me, a lot of the way I see the threat is through the eyes of young people. They are really there on the line.

Mennonite Leader. They're concerned.

Mr. Bennett. And I wonder what they are telling you in terms of things. Are things better than they were 5 years ago? Are they worse than they are?

Mennonite Leader. In my opinion, it would be worse, because our two oldest sons work at public places and they both were exposed to drugs and had opportunity to buy. Now, what I'm concerned about is, like I said, the four-year-old. By the time he comes of age, will he be able to say no?

Mr. Bennett. Yes.

Mennonite Leader. Will he continue to maintain that value that we are trying to plant into our children that was implanted into us, as President Bush just said about values. This is what we uphold more than money. I don't want to take much of your time, but we want to teach our children there's more of a greater value to go to bed with a clear conscience than to make money on drugs or to get high on it.

Mr. Bennett. Well, we have found in all the drug studies that the best community, the best protection for a young person, is what one of the people writing has called the internal compass in the sense of high aspiration: deeply rooted values, faith, and a closeness to family. These are the things, if you wanted to design a system which would protect the children.

And I don't think, whatever kind of drug we see, whatever kind of onslaught you see, that those rules will change. It seems to me that has been the case throughout history in terms of the best things we can do for our young people. One of the things that we see is a very strong affirmation on the part of young people who have experimented with drugs, in many cases, have almost been destroyed—they come back and reaffirm what we've seen. They tell us, having gone through the trial, having gone through the fire, that what was missing in their lives was this.

The President. May I tell you one other additional—this gets a little bit off, but it gives you an idea of how we're looking at this. I don't want to see Federal legislation that diminishes the family. We've got a big, new thing on child care now. And I think the Federal Government does have some responsible role in child care. But our approach is to give the families the choice, to give the families—well, put it this way, some religious institutions are new day-care services. I don't want to see the Federal law defined so narrowly by the bureaucracy in Washington that it erodes out the community, religious institutions, or family from child care. And yet I do think the Federal Government has a role in helping the private sector, helping the States in the question of child care.

So, philosophically, you say what does this have to do with drugs? Because I think you are a shining example of what family and faith can do. Where we have responsibilities at the Federal level, we must see that inadvertently we don't weaken the role of family or weaken the role of, I'd say, faith in our country. I believe in separation of church and state; but I don't want to see the church people get together in a church community and take care of the other guy's kids—work from whatever it is, and then have them denied that because of Federal money serving as a magnet that has to go into some federally certified, rubber-stamped institution down the street. So, we will be working at the Federal level to see that we don't impose on communities legislation that, even though it isn't intended that way, would diminish and weaken the family. And it isn't easy, but there are other areas, I think, where we're going to be able to—Dick, you want to say something?

Attorney General Thornburgh. Well, I, as you know, am in the law enforcement side of the effort to deal with drugs. President Bush—I'm sure you've heard it said—has established a goal of providing a kinder and gentler America. And I think that's one that we support to a man or woman throughout this country. But a kinder, gentler America is not one where drugs are abused and where drug traffickers rule the streets of some of our communities. I've told the President that if we're going to have a kinder, gentler America, we're going to have to be rougher and tougher with some Americans: those who are drug traffickers, those who are the urban terrorists that have captured so many of our communities. And that's a job for law enforcement. The President's supporting tougher laws. He's supporting more resources for our police and prosecutors, and supporting a tougher attitude toward those countries in the international community where these substances are grown and produced. And we'll do our share in helping to interrupt the flow of drugs into your community.

But for my two cents' worth, I just want to underscore what the President has said: even from a law enforcement view, how important it is for the types of values that you've enunciated and practiced in your communities to gain currency in every community across the United States so that the appetite for drugs and the consumption of drugs, the demand for drugs, is diminished to a point where we don't have this problem.

But we're very grateful for the opportunity to visit with you, learn from you, and carry the message that's exemplified by your communities elsewhere. Thank you.

Mennonite Leader. We're very happy for your concern and what you're doing for the sake of the young people of the U.S. And I think the fact that we have no trouble with drug addiction is because of the close family ties; and the children are taught obedience at a very young age and self-denial, that they don't have everything they wish as they're growing up; and because they are taught of God, and urged to pray, and in school have prayer and Bible reading. And as they grow up, they have a sense of value that they're not just out seeking thrills and drugs or any other. We appreciate it much for the warnings on the tobacco ads: harmful to the body—wish it were on the alcoholic drinks. And we surely appreciate your efforts.

Another thing that I think why we have no drug problem is for things we do not do. We do not have television, radio; and as I understand, almost—coming into the homes of sexual things and robbers, and children growing up in that atmosphere. It's just that they're at a disadvantage, I think.

You read in the Bible of the people who do not seek after God, and that God is not in all their thoughts. I think that is why the young people of America are going astray with drugs. We wish God would be more in their thoughts, and you respond to a higher power.

Mennonite Leader. I also welcome President Bush. We feel kind of honored to be here. And as for us, as a people, as we are—it's one advantage that we have strived for, and that is like Aaron there said, that we don't have television and recorded music. We feel sorry that our Constitution or our courts have taken the prayer and Bible reading out of schools. Then, after that has left, we also have this rock music. And those things just enter into the mind, that the child will do things that they had not intended to do, and then they are turned to drugs. It leads to that.

Now, if our moral fiber—not ruin it through removing the prayer and Bible, we'd have a stronger America today. But that is the thing. This is why we feel what we have is because we try to avoid this recorded music, rock music, and those things that the child has control—the spirit can be—rather than it being entertained by the music of the world and some of the—as you all know, that hard music is—well, you know all about it. And that's where we shy away strongly, because it just does something to a person. And that's from our stand of viewpoint. That's where we feel we have some advantage with our children, because they are not exposed to that point, that they have more self-control.

The President. You know, it's interesting on the music. I think of the action that Susan Baker, who is the wife of our Secretary of State, and Tipper Gore, who is the wife of a man who ran for President last year and a United States Senator—they got outraged by just some of the really bad lyrics in this music. And they took their fight—aware of the right of people to speak out and the freedom of speech amendment—but they took this fight to the public, and indeed they were ridiculed for this in a lot of high, sophisticated quarters, even though the lyrics were so bad and so awful that they would challenge any family. And they went through a real tough time, but they have not let up on it. And they've got the most sophisticated, liberal communities—get all over them, thinking that they're violating somebody's right to speak. And I was quite supportive in talking to them and know what they're doing.

I think we have an obligation as President—you do have to be careful of violating somebody's freedom of speech. But I think there are some certain excesses that have cropped in now that we've come to condone, that under the same Constitution would have been condemned years ago.

So, I think these are interesting warnings you're putting out here. I want to preserve freedom of speech and freedom of expression. But I think it's fine when citizens are up in arms about it and try to express their viewpoint. Maybe we've gone too far in some things. I mean, I don't like seeing the American flag down on the floor, either. I know how this President looks at it. But maybe that's a little reactionary, but that's exactly the way I feel about it. And so, we'll see.

Mennonite Leader. President Bush, of course, we don't want you to leave here feeling we are making demands or telling the bad side. We also wanted to express appreciation for what you and former Presidents have done for us in the past. We want you to realize that we do feel grateful for what has been done for us. I thought maybe we could just relate a thought that seemed to be some of our teaching, that the hand that rocks the cradle, it rules the Nation. Not only speaking to the young people, maybe the parents, if they could some way—that parents could plant this in their children at a younger age—would often go a far way.

Mennonite Leader. We are not so politically involved as some groups are, but we spiritually support our country, and we pray for them at every church service. We pray for our government and thank God for the freedom we have in religion and so forth. And I'm afraid we do not appreciate this as much in our thoughts or in our actions as far as confessing to be Christians in our way of looking at things.

Mr. Bennett. If I may, I know you wouldn't say it—I think that we could all take pride—I'm not sure there's ever been a President or a First Lady who were better parents to teach by their example what it means to be parents and grandparents. And I think this is a lesson in all these areas, whether you're talking about drugs or alcohol or anything else. I know I learned at the Department of Education—not every teacher is a parent, but every parent is a teacher, a child's first teacher. So, I think we have a special blessing that this President and this First Lady are as splendid parents, very splendid teachers, as well—if you'll allow me, Mr. President.

The President. These things are important, and you have to find the balance, I mean, in the Presidency or in the responsibility as an Attorney General. And now we don't want to be disrespectful of people's right to differ and people's right, as I say, of freedom of expression. But I know, I am absolutely certain, that family values and community and faith—where those abound, the problems that we're talking about over in that school of fighting narcotics, the fight is easier and the problem less big.

No one's immune. You mentioned the kid of yours, driving along with the pressure. Who knows who's going to succumb, no matter how strong their faith. And this is what—I mean, everybody's waxing philosophical here, but when you see kids born into this world with really one-part family with very little love and very little hope—I mean, it's tough for a child. Then off in the school system, and it's very, very tough. I'm not suggesting that it's easy and that everybody that is not blessed with the faith of your community should automatically be perfect. But somehow, we have got to find ways to strengthen the American concept of family and faith. And it can't be legislated. Once we start legislating, there's a threat to you in that kind of thing, threat to your kind of community. But somehow we've got to find ways to point out our nation's historic reliance on these things.

Did I interrupt? You were going to say something.

Amish Leader. No.

The President. No? Anybody else?

Amish Leader. I think perhaps the public should be urged, as well as ourselves, to probably get back to the Bible.

Amish Leader. I'm about worn out. I'm 90 years old. But I thank you for coming to Pennsylvania, Lancaster County. The President visits Lancaster County—I thank you.

The President. Don't sound worn out at all.

Mennonite Leader. He can't understand much.

The President. Really? That's loud and clear. There's something about the Presidency—leave out the fact that George Bush is President—that when you go around in that big automobile and you see people who may vote for you or may have not voted for you turning out to salute the Presidency, it is a very emotional experience, and it's a wonderful thing. I remember as a young guy, rushing out to see Presidents of another party. It has nothing to do with party. It has to do with the respect for the institution or an emotional commitment to the institution of the Presidency.

So, when we see those kids and those signs—we were talking about that coming over with the Senator and the Governor and the Secretary and John Sununu—it's very emotional. You almost get tears in your eyes. But it always has to be that. It always has to be—we fight in these elections and then we come together as a country. And as you mentioned coming here, sir—but it's a great pleasure for us to be here.

Amish Leader. That's my father.

The President. Is that your dad? Ninety years old. Well, my mother is 87. She's going pretty strong, not quite as strong as you are, though.

Mennonite Leader. I think the fact—going across the U.S.—that you're against drugs will help a lot. Just that fact. We just hope the people will stand to you. Years ago, Israel had a good King Solomon—the Lord spoke to the people: "My people that are called by my name, humble themselves and pray and seek my face and confess—and turn away from their sins, them I will hear from in Heaven and heal their name." I think a great responsibility is in the families to help you along in your wonderful work.

The President. You know, I'll share with you something. We're getting philosophical near the end of our visit here. But Barbara and I went to China as your emissary—not ambassador then, because we didn't have, as you remember, full relations with China. And we went there in 1974, and then I was there in '75. And we had wondered about the family in China—Communist country, totalitarian—and the common perception was that there had been an erosion of the strength of family. We knew that there had been a banning—almost entire banning on practicing and teaching Christianity. That was a given. But I wondered more fundamentally about family.

Then we got there. And then you'd see on their festival days—you'd see the granddad and the grandson and the sons and daughters all together—strong. And finally, when they dared talk to you—and they didn't do much then because this was right after the Cultural Revolution—they kept separating out from Westerners—but when you did, when you'd get a little glimpse of it through sports or through somebody—my language teacher—it was family. My son is sick; we care about that. My husband is in the hospital. I mean, it was a family thing.

And we'd go to a little church service there. Indeed, our daughter was christened in a church service where there was maybe 10 or 12 Westerners and 5 or 6 faithful Chinese who were permitted in what used to be the YMCA to have this Sunday service, mainly for diplomats, you see. Now, that was in 1975 that she was christened there. In 1989 I went back there as President of the United States. The church had moved even. Now it was in what they call a *hutong*, an alley. But it moved into an even bigger building. There was close to 1,000 people in it. The choir had vestments. They were able to have hymn books. And the Bible was read from. And the message that I got from all of this is not that there's freedom of worship in China yet—there's not—but that it is moving. The family has never been weakened in China; it's always been strong. A totalitarian state can't stamp that out, and that faith can't be crushed by a state doctrine. It can't be crushed by it. And you're beginning to see more expressions of worship there. And I am absolutely convinced it's going to continue. And you see it in the Soviet Union.

So, what molds you together in the community, your family and your faith, is something that transcends—my point is: It transcends liberal-conservative, Republican-Democrat, American-Soviet. I mean, it is there, and it is strong. And maybe it's what you said, sir: We've got to keep talking about values, and hopefully, that will help the enforcement end and the education end and the interdiction and all these kinds of things that we have to continue to do on the drug fight.

But that China thing—every family has experienced something that sticks in their hearts. And this one is something that—I tell you, when I got up to speak there, I was all choked up. They welcomed me back, and they said, "How is our sister, Dorothy?"—that's our daughter who was baptized in that faith. And it was a great lesson for me: the strength of faith. Somehow it just keeps coming up.

Amish Leader. We appreciate that feeling for our leader of the country.

The President. Well, thank you all.

Attorney General Thornburgh. Mr. President, my fellow Pennsylvanians and I have a sentiment that I think they would permit me to share with you during your visit. *Astan un freund* [You've got a friend] in Pennsylvania.

The President. I understand that. I studied German I, II in school. But "You have a friend in Pennsylvania." [*Laughter*]

Amish Leader. A lot of friends in Pennsylvania.

The President. Thank you all for taking the time.

Mennonite Leader. Say "hello" to the Fletcher family. They came—my parents—one that's the head of the shuttle.

The President. Oh, Jim Fletcher.

Amish Leader. Make a greeting to Mrs. Bush.

The President. Well, she is working hard, and she's into—works a lot with the Secretary on literacy. Learned a lot from him, and now she is continuing her interest in literacy because, again, it gets down to how you appreciate these things. When you can't read, it's pretty hard to——

Mennonite Leader. We want to appreciate our government more than we ever did because of your interest.

The President. Well, we want to give you something to be proud of. We want to set examples where we can. We've talked about some of the problem areas, but we're living in tough fiscal times and all of that. I think we're in optimistic times in terms of peace. If we can keep ourselves vigilant, I think we have a good chance now, with the changes in the Pacific, but in the Soviet Union—that if we find a way to move properly, I think we could ensure the kid you were talking about and the other seven a more peaceful future. And that, of course, a President has to be thinking about.

Mennonite Leader. God bless you, those in the family. The family that prays together stays together.

The President. That's right.

Mennonite Leader. We want to keep that theme, "In God We Trust," which is stamped on our money.

The President. It's staying there. Nobody can knock that off. And I very openly advocated the fact of prayer in the schools. And it's got to be voluntary so some minority kid doesn't feel discriminated against. It's got to be obviously nondictated by the state. But I am not going to change my mind about it. I'm absolutely convinced that it is right. It drives political opponents right up the wall. They just don't understand it, but I feel strongly about it—end of speech. Thank you all.

Note: The President spoke at 10 a.m. in the meeting room at Penn Johns Elementary School. In his opening remarks, he referred to Attorney General Dick Thornburgh. Following his remarks, the President traveled to Wilmington, DE.

Question-and-Answer Session at the Wilmington Cluster Against Substance Abuse Program in Delaware

March 22, 1989

Mr. Mustafa. Mr. President, I'm sure the kids have some questions they'd like to ask you, so why don't you have a seat.

The President. Okay, now, what's happening here, you guys? Who's got a question, or tell me something about how this is working. I mean, this is wonderful.

War on Drugs

Q. What can I do to stop drugs?

The President. Well, that's a good question, and the answer is to stand—I mean for your individual self—is to avoid the pressure that comes when those guys come around with the drugs, I mean, just to encourage yourself and the guys like this that are in training here to stay away from it—to stay totally away from it. And then get other friends, and get them to turn down drugs. So, when the guy comes into the neighborhood peddling the drugs, why, you take a role like an individual leader, and you say no, I'm not going to do that. I'm going to go the clean way. I'm going to go that—and then you want to help other guys do it.

And what we've got to do in the Government—like in Washington and then Governor Castle here and the State government and your mayor and the local police guys—

we've got to help as private citizens. We've got to help you in the law enforcement side of things. And then, our drug czar, who is with us today, Bill Bennett—he's the big guy over here, and he was in education. He was the Secretary of Education and in charge for the Federal Government in education. And he's going to help work with the schools and others in terms of the education side for all kids, in the classrooms, to just say, "Look, this is wrong; this is bad; don't come in here telling me it's okay."

You've got to listen to Rashid, your able instructor here. It's his whole life. He's given a lot out of his own life to not only train you and discipline you guys but help on the education side himself, just by his time that he gives you guys. So, it's kind of hard for one individual, but every guy can make a difference. And if somebody in your family does it, you've got to say, "Hey, that's wrong." Even sometimes when it's unpopular. You know, they say, "Hey, come on, you. What's the matter with you? Come on." And you've got to be the guy that stands up to it, says, "No, I don't want that." Come on over here and work out and do what you've got to do.

Q. Have you ever been offered drugs?

The President. No. See, you know, I'll tell you something. They had drugs around when I was a little guy, but I hate to tell you how old I am. It wasn't as much—there wasn't the pressure on the kids in schools. It's just kind of come in more lately, you know? And so, when I was your age, the pressures and the temptations on all kids was much less in terms of the drug threat you guys face up to now. Have you ever been offered them?

Q. Yes, once.

The President. Did you? Did you tell the guy to bug off?

Q. Yes.

Athletics

Q. When you were younger, have you ever been in an activity like karate or a different—other things—basketball, gym?

The President. A lot of athletics, not karate. I watched you guys. I'm not sure I could have done that. [*Laughter*] That was pretty good, and——

Q. Do you know where drugs come from?

The President. Yes, I know that. I'll get to that one in a minute. But sports—yes, I love sports—still do play. I love to play baseball, and I played soccer. I don't know whether you've ever played that, but I did a little bit of football in grade school. So, sports I think helps. It keeps your body going good and keeps your mind cleaned out for you.

What did you say?

War on Drugs

Q. Do you know where drugs come from?

The President. Yes. They come from all over the world, unfortunately. Picture a map and see where you are in Delaware. And then you go way down south to the Rio Grande River, and then on down south into South America. A lot of them come from down there.

And our Attorney General [Richard L. Thornburgh] right here, he can tell you where he was for some of this. Tell him where you were, Dick, just recently.

The Attorney General. I was in three countries where they grow drugs. If you look at the map of South America, one of them is Bolivia—high in the Andes Mountains. And then right next door to that is Peru. And then just north of that is Colombia. In all three of those countries, they grow the plants that produce the materials that are made into drugs, and they sell them for a lot of money in this country. But they wouldn't be able to sell any of them if nobody wanted to use drugs. And that's what the President is saying. He says the best thing we can do is to turn our back on those people who want us to use drugs and put the money into the pockets of the crooks who handle the drugs.

The President. Some people, they grow it here sometimes in the United States, too. It's terrible. So, then the law enforcement guys have to go out and try to crack down on them and stuff.

Q. Are they legal in the other countries?

The President. I don't think they're ever legal. I don't know for sure. Bill, maybe you can tell them. I don't think they're legal. They turn their back on it in some places and condone it—well, we did in this country for a while.

Attorney General Thornburgh. There are

108 countries that signed the U.N. drug convention, Mr. President, and that means there are 108 countries that are your working partners in the effort to deal with the drug problem around the world. There aren't many places where the drug dealers or the drug traffickers are going to get much in the way of approval.

The President. Here's another one for this guy. How about these quiet guys down there? Go ahead.

Q. Mr. President, as I learned as I was in school, they took a lot of drugs that were good, like narcotics and stuff that heal some people's wounds, like cocaine and stuff that numbs.

The President. Yes. Like morphine to keep the pain away and stuff.

Q. Yes, keep your pain away, and sometimes marijuana for different things. But as my teacher told me, drugs were good until somebody took them and abused the drugs. They used them on their body as the wrong thing.

The President. Good point. Good point. You know, when a guy lying out on the battlefield was shot, fighting for his country or something, and they'd give him a shot of morphine to take the pain down, well, that was some kind of narcotic effect on them. And so, there are some uses—very narrow medical uses—that people, well, doctors would say this could help save a life or help a person bear the pain of a wound. But then it got abused. Your teacher was absolutely right about that.

Q. Do you know exactly how long the drugs have been around?

The President. No, because you go back in history and you look in the opium wars that go over into China years ago, and you've got—so, I don't know, but I expect long, long ago in history it started. But whether society condones it, whether there's a growing—what they call permitting it—permissiveness that permits that to happen to a society. You know, you go back into ancient history now—Rome, and when Rome got corrupt with a lot of alcohol abuse and that kind of thing. And so, it isn't something brand new in our history, but it's something that's become because people have just turned the other cheek and just kind of let it happen in their neighborhoods. And then, when parents do it, why, then it's hard for the kid, even though he's taught the right things, right in this very room, right over there on those mats—taught the right thing. In the home, maybe the pressures are tough on you at home, and it's hard for a little guy to stand up. That's why you need to be company on this—stand together in fighting against it.

Q. Have you ever been offered drugs?

The President. I haven't. No. No, I haven't been offered that. Have you?

Q. No.

The President. Never did? How about you?

Q. Where do drugs come from?

The President. Well, you didn't hear. He asked it. A lot of the basic plants are grown in South America, sometimes over in Burma and in what they call the Golden Triangle over there. And some right here in this country—marijuana plants illegally grown out in the forests and out in the woods. And Alabama—the Governor was in to see me the other day—the Governor of that State. And he said it's hard to find the plants because people sneak out and cultivate them. And then it's hard. You have to find them from helicopters. So, a wide array of places they come from.

Mr. Mustafa. Well, Mr. President, I'd like to make a comment. I'd like to say that the WACASA program, or Wilmington Cluster Against Substance Abuse here in this State—we have made a pledge to live a drug-free lifestyle and to help these youth become the hope for the future. And they understand that a mind is a terrible thing to waste and that they are the hope of the future and that their present thoughts determine their future actions. And they all have made that pledge to live that lifestyle.

The President. That's wonderful, Rashid.

Q. Our teacher said when he was growing up, when he was a little kid——

The President. Yes, a little guy?

Q. Yes. He said while other little kids were wanting to buy drugs and they couldn't—he said they used to go to the store and buy airplane glue and sniff it.

The President. They did. That's right. Duco—what was it called? Something like that? Yes. And it would give you some drug effect. That's true.

The Attorney General. It's not good for you.

The President. No. And then they'd damage their brain, and it would be very bad.

Wilmington Cluster

Q. Mr. President, how do you feel about the WACASA program?

The President. Well, I'm going to talk about it at lunch. I don't know all of the details of it. But I feel that programs like that—and I'm going to mention it because the Governor and others have told us that it's making a real move, being successful—that in there lies a lot of the answer. Federal Government—Washington, DC—they can't design all these programs. I mean, what works here is good. Nobody can tell your instructor here, "You're going to have to do this nationwide. Everybody at 2 o'clock in the afternoon, or whatever it is, is going to have a karate lesson." But it's all different kinds of answers.

I talked about the concept of 1,000 points of light—1,000 different programs, multiplied by 1,000, all working in their own way and in their own community. So, I would just say, Hey, go for it. Participate. Get others to do it, too. And that's part of it.

Q. Do you think the WACASA program would be in existence at least another 4 or 5 years?

The President. Yes, because I don't think this whole program is going to be whipped. I mean, the whole drug thing is—I wish I could tell you differently, but we're going to make some moves. I've got 4 years as President, and I want to be able to look back—and not just for the country, but also I'd like to be able to say to my grandchildren—about the age of some of these guys here—we worked hard to make it better. It's not going to be solved. We need to keep these programs going.

War on Drugs

Q. Mr. President, how can I, one person, help?

The President. Out at schools and everyplace? Yes, you've got to encourage others not to use them. You've got to participate in the programs. And other kids that are down there, other kids in the neighborhoods, they'll see this, and they'll see you working out here, and they'll say hey, maybe these guys have got something.

Q. Mr. President, have you ever went to anybody's funeral that used drugs?

The President. Went to a funeral where the person died from drugs? I don't think so, but I've been to ceremonies honoring people whose lives were taken by the drug pushers and the drug criminals, like law enforcement people. And you go, and you give a medal—like when I was Vice President—you give a medal to a family, a widow, a woman whose husband had been killed trying to protect your neighborhood and mine from drugs. And that's sad, I'll tell you—people to give their lives, to fight so you guys can have a good environment and we all can.

What's that guy's name?

Q. Mr. President, what do you do to keep drugs out of your life?

The President. Keep them out of your life? Well, kind of getting along in my level of life here, the pressures aren't quite that big. You don't have a lot of guys coming up to you in daily life saying, hey. So, I don't have the temptations and the pressures that you've got, like young guys in school and all of that. But I think if I did I'd try to do what you're doing: I'd try to have that lifestyle going in such a way and helping the education programs and helping the law enforcement so people wouldn't be tempted to offer up those narcotics.

But I'm not saying it's the same. Now, like I'm President. It would be pretty hard for some drug guy to come into the White House and start offering it up, you know. It's different. We've got a lot of Secret Service guys there—hey, throw them right out of there. But it's different in a school or a community. And so, the pressures—I think I understand them, but I can't say that it's the same when you're in this job on that kind of thing. But I bet if they did, I hope I would say hey, get lost. We don't want any of that.

Mr. Smith. Besides the program they have set up here in Delaware, I think that you've really set the example by appointing one person in charge of it, which nobody has ever done before—to have somebody of the caliber of William Bennett, with his track record that he's done in education, to be in charge of it. I think he's going to inspire more people to start——

The President. And your Senators here, both Senator Roth and Senator Biden, have been in the forefront of that kind of battle. And so, it's a new office, and it's a tough deal for Bill because the statutory authority is blurred. Attorney General Thornburgh has direct responsibility as Attorney General, and yet, he's got to work cooperatively with the drug czar, the new leader of the fight. So, it's a job that is just being defined. This man is the first man in the whole country to have the responsibility under the law for coordinating all this drug policy and setting the policy. How would you like such a big job as that? [*Applause*]

Rashid, can I give you these to give to these kids? I guess we've got to go on. I'd much rather talk to you guys, I think. But that was wonderful.

Did you ever get kicked with a flying heel there when you're out there on the mat or anything? I'll be honest. I was a little nervous when I first got here, although I knew he wouldn't let you boot me around.

Thanks a lot.

Note: The President spoke at 11:55 a.m. in the gymnasium at the Young Men's Christian Association. Rashid Mustafa and Jeff Smith were karate instructors and counselors at the Wilmington Cluster Against Substance Abuse program. Prior to his remarks, the President viewed a karate demonstration. The President gave Mr. Mustafa patches that read "Kick Drugs Out of Your Life" for each child.

Remarks to the Law Enforcement Community in Wilmington, Delaware
March 22, 1989

Thank you, ladies and gentlemen, thank you all. Honored guests, thank you all very much. Thank you, Governor Castle, for the introduction, and all of you for the pleasure of your company. And let me say what an honor it is to be here among Delaware's finest and among friends.

I want to pay my respects to Lieutenant Governor Dale Wolf, and in particular, I want to salute four friends who share this platform. Bill Roth, your senior Senator—he's been a force for peace and prosperity. He and I were classmates in the Congress, both elected on the same day in 1966. We've been friends ever since, and I've been watching him in action. And not only is he known for his economic prowess and knowledge but he has been strong in fighting the use of crack and cocaine and other narcotics.

[Attorney General] Dick Thornburgh, America's chief law enforcement official, is here—say more about that in a minute. Our first Drug Control Policy Director—I'm trying not to say czar. [*Laughter*] There is something—I don't want to say un-American about it, but—[*laughter*]—it just doesn't ring why we set up a czar of baseball or a czar of the narcotics battle. But nevertheless, we've got a strong, tough guy; and if we were electing a czar, he might well qualify. [*Laughter*] But nevertheless, you're going to see him in action over the next 4 years. Both Dick and Bill are combating this menace which endangers us all.

And then as chairman of the Senate Judiciary Committee, your own Senator, Joe Biden. He was one of the principal architects of the legislation that created this new drug post. And he's been a tireless fighter out there, leading the way in the Senate. So, Bill Bennett, Bill Roth, Dick Thornburgh, Joe Biden, and I will work together to shape this drug strategy to really try to nurture a safer, fairer, and more decent land. I told Bill Roth, incidentally, if he didn't tell the ostrich joke, I wouldn't make him hear about Millie and the puppies.

[*Laughter*]

Earlier today, several of us were up over in Lancaster, Pennsylvania. And then I've just come right here now from your Y, from the Wilmington YMCA, where kids are learning karate and learning to avoid drugs through the Wilmington Cluster Against Substance Abuse program. And the message there in that group is: "Kick drugs out of your life." And sure enough, there they were. I almost got hit by a couple of heels flying by me. [*Laughter*] But I got a kick out of those kids. And come to think of it, the karate out there reminded me of a family dinner at Kennebunkport with our 11 grandchildren. I've never seen so much mayhem. [*Laughter*]

But there was a stronger message from those kids. You know, here they are, perhaps some of them out of underprivileged backgrounds, joined together, led by volunteers and others out there, teaching them to stay out of the drug culture. And I don't care whether you're President of the United States, a worthy citizen of Wilmington, just a plain guy coming off the street somewhere, it couldn't help but make a tremendous impression on anyone if you had a chance to see that program, see these little guys out there with discipline and energy and spirit, trying to do their part in this fight on drugs. It was an inspiration to me, and I won't forget it.

Getting ready for this visit, I thought of a poem that captured the spirit of this gathering and the true genius of America. The poet was Carl Sandburg, the poem entitled, "The People, Yes."

> "The People, Yes." They're retired laborers, textile workers, and pillars of the law.
> "The People, Yes." They live on the prairies in Nebraska, in the central valley of California, in the small burgs and factory towns of the first State of Delaware.
> "The People, Yes."

These Americans support their police and respect our legal system. And they cherish the decent stability which makes justice possible and our lives secure. My friends, nothing—nothing—threatens the stability of our families and our nation more than the scourge of drug abuse. And as a candidate for the office I now hold, I pledged to undertake a mission to try to make America free from drugs. Well, my selection of Secretary Bennett to direct the newly created Office of the National Drug Control Policy shows that I meant exactly what I said. As Secretary of Education, Bill was a crusader for excellence, challenging the educators all across this country to do better. And as America's first Drug Control Policy Director, he's engaged in an even greater struggle: America's war on drugs. He's going to do just fine.

This war seeks to educate all Americans on the inherent evils of drug abuse, and it'll encourage those caught in the trap of drug addiction to get clean and stay clean. And this war pledges increased support for those tasked with the dangerous job of stopping the flow of drugs into America. And it vows to enforce our drug laws.

Last month before a joint session of Congress, I spoke about four critical areas in the war on drugs: education, treatment, interdiction, and enforcement. And I asked for an increase of $1 billion in budget outlays—to nearly $6 billion in 1990 to escalate this war. Some money will be used to expand treatment to the poor and addicted young mothers. Some money will be used to cut the waiting time for treatment and to help urban schools where the emergency is the greatest. And $1.1 billion of my request will go for education.

And here in Delaware, you have shown the way. And it hasn't been easy. After all, Interstate I–95 is a major, major avenue of illicit drug trafficking—intersects the greater Wilmington area right here. But Delaware law enforcement officers—like one who is with us today, I'm told, Delaware State Police Corporal Durnan and many of you—are aggressively fighting this war. Where is the Corporal? And all the rest of them. I single him out, but I know he'd say it's everybody here, and all across this State, that are waging this fight. Under Governor Castle, your "Above the Influence" campaign is combating alcohol and drug abuse. And the Wilmington Cluster program aims to pull students together and help the communities help themselves. And for that, I congratulate you.

Delaware is waging war against drugs. And it's a war we must and will win. For while more than 200 million Americans didn't use illegal drugs last year, over 23 million Americans did. And that means we must stop those who produce and buy and traffic drugs. And that, in turn, means an all-out fight in enforcement and interdiction.

As you know, in the last year, the global production of coca and marijuana, opium poppies, hashish, increased sharply. And that supply abroad imperils our kids at home. It threatens countries like those that have been long friendly to the United States, and it reaffirms the need to stop drugs before they reach our borders and to eradicate them at their source.

I mentioned Bill Bennett, but let me just say a word about your neighbor, Mike Castle's former compadre, Governor Thornburgh. He's been on the cutting edge as the Governor, you see, fighting the problem at the State level. And the Governors are those out there delivering the services and working the problems of backing their law enforcement people. So, he's been through all that. And there is no one I can think of in the United States better suited now to be the chief law enforcement officer of the United States than Dick Thornburgh, your neighbor and our friend.

Two weeks ago, I asked Attorney General Thornburgh to go to South America to meet with the Presidents and top officials in Colombia and Bolivia and Peru. And the topic? How to curb drug production and arrest, convict, and destroy trafficking cartels. He came back with a very interesting and, in ways, troubling report. The Presidents may want to cooperate, and yet some of their communities are so wrecked by crime that it is extraordinarily difficult for them, no matter how good their intentions, to stand up against these illegal cartels and these armed gangs that seem to control the crops that destroy the lives of our kids. We hope to work more closely with our hemispheric neighbors in this vital effort. We're not going to give up on that at all.

And I'm glad to tell you that Dick reported to me that in these countries—and then through his contacts in others—they are much more eager now to get on with the task. Heretofore, I believe that the Presidents of the South American countries always felt that it was our problem and if it weren't for the rich Norte Americanos consuming the product, that then the problem would go away. But today, sadly, their own societies are adversely affected by drug use. And so, it isn't just the consuming United States. We are in this with our friends south of the border, and we're going to fight it in an international multilateral concept. We've got to destroy the crops and the labs that process the crops in these drug-producing countries. We've got to protect our borders; and that isn't easy, as you know, given the enormous length of the borders.

Our budget proposes $690 million for Coast Guard drug interdiction, which plays a major role in coordinating the identification and search of suspicious planes and vessels. We've also proposed more than $300 million in interdiction funds for the Department of Defense. All told, fully 70 percent of our drug budget is for law enforcement purposes. In particular, we want to significantly increase funding for Federal prisons. Why? Because prison overcrowding has caused too many convicts to go scot-free. And I will act also—and I'll need your help and backing—to enforce tougher sentences.

You know, I've talked a lot about zero tolerance. "Zero tolerance" is not a catchword. It means, quite simply, if you do crime, you do time. And that means judges who strictly apply the law to convicted drug offenders and severe sentences for dealers who hire children. And it means increasing Federal drug prosecutions. And, yes, it means strict enforcement—and I mean strict enforcement—of the Antidrug Abuse Act of 1988. I want increased prison sentences for drug-related crimes and, yes, the death penalty for drug kingpins and those who commit these drug-related murders. We owe our police officers nothing less than that. I was very pleased that yesterday the Supreme Court validated drug testing. I hope this will help achieve our goal of a drug-free workplace.

A secure community is the right of every American. Toward the end, guns can be imported under current law only if they are adapted for sporting purposes. That's the way the law reads now. We've recently taken a step and temporarily suspended the import of these AK–47's and certain other semiautomatic weapons into this country, as we continue to search for a solution to this difficult and complex problem.

I do believe—and I expect many in the room like me are sportsmen—I do believe in the legitimate right of sportsmen and others who own guns. But I also believe in supporting our police officers who lay their lives on the line. And I am convinced that the vast majority of sportsmen want to find a way to support our law enforcement officers, and I want to be with them in finding a solution to this problem. I said yesterday that I'm a member of the NRA [National Rifle Association], and I am. I have nothing to be ashamed of there. But I happen to believe that the vast majority of NRA members support the position I've just taken: that the time has come to do something about these automated weapons that are threatening the lives of these people behind me. And I'm going to see that it takes place.

You know, many issues involve shades of gray. Crime is not among them. Drug trade is not among them. It involves good guys and bad guys, white hats and black hats, good and evil. And many of you, I'm sure, have heard of Everett Hatcher—I'll bet these guys have—Federal agent involved in an undercover drug investigation. He was only 46 years old, the father of two. Barely 3 weeks ago, an hour after radioing colleagues that he was driving to a new site to meet a drug dealer, he was found shot to death in Staten Island. And earlier this month I met with his widow, Mary Jane—a very emotional moment. And we have offered $250,000 for information leading to the apprehension of the man wanted in connection with this murder. But it brought it home to me, loud and clear: We have got to win the war on drugs for Everett Hatcher and all those of your profession who have given their lives to free America of drug abuse.

To build a better life, to make tomorrow free of drugs, will require the will and spirit of the American people—people like Everett Hatcher, people like Corporal Durnan, people like you. And of this I am certain: As Americans, nothing lies beyond our reach. The people, yes. The future, yes. By serving one, let us seize the other.

And thank you for inviting me and for your many kindnesses. And God bless you all, and God bless the United States of America. Thank you very, very much.

Note: The President spoke at 12:35 p.m. in the Delaware Ballroom at the Radisson Hotel. He was introduced by Gov. Michael N. Castle. Following his remarks, the President returned to Washington, DC.

Statement by Press Secretary Fitzwater on President Bush's Telephone Conversation With President-Elect Alfredo Cristiani of El Salvador

March 22, 1989

President Bush spoke earlier today with Alfredo Cristiani, the winner of the Salvadoran Presidential election, to congratulate him on his victory. The President assured Mr. Cristiani that the United States would continue to work closely with El Salvador to help the Salvadorans create and protect a durable democracy there. Mr. Cristiani affirmed his recent public statements that he and his administration will be committed to respect for human rights. President Bush invited Mr. Cristiani to visit Washington at an early date.

On Sunday, March 19, hundreds of thousands of Salvadoran peasants, working people, business men and women, and citizens from every walk of life defied threats of death and terror from Marxist guerrillas to vote in that country's Presidential election. This was the sixth national election El

Salvador has held under international supervision in the last 7 years. What we witnessed last Sunday should leave no doubt: The people of El Salvador are passionately committed to the democratic rights and liberties they have fought for and won with U.S. support in recent years.

Our policy in El Salvador, forged through bipartisan consensus and with bipartisan support, is clear: We are committed to continue democratic progress and the defense of human rights. There must be no turning back to the dark and terrible past. We expect, and the Salvadoran people clearly desire, continued steady progress toward establishing the rule of law, an effective judicial system, and security against political violence from either the right or the left. There is also a message for the FMLN [Farabundo Marti National Liberation Front] guerrillas in Sunday's election: The Salvadoran people clearly yearn for an end to the terrible violence to which they have been subjected.

The time has come to end the violence and secure an honorable peace that will protect the rights and security of all Salvadorans, regardless of their political views, to participate in a safe and fair political process. If the FMLN would embrace that goal, we are confident that this tragic war can come to an end. The President welcomes Mr. Cristiani's stated commitment to continue the dialog with the FMLN guerrillas and hopes the guerrillas accept his offer. Moreover, the guerrillas will not succeed in obtaining the political victory in the United States that they cannot win among the people of El Salvador. The United States is committed to the defense of democracy and human rights in El Salvador. So long as El Salvador continues on that path, the United States will remain a firm and steady ally.

A final note: Last Sunday's election heralds the final months of the Presidency of José Napoleón Duarte, a great patriot and champion of democracy. The President salutes President Duarte for his courage, his patriotism, his steadfast commitment to democracy, and for his enormous and lasting contribution to building an authentic democratic process in his country.

Nomination of Kenneth W. Gideon To Be an Assistant Secretary of the Treasury

March 22, 1989

The President today announced his intention to nominate Kenneth W. Gideon to be Assistant Secretary of the Treasury (Tax Policy). He would succeed O. Donaldson Chapoton.

Since 1986 Mr. Gideon has been a partner with Fried, Frank, Harris, Shriver, and Jacobson in Washington, DC. Prior to this he was in practice with Fulbright and Jaworski, 1983–1986. He served as Chief Counsel for the Internal Revenue Service, 1981–1983. Mr. Gideon has served in several capacities on the American Bar Association including council member elected for a term to end 1990; chairman of the committee on government relations, 1984–1986; and chairman of the committee on court procedure, 1979–1981. He was the cochair of the task force on civil tax penalties, 1988.

Mr. Gideon graduated from Harvard University (B.A., 1968) and Yale Law School (J.D., 1971). Mr. Gideon resides in Washington, DC.

Nomination of Quincy Mellon Krosby To Be an Assistant Secretary of Commerce
March 22, 1989

The President today announced his intention to nominate Quincy Mellon Krosby to be Assistant Secretary of Commerce (Export Enforcement). She would succeed G. Philip Hughes.

Since 1982 Mrs. Krosby has been with the Department of State, serving in several capacities, including economic officer (energy attaché) for the U.S. Embassy in London; Special Assistant to the Under Secretary for Security Assistance, Science and Technology; Special Assistant to the Counselor of the Department; economic counselor for the U.S. Embassy in Bulgaria; and political/economic officer in the Office of East European and Yugoslav Affairs. Between 1973 and 1981, she was a consultant in London and Oslo for private firms and U.S. Government agencies and served as an adjunct college teacher for Union College, University of Minnesota, the London School of Economics, and Oslo University.

Mrs. Krosby received a bachelor of arts and a master of arts degree from the University of Minnesota and the London School of Economics and Political Science (Ph.D., 1979).

Nomination of Edward Martin Emmett To Be a Member of the Interstate Commerce Commission
March 22, 1989

The President today announced his intention to nominate Edward Martin Emmett to be a member of the Interstate Commerce Commission for a term expiring on December 31, 1992. He would succeed Frederic N. Andre.

Since 1986 Mr. Emmett has been executive director of the Texas Association to Improve Distribution. Prior to this he was executive director for the North Houston Association, 1983–1986. From 1979 to 1983, he was the owner of the Public Affairs Group. He was a State representative from Texas, 1979–1987, serving as chairman of the House Committee on Energy, 1985–1987, and a member of the House Committee on Transportation, 1979–1987. From 1976 to 1979, he was a policy analyst for Exxon Corp.

Mr. Emmett graduated from Rice University (B.A., 1971) and the University of Texas at Austin (M.A., 1974). He was born August 14, 1949, in New London, TX. Mr. Emmett is married, has four children, and resides in Round Rock, TX.

Nomination of Shirley D. Peterson To Be an Assistant Attorney General
March 23, 1989

The President today announced his intention to nominate Shirley D. Peterson to be Assistant Attorney General (Tax Division). She would succeed William S. Rose, Jr.

Since 1969 Mrs. Peterson has been in practice with Steptoe and Johnson and has been a partner since 1978. She currently serves in several capacities on the American

Bar Association, including chair of the estate and gift tax committee of the tax section and member of the real property, probate and trust law section committee. She is also a fellow of the American College of Probate Counsel, serving on the board of regents, the nominating committee, the estate and gift tax committee, and as chair of the transfer tax study committee. In addition, Mrs. Peterson served on the Assistant Attorney General's Advisory Committee on Tax Litigation, Department of Justice, 1982–1984.

Mrs. Peterson graduated from Bryn Mawr (A.B., 1963) and New York University School of Law (LL.B., 1967). She was born September 3, 1941, in Holly, CO. Mrs. Peterson is married, has two children, and resides in Bethesda, MD.

Nomination of E. Patrick Coady To Be United States Executive Director of the International Bank for Reconstruction and Development

March 23, 1989

The President today announced his intention to nominate E. Patrick Coady to be U.S. Executive Director of the International Bank for Reconstruction and Development for a term of 2 years. He would succeed Robert Brendon Keating.

Mr. Coady was chief financial officer for the Acacia Group in Washington, DC, 1985–1988. Prior to this he was managing general partner with the investment banking firm of Coady and Co. in New York City, 1981–1985. Mr. Coady was senior vice president with Dillon, Read and Co., Inc., in New York City, 1966–1980.

Mr. Coady graduated from Massachusetts Institute of Technology (B.S., 1960) and Harvard Graduate School of Business (M.B.A., 1966). He served in the U.S. Navy, 1960–1964. He is married, has three children, and resides in Great Falls, VA.

Remarks to the National Association of Manufacturers

March 23, 1989

Thank you, Dick, and thank all of you. Thank you very much for that warm welcome. Thank you for that warm welcome back. And Dick, thank you, sir, for introducing me and for what you're doing leading the NAM. I want to pay my respects to your president, former secretary, Sandy Trowbridge, who continues to do an outstanding job. Harry Truman used to say: "If you want a friend in Washington, buy a dog." [*Laughter*] And I'm here to disagree with him, because I feel in Dick, your chairman, and in Sandy, your president, and in the membership of this illustrious organization, that our administration has a friend not only in Washington but all across the country.

And I am very grateful for that, and I normally would not dare to speak for our new illustrious Secretary of Commerce, Bob Mosbacher, but in this regard I expect I'm saying exactly what he feels. And I might say to you, the members of the NAM, it is a wonderful thing to have him at my side, a successful businessman who knows what it means to take risks, knows what it means to try to keep the costs down, and knows what it means to add to the productivity of this country. And Bob Mosbacher is already doing a superb job.

After one tough football game, somebody asked Knute Rockne why Notre Dame had lost. And he answered, "I won't know until my barber tells me on Monday." [*Laughter*] Well, nobody is second-guessing American manufacturing anymore. And clearly, you all are playing a winning game.

And I'm here today to tell you that deindustrialization that we read about is a myth. And manufacturing, as a share of our national output, is as strong today as it has ever been. And I think many people in this room deserve great credit for that. Thanks to the hard work of you people, who are the brains and the muscle of our basic industries, we're producing more products with a smaller percentage of our population than ever before. And that, my friends, is productivity. And that is why since 1982 our manufacturing output has gone up twice as fast as Western Europe and has kept pace with Japan. You're the producers—is somebody's heart beating very fast over there or what the heck's going on? [*Laughter*]

[*The President referred to a thumping noise coming from the back of the room.*]

In the technological age in which we're living, I'm sure we can—[*laughter*]. No, but you are the producers who are building a better America. And I think that your presence demonstrates that you are fighting to win the international struggle for continued growth. You've demonstrated that you can make America more competitive and that you can keep America more competitive.

So, I'm not saying you're going to have to do it alone. There's a role for government; sometimes political leadership is needed, for example, to keep international trade free and fair. But I will tell you that this government will not confuse involvement with interference.

And there's a lot of talk about competitiveness going around these days, and in a way that's a very good thing. But competitiveness is more than just the latest trade figures or the latest quarterly earnings or the latest poll—or the latest election, for that matter. Surely our success can be measured by better methods than these. This is a good time for us to look towards a larger horizon. And we stand at a special moment in our history. We're prosperous. We are at peace. And at such a point, we've got to set our sights higher. And we must look farther ahead. It's hard for us to believe, but the 21st century is only 11 years from now.

And you've called this conference the New Leadership Summit. Leadership is certainly found in those like you who keep the great engines of American industry turning. In creating jobs and building businesses and meeting needs, our nation's manufacturers have shown the qualities that will carry us into the future. And make no mistake, the challenges we face will test your vision and your capacity to define an agenda for action. So, today I'd like to address that very point by outlining my agenda for the next American century.

To build a better America, one of the most important priorities for this government will be to encourage savings and long-term investment, to get our fiscal house in order—and that means, priority, bringing down the Federal budget deficit.

And last month, one of the very first things we did was to submit a budget to Congress with a clear agenda to cut the Federal deficit and enhance business' ability to plan, expand, and build. And next year, under current law—there are no changes in the revenue laws—the economic growth we are currently enjoying will increase Federal revenues by more than $80 billion without increasing the tax rates. And our plan will hold the line on spending, using some of those new revenues to slash the deficit by more than 40 percent and meeting those Gramm-Rudman-Hollings targets.

To encourage long-range investment in businesses of all sizes, it's time that we restored the capital gains differential by reducing the capital gains rate to 15 percent on long-held assets. And this really is a case where less means more: more revenue to the Federal Government. The Treasury now estimates that my proposal would bring in $4.8 billion of new revenues in 1990. That's the Treasury estimate. And the critics all say, and have climbed on us in saying, "This is a tax cut for the rich." I say, cut the capital gains rate, and you'll have more jobs for the poor and others, and more growth and opportunity for the whole country. Competitiveness, opportunity, saving and investing for the long term—this is why we need a capital gains tax rate cut. And it's why we need one now. And I am going to keep on fighting to see that the Congress gives the people that which they deserve: more opportunity and more jobs.

To spur investment in basic research, we've proposed a permanent research and experimentation tax credit. We've also proposed a 13-percent increase for science and technology programs and intend to double the National Science Foundation's budget by 1993 to guarantee that America's technology is number one.

A strong economy needs a safe and secure banking system. And that's why we proposed a comprehensive plan to solve the difficulties of our savings and loan industry; and I'm delighted that our very able Secretary of the Treasury, Nick Brady, was over here this morning talking to you about the broad principles of that plan. Frankly, the plan has been pretty darn well received on both sides of the aisle on Capitol Hill. And in my speech to the Congress I challenged the Congress to act within 45 days. This is a matter of considerable national urgency.

We want to ease the pressures now building on the most important organization in America—the family—by promoting choice on issues like child care. So, last week I sent legislation to Congress that puts money and options in the hands of parents rather than in the hands of the bureaucracies. And we are going to keep on pushing for that concept. I do not want to have my administration identified with one single initiative that diminishes parental choice or in any way weakens the family. The Government must do what it can to strengthen family.

I'd say, though, that the most powerful key to long-term competitiveness is education. A strengthened education system is the essential ingredient for America's prosperity into the next decade, into the next century. But no one suggests that education is a minor matter on the national agenda. It is vital to everything we are and can become. Make no mistake about it, I understand the historic role of the communities and of the States, and I understand the limited role that is properly assigned the Federal Government. So, I don't want you to feel that I'm moving towards centralizing control over our schools in Washington, DC.

There are no quick fixes in education. Like most of the long-term issues on the national agenda, American education won't be fixed with a bolt of lightning or a puff of smoke. It's going to take collective effort at all levels, public and private, to get it right. And those businesses that are involved with local schools—developing the work force at its source—are making fail-safe investments. And they stand to reap the greatest rewards.

I wish Barbara were here to talk to you a little bit about her interest in literacy and to salute as she does the business community for its involvement. I talk about a Thousand Points of Light. And if there's ever an example of that, it is the wide array of business people and business interests that are out there helping in the field of education. I didn't much like it when I talked about a Thousand Points of Light and some cynic around here made some reference, "What he really is talking about is a thousand pints of Lite." [*Laughter*]

But I do salute you for your outreach. For those workers that are already on the line, we must build new skills and flexibility, as jobs change, through training and retraining. The NAM policy position that you adopted last year said that "investment in human resources is at least as important as investment in equipment and technology." And you're absolutely right on that one. Machinery and technology alone don't improve productivity; people do.

Another issue where we plan to play for keeps—we're determined, and we are going to keep working at this one—to get the drugs out of the workplace. Drug and alcohol abuse in the workplace costs $60 billion every year, putting productivity and lives at risk.

Drug abuse in America really must stop, and we're off to a fast start. Last month I talked to the Congress about four decisive issues: education, treatment, interdiction, and enforcement. And I asked for an increase of $1 billion in budget outlays—to nearly $6 billion in 1990—to escalate this effort. But we'll also be looking to you to set effective, well-reasoned drug policies in your businesses.

Employers can teach their people to recognize the signs of substance abuse in their coworkers and understand how drug abuse hurts the nonusers on the line. I've called for a drug-free workplace. And Tuesday's Supreme Court decision, one that just came down the day before yesterday, affirms drug testing. And that's going to give this concept of a drug-free workplace a much better chance of success.

Any long-term agenda must also ask how we can leave the Earth we've inherited a little better than when we found it. And I was delighted to see Russ Train here, Bill Ruckelshaus here, and I understand they did a first-class job in addressing themselves, with their background of experience, to this question.

We've got to devise answers to the problems of ozone depletion and global warming and acid rain. We've already joined with other nations to call for the elimination of CFC's [chlorofluorocarbons] and the development of environmentally safe substitutes, as well as adopting a tough new policy on the export of hazardous waste. We can do these things without stifling the economic growth that is necessary, indeed, essential for our nation's economic health. The time has come to set aside partisan approaches to these and these other enormous environmental questions. We've got to ensure that our grandchildren can fish on the same lakes we've enjoyed.

And in this agenda for the new American century, I've asked you to consider a broad vision, a vision that relies on the dynamic spirit that is America: the spirit that says buildings should not stand empty while people lack shelter; jobs should not go unfilled while young men and women stand idle on the street corners; no one should go hungry in the richest Nation on the face of the Earth. And we must promote local efforts to assure that every American can seize a share of this prosperity and help to create more of it, whether through the constellation of local community groups already at work or through new ideas, like our program to encourage our nation's youth to become involved in community service. I'm absolutely convinced that, with the proper leadership from the White House and across the business community and elsewhere, we can encourage those young people who are more fortunate than some of their peers to pitch in and help those that are less fortunate.

We're going to rely less on the collective wallet—we have to, to do what I told you I want to do on the budget—less on the collective wallet and more on the collective will. But this does not mean lowering our sights or our expectations. It's just exactly the opposite of that. In the era of tight budgets, we're not going to simply "make do with less." We're going to learn how to do more with less—and do it better. In the factory, you call it productivity. Across our country, I call it the national spirit.

And, yes, we're a prosperous country, and we are at peace. But such quiet moments often become pivotal in the Nation's history. The choices we make now are going to determine whether the door to the next American century is closing or opening wide, for all who dare to dream.

Thank you for your leadership. Thank you for the support of our administration. And aren't we lucky to be living in 1989 in the United States of America, the best, the freest, the greatest country on the face of the Earth? Thank you all, and God bless you.

Note: The President spoke at 1:23 p.m. in the Grand Ballroom at the Mayflower Hotel. In his remarks, he referred to Richard E. Heckert and Alexander (Sandy) B. Trowbridge, chairman and president of the association, respectively; and Russell E. Train and William D. Ruckelshaus, former Administrators of the Environmental Protection Agency.

Nomination of Walter J.P. Curley To Be United States Ambassador to France

March 23, 1989

The President today announced his intention to nominate Walter J.P. Curley to be Ambassador Extraordinary and Plenipotentiary of the United States of America to France. He would succeed Joe M. Rodgers.

Since 1977 Ambassador Curley has been with W.J.P. Curley, Venture Capital, in New York City. Prior to this he was U.S. Ambassador to Ireland, 1975–1977. From 1958 to 1975, Ambassador Curley was with J.H. Whitney and Co., Venture Capital, in New York City. He was with California Texas Oil Co. in India and Italy, 1948–1957. Ambassador Curley also served as commissioner of public events and chief of protocol for New York City, 1973–1974.

Ambassador Curley attended Yale University (B.A., 1944); the University of Oslo in Norway, 1947; Harvard University (M.B.A., 1948); and Trinity College (LL.D., 1976). He served as a captain in the U.S. Marine Corps, 1943–1946. He is married, has four children, and resides in Bedford Village, NY.

Nomination of Franklin Eugene Bailey To Be an Assistant Secretary of Agriculture

March 23, 1989

The President today announced his intention to nominate Franklin Eugene Bailey to be Assistant Secretary of Agriculture (Government and Public Affairs). He would succeed Wilmer D. Mizell, Sr.

Since 1987 Mr. Bailey has been a government relations representative of the National Cotton Council of America in Washington, DC. Prior to this he was executive director of the southeast area for the Agriculture Stabilization and Conservation Service of the Department of Agriculture in Washington, DC, 1985–1987; Deputy Director of Administration, Personnel Policies and Budget, 1983–1985; agricultural programs coordinator, 1981–1983; and a senior policy specialist, 1978–1981.

Mr. Bailey received a bachelor of science degree and a master of public administration degree from James Mason University. He was born July 31, 1949, in Phenix, VA. He is married, has two children, and resides in Fredericksburg, VA.

Nomination of Jo Ann D. Smith To Be an Assistant Secretary of Agriculture

March 23, 1989

The President today announced his intention to nominate Jo Ann D. Smith to be Assistant Secretary of Agriculture (Marketing and Inspection). She would succeed Kenneth A. Gilles.

Since 1958 Mrs. Smith has been an operating partner, secretary, and treasurer of Smith Brothers Farming and Ranching in Wacahoota, FL. In addition she served as vice president of Smith Construction Co., 1962–1988, and as a marketing and public relations consultant for White Meat Packers, 1981–1988. Mrs. Smith served as chairman of the Cattlemen's Beef Promotion and Research Board from 1986 to 1988 and president of the National Cattlemen's Association in 1985. She has also served as chairman of the board for the Federal Reserve Bank of Jacksonville, FL, 1984–1986, and as a member of the board of governors for the Chicago Mercantile Board of Trade, 1985–1987. She was a member of the U.S. Advisory Committee for Trade Negotiations, 1985–1987, and a member of the Governor's Task Force on the Future of Florida Agriculture, 1984–1986. Mrs. Smith has served on the executive committee of the National Cattlemen's Association, 1982–1988.

Mrs. Smith was born May 9, 1939, in Gainesville, FL. She is married, has two children, and currently resides in Micanopy, FL.

Nomination of James E. Cason To Be an Assistant Secretary of Agriculture

March 23, 1989

The President today announced his intention to nominate James E. Cason to be Assistant Secretary of Agriculture (Special Services). He would succeed George S. Dunlop.

Since 1985 Mr. Cason has been Principal Deputy Assistant Secretary for Land and Minerals Management at the Department of the Interior in Washington, DC. Prior to this he was Special Assistant to the Director for the Bureau of Land Management, 1982–1985. Mr. Cason was operations manager for Fred Meyer, Inc., in Portland, OR, 1981–1982; a partner, office manager, and salesman for ACM Real Estate, Inc., 1979–1981; and campaign manager with the committee to elect Lynn Engdahl, 1979–1980. Mr. Cason has also served as vice president for Cascade Overview Development Enterprises, Inc., 1978–1979, and project manager with the Western Environmental Trade Association, 1976–1978.

Mr. Cason graduated from Pacific University (B.A., 1976). He currently resides in Falls Church, VA.

The President's News Conference

March 24, 1989

The President. Well, let me first welcome the congressional leadership—Speaker, majority leader, and Senator Dole, Senator Michel, Congressman Foley—to the White House.

In my Inaugural Address, I advocated a bipartisan foreign policy; and today we, the Executive and the Congress, Republicans and Democrats, will be speaking with one voice on an extremely important foreign policy issue: Central America. We've signed today in the Cabinet Room a bipartisan accord on Central America which sets out the broad outlines of U.S. policy toward the region. We're seeking the same goals as those of the people of Central America: democracy, security, and peace.

In order to meet the challenge of realizing those goals, we must work together with Latin American democratic leaders, with the support of our European friends. Under the Esquipulas accord, insurgent forces have the right to reintegrate into their homeland under safe, democratic conditions with full civil and political rights, and that is the desire of the Nicaraguan resistance.

To achieve our objectives the bipartisan leadership of Congress has agreed to support my request for continued humanitarian assistance at current levels through the elections in Nicaragua scheduled for February 28, 1990. We do not claim the right to order the politics of Nicaragua; that is for the Nicaraguan people to decide. The Esquipulas accord requires a free, open political process in which all groups can participate. The playing field must be level. The burden of proof is on the Sandinista government to comply with the promises that it has made since 1979. And if they comply, we have an opportunity to start a new day in Central America.

The Soviet Union also has an obligation and an opportunity to demonstrate its "new thinking." In other regional conflicts, it's adopted a welcome new approach, but in Central America, what we've seen to date is only "old thinking." The Soviet Union has no legitimate security interests in Central America; the United States has many. We reject any doctrine of equivalence in the region. The Soviet Union and Cuba have an obligation to stop violating the provisions of Esquipulas.

Some see violence and despair in Central America, but I have a different view of its future. I can see a democratic Central America in which all nations in the region live in peace, where resources are devoted to social ends instead of military defense. I hope the Esquipulas accord and the bipartisan accord that we've signed here will someday be seen as the first step toward that future.

And now I'd like to ask Secretary Baker to say a word, and then I think the leaders would each like to say something. And they will respond to your questions.

Mr. Secretary, and thank you gentlemen, very much. Mr. Speaker, thank you, sir.

Speaker Wright. It's been a pleasure.

The President. Bob, thank you.

Reporter. Mr. President, does this mean the end of the war in Nicaragua?

The President. I'd refer the questions to the leadership and to the Secretary of State.

Note: The President's ninth news conference began at 10:25 a.m. in the Briefing Room at the White House.

Bipartisan Accord on Central America
March 24, 1989

The Executive and the Congress are united today in support of democracy, peace, and security in Central America. The United States supports the peace and democratization process and the goals of the Central American Presidents embodied in the Esquipulas Accord. The United States is committed to working in good faith with the democratic leaders of Central America and Latin America to translate the bright promises of Esquipulas II into concrete realities on the ground.

With regard to Nicaragua, the United States is united in its goals: democratization; an end to subversion and destabilization of its neighbors; an end to Soviet bloc military ties that threaten U.S. and regional security. Today the Executive and the Congress are united on a policy to achieve those goals.

To be successful the Central American peace process cannot be based on promises alone. It must be based on credible standards of compliance, strict timetables for enforcement, and effective on-going means to verify both the democratic and security requirements of those agreements. We support the use of incentives and disincentives to achieve U.S. policy objectives.

We also endorse an open, consultative process with bipartisanship as the watchword for the development and success of a unified policy towards Central America. The Congress recognizes the need for consistency and continuity in policy and the responsibility of the Executive to administer and carry out that policy, the programs based upon it, and to conduct American diplomacy in the region. The Executive will consult regularly and report to the Congress on progress in meeting the goals of the peace and democratization process, including the use of assistance as outlined in this Accord.

Under Esquipulas II and the El Salvador Accord, insurgent forces are supposed to voluntarily reintegrate into their homeland under safe, democratic conditions. The United States shall encourage the Government of Nicaragua and the Nicaraguan Resistance to continue the cessation of hostilities currently in effect.

To implement our purposes, the Executive will propose and the bipartisan leadership of the Congress will act promptly after the Easter Recess to extend humanitarian assistance at current levels to the Resistance through February 28, 1990, noting that the Government of Nicaragua has agreed to hold new elections under international supervision just prior to that date. Those funds shall also be available to support voluntary reintegration or voluntary regional relocation by the Nicaraguan Resistance. Such voluntary reintegration or voluntary regional relocation assistance shall be provided in a manner supportive of the goals of the Central American nations, as expressed in the Esquipulas II agreement and the El Salvador Accord, including the goal of democratization within Nicaragua, and the reintegration plan to be developed pursuant to those accords.

We believe that democratization should continue throughout Central America in those nations in which it is not yet complete with progress towards strengthening of civilian leadership, the defense of human rights, the rule of law and functioning judicial systems, and consolidation of free, open, safe, political processes in which all groups and individuals can fairly compete for political leadership. We believe that democracy and peace in Central America can create the conditions for economic integration and development that can benefit all the people of the region and pledge ourselves to examine new ideas to further those worthy goals.

While the Soviet Union and Cuba both publicly endorsed the Esquipulas Agreement, their continued aid and support of violence and subversion in Central America is in direct violation of that regional agreement. The United States believes that President Gorbachev's impending visit to Cuba represents an important opportunity for both the Soviet Union and Cuba to end all aid that supports subversion and destabilization in Central America as President Arias has requested and as the Central American peace process demands.

The United States Government retains ultimate responsibility to define its national interests and foreign policy, and nothing in this Accord shall be interpreted to infringe on that responsibility. The United States need not spell out in advance the nature or type of action that would be undertaken in response to threats to U.S. national security interests. Rather it should be sufficient to simply make clear that such threats will be met by any appropriate Constitutional means. The spirit of trust, bipartisanship, and common purpose expressed in this Accord between the Executive and the Congress shall continue to be the foundation for its full implementation and the achievement of democracy, security, and peace in Central America.

George Bush
President of the United States

James C. Wright, Jr.
Speaker of the House

George J. Mitchell
Senate Majority Leader

Thomas S. Foley
House Majority Leader

Robert Dole
Senate Republican Leader

Robert H. Michel
House Republican Leader

The White House,
March 24, 1989.

Statement on the Bipartisan Accord on Central America
March 24, 1989

The President of a Central American democracy was asked recently what is the most important step the United States can take. He said: "Speak with one voice." Today, for the first time in many years, the President and Congress, the Democratic and Republican leadership in the House and Senate, are speaking with one voice about Central America.

In my Inaugural Address I reached out my hand to the leadership of Congress in both parties asking them to join with me to rebuild a bipartisan foreign policy based on trust and common purpose. Today I am gratified that the Speaker and the majority and minority leaders of the Senate and House have extended their hands back to me.

We have signed today together a bipartisan accord on Central America. It sets out the broad outlines of U.S. policy towards that troubled region and commits both the Executive and Congress to work together to achieve it.

The goals we seek are the goals which the people of Central America yearn for: democracy, security, and peace. Those are the pledges made by the Central American Presidents in the Esquipulas II accord. That agreement is an integrated whole: All of its provisions must move forward together if any of them are to be fulfilled. Our challenge now is to turn those promises into concrete realities on the ground.

The only way we can meet that challenge is if Latin democratic leaders and the United States work together, with the support of our European friends and allies, as true partners with candor and mutual respect. I believe Latin leaders are asking for that kind of relationship as we confront together the many challenges facing our hemisphere. As President, I pledge the United States is ready to respond.

Under this Central America agreement, insurgent forces have the right to reintegrate into their homeland under safe, democratic conditions with full civil and political rights. That is the desire of the Nicaraguan resistance. It is what they are fighting for. We hope and believe it can be achieved through a concerted diplomatic effort to enforce this regional agreement. To achieve these goals, the bipartisan leadership of Congress has agreed to support my request for continued humanitarian assistance to the Nicaraguan resistance through the elections scheduled in Nicaragua for February 28, 1990.

There will be extensive consultations and review with respect to these funds effective November 30, 1989 by the bipartisan leadership and relevant committees. However, I have been assured that the leadership in both Houses supports the extension of this assistance through the Nicaraguan elections, barring unforeseen circumstances.

There is no shortcut to democracy, no quick fix. The next weeks and months will demand patience and perseverance by the democratic community and the hard, technical work of ensuring compliance with the Esquipulas accord. The United States will work in good faith to support that kind of diplomatic effort, but we will not support a paper agreement that sells out the Nicaraguan people's right to be free.

We do not claim the right to order the politics of that country; that is for the people of Nicaragua to decide. We support what the Esquipulas accord requires: free, open political processes in which all groups can fairly and safely compete for political leadership. That means the playing field must be level; all, including the current government, must respect the majority's decision in the end; and the losers must also retain the political rights to operate as a legal opposition and contest again for political authority in the next recurring election contest.

The burden of proof is on the Sandinista government to do something it has steadfastly refused to do from 1979 to 1989: to keep its promises to the Nicaraguan people to permit real democracy, keep its promises to its neighbors not to support subversion in Central America, and keep its obligation to this hemisphere not to permit the establishment of Soviet-bloc bases in Central America. If those promises are kept, we have an opportunity to start a new day in Central America; but if those pledges continue to be violated, we hope and expect that other nations will find ways to join us to condemn those actions and reverse those processes.

The Soviet Union also has an obligation and an opportunity: to demonstrate that its proclaimed commitment to "new thinking" is more than a tactical response to temporary setbacks, but represents instead a new principled approach to foreign policy. In other regional conflicts around the world, the Soviet Union has adopted a welcome new approach that has helped resolve longstanding problems in constructive ways. In Central America, what we have seen from the Soviet Union and Cuba can only be described as "old thinking."

In the last decade, the Soviet bloc has poured at least $50 billion in aid into Cuba and Nicaragua. Soviet and Cuban aid is building in Nicaragua a military machine larger than all the armies of the other Central American nations combined and continues to finance violence, revolution, and destruction against the democratically elected government of El Salvador. Indeed, Soviet-bloc military support for the Marxist guerrillas has increased since the United States ended military support for the Nicaraguan resistance, and Soviet military aid to the Government of Nicaragua continues at levels wholly uncalled for by any legitimate defensive needs. The continuation of these levels of Soviet-bloc aid into Central America raises serious questions about Soviet attitudes and intentions towards the United States.

The Soviet Union has no legitimate security interest in Central America, and the United States has many. We reject any doctrine of equivalence of interest in this region as a basis for negotiations. Instead, the Soviet Union and Cuba have an obligation to the leaders of Central America to stop violating the provisions of the Esquipulas accord, which the Soviet Union and Cuba both pledged to uphold. The time to begin is now.

In signing the Esquipulas accord, President Oscar Arias of Costa Rica said: "Without democracy, there can be no peace in Central America." He is right. But with democracy and peace in Central America can come new hope for economic development in which all of the people of the region can share. One can look at the terrible violence ravaging Central America and despair, but I have a different vision of its future. I can see a democratic Central America in which all of the Nations of the region live in peace with each other; where the citizens of the region are safe from the violence of the state or from revolutionary guerrillas; where resources now devoted to military defense could be channeled to build hospitals, homes, and schools. That is not a dream if all the people and nations of the Americas will it to be true. I hope the Esquipulas accord and perhaps, also, the bipartisan accord will someday be seen as the first step toward its fulfillment.

Remarks on Greeting the Crew of the Space Shuttle *Discovery*
March 24, 1989

The President. Dr. Fletcher and Admiral Truly, Commander Mike Coats and crew, friends and families: First, let me just take a second to salute Dr. Fletcher, whose name has become almost synonymous with NASA's. And as you know, he will be retiring on April 8th, and I want to thank him for his example, for his leadership, and for his commitment to this space program. He's been an inspiration to everybody not just in this administration and in government but all across the country, and we all owe him a vote of great thanks. [*Applause*]

And I think Jim, like these gentlemen with me, show that America is a family. And there are moments when we celebrate as a family would—moments of remembrance and moments of pride. And last Saturday, nearly half a million people welcomed these gentlemen's return to Andrews—Andrews—Freudian slip—[*laughter*]—Edwards Air Force Base. And they were there to pay America's respects to your courage and to your enterprise. And today, we, too, salute the story that you've written. You've shown once again that teamwork works. And in a sense, though, your triumph is personal. After all, it's you who braved the elements and performed the tasks which made this mission such a success.

But in a larger sense, the story of *Discovery* is as American as "Opening Day," timeless as our history. And it says that, to Americans, nothing lies beyond our reach. It speaks to our capacity to dare and to dream the impossible. My friends, this quality has graced every great moment of the American story. And by enriching our lives and our children's lives, it can shape America's dreams of the 21st century.

On the flight of *Discovery,* you showed anew America's genius in science and technology. By conducting the protein crystal growth experiments, you furthered advancements in medical research. And you used the IMAX camera to study this planet's environmental damage. And I hope that this will lead—I'm confident it will—to our knowledge base and that that, in turn, will lead to reducing the threat to our Earth's environment. And you launched a TDRS [tracking and data relay] satellite, which completes the satellite communications network that will allow us more effectively and efficiently to relay data from all of our scientific satellites to Earth. And in short, you showed exactly where we are going and why. And we're exploring the new horizons of this nation's technological future. For as Americans, we are driven always by a restlessness to do better. This desire links the generations and has pushed back the frontiers of research and exploration.

For evidence, I point to two students here today. They show how tomorrow's technological promise lies in the youth of today. John Vellinger was in ninth grade when he started work on an experiment using chicken embryos to study how tissues develop in weightlessness. And last week his experiment flew on shuttle *Discovery.* And so did the work of Andrew Fras. His experiment studied microgravity's effect on the healing of bones. John and Andrew show how America's future will depend, in space and on Earth, on our most precious resource: our youth.

You know, Adlai Stevenson once spoke of the awful majesty of outer space. This voyage of the shuttle *Discovery* is over, but its spirit lives, linking the majesty of outer space with the greatness of America. And we're going to forge even stronger links as we reaffirm our commitment to the shuttle program, as our science missions open up new horizons of knowledge, and as space station *Freedom* symbolizes the promise of man. As we do, we will honor the spirit of *Discovery,* the spirit which throws open the possibilities of tomorrow and which points us toward the stars.

Gentlemen, your mission is accomplished. Your nation says, well done! Thank you, God bless you, and God bless America. Thank you, fellas.

Commander Coats. Well, thank you, Mr. President. We deeply appreciate your words of support for our country's space program. We represent thousands of people that work very hard to get the shuttle off the ground each time. And the encouragement you've shown is deeply appreciated.

We also appreciate your words talking about family and the importance of youth. All of us on this crew are very proud of our wives and of our children. And when we're not working in the space program, we're talking about our families. And it's been very encouraging to us to see you and Mrs. Bush and the emphasis that you place on family. We think it's wonderful, and we applaud that, sir.

We presented Mrs. Bush with a gold shuttle charm on a necklace earlier this morning. When it became obvious that we would be flying the first flight of this administration, we had a lot of discussion about what to fly for the President. And it became apparent quickly that we really wanted to fly something for Mrs. Bush as well. She's obviously a very special lady and she's very special to us. And we presented that with her this morning, and we'd like to thank you for a very special First Lady.

When we discussed what to fly for our new President, most of us, of course, being home-ported in Houston, Texas, wanted to fly a Texas flag. It became obvious that, as proud as we are of our new President being from Texas, it probably wasn't appropriate to give you a Texas flag, sir, since you're now President of all these United States. So, we did fly a United States flag, and we'd like to present that to you right now, sir. And with it goes this plaque that says, "Presented to the President of the United States of America, George Bush. This United States flag was flown in the official flight kit aboard the orbiter *Discovery*, STS 29, March 13th through 18th, 1989." And each of the crew members have signed it. Sir, thank you very much.

The President. That's lovely. Well, thank you for the special—that actually went? Thank you all. Let me get the wives to come up. Come up here, ladies, so they can get a fitting group picture here. Pick out a husband. [*Laughter*]

I'd like to ask the Members of Congress that are here to come and say hello to these gentlemen before they head on back to Houston, Texas, which I understand they're fixing to do right after this. So, I see some right here. Come on, you guys. Jim, Jamie, and the Senator—come on. We'll just say a quick hello to these people, because I don't know if they're going to have the chance—Congress is out—to go up to the Hill. Here's Jim Sensenbrenner here. This is the chairman. Be nice to this guy. [*Laughter*]

Note: The President spoke at 11:30 a.m. in Room 450 of the Old Executive Office Building. In his closing remarks, he referred to Representatives F. James Sensenbrenner, Jr., of Wisconsin and Jamie L. Whitten of Mississippi, and Senator Quentin N. Burdick of North Dakota. The space shuttle "Discovery" was launched on March 13 from the Kennedy Space Center in Cape Canaveral, FL, and returned to Edwards Air Force Base, CA, on March 18. The members of the crew were: Capt. Michael L. Coats, USN, flight commander; Col. John E. Blaha, USAF, mission pilot; Col. James F. Buchli and Col. Robert C. Springer, USMC, mission specialists; and James P. Bagian, physician and mission specialist.

Nomination of William H. Taft IV To Be United States Permanent Representative to the North Atlantic Treaty Organization Council

March 24, 1989

The President today announced his intention to nominate William H. Taft IV to be the U.S. Permanent Representative on the Council of the North Atlantic Treaty Organization with the rank and status of Ambassador Extraordinary and Plenipotentiary. He would succeed Alton Keel.

Since 1984 Mr. Taft has been Deputy Secretary of Defense in Washington, DC. Prior to this he was General Counsel at the Department of Defense, 1981–1984. Mr. Taft was a partner with the law firm of Leva, Hawes, Symington, Martin and Oppenheimer in Washington, DC, 1977–1981; General Counsel at the Department of Health, Education, and Welfare, 1973–1976; Executive Assistant to the Director in the Office of Management and Budget, 1972–1973; and Special Assistant to the Deputy Director in the Office of Management and Budget, 1970–1972. He was attorney adviser to the Chairman of the Federal Trade Commission, 1970, and an associate with Winthrop, Stimson, Putnam and Roberts of New York City, 1969–1970.

Mr. Taft graduated from Yale College (B.A., 1966) and Harvard Law School (J.D., 1969). He was born September 13, 1945, in Washington, DC. He is married, has three children, and resides in Lorton, VA.

Nomination of Joseph B. Gildenhorn To Be United States Ambassador to Switzerland
March 24, 1989

The President today announced his intention to nominate Joseph B. Gildenhorn to be Ambassador Extraordinary and Plenipotentiary of the United States of America to Switzerland. He would succeed Philip D. Winn.

Since 1962 Mr. Gildenhorn has served as president and director of JBG Real Estate Associates, Inc., in Washington, DC. He has also been a senior partner with Brown, Gildenhorn, and Jacobs in Washington, DC, 1958 to present. Prior to this Mr. Gildenhorn served as an attorney with the Office of the General Counsel of the Securities and Exchange Commission in Washington, DC, 1956–1958. Mr. Gildenhorn has served in several capacities with the United Jewish Appeal Federation of Greater Washington, including president, 1987–1989; vice president, 1986–1987; and major gifts chairman, 1981–1983.

Mr. Gildenhorn graduated from the University of Maryland (B.S., 1951) and Yale University Law School (LL.B. and J.D., 1954). Mr. Gildenhorn was born September 17, 1929, in Washington, DC. He is married, has two children, and currently resides in Washington, DC.

Nomination of Paul Matthews Cleveland To Be United States Ambassador to Malaysia
March 24, 1989

The President today announced his intention to nominate Paul Matthews Cleveland to be Ambassador Extraordinary and Plenipotentiary of the United States of America to Malaysia. He would succeed John Cameron Monjo.

Since 1986 Mr. Cleveland has served as Ambassador to New Zealand and Ambassador to Western Samoa. Prior to this Mr. Cleveland served as Deputy Chief of Mission at the U.S. Embassy in Seoul, South Korea. Mr. Cleveland has served in several capacities at the Department of State, including Director of Korean Affairs, 1981–1982; Director of Thai Affairs, 1980–1981; Deputy Director and Director of Regional Affairs, East Asian Bureau, 1977–1980; political counselor in Seoul, South Korea, 1973–1977; Special Assistant to the Assistant Secretary for East Asian Affairs, 1970–1973; economic officer at the Office of Fuels and Energy, 1968–1970; and economic officer in Jakarta, Indonesia, 1965–1968.

Mr. Cleveland graduated from Yale University (B.A., 1953) and Fletcher School of Law and Diplomacy (M.A., 1965). He was born August 25, 1931, in Boston, MA. Mr. Cleveland is married, has four children, and resides in McLean, VA.

Nomination of Chic Hecht To Be United States Ambassador to the Bahamas
March 24, 1989

The President today announced his intention to nominate Senator Chic Hecht to be Ambassador Extraordinary and Plenipotentiary of the United States of America to the

Commonwealth of the Bahamas. He would succeed Carol Boyd Hallett.

Senator Hecht served in the United States Senate, representing the State of Nevada from 1983 to 1989. Senator Hecht served in the Nevada State senate and was senate minority leader, 1967–1975. He also served as a special agent in the U.S. Army Intelligence Corps, 1951–1953.

Senator Hecht graduated from Washington University (B.S., 1949). He was born November 30, 1928, in Cape Girardeau, MO. He is married, has two children, and resides in Las Vegas, NV.

Nomination of Richard H. Solomon To Be an Assistant Secretary of State
March 24, 1989

The President today announced his intention to nominate Richard H. Solomon to be Assistant Secretary of State (East Asian and Pacific Affairs). He would succeed Gaston Joseph Sigur, Jr. Richard L. Armitage, who was previously announced for the position as Assistant Secretary of State (East Asian and Pacific Affairs), has been asked by the President to remain at the Department of Defense in a senior position which will be announced at a later date.

Since 1986 Dr. Solomon has been the Director of the Policy Planning Staff of the Department of State. He previously served from 1976 to 1986 as head of the Rand Corporation's political science department and also directed the corporation's research program on international security policy from 1977 to 1983. From 1971 to 1973 he was senior staff member for Asian Affairs on the National Security Council and was professor of political science at the University of Michigan from 1966 to 1971.

Dr. Solomon graduated from the Massachusetts Institute of Technology (S.B., 1960, and Ph.D., 1966). He was an international affairs fellow of the Council on Foreign Relations in 1971 and served as a consultant to the President's Commission on Foreign Language and International Studies from 1978 to 1980.

Accordance of the Personal Rank of Ambassador to John J. Maresca While Serving as Chief of the Delegation to the Conference on Confidence and Security Building Measures and Disarmament in Europe
March 24, 1989

The President today accorded the personal rank of Ambassador to John J. Maresca, of Connecticut, a career member of the Senior Foreign Service, Class of Minister-Counselor, in his capacity as Chief of the United States Delegation to the Negotiations on Confidence and Security Building Measures.

Since 1986 he has been serving as the Deputy Assistant Secretary for European and NATO Policy at the Department of Defense. Mr. Maresca graduated from Yale University (B.A., 1959). He served in the U.S. Navy from 1959 to 1965, and his foreign languages are French, Italian, and Dutch. Mr. Maresca is married, has one child, and resides in Chevy Chase, MD.

Nomination of Edward Noonan Ney To Be United States Ambassador to Canada
March 24, 1989

The President today announced his intention to nominate Edward Noonan Ney to be Ambassador Extraordinary and Plenipotentiary of the United States of America to Canada. He would succeed Thomas Michael Tolliver Niles.

Since 1986 Mr. Ney has served as the chairman of PaineWebber/Young & Rubicam Ventures and vice chairman of PaineWebber, Inc. Prior to this he was chairman, president, and chief executive officer of Young and Rubicam, Inc. In April 1984, Mr. Ney was appointed to the Board for International Broadcasting. He was a member of the Grace commission and the Commission on National Elections. He is a member of the services policy advisory committee of the United States Trade Representative and serves on the advisory board of the Center for Strategic and International Studies.

Mr. Ney graduated from Amherst College and served as an ensign in the Navy Air Corps during World War II. He currently resides in New York City.

Nomination of Charles Edgar Redman To Be United States Ambassador to Sweden
March 24, 1989

The President today announced his intention to nominate Charles Edgar Redman to be Ambassador Extraordinary and Plenipotentiary of the United States of America to Sweden. He would succeed Gregory J. Newell.

Since 1986 Mr. Redman has served as the Assistant Secretary of State for Public Affairs. Mr. Redman entered the Foreign Service in June 1974. He served first in the State Department Operations Center and then as staff assistant in the Bureau of European Affairs. In December 1976 he began a tour of duty as political officer at the U.S. Embassy in Paris. He then served from 1979 to 1982 on the NATO international staff as Deputy Director of the Private Office of the Secretary-General of NATO. Following a 2-year assignment as political officer in Algiers, he returned to Washington in August 1984 to become Deputy Director, and then Acting Director, of the Office of European Security and Political Affairs. Since July 1985 Mr. Redman has served as Deputy Spokesman for the Department of State. On October 12, 1986, he also became the Deputy Assistant Secretary for Public Affairs at the Department of State.

Mr. Redman graduated from the United States Air Force Academy (B.S., 1966) and Harvard University (M.A., 1968). He served in the U.S. Air Force until 1974, including assignments in Vietnam and on the air staff in Washington as Special Assistant to the Assistant Chief of Staff for Intelligence. Mr. Redman was born December 24, 1943, in Waukegan, IL. He is married, has three children, and resides in Bethesda, MD.

Nomination of William G. Rosenberg To Be an Assistant Administrator of the Environmental Protection Agency
March 27, 1989

The President today announced his intention to nominate William G. Rosenberg to be Assistant Administrator of the Environmental Protection Agency for Air and Radiation. He would succeed J. Craig Potter.

Since 1982 Mr. Rosenberg has been chairman of the Investment Group in Ann Arbor, MI, and Washington, DC. Prior to this he was president of Rosenberg, Freeman and Associates, 1977–1982. He was Assistant Administrator for Energy Resource Development at the Federal Energy Administration, 1975–1977, and chairman of the State regulatory commission of the Michigan Public Service Commission, 1973–1975. Mr. Rosenberg was executive director for the Michigan State Housing Development Authority, 1969–1973, and an attorney with the law firm of Honigman, Miller, Schwartz, and Cohn in Detroit, MI, 1965–1969.

Mr. Rosenberg graduated from Syracuse University (B.A., 1961), Columbia University School of Law (J.D., 1965), and Columbia University Graduate School of Business (M.B.A., 1965). He was born December 25, 1940, in New York City. He is married, has three children, and resides in Chelsea, MI.

Nomination of Alfred A. DelliBovi To Be Under Secretary of Housing and Urban Development
March 27, 1989

The President today announced his intention to nominate Alfred A. DelliBovi to be Under Secretary of Housing and Urban Development. He would succeed Carl D. Covitz.

Since 1987 Mr. DelliBovi has been Administrator of the Urban Mass Transportation Administration at the Department of Transportation in Washington, DC. He has served as Deputy Administrator, 1984–1987, and as Regional Administrator in New York, 1981–1984. Mr. DelliBovi served four terms as a member of the New York State Assembly, 1971–1978, and director of the public relations unit, 1969–1971.

Mr. DelliBovi graduated from Fordham College (B.A., 1967) and Baruch College (M.P.A., 1973). He is married, has two children, and currently resides in Burke, VA.

Nomination of John C. Weicher To Be an Assistant Secretary of Housing and Urban Development
March 27, 1989

The President today announced his intention to nominate John C. Weicher to be Assistant Secretary of Housing and Urban Development for Policy Development and Research. He would succeed Kenneth J. Beirne.

Since 1987 Dr. Weicher has been Associate Director for Economic Policy in the Office of Management and Budget. Prior to this, he was Deputy Staff Director for the President's Commission on Housing, 1981. He has served in several capacities at the Department of Housing and Urban Development, including Deputy Assistant Secretary for Economic Affairs, 1975–1977; Director for the Division of Economic Policy, 1973–1974; and prepared the National Housing Policy Review, 1973. He has also served as an associate and assistant professor of economics at Ohio State University, 1967–1977, and an assistant professor of economics at the University of California at Irvine, 1965–1967.

Dr. Weicher graduated from the University of Michigan (A.B., 1959) and the University of Chicago (Ph.D., 1968). He was born March 8, 1938. He is married, has two children, and resides in Washington, DC.

Nomination of Francis Anthony Keating II To Be General Counsel of the Department of Housing and Urban Development

March 27, 1989

The President today announced his intention to nominate Francis Anthony Keating II to be General Counsel of the Department of Housing and Urban Development. He would succeed J. Michael Dorsey.

Mr. Keating is currently Associate Attorney General at the Department of Justice in Washington, DC, and serves as chairman of the law enforcement coordinating group of the National Drug Policy Board. Prior to this, he was Assistant Secretary of the Treasury for Enforcement, 1985–1988. In 1981 he was a United States Attorney for the Northern District of Oklahoma. Mr. Keating was a member of the law firm of Blackstock, Joyce, Pollard and Montgomery in Tulsa, OK, 1972–1981.

Mr. Keating graduated from Georgetown University (B.A., 1966) and the University of Oklahoma Law School (J.D., 1969). He is married and has three children.

Nomination of Ronald Frank Lehman II To Be Director of the United States Arms Control and Disarmament Agency

March 27, 1989

The President today announced his intention to nominate Ronald Frank Lehman II to be Director of the U.S. Arms Control and Disarmament Agency. He would succeed William F. Burns.

Ambassador Lehman is currently serving as Assistant Secretary of Defense for International Security Policy. He has served as the U.S. chief negotiator for strategic nuclear arms (START) at the U.S.-Soviet nuclear and space arms talks in Geneva. Prior to this, he served as Deputy Assistant to the President for National Security Affairs (Defense Policy) at the White House, deputy U.S. negotiator on strategic nuclear arms, Special Assistant to the President for National Security Affairs, and Senior Director for Defense Programs and Arms Control on the National Security Council staff at the White House. Ambassador Lehman has also served as Deputy Assistant Secretary of Defense and as a senior adviser to the United Nations Special Session on Disarmament.

Ambassador Lehman graduated from Claremont Men's College (1968) and Claremont Graduate School (Ph.D., 1975). He is married and currently resides in Arlington, VA.

Remarks and an Informal Exchange With Reporters Following a Meeting With Administration Officials
March 28, 1989

The President. Well, let me just say that we've had a very good meeting here, and I've asked the Secretary of Transportation, Sam Skinner; Mr. Reilly, who's the head of the EPA; and the Commandant of the Coast Guard [Adm. Paul A. Yost]—all three of whom are here with us now—to go up to Alaska to take a hard look at where this disaster stands.

There are many Federal agencies involved—some 14 Federal agencies—under the national response team, which is cochaired by the Coast Guard and by EPA. And so, a lot is going on. Exxon is in charge, at this moment, of the cleanup, but many of the facilities, much of the equipment that is being used has been promptly furnished by the Coast Guard. And some of the top Coast Guard people in charge of this kind of matter are on the scene.

But I think it's important that these top officials now—Federal officials—accompanied by the Commandant, go there, and then they will report to me after they've had a chance to assess the situation on the ground. The congressional delegation and the Governor, of course, have strong feelings on these matters, and we've been in touch with them. But this is a matter of tremendous concern to Alaskans and, indeed, to all of us. The conservation side is important; the energy side is important. And I'll feel much better after Sam Skinner and Bill Reilly and the admiral get a chance to report back.

Alaskan Oil Spill

Q. Mr. President, is Exxon doing enough, do you think, in the cleanup?

The President. Well, I've just had a report that they're certainly making a good beginning here. But there's been some conflicting reports on that, and I don't want to prejudge that. I think one of the things we're interested in hearing is exactly how our top officials feel the cleanup is going.

Q. Mr. President, can civil penalties be imposed against Exxon in addition to having to pay for the cost of the cleanup?

The President. I don't know the answer to that.

Q. Can the Government bring suit?

The President. Sam?

Secretary Skinner. Yes, they can; they can do that. There are civil penalties. There's a variety of legal options that are available. But right now the primary consideration is to make sure everything is being done possibly, and the President has directed us to assess that the oil is being contained and that the oil that remains on the tanker is being off-loaded as quick as possible. That is our primary objective, as mandated by the President—to assess how that is going. We'll then, later on, worry about who's going to pay for the damage. But there are significant penalties and provisions for reimbursement.

The President. The main thing is to get it cleaned up, to protect a very precious environment up there, and to be sure that everything is being done to clean up this disaster, and then figure out all these penalties and all that other——

Q. Does this demonstration——

Q. Mr. President, has this changed your opinion on development of the Alaska National Wildlife Refuge?

The President. No. I see no connection.

Q. So, you consider this as being an isolated incident?

The President. Well, they've been shipping oil out of here for a long, long time and never had anything of this magnitude or this concern. So, the big thing is to correct it. I don't know how you design against what appears to be the cause here. You have a ship that's out of the channel, going 12 knots, and ripping the bottom out of the most modern tanker that's ever been built to haul this oil. But I think we need to assess the matter and judge it on its demerits and make our conclusions later on.

Q. Is the Government taking over the cleanup one of the options that you're considering?

The President. There is an option for federalization. And then the question is: Is that the most prudent way to go? And that's one of the recommendations I'll be awaiting from Secretary Skinner, Mr. Reilly, Admiral Yost.

Q. When do you anticipate a report, Mr. Secretary, to the President on this?

Secretary Skinner. Our plan is to report by phone as soon as we get up there and get an assessment. We'll be departing in the not-too-distant future, within hours, and hopefully, we'll be reporting to him late this evening or early in the morning, at the very latest.

Q. How long do you expect to be up there at this point?

Secretary Skinner. We're going to be up there as long as it takes to find out what the President has asked us to find out so we can report back to him.

Bipartisan Accord on Central America

Q. Mr. President, can you give us your reaction when you read Boyden Gray's [Counsel to the President] comments in the New York Times Sunday morning—his public dissent about the Central America agreement?

The President. No, but I shared my reaction with Boyden, which is the way I handle things. [*Laughter*]

Japan-U.S. Jet Fighter

Q. What's the state of play on the FSX, Mr. President?

The President. Still churning around out there, but we're not ready to say where it stands. We've asked for certain—insisting on certain clarifications, and we'll let you know. But we're not ready to have an announcement.

Q. Still expect it to be nailed down by Friday?

The President. I don't know, Norm [Norman Sandler, United Press International], whether it will be done by then or not. It's going back and forth a little bit. But all I want to know is that the agreement is clear—no point in having an unclear agreement. And we have a lot at stake here, a lot at stake in terms of the common defense; we have a lot at stake in terms of commerce; we have a lot at stake in terms of technology. And so, all I'm asking is to be clear. The United States will keep its word, but the United States, properly, is insisting on clarity in the agreement. And that's about where we stand right now. And I just can't give you my view as to when that will be completed.

Q. Well, there are these reports of increasing Japanese concern that this is going to cause some kind of severe damage to relations between the United States and Japan. Are you troubled by those reports?

The President. No, I'm not troubled by them.

Note: The President spoke at 9:40 a.m. in the Oval Office at the White House.

Remarks and a Question-and-Answer Session With Students at James Madison High School in Vienna, Virginia
March 28, 1989

The President. I happen to believe that education is going to be the key to our future. You look at the whole world, and you see our need to compete, and it gets right back down to education. And then you see some of the problems in the less affluent areas in the country, and then you find out, well, the way to give a guy a break that's trying to get out of poverty is education. And it goes for everything. It goes right across the board. And you're hearing a lot more now on math and science, and I wanted to ask you about that because it is important. But I really kind of—you learn from these visits.

Last week we were in a rural school out in Lancaster, Pennsylvania, and then we went to a school attended mainly by the

Amish kids, coming out of a very closely knit religious and family background. And who knows where we'll be next week? But I'm delighted to be here. And what I really wanted to do is ask you all how you view the importance of what you're doing, answer any questions that you might have. We can have a two-way street. I don't know how we want to get this thing going, but I'll be glad to respond to questions on the Government.

But let me ask you: How many of you all take math and science? Does everyone have to do that here, or is that——

Audience. Yes!

The President. You do. And is that considered among the tougher disciplines, or not necessarily? Is it hard?

Audience. Yes!

The President. How many do the computer stuff? How many are computer literate? About half. Is that considered hard, or is that considered advanced, or is it considered average kind of——

Audience. Average.

The President. Average kind of a course. Because as you look at it, I was impressed by what they're doing, the programming of some of your classmates, I guess. But the importance of it in the future is just—you can't underestimate that.

How about questions? Anybody got any questions about my line of work? [*Laughter*]

President's Dog

Q. How are the puppies?

The President. They're doing just fine. [*Laughter*] They're doing fine. I'll tell you something about that. I don't want to get too clinical, but it was a very emotional experience seeing that take place.

President's Schedule

Q. How does the President have time to come to a high school?

The President. The question is: How does a President have the time to come to a high school? Very good question, because a lot of what you do is trying to formulate—take education—formulate the legislation or see that the various Departments of Government that have an input on this have the education package ready.

We're perfecting now an education package. I'll tell you how it works. In a campaign, you give certain themes of what you think is right for education. The reason I mentioned computers—I think it is important that people be computer literate. I think math and science are important. I favor magnet schools. We favor trying to set up a system to reward the better teachers, even though the teacher pay and all is the responsibility of the local school boards.

But I think you learn something from every step outside of the White House that you take, and it's more that. It's symbolic in some sense, but you also pick up information as you go along. And last week we were in this school I mentioned in Pennsylvania, and here was a rural area where people think—well, they don't have much to do about narcotics out there. And yet we found, in talking to some of the kids, that the pressures on the young people in that school were very high when it comes to this stupid use of drugs and substance abuse. So, you have to take the time to get outside of the White House, but you have to balance that in terms of your overall responsibilities.

Next week we're going to probably have several foreign leaders here, in that venue—shift the emphasis to foreign affairs. But all the time—every morning—I meet, for example, with our national security adviser. So, we have an ongoing input on foreign affairs and what we're going to do and how we're going to handle our relations with the Soviet Union, or in this case next week, the emphasis will be on the Middle East. So, all of that goes on every day. This morning, I was talking to Brent Scowcroft [Assistant to the President for National Security Affairs] about the visit of these Middle Eastern leaders that are coming.

But you have a great responsibility in terms of taking the point on questions like education, so you have to find time to get out of there. It's not easy to balance, as a matter of fact.

Q. Do you enjoy getting out and being able to meet all the students and want to see——

The President. I do. I do. There's a certain recognition on my part that it's not the same as if a parent dropped in on a class or something. [*Laughter*] They don't come with this much attention. So, it's different. But you know, you can get a feel for things, whether it's in sports or education or wide array of other subjects.

I'll tell you one that really moved me—and I think they liked the visit—it was these DEA, Drug Enforcement Agency people that are working on the streets of New York. And I went up there and talked to 300 or 400 of them, people that are out there fighting the drug battle under DEA's banner, you see. But then afterwards, you meet with 6 or 8 of them—some of them not much older than you—who are people that, just out of belief they can help society, are out there putting their lives on the line trying to bust up these drug rings and trying to intervene in the sale of all these narcotics.

And some would say, well, there's a little show business in that—the President meeting with these 8 agents, but I learned from that. I learned just from listening to this guy tell me about his software that he put in on a car rental business now into that computer. So, you pick something up at each stop of the way. And the President has to do certain things of that nature to be sure that you just don't get it all from your own staff.

Regional Conflicts

Q. You said, like, next week you're going to deal with the Middle East. Is that, like, the main issue with that chemical plant in the Middle East?

The President. No, it's a very important issue, but it's a peripheral issue. You're thinking of the chemical plant in Libya. And that Libyan leader, Qadhafi, does have a role, a very disruptive role, as a matter of fact, in Middle Eastern affairs. But what we're talking about next week is the—Mubarak of Egypt and Shamir of Israel, the two top—President Mubarak and the Prime Minister of Israel coming here. And we will be probing as best we can and making suggestions to them as to what the U.S. can do in trying to bring about peace in the Middle East.

As you know, and all of you know, I'm sure, that has just been in turmoil for years and years, particularly since the '67 war—war that took place in 1967, and the resolution of which has escaped us all, escaped the world, even though things moved forward with the Camp David accords. Remember the Camp David accords? That was something that happened under President Carter. It was a step in the right direction, but you still see a lot of killing. You see on the television the *Intifada* [Palestinian uprising in the West Bank and Gaza] fighting on the West Bank.

And so, we have a particularly important role there. We are the only country that can be a substantial catalyst for peace there, and it's difficult. And so, I sit and talk—the way it works on the thought process, the State Department will be coming with strong ideas, and our national security adviser, the trade people, and the Treasury fits into this in some ways, as we look at the economic problems of the countries involved. And then the administration comes together, and then the President is given some good thoughts as to what to present to the leaders. And they'll come in; we'll have one-on-one meetings with them. And then we'll meet with a group of our top Cabinet people and the top leaders from Israel or from Egypt.

And recently, there was an election down in El Salvador that you may have seen. And we are determined that that democratic process go forward. They had certifiably free elections. I say certifiably—the President chooses a delegation in this case to go down to Nicaragua—I mean, in this case, to Salvador, and watch the elections. And they came back, and Democrats and Republicans on the delegation all saying this was a very good election, very free.

Now we've got to deal with the newly elected President of Salvador and convince him that he should go down the democratic road, turn his back on the death squads, but give the man a chance, give him an opportunity to follow through on what he said in his campaign. And so, he'll be coming up here—Mr. Cristiani.

That part of it is all very interesting, and it takes a lot of teamwork.

Congressional and Judicial Pay Raise

Q. How did you justify giving Congress a 51-percent pay raise when the budget and deficit are so huge right now?

The President. Very hard to do, and a lot of my thinking on it was that it was connected to the pay raise for the judiciary. My feeling is—and I would like to have some proposal on this—that the judiciary, particularly, needs an increase in pay. The justification for that very large increase was made on the basis of inflation. In my view, in retrospect, it was too big a bite at once, and the country didn't support it at all. So, to accommodate the legitimate needs for a raise it has to be done differently. And that was a good lesson out of that one.

War on Drugs

Q. Are you thinking of working to get—like, in Washington, people were just killed——

The President. Oh, yes, question on the—what do you do about fighting to see that more people don't lose their lives on this drug fight? This young—well, fairly young—in my school of thought, young; in yours, old—guy that lost his life the other day in that hostage thing—and it's happening, regrettably, across the country.

I had to hold my arm around the shoulder of a woman whose husband had—at this DEA thing I mentioned—whose husband had been gunned down the week before, just blown away by these narcotics people. And we just have got to keep working on not only the interdiction side, which is to try to keep the drugs from coming in, but on the education side. If as more people get caught up in the view that this is wrong and bad and terrible, then the problem will be well on its way to solution.

And we got to change the way this problem has been looked at. For a while in our country, it seemed to be we condoned those things we should condemn. And we went through a period where the treatment, for example, of the use of cocaine in movies was done in a humorous vein or some kind of, well, harmless—but made the user look like some kind of silly idiot, but nothing, not condemnatory. And so, we've got to mobilize the entertainment media, and say, "Look, don't put out great emotion in favor of—or treat these—in favor of cocaine or other drugs."

So, a lot of it is educational because this is not going to be solved from the White House. It's going to be solved by the American people, young and old, saying enough is enough. This is poisoning our society. So, when it comes to people that have lost their lives, we've got to show support for the police officers.

We're having a lively debate now about these automated weapons. And there's a lot of laws on the books that need to be enforced, and maybe there's a need for more laws. But you have to balance out all these interests. But the White House has a role; the President has a key role. But it's got to be a shared responsibility, with all the people in this country working the problem. And I think we can make headway on it. We've got to; we cannot permit narcotics and substance abuse to undermine the fabric of our society.

Education

Q. Madison High School seems to be one of them that has been lucky about this, but in America the student dropout rate is 25 percent. What are your proposals to try and curb this number—a quarter of our students not even completing high school?

The President. It's outrageous, and the answer is: Encourage people to stay in school, and excellence in education. And what we're doing at the Federal level—you see, about 7 percent of the funds that go for schooling comes from the Federal Government, and the rest from State and local governments. For our part, we are emphasizing parental choice; we're emphasizing magnet schools. We're trying to use an award system for excellence so others will aspire to excellence. And we've got a program of about—more emphasis on Head Start, more funding—and a very difficult period for Federal money because of the question that was asked over here on, got close to asking, about the deficit. Very complicated, we've got to get the Federal deficit down. We do not have the money to spend on everything we want.

But in spite of that, we are proposing substantially more money for Head Start, which is the best antidote, I think, from the Federal level, for dropouts. And a lot of it happening in some of the minority communities. I know in the Hispanic communities in our State, my State of Texas, the dropout rate is disproportionately high. And that's one of the reasons I'd like to see continued support for bilingual education. You bring a kid in whose family speaks only Spanish, throw him into a school where he instantly has English only, and it's hard for him to keep up. And the dropouts have been high. I think we can do better in both Head Start, which gradually gets them into the system, starting early, and bilingual.

Q. What would you like to see students and faculty members in public schools do to help you curb the drug problem? What can we do for you?

The President. I think you can put the emphasis on the peers of the students, and indeed, the faculty can be very helpful in this: each student on his peers, in just rejecting this concept of drug use. I mean, we have condoned that which we could condemn. People used to talk about legalizing narcotics, and that was some very serious people. And I just think it's 180 degrees wrong.

And I know what peer pressure is, and I think a lot of it is education in the schoolroom itself about the damage that comes from substance abuse. And I really believe a lot of the answer is here. We're going to have a new proposal that I talked about in the campaign that we're just fleshing out now called Youth Entering Service. And it is a concept that appeals to the best in American kids, which is: Look, you're doing pretty good; now you ought to really get in and help those who aren't. It's the old propensity of one American to help another that De Tocqueville talked about when he came to America years ago. And it's this concept that young people who have the advantage of family—good teachers teaching them against substance abuse, then they themselves taking that concept to others in other areas, in other school districts. So, the resistance to peer pressure, if peer pressure is leaning towards drug use, is very important; and then the outreach, reaching out to others, both in the education side and in the exhortation side.

Easter Balloons

Q. Just yesterday my church volunteered, and we were working on the balloons at the Easter Egg Roll. And we wanted to take some of the balloons to Ghana for our mission trip that we're going on. And they wouldn't let us take them because they were government property. I was just wondering what you do with 10,000 balloons that say, "A Family Easter at the White House, 1989"? [*Laughter*]

The President. If only I had known about it, you'd have been able to carry more than that one with you.

Q. Can you sign my card for me?

The President. Sure. Bring it over here. No, I don't know what the bureaucratic hangup was on that because you're right. I saw a lot of them soaring off into the sky, so you might as well have them with you. They really wouldn't let you take them out? What did they say? What did they say the reason was, just for the heck of it?

Q. Government property.

The President. Government property?

Q. So, a bunch of bureaucratic——

The President. I see.

Terrorism

Q. In many of our government classes we've been studying a book called "Profiles in Terrorism." And in that you gave your definition of terrorism. I was wondering what type of programs you have in mind to combat terrorism overseas and if you have any worries that terrorism will start to occur on a larger scale within our own borders?

The President. We're always concerned about it. We have been through a period in our history where we had what I would call terrorism, and it's probably before you were born, or maybe about that time. You remember the hijackings of airplanes in this country to go to Cuba? We forget that, we forget that we went through a rash of those hijackings, which indeed are—it's not international terror so much, but it's domestic terror. To hijack an airplane at gunpoint and instruct the pilot to go elsewhere, fly to Cuba—that's international terror. So, we have been through that.

I want to get your name and how to get to you what I'm going to send you, because we have a good antiterrorist program. And a lot of it is insisting that we do better on interdiction—I mean, on having people sent out from the countries where they're caught. It is very hard. Extradition it's called. It's very hard, for example, to get drug kingpins in Colombia extradited to the United States when the cartel down there goes in and murders a supreme court justice. I think you had 9 or 10 justices killed there. You had an attorney general fleeing for his life in Colombia, caught somewhere over in Hungary or somewhere in Eastern Europe and gunned down.

And so, we've got to do more in extradition. We've got to do more in the sharing of intelligence. We've got to do more in punishing those who practice international terror, if you can find them. It's pretty hard to track it down with definition. It is very hard to single out and punish the state leader that condones it. The attack on Libya did that, and I strongly support that. But in the rest of these cases, a lot of these cases, it is very hard to do. But we do have a good program, and yet I wish I could tell you I thought it alone would solve the problem of international terror. As long as you have a handful of people or a large group of people that use this relatively new instrument to effect political change, it's going to be hard to control, because it's like dealing with fog: You can't get a hold of it very well. And they're protected at times by governments, although the governments themselves don't sponsor it.

But let me send you—if Tim will get the address, and maybe you can share it with others—this policy. It will show you—and a lot of good people went—this was last year it came out, but it's still valid, as to what governments contend with when they try to formulate an antiterrorism policy. It's tough, but we've got to keep doing it.

We've got Americans held against their will right now—hostages. Hard to even know where they are, as good as our intelligence is. And incidentally, it is still the best in the world, in my view. But when you're dealing with something like this, this new approach to changing things, it is very difficult for any government to singlehandedly cope. And even when you're working with friendly governments, it's hard to cope.

She has what they call a followup.

Q. Do you think by fortifying our own borders you'll be able to keep terrorism out of—at least out of—occurring within our boundaries?

The President. By what we're doing? You said——

Q. By fortifying our borders.

The President. No, I don't think that is an answer. I think being sure that the intelligence is widely shared of people coming in is very important. But I don't think fortification—if I'm using the right picture of fortification—of our borders is feasible, and I don't think it's appropriate. But interdicting at the borders in a better way, a more efficient way, of terrorists is very important. And that's where this sharing of intelligence is a key to doing what you've suggested. But I don't think living inside a fortressed America concept, where you have bristling armaments along the Rio Grande River, for example, or across Canada, makes sense for the United States.

Principal Ryan. We have time for one more question.

The President. Then I want to know what's on for lunch. [*Laughter*] All right, I saw two hands up there—one and then two, and then we'll go peacefully.

Aviation Safety

Q. I was wondering, this concern over the recent incidents in the aviation industry, I was just wondering what your thoughts were on our industry and aviation?

The President. Aviation generally, you mean? Or are you talking about the safety of the skies for international travelers?

Q. Yes, I guess so. [*Laughter*] I can't believe I'm talking to you, that's why I'm just—[*laughter*].

The President. No, but you ask a good question, because modernization of the facilities for air control is very important. And there's funds now in our budgeting to accomplish that. In terms of one of the hot subjects, of warnings of—you know, when you get a phone call saying that some terrorist act is going to take place, you have to sort through that in an intelligent way, because you cannot have some crackpot shutting down the air travel in this country, some prankster calling in, and thus the

Government insisting that flights not take off. So, again, I come back to the sharing of intelligence, and the best possible intelligence is the answer to that, to the tranquillity of the skies, and in terms of securing for the traveler not only the best information available but not scaring them to death in the process.

Voluntarism

Q. During your campaign I heard a lot of people wonder and talk about what exactly you mean by the Thousand Points of Light? [*Laughter*]

The President. Some of the opposition weren't quite bright enough to get it, so let me help—[*laughter*]—I want to help them.

Q. All right.

The President. A Thousand Points of Light—you could make it a million. It's a good—no, it's a very good question she asked, because what I'm talking about in a Thousand Points of Light—I talked about it just a minute ago—didn't define it as such. You going out and helping some kid that may be tempted to use narcotics. Somebody else mentioned her church group doing something. There's a second point of light. And you can go on and on and on. It's the Red Cross; it's day care centers of a voluntary nature; it is the Boy Scouts; it is Christian Athletes. It is almost anything you can think of that comes under the heading of voluntarism.

Now, when a President talks about voluntarism, there are a few cynics around who suggest he's trying to escape the responsibility of the Federal Government, he's trying to say let somebody else do it. I'm saying, and I believe it with fervor, that this narcotics problem in this country is not going to be solved without the Thousand Points of Light. Not just a thousand organizations, but literally a million efforts to get out there and try to work the problem. It isn't going to be done by the Government. We aren't going to care for the poor. And in education, there's a lot of room. As I mentioned, this Youth Entering Service—that's a point of light. It's a new concept; it's a government-private foundation that we're going to be proposing here very soon, which I've already talked about in the campaign.

But you're right, and the reason you have that in your mind is that it was somewhat ridiculed. And maybe I didn't express it clearly in the campaign. It was somewhat ridiculed in one of the debates we had. And yet I have a feeling the American people know what I'm talking about, because family is involved in this, religious institutions are involved in it, outreach of all kinds in the communities are involved—one American helping another; groups of Americans helping others. And it's true in the law enforcement; it's true in the poor; it's true everyplace—this idea that we are a giving nation, we're a caring nation, and we're going to help each other. And that's what I mean by it. And I think it's getting a little better focus now than it did in the campaign. I think people are beginning to understand it more. And I'll be talking about it a lot from the White House, because it is very, very important.

And every time you bring in somebody—I had a group of marines in there that help with presents for kids, underprivileged kids—it's a point of light. And then they'll leave, and it will be somebody else with something. So, we've got to keep emphasizing it. We can't make you; we can't say you've got to go out after school and help this kid learn to read. But somehow it's moving, and people say, "Look, we're a giving nation; we're a caring nation; we're going to help."

Persistence gets the last one.

Q. It's just a quick question. How busy is your schedule around the 15th of June? Because if you're not too busy, we'd really be honored if you'd speak at our graduation. [*Laughter*]

The President. Thank you for the invitation. I don't know how busy it is. I don't even dare look till tomorrow, but thanks for the invite. Thanks a lot.

Note: The President spoke at 11:20 a.m. in the school library. Prior to his remarks, he visited an advanced-placement computer science class. In his remarks, the President referred to Special Assistant to the President Timothy J. McBride. Following his remarks, the President had lunch in the cafeteria and then returned to the White House.

Nomination of Carol T. Crawford To Be an Assistant Attorney General

March 28, 1989

The President today announced his intention to nominate Carol T. Crawford to be Assistant Attorney General for the Office of Legislative Affairs. She would succeed Thomas M. Boyd.

Since 1985 Ms. Crawford has been Associate Director for Economics and Government at the Office of Management and Budget at the White House. She has served at the Federal Trade Commission as Director of Bureau of Consumer Protection, 1983–1985, and as executive assistant to the Chairman of the Federal Trade Commission, 1981–1983. Prior to this she was an attorney at Collier, Shannon, Rill and Scott, 1979–1981. Ms. Crawford has been a trustee with the Barry Goldwater Chair of American Institutions, Arizona State University since 1983, and she served as a senior adviser to the Reagan-Bush transition team, 1980.

Ms. Crawford graduated from Mount Holyoke College (B.A., 1965) and American University, Washington College of Law (J.D., 1978). She was born in Mount Holly, NJ, on February 25, 1943. She resides in McLean, VA.

Nomination of Roger Bolton To Be an Assistant Secretary of the Treasury

March 28, 1989

The President today announced his intention to nominate Roger Bolton to be Assistant Secretary of the Treasury for Public Affairs and Public Liaison. He would succeed Edith E. Holiday.

Since 1988 Mr. Bolton has served as a Special Assistant to the President for Public Liaison and Director of the Economic Division at the White House in Washington, DC. Mr. Bolton has also served as Assistant U.S. Trade Representative for Public Affairs, and private sector liaison for the Office of the U.S. Trade Representative, July 1985–1989. Prior to this he was Deputy Assistant Secretary for Public Affairs at the Department of the Treasury, 1984–1985. Mr. Bolton was director of speechwriting for Reagan-Bush '84, 1984; press secretary for the Joint Economic Committee of Congress, 1983; and Deputy Director of Government Affairs for the National Transportation Safety Board, 1983. Mr. Bolton has also served as administrative assistant for Congressman Clarence J. Brown, 1977–1983, and as press secretary, 1975–1977. From 1972 to 1975, he was a political reporter for the Marion (Ohio) Star.

Mr. Bolton graduated from Ohio State University (B.A., 1972). He is married to the former Lynne Melillo. He was born June 12, 1950, is a native of Cincinnati, OH, and currently resides in Reston, VA.

Continuation of Henry Anatole Grunwald as United States Ambassador to Austria

March 29, 1989

The President today announced that Henry Anatole Grunwald will continue to serve as United States Ambassador to the Republic of Austria.

Since 1987 Ambassador Grunwald has been the United States Ambassador to the Republic of Austria. Prior to this he was with Time, Inc., in New York City serving in several capacities: editor-in-chief, 1979–1987; corporate editor, 1977–1979; managing editor, 1968–1977; assistant managing editor, 1966–1968; foreign news editor, 1961–1966; senior editor, 1951–1961; and staff writer, 1945–1951.

Ambassador Grunwald graduated from New York University (A.B., 1944). He was born December 3, 1922, in Vienna, Austria. He is married, has three children, and resides in New York City.

Nomination of John Cameron Monjo To Be United States Ambassador to Indonesia

March 29, 1989

The President today announced his intention to nominate John Cameron Monjo to be Ambassador Extraordinary and Plenipotentiary of the United States of America to the Republic of Indonesia. He would succeed Paul Dundes Wolfowitz.

Since 1987 Ambassador Monjo has been the United States Ambassador to Malaysia. Prior to this he was Senior Deputy Assistant Secretary for East Asian and Pacific Affairs at the Department of State, 1985–1987. He was Deputy Assistant Secretary for East Asian and Pacific Affairs, 1983–1985. He has served in several other capacities at the Department of State: Deputy Chief of Mission in Jakarta, Indonesia, 1982–1983; and Deputy Chief of Mission in Seoul, Korea, 1979–1982. Ambassador Monjo was country director in the Office of Philippine Affairs, 1978–1979; principal officer for Casablanca, Morocco, 1976–1978; and a political officer in Jakarta, Indonesia, 1971–1976. From 1969 to 1971, he was a special assistant in the Office of the Under Secretary for Political Affairs; an international relations officer in the Office of Japanese Affairs, 1967–1969; and a political officer in the Department of the Army in Naha, Okinawa, 1965–1967. Ambassador Monjo has also served as an economic officer, 1964–1965; a commercial officer in Tokyo, Japan, 1961–1962; and a political officer in Phnom Penh, Cambodia, 1958–1961.

Ambassador Monjo graduated from the University of Pennsylvania (B.S., 1953). He served in the United States Navy, 1953–1956. He was born July 17, 1931, in Stamford, CT. He is married, has two children, and resides in Bethesda, MD.

Nomination of Peter F. Secchia To Be United States Ambassador to Italy

March 29, 1989

The President today announced his intention to nominate Peter F. Secchia to be Ambassador Extraordinary and Plenipotentiary of the United States of America to

Italy. He would succeed Maxwell M. Rabb.

Currently Mr. Secchia serves as chairman of the board of The Universal Companies, Inc.; and as vice chairman of the Republican National Committee in the Midwest. He also served as host chairman of the 1985 Republican National Committee midwest leadership conference in Grand Rapids, MI. Mr. Secchia founded the Lake Michigan conference and is a member of the executive committee of the Gerald R. Ford Foundation. In addition, he was the founding president of the West Michigan Lodge of the Order Sons of Italy.

Mr. Secchia received a business administration degree from Michigan State University. He is married, has four children, and resides in East Grand Rapids, MI.

Remarks and a Question-and-Answer Session With High School Students From the Close Up Foundation

March 29, 1989

The President. Welcome to the White House. Famous personalities roam the corridors of this famous house. Play your cards right and you can see our dog, Millie, in a few minutes, coming down the stairs. [*Laughter*] But I'm delighted that you all are here in Washington. And I hope you're gaining an understanding of something that really matters, and that is good government.

I met today with a very prestigious group headed by Paul Volcker, and many others—the former Secretary of State, Mr. Muskie; and several Ambassadors; and Bruce Laingen, who you may remember was held hostage for a while over there in Iran. And the thrust of their report was the need to encourage more people to be involved in government service. And I hope you'll have a chance to see it. I'm sure there will be some press on it tomorrow.

But in addition to that—and I want to encourage in every way I can those who serve their country, whether it's military or civilian, in the civil service, or wherever else—I want to encourage that kind of service. But also, particularly in a group like this, to urge you to save some time in your lives for the political process. Some feel it's a demeaning line of work, and I happen to think that it is absolutely fundamental. Because 200 years ago, a great experiment really began on this continent that began with the profound idea that the power should reside with the people. And that sounds, I'm sure, to you who are bright and able students, as perhaps trite or a cliche. But it isn't when you look at today's world.

We take for granted that the power comes from the people in this country. But it isn't true in some of the totalitarian systems. Certainly, it's not true in the Marxist system. And it's fascinating now to see what's happening in the Soviet system as they lighten up a little and begin to have the elective process that we've taken for granted throughout our history. But the fundamental principle of freedom that built our democracy has served us well for these two centuries, and it's all the more vital that we preserve the freedom as we look to the future.

Some historians have called the 20th century the American century, but the 21st century is less than a dozen years away. And I've been talking with several different groups now about the future, charting a course for the next American century. And really, it's your future and your century. And so, we've been talking about what we as a government can do to not only set the agenda but what we can accomplish now that will guarantee that that century be more peaceful, more productive, and certainly a century in which the freedoms that I talked about earlier are provided—or preserved.

So, I guess we could say that everything we do now today with the Congress in terms of legislation is investing in your future. And we've got to solve some short-range problems that I'm sure you've heard a lot about—the budget deficit, because it does affect your future—how big a mortgage on your future if we continue to spend beyond our means today. Drugs in the streets: If we don't do better in battling this scourge of narcotics, it has an adverse affect on your future. Threats to the environment: We're seeing now an oil spill up in Alaska. But there's many, many other—global warming and things—that really do seem remote, but have a vital affect on the kind of century you're going to be living in. So, we have to address those problems, and that's the role of a President, and certainly it's the role of the Congress. And I'm still intent on working with the Congress to move forward as we get closer and closer to the next century.

I think from what I'm told about you all that you are much more aware of these things than the average young person in this country. This Close Up program is a great place to hone your ability to think, to question, to form reasoned opinions. And I want to find out about that in a minute because I'm told this has been billed for me at least as a listening session. And so I hope you will give me your ideas, and I'll try to conduct the discussion in such a way that you feel free to do that.

When you understand our political traditions and the questions of public policy, you can ensure that we preserve what works and that we work for change where it's needed. In my book, that's the best kind of citizenship. Government is not a spectator sport. You've got to be involved—needs people, bright people like you to make it succeed. And so, you have it within you all to be leaders in the next century wherever you decide to apply these talents. I don't want to say just public service or just politics because one of the themes that I'm talking about a lot and believe in is this concept of a better educated America. And that leads me to encourage those in the teaching profession to be the very best and then to encourage people to go into that profession as well. It takes hard work; it means asking questions of people; it means looking deeper. It means investing time and energy to learn all you can, now and in the future. You never stop learning. Heaven knows, I hope I don't. We've had fascinating meetings today on a wide array of subjects that—important to expand your horizons, and they've been very helpful to me.

Education is all about this. And I've been proposing new ways to make the schools more responsive. I really believe that choice is important. Choice—parental choice, student choice—can lead to excellence not just in the school that's chosen, but in those that maybe aren't chosen. So we've got to find ways to encourage choice.

I want to encourage excellence through programs like merit schools that some of you are familiar with—giving awards to outstanding teachers. The major responsibility, incidentally, as you know, in education lies at the local and State level. An overwhelming percentage of the funds come from the local and the State level. But we can, even in these tough budget times, give a system of awards for the outstanding teachers, thus giving them hope, and others seeing them trying to aspire to higher levels of production and levels of concern for the kids.

So, I believe in accountability. I think the educational process is somewhat—been somewhat devoid of accounting for its successes and failures, and I would like to see that. Over the past year, I've asked teachers and parents and administrators, political leaders at all levels to get involved. And they are. And I think it's beginning to show what's been going on the last few years in striving for excellence.

But you know, these are your schools, and they exist to serve you. And you have the right to demand the best from your teachers and from your schools. And you can expect excellence from your schools, and you can make them work for you. So where school is concerned, it's not a matter of like it or leave it. It's like it or help change it. And you're the bright ones; I hope that you'll never lose interest in the school system itself.

I wanted to meet with you. I have some ideas—these are what I've spelled out here on education and others, as well. I am told that you have ideas of your own, so why don't we get ahead with the give-and-take part of this, where you tell me what's on your minds. I noticed some notes. It's always formidable when you see notes having been written down here. [*Laughter*] But it's a good time to speak to me and I guess, with these cameras listening, be sure never to end a sentence with a preposition, because it will be duly reported all across the country by these guardians of the—[*laughter*].

But nevertheless, really, feel relaxed about it, and I hope you'll fire away. And I guess I get to sit down and listen. I'll conduct this, but just go ahead.

Q. Thank you, Mr. President. My name is Molly Evans, and I'm from Wooster High School in Wooster, Ohio. I'd like to thank you first for allowing Close Up the opportunity to question you and thank you——

The President. No, I'm questioning you. You've got it wrong, Molly. Go ahead. [*Laughter*]

Federal Role in Education

Q. Okay. Mr. President, in the past, the schools have traditionally held jurisdiction over the educational issues. But now that it's become a serious national problem, do you believe that the Federal Government should have more power on making decisions over the educational issues?

The President. No. I don't believe that the power in determining curriculum, in determining teachers' pay, in determining standards for schools ought to be set by the Federal Government. I believe in the genius of diversity. I believe that one set of standards has much more applicability to one area than to another. And so I don't think the Federal Government should be looked to as the final arbiter, or the one that's going to set the policies for the local school districts.

I believe instead in more parental participation. I believe in local school boards having the final authority and State departments of education having their say. And the Federal Government, which I think provides 7 percent of the funding, as opposed to 93 percent coming from other sources, has about that percentage in terms of dictating things. I don't see the Federal Government in a dictatorial role; I don't see it as the dominant role. I see this pulpit here—what Teddy Roosevelt referred to as the bully pulpit—being used to encourage excellence, encourage choice, encourage the good teachers, but not dictate to the schools.

Illiteracy

Q. My name is Jennifer Bean. I'm from Danvers High School, Danvers, Massachusetts. I know Mrs. Bush is involved in the campaign against illiteracy. There are many high school students that graduate from high school and are functionally illiterate. As the "Education President," what are you going to do to eliminate this problem?

The President. Again, I don't think the Federal Government can eliminate it. I do think it becomes the responsibility of everybody. And we are unveiling a program in a week or two that I've talked about earlier called Youth Entering Service. It's a concept, a concept of one kid, a bright kid—you perhaps—helping somebody in another area that doesn't have the advantage that you've had in terms of education.

My wife is involved in this whole concept of fighting against illiteracy, and in that, she's encouraging corporations and others to be thoroughly involved. You may have seen some of the pro bono advertising on a couple of the networks in terms of fighting against illiteracy.

So, I think the Federal Government has a substantial role. I think in the programs the Federal Government does do, that it can put emphasis on stamping out illiteracy. But again, I'd be misleading you if I had you believe that the problem could be solved from the White House or from Congress, itself. It can't be; it's got to have—scratch one newsman—[*laughter*]. Did anybody get hurt? But that's the way I look at it. And so I will be encouraging this hortatory, encouraging in every way we can.

And when I talk about accountability—promoting those who—you might be classmates—that you know can't read. It doesn't do that kid any good—needs special training, special help, special concern. So we've got to do better on it, but the Federal Government can help, can exhort, but can't solve it alone.

Q. Thank you, Mr. President. My name is David Hardin. I'm from Horizon High School in Scottsdale, Arizona.

The President. Where's your suntan? [*Laughter*]

Q. I get sunburned. [*Laughter*]

The President. Do you?

War on Drugs

Q. The drug problem that's infiltrated the United States educational system has proven to be a catalyst that's destroying the American youth. What do you think needs to be done to solve this problem?

The President. Well, we're making a whole new push against the scourge of drugs. The Congress passed legislation calling for a drug czar. You're all bright students of history, I'm sure. And why we use the term "czar" in the United States to determine a strong leader, I don't know.

But nevertheless, we're implementing that legislation as best we can in the executive branch. The appointment of Bill Bennett, who, I think set very high standards for education, shows that I think that a lot of the drug problem can be solved through the demand side of the equation—through teaching, through education, through getting peer to stand with peer and say, "No, we can't go forward with it."

We've got to change the culture that condoned the use of narcotics. Yesterday, I challenged through a meeting somewhat like this, challenged the entertainment media who, heretofore, has almost condoned narcotics by emphasizing the silly side of somebody being high on some substance or another. So we've got to change the culture, we've got to change the demand, and at the same time we've got to have much more enforcement of laws. We may need new laws, but we have existing laws that have not been enforced in terms of drug use. We're going to have to expand our prison space because it is frustrating to a law enforcement official who lays her or his life on the line to make a bust and then see that person out on the street again because there is no room in the prison. I believe severe sentencing is called for for drug kingpins. We've got to do more on the sentencing side, more on the enforcement side, and then we've got to do—and education side—and then we're trying to step up our cooperation with South American countries, particularly in terms of interdiction.

Somebody asked the question yesterday, and maybe it's on you all's minds about closing the borders, of fortifying the borders. We can't do that in the United States. In the first place, the borders are too long; we don't have that much money. Secondly, that isn't the concept we want with friendly countries—Mexico to our south, Canada to the north. But we've got to do better in terms of interdiction.

Last point—we are not going to solve the drug problem by stopping the flow. It's not going to be solved—in my view, it's going to be—that'll help, but we've got to do more on the demand side. Both sides, incidentally, our new drug czar, Bill Bennett, is working on. And for those of you who follow the intricacies of government, it isn't that easy because he is dealing with the Secretary of Defense and the Attorney General and the Secretary of State. And they are statutorily in command of their departments. So, he comes in, working for the President with a Cabinet rank, but without the statutory power of some of the Cabinet officers. So, he's got a job of persuasion and coordination. But we've got a man—if anybody can do it, he can.

Federal Role in Education

Q. Thank you, Mr. President. My name is Shawndra Miles. I attend Crenshaw High School in Los Angeles, California. In recent years, there have been significant cutbacks in Federal money for education. I would like to know how would you address this problem, since the students today are leaders of tomorrow?

The President. In the first place, we have a crunch. I think your figures are wrong. I don't think there have been substantial cutbacks. I don't think there have been cutbacks. I think the budget for the Department of Education is higher than it was 8 years ago—or 6 years ago—and will be this time. There have been some programs that have been curtailed. There has been some means testing in terms of student loans.

Let me give you an example of that. I don't believe as President that the Federal Government has an obligation to pay for the education of all kids that are qualified to go to college. That's my philosophy.

That's what I ran on with this kind of an underpinning of that in terms of being elected by the people of the United States to be President. I do think that the Federal Government has a role in helping those who can't afford to get to college. And so, tightening up on the means test for student loans, for example, was considered by some to be cutting educational funds. And I'm sure some programs have been taken out.

But generally speaking, I just come back to the fact—and I don't know that you all knew this, and I'm pretty sure I'm right on the figure—93 percent comes from all sources, and 7 percent of the funds come from the Federal Government. So in times of tough budget money, I've got to get this budget deficit down. The best hope, antidote to poverty, is a job, and the best way to have a job is to have a vibrant economy. And the way to do that is to be sure these interest rates don't go sky high. And this gets into the whole economic question, but all of which—it comes back to me as President in terms of priority: Get the budget deficit down. And that means we can't spend all the money that I'd like for that 7 percent.

There are some programs I'd like to fund more. But somebody asked me yesterday—I don't think it's come up yet today—on the question of dropouts. One of my answers to that is, do as much as we possibly can for Head Start. I think Head Start is a good program. And so we've increased, in tight financial times, the funds for Head Start. So, you know, it's like—I don't know what would be a parallel in your lives—is how you sort out priorities. But I am faced with a strong Secretary of Education who says we've got to spend more for this program or that. I've got a strong budget director on the other hand saying, "Wait a minute! We can't do that if your objective is to get the budget deficit down." So, you just do the best you can, and then you exhort. You encourage the private sector and the States and everybody to do as much as they can. No clear answer, and a very tough and good question.

You had one here, and then I'll go in the back. We're cutting out all the back bench guys. Go ahead. Did you have a question?

Q. Me?

The President. Yes, I thought I saw your hand. Yes?

Q. Thank you, Mr. President.

The President. Janel, if you're too polite in life you get stomped on. [*Laughter*] You're doing just great, but I didn't want you to have it. I thought you thought I had recognized you. Go ahead.

Q. My name is Janel McCurtis. I'm from Business Management Center in Dallas, Texas. And I was wondering how you feel about the Federal Government playing a more—a role in education.

The President. More of a role? Well, as I say, I think it's got to be State and local, the way our system works, because I don't want that highly centralized control. I've confessed here to Shawndra I'd like to see us be able to do more things, but I don't want the role—I don't want education to be federalized. That's the fundamental philosophical underpinning that I have with me as I approach public education and private education. I don't want the Federal Government to tell you, your school board, or your teachers what you're going to get taught in class. I don't want them to set the pay from on high—Washington, DC. We don't know much about Dallas. I do, coming from Houston.

But that's my philosophy, and I think it's right. I think—it's federalism, decentralization. We're strong that way. And I probably, when I was little, was wondering, why do we have all these different overlapping functions of the State government? And then I realized that it preserves our Union and strengthens our system by diversity—Scottsdale having a different answer than Los Angeles, and a different answer than Dallas and wherever else it is.

Who's got some in the back? We've got to—fire away, you two guys back there.

Q. Hello, Mr. President. My name is Joseph Thrill, and I go to the Hawaii Preparatory Academy in Hawaii. And I was wondering, I go to a private school and my parents pay tuition directly to the school. But yet part of their taxes which they pay to the Federal Government go to the public school system, even though I do not attend a public school. Should they get a tax break on that?

The President. No, they shouldn't. And I think it is the obligation of all taxpayers to support a public education system. We want it to be the best. And I think in many ways it is the best, although I'm disturbed when I see some kids underachieving—not being able to identify where the United States is on a globe or something of that nature. But, no, I think that that's your parents' choice, and I think that they shouldn't.

I have been intrigued with the concept of tuition tax credits. And some say, "Well, should that include parochial schools?" And I've said yes, but the problem again is that we are—and that gets really to your philosophical underpinning of your question—we can't afford to do that. So, I think that everybody should support the public school system. And then, if on top of that, your parents think that they want to shell out, in addition to the tax money, tuition money, that's their right, and that should be respected. But I don't think they should get a break for that.

Study Abroad

Q. Thank you, Mr. President. I'm Max Kalhammet, from Cairo, Egypt. And recently there's been a lot of publicity about the advantages of studying abroad, especially in your college career. The advantages would be traveling, being exposed to new cultures, et cetera. With your interest in reviving education domestically, do you support this?

The President. Yes, I support it, but again, we're talking about sparse funds. Not only do I support it, but I think it is enormously useful for our foreign affairs, and for understanding around the world about the United States of America. So, I strongly support it.

One of the things in my background that really helped shape my life a lot was living in China. Right after the Cultural Revolution, or right before the renaissance, or before the capitalistic—or quasi—you've got to be careful when you talk about China—quasi-capitalistic experimentation—incentive, moving away from the commune system for farm. And living there was very helpful to me and broadening—I was then Ambassador—but broadening out my own horizons, understanding the importance of China in the world scheme of things.

And I think it's true for students. I think not only does the student himself or herself gain a dimension on the world it might not have otherwise, but I think the people with whom you interact abroad do. And I strongly favor, as much as we can afford it, bringing kids from other countries over here. I believe firmly that any student that comes to the United States can no longer return to his or her country without some respect for democracy—for the underpinnings that I talked about in the remarks—you can't do it. You come out of a totalitarian system and you see the freedoms that you and I take for granted every day in our lives—see them every day one way or another. You see the bounty of this country, and you see the concern that Americans have for their fellow American, and it's bound to make an impact on them.

And I hear all kinds of griping about the United States all over the world. And I've traveled to I don't know how many countries. Now, I would guess—well, as Vice President, it was 85 just in that one job. And then I did business all around the world, from Brunei to the Persian Gulf to South America. And you hear complaints about the Americans, and you sit around and you interact. But you also have the sense that people say, yes, we may be griping about it or criticizing, but we'd like a little piece of the action.

And the more those students come here on the kind of thing you're talking about, the more understanding they have about us. And it is a really remarkable, remarkable thing. And I saw that most when I was the Ambassador at the United Nations, interacting with then the Ambassadors from 134 countries. And we were, you know, the host country. You got to know a lot of them.

I know the point you're bringing up is, I guess by the question, is very, very important. And so I would encourage not only travel abroad, but I would try in every way I can to do as much as we can do in terms of support for these people going to different countries and bringing students here. A lot go to the Soviet Union. They have a very active program of taking people, particularly from Eastern Europe—but it's much more widely spread than that—to the Soviet Union. And until recently, I think that could have been in some ways counterproductive. They have a big propaganda thing in their education, major propaganda offensive. But then, when those kids get back home and then they interact with freer countries, it rubs off pretty easily. Today, in the Soviet Union, they're still doing quite a bit of this, and I'm sure that the students going there see it ferment a change that's taking place through both *perestroika* and the openness and *glasnost*.

So, I would encourage people doing it. I would encourage those foundations—International Education Institute, and those things that help bring people to live with American families. The Federal Government has some role in this, and I think it's very important. And I wish I had time to ask you what your view is because I would expect it would parallel.

I mean, I have been to Egypt, and I think there is a good feeling in Egypt about the United States. There are some concerns about certain aspects of our policy that I'll hear about next Monday and Tuesday when President Mubarak is here right in this very house. But I can tell you—here he is, the President of that country, coming in for Sadat, and there's a certain feeling—the United States can effect change. The United States can move things forward in the peace process. The United States has a certain economic system that we'd like to aspire to in Egypt.

And so never apologize for it. And share it, spread it around as best you can—goodwill that comes from being very bright, bright kids. Share it with foreigners as much as you can because we are, I'll still say—and I got accused of being a little bit overly patriotic, but I've been to these, a lot of them—we are the freest, we are the most honorable and caring country, I think, in the whole world. And so we ought to have others understand that.

And I will say this, that as President—you know, they ask, "Well, what is your aim, priorities?" We talk here about education and civics and all of that, but I want to try hard to enhance world peace. We talk about a new century. How old are you, Eric?

Q. I'm 17.

The President. Okay, 17. In the year 2000, you'll be 28. I'd like to think that because we were here and worked the problem hard, that the world will be somewhat more peaceful. And let me say this: The changes in the Soviet Union are encouraging. I'm an optimist about it. But if those changes keep going forward, you guys have a much better chance to—I don't need that—[*laughter*]—to live in a more harmonious world. So we'll try our hardest, and you all stay involved.

Mr. Janger. Mr. President, on behalf of all of us at the Close Up Foundation, these young people and young people throughout the United States, I know you understand how wonderfully motivating your exchange of ideas has been. Your special focus on education is inspiring, and we thank you for your time today.

Note: The President spoke at 2:18 p.m. in the East Room at the White House. In his opening remarks, he referred to Paul Volcker, Chairman of the National Commission on Public Service. The event was broadcast live on the Cable Satellite Public Affairs Network. The participants were part of the Close Up Foundation program, a nonpartisan educational foundation providing secondary school students opportunities to study the American political system. Stephen A. Janger was president of the foundation.

Remarks to Members of the American Association of Community and Junior Colleges
March 30, 1989

To Dale Parnell and Jess Parrish, others, thank you for that warm reception for Barbara and for me. And I'm just delighted to be here. I understand we do have two Governors here: Jim Martin, whom I saw over here, and somebody told me Carroll Campbell was here. And I want to pay my respects to them, both leaders in the field of education.

Before making my remarks, I do want to make a comment on a subject that is of concern to all Americans today. I know that you, like most Americans, are concerned about this massive oil spill off the coast of Alaska. And there's no doubt this is a major tragedy, both for the environment and for the people up there.

This morning I met with the Secretary of Transportation, Sam Skinner; with our new able EPA Administrator, Bill Reilly; with our Coast Guard Commandant, Admiral Yost. And they've just returned from surveying the damage and assessing the progress of the cleanup effort. And we're doing all we can at the Federal level to speed up this undertaking.

I've directed the Department of Transportation and the Environmental Protection Agency and the Coast Guard to continue to give this matter top priority. I've directed Bill Reilly to report back to me as soon as possible regarding the severity of damage to the environment, particularly to marine life and the Alaskan coastline, with suggestions as to what we might do to ameliorate the situation. The cleanup will not be easy. It's in remote areas, and it's very complicated. But as with other serious disasters, we must and we will work together at all levels, public and private, to remedy the damage that has been done, and then to safeguard the precious environment for the future.

But I wanted you to know that we did have a good meeting. The report was not all negative, but there—lets be frank, there's some very serious problems up there right now. But I'm confident with this able team and with the work of the Alaskan citizens there who are concerned, that we can do our very best to see that the damage is restricted.

Now on to the business at hand. I am delighted, Barbara, that this distinguished group has recognized your efforts. Or put it in the third person—I'm grateful to all of you that have recognized her efforts to promote literacy. And to think, all this time I thought she was cheating at Scrabble. [*Laughter*] It has been said by some cynic—maybe it was a former President—"If you want a friend in Washington, get a dog." [*Laughter*] Well, we took them literally—that advice, as you know. [*Laughter*] But I didn't need that because I have Barbara Bush—your honoree.

As you know, Bar has taken the lead in promoting literacy, as you so, I think, properly pointed out, for more than 8 years now, traveling to the schools across this country. And one day she came back from Boston and told me that she'd seen a gentleman sitting in a chair in the corner of a schoolroom surrounded by children who were enraptured by his storytelling and his good-natured kidding. Every now and then, this man would ask a child to spell a word by tracing the letters in the palm of his hand, and he would tell them whether they got it right or not. Barbara thought that this is strange—wondered if this was some new kind of teaching technique that you may have designed. And, no, the superintendent told her, "He has to teach this way. You see, he's blind." Think of it. He's retired. He could have found a thousand excuses to retreat into his own world of darkness. And yet, he ventured out into the light to teach children to read books that he would never again see. And it's moments like these that make her efforts on behalf of literacy so very rewarding.

We are deeply moved by the plight of those who lack the skills that most of us just simply take for granted. And rest assured, we're going to continue to work with you, those of you out there on the cutting edge, to promote literacy skills. You've bestowed on Barbara an honor that will be treasured by all in our family for years to come. And still, she and I can't get over the feeling that we should be giving you, the people in this room, an award. After all, you provide adult basic education on a scale that is nothing short of heroic.

This nation grew into greatness because early Americans met the challenge of building an educational system second to none. And with the dawn of a new century only

11 years away, we're faced with a new challenge: to revitalize and restore that system that our forebears bequeathed to us; to ensure that an American education is once again the best, the very best in the world. In this important mission, we can look to leadership from an American innovation in education—our nation's community colleges, more than a thousand strong.

Whole communities are enriched and enlightened by the cultural resources you provide: vast libraries and night schools and stages for local theatrical productions and on and on it goes. This attitude toward education as something more than a requirement of an industrial society, as an embellishment of life, rather, is uniquely American.

I believe secondary and even elementary schools can learn a lot from your success, starting with your policy of flexibility. And by this I mean the way in which you tap local talent and draw on the knowledge of experts from the private sector. When a Ph.D. on sabbatical cannot volunteer as a teacher in many of our schools, something's wrong. And that's why I've proposed alternative teacher certification, to open classrooms to every qualified person with the talent, and the knowledge, and mainly the desire to help the kids, to teach.

We must all pitch in to restore our educational system. Business must get involved, work with our schools to ensure American competitiveness. Students must understand the value of a solid education and personal responsibility in today's market. And education at all levels must follow the example set by you, by the community colleges, which are directly accountable to the needs of students, communities, and businesses. This principle of accountability should be universally applied to all educational institutions. You also serve a particular need with the disadvantaged and the disabled—providing opportunity and choice for older citizens, women, minorities, and the handicapped.

But excellence in education is our most basic shared principle. We share the conviction that there is no such thing as an expendable student. We will never accept the notion that vast numbers of illiterate and undereducated Americans can be offset by a well-educated elite. That is not the American way. For years, rescuing underachieving students has been a quest of the heart. And today, it's also a test of our national will, a test critical to the very future of America. This may sound like an overstatement. America, after all, is still a world leader when it comes to producing Nobel Prize winners in physics, in economics, and literature. But what's the advantage for a nation with Nobel Prize-winning novelists, if their books cannot be read by 27 million functional illiterates in their own country?

I am committed to increased investment in basic research, but America can continue to lead the world in theoretical science and still lose the race in the application of knowledge. H.G. Wells wrote that "Human history becomes more and more a race between education and catastrophe." Catastrophe may not be around the corner, but what had a ring of truth in the 1920's sounds ominously true in the 1980's, with our highly competitive international market. Let me share a few stark facts with you.

In Japan, levels of functional literacy and student achievement are extremely high, while the Japanese drop-out rate remains very low. In America, however, functional literacy is much lower. About one in five American high school students drop out. And of those Americans who do graduate from high school, almost one in five cannot read or write at the intermediate level.

While many Americans become less educated, the standards of the workplace are becoming ever more rigorous. And the balmy days of the baby boom are passing us by. Between now and the year 2000, we're going to face a baby bust; a shrinkage of the basic labor pool for this country. According to Business Week, we will have to train or retrain as many as 50 million workers in the next dozen years alone. Think of it—50 million.

There is more opportunity today than ever before, but only for those who are prepared to take advantage of it. For those workers who lack skills and basic education today, a comfortable middle-class existence will be harder and harder to come by. And when some high school grads can't find jobs in a market begging for workers, then we've got a serious social imbalance; we have an education gap. Let's bridge that gap. Let's bridge it as fast as we possibly can.

You're doing it. Community colleges provide such a bridge to higher education, a ready resource for vocational training and adult remedial education. You provide access for precisely the very people who are being summoned to alleviate the coming labor shortage. Some of your programs spell opportunity for the most disadvantaged members of the work force. But they also spell opportunity for business at the same time. The disadvantaged and business are coming together in hundreds of programs—from Colorado to Kansas to Kentucky—called employer-college partnerships. And this friendly merger of business and academia is a sweeping force for social improvement. Everyone must work together if America is to remain prosperous and competitive in the years ahead.

Let me conclude by paraphrasing a few words of advice offered at the turn of the century, but so appropriate for our modern quest for excellence in education: "Make no little plans. They have no magic to stir men's blood and probably in themselves will not be realized. Make big plans; aim high in hope and work, remembering that a noble idea once recorded will never die, but long after we are gone will be a living thing."

These are the words of Daniel Burnham, who was the architect of such a big plan—Washington's Union Station, which stands out as a visual delight in a city already crowded with great monuments and statuary. Burnham's legacy is a truly living monument, with its vaulted ceilings and its gilded geometry above bustling crowds of shoppers and commuters. But it would be nothing but a wreck, an eyesore, if it had not been lovingly restored. As important as it is to reclaim our civic capital of burnished brass and polished marble, how much more important it is to reclaim our human capital.

Think, then, of our educational system in this way: as a vast and beautiful inheritance which must be lovingly restored—not once, but every generation. And in this effort, make no little plans. Think big; aim high in hope and work. Continue to work together as a community, to help your students, to lift their vision and lengthen their horizon.

For this, and all you are doing, and for those that walked across this platform, a hearty thanks for all you have done. For this, for all you do and for what you have done, you have earned and you are earning the gratitude of a nation. Thank you. God bless you. And God bless America. Thank you all very, very much.

Note: The President spoke at 1:42 p.m. in the International Ballroom at the Washington Hilton Hotel. In his opening remarks, he referred to Dale Parnell, president of the association; Dr. Jess H. Parrish, president of Midland College; Governors James G. Martin of North Carolina and Carroll A. Campbell, Jr., of South Carolina.

Nomination of Richard Anthony Moore To Be United States Ambassador to Ireland
March 30, 1989

The President today announced his intention to nominate Richard Anthony Moore to be Ambassador Extraordinary and Plenipotentiary of the United States of America to Ireland. He would succeed Margaret M. O'Shaughnessy Heckler.

Since 1975 Mr. Moore has been associate producer for the McLaughlin Group in Washington, DC. He served as Special Counsel to the President at the White House, 1971–1974. In 1970 Mr. Moore was a confidential assistant to the Attorney General. From 1962 to 1970, he organized and was head of a number of television enterprises. He also served as chief executive officer for the Times Mirror Broadcasting Co., 1951–1962. He is also cofounder and chairman of the Television Bureau of Advertising.

Mr. Moore graduated from Yale College (B.A., 1936) and Yale Law School (LL.B., 1939). He served in the U.S. Army, 1942–1946. He was born January 23, 1914, in Albany, NY. Mr. Moore has five children and resides in Washington, DC.

Nomination of Della Newman To Be United States Ambassador to New Zealand and Western Samoa

March 30, 1989

The President today announced his intention to nominate Della Newman to be Ambassador Extraordinary and Plenipotentiary of the United States of America to New Zealand and to serve concurrently as Ambassador to Western Samoa. She would succeed Paul Matthews Cleveland.

Currently Ms. Newman is president and owner of Village Real Estate, Inc., in Seattle, WA; treasurer of Pacific Factors Ltd., Inc.; and proprietor of Braemar Associates. She has served as international corporate president of Executive Women International. Ms. Newman has been actively involved in various political activities on the national and State level, including Republican National Convention delegate, 1988; chairman of the Washington State George Bush for President campaign, 1987–1988; cochair Reagan-Bush finance committee, 1984; special events director for the Washington State Reagan-Bush campaign, 1980; and Republican National Convention delegate, 1980. In addition, Ms. Newman serves on the board of directors for the Washington Institute for Policy Studies.

Ms. Newman is married to Wells B. McCurdy, and she resides in Seattle, WA.

Remarks and a Question-and-Answer Session at a White House Luncheon for Journalists

March 31, 1989

The President. Well, first, let me just say, welcome to Washington. And I've been traveling some, but I like this much better—you all coming here. And we're delighted that you are here.

We've got a broad cross-section of both print and broadcast journalists here, and what I really want to do is to take your questions. I'm delighted that you heard from our drug czar, Bill Bennett, this morning, and Roger Porter, as well. And I'll be glad to follow on to any subjects that you have taken up with them. Our Chief of Staff John Sununu came over here with me—hey, you don't get off that easy, Joe. You haven't heard my speech. [*Laughter*]

No, I'm not going to spend a lot of time, but I do want to indicate that certain important things have taken place at the outset. We went up with a good budget agreement—we hope we'll get an agreement—a good budget proposal. We've thrown an idea, a plan out there for the savings and loans, and I think that is an important thing to have happen. We've introduced a child-care initiative in keeping with the philosophical approach that I talked about in the campaign: parental choice. We've done that one. We've made a vigorous start in the narcotics area, and I want to congratulate Bill Bennett, who really—antinarcotics area—hit the ground running. And he has to formulate under the law a specific plan, but we're not going to wait for that to move forward in various ways.

Next week, we'll be sending up new legislation on ethics and education. The ethics guidelines will enable us to sustain an honesty and integrity in public service. I've been talking some about my belief in public service: those not that are in and out on the political basis, but those who serve in a career basis. Though we have no legislation on that, I want to keep saying how important I think that is.

We recognize that the major problem facing us is the budget deficit. And Dick Darman is doing a very good job. Nobody declared our budget dead on arrival, which pleased me very, very much. Nobody has anointed it, either, in every possible way. [*Laughter*] But nevertheless, we are making progress.

On the national security-foreign affairs side, we're going to have a vigorous week next week with President Mubarak here, Prime Minister Shamir here. And then we're going to have several of the Central Americans up here very soon. You've seen our new approach, you might say, on Nicaragua, where we are working with the Congress, we're together with Congress. One of my regrets is that we were sending two signals. We'd have one signal out of the executive branch and then another signal coming out of Capitol Hill. And I think that now we've laid that to rest, and we're going to do what we can to move forward—help move forward the democracy that I believe the people of Nicaragua want and the democracy that they've been denied.

So, we've got a big agenda there with forthcoming meetings on Europe, on the NATO summit coming up at the end of May, and then, of course, we'll have a big meeting in Paris in July. So, the agenda is full. We're moving forward on our national security reviews. I remain optimistic about working with the Soviets, but I've said and I'll repeat to you all: I'm not going to precipitously move just to have some meeting going on out there. There's a lot happening, and when I come forward with a proposal, I want it to be sound. I want it to have the full support of the NATO alliance, and I want it to have a credibility, an instant credibility that shows our commitment, not only to enhancing the peace but to preserving the alliance and keeping it strong.

So, there's a lot happening out there. I'm just delighted all of you are here. And now let's just go to the questions.

Substance Abuse and Alaskan Oil Spill

Q. Mr. President, I was wondering whether you, in the light of the Alaskan oil spill, whether you think the Federal Government should take measures in perhaps two areas: one, to tighten up the requirements—the restrictions on alcohol and drug abuse by the people who are in charge of these ships, and perhaps more importantly, to ensure that there is a quicker response on the cleanup efforts?

The President. I would certainly support constitutional steps in the former area. I feel that substance abuse is wrong. I want to see a drug-free workplace, and I would certainly think we could expand that to reasonable requirements in terms of people who are fulfilling important functions like taking crude oil through straits.

I will say it's awful hard to guard against abuse of this nature when you're making laws. And I think one of the things I learned from our meeting with our EPA Administrator [William K. Reilly] and the head of the Coast Guard [Adm. Paul A. Yost] and our able Secretary of Transportation [Samuel K. Skinner] was that this strait was pretty wide and that I don't think there is any way you could plan, as you're making the pipeline, against this kind of abuse. But in terms of testing, I do favor that. You noticed I used the word "constitutional."

What was the second part, Joe? [Joseph Day, WNEV–TV, Boston]

Q. Regarding the cleanup, sir. There's been criticism in Alaska that, for a number of reasons, that the cleanup didn't begin——

The President. I think there were some reasons that it didn't go fast enough, and yes, I think we will have to do everything we can to see that the Federal Government, working with the States and private industry, has as rapid response time as possible. And I will say, I feel very concerned about the environmental damage up there.

When you look at those pristine shores and then see the threat to the fisheries and certainly the loss of life that's taken place so far—birds and animals—you have to be concerned about the environmental damage. And we have a very able Administrator of EPA, a man with unquestioned credentials in environment. And I expect that he and his people will learn from this, and then maybe there are things we can do to guarantee quicker cleanup. Gabe? [Gabe Pressman, WNBC–TV, New York]

Nuclear Proliferation

Q. Mr. President, Iraq is reported as seriously engaged in a program to build nuclear warheads and missiles. Does the prospect of this tiny, sometimes warlike nation being able to wage nuclear war—does it give you great concern for the future?

The President. Well, one, I don't want to give credibility to the reports. Two, I strongly stand against the proliferation of nuclear weapons. We must strengthen IAEA [International Atomic Energy Agency] safeguards to be sure that there is as much inspection as possible. But I don't want to give credence to the fact that Iraq is in the process of building nuclear weapons. I cannot confirm that. And so, I don't want to go beyond that, Gabe. Anytime you see representations that there will be nuclear proliferation it has got to concern us. And we will be making those representations, if we feel it's about to take place, to any country.

Q. Is it a matter that you feel that the Soviet Union and the United States should take action on in connection with small countries developing—other countries developing those weapons?

The President. Well, I think we do agree with the Soviet Union, who has also made its statements against proliferation. And you look around the world and there's some very worrisome areas. You know our position on Pakistan. Pakistan's very concerned about Indian proliferation. And so you can just keep going and find areas that we have to be alert to the dangers, and then try to find ways to see that nuclear proliferation does not happen. But I just don't want to be pushed into giving credence to the reports.

Oil Exploration and Drilling

Q. Mr. President, if I might follow up on the Alaskan situation for just a moment.

The President. Please.

Q. Might this cause you to review and possibly change your support for oil exploration and/or drilling in the northeastern part of Alaska, near that wildlife refuge up there? Might you now review the policies on this because of this oil spill?

The President. No.

Q. No? [*Laughter*]

The President. You asked me if I would review the policies about ANWR [Arctic National Wildlife Refuge], about somebody bringing oil out of a strait 10 miles wide who was allegedly intoxicated. And the answer to your question is no.

Q. The reason I ask is because environmentalists now are very concerned, as they were after the Santa Barbara spill of 1969, which I think you remember——

The President. I do.

Q. ——about transporting this oil from Alaska down the coastline.

The President. Well, we have to transport oil. We are becoming increasingly dependent on foreign oil. And that is not acceptable to any President who is responsible for the national security of this country. So what we will do is not go backwards; what we will do is redouble every effort to provide the proper safeguards. And I think most people are reasonable enough and fair enough to look back at the record over the years in terms of the pipeline, and found that there had been very little damage, if any. Certainly there's been no lasting environmental damage.

Now you have a ship that runs on a reef at 12 knots and driven by somebody or in command by a person who allegedly had been under the influence. And I'm not sure you can ever design a policy anywhere to guard against that. The logical suggestion would be, well, should we shut down the Gulf of Mexico? Should we shut down the oil fields off of Louisiana because of this? And the answer would be no, that would be irresponsible.

So what you do is do the best you can, express the genuine concern that you feel on the environment—and I do feel a concern—but not take irresponsible action to guard against an incident of this nature.

War on Drugs

Q. Mr. President, I'll ask you a question I asked Mr. Bennett earlier today. We've seen a number of antidrug programs——

The President. You didn't like his answer? [*Laughter*]

Q. ——in the last couple of decades, and my question is: Are you confident that the Federal Government, working with local governments and—I'm here in Washington at WMAL—that you will be able to come up with something this time that will actually have an impact on the Nation's drug problem?

The President. I hope so. I would never suggest that the Federal Government will design a program and implement it that will be imposed on every locality. We can't do that. I believe the Federal Government has a certain role, and I believe that the control and power rests with the States and the localities.

But we have a responsibility, and there's no better person to fulfill that responsibility than Bill Bennett in making suggestions in terms of training programs, or educational programs, or enforcement programs, or programs that relate to prison space, programs that relate to utilization of the military assets—and we are using them in the interdiction field—than Bill Bennett.

American Hostages in Lebanon

Q. Mr. President, what is the administration's plan to obtain the freedom of the American hostages in Lebanon?

The President. The plan to do it?

Q. Well, what is the plan? What is the administration's plan——

The President. The administration's plan is to do its level best to try through intelligence to find who is holding these hostages and where they are, and then to do what we can to release them. The plan is not to knuckle under to demands that will put American citizens at risk all around the world. That's the plan.

Two Forks Dam

Q. Mr. President, I gather you had a meeting this morning with Senator Armstrong of Colorado about the Two Forks Dam. Are you willing to ask the EPA to change its decision on that dam at all? What do you have to say to the people who feel they haven't been given a fair shake by the EPA?

The President. Well, I have a feeling that—you ask what I plan to do—I heard from Bill Armstrong a very strong presentation representing the need to go forward with the dam. And what I have asked is that our Administrator, Bill Reilly, be there for that presentation. He was, and he will be back in touch with me. It is a matter that is decided by the EPA Administrator, and I was very anxious that Bill Armstrong have him in attendance so that he hear this side of it. And I have confidence that Bill Armstrong, a very fair individual—and we'll just see what is recommended. But it was a good meeting, and I was given a lot more detail on it than I had had before. But there's—no final decision has been taken on that matter.

Dependence on Foreign Oil

Q. Mr. President, during the campaign, the general and primary, you were asked several times to protect the textile industry from foreign imports. Invariably, your response was that you would enforce existing laws. Since you've come into office, can you point to a single specific instance in which you have taken some action to——

The President. No, no, I can't.

Q. The question is on U.S. dependency on foreign oil. Would——

The President. Let me go back. Existing laws, to my knowledge, are being enforced. I can't think of any new existing law that's in force that wasn't before.

Q. Okay. On the question of U.S. dependency on foreign oil, can we reach a point where your administration would take steps such as an oil import fee or other stances that would help the domestic oil industry?

The President. Well, the domestic oil industry is doing a little better now, the price of crude oil having risen to some $20 or $18—I don't know what west Texas crude is today—$18.50, something of that nature. The industry is doing a little better; the rig count is still very low. I repeat: There is no security for the United States in further dependency on foreign oil. I have made proposals that would stimulate domestic production and I'd like to see the Congress move on those proposals. And so I have not changed my view on the oil import tax.

Drug Abuse Education

Q. Mr. President, what do you envision for the role of education, especially in the fight against drug abuse? Do you see a blending together of the two?

The President. I think it is absolutely essential. We are not going to win the fight against narcotics on the interdiction front alone. And I think Bill Bennett agrees with me that the demand side is the place where we've got to do better, and that means education.

Representative Gingrich of Georgia

Q. Mr. President, we've been hearing about the new whip in the House, and all we hear is: He's a pretty tough guy. Are you going to meet the Congressman, and are you going to talk to him—I mean, talk to him about the style that he's known for with respect to what you have at stake in legislation over there?

The President. I am absolutely convinced, having known Newt Gingrich, that we are going to work together very, very well. I don't think he needs any lectures from me. I think that every Congressman that I've talked to since then feels that he'll be what he said he'd be: a team player. He's not going to suddenly become a shrinking violet, but we don't want that. He's going to be a good leader. And I'm going to work with him, and I'm going to work with him productively. He's got his style, and I got mine.

Private Enterprise and the Space Program

Q. Mr. President, a few days ago, a small company out of Houston called Space Services launched a private rocket. What are your plans to incorporate private enterprise in space? How is that going to work with NASA?

The President. It's going to work that we're going to encourage it. I've had a feeling—and I can't document this—that there has been some reluctance in some quarters of the government against privatization, against the commercial aspects of this. David Hannah, who was the founder, certainly one of the key honchos in that company, has risked a lot of capital. He's gone out and done what he believed in. He had one dramatic failure—and a lot of people were giving him grief over that—and he stayed with it. And he's had a successful launch—he and Deke Slayton and others—and I applaud them.

My role will be to tell the bureaucracy, NASA, that we want to encourage the privatization. NASA has a role that's a government role, and it'll continue to be a government role. But when you have enterprise like this, I think it is nothing but good for the United States. And we need alternate ways to put things into space, and this is good.

Q. Can I just follow that up, Mr. President?

The President. Yes.

Q. Are you saying then, that at some time private enterprise will take over NASA's role of the R&D?

The President. No.

Q. Do you see that coming?

The President. No. No, I don't. But I see NASA making room for a significant private role in terms of putting things into space. And I don't sense, at the highest levels of NASA, a total resistance to this. But I've had a feeling that some involved in the process, not just in NASA but along the way, have not been pushing the concept of privatization—not being as cooperative as we might. So, I see NASA's role continuing in R&D. And I see it continuing in its shuttle business, space station business. I hope to see come to fruition, but I just think that we need to support and applaud those who, in the private sector, have big dreams like David Hannah has had.

Aid to the Contras

Q. Mr. President, you have come under criticism in some conservative circles due to your policy toward the Nicaraguan *contras.* The fact that apparently you have no plans to request military aid for the *contras*—is that a tacit admission on your part that the Reagan administration policy, which you had a part in for 8 years—of asking for military aid for the *contras*—was a failure in forcing out the Sandinista government or making it make reforms in Nicaragua?

The President. No, I think the Reagan policy brought the Sandinistas to the table. And I think, had there been no pressure, the Sandinistas would have gone about their merry revolutionary ways without keeping their commitment to the Organization of American States, a commitment for free press, for freedom of worship—democratization, if you will. So, I think now we are—the problem we had is you go to recommend aid and you have a different foreign policy set on Capitol Hill. Now we're saying—and my own view is there was no way, not a snowball's chance in hell, of getting a dime for lethal aid—military aid—from Congress. And I think anybody that's familiar with Congress would acknowledge that.

So, what we've done is get together with the Congress—with strong conservative support, I might say. I'm not suggesting your question is wrong, because I hear some voices out there hitting us. But it's not bad; the policy has been well received. And we're speaking with one voice, and we are going to push for democratization. And by getting humanitarian aid that goes through this election, I am hopeful that the Nicaraguans will go forward and do that which they give rhetorical support for, but that which they've failed to implement, and that means democracy—free, certifiable elections.

And you hear some criticism of Salvador and what's taken place down there recently. You don't hear it from me because I want to give Cristiani a chance. Those elections were certifiably free—Democrats and Republicans on our commission going down there and saying that. So, we will treat the Salvadoran winner on his word: that he wants to continue the democracy; that we salute Duarte for moving forward; that he stands against the extremes. And I think he's got some big problems with these Marxist-backed guerrillas coming at him. But we're going to support that, just as we're going to support the Central American Presidents as they now, hopefully, push Ortega to do what Ortega should have done long before now.

Foreign Trade

Q. Secretary Yeutter and Ambassador Hills, Mr. President, go to Geneva next week for very important trade negotiations that I've been told will determine the shape of the U.S. foreign policy in the next decade and how the world reads it. What are your expectations from that meeting? Are you optimistic?

The President. Well, it's hard to say. So far, I've been pleased with what came out of Canada, for example. I had a talk with both Clayton Yeutter and Carla Hills two days ago. I would say that Carla expressed a certain optimism about moving forward with the agenda, and that would include agriculture. But I'd just say I'm reserved on it. I'm reserved on how that's going to come out. But I think it is very, very important, if you believe as I do in free trade. I also think we need to get the emphasis on fair trade. And so I'm hopeful that they can make more progress. But I think they think there will be progress, if I had to give you the judgment of both the Secretary of Agriculture and the USTR.

Q. Did you give them any advice that you could share with us?

The President. No. I just said I hope they're right, and they're both professionals. They know my view on opening up agricultural markets. They know my view on fair trade. They know my abhorrence to more protectionist measures, but they also know that I support selective shots. I supported the wheat flour shot that was fired several years ago. And where the United States is being unfairly treated, I think we have every right to fire a selective shot, but I don't want to see us unleash the hordes of protectionist legislation. It gets back to the textile question: I'm not supporting legislation. Fortunately, that industry is doing fairly well right now.

District of Columbia War on Drugs

Q. Can you be more specific about your intentions in dealing here in Washington with drugs and drug-related crime?

The President. Well, I'd have to defer to Bill Bennett in more specificity. But it's going to be across the board where we can help: education, law enforcement, prison—maybe expansion of prisons and prosecutors and judges, if we can help on that area. I'd say those are some broad fields, but I really would have to, on a 5-point program, defer to Bill Bennett on that.

Tritium Production

Q. The Department of Defense has expressed concern over tritium supply to fuel nuclear weapons and such.

The President. What was that?

Q. The tritium supply to fuel nuclear weapons.

The President. Yes, sir.

Q. Do you plan to have the Savannah River Plant be started this year, and what is——

The President. I'm waiting to hear from Secretary [of Energy] Watkins on that, but I do share the concern about it. I am one who believes that it is important that we not—in this era where some are proclaiming no need, almost, to keep our guard up—that we not succumb to that and that we recognize we have got to have a tritium production capability. But I can't give you a time frame yet or anything of that nature.

Illinois Foreign Trade

Q. Mr. Bush, thank you for calling on me. I have a regional question to ask you. Governor Thompson [of Illinois] is in Moscow to establish a trade bureau with the Soviets there. I'd like to know if he went with your blessing, and do you encourage similar initiatives on the parts of other States? And why didn't the Republican Party support Ed Vrdolyak in the Chicago mayoral race?

The President. Very good questions—somewhat unrelated, but let me try to help. [*Laughter*] I have absolutely nothing but admiration for those Governors that try to expand trade between their States, thus the country, and other countries. We have certain laws governing them and Jim Thompson is very familiar with them. I must confess that I personally did not bless this mission because I wasn't familiar with it. He's done other such missions that he's done on his own, as a Governor of a State should do. So that would handle the Thompson one. The other one was on Ed Vrdolyak?

Chicago Mayoral Race

Q. Fast Eddie.

The President. Fast Eddie?

Q. ——support of the Republican National Party as Rich Daley with—be a—Democrats. So, we were wondering why didn't the committee support him——

The President. Well, I don't know. We'd have to refer that to Lee Atwater. If you want to know whether I'd support the Republican nominee, I do—Ed Vrdolyak amongst the nominees. And he supported me, and I don't forget those things. If the question is, how much in the way of assets or stuff, I really would have to refer you to the National Committee.

Federal Aid to Cities

Q. Mr. President, I've just come from Philadelphia, where the mayor last night unveiled the most austere budget they've seen in decades, and he's planning on eliminating city services that have been long protected. And the feeling is that much of the problem is the elimination of revenue sharing and other forms of Federal aid, that cities are being abandoned by Washington. What hope can you offer the mayor of Philadelphia and the citizens there that Washington will begin to help them with some of the social problems they're trying to deal with?

The President. Well, first, I'd tell there isn't any revenue to share, and say it respectfully, but make sure he understands that. And the best hope that we can do for Mayor Goode or for anybody else, is to get our Federal deficit down, because that's going to have a major impact on interest rates in this country. So we've got to get an agreement. And I would ask people who are pressed for funds and certainly a majority of a major urban area would fit that description—not just Philadelphia, a lot of cities—but you say what can we do? What we can do is get the Federal budget deficit solved and get the deficit going downward in accordance with Gramm-Rudman-Hollings.

And that is the best thing to do because if we do that we keep the economic growth going—the longest in a long, long time in American history. That means job creation—the new job creation reached, I think it was 20 million jobs, in the last announcement that I have seen. Interest rates have been creeping up, and this worries me. We've got to always be on guard against inflation, but I don't want to see an interest crunch slow down this economy. And that means then that we are going to have to do the best we can on the spending side. And we are going to have $80 billion more revenue to the Federal Government this year than last—under existing law, no change in law—$80 billion more coming in.

Now some programs have claim on that, many in the entitlements area, I will concede that. But we've got to take that money and use some of it to meet our obligations to get this deficit under control. And that is the best thing—that is the priority thing that the Federal Government can do for any city. And there are a lot of programs that are still amply funded or well funded, and we're going to try to continue as many of those as possible.

Medicare

Q. Mr. President, you promised a kinder, gentler nation, yet your budget calls for a $5 billion cut to Medicare beyond the current law. How can that help but not adversely affect beneficiaries?

The President. Well, what we want to do is take it out of the side on terms of efficiency, of delivering services, and that's what the proposals that we have sent up to the Congress and that Dick Darman is discussing with the various committees—that's the emphasis that our recommendations take. And I hope they'll be implemented. There will probably be some give-and-take on that recommendation, I think.

Q. Won't there be adverse effects, though, to beneficiaries with such a deep cut?

The President. Well, as I'm saying, it needn't be. It depends what's worked out with the Congress. Our proposal took it out mainly on the side of services, so we're not talking about drastic cuts of monies to families.

Last one. Once, twice, then I'll go peacefully.

Former Presidents

Q. Your resident scholar, Dr. Porter, gave us a brief history lesson this morning on the Presidency. And he recalled a conversation he had with you about the great Presidents of the past, and why we don't have great leaders today—talking about Jefferson and Monroe and Madison. Who are your two favorite great Presidents?

The President. First, I'd make a point that everybody looks better over time. [*Laughter*]

Q. But who are your two?

The President. Herbert Hoover looks better today than he did 40 years ago, doesn't he?

Q. No.

The President. People remember—[*laughter*]—not to you, but to a lot of people, they do. They remember the compassionate side of the man. You couldn't even talk about that 30 or 40 years ago.

Q. Is he your model?

The President. No he's not. [*Laughter*] But I was trying to make the point that time is generous to people. I remember the hue and cry around Harry Truman from guys like me and Republicans. Now we're all kind of moderated and think the good things and leave out some of the contentious matters.

So history is basically kind to American Presidents. A model, I think—I was talking to some people the other day about it—would be Teddy Roosevelt. He comes out of the same elitist background that I do. [*Laughter*] And he had the same commitment to the environment I did, although the rules on hunting have changed dramatically since he used to shoot with no limits out there in South Dakota, or North Dakota.

But he was a man of some action; he was a person that understood government, didn't mind getting his hands dirty in government. I remember part of his life being on the Police Board in New York City. Ask Gabe Pressman about that. Probably combat pay was required in those days. So, he was an activist.

I have great respect for Eisenhower. I'm not trying to compare myself to any of these people, but in Eisenhower's case, he was a hero. He was a man that, I'm old enough to remember, was our hero. He led the Allied Forces, and helped free the world from imperialism and nazism. And he brought to the Presidency a certain stability. Others may have had more flair, and he presided, I will concede to you—and I take it you're a student of history—in fairly tranquil times, but he did it. He was a fair-minded person, strong leader, and had the respect of people. And I think he was given credit for being a compassionate individual. So, those are two who I would throw out there. And you can't live in this house and do as I do: have my office upstairs, next door to the Lincoln Bedroom in which resides one of the signed, handwritten copies of the freedom doctrine that will live forever—Emancipation Proclamation—right there in our house. So I think all of us—I think almost all Americans put Lincoln on that list some place.

Q. Any Democrats in your pantheon, sir?

The President. Well, there could well be. Sure.

Q. One?

The President. Well, I respect certain things about Harry Truman. He liked to go for walks. [*Laughter*] But he was tough—said what he thought and had respect from people. Won them over, did it his way, and I respect him being a fighter. They had him written off in '48. I bet 10 bucks against him and on Tom Dewey. And I lost. So did a lot of other people who thought that the polls were going to be correct. So I respect a guy that fights back, and Truman did that.

So there's—and you can walk down—I had a lot of differences with Lyndon Johnson, but there are certain things about him that were good. And he was certainly a very gracious freshman Congressman in those days to Barbara and me. So, we had a little insight that came from a personal knowledge of the man. And he got all caught up in Vietnam, but people forget that—for his legislative agenda—he got through what President Kennedy couldn't get through. We ought to give a little credit for somebody that can do that. He controlled both Houses of the Legislature, which is slightly different than the 41st President is facing.

But it's interesting, because when you live in the house here, you think about the question that you just asked. And again, I'm no student of history. You can't live here without becoming more of a student of history, but you learn the redeeming features. You begin to pick up the redeeming features of those that maybe you hadn't had down as a hero, or hadn't even thought much about in the history of this country.

So I don't think that—I would argue with your premise. I could just go on forever here—[*laughter*]—but I would argue with what I thought was the premise that great leaders were all back there somewhere. I'm not sure of that.

Let me just end on one that—I learned a lot from Ronald Reagan. And one thing I was telling these guys at lunch here: One thing I learned from him is, I never once in 8 years, no matter how difficult the problem, heard him appeal to me or to others around him for understanding about the toughest, loneliest job in the world—how can anybody be asked to bear the burden singlehandedly? Never—and when Reagan left office, you never heard the Presidency is too big for one man—never heard it.

Back in 1980, people like Lloyd Cutler, for whom I have great respect, were saying, look, this is so complex today that maybe we need a parliamentary system. He wasn't proposing it; he was saying it ought to be looked at. Reagan came in, stood on certain principles, stayed with them, and never asked for sympathy or never asked for understanding of the great overwhelming burden of the Presidency, and left with 61 percent of the people saying, "Hey, wait a minute! He did a good job." Good lesson right here in modern history.

Last one.

Federal Drought Relief

Q. Thank you, Mr. President. In the State of Kansas, about a third of the wheat crop has already been destroyed by drought, and there were indications that the rest may be in jeopardy. Given the current budget problems, what's realistic for those farmers to expect in the way of disaster aid?

The President. I can't give you any numbers on it. Current law addresses itself to disaster aid, and we can fulfill our obligations there. But I really am not up to speed enough to tell you exactly what I can propose on that, or what will be proposed in terms of disaster aid.

Q. Are you aware Senator Dole and Senator Kassebaum are trying to get some——

The President. Well, they're talking to our Secretary of Agriculture right now in terms of trying to come up—but I just can't tell you what the administration is going to come up with on it.

Fairness Doctrine

Q. Are you going to sign the fairness doctrine—passed by Congress—expect to veto?

The President. I never talk about what I'm going to sign until I know exactly what's in it—read the fine print. Or better still, given the size of some of this stuff that comes around, have somebody else read the fine print that you have confidence in.

Thank you all. Listen, I've got to run. Thank you all very, very much. Hope you've enjoyed your stay.

Note: The President spoke at 12:45 p.m. in the East Room at the White House. Roger Porter was Assistant to the President for Economic and Domestic Policy.

Statement by Press Secretary Fitzwater on President Bush's Meeting With President Carlos Andrés Pérez of Venezuela

April 1, 1989

President Bush this morning had breakfast in the Residence with Venezuelan President Carlos Andrés Pérez. The breakfast and meeting focused on the Venezuelan debt situation. President Pérez described the economic reforms being undertaken in Venezuela. President Bush encouraged President Pérez to continue those reforms. The two leaders also discussed the situation in Central America and the new United States bipartisan agreement. President Bush emphasized keeping diplomatic pressure on the Sandinistas, and he asked for Venezuelan support in that effort.

The breakfast and meeting began at 8 a.m. and lasted approximately 90 minutes. Participating on the U.S. side were the President; Vice President Quayle; Secretary of State James Baker; Secretary of the Treasury Nicholas Brady; Chief of Staff John Sununu; National Security Adviser Brent Scowcroft; Bernard Aronson, Assistant Secretary of State-designate for Latin American and Caribbean Affairs; and Robert Pastorino from the National Security Council staff. Participating from the Venezuelan side were President Pérez, Foreign Minister Enrique Tejera-Paris, Minister of Planning Miguel Rodriguez, Chief of Staff Reinaldo Figueredo, Ambassador to the United States Valentín Hernández, and Ambassador-designate to the United States Simón Alberto Consalvi.

Statement by Press Secretary Fitzwater on the President's Meeting With the Families of the Victims of Pan American Flight 103

April 3, 1989

President Bush met this morning for approximately 1 hour and 5 minutes with representatives of the families of victims of Pan Am Flight 103. President Bush expressed his sorrow and deep concern with respect to the families of the victims of this tragic incident. President Bush said he had read some of the letters from families and was generally aware of their concerns.

The following representatives attended:

Burt Ammerman, Joe Horgan, Paul Hudson, Wendy Geibler, and Vicki Cummock. The group discussed their concern for airport security and various efforts that might be taken to improve it. They had discussed these matters with Secretary of Transportation Samuel Skinner. Secretary Skinner will address many of these concerns, along with other announcements on airport security, at a press conference later today. The group also discussed the Government's liaison with them in the aftermath of the incident.

President Bush asked Secretary Skinner to remain in contact with the group and to keep them advised of security issues of concern to them. The meeting was sensitive, solemn, and productive. The families appreciated the President's sincerity and the opportunity to discuss the issue with him. Also attending the meeting were Secretary Skinner, Governor Sununu [Chief of Staff to the President], and General Scowcroft [Assistant to the President for National Security Affairs].

Remarks Following Discussions With President Mohammed Hosni Mubarak of Egypt

April 3, 1989

President Bush. Well, it was a special pleasure for me to welcome our good friend, President Hosni Mubarak, to the White House this morning. Our personal relationship goes back several years, from the days we were both Vice Presidents, then through my visit to Cairo in 1986, and then our most recent meeting in Tokyo in February. I am glad for this early opportunity to discuss with President Mubarak the vital interest of my administration in moving the peace process forward.

Egypt's pivotal role in the Middle East and our strong bilateral partnership remain key to achieving that goal. President Mubarak's visit is particularly timely. For over 15 years, Egypt has been our partner in the peace process, and 10 years ago, Egypt and Israel signed their historic treaty of peace. Egypt's continued commitment to expanding that peace is a source of great encouragement for all of us who seek a comprehensive resolution to the Arab-Israeli conflict. The reemergence of Egypt as a respected leader of the Arab world attests to President Mubarak's statesmanship and ability, as well as to Egypt's wisdom in pursuing the path of peace. In our discussions, we spent a considerable amount of time talking about the Middle East peace process. We share a sense of urgency to move toward a comprehensive settlement through direct negotiations.

Ten years of peace between Egypt and Israel demonstrate that peace works, and it can work for Israelis and Palestinians as well. There's a need now for creativity, demonstrable commitment and the application of sound principles—creativity in order to look again at old problems and then devise imaginative ways of solving them; commitment to face the challenges and risks of making peace rather than throwing up our hands and giving up; and adherence to sound principles, like the United Nations Security Council Resolutions 242 and 338. A new atmosphere must be created where Israelis and Arabs feel each other's willingness to compromise so that both sides can win. Violence can give way to dialog once both sides understand that the dialog will offer political gain. Egypt and the United States share the goals of security for Israel, the end of the occupation, and achievement of Palestinian political rights. These are the promises held out by a sustained commitment to a negotiated settlement, towards which a properly structured international conference could play a useful role at an appropriate time.

We also had a chance to review some important elements of our own bilateral relationship. They've been sealed at the highest levels, these special ties that we have with Egypt. They're forged by the global imperatives of peace, stability, and development in the region. They are strong and flexible, reaffirmed by every administration, and resilient to withstand turbulent times for the region and for the world.

President Mubarak enjoys our full support as he implements courageous reform measures to strengthen Egypt's economy for future generations. And under the inspired stewardship of President Mubarak, Egypt has grown in stature and in strength, and we in the United States welcome this development. We are proud of our partnership with Egypt, and I look forward to working closely with President Mubarak in carrying out our common vision of peace, stability, and development in the Middle East.

Mr. President.

President Mubarak. Once again, I meet with my old friend, President Bush, in an atmosphere of genuine friendship and mutual understanding. I have known the President for many years, and I have always found him a man of honor and commitment. His vast experience and profound understanding of international problems have been skillfully employed for the good of his country and the cause of world peace.

Today we discussed a wide range of issues of common concern. Naturally, we focused on matters related to the bilateral relations and the situation in the Middle East. I'm happy to say that we concluded this round of talks with a note of optimism and hope. We are quite satisfied with the state of U.S.-Egyptian cooperation. Our steadily increasing interaction between our two peoples constitutes a cornerstone of the policy of our two countries. We are equally determined to cement this friendship even further.

As President Bush said, our commitment to the promotion of peace in the Middle East is a paramount one that takes priority over any other concern. To us, peace is not only a cherished ideal but also a practical necessity. We believe that the area stands at an historic crossroads that is certain to affect the future of many generations. It's our sacred duty to exert maximum effort in order to widen the scope of peace and remove the remaining obstacles to a just and a comprehensive settlement.

The past few months have witnessed several breakthroughs. The PLO [Palestine Liberation Organization] has accepted unequivocally the requirements for peace. An Arab consensus has emerged in favor of peace and reconciliation. The United States initiated a dialog with the PLO, thus enabling itself to communicate directly with all parties to the conflict. A majority of the Israeli people is shaping up in support of peace. Worldly powers are adopting constructive policies designed to help the parties reach agreement. In short, the situation is right for an active effort more than ever before. The United States has contributed greatly to the process of bringing about this remarkable change. It remains highly qualified to play a pivotal role during the months ahead.

We found ourselves in agreement on most issues at stake. Together, we believe that for any settlement to be durable it should be a comprehensive one that addresses all aspects of the dispute, particularly the Palestinian problem. That settlement should be achieved through direct negotiations between Israel and all Arab parties within the framework of the international peace conference. The basis of the negotiation is Security Council Resolutions 242 and 338: the principle of land for peace, security for all parties concerned, and the realization of the legitimate national rights of the Palestinian people. We are both opposed to the annexation of the occupied territories as firmly as we stand against any irredentist claims and vengeful acts. We reject the policies that result in the continuation of violence and escalation of tension.

I discussed with President Bush some ideas designed to activate the peace process and to facilitate starting the negotiations. On the other hand, we expressed deep concern over recent developments in Lebanon and agreed to double our efforts in order to help the Lebanese people put an end to their tragedy and resume their peaceful mission.

Last, but not least, we discussed certain African problems. And I was pleased to find President Bush aware of the urgent need for a concerted action on southern Africa and the debt problem.

Again, I enjoyed the meeting with our dear friend President Bush today, and I'm looking forward to pursuing with him our friendly talks tomorrow. Thank you.

Note: President Bush spoke at 12:10 p.m. in the Rose Garden at the White House, following a meeting with President Mubarak in the Oval Office. After their remarks, the two Presidents traveled to Baltimore, MD, to attend the opening game of the baseball season.

Nomination of Alan Charles Raul To Be General Counsel of the Department of Agriculture

April 3, 1989

The President today announced his intention to nominate Alan Charles Raul to be General Counsel of the Department of Agriculture. He would succeed Christopher Hicks.

Since 1988 Mr. Raul has been General Counsel for the Office of Management and Budget in Washington, DC. Prior to this he was Associate Counsel to the President at the White House, 1986–1988. He was an associate with Debevoise & Plimpton in New York City and Washington, DC, 1981–1986. He has also served as a law clerk to the Honorable Malcolm R. Wilkey, U.S. Court of Appeals for the District of Columbia Circuit, 1980–1981.

Mr. Raul graduated from Harvard College (A.B., 1975), Harvard University's Kennedy School of Government (M.P.A., 1977), and Yale Law School (J.D., 1980). He was born September 9, 1954, in the Bronx, NY. Mr. Raul is married to Mary Tinsley Raul, and they currently reside in Washington, DC.

Remarks at a Ceremony Commemorating the 40th Anniversary of the North Atlantic Treaty

April 4, 1989

Your Excellencies and fellow citizens, 40 years ago today, some of the most accomplished and farsighted statesmen of their or any other generation—men such as Robert Schuman and Lester Pearson, Paul-Henri Spaak, Dean Acheson, Ernest Bevin—gathered here in Washington under the watchful eye of Harry Truman to take an historic step. They signed a solemn declaration of collective security, a treaty to safeguard the peace and the prosperity of the community of free nations. That treaty proved to be the foundation of the most successful alliance in modern history. And gathered here today are many distinguished Americans who as officials or Members of Congress or private citizens have served the Atlantic community and the ideals that it embodies; and we pay tribute to them.

The North Atlantic Treaty at its signing symbolized a bold commitment to safeguard against new dangers the very freedoms for which we had fought so hard only a few years earlier. Equally, it embodied the shared values of our civilization, values which have given form to many other historic political milestones of the postwar period, from the U.N. Charter to the Helsinki process. And while planting firmly the banner of freedom, the North Atlantic Treaty, because of the strength it mobilized, became the basis of the longest peace—matched by an unparalleled prosperity—that Europe has known. By any standard, NATO has been a resounding success. Like any human institution, it is continually tested and challenged; but we've held together.

And next month, I'll travel to Europe to

attend the NATO summit in Brussels, as well as to visit allied leaders in Rome, Bonn, and London. This will be an historic occasion not only for the anniversary it commemorates but also for the hopeful changes it can mark, changes made possible by the strength and solidarity of the Atlantic alliance.

Today in a changing world, our alliance not only keeps the peace and freedom of the Atlantic world, it has made possible the common effort to build a more constructive relationship with the East. Europe is entering a period of unprecedented change and enormous hope. Without our moral and political unity over four decades, this would never be happening.

Our values of freedom and democracy turn out to be the most powerful political force around the world today, most particularly in Europe. On this anniversary, I join my fellow Americans and citizens of the 15 other allied countries in saluting what has been accomplished. Equally, we salute a bright future and recommit ourselves to the shared vision of a Europe undivided in which security and peace are assured for all the nations of the continent on the basis of freedom, true democracy, human rights, and the rule of law, fulfilling the dream and vision of 40 years ago.

And now I would like to invite the NATO Ambassadors to come forward for a group photo, and then I hope we'll all have a chance to say hello. Please?

Note: The President spoke at 11:04 a.m. in the Rose Garden at the White House.

Designation of Joseph E. DeSio as Acting General Counsel of the National Labor Relations Board

April 4, 1989

The President today designated Joseph E. DeSio to be Acting General Counsel of the National Labor Relations Board. He would succeed Rosemary Collyer.

Since 1972 Mr. DeSio has been Associate General Counsel in the Division of Operations-Management of the National Labor Relations Board in Washington, DC. He has served in several capacities for the National Labor Relations Board since 1955, including Deputy Associate General Counsel in the Division of Operations-Management; Assistant General Counsel of the Time and Performance Branch; serving in the Division of Law, the Appeals Branch, and as a field attorney in the Kansas City Regional Office. In 1979 Mr. DeSio became a charter member of the Senior Executive Service. He is a recipient of the President's Meritorious Rank Award for Senior Executives.

Mr. DeSio graduated from Fordham University (A.B.), Fordham University Law School (LL.B., 1947), and New York University Law School (LL.M., 1955). He was born October 11, 1916, in Geneva, NY. He has four children and currently resides in Springfield, VA.

Remarks at a White House Briefing for Members of the American Business Conference

April 4, 1989

The President. Welcome. Thank you for the welcome, and welcome to all of you. Roger Porter told me he'd had a chance to visit with you all, and I'm just delighted to be with you again. I think I've met three times with this group over the last 8 years. As far as I'm concerned, at least, every meeting has been, for me, helpful, either from garnering what's on your mind from the question or, in one or two more kinder and gentler meetings, we had a chance to visit around a little bit.

But among the friends—I think many friends—that I have in this organization, I want to single out your former Vice Chairman, now the Secretary of Commerce, Bob Mosbacher. And like everyone in this room, he knows what it means to take risks, start a business, make it grow, and keep competitive. And I am just delighted that he is here in Washington with us, giving up his private enterprise, for a while at least, to be Secretary of Commerce. He's on the cutting edge of our national effort to build a better America. And for those of you who were with him in this organization—that's most in the room—he's really doing a superb job.

To be sitting in this room today, you've had to keep your earnings at three times the growth of the economy, I'm told—three times the growth of the economy plus inflation—a tremendous goal. I hope that last category will not make it more difficult for you to achieve—[*laughter*]—but we can talk about that later on. But now we're relying on Mosbacher to make that happen not just for ABC but for every business in America. And so, in a time where the United States creates positions of czar—something that escapes me as to why we turn to that nomenclature to solve our problems—we have a drug czar—we will anoint Bob Mosbacher as the business czar, and then the rest of us can all pursue our favorite pastimes. Mine is fishing, and you guys can speak for yourselves. [*Laughter*]

I don't know—Mike, have you talked to this distinguished group yet?

Dr. Boskin. Tomorrow morning.

The President. Tomorrow morning. I see Dr. Michael Boskin [Chairman of the Council of Economic Advisers] here, and I am very proud to have him on our team. He and I have a very direct relationship, a personal relationship. And he calls them as he sees them, as the umpires over in Baltimore said yesterday. And he's very knowledgeable on how the private sector works. So, he combines that knowledge and the gut instincts that come from that with his enormously good credentials in academia. And so, I think here in this CEA, with him heading it, we have a sensible approach to economics. And I can just tell you that I already have valued the advice and experience we're getting from him. And I'm glad that tomorrow you can have a give-and-take.

Now, you run these high-growth businesses that do represent the most dynamic entrepreneurial segment of our economy. And we know better than to try to fix that which is not broken. So, this afternoon, let me just mention a couple of areas: the economics of enterprise and then the need for education reform.

You know the same lessons that I learned as a businessman. You've got to have capital to grow. And what you don't need, in my view, is higher taxes on the earnings or higher taxes on the workers or higher taxes on those who invest money in the businesses. And right now the Government is making too big a claim on America's capital to cover our deficit. And that capital should be invested in American businesses. And the best way to channel more capital into productive investment is not through higher taxes.

And we're going through a real struggle right now: trying to have enacted a budget which I sent to the Hill a while back that did hold the line on taxes. And it's tough; it's a difficult negotiation. But I can tell you, I have been pleased with the way the budget document was received by the Congress. Nobody jumped up and seconded the motion and agreed that it ought to be passed exactly as it was presented by me and then by Dick Darman. But the response has been good. And I think that signifies that the Congress, as well as the executive branch, are listening to the American people—people saying we've got to do something about the deficit.

So, the answer: spending restraint. And again, I would readily tell you that it's very, very difficult. The working paper that you released last month was another reminder that the deficit ought to be brought under control. Accountability in government demands that we put an end to the spending spiral.

You know, when George Kaufman, that famous wit from the Algonquin Round

Table, was at a party, he heard a self-made millionaire boasting to a circle of people, "I wish I was born into the world without a single penny." And Kaufman answered, "Oh really? When I was born, I owed $12." [*Laughter*]

Well, we don't have to let the deficit play a cruel joke on future generations. Next year alone, fiscal year 1990—and most of you are familiar with this figure—but Federal revenues will rise by more than $80 billion with no tax increase—$80 billion more coming into the Government just under the existing tax structure. And so, what we're going to do is meet or beat the Gramm-Rudman targets.

Our budget consultations with Congress so far have been going well. We're determined to work with the Congress, as I said, and we're going to continue to approach the matter in one of cooperation. There will be some tough, you know, dividing points along the way. But I think Dick Darman [Director of the Office of Management and Budget] would tell you that so far we've been pleased.

To spur greater investment, there is one area where we need to bring taxation down—and I remain convinced that'll mean more revenues to the Federal Government—and this is our proposal to bring down the rate on capital gains. We've got to get it more in line with our trading partners. In the budget we've proposed, we want to restore the differential to 15 percent on long-held assets.

And I think many of you know, as you built your businesses, that you could not walk up to a bank and automatically get startup costs. You can't do that—or at least, you couldn't when I started a small business. Most of you probably raise capital by offering people a share of the business, a stake in the outcome.

And cutting the capital gains rate means more of that can happen. It'll give businesses much more of the capital they need to grow, and it'll bring in $4.8 billion—this is the estimate now, with no arm-twisting, I might add, of the Treasury—this is their estimate—that'll bring in $4.8 billion more in tax revenues in 1990. It will in the process—and this is preaching to the choir—create new jobs. And that is no tax break for the rich. That's a fair shake for every American. And they all come after me, saying this is a tax break for the rich. And I'm going back saying, Steiger amendment, 19—what was it, '78—worked just the opposite: it brought in more revenues to the Federal Government and created more jobs.

We want to build on the energy and the initiative of American business without burdensome mandates that only enforce solutions of uniform mediocrity. Now, we don't want to limit the flexibility of managers and workers, who are trying to find their own best solutions. Many are already succeeding, as you know.

The Chamber of Commerce estimates suggest that workers are receiving more fringe benefits than ever before. Total benefits in 1987 were up 163 percent in a decade. And it is the market, in our system—it is the market, not government, that is responsible for most of this growth. Nearly 70 percent of growth in benefits is due to voluntary action by employers, only 30 percent mandated government requirements. And I want to keep it that way. Our friends in Europe have tried mandated benefits, and they haven't had much success. And I've talked to the political leaders, and I'm sure you've talked to many of the business leaders. And I expect almost to a person, man or woman in business, they agree with that. They're now looking for ways over there to free up enterprise American-style and make it more flexible, not less. And for us to go toward mandated benefits would be, as Yogi Berra put it, "Like deja vu all over again." [*Laughter*]

America is going to be more competitive if we continue to resist the temptation to heap burdensome mandates on the productive private sector. And so, they go after me for an unwillingness to support a wide menu of mandated benefits. But I don't think there is anything kinder and gentler about rendering businesses noncompetitive in world markets, because that will mean fewer jobs. And that is the worst thing that we need in economic times such as these.

A hallmark of this administration, I hope, will be our focus on the future: the importance we attach to making the right kinds of investment. There can be no investment more urgent than education. And in this, all of us have a stake. So, a word about that.

As labor markets continue to get tighter in the coming years, many of you are going to be facing shortages of skilled people. Some managers are already worried about a scarcity of science and engineering graduates. And you've all read the surveys that show many foreign students outperforming our own. Although our best students can compete with anyone in the world, the challenge we face is to adapt our educational system so that all of our students receive the skills they need to share in that prosperity.

My administration has made, rhetorically, and now wants to make in terms of action, education a national priority. Our program is based on four principles: rewards excellence; helps those most in need; demands accountability; and supports greater flexibility in parental choice. And tomorrow, we're going to send to the Congress our education package. We want to reward merit schools that make progress in terms of raising student achievement and reducing drug use and dropout rates. We're promoting parental choice and educational quality through these magnet schools of excellence that some of you are familiar with in your own communities. We want to provide alternative certification of teachers and principals to broaden the pool of talent that's available, President's awards to outstanding teachers, urban emergency grants to provide comprehensive help in fighting drugs for school districts that are literally under siege today, and then a National Science Scholars program for high school seniors, and additional endowment matching grants for these historically black colleges and universities which do occupy—I believe we would all agree—a unique and vital position in American higher education.

We're committed to a program of reform that will give our young people a solid foundation for the future. But to make lasting improvements, we need to get all of the players—administrators, school boards, local business leaders, parents, teachers' unions—around the table working together, and this will demand accountability from all of us. It's going to require the best kind of collective effort from all directions, but it holds the promise of real progress.

Many of you have been prime movers, spending a remarkable amount of your own time making good on that promise. More than a third of you serve on local school boards, public or private, on the board of a local college or a university. We talk about funds at the Federal level. The Federal Government puts up 7 percent of the total tab for educational funding, and the total—I just came from lunch with Larry Cavazos, our Secretary of Education—I believe the figure he used, the amount that's being spent on education today, is something like $330 billion.

So, it isn't necessarily a shortage of funds, and that's what some of these ideas that I'm talking about here take into consideration. Several of you have established a program with a local community college or you've adopted a school or taught part-time or promoted science education across a school district. And that is the kind of involvement that, while it isn't always easy, leads to the kind of educational reform that lasts. And it places you among the Thousand Points of Light that I talk about that do spread hope and opportunity. We're not going to whip the educational problem in this country by everybody running over to the Department of Education. It is a Thousand Points of Light. It is parents that care and school boards and PTA's and good administrators and teachers at the local level.

And so, I would simply encourage you to continue an active role in your communities. There isn't a better answer. By investing your time and talents towards the education of our young, you're helping to bring about something vital: a fundamental cultural shift that reasserts the value of learning in this country. You're breathing new life into an idea that's always been a testament to the American spirit: that doing well demands doing good. So, nothing I might tell you would say it better than your own mission statement, which says ABC executives "believe their own business success carries with it a responsibility to help expand economic opportunity throughout the economy." As leaders not only in business but all across the board in every sector of our society, you know that the national interest requires us to invest in the future. Education is the best investment we can make if we really want to build a better America. And I want to do my part in all of that.

Thank you all for coming, and I'd be glad to take a few questions. Who is first?

Baltimore Orioles Opening Game

Q. Mr. President, Red Scott from southern California.

The President. Yes, sir?

Q. Was that pitch a curve or wasn't it, yesterday?

The President. That pitch—you mean at the Baltimore game? [*Laughter*] I got into the locker room and warmed up with Mickey Nettleton [Tettleton], the catcher. Sixty-four—your old arm gradually got a little looser. But it was high and outside. But here's my problem. [*Laughter*] He stepped in front of the plate before it could break down across the inside. That's my side of it, and I'm going to stick with it.

I'll tell you, there's a little Walter Mitty in me, and I've always loved sports. Walk out there, and you're always wondering about getting booed when—any politician that goes to a ballgame. I don't want to get diverted here, but Reggie asked a good question. So, last year, I go to the All Star Game in Cincinnati—and we're in the middle of the campaign—saying this is suicide, man, what are you doing going out here? You know you're going to get booed. So, right there as I was about to walk out, I saw two little leaguers—one 11-year-old kid, big, tall guy, you know, and a little 8-year-old blonde girl. And I said, "Who are these?" And they said, "Well, these are the little leaguers. They're going out first." So, I got with them, and I said, "You guys nervous?" [*Laughter*] And I said, "Well, why don't we all walk out together?" [*Laughter*] There wasn't a boo in the house—[*laughter*]—it worked!

Okay. Sir?

Minimum and Training Wages

Q. Mr. President, do you believe the training wage proposal will pass?

The President. For the first time, the training wage—well, I refer to it also as a differential—is getting strong support on both sides of the aisle. The problem I face as President is that I went up with a 6-months training wage and a $4.25 minimum wage. And we've talked about it, Michael Boskin and I and Roger Porter and others, and we wrestled with the economics of it. And we figured this is the best offer. And so, unlike the normal trading that goes on here, we said, let's—and our Secretary of Labor wanted us to do it this way, too—Liddy Dole, a very able woman—let's go with our best shot, and let's make very clear in the testimony that that is our best shot. Now, what we saw in the Congress was a pretty good bipartisan support for our proposal—not enough to get it through, but I've got to hold the line on the grounds of economics, on the grounds of making people understand that I was serious about that being the best offer.

And so, I think that if I do what I've just told you I will do, that there is a good chance to get a differential with a reasonable increase on the minimum wage. But I talked here about—I don't want to see a proliferation of new mandated benefits. This is a—you might say mandated, but I think we've got to be very concerned about the inflationary aspects. I think we have to be concerned about the counter-job aspects in some of these low-paying, labor-intensive businesses, particularly in the service sector.

And I think our proposal would make a necessary adjustment, but having the minimum wage would lessen the likelihood of more unemployment. So, I hope it works. I know we're going to have to go through some kind of a disagreement with Congress, because the House has passed a bill that frankly is unacceptable to me. But at least we told them the truth ahead of time: look, we can't go with that.

Relations With Congress

Q. Mr. President, it's been suggested by some of our meetings with Members of Congress that a far greater use of the Presidential veto might be exercised, particularly when spending plans are proposed that obviously are going to not meet either Gramm-Rudman or your own targets. Like, as I understand it, President Reagan only vetoed 5 bills out of 170 in 8 years.

The President. I'm not sure that's correct—the numbers. I do know that—as a member of the previous administration, a proud member—that part of the problem was the size of the bill that comes down here. The one that comes to mind that he did veto was the defense appropriations bill. And there were all kinds of statements of concern that that would unravel the military and all of that. And it didn't; the Congress went back and made an adjustment.

So, we do not control—my party—either side of the Congress. And I think there will be times when we have to say, look, this is what I believe, and then rally our third to defend the President's position, and then go back.

I was using some rhetoric that was kinder and gentler than veto when I described my standing on the minimum wage just a minute—but let the Congress not misunderstand my determination. And this one will be one where we have said, this is what we can do. And I, with respect, would recognize the position of other Members of Congress on it, but I've got to stay with this. And I'm going to stay with it. And I hope it'll send the kind of signal that will have an ameliorating effect on other pieces of legislation.

I'll tell you, there is an ingredient out there today that's quite different. There's a recognition on the part of Members—both sides of the aisle—that the deficit really has to be brought down and that some of the programs—we're going to have to constrain the spending growth.

Now, I was in Congress 20 years ago, and I really see a different mood on the Hill. And the Secretary—again, the Secretary of Education and I had lunch—we talked about the propensity of Congress to add, you know—if you're for education, you propose $1 billion; if you're really for education, make it $2 billion; you're for clean water, where you propose $11 billion, make it $12 billion. I mean, there's a tendency now on both sides to recognize we cannot go down that road. I will have to do some of what you suggest, I know, because they're not going to, obviously, want to do it just exactly my way. But if we demonstrate a fairness, in some areas, a place for compromise—but when there is no room for compromise, be very frank about it, and be up front about it. I hope that we can get along together. But it's going to take doing some of what you talked about here.

President's Agenda

Q. Mr. President, is there any chance that your administration might lead the way towards a tax on consumerism rather than taxes on savings, such as a value-added tax or something of that type?

The President. Well, I don't want to even discuss the tax on consumerism. There's a wide array of suggestions been made, including a horrendously prolific value-added tax, which kind of is painless at first, and then you wake up and realize that you've increased the cost of a lot of goods out there. You have the suggestion that people put a fuel tax on, or an import tax on oil coming into this country. But I really don't believe we should do that.

I have got to get this 1990 budget down without increasing taxes. There's a lot at stake. I think, in fairness, most Members of Congress, whether they agree with me or not, recognize that; and thus they'll understand my fighting for a budget that does not include a consumer tax or a tax on investment-saving capital or anything else. If you want to have a philosophical discussion, I take your point, because I think it is important that if you presented me a hypothesis—you've got to do that, or you've got to do that—and I would accept it and understand the political risk I'd be involved if I showed any flexibility at all in even discussing it. [*Laughter*]

I would have to say that you make a very valid point in your question, because as I tried to indicate in my remarks, it's job creation—and that is subtraction of capital—that is really the best antidote to poverty. The best poverty program is a job in the private sector, where a family can hold their heads up with a certain dignity.

And so, I have got—and that's why when these mandated benefits come down here they have good titles on them, they have things we're concerned about: parental leave or child care, whatever it is. And I'm sympathetic with many of the objectives.

But as I weigh them, I have a responsibility to say what kind of an effect are they going to have on this best antidote to poverty, and that's a job. And so, we've got to resist some of the call for these good things that have good titles if they undermine the fundamental thing, which is our ability to create jobs. So, I will keep trying, keep that philosophy in mind, as we try to answer these pressing social problems.

One word on child care, and then I promise to go peacefully, Bobbie [Bobbie G. Kilberg, Deputy Assistant to the President for Public Liaison]. [*Laughter*] But you know, business and religious groups and family groupings and communities have started moving pretty actively into the child-care business. And you have a different family structure now. You have many two-parent workforce people there—husband and wife at work. And so, I recognize this, and I recognize the demand for child care. But as we formulated our policy, we wanted to get something that would fit within the budget, but we wanted to get something that would not rule out the diverse answers that I mentioned in the beginning: crowd businesses out because they had to turn to highly regulated, centralized child-care centers. Say to a religious group, you can't do this any more; that violates the ABC child care act. Say to a cluster of parents in a neighborhood that alternate taking care of the kids, you can't do any of that because you're not subject to our regulation. And so, what I want to do on something—a mandated benefit of this nature, if you will, is keep it as flexible as possible, preserve parental choice, and recognize this genius of diversity that is our American way.

And it's not just child care; there's a whole array of other mandated benefits that are coming down the pike that we have to address ourselves to. Some we just say, look, we can't do it; we can't afford that. And others we're going to have to say, well, we can do a little here, but it's got to preserve this diversity, and it's got to strengthen family. I am tremendously concerned about the erosion of the family unit in this day and age. And when you look at some of the troubles we have on dropouts or look at some of the troubles we have in keeping our kids out of the grips of these crack pushers, you really have to go right back to the fundamentals in terms of the family unit.

And you know, people say, well, you're privileged; you're blessed in that area. I am. And so, I can't profess to know what it is just from firsthand experience in the inner city, when a family is divided and there's only one parent. But whatever we do at the government level has got to see that we don't diminish family units and, frankly, find a way to strengthen them. And that's why this concept of parental choice, I think, is absolutely essential, that it be woven into everything we do, wherever possible.

Listen, thank you all very much. Didn't mean to end with a sermon, but thanks a lot for coming.

Note: The President spoke at 2:10 p.m. in Room 450 of the Old Executive Office Building. In his opening remarks, he referred to Roger B. Porter, Assistant to the President for Economic and Domestic Policy. The President also referred to the Algonquin Round Table, an informal literary circle that met at the Algonquin Hotel in New York City. Charles R. (Red) Scott, president and chief executive officer of the Intermark Corp. in La Jolla, CA, asked the first question.

Nomination of Delos Cy Jamison To Be Director of the Bureau of Land Management

April 4, 1989

The President today announced his intention to nominate Delos Cy Jamison to be Director of the Bureau of Land Management at the Department of the Interior. He would succeed Robert F. Burford.

Since 1985 Mr. Jamison has been a legislative adviser on the National Parks and Public Lands Subcommittee for the Committee on Interior and Insular Affairs for the U.S. House of Representatives. Prior to this he was district field director for Congressman Ron Marlenee from Montana. He has been a House liaison for the Secretary of the Interior, 1983–1984, and a Republican consultant on the Oversight and Investigations Subcommittee for the Committee on Interior and Insular Affairs for the U.S. House of Representatives, 1981–1983. He was a legislative affairs specialist for the Montana State Office of the Bureau of Land Management in Billings, MT, 1980–1981.

Mr. Jamison graduated from Eastern Montana College (B.S., 1971). He was born April 12, 1949, in Billings, MT, and currently resides in Washington, DC.

Nomination of Richard Schmalensee To Be a Member of the Council of Economic Advisers
April 4, 1989

The President today announced his intention to nominate Richard Schmalensee to be a member of the Council of Economic Advisers. He would succeed Thomas Gale Moore.

Since 1967 Dr. Schmalensee has served in various capacities at the Massachusetts Institute of Technology, including Gordon Y. Billard professor of economics and management, 1988 to present; professor, department of economics, 1986 to present; professor, school of management, 1979 to present; associate professor, school of management, 1977–1979; assistant professor, school of management, 1970; and an instructor, school of management, 1967–1969. Prior to this he was with the University of California at San Diego as an associate professor, department of economics, 1974–1977, and assistant professor, department of economics, 1970–1974. He also served on the President's Council of Economic Advisers as a junior economist, 1967.

Dr. Schmalensee graduated from the Massachusetts Institute of Technology (S.B., 1965; Ph.D., 1970). Dr. Schmalensee resides in Brookline, MA.

Nomination of Thomas Michael Tolliver Niles To Be United States Representative to the European Communities
April 4, 1989

The President today announced his intention to nominate Thomas Michael Tolliver Niles to be the Representative of the United States of America to the European Communities with the rank and status of Ambassador Extraordinary and Plenipotentiary. He would succeed Alfred Hugh Kingon.

Since 1985 Ambassador Niles has been the United States Ambassador to Canada. Prior to this he was Deputy Assistant Secretary of State for European and Canadian Affairs, 1981–1985. He was Director for Central European Affairs, 1979–1981, and served in the United Nations Office for International Organizations at the Department of State, 1977–1979. From 1976 to 1977, Ambassador Niles was a student at the National War College. He was director of commercial affairs in Moscow, 1973–1976; a political officer for the U.S. mission to the North Atlantic Treaty Organization (NATO) in Brussels, 1971–1973; and an economic officer in Moscow, 1968–1971. He also served at the U.S. Embassy in Belgrade, Yugoslavia, 1963–1965.

Ambassador Niles graduated from Harvard University (B.A., 1960) and the University of Kentucky (M.A., 1962). He was born September 22, 1939, in Lexington, KY. He is married, has two children, and resides in Washington, DC.

Nomination of Melvyn Levitsky To Be an Assistant Secretary of State

April 4, 1989

The President today announced his intention to nominate Melvyn Levitsky to be Assistant Secretary of State for International Narcotics Matters. He would succeed Ann Barbara Wrobleski.

Since 1987 Ambassador Levitsky has been Executive Secretary and Special Assistant to the Secretary at the Department of State in Washington, DC. Prior to this he was U.S. Ambassador to Bulgaria, 1984–1987. He has been Deputy Director for the Voice of America, 1983–1984. Ambassador Levitsky was Deputy Assistant Secretary for Human Rights and Humanitarian Affairs at the Department of State, 1982–1983; Director of the Office of U.N. Political Affairs, 1980–1982; and Deputy Director, 1978–1980. He was an officer-in-charge for bilateral relations in the Office of Soviet Union Affairs, 1975–1978, and a political officer in the U.S. Embassy in Moscow, 1972–1975. He entered the Foreign Service in 1963 and has served in Germany and Brazil. Ambassador Levitsky also received the Presidential Meritorious Service Award in 1986.

Ambassador Levitsky graduated from the University of Michigan (B.A., 1960) and the State University of Iowa (M.A., 1963). He was born March 19, 1938, in Sioux City, IA. He is married and has three children.

Nomination of Catalina Vasquez Villalpando To Be Treasurer of the United States

April 4, 1989

The President today announced his intention to nominate Catalina Vasquez Villalpando to be Treasurer of the United States. She would succeed Katherine D. Ortega.

Since 1985 Ms. Villalpando has been a senior vice president and partner of Communications International, Inc., in Washington, DC. She is currently national chairman for the Republican National Hispanic Assembly and has served in this capacity since 1987. Prior to this Ms. Villalpando served as Special Assistant to the President for Public Liaison at the White House, 1983–1985. She was the voter groups coordinator for the Republican Party of Texas, 1981–1983; Staff Assistant in the White House Office of Presidential Personnel, 1980–1981; and vice president of Mid-South Oil Co., 1979–1980.

Ms. Villalpando was born April 1, 1940, in San Marcos, TX. She currently resides in Washington, DC.

Toasts at a State Dinner Honoring President Mohammed Hosni Mubarak of Egypt
April 4, 1989

President Bush. Ladies and gentlemen, it is an honor to welcome the President and First Lady of the Arab Republic of Egypt to the United States. And it's a pleasure for me to greet an old friend and colleague as one of my first visitors to the White House and to this, our first dinner in the State Dining Room.

These last 2 days have been productive, a time for seeking common ground in approaching the peace process, as well as a good time to discuss the bilateral issues. We've also shared some insights into each other's cultures, including the most American of pastimes, baseball. [*Laughter*] And my dear friend, President Mubarak, there's a great philosopher in baseball, a great baseball player named Yogi Berra. [*Laughter*] And Yogi Berra once said, "You can observe a lot by just watching." [*Laughter*] And, Mr. President, baseball is a game in which coordinated effort, patience, and a spirit of teamwork provide the winning edge—in a phrase, the spirit of teamwork.

And you and I share a special bond. Both of us have been tested as seconds-in-command. Both of us have assumed the Presidency at a time when we are challenged to fulfill the promise of past diplomacy.

In fact, there have been favorable developments since your last visit to the United States, just 15 months ago. In Afghanistan, 10 years of foreign occupation have been swept away by a brave people. The cease-fire between Iran and Iraq is a first step towards lasting peace. And we have recently seen an enhanced and well-deserved recognition of Egypt's leadership role in the Arab world, a role that has been enhanced by your perseverance and your commitment to peace. And as I said yesterday, we must work to create a new atmosphere where Palestinians and Israelis put aside violence in favor of words. A dialog for peace is the best way to establish Israeli security and give the Palestinians their legitimate political rights.

Mr. President, just 1 week ago we observed the 10th anniversary of Egypt's historic peace treaty with Israel. And our task today is to extend that peace to all the nations in the Middle East. Such an undertaking will require great patience and immense trust. But I firmly believe that peace will prevail if we continue to work with a common purpose, in the spirit of teamwork. The United States, I assure you, remains willing to help in this important quest.

Mr. President and Mrs. Mubarak—your beautiful Suzanne, I raise my glass in your honor, proud of your friendship, thankful for your leadership. And God bless you, and God bless the peoples of America and Egypt.

President Mubarak. Mr. President, Mrs. Bush, dear friends, let me first express my sincere appreciation for the warm and the friendly reception which we received since we came to your lovely capital, Washington.

My meeting yesterday with you, Mr. President, has a special significance, for it is a beginning of a new era in our friendship and cooperation over the years. Over the years, and in the different roles you assume, Mr. President, you have been a great friend of Egypt and an active participant in the shaping of the Middle East future. Your thoughtful gesture of inviting me to meet with you here in Washington at this early stage, after we had met only a few weeks ago in Tokyo, did not go unnoticed. As we met with you yesterday, and with your able assistants, we look to the future with great optimism. Your deep knowledge of the region and your keen interest in promoting peace assure us of a better and safer future for the whole area.

The American people have chosen you as the torchbearer at a unique and historical junction. The whole world is yearning for an easing of tensions. People in all four corners of the world are seeking a just resolution to disputes and termination of all wars. They want to be better equipped to cope with the awesome challenge they confront today and tomorrow. Issues like underdevelopment and environment require urgent remedies.

Your pledge to make this great land a kinder and gentler nation will certainly contribute to making the whole world a kinder and gentler place for our children and the generations to come. We appreciate your role and the role of the American people as partners in peace and development in the area.

A few days ago, we celebrated, as you mentioned, Mr. President, the 10th anniversary of the peace treaty which was signed here in Washington. That event coincides with the successful conclusion of the Taba dispute, with your help and assistance. These events constitute a living testimony to the validity of the premises that nations can solve all their differences throughout negotiations and other peaceful means. On the other hand, they represent a tribute to the American role as a peacemaker and conciliator.

Over the last two decades, four distinguished Americans, namely former Presidents Richard Nixon, Gerald Ford, Jimmy Carter, and Ronald Reagan—and their assistants played a pivotal role in order to help the parties of the Middle East conflict achieve peace. We are grateful to these men and to every American for their genuine concern and moral commitment. Today President Bush has already begun to put the mark on the peace process, only a few weeks after he had assumed office. We have full faith in President Bush, his sense of fairness and sound judgment. Your leadership, Mr. President, and your commitment as an active partner in the peace process reinforce hope in the heart of every Arab and Israeli who yearn for peace. No one is better equipped than yourself, Mr. President, to influence the course of events in this troubled region.

Egypt is ready to work hand-in-hand with you in the pursuit of that worthy goal. With your knowledge and vision, we can develop all our friendship to a higher plateau of shared views and the common interests. Above all, we share a vision of a Middle East where all countries and people coexist in harmony and cooperate as good neighbors, ushering in a new era in which the enemies of yesterday become partners in the pursuit of peace and prosperity.

Mr. President, our bilateral relations and friendship have been growing over the years, as we talked yesterday about the consolidation of our cooperation in all fields. I am glad to state that our relations have never been better and that our cooperation is proceeding steadily and very smoothly. We value your cooperation, especially at a time when we are exerting great efforts in order to achieve both economic reform and growth. Our cooperation in various economic fields is essential for achieving our goal of improving our economic performances and enhancing productivity.

In our discussions yesterday, Mr. President, as in our previous meetings in Washington, Cairo, and elsewhere, I have sensed the depth of your sentiments towards the friendship that binds our two countries. We in Egypt share those feelings. We are both nations that attach a great value to friendship and loyalty to our friends. Together, we have an opportunity to make the Middle East a much safer and more stable place, to the benefit of all its people and that of the entire world.

Let me, Mr. President, extend my invitation to you and to Mrs. Bush to visit Egypt when you find it convenient and at a suitable time for you, Mr. President and Mrs. Bush. We share with you a great vision of the future for a better and safer world which is within our grasp. We count on your partnership and on your leadership to sail together to that bright destination.

In conclusion, permit me to ask you, ladies and gentlemen, to raise in tribute to President and Mrs. Bush, who are leading this great nation in a new era of hope and dynamism, in tribute to all friends present here, and in tribute to each American on this land, and in tribute for the good friendship between the United States of America and Egypt.

Note: President Bush spoke at 9:35 p.m. in the State Dining Room at the White House.

Remarks at the Presentation Ceremony for the National Teacher of the Year Award
April 5, 1989

Thank you, ladies and gentlemen, Governor, distinguished Members of the Congress. Well, it is my pleasure to welcome so many distinguished guests here to the White House, to honor a teacher who epitomizes excellence in education.

What goes on in the schools is important to me, and I like to get out of the office and talk with the kids whenever the chance presents itself. Last week I was over here in James Madison High in Vienna, Virginia, and had lunch in the cafeteria there. I found the students interested and well informed, the teachers engaged and energetic, but the pizza—[*laughter*]—enough said!

But to the business at hand. The 1989 National Teacher of the Year has made the journey to Washington from Bethel High School in Hampton, Virginia, many times before to give her social studies students a firsthand look at how government really works. But in a more important respect, the journey for this year's winner, Mary Bicouvaris, began almost 30 years ago and 5,000 miles away. Mary, or Mrs. Bic, as her students call her—and I will, too—was born in Greece, came to the United States as a college student, and then chose to stay. Ms. Bic was inspiring good citizenship in her students before she herself was an American citizen. And her secret is using the real world as her classroom: getting her students involved in programs like the model U.N. and in political campaigns and bringing people involved in politics in to speak to her students.

And so, now I'd like to ask Barbara to bring Mrs. Bic up here and present this award. Congratulations!

[*At this point, Mrs. Bush gave Mrs. Bicouvaris a crystal apple.*]

And now let me just take this opportunity, with so many distinguished educators, and Governors, Members of Congress present, to lay out a plan for what we on the Federal level can do to improve our nation's schools.

Six years ago this month, this report that all of us remember, "A Nation At Risk," was first published, and America awakened to the crying need for fundamental change in our educational system. We're at a point today where there's an emerging consensus on education reform and an energy of purpose to take up the challenge. The stakes could hardly be higher. Today's first graders will be high school graduates in the year 2000, a generation on the threshold of a new century. And so, we ask ourselves what can we do today to build accountability into our education system to make sure we don't pass the problem kid who need extra help up through the system, out of the schools and then into the society without the skills that they need? What can we do to make sure our children stay in school, graduate, and get that diploma instead of dropping out and falling into a cycle of chronic joblessness?

I had lunch yesterday with Secretary Cavazos and talked about some of the problems in the severely disadvantaged areas and some on reservations and others where the dropout rates are simply intolerable. What can we do to make sure America has the additional 400,000 scientists—the National Science Foundation say that we're going to need by the year 2000? What can we do to guarantee that graduates in the year 2000 have the skills and knowledge to make this nation competitive in the global marketplace? And all of these are good questions. And then there's the one I often hear when education is the issue and budget constraints becloud everything on the horizon. And the question is: Well, what are you going to do about it? A fair question. We're going to take action to make excellence in education not just a rallying cry but a classroom reality. And we can start by rewarding what works. We can help those most in need. We can promote choice and flexibility for parents and school administrators. And we can raise expectations and hold ourselves accountable for the results.

These four simple ideas—rewarding excellence, helping those in need, choice and flexibility, and accountability—are at the heart of the legislation that I'm sending to the Congress today: Educational Excellence Act of 1989. And I want to take a moment to detail this seven-point plan.

First, merit schools—if our aim is excellence in education, we've got to single out excellence and reward it, whether that means raising test scores, lowering that dropout rate, or making progress of another kind. My merit school proposal will provide cash awards to schools with a proven formula for success and serve as a powerful incentive to encourage other schools to follow their lead.

Second, merit awards for our top teachers—I'm asking Congress to fund a President's Award for Excellence in Education, to recognize first-rate teachers in every State and reward them for a job well done.

Third, science scholarships for our best high school seniors—these awards will go to 570 of the best young scientific minds, at least one from every congressional district across the country. National Science Scholars will receive up to $10,000 a year for 4 years, to be used at the schools of their choice.

Encouraging excellence means more than rewarding successful schools and teachers and students. It means introducing into our educational system elements of flexibility, choice, and competition that will help promote quality education. And that's the idea behind the next two initiatives: magnet schools and alternative certification for teachers.

Magnet schools are an important instrument of choice, a means of promoting healthy competition to attract students and create an incentive for educational innovation. My initiative calls for $100 million a year for each of the next 4 years to help with magnet school start-up or the expansion costs.

Alternative certification is a way to expand the pool of talented teachers and administrators. Not all people who can teach are teachers by training. Whether you're an acclaimed author like Alex Haley or John Updike, who aren't certified to teach the literature courses in which their books are read, or a businessman from Odessa, Texas, anxious to go into the classroom to share what you know, our schools ought to offer that opportunity. And that's why my education package includes $25 million to fund State efforts to encourage more flexible certification systems for teachers and principals.

Above all, our children deserve a chance to learn, especially the least advantaged among us. And the final two initiatives, then, are aimed at securing that change for children in schools plagued by the drug problem and for college-age minority youth.

Drug-free schools—now, this initiative involves funding urban emergency grants to help our hardest hit school districts rid themselves of drugs. The plain fact is kids can't succeed in the classroom if there's drug dealing in the corridors. Our aim must be to get the drugs out, get back to basics, and let students and teachers get down to the business in an environment where learning can take place.

And the last and not the least of initiatives is expanded Federal help to these historically black colleges and universities in the form of matching grants to build the endowments at these vital institutions, endowments that are lagging far behind many other schools. Historically black schools have served as an avenue of opportunity for millions of young men and women, and they do deserve Federal help.

Each of these seven initiatives are going to make a difference. Let me just mention quickly three more efforts: one, Head Start program for disadvantaged preschool children; the tax-free college savings bond program to help our low- and middle-income families cope with the costs of sending a child to college; and the reauthorization of the Carl D. Perkins Vocational Education Act.

The budget I introduced a couple of months ago calls for a $250 million increase to expand Head Start so that more children from disadvantaged backgrounds enter school ready to learn. I'm pleased to say that the House has moved very swiftly to approve the increase. The college savings bond plan that I called for over a year and a half ago is already on the books, and that's a tribute to the foresight of many of the Members of Congress that are here today. And the legislation we will soon propose for voc-ed, for vocational education, will advance the principles of accountability and flexibility and excellence. Good work was done in the 100th Congress. The 101st can build on that work and advance education reform another step.

These education initiatives don't constitute a cure-all, a quick fix for whatever ails our education system. Real reform, lasting improvement, occurs one step at a time, one student at a time.

And I don't have to tell you about the current Federal budget situation. Money is tight. And we wish that more funds were available to spend on all levels of education. I'm one who recognizes the Federal role and, I think, got it properly in my mind that the States and local governments and private institutions across the country bear the significant responsibility. But the Federal Government has a role. It's important that we measure our success, though, not simply by the resources that we put into the effort but by the kind of students that our schools turn out. For our schools, that's the only test that counts.

I've said before that education is long-term planning at its best. And we'll see the payoff from the work we do in schools today years from now. But there are few tasks that demand more urgent attention than the education of our kids.

Let me share a story with you, a story about two ways to look at the future, told by the French. The master of a house was planning his garden and told his gardener to plant a certain kind of tree. And the gardener objected. And he explained that the tree was slow growing and would take 100 years to reach its full growth. It's the master's response that I find interesting. "In that case," he said, "there's no time to lose. Plant it this afternoon." [*Laughter*]

And that's why I really do believe that's the way we ought to look at education. As the teachers here today know, the work you do, the seeds you plant, bear fruit across a lifetime. And there's no time to lose in shaping the next generation and no better time to begin than today. And so, we're taking a step forward, and I ask all of you to work with me to advance excellence in education in every possible way.

Secretary Cavazos, why don't you, if you would, sir, bring Senator Kassebaum and Congressman Goodling and our distinguished Governors up here. And Mrs. Bic, if you'll join us, too. And we will sign this, and then I'll have a chance to say hello.

Note: The President spoke at 11:41 a.m. in the Rose Garden at the White House. In his remarks, he referred to Governors Thomas H. Kean of New Jersey, Michael N. Castle of Delaware, Rudy Perpich of Minnesota, and Gerald L. Baliles of Virginia. At the close of his remarks, the President signed the message transmitting his legislative proposal to the Congress.

Message to the Congress Transmitting Proposed Legislation on Educational Excellence

April 5, 1989

To the Congress of the United States:

I am pleased to transmit today for your immediate consideration and enactment the "Educational Excellence Act of 1989," a bill to provide incentives to attain a better-educated America. I believe that greater educational achievement promotes sustained economic growth, enhances the Nation's competitive position in world markets, increases productivity, and leads to higher incomes for everyone. The Nation must invest in its young people, giving them the knowledge, skills, and values to live productive lives. The "Educational Excellence Act of 1989" would move us toward this goal.

The initiatives included in this bill

embody four principles central to my Administration's policies on education and essential for further education reform. These principles are:

1) *Recognition of excellence.* Excellence and achievement in education should be recognized and rewarded.

2) *Addressing need.* Federal dollars should be targeted to help those most in need.

3) *Flexibility and choice.* Greater flexibility and choice in education—both for parents in selecting schools for their children and local school systems' choice of teachers and principals—are essential.

4) *Accountability.* I support educational accountability, and toward this end, I am committed to measuring and rewarding progress toward quality education.

This legislation builds on the accomplishments of the last Congress, which enacted into law the Augustus F. Hawkins-Robert T. Stafford Elementary and Secondary School Improvement Amendments of 1988. That law took significant steps toward improving elementary and secondary education by improving program accountability, reauthorizing the magnet school program and expanding parental choice, providing greater flexibility to local school districts in the implementation of bilingual education programs, enhancing parental involvement in programs for disadvantaged children, and stimulating education innovation and reform. My proposals have distinct differences from current law, but complement in numerous ways the important work of the 100th Congress in pursuing educational excellence.

The Educational Excellence Act of 1989 includes seven specific legislative initiatives aimed at fulfilling these important principles:

(1) The *Presidential Merit Schools* program would reward public and private elementary and secondary schools that have made substantial progress in raising students' educational achievement, creating a safe and drug-free school environment, and reducing the dropout rate. This program would provide a powerful incentive for all schools to improve their educational performance.

(2) A new *Magnet Schools of Excellence* program would support the establishment, expansion, or enhancement of magnet schools, without regard to the presence of desegregation plans in applicant districts. Magnet schools have been highly successful at increasing parental choice and improving educational quality.

(3) The *Alternative Certification of Teachers and Principals* program would assist States interested in broadening the pool of talent from which to recruit teachers and principals. Funds would assist States to develop and implement, or expand and improve, flexible certification systems, so that talented professionals who have demonstrated their subject area competence or leadership qualities in fields outside education might be drawn into education.

(4) *President's Awards for Excellence in Education* would be given to teachers in every State who meet the highest standards of excellence. Each award would be for $5,000.

(5) Drug-Free Schools *Urban Emergency Grants* would provide special assistance to urban school districts that are disproportionately affected by drug trafficking and abuse. These funds would be used for a comprehensive range of services appropriate to the needs of individual communities.

(6) A *National Science Scholars* program would provide scholarships to high school seniors who have excelled in the sciences and mathematics. These scholarships, of up to $10,000 a year, would recognize recipients' academic achievement and encourage them to continue their education in science, mathematics, and engineering. The President would select recipients after considering recommendations made by Senators and Members of the House of Representatives.

(7) I am proposing to provide additional endowment matching grants for *Historically Black Colleges and Universities*, institutions that occupy a unique position and have a major responsibility in the structure of American higher education.

I urge the Congress to take prompt and favorable action on this legislation. Taken together, these seven initiatives, for which I have proposed adding $422.6 million in the

1990 budget, would help us advance toward the goal of a better-educated Nation.

In addition to these initiatives, I have proposed a budget amendment for $13 million in new funds for experiments and data collection in support of education reform. I am also asking the Congress to fund fully the authorization in the Stewart McKinney Homeless Assistance Act. This includes $2.5 million to fund for the first time the Exemplary Grants program and $2.7 million in additional funding for literacy programs for homeless adults.

GEORGE BUSH

The White House,
April 5, 1989.

White House Fact Sheet on Proposed Educational Excellence Legislation

April 5, 1989

The President outlined today a program for fostering excellence in education. The need for reform is evident:

• America is in an increasingly competitive world, where investment in people, in human capital, is becoming a critical factor in a country's potential for economic growth and prosperity.

• Many of our young people are performing well below their capacity and below the levels of young people in other countries in such important subjects as science and math.

• Outstanding achievement by schools, teachers, and principals too often goes unrecognized and unrewarded.

• Achieving excellence in education requires high expectations, low dropout rates, and safe and drug-free schools.

• Parents lack adequate choice in the education of their children.

• Schools often find that it is difficult to hire capable teachers and administrators, even though many people possess outstanding subject matter knowledge and management skills.

• Projections of the future indicate an increasing shortage of people with advanced training in science and mathematics.

• Our country's historically black colleges and universities struggle to maintain their commitment to educational excellence.

The Educational Excellence Act would authorize several initiatives designed to address these problems.

This legislation builds on the accomplishments of the last Congress, which enacted into law the Augustus F. Hawkins-Robert T. Stafford Elementary and Secondary School Improvement Amendments of 1988. That law took significant steps toward improving elementary and secondary education by improving program accountability, reauthorizing the magnet school program, and expanding parental choice, providing greater flexibility to local school districts in the implementation of bilingual education programs, enhancing parental involvement in programs for disadvantaged children, and stimulating education innovation and reform. The President's initiative proposes new efforts, but complements in numerous ways the important work of the 100th Congress in pursuing educational excellence.

This legislation is based on four basic principles. These are:

1. *Recognition of Excellence.* Recognizing and rewarding our best schools, teachers, and students will serve as an incentive for all schools, teachers, and students to improve their performance.

2. *Addressing Need.* This administration believes that Federal dollars should assist those most in need.

3. *Flexibility and Choice.* Greater flexibility and choice in education, both parental choice in selecting schools for their children and local school systems' choice of teachers and principals, are important to providing

the means and incentives for achieving educational excellence.

4. *Accountability.* The administration supports objective measurement and reward of progress toward quality education.

The Educational Excellence Act includes seven legislative initiatives aimed at fulfilling these important principles. Highlights of the individual initiatives follow.

Presidential Merit Schools

Program

• The Presidential Merit Schools program would provide cash awards to public and private elementary and secondary schools that have made substantial progress in raising student educational achievement, creating a safe and drug-free school environment, and reducing the dropout rate. This program would provide a powerful incentive for all schools to improve the educational achievement of their students.

Funding

• The legislation would authorize $250 million for fiscal year 1990, increasing to $500 million by 1993. These funds would be allocated by formula to the States, with State allocations based on school-aged population and State shares of funding under the Chapter 1 Basic Grants program.

• The amount of each merit award would depend on State-established criteria, including criteria related to the size of the school and the composition of the student body.

Implementation

• Presidential Merit Schools would be selected by the State, assisted by a special State review panel, using State and Federal criteria. These criteria would focus on schools' progress in improving students' educational performance, creating or maintaining a safe and drug-free environment, reducing the dropout rate, and other State-determined factors. States could also give special consideration to schools enrolling substantial numbers or proportions of children from low-income families.

• A school selected as a Presidential Merit School would use its award for any purpose that furthers its educational program, including development or implementation of special educational programs, purchase of computers and other materials and equipment, and bonus payments to teachers and administrators. Private schools would be prohibited from using Presidential Merit Schools funds to provide religious instruction or for other sectarian purposes.

• The bill would also prohibit the reduction of other Federal, State, or local support to a school because of its receipt of a Presidential Merit Schools award.

Magnet Schools of Excellence

Program

• Currently, the Department of Education makes Magnet Schools Assistance grants to school systems undergoing court-ordered or voluntary desegregation. Because of the success of magnet schools in increasing parental choice and improving educational quality, the bill would create a Magnet Schools of Excellence program to support the establishment, expansion, or enhancement of magnet schools, without regard to the presence of desegregation plans.

Funding

• The bill would authorize $100 million for Magnet Schools of Excellence for fiscal year 1990 and each of the 3 succeeding fiscal years.

Implementation

• Local educational agencies, intermediate educational agencies, or consortia of such agencies would apply directly to the Department for competitive grants. Applications would be selected for funding on the basis of the quality of the proposed project, the likelihood of its successful implementation, and the likelihood of its strengthening the educational program of the district or districts.

• The Department would encourage applications that recognize the potential of educationally disadvantaged children to benefit from magnet school programs and applications to establish, expand, or enhance magnet schools which enhance the diversity of educational offerings to students.

• No magnet school could be supported under the program for more than 2 years or if the award would result in segregation or impede the process of desegregation.

ALTERNATIVE CERTIFICATION OF TEACHERS AND PRINCIPALS

Program

• The bill would provide assistance to States interested in expanding the pool of talent from which to draw teachers and principals. Funds would support such activities as training, program development, and evaluation. The bill would provide incentives for States to develop, expand, or improve flexible certification systems designed to draw into education talented professionals with demonstrated subject-area competence or leadership qualities.

Funding

• The legislation would authorize $25 million for fiscal year 1990 only, for one-time grants to the States. States would apply for the amount of funds they need or an amount that is proportional to their school-aged population, whichever is less; excess funds would be reallocated on the basis of demonstrated need.

Implementation

• Grants could support the design, development, implementation, testing, and evaluation of strategies for the alternative certification of teachers and principals, as well as training and recruitment activities.

• States would be required to consult with teachers, principals, parents, and others in developing their applications. Subgrants to school districts, intermediate educational agencies, colleges and universities, and consortia of these agencies would be authorized.

PRESIDENT'S AWARDS FOR EXCELLENCE IN EDUCATION

Program

• The success of American education depends heavily on the Nation's teachers. Because teachers who meet the highest standards of excellence deserve public recognition, respect, and appropriate financial rewards, our bill includes authorization for a new program of Presidential awards for excellent public and private school teachers. The amount of each Presidential award would be $5,000. Teachers receiving awards would be permitted to use their awards for any purpose.

Funding

• The bill would authorize $7.6 million for each of the fiscal years 1990 through 1993. Funds would be allocated to the States on the basis of the number of full-time equivalent public school teachers in each State.

Implementation

• In each State, winners of Presidential awards would be selected by a statewide panel, selected by the Governor, from nominations made by local educational agencies, public and private schools, parents, teachers, teacher associations, associations of parents and teachers, private businesses, business groups, and student groups. In making selections, the panel would use selection criteria developed by the State, subject to approval by the Secretary.

• Each State would be permitted to use up to 5 percent of its allocation for administrative expenses, including the cost of convening the statewide panel.

NATIONAL SCIENCE SCHOLARS

Program

• The National Science Scholars program would encourage achievement in the sciences by providing scholarships to graduating high school students who have excelled in the sciences and mathematics and engineering. The scholarships would recognize the academic achievement of these students and would encourage them to continue their education in these academic areas at the postsecondary level.

Funding

• The bill would authorize $5 million for fiscal year 1990. The amount authorized would increase in increments of $5 million per year to a total authorization of $20 million for fiscal year 1993. These funding levels would ensure that the scholars would be supported throughout their undergraduate study and that a new group of 570 scholars would be selected each year.

Implementation

- National Science Scholars would receive up to $10,000 a year for each year of undergraduate education.
- Each State would nominate between 4 and 10 students per congressional district to receive scholarships. The President would select a total of 570 scholars, after considering the recommendations of an advisory board (30 scholarships) and the recommendations of Senators and Members of the House of Representatives (540 scholarships). The scholars would be nominated in accordance with specific academic achievement criteria that would be developed by the Secretary in consultation with a panel of experts in the sciences, mathematics, and engineering.

DRUG-FREE SCHOOLS URBAN EMERGENCY GRANTS

Program

- Prevention and education programs are frequently inadequate in urban areas with the most severe drug problems. More concentrated and comprehensive approaches are required. The bill would amend the Drug-Free Schools and Communities Act of 1986 to authorize a program of Urban Emergency Grants.

Funding

- The bill would authorize $25 million for each of the fiscal years 1990–1993 for Urban Emergency Grants.

Implementation

- This amendment would authorize a small number of special, competitive grants to urban districts that have the most severe drug problems so that these districts can develop and implement comprehensive approaches to solving those problems.

HISTORICALLY BLACK COLLEGES AND UNIVERSITIES

Program

- Historically Black Colleges and Universities (HBCU's) play a vital role in the American system of higher education. In the past, these institutions offered many Black Americans their only opportunity for a higher education. Today HBCU's enrich the range of educational choice. These institutions enroll approximately 220,000 students.
- Many HBCU's are financially weaker than comparable institutions. This bill would strengthen HBCU's by providing additional support for endowment matching grants. Endowment building is an especially effective way to create financial strength and long-term financial security for HBCU's.

Funding

- The bill would provide additional authorizations of $10 million for fiscal year 1990, $20 million for both fiscal year 1991 and fiscal year 1992, and $10 million for fiscal year 1993.

Implementation

- Federal funds would be available to match private sector contributions to the school's endowment fund. Income from the endowment fund could be used to improve academic programs as well as administrative management.
- All HBCU's currently eligible under title III of the Higher Education Act of 1965 would be eligible to apply for grants.

Message to the Congress Transmitting the Annual Report on International Activities in Science and Technology
April 5, 1989

To the Congress of the United States:

In accordance with Title V of the Foreign Relations Authorization Act for Fiscal Year 1979 (Public Law 95–426), I am transmitting the annual report on international activities in science and technology (S&T) for Fiscal Year 1988.

I firmly believe that the economic advances of the 21st century are rooted in the research and development (R&D) performed in laboratories around the world today. Innovation and dedication of resources and people, both public and private, to scientific and technological advances are essential to economic progress. Our future well-being as a nation is dependent upon the continuous transfer of technology from basic science into commercial goods and services.

Over the past 5 years, this concept—the linkage of our science and technology enterprise to our future global competitiveness—has become a dominant theme in the United States. Because of this linkage, some have challenged our historical subscription to an open, unimpeded R&D system, claiming that such a system transfers valuable R&D results to other countries for commercialization and eventual sale in the United States. I, and President Reagan before me, believe that the United States benefits, and our global competitive position is improved, by international cooperation in research and development based on balance, reciprocity, and comparable access. We have actively promoted this policy through multilateral fora and bilaterally with our trading partners and advanced developing countries.

For example, a major accomplishment of FY 1988 was winning multilateral endorsement for key themes of President Reagan's Executive Order No. 12591 of April 10, 1987, on "Facilitating Access to Science and Technology." At the Ministerial Meeting of the Organization for Economic Cooperation and Development (OECD) in Paris in May 1988, the ministers endorsed a new framework of common principles for international S&T cooperation, originally introduced by the President's Science Adviser, Dr. William R. Graham. The framework endorses adequate investment and excellence in basic sciences; reciprocity and balanced access as a solid foundation for science and technology cooperation; improved universal protection of intellectual property rights (IPR); and effective protection of sensitive knowledge. I am convinced that the new OECD framework establishes a firm, future-oriented foundation for sustainable cooperation in science and technology.

On the bilateral front, under the guidance of the Economic Policy Council, the Administration developed a coordinated policy to reshape our S&T relationship with Japan based on the principles of shared responsibilities, equitable contributions, adequate protection and fair disposition of intellectual property rights, acknowledged security obligations, and comparable access to government-sponsored and -supported R&D facilities and programs. The culmination of this effort came in Toronto in June 1988, when President Reagan and Prime Minister Takeshita signed the new umbrella S&T Agreement. We view this as a model agreement and now are incorporating its principles into all our science and technology bilateral agreements.

Maintenance of our global competitiveness requires adequate and effective protection and equitable allocation of intellectual property rights. The commercial development of a new technology requires large investments of time, money, and talent. Continued investments in research and development require the ability to derive economic benefits from the new technology. Therefore, in FY 1988, we initiated numerous bilateral and multilateral dialogues on the benefits accruing to all partners from effective protection and equitable disposition of IPR.

With the view that balanced and reciprocal cooperation in S&T benefits the United States and the world at large, at the December 1987 Washington Summit, President Reagan and General Secretary Gorbachev agreed to further cooperation in the areas of transportation, global climate change, ocean studies, and nuclear reactor safety, as well as to continue a multilateral conceptual design effort in thermonuclear fusion. As a result, in April 1988, we signed a protocol with the Soviets on cooperation in maintaining the safety of civilian reactors. This agreement, which was stimulated by Chernobyl, covers the design and operation, health, environmental, and regulatory aspects of the reactor safety problem. In addition, in January 1989, we signed a U.S.-USSR Framework Agreement for Cooperation in Basic Scientific Research, which is serving as the model for other U.S.-USSR agreements to ensure policy consistency among all our extensive interactions with the Soviets in science and technology.

Sustainable international cooperation in science and technology is good for the Nation, particularly when projects that are in the national interest are enhanced by or intrinsically require multilateral effort. Examples are the Space Station Freedom, the superconductor super collider (SSC), AIDS research, and global climate change.

In December 1987, the Secretary of Energy invited our major allies to contribute to building the world's most advanced high-energy particle accelerator, the SSC, and to participate in its utilization. We now look forward to extensive collaboration in the project.

In September 1988, a final agreement was signed among the United States, member states of the European Space Agency (ESA), and the Governments of Japan and Canada on the Space Station Freedom's design, development, and operation.

AIDS is a major worldwide public health concern. The United States Government, particularly the Agency for International Development and the Public Health Service, is engaged in a substantial international program working with the World Health Organization and others to develop national plans to combat AIDS and to utilize research findings and technologies as they become available.

The policy question of human impact on the global environment in the past few years has moved out of the confines of scientific papers and conferences to become a front-page issue. Recent events, such as the 1985 discovery of the Antarctic "ozone hole" and the 1988 North American drought, have created much debate regarding the relative contributions of human-induced and natural processes on global climatic and environmental change. Bearing these concerns in mind, in April 1988, the United States ratified the Montreal Protocol on Substances that Deplete the Ozone Layer, which provides for reductions in production and consumption of principal ozone-depleting chemicals.

Significant uncertainties remain about the magnitude, timing, and regional impacts of global climate change. During FY 1988, the United States has made major contributions to international plans to reduce those uncertainties. The FCCSET Committee on Earth Sciences prepared a strategy for the U.S. Global Change Research Program, which I have endorsed. Prepared in close collaboration with other national and international planning groups and activities, the U.S. research strategy calls for an integrated approach in partnership with international organizations such as the World Meteorological Organization, the United Nations Environment Programme, and the International Council of Scientific Unions. The Intergovernmental Panel on Climate Change launched its multilateral effort in November 1988 with U.S. participation and support.

Believing that the R&D of today is the goods and services of tomorrow, and believing that further discoveries in superconductivity hold enormous potential for applications, President Reagan signed into law on November 19, 1988, the "National Superconductivity and Competitiveness Act of 1988," which establishes a framework for a national program in superconductivity. He also named a National Commission on Superconductivity to provide guidance over the long term, as the real benefits from superconductivity may take years or decades to fully realize. Our goal as a nation is to lead the world in superconductivity R&D and in translating this new technology into useful products.

Strong U.S. involvement in international S&T requires excellence in the administration and implementation of our S&T policies around the world. Therefore, in response to President Reagan's Executive Order No. 12591 of April 10, 1987, the Department of State has sought to strengthen the technical expertise of its S&T officer corps by intensified recruitment from United States Government technical agencies, academia, and industry, and has recently established a specific career track for S&T officers. In addition, the Department of State, in cooperation with the National Science Foundation and the Department of Commerce, initiated the S&T Reporting and Information Dissemination Enhancement Project (STRIDE) in order to improve international scientific reporting.

As President, I intend to continue to build on the solid foundation in science and technology laid by President Reagan and his Administration. I believe that sustainable cooperation in science and technology is good for America and good for the world. Therefore, as the technology gap narrows, as internationalization of scientific and technological progress becomes the accepted norm, we must be concerned that the competitive drive for technological leadership not lead to protectionism in science, even as we are removing barriers to free and open trade. The challenge facing us in the years ahead is how to maintain and expand an open, mutually beneficial world system of exchange and cooperation in science and technology without undercutting our national competitiveness or jeopardizing our security interests and responsibilities. Articulating and responding to that challenge is a high priority of my Administration.

GEORGE BUSH

The White House,
April 5, 1989.

Statement by Press Secretary Fitzwater on the Polish Roundtable Accords
April 5, 1989

Seven years ago, Americans lit candles in support of Poland's freedom in the hope that darkness of repression would someday be lifted. Today Solidarity signed accords which will lead to its relegalization and which will allow it to resume its rightful place in Polish life.

This is a great day for the Polish people and for freedom. The discussions have been long and arduous. We welcome the roundtable accords and see them as an historic step towards pluralism and freedom which we hope will eventually take Poland far from totalitarianism and towards a better political and economic future.

We are following the developments in Poland closely and are consulting with Congress and our friends and allies on this issue. In September 1987, then Vice President Bush visited with Lech Walesa and General Jaruzelski concerning the Polish political situation. The Vice President at that time urged dialog and reconciliation to bring about economic growth and political freedom.

The President today is very pleased by the accords that started Poland on this new path of reconciliation.

Note: Marlin Fitzwater read the statement to reporters at 1:32 p.m. in the Briefing Room at the White House.

Statement by Press Secretary Fitzwater on Soviet Policy in Central America
April 5, 1989

We listened carefully to what President Gorbachev had to say in Havana yesterday. While his words about not exporting revolution are welcomed, they are not matched by deeds which would give those words credence.

Today we call upon the Soviets to cut off their half-billion-dollar annual military aid to Nicaragua. The Soviets continue to pour arms into Nicaragua, a country whose army is already larger than those of all their neighbors combined. This is hard to fathom. It is a key issue in resolving the conflict in Central America. Our bipartisan plan for peace in Central America has the support of the Central American democracies. It is time for the Soviet Union to join us in supporting that plan.

If President Gorbachev means his words, the Soviets should demonstrate through their behavior that they are adhering to this principle, and they should pressure their client states and revolutionary groups that they support to do the same. We note that the Soviets and Cuba have concluded a friendship treaty that apparently commits both parties to the peaceful resolution of conflicts in the region. We trust that the Soviets will follow these words with concrete actions.

We believe, however, that to demonstrate his commitment to Esquipulas, President Gorbachev could have proposed a cutoff of military supplies to all irregular forces in the region. That is what Esquipulas calls for: an end to outside support to the guerrilla forces. This would have suggested a "new thinking" in Central America.

The United States is in compliance with Esquipulas. We are not providing military aid to the Nicaraguan resistance. The Soviet bloc, particularly Nicaragua and Cuba, continue to supply military and logistical support to the FMLN [Farabundo Marti National Liberation Front, El Salvador] and other irregular forces in Central America.

As the President and the Secretary of State have said, we reject the idea of equivalence between legitimate U.S. interests and the Soviet presence in Central America. We provide support, including military assistance, to the democratic Governments of Central America. These governments are not involved in subversion of their neighbors.

Note: Marlin Fitzwater read the statement to reporters at 1:32 p.m. in the Briefing Room at the White House.

Statement by Press Secretary Fitzwater on the Suspension of Semiautomatic Weapons Imports

April 5, 1989

I want to announce an action that the Treasury Department is taking today with regard to suspension of imports of certain semiautomatic weapons.

In recently approving a temporary suspension of imports of certain semiautomatic weapons, the President sought to foster a climate in which reasonable, well-intentioned people on all sides of the firearms issue could work out a solution without infringing on the rights of law-abiding hunters and sportsmen. In an effort to ensure that existing laws are being enforced to the fullest extent possible, he ordered the Treasury Department to review the suitability of these weapons for sporting purposes. To date, the Treasury review has disclosed 24 additional types of imported firearms which, by virtue of their general appearance and capabilities, compete directly with those firearms for which import permits were previously suspended. To ensure an orderly and fair review process, the President has authorized the Secretary of the Treasury to expand the temporary import suspension to include these additional 24 types of weapons.

This action will accomplish two things. First, those importers whose permits have already been suspended will not suffer a loss of market to importers of similar weapons during the review period. Second, this action will preclude imports of firearms which might later be found unsuitable for sporting purposes.

The President believes that by working closely with law enforcement groups, sportsmen, concerned citizen groups, and the Congress, we can reach a solution to these problems.

Note: Marlin Fitzwater read the statement to reporters at 1:32 p.m. in the Briefing Room at the White House.

Remarks Following Discussions With Prime Minister Yitzhak Shamir of Israel
April 6, 1989

The President. Well, the Prime Minister Shamir and I have had a very productive meeting. My message to him and, through him, to the Government and the people of Israel was clear: We are friends, strategic partners, and allies. And the mutual interests that bind together the people of the United States and Israel are broad and deep. The Prime Minister and I dedicated ourselves to maintaining and, where possible, improving the relationship between our two countries. Both of us are committed to this goal.

Throughout the world, old enemies are finding ways to talk to one another and to end conflicts in a manner that preserves the basic interests of all concerned. This can and must happen in the Middle East. The Arab-Israeli conflict can be resolved. Peace, security, and political rights can be attained through direct negotiations. The status quo serves the interests of no one. In this spirit, I reiterated to Prime Minister Shamir the resolve of the United States to assist the parties of the Middle East in their pursuit of a comprehensive settlement of the Arab-Israeli conflict. Our responsibility as friends and as partners in the search for peace is to help develop approaches that enhance peace prospects. Problems do not resolve themselves; leaders acting with courage and vision solve problems. Menachem Begin and Anwar Sadat demonstrated this truth a decade ago at Camp David. Today's leaders can afford to do no less.

I reassured the Prime Minister that the fundamental basis of our approach to a Middle East settlement has not changed. The United States is committed to a comprehensive peace achieved through direct negotiations based on U.N. Security Council Resolutions 242 and 338. This remains the building block for a viable negotiation for a durable settlement. This is our goal. With regard to final status issues, I reaffirmed to the Prime Minister that we do not support an independent Palestinian state nor Israeli sovereignty or permanent occupation of the West Bank and Gaza.

To move the peace process forward, I discussed with the Prime Minister, as I had earlier this week with President Mubarak, an ambitious but realistic approach. Progress will require meaningful steps to reduce tensions, political dialog between Israel and Palestinians, and clear indications that all concerned are prepared to think creatively about key substantive issues. Israel has an obligation to contribute to this process, but it cannot be expected to assume the entire burden. The Palestinians, the Arab States, and other interested parties must demonstrate that they, too, are willing to make peace a reality.

I stressed that no peace process can succeed in a political vacuum. I believe it is in Israel's interest to engage in a serious dialog with Palestinians that address their legitimate political rights. The United States believes that elections in the territories can be designed to contribute to a political process of dialog and negotiation. We urge Israel and the Palestinians to arrive at a mutually acceptable formula for elections, and we plan in the days and weeks ahead to work toward that end.

In negotiations, Israel understands that Palestinians will be free to bring their own positions and preferences to the bargaining table. The Prime Minister assured me that Israel is committed to negotiating an agreement on final status that is satisfactory to all sides. And he made it clear that interim arrangements on Palestinian self-rule are not the end of the road but are directly linked to a broader political process that includes negotiating and concluding an agreement on final status.

I'm encouraged by the Prime Minister's assurance that all options are open for negotiation. The Prime Minister and I agreed that our governments would remain in close touch to ensure that everything possible is being done to promote the prospects for peace in the Middle East. And speaking for myself and for the American people, I want to assure everyone that the United States is committed to promoting this goal.

Mr. Prime Minister, we're delighted you're here. The floor is yours, sir.

The Prime Minister. Thank you, Mr. President. I am honored to be here today. Let me first, on behalf of the people of Israel and on behalf of my wife and myself, express our warm wishes on your assuming the mantle of leadership of the United States and the free world. We have cherished your personal friendship and warm humanitarian concern for many years. We shall never forget the help you have extended our brothers and sisters in distress, just as we shall always remember the role the United States has played in our history.

Our alliance is based on common values and shared interests. Our agreements on strategic cooperation and free trade area benefit both countries. They help us continue as a vanguard of democracy in the Middle East. I am confident that under your administration our bonds of friendship and cooperation will grow even stronger.

Our two nations share the values and ideas of the free world and the ideals of democracy and freedom. What we do not share is a neighborhood. For us the carnage in Beirut, the use of poison gas against civilians, and acts of terrorism and fanaticism are not news from afar, for as they are events happening around the corner, they are our daily reality. If there is one mistake Israel cannot afford to make, it is the mistake of forgetting where we live.

I would like to reiterate here what I said to you in private: We shall make the greatest possible efforts to achieve peace, short of endangering the security of our state. We consider the establishment of a Palestinian state west of the Jordan River, which is an objective of the PLO [Palestine Liberation Organization], a mortal threat to our security. I have assured you that we would sit with anyone, anytime, anywhere, without preconditions if we thought it would advance the cause of peace. But we cannot lend ourselves to any steps that will result in a Palestinian state, which is a prescription not for peace but for war. I can assure you we will be forthcoming. We believe the Camp David accords based on Resolutions 242 and 338 are the cornerstone of peace in our region. We faithfully abide by your agreements, and we expect others to do so as well.

Mr. President, to advance the cause of peace, we have put forward a four-point peace initiative. First, we propose an effort to make the existing peace between Israel and Egypt based on the Camp David accords a cornerstone for expanding peace in the region. We call upon the three signatories of the Camp David accords at this 10th anniversary of the treaty of peace to reaffirm indeed their dedication to the accords.

Second, we call upon the United States and Egypt to make it clear to the Arab Governments that they must abandon their hostility and belligerency toward Israel. They must replace political warfare and economic boycott with negotiations and cooperation.

Third, we call for a multinational effort under the leadership of the U.S. and with substantial Israeli participation to finally solve the Arab refugee problem perpetuated by Arab Governments, while Israel absorbs hundreds of thousands of Jewish refugees from Arab countries. All these refugees should have decent housing and live in dignity. This process does not have to await a political solution or to substitute for it.

Fourth, in order to launch a political negotiating process, the proposed free democratic elections, free from an atmosphere of PLO violence, terror, and intimidation among the Palestinian Arabs of Judea, Samaria, and Gaza—their purpose is to produce a delegation to negotiate an interim period of self-governing administration. To shape modalities and participation in the elections will have to be discussed. The interim phase will provide a vital test of coexistence and cooperation. It will be followed by negotiations for a permanent agreement.

All proposed options will be examined during these negotiations. This is an outline of our comprehensive plan for peace. It is based on democratic principles. It addresses the real issues. Together, I believe we can achieve these goals.

May God lead us to the right decision. Thank you, Mr. President.

Note: The President spoke at 12:15 p.m. at the South Portico of the White House. Prior to their remarks, the President and the Prime Minister met in the Oval Office.

Notice of the Continuation of the National Emergency With Respect to Panama
April 6, 1989

On April 8, 1988, by Executive Order No. 12635, the President declared a national emergency to deal with the unusual and extraordinary threat to the national security and foreign policy of the United States constituted by the actions and policies of the Noriega/Solis regime of Panama. Because the Noriega/Solis regime has continued its actions and policies, the national emergency declared on April 8, 1988, must continue in effect beyond April 8, 1989. Therefore, in accordance with section 202(d) of the National Emergencies Act (50 U.S.C. 1622(d)), I am continuing the national emergency with respect to Panama. This notice shall be published in the *Federal Register* and transmitted to the Congress.

GEORGE BUSH

The White House,
April 6, 1989.

[*Filed with the Office of the Federal Register, 2:36 p.m., April 6, 1989*]

Note: The notice was printed in the Federal Register of April 7.

Message to the Congress on the Continuation of the National Emergency With Respect to Panama
April 6, 1989

To the Congress of the United States:

Section 202(d) of the National Emergencies Act (50 U.S.C. 1622(d)) provides for the automatic termination of a national emergency unless, prior to the anniversary date of its declaration, the President publishes in the *Federal Register* and transmits to the Congress a notice stating that the emergency is to continue in effect beyond the anniversary date. In accordance with this provision, I have sent the enclosed notice, stating that the Panamanian emergency is to continue in effect beyond April 8, 1989, to the *Federal Register* for publication.

The actions and policies of the Noriega/Solis regime in Panama continue to pose an unusual and extraordinary threat to the national security and foreign policy of the United States. If the Panamanian emergency were allowed to lapse, the current sanctions imposed against the Noriega/Solis regime, including the blocking of Panamanian governmental assets, would also lapse, impairing our Government's ability to apply economic pressure on the Noriega/Solis regime. In these circumstances, I have determined that it is necessary to maintain in force the broad authorities that may be needed to deal with the situation in Panama.

GEORGE BUSH

The White House,
April 6, 1989.

Message to the Congress Reporting on the Economic Sanctions Against Panama
April 6, 1989

To the Congress of the United States:

1. I hereby report to the Congress on developments since the last Presidential report of October 14, 1988, concerning the national emergency with respect to Panama that was declared in Executive Order No. 12635 of April 8, 1988. This report is submitted pursuant to section 401(c) of the National Emergencies Act (50 U.S.C. 1641(c)), and section 204(c) of the International Emergency Economic Powers Act (50 U.S.C. 1703(c)).

2. Since the last report of October 14, 1988, there has been one amendment to the Panamanian Transactions Regulations, 31 C.F.R. Part 565 (the "Regulations"), administered by the Office of Foreign Assets Control ("FAC") of the Department of the Treasury. Effective January 3, 1989, persons owing funds to the Government of Panama may apply for a specific license authorizing the crediting of the amounts owed, plus applicable interest, to a blocked reserve account on their books or with a commercial bank. These procedures are designed to serve as alternatives to payment of the amounts owed into a blocked account at the Federal Reserve Bank of New York (the "FRBNY"). At the same time, they will enable FAC to maintain a record of payments withheld from the Noriega/Solis regime. Any persons who have already made payments into the FRBNY and who wish to credit the funds instead to a blocked reserve or bank account may also apply for a license authorizing such a transfer.

With this report, I am enclosing a copy of the amendment to the Regulations. 54 *Fed. Reg.* 21 (Jan. 3, 1989).

3. FAC continues to monitor compliance with the Regulations and advise affected parties of their provisions. FAC is currently in the process of notifying by letter over 170 companies with subsidiaries in Panama of the latest amendment to the Regulations permitting the establishment of blocked reserve or bank accounts and advising them that they must either establish such an account on their books or with a commercial bank by license from FAC or transfer monies owed to the Government of Panama to the FRBNY. Information received from Panama indicates that certain U.S. firms with operations in Panama may have failed to withhold Panamanian taxes from employee paychecks in possible violation of the Regulations. FAC has notified the responsible corporate officers that a written explanation of company practices would be required. Responses are due in the near future.

4. The objective of Administration policy remains support for a return to civilian constitutional rule and the development of an apolitical military establishment in Panama. In furtherance of our policy, the Administration has imposed economic sanctions against the Noriega/Solis regime. Our judgment remains that the root cause of the current crisis is the fact that the Panamanian people have lost confidence in a political system widely perceived as corrupt, repressive, and inept. A genuine Panamanian resolution of the political crisis is necessary to restore confidence in the Panamanian economy, a precondition to the return of economic stability and growth in Panama. Accordingly, our efforts have been directed at supporting Panamanian efforts to resolve the underlying political crisis as rapidly as possible.

5. The expenses incurred by the Federal Government in the 6-month period from October 14, 1988, through April 1, 1989,

which are directly attributable to the exercise of powers and authorities conferred by the declaration of the Panamanian national emergency are estimated at $411,960, most of which represents wage and salary costs for Federal personnel. Personnel costs were largely centered in the Department of the Treasury (particularly in the Office of Foreign Assets Control, the Office of the Assistant Secretary for Enforcement, the Office of the Assistant Secretary for International Affairs, and the Office of the General Counsel), the Department of State, the Federal Reserve Board, the National Security Council, and the Department of Defense.

6. The policies and actions of the Noriega/Solis regime in Panama continue to pose an unusual and extraordinary threat to the national security and foreign policy of the United States. I shall continue to exercise the powers at my disposal to apply economic sanctions against Panama as long as these measures are appropriate and will continue to report periodically to the Congress on significant developments, pursuant to 50 U.S.C. 1703(c).

GEORGE BUSH

The White House,
April 6, 1989.

Appointment of Mary McClure as Special Assistant to the President for Intergovernmental Affairs
April 6, 1989

The President today announced the appointment of Mary McClure to be Special Assistant to the President for Intergovernmental Affairs with responsibility for liaison with State legislators.

Senator McClure was elected to the State senate of South Dakota in 1974. She was the first woman to serve as senate president pro tempore, as well as national chairman for the Council of State Governments, since 1979. Senator McClure has served on the executive board of the Legislative Research Council since 1977, and was on the executive committee of the National Conference of State Legislatures (NCSL), 1982–1985 and in 1988. She also chaired the NCSL education committee in 1986 and the NCSL government operations committee in 1987. Prior to her service in the South Dakota legislature, Senator McClure was a teacher.

Senator McClure received a bachelor of arts degree from the University of South Dakota; a Fulbright Scholarship to the University of Manchester, England; and a master's of public administration in 1980 from Syracuse University. She was born April 21, 1939, in Milbank, SD. She is married to Donald James McClure, and they have one daughter.

Continuation of Leonard H.O. Spearman, Sr., as United States Ambassador to Rwanda
April 6, 1989

The President today announced that Leonard H.O. Spearman, Sr., will continue to serve as Ambassador Extraordinary and Plenipotentiary of the United States of America to the Republic of Rwanda.

Since 1988 Ambassador Spearman has been the United States Ambassador to the Republic of Rwanda. Prior to this he was a distinguished professor of psychology at Texas Southern University, 1986–1988. He was president of Texas Southern University, 1980–1986, and a professor of psychology at Southern University, 1960–1970. From 1970 to 1980, Ambassador Spearman worked for the U.S. Office of Education, Department of Health, Education, and Welfare in the following capacities: Associate Deputy Assistant Secretary for Higher and Continuing Education, 1980; Associate Deputy Commissioner for Higher and Continuing Education, 1978–1980; Acting Deputy Commissioner for Higher and Continuing Education, 1976–1978; Associate Commissioner for Student Assistance, 1975–1978; Director of the Division of Student Financial Assistance, 1972–1975; Director of the Division of Student Special Services, 1970–1972.

Ambassador Spearman graduated from Florida A&M University (B.S., 1947) and the University of Michigan (M.A., 1950; Ph.D., 1960). He was born July 8, 1929, in Tallahassee, FL. He is married and has three children.

Toasts at a Dinner Honoring Prime Minister Yitzhak Shamir of Israel

April 6, 1989

The President. Mr. Prime Minister, it has been my pleasure—our pleasure—to welcome you to Washington and to renew a friendship that I cherish—that we all cherish—and to reaffirm, more importantly even, the friendship between our two nations. And the value of these visits goes beyond the meetings of state to the experience we gain from the time spent among the people of Israel and America.

I recall the trips that I've made to your country—first, I think, Barbara and I in 1979 and then in the summer of 1986. And I recall the deep longing for peace that I found on the part of the people there in Israel. And I'm grateful for your visit now in the first days of our brand new administration; and also, because you see Washington in springtime, which some say is its most beautiful season, and because you had a chance to go to the Air and Space Museum today, where we saw many American tourists. And for those of you who weren't with us, it was a wonderful thing, because you heard people saying to the Prime Minister, *Shalom.* You know, I thought they were all tourists from Texas. But no—[*laughter*]—they knew that much. And I think they expressed the affection that we all feel for Israel and for you, sir.

But the friendship, the alliance between the United States and Israel is strong and solid—built upon a foundation of shared democratic values, of shared history and heritage that sustain the moral life of our two countries. The emotional bond of our peoples goes—it transcends politics. Our strategic cooperation—and I renewed today our determination that that go forward—is a source of mutual security. And the United States' commitment to the security of Israel remains unshakable. We may differ over some policies from time to time, individual policies, but never over this principle.

Mr. Prime Minister, the great unsolved challenge that concerns us both is peace in the Middle East, and we know peace is possible. Last month we marked the 10th anniversary of the treaty between Israel and Egypt, and that treaty was the product of the remarkable courage and leadership of two men—and also—I want to say right here in this White House—and also will give credit to the strong-principled, mediating efforts of President Carter, too. Those qualities, courage and leadership, are no less necessary today in the effort to advance the cause of peace in the Middle East. We also know there's much more to do. Mr. Prime Minister, the discussions that we've had and then those I had earlier this week with President Mubarak give me reason to hope that in the Middle East today, there is leadership, courage, and vision, capable of transcending the historic animosities that have long stood as obstacles on the path towards peace. The United States is proud of the role it has played in the search for peace. We know a partnership with Israel in peace can work, and we stand ready today to take another step for the cause of peace in the Middle East.

Mr. Prime Minister and Mrs. Shamir, I raise my glass to the abiding friendship between our two nations and lasting peace among the peoples of the Middle East, and to life—*L'Chaim.*

The Prime Minister. Mr. President, Mrs. Bush, distinguished Secretaries, Members of the Senate, the House of Representatives, judges, ambassadors, ladies and gentlemen. It is almost exactly a year ago since you, Mr. President, graciously entertained my wife and me and my colleagues at dinner in your previous capacity as Vice President. At that time we were both facing elections. [*Laughter*] You were already very much on the campaign trail, and I was preparing to set out on mine. It was a demanding but interesting experience. And here we both are. [*Laughter*]

Permit me, Mr. President, to extend the heartfelt congratulations of all the people of Israel on your election to the most important office in your country and, I venture to suggest, in the world. The people of Israel know you and Mrs. Bush. They respect and admire you. They are grateful for your longstanding friendship, support, and efforts for our people, especially those who have been struggling for the right to leave the Soviet Union and return to their homeland. And, Mr. President, your name is permanently linked with the saga of the rescue of many thousands of Ethiopian Jews who 5 years ago started out on an exodus and returned to their ancient homeland after a very long separation. But several thousand Ethiopian Jews remained behind, and we must solve their problem and especially the human tragedies of family separation. I hope that we will soon find an answer.

Mr. President, an awesome responsibility rests upon you as you set out on the new road that lies before you. As leader of the United States of America, you are the leader of the free world who has to find a way to prevent global conflicts. We acknowledge and applaud your efforts to ensure that the great advances in technology are not abused and exploited for evil designs that could cause devastation to millions of people. In your Presidency, it will be necessary, I am sure, to reach further agreements on the elimination of the new and growing threat of gas, chemical, and biological weapons which are being developed at an alarming pace, especially in our part of the world.

My responsibility is more limited, but equally awesome. I must find a way to achieve comprehensive and lasting peace for my nation and country. That is my overriding goal and ambition. We are not content with the status quo, because we firmly believe that peace is achievable.

Mr. President, 10 days ago, we completed a decade of peace between Israel and the leading Arab country, Egypt. That peace was the first and, so far, still the only breakthrough in the otherwise ongoing hostility of Arab States against Israel. Ten years ago not many believed that we would be standing here today and looking back on a decade of peace with all its shortcomings and deficiencies. Our relationship with Egypt is not yet regular and normal. It must be deepened. It must be enriched.

Mr. President, ladies and gentlemen, it is now almost 50 years since the start of World War II, in which we were the principal victims and paid relatively the highest price. And it is now 40 years since we renewed our national life in our ancient homeland. In that period, six wars were forced upon us, and we have faced permanent terrorism against our civilian population. Few nations in the annals of humanity had to endure such perils and to pay such a price. It is, therefore, only natural that we never stop searching for the road to peace.

The yearning for peace is ingrained in the national tradition and character of our people. We pray for peace three times every day. We despise violence and war. We refuse to believe that a military confrontation is a valid way to solving disputes, but we cannot permit our abhorrence of war to be used against us by terrorists and dictators to force us to submit to their demands. We want to devote and utilize the talents and skills of our people for creativity, for scholarship, for science, for medicine—not for developing more and more sophisticated instruments of war. But until today we have had no choice. Therefore, in the absence of peace, we must be strong as you are.

In one of our prayers we use the words, "The Lord will give His people strength. The Lord will bless His people with peace." First strength, then peace.

We are grateful to the United States for its great contribution to enable our small nation to develop a deterrent capacity in the face of a bloc of 20 Arab countries with a population of 120 million people and a land mass twice the size of the United States. In our view the United States can play a useful role in advancing the search for peace because it enjoys the confidence of the parties in the Middle East. We are ready at all times to explore new ideas and study new proposals together with you and to reach understanding on how to proceed.

Mr. President, today we celebrate the beginning of the month of Nisan. Nisan is the month of miracles, the month of deliverance, because it was established in the Jewish calendar some 3,500 years ago, on the eve of the great Exodus of the 12 tribes of Israel from bondage in Egypt. Since then our people have carried an eternal message to humanity. The message is that all human beings are equal and were created in the image of God, that no man should be enslaved by his fellow men, that human life is sacred, and that peace on Earth is the loftiest of goals. Our people have lived by these principles through triumph and exile, from Babylon to Auschwitz. We were ravaged but never destroyed, because our message and our spirit are eternal and indestructible. And now, in our renewed homeland, we aspire to nothing more than the total achievement of these same principles. Our two democracies, our two peoples, share these values, cherish these ideals, long for similar objectives.

Mr. President, I wish you a successful term of office. May the United States prosper under your leadership. May it enjoy peace and avoid conflict. May it continue to stimulate and lead the free world and stem the tide of evil. We pray, Mr. President, that under your leadership the relationship between our two countries will continue to be solid, strong, deep, and enduring.

Ladies and gentlemen, please join me in this toast to the President of the United States and Mrs. Bush, and the people of this great country: *L'Chaim.*

Note: The President spoke at 9:35 p.m. in the State Dining Room at the White House.

The President's News Conference
April 7, 1989

The President. I have a statement, and then would be glad to take a few questions, and then refer them to our experts here.

But virtually every American is familiar with the tragic environmental disaster in Alaskan waters. And more than 10 million gallons of oil have been spilled, with deadly results for wildlife and hardship for local citizens. We all share the sorrow and concern of Alaskans and a determination to mount a sustained cleanup effort. Our ultimate goal must be the complete restoration of the ecology and the economy of Prince William Sound, including all of its fish, marine mammals, birds, and other wildlife.

The Exxon Corporation has acknowledged responsibility for this spill and its liability for the damages. Exxon should remain responsible for both damages and for employing civilian personnel necessary to control further damage. However, Exxon's efforts standing alone are not enough. And after consulting with the congressional delegation—Senator Ted Stevens, Senator Frank Murkowski, Congressman Don Young—I have determined to add additional Federal resources to the cleanup effort, in addition to the considerable Federal personnel and equipment already on the scene. And this new effort will focus on the job of helping recover oil now in the water and restoring beaches and other damaged areas. This effort should not in any way relieve Exxon from any of its responsibilities or its liabilities.

I've asked Sam Skinner, our Secretary of Transportation, to serve as the coordinator of the efforts of all Federal agencies involved in the cleanup and to work with the Alaskan authorities and Exxon. Admiral Paul Yost, the Commandant of the Coast Guard, will return to Alaska to assume the personal oversight of developments. As we all know, the Coast Guard has many assets in place right now. Also at my direction, Defense Secretary Dick Cheney will make available U.S. Armed Forces personnel and equipment to assist in the cleanup. The military will provide personnel for direct cleanup activities, as well as assisting with the needs of logistics related to the cleanup.

And of course, these efforts must be undertaken carefully, so that further damage to fragile areas will not occur. Intensive planning now going on, as well as appropriate cleanup training, will be completed before ground units are actually deployed. In addition to the Department of Defense personnel, I've asked my staff to develop plans to enable volunteers to participate in cleanup activities. By summer we hope to have developed facilities to enable us to accommodate a corps of Alaskan volunteers. And when I say develop facilities, as these gentlemen will tell you, we're dealing with very remote areas in some cases here.

I've asked EPA Administrator Bill Reilly to coordinate the long-range planning to restore the environment of the Sound. EPA will draw on the expert of leading scientists and oil spill experts in this work, and it will also consult with other Federal agencies that are assessing scientific data regarding the effects of the spill.

We'll not forget the residents of Alaska who have suffered extraordinary economic loss. And when you talk to these Congressmen, as I have, and get it brought home on a case-by-case basis, we have to be concerned, and we are concerned. In addition to paying damage claims against it, we encourage Exxon to increase its local hiring for the cleanup efforts. Secretary Skinner will also work with Exxon and appropriate agencies to develop appropriate loan assistance programs to assist those who have suffered economic injury. This situation has demonstrated the inadequacy of existing contingency plans. And consequently, I have directed a nationwide review of contingency plans of this type to determine improvements that may be necessary.

In describing these measures, we should not be under any illusions. The job of cleaning up the oil from both the sea and the affected land areas will be massive, prolonged, and frustrating. Nothing we can do will totally resolve this problem in the short term. Rather, we must be prepared for a long, sustained effort.

Learning from this experience, we also rededicate ourselves to transportation safety and to realistic planning for accidents that do occur. At the same time, our national security interests in the domestic energy supplies should not be forgotten. The excellent safety record that was recorded prior to this incident must be restored and maintained consistently into the future.

Secretary Skinner and Administrator Reilly will make brief statements and they, Secretary Cheney, and others will be available to answer questions. Prior to that, let me just take a couple of questions, and then I want to keep the focus, if possible, on this. So, fire away.

Q. Mr. President, if——

The President. My protocol—sorry, about that.

Iran Arms and Contra Aid Controversy

Q. Thank you, Mr. President. If I could try another subject: How do you reconcile your efforts to arrange third-country military aid for the *contras* with the spirit of the ban by Congress on aid to the rebels?

The President. Look, I am not going to comment on any aspect of the North trial while it's in progress. If I even commented on your question, it could prejudice the trial. That would be totally unfair. And I would note that of all the material that you seem to be referring to and has been introduced, all the material that was introduced yesterday, material you're referring to, has been available to the Independent Counsel and the Iran-*contra* committee and has been reviewed by them for any special significance. So, I believe the legal process ought to run unfettered, without you or me endangering the trial process that's going on right now. And that's the last question I'll take on that subject.

U.S. Foreign Policy Review

Q. Do you have any reply to Mr. Gorbachev's contention that the foreign policy review is taking too long?

The President. This is an environmental briefing here, and we're concerned about the Alaska oil spill. But the answer is no. Let me simply say we're the United States of America; we're making a prudent review, and I will be ready to discuss that with the Soviets when we are ready. And Mr. Gorbachev knows that there is no foot-dragging going on, so I am not concerned in the least.

Alaskan Oil Spill

Q. A number of local officials in Alaska, as well as Alaskan residents, have been complaining, virtually since this spill took place, for a greater Federal role. I guess my question would be, why has it taken so long to reach this conclusion, and hasn't valuable time been lost during your deliberations?

The President. Well, as you may recall, action started immediately. The big thing was to stop the hemorrhaging and get that ship moved. I immediately asked the head of the Coast Guard, the head of the Department of Transportation, and Bill Reilly to go up there. They came back and, upon sound advice, recommended that we not federalize. And let me be clear: We are not federalizing this operation. There is no demand from reasonable people to federalize this operation. And that is not going to be done.

So, what have we done? The flow was stopped. And let me be very clear: I give great credit certainly—and some of those that are working out there—volunteers, private side, local citizens, company and everything else—for stopping. But I also give great credit to the Coast Guard and to military assets that have already been used in moving equipment thousands of miles to stop the flow. And I'll tell you, a lot has been done. I've had a talk here with Bill Reilly about protecting the hatcheries. And I don't want to make premature judgments on this, but it looks like the five hatcheries may have been saved. And now—is that an overstatement? And now the cleanup phase comes, and it's the time when we can step up some activity.

So, something has gone on. I'm not about to defend the status quo, but there is no desire on our part to federalize. We're not going to do it. And I think it's fair to point this out: I think the priorities were right. There is four times as much oil in that ship as spilled out of that ship. And it was important to guarantee, even in rough elements up there, that no more escape. And so, some things have happened. It was prudent to contain that spill. And so, the process is going forward.

Q. Mr. President, do you have a sense yet of how much this Federal effort is going to cost? And will you try to recover from Exxon that amount?

The President. As I said, Exxon is liable, and they will continue to be liable. And we don't, at this point, have a full assessment.

Q. Are you going to take them to court on that, sir?

The President. Sir?

Q. Does that mean you're going to follow up—you would take them to court or do whatever——

The President. I think Exxon has assumed liability, and I'm not going to stand here and suggest otherwise.

Q. Mr. President, Mr. Gorbachev today made another arms control gesture, saying that he'll stop production of weapons-grade uranium and shut down two plutonium plants. What's your response or reaction?

The President. I've given you my response. We'll be ready to react when we feel like reacting and when we have prudently made our reviews upon which to act.

Q. I meant: What do you think of his proposal or his offer? Is this a big step forward? Are you impressed?

The President. I haven't seen it analyzed, Lesley [Lesley Stahl, CBS News] so I honestly can't tell you that I know the full significance.

Iran Arms and Contra Aid Controversy

Q. Sir, I know you don't want to talk about it, but former Senator Muskie, who was a member of the Tower commission, says he was not aware of this effort to involve the Hondurans or of your role. You have said this was available to the Tower commission. Do you want to reply to that without prejudicing Oliver North?

The President. No, because I don't want to prejudice a trial, John [John Cochran, NBC News]. It would be imprudent for us to do that, and we're not going to do it. And I stand by my statement about the Iran-*contra* Committee.

Q. Will you speak after the trial, then?

The President. That's it.

Middle East Peace Process

Q. Mr. President, the conventional wisdom is that an American President never has much to gain by getting personally involved in the Middle East. But I was thinking that maybe you were an exception, given your initial round this week. Can you tell us what's in your mind about the Middle East, if you see yourself getting very personally involved over the course of your Presidency in trying to solve this?

The President. Look, if I felt that being immersed in it would help solve the problem of peace in the Middle East, I would do that. And I think you're right: there have been times when it appears that the President shouldn't be fully involved. But we've had two visits here now this week—President Mubarak [of Egypt], Prime Minister Shamir [of Israel]. We'll have a forthcoming visit from King Hussein [of Jordan]. And I'm going to give the same assurances to him I've given to Mubarak and Shamir, and that is that if I personally can be helpful, I want to do it. And in the meantime, why, I will say that—I can't say I'm elated, but in the Middle East, a little step sometimes can prove to be fruitful. And I think the climate is better than it's been in a while. But I would simply say it is not a time where a lot of high-visibility missions on the part of the President can be helpful in the process. But I want to leave you with the view that it is of deep concern to us, particularly the violence in the West Bank. And so, I think both leaders that I've talked to so far know my personal feelings on this, and we're not despairing. In fact, I hope the two visits have moved things forward a little bit.

Saul [Saul Friedman, Newsday]?

Iran Arms and Contra Aid Controversy

Q. Yes. Do your statements today mean that you won't discuss this *contra* affair——

The President. Yes, it means I've said all I want to say about it. Look, we're having a briefing on Alaska, and with all respect—did I cut you off? [*Laughter*]

Q. Mr. President, does this mean——

The President. Come on, Saul. [*Laughter*]

Q. Does this mean you won't discuss it until the end of the Ollie North trial or——

The President. It means I've said all I want to say about it, because I really believe, on the advice of lawyers, that that's the last thing we ought to do—is even be kicking it around to this end. So, please accept it when I said I don't want to talk about it anymore. And I'm not going to. So, nice try. [*Laughter*]

Q. Until after——

The President. No, just let it stand. Go back and interpret what I said.

Middle East Peace Process

Q. Do you believe the PLO [Palestine Liberation Organization] should have a role in those independent elections in Israel—or in the West Bank?

The President. I think that the answer is to get on with the elections. And I'd like to. We haven't fully resolved exactly who's going to have a role, but I think that's a matter to be determined between the parties. But I'd leave it right there. I'd leave it right there. The PLO has people living on the West Bank, as you know, and we want to see elections that are free and fair there.

Yes, David [David H. Hoffman, Washington Post]?

Q. Mr. President, was your statement this week about Israel ending the occupation intended as sort of a diplomatic nudge to Prime Minister Shamir? Should we read something into that?

The President. I wouldn't read anything into it. I do not feel that the provisions of Security Council Resolution 242 and 338 have been fulfilled, and I wanted to be clear to all the parties in the Middle East that that is my view. And I will hold the—as best the U.S. can—hold the parties to a full implementation of those resolutions. And so, what I was signaling is that the territory that has been ceded for peace is not the end; it simply isn't.

Yes, Ellen [Ellen Warren, Knight-Ridder Newspapers]? And then Tom. And then we'll go up here.

Oil Drilling and Exploration

Q. Mr. President, you've used words like "deadly," "tragic," "disastrous" to describe the oil spill. During the campaign you said you were an environmentalist. Have you had any opportunity to rethink your commitment to drilling in the Arctic Wildlife Refuge as a result of this disaster?

The President. Yes, I've had the opportunity.

Q. And what have you decided, sir?

The President. No, I don't think that you compromise the genuine national security interests of this country. And I don't think that you can predicate a sound national energy policy on an aberration that seemed to have taken place in Prince William Sound. And my—if for those that do, I say, please let me follow logically: Are you suggesting, because of the alleged human error of a pilot of a ship in Prince William Sound, that we shut down all the offshore production in the Gulf of Mexico? Is that the suggestion? If so, I oppose it. And I think we've got to do what I said in this statement: do everything humanly possible here and elsewhere, on land and on sea, to see that we have the soundest environmental practice and reserve in terms of putting out fires or stemming the flow of oil that leaks out, gets away. But I am not going to suggest that because of this we should rethink a policy of trying to get this country less dependent on foreign oil.

Alaskan Oil Spill

Q. Mr. President, you said earlier that you don't want to defend the status quo in Alaska. You sounded sometimes like you're defending Exxon. Are you satisfied with their performance since the spill?

The President. No.

Q. What have they done wrong? What could they have done better?

The President. Let these experts tell you.

Q. Mr. President, you have said——

The President. I'm not satisfied with anything about it when we have a risk to the environment like this. Because Ellen was telling you correctly: I feel very, very strongly about the damage to our environment there—to the fisheries, to the lives of people involved there, and to all of that. So, I am not totally satisfied.

Yes. I'm going to take two more. We're taking too much time away from the people that are really most thoroughly involved with this. And besides that, we're getting off Marlin's schedule.

Q. Oh.

The President. Thank you for your understanding. [*Laughter*] Go ahead.

Minimum and Training Wages

Q. Let me make one more subject change, if I may, sir. You've said a couple of times your minimum wage offer is your last and best. Does that mean you feel that the package being debated on the Hill now, the Democrats' package, is worse than no bill at all, sir?

The President. Well, there are several packages being debated. But I've told you, in terms of the increase and the length of time for the training wage, we did something unusual. We fired our best shot and last shot and only shot first. And I'd like to take this opportunity to say what I heard several of our leaders saying yesterday after the meeting: I have no intention of budging 1 inch on this, and I've got too much at stake to change right now, and I'm not going to. And so, that's what we've done, and I know it's an unusual procedure. The Secretary of Labor made her position very, very clear in this, and there we are.

Alaskan Oil Spill

Q. I was just going to ask one last question on this spill. You said that the cleanup would be protracted. How long do you think it's going to take—number of years—and is there any real expectation this will ever be cleaned up?

The President. Well, I think we've got to hope that it is. I think Santa Barbara, I would say, has been pretty well cleaned up. I'd say that the spill, the *Amoco Cadiz*, which was six times as big as this, has been cleaned up. And so, we've got to aspire to standards that make me able to tell the people of Alaska and people that are concerned all over this country: Yes, we can shoot for that standard, and we have history to point to. But I think what we do now will determine how fast we can say that it has been done. And that's why we want to move as quickly as—we've got to.

All right, last one. In the middle. Owen [Owen Ullmann, Knight-Ridder Newspapers]? Sorry, Tom.

Polish Roundtable Accords

Q. Can you tell me if you believe the political agreement reached in Poland this week could be a model for political reforms throughout Eastern Europe? And can we anticipate another visit to either Poland or Eastern Europe by you this summer or this spring?

The President. No two Eastern European countries are the same. The striving for change in some, if not all, of these countries is the same. But I would say that the roundtable development there in Poland is very positive, and I would certainly commend the parties getting together there. I go back to when we were there not very many months ago, and many of you were with me on that trip. I think the situation has moved so fast since that trip that I took a year or two ago that it's mind-boggling.

And to think that you'd see Jaruzelski [Chairman of the Council of State] shaking hands with Lech Walesa [Solidarity leader]—we couldn't have predicted that a couple of years ago. Why? Because I was lectured very firmly about the *Solidarność* being "outlawed." So, things are moving. And I think it's a sign of the change that democracy and democratization, if you will—and elections and parliaments and congresses—is on the move. And this is recognition of a trade union's rights to bargain.

This is all very encouraging. But what it means to the other Eastern European countries, Owen, I simply can't tell you. In terms of my own plans, we have not formulated any plans yet. I'd love to go back to Poland sometime. I'd love to go back there, but there's no such plans.

I really do have to run. And I'll just turn this over now to Sam Skinner and the Congressmen and Senators.

Note: The President's 10th news conference began at 10:50 a.m. in the Briefing Room at the White House.

White House Fact Sheet on Federal Assistance for the Alaskan Oil Spill Cleanup

April 7, 1989

The oil spill in Prince William Sound, simply put, is one of the greatest environmental tragedies in American history. More than 10 million gallons of oil went into the waters of the Sound. The spill has been deadly to marine life, mammals, and birds on a substantial scale. Adding to the threat of the situation was the possibility that more than 40 million additional gallons of oil still in the ship might have been discharged if further damage to the ship, still on the reef in exposed waters, had occurred.

The remaining oil on the *Exxon Valdez* has now been unloaded to the extent possible and the tanker refloated. Thus, the danger that this tragedy could have been magnified by several times in size has now been removed. Now it is time to focus private and public resources on the job of cleaning up the oil, protecting fragile areas from the spreading pollution, and restoring damaged areas.

The Exxon Corp. has acknowledged its responsibility, and it will be held strictly accountable for all damages caused by this incident to the maximum extent of the law. Exxon is currently conducting extensive operations designed to recover spilled oil. In addition to Exxon's current efforts, a substantial Federal response has been mounted, coordinated by the United States Coast

Guard. At present, this effort involves almost 400 Coast Guard personnel, as well as vessels, aircraft, helicopters, and large quantities of equipment.

The President has determined, however, that this effort should be expanded; and he has today directed a series of additional measures.

Accelerating Cleanup

1. The President has asked Secretary of Transportation Samuel Skinner to serve as the President's personal liaison to the cleanup efforts. Secretary Skinner will be responsible for mobilizing and coordinating all Federal Government Departments and Agencies as necessary. Adm. Paul Yost, Commandant of the U.S. Coast Guard, and Vice Adm. Clyde Robbins will assume personal oversight direction of the cleanup effort, working with Exxon and the Governor of Alaska.

2. The Department of Defense has been directed by the President to make available all facilities, equipment, and personnel that can be effectively utilized in assisting the cleanup of spilled oil. Planning for this effort, which will be coordinated by Maj. Gen. J.D. Smith, the Director of Military Support, has already begun. Elements of all military services will be available as necessary to support oil cleanup operations.

- The operations that are anticipated will include utilization of Armed Forces ground personnel in the cleanup of affected beach areas, additional personnel and equipment to assist in skimming and booming activities related to oil in the Sound, and construction of facilities for civilian and military personnel participating in the cleanup efforts.
- As on-site coordinator of cleanup efforts, the Coast Guard has been assured of the availability of necessary Department of Defense assets. It has been charged by the President with the responsibility of utilizing the maximum practicable effort to begin the restoration of affected land and water areas.
- Use of military forces will not displace civilian employment by Exxon or by Federal Agencies. By constructing facilities in remote areas, the military effort will facilitate future use of civilian personnel in cleanup-related work.

3. The President calls on Exxon to increase the number of civilian employees and locally owned vessels employed in oil cleanup operations. The President believes that simple, expeditious, and nonexclusive claims procedures should be established by Exxon for those damaged as a result of the spill. This assistance should include temporary funds pending resolution of permanent claims.

4. The President has directed that a program for volunteers willing to assist cleanup efforts be established during the coming summer months. Volunteers and other civilian assistance will supplement military personnel in cleanup operations.

Promoting Recovery

5. In addition to these immediate cleanup efforts, the President has named EPA Administrator William Reilly to coordinate efforts to promote the long-term revival of the ecology of Prince William Sound. EPA will draw on the expertise of leading scientific and oil spill experts in developing long-term recovery plans.

6. The National Oceanic and Atmospheric Administration (NOAA) of the Department of Commerce, the Department of Interior, and the Department of Agriculture have already commenced a scientific assessment of the ecological damage from the oil spill and the development of a plan for long-run restoration, rehabilitation, and replacement of the damaged natural resources. As a part of this effort, the Departments will assist in the development of plans for restoring fish and wildlife stocks and habitats.

7. The President will shortly submit comprehensive oil spill liability and compensation legislation, and he urges Congress to consider and act upon such legislation promptly. In addition, the President believes ratification of pending international oil spill agreements should receive priority attention by the Senate.

8. The President has directed Secretary Skinner, working with Exxon, the Alaskan congressional delegation, State authorities, and other agencies, to develop appropriate loan programs to assist those who have suffered economic losses, and to report back to

the President on such programs within 10 days.

9. Finally, the tragic consequences of the *Exxon Valdez* situation have demonstrated the inadequacy of contingency planning for emergencies of this type. As a result, the President has directed a review of contingency plans of this type nationwide to determine their adequacy in light of the lessons of this situation and the critical importance of an adequate capacity for a timely response. The National Response Team, established pursuant to the Clean Water Act and the Comprehensive Environmental Response, Compensation, and Liability Act, has been directed to undertake this reevaluation of existing planning and to report findings and recommendations within 6 months.

Statement by Press Secretary Fitzwater on President Bush's Meeting With President-Elect Alfredo Cristiani of El Salvador

April 7, 1989

President Bush met with Salvadoran President-elect Alfredo Cristiani and Vice President-elect Francisco Merino in the Oval Office for 30 minutes today. The President again congratulated Mr. Cristiani for his first-round electoral victory on March 19. The President said he looked forward to establishing the same sort of working relationship that he and President Reagan had with President Duarte. In furtherance of that goal, the President issued an invitation to Mr. Cristiani to come to Washington in late summer for an official working visit. Mr. Cristiani accepted the President's offer and expressed his hope of enhancing our mutual cooperation.

The President stated in strongest terms his commitment to support Salvadoran democracy and his admiration of the commitment of the Salvadoran people who risked death or injury by guerrilla threats to interrupt the vote. A U.S. observer team from both political parties, as well as electoral observers from other countries, have certified the election as free and fair. The President noted that El Salvador's democratic institutions stand in marked contrast to those of Nicaragua. The Salvadoran press is free. Political groups mount demonstrations without government interference. And the Government has granted a total amnesty.

For the past 8 years, our commitment to El Salvador has reflected a bipartisan consensus. Nevertheless, there have been some voices that have prejudged Mr. Cristiani and who are pessimistic about the future. The President stated his view that Mr. Cristiani should be given the chance to prove his dedication to democracy, peace, and human rights. Mr. Cristiani has already proven his ability to run a fair campaign, which inspires our confidence about the future.

The President and Mr. Cristiani noted the importance of human rights in El Salvador. The President noted with satisfaction Mr. Cristiani's role in helping to overturn the decision of a judge who released rightwing elements accused of involvement in kidnappings. The President offered continued U.S. assistance to improve Salvadoran judicial institutions.

Mr. Cristiani warmly endorsed the bipartisan accord on Central America as a contribution to peace and said that the focus must remain on Nicaraguan democratization. The President indicated that we would consult El Salvador, as well as the other Central American democracies, on peace issues.

Letter to Congressional Leaders on the Release of Additional Funds for the ICBM Rail Garrison Program
April 7, 1989

Dear Mr. Chairman:

As you know, I am committed to an open and full review of the ICBM modernization issue. I am confident the review will provide the basis for development of consensus on ICBM modernization. To this end, I want to ensure nothing is done to prejudge the results of the review by favoring one or the other of the alternatives.

As I indicated in my February 17, 1989 letter regarding the ICBM modernization program, we have ensured obligations for the Rail Garrison program will not exceed $250 million before April 3, 1989. Since the national security strategy review will not be completed by that date and since the FY 1989 Authorization and Appropriations Acts allow release of additional ICBM modernization funds after February 15, 1989, I intend to release $120 million to the Rail Garrison program in April.

This will ensure the viability of the Rail Garrison program while not affecting the Small ICBM program, which can proceed without additional funds until the national security strategy review and amendments to the FY 1990/1991 budget are completed.

This obligation of additional funds for Rail Garrison must occur in order to prevent program disruption, substantial cost increases, or significant schedule delays.

This action keeps both programs viable and provides us the flexibility to proceed with the programs as deemed appropriate after completion of the strategy review.

Sincerely,

GEORGE BUSH

Note: Identical letters were sent to Robert C. Byrd and Jamie L. Whitten, chairmen of the Senate and House of Representatives Committees on Appropriations, respectively, and Sam Nunn and Les Aspin, chairmen of the Senate and House of Representatives Committees on Armed Services, respectively.

Remarks on Signing the National Volunteer Week Proclamation
April 10, 1989

Well, what a great privilege it is to have you here in the Rose Garden. You're taking on the most difficult challenges that we face as a nation. You're fighting poverty, drug abuse, illiteracy, teen pregnancy, the alienation of young and old. And you're winning because you refuse to believe that it can't be done. And so, I'm here to thank you. You've lived up to an ideal, once given voice by Horace Mann, that I've always admired: "Be ashamed to die," he said, "until you have won some victory for humanity."

Well, recently I received a letter from a man in Indiana who was forced to retire on disability because of heart problems. He was only 45 years old. And he wrote to explain that, while he couldn't take a job, he was giving his time to a nearby mental health center, a local school, and his county environment department. And he wrote this: "I guess what I'm trying to say is this: I'm disabled, but not an invalid. And I enjoy being able to be of help." Then he went on, "I hope in some small way that I'm still able to make a contribution to this great nation of ours and, indeed, to the world as a volunteer. I hope and pray that you and I and, indeed, millions of others will strive to truly make this a kinder and gentler nation. We need that very much."

What an inspiration! The good that voluntarism does in this country every year wins countless victories for humanity, large and small. And here at the White House, we benefit from the tireless efforts of volunteers. And seated to my right are people motivated much the way you are. And I include my wife, Barbara, in that. And then there's Ella Miller sitting in the front row, who continues to serve her community, her church, and in local schools. And she is 108 years old.

And I'm told that over half of adult Americans, 80 million, actively volunteer in some way in their communities. And last year that was worth almost $150 billion in man- and woman-hours. But what you're doing goes above and beyond dollars and cents. Your work and the work of many others as motivated as yourselves is a testament to a powerful idea: that along with the many rights and privileges that distinguish us as Americans is the shared responsibility to look after one another. I always like to remember that there is no exercise better for the human heart than reaching down and lifting someone else up. You understand that helping the less fortunate is in everyone's best interest; that the most powerful gift we can offer anyone is a sense of purpose, a path to self-esteem; that the fabric of the family, like that of society, must forever be renewed and rewoven.

At the Inaugural, I spoke of a new engagement in the lives of others. We must seek common points where the practical and the compassionate converge. Yours is an example we seek to spread across every community, every town, every city in America.

This week I challenge every American who cares about the future of this country to get involved. Find a place or an organization or even a single life where you can make a difference for someone else. From now on in America, any definition of a successful life must include serving others. It's not simply volunteering but the personal act of helping another individual in need which gives us membership in a community. Giving and expecting nothing in return is what it means to be a citizen. When you volunteer, you confirm your citizenship. Volunteering is an act—it's an act of heroism on a grand scale, and it matters profoundly. It does more than help people beat the odds; it changes the odds. You might say it puts the unity in community.

And today I'll be signing a proclamation to make this National Volunteer Week. But week in and week out, it will be people like you who bring the era of the offered hand to life. And I'll be establishing a program encouraging youth enterprise and service to America. But it will be your challenge to open your organizations to young people seeking meaningful service to their communities; to match need with need; to find a calling for every volunteer; and to keep reminding us that each one of us has something to give, each one of us has a gift to give—which reminds me of an old story that Barbara likes to tell about a minister who was given a jar of peaches soaked in brandy by one of his admiring parishioners.

This minister opens the jar, takes a whiff, and says, "Oh, dear lady, you don't know how grateful I am for this gift." "Really," says the lady, "it's such a small present." "Ah," says the minister, "it's not the gift that counts. It's the spirits in which it's given." [*Laughter*]

Well, the spirit of voluntarism in America is stronger than ever—stronger than it's ever been. You know, Alfred North Whitehead once said, "With all its limitations, life in America is better and kinder than anywhere on Earth that I've ever heard of." And that's true, but we can make it better still. We must lift away more of the limitations that remain and tap the limitless potential of the American people through countless small victories for humanity. Together, let us give honor to the phrase, "I volunteered."

And now I'd like to ask Barbara and the group of kids and volunteers on the dais here to join me as I sign the proclamation making this National Volunteer Week. And I do it with great respect for everybody here and gratitude in my heart, as well. Thank you.

Note: The President spoke at 11 a.m. in the Rose Garden at the White House. The proclamation is listed in Appendix E at the end of this volume.

Remarks on Signing the Whistleblower Protection Act of 1989
April 10, 1989

Well, today I am pleased to sign S. 20, the Whistleblower Protection Act of 1989. We used to think of a whistleblower as some guy in a funny hat running around on a field with a black and white shirt on, always throwing down the flag. But that might well be an apt comparison for the business at hand because whistleblowing is, after all, the one who cries foul to waste, to fraud, and to abuse. And in short, a true whistleblower is a public servant of the highest order. And I share the determination of the Congress that we do everything possible to ensure that these dedicated men and women should not be fired or rebuked or suffer financially for their honesty and good judgment.

This bill will go a long way toward this goal by strengthening the protections and procedural rights available to those Federal employees who report misdeeds and mismanagement. Toward this end, the bill I am signing today is a significant improvement over legislation enacted by the Congress last year. Indeed, the fact that the legislative and executive worked together to eliminate major constitutional flaws in this bill is, indeed, a reflection of our joint commitment to good government.

Through their diligence and hard work, the Attorney General, along with Senator Levin and Congressman Frank Horton and others in the Congress, were successful in clarifying the burden of proof on employees; eliminating independent litigating authority in the Office of Special Counsel; and then, thirdly, retaining current law which provides that the Special Counsel may only be removed for inefficiency, neglect of duty, or malfeasance. These three issues were at the root of last year's disagreement over this legislation. And I am tremendously pleased that these valid constitutional concerns were addressed in the bill that I am signing here today. As a result, this legislation will enhance the authority of the Office of Special Counsel to protect whistleblowers and other employees victimized by prohibited personnel practices. Whistleblowers will also now be allowed to take their cases to the Merit System Protection Board.

Let me also reaffirm my confidence in the competence and skill of our senior executive and career managers and supervisors, both civilian and military. And let us remember that most government managers respond promptly and effectively to problems like those disclosed by whistleblowers, even without special provisions of the law.

And finally, this bill is an example of how the Congress and the administration can work together to sharpen and to improve legislation.

For this and many other reasons, I am delighted to now sign S. 20, and I would invite the members of the Congress that are with us today to come forward as I do so. And I appreciate very much you all being here.

Note: The President spoke at 2:05 p.m. in Room 450 of the Old Executive Office Building. S. 20, approved April 10, was assigned Public Law No. 101-12.

Statement on Signing the Whistleblower Protection Act of 1989
April 10, 1989

Today I am pleased to sign S. 20, the "Whistleblower Protection Act of 1989." This bill will strengthen the protections and procedural rights available to those Federal employees, often called "whistleblowers," who report waste, fraud, or abuse in Federal programs. It will ensure that those employees will not suffer adverse personnel actions because of their whistleblowing activities.

Federal employee whistleblowers can make a valuable contribution to the Administration's commitment to ensure effective and efficient use of tax dollars by the Government. My Administration shares the view in the Congress that whistleblowers should be protected from punitive action against them in reprisal for their disclosures.

The bill I am signing today will enhance the authorities and responsibilities of the Office of Special Counsel to protect whistleblowers and other employees victimized by prohibited personnel practices. It also provides whistleblowers with a new independent right to take their cases to the Merit Systems Protection Board.

S. 20 addresses the chief constitutional concerns raised by earlier versions of this legislation. The most substantial improvement in the bill is the deletion of provisions that would have enabled the Special Counsel, an executive branch official, to oppose other executive branch agencies in court. Under our constitutional system, the executive branch cannot sue itself. Article II and Article III of the Constitution require that disputes between executive branch officials or agencies be resolved within the executive branch.

The second major improvement in the bill is its clarification of the burden of proof that an employee must meet in establishing a claim that an adverse personnel action was taken because of whistleblowing. The bill clarifies that an employee must show that whistleblowing activity was a "contributing factor" in the decision to take the personnel action. The employee must demonstrate that his or her whistleblowing actually contributed to the agency's decision to take the adverse personnel action. The agency may rebut proof that whistleblowing was a "contributing" factor in the decision by showing that it would have taken the action in the absence of any whistleblowing.

Several provisions of the bill must be construed carefully in order to avoid constitutional problems. Among these is new section 1217 of title 5, United States Code, which provides that information transmitted by the Special Counsel to the Congress "shall be transmitted concurrently to the President and any other appropriate agency in the executive branch." New section 1213(j) similarly provides that certain information that comes into the hands of the Special Counsel shall be transmitted to the President's National Security Advisor as well as specified committees in the Congress. I do not interpret these provisions to interfere with my ability to provide for appropriate prior review of transmittals by the Special Counsel to the Congress.

In signing S. 20, I wish to reaffirm my confidence in the competence and skills of our senior executive and career managers and supervisors, both civilian and military. These individuals' day-to-day devotion to duty is what makes the Government work. Although whistleblowers clearly can and do contribute to better government, these managers respond regularly to a variety of problems, including those disclosed by whistleblowers, without special statutory provisions and procedures.

I also have confidence that agency heads and the Special Counsel will help address the problems of fraud, waste, or abuse by ensuring that reprisals for whistleblowing will not be tolerated.

S. 20 will contribute to this effort, and I believe it is a constructive measure that will serve the public interest. I am pleased that the Administration was able to work in a spirit of cooperation and bipartisanship with both Houses of Congress to resolve our differences and enact this important legislation.

GEORGE BUSH

The White House,
April 10, 1989.

Note: S. 20, approved April 10, was assigned Public Law No. 101–12.

Designation of John Charles Gartland as Chairman of the National Commission for Employment Policy
April 10, 1989

The President today designated John Charles Gartland as Chairman of the National Commission for Employment Policy. He would succeed Trudy McDonald. Mr. Gartland has served as a member since March 3, 1987.

Since 1979 Mr. Gartland has served as director of Washington affairs for the Amway Corp. in Washington, DC. From 1974 to 1976, he served as Executive Assistant to the Secretary of the Treasury, and as a congressional administrative assistant, 1977. He currently serves as chairman of the Jefferson Foundation.

Mr. Gartland graduated from Villanova University (B.S., 1963) and received a master of arts degree in financial management from George Washington University. He is a native of Cleveland, OH.

Nomination of Diane Kay Morales To Be an Assistant Secretary of Energy
April 10, 1989

The President today announced his intention to nominate Diane Kay Morales to be an Assistant Secretary of Energy (Environment, Safety and Health). She would succeed Ernest C. Baynard.

Most recently, Ms. Morales has served as head of her own firm, analyzing legislative and national policy issues concerning complex weapons systems and arms control issues. She has also coauthored a long-term acquisition plan for ICBM modernization. From 1986–1988, Ms. Morales has served as vice president for government affairs for the Earth Technology Corp., a geotechnical and environmental services firm in Alexandria, VA, and Los Angeles, CA. Between 1981 and 1986, she was a Board Member of the Civil Aeronautics Board and Committee Chairman of the Native Hawaiian Study Commission. She has served as Deputy Assistant Secretary for Policy at the Department of the Interior, and was a consultant for the Office of Information and Regulatory Affairs in the Office of Management and Budget and for the Consumer Product Safety Commission.

Ms. Morales graduated from the University of Texas at Austin (B.A., 1968). She was born in Houston, TX.

Remarks at the Presentation Ceremony for the President's Volunteer Action Awards
April 11, 1989

The President. Welcome, honored guests, ladies and gentlemen. First, I'm pleased to see so many members of our Cabinet present here today, Members of the United States Congress, Senator. And welcome to all of you, our most honored guests.

Let me add that I have a slight confession to make. It's been said—and I know this will shock you—that sometimes I don't speak in very good English and that I have a hard time being understood. I'll admit it; it's true. And all I can say is that I'm in pretty good company, though. Look at Yogi Berra. [*Laughter*] When asked if he had seen "Dr. Zhivago," he said, "No, I feel fine." [*Laughter*] And Danny Ozark, baseball's master of the malaprop, once observed of his ballplayers, "Contrary to popular belief, I've always had a wonderful repertoire with them." See what I mean? It's not just me. Everybody does it; even these silver-tongued orators have the meaning blurred.

But today this group here makes me realize the message isn't blurred—certainly not the message that brings us together. Let it ring loud and clear: America is great because America is good. And America's greatest deeds come from the basic decency and compassion of her people, each of you here today. And we see that decency and compassion everywhere—in a child-care center, the Rotary, the Little League, synagogue or church. It means lending a hand, tending a wound, and helping the less fortunate.

And this is Volunteer Week, a time to celebrate those qualities. And it's my honor today to present the 1989 President's Volunteer Action Awards. These awards were first presented in 1982, and since then 148 Americans have been recognized and honored. And I've said that from now on any definition of a successful life must include serving others. And today's award recipients embody that definition.

Eleven years ago, Rose Tichy began tutoring adults through a church-sponsored literacy program in Middleburg Heights, Ohio. And she loved her work, but there weren't enough adult-level books to fit her students' needs. So, she got out her pen and enriched the printed page, and since 1978 she's written 32 books and edited the more than 100 books developed by her writers group.

Down in Huntsville, Alabama, my dinner partner, my very same Chessie Harris, once took several abandoned children into her two-bedroom home. And when the welfare department demanded a boarding license, the Harrises built a house on land purchased with money from the sale of a family farm. And since 1958, that site has been a home for more than 800 children, or about 10 for each of Chessie's 82 years. Eight hundred children—sounds like a weekend with my grandkids in Kennebunkport, Maine, but nevertheless—[*laughter*].

Allison Stieglitz, 15 years old—listening to her at lunch, sounds a little older than that. But nevertheless, she was only 12 when she asked her parents to use the money they had planned to spend on her Bat Mitzvah to provide Thanksgiving baskets for needy families. And that first year, she gave out 15. In 1980, she donated 75. And in Miami, Allison has begun a Sunday breakfast and bag lunch program in two local temples.

Rose and Chessie and Allison and this year's 15 other President Award winners were chosen from nearly 1,500 nominations. And let's face it, the 15 just barely scratched the surface of people that are volunteering and helping all across the country. You know that prosperity without purpose means nothing. Instead, you revere what matters: simple, fundamental values like decency, goodness, self-discipline, compassion, caring.

And as President, I want to promote those basic values because they form the heart of voluntarism and of these President's Awards. And that is why we have opened the Office of National Service, which is leading our administration's national service movement. This Office will encourage partnerships between all levels of government, private enterprise, and the voluntary organizations. It's going to take things that work and carry them to the Nation. And it will enlist new volunteers in community-based efforts to combat urgent social needs. And toward that end, soon I will announce our administration's Y-E-S, or YES to America program—Youth Entering Service. Here American youth can give of, not to, themselves. By saying yes to America, they can define a successful life.

Of course, that's what you already have done. And you know that voluntarism never asks, "What can I do for myself?" It asks, "What can I do myself for others?" And, yes, government can and should be a catalyst of caring. Its role is critical. But we have surpassed—far surpassed—the limits of what government alone can do. Voluntarism says that it is the private sector which has the responsibility, the understanding and, yes, the resources to confront issues like hunger, health care, homelessness, illiteracy, teen pregnancy, and drug abuse. Our challenge is to use that understanding and those resources to meet our responsibility. For we are a nation and a family, helping, enriching, and caring for each other. And as a family, we are committed to a nationwide effort. Voluntarism says that individuals, like communities, can join hands and exchange talents for the good of America. One person can tutor an inner-city student. That boy or girl can someday become an engineer or an artist. The child-turned-adult will then become a role model to others.

Fellow volunteers, each of you has been a role model. You have enriched the American spirit. And in that spirit, let me close on a personal note—about a hero, if you will.

Lou Gehrig was a Hall of Fame first baseman in the 1920's and the 1930's. He played in 2,130 straight games, a record which still stands. But more than that, he was a good and decent man about whom a teammate said, "Every day, any day, he just went out and did his job." Fifty years ago, Lou Gehrig was stricken by a form of paralysis which today bears his name: Lou Gehrig's disease. And even so, he told the crowd at Yankee Stadium, "I consider myself the luckiest man on the face of the Earth."

This story has become—certainly among sportsmen and, I think, even more widely—an American parable. But less known is that after he left the Yankees, for much of the last 2 years of his life, he served his fellow man. He was dying, weaker by the day; he could barely move his body. But as a parole commissioner for the City of New York, he counseled and inspired kids. And they called him the Iron Horse, the Pride of the Yankees. And he was a hero.

To serve others, to enrich your community—this truly defines a successful life. For success is personal, and it is charitable, the sum not of our possessions but of how we help our neighbors. My friends, on that score, you all have hit a grand-slam home run. Congratulations to each of you, the award-winners, and thank you for coming today. And may your example inspire and uplift others.

And now it is my distinct pleasure to present the 1980 awards. And to help me is another real volunteer, certainly the lead one in our family, Barbara Bush.

And I'd like to ask Donna Alvarado, the head of ACTION, and my dear friend, Mr. Volunteer himself, Governor George Romney, to come forward to help Barbara with these presentations. And then to all of you, our most heartfelt thanks.

Mrs. Bush. The United Auto Workers, Local 31, of Kansas City, Kansas—Bud Carroll, Local 31 president, accepting. The United Auto Workers, Local 31, of Kansas City, Kansas, joined forces with General Motors, the city council, and other union locals to raise $100,000 and remodel its former union hall into a facility for the homeless. UAW members and retirees now volunteer at the center.

Samuel and Nanette Evans. Samuel and Nanette Evans, of Arlington, Virginia, formed the Northern Virginia Patriots, an award-winning marching band whose 450 young members perform in colonial costumes at many nationally known parades and events.

Senior Master Sergeant Apolonio E. (Ed) Garcia, of Enid, Oklahoma, tutors Spanish-speaking immigrants in English as a second language and has assisted over 50 Hispanics to get their temporary resident papers.

Chessie Harris. Chessie Harris, of Huntsville, Alabama, founded Harris Home for Children in 1958, a facility which has provided a home for over 800 abandoned children. She and Mr. Harris, who died in 1988 at the age of 93, raised the building and operating funds and managed the home.

The Judeo Christian Health Clinic—Rhea Hurwitz accepting. The Judeo Christian Health Clinic, Tampa, Florida, organized in 1972 by a Presbyterian church and now managed by a group of local churches, involves over 400 volunteer physicians and other professionals in providing health care to low-income people who do not qualify for public assistance.

The Great American First Savings Bank, You Miss School—You Miss Out program—James Schmidt, vice chairman, accepting. The Great American First Savings Bank, You Miss School—You Miss Out program, San Diego, is designed to increase school attendance by involving bank employees in school activities through Adopt a School programs, drawings for cash incentives for perfect attendance, and special community events.

Walter Maddocks, of Lancaster, Kentucky. Walter Maddocks headed Rotary International's Polio Plus program, a long-term commitment to eradicate polio in developing countries. Polio Plus has raised over $168 million in cash and provided vaccines for children in 79 countries to date.

The Association of Junior Leagues, New York City—Maridel J. Moulton accepting. The Association of Junior Leagues, New York City, founded in 1921, provides personal development and issues training for members, advocacy at the national level on subjects of interest to women and children, and special programs emphasis on such topics as teen pregnancy and women and alcohol.

Habitat for Humanity, International—Amy Parsons accepting. Habitat for Humanity, International, based in Americus, Georgia, involves over 35,000 volunteers in 324 sites, who develop simple, decent, affordable housing for low-income families. Habitat provides no-interest loans, and the buyers provide sweat equity.

Inner City Development, Incorporated—Patti and Rod Radle accepting. Inner City Development, Incorporated, organized to offer hope to the Hispanic residents of San Antonio's inner city, provides a food and clothing bank, a tutoring program, family counseling, the city's largest recreation program, and a Christmas toy program that allows parents to purchase toys for 10 percent of their actual price.

The Virginia Power Volunteer Program—Dr. James T. Rhodes, president and chief executive officer, accepting. The Virginia Power Volunteer Program provides an organized way for company employees and retirees to volunteer in community activities through 60 volunteer team councils. Employees participated in more than 1,500 projects, totaling over 100,000 hours of service in 1988.

Covenant House—Father Bruce Ritter accepting. Covenant House, founded in New York in 1968 by Father Bruce Ritter to provide shelter to runaway and abandoned children, involves over 300 volunteers a month as tutors, staffing recreation programs, providing counseling and operating outreach programs, There are also Covenant Houses in Houston, Fort Lauderdale, New Orleans, and Toronto.

Compeer, Inc.—M. Norton Rosner, chairman of the board, accepting. Compeer, Inc., based in Rochester, New York, matches training caring volunteers in one-to-one relationships with over 10,000 mental health clients in 120 communities.

REACH—David Schaff, vice president of REACH program accepting. REACH—Responsible, Educated Adolescents Can Help—of Scottsbluff, Nebraska, involves 30 junior and senior high school students who develop and deliver a strong drug and alcohol abuse message to elementary school students.

The California Marine Mammal Center—Mary Jane Schramm accepting. The California Marine Mammal Center, based in Sausalito, involves over 330 volunteers out of a staff of 350 in rescuing, rehabilitating, and returning to their environment sick, injured, and distressed marine mammals.

The Clothing Bank: New Clothes for the Homeless—Edward Shapiro accepting. The Clothing Bank: New Clothes for the Homeless was developed in 1986 by the J.M. Kaplan Fund and New York City Mayor's Voluntary Action Center. The Clothing Bank has provided over 1.25 million items of new clothing worth over $6 million to the city's homeless through 250 nonprofit agencies.

Allison Stieglitz. Allison Stieglitz, of Miami, Florida, developed the Thanksgiving Basket program when she was 13 years old, a program that now provides 75 baskets each Thanksgiving. She also helped to develop a Sunday breakfast program that feeds 250 homeless people each week.

Rose Tichy. Rose Tichy, of Middleburg Heights, Ohio, began her work in literacy as a tutor and has since written 32 books geared to the skills of a beginning adult reader on topics such as obtaining a driver's license, AIDS, and books of interest to Ohio readers.

The President. Congratulations, but much more important, thanks for what you do to set this example in our great country.

But finally we come to a man I'm pleased to honor now. Twenty-two years ago, having moved to the East Village in New York to help the urban poor, Father Ritter opened his door one night to see six children; and they were asking for a place to stay. And eventually, as you heard, Father Ritter founded Covenant House to provide a shelter for abandoned and runaway children. Today his program involves over 1,200 volunteers each month, and it offers shelter to more than 25,000 children each year. My friends, because of Covenant House, a child has escaped heroin addiction; another no longer yearns for a decent meal; still another views the world as a warm, not sullen place. And it is an American success story almost without parallel.

Last year a new award was created to honor the individual or organization whose contribution to voluntarism is greatest among those winning the Volunteer Action Awards. And so, I am pleased to announce Father Ritter as this administration's first recipient of an award named for a great President and our dear friend, the Ronald Reagan Award for Volunteer Excellence.

And to Father Ritter and all of you, our warmest congratulations. Thank you all very much for coming.

Note: The President spoke at 1:20 p.m. in the East Room at the White House. In his opening remarks, he referred to Senator Dave Durenberger of Minnesota.

Continuation of Eugene J. McAllister as an Assistant Secretary of State

April 11, 1989

The President today announced that Eugene J. McAllister will continue to serve as Assistant Secretary of State (Economic and Business Affairs) at the Department of State. He was appointed on April 1, 1988.

Mr. McAllister was an Assistant to the President at the White House in Washington, DC, 1986–1988, and Executive Secretary for the Economic Policy Council, 1985–1988. Prior to this he was Deputy Assistant Director for Economic Affairs at the Office of Policy Development, 1983–1985. He was senior policy analyst at the Office of Management and Budget, 1981–1982. Mr. McAllister has also served as a Walker fellow in economics at the Heritage Foundation in Washington, DC.

Mr. McAllister graduated from Loyola University of Los Angeles (B.A., 1974) and the University of California at Davis (M.A., 1976). He was born May 20, 1952, in Bronx, NY.

Statement by Press Secretary Fitzwater on President and Mrs. Bush's 1988 Income Tax Return

April 12, 1989

The President and Mrs. Bush's 1988 tax return shows that they paid $62,106 in Federal income tax on an adjusted gross income of $287,171, of which $115,000 was the President's salary as Vice President. In addition to the Vice Presidential salary, the Bushes also reported $155,662 in income from their blind trust: $7,147 in interest income and $12,362 in income from other sources. A capital loss from the blind trust of $3,000 also was reported.

The President and Mrs. Bush claimed $65,365 in itemized deductions, which included $12,250 in contributions to 39 charities and $218 to charities through the blind trust. The blind trust is managed by Bessemer Trust Company, N.A., New York City.

The President and Mrs. Bush's tax return has been reviewed by the Office of Government Ethics and will be filed in the Philadelphia Regional Office of the IRS.

Remarks Congratulating the University of Michigan Wolverines on Winning the NCAA Basketball Championship

April 12, 1989

The President. Where's Bo? Is your Athletic Director here?

Coach Fisher. Bo's not here. We have our Associate Athletic Director.

The President. All right. Please, be seated. My briefing paper was wrong. [*Laughter*] Glad to see you back.

Well, President Duderstadt and Coach Fisher and all you Wolverine players and staff; and members of the Michigan congressional delegation; and players and coaches of the Dunbar, Highpoint, and Archbishop Carroll High School teams; above all, friends, welcome to the White House. Let me recall, first, that this was once the home of a Michigan alumnus—the home court, you might say. [*Laughter*] And I know that this morning—that Gerald Ford would join me in saying that Michigan basketball, like America, is truly number one. And secondly, let me welcome you here to 1600 Pennsylvania Avenue. For nearly 200 years, this has been America's house. And in 1989, you have become America's sports heroes.

And you know, it was another sports hero, Yogi Berra—I love to quote Yogi—who once said at a state dinner right here in this building: "How could you get a conversation started in there? Everybody was talking too much." [*Laughter*] Well, today America is talking, and they're talking about you all and your incredible championship. And they're calling it Wolverine Wonder or the Michigan Miracle or basketball's Impossible Dream. And the 1989 Wolverines, indeed, had it all: depth and quickness, shooting and intelligence, and that strength of character which embodies a champion.

For example, there's Terry Mills and Loy Vaught and Mark Hughes, who combined for 27 points in that great semifinal game against Illinois; or Sean Higgins, who scored the winning basket against the Fighting Illini; and, yes, Bo Schembechler, you did get Illinois, and I wish you were here to join us today. [*Laughter*] And then there's Rumeal Robinson, of whom Sports Illustrated said—and Jerry Ford would love this one—"He looks and plays like a fullback." And against Seton Hall, your two free throws—I expect the sports fans in the country will never forget them—those two free throws with 3 seconds left won Michigan's first-ever national basketball championship.

And don't worry. I'm not forgetting Glen Rice. [*Laughter*] This year he became the Big Ten all-time leading scorer and the NCAA tournament's most valuable player. And, Glen, in the tourney's 6 games, you scored 184 points to break the old record held by a guy who works up the Hill here: Princeton's Bill Bradley.

And finally there's Steve Fisher, new permanent coach at Michigan. Steve, compared with you, Walter Mitty was a humdrum existence—[*laughter*]—and your success even Ripley would disbelieve. But in 3 amazing weeks, you became the first rookie coach to win a national basketball championship. And you helped Michigan become the first school to win the Rose Bowl and NCAA basketball title in the same year. And last Monday night, surrounded by your wife and two boys, you showed that nice guys can finish first. And Thursday night, Steve and his wife were here walking the dog at the White House—[*laughter*]—and he did a good job on that. [*Laughter*] So, we're glad you're back. And 8 weeks ago, following a last-second loss to Indiana—forgive me—Dan Quayle insisted that I bring that one up. [*Laughter*]

The Vice President. Yes, you guys remember that? [*Laughter*]

The President. Glen Rice said that every Michigan player was "going on a mission." Well, last week, in Steve Fisher's words, that mission reached basketball's "promised land." And today, schools from Syracuse to North Carolina to UCLA salute your story. And today, "Hail to the Victors" is the number one basketball hit parade song. Mission impossible? Yours has been a mission accomplished.

And thanks for coming here. God bless you all, and God bless the United States.

And now, Rumeal, I have a prop for you—a basketball. And where is it? Here. All right. Go for it. Right here, we've got a little demonstration. [*Laughter*] You want to fire one off? Oh, wait a minute, hold off. I'm getting something, don't go away. [*Laughter*]

[*At this point, Rumeal Robinson and the President each shot basketballs into a hoop.*]

That pressure must have been something.

Coach Fisher. Mr. President, it's with great pride that our basketball staff, coaches, and administrators present you with a Michigan Number One jersey to join us and these high school athletes to let you know how proud we are to be here. And we are all number one today alongside you. Thank you very much.

The President. Thank you, Steve.

Note: The President spoke at 11:05 a.m. in the Rose Garden at the White House. Dr. James J. Duderstadt was president of the university.

Remarks Announcing the Nomination of Richard Harrison Truly To Be Administrator of the National Aeronautics and Space Administration

April 12, 1989

The President. Mr. Vice President and distinguished Members of the Congress and Admiral Truly and Dr. Fletcher and Dale Myers and NASA officials: today I'm pleased to announce my intention to nominate Admiral Dick Truly to serve as the Administrator of NASA.

This marks the first time in its distinguished history that NASA will be led by a hero of its own making, an astronaut who had been to space, a man who has uniquely experienced NASA's tremendous teamwork and achievement. And Dick has given 20 years of his life to NASA's work. In April '81, he piloted shuttle *Columbia* in America's first shuttle flight. And since 1986 he served as the Associate Administrator for Space Flight. He led the recovery team immediately following the *Challenger* accident and headed the return to flight team that redesigned the solid rocket boosters and then revamped NASA's safety and quality assurance efforts.

I am fully mindful that because Dick Truly is an active duty naval officer that I will need the assent and cooperation of the Congress to make this appointment. And I would like to say thanks in advance to the congressional leaders here today for their willingness to assist in moving this important nomination forward. Dick is already a busy fellow. He's going to leave this ceremony to go down to the flight readiness review for the next shuttle launch. He's going to the Cape, I believe.

Admiral Truly. Yes, sir.

The President. And on that mission, the shuttle *Atlantis* will carry the Magellan Venus Radar Mapper which will revolutionize knowledge about Earth's sister planet. The launch of Magellan is the first in a series of long-planned space science missions scheduled for 1989. I personally place a great deal of importance in our nation's civil space program. And NASA's scientific achievements have been enormous, and its future promises equally important discoveries. NASA's work is a source of inspiration and a challenge to the young people in this country. And the excitement and interest of space exploration has encouraged many young Americans to study technical fields. NASA's accomplishments are a source of pride to all Americans.

And in closing, I would be remiss, indeed, if I didn't thank Dr. Fletcher once again for an outstanding job as NASA Administrator. I can tell you, I seldom speak for the Congress, but he has been an inspiration to all of us. Jim, your return there gave NASA the stability and leadership that it needed to believe in itself again. And for your sacrifices and those of your family, too, we thank you.

So, Dick, you know you've got a tough act to follow, and I certainly know something about following a class act myself. [*Laughter*] But you are going to do a terrific job. And we are very, very grateful at your willingness to undertake this. And Dan and I look forward to working with you. Congratulations!

Admiral Truly. Mr. President, let me first just thank you for the faith you show in me to take over from a person of Jim Fletcher's caliber in running NASA. NASA is premier in aeronautics and space science and exploration and taking men and women to space to do important jobs for our country. And I really look forward to—with your leadership, in working with the Vice President at the space council and contributing what I can. And thank you so very much.

Note: The President spoke at 2:35 p.m. in the Roosevelt Room at the White House. In his opening remarks, he referred to James C. Fletcher and Dale D. Myers, former Administrator and Deputy Administrator, respectively, of the National Aeronautics and Space Administration.

Nomination of Richard Harrison Truly To Be Administrator of the National Aeronautics and Space Administration

April 12, 1989

The President today announced his intention to nominate Richard Harrison Truly to be Administrator of the National Aeronautics and Space Administration. He would succeed Jame C. Fletcher.

Since 1986 Rear Admiral Truly has served as Associate Administrator for Space Flight at the National Aeronautics and Space Administration in Washington, DC. Prior to this he was first Commander of the Naval Space Command in Dahlgren, VA, established on October 1, 1984. Rear Admiral Truly began his career in 1959 as a Navy ensign and was designated a naval aviator in 1960. From 1963 to 1965, he was first a student and later an instructor at the U.S. Air Force Aerospace Research Pilot School at Edwards Air Force Base in California. In 1965 he was among the initial military astronauts selected to the USAF manned orbiting laboratory program in Los Angeles, CA. He became a NASA astronaut in August, 1969 and was a member of the astronaut support crew and capsule communicator for all three of the manned Skylab missions in 1973 and the Apollo-Soyuz test project in 1975. In 1977 he was a pilot for one of the two-man crews that flew the 747/Space shuttle *Enterprise* approach and landing test flights. His first flight in space was November 12–14, 1981, as the pilot of the space shuttle *Columbia,* the first manned spacecraft to be reflown in space. August 30, 1983, to September 5, 1983, he was commander of the space shuttle *Challenger,* the first night launch and landing in the shuttle program.

Rear Admiral Truly has received the American Astronautical Society's Flight Achievement Award, 1977; the Air Force Association's David C. Shilling Award, 1978; and the Society of Experimental Test Pilots'

Ivan C. Kincheloe Award, 1978. He has also received the Defense Distinguished Service Medal, the Defense Superior Service Medal, the Navy Distinguished Flying Cross and the Meritorious Service Medal; and the NASA Distinguished Service Medal.

Rear Admiral Truly received a bachelor of aeronautical engineering degree from the Georgia Institute of Technology in 1959. He was born November 12, 1937, in Fayette, MS. He is married and has three children.

Nomination of James R. Thompson, Jr., To Be Deputy Administrator of the National Aeronautics and Space Administration
April 12, 1989

The President today announced his intention to nominate James R. Thompson, Jr., to be Deputy Administrator of the National Aeronautics and Space Administration. He would succeed Dale D. Myers.

Since 1986 Mr. Thompson has served as Director of the National Aeronautics and Space Administration's Marshall Space Flight Center in Huntsville, AL. He has served in various positions with NASA at the Marshall Space Flight Center, including associate director for engineering in the science and engineering directorate; manager of the space shuttle main engine project in the shuttle projects office; liquid propulsion system engineer, 1963; lead engineer in the space engine section; and chief of the space engine section, 1968. He was chief of the man/systems integration branch, 1969–1974; manager of the main engine project of the shuttle projects office, 1974–1982; and associate director for engineering directorate, 1982–1983. He was deputy director for technical operations at the Princeton Applied Physics Laboratory, 1983–1986. He served as the vice chairman of the NASA task force inquiring into the cause of the space shuttle *Challenger* accident.

Mr. Thompson graduated from the Georgia Institute of Technology (B.S., 1958) and the University of Florida (M.S., 1963). He received the NASA Medal for Exceptional Service in 1973, and the NASA Medal for Distinguished Service in 1981. He was born in Greenville, SC.

Message to the Congress Transmitting Proposed Legislation on Government Ethics
April 12, 1989

To the Congress of the United States:

I am pleased to submit for your consideration and enactment a bill entitled the "Government-Wide Ethics Act of 1989." This legislation reflects my commitment to ensuring the protection of the public interest in the integrity of the Government.

The "Government-Wide Ethics Act of 1989" would constitute the first major revision of the Ethics in Government Act of 1978 and covers a broad spectrum of ethics issues. Federal personnel financial disclosure reporting requirements would be revised to strengthen the public disclosure process. The general conflict-of-interest and post-employment restriction statutes would be strengthened and expanded to cover, with stated exceptions, officers and employees in all three branches of Government. The bill also includes numerous other important provisions addressing such matters as: deferral of tax liability associated with divestiture of assets in order to avoid conflicts of interest; outside earned income limitations for senior officials; extension to the Congress of the independent counsel statute; and restrictions on the use of excess campaign contributions.

The proposals represent an effort to communicate definitive ethical standards to Federal employees throughout our Government. The people who dedicate their lives selflessly to serving this country and the citizens who rely on the integrity of their public servants deserve no less.

GEORGE BUSH

The White House,
April 12, 1989.

White House Fact Sheet on the President's Ethics Reform Proposals
April 12, 1989

Today the President sent to the Hill his ethics reforms legislation and signed an Executive order establishing strict ethical standards for the executive branch. The bill and order reflect the President's strong commitment to integrity in government and incorporate many of the recommendations of the President's Commission on Federal Ethics Law Reform, established by President Bush in January 1989. These proposals follow the four principles the President had set forth to guide the Commission:

1. Ethical standards for public servants must be exacting enough to ensure that the officials act with the utmost integrity and live up to the public's confidence in them.
2. Standards must be fair, objective, and consistent with common sense.
3. Standards must be equitable all across the three branches of the Federal Government.
4. We cannot afford to have unreasonably restrictive requirements that discourage able citizens from entering public service.

The President recognizes that the order may need to be amended, depending on what is ultimately enacted as law, but he signed the order today to avoid any delay in implementing ethics reform in the executive branch.

In separate legislation sent to the Hill today, the President proposed a 25-percent pay increase for judges, and the proposed ethics bill itself includes a limitation on receipt by judges of honoraria. The President will be working with the Congress separately on the questions of honoraria for Members of Congress, a possible congressional pay raise, and a pay raise for certain executive branch positions, including specialized jobs like those at the National Institutes of Health.

GOVERNMENTWIDE ETHICS ACT OF 1989

Financial Disclosure

• Financial reporting and review requirements would be uniform across the three branches of government.

• In place of the current system in which individuals disclose only the category of value of their assets and income, the bill would require individuals to disclose the actual value of each asset and source of income rounded to the nearest thousand dollars. (Where the actual valuation is unknown or not easily determined, a good faith estimate could be supplied. In the case of stock, an individual could report the number of shares held.)

• Employees would no longer be exempted from reporting liabilities for home mortgages and loans from relatives other than spouses, parents, brothers, sisters, and children.

• Commissioned officers in the Executive Office of the President (not including advisory committee members) would be added to the list of those required to file public financial disclosure reports.

• To reinforce the independence of the trustee of a qualified blind trust, such a trustee could not be an individual or an entity owned in its entirety by an individual.

• The legislation would create an advisory commission to study ways of simplifying the forms that need to be filled out in the Presidential appointment process and to report back to the President within 90 days.

Conflicts of Interest

• The proposal would extend coverage of the general conflict-of-interest statute, 18 U.S.C. 208, to the judiciary and to non-Member officers and employees of the Congress (but not to Members themselves).

• Members of Congress would be included in the portion of 18 U.S.C. 208 that prohibits an official from taking actions that affect entities with which he is negotiating for employment.

• The Internal Revenue Code would be amended to authorize deferral of tax liability when an individual is required by his/her agency to divest assets in order to avoid conflicts of interest.

• The President would be given the authority to grant conflict-of-interest waivers when the national interest so requires.

• Advisory committee members would be allowed conflict-of-interest waivers if the appointing official determines, after review of confidential financial disclosure reports, that the need for a member's expertise outweighs the potential of conflict of interest. The proposal would require public disclosure of the waiver and the information from the report about the financial interest necessitating the waiver.

• The Office of Government Ethics would receive the authority to issue regulations providing for waivers, across-the-board, for inconsequential and remote financial interests.

Honoraria, Outside Activities, and Gifts

• The current statute barring supplementation of the salaries of executive branch officials would be extended to the judicial branch; this would have the effect of barring the receipt of honoraria for speeches, writings, and other appearances in their official capacity by judges and other judicial branch employees.

• The legislation would impose a cap—set at 15 percent of an Executive Level I salary—on the outside income that could be earned by senior officials in all three branches. (In view of the pending discussion with Congress regarding honoraria, congressional honoraria would not count against the cap.)

• The legislation would bar senior officials in all three branches of government from serving on the board of directors of a for-profit enterprise. Requests by such employees to serve on the boards of nonprofit organizations would be subject to case-by-case review to avoid conflicts of interest.

• The legislation would include uniform governmentwide rules for agencies and individuals concerning the acceptance of reimbursement of travel expenses.

• The legislation would prohibit employees in all three branches, except pursuant to reasonable exceptions provided by regulation, from accepting a gift or other item of monetary value from anyone seeking official action from their agency or whose interests may be substantially affected by the performance or nonperformance of the employee's official duties.

Postemployment Restrictions

• The lifetime prohibition against making representations to the Government in a particular matter involving specific parties would be extended to the judicial branch.

• The bill would abolish "compartmentalization" of the Executive Office of the President (EOP) for postemployment purposes. Thus a senior employee leaving a job in any agency within the EOP would be subject to a 1-year cooling-off period before he or she could attempt to influence any official anywhere within the EOP.

• The existing 1-year postemployment cooling-off period for senior executive branch employees would be extended to cover senior personnel in the legislative and judicial branches. (During the cooling-off period, former employees are generally not permitted to contact their former agencies.) Members of Congress and legislative staff would be barred from contacting Members or staff in either House of Congress during the cooling-off period. Compartmentalization rulings would be possible for legislative staff, but not for Members.

• A proposed new provision would limit damaging "side-switching" by Government employees by prohibiting former executive and legislative personnel, for 2 years after leaving the Government, from disclosing specified nonpublic government information, including specified information pertaining to U.S. strategy in international negotiations.

Enforcement and Structure

• The independent counsel statute would be extended to cover the Congress. Other changes to the statute would include the selection of an independent counsel from a list of 15 individuals submitted by the Attorney General.

• Misdemeanor and civil penalties would be included as sanctions for violations of the criminal conflict-of-interest statutes, while retaining and enhancing felony sanctions for willful violations of these laws.

• The Attorney General would be given authority to seek injunctive relief for violations of these laws, and administrative debarment authority against former Government employees who violate the postemployment restrictions would be expanded.

• The bill would authorize an exemption from the Federal Advisory Committee Act facilitating the creation of a White House Ethics Council to advise White House and Cabinet officials, in conjunction with the Counsel to the President, on ethics matters.

Campaign Financing

• The bill would prohibit the use of excess campaign contributions for personal use and office expenses.

EXECUTIVE ORDER

• The new Executive order would set forth 14 fundamental principles of ethical conduct for the executive branch.

• Full-time noncareer Presidential appointees in the executive branch would be prohibited from receiving any earned income for outside employment during their Presidential appointments.

• The Office of Government Ethics would be responsible for administering the order by:

—Consolidating all executive branch standards of conduct regulations into a single set of regulations, and developing and periodically updating a comprehensive executive branch ethics manual.

—Issuing regulations (with the concurrence of the Attorney General) interpreting the general statute prohibiting actions in matters in which employees have financial interests (18 U.S.C. 208) and the statute prohibiting supplementation of salaries (18 U.S.C. 209).

—Issuing regulations (as previously authorized) setting forth a system for nonpublic (confidential) financial reporting for executive branch employees to supplement the public disclosure system.

• Agency responsibilities include:

—Supplementing the standards provided by law, the Executive order, and the comprehensive regulations issued by the Office of Government Ethics. Any supplements must be prepared as addenda to the comprehensive branch-wide regulations, and be approved by the Office of Government Ethics.

—Consulting with the Office of Government Ethics, where practicable, prior to granting waivers of conflict-of-interest requirements, and providing that office with a copy of any waiver granted.

—Obtaining approval from the Office of Government Ethics for annual plans for training and awareness activities.

—Providing mandatory annual training briefings on ethics for all senior officials as well as other designated employees. All Executive Office of the President staff would be included.

—Assessment of the ethics program in each agency and provision of adequate support, including the use of a separate line item in the budget, where practicable.

• The order would provide that the Executive Office of the President may not be compartmentalized for the purpose of the 1-year postemployment cooling-off restriction.

• The order reaffirms existing delegations of authority to issue conflict-of-interest waivers for certain Presidential appointees.

Remarks to the American Society of Newspaper Editors
April 12, 1989

The President. Thank you all very much. John, thank you—please. Well, I'm delighted to be here and look forward to taking a few questions. I've been getting such a ribbing about my highly stylized prose; I thought it only appropriate for me to share a few recent headlines with you. [*Laughter*] I'm sure nobody here would write things like this, but—"Dentist Receives Plaque"—that was one—[*laughter*]—"Actor Sent to Jail for Not Finishing Sentence"—[*laughter*]—and "The Rest of the Year May Not Follow January." I'm tempted to gloat. If that's the standard, I'm not doing too bad. [*Laughter*]

Adlai Stevenson said: "An editor is a person who separates the wheat from the chaff and prints the chaff." [*Laughter*] So, I know I'm probably responsible for providing my fair share of chaff, but after all, I am the guy that said during the campaign, "A kitchen in every pot"—[*laughter*]—and also that "America's freedom"—I was reminded by some of these back here—"America's freedom is the example by which the world expires." [*Laughter*]

So, let no one miss the message: As editors you uphold a certain ethical standard in your newsrooms, and you've got to do that because a newspaper is only as good as its word. And I think this is no less true of government. High ethical standards are central to this administration, and we're going to enforce them strictly, comprehensively, fairly, and to the letter and spirit of the law.

And we've got to work together to reform a public code of conduct that at times appears to be in disarray. And it's not logical or fair—a code—it's both too harsh and too lenient. And it elevates detail over substance, precept over principle.

And so, today I want to talk to you about some proposals of our administration, because such a system as now constituted ultimately breeds cynicism and contempt for the law. To truly reform it, we must remember that standards of trust and honesty are not dictated from regulations written in Washington, DC. Ethics in public service derive from the natural integrity of the American people. They are to be found in the everyday conduct of working men and women, in the postman checking up on the elderly resident at home or in the cashier who runs after the customer that's been overcharged. The millions of Americans who meet their obligations honestly and teach their kids to do it the same way see nothing extraordinary about asking the same of their government. The American people are troubled when they hear of officials in every branch of government, at whatever level of government, who show a brazen contempt for the letter or spirit of the law. And the American people do not understand why certain behavior is considered criminal when committed by an executive branch official—are perfectly legal when committed by someone in another branch of government. Is not a crime a crime? Should there not be an underlying standard of integrity for all?

And as President-elect, I heard about talented men and women who, though perfectly honest, declined to come to serve in government out of fear—fear of the sheer complexity of Federal ethics laws, fear that a simple, honest mistake could lead to a public nightmare. And these concerns led me to issue an Executive order [No. 12668] creating the President's Commission on Federal Ethics Law Reform. And I asked its members to recommend steps to foster full confidence in the integrity of all Federal public officials and employees.

And on March 9, as you may remember, this Commission filed its report and its recommendations. It was chaired by Judge Wilkey, co-chaired by former Attorney General Griffin Bell. In fact, the legislation now resulting from their recommendations and other ideas that I have—the legislation is being sent to the Congress today. And just this morning, I issued an Executive order [No. 12674] announcing ethical principles for the conduct of executive branch employees.

Both actions seek a common end: to raise ethical standards, to avoid conflicts of interest, and to ensure that the law is respected in fact and in appearance.

There are those, of course, who say that public ethics and values cannot be legislated—and I'm inclined to agree. You're never going to legislate away impropriety or through legislation guarantee that everybody lives beyond the, you know, perception of criticism—but these values and ethics can be encouraged, respected, and adhered to in government. Public service must reflect the best values of America. And let me add that most public servants, in my view, do that. And I have served in the Congress, and I have served in the executive branch as well.

Jefferson said: "The whole art of government consists in being honest." And yet too often, simple honesty is not enough. Government rules have worked at cross-purposes. Our regulations have been complicated and unequally applied. Our laws have been contradictory and unclear. And we've spent more time trying to understand Federal ethics laws than we have trying to live by them.

My ethics program seeks to remedy these defects. How? By setting four objectives: first, to establish clear ethical principles; second, to ensure uniform standards among all three branches of government; third, to insist that these standards be fair and reasonable; and fourth, to ensure that these standards attract, not drive out, talented men and women to government.

My ethics program first insists that ethical standards must be exacting enough to ensure that officials act with the utmost integrity, for the public's confidence is not ours to inherit. We must earn that confidence, and it must be constantly renewed. With this in mind, I have placed a ban on outside income for noncareer Presidential appointees in the executive branch, including all employees in the immediate White House Office. I am proposing expanded financial disclosure for all three branches of government. And I have instructed my staff to perform a comprehensive review of Federal campaign finance laws.

Regarding the last, I have already reached one determination. Congress should extend for all Members the prohibition against the conversion of political contributions for personal or office use. Political donations should not become a sort of individual retirement account for Members of the United States Congress. And I call on Congress to close this loophole, and to close it this year.

Modern democratic government works best when organized by strong political parties. And yet we've allowed our parties to become weakened and overshadowed by special interests. And we can best restore the role of the parties by limiting political action committees. PAC's weaken the parties, restrain competition, and deaden the political debate. And I believe we should eliminate contributions to candidates by political action committees, and I'll be consulting with the Congress about that. And I also oppose Federal funding of congressional campaigns. My legislative proposal also strengthens the rules against abusing the revolving door for private gain at the expense of public trust. These rules must not make Government service a bar to productive work in the private sector, but they must prohibit the appearance of profiting from Government service, and this must include the legislative branch as well.

I'm proposing a 25-percent pay raise for Federal judges, while restricting their acceptance of honoraria. I also believe that honoraria for Members of Congress should be banned. And I believe Congress should have a pay increase. And I will not make a formal proposal on Congress until after I consult with the leaders of Congress on the issue of congressional pay. There is no point, absolutely no point, in putting Congress through another traumatic bashing like the one just completed. And I will include in those consultations the question of a pay increase for certain executive branch positions, including specialized jobs like those out there at the National Institute of Health. And I will strongly support pay increases for these jobs which are so important to this country.

My ethics program's second goal recognizes that ethical consistency demands equitable standards across all three branches of government. And under our Constitution, every branch of government is equal and none warrants preferential treatment. The same standard that applies to a staff person at HUD should also apply to housing subcommittee staff on Capitol Hill. And a practice is either ethical or it is not. And if Washington is to be a level playing field, then every player should be treated the same. And therefore, I am proposing that we must extend the independent counsel statute to cover the Congress. I am also proposing that the Federal statute that prohibits employees from taking actions that enhance their own financial interest be extended to cover legislative and judicial branch employees. There should also be an independent ethics office for Congress, to be headed by a clearly nonpartisan official, confirmed by both Houses. And I ask that the existing 1-year postemployment cooling-off period for the senior executive branch employees also apply to the legislative and judicial branches.

And then there's the third objective of this ethics program. It insists that standards be reasonable and reflect good old-fashioned common sense. Some financial interests, for example, are too minor to create any meaningful conflict of interest at all. So, I want the Office of Government Ethics to have the authority to issue regulations authorizing waivers from these conflict of interest statute. But at the same time, we're urging tougher penalties when intentional violations of criminal conflict of interest laws occur. We're asking officials from all three branches to simplify the forms that must be completed by prospective appointees. And I'm also requiring mandatory annual briefings on ethics for Presidential appointees.

My program's fourth objective is to attract and keep the best people in government by keeping Federal ethics laws fair and balanced.

An ethics law is not a weapon—a blunt instrument with which to pound a public servant. It's not a gag with which to silence the outspoken. It's a tool to ensure a government as honest as the American people. We must not allow overly restrictive requirements to be abused or to keep talented people from entering public service. And that is why we have carefully crafted new postemployment restrictions. And that's why we want to allow persons who are required to divest assets to defer their tax liability.

My ethics program shows exactly where we are going and why. We seek to attract and keep the best and brightest in government. And by helping others, by building a better America—honorably, ethically—we seek to show how public service is not the sum of our perks or possessions but a measure of how we conduct ourselves and what we achieve.

Come to think of it, this is a good code for all occupations, from high school to the highest callings in journalism and government. I am delighted to have the opportunity to present to you the principles of this ethics package and obviously—I don't want to see this powerful crowd escape without a pitch—I'd like to have your editorial support for the objectives that I've outlined here today.

Thank you all very much, and I'd be glad to take your questions.

Political Opportunities for Minorities

Q. Mr. President, my daughter thanks you for the autograph you gave us last week, and I'm asking this question on her behalf. She is a 12-year-old 6th grader—and I'm a little nervous here—12-year-old 6th grader at Shepherd Elementary School. And she asked me after I left the White House, "Daddy, will I ever be President? Will I have a chance to be President like Mr. Bush?" She's black and also female. Do you envision, sir, a time when this country might be prepared to elect a black and/or female as President?

The President. Yes, I do. I'd say to her: If I can make it, she can make it. But nevertheless—[*laughter*]—no, but seriously, Ben

[Benjamin Johnson, Jr., managing editor of the Columbia-Missourian], of course we're in changing times here; and the great thing is that she might, by her question, aspire to be President. And I hope that I can keep alive, for at least the time I'm in the White House, the concept—the honor of public service, the obligation to put something back into the system, and also the fact that if you get into the arena you get a very different perspective than when you're sitting outside.

I'll always love what Sam Rayburn said. And this is a little off your question for your daughter. But as he was listening to some debate with a bunch of staffers, I think it was, up on the Hill, he said, "Well, the problem is they never ran for sheriff." And it makes a difference. So, I hope that the question means she is interested, and I hope that the progress this country has made and will make in the future will guarantee that a black teenager today, female, might well be President of the United States.

Secretary of Defense-Designate Tower

Q. How do you square that excellent program you've just outlined to us, sir, with the Tower nomination and your support right to the end?

The President. I see no contradiction whatsoever. As you know, I don't want to relive the Tower question, but I believe that judgments should be made on reality, not on perception. I didn't like what happened, and I don't think that it is any conflict at all with any of the four points I made here today. So, I'd simply—and nothing convinced me from the hearings of that, because I don't think that there was anything that was pointed out to definitively—that conflicts with what we've talked about here. So, I just would respectfully disagree with the conclusion that the United States Senate reached. And I'm going to work with them. We're going forward now. And they promptly confirmed Dick Cheney. But I just don't see any there at all.

Fairness Doctrine

Q. Mr. President, this week the House committee reported out a bill which most of the people in this room think would severely limit and hamper the first amendment. It would pass into law the so-called fairness doctrine. The head-counters say that it will probably go through both chambers quite comfortably. Will you stand with your predecessor in vetoing that bill should it come to you?

The President. Well, I don't want to indicate a veto would be necessary, but I will stand with the previous position that I was a part of in the last administration.

Press Coverage of Presidency

Q. Mr. President, since you've taken office, you've greatly increased the access to the Presidency on the part of the press, and you've taken such initiatives as hosting small dinners in your private residence with reporters and editors. This has sparked some debate, and if I can frame it, if you'll permit me to frame it in the spirit of our morning session with Morton Downey and Geraldo Rivera [television talk-show hosts] and others: Is he trying to woo us, and may he succeed in seducing us? Mr. President, if you would explain your philosophy to press coverage of the Presidency and the relationship with your administration? I realize that some of the debate is probably our ability to complain, no matter what kind of access we get. But I'd like to hear your views of your relationship to the media.

The President. Well, in the first place, when Barbara and I invite a reporter and her spouse or a reporter and his spouse to the White House for an upstairs dinner, we're doing that not to seduce the press—[*laughter*]—treating them as human beings. And one of the reasons—you've asked my press policy—one of the reasons I don't take questions over the sound of the helicopter blades out there is: I want to treat the press with the dignity to which it is entitled. And if you have to get your question answered by screaming at me when I don't want to answer it, you don't look very good. And I don't think it's very good for the White House.

And so, what I've tried to do is have enough availability. In fact, I'm going to cross this one up as a press conference for the record. One more notch so I can go to those doubters—[*laughter*]—and say, look, we want to be accessible. But I would separate out—you know, I don't know what we'll do at Christmas. So, what Barbara and I try to do at our house is say, hey, you and Joan and Gene, or whoever it is, come on to the Christmas party—and not have to have it all categorized and so afraid that somebody thinks I'm trying to seduce some reporter that you have to be treated as something so different than anybody else. And so, availability—don't get mad when they ask stuff you don't like, and treat people as you would whatever walk of life or whatever occupation they come from. And if it's misinterpreted, fine. You don't have to come.

And so, I understand. I remember back a few years ago when one of the great news organizations said, "Okay, we're no longer going to be used. We're not going to any backgrounders or off the record." It lasted about 30 seconds, and those reporters came trooping back in. [*Laughter*] But I respected that if they want to do it; but please believe me that when we do it this way, it's what we feel is appropriate. And if it's not, I'll sure—I think we'll take a hit, but I'm unpersuaded by the gentle logic of Morton Downey—[*laughter*]—and whoever that other guy was that was here.

Speaker of the House Wright

Q. Mr. President, since you've announced this ethics program for the executive branch, I'd like to ask your comments about another situation involving ethics.

The President. Oops. Nice try, Jack [Jackson B. Tinsley, editor and vice president of the Fort Worth Star-Telegram]. [*Laughter*] Go ahead.

Q. That is the long running Ethics Committee investigation of House Speaker Jim Wright. The Washington Times reported this morning that the findings of this committee would be turned over to the Justice Department for investigation of possible Federal law violations. And also, there is a belief by some in Texas that since the rejection of John Tower as your first nominee for Secretary of Defense, that there might be an attempt by the Republican Party to retaliate against Speaker Wright. Would you comment on that, please?

The President. Well, let me comment on the last part first, and I know of no such retaliatory action. I think it would be impossible to do anyway. And it would be wrong, and certainly I would condemn anyone in our administration that had any hand in anything of that nature. Secondly, there is nothing in this ethics package—when I call for an even playing field—Congress, executive branch, and judicial branch do have the same standards that should in any way, directly or indirectly, be interpreted as intervening in the matter now before the House Ethics Committee. And surely, Jack—and I know there's this interest, particularly in your area and in my State. And I think it's wider than that now in the matters that are going forward there. But the last thing I want to do is involve myself in any way.

And please believe me, there is no—on my view, I answered the first question as frankly as I could about the John Tower matter. But in terms of getting even or something of that nature by unfairly intervening into a process that is now being handled by the Ethics Committee in the House, I simply wouldn't condone that at all, and I would condemn it. So, I want to separate out what's happening there from this package, and certainly, in response to your question, from any politics of retaliation because of my view that the Tower matter was not handled the way I would like to have. seen it handled.

Oliver North

Q. At this point in time, would you call Ollie North a real American hero?

The President. Anybody that gets a Purple Heart and sheds his blood fighting for his country deserves to be called an American hero. And it was in that context that I made those claims, and in that context that I will repeat them. And the last thing I want to do is intervene in that matter that is now before the courts. But that's how I feel about those who risk their lives to save this country.

Texans in Government

Q. In view of the fact that there's a program on the table to put a space establishment in Houston and the supercollider is going to be built in Jack's backyard, or has been selected to be built in Jack's backyard, and two or three of the top administrative officials are from Texas, is there a real backlash developing because of that? We saw the Georgia Mafia. We saw the California Mafia talked about by the press. Is this going to happen? And is it going to hurt your program?

The President. No. [*Laughter*] No, we've made appointments that are excellent in my view, men and women of standing. And the fact that some of them come from my home State—hey, what's wrong with that? And the supercollider decision was made by President Reagan. It's a good decision. I want to support it. The space center was made by—I guess when President Johnson was in office, or maybe under President Kennedy—I'm not sure. And it should have strong support. But I don't see any risk of backlash at all, provided you get people that measure up. And that's what I'm trying to do.

Q. Mr. President, I apologize. I've neglected the far left, which some would say is out of character for me. [*Laughter*]

The President. Note that he said that, not I. [*Laughter*] Go ahead.

Alaskan Oil Spill

Q. Mr. President, I live and work in a State with a 2,500-mile coastline, a coastline that includes an oil terminal as well as the village of Kennebunkport. I'm wondering why it took so long for the Government to move on the Alaskan oil spill. Why didn't the Government—the Federal Government—move more boldly, more quickly to clean up the spill?

The President. I think the Federal Government moved much more quickly and more boldly than it gets credit for. I consider the United States Coast Guard a part of the United States Government. And the Coast Guard moved very rapidly. What we did not want to do—and I'm convinced now, even in retrospect, that this decision is correct—was to relieve the Exxon Corporation of its liability by federalizing. And when I promptly sent our able EPA Administrator [William K. Reilly] and our head of the Coast Guard, Admiral Yost, and Sam Skinner, the Secretary of Transportation, up there, they came back with the unanimous recommendation that federalizing wasn't appropriate. The Federal assets—we have moved forward now on the cleanup. The first was containment, and now it's mainly in the cleanup phase, although there still are some containment problems.

Subsequently—and maybe I should accept some criticism on whether I should have done this a week before we did, or something of that nature; I'm giving you the reasons—but I think that the Federal Government is properly involved, but we should not have done what some are urging upon us: federalize that whole cleanup. And you know, it's a tough one. I do know the corner of the Maine coast you're talking about and something about the pristine nature of Prince William Sound. And I do have a great concern about the environment. I want to do better. I want to do better and set higher standards in the environment. But I also happen to believe that the national security needs of this country are served by having a production offshore and by producing oil from the North Slope. And it is awful hard to guarantee against a contingency in a 10-mile-wide channel after thousands and thousands and thousands are—put it millions of barrels have gone through there safely, and now, apparently, what human error seems to have caused this aberration. It's hard to have a contingency plan against that.

And the other day, they asked me about that and said—well, you know, because there were some saying, "Well, you ought to shut down the oil coming out of Prince William Sound, coming out of the Port of Valdez." And I said, "Well, to guarantee against what happened, should shut down all the production off of Louisiana and Texas." I'm not sure I understand the difference. And I think we have got to do everything we can to learn from this. We've got to do everything we can to have a plan that is based not on a third of this bill but on the totality of this bill in terms of recovery. But I simply do not want this disaster to—this isn't all your question, but projecting a little—to weaken the national security interest by making us further and further dependent on foreign oil. We're about up to

50 percent now, and that is not a good enough standard. So, let's learn from this; let's do better in protecting the environment. If there's a lesson here that one agency or another might have moved faster, I will be the first to learn from that. But we've got to keep a certain perspective.

And I am very pleased that the Federal Government is as involved as it should be now. I also would like to see more volunteers involved. And therein, I would make a pitch for strong support for revision of our liability laws. Some, I am told, in volunteer groups, are kept from helping out—maybe not on this one but in many other areas—because of the fear—outrageous liability claims. So, this is a good—we can maybe learn that much from this disaster up there. But I think maybe we should take some blame. But I think we've had prudent action, and I hope it's been timely.

Iran Arms and Contra Aid Controversy

Q. Mr. President, when the North trial is over, will you tell the American people if you were the so-called discreet emissary sent to Honduras during the Iran-*contra* affair and, if you were, give a full accounting of what you did there?

The President. I think I've given a full accounting. I would refer you, sir, to what—incidentally, in today's paper—to what was said by Ambassador Negroponte [U.S. Ambassador to Mexico] and also Tony Motley [former Assistant Secretary of State for Inter-American Affairs], who sat in on that meeting. And having said that, every attorney that advises the President has advised me not to do something that inadvertently would cause a mistrial or would disturb the process that is underway. And so, I don't like reading charges that I happen to feel are untrue, but I have to stand on that. And that just goes with the territory. And I am confident that the process that has gone on, and the process that undoubtedly will go on after this trial is over, will say that anything I have heretofore said is correct. But I do not want to be pushed into doing something for self-aggrandizement that would be ruled by some judge to have aborted a trial that is underway.

Well, thank you all very much.

Note: The President spoke at 1:35 p.m. in the Grand Ballroom at the J.W. Marriott Hotel. He was introduced by John Seigenthaler, president of the American Society of Newspaper Editors.

Remarks at the Congressional Fire Services Institute Dinner
April 12, 1989

The President. Members of the fire service community and ladies and gentlemen and friends, what a wonderful evening this is. Let me say, it's a great privilege to be, as Yogi Berra might say, in such extinguished company—[*laughter*]—all fired up. [*Laughter*] I want to thank you, though, for that warmth of your reception here and for your kindness. And let me just first congratulate some who are responsible for this first, massively successful event. I'm referring, of course, to the International Associations of Fire Chiefs and Fire Fighters, the International Society of Fire Service Instructors, the National Fire Protection Association, the National Volunteer Fire Council, and the Volunteer Firemen's Insurance Services.

And I want to also salute the individual representatives of the fire service community and then the members of the Congressional Fire Service Caucus, now the third-largest, I believe, technically. But if I know Congressman Curt Weldon, you're going to be number one. Let me salute the members of Congress that are gathered here, and particularly singling out not only the firefighter's best friend, Congressman Curt Weldon—he talked about a sleeping giant awakened; you try sleeping—[*laughter*]—with Curt Weldon on your case, giving you a hot foot—but Congressman Doug Walgren here and Sherry Boehlert on this side here at the head table. I single them out for their special leadership and interest in the affairs that bind us all together tonight here.

And finally, I want to say that you've chosen a wonderful time of year to hold this first annual Congressional Fire Services Institute dinner. After all, just think of it. Spring is in the air. Washington is alive with visitors. Baseball's Orioles are still in the pennant race—something we couldn't have said last year at this time—[*laughter*]—the season's a week old. [*Laughter*] Our dog has had her puppies. [*Laughter*] And my wife got a nice clean bill of health today out of Walter Reed Hospital.

So, we meet together in a special week, for this is Volunteer Week, a time which celebrates the selfless character of the American people. And looking toward tonight, I was struck by the fact that 85 percent of our nation's fire protection is indeed supplied by volunteers. And it occurred to me that both you and your paid colleagues—professionals—for both give time and of yourselves—provide the definition of a successful life. For any definition of a successful life, it seems to me, must include serving others. A successful life means that we're partners, not islands unto ourselves, the sum not of our possessions but of how we treat our neighbors. For more than 200 years, firefighters have been this nation's neighbor in word and deed, the backbone of America. And you've met local emergencies through volunteer and paid fire and emergency service networks. And today, you meet them still—three million members strong.

And you know, being here tonight reminds me of a story that I heard which happened back in Prohibition days. It seems that 25 of Boston's top bootleggers were rounded up in a surprise raid. And as they were being arraigned, the judge asked the usual question about occupation. And the first 24 men were engaged in the same profession: each claimed to be a firefighter. Well, naturally, the judge asked the last prisoner, "And what are you?" And "Your Honor," he replied, "I'm a bootlegger." And surprised, the judge laughed and asked, "Well, how's business?" The guy said, "Well, it'd be a hell of a lot better if there weren't so many firefighters around." [*Laughter*]

What I'm getting at—even back in Prohibition, your numbers turned the tide. [*Laughter*] And so, they can today, and must, too, in the future. We've come a long way since Benjamin Franklin founded one of the first volunteer fire companies in 1736. And now, let's go forward and help achieve your goal: a better, more secure, more firesafe America.

Let me just share a few thoughts with you, and then you can get on with the dinner. First, this administration believes the fire service network deserves a Federal Government which understands and values its place in the American community. Almost every municipality has some sort of emergency fire organization. At the 4th of July celebration or Memorial Day parade, the fire service is there. At senior citizens centers and service clubs, the fire service is there. And when fire raged at Yellowstone, the fire service was there. And so, too, when you become the first responder not only to fire but to accidents and floods and cave-ins and collapsed buildings, you deserve the Government's respect. And in my administration, you have it.

Second, this administration believes that you deserve the Government's support. Fifteen years ago, the National Fire Prevention and Control Administration was created to ensure that your concerns would be heard by every level of government. I intend for those concerns to be heard. And tonight, I commend the U.S. Fire Administration for pursuing with vigor its rightful role as the fire services Federal advocate and for providing a national clearinghouse to deal with these fire service issues. We want the National Fire Academy to retain its prominence as a national training center. And like the previous administration, we want the original intent of the Federal Fire Act of 1974 to be maintained.

You know, every profession—you know this and I know it—every profession has its ups and downs. And perhaps former hockey coach Harry Neale put it best: "Last season we couldn't win at home, and we were losing on the road." He said, "My failure as a coach was that I couldn't think of anyplace else to play." [*Laughter*]

Well, the difference is that few professions display that special brand of skill and heroism that is found in the fire service. I'm thinking, for example, of how last May, Richard Shiah, an off-duty battalion chief, arrived at the scene of a burning pickup truck that was overturned in a ditch. And with no protective clothing on, risked his life—suffered second-degree burns on his face and wrists—to save a father and two sons. Chief Shiah shows, like every firefighter, that heroism American-style is not going out of style, and tonight let us pledge that it never will. And to achieve that goal, let us act specifically to help the fire services in protecting our citizens from loss of life and property.

Each year, more than 6,000 lives are lost in fires, and over $10 billion lost in property damage. And to combat such tragedy, we must foster greater public awareness of fire problems by supporting the Federal fire safety program. But we must also act when tragedy does occur. And toward that end, last year, as part of the Omnibus Drug Act of 1988, we raised the death benefit for fallen firefighters from $50,000 to $100,000.

We've done much, but we must do more. And as we do, we'll show how voluntarism can join hands with government to renew the promise of America. And that's why I have opened at the White House the Office of National Service. This office is leading my administration's community and national service efforts. And yesterday, I saluted the 18 recipients of the 1989 President's Volunteer Action Awards. And soon, I will announce our administration's Y-E-S, or YES Program, Youth Entering Service. And this program will encourage all young Americans to get involved in community service, to reignite the concept of one young person helping another.

And I have said I like what works. Well, voluntarism works. In a recent Gallup Poll, nearly 50 percent of the population was involved in community service. And today millions of people are lending a hand, tending a wound, helping the less fortunate, in a homeless shelter, in an inner-city school, or in our fire and emergency services.

And some of you may know, Teddy Roosevelt is among my favorite Presidents. Let me relate what his dad said to him on the eve of his 16th birthday: "All that gives me most pleasure in the retrospect is connected with others. We are not placed here to live exclusively for ourselves." And my friends, you, as well as anyone, embody those words. By saving lives, you have defined a successful life. And for that, I thank you. And yet I challenge you, too. And so, let us build on our beginnings. Let us continue to strive for a firesafe America. And as we do, all Americans will say, as I do tonight: The horizons of America have no limit. The best for America still does lie ahead.

Thank you for this evening. Thank you for inviting me. God bless you, and God bless the United States of America. Thank you all very much.

Note: The President spoke at 7:08 p.m. in the Sheraton Washington Ballroom at the Sheraton Washington Hotel.

Letter to the Speaker of the House of Representatives and the Chairman of the Senate Foreign Relations Committee on the Continuation of Arms Sales to Saudi Arabia
April 12, 1989

Dear Mr. Speaker: (Dear Mr. Chairman:)

I am writing to you with respect to Section 1307 of the National Defense Authorization Act, Fiscal Year 1989, which prohibits the sale of any defense articles subject to Section 36(b) of the Arms Export Control Act to any nation which has acquired intermediate-range ballistic missiles made by the People's Republic of China. Section 1307(b) includes a provision that this restriction will cease to apply if the President certifies to the Congress that the nation which has purchased the missiles does not have chemical, biological, or nuclear warheads for those missiles.

After a review of the information available to the United States Government, I have certified that Saudi Arabia does not possess chemical, biological, or nuclear warheads for its intermediate-range ballistic missiles purchased from the People's Republic of China.

A copy of my certification pursuant to Section 1307 of the National Defense Authorization Act, Fiscal Year 1989, is enclosed. Additional information concerning this action is contained in the enclosed justification.

Sincerely,

GEORGE BUSH

Note: Identical letters were sent to Jim Wright, Speaker of the House of Representatives, and Claiborne Pell, chairman of the Senate Foreign Relations Committee. The letter was released by the Office of the Press Secretary on April 13.

Presidential Determination No. 89–13—Arms Sales to Saudi Arabia
April 12, 1989

Memorandum for the Secretary of State

Subject: Certification with Respect to Section 1307 of the National Defense Authorization Act, Fiscal Year 1989

Pursuant to Section 1307 of the National Defense Authorization Act, Fiscal Year 1989, I hereby certify that Saudi Arabia does not possess biological, chemical, or nuclear warheads for the intermediate-range ballistic missiles purchased from the People's Republic of China.

You are hereby authorized and directed to publish this certification in the *Federal Register.*

GEORGE BUSH

Note: The Presidential determination was released by the Office of the Press Secretary on April 13. It was printed in the "Federal Register" of April 25.

White House Statement on Arms Sales to Saudi Arabia
April 13, 1989

Although Saudi Arabia has acquired intermediate-range ballistic missiles from the People's Republic of China, based on information available to the U.S. Government, there is no credible intelligence reporting indicating that Saudi Arabia possesses nuclear, chemical, or biological weapons. We are not aware of production facilities for chemical munitions, chemical warfare agents, or biological warfare agents in Saudi Arabia. Saudi Arabia possesses no significant nuclear facilities. In addition, the Saudis and the Chinese have told us that the missiles will not be equipped with nuclear warheads. The Saudis have also assured us that the missiles will not be equipped with chemical warheads. This commitment is reaffirmed by Saudi Arabia's adherence to the Nuclear Non-Proliferation Treaty, the 1925 Geneva Protocol, and the Biological Weapons Convention.

We remain concerned about the possible proliferation of these types of weapons in the Middle East and will continue to watch developments closely. Any evidence that Saudi Arabia has acquired chemical, biological, or nuclear warheads after the date of certification will be notified to the Congress, as required by section 1307(a)(2) of the National Defense Authorization Act, Fiscal Year 1989.

Nomination of H. Lawrence Garrett III To Be Secretary of the Navy
April 13, 1989

The President today announced his intention to nominate H. Lawrence Garrett III to be Secretary of the Navy. He would succeed William Lockhart Ball III.

Mr. Garrett is currently the Under Secretary of the Navy. Prior to this, he served as General Counsel of the Department of Defense, 1986–1987; Associate Counsel to the President, the White House, 1983–1986; Regional Director, Merit Systems Protection Board, 1982–1983; executive assistant to the president and chief operating officer, U.S. Synthetic Fuels Corp., 1981–1982; and Assistant Counsel in the Office of the Counsel to the President, 1981. Mr. Garrett also served as a member of the President's Commission on Compensation of Career Federal Executives, 1987–1988.

Mr. Garrett graduated from the University of West Florida (B.S., 1969) and the University of San Diego School of Law (J.D., 1972). He enlisted in the U.S. Navy in 1961, was commissioned in 1964, and retired in 1981. Mr. Garrett was born June 24, 1939, in Washington, DC. He is married, has two children, and resides in Oakton, VA.

Nomination of Frank Henry Habicht II To Be Deputy Administrator of the Environmental Protection Agency
April 13, 1989

The President today announced his intention to nominate Frank Henry Habicht II to be Deputy Administrator of the Environmental Protection Agency. He would succeed A. James Barnes.

Mr. Habicht is currently a principal with William D. Ruckelshaus Associates and a senior attorney in the environmental and natural resources department of Perkins Coie in Washington, DC. Prior to this he served as Assistant Attorney General of the United States for the Land and Natural Resources Division, 1983–1987. From 1982 to 1983, Mr. Habicht was Deputy Assistant Attorney General for the Land and Natural Resources Division. He was Special Assistant to Attorney General William French Smith, 1981–1982, and an associate with Kirkland and Ellis, 1978–1981.

Mr. Habicht graduated from Princeton University (A.B., 1975) and the University of Virginia (J.D., 1978). He was born April 10, 1953, in Oak Park, IL. He is married and has two children.

Nomination of Eddie F. Brown To Be an Assistant Secretary of the Interior
April 13, 1989

The President today announced his intention to nominate Eddie F. Brown to be Assistant Secretary of the Interior for Indian Affairs. He would succeed Ross O. Swimmer.

Since 1987 Dr. Brown has been director

of the Arizona Department of Economic Security in Phoenix, AZ. Prior to this he was director of community affairs and associate professor for Arizona State University in the office of the vice president of academic affairs and the school of social work, 1986–1987. From 1985 to 1986, he was Division Chief for the Bureau of Indian Affairs, Division of Social Services, at the Department of the Interior. He has also served as assistant director for the Arizona Department of Economic Security, 1979–1985; an associate professor for the graduate school of social work for Arizona State University, 1975–1979; and an assistant professor for the school of social work and Native American studies at the University of Utah, 1972–1975. He has also served as director of the United Council on Urban Indian Affairs in Salt Lake City, UT, 1972.

Dr. Brown graduated from Brigham Young University (B.S., 1970) and received a master of social work degree, 1972, and a doctor of social work degree, 1975, from the University of Utah. He was born December 26, 1945, in Ajo, AZ.

Nomination of Martin Lewis Allday To Be Solicitor of the Department of the Interior

April 13, 1989

The President today announced his intention to nominate Martin Lewis Allday to be Solicitor of the Department of the Interior. He would succeed Ralph W. Tarr.

From 1959 to 1988, Mr. Allday has been with the law firm of Lynch, Chappell, Allday and Alsup in Midland, TX, and a managing partner, 1971–1983.

Mr. Allday graduated from the University of Texas Law School at Austin (J.D., 1951). He served in the U.S. Army, 96th Division, 1944–1946. He received the Good Conduct Medal, the Purple Heart, and the Combat Infantryman's Badge. Mr. Allday was born May 30, 1926, in Eldorado, AR. He is married, has three children, and resides in Midland, TX.

Nomination of Frank A. Bracken To Be Under Secretary of the Department of the Interior

April 13, 1989

The President today announced his intention to nominate Frank A. Bracken to be Under Secretary of the Interior. He would succeed Earl E. Gjelde.

Since 1987 Mr. Bracken has been chairman of the board of directors for Ball-InCon Glass Packaging Corp. in Muncie, IN. He has served in several capacities with the Ball Corp., including group vice president for the glass containers division, 1981–1988; vice president and general manager for the commercial glass division, 1980–1981; vice president of administration, 1979–1980; vice president and general counsel, 1974–1979; general counsel and assistant secretary, 1973–1974; and associate general counsel, 1972–1973. He was Legislative Counsel at the Department of the Interior, 1969–1972, and was in the private practice of law, 1960–1969.

Mr. Bracken graduated from Carleton College (B.A., 1956) and the University of Michigan (J.D., 1960). He was born March 29, 1934. He is married, has four children, and resides in Muncie, IN.

Remarks to Participants in Project Educational Forum in Union, New Jersey
April 13, 1989

Thank you, ladies and gentlemen. Thank you very much, Secretary Cavazos. Dr. Cavazos is doing an outstanding job as our Secretary of Education, and I'm so pleased he came up here with me today.

I want to pay my respects to your Governor, who has been a great inspiration to me, not just in education but in many other ways. And when I think of the Governors across this State, no one has a greater claim on doing a lot for education than your own Tom Kean. He has been outstanding, and I'm delighted to have him here today.

I want to salute the three Members of Congress who are here today and those who are actively involved. I know some are here who are actively participating in the political process—Democrats and Republican alike. You have a Governors' race up here, and several of those candidates—here with us. And I want to congratulate them and say to the young people here: I hope when you finish school and then go on and finish your education that you will save time for public service and participating in politics. So, let's welcome those who not only are Members of Congress but others who are so—participating right here with us today. [*Applause*]

And of course, I listened carefully to the four superintendents who were selected to represent the point of view of the superintendents. And I can understand why there's a great new hope in the United States today for quality education. They did an outstanding job, and thank you, gentlemen. Thank you very, very much.

You know, when you come here, walking into the building or being here in the room, you can't help but feel that you don't really have to worry about the future of our young people. I see staunch advocates—met with some dedicated professionals and determined students—who know what an education in America can be. And today is about excellence—and I am told that the brightest and best achievers, many of them in the school level, are right here in this room—but it's also about hard work.

And I wanted to mention a little visit we had on the corner with one of Union's own, Gina Marie Sisco. She wrote me a letter. It's a surprise I got the mail. That's the way it's working these days. [*Laughter*] But nevertheless, she said, "I'm a resource room student for math and English, and I have a learning disability. And there are many kids like me," she goes on, "and we all have to work harder than most kids." But she said, "Union is showing you their best in intelligence, but Union also has the best in trying the hardest, like us kids in resource room." So, it's excellence, and it is hard work.

I'm delighted that Barbara Bush is with me today. She got a good, clean bill of health yesterday from Walter Reed Hospital, I might add. But I'm taking another look at our doctor. He told her, "It's okay to kiss your husband, but don't kiss the dogs." [*Laughter*] So, I don't know exactly what that means. [*Laughter*]

No, America can be the very best in education. I know a few skeptics have doubted that. For instance, somebody once asked Mahatma Gandhi what he thought in general about Western civilization, and he said, "I think it would be a good idea." [*Laughter*]

You know, this nation was founded by people who sought out unexplored frontiers. At first that meant, as you history students know, perilous ocean crossings. And then the West in the United States offered the challenge of vast, new, uncharted lands, expanses. And recently, we've found new directions in space exploration and astrophysics, taking us to the farthest reaches of the universe. And we've always taught our children about these frontiers. They're part of the American world view, part of our idea of human progress, part of our picture of ourselves. But we must now draw the attention of a new generation to a larger, almost limitless horizon: the frontier of the mind. Our goal for education must be as ambitious as it's been for the West or for space or for any other American frontier. And we have a new manifest destiny: to develop America's young minds to their fullest, because if we lose the mind and we lose the spirit of even one young person, we will have lost something precious, forever.

Many of our students are among the best in the world, and I'm told many right here in this room fit that description. Let's hear it for yourself. You've got it. [*Applause*] But all aren't so fortunate, and Barbara knows this because of her dedicated work for literacy. Too many still graduate unable to read their own diplomas. Too many don't get the skills they'll need to fill the jobs for the future. And let's not forget, as well, that there's a lot that's right about American education, and we heard from four superintendents that spelled that out loud and clear right here today.

So, how do we build on the good and eliminate the bad? The way to do it is with people like you in this room, through partnerships at the State level, with the National Governors' Association, teachers, administrators, parents, private industry councils, local businesses, and then the students themselves. And by thinking ahead, by working creatively, we can build a culture of high expectations. We can open up the frontier of the mind to every kid who enters a classroom.

And you know, somebody once asked Mae West what she wanted to be remembered for. And she said, "Everything." [*Laughter*] Well, my goal is a little more modest. But I do want to be remembered, as Secretary Cavazos mentioned, as the education President—someone who used the bully pulpit of the White House, the bully pulpit of the Presidency of the United States, to help you all improve American schools. And my ideas about education are based on four principles—tapping the kind of creativity that's already at work in local communities like this one.

First, our administration will reward excellence through awards to schools that demonstrate significant improvement, rewards for good teachers—and God bless our teachers—and a new scholarship program for outstanding math and science students. Our schools have always recognized athletic excellence. And that's great. But it's also good to hear about groups like the Montrose Academic Booster Club and the Presidential Academic Fitness Awards, which reward excellence in scholarship. Some of those winners are with us today.

And second, we want to promote flexibility and choice through magnet schools and by removing some of the overregulation of education. And I listened to those superintendents as they called for regulatory simplification. We seek alternative certification for good people who want to teach, but are now kept out of the classroom by needless regulations. And we're considering more school-based management to give the local control that you heard these superintendents call for. This government will in no way—the Washington administration will in no way try to dictate curriculum. Let's not get too experimental. I worry that somebody is going to produce a new-age "Hamlet." [*Laughter*] And the famous oration will start like this: "To be, or what?" [*Laughter*] We don't need to set the curriculum in Washington, DC. It's better done right here.

And third, we want to help those most in need, targeting Federal resources—restricted and limited though they must be in these days of budgetary deficit—targeting those where they can do the most good. And we want to waive some of the regulations for poorer communities, allowing them to pool State and Federal funds in exchange for higher accountability and performance—a kind of performance-driven, partial deregulation of education, if you will. And we'll give you the flexibility, and you show us the results. And I bet they'll be outstanding.

And fourth, we need to promote accountability in education for everyone. And that means teachers. Yes, and we want to work with educators—how to objectively and fairly measure results. But it's much broader than that. The problems our schools face won't be solved by assigning blame or applying a puff of smoke here, some bolt of lightning there. Only a united effort can lead to the kind of education reform that lasts.

And this means that all of us are accountable for the quality of American schools.

And that means business leaders, who understand that their ability to compete depends on the quality of the new talent that they help develop and who set up outstanding public-private ventures, like the Sci-Tech Center in Liberty State Park, where students will learn about science and engineering, but in a hands-on way. Accountability also extends to superintendents who can create a clear mandate for improvement and gain support for their priorities. And parents who get involved through programs like "Books and Beyond" in Paramus, where reading at home to the kids has cut time in front of the TV by over 70 percent, or the "Very Important Parent" award to Jersey City parents who get involved with their kids' local schools.

And there are other unexpected sources of untapped talent that can help improve our schools. In New York City, where thousands of volunteers are helping in hundreds of schools, my wife Barbara met with a group helping Cambodian children learn English. And while she was there, one older lady told Barbara how desperately lonely she had been until she volunteered. And her eyes filled up with tears at the memory. Then her face lit up as she told Barbara, "I have never been lonely a day since." Helping others made this woman's life have so much more meaning.

One need matches another, and a wonderful thing happens: you come up with an answer that money simply cannot buy. And that's one reason we need to rely less on the collective wallet, and more on our collective will. A society that worships money or sees money as a cure for all that ails it is a society in peril. But we're not that kind of people. And we must do more than wish we had more to spend, because the challenge of education reform suggests something much more fundamental than money.

As a nation—this may surprise you—but as a nation, we already spend $330 billion a year on education. And that's more than we spend on national security, on defense. We devote more money per capita to education than any of our most advanced competitors. That includes France and Germany, Great Britain, the Soviet Union, and Japan. A billion here, a billion there—as Everett Dirksen once said, "It all someday—pretty soon adds up to real money." [*Laughter*]

One lesson I learned in school is that sometimes there's more than one right answer. More spending isn't the only right answer or even the best answer. What we need is a better value for what we spend. And what we need, and what this conference is all about, is a shared determination on the part of every American to get involved with our schools. We must reestablish the value of teaching and learning in this country.

Like every new landscape we've explored in American history, the frontier of the mind will be won by individuals of courage and determination. And you know, frontier stories are full of tales about brave individuals. So, let me just share one little story with you that I heard—a study, if you will, in determination.

This week I heard about a young woman who'd been poor and on welfare all her life. And she enrolled in a program for pregnant high school girls in Memphis. And things were going fine until the last day of the exams, when she realized that her baby had other plans for her that day. And she wouldn't leave. And she took her last two final exams in the nurse's office. And only then did she let them rush her off to the hospital. And she made B's on the two exams. And she had a boy. And she'll graduate in May. And she's landed a job at a university, with child care, where she's also going to take classes. Now, if the rest of us can summon even a fraction of that kind of courage against the odds, we can make sure that every young American gets a solid education.

Good schools in America are a social responsibility and, yes, in this competitive age we're living in, an economic necessity. And we share the conviction that there is no such thing as an expendable student. We will never accept the notion that vast numbers of illiterate and undereducated Americans can be offset by a well-educated elite. That is not the American way. You know, every young American deserves the best chance. And I'm asking you to join me, in renewed determination, to help this generation—and every generation—develop and triumph in the frontier of the mind.

Thank you for what you are doing, and thank you for what you will do. And God bless you all, and God bless the United States of America. Thank you very much.

Note: The President spoke at 1:40 p.m. in the gymnasium of Union High School. In his opening remarks, he referred to Representatives Marge Roukema, Jim Courter, and Matthew J. Rinaldo; and school superintendents James Caulfield, of Union, NJ; Harry Galinsky, of Paramus, NJ; James Wilsford, of Orangeburg, SC; and Edgar Melanson, of White Mountain, NH. Following his remarks, the President traveled to Kennebunkport, ME, for a weekend stay.

Letter to the Speaker of the House of Representatives and the President of the Senate Reporting on the Generalized System of Preferences

April 13, 1989

Dear Mr. Speaker: (Dear Mr. President:)

I am writing concerning the Generalized System of Preferences (GSP) and two current beneficiary countries, Burma and the Central African Republic. The GSP program is authorized by the Trade Act of 1974, as amended.

I intend to suspend indefinitely Burma and the Central African Republic from their status as GSP beneficiaries for failure to comply with section 502(b)(7) of that Act concerning internationally recognized worker rights. My decision will take place at least 60 days from the date of this letter.

Sincerely,

GEORGE BUSH

Note: Identical letters were sent to Jim Wright, Speaker of the House of Representatives, and Dan Quayle, President of the Senate.

Memorandum on Amendments to the Generalized System of Preferences

April 13, 1989

Memorandum for the United States Trade Representative

Subject: Actions Concerning the Generalized System of Preferences

Pursuant to subsections 502(b)(4) and 502(b)(7) and section 504 of the Trade Act of 1974, as amended (the Act) (19 U.S.C. 2462(b)(4), 2462(b)(7), and 2464)), I have determined to modify the application of duty-free treatment under the Generalized System of Preferences (GSP) currently being afforded to certain beneficiary developing countries, to make a determination concerning the alleged expropriation without compensation by a beneficiary developing country, and to make findings concerning whether steps have been taken or are being taken by certain beneficiary developing countries to afford internationally recognized worker rights to workers in such countries.

Specifically, after considering a private sector request for a review concerning the alleged expropriation by Venezuela of property owned by a United States person allegedly without prompt, adequate, and effective compensation, without entering into good-faith negotiations to provide such compensation or otherwise taking steps to discharge its obligations, and without submitting the expropriation claim to arbitration, I have determined to continue to review the status of such alleged expropriation by Venezuela.

Second, after considering various private sector requests for a review of whether or not certain beneficiary developing countries have taken or are taking steps to afford internationally recognized worker rights (as defined in subsection 502(a)(4) of the Act) to workers in such countries, and in accordance with section 502(b)(7) of the Act, I have determined that Israel and Malaysia have taken or are taking steps to afford internationally recognized worker rights, and I have determined that Burma and the Central African Republic have not taken and are not taking steps to afford such internationally recognized rights. Therefore, I am notifying the Congress of my intention to suspend the GSP eligibility of Burma and the Central African Republic. Finally, I have determined to continue to review the status of such worker rights in Haiti, Liberia, and Syria.

In the case of Israel, I did not review worker rights matters concerning the West Bank and Gaza Strip because they are not a part of the "country" of Israel as contemplated in section 502(b)(7) of the Act. The United States has consistently refrained from formal determinations that would have the effect of recognizing, either impliedly or expressly, the de jure incorporation of the occupied territories into Israel.

Further, in order to convert and implement prior decisions taken in terms of the Tariff Schedules of the United States (TSUS) into the nomenclature structure of the Harmonized Tariff Schedule of the United States (HTS) and after consideration of a private sector request for a waiver of the application of section 504(c) of the Act (19 U.S.C. 2464(c)) with respect to certain eligible articles from Mexico, I have determined to modify the application of duty-free treatment under the GSP currently being afforded to certain articles and to certain beneficiary developing countries.

Specifically, I have determined, pursuant to subsection 504(d)(1) of the Act (19 U.S.C. 2464(d)(1)), that the limitation provided for in subsection 504(c)(1)(B) of the Act should not apply with respect to certain eligible articles because no like or directly competitive article was produced in the United States on January 3, 1985. Such articles are enumerated in the list of HTS subheadings in Annex A.

Second, pursuant to subsection 504(c)(3) of the Act, I have determined to waive the application of section 504(c) of the Act with respect to certain eligible articles from certain beneficiary developing countries. I have received the advice of the United States International Trade Commission on whether any industries in the United States are likely to be adversely affected by such waivers, and I have determined, based on that advice and on the considerations described in sections 501 and 502(c) of the Act (19 U.S.C. 2461 and 2462(c)), that such waivers are in the national economic interest of the United States. The waivers apply to the eligible articles of the beneficiary developing countries that are enumerated in Annex B opposite the HTS subheadings applicable to each article.

Finally, I have determined, pursuant to subsection 504(c)(2) of the Act and after taking into account the considerations described in sections 501 and 502(c) of the Act, that certain beneficiary developing countries have demonstrated a sufficient degree of competitiveness (relative to other beneficiary developing countries) with respect to certain eligible articles. Therefore, I have determined that subsection 504(c)(2)(B) of the Act should apply to such countries with respect to such articles. Such countries are enumerated in Annex C opposite the HTS subheadings applicable to each article.

These determinations shall be published in the *Federal Register*.

GEORGE BUSH

[*Filed with the Office of the Federal Register, 10:43 a.m., April 14, 1989*]

Note: The determinations were printed in the "Federal Register" of April 18.

Remarks Announcing the Bipartisan Budget Agreement
April 14, 1989

The President. Well, I'm joined here by the Speaker, the majority leaders of the Senate and House; the Republican whips of the Senate and House; the chairmen and ranking Republican members of the Appropriations, Finance, and Budget Committees; and members of the bipartisan budget negotiating group. And we've come together in support of a bipartisan budget agreement for fiscal year 1990.

When I presented my budget to the Congress on February 9th, I said we could and should meet several tests. We should meet fundamental obligations for protection of national security and the support of the needy. We should provide sufficient funds to advance high priority initiatives. And we should, at the same time, restrain the overall growth of spending so that we can meet the Gramm-Rudman-Hollings targets on time without tax increases. And this plan allows us to meet those tests.

It would provide for the same revenue level as I requested in my February 9th budget. It would provide $299.2 billion in defense outlays, compared with the $300.6 billion that I requested—very close—and $17 billion in outlays for international affairs, compared with my request of 17.3—again, very close. And it would save $7.3 billion through entitlement reforms. And it would firmly cap domestic discretionary program growth at an overall growth rate of 5.9 relative to the previous year. In total, it would reduce the estimated fiscal year 1990 deficit by about $24 billion, as OMB would estimate the savings, and $28 billion, as the CBO [Congressional Budget Office] would estimate, relative to the Gramm-Rudman-Hollings baseline. It would thus bring the deficit down to $99.4 billion and that, of course, would be a $64 billion reduction relative to the current estimate of the fiscal year 1989 deficit.

The budget agreement does not complete the whole deficit reduction job that is to be done by fiscal year 1993, not by a long shot. But I am convinced that we will only be able to complete that job if we tackle it in manageable steps, on an orderly basis, in a constructive, bipartisan spirit. And this is a first manageable step, and this budget agreement is the first such agreement reached ahead of schedule and not framed in the context of crisis. This is not an insignificant point; it shows that we can make the system work, even with the branches of government controlled by different parties, and if we approach our jobs responsibly and are willing to stay with it, to stick with the task.

On February 9th, I said that we were prepared to negotiate day and night, in good faith, in a true bipartisan spirit, recalling that the American people wanted us to rise above partisan bickering and to produce. And Mr. Speaker and Mr. Majority Leader, you have joined us in good faith and in bipartisan spirit, for which we are grateful; and I believe the American people will be grateful. And I'm particularly grateful to the negotiators, the chairmen, the members, ranking members, who participated in these long, long negotiations. And I commend them for their spirit of bipartisanship and I'm grateful to each and every one.

And so, may I ask you, Mr. Speaker and Mr. Majority Leader, as well as the ranking Republicans here, the Republican whips, and the majority leader of the House, to say a few words; and then the negotiating group will be glad to take questions inside.

Mr. Speaker?

Speaker Wright. Mr. President, thank you. This is not an heroic agreement. It's quite austere. It is not really adequate to address some of the truly serious domestic problems of our country, such as affordable housing, a crumbling public infrastructure, and a need to revitalize American industry through encouragements to additional research and development and modernization of American plant and machinery. But if we begin with the assumption that there can be no significant major increase in revenue, this agreement is probably about as good as we could do.

It is bipartisan; both ideological extremes have yielded. It does provide funds for some of the specific priority initiatives that the President has recommended and Congress wholeheartedly embraces, things like day care, Head Start, funding for the drug war, and a few of those specific priority initiatives. It does reach the Gramm-Rudman deficit reduction targets. And it does permit us to stay on schedule and begin our process immediately for our appropriations bills and pass them again, as we're determined that we shall, on time. So, in those ways, it's a very good start in the direction of better cooperation and better performance.

Senator Mitchell. The most significant aspect of this agreement is its existence, and that is no small accomplishment. For the first time, early in the process, outside the atmosphere of last-minute crisis, a genuine, good-faith effort has been made, and an agreement has been reached on significant deficit reduction. It does not go as far and do as much as any of us would like. But in establishing an atmosphere of cooperation and bipartisanship, for which the President deserves great credit, it sets us on the right course.

No one should be deluded into thinking that this is the end of a process. It is the beginning of a process. Very hard choices lie ahead; much sterner measures will be required in the future. But if we approach those difficult tasks with the same positive spirit that has been exhibited in reaching this agreement, then we will solve them, for there is no problem that Americans cannot solve if they work together in good faith.

And, Mr. President, we commit ourselves to implementing this agreement in good faith and to working with you in the future, when you and we will face much more difficult decisions.

Representative Foley. Mr. President, I want to express our appreciation to you, sir, to the Speaker, to Senator Mitchell, to the Republican leadership of the Senate and the House for authorizing the efforts to come together with a budget negotiating group. Secretary Brady and Mr. Darman, the leadership of the Senate and House, budget committees on both sides of the aisle have taken several weeks to hammer out this agreement. It's been said before—I'll repeat it: It's not as much as each of us individually might have wished; it does represent a very important movement on the part of the Congress and the executive branch, Republicans and Democrats, to establish an early consensus on the budget resolutions which will make possible the action on the appropriation bills in a timely manner.

Beyond that, it represents our continued determination to work together to deal with the tough budget issues that lie ahead that have been mentioned by others before me. But I particularly want to underscore the cordiality and cooperation of our efforts, which I think express a new mood of bipartisan determination to make this government—a Republican administration, Democratic leadership in the House and the Senate, with their Republican colleagues—prove that we can address serious problems of the country productively and well.

Thank you, sir.

Senator Simpson. Mr. President, I appreciate your not letting me slip completely into the tulip patch there. And sometimes in these kinds of things we forget the beauty of days like this. This is really an extraordinary day of beauty in the blossoms and the Sun, but that's not why I'm here. [*Laughter*] I'm just here on behalf of—no, don't look at your watch, that's all right. It shouldn't take over 45 minutes. I'd like to talk about the fate of the domestic uranium industry in America. [*Laughter*] No, it's all right.

Let me say on behalf of Senator Dole, who could not be present today, that this is a very significant thing. We take it seriously; it is the beginning. Senator Byrd described it as that this morning. It is a first step, and that is indeed what it is. So, I'm very proud and pleased to be a part of it. The Republicans will be participating and doing everything they can to see it come to fruition.

It will take a great deal of pressure off of us who legislate. We are legislators, that's our job. And with this pressure off of us, we can go about our work, as we have done in recent days, with a bipartisan agreement on

Central America, other things out there—so many things need to be addressed. And every one of us here know exactly what we have to do with the budget, and this is a start toward the honesty of doing it—entitlements and things like that that must be dealt with.

So, thank you, and on behalf of the Republican leader, thanks to all of those who have worked so hard. It is a daunting and terrible job and a tremendous physical and mental drain that it takes on the Democrat and Republican chairmen of these committees. I thank them.

Representative Gingrich. Thank you, Mr. President. On behalf of Mr. Michel, the Republican leader in the House, who could not be here, I want to say that we are very strongly supportive of this agreement. We agree with the sentiments that have been expressed; it is a very important bipartisan step towards a balanced budget. And I just want to say, for a moment, for the more conservative viewpoint, it is very solid on defense; those who care about defense should be supportive of this agreement.

It is a major step towards a balanced budget, recognizing that we're going to need bipartisan cooperation over the next several years to get there. It is a very prudent agreement, and I would hope that most Americans would be grateful for this kind of bipartisan teamwork which has, in fact, taken us one more step in the right direction towards a balanced budget. And we'll do all we can in the House to help pass it.

Thank you, Mr. President.

The President. There's been one oversight, and that is that I did not properly thank Dick Darman and Secretary Brady for their representing the administration so effectively in these negotiations.

Again, Mr. Speaker and Mr. Leader, my thanks to you as leaders of the Congress for their cooperation. And they will be available for questions in a bit. Many thanks.

Note: The President spoke at 10:24 a.m. in the Rose Garden at the White House. In his remarks, he referred to Senators George J. Mitchell, majority leader; Alan K. Simpson, Republican whip; James R. Sasser, chairman of the Budget Committee; Pete V. Domenici, ranking Republican of the Budget Committee; Robert C. Byrd, chairman of the Appropriations Committee; Mark O. Hatfield, ranking Republican of the Appropriations Committee; Lloyd Bentsen, chairman of the Finance Committee; and Bob Packwood, ranking Republican of the Finance Committee; Representatives Jim Wright, Speaker of the House of Representatives; Thomas S. Foley, majority leader; Newt Gingrich, Republican whip; Jamie L. Whitten, chairman of the Appropriations Committee; Silvio O. Conte, ranking Republican of the Appropriations Committee; Leon E. Panetta, chairman of the Budget Committee; and Bill Frenzel, ranking Republican of the Budget Committee; Secretary of the Treasury Nicholas F. Brady; and Richard G. Darman, Director of the Office of Management and Budget.

White House Statement on the Bipartisan Budget Agreement
April 14, 1989

In March 1989 the President, the Speaker of the House, the majority leaders of the Senate and House, the Republican leaders of the Senate and House, joined by the chairmen and ranking Republican members of the Appropriations, Ways and Means, Finance, and Budget Committees, and by the Secretary of the Treasury, the Chief of Staff to the President, and the Director of the Office of Management and Budget, concurred in a recommendation to establish a special budget negotiating group. The group was charged to explore the possibility of reaching an agreement on a budget framework for fiscal year 1990 and to report upon its progress to the President and the joint leadership of Congress. The group was composed of the chairmen and ranking Republican members of the Senate and House Budget Committees, the Majority Leader of the House, the Secretary of the Treasury, and the Director of the Office of Management and Budget. The attached agreement is the product of that negotiating group, as developed in accordance with the guidance of the leadership group.

Bipartisan Budget Agreement Between the President and the Joint Leadership of Congress

1. The elements of this agreement provide for deficit reduction amounts that, for fiscal year 1990, are currently estimated to meet the deficit target of the Balanced Budget and Emergency Deficit Control Reaffirmation Act of 1987.

2. The budget framework is approved by the President, the Speaker, and the Majority and Republican Leadership of Congress.

3. The President and the Leadership of Congress will carry out this agreement.

4. The following procedures will be utilized to implement this agreement: Congressional implementation will follow, as much as possible, the regular budget and legislative procedures. The House and Senate Budget Committees will each report a concurrent resolution on the budget for fiscal year 1990 consistent with this budget agreement. The budget resolution will contain reconciliation instructions and 302(a) allocations consistent with this budget agreement. The House and Senate Committees with jurisdiction over matters necessary to implement the agreement will be responsible for developing 302(b) allocations, legislation, and budget levels consistent with this budget agreement. Regular House and Senate procedures applicable to the consideration of budget resolutions, appropriations bills, reconciliation legislation, and other measures will apply.

5. Congress shall present the revenue portion of the reconciliation bill to the President at the same time as the spending reduction provisions of the reconciliation bill.

6. Agreed-upon fiscal year 1990 budget levels are as follows for each of the three discretionary appropriations categories:

[In billions of dollars] *

Category:	BA	0
Domestic	$157.5	$181.3
Defense (050) **	305.5	299.2
International Affairs	19.0	17.0

* Congressional enforcement of these discretionary levels in the legislative process will be based on CBO scoring.

** Functional total includes mandatory spending.

7. The Budget Committees, CBO, and OMB shall use the "Scorekeeping Guidelines for the Bipartisan Budget Agreement of April 14, 1989," and shall work together to resolve any new scorekeeping issues that may arise.

8. Within the domestic discretionary amount, the budget resolution will provide sufficient funding for subsidized housing contract renewals (without prejudice to the form or length of such renewals).

9. Deficit reduction to be implemented in accordance with this agreement is specified in the attached "Deficit Reduction Plan." For both budget scorekeeping and Gramm-Rudman-Hollings, final scoring will necessarily depend on the review of legislation by the scorekeepers, as provided in the Congressional Budget Act and Gramm-Rudman-Hollings.

10. The specific measures composing the governmental receipts figure will be determined through the regular legislative and Constitutional process. Agreements reached between the Administration and the Congressional tax-writing committees on revenue legislation reconciled pursuant to this agreement will be advanced legislatively when supported by the President of the United States.

11. Neither the Congress nor the President shall initiate supplementals except in the case of dire emergency. When the Executive Branch makes such a request, it shall be accompanied by a presidentially-transmitted budget amendment to Congress.

12. Both the President and the Congress have addressed the need for additional domestic discretionary spending priorities for the fiscal year 1990 budget. It is agreed that any funding of priorities will be within the

domestic spending levels set forth in paragraph 6 of this agreement.

13. The President and the Congressional Leadership will continue to consult closely to seek opportunities for further deficit reduction and to explore policy and process changes which would reduce the deficit to meet the deficit targets of the Gramm-Rudman-Hollings law and balance the Federal budget by fiscal year 1993. In order to facilitate progress toward that objective, the bipartisan Budget Committee Leadership, the Secretary of the Treasury, and the Director of Office of Management and Budget shall continue discussions in consultation with the bipartisan leadership of the appropriate committees of the House and Senate.

Attachments:
Deficit Reduction Plan
Estimated Budget Levels

DEFICIT REDUCTION PLAN *

[Fiscal Year 1990, in billions of dollars]

	CBO scoring	OMB scoring
Baseline Deficit	$147.3	$126.6
Adjustment for estimating differences	−19.9	−3.5
Adjusted Baseline Deficit	127.4	123.1
Revenues:		
Revenue Measures	−5.3	−5.3
IRS Compliance **	−0.5	−0.5
User Fees and Offsetting Collections	−2.7	−2.7
Subtotal, revenues	−8.5	−8.5
Spending:		
Defense (Function 050)	−4.2	−1.7
International Discretionary	−0.0	+0.1
Domestic Discretionary	−0.3	+2.4
Entitlements/Mandatory:		
Medicare	−2.7	−2.7
Agriculture	−1.9	−2.2
Veterans' Loan Sales	−0.5	−0.6
Federal Pension & Postal Reform	−1.1	−1.3
Other Entitlements	−0.6	−0.5

DEFICIT REDUCTION PLAN *—Continued

[Fiscal Year 1990, in billions of dollars]

	CBO scoring	OMB scoring
Subtotal, Entitlements/Mandatory	−6.8	−7.3
Pay Offset, Retirement Contributions	+0.4	+0.3
Adjustment: Postal Budgetary Treatment ***	−1.8	−2.2
Debt Service	−1.1	−1.1
Subtotal, spending	−13.8	−9.5
Asset Sales	−5.7	−5.7
Total Deficit Reduction Measures	−28.0	−23.7
Final Deficit	99.4	99.4

* Estimates as of April 14, 1989.
** Predicated on IRS compliance funding sufficient to achieve the additional revenues specified.
*** Predicated on postal reforms.

BUDGET LEVELS

[Fiscal Year 1990, in billions of dollars]

	CBO estimates	OMB estimates
Budget Authority:		
Domestic Discretionary	$157.5	$157.5
Defense (Function 050)	305.5	305.5
International Discretionary	19.0	19.0
Estimated Outlays:		
Domestic Discretionary	181.3	181.3
Defense (Function 050)	299.2	299.2
International Discretionary	17.0	17.0
Entitlement/Mandatory	556.4	539.7
Net Interest	181.0	173.2
Offsetting Retirement Receipts	−32.8	−33.4
Fees, Collections, and Asset Sales	−8.4	−8.4
Total Estimated Outlays	1,193.8	1,168.7
Estimated Receipts	1,074.4	1,065.7
Adjustment for estimating differences	−19.9	−3.5
Deficit	99.4	99.4

Nomination of Paul Dundes Wolfowitz To Be an Under Secretary of Defense
April 14, 1989

The President today announced his intention to nominate Paul Dundes Wolfowitz to be Under Secretary of Defense for Policy. He would succeed Fred Charles Ikle.

Since 1986 Ambassador Wolfowitz has served as the United States Ambassador to the Republic of Indonesia. From 1982 to 1986, Ambassador Wolfowitz was Assistant Secretary of State for East Asian and Pacific Affairs. Prior to this he was Director of Policy Planning for the Department of State, 1981–1982. He was Deputy Assistant Secretary of Defense for Regional Programs, 1977–1980. He has also served in several capacities for the Arms Control and Disarmament Agency, including Special Assistant for SALT in the Office of the Director, 1976–1977; deputy assistant director for the Verification and Analysis Bureau, 1976; special assistant to the Director, 1974–1975; and a staff member in the Evaluation and Policy Division of the Plans and Analysis Bureau, 1973–1974. From 1970 to 1973, he was an assistant professor of political science at Yale University.

Ambassador Wolfowitz graduated from Cornell University (A.B., 1965) and the University of Chicago (Ph.D., 1976). He was born December 22, 1943, in New York. He is married and has three children.

Nomination of David George Ball To Be an Assistant Secretary of Labor
April 14, 1989

The President today announced his intention to nominate David George Ball to be an Assistant Secretary of Labor (Pension and Welfare Benefit). He would succeed David M. Walker.

Since 1974 Mr. Ball has been with Amex, Inc., in Greenwich, CT, serving in several positions, including senior vice president and president, Amex Central Services, 1987–1988; senior vice president and secretary, 1983–1987; vice president for investor relations and secretary, 1977–1983; and secretary, 1974–1977. He was assistant secretary and assistant counsel for the Babcock and Wilcox Co., 1970–1974, and general counsel for the Southeastern Public Service Co., 1969–1970. He has also served as an attorney with White and Case, 1964–1969.

Mr. Ball graduated from Yale College (B.A., 1960) and Columbia Law School (J.D., 1964). He is married, has five children, and resides in Greenwich, CT.

Nomination of Bryce L. Harlow To Be Deputy Under Secretary of the Treasury, and Designation as an Assistant Secretary
April 14, 1989

The President today announced his intention to nominate Bryce L. Harlow to be Deputy Under Secretary of the Treasury (Legislative Affairs). He would succeed John K. Meagher. Upon confirmation the President intends to designate him as an Assistant Secretary of the Treasury (Legislative Affairs).

Since 1986 Mr. Harlow has served as Special Assistant to the President for Legislative Affairs at the White House in Washington, DC. Prior to this he was Associate Director for Legislative Affairs for the Office of Management and Budget, 1985–1986. He has also served as Special Assistant to the President for Legislative Affairs at the White House, 1985, and Director of the Office of Congressional Relations for the Federal Trade Commission, 1981–1985. He was Special Assistant to the Administrator and Acting Director of the Office of Legislation, 1981; director of governmental relations for the Grocery Manufacturers of America, Inc., 1976–1981; and a legislative specialist for the Environmental Protection Agency in Denver, CO, 1972–1976. From 1969 to 1971, Mr. Harlow was a staff assistant to Senator Howard H. Baker, 1969–1971.

Mr. Harlow graduated from George Washington University (B.A., 1971). He was born January 21, 1949, in Oklahoma City, OK. He is married, has two children, and resides in Vienna, VA.

Nomination of Thomas D. Larson To Be Administrator of the Federal Highway Administration
April 14, 1989

The President today announced his intention to nominate Thomas D. Larson to be Administrator of the Federal Highway Administration, Department of Transportation. He would succeed Robert Earl Farris.

Since 1987 Dr. Larson has been a faculty member and administrator at the Pennsylvania State University. Prior to this he was secretary of transportation for the Commonwealth of Pennsylvania, 1979–1987. From 1962 to 1979, he served as a faculty member and administrator at the Pennsylvania State University: professor of civil engineering, 1969; director of the Pennsylvania Transportation Institute, 1968; an associate professor of civil engineering, 1964; and an assistant professor of civil engineering, 1962. Dr. Larson also served in the U.S. Navy Civil Engineering Corps, 1954–1957.

Dr. Larson graduated from the Pennsylvania State University (B.S., 1952; M.S., 1959; Ph.D., 1962). He currently resides in University Park, PA.

Nomination of Brian W. Clymer To Be Administrator of the Urban Mass Transit Administration
April 14, 1989

The President today announced his intention to nominate Brian W. Clymer to be Administrator of the Urban Mass Transportation Administration, Department of Transportation. He would succeed Alfred A. DelliBovi.

Mr. Clymer currently serves as vice chairman of the board of directors for the Southeastern Pennsylvania Transportation Authority, and he has served in various capacities for SEPTA, including chairman of the budget and audit committee, 1983 to present; member of the committee, 1981 to present; member and former chairman of the pension committee, 1980 to present; member of the transit committee, 1980 to present; former chairman of the professional services committee, and member of ad hoc privatization. He also founded Clymer, Merves & Amon, Certified Public Accountants, 1982.

Mr. Clymer graduated from Lehigh University (B.S., 1969). He is married, has two children, and resides in Swarthmore, PA.

Nomination of Jacqueline Knox Brown To Be an Assistant Secretary of Energy
April 14, 1989

The President today announced his intention to nominate Jacqueline Knox Brown to be an Assistant Secretary of Energy (Congressional and Intergovernmental Affairs). She would succeed C. Anson Franklin.

Mrs. Brown most recently served as a senior policy analyst with the Commission on Executive, Legislative and Judicial Salaries in Washington, DC. Prior to this she was a senior policy analyst for the Presidential Commission on the Human Immunodeficiency Virus Epidemic, 1987–1988. Mrs. Brown has also served as staff director for the Minority Subcommittee on Aging, Committee on Labor and Human Resources, of the United States Senate, 1986–1987; and a legislative assistant to the Honorable Thad Cochran (R–MS), 1979–1986.

Mrs. Brown graduated from Howard University (B.A., 1983). She was born November 20, 1952, in Washington, DC. She is married and has one daughter.

Nomination of Joseph G. Schiff To Be an Assistant Secretary of Housing and Urban Development
April 14, 1989

The President today announced his intention to nominate Joseph G. Schiff to be an Assistant Secretary of Housing and Urban Development (Public and Indian Housing). He would succeed J. Michael Dorsey.

Since 1985 Mr. Schiff has been manager of the Louisville Office of the U.S. Department of Housing and Urban Development in Louisville, KY. Prior to this he was managing partner of Elaine Schiff Realtors in Louisville. He has served as deputy county judge-executive for Jefferson County, KY, and as a legislative assistant to Congressman William O. Cowger.

Mr. Schiff received a bachelor of arts degree from American University and a juris doctorate degree from the University of Louisville. He is married to the former Polly Sherman. They have two sons and reside in Louisville, KY.

Continuation of Frank E. Young as Commissioner of Food and Drugs at the Department of Health and Human Services
April 14, 1989

The President today announced that Frank E. Young, M.D. will continue to serve as Commissioner of Food and Drugs at the Department of Health and Human Services.

Dr. Young has served as Commissioner of the Food and Drug Administration since July 15, 1984. While Commissioner he has served as a member of the U.S. delegation to the world health assembly in Geneva, Switzerland, 1985–1986, and led the U.S. delegation to the third U.S./Israeli symposium on health in Jerusalem, 1985. He has served as chairman of the executive hospital committee of Strong Memorial Hospital, 1979–1984; chairman of the medical advisory committee for Monroe Community Hospital, 1979–1984; and a pathologist for Strong Memorial Hospital, 1974–1984. He was dean of the school of medicine and dentistry, and director of the medical center of the University of Rochester, 1979–1984, and vice president for health affairs, 1981–1984.

Dr. Young graduated from Union College, the medical center of the State University of New York (M.D.), and Case Western Reserve University (Ph.D). He is married and has five children.

Remarks to Citizens in Hamtramck, Michigan

April 17, 1989

Cardinal Szoka, your Eminence. Bob, thank you for the warm greeting to your wonderful community. Governor Blanchard—it's an honor to have the Governor of the great State here. And I want to pay my respects to the members of the Michigan congressional delegation that came out here with me—Senator Riegle and several distinguished Members of the House of Representatives sitting over here—and also to Senator John Engler, who is the majority leader of the Michigan State Senate, and to other elected leaders not only from your community but in other parts of this State.

I'm delighted to be here. Bread and salt are both of the Earth, an ancient symbol of a life leavened by health and prosperity. And in this same spirit, I wish you all the same. And now, if I may, I want to address, at this important gathering, the health and prosperity of a whole nation—the proud people of Poland. You know, we Americans are not mildly sympathetic spectators of events in Poland. We are bound to Poland by a very special bond: a bond of blood, of culture, and shared values. And so, it is only natural that as dramatic change comes to Poland we share the aspirations and excitement of the Polish people.

In my Inaugural Address, I spoke of the new breeze of freedom gaining strength around the world. "In man's heart," I said, "if not in fact, the day of the dictator is over. The totalitarian era is passing; its old ideas blown away like leaves from an ancient leafless tree." I spoke of the spreading recognition that prosperity can only come from a free market and the creative genius of individuals. And I spoke of the new potency of democratic ideals: of free speech, free elections, and the exercise of free will. And we should not be surprised that the ideas of democracy are returning with renewed force in Europe, the homeland of philosophers of freedom, whose ideals have been so fully realized in our great United States of America. And Victor Hugo said: "An invasion of armies can be resisted, but not an idea whose time has come." My friends, liberty is an idea whose time has come in Eastern Europe, and make no mistake about it.

For almost half a century, the suppression of freedom in Eastern Europe, sustained by the military power of the Soviet Union, has kept nation from nation, neighbor from neighbor. And as East and West now seek to reduce arms, it must not be forgotten that arms are a symptom, not a source, of tension. The true source of tension is the imposed and unnatural division of Europe. How can there be stability and security in Europe and the world as long as nations and peoples are denied the right to determine their own future, a right explicitly promised by agreements among the victorious powers at the end of World War II? How can there be stability and security in Europe as long as nations which once stood proudly at the front rank of industrial powers are impoverished by a discredited ideology and stifling authoritarianism? The United States—and let's be clear on this—has never accepted the legitimacy of Europe's division. We accept no spheres of influence that deny the sovereign rights of nations.

And yet the winds of change are shaping a new European destiny. Western Europe is resurgent, and Eastern Europe is awakening to yearnings for democracy, independence, and prosperity. In the Soviet Union itself, we are encouraged by the sound of voices long silent and the sight of the rulers consulting the ruled. We see new thinking in some aspects of Soviet foreign policy. We are hopeful that these stirrings presage meaningful, lasting, and far more reaching change. So, let no one doubt the sincerity of the American people and their government in our desire to see reform succeed inside the Soviet Union. We welcome the changes that have taken place, and we will continue to encourage greater recognition of human rights, market incentives, and free elections.

East and West are now negotiating on a broad range of issues, from arms reductions to the environment. But the Cold War began in Eastern Europe, and if it is to end, it will end in this crucible of world conflict. And it must end—the American people want to see east and central Europe free, prosperous, and at peace. With prudence, realism, and patience, we seek to promote the evolution of freedom—the opportunities sparked by the Helsinki accords and the deepening East-West contact. In recent years, we have improved relations with countries in the region. And in each case, we looked for progress in international posture and internal practices—in human rights, cultural openness, emigration issues, opposition to international terror. While we want relations to improve, there are certain acts we will not condone or accept, behavior that can shift relations in the wrong direction—human rights abuses, technology theft, and hostile intelligence or foreign policy actions against us.

Some regions are now seeking to win popular legitimacy through reforms. In Hungary, a new leadership is experimenting with reforms that may permit a political pluralism that only a few years ago would have been absolutely unthinkable. And in Poland, on April 5th, Solidarity leader Lech Walesa and Interior Minister Kiszczak signed agreements that, if faithfully implemented, will be a watershed in the postwar history of Eastern Europe.

Under the auspices of the roundtable agreements, the free trade union *Solidarność* was today—this very day, under those agreements—*Solidarność* was today formally restored. And the agreements also provide that a free opposition press will be legalized, independent political and other free association will be permitted, and elections for a new Polish senate will be held. These agreements testify to the realism of General Jaruzelski and his colleagues, and they are inspiring testimony to the spiritual guidance of the Catholic Church, the indomitable spirit of the Polish people, and the strength and wisdom of Lech Walesa.

Poland faces, and will continue to face for some time, severe economic problems. A modern French writer observed that communism is not another form of economics: It is the death of economics. In Poland, an economic system crippled by the inefficiencies of central planning almost proved the death of initiative and enterprise—almost. But economic reforms can still give free rein to the enterprising impulse and creative spirit of the great Polish people.

The Polish people understand the magnitude of this challenge. Democratic forces in Poland have asked for the moral, political, and economic support of the West, and the West will respond. My administration is completing now a thorough review of our policies toward Poland and all of Eastern Europe, and I've carefully considered ways that the United States can help Poland. And we will not act unconditionally. We're not going to offer unsound credits. We're not going to offer aid without requiring sound economic practices in return. And we must remember that Poland still is a member of the Warsaw Pact. And I will take no steps that compromise the security of the West.

The Congress, the Polish-American community—and I support, I endorse strongly Ed Moskal and what he is doing in the Polish American Congress, I might say; and I'm delighted he's here, good Chicago boy right here in Hamtramck—that the Congress, the Polish-American community, the American labor movement, our allies, and international financial institutions—our allies all must work in concert if Polish democracy is to take root anew and sustain itself. And we can and must answer this call to freedom. And it is particularly appropriate here in Hamtramck for me to salute the members and leaders of the American labor movement for hanging tough with Solidarity through its darkest days. Labor deserves great credit for that.

Now the Poles are now taking steps that deserve our active support. And I have decided as your President on specific steps to be taken by the United States, carefully chosen to recognize the reforms underway and to encourage reforms yet to come now that *Solidarność* is legal. I will ask Congress to join me in providing Poland access to our Generalized System of Preferences, which offers selective tariff relief to beneficiary countries. We will work with our allies and friends in the Paris Club to develop sustainable new schedules for Poland to repay its debt, easing a heavy burden so that a free market can grow.

I will also ask Congress to join me in authorizing the Overseas Private Investment Corporation to operate in Poland, to the benefit of both Polish and U.S. investors. We will propose negotiations for a private business agreement with Poland to encourage cooperation between U.S. firms and Poland's private businesses—both sides can benefit. The United States will continue to consider supporting, on their merits, viable loans to the private sector by the International Finance Corporation. We believe that the roundtable agreements clear the way for Poland to be able to work with International Monetary Fund on programs that support sound, market-oriented economic policies. We will encourage business and private nonprofit groups to develop innovative programs to swap Polish debt for equity in Polish enterprises, and for charitable, humanitarian, and environmental projects. We will support imaginative educational, cultural, and training programs to help liberate the creative energies of the Polish people.

You know, when I visited Poland in September of 1987, I was then Vice President, and I told Chairman Jaruzelski and Lech Walesa that the American people and Government would respond quickly and imaginatively to significant internal reform of the kind that we now see—both of them valued that assurance. So, it is especially gratifying for me today to witness the changes now taking place in Poland and to announce these important changes in U.S. policy. The United States of America keeps its promises.

If Poland's experiment succeeds, other countries may follow. And while we must still differentiate among the nations of Eastern Europe, Poland offers two lessons for all. First, there can be no progress without significant political and economic liberalization. And second, help from the West will come in concert with liberalization. Our friends and European allies share this philosophy.

The West can now be bold in proposing a vision of the European future. We dream of the day when there will be no barriers to the free movement of peoples, goods, and ideas. We dream of the day when Eastern European peoples will be free to choose their system of government and to vote for the party of their choice in regular, free, contested elections. And we dream of the day when Eastern European countries will be free to choose their own peaceful course in the world, including closer ties with Western Europe. And we envision an Eastern Europe in which the Soviet Union has renounced military intervention as an instrument of its policy—on any pretext. We share an unwavering conviction that one day all the peoples of Europe will live in freedom. And make no mistake about that.

Next month, at a summit of the North Atlantic alliance, I will meet with the leaders of the Western democracies. The leaders of the Western democracies will discuss these concerns. And these are not bilateral issues just between the United States and the Soviet Union. They are, rather, the concern of all the Western allies, calling for common approaches. The Soviet Union should understand, in turn, that a free, democratic Eastern Europe as we envision it would threaten no one and no country. Such an evolution would imply and reinforce the further improvement of East-West relations in all dimensions—arms reductions, political relations, trade—in ways that enhance the safety and well-being of all of Europe. There is no other way.

What has brought us to this opening? The unity and strength of the democracies, yes, and something else: the bold, new thinking in the Soviet Union, the innate desire for freedom in the hearts of all men. We will not waver in our dedication to freedom now. And if we're wise, united, and ready to seize the moment, we will be remembered as the generation that made all Europe free.

Two centuries ago, a Polish patriot, Thaddeus Kosciusko, came to these American shores to stand for freedom. Let us honor and remember this hero of our own struggle for freedom by extending our hand to those who work the shipyards of Gdansk and walk the cobbled streets of Warsaw. Let us recall the words of the Poles who struggled for independence: "For your freedom and ours." Let us support the peaceful evolution of democracy in Poland. The cause of liberty knows no limits; the friends of freedom, no borders.

God bless Poland. God bless the United States of America. Thank you all very much. *Niech Zyje Polska!* [Long live Poland!] Thank you very much.

Note: The President spoke at 11:53 a.m. at Hamtramck City Hall. In his opening remarks, he referred to Cardinal Edmund C. Szoka, the Archbishop of Detroit, and Robert Kozaren, mayor of Hamtramck. He also referred to Edward Moskal, president of the Polish-American Congress. Following his remarks, the President attended a luncheon at the Eagle Restaurant. Following the luncheon, he returned to Washington, DC.

A fact sheet entitled "Support for Polish Reforms" was also released by the Office of the Press Secretary. In addition to covering the material on this subject found in these remarks, the fact sheet also contained the following points concerning U.S. policy toward Poland:

"Once authorized, OPIC [Overseas Private Investment Corporation] and the Polish Government will negotiate an investment incentives agreement detailing OPIC's rights and the GOP's [Government of Poland's] responsibilities for OPIC-assisted investment.

"In the absence of GSP [Generalized System of Preferences], OPIC would make an independent determination that Poland is taking steps to adopt and implement worker rights. We will work closely with Solidarity."

Remarks at the National Conference of the Building and Construction Trades Department of the AFL–CIO
April 18, 1989

Thank you for that warm welcome. Thank you, Bob Georgine, for that warm welcome. Since the election is over, the story can now be told: a proud story about all the help this guy gave me in the last two elections. [*Laughter*] No, here's the way it worked, really. [*Laughter*]

In this very room, I'm at an Italian-American dinner in 1984, sitting up here at the high—you know, the big dais here and everything. Georgine comes over—very pleasant to my wife, who could well be his campaign manager if he has higher aspirations. [*Laughter*] And he says, "You've got to understand, George," he tells me, "you've got to understand. Don't you realize Geraldine Ferraro is an Italian? Don't you understand that?" I said, "Yes, I understand, so I was waiting for 1988." [*Laughter*] See him at the same dinner, same place, looking at him. "Hey, come on." And he says, "You've got to understand." I looked at his nametag. I'm running against Michael Dukakis, famous Greek-American. I see his nametag—Bob Georgapolis—[*laughter*]—little much.

But look, here I am, and I appreciate very much the tone with which your outstanding leader set the agenda here today and the warm welcome that you gave me. And I do have great respect for Bob Georgine. I've told him this. The door will be open over there to him, to the leaders here, and to all of you, whom he represents so well. And he doesn't hide behind the differences. We get them out there on the table.

But there's a lot more to the relationship between the White House and the labor organizations than one issue or another.

And I think of this group, and I think of patriotism. I think of love of country. I think of family and the values that have always made this country great. And so, I came over here to salute you and to express my great appreciation and to tell you a couple other things. The puppies are fine. [*Laughter*] And even more important, my wife's health is great, and I appreciate that.

So, I think we all have a lot to be grateful for, and I'm honored by the presence of many friends here today. I have great confidence in and respect for and obvious friendship with our Secretary of Labor Elizabeth Dole, who's with me here today and who's going to speak in just a minute. And I appreciate the cooperation so many of you have given her already. I want to salute Tom Ridge, a friend of mine of long standing, and I don't think labor has a better friend in the Congress. Of course, there's others up here: the Teamsters president Billy McCarthy down there, a friend of mine; and Buddy Ruel and John Bowden of the Iron Workers; Bill Dugan and John Bertrand of the Operating Engineers; Eddie Brubeck, Indianapolis Building Trades, and many, many others. I'm going to make an omission and thus hurt feelings, and I don't want to do that. But I want to thank everybody.

We hold elections in this country—it's a good thing—and then we move on. Leadership assumes office; it exerts its influence. But it must never presume that it does any more than speak and act for the people, and we have had honest differences. But we agree on goals, and what matters is that we make progress on issues of shared concern.

So, I begin today with a special word of thanks. Your Dad's Day event is a shining example of voluntarism in action. And it's a reminder of how we in America must learn to measure success: not by the sum of our possessions but by the good we do for others. And on Father's Day, the Building Trades will be winning a victory for humanity, large and small.

Your theme for this magnificent conference is "Building for the Future." And so, today I want to share just a few thoughts on how we can build a better America. We're a prosperous nation. Thank God we're at peace. And you've heard the numbers: 76 months of recordbreaking economic growth—a growth rate that outstrips the nations of Europe, exceeding all expectations—and nearly 20 million new jobs. Unemployment at a 15-year low; real family income at all-time high; output of goods and services up over 27 percent since the end of '82. But we have to remember what's driving the economic growth: the enterprise and the energy of people like yourselves. You build a better America every single day.

Anyone who forgets that the working men and women drive this economy ought to take a lesson from the guy with the circular saw who runs over his own power cord. The guy may think he's headed in the right direction, but he's headed for a real shock. [*Laughter*]

Our economy is healthy. But to keep the momentum going, to keep America competitive, and to keep the building trades strong, we must keep inflation and interest rates down; and moreover, we must bring them down further. The way to do that is to bring the budget deficit down. And it isn't fun working at it, but I am going to succeed. We've got to bring that deficit down.

I'm pleased to say that we've reached a budget agreement with Congress. And I'd add that this is the first such agreement reached ahead of schedule and not framed in the context of crisis. This is only a first step, but it is an important step. This budget agreement meets our fundamental obligations to protect national security and support the needy. It provides funds to advance high-priority initiatives, but it also—and this is the hard part—it restrains the overall growth of Federal spending so that we can meet these Gramm-Rudman-Hollings deficit targets. Next year alone, Federal revenues will rise by more than $80 billion, with no tax increase. And that's an agreed revenue increase—I believe it's agreed by both the CBO [Congressional Budget Office] and our own estimates. This agreement should bring the deficit for 1990 down to $99.4 billion, and that is a $64 billion reduction in 1 year.

And let me say this—I did keep a promise I made, and it was alluded to by Bob Georgine: We have not raised taxes on the working men and women of this country. And I'm going to hold the line on those taxes. What the budget does do is put our priorities in the right place. It puts the focus on the kind of investment we need to build on economic growth and stimulate competitive enterprise, and that means—and I know this one is controversial—but it means restoring the capital gains differential to 15 percent.

Whatever else you've heard, the capital gains cut will make us more competitive with our major trading partners who tax capital gains lightly, if at all. It will bring in $4.8 billion more in tax revenues in 1990, according to the Treasury Department, and it will help American enterprise grow. But the big thing about it is: More people will start businesses; more people will help join in creating jobs and competitiveness, opportunity and growth, saving investment for the long-term, and more jobs. And that is what we are all fighting for. So, I must make clear why it is I am fighting for that one provision, that change in the Tax Code.

Construction-related jobs are vital to a strong economy; but as we work to create those jobs, we need to make sure that every person who takes a construction job is as safe as we can make them. And one step—we've established a new Office of Engineering Support in OSHA [Occupational Safety and Health Administration] to work more closely with you for better accident investigation and prevention.

Along with keeping workers safe, building a better, more competitive America demands that the workers are skilled. And we need to ease some of the shortages of talent already developing in your trades and many others. So, we're looking to the only long-term solution: comprehensive education and training. Over 50 million Americans—this is a mind-boggling figure—50 million Americans will need some kind of training or retraining before the end of this century, and meeting that need will demand real partnerships between employers and workers and between government and industry.

The construction trades have a history of outstanding training and development efforts. Job Corps, the Job Training Partnership Act have also had outstanding results. And I'll be looking to Secretary Dole, as she finds new solutions, to help those who aren't yet prepared for the jobs of the future because of skills gap and family pressures or a lack of supportive policies. Let me say she has in this my full support.

You know, back a thousand years ago, when Barbara and I left the East and moved out to west Texas—Odessa-Midland area—in the late forties, I learned something about building a business and meeting a payroll, and lived a few of the lessons that you're supposed to get out of books about supply and demand and risk and reward and profit and loss. But I also learned something about the trust that must exist between workers and managers. And our working men and women face real challenges now. And to meet them, our spirit has got to be one of cooperation, or motivation, if you will, for the common good. And there will be honest differences, and that's why we need a National Labor Relations Board of knowledgeable individuals whose neutrality and integrity are above reproach. And let me assure you: People I'm going to nominate meet these standards. My appointments will not be antilabor or antibusiness—or, as I say, antibusiness. They will be based on fairplay.

We must keep the ball in play. Like Mark Twain said: "It's not good sportsmanship to pick up lost golf balls while they're still rolling." [*Laughter*] I can't figure out who was the better philosopher, Yogi Berra or Mark Twain. You remember Yogi: "Okay, now pair them off in threes." [*Laughter*]

Yesterday, I saluted the members and leaders of the American labor movement for hanging tough with Lech Walesa in *Solidarność* through the darkest days. Democratic forces in Poland have asked for the support of the West, and the West will respond. The Congress, the Polish-American community, the American labor movement, our allies, and international financial institutions all must work together if Polish democracy is to take root and to endure. Brighter days may be dawning in Eastern Europe, in Poland, in Central America.

Wherever the free trade movement is threatened, so, too, is democracy and freedom itself. And I put this in here about Poland and the changes that are taking place because when I think of freedom and the American people's understanding of freedom, I do think of your great organizations—you understand it.

One of the things I most admire when I talk with members of the building trades is this underlying sense of patriotism. Among you here today are many veterans—World War II, Korea, and Vietnam. And you want to talk about freedom? No one appreciates it more than someone who's put their lives and limbs at risk in its defense, and many of you in this room have done just exactly that.

And, now, you may figure that politicians come and go. Well, the kind of people that are essential to a free and prosperous society with a competitive economy are people like yourselves. You bear the tools, the skills, and the will to build a better America and to keep this great nation free. I want this door at the White House to stay open. I want to work with you to advocate, to negotiate—and to count on you, most importantly, as neighbors and friends who share the family values that I think are so vital to the survival and strength of the United States of America.

You know, speaking of Yogi Berra, again, someone once asked him if he was a fatalist. And he answered, "No, I never collected postage stamps." [*Laughter*] We are the United States of America. We have no time for fatalism in the face of our good fortune. And like every American, I am grateful for all of the blessings that the builders of America have built as monuments to our labor and our freedom. I came over here to salute your leadership and to thank each and every one of the building trades members.

Thank you all. God bless you, and most of all, God bless the United States of America.

Note: The President spoke at 10:16 a.m. in the International Ballroom at the Washington Hilton Hotel. In his remarks, he referred to Robert Georgine, president of the department, and Representative Thomas J. Ridge of Pennsylvania.

Message to the Congress Reporting Budget Deferrals
April 18, 1989

To the Congress of the United States:

In accordance with the Impoundment Control Act of 1974, I herewith report five revised deferrals of budget authority now totaling $649,663,811.

The deferrals affect programs in the Departments of Agriculture, Defense-Civil, Energy, Health and Human Services-Social Security Administration, and Justice.

The details of the deferrals are contained in the enclosed report.

GEORGE BUSH

The White House,
April 18, 1989.

Note: The attachments detailing the deferrals were printed in the "Federal Register" of April 27.

Remarks and a Question-and-Answer Session With Agricultural Journalists
April 18, 1989

The President. Thank you, Clayton Yeutter, our distinguished Secretary of Agriculture. And, Gary, thank you for monitoring us here and, Brenda, thank you for those words of welcome.

You know, American farmers got good news at the GATT [General Agreement on Tariffs and Trade] agricultural talks in Geneva a couple of weeks ago. G-A-T-T, known as GATT, was set up to provide these international rules of trade. And there was a renewed commitment by the 96 participating nations to long-term agricultural reform, benefiting farmers, consumers, and taxpayers all around the world. And there was a new road map for the final 2 years of negotiations.

America's goals for this trade round have not changed. Clayt, you fought for this when you were the U.S. Trade Representative and now as Secretary of Agriculture. The goals haven't changed; the bottom line is fairness for the American farmer. And we seek a level playing field for our farmers: the eventual elimination of export subsidies, import barriers, and other devices that distort trade and create bogus incentives to grow products for which no markets exist. On a level playing field, where neither side has the home team advantage, American farmers can compete with anybody in the world. And we'd have an export boom if we had that kind of international market.

The American people are behind you in these negotiations. We will not take actions, short-term or long-term, that aren't matched by the European Community and the other developed nations. We're not about to disarm unilaterally in agriculture. And we want to get rid of the impediments that keep us from exporting.

The American public is also deeply concerned about economic conditions in our rural communities. And that means, need to diversify in our rural economies—creating more jobs in these rural areas. In a response, we're developing a new working group on rural development. It's chaired by the Secretary of Agriculture, and I know he'll be glad to talk about that. It'll have senior leaders from every arm of government with outreach to rural America. And to the listeners today, we would welcome your ideas. Economic stress in rural areas is not just numbers and statistics and bushels of wheat: It's people and pride and sweat and families that need help now.

And then lastly, to provide some extra money to farmers early in the crop year, today we are announcing additional advance deficiency payments for farmers who sign up for the 1989 wheat, feed grain, rice, and upland cotton programs. This will mean an additional 10 percent of projected deficiency payments, or a total of about $850 million for American farmers.

And this the final thought, before we go to the questions from the farm broadcasters: A breakthrough budget compromise was reached with Congress on Friday. It came early, and that's good news for all Americans.

We're listening. We are with the American farmer in these tough times. And we're here today to take some questions, and thank you very much.

Agricultural Exports

Q. Mr. President, I'd like to pursue the area of agricultural trade. Until this morning, we had been using our agricultural trade through the Export Enhancement Program to maintain, and perhaps to gain, some new markets. There are those who say that we should use our food exports as a foreign policy tool as well. Do you and your administration see using the food that we can produce for other countries as a foreign policy tool?

The President. No, sir, not if I'm interpreting your question correctly, because when I think of foreign policy tool, my mind goes back to singling out agriculture in a trade embargo against the Soviet Union. And I will not do that as President of the United States. I know our able Secretary of Agriculture is on the same side of this one. We will not use food as a diplomatic tool. We are rebuilding confidence in American agriculture in terms of reliability in foreign markets, and we're going to have to continue to do that. And one way to reverse that out and set back exports would be to use food as a diplomatic tool. And I'm not going to do that.

Drought Relief

Q. Mr. President, all the farm broadcasters appreciate your openness and Secretary

Yeutter's openness to American agriculture. You mentioned the advanced deficiency payment increases, and being the fact that Kansas crop, especially wheat, so devastated by the drought conditions—will this be the sum total of Federal action for producers who've lost crops to drought—increase in deficiency payments?

The President. Well, I wouldn't say the sum total. And I'd let Secretary Yeutter share with you, as he did with me in the Oval Office, his views on his recent trip to Kansas, where he saw firsthand the suffering and the concern of American farmers. So, I wouldn't say this will be all that can be done. I do think that because farmers are still experiencing these dry conditions in the Midwest and in other parts of the Nation that this program will help—advancing the payments. But on the other hand, I'd leave to Clayton what steps further we might take, but I can tell you this: Because of his standing in the agricultural community and his day-to-day contact with farmers, I will be very openminded over in the White House if he comes over with additional suggestions or recommendations. So, this should not be viewed as the definitive answer. We hope it is something that will help the farm family.

Secretary Yeutter. I'll do just a quick supplement to that so that we don't cut into the valuable time of the President of the United States. But just to say, as you know, Mark [Mark Vail, Kansas Agriculture Network, Topeka, KS], I visited Kansas, along with Senators Dole and Kassebaum and Congressman Roberts, on Friday. Governor Hayden [of Kansas] accompanied us. The Governor has submitted a followup letter already. It came in today. We're going to analyze all that very carefully over the next few days, and we'll see what we can do. Clearly, we don't have an open spigot that just spits out Federal dollars in any situation today. I made that point clear when I was in Kansas. But we'll be as sympathetic and accommodative as we can be within rather severe budgetary constraints.

Agriculture Budget

Q. Good afternoon, Mr. President. And by the way, greetings from the Concho Valley and the Permian Basin. Since your budget announcement Friday, there has been a lot of concern voiced by Congressmen de la Garza and Stenholm on the House Agriculture Committee that agriculture is being asked to take more than its fair share of cuts in spending. Now, in your campaign, you assured farmers that the budget would not be balanced on their backs, and I just wonder, how do you react to these concerns?

The President. Well, Roddy [Roddy Peeples, Southwest Agriculture Network, San Angelo, TX], first, greetings to Tom Green County out there, and I'm delighted to be talking to you. Secondly, my view is this: We are in perilous budget deficit times. We have got to get the deficit down, and the best thing we can do to help the American farmer is to get these interest rates down. And the best way to do that is to make the tough decision on the spending side of our budget. Now, having said that, I feel that farmers are fairplay. I mentioned earlier the grain embargo. One of the things that irks the farmers—properly—is that they were asked to carry the whole burden, and here we're not. Yes, ag has taken a hit, but so has a wide array of programs across the board. And I think what we've done here is fair.

The program is still there and vigorous and high levels of spending—$11 billion I think is the figure. And so, I hope that nobody feels that this is an unfair approach to getting the deficit down. But I can guarantee you that if we are successful—and I've done this, incidentally, this first step, without raising taxes on the American farmer—if we are successful here, then you're going to have the biggest benefit to the farmers at all: You're going to have a lower interest rate, a continued growing economy. And then, if we succeed overseas, you're going to have a vigorous new market for ag products. So please, I can understand Chairman de la Garza, my friend from south Texas, and—who was it?—Charlie Stenholm, who is out there from east and north of you; but I'll tell you I think in the final analysis, we'll convince them that this is an equitable approach to our budget.

Agricultural Exports

Q. Mr. President, it's a real privilege to have this opportunity to visit with you today. And I'd like to return to what you opened with, and that's the good news of the GATT talks and the effect that might be seen on the new farm bill. I know that Secretary Yeutter has referred to that; he said he may want to alter the content, have more leverage in the GATT negotiations. Would you comment on that, please?

The President. Well, Dix [Dix Harper, Tobacco Network, Raleigh, NC], first, thank you, sir, for the greeting, and I'll let Clayton in a minute go into a little more detail. But what happened over there was that an international community reluctant to discuss agriculture has finally understood that we've got to go forward. Now, we have agricultural Export Enhancement Program. Others have had that for a long time. Others gripe when the United States farmer gets the same incentive built into the system that they themselves have enjoyed for a long time. We understand that. We understand the screams coming from them. But the good news is we've got this on the agenda; we will be able to move forward now to freer markets and to less protection.

And so, the upcoming farm bill can indeed be used as leverage, you might say, because we are not going to unilaterally disarm, if you will. We're not going to take cuts unilaterally based on some verbal assurance from people that have excluded our products from their market. So, we've moved forward at GATT. We've got a farm bill where we're not going to back away and make unilateral concessions to others. But the climate is better. And I'll let Clayton, if he will, fill in a little bit more detail on that.

Secretary Yeutter. As you know, we've got 20 months to go in these negotiations, as they wrap up on time at the end of 1990. We hope they will, and we believe that the agreement that was reached in Geneva just a few days ago is going to contribute to that end. We had a good week in Geneva. We got the kind of long-term commitment we wanted, and now we simply have to fight this out at the negotiating table.

But as President Bush said, we certainly want to do the right things in next year's farm bill to contribute to that negotiating environment. In other words, we sure don't want to give away any negotiating leverage, and if possible, we've got to try to enhance it. In that regard, by the way, I'm going to be testifying to the Senate Ag Committee tomorrow morning in the first hearing that'll be held on the farm bill. You may want to take a look at my testimony when it's available tomorrow, because it'll have some statements on this subject that'll be quite definitive and specific.

Q. Mr. President, you frequently linked ag and exports in public comments and once suggested that Secretary Yeutter was hardly changing his job in moving from USTR [U.S. Trade Representative] to Agriculture. With the steep debt we've got and with the favorable import balance agriculture brings, should U.S. producers be worried the Government's use for them now is strictly as earners of currency to stanch the flow of assets out of this country?

The President. No, they shouldn't have any concern on that because we are—let me just repeat, using this phrase "unilateral disarmament"—we are not going to unilaterally disarm. And I still feel deep in my heart that if we can get fewer barriers the American farmer can compete in all kinds of areas. And I'm including dairy in this, where we haven't competed much before. And so, we're not going to take unilateral hits in agriculture, because agriculture in many areas is benefiting our whole international trade position.

Secretary Yeutter. And we do want to be big export earners, as a matter of fact. Gary [Gary Digiuseppe, Brownfield Network, Centertown, MO], as you well know, the more markets we can open up overseas, the more exports we'll have. And agriculture will continue to make a very positive contribution to the trade balance. And that'll be good because that'll also result in higher farm incomes. And that's what all of us want, and the President's strongly supportive of that.

Secretary of Agriculture Yeutter

The President. Gary, there was one person that wasn't sure that Secretary Yeutter was doing exactly the same thing, and that was Mrs. Yeutter. Because I think they had had plans to go back to the private sector. And I got with Clayton, and I said, "Look, it is absolutely essential to our country that you agree to serve as Secretary of Agriculture." And it was one of the best decisions, I think, that I've made. And of course, I was grateful that he set aside his private-sector plan—and his wife very graciously understood this—so he once again could serve, and did it in a portfolio here that is just vital, and not just in your area of question, international trade, but to our whole economy. So, I'm grateful the Secretary did differentiate here.

Secretary Yeutter. Thank you, Mr. President. That's a very gracious and generous comment and a true story. Your time with us is up, I'm sorry to say, Mr. President. But on behalf of everybody in American agriculture, I want to thank you for coming, and then I'll stay on and answer a few more questions.

The President. Well—and I would apologize to those whose questions I didn't get to take. And I was talking to Clayt—he came over to the White House. And I wish that all of you who love nature and love the Mother Earth could have been with Clayton Yeutter and me as we walked through the beautiful Rose Garden area of the White House. It is at its most beautiful this time of year. And I get a kick out of seeing all the tourists from middle America and agricultural America and everyplace coming to the "people's house."

But having said all that, we were talking about this first program of this nature. And I told Clayt that, if agreeable and if we didn't foul it up too bad in this first session, that I would welcome coming back here to this little studio in the Ag Department to take questions from you, the important voices of agriculture in America. So, thanks for your hospitality. And as Douglas MacArthur said, "I shall return." Thank you very much.

Note: The President spoke at 1:18 p.m., during the Farm Radio Broadcast, in the Department of Agriculture broadcasting studio. In his opening remarks, he referred to announcers Gary Crawford and Brenda Curtis.

Remarks Upon Signing the Bill Implementing the Bipartisan Accord on Central America

April 18, 1989

Please be seated. And distinguished leaders of the Congress here today, my thanks for joining us. Four weeks ago, for the first time in many years, the President and Congress, the Democratic and Republican leadership in the House and Senate, spoke with one voice about Central America. And by signing a bipartisan accord on Central America, we joined hands for the good of that troubled region, and by placing principle above party, we reaffirmed the cornerstone of America's foreign policy.

Last week the Congress passed legislation to implement the bipartisan accord, and today I am very proud to sign this legislation. My friends, you've shown that bipartisanship works. And I want to thank you for acting quickly, honorably, and in the national interest.

Our objective in Central America is a democratic Nicaragua which does not subvert or threaten its neighbors and whose people enjoy the social and economic fruits of a free society. Our continued assistance to the Nicaraguan resistance represents the commitment of the United States both to Esquipulas—the peace process—and to sustain those who struggle for freedom and democracy. Under the Esquipulas accord, insurgent forces have the right to reintegrate into their homeland under safe, democratic conditions with full civil and political rights. And that's the desire of the Nicaraguan resistance. And we will support it through concerted diplomatic efforts to reinforce this regional agreement.

Here, in particular, let me thank the Congress. For by supporting my request for continued assistance at current levels through the elections in Nicaragua, scheduled now for February 28, 1990, you have reaffirmed the will of this government to ensure peace and freedom in Central America.

The success of the Central American peace process and the prospects of national reconciliation in Nicaragua depend on full and honest Sandinista compliance with their repeated pledges of democracy and freedom. We've yet to see genuine Sandinista compliance; thus far, they've refused to negotiate with the opposition regarding the necessary conditions for fair elections. It's clear that close international scrutiny and sustained pressure will be critical to induce Sandinista compliance. It's also clear that the Soviet Union must match its rhetorical support for the peace process with concrete action to halt military aid, to end subversion in that region, and to promote genuine democracy in Nicaragua.

It is fitting to recall what Franklin Roosevelt said when he addressed the Nation in 1940: "Today we seek a moral basis for peace. It cannot be a lasting peace if the fruit of it is oppression or starvation or cruelty or human life dominated by armed camps."

Our accord envisions a democratic Central America and a more just and tranquil hemisphere. And above all, it points us toward the future—for America and for the people of Central America.

So, let us seize the moment. Thank you, Mr. Speaker and Mr. Majority Leader, minority leaders, distinguished Members of the Congress; and thank all of you for being here. And now it's my pleasure to sign the legislation implementing the bipartisan accord on Central America. Thank you all.

Note: The President spoke at 2:18 p.m. in the Rose Garden at the White House. In his closing remarks, he referred to Jim Wright, Speaker of the House of Representatives; George J. Mitchell and Robert Dole, majority and minority leaders of the Senate, respectively. Thomas S. Foley and Robert H. Michel, majority and minority leaders of the House of Representatives, respectively. H.R. 1750, approved April 18, was assigned Public Law No. 101-14.

Statement by Press Secretary Fitzwater on the Situation in Lebanon
April 18, 1989

President Bush is deeply concerned about the growing violence in Lebanon and the escalating suffering of the Lebanese people. The President calls for all internal parties and Syria to cease shelling and to step back from confrontation. The President strongly supports efforts currently underway, such as the one by the Arab League, to bring about a cease-fire and an end to the violence.

In addition, yesterday President Bush and President Mitterrand of France discussed by telephone steps that the United Nations could take to calm the situation. Both Presidents stressed their concern about the loss of life, injuries, and deterioration of the situation in Beirut. The two Presidents stressed the need for international support for efforts to bring about a peaceful solution.

Statement on Maternal and Child Health Care Proposals
April 18, 1989

I look forward to meeting today with Secretary Sullivan to discuss our effort to improve the health of mothers and children.

As part of that effort, we are today forwarding to the Congress our maternal and infant health proposals. I hope the Congress will enact this legislation and will also act on my other Medicaid commitments: full funding of the ongoing Medicaid program in FY 90 and an additional appropriation of $20 million to build our understanding of how best to improve maternal and infant health.

Infant and maternal health is an area where we must invest in the future. It is also an area where we must all be committed to improvement. I am particularly disturbed by the fact that the infant mortality rate for black infants is nearly twice that for whites.

This legislation does not do all that we want to do, but it does do what we can do at this time. In my February 9 address to the Nation, I said the budget we were submitting represented my best judgment of how we can address our priorities. This legislation shows that principle at work. Investing in the health of pregnant women, infants, and children is our highest priority for the Medicaid program. And that is why, at a time like today when resources are tight, when we have more desires than funds, we must move resources from certain lower priorities to the higher priority of maternal and infant health.

Maternal and infant health is equally important to Secretary Sullivan. He knows the issues; he knows the problems. I'm confident that his effort to put all the knowledge and talent in the Department of Health and Human Services behind this issue will yield substantial rewards for our nation's effort to improve maternal and infant health.

White House Fact Sheet on Maternal and Child Health Care Proposals
April 18, 1989

The administration today forwarded to the Congress proposed legislation to make Federal programs better serve pregnant women, infants, and children. The legislation carries out commitments the President made in his February 9 address, "Building a Better America." The President's proposals also include funds for improving the delivery of health care services; this request does not require new legislation.

The legislation would expand significantly the population Medicaid serves, making Medicaid available to 1.9 million more women when they become pregnant. The legislation also takes steps to make Medicaid more effective by bringing more eligible women and infants into the program. The legislation is part of an overall approach to health care for the disadvantaged that calls for full funding for Medicaid, $37.6 billion for FY 1990, an increase of $3.3 billion or 9.6 percent over the FY 1989 level.

The President's Principles

- The President is committed to improving health care for lower income Americans by focusing first on the populations most at risk: mothers and their babies. Expansions in the Medicaid program contemplated under current law will do much to meet these needs.
- The most cost-effective means must be used to achieve our goals. Adequate prenatal care and immunization against childhood diseases are both the most effective and least costly means to good health early in life.
- Greater personal responsibility for

good health must be fostered. Mothers must be encouraged to seek prenatal care; to avoid the use of cigarettes, alcohol, and drugs; and to obtain good nutrition. The effects of the expanded Medicaid eligibility in the administration proposal will be undermined if mothers make unhealthy choices.

• States and community groups have a vital role in improving child health care and must be given flexibility in using their resources to meet their own specific problems. The Federal Government should continue to provide support through State-administered programs such as Medicaid.

The President's Proposals

The legislation transmitted to the Congress today would:

- increase by 374,000 the number of pregnant women and children eligible for Medicaid.
- foster greater participation in Medicaid by eligible pregnant women by providing services to pregnant women who are presumed eligible for Medicaid before a formal eligibility determination is made, and requiring States to operate outreach programs in areas of high infant mortality.
- entitle all children under age 6 who are receiving food stamps to Medicaid coverage for immunizations.
- make the Federal match rate for State administrative expenses a uniform 50 percent by gradually reducing special administrative match rates ranging from 75 to 100 percent. The savings that result would allow the legislative eligibility changes proposed by the President to be implemented within the current programs' spending level.

The President has also proposed investing $20 million in both FY 1990 and FY 1991 for a new demonstration program. The demonstrations would implement improved coordination among three Federal programs: Medicaid; Maternal and Child Health; and the Women, Infants, and Children (WIC) nutrition programs. The results of the demonstrations are intended to serve as the basis for future reform of service delivery under these programs.

Infant Health in America

Progress in improving infant health is most often described in terms of infant mortality statistics. The United States has made significant progress since World War II in reducing infant mortality. Infant mortality has dropped from 29.2 deaths per thousand births in 1950 to 10.4 in 1986, the most recent year for which final data is available.

In recent years, the United States has not made as much progress as other countries. As a result, the United States has dropped from 19th in 1980 to 22d in 1985 among the nations of the world when ranked by infant mortality rates.

Infant mortality rates for black Americans have been and remain higher than those for whites. The black infant mortality rate stood at 43.9 deaths per 1,000 births in 1950; in 1985 it was 18.2 deaths. While this is a significant improvement, it remains nearly twice the 9.3 deaths per 1,000 births among white Americans.

Medicaid alone is not sufficient to assure proper medical care. In a survey of the poorest areas of New York City, where infant mortality is high, 68.5 percent of the mothers were Medicaid recipients, but 39 percent of the mothers received late or no prenatal care. In such areas, drug and alcohol abuse are often the greatest threat to maternal and infant health.

The goal of healthier babies depends on mothers making intelligent choices during pregnancy: avoiding smoking, drugs, and alcohol. The President's proposal to fund demonstrations that encourage better coordination of Federal programs will lead to more effective program designs and form the basis for future Federal program changes.

Medicaid and Infant Health: Current Law and the Administration's Proposals

Under current law, by July 1, 1990, every State Medicaid program must cover pregnant women and infants (up to age 1) with incomes not exceeding 100 percent of the Federal poverty line. States may elect to cover women and infants with incomes up to 185 percent of the poverty line.

Under the administration's proposal,

States would be required, by April 1, 1990, to provide coverage to pregnant women and infants whose income does not exceed 130 percent of the poverty line. The option for coverage up to 185 percent of the poverty line would remain unchanged.

Under the President's proposals, a single pregnant woman with an income of up to $10,426 would be eligible; $13,078 for a household of two; $15,730 for a household of three; and $18,382 for a household of four.

Current law provides that States may grant presumptive Medicaid eligibility to pregnant women. Under this option, States designate qualified providers who, based on a preliminary assessment of the woman's income, may determine her to be eligible. These providers are facilities that have a high proportion of eligible women in their clientele and include community health centers, public health departments, and maternal and child health clinics. A woman who is presumptively eligible is entitled to ambulatory care for up to 45 days, during the first 14 of which she is expected to apply for Medicaid. Twenty States have adopted this option.

The administration proposes to require that all States offer presumptive Medicaid eligibility. This will increase the number of pregnant women who will receive coverage and obtain prenatal care early in their pregnancies. Any woman with a valid food stamp card would be presumptively eligible. The period of presumptive eligibility would be set at 60 days. States would be required to demonstrate efforts to make the presumptive eligibility process work in all areas of the State. In addition, the State would be required to demonstrate outreach and public education efforts in areas with high rates of infant mortality.

Remarks Following Discussions With King Hussein I of Jordan
April 19, 1989

The President. Well, I've had the pleasure and honor of an intimate discussion with an old friend, His Majesty King Hussein of Jordan. The relationship between Jordan and the United States has deep roots; it's founded on a commonality of interests and mutual respect. And it is in this spirit that His Majesty and I reviewed the situation in the Middle East and, in particular, the search for Arab-Israeli peace. We talked also of the concerns that we both have about Lebanon.

Few individuals can match the dedication of His Majesty King Hussein to the cause of peace, for his is a commitment to explore opportunities, examine options, pursue possibilities. And I explained to him our thinking on the need to diffuse tensions, to promote dialog, to foster the process of negotiations that could lead to a comprehensive settlement. And I reiterated my belief that properly designed and mutually acceptable elections could, as an initial step, contribute to a political process leading to negotiations on the final status of the West Bank and Gaza. I also reaffirmed to His Majesty our longstanding commitment to bring about a comprehensive settlement through negotiations based on U.N. Resolutions 242 and 338 and the principle of territory for peace. Through these negotiations, peace and security for Israel and all states, and legitimate Palestinian political rights, can be realized. In addition, a properly structured international conference could serve, at the appropriate time, as a means to facilitate direct negotiations between the parties.

The time has come to encourage fresh thinking, to avoid sterile debate, and to focus on the difficult but critical work of structuring a serious negotiating process. His Majesty committed Jordan to this task, and I commit the United States to this task. An important part of this effort and of the stability of the Middle East as a whole will be the continued economic and military strength of Jordan. Jordan's security remains of fundamental concern to the

Photographic Portfolio

Overleaf: Being sworn in as the 41st President at the West Front of the Capitol, January 20. ***Left:*** Walking along the Inaugural Parade route, January 20. ***Right:*** Reviewing an address to Congress in the Oval Office Study, February 8. ***Below:*** Meeting with Pope John Paul II at the Vatican, May 27.

Left: With Millie and her puppies on the South Lawn, April 20. *Below left:* Meeting with Cabinet members at the White House, June 5. *Right:* Signing the Executive order on Historically Black Colleges and Universities in the Rose Garden, April 20. *Below:* Touring the American Cemetery in Nettuno, Italy, May 28.

Left: With Queen Elizabeth II and Prince Philip at Buckingham Palace in London, June 1. ***Below:*** Interview with members of the White House press corps on the patio outside the Oval Office, April 20. ***Right:*** Speaking to naval personnel on the U.S.S. *America* in Norfolk, VA, January 30. ***Overleaf:*** Arriving at Texas A&M University in College Station, May 12.

United States, and I have reassured His Majesty that the United States will do its utmost to help meet Jordan's economic and military requirements. His Majesty King Hussein and I delved deeply into the broader regional and internal problems, and as always, I benefited greatly from the wisdom of my friend. Together we pledge to continue the close cooperation and coordination that mark the relations between Jordan and the United States.

And in closing, I would like to express my best wishes to King Hussein and to the people of Jordan for an auspicious month of Ramadan and a blessed 'Id holiday. Thank you.

The King. Thank you, Mr. President. It's a great pleasure, as always, to return to the United States, a country with whom Jordan has enjoyed a special relationship for so many years. It is even a greater pleasure on this occasion to be meeting with you, Mr. President, a treasured friend of long standing. Your dedication to the service of your great country has been a source of inspiration, respect, and admiration to me, as it is to all who know you.

Mr. President, I know how devoted you are to the cause of peace. I share this devotion. I sincerely hope that through our common devotion to peace we can, with those who are equally devoted, finally bring peace to the Middle East.

You are the sixth President with whom I've joined to pursue that peace. I first visited this historic house in 1959 to meet with President Eisenhower. It marked the beginning of a warm and productive relationship between our two countries, a relationship which has flourished because of our shared values, shared interests, and shared goals. It is a relationship which my country and I cherish. I am heartened that the talks we are engaged in will contribute to a deepening of this relationship.

One of our goals, which despite 22 years of efforts we have yet to achieve, is a comprehensive settlement of the Arab-Israeli conflict. The principles for that settlement were established many years ago: United Nations Security Council Resolutions 242 and 338. These resolutions provide for the withdrawal of Israeli forces from the territories occupied in 1967 in return for the establishment of peace, arrangements for secure and recognized borders, and negotiations under appropriate auspices to implement these provisions.

Your recent expressed reaffirmation of American support for the end of Israeli occupation in return for peace and for the political rights of the Palestinian people—integral part of any comprehensive settlement—both constructive and commendable. As a result of a recent decision by the Palestine Liberation Organization to accept the right of Israel to exist, to negotiate a settlement with Israel based on Security Council Resolutions 242 and 338, and to renounce terrorism, a significant contribution to peace has been made.

This historic decision has the overwhelming support of the Arab world. The decision by the United States to undertake substantive discussions with the PLO has further improved the prospects for peace. I hope this will prompt Israel to respond similarly to the requirements of peace and recognize the legitimate representative of the Palestinian people. Peace can neither be negotiated nor achieved without PLO participation.

Mr. President, I believe the bases for peace are already established. What is required is to implement them. The forum for a negotiated comprehensive settlement is a peace conference under the auspices of the United Nations. In my opinion, any steps taken should lead to such a conference, if our efforts to arrive at a comprehensive settlement are not to be diverted. All the people in the Middle East need peace and an end to this tragic and interminable conflict. The rewards of peace are limitless and far outweigh any advantage which might be gained by any party from continued controversy and conflict. The conditions for peace exist. We all must display the vision and determination to capitalize on them.

Mr. President, allow me to say, as one of your many friends and as one who knows well your qualities, abilities, devotion and dedication to the cause of peace, that you are the right leader in the right office at the right time. I know the high esteem with which you are held throughout the Middle

East. You are in a unique position to help the protagonists in our area to engender the needed trust and hope and to assist us in bringing the conflict to a just and durable conclusion. I can assure you that I fully support you and all your efforts in this regard.

May God bless you, Mr. President, your dear family, and the friendly people of these great United States. Thank you.

Note: The President spoke at 10:34 a.m. in the Rose Garden at the White House. Prior to their remarks, the President and the King met in the Oval Office. Following their remarks, the President and the King toured Mount Vernon and took a cruise on the Potomac River, which ended at Bolling Air Force Base.

Message on the Observance of National Nursing Home Week, May 14–20, 1989

April 19, 1989

National Nursing Home Week is a time for us to remember in a special way the millions of older Americans who reside in the 19,000 nursing homes and long-term care facilities throughout the United States. This week we also salute the thousands of dedicated healthcare professionals and volunteers who work tirelessly to provide care and support to residents and their families.

This year's theme: "Nursing Homes: A Tradition of Caring," is a succinct description of the history and focus of these institutions. The residents of our nursing homes are men and women who helped make the 20th century the American Century. They are our mothers and fathers, our aunts and uncles—people who raised strong families, who plowed fertile fields, who built great cities and defended the free world from the threat of totalitarianism. Now in their senior years, these generous, hardworking men and women need special care and attention. Nursing homes provide that care, helping to ensure that ill or infirm seniors are able to live with the dignity and comfort they deserve. Such service—while in the finest American tradition of compassion and concern for all members of our society—is but small repayment toward the tremendous debt we owe older Americans.

I encourage all Americans to join in observing National Nursing Home Week and saluting the unsung heroes who care for our Nation's elderly. I also urge every American to remember those who live in our Nation's nursing homes—to show them our love and appreciation—not only this week but also throughout the year.

Let it always be said that America honors and cares for her citizens in their golden years.

GEORGE BUSH

Nomination of Morton Isaac Abramowitz To Be United States Ambassador to Turkey

April 19, 1989

The President today announced his intention to nominate Morton Isaac Abramowitz, a career member of the Senior Foreign Service, Class of Career Minister, as Ambassador Extraordinary and Plenipotentiary of the United States of America to Turkey. He would succeed Robert Strausz-Hupe.

Since 1986 Ambassador Abramowitz has been Assistant Secretary of State for Intelligence and Research. Prior to this, he was

Director of the Bureau of Intelligence and Research, 1984–1985, and representative of the United States of America to the mutual balanced force reduction negotiations, with the rank of Ambassador, 1983–1984. He joined the Foreign Service in 1960 as consular/economic officer and served in this position until 1962. From 1962 to 1963, he took language training in Tai Chung. From 1963 to 1966, he was political officer at the U.S. Consulate General in Hong Kong. He served as an international economist at the Department of State, 1966–1968, and as special assistant in the Office of the Secretary, 1969–1971. He was a student at the Institute for Strategic Studies in London, England. From 1971 to 1972, he was a Foreign Service inspector, and foreign affairs analyst at the Department of State, 1972–1973. He served as political adviser to CINC-PAC [commander in chief, Pacific Command] in Honolulu, Hawaii, 1973–1974. From 1974 to 1978, he was on detail as Deputy Assistant Secretary of Defense for International Affairs. He has served as Ambassador to the Kingdom of Thailand, 1978–1981; served in the Bureau of East Asian and Pacific Affairs, 1981–1982; and was a foreign affairs fellow at the Rand Corp., 1982–1983.

Ambassador Abramowitz was born January 20, 1933, in Lakewood, NJ. He graduated from Stanford University (B.A., 1953) and Harvard University (M.A., 1955). He served in the U.S. Army in 1957. He is married and has two children.

Toasts at a State Dinner Honoring King Hussein I of Jordan
April 19, 1989

The President. You are among friends, sir, your lovely Queen, and among admirers. And your visit here gives me and Barbara a chance, in a very small way, to tell you how much we appreciated your special hospitality to us when we visited you at your lovely home at Aqaba, as well as your beautiful home in Amman itself, not so many months ago.

This magnificent picture of Abraham Lincoln that I know you're all admiring was painted by George Healy in 1869. Upstairs in my office—excuse me, a little slight cold—upstairs in my office there's another marvelous picture of Abraham Lincoln, and that was also painted by George Healy 4 years earlier. And I took His Majesty to see it today. It's called "The Peacemakers," and the picture shows Lincoln in exactly the same pensive pose as this magnificent picture. But in the picture upstairs, there's a window right over his left shoulder, and out that window one can see this beautiful rainbow. And the picture depicts Lincoln with his generals—three generals—right near the end of the war that threatened our Union and pitted brother against brother. The rainbow in the picture by Healy symbolized the hope of peace, the imminent end to hostilities that near bled us as a nation to death. And so, Your Majesty, it is my fervent hope that by working together we can guarantee that there will be a rainbow over the Middle East. And war must give way to peace. And whether it's the turmoil or the fighting in the West Bank that plagues us all or the heart-rending hostilities that we now all feel so strongly about in a fractured Lebanon, we must all recommit ourselves to lasting peace in the Middle East.

And this visit today by the King of Jordan comes at a crucial moment in your region's history that—we feel it, we in the United States feel it. And I think the King summed it up well when he told me today that the time is right. But let me assure you, sir, that we can sense an urgency to the quest for peace now. Our task is to use that urgency to seize the moment. And toward that end, Your Majesty, I look forward to working with you as old friends. And I mean that; it's not a diplomatic use of the word. Let us find new ways to bridge the deep differences that exist. Let's reduce suspicions and prepare the way for negotiations that will lead to the comprehensive settlement that everybody wants. And I pledge to work with you, sir, first to bring the rainbow of hope to the wonderful people of Jordan, and to all your neighbors, and then, with that rainbow clearly in view, to finalize a peace so secure that not a single child will know the horrors of battle.

And so, my friends, I ask you to join me in a toast to the goal of peace and to raise your glasses to the health of His Majesty King Hussein and to Queen Noor, of whom America is so especially proud, and to the lasting friendship between Jordan and the United States of America.

The King. Mr. President, Mrs. Bush, distinguished guests, and dear friends. I thank you, Mr. President. I am deeply moved by the generosity of your remarks and the affection and hospitality with which you and Mrs. Bush received Noor, myself, and my colleagues. We are most appreciative. It is clear that the kinder, gentler America of which you have spoken begins in this house. I was also genuinely gratified, Mr. President, by the assurances you gave this morning of your commitment to the security and well-being of Jordan. We, indeed, feel very much at home, which befits friends.

The friendship between Jordan and the United States has indeed been special. It began 30 years ago when I first came to the White House to meet President Eisenhower. I have since dined in this lovely room as the guest of Presidents on more occasions than I can count. If that is a record, it is one of which I am proud. These have all been memorable occasions, but none more so than tonight as your guest, Mr. President, and the guest of Mrs. Bush.

But our friendship is not only personal, which I treasure, it is based as well on the common values which our two nations share: freedom, equality, and human dignity. Friendship deserves the most serious consideration of those who enjoy it. When there is joy, one calls upon friends to celebrate. When there is sorrow, friends come to comfort one. When there is a task to be done, friends join together in common effort. There is honor and pride and true friendship, as is evident here tonight.

One of the sorrows which we share is the continuous tragedy of that of the Arab-Israeli conflict. To end this tragedy is the focus of our visit. I was interested in your explanation this morning, Mr. President, of the American viewpoint regarding steps to further the cause of peace in our area. And as I assured you this morning, Jordan will cooperate closely with the United States to achieve a just, durable, and comprehensive peaceful settlement. We will support you in all your endeavors to achieve a comprehensive, just, and lasting peace in the Middle East. And God willing, we will see that rainbow, and so will people in our part of the world. And God willing, it will be our contribution for a better future for generations to come on all sides in that area of the world.

Mr. President, we share with you an unusual fact: the names of our founding capitals. Philadelphia was the birthplace of your independence. Philadelphia was, as well, the ancient name of our capital, Amman. The meaning of both is the same: brotherly love. In this spirit, I would like to convey the best wishes and warmest greetings from the people of Jordan to you, Mr. President, and Mrs. Bush, and to all of your fellow Americans.

Ladies and gentlemen, my dear friends, may I ask you to join me in a toast to the President of the United States and Mrs. Bush.

Note: The President spoke at 9:42 p.m. in the State Dining Room at the White House.

Letter to the Speaker of the House of Representatives and the President of the Senate Transmitting the Report on Activities of United Nations Member Countries
April 20, 1989

Dear Mr. Speaker: (Dear Mr. President:)

Pursuant to title V, section 527 of the Foreign Operations, Export Financing, and Related Programs Appropriations Act, 1989, as contained in Public Law 100–461, I am transmitting herewith the report on the activities of countries within the United Nations and its specialized agencies.

This report assesses the degree of support of United States foreign policy in the United Nations context by the governments of countries that are members of the United Nations.

In addition, this report includes the report required of the Secretary of State under section 117 of Public Law 98–164 on the performance of U.N. member countries in international organizations.

Sincerely,

GEORGE BUSH

Note: Identical letters were sent to Jim Wright, Speaker of the House of Representatives, and Dan Quayle, President of the Senate.

Interview With Members of the White House Press Corps
April 20, 1989

Iran Arms and Contra Aid Controversy

The President. Fire away.

Q. Mr. President, what are you going to do about the fact that sensitive and relevant documents were not reviewed by the Iran-*contra* committees?

The President. In the first place, I have great confidence that A.B. Culvahouse [Counsel to President Reagan] and those charged with cooperating with Congress were cooperative; I've seen nothing to indicate they weren't. Secondly, I would offer full cooperation to any request made of this administration, and I just can't confirm the hypothesis of your question at all.

Q. But you mean you would turn over any documents that they now want to see? Is that what you're saying by "full cooperation"?

The President. Well, procedures were set up to determine what documents would be made available. Those procedures were agreed to by the Congress. Certainly, I would see that if any documents are in control of this administration—relevant documents—that we would live assiduously by those guidelines. But I have no reason to believe that the previous administration, the lawyers in it who worked closely with Congress, did not fulfill their obligations.

Q. Mr. President, were you an emissary to Honduras, as has been alleged?

The President. I went to Honduras, sure. That's a matter of public record.

Q. And did you have a quid pro quo deal?

The President. I've told you that I am not going to discuss that until the trial with North is over.

Q. But the jury is being sequestered today, sir, and it's——

The President. No, I might have something to say on it when the trial is over, but I would simply ask you to understand that this is a request of the lawyers. And I'm not going to do something that inadvertently will—but put it this way: My conscience is clear.

Q. Well, there have been suggestions that—on the documents—that there might have been an oversight, either on the part of the FBI, the part of the White House staff. As far as you can tell, was there an oversight by any of those two bodies, or was it a question of—the Congress was not pushing the right buttons to get the documents?

The President. Well, I'm not sure. I don't know. All I can just state is the confidence that I feel in Culvahouse and company. But we've received the letter down here, and I will take this opportunity to tell them we'll cooperate fully. But who controls the documents and all of that—you'll have to talk to the lawyers about that.

Q. Mr. President, when you say——

The President. I think they're in the control and in the custody of the Archives archivists, but I'm not sure.

Q. When you say you'll cooperate fully with—I presume you mean Senators Mitchell and Inouye [member and chairman of the Select Committee on Secret Military Assistance to Iran and the Nicaraguan Opposition, respectively]. In their letter——

The President. Everybody.

Q. Does that mean—they've asked you, I think, to launch an investigation to find out exactly what happened. Are you saying you will launch an investigation or that you have?

The President. I don't remember "launching an investigation." Was that part of their request?

Q. I think the language is "an immediate and thorough investigation" which essentially asks whether and why documents were not provided.

The President. Well, I would refer them to the people that were in charge of the documentation, which would be Mr. Culvahouse and company, in whom I have great confidence. But if there's anything we can do to encourage that—absolutely.

Q. Mr. President, when you say your conscience is clear, do you mean that the interpretation that has been made of the documents in this trial, which I gather were made by Mr. North himself, are not entirely accurate?

The President. I'm not discussing anything about my role in this except to say that everything I've said I'll stand behind.

Q. You won't even—since they're sequestered—just give us a——

The President. I've just told the gentleman that I'm not going to go into that. So, please, don't ask me to do that which I've just said I'm not going to do, because you're burning up time. The meter is running. Throw the sand on you——

Semiautomatic Weapons

Q. Right. Assault weapons.

The President. And I am now filibustering, so—[*laughter*].

Q. Sir, can I ask you about assault weapons?

The President. Oh, no, you've already used up your time.

Q. No, no, no. Assault weapons. You know, William Bennett, your drug czar, has made a proposal that you treat them like machineguns, which would mean people would register and they'd have their names on file and so forth. First off, what do you think of that idea? And secondly, when are you going to tell us your next step on that?

The President. Well, we're having a meeting this afternoon with certain Members of Congress on this. The standards that are set up in existing law about import are: "suitability for sporting purposes." And we're being very careful here, but we're going to make a determination using that as a standard. And, Lesley [Lesley Stahl, CBS News], I can't say exactly when it will be, but I've expressed my concern about these weapons and their suitability. So, stay tuned. I don't know exactly when it will be, but there is a meeting here today that's just ongoing, and I have great confidence in Bill Bennett.

We've talked to a wide array of people on this. We've gone to some of the think tanks—that very intelligent, thoughtful paper from Ed Feulner's [president, Heritage Foundation] group over at Heritage, very thoughtful. And so, our package will be—I guarantee it will include more on law enforcement. And I'm sure that Bill Bennett will be totally on board. But we haven't gotten the final administration position yet.

Q. Mr. President, will you apply the same standard to domestically made weapons that you apply to imported weapons?

The President. We're in the process of discussing that now and what role the administration has—whether it's strictly restriction of imports or something broader than that.

Q. At this point, are you convinced that any package that deals with drug violence and crime must also include some aspect that deals with assault weapons?

The President. Well, no, I can't say that. I can't go that far, because we really haven't gotten that far in determining it.

President's Popularity

Q. Mr. President, the CBS-New York Times poll this morning puts your approval rating at about 61 percent but suggests there is more style than substance. What do you think about that evaluation? And I think that you and Governor Sununu have been briefed by a Teeter poll that's been taken. Does that contain the same sort of information?

The President. No, the Teeter poll—I'm not sure it's just because the committee paid for it—is much stronger. [*Laughter*]

Q. Higher ratings?

Q. What about the *Iowa*?

The President. Higher, higher, higher. I'm not sure. I don't want this to be considered a vicious assault on CBS. [*Laughter*] They're entitled to their polling figures. But the others were—look, these things—you know me on polls, John [John Mashek, Boston Globe]. You've heard me on this subject before, and I haven't changed my view. It's not a question of polls, but a question of what's going on, achieving what you're trying to do.

And we're making some progress here. I'm very pleased that the Senate did what it did on the savings and loan bill, pleased that we got a budget agreement that many cynics thought we could never achieve at all, no matter of what scope, whatsoever—that took place. And so, I've been very pleased with the recent talks on the Middle East with three leaders there. And so, things are moving. But I don't feel under any pressure to meet somebody else's standard on what is progress or not. I know what I'm doing, and I think one thing is the country senses that. Otherwise, there wouldn't be that kind of support.

Aid to Cambodian Non-Communists

Q. Mr. President, are you going to offer military aid to the non-Communist resistance in Cambodia?

The President. No, no discussion of that yet, no decision taken on that yet.

Q. Mr. President, we're coming——

The President. I'll continue to give good support to the process and certainly to [President] Sihanouk's efforts.

Q. Did you say no decision or no discussion on that?

The President. No decision and—not with me—can't recall, but I'm not anywhere close to making a decision of that nature.

Administration Accomplishments

Q. We're coming up to the 100-day mark on your Presidency, which—if you'll look over the past 50 years, every other President, or almost every other President, has come into office at times of crisis, and crisis has been kind of a stage on which we watch Presidents perform. How would you assess your first 100 days so far?

The President. About the same as Martin Van Buren's.

Q. Uh-oh.

Q. Can you elaborate on that? [*Laughter*]

The President. Martin came in; he was not radically trying to change things. But then, that's about where the parallel ends, because I don't know what he did in his first 100 days. [*Laughter*]

Q. ——or any of the other 900 days.

The President. We got an agenda, and I've clicked off things that I think demonstrate progress. And I left out the whole question of an ethics package that I think is a very good one. We've had many visitors from foreign lands. We've moved forward on—I want to add now to what I was saying—moved forward on Third World debt in a positive way.

So, I think that we're moving reasonably well. And I don't even think in terms of 100 days because we aren't radically shifting things; this is the Martin Van Buren analogy. We didn't come in here throwing the rascals out to try to do something—correct all the ills of the world in 100 days. Now, there's some ills of the world; there's some unsolved problems. And I'm methodically, I think, pragmatically moving forward on these. So, I really don't measure it in terms of 100 days.

Q. I guess we are the ones who measure the 100 days.

The President. You are.

Foreign Policy

Q. Foreign policy has been kind of held back. You've had visitors, but do you expect the pace of your foreign policy to pick up after this?

The President. I'm not sure I understand the question.

Q. Well, the pace——

The President. The pace of it? No, I don't. The pace of it is pretty intense—numbers of visitors, amount of time I spend on foreign policy, initiatives taken by the Secretary of State, attention given to this in the White House, every single day. So, you see, I think we've got prudent foreign policy. We've set into forward motion certain reviews that are moving towards completion. And so, I don't feel a need for some precipitous and dramatic initiative in order to salve the consciences of those who are saying you've got to do something in 100 days.

Q. Let me go back——

Q. These reviews won't trigger something then?

The President. It could; it might. But I think Gorbachev—on the Soviet East-West relations—understands what we're about. I, frankly, thought that what we said on Poland the other day was new and a strong initiative. But that takes time to sort out these things. But I didn't do it because I wanted to get in under the 100-day wire. Now, the question is: We've spelled out what we want to do, and I've got to move our bureaucracy to see that we do it.

And you know, it's that kind of concept on the Middle East—spent a lot of time on the Middle East. And I think King Hussein was right when he said yesterday that the time is right for some kind of action. But now we've got to assess, after he leaves here, where we go, what next step we take. We've got something out there on elections that offers some promise. We haven't backed away from historic positions on conference or whatever. And so, we move—we take whatever the next step is.

I wish I could give you a more dramatic answer to the Lebanon, because this is one that really does hurt. And I'm very, very concerned about it. And here all I can say to you is that we have encouraged the Secretary-General to go forward, to try this mission of peace. There's some stumbling blocks to that; I'm told we will renew our call for removal of all foreign troops and for a cease-fire.

But here is one where I wish that there was some dramatic plan in which the players in the area could agree to, and it's not there. And we've talked to the Middle Eastern leaders. But I cite this one because I really feel it—about the Lebanon, of the divisions in Lebanon. We've talked to the Brits about it. We've talked to the French about it—and President Mitterrand the other day. And the people at the U.N. are trying to figure. But there is not a dramatic plan that can bring peace to Lebanon right now.

Q. Is that a problem that defies solution?

The President. The problem—the short-run of it—how you stop this firing, the shelling, how you get factions to stop warring—has certainly in recent times defied solution. But we can't give up on it. We simply are not going to——

Q. How has the U.S. managed to provide any kind of influence in the situation?

The President. That's the problem: We don't have great influence in Lebanon, with the factions that are fighting. We do have good influence with many of the countries out there. In fact, I think our standing with the moderate Arab countries is as good today as any time in recent history. And I feel strongly about that. And back to the Martin Van Buren theory—I mean, we're building still, coming back out of a time that hit a bit of a low 3 or 4 years ago. Then we restored some prestige by the way we acted in the Gulf. Then you see a cease-fire in the Gulf. We have, I think, much better communication now with Jordan. We've kept good cooperation and coordination with the Egyptians. The Israelis themselves attest to the fact that they have great confidence in our administration. We have some differences with all three of those countries, but, no, I think it's moving. But, Norm [Norman Sandler, United Press International], I wish there was a short-term answer to stop the killing in Lebanon.

Strategic Weapons Modernization

Q. ——you missed a couple of deadlines——

Q. Mr. President, could I——

Q. You've missed a couple of deadlines on the MX missile, on what you're going to do to modernize the strategic arsenal—go MX, Midgetman. And Mr. Cheney gave you some recommendations this week, and a decision is expected this week. What are you going to do on that?

The President. Don't know yet. We'll obviously be talking to Cheney when he comes back from NATO. But no decision has been taken.

Q. Any leaning?

The President. Well, can't tell you that. I'm listening—because this exercise yesterday in this Cabinet Room was not just a semantic drill of some sort. When I talk about cooperation with Congress, I mean it—consultation with Congress, I mean it. And some of what yesterday was about was getting the views of various Members of Congress on this decision that's facing the President. But how do you—you know, what do you do about SDI and levels of funding? What do you do about MX or Midgetman? And I have to make the call, the recommendation, from here; but I wanted to get their input. Now I want to get renewed talks with Dick Cheney when he comes back. The national security adviser has provided me with a lot of thinking on this, had several important briefings on it. And I will be prepared very soon to make a decision on it. But we haven't—I can't go any further than that.

Middle East Peace Process

Q. Mr. President, you met now with [Egyptian President] Mubarak, [Israeli Prime Minister] Shamir, and [Jordanian King] Hussein. What is the next step in the Middle East peace process?

The President. Not sure now. On the table is the election process, and one other thing would be how we flesh that out, taking into consideration the concerns about it that have been expressed by Mubarak and by King Hussein and also by Mr. Shamir. So, how we do that—what the modalities are of that—a lot of thought will be going into that: who's represented; making clear that this isn't a final step, that that isn't going to solve the Middle East problem; making clear that it's a step, but we want it to be a constructive step; and exploring other options as well.

Q. What is the structural procedure for doing that?

The President. On the U.S. side, we'll use the National Security Council procedures to do that. And of course, I plan to be in touch with the various leaders. I've told them I want to do that as President. And I do plan to talk personally with some of the leaders out there on these matters——

Q. Is this a high priority?

The President. ——in addition to the ones I've already talked to. For example, I talked to King Fahd [of Saudi Arabia] the other day, and think that that is useful, to be sure. Now, after this round of visits, what do they think? A lot of these countries can be important players here, and the more agreement we can get on the next step, the more likely it is to succeed.

U.S.S. "Iowa"

Q. Mr. President, on the *Iowa*: Is it time to say that 50-year-old battleships are, in fact, obsolete and begin taking them out of service? Is that the lesson here?

The President. No, that's——

Q. Or if not, what's your lesson on it?

The President. That's not—well, my lesson is that—to find out what happened in infinite detail, check all procedures to be sure that safety is at the highest point, and—but not—I wouldn't jump to the conclusion that because that kind of powder was put into these turrets in that way that that makes a useful platform obsolete. I'm not going to go that far.

Drug Testing

Q. Could you indulge me one quick question because of a conflict that the Attorney General suggested yesterday?

The President. John, give me a break.

Q. One quick one. The Attorney General——

The President. Is this for TV or is this for the print?

Q. TV.

Q. Both. The Attorney General suggested

yesterday that it might be appropriate to drug-test people in public housing. HUD took immediate exception to that. What do you think?

The President. I'd have to talk to him about it because I don't know, and I'm not going to go off on some tangent here until I know exactly the thinking of our key Cabinet people. We've got a good Cabinet system, and I encourage people to speak out. But the decisions on something of that nature will be made right here in that room, and they're not going to be made until I have all the facts.

Q. You don't favor a drug——

Interest Rates

Q. Do you expect interest rates to come down now that you've got a budget agreement?

The President. I was very pleased at the market reaction to the budget agreement. It seems to have been underreported, but nevertheless, it's very heartening, Terry [Terence Hunt, Associated Press].

Q. How about the interest rates? You said you were going to campaign——

The President. I'm not heartened by the interest rates. [*Laughter*]

Drug Testing

Q. Is there still going to be those drug tests for the Federal employees?

The President. Selectively, yes, absolutely.

Q. Selectively? To everybody?

The President. Well, we've already got some patterns out there—well, widely. If we're talking about a drug-free workplace, we've got to have some testing, and I support that. This idea that this is a total infringement on everybody—I don't agree. Now, in some cases—I mean, I don't want it to be so widespread, but I do think that selective drug testing is very important, and nobody will change my mind on that one.

Q. Civil rights? Human—no?

The President. Civil rights is very important, too—and so is the law.

Note: The interview began at 10:20 a.m. on the Oval Office patio at the White House. The following journalists participated in the interview: Lesley Stahl, CBS News; James Angle, National Public Radio; Terence Hunt, Associated Press; Norman Sandler, United Press International; Lawrence McQuillan, Reuters; Pascal Taillandier, Agence France-Presse; Michael Duffy, Time; John Mashek, Boston Globe; and Tim McNulty, Chicago Tribune.

Remarks Congratulating the University of Tennessee Lady Volunteers on Winning the NCAA Basketball Championship

April 20, 1989

The President. Well, beautiful Rose Garden day—sorry we're a little late getting started. I heard that there was a little security problem, a little backup going through these devices that—Bridgette Gordon's jewelry getting through the metal detectors out there. [*Laughter*]

No, we're just delighted you all are here, and I'm particularly pleased to see the president, former Governor Lamar Alexander, here with us today. I know I speak for Dan Quayle when we give him a warm welcome back to Washington. Coach Summitt, Athletic Director Cronan, families and friends and fans, Members of Congress, and then our own local teams that are here today, the White House is proud to host Tennessee's Lady Volunteers, the 1989 NCAA champions. It's a great pleasure having you here.

After you won in Tacoma and after the tears of joy and victory and remembrance, Pat Summitt told a cheering nation that "This one belongs to the family." And it's quite a family, these Lady Volunteers—five freshmen, two sophomores, three seniors. And before this season, only the seniors had ever played college ball. And the L.A. Times called your victory "beyond the imagination of most." And archrival Auburn's coach dubbed the Lady Vols a "Who's Who roster of excellence": Melissa McCray, Sheila Frost, Daedra Charles; players like Carla McGhee, who came back from a 1987 car accident after they said she'd be lucky ever to run again; and there's Tonya Edwards and Dena Head.

And now, I admit, the Bush family is generally pretty happy when Texas wins something. But your midseason loss to Texas is also when—it proved that this team had character as well as talent. Tonya, the 1987 Most Valuable Player, who led the Vols to Tennessee's first championship, got hurt. Dena, a little-known freshman, came off the bench and emerged as SEC Rookie of the Year. And don't worry, I'm not forgetting Bridgette Gordon, All American, Most Valuable Player, MVP. The papers call her the best woman in college basketball. And when Auburn closed to within three in that final game, she stepped in and sank three straight jumpers. Maybe you heard what the losing coach said about her: "God bless her, graduate her, and get her out of Tennessee." [*Laughter*] You'll note there is no basket here today in the Rose Garden. That's on purpose. I'll be darned if I want to go head-on-head with her out there on the foul line. [*Laughter*]

And then the coach, a silver medalist as a player in 1976, Coach Summitt—she coached America's Olympic team to a gold in 1984. And in 13 years she brought Tennessee to the final four 10 times, winning it twice. Later on we're going down to that fountain over here that you all can see, to see if literally she can walk on water. [*Laughter*] There's been some speculation about that. And the most rare, the most important stat of all: in 14 years as coach, her players have a 100-percent graduation rate. And all five—Lamar would kill me if I didn't point this out—all five of this year's freshmen are on the dean's list. One, Debbie Hawhee, has a 3.95 GPA in medical technology. What in the world did she get the A-minus in? [*Laughter*]

Ms. Hawhee. English.

Mr. Alexander. English.

The President. Well, she speaks Tennessean. And so, we're going to get her a—every sport has legendary teams from its early days, and I have a feeling that, years from now when they go back—as sports fans do and historians do—and talk about the legends of women's basketball, it'll be this team, your team, the 1989 NCAA champions from Tennessee, that sets the highest standard. As the years unfold, you will always remember that championship season that brought you to the White House. Tomorrow's news clippings that'll be yellowed with age are going to be read by grandchildren born in a different century. And it's a story that began on summer nights, not so long ago—years before college, though—when these champions were themselves kids, shooting until twilight in obscure barns or out in driveways scattered across the deep South and the Middle West—young girls unknown to one another, but dreaming the same dream that this month became real.

So, this is a great opportunity to say thank you all for coming here. Hold fast to your dreams yet to come. Congratulations to all of you. And God bless you, and God bless the U.S.A. Thank you all very, very much.

Coach Summitt. This is a great honor for us. And I think throughout this year, this has been a real special team because we have been family. And we talked about all the highlights that we experienced as a team and as a staff and as a family. And certainly, winning a national championship was a great highlight. I know Debbie Scott, one of our freshmen, said her highlight this year was getting lost in New York City—[*laughter*]—until she found out we got to come here, and she said it would be to see the puppies. [*Laughter*]

So, we are delighted and honored to be here. I am extremely proud of our academic success. We have won two national championships in the last 3 years, but the most important statistic for our team and our program is 100-percent graduation rate, of which we will hold our heads very proudly. And I know Lamar's excited about that too, but we all are. We have had great leadership, and I don't think you win without leadership. And you don't win without great people, and we've had both. And today we'd like for our three seniors, who have been very instrumental in leading the University of Tennessee to four consecutive

NCAA appearances, to come forth and present you with a little gift. And that's Bridgette Gordon—she wants to deposit her gold, I think, today—[*laughter*]—Sheila Frost, and Melissa McCray.

The President. Come on—here we go—who is which, now?

Ms. McCray. I'm Melissa McCray. Nice to meet you.

The President. That's Bridgette. Good to see you all. Who's going to give the speech?

Ms. McCray. Okay, I will. [*Laughter*] I certainly want to echo what our coach has said. I think it's indeed an honor and a privilege to be here. It's nice to see Mrs. Bush out and certainly nice to see Dan Quayle, the Vice President. We have a jacket here for you. Now, I realize you're not going to be playing any basketball. But maybe once when you're out walking through the garden and playing with your puppies, you might think about the Lady Vols from Tennessee, all right? I hope you enjoy it.

The President. Oh, yes, that's beautiful. Thank you so much. She'll come—come on, Bar.

Ms. Frost. Mrs. Bush, we have something for you also. I'd like to echo just about the same thing that Melissa said. Thank you for inviting us out. And this is a little something—when you both go out to see the puppies, you'll be matching. [*Laughter*]

Mrs. Bush. That's so sweet. Thank you.

Ms. Frost. Thank you.

Coach Summitt. Yes, oh, they want to see the puppies.

The President. They really do want to see them?

Mrs. Bush. You're all invited to see the puppies, but they're not. [*Laughter*]

Coach Summitt. Okay, we got that. It's our secret.

Ms. Gordon. I have "The Summitt Season" here. It's a book written about Pat and our team.

The President. Great.

Ms. Gordon. The year that we lost to Louisiana Tech, but—[*laughter*].

The President. There she is.

Ms. Gordon. And this is for Mr. Quayle—a T-shirt.

The President. Great.

The Vice President. Thank you.

Ms. Gordon. And I have an autographed poster of myself. [*Laughter*]

The President. Let's see that. Hey! Oh, this is neat. Thank you.

Ms. Gordon. You're welcome.

The President. Here, we've got to get this all set for our—here, I'll hold it so it doesn't get bent.

Ms. Gordon. Okay.

The President. Loaded up with—well, I think that I want to ask the Members of Congress that are here to come up and congratulate you all. We've got some good Tennesseans out there. And congratulations to all of you. And Barbara means it. She'll arrange to take you over to see the—if you're really interested. You don't have to be interested, but you——

Team Members. Oh, yes, we are, we are.

The President. They are so cute.

Coach Summitt. There's one thing—I want you to meet my mom.

The President. Oh, we want to see her. Now, you guys come say hello.

Note: The President spoke at 11:05 a.m. in the Rose Garden at the White House. In his remarks, he referred to Athletic Director Joan Cronan and Representatives John J. Duncan, James H. Quillen, Jim Cooper, Bob Clement, Bart Gordon, and Don Sundquist.

Remarks on Signing the Executive Order Establishing the National Space Council
April 20, 1989

The President. Well, to the Members of Congress here and Members of the Joint Chiefs, distinguished guests, thank you. It's a great pleasure to be here on an occasion of this nature. And I want to thank all of you for being here. You're helping to fulfill a promise that I made 18 months ago in Huntsville, Alabama, at the George C. Marshall Space Flight Center. I pledged then, and I'm proud now, to reestablish the National Space Council.

I've asked Vice President Quayle to serve as Chairman. Under his able leadership, I'm confident that the Space Council will bring coherence and continuity and commitment to our efforts to explore, study, and develop space. I look to the Council to coordinate our civil, military, and commercial efforts. We must establish a permanent manned presence in space by building the space station *Freedom.* We must encourage private initiatives in investment, and we must ensure our national security through effective defense activities in space.

You know, when people talk about space exploration, what it represents to us in this country, some say that it captures the American imagination. But it's much more than that. Our efforts in space unleash the imagination. And 20 years ago, an entire generation of Americans was inspired by the space program. We must continue on the path we've blazed in earlier decades with a renewed dedication.

Space is vitally important to our nation's future and, I would add, to the quality of life here on Earth. And it offers a technological frontier, creating jobs for tomorrow. And space programs inspire an interest in math and science, engineering in young people, knowledge so important for a competitive future. Space offers us the chance to unlock secrets billions of years old and billions of light years away. Space is the manifest destiny of a new generation and a new century.

Mr. Vice President, I plan to sign this Executive order with one objective in mind: to keep America first in space. And it's only a matter of time before the world salutes the first men and women on their way outward into the solar system. All of us want them to be Americans.

And now I'd like to ask the Vice President to say a few words, and then I'll be honored to sign this declaration.

The Vice President. Thank you very much, Mr. President, and welcome back to your former office. It's about 100 days ago, a little less, that you were here to witness the official signing of the Vice President's desk, and we welcome you back today as you establish the Space Council.

I certainly look forward to getting involved with the Space Council, working with the Members of Congress to develop a coherent space policy and space strategy for this country. Space is certainly the frontier. It is a frontier that we understand, and we're going to be there. Space is important to us from an economic point of view, from a national security point of view, and certainly from a point of view of technology. So, Mr. President, we take your charge with a great deal of seriousness. We will be working with all deliberation and cooperation with Members of Congress and the space community—that we will work and present a very good space policy and strategy for the future of this nation.

Thank you very much.

Note: The President spoke at 1:08 p.m. in the Vice President's office in the Old Executive Office Building. The Executive order is listed in Appendix E at the end of this volume.

Nomination of D. Allan Bromley To Be Director of the Office of Science and Technology Policy
April 20, 1989

The President today announced his intention to nominate D. Allan Bromley to be Director of the Office of Science and Technology Policy. He would succeed William R. Graham.

Since 1972 Dr. Bromley has been a

Henry Ford II Professor of Physics at Yale University in New Haven, CT. Since 1960 he has served in several capacities at Yale University, including chairman of the physics department, 1970–1977; director of the A.W. Wright Nuclear Structure Laboratory, 1963 to present; professor of physics, 1961 to present; associate director of the Heavy Ion Accelerator Laboratory, 1960–1963; and associate professor, 1960–1961. Prior to this, he served as a senior research officer and section head of Atomic Energy of Canada, Ltd., in Chalk River, Ontario, Canada, 1958–1960, and associate research officer, 1955–1957. He has served as assistant professor in the physics department of the University of Rochester, 1953–1954, and as an instructor, 1952–1953.

Dr. Bromley graduated from Queen's University at Kingston, Ontario (B.S., 1948; M.S., 1950) and the University of Rochester (M.S., 1951; Ph.D., 1952). He has been a recipient of the National Medal of Science, 1988. He has served as a member of the White House Science Council, 1981 to present, and as a member of the Advisory Board for the National Academy of Sciences and the National Science Foundation. Dr. Bromley was born May 4, 1926, in Westmeath, Ontario, Canada. He is married, has two children, and resides in New Haven, CT.

Statement by Press Secretary Fitzwater on the Assassination of Lieutenant Colonel James N. Rowe in the Philippines

April 21, 1989

This was a cowardly and heinous act. Colonel Rowe was in the Philippines to help the Filipino people in their efforts to defend democracy. We will work closely with the Filipino Government in their efforts to track down and bring to justice those responsible for this assassination.

The U.S. Government support for Philippine democracy is unshaken. As President Bush has said, "President Aquino has our total support in her effort to maintain national unity, revitalize democracy, and counter the Communist insurgency." President and Mrs. Bush extend their deepest sympathy to the family and friends of Colonel Rowe.

Note: Marlin Fitzwater read the statement to reporters at 9:39 a.m. in the Briefing Room at the White House.

Remarks on Signing the Law Day, U.S.A., Proclamation

April 21, 1989

Well, let me welcome Senator Thurmond and Congressman Jack Brooks, representing the Judiciary Committees on the Hill, and Bob Raven, the president of the ABA, American Bar Association. For more than 30 years, Presidents have designated May 1st Law Day, and I'm honored to continue that tradition. On that day, we celebrate the American legal system's vital role in helping to maintain the balance between freedom and order, the principled and yet practical balance that makes democracy possible.

And this year, our Law Day celebration will focus on access to justice. Let me quote the oath that every Federal judge takes before assuming office: "To administer justice without regard to person and do equal right to the poor and the rich." Now, that oath reflects our nation's deep commitment to equal justice for all, a commitment that every citizen's claim shall be judged on its merit, not on the basis of his status or place or standing in society. It's the very core of the democratic idea, the distinction that sets democracy apart from all other systems of government. And we can all take pride in our nation's ability to give life to that ideal.

And yet our work is not done—the work of ensuring that recourse to justice is within the reach of every individual in this nation. For the poor, especially, the legal process can be a costly, complex, and extremely cumbersome route to the justice that they deserve. And today I call on all of you—on all Americans—to perfect the promise of that judicial path. Each of you can contribute. Each of you can help people understand the legal system and to use it responsibly. You can encourage the resolution of disputes without recourse to the legal system when that serves the interests of the parties involved. And each of you can make the highest standards of justice your own standard.

But access without quality is in the interests of no one. We must recruit and retain this nation's best legal talent on the Federal bench. I have submitted to Congress a legislation that would raise the salary of the judges by 25 percent, an increase that, in my view, is long overdue. I urge each of you and all those out there listening to give your strongest possible support to see that that measure wins quick approval.

The rule of law—equal for all—is the central concept of our democratic system. I'm pleased to sign the proclamation declaring May 1st as Law Day, 1989. And thank you all for coming.

Note: The President spoke at 11:05 a.m. in the Roosevelt Room at the White House. The proclamation is listed in Appendix E at the end of this volume.

Designation of James J. Carey as Acting Chairman of the Federal Maritime Commission
April 21, 1989

The President today designated James J. Carey to be Acting Chairman of the Federal Maritime Commission. He would succeed Elaine L. Chao.

Since 1981 Mr. Carey has been Federal Maritime Commissioner, and Vice Chairman since 1983. Prior to this, he was an international business development manager for Telemedia, Inc., in Chicago, IL, and a management consultant for Telemedia, Inc., and Coordinated Graphics, 1978–1979. He was president and chief executive officer for Coordinated Graphics, 1976–1978; executive vice president for Total Graphic Communication, Inc., 1974–1976; and president and chief operating officer of Chicago Offset Corp., 1972–1974. He was senior account executive for I.S. Berlin Press, 1966–1972. Mr. Carey served in the U.S. Navy, 1962–1965, and is a rear admiral in the Naval Reserve. He has received the Meritorious Service Medal, the Navy Commendation Medal, and the Naval Reserve Association National Award of Merit.

Mr. Carey graduated from Northwestern University (B.S., 1960). He was born April 9, 1939, in Berlin, WI. He is married, has two daughters, and resides in Alexandria, VA.

Designation of David W. McCall as Chairman of the National Commission on Superconductivity
April 21, 1989

The President today designated David W. McCall to be Chairman of the National Commission on Superconductivity.

Dr. McCall has served in various capacities at AT&T Bell Laboratories since 1953, including director of the chemical research laboratory, 1973 to present; assistant chemical director, 1969–1973; head of the department of physical chemistry, 1962–1969; and a member of the technical staff, 1953–1962. Dr. McCall is a member of the American Chemical Society, and he has served on the executive committee of the division of physical chemistry, 1967–1969; and as program chairman, 1971; chairman, 1971–1972; and alternate councilor, 1973.

Dr. McCall graduated from the University of Wichita (B.S., 1950) and the University of Illinois (M.S., 1951; Ph.D., 1953). Dr. McCall was born December 1, 1928, in Omaha, NE.

Notice of the Continuation of the National Emergency With Respect to Nicaragua
April 21, 1989

On May 1, 1985, by Executive Order No. 12513, President Reagan declared a national emergency to deal with the threat to the national security and foreign policy of the United States constituted by the situation in Nicaragua. On April 25, 1988, the President announced the continuation of that emergency beyond May 1, 1988. Because the actions and policies of the Government of Nicaragua continue to pose an unusual and extraordinary threat to the national security and foreign policy of the United States, the national emergency declared on May 1, 1985, and subsequently extended, must continue in effect beyond May 1, 1989. Therefore, in accordance with section 202(d) of the National Emergencies Act (50 U.S.C. 1622(d)), I am continuing the national emergency with respect to Nicaragua. This notice shall be published in the *Federal Register* and transmitted to the Congress.

GEORGE BUSH

The White House,
April 21, 1989.

[*Filed with the Office of the Federal Register, 4:55 p.m., April 21, 1989*]

Letter to the Speaker of the House of Representatives and the President of the Senate on the Continuation of the National Emergency With Respect to Nicaragua
April 21, 1989

Dear Mr. Speaker: (Dear Mr. President:)

Section 202(d) of the National Emergencies Act (50 U.S.C. 1622(d)) provides for the automatic termination of a national emergency unless, prior to the anniversary date of its declaration, the President publishes in the *Federal Register* and transmits to the Congress a notice stating that the emergency is to continue in effect beyond the anniversary date. In accordance with this provision, I have sent the enclosed notice, stating that the Nicaraguan emergency is to continue in effect beyond May 1, 1989, to the *Federal Register* for publication. A similar notice was sent to the Congress and the *Federal Register* on April 25, 1988, extending the emergency beyond May 1, 1988.

The actions and policies of the Government of Nicaragua continue to pose an unusual and extraordinary threat to the national security and foreign policy of the United States. If the Nicaraguan emergency were allowed to lapse, the present Nicaraguan trade controls would also lapse, impairing our Government's ability to apply economic pressure on the Sandinista government and reducing the effectiveness of our support for the forces of the democratic opposition in Nicaragua. In these circumstances, I have determined that it is necessary to maintain in force the broad authorities that may be needed in the process of dealing with the situation in Nicaragua.

Sincerely,

GEORGE BUSH

Note: Identical letters were sent to Jim Wright, Speaker of the House of Representatives, and Dan Quayle, President of the Senate.

Letter to the Speaker of the House of Representatives and the President of the Senate Reporting on the Economic Sanctions Against Nicaragua

April 21, 1989

Dear Mr. Speaker: (Dear Mr. President:)

I hereby report to the Congress on developments since President Reagan's last report of November 9, 1988, concerning the national emergency with respect to Nicaragua that was declared in Executive Order No. 12513 of May 1, 1985. In that order, the President prohibited: (1) all imports into the United States of goods and services of Nicaraguan origin; (2) all exports from the United States of goods to or destined for Nicaragua except those destined for the organized democratic resistance; (3) Nicaraguan air carriers from engaging in air transportation to or from points in the United States; and (4) vessels of Nicaraguan registry from entering United States ports.

1. The declaration of emergency was made pursuant to the authority vested in the President by the Constitution and laws of the United States, including the International Emergency Economic Powers Act, 50 U.S.C. 1701 *et seq.*, and the National Emergencies Act, 50 U.S.C. 1601 *et seq.* This report is submitted pursuant to 50 U.S.C. 1641(c) and 1703(c).

2. The Office of Foreign Assets Control (FAC) of the Department of the Treasury issued the Nicaraguan Trade Control Regulations implementing the prohibitions in Executive Order No. 12513 effective May 7, 1985, 50 Fed. Reg. 19890 (May 10, 1985).

3. Since the report of November 9, 1988, fewer than 40 applications for licenses have been received with respect to Nicaragua, and the majority of these applications have been granted. Of the licenses issued in this period, some authorized exports for humanitarian purposes, covering donated articles beyond the scope of the exemption to the export ban to assist in the rebuilding of houses and churches that were destroyed by Hurricane Joan in 1988. Many more exports intended to relieve human suffering caused by Hurricane Joan were deemed to fall within the exemption to the export ban and were cleared for export without application for or receipt of a specific license from FAC. Other licenses extended authorizations previously given to acquire intellectual property protection under Nicaraguan law. Certain licenses were issued that authorized the exportation of equipment to *La Prensa,* the major opposition publication in Nicaragua, as well as to other opposition press groups.

4. Since the last report, the Department of the Treasury completed two significant enforcement actions. The U.S. Customs Service seized a U.S.-controlled Panamanian-flag oil tanker for its role in transshipping U.S.-origin aviation fuel to Nicaragua. A second seizure of the same tanker was effected on the basis of a separate transshipment of aviation fuel from the United States to Nicaragua. Civil forfeiture action against the vessel has been initiated in the United States District Court for the District of Puerto Rico.

The second action involved four principals of two U.S. trading and investment firms who pleaded guilty to criminal charges related to the operation of several front companies that exported computer software and other commercial goods to Nicaragua through Panama. The case was brought in the United States District Court for the Southern District of Florida. One principal received 4 years' incarceration (3–½ years suspended), 5 months' attendance at a community training center, and 225 hours of community service. The other three individuals were each sentenced to 3 years' incarceration (2–½ years suspended), 5 months' attendance at a community training center, and 225 hours of community service.

5. The Treasury and State Departments were sued in the United States District Court for the Southern District of Texas by an organization and certain individuals seeking to donate food, medicine, clothing, vehicles, and other items to Nicaragua. Under the International Emergency Economic Powers Act, articles such as food, clothing, and medicine, intended to be used to relieve human suffering, are exempt from export prohibitions. The Government took the position that vehicles, such as passenger cars, trucks, and buses, are fit for a variety of uses and thus do not automatically fall within the exempt category for food, medicine, clothing, and other articles whose intended use is confined to the relief of human suffering. Consequently, Treasury would not permit the transfer of the vehicles to groups in Nicaragua without a specific license. The trial court rejected the Government's position and on September 29, 1988, issued a judgment declaring that the President has no authority to regulate or prohibit, directly or indirectly, donations to an embargoed country of articles that the donor intends to be used to relieve human suffering and that can reasonably be expected to serve that end. The Government has decided against seeking an appeal of this adverse decision and is currently conducting a policy review of the humanitarian relief area.

6. The trade sanctions are an essential element of our policy that seeks a democratic outcome in Nicaragua by diplomatic means. The Sandinista regime made numerous commitments to democratization and national reconciliation when it signed the Esquipulas Agreement in 1987. The Government of Nicaragua reiterated these commitments February 14 at Tesoro Beach, El Salvador, and, in addition, promised to hold free, fair, and open elections in February 1990. I do not believe that current conditions in Nicaragua justify lifting the trade sanctions. If Nicaragua implements its Esquipulas commitments and holds free, fair, and honest elections, I believe the emergency that prompted the prior administration to impose the trade sanctions would largely be resolved.

7. The expenses incurred by the Federal Government in the period from November 1, 1988, through May 1, 1989, that are directly attributable to the exercise of powers and authorities conferred by the declaration of the Nicaraguan national emergency are estimated at $213,577.62, all of which represents wage and salary costs for Federal personnel. Personnel costs were largely centered in the Department of the Treasury (particularly in the Customs Service, as well as in FAC and the Office of the General Counsel), with expenses also incurred by the Department of State and the National Security Council.

8. The policies and actions of the Government of Nicaragua continue to pose an unusual and extraordinary threat to the national security and foreign policy of the United States. I shall continue to exercise the powers at my disposal to apply economic sanctions against Nicaragua as long as these measures are appropriate and will continue to report periodically to the Con-

gress on expenses and significant developments pursuant to 50 U.S.C. 1641(c) and 1703(c).

Sincerely,

GEORGE BUSH

Note: Identical letters were sent to Jim Wright, Speaker of the House of Representatives, and Dan Quayle, President of the Senate.

Statement by Press Secretary Fitzwater on the President's Meeting on the Situation in Lebanon

April 21, 1989

President Bush met at 2:15 p.m. today with Lebanese-American leaders and Lebanese officials to discuss the current situation in Lebanon. President Bush expressed the deep concern of the United States for the violence now going on in Lebanon. He expressed his personal anguish over the many victims of the war that permeates through many parts of that country. The President referred to his telephone conversation with President Mitterrand of France and their mutual interest in finding a solution to the Lebanese problem.

President Bush said that the United States remains committed to an independent, free Lebanon and the restoration of Lebanon's unity, sovereignty, and territorial integrity, with the disbandment of militias and the withdrawal of all foreign forces. The President expressed his support for a cease-fire.

Remarks on Presenting the Congressional Gold Medal to Mary Lasker

April 21, 1989

The President. Welcome, Mrs. Lasker. Mr. Speaker, it's nice to have you back. Distinguished Members of Congress—pleased to greet Congressmen Early and Conte and our other friends who are here. And a very special welcome, Tip, to you, sir.

You've heard me talk about a Thousand Points of Light, a metaphor that I've used to celebrate the extraordinary selflessness of Americans who give so much to the service of others. And we're here today to honor a veritable beacon of light, a woman who has focused an enormous amount of energy on finding solutions to life-threatening diseases, Mary Lasker. She's president of the Albert and Mary Lasker Foundation, which she started with her husband in 1942 to encourage medical research and to raise public awareness of major diseases which cripple and kill. Today the Lasker Foundation's Medical Research Award is one of the most prestigious honors in American medicine.

Mary's contribution to medicine—they've not stopped with the important work of the Lasker Foundation. Dr. Jonas Salk said: "When I think of Mary Lasker, I think of a matchmaker between science and society." Business Week magazine called her the fairy godmother of medical research. And she's worked extensively in many diverse causes, from supporting cancer research to preventing heart disease to working with those with cerebral palsy—and believe me, I am only naming a few here. And the list is so long because her good works and tireless efforts are legion.

And I cannot resist a special word of thanks and praise for Mary's leadership here in Washington. Senator Claude Pepper calls Mary the driving force behind the creation of the National Cancer Institute, the first of the National Institutes of Health, and of subsequent institutes. Her generosity and association with NIH continues today. Her work in urging legislation to expand Federal cancer research culminated in a 1971 bill that made the conquest of cancer a national goal. In 1984 Congress honored Mary Lasker by naming a center for her out at NIH: the Mary Woodard Lasker Center for Health Research and Education.

Not only is she well-known for advancing medical research but for her contributions to the arts and for her many public plantings that allow others to share her love of flowers. Through the Society for a More Beautiful Capital, she's donated extensive plantings in Washington, including over a million daffodil bulbs for Rock Creek Park and Lady Bird Johnson Park.

Mary, your gifts of health and beauty have left the country very much in your debt. In 1987 it was with gratitude and great pride that the United States Congress voted to honor your humanitarian contributions to the areas of medical research and education, urban beautification, and the fine arts.

Now it is my pleasure to thank you on behalf of the Nation and to present you with this token of our gratitude, the Mary Woodard Lasker Congressional Gold Medal. Congratulations.

Mrs. Lasker. Mr. President, "thank you" is much too small a word to describe this honor. Without your help and that of Congress, no success would be possible. This medal belongs to so many people, for the triumph and hope that medical research brought to this country. Mr. President, you know how and why medical research is so important. We look to you now, Mr. President, for leadership in helping to support research at the National Institutes of Health.

Cancer still kills 500,000 people a year in this country—more people than have been killed in all our wars combined. The strength of our nation depends on the health of our people. This medal recognizes the priority which we must once again place on research. It's good for trade, good for jobs, and vital for all Americans. Medical research is our hope for our children and for the building of a healthy America. Thank you.

Note: The President spoke at 2:59 p.m. in the Rose Garden at the White House. In his remarks, he referred to Jim Wright, Speaker of the House of Representatives, and Thomas P. O'Neill, Jr., former Speaker of the House of Representatives.

Remarks at the Memorial Service for Crewmembers of the U.S.S. *Iowa* in Norfolk, Virginia

April 24, 1989

We join today in mourning for the 47 who perished and in thanks for the 11 who survived. They all were, in the words of a poet, the men behind the guns. They came from Hidalgo, Texas; Cleveland, Ohio; Tampa, Florida; Costa Mesa, California. They came to the Navy as strangers, served the Navy as shipmates and friends, and left the Navy as brothers in eternity. In the finest Navy tradition, they served proudly on a great battleship, U.S.S. *Iowa.*

This dreadnought, built long before these sailors were born, braved the wartime waters of the Atlantic to take President Roosevelt to meet Winston Churchill at Casablanca and anchored in Tokyo Harbor on the day that World War II ended. The *Iowa* earned 11 battle stars in two wars. October of '44, off the coast of the Philippines—I can still remember it—for those of us serving in carriers and Halsey's Third Fleet, having *Iowa* nearby really built our confidence. And I was proud to be a part of the recommissioning ceremony in 1984. And now fate has written a sorrowful chapter in this history of this great ship.

Let me say to the crew of *Iowa*: I understand your great grief. I promise you today we will find out why, the circumstances of the tragedy. But in a larger sense, there will never be answers to the questions that haunt us. We will not—cannot, as long as we live—know why God has called them home. But one thing we can be sure—this world is a more peaceful place because of the U.S.S. *Iowa.* The *Iowa* was recommissioned and her crew trained to preserve the peace. So, never forget that your friends died for the cause of peace and freedom.

To the Navy community, remember that you have the admiration of America for sharing the burden of grief as a family, especially the Navy wives, who suffer most the hardships of separation. You've always been strong for the sake of love. You must be heroically strong now, but you will find that love endures. It endures in the lingering memory of time together, in the embrace of a friend, in the bright, questioning eyes of a child.

And as for the children of the lost, throughout your lives you must never forget, your father was America's pride. Your mothers and grandmothers, aunts and uncles are entrusted with the memory of this day. In the years to come, they must pass along to you the legacy of the men behind the guns. And to all who mourn a son, a brother, a husband, a father, a friend, I can only offer you the gratitude of a nation—for your loved one served his country with distinction and honor. I hope that the sympathy and appreciation of all the American people provide some comfort. The true comfort comes from prayer and faith.

And your men are under a different command now, one that knows no rank, only love, knows no danger, only peace. May God bless them all.

Note: The President spoke at 9:23 a.m. in Hangar LP–2 at the Norfolk Naval Air Station. Following his remarks, the President traveled to Chicago, IL.

Remarks at the Associated Press Business Luncheon in Chicago, Illinois

April 24, 1989

Thank you all for that warm welcome. And my friend, Bill Keating—friend from Congress days—thank you for that most generous introduction. I also want to thank your able—I don't know whether I should say leaders or deputies of the Associated Press. Lou Boccardi, sitting over here, and Jim Tomlinson—and thank them and you for including me in this AP luncheon, given at the time of the Newspaper Publishers Association meeting. And I also want to say how pleased I am to be with you once again.

I've just come from Norfolk, a very moving ceremony paying tribute to the 47 young men that died in the turret aboard *Iowa*—and it was indeed moving. And it made me once again realize how precious human life is and how sometimes you can't control things the way you'd like. And that leads me to just say a word about Terry Anderson, because in a meeting just now, the greeting by Lou and Bill Keating, they brought up with me, once again, with this sense of urgency that all in the Associated Press feel about Terry Anderson—the question of the hostages [in Lebanon].

And I just want to say, without being able to give you any good news, that we are concerned; we will follow every intelligence lead; we will go the extra mile to do what we can. And I vowed when I came into the Presidency not to talk about the burden of the Presidency, the loneliness of the job or the great toughness that nobody understands. I learned that from my immediate predecessor—8 years and I never once heard a call for sympathy or a call for understanding along those lines. But I will say that when you do take that oath of office you do feel perhaps a disproportionate concern for a fallen sailor or an individual held hostage against his or her will anywhere in the world. And so, we will continue to keep this question of these hostages on the front burner.

I know the news business is a serious and sometimes extraordinarily dangerous business. Mark Twain liked to recall that Napoleon once shot at a magazine editor. He missed him, but he killed a publisher. [*Laughter*] Twain says: "It seems his aim was bad, but his intentions were good." [*Laughter*]

You all know Jefferson's tribute to the importance of the press: "Were it left for me to decide whether we should have a government without newspapers or newspapers without a government, I should not hesitate a moment to prefer the latter."

And now, despite the fact that there are days when I think that all we really need is a sports page—[*laughter*]—both of us, government and the news media, need one another; we owe each other a measure of respect, honesty, and integrity equal to the work we're engaged in.

It's been a little over 3 months since I took the oath of office, and I am pleased with the progress that we've made in a short time. And I'll say more about that shortly, but before I do, I'd just like to share with you some impressions of the past 3 months.

People often ask me, understandably, what's it like—how the Presidency compares to the expectations you bring to it. I can sum up the thing that's made the deepest impression on me so far, in one word, and it's history, a sense of history all around you. And you can't live in the White House and you can't sit at the desk in the Oval Office, or upstairs in the office that I have now right next to the Lincoln Bedroom, without constantly experiencing the history of the place, without thinking of the Presidents we all know, but perhaps in a different light.

And I think of Washington, working to define the Presidency, to mix power and restraint in a way that created a Chief Executive consistent with democratic government. This Sunday I'm going to go up to New York to join in the ceremonies marking the 200th anniversary of Washington's swearing in. Each of those 200 years is lasting testimony to the solid foundation laid by Washington.

And I find myself thinking a lot of Teddy Roosevelt—his limitless energy; his mental, moral, and physical toughness. I want the record to show it's not just that he was an elitist, like me. [*Laughter*] I think of his dedication to serve his nation, a dedication instilled in earliest childhood, this sense of service, and then, I guess most of all, his love of nature, passion for reform and preservation.

I think of Harry Truman, a man who spoke his mind, a practical problemsolver, a fighter who never gave up. And I learned that one the hard way, because I'm old enough to have bet 10 bucks on Tom Dewey back in 1948.

And there's Ike, Dwight Eisenhower, hero to a generation, a man who, once he became President, didn't appear to seek the spotlight. He understood the value of quiet, steady leadership and led this nation through a decade of growth and progress and prosperity.

And of course, I do think of the man that I served for 8 years, Ronald Reagan—his commitment. People wondered: What was it? Why was he successful? It was his commitment to a handful of principles, a commitment to his beliefs, plus his great faith in the American people and then this unshakable optimism that he brought to the job. The opportunities open to us today, to my administration today, were made possible by the peace and prosperity that Ronald Reagan left as his legacy.

We used to hear a lot about the Presidency being too big for one man. Indeed, a very distinguished Washington lawyer wrote just at the end of the Carter Presidency, just as President Reagan was coming in—there was talk, because of the frustration abounding, that what we might need is a parliamentary system. That talk stopped when Ronald Reagan became President. Different men, different methods, different circumstances—proof, as I see it, that the Presidency is ample enough to accommodate the strengths and styles of our nation's rich political history.

In the past 3 months, these thoughts have framed my own approach in dealing with the pressing problems that confront us—some of them decades in the making—and in working to put the United States on a steady course for the decade ahead and the new century beyond it. I do not feel compelled or pressed because of a column here or a column there to reach out for something dramatic. The first step in every initiative that I've undertaken is to square our action with enduring American principles. Whatever the problem, we can count on public support so long as our policy and principles share a common root.

And these principles are: freedom for individuals, for nations—self-determination and democracy; fairness—equal standards, equal opportunity—a chance for each of us to achieve and make our way on our own merits; strength—in international affairs, strength our allies can count on and our adversaries must respect—and at home, strength and a sense of self-confidence in carrying forward our nation's work; excellence—the underlying goal in the collective efforts that we undertake, and accountability for the work we do; and in the workings of government, a firm sense of the responsibilities and powers of government and the private sector that lies beyond its limits.

My starting point has been a respect for American institutions—for Congress, for the dedicated civil servants in the executive branch, for State and local governments, for the concept of public service—and a firm belief in the constitutional powers of the Presidency. Each has its role; each can be enlisted in the work at hand. The emphasis is on cooperation, not confrontation, as the surest route to progress.

I've read more than a few news stories before and after the election—you can remember them—said that the new President and the Congress could not possibly work together after a bitter campaign that made cooperation impossible. I didn't believe that then, and I think we're proving it wrong now. When I took office, I told the Congress that the American people hadn't sent us to Washington to bicker. They sent us to govern, to work together to solve the urgent problems that confront us, and to shape the long-term strategies to ensure peace and prosperity in the future. I think the work we've done these past 3 months demonstrates the value of tough, principled negotiations between this administration and the Congress.

The bipartisan budget agreement that we worked out 10 days ago is a key example. That agreement—ahead of schedule, on target with Gramm-Rudman, and with my "no new taxes" pledge intact—is a strong first step towards dealing with the deficit problem and keeping our economy—76 straight months of expanding, uninterrupted growth—on track. Difficult decisions lie ahead. I'm well aware of that, but the important first step, an important agreement, has been reached.

And of course, there's the accord we reached on Central America. The people of Nicaragua—like their neighbors in the region, like people everywhere—deserve to live in peace, with freedom. The United States is now speaking with one voice and standing behind a plan that will put the Sandinistas to the test. And this unity has encouraged leaders like President Oscar Arias of Costa Rica to support—strongly support—the U.S. policy. And the support of the leaders in that area, in Central America, those democratic leaders surrounding Nicaragua, is vital if we're to succeed.

And in 3 short months, we've made a good start coming to grips with issues demanding urgent attention and decisive action, and we've taken that action.

Action to stabilize the troubled savings and loan system—the reform plan that I sent to Congress will restore stability and put the savings and loan system back on its feet in sound fiscal order. My plan guarantees that depositors will be fully protected—they are today, and they will be in the future. The S&L system must be reformed so that the questionable practices and outright illegalities that caused the crisis will not happen again. And those S&L officials found guilty of criminal actions will be punished for the losses that they have caused. Last week the Senate passed my plan by 91 to 8, and I urge the House to act promptly and pass this S&L reform bill with its central provisions intact.

Action to strengthen ethics in government—the ethics reforms that I've sent to Capitol Hill this month will uphold honesty and integrity in government service, and they will apply an evenhanded ethics standard across all branches of government.

Action in the war on drugs, where we're advancing on all fronts—education, treatment, interdiction, and tougher law enforcement—the antidrug effort, even in these tight budget times, will receive almost $1 billion in additional funding in 1990, a 21-percent increase in the outlays over what we'll spend in 1989. We've imposed a temporary ban on the import of certain semiautomatic rifles, weapons all too often used in drug-related killings. And we're tackling the drug epidemic in the District of Columbia, a test case for a full range of innovative antidrug measures.

Of course, dealing with problems that demand immediate attention is only part of the picture. We need to look to the long-term as well, to focus now on the kind of future we want to see for ourselves and our nation. And investing in that future is high on our national agenda.

First and foremost, that does mean improving education. Investing in the rising generation is long-range planning at its best. Our future in this technological age depends upon the qualities and capabilities of the American worker, and not just the most talented among us but each individual member of the work force. The seven-point program on education reform that I sent to Congress early this month will help us reward excellence, reach out to students most in need, increase choice, and introduce a healthy element of competition and accountability that will promote quality in our schools.

I have no intention of shifting the emphasis to Washington, away from the localities, away from the States, away from the diversity that is one of the hallmarks of our educational system. But I do want to use the White House as a bully pulpit to encourage excellence in every way and to encourage the private sector in every way. And I would say to you publishers here: I salute those of you who have already taken up the cause of education—be it literacy or dropout rates or whatever it is—you can do the Lord's work in no better way. The seven-point program is going to help us reward excellence, and you can do an awful lot as well.

Preparing for the kinder, gentler future I've spoken of means helping Americans cope with the changing nature of society, helping fundamental institutions like the family remain strong and prosper. We have big differences. We talk now about child care. I want the family to remain strong, and that's the guiding aim of my child-care initiatives: a tax credit proposal designed to expand the options of low-income families, keeping the ultimate choice of who will care for the children in their hands. One of my greatest concerns as President of the United States is the diminution, the denigration in some ways of the family structure. We in government must see that everything we do is aimed at strengthening, not weakening, the families.

Preparing for the future has got to mean protecting our environment. Teddy Roosevelt put it best when he said: "I do not recognize the right to rob, by wasteful use, the generations that come after us." Roosevelt spoke those words almost 80 years ago. And now, a little more than a decade away from the 21st century, safeguarding our environment is a national and international imperative. And we've taken the first important steps. We've urged Congress to enact legislation enabling us to ban the export of hazardous wastes to nations where safe handling of those dangerous substances cannot be guaranteed. And in response to growing concern about global warming, the U.S. will work in concert with other nations to end the discharge of CFC's [chlorofluorocarbons] into the atmosphere by the year 2000. And in the case of this Alaskan oil spill, we've taken steps to ensure a Federal role that is strong—a Federal role in oversight of the cleanup effort and to explore ways to prevent such spills in the future or to react more promptly if they should occur.

And finally, we've launched an initiative to strengthen the international strategy on Third World debt, which has already received broad international support from both the industrialized and the developing countries. We've set our course with this policy, and now I want to see this Third World debt a success on a case-by-case basis. I want to see us successful as we negotiate with Mexico, with Venezuela, and with other countries as well.

We've examined and I've made decisions on U.S. strategy for Afghanistan, Poland, Central America, and other problems and opportunities needing prompt attention. We have moved there. Within a few weeks, nearly all of the far-reaching and systematic defense and foreign policy reviews will be complete. And I've already made some decisions. Others, including arms control, will be forthcoming soon.

We're mapping strategies for a period of remarkable change in international affairs, change more wide-ranging and rapid than at any time in the postwar period. While we will lead, we also intend to consult and listen to our friends abroad and to consult and work with—listen to the United States Congress. I've met with the leaders of 34 nations, renewing my acquaintance with many of them, establishing a working relationship with the others. Secretary of State Jim Baker has met once with Foreign Minister Shevardnadze of the Soviet Union. He will meet again next month in Moscow to continue that dialog. And as with the bipartisan agreement on Nicaragua, I will work closely on all international matters with the Congress. We have had several meetings already with the leaders of Congress to discuss, in a nonstructured way, consultation—not only the process of consultation but we've begun it on individual areas around the globe.

Last Monday in Michigan I announced a new policy towards Poland in recognition of the positive changes taking place there. We'll be watching events in Poland closely—the fate of *Solidarność*, the follow-through on the free elections promised by the Polish Government. Freedom is proving a powerful force in world affairs, a force for peace and stability. The United States must seize opportunities to strengthen and support developments that advance the cause of freedom, and we will do exactly that.

I think we've made a good start these first 3 months, and there's more to come. The completion of our defense and foreign policy reviews in late May, draft legislation for a new Clean Air Act, a new strategy to curb the increased use of lethal weapons by drug dealers and other criminals, and new initiatives to combat the problem of homelessness—all are on the near horizon.

You know, some of my toughest critics are not in your line of work. Quite often, they're the kids, the children who write to me at the White House. I want to share with you a letter from a young seventh-grader from Torrance, California. He wrote asking me to take action on pollution, toxic waste, smog, littering—and a very detailed list, if you will, of environmental concerns. And he says in his letter: "I'm not saying you're doing a bad job, but could you put a little more effort into it?" [*Laughter*] That letter was written on January 20, 1989—Inauguration Day. [*Laughter*] And I have no way—maybe I ought to check on it as we go to California—I don't know whether I've satisfied that guy or not. But I can say, I got his message. And as I said before, I'm a practical man; I like what's real. I'm not much for the airy and the abstract, and I like what works.

And there's a running debate now on what it takes to move a nation forward. Some will tell you it's ideology that matters. Some say it's a question of competence. And others say that issues are the issue. But the fact is, what it takes to move a nation can't be captured in one word. It's a matter of principles and performance, ideology and action on the issues. And this administration understands that the American people expect all of this and something more: They expect results.

And so, while I'm pleased with what's been done and what we've accomplished in these 3 months, there is a long road ahead of us. And I am optimistic that our reforms will produce lasting results, that the long-range planning we do today will pay off in the future, that our consultations with Congress will result in progress in domestic and international affairs as well. But most of all, this nation is ready to move forward to meet the central challenges that we face: keeping America free, prosperous, and at peace—tomorrow and into the century ahead. Thank you very, very much.

Note: The President spoke at 12:17 p.m. in the Grand Ballroom at the Hyatt Regency

Hotel, during the annual conference of the American Newspaper Publishers Association. In his opening remarks, he referred to William J. Keating, chief executive officer of the Detroit Newspaper Agency; Louis D. Boccardi, president and general manager of Associated Press; and James F. Tomlinson, vice president and assistant to the president of Associated Press. Following his remarks, the President traveled to Bismarck, ND.

Remarks at the Dedication Ceremony for the Centennial Grove in Bismarck, North Dakota
April 24, 1989

I'm so pleased to be here. Thank you, Tom Kleppe. When Secretary—and I say "Secretary" because North Dakotans know that Tom served so well as Secretary of the Interior—former Congressman, but called me about this marvelous project of yours, he's right, I accepted in a hurry. And I'm very grateful to Governor Sinner and all involved in the preparations for this wonderful visit. I want to pay my respects not only to Governor and Mrs. Sinner, [former] Governor Link, Senator Conrad, Congressman Dorgan, and other distinguished leaders of the North Dakota Legislature. Thank you for inviting me.

It has been a very emotional day for me. I understand that lost on the *Iowa* was the grandson of a Bismarck family, and if that family didn't attend today's services, I can attest firsthand how moving it was and what a wonderful job our Navy did in holding the loved ones close to them, giving them comfort that I know all Americans would want given to these families. It was a very moving day. And the flags I see at half-mast here are appropriate tribute to those young men who lost their lives. I'm also proud to see that POW and MIA flag flying, Governor, right here at this magnificent State capital, because we must never forget the POW's and the MIA's.

When I accepted your invitation to come here, I had no idea that part of the program was to put me to work. "A sapling," they said, "all you'll have to do is to plant a sapling." No one told me that the sapling is about 12 feet tall over there. But I think we can figure it out. This hardy elm is a descendant of a tree planted on the White House lawn by John Quincy Adams. And now, its seedlings will be a part of North Dakota forever.

And just a few years before this State was carved out of the Dakota territory, a young man from New York City set aside a prominent career in politics to become a North Dakota rancher. Having lost his wife and mother in one single day, he came to these parts almost insane with grief. No tenderfoot, he worked the range in the harshest weather, always leading and never following. And he wore a sheriff's badge, and he roamed the Badlands to singlehandedly bring the worst characters to justice. And, in short, Teddy Roosevelt became a man in North Dakota; and he became something else, a guardian of nature. When he went back East and back to politics, Teddy Roosevelt took with him an understanding that the seemingly endless resources of the West were threatened by the unfettered exploitation of man. As President, Teddy Roosevelt wrote these words to schoolchildren on Arbor Day, 1907: "A people without children would face a hopeless future; a country without trees is almost as hopeless."

So, let us honor the coming 100th birthday of North Dakota and the memory of the Nation's first true environmentalist by dedicating this centennial bur oak along with this White House elm. Before the year 2000, your State will plant 100 million trees, almost half as many new trees in one State as there are Americans in the Union. May each tree add to the abundance of the good life in North Dakota, cleaner air for North America. This forestation effort is just one of 600 ambitious centennial projects North Dakotans are taking on. You are fulfilling the spirit that I call One Thousand

Points of Light: the spirit of voluntarism, from projects to help senior citizens, to the building of local and community centers, to a memorial for the North Dakotans who fell in the war.

This year you're also honoring those who settled here before North Dakota became a State by honoring their children: the sons and daughters of the pioneers, some 3,000 strong. And let us especially remember, in word and deed, those great peoples and great cultures here well before anyone else—the Native Americans of North Dakota. These Americans knew the Plains when buffalo ranged in the millions. We can learn then from a special, poignant knowledge that they taught us, that nature once violated is forever altered.

Around the world there's a growing recognition that environmental problems respect no borders. In these first few months in office we've begun to act on our own and in concert with other nations to face up to this fundamental fact. We've agreed that all nations must get together to ban CFC's [chlorofluorocarbons] and to prevent global warming. And as the world wakes us to these problems—and believe me, it is awakening—North Dakota, you're already at work planting trees that exchange carbon dioxide for fresh oxygen. What a fitting way to celebrate this magnificent centennial—by getting ready for the next 100 years.

As you've shown, we do not have to accept as inevitable the spoiling of our air, our rivers, our wetlands, and our forests. When North Dakotans celebrate their bicentennial, these 2 trees will be mammoth, almost 50 feet tall, as hardy and strong as the people they represent. Let them stand as a symbol of our commitment to a clean and healthy environment. May we always have the priceless resource of the outdoors for the enjoyment of our children and our children's children.

Thank you for asking me to be with you today at this wonderful celebration. I just can't tell you how moved I was when I came in from the airport to be greeted by so many of your neighbors, so many citizens of this great State. The respect for the institutions that we hold dear, in this case, the Presidency. It has nothing to do with the President—the respect for the institution was clear and evident for all to see, and I am grateful for that warm welcome. And so, I will watch with interest and lend a hand where I can, as this tree grows and develops, just like the Peace Garden State.

Happy birthday North Dakota! God bless you, and God bless the United States of America. Thank you all very much.

Note: The President spoke at 4:35 p.m. in the Great Hall of the State capitol. Following the remarks, he participated in a tree planting ceremony on the capitol lawn. Following the ceremony, the President traveled to San Jose, CA, where he stayed overnight.

Remarks to Ford Aerospace Space Systems Employees in Palo Alto, California

April 25, 1989

The President. Thank you, Don, very much. And my respects to our congressional representatives that are here today—Pete Wilson, our United States Senator with us today; and Congressman Campbell especially; other Members of Congress that are here—and all of you at Ford. I want to thank Don Petersen for coming from Detroit for this occasion and thank everybody involved in this visit. And I know what a logistical headache a visit like this might be. [*Laughter*] So, we promise to go on time. [*Laughter*] Thank you, gentlemen from the Navy. And, Don, thanks for the introduction, and all of you for the generous welcome. It's a pleasure to be back in the Bay Area, among friends. I'm taking a chance by quoting him in north California, but it was that noted gourmet, Dodger manager Tommy Lasorda—[*laughter*]—who conceded——

Audience. Oh!

The President. I knew I was taking a chance. [*Laughter*] "I'm on a seafood diet. I eat all the food I can see," he said. [*Laughter*] Well, he's not like most of us; he never met a meal he didn't like. And if you ask, he'll insist that food ranks among his most precious investments. It uplifts his performance, mentally and physically. It enhances his ability to compete and, indirectly, to keep his ball club in contention. And I'm sure you've all heard the old saying: "Never invest your money in anything that eats or needs repainting." [*Laughter*]

Well, today I want to talk briefly about a different kind of investment—investments which prize the new horizons of America's technological future; investments which can create new jobs, unlock new markets and unleash new technologies; investments, in short, which will make us more competitive and keep America number one.

In a sense, this attitude is typically American. For we are, at heart, a very competitive people. We measure life by today's Dow Jones average or by how our ball club did most recently, or whatever the statistic. And as Americans, we expect short-term results, and historically, we get them. Government's role is to unleash America's ambition, to make us more competitive, by pointing toward the 21st century, ensuring long-term results.

The best investment in the future is to slash the Federal budget deficit. And every dollar the Government does not borrow means more capital available for sound, productive investment. Recently I unveiled an important bipartisan budget agreement with Congress to reduce the deficit. It is but a first step, but the very fact of it was important—agreement between the executive branch and the Congress. And our accord will narrow this deficit to $99.4 billion in the fiscal year that began October 1st. And that's far below the $163 billion estimated for the current fiscal year. And now, this plan's an agreed outline—tough talks still lie ahead. And we will resume consultations soon on a plan aimed at balancing the budget by 1993.

Think of the deficit reduction as exercise, like walking the dog every day. Believe me, I know: Exercise keeps you at the top of your game. And so will another investment to build a more competitive America, one of many that I'll be asking Congress to make. And I am talking about getting Congress to restore the capital gains differential, a step which, according to Treasury estimates, will raise $4.8 billion in new revenue.

I listen to all the criticism, and I've heard, as you have, the criticism of people who ridicule cutting the capital gains tax as somehow a tax break for the rich. Well, they couldn't be more wrong. Lower capital gains taxes will create jobs for those who don't have jobs, will help build a better America. It worked once before, and it will work again. So, I would urge everybody here to give strong support, contacting your Members of the United States Congress to help me restore the capital gains differential.

Consider, on the one hand, those countries that cripple opportunity. They know firsthand the damage caused by excessive taxation on capital gains. And then consider that our second-largest trading partner, Japan, with whom you are working very closely, has taxed them little, if at all. And so, the lesson then, again, is self-evident: Restoring the capital gains differential will make America more competitive. Our plan supports reducing it to 15 percent on long-held assets. So, let us act to lift revenue, help savings, and free American businesses without distorting world markets.

You know, ordinarily, I take statistics with a grain of salt. I've seen too many of these polls. These political polls go up and down. And I guess if I'd have listened to them and gotten discouraged by them I wouldn't be standing here as President of the United States of America. But I like what Woody Hayes said—remember Woody Hayes, the coach at Ohio State? He put it best: "Statistics always remind me of the fellow who drowned in a river whose average depth was only three feet." One statistic, though, does bear reciting. Since November 1982, nearly 20 million new jobs have been created in this country. And many have been created right here in the Silicon Valley. Well, through investments to increase competitiveness, I know that we can do even better.

For instance, we have proposed a permanent extension on the research and experimentation tax credit. America must remain in the front lines of technological innovation. And we want to actively increase domestic research by multinationals and end the uncertainty of expiring temporary rules. These steps and others can help us walk the unexplored frontiers of high technology. For high tech is potent, precise, and in the end, unbeatable.

The truth is it reminds a lot of people of the way I pitch horseshoes. Would you believe—[*laughter*]—would you believe some of the people? [*Laughter*] Would you believe our dog? [*Laughter*]

Look, I want to give the high-five symbol to high tech, and I want to do it by investing in competitiveness. And that's why I've asked Congress for an increase of $2.4 billion for NASA, as it moves ahead with the space station *Freedom.* We have selected a new Science Adviser, and I will elevate his status. It is important that the President's Science Adviser have access to the President and that his views be considered in a wide array of important issues. I've also just reestablished the National Space Council, headed by the Vice President, to coordinate our future space efforts.

But we can't stop there; our future won't allow it. So, let us also invest in the superconducting supercollider, a bold new experiment fusing science, technology, and education. Because science is so critical, let us double the National Science Foundation budget by 1993. And let us use our own technological prowess to expand free and fair trade. I'm talking about excellence in such fields as microcomputers and superconductivity and, yes, aerospace.

In aerospace, we can point to satellites whose technology is American, point with pride to satellites like the Superbird satellite, among the largest, 5,500 pounds. The most powerful communications satellites yet developed—5,500 pounds—that's even bigger than the 49'ers' offensive line. [*Laughter*] Today America's satellites are among the most competitive spacecrafts for customers who want affordable high-powered communications satellites. And they are providing regular and cable television access, telephone lines, newspaper transmission, and other telecommunications services. And best of all, they're just a preview of the next generation of satellites. In the 21st century, they will keep America as number one.

You know—remember Satchel Paige—great black pitcher, self-proclaimed philosopher? They asked him what was the secret of his competitiveness. You remember what he said. "Don't look back. Somebody might be gaining on you." Well, Satchel, like high technology, knew that as Americans we do look ahead and not back. We always have, and we must now, more than ever. For the coming decade will see and shape a rapidly changing work force. To invest its talents will be our challenge as a nation.

According to the National Science Foundation, for instance, by the year 2000 the college-age population will have shrunk almost 20 percent. Among college-age youth, minorities will comprise one-third. And women, minorities, and immigrants will total almost two-thirds of the new entrants into the labor force. These facts demand a new investment to build a more competitive America. It's an investment different from lower capital gains taxes or more funds for space and other high tech, but it is vital. And I'm referring, of course, to child care.

At Ford Aerospace, officials are responding to changing demographics and the needs of its employees. By increasing parental options, Ford's Employee Assistance Program is helping to keep us competitive. And it is involving community agencies as child care resource referrals, like the YMCA Child Care Center in Palo Alto, approved and supported by the United Way.

Now, I salute this example, and I applaud its emphasis on choice. There are some congressional child-care initiatives, well-meaning, I am sure, but which don't reflect this emphasis. Our new child-care initiative—mine, the one that I've sent up to the Congress—does. And our proposal urges a new tax credit to make child care more affordable. And it puts money in the hands of the low-income parents, limits Federal intervention, and increases options. A church can help, or grandparents or professional nursery. When it comes to child care, we say: Let the parents decide. Keep the family strong. And we must do that.

For in the end, it's decisions we come down to: decisions to say yes to child care, more funds for space and other high technology; decisions which serve the entire community—workers, investors, students, parents; decisions to invest in America so that we can create a more competitive America.

As Californians, you know what I'm talking about. You've always believed in daring, aspiring, and charting unexplored frontiers. And you look ahead, not back. And you know that nothing is impossible. And by giving of yourselves and to your country, you give lift to the American dream.

Thank you for that. Thank you for a fascinating day in the laboratories here. Thank you for your kindness and your generosity. God bless you, and God bless the United States of America. Thank you all very much.

Note: The President spoke at 9:27 a.m. in the facility's cafeteria courtyard. He was introduced by Donald Rassier, president of Ford Aerospace Space Systems Division. Donald E. Petersen was chairman of the board of the Ford Motor Co. Following his remarks, the President traveled to Los Angeles, CA.

Remarks to Law Enforcement Officers in Orange County, California
April 25, 1989

Thank you very much, Sheriff Gates. And thank all of you, the supervisors, law enforcement community, thank you for that warm Orange County welcome. And it's good to be here. And I'm very proud that our great Attorney General is with me, Dick Thornburgh, who's doing a superb job in this battle against drugs and against crime all across the board. Dick, welcome. To Willie von Raab, the Commissioner of the Customs, I am delighted he is here. Sheriff Gates very generously telling me of the superb cooperation between the U.S. Customs and the sheriff's office here. And that's what it's going to take if we're going to have further victories in this war.

I'm delighted to be here with Senator Pete Wilson, an outstanding leader in the Senate, a man who has been really a conscience of the Senate in terms of antinarcotics, and Mike Hayde as well. And may I pay my respects to—I know four Members of the United States Congress are here today—Bill Dannemeyer and Congressman Cox. I believe I'm a little insecure in my lines here. I think we're in Chris' district, unless we flew over it. So, I'm glad to be hosted by Congressman Cox and then Congressman Bob Dornan, Congressman Gallegly as well.

So, I'm delighted again to be here. And let me just say this: that somewhere out here are 50 undercover narcotics agents; and let me say to you, you are the unsung heroes in this war, risking your lives almost every single day behind enemy lines, if you will, to save our kids' lives. And you know who you are, and we salute you and thank you for laying your lives out there for the rest of us. All of you are fighting fierce battles in one of the largest and toughest drug markets in the country. And somebody dies every other day in Orange County as a result of drugs. I don't know how many of you have seen the visuals, the display, but there is a penetrating chart that demonstrates dramatically the amounts of lives that are lost in Orange County from narcotics. And these people that have lost their lives—they've ranged from an 82-year-old man to a 1-month-old child. It doesn't spare anyone. But you're not backing down; you're not giving up.

And that's one of the reasons I wanted to come here today. The communities here in Orange County are united. Law enforcement agencies crossed over sometimes competitive lines and banded together. And you're an example of hope, determination, and the true American spirit. You know, we won't build a better America until we win this war on drugs. And so, today I want to touch on both sides of the equation—education, to cut off demand for drugs, and enforcement, to cut off the supply.

And I might say, parenthetically, that our new drug czar, Bill Bennett, former Secretary of Education, is tackling the problem on both sides of the equation—education and interdiction. And I'm just delighted that he is doing the job he is in Washington. I wish he were here with us today so I could brag on him in public.

Demand for drugs is driven by a sense of hopelessness. Last year—this is so sad—an 18-year-old member of one of these gangs, in this instance the L.A. Crips gang, was asked: "If you could change the world, how would you do it?" And he said: "I wouldn't know what to do. I wouldn't know what to change." And later he was asked: "What do you think you'll be doing in 10 years?" And he said: "I don't think I'll be alive in 10 years." And that is life without hope, without meaning. And we're looking at a desperation that money alone will never cure. We won't win this one with our wallets alone. We will only win it through our collective effort and our collective will. And that means education—cutting off demand through community involvement at all levels.

Mike Hayde and Sheriff Gates and so many others, your Drug Use Is Life Abuse Program is one outstanding community awareness effort. And you've got business, government, schools, religious groups, families, and law enforcement all personally committed to halting demand. There are the students that Brad was telling me about who produced the antidrug video that runs before the movies start, the workers who roll by on a sanitation truck painted on its side "Drugs Are Garbage," and every L.A. Ram—no matter who you're for—but I commend the Rams in this one—every L.A. Ram with a Drug Use Is Life Abuse patch on his uniform, over 22,000 student athletes on teams in Orange County who will wear the same patch. And then there's my friend, Reverend Robert Schuller, who's got churches all over the county delivering a sermon on drug abuse every 3 months, and again the students, distributing tens of thousands of cards for people to sign, making a personal commitment against drugs. And that idea came from a 16-year-old girl who says: "The only thing I own is my name. I don't take signing my name lightly." Well, I want to join her. I want to proudly sign one of these cards, too, and I hope we can after this.

So, many are getting the word out. But I'd like to enlist one other group in the L.A. area that has a special responsibility: those in the entertainment industry. Television, films, and music are a positive influence. And my advice to them—my entreaty is: Use that influence wisely to do good. I know that many in the business are already concerned and active, but I never want to see a movie again that makes drug use into something humorous. It is time that they got behind this crusade. This community has raised your voices; you've raised your voices so effectively in the cause of so many issues. Can you not raise them once more in support of a cause so important? In the work you do and the lives you lead, help us send a strong message, the right message, to a new generation of Americans: We want a drug-free America!

You get some marvelous mail in my line of work here as President, unbelievable. I quoted one yesterday from some kid, an eighth-grader or something, who said: "Well, you've got to do better. You've got to do better on the fight against drugs and helping the environment." He wrote it on January 20th, the day I was sworn in. [*Laughter*] But nevertheless, he has a point. But here's one, a young woman: "I have a brother who has wasted time, opportunity, and finally his mind. I've watched my mother and father cry and spend years of energy and effort on their addicted son instead of themselves. I hate drugs. Drugs have virtually destroyed my family." She deserves better; we all do. With the strongest means of enforcement we can devise, we must disarm, dismantle, and destroy the drug market in America.

You heard Brad Gates, the sheriff, tell us something of the history of this ground that we stand on. It was the core of an international marijuana and cocaine smuggling ring. How many lives, how many families, how many hopes and dreams have been destroyed with these chemical weapons of death and destruction—drugs? Death bought and sold by the ton—this operation had commercial packing equipment, underground storage vaults, large vans with hidden compartments, jet aircraft, oceangoing vessels. Once a warehouse of death, now it is a source of hope. Rancho del Rio has been reclaimed. Thanks to the Comprehensive Crime Control Act of 1984, pushed through by your former Congressman, Dan Lungren, we can now seize drug dealers' assets and use them in the war on drugs. And this is the first piece of forfeited drug property turned over for use by local officials in Orange County. It's going to serve as an International Narcotics Training Center and as a reminder to these merchants of death: Your money won't help you; in fact, we're going to use it against you.

So, what you see on these tables behind us is over $4 million—line up—[*laughter*]—$4 million of laundered drug money recently seized by U.S. Customs and the regional narcotics suppression program in Operation Shackle. And today I'd like to formally turn these funds over to Sheriff Gates to help fund the Rancho del Rio project. I hope that all of you can help make this project a reality. I'm also pleased to present another $6 million in drug money—confiscated through a joint DEA-local sting operation in California and Arizona—to fund more effective, cooperative efforts between local, State, and Federal enforcement agencies. This money then, totaling $10 million, is the bounty of defeated drug criminals. And we won't stop until we nail every coward who deals in death and put them where they belong.

Now, you have had outstanding results over the last 2 years, thanks to the team efforts of local, State, and Federal agents: nearly 40 million in cash confiscated, the equivalent of 9 million injections of heroin and 38 million doses of cocaine seized. And that's 15 doses for every man, woman, and child in Orange County. Do we need any other reason than that to win this war? Let these funds go then to fighting the war they once financed. Let us raise awareness and build strength through a constellation of concerned Americans in every town, city, and community in this country. And let us send a message, loud and clear, to every drug merchant in America: You're going to be out of business! That is our message. That is my message to you today. Keep up the good work and continue to set an example for the rest of our great country.

Thank you. God bless you. And God bless the United States of America.

Note: The President spoke at 12:23 p.m. outside of the main house at Rancho del Rio. He was introduced by Orange County Sheriff Brad Gates. In his remarks, he referred to Michael K. Hayde, president of Drug Use Is Life Abuse, and Robert Schuller, pastor of the Crystal Cathedral. Prior to his remarks, the President toured the facility. Following his remarks, he attended a working luncheon with law enforcement officers at the ranch.

Remarks to Members of the Hispanic-American Community in Los Angeles, California
April 25, 1989

Thank you very much. And, Mr. Schwartz—Murray, thank you, sir, for the warm welcome back to this campus, and I am so delighted to be here. This is a nonpartisan appearance. And therefore I will resist any partisan commentary except to make note that it was here, not in this very room, but right on this campus—Murray Schwartz referring to my last visit here that was highly politicized, perhaps one of the most dramatic moments in our whole campaign cycle, but certainly in my life. And so,

I have a feeling, a good feeling, and very pleased to be welcomed back by two people who give so much to UCLA.

I would just give a word of welcome to all of you. And I'm delighted to salute UCLA, one of our great universities. I would simply say that expressing gratitude is not always easy. But I do want to express my gratitude for this warm reception. I had a chance to meet with some of the organizers early on to tell them how grateful I am for this wonderful get-together on relatively short notice.

You know, a Hispanic patriot of our hemisphere once said: "I am America's son. To her I belong." Well, let me speak for Barbara, who regrettably is not with us here tonight. I feel that we belong, for we've spent a lot of our adult lives in—Barbara and I—in Texas, seeing close up, firsthand, the strength of the Hispanic communities there. Hispanic values touched us: discipline, caring, patriotism, love of God. And of course because of Jeb's wife, Columba, we feel doubly blessed as a family because the Hispanic culture is our culture, too.

And tomorrow I'm going to meet with one of our greatest Presidents. And I'm talking about California's always-favorite son and my good friend, Ronald Reagan. And I can't help recalling the words that he once said about Hispanic-Americans: "Just as their forefathers sought a dream in the new world, Hispanic-Americans have realized their dream in our great nation and will continue to do so. Their dedication to higher purposes reflects what is best in the American spirit."

Well, my friends, that spirit brought your parents and your grandparents and some of you to the United States. And they and you came in search of a better life, and you're finding it. And you came to build a better America, and you're sure helping build it. And you're building it through family, through church, through love of country and belief in the value of hard work—you know, building it in the school also, a new spirit, I'd say, of public service that is sweeping our educational system, from grade school to grad school, building it through excellence and through such leaders now as we have in Washington: Secretaries Lujan [Interior] and Cavazos [Education], who so enrich our administration.

It was over a year ago at a LULAC [League of United Latin American Communities] meeting in Texas where I said time had come, long since, that we have Hispanics in the President's Cabinet. And now we have two outstanding Secretaries: Manuel Lujan and Lauro Cavazos.

I don't want to embarrass this guy, but it was here at UCLA, on one of these questions they ask you at these debates out of a clear blue sky—and they asked me: Name a couple of contemporary heroes, or who are your heroes? I've found that in this line of work you always get psychoanalyzed—[*laughter*]—and you're stretched out on a theoretical couch for people to figure out what makes you tick—that just goes with the job. But this question came out of the clear blue sky, and it had something to do with your heroes. And I cited, quite proudly, Tony Fauci, who is one of the researchers and now top people at the National Institutes of Health who is doing so much in AIDS and cancer research and all of this. What immediately came to my mind was Jaime Escalante, who is here with us today. And I—here he is—I told Jaime—I said, "Look"—I saw him later; I think it was back at the White House or somewhere—I said: "I hope I didn't throw you into some kind of partisan limelight there because what I really wanted to do, though, is express my feeling of contribution, my feeling of respect for the contribution that you have made in this—what we're talking about here today—excellence in education." So, right amongst us again is one of my genuine heroes.

I see many business people here, people that know what entrepreneurship means and have taken the lead in starting businesses and building them. And you are creating new jobs and cutting unemployment in the process—here, California, many of you from across the country. And as America's fastest growing minority in the 21st century, you, more than ever, will help tell the American story. And so is the promise that our kids will inherit a better land than we inherited true. It is very, very true—and I'm convinced of it.

And I haven't been President very long,

but I remain an optimist about the United States of America. The problems are big, but we can solve them. And when I look to the values that give us the underpinning for everything we do in society, I come right back to the Hispanic community. And I'm grateful to you.

Some people say that the younger generation is selfish. I don't believe this. I have much more confidence in the young people than to say they're selfish. And young people of this country hunger to return to America a measure of what America has given us all. The people in this room care about the disadvantaged, about the environment. And under this administration, we are going to work together to transform our caring into a commitment for action. Let us pledge, then, not simply to knock at the door of opportunity, let's throw that door wide open and keep it open! And let's remember that we are one nation under God and that we honor Him with the lives we lead.

People are asking me now that you've been President, what are some of your major concerns? And one for me is the diminution of American family. It's more than a sociological textbook kind of a concern. I worry about it. And I want to say to you in this room—because I think of the Hispanic culture in America, in the United States, is family-oriented; strength coming from the family—I will have nothing to do with any Federal legislation that diminishes the strength of the American family. We've got to find ways to strengthen it, and I think I've learned a lot of that right here from people in this room.

We are rural and urban; native-born and foreign-born; Hispanic and non-Hispanic; brown, black, white—but most of all, we are Americans. So, my plea is: Let's join our hands together, for the future is ours. And as we do, please accept my thanks for this wonderful occasion. I do want to have an opportunity now to come and greet as many as I possibly can. God bless you. Thank you all, and God bless the United States of America. Thank you very, very much.

Note: The President spoke at 5:28 p.m. in the Galleria at the James West Alumni Center on the campus of the University of California at Los Angeles. In his remarks, he referred to Murray Schwartz, executive vice chancellor of the university; John and Columba Bush, his son and daughter-in-law; and Jaime Escalante, a calculus teacher at Garfield High School in east Los Angeles. Prior to his remarks, the President attended a reception in the alumni center for leaders of the Hispanic community. Following his remarks, he stayed overnight at the Four Seasons Hotel.

Nomination of Richard L. Armitage To Be Secretary of the Army
April 25, 1989

The President today announced his intention to nominate Richard L. Armitage to be Secretary of the Army. He would succeed John O. Marsh.

Mr. Armitage has served in several capacities at the Department of Defense, including Assistant Secretary of Defense for International Security Affairs, 1983 to present, and Deputy Assistant Secretary of Defense for International Security Affairs for East Asia, 1981–1983. From 1979 to 1983, Mr. Armitage established a Washington-based consulting firm specializing in Asian affairs, and he worked in the foreign policy office of the Reagan Presidential campaign. Mr. Armitage has served as administrative assistant to Senator Robert Dole of Kansas, 1978–1979; consultant to the Pentagon, 1975–1976; and Naval and Marine Corps adviser with the U.S. Defense Attaché Office in Saigon, 1973–1975. He is a member of the Association of Asian Studies and the World Affairs Council.

Mr. Armitage graduated from the U.S. Naval Academy in 1967, where he received a commission as an ensign in the U.S. Navy.

Mr. Armitage was born in 1945, in Boston, MA. He is married, has seven children, and resides in Vienna, VA.

Nomination of William Lucas To Be an Assistant Attorney General
April 25, 1989

The President today announced his intention to nominate William Lucas to be an Assistant Attorney General (Civil Rights Division). He would succeed William Bradford Reynolds.

Since 1987 Mr. Lucas has been an attorney with Evans and Luptak in Detroit, MI. He served as chief executive officer in Wayne County, MI, 1983–1987, and he served in the Wayne County Sheriff's Department, 1968–1983. Mr. Lucas served as a Special Agent in the Federal Bureau of Investigation, 1963–1968; Civil Rights Division of the Justice Department, 1962–1963; and in the New York City Police Department, 1954–1962. He was a teacher and social worker in New York City, 1952–1954. In addition, Mr. Lucas was chairman of the Republican National Committee Coalition Outreach Committee.

Mr. Lucas graduated from Manhattan College (B.S., 1952) and Fordham Law School (J.D., 1962). In addition, he was a fellow at the John F. Kennedy School of Government at Harvard University. Mr. Lucas resides in Detroit, MI.

Nomination of Robert Davila To Be Assistant Secretary of Education and Nell Carney To Be Commissioner of the Rehabilitation Services Administration
April 25, 1989

The President today announced his intention to nominate Robert Davila to be Assistant Secretary for Special Education and Rehabilitative Services and Nell Carney to be Commissioner of the Rehabilitation Services Administration. Both positions are in the Department of Education. Dr. Davila would succeed Madeleine Will, and Dr. Carney would succeed Susan Suter.

Concurrently, the Department of Education announced today the appointment of Michael Vader as Deputy Assistant Secretary in the Office of Special Education and Rehabilitative Services and Judy Schrag as Director of the Office of Special Education Services.

Robert Davila has served in several capacities at Gallaudet University, including vice president for precollege programs, 1978 to present; professor, department of education, 1980 to present; acting dean, Model Secondary School for the Deaf, 1979–1980; and director, Kendall Demonstration Elementary School, 1974–1978. Dr. Davila graduated from Gallaudet University (B.A., 1953), Hunter College (M.S., 1963), and Syracuse University (Ph.D., 1972). He is married, has two children, and resides in Washington, DC.

Since 1987 Dr. Carney has served as assistant director at the Virginia Department for the Visually Handicapped and as assistant regional manager, 1985–1987. She has also served in several other capacities in the education field, including instructor, Washington, DC, public schools, 1984–1985; vocational rehabilitation administrator, Washington State Department for the Blind, 1979–1984; rehabilitation counselor, 1978–1979; and instructor, Nashville public schools, 1975–1978. She graduated from Peabody College for Teachers (B.S., 1974; M.A., 1975). She is married and resides in Richmond, VA.

Appointment of Bonnie Guiton as Director of the Office of Consumer Affairs at the Department of Health and Human Services
April 25, 1989

The President today announced his intention to appoint Bonnie Guiton to be Director of the Office of Consumer Affairs at the Department of Health and Human Services. In that capacity she will be the principal adviser to the President on consumer issues. She would succeed Virginia H. Knauer.

Dr. Guiton was appointed by President Reagan on June 18, 1987, as Assistant Secretary for Vocational and Adult Education at the Department of Education. Prior to the appointment, she served as vice chairman of the U.S. Postal Rate Commission, 1984–1987. She also served as vice president and general manager of Kaiser Center, Inc., and Kaiser Center Properties. She has served as the executive director of the Marcus A. Foster Educational Institute and was formerly an assistant dean of students, interim head of the ethnic studies department, and a lecturer at Mills College.

Dr. Guiton received a bachelor's degree from Mills College, a master's degree from California State University at Hayward, and a doctorate in education from the University of California at Berkeley. She was born in Springfield, IL, on October 30, 1941, and she resides in Falls Church, VA.

Question-and-Answer Session With Reporters Following a Meeting With Former President Reagan in Los Angeles, California
April 26, 1989

President Bush

Q. President Reagan, how do you think your successor is doing in his first hundred days? There seems to be some discussion about that.

President Reagan. Well, I'm not a part of that discussion because I think he's doing just fine. And he was a major part of everything that we did for the preceding 8 years. I'm very pleased to have him here.

Q. President Reagan, there's been some suggestion that President Bush has been a little slow in reacting and responding to Mr. Gorbachev. How do you feel about that, sir?

President Reagan. As I say, I think he's doing just fine.

Iran Arms and Contra Aid Controversy

Q. Mr. President, what do you feel about Ollie North these days, now that he's built a legal defense on an assertion that he was only following orders the entire time in the Iran-*contra* affair?

President Reagan. Here's one where I think we're both in the same boat. With this before a jury now, I don't think any comment is appropriate or proper with regard to that.

Q. Were you aware, Mr. President, that documents were not seen by the Iran-*contra* committees on the Hill?

President Reagan. Well, again, as I say, I just don't think this is a time to comment.

Death of Lucille Ball

Q. President Reagan, would you comment on the passing of Lucille Ball today?

President Reagan. Well, yes, I've issued a statement on that. I think it's a great tragedy, and all of us are affected. She was a friend; we loved her dearly, and she's truly going to be missed.

Defense Budget

Q. Mr. President, what do you think of President Bush's decision to cut money for Star Wars and military aid to the *contras*?

President Reagan. Well, having had, for 8 years, some of the same problems he's facing now, I'm not going to comment on that. I think that I can rest assured that he means to maintain our national security. There are many problems to contend with.

Abortion

Q. President Bush, the Supreme Court today will be considering an abortion case. Would you like to see that be the first step in a move to ban abortion in this country?

President Bush. Yes.

Q. President Reagan? Same question.

President Reagan. I think we've been agreed on that. You know my position on abortion.

Advice From President Reagan

Q. President Bush, are you looking for any tips today or anything in this meeting?

President Bush. Always.

Q. On what?

President Bush. "Life its own self," as Dan Jenkins said—"life its own self." Figure that one out, Norm [Norman Sandler, United Press International]. But what it means is: I have a lot more to learn from President Reagan. As I've told you all over and over again, I learned a lot in 8 years. I learned a lot about principle; I learned a lot about the world as it really is. And so, I want to talk to him about the changes that are taking place abroad—Japan, NATO [North Atlantic Treaty Organization], Europe, all over the place—and get his advice. So, that's what I hope this visit will be about.

Q. Can you give us a sense of what he's told you here today, sir?

President Bush. Well, we just started. He told me you were coming in. He said there would be two waves and we were going to take questions at the second wave. That was all we've said so far after we said "hello."

Q. Would you like to enlist President Reagan's support for anything in particular—missions, special——

President Bush. Yes.

Q. Can you tell us about it?

President Bush. No specific mission, but strong support. And I want to keep him fully informed. The respect for him around the world knows no bounds, and I've encountered that when I've met with 36, I believe it is, heads of state so far. And so, I hope I can talk him into various missions or assignments as time goes by. But I'm respectful of his own private life and what he's doing, but there will be plenty of opportunity to stay in touch, and that I'm determined to do.

White House Press Corps

Q. President Reagan, do you think your successor has a kinder, gentler press corps? More so than you had? [*Laughter*]

President Reagan. Oh, I think we're familiar with that. One thing I want to tell you that I proved to him before you came in, if you're curious about that—I proved to him I was a Californian. We stood in the window, and I showed him that you could see Catalina from here.

President Bush. That's right. That's right. What a view! Have you all checked it? It's worth a look out there.

Offshore Oil Drilling

Q. You don't want any offshore oil drills out there, do you?

President Bush. Any what?

Q. Offshore oil drills out there.

President Bush. Out where?

Q. Out there at that view?

President Bush. Well, I don't know that anyone is proposing that right now, but you know my position on that—strong environmental concerns and strong concerns about this country becoming further dependent on foreign oil. And I'm convinced that the proper balance can be found.

Views on the Presidency

Q. Do you miss the White House, sir?

President Reagan. No, it's in good hands.

President Bush. I can tell you they miss him, because the people there are the same. They're the same wonderful group that you told me were first-rate, and they talk very fondly about you and Nancy.

Note: President Bush spoke at 9:48 a.m. in the Office of former President Ronald Reagan at Fox Plaza. Following their meeting, President Bush traveled to Austin, TX.

Remarks to the Texas State Legislature in Austin
April 26, 1989

Thank you very, very much for that warm welcome. Mr. Speaker, thank you, sir, for presenting me to this esteemed body. And, Lieutenant Governor Hobby, my respects and thanks to you and to Bill Clements. It's a good thing it isn't his birthday. *[Laughter]* I'm not sure another plaid day in the Texas Legislature is in order. But a belated happy birthday, anyway.

I'm delighted to be back in Austin with so many friends. And I'll want to discuss a few issues facing Texas and all of America. But let me just say a few words about what it means to be a Texan. My credentials: I have my driver's license here, and I have my Texas hunting license here, and, somewhere, my voter registration slip. And it is true, I like Kennebunkport, but I am a Texan. And so, I just want to clear the air and say a few words about that.

You know, like the former kingdom of Hawaii, Texas is a nation that had to reconcile itself to being a State. But like Hawaii, we'll never reconcile ourselves to being ordinary. From the Pecos to the Pedernales, from the Rio Grande to the Red River, there is no place on Earth like Texas, nor is there another capitol in America quite like this one, built of this rose-tinged granite that blushes in the low sun. And this being Texas, we had to build a capitol that is exactly one foot taller than the one in Washington. And so, I hope it's not too much of a cliche to say that Texas stands tall in the heart of this President.

Perhaps for this reason, Larry McMurtry, who was at the White House the other day—he's one of my favorite writers—in "Lonesome Dove" he describes the mythic Texas and conjures that sense of the place we all know so well. And I'm inspired by a man of letters who can convincingly adopt the voice of the cowboys and the outlaws, men whose only schooling was in dodging bullets, whose only lessons were in how to run or rustle cattle.

But unlike Davy Crockett, I first set out for Texas not on horseback from Tennessee but from Connecticut in a red Studebaker in June of 1948. And more than 40 years later, that trip is still a vivid memory: Highway 80, neon Pearl Beer signs appearing in the desert twilight—and see, I've got a note here—and stopping at a cafe—I'll admit it I didn't know if chicken-fried steak was a chicken fried like a steak or a steak that tasted like a chicken, but I've learned. *[Laughter]*

And still, Bar and I settled in Texas, as did many before us. We raised five kids and helped get into the business world—helped start a business. And in that span of 40 years, I've watched with pride as this State has grown into even greater glory. And in my lifetime, I've seen the oil wealth of west Texas help finance the building of great cities, the expansion of great universities and colleges—the origins of a Texas renaissance, if you will. The energy business helped make Texas what it is today: the third coast of the United States.

This Texas renaissance lasted for years, even decades. But you also know another more recent chapter of the Texas story: oil cheaper than some of this fancy mineral water, skylines of sometimes empty buildings, expensive homes to be had just for the monthly payments, and thousands of laid-off workers. Now, I'm no cowboy; I pitch horseshoes for a living, but I don't ride these broncos. I understand, though, that cowboys have a term for the most dangerous and cunning bronco of all, and they call it a sunfisher. And those broncos will rebel against a rider by adopting a motion not unlike the sunfish: a full-force leap into the air, back arched high, flank twisting the rider to the left, head and upper torso twisting the rider to the right in an attempt to tear him apart. And let me suggest that not so many months ago, the whole State of Texas, our State, felt like it had been on just such a ride. But strong men and women are challenged by adversity, and I believe Texas has proven that. And there may be a few more bumps and bruises ahead, but make no mistake: Texas is back—back in the saddle, strong in every way.

State unemployment has dipped to its lowest level in 4 years, signaling, I think, the diversification of the Texas economy. In 1970 the energy sector accounted for nearly 25 percent of State output—25 percent. And last year it accounted for 11.4 percent. And yet Texas has more than regained the 208,000 jobs it lost from 1986 to 1987, with employment in plastics and aviation, electronics, space, and computer programming leading the way. More people are at work in Texas today than ever before in our history. And the Dallas-Fort Worth Metroplex leads in defense and aviation and technology; Houston in space and biomedical research; Austin, microelectronics. Another sign that Texas is becoming a world center of technology is the selection of Ellis County as the site of the Superconducting Supercollider. And when built, the SSC will enable us to study elemental particles with names like quarks and mesons and neutrinos—sounds like a breakfast cereal that these grandkids of ours are into these days.

But as Tom Luce, chairman of the Texas National Research Laboratory Commission, said: "With a little imagination, you can conclude that future research in the field of high energy could some day help us conquer cancer or discover a way to boost the amount of information on a microchip or answer questions that eluded Einstein, giving us a glimpse of the forces that bind the universe together." The SSC is a key to understanding nature and to developing the technologies and industries of the 21st century. Let me assure you: I will back the construction of the SSC because it is good for the entire United States of America. And let me also salute you, the members of the Texas house and senate, and the voters of this State, for having the vision to take an early lead on this project. Texas got its act together and made an outstanding presentation early on.

Still, no matter how diversified and high tech that we become, a strong domestic energy industry is important, still important, to the future of this State and, in my view, to the future of all America. I find it disturbing that nearly 50 percent of America's oil is imported. This is not good for the national security of the United States of America. And now some are questioning the future of America's energy production in the aftermath of the wreck of the *Exxon Valdez* off Alaska. I am as concerned as anyone, as all Americans are, by the environmental tragedy in Prince William Sound. We're using Federal resources intelligently to clean it up. We're working with industry to develop an improved plan in the event of a future spill. But shutting down our domestic energy production is no answer and would merely increase our dependence on foreign oil. We must, and we will, maintain a strong domestic energy industry.

To reduce our dependence on foreign oil, we must return to high levels of exploratory drilling. I propose to stimulate domestic drilling with tax credits and other incentives. We need more research—this isn't just a function of the Government, incidentally—but we need more research to learn how to recover more of our secondary and tertiary oil. And I want to do something else. Texas has a 65-year supply of one of the cleanest forms of energy known to man: natural gas. And I call on the United States Congress, at long last, to fully decontrol natural gas. And I believe that's going to happen soon.

We need a national energy policy that relies not only on oil but on other sources as well. I believe we can and must use safe nuclear power. I believe that coal has a bright future. And you know my confidence in natural gas. As we all become increasingly concerned about the need for clean air, we must look more to natural gas and to nuclear power. We must press forward with clean-coal technology, and we must produce more of our corn crop to produce—switch more of our corn crop to produce ethanol; more of our natural gas to produce methanol. And the greater use of these alternate fuels will rapidly improve the air quality of our most heavily polluted cities. And I'm talking about Los Angeles, Denver; I'm talking about Houston, Texas, and other heavily impacted areas.

I know there are still a few dark clouds remaining on our economic horizon. I know that you're concerned about the continuing crisis in many of the savings and loan institutions. And I've asked for measures to restore these institutions to financial health.

And I've asked for $37 million in 1989 funds for the Justice Department so that those who willfully abuse the trust of the small savers can expect to be pursued, tried, and, if guilty, put into prison. We must go after the white-collar criminal in this country as well as the others. The United States Senate has acted expeditiously on the savings and loan bill that I put forward—strong support on both sides of the aisle, Democrats and Republicans alike. And I now call on the House of Representatives to pass a responsible savings and loan bill as soon as possible.

Texas, like all America, faces many challenges. But I believe that by working together, as Republicans and Democrats, as Federal and as State officials, we can lick any problems down the path. Federalism works; federalism works because of your leadership and your initiative. The old dictum of the best government being that which is closest to the people applies here, right here in this chamber, right here in Austin, Texas—right here at the Capitol. True, some problems of the recent past linger on. Some areas of the State are recovering more slowly than others.

But the way is clear to a future as bright and promising as the blue Texas sky: a new reliance on a diversified economy and the technologies of the next century. And this is the secret of the Texas turn around, and its unfolding is a tribute not just to the entrepreneurial spirit of Texans themselves but to the leadership of Governor Clements, Senators Gramm and Bentsen, the congressional delegation, and the men and women of the Texas legislature. Texas is starting to feel like its old self again. And there's a feeling now that anything is possible. I'm not standing here trying to underestimate the problems of education or health or urban blight, but there is a new feeling abroad. Who knows, the Astros might win in the National League, and, yes, under enlightened new leadership—*[laughter]*—the Texas Rangers might even win in the American League. Good luck!

Seriously, as we face our future in the White House, Barbara and I take with us memories of people and places from a State that has been home for most of our lives—all of my adult life, if you will. We remember those 12 years in west Texas. It's a dry heat. You don't feel it—[*laughter*]—my eye! We were there for 12 years. But the people—I feel their strength and fierce independence to this very day. And I remember driving the kids across Texas. We moved down from west Texas down to the gulf coast, slowing down to take in the fields of the blue bonnets and Indian paintbrush. I don't think you can drive through that country without thinking of yourself as a naturalist or an environmentalist, or at least counting your blessings. And I remember the people of Houston, many of them mature and skeptical, but who nonetheless listened to a very green young man and sent him to Congress in 1966. And I remember Lyndon Johnson at his ranch back in 1969, when I went over there—an elder Democrat, retired from the Presidency, giving neighborly advice to a young Republican, while his very special Lady Bird held out her hand in hospitality.

Barbara and I treasure these 41 years as Texans—the sights and sounds of our adult lifetime, the trust of many friends, and the love of a family. And all this and more we remember when we think of home.

You know, I've been thinking about it. Ann Richards was right. [*Laughter*] Why do you think that I said we could cancer conquer? [*Laughter*] Look, I kept putting that silver foot in my mouth—[*laughter*]—all along the way. But the bottom line is when they ask, "Where's George?", say he's in Austin, among friends. And I'm very proud to be back. Thank you all. God bless you. And God bless the United States of America.

Note: The President spoke at 4:35 p.m. in the house chamber of the State Capitol. He was introduced by Gib Lewis, speaker of the house of representatives. In his closing remarks, the President referred to State treasurer Ann Richards, who spoke at the 1988 Democratic national convention. Following his remarks, the President traveled to Miami, FL.

Statement on the Death of Lucille Ball
April 26, 1989

Lucille Ball possessed the gift of laughter, but she also embodied an even greater treasure: the gift of love. She appealed to the gentler impulses of the human spirit. She was not merely an actress or comedienne; she was "Lucy," and she was loved. I want to extend my deepest sympathy to the family of Lucille Ball. Their loss is immeasurable, but so is her legacy of laughter. It is timeless. It spans the generations.

No television program in history was better named than "I Love Lucy". Mrs. Bush joins me in mourning the death of this legendary figure. We, too, loved Lucy; so did the world.

Remarks at the International Drug Enforcement Conference in Miami, Florida
April 27, 1989

And let me, at the outset, pay my respects to Governor Martinez, the Governor of Florida, who's with me here today, with all of us here—and Senator Connie Mack, vitally interested, as is the Governor, in the war against drugs. And of course, my great respects to the Attorney General, who is taking a very prominent leadership role in this common fight. And it's a pleasure to see—out of Alaska for a change—the Commandant of the Coast Guard, Paul Yost, who is doing an outstanding job half a world away up there in Alaska, but whose organization is doing such a superb job for the United States in this whole concept of interdiction. And so, we have a distinguished group here.

"This scourge will stop." Those were the words that Dick alluded to; those were the words with which I opened my Presidency. And it's the continuation of that promise that brings me to Miami today. And I am honored to be here to talk with you. And I am very grateful to Jack Lawn and the—whose head of the, as you all know, head of the DEA—and the other distinguished enforcement chiefs who have come throughout the Americas, along with our friends and observers from Europe, to join forces in a new tradition of international cooperation. And I had a visit just a second ago with Jack—just took a minute, but he was filling me in on his hopes for this conference and telling me of the cooperation that his organization was receiving from all of you. And so, let me, at the outset, say thank you.

I'm here today to talk about war: first, to see cocaine trafficking for what it is—an attack aimed at enslaving and exploiting the weak; second, to confront what's become a world war; and third, I hope to help end a nasty chapter in that war—the diversion of precursor chemicals.

In the 19th century, the scourge of the Americas was slavery, a struggle of good and evil in which some sought to enrich themselves by enslaving the most downtrodden of their countrymen. Today the scourge of this hemisphere is called cocaine. As commanding officers, you know the havoc of which we speak. You see it every day on the streets of your cities and in mountain villages, in the haunted eyes and the broken dreams of a generation of youth, of children who have fallen victim to a seductive, nightmarish new form of dependency and slavery. Our countries have suffered a terrible toll, many far worse than the United States.

Drug traffic is called the world's second most dangerous profession. The most dangerous really is yours, law enforcement, drug enforcement. Earlier this year, I had a glimpse of what must be all too familiar to many of you sitting around this table. I joined Mrs. Everett Hatcher to grieve for the death of her husband, a veteran DEA agent who was executed by cocaine cowards in the back streets of New York. A woman of considerable dignity, she put responsibility for Mr. Hatcher's death squarely on those once naively excused as casual users of cocaine. Well, cocaine users can no longer claim noncombatant status. There is blood on their hands. And thanks in part to the demand-side programs like those you're going to be talking about later this morning, this message has begun to sear the consciences of the stockbrokers and the students, the lawyers and the homemakers and the athletes who finance our common enemy.

There are many ironies. Drug addiction does not discriminate against a person because of race, religion, or financial status. It's the great equalizer, sharing sons and daughters of the rich, the poor, the middle class. Sometimes the opposite occurs, and kingpins are reduced to paupers. The opulence of Carlos Lehder's lifestyle is but memory now, as he begins his journey to the grave—life without parole—in an Illinois penitentiary. The notorious Felix Gallardo, once boasting of his power and wealth, is also behind bars in Mexico. Stripped of blood money, they are nobodies, no longer the stuff of myth.

Your business, then—our business—is to pursue these outlaws to the ends of the Earth, to create a world without refuge, to leave no sanctuary, in your countries or in mine. And I've said it before: The war on drugs is no metaphor. We've been slower to recognize that it is also a world war, leaving no nation unscathed, one in which Hong Kong bankers and Bolivian growers and Middle Eastern couriers and west coast wholesalers all play insidious roles. And it is especially acute in this hemisphere, where an explosive cycle of drugs, dependency, and dollars has escalated clear out of control.

The time for blame—the time for assigning blame is behind us. For too long, a sharp divide has been drawn between producing and consuming nations. Well, denial is a natural part of human nature, and probably part of a country's nature as well. But let's face it; Americans cannot blame the Andean nations for our voracious appetite for drugs. Ultimately, the solution to the United States drug problem lies within our own borders—stepped-up enforcement, but education and treatment as well. And our Latin American cousins cannot blame the United States for the voracious greed of the drug traffickers who control small empires at home. Ultimately, the solution to that problem lies within your borders.

And yet good neighbors must stand together. A world war must be met in kind. And so, today, as this conference winds down and concludes, we are presented with an historic opportunity. Allies in any war must consult—as partners. And just as you have gathered on seven occasions for IDEC, I ask that the leaders of the Western Hemisphere, whose nations are afflicted by this scourge, join with me to work together toward a hemispheric compact on drugs, a mutual commitment of resources and energy to ensure a brighter day for the children of America. And I mean by that all the Americas. And I have directed that our nation's new drug czar, William Bennett, take the lead in coordinating this vital initiative.

IDEC demonstrates that we will put aside national differences to do what must be done. And together you have put cartels out of business, reduced the supply of cocaine, and increasingly educated our children about the dangers of drug use and trafficking. And I do commend Jack Lawn and each of you for having the foresight to establish this organization and for demonstrating the collective commitment to work together.

I've spoken often of the horrors of chemical warfare. Well, chemical abuse is also chemical warfare, poisoning our streets, as deadly as mustard gas. And today we're opening a new campaign to rid the world of these toxics. We're going to start right here in the United States, because all too often that's the original source of the basic industrial chemicals needed to produce cocaine. Now, U.S. chemical companies are justly proud of their products that vastly improve and help to extend life here and abroad. But few Americans are aware that illegally diverted barrels of dangerous chemicals—clearly marked with U.S. corporate logos—are routinely seized in the jungles of Colombia. IDEC held a panel discussion this Tuesday. And those gathered here—you understand its importance. Traffickers have hit us where it hurts. And now we're going to exploit their vulnerabilities, crimping the flow of the materials without which they cannot produce—no chemicals, no cocaine.

We know it works in the field. Many of you participated in IDEC Six, the operations last August, when the combined efforts of 30 nations saw the seizure of 155,000 pounds of highly flammable ether, almost 450,000 pounds of acetone, over 50,000 pounds of hydrochloric acid, and nearly 14,000 pounds of MEK. This past January, Colombian antinarcotics officers under General Muñoz Sanabria, who I understand is here today—is he? I hope—congratulations, General, for that, and thank you for what you're doing for all of us in that regard. They destroyed 25 cocaine laboratories and enough chemicals to make approximately 88 metric tons of cocaine.

The damage that's done when 88 tons of cocaine hits the United States streets is pretty obvious. What's not so well understood is the widespread environmental damage that precursor chemicals wreak when they are dumped in the forests of the Amazon Basin. One of today's delegates, the director of narcotics enforcement for Peru's national police, has told the DEA that as much as 175,000 pounds of sulfuric acid is dropped into the tributaries of the Upper Huallaga Valley each year. And anyone concerned about the legacy of defoliation in Southeast Asia ought to go see what illegally diverted chemicals are beginning to do the Andes right now.

Nor are these chemical timebombs unique to South America. The problem here is so severe that last year's drug bill authorized funds for the Environmental Protection Agency to clean up hazardous waste at clandestine U.S. drug labs. In January, DEA task force agents busted a heavily armed houseboat located on California's Sacramento River. And the lab—here it was, right on the Sacramento River—had been dumping hydrochloric acid and other raw waste directly into the water, within splashing distance of swimming kids and within casting distance of those out there fishing for salmon or stripers or whatever. And so, today I pledge to you that the United States will lead the fight against illicit shipments of precursor chemicals. And I have asked Dick Thornburgh, our able Attorney General, to take a principal role in this new effort.

By and large, the chemical industry has supported us. Let's be clear: We have been getting good support from most of the chemical industry. And as a result of last year's omnibus drug law, regulations are not being drafted to tighten controls on the chemicals needed to refine cocaine. And we are dedicating the resources necessary to the task. Whatever needs to be done will be done.

Of course, unilateral action by us is not going to solve this problem. And that's why we commend those governments, like Venezuela and Colombia, that have already adopted strict chemical controls. And we urge other nations to do so quickly, as well as to approve the landmark U.N. Convention, which includes precursor chemical controls.

You know, many U.S. companies, including some chemical companies, have long recognized how drug abuse threatens productivity, corporate image, and ultimately profits. And many in the American corporate community have donated countless hours and millions of dollars to stopping drug abuse. My Miami son, our son living here in Miami, Jeb, talks about the successful Business Against Drugs program right here in Miami. The American people are proud of these efforts, and I can tell you, our visitors from other countries, that breaking out all across this country are new such efforts, efforts by civilians, just plain concerned parents—others all around the country beginning to come together in their communities to join in this fight.

Industry has got to do more, and I hope that parents' groups and stockholders are listening today. We should demand that United States corporations act responsibly and that they not tolerate their chemicals ending up in criminal hands. We would like to see U.S. chemical manufacturers demonstrate their courage and civic responsibility by entering into a true partnership with our government as we try to stop narcotics at the source. These companies can make an important contribution to our nation's fight against illegal drugs. They should make it their job to join in. No one—not parents, not churches, not bankers, and certainly not chemical makers—can afford to be a.w.o.l. in the war on drugs.

With so many cultures represented right here in this room, it is inevitable that there are going to be differences. But we share at least one compelling experience. Wherever you call home—Bonn or Bogota or Boston—people around the world are beginning to hear the cries of the kids, the cries of our children, pleading with us to stop drugs. Here in Miami last month one elementary teacher told of a writing assignment that she gave to her sixth-grade kids in school. The topic was "If I Were In Charge Of The World." And every single one of these 36 children, those sixth-graders, wrote that they would get rid of drugs if they were in charge of the world. They'd get rid of those people who are breaking the law, and they would put more effective policemen on the streets.

My favorite speechwriter—I don't know how well-known he is in some of your countries, but he's well-known here—is a baseball great named Yogi Berra. And he's been kidded for describing the 1969 Mets as "overwhelming underdogs." Well, maybe that's not such a bad description for the good guys in the fight against drugs. Sure, tough challenges remain, but the children are with us, and the times are beginning to change—and Yogi's underdogs did win the World Series.

So, thank you for joining us here today; thank you all for coming to the United States. And please, tell your leaders, your Presidents, whoever else you need to have involved, that we are anxious to work with them. God bless you, and Godspeed in your noble work to save the children of the world. Thank you all very, very much.

Note: The President spoke at 9:55 a.m. in the Grand Ballroom at the Biscayne Bay Marriott Hotel. In his remarks, he referred to National Drug Control Policy Director William J. Bennett, and John C. Lawn, Administrator of the Drug Enforcement Administration.

Remarks at the Drug Command Coordination Control and Intelligence Center Dedication Ceremony in Miami, Florida
April 27, 1989

Commissioner Von Raab, my thanks to you, sir, for that warm introduction. My respects to Admiral Yost, who has not neglected the Coast Guard's significant role in interdiction, but has found time to take a crucial leadership role as we battle against the environmental disaster up thousands of miles away in Prince William Sound, where the Coast Guard has performed in a superb fashion. I'm delighted to see Admiral Kelso here, and of course, it is most appropriate that Dick Thornburgh, our outstanding Attorney General, be at my side today, as he was, along with the Commissioner, 2 or 3 days ago in California, where we were reviewing a site in a peaceful mountain area that had been taken over by a drug warlord in this country.

And the effort had been broken up by the cooperative efforts, some of which we see on display here today. And so, it's a pleasure, Dick, that you joined us once again. To my friend, Governor Martinez. I want to say to him I am grateful for the effort that Florida is putting into this effort. This war, this effort, will not be successful without the involvement of States and local communities and the private sector. And Bob Martinez has led the way and, I might say, ably assisted at the national level by Senator Gramm and Senator Mack, who are with us today, too. And I'd be remiss if I didn't single out two United States Congressmen—if I hurt feelings, sorry, I just missed you—but Congressman Bilirakis and Congressman Young, two of Florida's greats, are with us here today as well.

The dedication of this facility—I am privileged to have a part in that. And as I do, let me lay to rest just one popular misconception that's brought home to me by the drill we saw inside. You know, in this country, there's an image of a drug smuggler, some still think of as a grizzled character with some Hawaiian shirt, leather jacket, perhaps the long hair, beard tucked underneath an aviator's hat—beard tucked underneath his helmet from some secondhand shop—expected to be flying in a jump plane by the seat of his pants. And you know best, you here, how that popular image lacks reality. All too often, the drug smuggler is an excellent pilot or seaman, with a jet or an expensive boat equipped with the latest communications and other sophisticated equipment. In short, he has everything that drug money can buy. And junking an airplane at sea can just be the cost of doing business on one run.

To identify and interdict this new breed of sophisticated drug smugglers, we must do more than match the resources of the multibillion-dollar drug empire. And that's what we've done here, at C–3–I East, a nerve center in this war on drugs. Think of this as one of America's drug war situation rooms, as our early warning network against narcotics. This facility, jointly commanded by the U.S. Customs Service and the Coast Guard, is an important part of our grand strategy in the war on drugs. And from here, we will be able to detect, track, identify, and apprehend suspected smugglers operating vessels and aircraft. This is the second such facility to come on-line, joining one in Riverside, California, to guard more than 3,600 miles of our nation's southern flank. In time, this facility alone will watch the skies from Brownsville, Texas, to Puerto Rico and across the entire eastern seaboard.

Four years in planning and construction, this facility is dedicated to the principles of unity and cooperation, principles that are essential to repel the drug invasion of America. This facility provides the best example of how agencies will work together to wage the war on drugs. From this site, civilian and defense radars will work together, under the watchful eye of the Coast Guard and Customs duty officers, who will coordinate interception by Federal, State, and local law enforcement agencies—whether that means scrambling a jet fighter, Coast Guard cutter, speedboats guided by the Blue Lightning Strike Force.

America's response to airborne smuggling is especially dramatic, growing from a ragtag collection of twin-engine planes that were seized, in the first instance, from the smugglers into a highly sophisticated fleet of aircraft equipped with sensors designed for a unique law enforcement mission. And Customs has a fleet of chase planes and Black Hawk helicopters on loan from the Army. The Coast Guard operates Falcon jets with infrared sensors and interceptor radars just like those on the F–16. These are just some of the birds of prey that will relentlessly search the skies for drug smugglers.

As impressive as this high-tech effort is, it's only as effective as the men and women who manage it. And it is with this in mind that I salute those in the field, who are at risk every single day in the war against drugs. But I also want to salute the officers who will staff this post, for every technician in this room and this area knows that the lives of his colleagues will be on the line. This is a special responsibility that takes a special kind of courage.

Our purpose is simple and close to home: to keep drugs out of the lockers, the classrooms, and off the playgrounds of our schools; to redeem the children of America from the scourge of drugs. In the months and years ahead, you will count kilos of cocaine and mountains of marijuana seized from the ships and the planes. And you'll never know how many lives will be saved by your efforts. But never forget that saving lives is what this is all about; saving lives is exactly what you are doing.

So, Commissioner and Admiral, I thank you, and I salute from the bottom of my heart the men and women of Customs and the Coast Guard for all that they have done and for all that they will do. Thank you all, and God bless you. Thank you very much.

Note: The President spoke at 11:40 a.m. in front of the facility. In his opening remarks, he referred to William von Raab,

Commissioner of the U.S. Customs Service; Adm. Paul A. Yost, Commandant of the U.S. Coast Guard; and Adm. F.B. Kelso III, USN, commander in chief of the U.S. Atlantic Fleet. Prior to the ceremony, the President observed a simulated drug interdiction on the operations floor of the facility. Following his remarks, the President traveled to Clearwater, FL.

Remarks at the Dedication Ceremony for the Michael Bilirakis Alzheimer's Center in Palm Harbor, Florida
April 27, 1989

Thank you, Mike. Thank you very much for this warm welcome, and I am pleased to be here. Governor Martinez and Senator Mack and Congressman Bill Young, our neighboring Congressman from here, I'm just delighted to be here. And I want to congratulate Ed and Reverend Fresh and everybody else that has been instrumental, and so creative in this marvelous project that we're here to honor.

But first, I want to say how much Barbara and I treasure the friendship with your Congressman Mike Bilirakis and his lovely Evelyn. And in case you didn't know it, you're pretty lucky. And since we're in a wonderful health facility, I'll give you a report on the Silver Fox. She's doing very well. And so are the puppies, though I will be glad when they go on to their new owners. But, Evelyn and Mike, thank you for the warm welcome back.

I'm here today to really thank Mike for what he has done in this Thousand-Points-of-Light fashion and his private devotion in seeking support and solutions for Alzheimer's patients. And for his dedicated work, we are all very, very grateful. It's a special honor to be here on behalf of a cause that matters so deeply to so many.

Alzheimer's extracts a devastating toll on its victims and on those who love them. And by the time this century ends, more than one out of four Americans will be over 50 and will face some risk of being stricken with this disease. The Michael Bilirakis Alzheimer's Center is designed to care for Alzheimer's patients all the way from that original diagnosis to caring for them in their most difficult days. And this center will serve as a place of hope and a source of comfort until a cure is found. And while the disease may ravage its victims, it makes heroes and heroines, in my view, out of all who care for them. And while it challenges the very fabric of the family, it also demands a new strength—a strength in each other—that we might not have known we had.

But above all, this disease is a reminder of what ought to be the American birthright: that we should be able to live our lives as engaged, productive, and full participants in this community of citizens. In a nation that looks after its own, that birthright entails its own responsibility: that any definition of a successful life must include serving others. And that success is not, cannot, be measured by the sum of our possessions but by the good we do for others—and that whatever life and health and love we have within us, we must share with others.

Older Americans represent a phenomenal reserve of talent and experience—qualities that this country sorely needs. And so, even as I join you in dedicating a place of refuge and comfort for those stricken with this deadly disease, I would ask all of you who have health and determination to consider how much we gain when we give of ourselves.

In New York City—I'll never forget it; hearing about it from her—Barbara met with a group helping young Cambodians to learn English. And while she was there, an older lady told Barbara how desperately lonely she had been before she volunteered. And her eyes filled with tears at remembering it, and then her face lit up as she told my wife: "I've never been lonely a day since." Well, one person's need matches another's, and a wonderful thing happens. I always like to remember that there is no exercise better for the human heart than reaching down and lifting someone else up. The rest of your life really should be the best of your life.

At the Inaugural, which seems like months ago, but it wasn't that long ago—I keep getting reminded it was about 100 days ago—[*laughter*] I spoke of a new engagement in the lives of others. And today I challenge those of you who can to get involved and to stay involved. Find a place or an organization or someone else's life where you can make a difference. And so many of you here—I feel like I'm preaching to the choir—so many of you already have. Some of you do volunteer work at local hospitals or in one of the constellation of community groups in and around Palm Harbor. I understand a number of the people here today have been helping boys in trouble at the sheriff's youth ranch. And many of you at St. Mark's are donating your time to helping out on the Alzheimer's unit.

And to those of you who are making the lives of the less fortunate a little easier, I offer my admiration and my thanks. "The young know the rules," Oliver Wendell Holmes once said, "but the old know the exceptions." Many of you today already are exceptions—and exceptional. And I cheer you on, and I encourage you. And I thank you for what you do to help others.

Thank you. God bless you. And God bless the United States of America. Thank you very much.

Note: The President spoke at 2:11 p.m. in the courtyard of St. Mark Village, a senior citizen facility. In his opening remarks, he referred to Edgar E. Hutfliz II, executive director of St. Mark Village, and Rev. James H. Fresh, senior pastor of St. Mark Lutheran Church and chairman of the board of the village. Following his remarks, the President returned to Washington, DC.

Statement on the Presidential Elections in Panama
April 27, 1989

The people of Panama clearly yearn for a free and fair election on May 7th so that their country can again take its rightful place in this hemisphere's community of democratic nations. Only the threat of violence and massive fraud by the Noriega regime will keep the Panamanian people from realizing that aspiration for democracy.

Free and fair elections on May 7th, and respect for the results, can produce a legitimate government in Panama which will end that nation's political and economic crisis and international isolation. That is clearly what the people of Panama deserve and desire.

The Noriega regime promised that free and fair elections would in fact take place May 7th and that international observers would be permitted to observe them. In recent weeks, the Noriega regime has taken steps to commit systematic fraud. Through violence and coercion, it threatens and intimidates Panamanian citizens who believe in democracy. It is attempting to limit and obstruct the presence of observers from around the world and the ability of journalists to report freely on the election.

Nevertheless, many observers intend to travel to Panama to shine the spotlight of world opinion on the Panamanian elections just as they did previously in nations like the Philippines and El Salvador. We admire their commitment to democracy and their courage, and will fully support their efforts.

The days of rule by dictatorship in Latin America are over. They must end in Panama as well. There is still time for Panama to resolve its current crisis through free and fair elections. The people and Government of the United States will not recognize fraudulent election results engineered by Noriega. The aspirations of the people of Panama for democracy must not be denied.

Remarks to the American Legislative Exchange Council
April 28, 1989

Thanks for that welcome, and thank all of you for being here today. And, Representative Halbrook, Mr. Brunelli, and ladies and gentlemen, friends—Secretary Dole, who is doing an outstanding job for this administration, here she is—and of course sitting over my left shoulder, Deb Anderson, the former speaker out there in South Dakota—so, you'll have some kindred spirits here to talk to in the White House. And some of you may recognize Andy Card, who's our Deputy Chief of Staff, from Massachusetts—and also everybody performing so well.

But I'm delighted to once again meet with this group, one of our nation's largest organizations of State legislators and, in my view, one of the most sensible—[*laughter*]—but I'm entitled to my opinion on that. And congratulations on this marvelous turnout! And I also want to thank all of you for your past support and, really, for kind of keeping us together, everybody across the country—as best you can—the matrix, if you will, for traditional values.

Your "conservative in free enterprise agenda" is helping us return power to the people. And on issues like federalism, tax policy, education and, yes, the environment, you're helping keep our country number one. And you know, a politician once reminded me of the saying: "Problems are really opportunities in disguise." But then he added, laughing: "There are times I feel there are more opportunities running around in disguise than I really deserve." [*Laughter*] It's true. Problems can get the upper hand, and our task is to confront them, as you do daily, and turn them into opportunities that are real. And that means realizing that in terms of problemsolving Washington—unlike Robert Young—does not automatically know best.

And I have just come back from a swing that took me to the Texas—appearing before a joint session of the Texas legislature and then a marvelous, uplifting day in North Dakota and then several other events in California and Illinois and Florida. And it is a very important thing for a President to get outside the White House and move around this country. And some of the friends that were traveling with us didn't seem to understand that. But I can tell you, I learned a lot from it. [*Laughter*] And it was a good thing to do, and I'm going to keep doing that. But I learned from the legislators who are on the front line.

But cooperation between the public and private sectors, between the executive branch, Congress, and the States is vital. The one line—I readily confess I'm not the world's greatest orator—but the line in the Inaugural Address that seemed to evoke an instant response from the American people was that the people didn't send us here to bicker; they sent us here to get things done. And our problems are too severe for bickering. And we are seeing that kind of cooperation with the Hill. It's not going exactly the way I want it, but we've started off with some cooperation from the Congress. That bipartisan budget agreement you've read about is a good agreement. It reduces the deficit. It's going to narrow the deficit to $99.4 billion in the fiscal year. And that's coming down from $163 billion estimated for the current fiscal year. And I've said I like what works; this agreement works. And it's a very important step.

And I looked over my shoulder the other day to read how widespread the confidence was that we could reach this agreement 2 months ago, and I didn't find many voices thinking that this agreement could be achieved. So—it has been. And all of you know that at times you have to work with those that differ with you on issues to get something done.

And so, I like what works. But let's be clear—and I know all of you are interested in this—rough times lie ahead, rough go lies out there. Because though, ahead of schedule—we did meet the Gramm-Rudman taxes, and I kept that "no new taxes" pledge. But we still have a ways to go because we've got to move dramatically down in the next fiscal year to meet the Gramm-Rudman targets, which I'm determined to do. And that does mean we have to have fiscal restraint in a lot of areas where, very candidly, I wish we could do more. But we have set certain priorities in this budget agreement, and I'm happy with it.

You know, in America, nothing—I'm one who still believes—and I get kidded a little bit about it in the press—but I still am very optimistic about our country. And I believe that nothing is impossible. Craig Nettles, remember the former major leaguer, put it best. He says: "When I was a little boy, I wanted to be a baseball player and join the circus. With the Yankees, I've accomplished both." [*Laughter*]

Well, deficit reduction can help achieve our goals. It's going to lower interest rates—I'm confident—lift savings rates, and help business invest. And so will this second step I'm talking about that we must and can take together—and I really believe in this one—that an additional aspect of not just another budget agreement but a key to all of this, an additional step is restoring the capital gains differential. And I've heard, as you have, a lot of people criticizing cutting the capital gains tax, and jumping on everybody as a tax for the rich. It is not a tax for the rich when you separate that differential.

They just are wrong on the facts. Our plan—and I'm going to keep pushing it—supports reducing the capital gains differential to 15 percent on long-held assets, a step which, according to the Treasury, the estimators over there, will raise $4.8 billion in new revenue in fiscal year 1990. And lowering the capital gains rate and restoring the differential will encourage the savings and investment needed to create new jobs and reduce this budget deficit. It brings in revenue, and this is something that the critics simply are not willing to recognize. Ours is a struggle for a more prosperous America. We can win it, and I am determined that we will.

There's another struggle, and of course that's the one that I've been spending a fair amount of time on lately, feel strongly about, and that is one that everyone in this room is concerned about; and that's this war on drugs. And I've just returned from this 4-day trip, and in Los Angeles and Miami, particularly, I had experiences there and saw things there that just renewed my commitment to win this battle.

I told them that the scourge of drugs must stop, and it has got to. Two months ago, before a joint session of the Congress, I asked for an increase of $1 billion in budget outlays, bringing it up to nearly $6 billion in 1990. And that would be earmarked for escalating this war on drugs. Some money is going to be used to expand treatment to the poor, to addicted young mothers, and some money is going to be used to cut the waiting time for treatment. About a billion-one of this request is going for education. I still remain firmly convinced that we are going to win this fight on the demand side, on the education side. And because over 23 million Americans used illegal drugs last year, we've got to stop those who produce, buy, and traffic illegal drugs. And so, that means an all-out fight in law enforcement and backing up our local people as best we can in this. And of course, it means a renewed concentration on the interdiction side as well.

I've talked a lot about zero tolerance. Well, zero tolerance, I hope you all realize, is much more than just a catchword. It means, quite simply, if you do crime, you do time. And I think our law enforcement people really are out in front, with that very much in their mind. But they need to be backed up by some changes in the law. They need to be backed up in other areas—certain sentencing provisions in the law. And certainly, they need to be backed up by increasing the funding for Federal prisons. We want judges who strictly apply the law to the convicted offenders. And I want increased prison sentences for drug-related crimes. And I still am convinced that the death penalty for drug kingpins and those who commit drug-related murders will be an inhibition to future criminals.

My friends, I do believe that these actions will make America a safer place. But again, as in everything, we need your help. The Federal Government cannot do it alone. And that's why this week I've been talking about how the States and the localities can join in the crusade, because I am convinced that we can help America get clean and stay clean when it comes to these deadly narcotics. And I'm talking here really about cooperation, about America as one family and our role as family members.

The kind of a cooperation exists in a lot of areas. Incidentally, nobody—I think most people now know what I mean by the concept of a Thousand Points of Light. And when you get into this—they used to say—the wags around here—what he really means is a "thousand pints of Lite". But that's not what it is. It's a Thousand Points of Light. And you don't have to explain it anymore, because people understand that we are going to win this fight on drugs through a lot of local programs, a lot of community programs that I've been witnessing in the last few days and local law enforcement and State efforts. And it isn't all going to be done in Washington, DC.

But the kind of cooperation exists, I believe for another area; and that is our administration's new child-care initiative. And again, I salute [Secretary of Labor] Elizabeth Dole not only for this but for the sound position she has taken on many issues, including the minimum wage.

Let me just tell you on that one—we had a conference. I took her advice. And it was sound advice—that we do something that most of you all don't do. You fire your best. We fired our best shot and only shot, first. And we made it very clear to the Congress that I had made a commitment to raise the minimum wage, but we selected a prudent level, one that will not have deleterious inflationary effects. On the advice of my Secretary of Labor, we put in a 6-month training wage, which I strongly support—this minimum wage differential, we used to call it. And it is a good, sound package.

And now you see speculation on the Hill: Well, the President's going to cave in. He can't argue over a dime or 15 cents on this. And they are just as wrong as they can be. And I'm going to do it the way this Secretary told me. Both of us like our jobs and want to stick around. [*Laughter*] And so, we're going to do what we said we're going to do. And this may be a first: going up there with your best and only shot, first. But it's going to set a tone that I think will be important for the rest of our administration.

So, anyway, that exists—cooperation—maybe not on that one, but there does exist in child-care initiative. I feel strongly about that. We had a chance to talk with some of you all in the campaign about that one. Our proposal urges a new tax credit to make child care more affordable, starting for those who need it the most. And it puts money in the hands then of the low-income families. It limits the counterproductive Federal intervention with its long list of federally mandated regulations. And it increases options; it increases choice. And here we say: Let the parents decide. And I know Elizabeth agrees with me on this one, and Deb, too, and Andy and everybody. But the more you're in this area here of responsibility and all the areas that we have of Federal responsibility, the more important you realize is the underpinning of society that comes from the family. And I do not want to see one piece of legislation passed that diminishes the family choice or that weakens the family in any way, whether it's welfare legislation, child-care legislation, or whatever legislation.

The Federal role has got to be—when legislation is passed—to look at it to see that not only it doesn't weaken the family but if it can strengthen the family, as our child-care proposal does, by providing for alternate—groups getting together so a grandmother can maybe take care of one grandkid and then some other kids in the community—that's good. And we want to find ways to have it strengthen the family unit, and we want to leave the choice with the parent. So, any help you can give us on this concept, we really would appreciate it.

We unveiled an education program, incidentally, which does parallel many of your suggestions that we've gotten in. We want to reward achievement, demand accountability, and spur again flexibility and choice. And we support also alternative certification. This is a concept that really is in your hands more than mine as President of the United States. But somehow, it seems to me a little antiquated, a little out-of-date, that a physicist who wants to take a sabbatical leave and help in some elementary physics class in a public school, would be denied the ability to help out because of some antiquated certification rules. So, I would urge you who are on the cutting edge of local legislation and State legislation to back us as best you can in working towards this alternative certification.

We've also put forward a program to award the best teachers in every State—and again, the emphasis being the pursuit of excellence is central to America. And the Federal Government's going to help. We're going to lead in terms of setting objectives, but we are a partner in this question of education and in all these other issues. For America's genius—and I feel this one very strongly at the end of, or maybe it's 99 days, as opposed to 100—but America's genius doesn't lie solely, or even mostly, in Washington. It is out across the country.

And so, I wanted to come over here and wish you all well. Thank you for what you do. You know, Will Rodgers once said: "I love a dog. He does nothing for political purposes." [*Laughter*] Well, let's, too, rise above politics as we go to serve the public and build a better, more decent, more prosperous land. I am very excited about that prospect. I think things are going reasonably well. There are plenty of problems out there, but so what's new? If I start telling you mine, you'll tell me yours, and yours are going to be closer to the people you represent just by the nature of your jobs. So, let's just agree that we live in the greatest country in the world, and we can make things happen.

And thank you all very much for being here today.

Note: The President spoke at 11:28 a.m. during a briefing in Room 450 of the Old Executive Office Building. In his remarks, he referred to David Halbrook, chairman of the board of directors of the council; Samuel Brunelli, executive director of the council; Debra R. Anderson, Deputy Assistant to the President and Director of the Office of Intergovernmental Affairs, and actor Robert Young.

Remarks on Signing the Executive Order on Historically Black Colleges and Universities
April 28, 1989

First, my respects to our two Secretaries here today, Secretary Cavazos, our Secretary of Education; Secretary Sullivan of HHS; and to our special guests, all of you fit that description; and particularly to the presidents and supporters of a noble educational tradition who honor us with their presence this afternoon. All of you, welcome to the Rose Garden.

Graduations are coming up, and I know you're looking forward to the free advice you'll get from the parents. I suggest the response of one English schoolmaster: "If you promise not to believe everything your child says happens at this school, I'll promise not to believe everything he says happens at home." [*Laughter*]

For over 100 years, the historically black colleges and universities have been a special part of our heritage. At a time when many schools barred their doors to black Americans, these colleges offered the best, and often the only opportunity for a higher education. And today, thank heavens, most of those barriers have been brought down by the law. And yet historically black colleges and universities still represent a vital component of American higher education, enriching a great tradition of educational choice and diversity in this country. As one educator put it: "We must see that every child has an equal opportunity to become different, to realize their unique potential of body, mind, and spirit."

Nine days before I became President, a number of you met with me across the way in the EOB to discuss new ways to ensure that every black child has that chance. Several of your colleagues—Gloria Scott and Van Payton, Leroy Keith come to mind. They asked that, first and foremost, the administration establish an advisory committee to make sure that your voices continue to be heard. It was a sound idea and one that I am pleased to put into effect in a few moments when the new Executive order I'm signing creates the President's Board of Advisors on Historically Black Colleges and Universities. Staffed by the Department of Education, this new board will assist Secretary Cavazos in developing annual plans to increase participation by your schools in federally sponsored programs. It also guarantees that each of you, every president of a historically black college or university, be given an opportunity to comment on these plans before they reach my desk in the Oval Office. We will continue to listen. Your voices must and will be heard.

As many here have requested, today's order also incorporates the most useful provisions of its predecessor. But more importantly, it contains new initiatives that will increase the private sector role in ensuring the long-term viability of the distinctive institutions that you represent. Now, that's just bureaucratese for the volunteer spirit, a tradition of helping one's neighbors well-known to black Americans. This tradition was perhaps best exemplified by Bill and Camille Cosby's singular gift to Spellman last fall. The New York Times called the Cosby donation "as much a challenge as a gift." Well, we're trying to sweeten that challenge. Some of you reminded me in January that perhaps the most important support that the Government can provide is through incentives to increase endowments. And that's why we have requested a total of $60 million during the next 4 years over and above the existing programs for endowment matching grants for the special schools you represent.

They say the universities usual state can be summed up by the lady who noted, "I have enough money to last me the rest of my life, unless I buy something." Well, the new endowments program represents a commitment to the long-term. It's not a quick fix, and it's flexible, producing new contributions and ultimately new income, permitting each of your schools to decide where its money is best spent. These budget proposals, like the new advisory committee, our support for the crimes bill, and the appointment of capable officials like Lauro Cavazos and Lou Sullivan, are but another part of this administration's commitment to see that the promise of the civil rights movement—a fair society for all Americans—becomes real.

In that regard, I know that Dick Thornburgh, our Attorney General, and our nominee to head the Civil Rights Division, Bill Lucas, are unshakeable in their commitment to equal rights and to the vigorous enforcement of the laws which guarantee those rights to all Americans.

And finally, it doesn't do much good to educate our young people if they can't get good jobs when they get out. They need work opportunities while still students, which can also provide another way to help finance their education. By this order, we also direct that the Office of Personnel Management, working together with Secretary Cavazos and Secretary Dole, our Secretary of Labor, develop a program to improve recruitment of your students for part-time and summer positions in the Federal Government. America needs and wants their creativity, their talent, their diversity.

We've just returned from a journey across this great country, from Florida, North Dakota, to Texas—California, Virginia—something like 7,500 miles in less than 4 days. And as we circled the continent, I thought of the coming commencements at the schools across our land. And it is a time of new beginnings for those kids—new dreams. And they are exciting times for all young Americans, and especially, I think, for those black Americans—those young kids that you have nurtured with a wonderful education. Out of a century that began with their people still bound by the remnants of slavery, this generation is emerging into a time rich with opportunities unimaginable to their grandparents. And you and the teachers—oh, God bless the teachers that work with you—are the fulfillers of your students' dreams and of your nation's destiny.

And so, bless you in your mission. And now, with great pleasure and really a great sense of personal pride, I want to sign this Executive order to launch these new initiatives, recognizing it is only a beginning. I think it's a good one. I want to work with you. God bless you all.

Note: The President spoke at 2:10 p.m. in the Rose Garden at the White House. In his remarks, he referred to Gloria Scott, president of Bennett College, in Greensboro, NC; Benjamin F. Payton, president of Tuskegee Institute, in Tuskegee AL; and Leroy Keith, president of Morehouse College, in Atlanta, GA. The Executive order is listed in Appendix E at the end of this volume.

The President's News Conference
April 28, 1989

Well, I have a brief statement that I'd like to read. And then at the end of this, why, experts will be available to take your questions.

I'm pleased to announce that the Governments of the United States and Japan have reached understandings that will allow us to proceed with joint development of the FSX fighter aircraft. I'm ready to submit the FSX agreement to Congress for its review.

We've been conducting talks with the Japanese to clarify both sides' understandings of this agreement. I'm convinced that the codevelopment of this aircraft is in the strategic and commercial interests of the United States. And we weighed this matter from the standpoint of trade, of our industrial growth, and technology transfer, as well as strategic and foreign policy considerations.

This aircraft will improve the basic F–16 design and will contribute to the security of the United States and our major ally, Japan. There will be no cost to the American taxpayer, and at the same time, the Japanese will improve their ability to carry their share of the defense burden. The U.S. will have a 40-percent work share in the initial development stage of this aircraft, and we will have a similar share when the aircraft goes into production.

We did have several initial concerns about the agreement, but I want to assure you that sensitive source codes for the aircraft's computer will be strictly controlled, access will be granted to only those codes that are essential to complete the project.

In conclusion, the United States is the world's leader in aircraft manufacturing. I believe this aircraft will improve the defense of the United States and Japan, and this agreement also helps preserve our commitment that U.S. aerospace products of the future will continue to dominate the world markets.

That's the end of the statement, and thank you all very much.

Note: The President's 11th news conference began at 4:55 p.m. in the Briefing Room at the White House.

Remarks at the Bicentennial Celebration of George Washington's Inauguration in New York, New York
April 30, 1989

Thank you, Senator, and Chief Justice Burger, Secretary Lujan, Ambassador Pickering, Archbishop Iakovos, Senators Moynihan and Lautenberg, and Mayor Koch, fellow citizens of the United States. Two centuries ago, standing here, a man took an oath before a new nation and the eyes of God—an oath that I, like 40 before me, have since had the privilege to take. Everyone here today can still feel the pulse of history, the charge and power of that great moment in the genesis of this nation. Here the first Congress was in session, beginning a tradition of representative government that has endured for 200 years. Here the representatives of 13 Colonies struggled to find balance, order, and unity between them. And here our first President issued a solemn address.

One who was there wrote: "This great man was agitated and embarrassed more than ever he was by the leveled cannon or pointed musket. He trembled and, several times, could scarce make out to read." Well, as Representative Boggs pointed out, who wouldn't have felt some trepidation, undertaking a task which has never been tried in the world's history?

And on that day, Washington spoke of his conflict of emotions. He admitted his anxieties and deficiencies, as honest men will. But then, as his first official act, he turned to God fervently for strength. For he knew that the advancement of America, while it might rely on its Presidents, would surely depend on providence.

How unlikely it must have seemed then that we might become united States—how uncertain that a Republic could be hewn out of the wilderness of competing interests! How awesome the prospect must have seemed to the man charged with guiding the new Republic made possible by his leadership in battle.

But George Washington defined and shaped this office. It was Washington's vision, his balance of power and restraint as he watched over the Constitutional Convention in 1787, that gave the delegates enough confidence to vest powers in a Chief Executive unparalleled in any freely elected government, before or since. It was Washington's vision, his balance, his integrity that made the Presidency possible. The Constitution was, and remains, a majestic document. But it was a blueprint, an outline for democratic government, in need of a master builder to ensure its foundations were strong. Based on that document, Washington created a living, functioning government. He brought together men of genius, a team of giants, with strong and competing views. He harnessed and directed their energies. And he established a precedent for 40 Presidents to follow.

For all of the turmoil and transformation of the last 200 years, there is a great constancy to this office and this Republic. So much of the vision of that first great President is reflected in the paths pursued by modern Presidents.

Today we reaffirm ethics, honor, and strength in government. Two centuries ago, in his first Inaugural Address, Washington spoke of a government "exemplified by all the attributes which can win the affections of its citizens and command the respect of the world." Today, we say that leaders are not elected to quarrel but to govern. On that spring day in 1789, Washington pledged that "no party animosities will misdirect the comprehensive and equal eye which ought to watch over this great assemblance of communities and interests."

Today, we seek a new engagement in the lives of others, believing that success is not measured by the sum of our possessions, our positions, or our professions, but by the good we do for others. Two hundred years ago today, Washington said there exists "in the economy and course of nature, an indissoluble union between virtue and happiness, between duty and advantage." And so, today we speak of values. At his inauguration, Washington said that "the foundations of our national policy will be laid in the pure and immutable principles of private morality." And over the last 200 years, we've moved from the revolution of democracy to the evolution of peace and prosperity.

But so much remains constant; so much endures: our faith in freedom—for individuals, freedom to choose, for nations, self-determination and democracy; our belief in fairness—equal standards, equal opportunity, the chance for each of us to achieve, on our own merits, to the very limit of our ambitions and potential; our enduring strength—abroad, a strength our allies can count on and our adversaries must respect, and at home, a sense of confidence, of purpose, in carrying forward our nation's work.

My starting point has been a respect for American institutions—for Congress, and I salute the members of the House and Senate with us today; for the judiciary, and through Chief Justice Burger, I pay my respects to the judiciary; for the executive branch, represented here today by Secretary Lujan and Ambassador Pickering; and for government at all levels—and a firm belief in maintaining the powers of the Presidency. The Presidency, then as now, in oath and in office, derives from the strength and the will of the people.

George Washington, residing at Mount Vernon, felt himself summoned by his country to serve his country—not to reign, not to rule, but to serve. It was the noblest of impulses because democracy brought a new definition of nobility. And it means that a complete life, whether in the 18th or 20th century, must involve service to others. Today, just as Washington heard the voice of his country calling him to public service, a new generation must heed that summons; more must hear that call.

And today we stand—free Americans, citizens in an experiment of freedom that has brought sustained and unprecedented progress and blessings in abundance. As we dedicate a museum of American constitutional government, let us together rededicate ourselves to the principles to which Washington gave voice 200 years ago. Let our motivation derive from the strength and character of our forefathers, from the blood of those who have died for freedom, and from the promise of the future that posterity deserves. Let us commit ourselves to the renewal of strong, united, representative government in these United States of America.

God bless you, and may God forever bless this great nation of ours. Thank you all very, very much.

Note: The President spoke at 12:53 p.m. outside of Federal Hall. In his remarks, he referred to Senator Alfonse M. D'Amato; Warren Burger, former Chief Justice of the Supreme Court; Thomas R. Pickering, Ambassador to the United Nations; Archbishop Demetrios A. Iakovos of the Greek Orthodox Archdiocese of North and South America; Senators Daniel P. Moynihan and Frank Lautenberg; and Edward Koch, mayor of New York City. Following his remarks, the President returned to Washington, DC.

Remarks to the United States Chamber of Commerce
May 1, 1989

Thank you, ladies and gentlemen. I want to thank Bill Kanaga for those kind words and commend you on the fine job that you've done as chairman. And I also want to congratulate the chamber's incoming chairman, John Clendenin, and of course say hello to the chamber's long-time president, media star—[*laughter*]—household word around DC, Dick Lesher. What a job he does for the chamber!

And I also want to thank the chamber for providing me a chance to deliver a May Day message, American style. On May Day, I always think about the celebration in the Soviet Union—all those red banners, the big military parade. Even the Economic Planning Ministry had a unit in the parade: 200 economists marching along yelling, "May Day! May Day!" [*Laughter*] Today that is beginning to change. Even the Socialist world is beginning to see that socialism isn't just another economic system: it's the death of economics. And there is a new breeze blowing. Nations the world over are coming to realize and recognize that free enterprise is the wave of the future, and that's a promising forecast for prosperity and for world peace.

In the United States—let me just say in that regard, though, whenever in the world there is economic reform, the United States should be hoping that that reform succeeds. Economic reform, with its emphasis on incentive and market economics, leads to more freedom. You know, I made clear to Mr. Gorbachev up there in New York—Governors Island, when we met—that we wanted to see *perestroika* succeed in the Soviet Union. And likewise, we want to see success for the economic reforms in China. Incentive, economic reforms, market economies, private ownership are indeed replacing Socialist dogma in many countries, large and small. And that is an exciting trend, and in my view, it will continue.

In the United States, the single most significant economic indicator of this decade is up today. We've enjoyed 77 full months of the longest peacetime economic expansion in American history. Without a doubt, this long-running economic expansion has been good for American business and for the American worker. In the past 77 months—and the chamber has been very helpful getting this message out—we've added nearly 20 million new jobs. And more Americans have moved up on the pay scale. Since 1982 the number of jobs paying less than $5 an hour is down 25 percent, while jobs paying $10 or more an hour have increased by 95 percent. Unemployment is at its lowest point in the past 15 years. During the economic expansion, America's industrial output is up 33 percent, overall growth up 26 percent. For those with an eye on the international competition, that's more than double Europe's industrial output growth. And the expansion has been just as good to the average American family. Per capita personal income is up 19 percent, and that's take-home, after-tax pay, adjusted for inflation. Real median family income has reached a new high, and that's quite an economic success story.

Our challenge now is to keep it going. We can, and we will. We've all heard the nay-sayers. I think there are a few out there whose predictions of economic disaster are now in their 78th straight month. [*Laughter*] And the nay-sayers are wrong. But why? What they've underestimated is the resilience, the remarkable responsiveness of the free enterprise system. And you can focus on government so long that you forget that it's the private sector that's home to the innovation and the economic creativity that powers this expansion.

I've been a small businessman, starting out with an idea and then working with others and building it into a successful business. And I know the risks and the rewards and the payoff in pride when you succeed. Entrepreneurs know this simple truth: nothing wagered, nothing won. And that's why I want a government that prompts entrepreneurs to take risks, not a government that forces them to take refuge. That doesn't mean that government's only job is simply to stand back and step out of the way. There's plenty for the Government to do to make sure commerce is free and fair and to maintain a climate where free enterprise can take place and prosper.

And today the Federal Government's number one economic priority is dealing with the deficit. We've made a good start. The budget agreement Congress and my administration concluded 2 weeks ago can keep the Federal deficit below the Gramm-Rudman target. And we haven't sacrificed our social or national security responsibilities in the progress. The budget level we've agreed on will allow us to discharge the critical duties of government. We'll be able to provide for our national security, meet the needs of the disadvantaged, and fund high-priority programs.

Our agreement is a first, important step. It sends a signal to the American people and to our trading partners: We're serious about getting that deficit down. And the deficit is coming down not only in straight dollar terms but as a percentage of our annual gross national product. You know, by the end of this fiscal year, we will have cut the deficit in half, from 6.3 percent of gross national product in 1983 to an estimated 3.1 percent in 1989. I urge the two Houses of Congress to pass the bipartisan budget resolution so we can keep the deficit coming on down.

One word more about the budget agreement for 1990. We've agreed to $5.3 billion in new revenues as part of the deal. And let me say a word about that $5.3 billion. I mean to live by what I've said: no new taxes. And let me tell you what my favorite source of new revenue is—three guesses for this crowd. We don't have to raise taxes; we have to release the energies of free enterprise. In a growing economy, tax revenues will take care of themselves. In fiscal 1990 alone, thanks to the expanding economic activity, the Treasury will take in more than $80 billion in increased revenues not through higher taxes but under the existing tax structure—$80 billion more in 1 year.

So, let's not be hunting for ways to wring another dollar in taxes out of our economy.

Let's concentrate on creating conditions for continued growth. And that's why I've called on Congress to restore the capital gains differential. I am absolutely convinced that in 1990 alone this step would bring an extra $4.8 billion into the Treasury, and that doesn't count increased economic activity that is spurred by a lower tax rate. That $4.8 billion is the lion's share of the $5.3 billion we need in the way of new revenues under our budget agreement.

Let's take a look at what our competitors are doing. Canada's maximum capital gains rate is about half of the U.S. rate. And how about Japan's rate? For entrepreneurs who built their businesses from scratch, a scant 1 percent. West Germany exempts all long-term capital gains on securities from any tax whatever. And the newly industrialized economies of the Pacific Rim—Singapore, Hong Kong, South Korea—have no capital gains tax at all. Among our competitors, those low rates contribute to low capital costs. Cutting our own capital gains rate would encourage productive investment in addition to generating the new revenues that we need to meet our deficit reduction agreement.

I think the case for a capital gains cut is a strong one, but there are several other economic issues that I want to discuss here today. First, a pressing problem with important consequences for our long-term fiscal health, and that is the S&L situation—savings and loan. This administration recognized the immediate need to take action to stabilize the S&L system, and less than 3 weeks after taking office, we proposed a comprehensive S&L reform plan, one designed to stop the dollar drain and deal with the insolvent thrifts and restore confidence in the S&L system. The Senate passed an S&L package with a resounding majority. I think it was 91–8. I urge the House to move quickly to give us the tools we need to reform the savings and loan system by passing my bill quickly, with its central provisions intact.

Now, I have a second message for the Congress as it debates an increase in the minimum wage. I've indicated my support for increasing the wage over 3 years to $4.25 an hour. I also want to establish a 6-month training wage for new workers at the current $3.35 rate and expand the exemption for minimum wage requirements for all small businesses with annual sales under a half a million dollars. It's time for those who want a higher wage to move out beyond the rhetoric and take a look at the consequences. We all know the studies that show that each 10-percent increase in the minimum wage will cost America between 100,000 and 200,000 jobs, and they're jobs for those who need them the most. What happens when minimum-wage workers open that pay envelope expecting a fatter paycheck and find a pink slip instead? An irresponsible increase in the minimum wage will cost jobs, as employers cut back to compensate for increased costs—$4.25 is as far as I can go. It is my first and final offer, and I repeat that here today.

We must guard against conferring benefits by government mandate and leaving employers to cope with the costs. I share your concerns about legislative efforts to mandate medical and parental leave. I also believe that choice in child care is best made by parents and not by government. And I know, because I've talked to Dick Lesher and others, that the Chamber supports the concept of choice. There are some child-care initiatives up on Capitol Hill—well-intentioned, I would readily concede—well-intentioned initiatives that would increase government intervention and crowd out parental choice.

You know, as I look at government, I feel an obligation to look at every piece of legislation to see that it strengthens rather than weakens the family unit in this country. Now, cost is yet another issue. We're determined to hold the line on government spending, so it is important that money allocated for child-care assistance goes for child-care assistance. Under the ABC bill, for example, much of the money would be used to set up another Federal bureaucracy instead of getting financial help directly to parents. The child-care tax credit initiatives that I've proposed do preserve choice, letting parents decide whether to place their child in the care of a relative or in a church-run center or in a public day care facility or in their own home. Let's let parents decide what's right for themselves.

And finally, I'll close with a brief comment on an issue I know is vital to those of you here today—vital, in fact, to all Americans in our evolving economy—and I'm talking about international trade. The global economy is a fact of life. It is no longer possible to draw a sharp line between domestic and international markets. This administration is committed to securing an open and fair world trading system because fair trade provides opportunities for America's competitiveness to come to the fore. We have the ingenuity to be preeminent. We have the drive to succeed. Entrepreneurs like you are our ace in the hole. Our challenge, then, is to make the most of this competitive edge.

And that's why we will work vigorously to break down barriers abroad while keeping markets open here at home. If any country, including the United States, is fooled into thinking that a closed market can be a prosperous one, they're wrong. Closed markets mean closed doors to opportunity, and that means less prosperity. The Chamber of Commerce has always stood for economic freedom, and I know you share my view that there is no surer route to prosperity and progress than the system of free enterprise.

The message of the past 77 months is clear: We can keep the economy strong, sustain the longest peacetime expansion in American history, and ensure America a prosperous and productive future, provided that government policies preserve the greatest possible freedom for American enterprise to innovate, to create, and to compete. I am pledged to those goals.

Thank you. God bless you all. And God bless the United States of America. Thank you all very much.

Note: The President spoke at 10:20 a.m. at DAR Constitution Hall.

Remarks at the Swearing-in Ceremony for Susan S. Engeleiter as Administrator of the Small Business Administration
May 1, 1989

The President. Well, welcome, Susan and family and Members of the United States Congress—delighted you all are here. You know, I'm glad that you all could come as Susan takes the oath as Administrator of SBA. This is a very special occasion for Susan and for her husband and for her kids here, and it is for me as well. I have a wonderful place in my heart for small business people, having been in that category myself. And I think because I once was, I do understand the challenges and the opportunities that face the smaller firms in this country.

As President, I certainly understand, as do all of us, the vital importance of small enterprises to our nation's economic growth and to the employment statistics—so many jobs held by small business. Many of you are aware of the truly impressive contribution that small business makes to our overall economy: half of our workers employed by small business. During the last decade, small business has produced two out of every three new jobs. So, it's the SBA's mission to help the smaller firms to continue and expand this record. The SBA does play a vital role in our effort to keep America's economic engine strong.

And so, I am pleased that this agency will be led by such a strong, articulate advocate of small businesses. During her 14-year—I should have let this front row talk about this—but her 14-year career in the Wisconsin legislature, Susan has been a pioneer: the youngest woman in the country elected to a State legislature when she took office at 22, first Republican woman to serve in the Wisconsin Senate, first woman of any party to hold a major elected leadership post in the Wisconsin Legislature. And her talents, therefore, have been well-recognized early on. She was selected as one of the 10 best Republican legislators in the Nation by the

National Republican Legislators Association. She has also been justifiably honored for her contributions to small businesses, both rural and urban. And last year she was named Guardian of Small Business by the National Federation of Independent Business.

And that's not all. She grew up in a small business family, working alongside her brothers in the family's flooring business in Milwaukee. And so, she observed an ethos of hard work and success from youth onward, from the ground up. She was voted one of the outstanding women in Wisconsin history at one point, and I'm delighted to welcome this outstanding woman to our team. I am confident that she will soon be recognized as one of the truly outstanding members of this administration.

So, congratulations, Susan, on this important day. Congratulations to your family. And incidentally, thanks for making this grandparent—[*laughter*]—feel like he's right at home! And now let's go with the Oath of Office. We've asked Chase Untermeyer to do the honors.

[*At this point, Administrator Engeleiter was sworn in.*]

The President. Congratulations!

Administrator Engeleiter. Thank you very much, Mr. President, for choosing me. I'm very honored to be the new Administrator of the SBA, and I look forward to the challenge. And thanks to all of you for being here today, and I very much look forward to being part of your team, to being a champion of small business around the country. So, thank you all very much for being here on this very important day to me.

Note: The President spoke at 11:22 a.m. in the Roosevelt Room at the White House. Charles G. Untermeyer was Assistant to the President and Director of Presidential Personnel. In his closing remarks, the President referred to a child's voice in the background.

Message to the Congress Transmitting the Republic of Korea-United States Fishing Agreement
May 1, 1989

To the Congress of the United States:

In accordance with the Magnuson Fishery Conservation and Management Act of 1976 (Public Law 94–265; 16 U.S.C. 1801 *et seq.*), I transmit herewith an agreement effected by exchange of notes February 17, 1989, and March 27, 1989, extending for the period of 2 years from July 1, 1989, until July 1, 1991, the Agreement between the Government of the United States of America and the Government of the Republic of Korea Concerning Fisheries off the Coasts of the United States, signed at Washington on July 26, 1982, as amended and extended. The exchange of notes together with the present agreement constitute a governing international fishery agreement within the meaning of section 201(c) of the act.

Several U.S. fishing industry interests have urged prompt consideration of this agreement. Because of the importance of our fishing relationship with Korea, I urge the Congress to give favorable consideration to this agreement at an early date.

Since 60 calendar days of continuous session, as required by the legislation, may not be available before the current agreement is scheduled to expire, I recommend the Congress consider passage of a joint resolution.

GEORGE BUSH

The White House,
May 1, 1989.

Nomination of Donald B. Rice To Be Secretary of the Air Force
May 1, 1989

The President today announced his intention to nominate Donald B. Rice to be Secretary of the Air Force. He would succeed Edward C. Aldridge, Jr.

Since 1972 Mr. Rice has been the president and chief executive officer of the RAND Corp. Prior to this he was Assistant Director of the Office of Management and Budget, 1970–1972. He has served as a senior consultant to the Defense Science Board since 1984, and as a member, 1977–1983. From 1969 to 1970, he was Deputy Assistant Secretary of Defense for Resource Analysis; and was Director of Cost Analysis in the Office of the Secretary of Defense, 1967–1969.

Mr. Rice received a bachelor's degree in chemical engineering from Notre Dame in 1961, a master's degree in industrial administration from Purdue in 1962, and a doctoral degree in economics from Purdue in 1965. From 1965 to 1967, he served in the U.S. Army. He was born June 4, 1939, in Frederick, MD.

Remarks to the Council of the Americas
May 2, 1989

Thank you very much, Mr. Secretary. And I am pleased to find myself here, surrounded by friends and in such high-powered company, once again, to be with David Rockefeller, the chairman of this illustrious Council; Ambassador Landau and Jim Flower, Bernie Aronson. And also I want to point out that I was accompanied over here by a man who is doing a superb job, a friend to many in this room, Brent Scowcroft. They couldn't find a seat for him, but there he is, standing over there—and delighted he's here.

But looking around the world today, in developing countries and even in the Communist bloc, we see the triumph of two great ideas: the idea of free government and the idea of free enterprise. And certainly Latin America and the Caribbean are proving fertile ground for these ideas. Democracy, a decade ago the exception, I think we would all agree, is today the rule. And the symbol of this new breeze is the ballot box. And by year's end, 14 national elections will have been held across the Americas.

And let's remember what it means to vote in some countries when democracy itself is at stake. We're not talking about people who may stay home from the polls because it's raining or rush-hour traffic is heavy. We're talking, in some cases, about people literally risking their lives to exercise their democratic right.

And listen to the words of a Salvadoran man on the eve of last month's Presidential elections in that country—elections that guerrilla forces vowed to disrupt: "Of course I'm going to vote, although I have to admit it's very scary. Here, going to the grocery store can be dangerous, but you have to do it. And you have to vote, too. We just can't roll over and play dead each time we're threatened." That's the voice of democracy speaking, and it's the voice of courage and hope.

Economically, although there is mounting concern about international debt, there are encouraging signs as well. Mexico has joined GATT and is moving toward a more open and internationally oriented economy. In Costa Rica and Brazil and Venezuela, new ventures are creating export opportunities that promise a broader economic base for those countries. You in the business community are among the pioneers and partners in these changes. And you're contributing to Latin America's increased productivity; you're helping the region to fulfill its potential for progress.

The historic shift in political and economic thinking now underway in Latin America is good news for us all. Our task is clear: to make the most of the new opportunities open to us, we must improve our working partnerships in this hemisphere—between countries north and south; between government, business and labor; and in the U.S., between the different branches of the Federal Government. We share common interests—must work towards a common aim.

My administration will work to build a new partnership for the Americas, a partnership built on mutual respect and mutual responsibilities. And we seek a partnership rooted in a common commitment to democratic rule. The battle for democracy is far from over. The institutions of free government are still fragile and in need of support. Our battlefield is the broad middle ground of democracy and popular government; our fight, against the enemies of freedom on the extreme right and on the extreme left.

As a result of the recent bipartisan accord on Central America, the United States is speaking with one voice on a matter of crucial importance to peace in Central America: bringing democracy to Nicaragua and peace to the region. And I want to salute our Secretary of State for hammering out this bipartisan accord when many, 2 or 3 months ago, said that it could not be done. Let me take this opportunity to make several observations on steps that are vital to peace, security, and democracy in Central America.

First, Nicaragua's effort to export violent revolution must stop. We cannot tolerate Sandinista support—which continues today—for the insurgencies in El Salvador and Guatemala, and terrorism in Honduras as well. Peace in the region cannot coexist with attempts to undermine democracy.

And second, we call upon the Soviet Union to end Soviet-bloc support for the Nicaraguan assault on regional democracy. The United States ended military aid to the Nicaraguan resistance 2 years ago. And yet, since that time, the Soviets continue to funnel about a half a billion worth of military assistance a year to the Sandinista regime, about the same rate as before we stopped our military aid to the *contras.* And furthermore, Cuba and Nicaragua, supplied by $7 billion in Soviet-bloc aid, have stepped up the arms flow to the Salvadoran guerrillas. Soviet-bloc weapons, such as AK–47's, are now being sent through Cuba and Nicaragua to the guerrillas; and that aid must stop. The Soviet Union must understand that we hold it accountable for the consequences of this intervention and for progress towards peace in the region and democracy in Nicaragua. As the bipartisan accord makes clear, continued Soviet support of violence and subversion in Central America is in direct violation of the Esquipulas agreement, concluded by the nations of Central America a year and a half ago.

Finally, within Nicaragua, we want to see a promise kept: the promise of democracy, withheld by the Sandinista regime for nearly a decade. To this end, the United States will continue to supply humanitarian aid to the Nicaraguan resistance through the elections scheduled in Nicaragua for February of 1990. The conduct and the outcome of those elections will demonstrate to Nicaragua's neighbors and the international community whether it means to deliver on democracy.

But the Sandinistas' recent attacks are ominous. April 25th was the benchmark date for Nicaragua to have in place electoral laws consistent with free and fair elections. Instead, restrictive new election and press laws have been pushed through the Sandinista-controlled legislature. These laws have been unilaterally imposed, and the proposals of Nicaragua's opposition parties have been ignored. The result is a stacked deck against the opposition and stacked rules of the game.

The election law mandates unilaterally that half of all foreign political contributions go to the Supreme Electoral Council, which remains under Sandinista control, and ignores proposals put forward by the opposition to provide for unlimited freedom of access for international election observers. In effect, that is a stacked deck against freedom. The new law governing press conduct gives excessive controls to the Interior Ministry to police violations against what they call national integrity and continues the prohibition of private sector ownership of television stations.

If there's to be peace in Nicaragua, the Sandinista regime must work with the opposition, including the resistance, to put in place election and press laws that are truly free and fair. And that means to have free and fair elections with outside observers given unfettered access to all election places and to all proceedings. It means a secret ballot on election day, the freedom to campaign, to organize, to hold rallies and to poll public opinion, to operate independent radio and TV stations as well. It means the absence of intimidation either from a politicized Sandinista military or police, or from those neighborhood block committees that control people's ration cards. It means an end to the arrests and bullying of opposition leaders. It means freeing all political prisoners jailed under the Sandinista rule, not just a handful of former Somoza soldiers. And if the Sandinistas fail this test, it will be a tragic setback and a dangerous one. The consolidation of tyranny will not be peace, it will be a crisis waiting to happen.

I want to mention several other Latin American nations where elections can signal positive change. In El Salvador, last month's free and fair elections proved another ringing affirmation of that nation's commitment to democracy. We expect ARENA [National Republican Alliance] to exercise its political power responsibly. And I have conveyed personally to President-elect Cristiani our commitment to human rights in El Salvador. I honestly feel that he shares my concern, and he deserves our support.

In Paraguay—the only country whose dictator had held power longer than Fidel Castro—elections have just taken place, the first hopeful sign that Paraguay is on its way to joining the democratic mainstream. And we do congratulate President-elect Rodriguez on his electoral victory and look forward to working with him. This democratic opening must continue.

In Panama, however—Jim [Secretary of State James A. Baker III] spoke to you all about this yesterday—the forecast for freedom is less clear. A free and fair vote in the elections scheduled for this Sunday would enable Panama to take a significant step towards ending the international isolation and internal economic crisis brought on by the Noriega regime. And in spite of intimidation from authorities, Panama's opposition parties have, with great courage, taken their campaign to the Panamanian people. The Noriega regime's candidates are trailing in poll after poll by margins of two to one. Unfortunately, as Secretary Baker told you yesterday, it is evident that the regime is ready to resort to massive election fraud in order to remain in power. The Noriega regime continues to threaten and intimidate Panamanians who believe in democracy. It's also attempting to limit the presence and freedom of action of international observers and to prevent journalists from reporting on the election process in Panama.

Let me be clear: The United States will not recognize the results of a fraudulent election engineered simply to keep Noriega in power. All nations that value democracy—that understand free and fair elections are the very heart of the democratic system—should speak out against election fraud in Panama. And that means the democracies of Europe—they ought to be speaking out about this, as well as nations in this hemisphere struggling to preserve the democratic system they've fought so hard to put in place. It is time for the plain truth: The day of the dictator is over. The people's right to democracy must not be denied.

A commitment to democracy is only one element in the new partnership that I envision for the nations of Americas. This new partnership must also aim at ensuring that the market economies survive and prosper and prevail. The principles of economic freedom have not been applied as fully as the principle of democracy. While the poverty of statism and protectionism is more evident than ever, statist economies remain in place, stifling growth in many Latin nations. And that is why the U.S. has made a new initiative to reduce the weight of the debt, as Latin governments and leaders take the difficult steps to restructure their economies.

Economic growth requires policies that create a climate for investment—one that will attract new capital, one that will reverse the flight of capital out of the region. We welcome the broad, broad international support that has been expressed for our ideas to strengthen the debt strategy. We urge the parties involved—the international financial institutions, debtor countries, commercial banks—to make a sustained effort to move this process forward. We recognize the competing claims debtor governments must try to satisfy as they work to advance economic reform, service their debt, and respond to the needs of their citizens. However, we also understand that progress can be an incremental process, case by case, step by step, provided there is a clear commitment to economic reform. I want to see some case-by-case successes in this hemisphere. To that end, we've started discussions, as you know, with Mexico and Venezuela and other countries as well.

Finally, our common partnership must confront a common enemy: international drug traffickers. Drugs threaten citizens and civil society throughout our hemisphere. Joining forces in the war on drugs is crucial. There is nothing gained by trying to lay blame and make recriminations. Drug abuse is a problem of both supply and demand. And attacking both is the only way we can face and defeat the drug menace. I believe that there is much more understanding on this point in this hemisphere south of our border than there used to be. It is my view that countries to the south felt for many years that this was simply the problem of a U.S. market for this insidious product. Now, they see that their own societies are being undermined by drug use. Now, they see that their own sense of order is being undermined by those trafficking in narcotics. So, I would call for much more cooperation between the countries in this hemisphere to combat the menace of narcotics.

There's a place in this new partnership for all of you in the Council of the Americas. Thomas Paine said that "The prosperity of any commercial nation is regulated by the prosperity of the rest." Your efforts do contribute—they contribute directly to the greater prosperity of all of the nations of the Americas. The challenge I've spoken of today won't be easy. But all of us—north and south, in government and in the private sector—can work together to meet the challenges and master them. We know we've got a lot of work to do. And you know you've got a lot of work to do—work that won't wait—to ensure that all the Americas enjoy the peace, the freedom, and the prosperity that we cherish.

Thank you for what you're doing—redouble your efforts. And I promise you, we'll do our level best in the executive branch of this government. Thank you very, very much.

Note: The President spoke at 11:08 a.m. in the main auditorium at the Department of State. In his opening remarks, he referred to Secretary of State James A. Baker III; George W. Landau, president of the council; Ludlow Flower III, director of the Washington, DC, office of the council; and Bernard W. Aronson, Assistant Secretary of State for Inter-American Affairs-designate.

Nomination of David J. Gribbin III To Be an Assistant Secretary of Defense

May 2, 1989

The President today announced his intention to nominate David J. Gribbin III to be Assistant Secretary of Defense (Legislative Affairs). He would succeed M.D.B. Carlisle.

Since 1979 Mr. Gribbin has worked in the House of Representatives and has most recently served as chief of staff to the Republican whip. In 1987 he served as executive director of the Republican Conference, and in 1986 as executive director of the Republican Policy Committee. From 1979 to 1986 he was the administrative assistant to Congressman Dick Cheney. Between 1967 and 1979, Mr. Gribbin worked in a variety of managerial capacities for the National Automobile Dealers Association.

Mr. Gribbin graduated from the University of Wyoming (1966) and Wesley Theological Seminary (1976). He also served in the U.S. Army from 1961 to 1964. Mr. Gribbin was born in San Francisco, CA, in 1939. He is married and has two children.

Continuation of Keith Lapham Brown as United States Ambassador to Denmark

May 2, 1989

The President today announced that Keith Lapham Brown will continue to serve as Ambassador Extraordinary and Plenipotentiary of the United States of America to Denmark.

Since November 1988 Ambassador Brown has served as United States Ambassador to Denmark. From 1984 to 1988 he was self-employed. From 1982 to 1983 he was Ambassador to the Kingdom of Lesotho. He was president of Brown Investment Corp. in Denver, CO, 1970–1982, and a vice president for Caulkins Oil Co., 1955–1970. He was with the law firm of Lang, Byrd, Cross, Ladon, and Oppenheimer, 1949–1955.

Ambassador Brown graduated from the University of Texas Law School (LL.B., 1949). He was born June 18, 1925, in Sterling, IL. He served in the U.S. Navy, 1943–1946. He is married and has three children.

Continuation of William Andreas Brown as the United States Ambassador to Israel

May 2, 1989

The President today announced that William Andreas Brown will continue to serve as Ambassador Extraordinary and Plenipotentiary of the United States of America to Israel.

Since November 1988 Ambassador Brown has served as United States Ambassador to Israel. Prior to this he was Ambassador to the Kingdom of Thailand, 1985–1988. He served as Principal Deputy Assistant Secretary of State for East Asian and Pacific Affairs, 1983–1985. He was visiting professor at the University of New Hampshire, 1982–1983; Deputy Chief of Mission in Tel Aviv, Israel, 1979–1982; Deputy Chief of Mission, Chargé d'Affaires, and Acting Director of the American Institute in Taipei, Taiwan, 1978–1979. Ambassador Brown has also served as political counselor in Moscow, 1977–1978, and Special Assistant to the Administrator of the Environmental Protection Agency, 1974–1976. He attended the National War College, 1972. He was Deputy Director of the Office of Asian Communist Affairs at the Department of State, 1970–1972. He has also served as a political officer in New Delhi, India, and Moscow, and as principal officer in Kuching, Sarawak. He entered the Foreign Service in 1956.

Ambassador Brown graduated from Harvard College (B.A., 1952) and Harvard University (M.A., 1955; Ph.D., 1963). He served in the U.S. Marine Corps, 1952–1955, and the U.S. Marine Corps Reserve, 1954–1969. He was born September 7, 1930, in Winchester, MA. He is married and has four children.

White House Statement on Wheat Exports to the Soviet Union
May 2, 1989

The President today approved a proposed sale of 1.5 million metric tons of wheat to the Soviet Union under the Export Enhancement Program (EEP). The wheat is intended for delivery in May and June.

The EEP was created in 1985 to enable U.S. exports of commodities to be sustained in the face of subsidies offered by foreign governments. It is intended to support our efforts to negotiate an international understanding on the removal of subsidies and other impediments to trade in agriculture. The President concluded that the dual objectives of maintaining market share for our farm exports and advancing international negotiations warrant the use of the EEP in this case.

Nomination of Louis A. Williams To Be an Assistant Secretary of Defense
May 2, 1989

The President today announced his intention to nominate Louis A. Williams to be an Assistant Secretary of Defense (Public Affairs). He would succeed J. Daniel Howard.

Since 1986 Mr. Williams has served as press secretary and legislative assistant to Congressman Dick Cheney. Mr. Williams has been involved in the Wyoming Futures Project, a joint public-private effort to help Wyoming plan for its future economic needs, 1985–1986. He was a news director and a radio and television reporter in Wyoming for 10 years. He has also served as a member of the board of directors of the Radio-Television News Directors Association for 6 years. Mr. Williams has received the First Amendment Award of the Society of Professional Journalists of the Rocky Mountain Region. In addition he has served on the staff of former U.S. Senator Clifford P. Hansen of Wyoming.

Mr. Williams was born in 1952, in Casper, WY, and he graduated from Stanford University (1974).

Appointment of Zvi Kestenbaum as a Member of the Commission for the Preservation of America's Heritage Abroad
May 2, 1989

The President today announced his intention to reappoint Zvi Kestenbaum to be a member of the Commission for the Preservation of America's Heritage Abroad for a term of 3 years.

Zvi Kestenbaum has served as the leader of the Opportunity Development Association to assist the Hasidic community with the social and economic disadvantages suffered by this group. Rabbi Kestenbaum was born in Uyfeherto, Hungary in 1922. He studied as a rabbinical student until World War II, surviving a Nazi concentration camp. He served as chairman of the economic planning board in Azor, Israel, and chairman of the city council. He then immigrated to the United States in 1955 from Israel. He has also been involved in the preservation of the Jewish cemeteries and holy sites both in Eastern Europe and throughout the world, and served as a member of the Presidential Commission to

Preserve America's Heritage Abroad.

Mr. Kestenbaum has received the U.S. Small Business Administration Advocate of the Year Award, 1984; the Presidential Recognition Award, 1985; and the U.S. Secretary of Commerce William C. Verity Award for outstanding efforts on behalf of the Hasidic community in 1988.

Remarks Following a Meeting With Polish and Chilean Human Rights Leaders

May 3, 1989

Well, it's a great honor to welcome to the White House today two outstanding individuals, truly heroes of democracy. Jacek Kuron has been a key leader in Solidarity's struggle in Poland. Solidarity has just won an important victory in Poland, not only its own legislation but a program of other democratic reforms as well. As Poland moves towards more freedoms for all of its people, greater economic opportunity and strength, the world will be watching and applauding. And this is especially true for the United States.

Monica Jimenez de Barros founded and directed the Crusade for Citizen Participation in Chile. She educated and mobilized millions of voters in Chile's plebiscite election last October. Due in part to her efforts, Chile is on a road toward democracy. We do not deceive ourselves that this is an easy road, but we believe Chile is on an irreversible course. And Chileans who seek democracy deserve the support of everybody in the United States—everybody that loves democracy around the world.

Mr. Kuron and Mrs. Jimenez are in Washington this week to receive the Democracy Award from the National Endowment for Democracy. We salute you, and we salute the kind of personal courage that you both have shown in the face of great obstacles. You've shown that tenacity and faith and courage in the name of democracy can make a difference for millions of people.

As I said in my Inaugural, the day of the dictator is over. All over the globe freedom is a fact now, more than at any other time in modern history. The National Endowment for Democracy—in these awards and in its other good work—is giving expression to the oldest and noblest tradition of this country: the devotion to freedom for all humanity. And thus, it is a special honor today to welcome you two outstanding democracy builders.

Congratulations! Well done. Keep it up. Congratulations to both of you, and thank you for coming to the White House at the end of what I understand has been a very good conference.

Note: The President spoke at 9:45 a.m. in the Roosevelt Room at the White House.

Message to the Congress Transmitting the European Economic Community-United States Fishing Agreement

May 3, 1989

To the Congress of the United States:

In accordance with the Magnuson Fishery Conservation and Management Act of 1976 (Public Law 94–265; 16 U.S.C. 1801 *et seq.*), I transmit herewith an agreement effected by exchange of notes on September 15, 1988, and February 27, 1989, extending for the period of 2 years from July 1, 1989, until July 1, 1991, and amending to conform with current U.S. law, the Agreement between the Government of the United States of America and the European Economic Community Concerning Fisheries off the Coasts of the United States, signed at Washington on October 1, 1984. The exchange of notes together with the present agreement constitute a governing international fishery agreement within the meaning of section 201(c) of the act.

U.S. fishing industry interests have urged prompt consideration of this agreement, and, similarly, I request that the Congress give favorable consideration to this agreement at an early date to avoid disruption of ongoing cooperative ventures.

Since 60 calendar days of continuous session, as required by the legislation, may not be available before the current agreement is scheduled to expire, I recommend the Congress consider passage of a joint resolution.

GEORGE BUSH

The White House,
May 3, 1989.

Message to the Congress Transmitting the Iceland-United States Fishing Agreement
May 3, 1989

To the Congress of the United States:

In accordance with the Magnuson Fishery Conservation and Management Act of 1976 (Public Law 94–265; 16 U.S.C. 1801 *et seq.*), I transmit herewith an agreement effected by exchange of notes on November 23, 1988, and January 17, 1989, extending for the period of 2 years from July 1, 1989, until July 1, 1991, and amending to conform with current U.S. law, the Agreement between the Government of the United States of America and the Government of the Republic of Iceland Concerning Fisheries off the Coasts of the United States, signed at Washington on September 21, 1984. The exchange of notes together with the present agreement constitute a governing international fishery agreement within the meaning of section 201(c) of the act.

U.S. fishing industry interests have urged prompt consideration of this agreement, and, similarly, I request that the Congress give favorable consideration to this agreement at an early date to avoid disruption of ongoing cooperative ventures.

Since 60 calendar days of continuous session, as required by the legislation, may not be available before the current agreement is scheduled to expire, I recommend the Congress consider passage of a joint resolution.

GEORGE BUSH

The White House,
May 3, 1989.

Nomination of Sean Charles O'Keefe To Be Comptroller of the Department of Defense
May 3, 1989

The President today announced his intention to nominate Sean Charles O'Keefe to be Comptroller of the Department of Defense. He would succeed Clyde O. Glaister.

Since 1981 Mr. O'Keefe has been on the staff of the United States Senate Committee on Appropriations, and serves as the minority counsel for the defense subcommittee. He served as the staff director for the defense subcommittee until 1987. Mr. O'Keefe served in principal analyst positions on the staff for operations and maintenance, shipbuilding, and aircraft procurement appropriations. He has also served as a Presidential management intern in 1978.

Mr. O'Keefe graduated from Loyola University with a bachelor of arts degree in political science and received a master of public administration degree from Syracuse University. He was born January 27, 1956. He is married, has one daughter, and resides in Arlington, VA.

Remarks on the National Day of Prayer
May 4, 1989

Dr. and Mrs. Bright and reverend clergy, and members of the National Day of Prayer Committee, distinguished Members of the Senate and the House of Representatives, and ladies and gentlemen: You know, it's often said of a group or individual that he hasn't got a prayer. [*Laughter*] Well, those of us interested in sports keep hearing that all of the time. But I'm delighted to address an audience about which that will never be said.

And first, I want to say what a pleasure it is to welcome you on this special day. America's religious, civic, political leaders welcome you to this very special place, America's house. We come as friends, as believers in a humane and loving God, and we meet on a special day for America—a National Day of Prayer.

You know, a little boy once uttered this simple prayer: "God bless mother and daddy, my brother and sister, and, oh, God, do take care of yourself because if anything happens to you, we're all sunk." [*Laughter*] Well, I expect this George Healy portrait of Lincoln gets to the margins of that prayer, and I expect he felt that way—perilous times for our country. And I'm sure all of us have shared those sentiments at one time or another—something in our own lives, something facing our country.

Certainly the Continental Congress did, for it was they who in 1775 issued the first official proclamation of a National Day of Prayer. In 1952 Congress decreed that a specific date be set aside each year for Americans to gather in homes and places of worship in order to pray. And since then, every President has declared a National Day of Prayer. And so, this morning, like my predecessors, I am proud to continue that tradition. But I am pleased to note that today marks a departure from the norm, for 1989 marks the first year of an official permanent date of designation: from now on, the first Thursday of every May.

My friends, I'm glad that together we could commemorate this event, and just for a few moments let me focus on what to me, and I hope to you, this observance means. It does mean, I'm sure we would all agree, that we believe in separation of church and state, but not in the separation of morality, or moral values and state. While the government must remain neutral towards particular religions, it must not, certainly it need not, remain neutral toward values that Americans support. And yes, we believe in pluralism. And I just want to reassure you I believe in pluralism—certainly in mutual tolerance, for we are one nation under God. And we were placed here on Earth to do His work. And our work has gone on now for more than 200 years in the Nation—a work best embodied in four simple words: In God we trust. And it was to that higher being that George Washington looked when in 1776 he was addressing his troops, and he said, "The fate of unborn millions will now depend, under God, on the courage and conduct of this army."

Lincoln believed in divine providence. Leaving Springfield to take over, to assume the Presidency, he told the people of his hometown that the God which helped General Washington must now help him. "Without the assistance of the divine being," Lincoln said, "I cannot succeed. With that assistance, I cannot fail." And some of you may be too young to remember D-day. Not many of you, but some of you may be too young. [*Laughter*] Over a nationwide network, Franklin Roosevelt prayed for the safety and success of our invading force.

"Our sons," he said, "pride of our nation, lead them straight and true. Give strength to their arms, stoutness to their hearts, steadfastness in their faith."

Our history tells us what our hearts confirm: As Americans, we are a religious people. We prize compassion and self-sacrifice. We know that America is great because America is good, and as President, I am reminded of that constantly. Several weeks ago, I was sharing this with Mrs. Bright and Mr. Zeoli. Barbara and I went up to—or did you go to Lancaster, PA? She didn't make the traveling squad. [*Laughter*] I went to Pennsylvania, and I went to a local high school in a relatively affluent rural area, Lancaster, and there we discussed a problem which is America's problem—the rising use of drugs. If you ever need to pray about something and ask for strength and guidance, it is this: that we succeed in our antinarcotics efforts.

But then, after meeting with this relatively affluent group, and hearing that drugs were in their corridors and in their playgrounds, I went a few miles over—just the same community—to meet with the Amish and Mennonite leaders. And wonderful people, and kind—living their own lives—and they don't have a drug problem. And they made very clear to me why: family and faith. Against them, drugs don't have a chance.

And I am convinced that faith and family can help us honor God in a most profound and personal way—daily, as human beings—by the conduct of our lives. They teach us not only to revere but to practice the Golden Rule. And they also help us reflect the internal values of decency, humility, kindness, and caring. I thought of those values last Sunday when I was in New York to mark the 200th anniversary of George Washington's first Inaugural Address. For it was then that, like Washington two centuries ago, Barbara and I prayed at St. Paul's Chapel, there where in 1789 a prayer service was offered by the chaplains of Congress for the United States of America. To me that day—some of you may have seen it—was moving, intimate, but there was something special about that church service 200 years ago. This Washington realized that political values without moral values, without that moral underpinning, cannot sustain a nation.

And so, this strong yet gentle man knew that the advancement of America, while it might rely on its President, would surely depend on providence. And so, what Washington believed so strongly over 200 years ago—it really is just as true today. For without God's help, we can do nothing, and with it, we can do great things—for our children, for the world.

So, let me just thank you all for coming. Barbara and I are delighted to have you here. We will do our best in the people's house to hold these values high that are shared by everybody here regardless of our denomination, regardless of our own personal commitments. We welcome you, we are pleased you're here. And if you have an extra minute for a prayer when the going gets a little tough, remember the Congress. They need it, too. [*Laughter*] And Barbara and I know we do, too.

Thank you all very, very much. Thank you for coming.

Note: The President spoke at 8:45 a.m. in the State Dining Room at the White House. In his remarks, he referred to Vonette Bright, chairwoman of the National Day of Prayer Committee; and Billy Zeoli, president of Gospel Films.

Nomination of Reggie B. Walton To Be Associate Director for National Drug Control Policy
May 4, 1989

The President today announced his intention to nominate Reggie B. Walton to be Associate Director for National Drug Control Policy (Bureau of State and Local Affairs). This is a new position.

Since 1986 Mr. Walton has been deputy presiding judge of the criminal division for the Superior Court of the District of Columbia. He was an associate judge for the Superior Court of the District of Columbia, since 1981. He has served as executive assistant United States attorney for the District of Columbia, 1980–1981; assistant United States attorney for the District of Columbia, chief of the career criminal unit, 1979–1980. He was assistant United States attorney for the District of Columbia, 1976–1980; and a staff attorney for the Defender Association of Philadelphia, 1974–1976. He has also served as an instructor for the National Institute of Trial Advocacy of Georgetown University Law School, 1983 to present.

Mr. Walton graduated from West Virginia State College (B.A., 1971) and American University, Washington College of Law (J.D., 1974). He was born February 8, 1949.

Remarks and a Question-and-Answer Session With Reporters Following a Luncheon With Prime Minister Brian Mulroney of Canada

May 4, 1989

The President. May I just, at the outset of this scrum, in which we each answer questions, say what a joy it's been to have Prime Minister Mulroney back here with his very special Mila. Barbara and I froze them to death on the balcony. It's warm now, but 20 minutes ago, it was cold—temperature; warm in terms of the feeling that existed at that little lunch and, indeed, over in the Oval Office.

And I cite that because the relationship between the United States and Canada remains strong. Our respect for the Prime Minister and his objectives remains strong. The fact that he fought hard for this breakthrough free trade agreement has the respect for him at an altogether high level. And so, I can report that the conversations that we had that touched on a wide array of subjects—on the environment, and on the importance of the NATO meeting, and on the bilateral relations—was good. And we found that we can look each other in the eye and talk out any differences with no rancor. And we salute him and welcome him as a good friend.

And now, Mr. Prime Minister, the standup mike is all yours.

The Prime Minister. Thank you, Mr. President. We had a very delightful and effective meeting, I thought, with President Bush and his colleagues. And Mila and I had an especially delightful lunch with Barbara and the President.

Our discussions today on the agenda dealt with the environment, which is very important, and I applaud the leadership the President is giving to the environment, particularly on the question of acid rain.

We discussed, as well, something that Margaret Thatcher has described as a model for the rest of the world, and that's the Canada-United States free trade agreement, which is in its infancy, is growing and growing strongly, and I think to the benefit of both of our nations.

And we discussed the role of NATO and the importance of the Western alliance in the world—the role of the United States in that alliance. The position of Canada is unequivocal in that regard.

Thank you, sir.

Arms Control

Q. Mr. President, are you willing to compromise your position now on short-range missiles in terms of starting negotiations with the Soviet Union on that area?

The President. I want the NATO summit to be a success. And we will be working with the Germans and with others to see that there is a common NATO position. This is no time for one to compromise or somebody not to compromise. We've made proposals to the Germans; I expect we'll be hearing from them soon. And I'd prefer to do whatever negotiation amongst allies that is required in private, recognizing that we all want the NATO summit to be successful. And there's a lot of public discussion of this issue, and that's fine. I don't plan in detail to join in on that public discussion. The U.S. position is well-known. NATO's last stated public position is well-known. And we're prepared to go from there.

Q. It sounds like you're ready to negotiate.

The President. Well, I'm always willing to negotiate. But we're not going to go for any third zero or getting SNF [Strategic Nuclear Forces] out of whack in terms of negotiations. So, let's be clear on that. But certainly, I'll be willing to discuss these issues, as we did in a very constructive way with the Prime Minister.

Q. Prime Minister Mulroney, what did you say to the President about the SNF issue?

The Prime Minister. What I said to the President was that NATO was founded on, in my judgment, two concepts: first, solidarity; and secondly, the American leadership of the Western alliance. And it's the solidarity that has brought about the success that the West has engendered thus far. And we have to stick together on all of these fundamental questions, and we will.

NATO is a grouping of sovereign independent nations. There is going to be vigorous debate, unlike the Warsaw Pact. In NATO, there are independent nations who get together, and who come together willingly under a common shield to achieve common objectives. And so, while there has to be this kind of debate, in the end, there must be solidarity, total solidarity. And there must be a common view of leadership, which has served the world so well for 40 years. Now, we're going to Brussels to celebrate the achievements of NATO. And that's exactly what we are going to be doing, and that is why we look forward to President Bush's presence there—to celebrate that particular achievement in which the United States has played such a pivotal role.

Q. ——how public opinion in Europe to have NATO——

Q. Did you urge the President to begin negotiations on SNF reductions, sir? Did you urge the President to begin negotiations on SNF reductions?

The Prime Minister. I'm sorry?

Q. Did you urge the President to begin negotiations—to at least back negotiations on SNF reductions?

The Prime Minister. I've just said what the position of Canada is in regard to—there's one NATO position. This is not an association where everybody freelances.

Q. ——different views on this, though.

The Prime Minister. We have a common NATO position, and while there are divergence of views that emerge from time to time, the object of our getting together is to harmonize those views into one position. And that's what we're going to be able to do.

Q. You told us that NATO was very good——

Iran Arms and Contra Aid Controversy

Q. Mr. President, the Oliver North jury is supposed to return a verdict momentarily. I was wondering if now you would discuss with us your trip to Honduras—as they're about to come in, and you couldn't affect their verdict one way or the other—and what happened there—whether or not you made some arrangements to give a quid pro quo for Honduras help.

The President. How do we know the North—I haven't heard—it's going to be in at 2 o'clock with a decision? Honduras—there was no quid pro quo. Everybody that attended the meeting says there was no quid pro quo. And for those who suggest there was, the onus is on them. The word of the President of the United States, George Bush, is there was no quid pro quo. The records of the meeting demonstrate that there was no quid pro quo. Thank you for asking that question.

Q. Mr. President, was there any implication——

The President. No implication, no quid pro quo, direct or indirect, from me to the President of Honduras on that visit.

Q. Why did you go down there for then?

Q. In that meeting, did you discuss aid to the *contras*—the Hondurans' compliance with our request that they help the *contras* and——

The President. We are going to—I am going to insist that the congressional committees, now that the jury is in or out, be briefed fully on the confidential cables that bring up every fact of that meeting.

North Atlantic Treaty Organization

Q. Mr. President, can we go back to NATO a second?

The President. Yes. For me or——

Q. For you, sir. Mr. President, you were very careful, I thought, to say you didn't want the third zero. That still allows for the possibility of reducing the number of short-range nuclear weapons.

The President. Look, my emphasis will be on conventional force reductions. And we will be talking very soon with the Germans on a proposal we made to them. We've listened very carefully in a very—to the constructive suggestions that Prime Minister Mulroney has raised, and that's really all I care to say about it. I want the NATO meeting to be a success. And one way you guarantee success is not to go out and fine tune nuance differences that may exist between various staunch allies. And so, the German position was made public last week. And I will continue to work with the leaders of the NATO countries to see that we have a successful summit.

Q. Mr. President——

Q. Mr. Prime Minister——

Q. Mr. President, did you discuss a bilateral accord——

The President. Here's what we're going to do to be fair. We're going to rotate these questions. The next one is for the Prime Minister of Canada—if you want equal time. [*Laughter*]

The Prime Minister. I don't insist on equal time, Mr. President. [*Laughter*]

The President. You're entitled to it. You've got to have it.

Acid Rain

Q. ——any new commitments on acid rain?

The Prime Minister. I'll take it. [*Laughter*] All right. We'll rotate.

Q. How about bilateral accords?

The Prime Minister. We'll rotate, but I've got to get a chance to answer.

Acid rain—we had an excellent discussion on that. The President has made a very strong statement in regard to his intentions in acid rain, which will involve legislation and cooperation with the Congress. We look forward to that and once that is achieved, we look forward to the conclusion of a mutual accord which will allow our countries to bring to an end, hopefully, a problem that has been a major challenge to both of our governments and one that has blighted the environments of the United States and of Canada. So, we're moving along on that. I'm pleased with what the President had to say today. I met with congressional leaders, including Senator Mitchell, earlier this morning. And as the Prime Minister of Canada, I'm pleased with the manner in which this very important matter is going.

Q. Mr. President, do you support a bilateral accord, sir?

Fusion Energy

Q. President Bush, with regard to all of the reports of the new developments of fusion energy, which is a clean form of energy that could make the whole acid rain issue moot, do you plan to take any role in helping to determine whether this breakthrough or potential breakthrough is real, and the Government would play a role in helping to develop it?

The President. I will be talking to my National Science Adviser about that in the next few days.

Q. Prime Minister Mulroney—

[*At this point, a question is asked and answered in French.*]

Q. Mr. President——

Q. Mr. Prime Minister——

The President. My turn, my turn! The gentleman over here.

Q. Translation, Mr. President?

Elections in Panama

Q. Mr. Gingrich this morning suggested if the Panama election is as fraudulent as many think it will be that perhaps you shouldn't give back the Canal. What's your view on that? What's your response to him?

The President. My view on that is to warn

Panama that the world will be looking at them, not just the United States. In terms of these elections and deciding what to do if the elections are fraudulent—calling on them for free and fair elections—there will be international observers there, and then we will cross whatever hypothetical bridge we may have to cross later on. But it's too hypothetical, Charles [Charles Bierbauer, Cable News Network], at this point to go beyond that. But this does give me an opportunity to say that I have been very disturbed by the reports that the election will be less than free and less than fair and less than open. And I simply want to encourage the people in Panama to do everything they can to guarantee free and fair elections. And what pressures they can bring to bear on the PDF [Panamanian Defense Force] leader, Mr. Noriega, I don't know. But I would hope, with the world watching, they would insist on free and fair elections.

Health Care in Canada

Q. ——about the health system in Canada.

The Prime Minister. Pardon me?

Q. I want to ask you, are you worried about this exodus of doctors from Canada to the United States, where they make more money? Are you worried that that will hurt your wonderful health system in Canada?

The Prime Minister. Well, we're always—we don't like to lose any talented Canadians. But we're very proud of the special health care system that we've developed over the years. It's an integral part of our citizenship. We strengthen it every opportunity we can, and we don't see it under any challenge or attack.

Q. Could you explain that to Mr. Bush so we can get that same health system in the United States?

The Prime Minister. Well, Mr. Bush is very, very well acquainted with the Canadian system, as with others, and I can only speak for ours. I know of your interest in this area. And as far as we're concerned, we've developed our own system, which we prize very highly. Others have their own, of which they're proud, no doubt.

Iran Arms and Contra Aid Controversy

Q. Mr. President, Senator Mitchell and others among the congressional leadership are adamant in pressing for answers on why they did not get certain documents or certain versions of documents related to the Iran-*contra* matter during their investigation. What will you undertake to do to meet their inquiries? What role will you take?

The President. Well, I've made clear to the Congress that we will cooperate in every way requested and referred them to a man in whom I have great confidence, Mr. Culvahouse [Arthur B. Culvahouse, former Counsel to President Reagan], who handled those documents for the previous administration. And hopefully, they can resolve it between themselves.

Acid Rain

Q. ——about acid rain once again, sir?

Q. Senator Mitchell mentioned this morning that Canada should be pushing for a bilateral accord on acid rain consecutively, while the administration introduces its legislation on acid rain. Was there any talk about that and will you be pushing for that?

The Prime Minister. Well, I think the President knows my position full well. We know that there have to be legislative changes here in the United States to kind of equate the initiatives taken in Canada. And once that is done, or while—in the process of that being done, then there has to be an international accord that is an enforceable document, by which we can measure our progress and enforce delinquency in that event. And so, President Bush is known as a strong environmentalist. He's made some very significant statements in regard to not only acid rain but its impact on our bilateral relationship and his resolve to clean it up. So, I'm very encouraged.

Q. President Bush, can we ask you, sir, about acid rain? Did you make any undertakings in your lunch in terms of what's going to be in your clean air legislation that's going to help this acid rain problem?

The President. We didn't go into the specific amounts. As the Prime Minister said, he knows of my commitment. He knows now that we are in the final stages of formulating our recommendations to the Congress—the Clean Air Act. And indeed, we'll be prepared, after those recommendations go forward, to discuss in more detail the subject that you're asking about. So, we did have a chance to do what you asked about. And look, if there's anything that the Prime Minister of Canada has been clear with me about—and he's been clear with me on everything—it is this subject. So, I don't think there's any—he forcefully brings it up, and I tell him where we stand.

Arms Control

Q. Prime Minister Mulroney, the President said you made concrete suggestions on the issue of short-range missiles. Can you give us an idea, sir, what some of those suggestions entailed?

The Prime Minister. Well, Mr. Clark [Canadian Secretary of State for External Affairs] has been in touch with Secretary [of State] Baker and others in regard to how this matter might be broached. We don't—we discuss it privately with our allies and that's what we have tried to do. But the position of Canada—the one I've set out is—it deals with the effectiveness of NATO being predicated on our solidarity and the leadership, a very particular role of leadership, by the United States in that equation. And we think that within those parameters, we can resolve differences of degree and emphasis that will come up from sovereign states from time to time. And we think that this is what the President and I and Secretary Baker and Minister Clark have been working on and will continue to work on.

Iran Arms and Contra Aid Controversy

Q. Mr. President, when you say that there was no quid pro quo at the meeting that you had with the Honduran President, are you willing to give us the same assurances that there was no quid pro quo between this Government and the Honduran Government in that time period?

The President. As far as I know of, as far as I know—to my knowledge. But the allegation that's been made on me was that I went to Honduras and talked to President Suazo about some quid pro quo. I can now state declaratively, without any fear of contradiction, that there wasn't. And that's all I'm going to tell you.

[*At this point, a question was asked and answered in French.*]

Q. Mr. President, you've made it pretty clear there was no quid pro quo. Can we go beyond that to the whole question of Iran-*contra*? You have declined in the past to discuss that, sir, because of confidentiality vis-a-vis President Reagan. Now, you're the President, the Oliver North jury is now delivering its verdict on all the counts—is this the time to set this at rest? Just to go through and say——

The President. I think it was set to rest in the last election. I think I have been singled out for a specific question here that I've answered. Do you have a specific question? I'll be glad to try to respond to it at your next turn, which does not come now, however. [*Laughter*] But I would be glad to try to do that. And that's the way it's going to be. And we'll have plenty of opportunities to answer questions, and I may or may not, depending on what they are, answer them. I've answered this one, where there has been much needless, mindless speculation about my word of honor, and I've answered it, now, definitively.

Acid Rain

Q. Mr. President, your good friend Michael Dukakis said the other day to the Prime Minister that he expected—he thought that it was possible for an acid rain treaty between Canada and the United States to be signed within a year. I don't know what your feelings are on this, but could you give us kind of a timeframe? Do you think it's possible that there might be a treaty signed at least before you leave or the next election?

The President. Well, there will be great progress made. Whether the treaty proves to be the vehicle for demonstrating that progress, I don't know, and I can't say.

Environmental Issues

Q. Mr. Prime Minister, was there any discussion of a global warming convention, and if so, what direction did it take?

The Prime Minister. Yes, the President and I had an excellent discussion of the entire environmental formula. I expressed the view as well that there can be little progress in terms of the environment unless there's a very strong leadership role played by the United States. And I've already indicated to you President Bush's very strong commitment to the environment in all of its related and ancillary and principal dimensions, and this is a very, very important one. But you know, you can hold all the conferences you want, but if the principal players are not there, then progress can be fairly modest. So, President Bush indicated to me, as he did in Ottawa, his intention to play a very significant leadership role in all aspects of the environment, and I think we're all very encouraged by that.

Thank you very much.

The President. Last question for the President—the Prime Minister having handled his last one beautifully.

China-U.S. Relations

Q. Different subject, on China. Your administration has been very outspoken in promoting democratic efforts in places like Poland and Nicaragua and around the world. But you haven't really said anything about China. Do you have some words of encouragement for the students who are defying a government ban in order to protest in favor of freedom and democracy?

The President. I have words of encouragement for freedom and democracy wherever, and I would like to see progress in China, in the Soviet Union, and in other systems that have heretofore not been in the forefront, to put it mildly, of human rights or of democratic rights. And I wouldn't suggest to any leadership of any country that they accept every demand by every group. But I will say that as I reviewed what the demands are today, we can certainly, as the United States, identify with them. When they talk about more free press, we would encourage that, wherever it might be. When they talk about—I forget what the list was of every demand, but a lot of them had my enthusiastic backing, in a broad, generic sense. And I would like to encourage China or the Soviet Union or other totalitarian countries—countries that have not enjoyed democratic practices—to move as quick as they can down democracy's path.

And I've been pleased with some of the changes in China. It's changed dramatically since I was living there. But they've got a ways to go, and other countries in this hemisphere have a long ways to go, and countries over in Europe have a long way to go. And so, I would encourage them all: Democracy is on the move. And this is one thing that the Prime Minister and I talked about. When we go to that NATO meeting, we're going to be on the side that is winning and the side that is right, fundamentally right. Freedom, democracy, human rights, these are the things we stand for. So, I would encourage every government to move as quickly as they can to achieve human rights.

Thank you.

Note: The President spoke at 1:55 p.m. on the South Portico at the White House. Earlier, the President and the Prime Minister met in the Oval Office.

White House Statement on the President's Meeting With Violeta Chamorro of Nicaragua
May 5, 1989

The President today met with Mrs. Violeta Chamorro, publisher of the Nicaraguan newspaper *La Prensa*. Mrs. Chamorro is in Washington at the invitation of the National Endowment for Democracy. Mrs. Chamorro and *La Prensa* have become symbols of freedom of expression and the struggle against tyranny and dictatorship throughout Latin America, beginning with the struggle against the Somoza government.

During the meeting, the President expressed his deep regard for Mrs. Chamorro and her unceasing efforts to carry on the tradition of her assassinated husband over the last 10 years, in the face of Sandinista harassment and intimidation. The President told Mrs. Chamorro that he shared her disappointment and concern that the new media law promulgated by the Sandinistas does not guarantee the free functioning of the media and unrestricted political expression. The new law gives the Ministry of Interior wide latitude for prosecuting and punishing the media for such ill-defined concepts as violating "national integrity" and for publishing "injurious, defamatory and false news." Rather than relaxing existing controls and increasing freedom of expression, the law is a more systematic compilation of existing restrictions and sanctions.

The Sandinista media law, as well as the recently approved electoral law, do not comply with the letter or the spirit of the Esquipulas and El Salvador agreements signed by Central American leaders. The President and Mrs. Chamorro expressed their hope that international leaders would use their influence to persuade the Sandinistas to fulfill their commitment.

Remarks at a Cinco de Mayo Celebration
May 5, 1989

Welcome to this Rose Garden celebration. [*Laughter*] But even the weather couldn't put a damper on a wonderful event like this, and I'm delighted to be here. I salute Mexico's Ambassador to the United States, who honors us with his presence. And next to him, my trusted friend, John Negroponte, who is going to be our next Ambassador to Mexico. So, we're well-represented here today.

Secretary [of Education] Cavazos, thank you, sir, for, in a sense, sponsoring this wonderful program. But isn't it a great sight to see the folklore and the traditions of a proud past so refreshingly alive in these kids! And you're all from Toledo, Ohio? [*Laughter*] Are you? That's fantastic. The whole scene—the costumes, the music, the pageantry—reminds me of my days as a Congressman in Houston, or indeed, some of my times in West Texas. Cinco de Mayo is a big one down in Texas, as I'm sure many of you in this room know, just as it is throughout the United States. And, in my view, it's becoming more significant or more celebrated each year, and the reason is obvious: We and Mexico are bound by ties of family, culture, and friendship. This is keenly appreciated in the Bush family. Barbara and I have always felt at home in the Hispanic community, and living in Texas, we are impressed by those values—caring, patriotism, love of God.

What is true of a family is true of a nation. Hispanic culture is growing deep roots into American life, and that's why the Hispanic community plays such a pivotal role in our national culture and in this administration. Not only do we have two highly respected Hispanic leaders—Lauro Cavazos and Manuel Lujan [Secretary of the Interior] serving in the Cabinet—but key advisers, six senior members of the White House staff sharing your Hispanic heritage and pride. And I see that several of our new appointees are with us today—Hispanic Americans whose service to their country will add to that pride. We deeply respect your commitment to family, honor, and tradition. We need the advice and the involvement of everybody here. You are leaders, and this is the age of empowerment. Empowerment is economic as well as political. Since 1982 more than two-and-a-half million Hispanic Americans have joined the job market, but this is not enough. We will not be satisfied until every Hispanic man and woman can make the most of their drive and their talent in the United States of America.

And on this day we also recognize something else that binds together the United States and Mexico. We are two former European colonies whose independence has been hard won. Less than 1 week ago, I joined in the celebration of the 200th anniversary of the swearing-in of George Washington in New York. How appropriate it is for us to now observe the victory of another champion of liberty, Benito Juarez. Like Washington, he possessed a homespun dignity, a simple eloquence, and a commanding presence. Both were men of peace who were forced to fight for freedom.

So, this is a day for all of us to look southward—to memories of home and hearth for some, to memories of friendship and respect for the rest. Think of the 5th of May as not a national holiday of another country only but as the celebration of ideals that know no border—ideals of pride, family, and tradition. And this is the spirit of the Hispanic community, and this is the spirit of all Americans, north and south of the Rio Grande.

Thank you for being with us today. Happy Cinco de Mayo, and welcome.

Note: The President spoke at 2:15 p.m. in the East Room at the White House. In his remarks, he referred to Gustavo Petricioli, Mexican Ambassador to the U.S., and Benito Juarez, the first President of Mexico. A mariachi band performed prior to his remarks.

Message on the Observance of Cinco de Mayo, 1989
May 5, 1989

It is with great pleasure that I join the people of Mexico and all those of Mexican heritage in the United States in celebrating Cinco de Mayo.

The historic victory at the Battle of Puebla clearly showed the unbeatable determination of a people struggling for independence. Though badly outnumbered by the French, the Mexican people fought bravely for the freedom of their country. With the beacon of democracy giving them hope and inspiration, their cause could not be denied.

Every American immediately identifies with that cause and shares in the pride and happiness Mexicans feel on this day. Our country is proud of the long-standing friendship that has existed between the United States and Mexico and prouder still of the wonderful contributions Mexican Americans have made to our Nation.

On this special day, I send congratulations and good wishes to the people of Mexico and to our citizens of Mexican descent. May we remember in gratitude and admiration the sacrifices your ancestors made for liberty, and may their brave legacy be a reminder to us all of the eternal vigilance that freedom demands.

God bless you.

GEORGE BUSH

Message to the Congress Transmitting a Report on Radiation Control for Health and Safety
May 5, 1989

To the Congress of the United States:

In accordance with section 360D of the Public Health Service Act, I am submitting the report of the Department of Health and Human Services regarding the administration of the Radiation Control for Health and Safety Act during calendar year 1988.

The report recommends that section 360D of the Public Health Service Act that requires the completion of this annual report be repealed. All the information found in this report is available to the Congress on a more immediate basis through congressional committee oversight and budget hearings. This annual report serves little useful purpose and diverts agency resources from more productive activities.

GEORGE BUSH

The White House,
May 5, 1989.

Continuation of Malcolm Richard Wilkey as Ambassador to Uruguay
May 5, 1989

The President today announced that Malcolm Richard Wilkey will continue to serve as Ambassador Extraordinary and Plenipotentiary of the United States of America to the Oriental Republic of Uruguay.

Since 1985 Ambassador Wilkey has served as Ambassador to the Oriental Republic of Uruguay. From 1969 to 1973, he was a member of the Advisory Panel on International Law for the Legal Adviser at the Department of State. From 1970 to 1985, he was U.S. Circuit Judge for the DC Court. From 1975 to 1979, he served on the Judicial Conference of the U.S. Committee on Rules for Admission to Practice in the Federal Courts. Since 1985 Ambassador Wilkey has also been a visiting fellow at Wolfson College in Cambridge, England.

Mr. Wilkey was born December 6, 1918, in Murfreesboro, TN. He received his A.B. in 1940 from Harvard College and his J.D. in 1948 from Harvard Law School. He served in the U.S. Army from 1941 to 1945, and in the U.S. Army Active Reserve from 1948 to 1954. Mr. Wilkey is married to the former Emma Secul.

Statement by Press Secretary Fitzwater on the Resumption of Arms Control Negotiations in Vienna
May 5, 1989

Today marks the resumption in Vienna, Austria, of both the negotiations on Conventional Armed Forces in Europe (CFE), which involves all 23 nations of NATO and the Warsaw Pact, and the talks on Confidence and Security Building Measures (CSBM) among the 35 participants in the Conference on Security and Cooperation in Europe (CSCE).

In the CFE negotiations, the United States and its allies are seeking a stable and secure balance of conventional forces in Europe at reduced levels, the elimination of destabilizing disparities of forces, and the elimination of capabilities for surprise attack and large-scale offensive action. NATO's approach reflects a continuing commitment to realizing these goals through a realistic, militarily significant, and verifiable agreement. The work ahead is complex. The United States and its allies are, however, encouraged by the seriousness with which the Soviet Union and its allies have entered into this negotiation. What is needed now is for them to join NATO in exchanges that are frank and constructive and enhance the chances for success. In the CSBM's talks, NATO has tabled a set of proposals which build upon and expand the Stockholm document. The centerpiece of the NATO proposal is an annual exchange of information on military organization, manpower, and equipment in Europe, and a corresponding system to evaluate the information that is exchanged. These and other NATO proposals apply equally to all participating states, in contrast to the Eastern proposals that clearly seek to constrain NATO's ability to train and reinforce its troops.

During this second round, NATO will be elaborating the practical details of its proposals to demonstrate their effectiveness, feasibility, and the contribution they can make to furthering openness, transparency and predictability about military organization and activities in Europe.

Remarks on Signing the Asian/Pacific American Heritage Week Proclamation

May 8, 1989

Welcome to the Rose Garden, ladies and gentlemen and fellow Americans. You know, an Asian proverb says: "Intelligence consists in recognizing opportunity." Well, if that's true, it's clear that we are recognizing opportunity in putting the flag back where it belongs. [*Laughter*] No, intelligence consists in recognizing opportunity, and it's clear that you may be one of the most intelligent groups that we've welcomed to the White House, for you've recognized opportunity and seized it. And I am just delighted to be with you.

I'd like to welcome a very special visitor, President Hammer DeRoburt of Nauru out in the Pacific—a friend of the United States. Welcome, sir. And I think it's appropriate he's here, head of an island state in the Pacific—most appropriate that you join us here today, sir. Thank you.

We gather in a special week: Asian/Pacific American Heritage Week. And yesterday marked the 146th anniversary of the day the first Japanese immigrated to America; and Wednesday celebrates the 120th birthday of an event that Chinese-Americans made possible, the driving of the golden spike to complete the first transcontinental railroad. And we meet, too, as special friends. And in particular, I want to thank three people: Jeanie Jew, who created the idea for this week and is the granddaughter of a Chinese pioneer who helped build that railroad; Frank Horton, the chief sponsor of the Heritage Week legislation; and Ruby Moy, chairman of the Congressional Asia/Pacific American Heritage Week Caucus. Perhaps most of all, we assemble here for a special reason—to salute the millions of refugees and immigrants from Asia and the Pacific who braved the unknown and ventured to our shores, and to salute a community which has enriched America's community socially, culturally, economically, spiritually.

Ladies and gentlemen, as we proclaim this Asian/Pacific American Heritage Week let me observe that you have earned this recognition. You've done it through excellence, with the value of your lives. Those values are, of course, discipline and self-sacrifice, humility and compassion, an abiding belief in work, a soaring love of freedom—values which brought your parents, your grandparents, and some of you right here to America—values which are now uplifting America.

I think, for example, of pioneers like Gerald Tsai, Jr.; or Jenlane Gee, the California Teacher of the Year; or Henry Tang and I.M. Pei; of our own Sichan Siv, who fled the killing fields of Cambodia and a daring escape—now at work right here in the White House. Let me mention my trusted adviser, Lehmann Li, who's been at my side for a long time. You talk about a bright individual—he's a walking encyclopedia.

My friends, they—you—are building a better America and creating new jobs. You're enhancing our medical schools, the law, our small and large businesses—in short, honoring your heritage by the lives you lead; and for that I congratulate you.

And in a personal sense, I want to thank you, too, for as Chief of the United States Liaison Office in China, I came with Barbara to love that heritage and, in countless ways, with countless friends, to see and share what lies at its center: the family. Ten weeks ago on a trip back to Asia and to the Pacific Rim, Barbara and I visited the nondenominational church that we'd attended in Beijing. And it's different now—it's bigger; but the values, the heritage, are the same, and the memories are even better. And I'll never forget when our own daughter was baptized right there in China.

Yes, the Asian/Pacific community has a special place in my heart, and so does an old Chinese proverb which I've often cited. It goes: "One generation plants the trees, another gets the shade." For decades, Asian Americans have planted the trees of prosperity, opportunity, and human dignity. And in coming years, more than ever, I know that my children, America's children, will thank you for the shade.

And finally, before I sign this proclamation declaring this week as Asia/Pacific American Heritage Week, it gives me great pleasure to announce two nominations that I will submit to the Senate for confirmation to positions within my administration. I'll be sending the name of Julia Chang Bloch to the Senate to be the next—[*applause*]—United States Ambassador—please—[*laughter and applause*]—the next United States Ambassador to Nepal, and the name of Kyo Jhin to be Chief Counsel—Kyo—Chief Counsel for Advocacy in the SBA [Small Business Administration]. And I salute, also, Katherine Chang Dress, sworn in today as an Assistant Secretary of the Interior. We are so lucky. And we welcome these qualified, capable individuals to our team.

God bless all of you. Thank you for coming here to Washington on this beautiful day. And now, let's sign this proclamation. Thank you very much.

Note: The President spoke at 10:15 a.m. in the Rose Garden at the White House. In his remarks, he referred to Gerald Tsai, Jr., member of the board of directors of Primerica; Henry Tang, vice president of Solomon Brothers; I.M. Pei, architect; and Sichan Siv, Deputy Assistant to the President for Public Liaison. The proclamation is listed in Appendix E at the end of this volume.

Nomination of Julia Chang Bloch To Be United States Ambassador to Nepal

May 8, 1989

The President today announced his intention to nominate Julia Chang Bloch to be Ambassador Extraordinary and Plenipotentiary of the United States of America to the Kingdom of Nepal. She would succeed Milton Frank.

Since 1981 Ms. Bloch has served in several capacities for the Agency for International Development, including Assistant Administrator for the Asia and Near East Bureau, since 1987; Assistant Administrator for the Food for Peace and Voluntary Assistance Bureau, 1981–1987; and Special Assistant to the Administrator, 1981. Prior to this she was a fellow at the Institute of Politics of the Kennedy School of Government at Harvard University, 1980–1981. She has also served as Deputy Director of the Office of African Affairs for the International Communication Agency, 1977–1980; and chief minority counsel for the Senate Select Committee on Nutrition and Human Needs, 1976–1977. Ms. Bloch served as a staff member for the minority staff of the Senate Select Committee on Nutrition and Human Needs, 1971–1976. She served in various capacities with the Peace Corps, including evaluation officer, 1968–1970; training officer for the East Asia and Pacific Region, 1967–1968; and a volunteer in Sabah, Malaysia, 1964–1966. Ms. Bloch was awarded the Woman of the Year Award from the Organization of Chinese American Women, 1987; the Leader for Peace Award from the Peace Corps, 1987; and the Humanitarian Service Award from the Agency for International Development, 1987.

Ms. Bloch graduated from the University of California (B.A., 1964) and Harvard University (M.A., 1967). She was born March 2, 1942, in Chefoo, China. She is married and resides in Washington, DC.

Nomination of Kyo Ryoon Jhin To Be Chief Counsel for Advocacy at the Small Business Administration
May 8, 1989

The President today announced his intention to nominate Kyo Ryoon Jhin to be Chief Counsel for Advocacy at the Small Business Administration. He would succeed Frank S. Swain.

Since 1986 Dr. Jhin has been an international trade consultant for Metro Investment Group in Bethesda, MD. He served as assistant superintendent for educational technology for the District of Columbia Public Schools, 1983 to present. He was a senior associate in the Office of Educational Research and Improvement for the Department of Education, 1981–1983; and an administrative officer in the Office of School Improvement, 1979–1981. Dr. Jhin was executive director for the Top of Alabama Regional Education Service Agency, 1971–1979. He has served as a member of the National Advisory Council on Adult Education, and vice-chairman, 1977–1978; and chairman of the Committee on Legislative and Government Relations, 1978–1979.

Dr. Jhin graduated from David Lipscomb College (B.A., 1960), New York University (M.A., 1965), Boston College (M.A., 1967), and Auburn University (Ed.D., 1971).

Remarks at the Presentation Ceremony for the Small Business Persons of the Year Awards
May 8, 1989

To the Members of Congress here and all the distinguished guests, first let me welcome Susan Engeleiter, the Administrator of SBA [Small Business Administration], as well as all the State small business people and their families who came here today. I've participated in these ceremonies before, and I'm especially pleased and honored to present these awards today.

As you probably know, I—long ago—was a small businessman myself, and I think, therefore, I know some of the worries that you share—the what-ifs when you're the one in charge. And I know how it feels to start something from scratch, work with it day and night, and hopefully see it succeed. Success goes to those who work hard, refuse to give up, and learn from their mistakes. And there's a saying: If I had my life to live again, I'd make the same mistakes, only sooner. [*Laughter*] I think small business men and women can understand those words.

You don't have to sell me on the value of small business. The work you do is vital to this nation's economic well-being. And I brought along some statistics to back that up. Small businesses employ more than half of America's private sector work force. Small businesses account for over a third of our gross national product. And I've saved the best statistics for last. During the past decade, small businesses have created two out of every three new jobs in our economy. And for me, that's the bottom line. Small business is on the business end of growth and at the cutting edge of the economic expansion that's 77 months old and still going strong.

Let me take a moment right here to mention an issue that should be on the top of the list for all small business people: the question of child care. As you know so well, you're more likely to find small business owners sitting around a kitchen table than in a big corporate boardroom someplace. A small business is less a corporation than a family. And like a family, people engaged in a small business enterprise share common aims, a common outlook, and certainly have common interests. And that's the perfect workplace environment for innovative approaches to meet the concerns and needs of employees. I urge America's small businesses to take the lead in developing creative solutions in child care. I think, for example, of pioneers like Gerald Tsai, Jr., or Jenlane Gee and others who we honored out there today, Asians who have a strong bearing and support in their families for child care. I will do nothing as President of the United States, absolutely nothing, that weakens our family structure. And I encourage small businesses to do everything they can to strengthen the family structure by getting together in a cooperative fashion.

My child care tax credit program is going to benefit small businesses, I believe. I do not believe in these mandated government benefits. I think it has to be decided by the Federal Government, making as flexible as possible the use of child-care tax credits. So, I wanted to take this opportunity, a little off the beaten path, you might say, of honoring these honorees today. But it is very, very important that all of you who are out there trying to produce at competitive rates, competitive ways, help as best you can. You know the value of freedom and flexibility. And so, I just want to see us work together to preserve that freedom in child care and in other issues that affect the way we live and work.

A moment ago, I cited some statistics on the large impact of small business in the American economy. Ceremonies like this one are important because they honor the individuals behind the statistics—the small business people who conceive the idea, take the chance, and make it work. So, today we recognize the best that small business has to offer. And I want to turn now to the awards.

This year there is no fourth place finisher. Instead, we have a tie for third place. And I'll start with Chad Olson of Utah. Chad produces a highly successful line of professional and collegiate sports merchandise. He's marketed franchises in 40 States already. And I understand he's got his eye on all 50. He's got international ambitions as well, with franchise plans for Canada and U.S. military bases overseas. Now, do we do this right now? All right. Chad? Well done.

And sharing this third place award with Chad is Carolyn Stradley of Georgia. She started out as a bookkeeper for a paving company and left that company to do what many here have done—start out on her own. She used a loan from her brother to buy her truck, built her business by taking the small jobs that no one else thought worthwhile; and today she's a success, and equally important, an inspiration to businesswomen everywhere. And so, congratulations to you.

The winner of this year's second place award comes from Kansas—Richard Barlow. Dick is well-known to gourmet cookie makers as the manufacturer of REMA insulated bakeware. He started his business with a family friend just 6 years ago selling these cookie sheets in Oklahoma—in Kansas. And today REMA bakeware is sold in all 50 States and Japan. And so, congratulations to you, Richard. Well done.

And now the 1989 winner, this year's Small Business Person of the Year, Tad Bretting of Wisconsin. I wondered why Senator Kasten was over here. [*Laughter*] Tad's got business in his blood. His family has been in the machinery business for three generations—almost 100 years. He joined the family business in 1958. And those 30 years have seen the Bretting Company grow and prosper from 11 employees back in 1958 to 260 today, from $120,000 in sales each year to $30 million. And today his company is the world's leading producer of high-tech, custom-designed machinery for making paper products. And the secret of Tad's success is the one small business people know so well: it all comes down to taking good care of customers. And so, congratulations to you, Tad.

So, there you have our four winners. This room, though, is full of success stories today. It's in this nation's small businesses that the American spirit, entrepreneurial spirit, takes root and grows. And so, our nation needs you—your drive, your dynamism, your creativity, and your can-do attitude. Congratulations to all of you, and especially to you winners with us here today. Thank you all very much.

Note: The President spoke at 1:40 p.m. in the East Room at the White House. In his remarks, he referred to Gerald Tsai, Jr., member of the board of directors of Primerica, and Jenlane Gee, California Teacher of the Year, 1988.

Message to the Congress Transmitting the District of Columbia Budget Request
May 9, 1989

To the Congress of the United States:

In accordance with the District of Columbia Self-Government and Governmental Reorganization Act, I am transmitting the District of Columbia Government's FY 1990 Budget and FY 1989 Budget supplemental.

The District's General Fund 1990 operating budget request is $3,071 million. Total Federal payments anticipated in the District's budget are $498 million. The District's FY 1989 budget supplemental contains $106 million in cost increases and $79 million in budget authority rescissions, for a net increase of $27 million. This transmittal does not affect the Federal budget.

There are four District budget issues to which I would direct your attention. First, I would encourage you to continue the abortion funding policy that the Congress established in the District's 1989 appropriations bill that prohibits the use of both Federal and local funds for abortions.

Second, the 1990 Budget reproposes an initiative that would require the District of Columbia to charge Federal establishments directly for water and sewer services. The lump-sum appropriation provided in recent years to the District for water and sewer services in Federal buildings increases the deficit unnecessarily because Federal agencies' budgets already contain funds to pay these costs. I urge the Congress to enact this needed reform. Direct billing also reduces appropriated Federal payments for nongovernmental entities, such as the American Red Cross and the Pan American Union, as well as for entities outside the appropriations process such as the Postal Service and the Federal Savings and Loan Insurance Corporation. It would encourage Federal agencies to assure the accuracy of bills received and to pursue conservation policies.

Third, I request reinstatement of Presidential apportionment authority over the Federal payment to the District of Columbia. Directing immediate disbursement of the Federal payment at the start of the fiscal year increases Treasury's cost of borrowing. Further, the Congress very clearly did not intend to exempt the District of Columbia from sequestration in the original Gramm-Rudman-Hollings Act, and there is no reason for doing so via an appropriations bill.

Finally, in a related Federal Budget request, I will include a $1 million supplemental reimbursing the District Government for additional Presidential inaugural expenses incurred above the $2.3 million appropriated.

I look forward to working with the Congress on these matters.

GEORGE BUSH

The White House,
May 9, 1989.

White House Fact Sheet on the President's Child-Care Principles
May 9, 1989

Four basic principles underlie the President's approach to child care:

- Parents, who are best able to make decisions about their children's care, should have the discretion to make these decisions.

- Federal policy should not discriminate against parents who work at home.
- Federal policies should act to increase, not decrease, the range of child care choices available to parents.
- New Federal assistance should be targeted to families most in need.

Myths and Facts about Child Care Today

Myth: Religiously affiliated day care will benefit from new Federal day care programs such as the ABC bill.

Fact: As many as one-third of formal day care centers are religiously affiliated. ABC prohibits assistance "for any sectarian purpose or activity, including sectarian worship and instruction." This implies that to be eligible under ABC, the child care services provided by religiously affiliated centers might be required to be *indistinguishable* from those provided by wholly secular providers. To meet this standard, facilities could be required by the courts or by Federal or State regulatory bodies to remove religious symbols, end the teaching of religious values and avoid such practices as prayer before meals and the singing of religious songs. Furthermore, even those centers which adhered rigorously to these standards would be subject to potential litigation over their receipt of ABC funds.

Myth: Most young children are being cared for in day care centers.

Fact: Less than 11 percent of children under 5 are cared for in child care centers. Only 46 percent of children under 5 have employed mothers. Even among those mothers who are employed, the great majority use relatives or neighbors as child care providers. For parents with young children who prefer to care for their children themselves while their spouses work, the President's proposals will shift the economics of work and child care in their favor. The President's proposals discriminate neither against day care centers nor mothers caring for children at home.

Myth: Aiding child care centers will primarily help low- and moderate-income working families.

Fact: Subsidies biased toward center-based care will naturally tend to help those who are comparatively better off. In 1986 a majority of mothers in married-couple families earning less than $20,000 chose to stay at home to provide child care while less than one-third of the mothers in families making over $20,000 made the same choice. Furthermore, approximately 80 percent of children in center-based care come from two-earner families.

Myth: Federal day care standards are necessary because day care is largely unregulated.

Fact: All States currently regulate day care to some extent. Every State licenses child care centers, and all but one regulate some or all family day care homes. State and local governments are best able to determine what standards are needed for child care. Federal standards, proposed in the past, will not work. Congress, realizing this, prohibited implementation of Federal standards in 1980.

Myth: Unregulated child care is unhealthy and unsafe for children.

Fact: The typical "unregulated" day care provider is a mother caring for one or two other neighborhood children, along with her own child. In contrast, in day care centers, the average ratio of children to staff is five to one. According to an ABT Associates report, "The National Day Care Home Study," unregulated family child care is "stable, warm, and stimulating . . . it caters successfully to the developmentally appropriate needs of children in care; parents who use family day care report it satisfactorily meets their child care needs . . . [the study's] observers were consistently impressed by the care they saw regardless of regulatory status."

THE ABC BILL DOES NOT MEET THE PRESIDENT'S PRINCIPLES

The Senate is likely to turn soon to the "Act for Better Child Care," sponsored by Senator Dodd. This bill, "ABC," does not meet the President's principles for increasing child care options and parental choice:

Parental choice: ABC puts its trust in government, not parents. No money goes directly to parents. All money goes to the

States. The States then fund providers, not parents, through grants, contracts, and certificates that they, not parents, arrange or approve. It is the States, not parents, who have the ultimate decision-making power on the care children will receive under ABC.

Encourages options: ABC imposes Federal day care standards on all providers who receive public assistance. All States currently regulate day care to some degree, ensuring a healthy and safe environment for children. These costly Federal requirements will put some current child care providers out of business, keep potential providers from offering care, and drive up the cost of care available for all parents. Parents who want their children to be taught and guided by the religious values that are central to their lives would not be able to receive assistance: All caregivers, including relatives, are prohibited from engaging in sectarian activities, worship, or instruction in providing services under ABC.

In fact, parents could not use their ABC eligibility to have anyone other than a grandparent, aunt, or uncle care for their children unless (1) the State rules in each individual case that the person was an eligible child care provider, (2) the person and his/her home meets Federal standards, and (3) the person submits to governmental grant, contract and paperwork requirements.

Nondiscrimination: ABC serves two-parent families only if both parents are employed, perpetuating the discrimination against two-parent families in which one parent stays at home to care for the children.

Targeted to families most in need: ABC is not well targeted and would serve only a fraction of families most in need. Families with incomes as high as 4 times the poverty level are eligible for ABC. Only a small number of eligible children would actually receive care under ABC—6 percent in 1990 according to the sponsors' estimates, and there is no guarantee that they would be from families most in need. Only one million children, the sponsors say, would receive child care services from the States—far less than the number of children in the 3.5 million families that would initially benefit from the President's tax credit proposals.

Note: The fact sheet also contained information concerning the President's visit to the Shiloh Child Development Center.

Question-and-Answer Session With Teachers at the Shiloh Child Development Center

May 9, 1989

The President. Well, tell me how it's going. That's what I wanted to find out. And it seems—where are we? What are we in?

Ms. Omachonu. This is in the chapel——

The President. The chapel?

Ms. Omachonu. And this is a special place where many of our youth come——

The President. I see.

Ms. Omachonu. ——on Sundays.

The President. Lovely, isn't it? Then the big church is right on this side?

Ms. Omachonu. It's right on the other side, yes.

The President. I haven't been here in a while, but I've known your pastor for a long time. Tell me about how it's going. One reason we wanted to do this is that I do feel that there is a role, a national role, for the kind of child care center that you all have run for—what, how many years?—some years.

Ms. Omachonu. A long time.

The President. Yes, a long time—because I do not want to see the Federal legislation erode out this kind of participation—in this instance, by a church. And I worry that some of the legislation up there would say to a church, if you want to get Federal help, you can't have a religious underpinning to your day care center. And I don't think that's good.

But anyway, that's the Bush view. But I'm anxious—more interested in listening and getting your views on this. Who wants to start?

Ms. Omachonu. First of all, I would like to say that the traditional philosophy of the center is based on meeting the direct needs of young children. And this developmental program is designed to meet the child's physical, social needs. And we do plan activity in different learning areas, and also we do celebrate religious programs—for example, Christmas. And children do learn that Christmas means sharing, caring, and loving, besides celebrating the birth of Jesus Christ. And also we encourage our children to say their grace before each meal. And we have show-and-tell period: when they come to school on Monday, they tell us about their experiences at the Sunday school; they have opportunities to sing religious songs on Monday morning.

The President. Well, that's good, that's very good. Are the kids that come here all—their families all parishioners of Shiloh?

Ms. Omachonu. No.

The President. Not necessarily. Who else?

Ms. Nickerson. I believe we have one minister's child in the 4-year-old group. But we recognize and we also respect religious philosophies from——

The President. Diversity, yes.

Ms. Nickerson. Yes. We have different backgrounds——

The President. And do you have kids from different—obviously, nondenominational. But do you have kids that come out of religions that are not Christian? I mean, like——

Ms. Omachonu. Yes, we do. We have two children whose parents are Muslim. We also have another child whose parents belong to the Jehovah Witness, the whole family. But we do sort of—with activities, we seek their permission that their children participate in the activities or exclude them out of activities. They've been very supportive. They say, "Go ahead, let them participate."

The President. Well, it's a concept that is so important. And I believe strongly in separation of church and state, and so does the pastor; but we're not talking of that here. We're talking about your right to diversify—to do it in a diverse way and not have the central government dictate exactly what you can do on this. And you know, our—I won't go into detail on the proposals, but my thought is choice, to help the parents with choice. If they want to send a kid to this facility, fine. Give them a little help—those that need it the most. And if they want to go to some other kind of facility where there's no religious reference, fine, let them do that, too. But I worry that if we have one piece of legislation that defines all the standards and leans over so far backwards on the separation of church and state, that you just erode out the participation of one of the best forces in the community for teaching these kids values.

You didn't have a say. I've been doing too much of the talking.

Ms. Johnson. I'm Ms. Johnson, and I have the 2-year-old class. And I teach them finger play, a lot of songs—have to keep them busy, because they don't keep still at all. But you have to really keep them busy. And, you know, I love them—I love them.

The President. What's the time now, what do they do? Parents go into work, mother will bring the kid here—or dad—and leave them off at what time?

Ms. Omachonu. Okay, around 7 a.m.

The President. Seven?

Ms. Johnson. Yes, we open at 7 a.m.

The President. And then do they pick them up at different times or——

Ms. Johnson. Yes, they have different times. They start picking them up around 4:30 p.m., and we close at 6 p.m. So between 4:30 p.m. and 6 p.m., they're picking the children up.

The President. Yes. And they pay—I think my briefing paper—what did it say?

Ms. Johnson. Fifty-five dollars a week.

The President. Fifty-five dollars? And they have a meal in there?

Ms. Johnson. Yes, they have hot breakfast, and they have hot lunches. Nothing packed. Everything is straight from the stove.

Ms. Omachonu. And a 1 p.m. snack.

The President. ——p.m. snack? What, end of the day kind of thing?

Ms. Omachonu. End of the day.

Reverend Gregory. I think this is so important, too, because the focus is on the whole person. And our center strives to emphasize health and wellness, nutrition, skills development, and also values clarification—values education, so the children will learn the difference between right and wrong. And most of all, the community I think is so important, and they have a sense of identity—who they are—and the opportunities——

The President. Oh, yes.

Reverend Gregory. And the community becomes like a extended family member.

The President. Some probably have—like in any part of the society—divided families, so they get an extra dimension of love here that they might not be getting at home.

Reverend Gregory. Exactly.

Ms. Nickerson. Well, the parents are pretty supportive in our program also. They help out in whatever way—whatever we teach is extended to the family setting. So, moral standards are a very strong criteria that we concentrate on in terms of social skills; they're going to need to develop these in the future.

The President. What's the oldest kid—age—that you get in the day care, or child care?

Ms. Omachonu. Up to 5 years of age.

The President. Five would be—then they go off to regular?

Ms. Omachonu. Regular school. But we do have an after-school program where they come here in the afternoon.

The President. The little guys—I mean, 6, 7 years old? That kind of thing?

Ms. Omachonu. Yes.

The President. What's your end of all of this madhouse?

Ms. Gerald. I'm Ms. Gerald, and I work with the 3-year-olds.

The President. Three-year-olds?

Ms. Gerald. Yes. And we have our daily activities. In the morning, we have our opening. We do reading and sharing. And they have math—we do numbers. We do our finger plays and our songs. We just have—go through the day.

The President. Do most of the kids that come to your center—do they have a family that goes, if not to Shiloh, to some church, or not? Is there a church—like a religious theme that runs through these various families, or some of them just totally out of that?

Ms. Omachonu. I wouldn't say totally. They are definitely from religious families.

The President. They are?

Ms. Omachonu. Yes.

Reverend Gregory. Mr. President, would you like to see some of the children?

The President. I'm kicking myself. I should have brought a couple of the little puppies out of that basket.

Ms. Johnson. They would have loved that.

The President. Except I wouldn't want to clean up your rugs around here. [*Laughter*] I should have done that because kids just love those little fuzzy things. And we're about to—I was telling the Reverend, they're about to leave home.

Note: The President spoke at 10:45 a.m. in the chapel of the family life center. Participants in the session included: Florence Omachonu, director of the center; teachers Yvette Nickerson, Joan Johnson, and Justina Gerald; and Rev. Henry Gregory III, pastor of Shiloh Baptist Church.

Remarks by Telephone to Astronauts Aboard the Space Shuttle *Atlantis*
May 9, 1989

The President. Hello. Captain Walker, can you hear me?

Astronauts. [*Inaudible*]

The President. Well, I'm just checking in to wish you five the very best and to thank you for a mission so well done. I've got to make a slight complaint on our communications, because you guys can send something off to Venus, but I couldn't get ahold of you on the airplane flying back to Houston. But that's a minor complaint from the Oval Office.

But how are you feeling? And we are so proud of the job you all did.

Astronauts. [*Inaudible*]

The President. No, after——

Astronauts. [*Inaudible*]

The President. I mean, just on the physical side, is there any comparison to jet lag, or do you just really feel up to speed now?

Astronauts. [*Inaudible*]

The President. Mary, it sounds like you. But, look, how was the actual deployment thing? That went smoothly, as I recall.

Astronauts. [*Inaudible*]

The President. Yes, yes, yes.

Astronauts. [*Inaudible*]

The President. That's amazing—1990 arrival? Is that something like that?

Astronauts. [*Inaudible*]

The President. August of—is it true that the Soviets have had great difficulty probing out that far?

Astronauts. [*Inaudible*]

The President. What'd they do—lose communication? Was it Venus? It was, wasn't it?

Astronauts. [*Inaudible*]

The President. Mars. Yes, have they done anything towards Venus?

Astronauts. [*Inaudible*]

The President. Is that right? I know our expectations are very high on the degree of resolution on this. It sounds like—hey, tell me just a little—have you got a couple of more seconds—tell me a little about the computer lab you all are setting up—the repair shop up there. Did everything end up being okay?

Astronauts. [*Inaudible*]

The President. Yes, well, it was. I think that captured the imagination of a lot of Earthlings, to think that something like that could be accomplished up there. What's next for you all?

Astronauts. [*Inaudible*]

The President. [*Laughing*] Just so you don't find the flight instructor, because I saw a couple of those sheets, and I'm a little embarrassed for you all to see them, frankly. I hope that——

Astronauts. [*Inaudible*]

The President. Well, you may have trouble being that selective. But, listen, are you coming to Washington, because we'd love to see you here in the Oval Office or—and I know Barbara would like to say hello. And if there are no plans for that, why, I expect I'll be—well, I know I'm coming down to Houston at the end of the week. But I'd love to have you all here. Are there any plans for that?

Astronauts. [*Inaudible*]

The President. It is. Hey, listen, it's an invitation, and—well, let's work it out. I'll work through Admiral Truly [Administrator of the National Aeronautics and Space Administration] and set it up, because I'd like very much to have you here soon, and I'll talk you in the corner about hiding the flight sheets from my naval aviator days. But, really, you——

Astronauts. [*Inaudible*]

The President. Do I—sure I want to hear it?

Astronauts. [*Inaudible*]

The President. You got it—you got it. But the trouble is, unless you get here—well, you can't do it because I'm leaving Thursday. I was going to say, unless you hurry up, the puppies are gone. They're heading on out to their various—no, a couple of them will be here. Three of them will be in the neighborhood, but one's already gone to Texas—Texas Rangerette, they call her—and she's there with our son in Dallas. And then one heads to Florida; one goes to Kentucky Thursday; but the other three will be in the neighborhood. For you we might reassemble them. But we'll work this out; I want you to come here. And we're very proud of the job you all did. So, we'll check with Admiral Truly and see that we get a time that's convenient for all of you—you and spouses as well.

Astronauts. [*Inaudible*]

The President. Well, I believe very much—and my only worries—and they are worries that affect absolutely everything that I want to do—is the budgetary constraints. But we've got some, I think, reasonably good figures in here now for NASA in which I totally believe, so we'll try to do our part from this end.

But, anyway, I'll let you all go and get some rest, but we will look forward to seeing you.

Astronauts. [*Inaudible*]

The President. And well done, and thank you. We're very, very proud of all five of you. Over and out.

Note: The President spoke at 2:17 p.m. from the Oval Office at the White House. The remarks of the astronauts were not included in the White House press release, and a tape was not available for verification of the content of this conversation. The crew of the "Atlantis" included: Capt. David M. Walker, USN, commanding officer; Lt. Col. Ronald J. Grabe, USAF, pilot; Mary L. Cleave, mission specialist; Maj. Mark C. Lee, USAF, mission specialist; and Norman E. Thagard, mission specialist.

Interview With Members of the White House Press Corps
May 9, 1989

Panamanian Elections

The President. Well, let me first make a brief statement: I'd like to comment on the Panamanian elections. I met with the Murtha delegation to hear their report, and I have now received the preliminary report from President Ford and President Carter. President Carter and his whole delegation will be here shortly to give me a full report. In addition, we have the report of other observer groups, including that of the Archbishop of Panama, which demonstrate clearly that despite massive irregularities at the polls the opposition has won a clear-cut, overwhelming victory. The Panamanian people have spoken, and I call on General Noriega to respect the voice of the people. And I call on all foreign leaders to urge General Noriega to honor the clear results of the election.

And I might add that I applaud the statement by Peru's [President] Alan Garcia, who has spoken out against the fraud. I noted with interest that the Archbishop of Panama felt that 74 percent of the vote went to the opposition. And I understand that President Carlos Andrés Pérez of Venezuela is talking to some of the neighboring countries there to encourage a joint statement against the fraud that has taken place and calling on Noriega to honor the results of this election.

Q. What kind of military force are you considering? We were told that that's one of the options.

The President. The election results have not been handed in, formally announced, and until they are, I will not discuss the options of the United States. I will simply again call on General Noriega to honor the will of the people.

Q. Mr. President, you called on him a year ago to do precisely the same thing, as did Mr. Reagan, and nothing happened. Why should it be any different this time?

The President. Because there has been a massive voice of the people heard. There has been a statement for democracy so loud and so clear that perhaps even General Noriega will listen to it. And I would like to think that he will heed the call of the people and that he would listen to the international outcry that is building and that he would step down from office, in which case, the relations with the United States would improve dramatically and instantly.

Q. Have you spoken to foreign leaders? Do you plan to speak with foreign leaders?

The President. I probably will, and without going into who I've spoken to, the answer is yes. You know, we've had foreign visitors here and talked to them and——

Q. Do you really think you have a military option? And on what basis could you go into someone else's country?

The President. Helen [Helen Thomas, United Press International], I'm not going to say what our options are. I've not discussed that here today. I have obviously discussed options with my own top advisers. I listened very intently to the Members of Congress that came in, and some of them had specific suggestions. But I want to see General Noriega do what I've just encouraged him to do and what other foreign leaders apparently are encouraging him to do.

Q. Did you put yourself in a box here by making such a public point of being upset about these elections, and if Noriega decides to stay anyhow, that it looks like the United States has been ineffective?

The President. I don't think the United States is ever in a box when it speaks out in favor of free, fair elections and honoring the will of the people. That's what we stand for. And so, I don't think there's any box involved.

Q. Some Members of Congress have called for the abrogation of the Canal treaty. Is that in any way a possibility in your mind, an option?

The President. I want to see General Noriega do what I have just encouraged him to do. I want to see the will of the people honored.

Q. But under any circumstances would you——

The President. I'm not going to go into hypothetical questions at this point.

Q. Have you talked to him? Have you given him any personal ultimatum?

The President. Put it this way: General Noriega knows my position.

Q. How?

The President. Never mind. He knows. And it's been told——

Q. Did you call him up?

The President. ——in recent—he knows about it through recent contacts.

Q. Have you issued any orders regarding the military on the bases in Panama? Are they in a state of alert? And are you anticipating increasing their numbers?

The President. I will discuss at the appropriate time what course of action I will take. But I'm not going to do that now. What I want to do now is encourage this last moment for General Noriega to heed the appeal of those people who favor democracy and to heed the will of the Panamanian people. So, I don't want to go beyond that in terms of deployment of U.S. force.

Short-Range Nuclear Forces in Europe

Q. Are you any closer to an SNF agreement with the Germans?

The President. I have a good feeling that there's been a lot of smoke out there and that we'll have a smooth summit.

Q. Have you talked with [West German Chancellor] Kohl again?

The President. Oh, I never discuss all these talks I've had.

Q. That means you're willing to compromise, right?

The President. It might mean people are willing to do it our way—with the United States.

Q. Doesn't sound that way.

The President. Well, don't believe everything you read in the UP. [*Laughter*]

Q. Will it be settled tonight with the Dutch?

The President. I don't know. We'll be talking to Mr. Lubbers [Prime Minister of The Netherlands] over here, a friend of long standing and a man with whom I can talk very, very frankly about SNF.

Q. You can talk frankly with us.

The President. And I didn't talk to him this morning about it. We talked about other subjects. But I've added an additional hour so we can do just exactly that. But this alliance is not going to fall apart. It is going to stay together and be strong.

Iran Arms and Contra Aid Controversy

Q. What do you think about the North verdict, Mr. President?

The President. What?

Q. What do you think about the North verdict?

The President. As you know, I wanted all along to see him exonerated. And that matter is now under appeal, and thus, I will have nothing more to say about it while it is.

Q. Well, do you think he was innocent?

The President. Well, I'm not going to argue with the courts, but the process is being appealed. He's entitled to the right of appeal without a lot of editorial comment from me on it.

Q. You don't believe in shredding documents, surely?

The President. No, I believe in taking them with me. [*Laughter*]

Note: The interview began at 3:20 p.m. in the Oval Office at the White House. George

Condon, of Copley News Service; Julia L. Malone, of Cox News Service; Helen Thomas, of United Press International; and Charles D. Goodgame, of Time, Inc., participated in the interview.

Statement by Press Secretary Fitzwater on the President's Physical Examination
May 9, 1989

President Bush will undergo a routine physical examination at Bethesda Naval Hospital at approximately 8 a.m. on Wednesday, May 10, 1989. The President will depart the White House aboard Marine One at 7:50 Wednesday morning and return following the examination at approximately 12:30 p.m.

The President will undergo the following tests: chest x ray, hearing tests, eye examination, electrocardiogram (EKG), allergy examination, urinalysis, dermatology examination, and a complete history and personal examination by Dr. Burton Lee, the President's personal physician. Dr. Lee has taken several blood samples earlier in the week which will be analyzed as part of the examination.

The entire physical will be under the direction of Dr. Lee with assistance from the physician staff of Bethesda Naval Hospital, which will include Capt. Ralph Sawyer, ophthalmologist; Capt. Kevin O'Connell, urologist; Capt. Harry Parlette, dermatologist; and Capt.'s Cheryl Rosenblatt and William Ebbeling, allergists. A written description of the results will be available Wednesday afternoon.

Statement by Press Secretary Fitzwater on the Results of the President's Physical Examination
May 10, 1989

President Bush today completed a routine physical examination at Bethesda Naval Hospital and is in excellent health. The President's examination lasted approximately 3 hours. The physical was under the direction of Dr. Burton Lee, the President's personal physician.

"President Bush is in extremely sound physical condition," Dr. Lee said. "He keeps fit through a number of physical activities, which we recommend he continue on a regular basis. Today's examination shows him to be in excellent health. He has no significant symptoms related to any of his organ systems."

In general, the results of the tests are as follows: chest x ray, normal; x rays of hips show mild degenerative osteoarthritis, which has been present for several years; eye and ear examinations, unchanged; electrocardiogram (EKG), normal; urinalysis shows no abnormalities; blood samples all appear normal; allergy tests showed excellent protective antibody levels; and dermatology examination showed no significant problem or change.

A sebaceous cyst on the third finger of his right hand was drained. The President is wearing a Band-Aid on the finger, which he can remove within the next few hours. This cyst has been present for many years and does not present a medical problem.

Assisting Dr. Lee from the physician staff of Bethesda Naval Hospital were Capt. Ralph Sawyer, ophthalmologist; Capt. Kevin O'Connell, urologist; Capt. Harry Parlette, dermatologist; and Capt.'s Cheryl Rosenblatt and William Ebbeling, allergists.

Remarks and a Question-and-Answer Session With Reporters on the Situation in Panama
May 11, 1989

The President. Well, I have a statement here, and then I'll be glad to take a couple of questions, and then I will turn the meeting over to General Scowcroft for any followup.

The people of Latin America and the Caribbean have sacrificed, fought, and died to establish democracy. Today elected constitutional government is the clear choice of the vast majority of the people in the Americas, and the days of the dictator are over. Still, in many parts of our hemisphere, the enemies of democracy lie in wait to overturn elected governments through force or to steal elections through fraud. All nations in the democratic community have a responsibility to make it clear, through our actions and our words, that efforts to overturn constitutional regimes or steal elections are unacceptable. If we fail to send a clear signal when democracy is imperiled, the enemies of constitutional government will become more dangerous. And that's why events in Panama place an enormous responsibility on all nations in the democratic community.

This past week, the people of Panama, in record numbers, voted to elect a new democratic leadership of their country; and they voted to replace the dictatorship of General Manuel Noriega. The whole world was watching. Every credible observer—the Catholic Church, Latin and European observers, leaders of our Congress, and two former Presidents of the United States—tell the same story: The opposition won. It was not even a close election. The opposition won by a margin of nearly 3 to 1.

The Noriega regime first tried to steal this election through massive fraud and intimidation and now has nullified the election and resorted to violence and bloodshed. In recent days, a host of Latin American leaders have condemned this election fraud. They've called on General Noriega to heed the will of the people of Panama. We support and second those demands. The United States will not recognize nor accommodate with a regime that holds power through force and violence at the expense of the Panamanian people's right to be free. I've exchanged these views over the last several days with democratic leaders in Latin America and in Europe. These consultations will continue.

The crisis in Panama is a conflict between Noriega and the people of Panama. The United States stands with the Panamanian people. We share their hope that the Panamanian defense forces will stand with them and fulfill their constitutional obligation to defend democracy. A professional Panamanian defense force can have an important role to play in Panama's democratic future.

The United States is committed to democracy in Panama. We respect the sovereignty of Panama, and of course, we have great affection for the Panamanian people. We are also committed to protect the lives of our citizens, and we're committed to the integrity of the Panama Canal treaties, which guarantee safe passage for all nations through the Canal. The Panama Canal treaties are a proud symbol of respect and partnership between the people of the United States and the people of Panama.

In support of these objectives and after consulting this morning with the bipartisan leadership of the Congress, I am taking the following steps: First, the United States strongly supports and will cooperate with initiatives taken by governments in this hemisphere to address this crisis through regional diplomacy and action in the Organization of American States and through other means. Second, our Ambassador in Panama, Arthur Davis, has been recalled, and our Embassy staff will be reduced to essential personnel only. Third, U.S. Government employees and their dependents living outside of U.S. military bases or Panama Canal commissioned housing areas will be relocated out of Panama or to secure U.S. housing areas within Panama. This action will begin immediately. It will be completed as quickly and in an orderly a manner as possible. Fourth, the State Department, through its travel advisory, will encourage U.S. business representatives resident in Panama to arrange for the extended absences of their dependents wherever possible. Fifth, economic sanctions will continue in force. Sixth, the United States will carry out its obligations and will assert and enforce its treaty rights in Panama under the Panama Canal treaties. And finally, we are sending a brigade-size force to Panama to augment our military forces already assigned there. If required, I do not rule out further steps in the future.

The United States and all democratic nations in this hemisphere hope that a peaceful resolution can be found to the crisis in Panama. And we urge all those in Panama—every individual, every institution—to put the well-being of their country first and seek an honorable solution to this crisis. The way is still open.

Thank you. God bless.

Q. Mr. President, are you willing to drop the drug charges against Noriega if it will mean that he will leave the country or at least give up control in a quid pro quo?

The President. No.

Q. Mr. President, do you recognize Mr. Endara as the President-elect, and what steps should the United States take to help him get inaugurated?

The President. We have not made any formal recognition determination at this point.

Q. Mr. President, I understand that you've been trying——

The President. We have been talking to other countries in the hemisphere on that point, I might add, Terry [Terence Hunt, Associated Press], but we have made no official determination.

Q. I understand you've been trying today, sir, to get other leaders in the hemisphere to agree on a joint statement of condemnation of Noriega, and I wonder if you could give us a progress report on that diplomatic effort, sir?

The President. Well, one, I have not—by joint statement—encouraged a joint statement in which the United States would participate. Some of the leaders in this hemisphere are working on getting a joint statement, and indeed, I'm told authoritatively that there might be a joint statement out of some European countries. But we would encourage countries in this hemisphere to either jointly or personally make strong statements. And I believe that—I want to say 10 countries have already made individual statements. And now, I think the next collective diplomatic action is going to be at the OAS.

Q. Sir, how many troops will that mean, and will they be quartered in the military compound? Will they stay there quietly and just be there, or will they be out on the streets patrolling?

The President. We will assert our treaty rights, enforce our treaty rights. And I will let General Scowcroft answer the question, but my estimate of the troops would be about 2,000.

Q. Mr. President, what is your justification for sending the brigade of troops? What are you worried about?

The President. I'm worried about the lives of American citizens. And I will do what is necessary to protect the lives of American citizens. And we will not be intimidated by the bullying tactics, brutal though they may be, of the dictator, Noriega.

Q. Mr. President, your statement just now about defense forces—would that be a signal that the United States would look favorably on a coup attempt?

The President. I have asserted what my interest is at this point: it is democracy in Panama; it is protection of the life of Americans in Panama.

I'm going to take two more, and then I'm going to go.

Q. Sir, we've been calling around to these Latin American Embassies. We find no enthusiasm for the dispatch of American troops there, and the Mexican Embassy even said that they warned against intervention. Are you disappointed at the reaction you're getting from Latin America?

The President. We've had good reaction from the Latin Americans. I haven't talked to them on that particular point, but we have had very good reaction from them. And I have been impressed with the role of several of the Latin American leaders. I think for the first time there is a total understanding on their part of the threat to democracy from the stealing of this election, or the threat to democracy in the hemisphere from totalitarianism; and it's brought home by this theft of the election.

So, they don't—I might add, on the troops: I have a profound obligation as Commander in Chief of the Armed Forces and as President, and that is to protect American life. And I'm going to do what is prudent and necessary to do this. And so, we have a different obligation. We also have certain treaty rights and obligations. I'm prepared to fulfill our treaty obligations, and I am prepared to see that our treaty rights are exercised. And so, I'd leave it right there in terms of the troop deployments.

Last one.

Q. Mr. President, in the Reagan administration there was a very formal negotiating process with General Noriega over terms under which he might leave. Is there any possibility that that might repeat itself now, that there might be some sort of formal discussions between yourselves and the Panamanian Government and General Noriega about conditions under which he might leave?

The President. Oh, he knows my position on the fact that if he does leave we would have the instant restoration of normal relations with Panama. That has been conveyed to him very, very recently. But look, I will be openminded about seeing what it might take to see him leave. I'm not going to go back and do what Helen [Helen Thomas, United Press International] asked about in dropping these indictments. I'm not going to do that. That has profound implications for our fight against narcotics, which has got to be worldwide. But if there's something short of that, the door is open to understand what it is that would be required. But I don't think the Panamanian people should be asked to compromise in terms of their election, which was won 3 to 1 by those opposed to Noriega. So, there would be certain things, other nonnegotiable things, but I don't think—that's between Noriega and the Panamanian people.

Thank you all very much. And Brent will take the remaining questions.

Q. How is Endara? Is he in the hospital?

The President. He was out, and then I think he's back in. But now I don't know whether he's gotten out later on or not.

General Scowcroft. I think he's back.

Q. Is Noriega capable of——

Q. Are you concerned about him taking hostages?

The President. I'm concerned about protecting the lives of Americans, and that is exactly why I've taken the action I have here today.

Note: The President spoke at 4:07 p.m. in the Briefing Room at the White House.

Nomination of James Franklin Rill To Be an Assistant Attorney General

May 11, 1989

The President today announced his intention to nominate James Franklin Rill to be an Assistant Attorney General (Antitrust Division), Department of Justice. He would succeed Charles F. Rule.

Mr. Rill is currently a practicing attorney in Washington, DC, serving as an antitrust and trade regulation counsel to RJR Tobacco; lead counsel for Cyclops Corp., the Detroit Auto Dealers, and Safeway Stores, Inc.; and an antitrust counsel for various companies and trade associations. Mr. Rill has served in various capacities in the antitrust section of the American Bar Association, including chairman, 1987–1988; finance officer, 1984–1986; and council member, 1981–1984.

Mr. Rill graduated from Dartmouth College (A.B., 1954) and Harvard University (LL.B., 1959). He was born in Evanston, IL, on March 4, 1933.

Nomination of Janet Dempsey Steiger To Be a Federal Trade Commissioner, and Designation as Chairman

May 11, 1989

The President today announced his intention to nominate Janet Dempsey Steiger to be a Federal Trade Commissioner for the term of 7 years from September 26, 1988. She would succeed Daniel Oliver. After appointment she will be designated Chairman.

Since 1987 Ms. Steiger has been Chairman of the Commission on Veterans Educational Policy. Prior to this, she has served in several capacities for the Postal Rate Commission, including Chairman, since 1982; Acting Chairman, 1981–1982; and Commissioner, since 1980. She was vice president for the Work Place, 1975–1980, and a legislative correspondent in the office of the Governor of Wisconsin, 1965.

Ms. Steiger graduated from Lawrence College (B.A., 1961) and did postgraduate study at the University of Reading, England, 1961–1962, and the University of Wisconsin, 1962–1963. She was a Woodrow Wilson scholar and a Fulbright scholar, 1961. She was born June 10, 1939, in Oshkosh, WI. Ms. Steiger has one son.

Nomination of Deborah Kaye Owen To Be a Federal Trade Commissioner

May 11, 1989

The President today announced his intention to nominate Deborah Kaye Owen to be a Federal Trade Commissioner for the unexpired term of 7 years from September 26, 1987. She would succeed Margot E. Machol.

Since 1986 Ms. Owen has served as a managing partner with McNair Law Firm, P.A., in Washington, DC. Prior to this she served in various capacities, including Associate Counsel to the President at the White House, 1985–1986; general counsel to Chairman Strom Thurmond for the Senate Committee on the Judiciary, 1983–1985; minority counsel for the House Committee on the Judiciary, 1980–1982, and as an attorney with Piper and Marbury, 1977–1979.

Ms. Owen graduated from the University of Maryland (B.A., 1972) and Harvard Law School (J.D., 1977). In addition, she was a Marshall scholar in political philosophy at the University of Edinburgh in Scotland, 1972–1974. Ms. Owen resides in Columbia, MD.

Statement on International Discussions Concerning Global Climate Change

May 12, 1989

The United States delegation to the steering group of the Response Strategies Working Group on Climate Change carried instructions to move the international community forward in establishing a process for considering how to respond to climate change. I am pleased to note that the nations meeting in Geneva have agreed to a workshop this fall, looking at the range of financial, economic, technical, and legal issues for responding to climate change. The United States looks forward to playing a significant role in efforts to assess and respond to global climate change.

I expect that these efforts will lead to formal negotiations on the establishment of a framework convention on global climate. It is important that this process lead to international scientific consensus on the seriousness of the issue for the environment and for the world economy. At the same time, we should ensure that the interests of developing countries are taken into account in this process.

The United States will host a meeting under the auspices of the Response Strategies Working Group this fall that is intended to advance our understanding and promote consensus. I look forward, personally, to reviewing its results.

Remarks at the Texas A&M University Commencement Ceremony in College Station
May 12, 1989

Thank you, Governor. Thank you all very much for that welcome. Good luck, good luck to you. Thank you, ladies and gentlemen, thank you all. Chairman McKenzie and Dr. Adkisson and Dr. Mobley, thank you for having me here. And to the Singing Cadets, thank you for that very special treat. And to my Secretary of Commerce, Bob Mosbacher, I'm delighted that he's with me today.

I want to pay my special respects to our Governor, Bill Clements; to your Congressman from this district, Joe Barton; and then, of course, to Senator Phil Gramm. He said he taught economics here and in Congress. It's hard to be humble. But nevertheless—[*laughter*]—the point is the guy's telling the truth, and we are grateful to him every day for his leadership up there in Washington, as we are for Joe Barton as well. So, we've got a good combination—Phil Gramm in the Senate and today Joe Barton in the United States Congress—a wonderful combination, with these Aggie values in the forefront.

I was brought here today by an Aggie, and I brought him here to this marvelous ceremony with me. He was mentioned by Congressman Barton, but I would like to ask the pilot of Air Force One, Lieutenant Colonel Dan Barr, to stand up so you can see another Aggie all suited up, up there. And you met my day-to-day inside Aggie, Fred McClure. We work every minute of the day on matters affecting the legislative interests of this country, but I won't reintroduce Fred. But I am delighted to be back among my fellow Texans and friends. And for those of you who are Democrats, there is no truth to the rumor that Phil Gramm and I are ready to take our elephant walk. [*Applause*]

My sincerest congratulations go to every graduate and to your parents. In this ceremony, we celebrate nothing less than the commencement of the rest, and the best, of your life. And when you look back at your days at Texas A&M, you will have a lot to be proud of: a university that is first in baseball and first in service to our nation. Many are the heroes whose names are called at muster. Many are those you remember in Silver Taps.

We are reminded that no generation can escape history. Parents, we share a fervent desire for our children and their children to know a better world, a safer world. And students, your parents and grandparents have lived through a world war and helped America to rebuild the world. They witnessed the drama of postwar nations divided by Soviet subversion and force, but sustained by an allied response most vividly seen in the Berlin airlift. And today I would like to use this joyous and solemn occasion to speak to you and to the rest of the country about our relations with the Soviet Union. It is fitting that these remarks be made here at Texas A&M University.

Wise men—Truman and Eisenhower, Vandenberg and Rayburn, Marshall, Acheson, and Kennan—crafted the strategy of containment. They believed that the Soviet Union, denied the easy course of expansion, would turn inward and address the contradictions of its inefficient, repressive, and inhumane system. And they were right—the Soviet Union is now publicly facing this hard reality. Containment worked. Containment worked because our democratic principles and institutions and values are sound and always have been. It worked because our alliances were, and are, strong and because the superiority of free societies and free markets over stagnant socialism is undeniable.

We are approaching the conclusion of an historic postwar struggle between two visions: one of tyranny and conflict and one of democracy and freedom. The review of U.S.-Soviet relations that my administration has just completed outlines a new path toward resolving this struggle. Our goal is bold, more ambitious than any of my predecessors could have thought possible. Our review indicates that 40 years of perseverance have brought us a precious opportunity, and now it is time to move beyond containment to a new policy for the 1990's—one that recognizes the full scope of change taking place around the world and in the Soviet Union itself. In sum, the United States now has as its goal much more than simply containing Soviet expansionism. We seek the integration of the Soviet Union into the community of nations. And as the Soviet Union itself moves toward greater openness and democratization, as they meet the challenge of responsible international behavior, we will match their steps with steps of our own. Ultimately, our objective is to welcome the Soviet Union back into the world order.

The Soviet Union says that it seeks to make peace with the world and criticizes its own postwar policies. These are words that we can only applaud, but a new relationship cannot simply be declared by Moscow or bestowed by others; it must be earned. It must be earned because promises are never enough. The Soviet Union has promised a more cooperative relationship before, only to reverse course and return to militarism. Soviet foreign policy has been almost seasonal: warmth before cold, thaw before freeze. We seek a friendship that knows no season of suspicion, no chill of distrust.

We hope *perestroika* is pointing the Soviet Union to a break with the cycles of the past—a definitive break. Who would have thought that we would see the deliberations of the Central Committee on the front page of Pravda or dissident Andrei Sakharov seated near the councils of power? Who would have imagined a Soviet leader who canvasses the sidewalks of Moscow and also Washington, DC? These are hopeful, indeed, remarkable signs. And let no one doubt our sincere desire to see *perestroika*, this reform, continue and succeed. But the national security of America and our allies is not predicated on hope. It must be based on deeds, and we look for enduring, ingrained economic and political change.

While we hope to move beyond containment, we are only at the beginning of our new path. Many dangers and uncertainties are ahead. We must not forget that the Soviet Union has acquired awesome military capabilities. That was a fact of life for my predecessors, and that's always been a fact of life for our allies. And that is a fact of life for me today as President of the United States.

As we seek peace, we must also remain strong. The purpose of our military might is not to pressure a weak Soviet economy or to seek military superiority. It is to deter war. It is to defend ourselves and our allies and to do something more: to convince the Soviet Union that there can be no reward in pursuing expansionism, to convince the Soviet Union that reward lies in the pursuit of peace.

Western policies must encourage the evolution of the Soviet Union toward an open society. This task will test our strength. It will tax our patience, and it will require a sweeping vision. Let me share with you my vision: I see a Western Hemisphere of democratic, prosperous nations, no longer threatened by a Cuba or a Nicaragua armed by Moscow. I see a Soviet Union as it pulls away from ties to terrorist nations like Libya that threaten the legitimate security of their neighbors. I see a Soviet Union which respects China's integrity and returns the northern territories to Japan, a prelude to the day when all the great nations of Asia will live in harmony.

But the fulfillment of this vision requires the Soviet Union to take positive steps, including: First, reduce Soviet forces. Although some small steps have already been taken, the Warsaw Pact still possesses more than 30,000 tanks, more than twice as much artillery, and hundreds of thousands more troops in Europe than NATO. They should cut their forces to less threatening levels, in proportion to their legitimate security needs.

Second, adhere to the Soviet obligation, promised in the final days of World War II, to support self-determination for all the nations of Eastern Europe and central Europe. And this requires specific abandonment of the Brezhnev doctrine. One day it should be possible to drive from Moscow to Munich without seeing a single guard tower or a strand of barbed wire. In short, tear down the Iron Curtain.

And third, work with the West in positive, practical—not merely rhetorical—steps toward diplomatic solution to these regional disputes around the world. I welcome the Soviet withdrawal from Afghanistan, and the Angola agreement. But there is much more to be done around the world. We're ready. Let's roll up our sleeves and get to work.

And fourth, achieve a lasting political pluralism and respect for human rights. Dramatic events have already occurred in Moscow. We are impressed by limited, but freely contested elections. We are impressed by a greater toleration of dissent. We are impressed by a new frankness about the Stalin era. Mr. Gorbachev, don't stop now!

And fifth, join with us in addressing pressing global problems, including the international drug menace and dangers to the environment. We can build a better world for our children.

As the Soviet Union moves toward arms reduction and reform, it will find willing partners in the West. We seek verifiable, stabilizing arms control and arms reduction agreements with the Soviet Union and its allies. However, arms control is not an end in itself but a means of contributing to the security of America and the peace of the world. I directed Secretary [of State] Baker to propose to the Soviets that we resume negotiations on strategic forces in June and, as you know, the Soviet Union has agreed.

Our basic approach is clear. In the strategic arms reductions talks, we wish to reduce the risk of nuclear war. And in the companion defense and space talks, our objective will be to preserve our options to deploy advanced defenses when they're ready. In nuclear testing, we will continue to seek the necessary verification improvements in existing treaties to permit them to be brought into force. And we're going to continue to seek a verifiable global ban on chemical weapons. We support NATO efforts to reduce the Soviet offensive threat in the negotiations on conventional forces in Europe. And as I've said, fundamental to all of these objectives is simple openness.

Make no mistake, a new breeze is blowing across the steppes and the cities of the Soviet Union. Why not, then, let this spirit of openness grow, let more barriers come down. Open emigration, open debate, open airwaves—let openness come to mean the publication and sale of banned books and newspapers in the Soviet Union. Let the 19,000 Soviet Jews who emigrated last year be followed by any number who wish to emigrate this year. And when people apply for exit visas, let there be no harassment against them. Let openness come to mean nothing less than the free exchange of people and books and ideas between East and West.

And let it come to mean one thing more. Thirty-four years ago, President Eisenhower met in Geneva with Soviet leaders who, after the death of Stalin, promised a new approach toward the West. He proposed a plan called Open Skies, which would allow unarmed aircraft from the United States and the Soviet Union to fly over the territory of the other country. This would open up military activities to regular scrutiny and, as President Eisenhower put it, "convince the world that we are lessening danger and relaxing tension." President Eisenhower's suggestion tested the Soviet readiness to open their society, and the Kremlin failed that test.

Now, let us again explore that proposal,

but on a broader, more intrusive and radical basis—one which I hope would include allies on both sides. We suggest that those countries that wish to examine this proposal meet soon to work out the necessary operational details, separately from other arms control negotiations. Such surveillance flights, complementing satellites, would provide regular scrutiny for both sides. Such unprecedented territorial access would show the world the true meaning of the concept of openness. The very Soviet willingness to embrace such a concept would reveal their commitment to change.

Where there is cooperation, there can be a broader economic relationship; but economic relations have been stifled by Soviet internal policies. They've been injured by Moscow's practice of using the cloak of commerce to steal technology from the West. Ending discriminatory treatment of U.S. firms would be a helpful step. Trade and financial transactions should take place on a normal commercial basis.

And should the Soviet Union codify its emigration laws in accord with international standards and implement its new laws faithfully, I am prepared to work with Congress for a temporary waiver of the Jackson-Vanik amendment, opening the way to extending most favored nation trade status to the Soviet Union. After that last weighty point, I can just imagine what you were thinking: It had to happen. Your last day in college had to end with yet another political science lecture. [*Laughter*]

In all seriousness, the policy I have just described has everything to do with you. Today you graduate. You're going to start careers and families, and you will become the leaders of America in the next century. And what kind of world will you know? Perhaps the world order of the future will truly be a family of nations.

It's a sad truth that nothing forces us to recognize our common humanity more swiftly than a natural disaster. I'm thinking, of course, of Soviet Armenia just a few months ago, a tragedy without blame, warlike devastation without war. Our son took our 12-year-old grandson to Yerevan. At the end of the day of comforting the injured and consoling the bereaved, the father and son went to church, sat down together in the midst of the ruins, and wept. How can our two countries magnify this simple expression of caring? How can we convey the good will of our people?

Forty-three years ago, a young lieutenant by the name of Albert Kotzebue, the class of 1945 at Texas A&M, was the first American soldier to shake hands with the Soviets at the bank of the Elbe River. Once again, we are ready to extend our hand. Once again, we are ready for a hand in return. And once again, it is a time for peace.

Thank you for inviting me to Texas A&M. I wish you the very best in years to come. God bless you all. Thank you very much.

Note: The President spoke at 3:05 p.m. in G. Rollie White Coliseum. In his opening remarks, he referred to William McKenzie, Perry Adkisson, and William H. Mobley, chairman of the board of regents, chancellor, and president of the university, respectively. The President also referred to Frederick D. McClure, Assistant to the President for Legislative Affairs.

Nomination of Jerry M. Hunter To Be General Counsel of the National Labor Relations Board

May 12, 1989

The President today nominated Jerry M. Hunter to be General Counsel of the National Labor Relations Board for a term of 4 years. He would succeed Rosemary M. Collyer.

Since 1986 Mr. Hunter has served as the director of the Missouri State Department of Labor and Industrial Relations. Mr. Hunter served as labor counsel for the Kellwood Co., St. Louis, MO. He served with the Equal Employment Opportunity Commission in St. Louis as a senior trial attorney, 1980–1981, and as a trial attorney, 1979–1980. Mr. Hunter was a field attorney for the National Labor Relations Board in St. Louis, 1977–1979.

Mr. Hunter graduated from the University of Arkansas (B.A., 1974) and the Washington University School of Law (J.D., 1977). He was born July 5, 1952, is married, and currently resides in Jefferson City, MO.

Remarks at the Alcorn State University Commencement Ceremony in Lorman, Mississippi
May 13, 1989

Thank you all, and especially, my thanks to you, Dr. Washington. You know, last month we commemorated the bicentennial of the American Presidency. And, Walter, I have to tell you, after all these actors in powdered wigs, it is a relief to stand beside someone who really is President Washington. [*Laughter*] Good morning.

But to you and your wonderful faculty here at Alcorn, I just say I am delighted to be here. Incidentally, Dr. Washington's ears should have been burning, because when I rode down on the helicopter from Jackson with the two United States Senators from Mississippi, they were telling me in considerable detail—more than I knew from my briefing papers—of this man's commitment to excellence. And so, I salute him and his service to this wonderful university.

Lieutenant Governor Dye, it's a pleasure to be with you, sir. I'm, of course, delighted that Thad Cochran and Trent Lott are with us today, a tribute to all here. I'm very pleased that my good friend, Sonny Montgomery, a Congressman whose home is in Meridian, is here. We're in Congressman Mike Espy's district, and I salute him. Congressman Mike Parker is here, and many other distinguished guests. I also want to say thanks to all of them.

Congratulations also to the families and the friends and the fans of these students. But I think most of all, to the Alcorn State University Class of 1989, we salute you, and I'm proud to be with you. You've been part of what they call the Alcorn family. And this is a day for the family. But it's your own individual families, the mothers and fathers and grandparents gathered here, that I want to congratulate. In a very private way, your years of hard work and your years of sacrifice and, yes, love for your sons and daughters have brought this moment to pass. And although the first round of applause has died now, I think you all really deserve the first round of applause—the parents and the grandparents of the graduates here today.

I know how deadly long graduation speeches can be. I'll never forget Yale University where I went. A man got up, he says, "I'm going to give you a brief graduation speech. And I will choose, because our school has a short name, Y. Y is for youth." He went on for about 30 minutes. "And then it's A, altruism"—[*laughter*]—another 20; L, loyalty—rushed that off in about 18 minutes; and then, of course, E, for excellence. He concluded about an hour and a half after he started. And there was one person left, his head bent in prayer. And the minister, the speaker, very touched by it, said, "Well, sir, I see that you are praying for these values." The man said, "No, no." He said, "I wasn't praying for the values. I was giving thanks to the Lord that I did not go to Alcorn State University in Lorman, Mississippi." [*Laughter*] I'll try to be a little more considerate.

Dr. David Matthews, in his lovely invocation, alluded to family. He alluded to some of the problems that we face. And the American family has been under siege in recent times. But as the months unfold, I've become more and more certain that the answer to our problems can be found in the strength of the American family. Looking around this room, you can sense the feeling of pride, and it's a powerful force for good. And as President, I will do everything I can to promote the family: excellence in education, to protect the family in the fight against narcotics, and to reaffirm the family values that brought your kids through these 4 challenging years.

For some American families—those fortunate families where children are raised assuming that they'll have the opportunity to go to college—the drama of today's ceremony is difficult to appreciate. Many of you are the first, though, in your families ever to attend college, let alone stay the course through graduation. And the economic transformation wrought by the historically black colleges such as Alcorn is nothing less than astounding. While 85 percent of the United Negro College Fund alumni come from blue-collar families, almost all go on to professional or managerial positions, and in many cases, they're the first blacks to hold these particular positions. It's an exciting tradition and one of the most underappreciated success stories in America.

It's also a tradition that is close to my heart, because way back in 1948, when I was a senior at Y-A-L-E, 41 years ago, my wife, Barbara—still my wife, Barbara; then she and I had been married just a few years—we began participating in the United Negro College Fund. And in the 40 years since then, we've continued to try to do our small part. And even before becoming President, back in January, just a week before the inauguration, Dr. Washington and some of his colleagues came to Washington, DC, met with me to talk about how the new administration can best support this unique tradition. And some good ideas came out of that gathering, and several are already in effect—begun last month in the meeting that he alluded to, when Dr. Washington and others joined me in the Rose Garden to launch the President's Board of Advisors on Historically Black Colleges and Universities.

And now I understand that several of today's graduates are going to be joining in Federal service—in agriculture, defense, transportation, and other critical areas. And I'm proud of you, and we welcome you. And we need excellence in Federal service; America needs your talents. And that's not just idle talk. Last month's order also directed that the Federal personnel office develop a program to improve recruitment at Alcorn and similar colleges for part-time and summer positions to help people get started in the concept of Federal public service. And I understand that a campaign is underway here now to raise a half a million dollars through a Federal challenge grant program. Recently, I signed an order bringing $60 million in new funds to boost the endowment matching grants available to schools like Alcorn. As I told the college Presidents who gathered at the White House last month, these new initiatives are just a start. More must be done.

But on a day like today, there is much of which we can be proud. Alcorn has come a long way since 1948. That was the landmark year that Alcorn first earned its "A" rating as an accredited college. And that was the year "The Stretch" was finally paved, a milestone that was resoundingly cheered by the graduating class.

Do you know how many graduated back in 1948? Trivial Pursuit question—how many? Sixty in number, barely a fifth of the total receiving degrees today, a ceremony so small that it fit comfortably into the Oakland Chapel. And like my classmates in Connecticut, many of the men at Alcorn in 1948 were veterans, soldiers who had fought for democracy, many of them serving in segregated units. And like many of you today, the Alcornites of 1948 were graduating with skills that would enable them to feed the hungry, nurse the sick, and reach out to help the young through education.

Future Pittsburgh Steeler Jack Spinks, the first black pro athlete to come out of Mississippi, was getting ready to start his freshman year. He would soon be practicing in a ramshackle wooden building that everyone called the "Old Chicken Coop." And Jack says that when it rained during basketball games, the roof leaked so bad that people had to keep their umbrellas open. The modern field house in which we're gathered today was not then even a dream. And Jack, I am told, is somewhere out here today, and I understand that his youngest son is part of the graduating class.

But these 40 years of schooling that separate father and son—the years that separate them embrace an era of tremendous change for Alcorn and for the United States of America, a time of upheaval and, finally, a time of growth, and maybe something like wisdom.

Not everything has changed: the threads woven through the fabric at Alcorn, and anyplace where excellence is sought, are what used to be called simple family values. We're not talking about two sets of values; family values are the same regardless of race, color, or creed. Family values—they're not complicated: honesty, faith, frugality, acceptance of responsibility, the importance of work, a tradition of helping one's neighbor. Martin Luther King argued that "intelligence is not enough." He said, "Intelligence plus character—that is the goal of the true education."

Well, you here at Alcorn are lucky. This is a place where, as your old football coach put it, "the air is a little bit cleaner, the grass is a little bit greener, and the water is a little bit sweeter—it's just a little bit closer to heaven." You see, this place has character. It is a university with a mission. And to paraphrase a new song that's climbing the charts this month, this special, secluded college has been "the wind beneath your wings." And for you and for young Americans graduating all across this country this month, it is time for you to take that wind and soar. And for some of you, I hope there comes a day when you ride those winds into the political arena to fight for what you believe in, to grapple not only with your own dreams but also those of your countrymen.

But politics is hardly the only arena where a new breeze is blowing. Some of you will land in business, maybe even start a business where you can create jobs adding to the opportunity of other Americans. And that's public service, too. Now, business can be pretty rough-and-tumble. But America is successful because we're a nation of risk-takers. The Alcorn Braves know that you can't steal second base and keep one foot on first. That's profound. [*Laughter*] Others will teach the next generation and put wind beneath their wings. Your touchstone should be excellence, accountability, and choice. The educational system must offer parents quality choice in education. Alcorn's a good example. But our schools must also be more accountable, and those of you who will know the joy of helping a child learn are an important part of that responsibility. Others are headed for health care, agriculture, journalism, the professions. Whatever you choose, it is within you to change the world; and any definition of a successful life must, of course, include serving others.

As each of you begins a new life today, you may fairly ask, will my future be secure? This isn't just a domestic question; it's a foreign policy question. For the past 40 years, the United States and the Soviet Union have been engaged in a struggle because the Soviets have chosen to stand apart from and opposed to the world family of nations. Yesterday I announced a new policy for the 1990's, one that moves beyond our country just trying to contain the Soviet Union. It sets a goal of bringing the Soviet Union into the world community, a policy of reintegration, if you will. And if we succeed, I can guarantee to you and your kids that the future you know is going to be safer and the world you know will be freer. This I see as a primary objective of any President of the United States of America. As the Soviet Union moves towards greater openness and democratization and as they meet the challenge of responsible international behavior, we will match their steps with steps of our own.

Today every senior here is an educated man or woman, proud, self-assured. With all the cockiness of youth, some of you—I hope most of you—must be feeling like anything is possible today. Well, trust those instincts. Everyone has a dream. Everyone has something to give.

Last month I saw a new movie—maybe some of you all saw it—a movie about baseball and about faith, in which Burt Lancaster ponders the power of hope. And he asks: "Is there enough magic out there in the moonlight to make this dream come true?" Well, I have come to Mississippi today because the magic of America and the magic of our times means believing that your best days—that our best days—are still to come. Born in an era of peace and educated in times of relative prosperity, your generation can look to a new century rich with unimaginable opportunities.

And, yes, there is enough magic out there, enough for all Americans. And, yes, you can seize the magic with the power of your own hands and with the skills bequeathed to you by this special university. And, yes, just as Alcorn's 1988 yearbook was dedicated to Dr. King, you can honor his memory by doing what he taught this nation to do: to have a dream and to work every day to make that dream come true.

America is proud of you and of your families that you represent. God bless you in the challenge to come, and God bless the United States of America. I am honored to be your guest today. Thank you.

Note: The President spoke at 11:15 a.m. in the Health and Physical Education Building. In his remarks, he referred to Walter Washington, president of the university; Lt. Gov. Brad Dye; Senators Thad Cochran and Trent Lott; and David Matthews, president of the General Missionary Baptist State Convention of Mississippi.

Interview With Members of the White House Press Corps on the Situation in Panama
May 13, 1989

The President. Let me take a couple of questions. But first, a word about Panama, just to be very clear. And if I were speaking to the Panamanian people, I would tell them that the affection of the American people for the people of Panama is still very much intact, strong. Secondly, I would say to the Panama Defense Forces, the PDF, they have a useful role to play, and they will in the future of Panama have a useful role to play. The problem is not the PDF, per se; the problem is Noriega.

And if Noriega were to leave office, we would have good relations with Panama. We would have good relations with the Panama Defense Force. And clearly, the good feelings between the American people and the people of Panama would grow and prosper. And so, I would hope that Noriega would leave and that the results of this election would be recognized. The fraud in the election has been condemned by people all across the world; the European Community, leaders in our hemisphere, all the way to Japan—people speaking out in indignation against this thuggery and against what the man has done.

So, I just want to be sure that the people of Panama understand that relations can quickly return to normal if Mr. Noriega will leave and set aside his dictatorship and permit democracy to prevail.

Q. Do you think they have any doubt about that? And aren't you calling for a coup on the part of the PDF? I mean, the Catholic Church in Panama also has basically been saying the same thing to the PDF. Are you saying——

The President. That I just said?

Q. Are you saying that you would like the PDF to get Noriega out?

The President. I would love to see them get him out. We'd like to see him out of there—not just the PDF, the will of the people of Panama.

Q. It sounds like you're calling on the people of Panama to rise up and basically have a revolution. Is that what you're trying to say?

The President. A revolution—the people rose up and spoke in a democratic election, with a tremendous turnout, said what they wanted. The will of the people should not be thwarted by this man and a handful of these Doberman thugs. That's what I'm saying.

Q. What do you think the people should do now?

The President. The people should do everything they can to have the will of the people respected. They ought to heed the international calls, and they ought to just do everything they can to get Mr. Noriega out of there.

Q. Have you been in conversation and contact with President Cerezo and others? Venezuela apparently has offered Noriega asylum. Have you been in contact with the Venezuelans, and do you have thoughts on when and where Noriega should go?

The President. No, but I have no doubt that countries would receive him.

Q. Why, have you had any assurances indirectly on that?

The President. Well, I have a habit of not liking to go into detail with what I talk to others about. But I'm just confident that they would receive him, and I think Noriega knows this, too.

Q. You said the other day that you would not favor dropping the drug indictments. But if he were to go to someplace that, either through prearrangement or postarrangement, did not have extradition arrangements with the U.S., how would you feel about that?

The President. Well, that could well be an answer. That could be a solution.

Q. What? Going to a country that——

The President. Yes, because if he has—no, he was saying, if there was a country that prohibited extradition—and he ought to think about that.

Q. Would you allow him to go to a country——

The President. ——think we have any control over that.

Q. Would you allow him into a country that didn't have an extradition——

The President. He can go anywhere he wants. But I am obligated as the President of the United States to respect our laws and to go forward on fulfilling obligations under the law. But if he went to a place where there wasn't any extradition treaty, then that would be a different situation than if he went to a place where there was an extradition treaty.

Q. Do you care which one he does?

The President. Yes, I'd like him to—well, I care that he does whatever it is that it takes to get him out of there right now. And that's what I'd like to see happen.

Q. ——more than getting him——

The President. I think it's right for the people of Panama. It's right for the democracies in this hemisphere. You cannot have an election that is blatantly stolen, where people that win are beaten up by thugs.

Q. So far, you have struck out—and so did President Reagan—in trying to get him out of power. Do you have any other options?

The President. No.

Q. Well, they haven't been successful.

The President. Still at the plate, and we'll stay at the plate until we can help the people of Panama have the democracy for which they spoke so articulately in an election. And we're not going to give up on it.

Q. This effort will not be a success until he leaves, right?

The President. No effort can be a success until he leaves. That's right.

Q. A couple of days ago, you said that the goal of your sending those extra troops down there was to protect American lives. Now you seem to be adding a new, much more outspoken dimension to your intention here, which is to see Noriega leave and leave——

The President. I'm not changing the definition of the role of the American troops at all.

Q. Have you had any contact with him indirectly, sir, in the last 2 days?

The President. Last 2 days? No.

Q. How about directly——

The President. No, you asked the question properly.

Q. How does it feel personally, after over a year of seeing this drag on—[*inaudible*]—now this thing comes to a head? How does it feel when you read the accounts and see the pictures?

The President. See, I think there's a whole new ingredient in Panama, regarding the relationship with Panama. And the ingredient is the election. And I think the election made so clear that the people want democracy and made so clear that that democracy is being thwarted by one man that that in itself could be the catalyst for removing Noriega.

Now, why do I say that? Because, heretofore, you have not heard the neighboring countries around Panama speaking up. Now they're speaking up loud and clear. You have not heard the Church as indignant as it is now. You have not seen the EC [European Community], our friends in Europe, speaking up and denouncing what happened. And I think the Japanese weighed in on this. So, I think this is a very different climate now and one much more conducive to possible change, because the people spoke so overwhelmingly, and heretofore, that has not been quite as clear. Never underestimate the power of the people, even though their will seems to have been frustrated short-run.

Q. Do you think the OAS [Organization of American States] will do something on Wednesday?

The President. Helen [Helen Thomas, United Press International], I would hope so, and I think it would be helpful if they did. And I'd love to see a very powerful and strong statement coming out of there, and I'd like to see it as unanimous. But I'm not sure what will come out of it. But I think it's well worth the effort.

Q. Mr. President—you're worried about the people in Panama and what they've gone through, and it's in their hands. Are you concerned, though, about any violence that might be started by anything that the people would do to change the situation where innocent lives may be lost or children would be hurt and families disrupted as they try to make a change for democracy?

The President. I always worry about the loss of innocent human life. And I would be worried about that.

Q. What about American——

Q. Would you caution them against rising up in violence?

The President. American life? We will protect American lives in every possible way. That is a solemn responsibility of the President, and that's one of the reasons I augmented our forces in Panama—is *the* reason I augmented them.

Q. Are you concerned that the situation there—with your calls and mounting pressure internationally—would lead to a situation right now in Panama that might lead to violence that would, in fact, endanger American lives more than they would be otherwise?

The President. Well, it's too hypothetical. I mean, I would be concerned about any escalation of violence that would endanger American lives. And I think we're in a good position to protect our American lives and interests.

Q. Mr. President, your words could be seen, though, as inciteful, basically saying to the Panamanian people that it's up to them: Don't let it die. Your will seems to have been thwarted, but you've got to hang tough. The people could see that as inflammatory, like it's a call to—[*inaudible*]—to revolt. Would you add any words of caution——

The President. No, I would add no words of caution. The will of the people should be implemented. And if I wanted to increase the rhetoric, strengthen it, I would do so. But I think I've phrased it just about the way I feel.

Q. And the will includes——

The President. What?

Q. And the will includes—[*inaudible*]—demonstrations in the street? What form would you say——

The President. Look, I'm not about to get into proposing a three-point action plan for the people of Panama. All I want them to know is that if they get rid of Noriega they will have an instant normalization of relationship with the United States and there will be a useful role for the Panamanian Defense Force. And I think there has been some doubt about that, perhaps in the Panamanian Defense Force itself, as to how we now view the Force, because of the thuggery of its leader. And this gives me an opportunity to clarify that specific point, as well as to repeat my support for Endara and Calderon and Guillermo Ford, who was so brutally beaten.

Q. Are you contemplating sending even more American troops down there now?

The President. Well, if I were, it would be unlikely I would announce it here, just before landing in Starkville, only because I think it would be prudent to do it differently. But I'll answer your question, though: I have no short-run plans, but that doesn't preclude anything I'll do in the future.

Q. You know Noriega. Is it strictly power that he wants or is there a point where he could be negotiated out?

The President. I don't know, Helen. I think it's power that he has wanted, but I don't know what his view is now that he's seen a total repudiation of his rule. And you see, I keep coming back to the fact that what happened the other day in the election is something quite different than has been on the table before. So, I just don't know the answer to it. It might be now he'd like to find a way to get out. I would hope that would be the case, but I don't know that for a fact. He has lost all support, all respect—the man is considered just out of it, an outlaw, by the world community now as a result of what happened. But I don't know. It's a good question, yet I don't know how to answer. I don't have an answer for it.

Q. Are you saying that the United States at this juncture has, more or less, done what it could and that now what we're going to do is lend moral support to whatever the Panamanians decide? That we really can't from the outside do anything further?

The President. No, what I've said is that we've taken certain action to protect American lives. I have now spelled out, although I hope it had been understood before, what it would take to have good relations with the United States; and I will continue my own efforts internationally. You see, I do think it's important that it not be the United States, the Colossus of the North, coming down there to try to dictate to the people of Panama. And that's one of the reasons I spent a lot of time last week working with the international community and instructing the State Department to do the same thing. So, we will continue our international efforts.

Q. Are you disappointed in the response to that of the PDF and some of the Panamanians to why you sent the troops down there? Are you disappointed in their response?

The President. Well, I'm not sure I know what their response has been. The PDF response?

Q. Yes. I mean, you've come out here to clarify your views.

The President. No, I'm not disappointed in the response. What I'm trying to do is make clear to the Panamanian Defense Forces that there's no vendetta against the Panamanian Defense Forces as an institution. There is clearly the desire to see Mr. Noriega get out of office. I don't know how they've reacted to the American forces.

Q. Mr. President, how long can the people of Panama be expected to put up with Noriega?

The President. About 4 days ago—[*laughter*]—when they demonstrated loud and clear they don't want any more. They've had it; and their will should be respected and honored. So, we've got to find a way to have that magnificent expression of democracy be honored.

Q. Are there certain things that you and the administration are sending them immediately, once Noriega leaves?

The President. Oh, sure. We'd recognize immediately the Endara government. As soon as he's sworn in, we would return our Ambassador; we would remove our economic sanctions; we would, in essence, have normalized relations with a country for whom we have great affection and whose people have great affection for us.

If you talk to those two delegations that came back, both of them—the liberal members of the delegation, the conservative members, the Republicans, the Democrats—all of them certified, stipulated that the people of Panama have great affection for our country and for our people. So, you'd see an instant release of this oppression; and you'd see an effort by the United States to help Panama go down the road to democracy and to help them economically, as best we could, and to welcome them as they rejoin the family of democracies in this hemisphere. That would happen instantly. We wouldn't need a lot of delaying or thinking about it either. But it has to have the—with that—it's the departure of Noriega and the recognition of the people's will; those two have to go together.

It has been lovely. It has been delightful here.

Q. Was there some development this morning or some intelligence that you got that caused this today?

The President. No, but I know because I was talking to General Scowcroft [Assistant to the President for National Security Affairs] yesterday and talked to Secretary [of State] Baker this morning. And I've had an uneasy feeling that perhaps what I've told you here today was not known clearly there. And it gives me a chance to—well, the question as to how we view the Panamanian Defense Force itself, what would happen if Noriega left, vis-a-vis the United States of America, and I hope it's known that Endara——

Q. You think that——

The President. Well, I think in a situation of this nature, where the head of the PDF has become such a pariah, that there perhaps—been misunderstanding there as to how we view the institution itself and other of its officers. But if they come in there and Noriega goes and they respect the will of the people, I—you know, we see a very useful role for the Panamanian Defense Force, in their own internal security and for their own—any threat they might feel they had to the external security.

Q. Mr. President, has the PDF——

The President. I really do have to go.

Q. If the PDF asked for U.S. military help, how can we respond? What would we do?

The President. Asked for it to do what?

Q. If they asked for military support—if the PDF asks for military support from the United States.

The President. Support for what?

Q. Military troops.

The President. For what purpose?

Q. To move in on Noriega.

The President. If the PDF asks for support to get rid of Noriega, they wouldn't need support from the United States to get rid of Noriega. He's one man, and they have a well-trained force. That's my——

Q. What about if—[*inaudible*]—opposition asked for military support?

The President. I've outlined what we're doing. I've outlined what we're doing. I'd love to see this be resolved diplomatically. And when you have overwhelming world opinion on your side, maybe something is possible in the short-range future that has not been possible over the difficult past. It's been a great pleasure.

Q. Do you still expect a smooth summit in terms of resolving the missile issue?

The President. We'll work it out.

Q. This is Panama day.

The President. No, no, it's a good question. It will work out. This alliance is strong.

Note: The interview began at 1:21 p.m. on board Air Force One. Helen Thomas, United Press International; Rita Beamish, Associated Press; Frank Sesno, Cable News Network; Joe Walsh, NBC/Mutual Radio; and Steve Kurkjian, Boston Globe, participated in the interview.

Remarks at the Mississippi State University Commencement Ceremony in Starkville

May 13, 1989

Congratulations to you. Thank you all very much. President Zacharias and members of the board of trustees, members of the distinguished faculty, administrators, friends, soon to be graduates, I can't tell you how much I appreciate that warm Bulldog welcome. Before I get too far into these remarks, I don't believe I've ever heard a more beautiful or remarkable rendition of the "Star Spangled Banner." Richard Gaddis—just wonderful. And thank you all for the warmth of this welcome here today. And I am very honored and privileged to address your commencement.

I was at Alcorn State, another part of this great State, earlier on. And I told them that I was reminded of my own graduation, because I could see on the faces of some of these kids the apprehension about the President coming here and how long they might have to endure the message. And I was reminded of a graduation at Yale, and the speaker got up and went on and on. He finally—at the beginning he said, "Yale—Y is for youth." He talked about that for 20 minutes; "A is for altruism"—18; "L is for loyalty"—32 minutes; "E is for excellence." Finished his speech—there was only one person left, head down in prayer. And the speaker said, "Were you praying for those values?" He said, "No, sir, I was giving thanks that I didn't go to Mississippi State University." [*Laughter*]

I want to say what a great honor it is to see a long-time family friend, one of the great patriots of this or any other era, the Honorable John Stennis, who resides right here on this campus. Judge Stennis, Senator Stennis, call him what you will. He doesn't merely hail from Mississippi: He is Mississippi. And his service to the United States of America will not be forgotten. Now, I wondered whether we could ever fill those big shoes. But I say this not as a partisan but as an observer of some time, as President Zacharias said, of the public scene. And you have two great United States Senators in Thad Cochran and in Trent Lott, and I'm proud to be with them here today.

And I salute the two Members of Congress that are with us today. One of them, Congressman Montgomery, and I were elected to Congress on the same day. I'm delighted he's here. His great-grandfather, Colonel W.B. Montgomery, was instrumental in rebuilding Mississippi after the war, and he played a major role in founding this university. And so, this afternoon I want to recognize those pioneering efforts and to salute my dear friend, the colonel's great-grandson, your own Congressman, Sonny Montgomery. He always kids me that I win only when I'm wearing my Mississippi State shorts. I brought them along today with a plea: Can't we do better than this? [*Laughter*] Twenty years. If you don't do better than that by me, you're going to get this. [*Laughter*]

[*At this point, the President held up an old, worn pair of Mississippi State exercise shorts and indicated that if they were not replaced by something better that he would wear shorts from the University of Mississippi, a rival school.*]

You know, I come from a State where we like to sing "The Eyes of Texas Are Upon You." Well, today, my friends, the eyes of America are upon Starkville, Mississippi. For we meet, to begin with, at a special school, special because for 109 years MSU has made education a lasting legacy and opportunity its bequest. We gather, also, in a very special State, special for its people. You realize that who we are matters more than what we have. And you value home and family and tradition and service to country.

I thought of that today as Air Force One brought me to Mississippi, and of how, for me, this afternoon also marks another journey, back to some of my own pivotal years, the years I spent as an undergraduate. It was 41 years ago next month that I, too, received my degree, 1948. In 1948 there were only 172,000 television sets owned in the entire United States of America. Milton Berle was "Mr. Television," taking pies in the face. Harry Truman was Mr. President, giving 'em hell. And in many ways, it was a different America: less congestion, less pollution, less high tech. Pac Man was a camper, not a video game. [*Laughter*] And we had problems, sure: at home, gas shortages and housing problems and veterans adjusting to domestic life after World War II. Abroad, the Cold War had turned frigid. The Communist bloc was solidifying. China and the Middle East were rent asunder by war. And in a Europe torn by conflicting ideologies, the Soviets were blockading West Berlin.

And yet, with the end of World War II, America was unified as few could have imagined. I'm sure many of you have seen that famous Life magazine photo that captured the spirit of those times: the sailor in Times Square embracing a woman in the mass exultation of V–J Day, a victory for freedom that came after so much sacrifice. Like the woman swept off her feet, the spirit of rejoicing, and more importantly the limitless possibilities of America, swept us all. And I, too, felt that sense of idealism and opportunity and headed on out with Barbara—headed out to Texas to make the most of the American Dream.

But today I look back upon those times, and I am struck by the wonder of how much this country has achieved. What newly married vet in his early twenties could have envisioned just how wide the golden door of opportunity would swing in four short decades? And I ask myself, what made this achievement possible? What caused America's technological and scientific advance, a prosperity and power unprecedented in world history? One thing, I believe, is what Mississippi's own William Faulkner called "the old verities and truths of the heart." My friends, it is these verities that in 1948 allowed us to meet our problems together. We took pride in our identity as a nation and solace in our faith in God. And above all, we believed in the simple, the basic truths like kindness and civility, self-sacrifice and courage, compassion and concern for others, timeless values which span the generations, values which show that America is great because America is good.

An old saying notes how "the world has turned over many times." It has since I graduated. The postwar period has given way to a new world, a world still perilous, but alive with prospects for peace and with the certainty of change. Yesterday at Texas A&M in Bryan, Texas, I talked of that change, of a new policy that moves beyond containment of the Soviet Union. And the new policy seeks to bring the Soviet Union into the family of nations, a policy, if you will, of reintegration. And as the Soviet Union moves toward greater openness and democratization, and as they meet the challenge of responsible international behavior, we will match their steps with steps of our own. And if we succeed, the future of every graduate today is going to be safer. The world we know will be more free. We can dedicate ourselves then to helping others even more.

Yet there are some things that haven't changed since 1948. Our values haven't. We see these values everywhere: a church-based child-care center, choir practice, or the PTA. And they uplift American society, for they reflect the tenets of "do unto others," tenets I respect and which I will try hard to serve as President of the United States. And they are the values of America's good, quiet, decent people, Americans who know that we are not the sum of our possessions but of how we conduct ourselves. And these people form the heart of our society, and they enrich its central unit, the family. Here these values play a special role, for they teach that life is not a celebration of self and our fate is not divisible.

As I mentioned to the graduating class at Alcorn, I will do nothing as President, nothing at all, to weaken our society by weakening the fundamental role of family in our society. Instead, I will do all I can to emphasize its importance and to reinforce its role. I've been very lucky—a wonderful wife and five great kids. They're through college. And I remember receiving letters from them, and there would always be that "P.S." at the bottom, those three little words, "Please send money," that special bond between parents at home and kids away at school. I expect these parents have never, ever received a letter like that.

Five kids and 11 lively grandkids—and by themselves, they could field the Bulldogs' entire pitching staff. And I understand you people with the earphones staying plugged in to the baseball game. [*Laughter*] If I were sitting up there, I'd be doing exactly the same thing. [*Laughter*] Never say that Mississippians do not have their priorities sorted out right. [*Laughter*]

But like all kids, ours provide a Rubik Cube of questions. And like most families, they supply that love and allegiance which make us more fulfilled. And, believe me, sometimes we need that loyalty. I'm reminded of the alumnus who sent his coach a telegram before the big game. It read: "Remember, coach, we're all behind you—win or tie." [*Laughter*]

The individual is important, but the family unit can be our secret weapon and our shield. And as President, I want to strengthen it. To help the family, we must keep America prosperous, strong, and free. We must stop the scourge of drug abuse, and we will. We must build an educational system which invests in our children. And for those who, for whatever reason—sickness, poverty, the death of a loved one—feel alone and isolated, let us become their family, not in a legal sense but in a human sense: helping, supporting, caring for our neighbor.

Today millions of Americans are doing just that: giving of themselves and helping others. And we term their work voluntarism, or community service. For they show how the definition of a successful life must include serving others.

The French writer Jean Cocteau was once asked what he would take if his house were on fire and he could remove only one thing. "I would take the fire," he replied. [*Laughter*] He liked what worked. Well, so do I. Community service works because it's real, not abstract. It makes achievements feasible. Compassion helps one child escape heroin addiction. Generosity allows another to eat a decent meal. And through faith in God, still another overcomes the curse of bigotry and hatred.

And that's why I have created the Office of National Service, which will enlist new volunteers to help meet unmet social needs. Project Victory, or Mission Impossible? Look to the heroes of today for an answer—look to David Pettry, an MSU agronomist who has traveled around the world to nurture soil management; or Steve Cooper, who works in Starkville's Help Find the Children campaign; or Donnie Prisock—Dr. Donnie—a quadriplegic who earned his Ph.D. and who counsels handicapped students right here at this school. Heroes? Every one; for they know that the private sector—and individuals—have the resources and the responsibility to confront issues like hunger and health care, drug abuse and teen pregnancy. A famous adage says that "Luck is the residue of design." Well, America's luck can be the residue of voluntarism's design.

My friends, you've worked hard and studied and struggled for 4 years, and now you've endured the hardest part: listening to the commencement address. [*Laughter*] And I haven't even begun. Let's see, Y–M–I–S. [*Laughter*]

But let me leave you with the thought that Mississippi has given America some indelible leaders: in politics, John Stennis; in publishing, Eugene Butler; in entertainment, country's Jerry Clower. And always, you've treasured Faulkner's "verities and truths of the heart." Community service—national service—reflects those verities: "love and honor and pride and compassion and sacrifice," values which can ennoble the family and American society at large. So, let Faulkner's "verities of the heart" be our values, not merely for this generation but for future generations. And inspired by America's good, quiet, decent people, let us help enrich America so that America can continue to enrich the world.

Good luck to each one of you. My heartfelt congratulations! May your future be worthy of your dreams. And may you always say, as I do now, God bless the United States of America. Thank you for inviting me. Thanks a lot.

Note: The President spoke at 3:22 p.m. on Thurman field. He was introduced by Donald W. Zacharias, president of the university. Following his remarks, the President traveled to Lexington, KY.

Remarks at a Fundraising Reception for Senator Mitch McConnell in Lexington, Kentucky

May 13, 1989

What a great United States Senator you have, and how impressive this turnout is, which will guarantee his reelection! I couldn't be more pleased to be here, and I'm pleased to see these three distinguished Members of the Congress here. You may not remember this ancient history, but Hal Rogers was my Kentucky State chairman in my quest for the Presidency. And what a job that guy did, I'll tell you. And I want to pay my respects to your own Congressman—your own on the turf right here, those of you from the Lexington area—Larry Hopkins, who's with us tonight and doing a great job in Washington. And long before he got into politics, I was a Jim Bunning fan. And now I'm even more of a Jim Bunning fan, I'll tell you. And I want to pay my respects to Bob Gable, our current State party chairman. I'm delighted he's here, and the other party officials. And of course, I'd be remiss if I didn't in a personal way pay my respects to Will and Sarah Farish and to my old friend, Lee Brown—give them a job to do, and it gets done. And I am just delighted to be here with all three of them.

Spring in the Bluegrass State, racing at Churchill Downs, and voting for Mitch McConnell—it doesn't get much better than that, wherever you are. Senator, your supporters have tonight given very generously to your campaign, and I know what it is that everyone here wants from me in return. Too late—all six puppies are spoken for. [*Laughter*] But I'll let you in on a secret. The biggest secret in town is that Will Farish's springer spaniel—or English spaniel—is actually Millie's boyfriend. [*Laughter*] Up to now we've tried to keep his name out of the press, though. [*Laughter*] I think it's okay now, though, to reveal his name—Tug Farish III. [*Laughter*] Just what my elitist image name—puppies with Roman numerals after their names. [*Laughter*]

But here we are in Kentucky. You may have read that the pups are sleeping, or have been, on the Washington Post and the New York Times—[*laughter*]—the first time in history that those papers have been used to prevent leaks. [*Laughter*]

Will and I—you got to—we'll confess it: we're partial to those English spaniels—Millie, Tug, the puppies, and all that. But when I arrived in Kentucky tonight, I saw the strangest thing: bloodhounds, everywhere, searching for your former Senator still. They have not found him yet. But they know where this one is. He's in Washington, doing the people's business, and I've never seen a guy work harder for the people that sent him up there than Mitch McConnell. He's never forgotten how he got to Washington.

And I might say—and this is a matter of at least note to me—and that is that Mitch McConnell was the first United States Senator to be in my corner to endorse me when I ran for the Presidency of the United States—the very first one. And I say that because he has always stood up for his convictions, a man of principle and character, the courage of those convictions. One of the reasons I am here tonight is—I will never forget and will always appreciate—the fact that Mitch McConnell stood out early, took a position, and stayed with it. He's that kind of guy; he's that kind of Senator.

In a very short time in the U.S. Senate, he's gained the kind of clout that Kentucky needs in Washington. And he's achieved the stature that caused me to choose him as chairman of our delegation to El Salvador to monitor those very important elections. And I knew I could count on Mitch for this sensitive foreign policy assignment. And I'll be looking to him for his advice and counsel as we chart America's course in the years ahead.

And speaking of delegations monitoring elections, let me just make a reference to Panama, because we had two delegations down there monitoring these elections—one headed by former Presidents Ford and Carter; one headed by Congressman Murtha of the United States House of Representatives and Senator McCain of Arizona. And both of them came back and said the following: One, the affections of the people of Panama about the United States is intact. Two, the election was clearly fraudulent. There's nobody that's looked at the election down there that has anything to say other than that it was fraudulent and free. They made the point that it would be in the interests of peace and freedom and democracy around the world if the Panamanian people could be granted their wish to have Mr. Endara be the new President of Panama.

And let me just assure you of this: I will act prudently in Central America. I will act as much as we possibly can in concert with the nations of Central and South America. We do not want to return to the days of the imperialistic gringos of the North. But let everybody be clear on one point: I will protect the lives of Americans in Panama, whether they're military or civilian. We will not let Americans' lives be put at risk by a dictator down there.

I mentioned Mitch's interest in foreign policy and his leadership there. But on domestic issues as well—important issues like keeping the economy strong—he's right out there. You see, there is great mutual respect between us. Mitch understands words like principle and loyalty. And as you know, those words are very, very important to all of us. Certainly, I say they're very important to me. So, take it from me, I know from experience you can count on Mitch McConnell.

Let me simply say, I know you haven't even eaten yet, and I've had two graduation speeches and a couple of miles of running over in Houston before going to Mississippi, and I'm just really delighted to be here. But let me just say a word about—[*laughter*]—let me just say one other serious word, because yesterday I gave a speech over at Texas A&M in Bryan, Texas, about our relationship with—do I hear a couple of Aggies in the crowd down there?—a speech about our relationship with the Soviet Union. And there are some young people here tonight, and I'd like to address myself to them and say I think you've got a wonderful chance to live in a more peaceful world, to grow up without the fear that some of your parents have had about nuclear holocaust or a world at war. And yesterday I made this proposal that we offer to the Soviets a chance to be reintegrated back into the family of nations. And that is going to be a driving goal of my Presidency. But we're not going to do it from naivete. We're not going to do it based on promises or bold proposals. We're going to do it on the facts. And I'm going to keep the United States of America strong, but I am not going to miss an opportunity to discuss global peace and to work for the relief of regional tensions with Mr. Gorbachev. We are going to do that, but we're going to do it in a timely fashion, a prudent fashion, with the interests of the free world foremost all the time.

These are exciting times, and we are the United States of America. And we have always led the alliance, and we're going to continue to lead the alliance. But I would conclude I am optimistic not only about the future of the alliance but I am optimistic about the changes that are taking place in the Soviet Union. And I'll do my level best—working with the three Congressmen that are here, with the Senator that is here—to enhance United States standing and to make clear to everyone in the world that we are committed to world peace, that we're going to stay strong in the pursuit of that peace.

Thank you all very much. Thank you very, very much for your support of this outstanding Senator. I'm delighted to be with you. God bless you, and God bless the United States of America. Thank you very, very much.

Note: The President spoke at 9:25 p.m. in the reception tent at Lane's End Farm. Following his remarks, the President returned to Washington, DC.

Message on the Observance of Police Week and Police Officers' Memorial Day, May 1989

May 13, 1989

America has a long tradition of excellence in law enforcement. Throughout the country, in each and every community, citizens expect the highest standards of conduct and character in those men and women who work in this field: honor, integrity, diligence, bravery, and professionalism. Police Week is a fitting time to show our special appreciation for these individuals who render an indispensable service to all of us and who set a splendid example of selflessness and valor.

Police Officers' Memorial Day poignantly reminds us that law enforcement officials face great danger every day of the year. Whether responding to an accident on a dark snow-covered rural highway, or arresting drug dealers in the inner-city, police officers save lives—often at the risk of their own. Today, we honor those who have fallen in the line of duty. They have paid the greatest price possible for our safety, and this observance is but a small repayment toward the lasting debt we owe to each of them.

I encourage all Americans to join me in expressing our heartfelt respect and gratitude to the Nation's law enforcement officers, not only during Police Week and Police Officers' Memorial Day, but also throughout the year. These dedicated individuals who uphold the law and protect our lives and property deserve our constant support.

GEORGE BUSH

Remarks at the National Peace Officers' Memorial Day Ceremony
May 15, 1989

Thank you, Suzy. If it doesn't start clearing up, we're issuing snorkels to everybody out there. [*Laughter*] Thank you, Suzy Sawyer, and of course, to Dewey Stokes and Craig Floyd, my respects as well. You have great leadership, and I salute them. I want to say how pleased I am that the Secretary of the Treasury is with me, Nick Brady; our Attorney General, the able Dick Thornburgh; and our drug czar, Secretary Bill Bennett. The fact that we four are here is intentional. It sends the signal of our commitment and of our interest. And I know Members of Congress are here as well. I spotted my own Senator, Senator Phil Gramm of Texas, and Senator Pete Wilson. But I'm going to be in trouble because I can't see over there—who else is there. But I know many are sitting right over here, and we salute them. I see Senator Ford and others, and we're just delighted that they are here today.

Last fall a retired New York police lieutenant gave me badge number 14072, and I have it with me today—the badge his son wore the day he was gunned down by a gang of cocaine cowards. Matt Byrne asked me to keep Eddie's badge as a "reminder of all the brave police officers who put their lives on the line for us every single day." Matt, your son's badge, as I have told you, is kept in my desk at the Oval Office. And during the debate on gun-related violence that has raged in this country the past several months, neither it nor what it represents has ever been far from my mind. I've heard the many voices, the courageous and the compassionate, the wounded and the widowed, and I salute the survivors that are here today.

We gather today to respond to those voices and to honor the fallen by launching a national strategy, a partnership with America's cities and States, to take back the streets. It calls for a return to common sense. And it begins with a clear-eyed vision of the kind of problems we face, the kind of people we are, the kind of values that we hold, and the kind of nation we intend to bequeath to our children.

The problem is violent crime, and in particular, the blood that's been shed by increasingly sophisticated guns in the hands of a new class of criminals. Usually, but not always, the deaths are tied to a cycle of dollars and drugs and dependency. The principles are simple. My generation well remembers what some believe was FDR's finest speech: the "Four Freedoms," an address to a joint session of the Congress. And the last, often forgotten, but arguably the most fundamental of those freedoms was simply this: freedom from fear. Our sworn duty to "insure domestic Tranquility" is as old as the Republic, placed in the Constitution's preamble even before the common defense and the general welfare. And so, when we ask what kind of society the American people deserve, our goal must be a nation in which law-abiding citizens are safe and feel safe.

To achieve this goal, people must be held accountable for their actions, and that's common sense. Most Americans are law-abiding, and most believe that there is such a thing as right and wrong, good and evil. And whether it's the brutalization of a young runner in a park or terrorizing a young man onto a crowded highway, these are acts that cannot be excused or explained away. A commonsense approach to crime means that if we're going to affect people's behavior we must have a criminal justice system in which there is an expectation that if you commit a crime you will be caught; and if caught, you will be prosecuted; and if convicted, you will do time. For far too long, a privileged class of violent and repeat offenders have calculated that crime really does pay, that our criminal justice system is a crapshoot where the risks are worth the rewards. Well, it's time we change the odds and up the stakes enormously.

And we will lead the way. We'll do our part and then some. But no Federal effort can succeed without the full partnership of the cities and the States that you so nobly represent. Unfortunately, nowhere is your front-line role more evident than in the honor roll that will be read today: of 161 officers killed in the line of duty last year, 152 were State or local cops. And you are the first line of defense, and your respective governments have an obligation to adopt tough legislation and provide the resources—in police, prosecutors, and prisons—to fully back you up.

At the trial of Eddie Byrne's executioners, there was testimony that the hit was ordered from prison to send a message to the people behind the badge. And one witness said that they hoped to see the attack on the television news at Riker's Island. Well, today we have a message of our own: We're going to take back the streets by taking criminals off the streets. And it is an attack on all four fronts: new laws to punish them, new agents to arrest them, new prosecutors to convict them, and new prisons to hold them.

I am announcing today—and there is no more fitting place than right here—a comprehensive new offensive for combating violent crime—for Eddie Byrne, for every officer we honor here today, and for America. The first front of this campaign, new laws, starts with the semiautomatic and so-called assault weapons that criminals have taken as their gun of choice. And again, common sense has to play an important part in this discussion. The fact of the matter is, nearly half the households in this country have guns, and guns are already out there. And the overwhelming majority are legitimately owned, for legitimate purposes. But in contrast to legitimate gun ownership is the chilling fact that something like 80 percent of all firearms used by felons are stolen or otherwise unlawfully obtained. Throughout our nation's history, the hard lesson we've learned is that criminals will get guns. And so, let me be very clear about our response: The right to own a gun is not a license to harm others.

And so, first I am calling on Congress today to do for dangerous firearms what it has wisely done for dangerous drugs: to double the mandatory minimum penalties for the use of semiautomatic weapons in crimes involving violence or drugs. And the math is simple. Anyone who uses a semiautomatic for crime, or so much as has one on them during a crime, will do an automatic 10 extra years in Federal prison—no probation, no parole, no matter which judge they get.

And secondly, we just can't plea-bargain away the lives of your loved ones, the lives of our cops and kids. And I'm directing the Attorney General to advise America's prosecutors to end plea bargaining for violent Federal firearms offenses. Those who use guns will do time—hard time.

And third, when a criminal carries a gun and someone dies, they must pay with their own lives. We are calling on Congress today to enact the steps necessary to implement the death penalty and to newly designate the use of a firearm as an aggravating factor for determining whether the death sentence should be imposed.

And I call on America's Governors to match this Federal initiative and propose these same three standards at home: mandatory time, no deals without cooperation, and the death penalty where appropriate. Your States owe it to those here today, and to the American people.

And fourth, 2 months ago, at my direction, the Bureau of Alcohol, Tobacco and Firearms suspended the importation of certain so-called assault weapons. ATF is continuing its examination to determine which, if any, of those weapons are not acceptable under standards in existing law. And at the conclusion of this study, and after careful consideration, we will permanently ban any imports that don't measure up to these standards.

Recently the U.S. News cover story on guns summed up a related challenge: "the difficulty in drafting laws that will separate assault weapons used in crime from semiautomatics frequently used for legitimate hunting and sport." And there is substantial controversy and debate on this point. You're all well aware of that. But one thing that we do know about these assault weapons is that they are invariably equipped with unjustifiably large magazines. The notorious AKS–47, for example, comes with a magazine that pumps off 30 explosive bullets without reloading. And that is why—fifth—we stand on the steps here in front of the Capitol and ask its support for legislation prohibiting the importation, manufacture, sale, or transfer of these insidious gun magazines of more than 15 rounds.

The current debate was first sparked when an unstable gunman in Stockton, California, purchased an AKS–47 over the counter and used it to lay waste to an elementary school playground. Patrick Edward Purdy had no business buying that gun. He was arrested on his first weapons charge before his 15th birthday. And by his fourth firearms arrest, Purdy had finally turned 18, and with it chalked up the first of two adult convictions. Although for violent and weapons offenses, both convictions were misdemeanors. Purdy crawled through the loophole that bars only felons from buying guns and got that deadly AKS–47. That is outrageous.

And therefore, we also propose that Congress close this Purdy loophole and others like it that allow deadly weapons to fall into deadly hands. Again, that's just plain common sense. We must not allow deadly weapons to fall into deadly hands.

But we need to do more than just enact new laws. And in a recent movie about the L.A. gang wars, a woman shouts encouragement to a cop on patrol, telling him: "You get them off the street." And he answers: "Lady, we're trying." And the woman offers a four-word solution: "You need more help." And believe me, we know it. Our police need more help. And I'm here today to tell you that we're prepared to match rhetoric with resources and call on our cities and States to do the same.

The second front, if you will, of our new offensive calls for increased manpower and a new strategy on guns, a strategy based on models of proven effectiveness. I have directed the Attorney General and the Treasury Secretary, working together with State and local enforcement, to launch a comprehensive, coordinated offensive against our nation's most violent criminals. And I am requesting funding for hiring 825 new Federal agents and staff—375 at ATF, 300 at the FBI, and 150 Deputy U.S. Marshals. Many of these hirings will permit experienced investigators from all three agencies to promptly combat violent crime in the field.

Of course, arresting these thugs doesn't help if we don't have the muscle to prosecute each criminal to the fullest extent of the law. And that's why the third front of this campaign calls for Congress to back up these new troops with 1,600 new prosecutors and staff. And now, there probably isn't a police officer here who hasn't seen a case where a dangerous felon—properly arrested, fully prosecuted, and sentenced to the maximum—walked out of jail early, sometimes years early, because prisons are bursting at the seams. That is not right.

Part of our commonsense approach is a simple recognition that it doesn't do any good to provide new Federal agents, new assistant U.S. Attorneys, and new laws with long-term penalties if we don't have the prison cells to keep criminals where they belong. A chain is only as strong as its weakest link. And so, as the fourth front in this comprehensive effort, I am calling on the Congress to authorize an additional $1 billion, over and above the $500 million already slated for 1990, for Federal prison construction. These 24,000 new beds will boost Federal prison capacity by nearly 80 percent.

Not since Lincoln has a President stood in front of the Capitol and been just a few miles from the front lines of a war. Never was the toll more visible than in the faces of the brave men and women, the families, gathered here today. And when I first stood here as President, over there, only moments after taking the oath of office, I made a promise: "This scourge will stop." And that's a promise that we intend to keep.

Ladies and gentlemen, I offer my condolences for your fallen loved ones and for your fellow officers. And I salute your commitment, and I salute your courage, and as a citizen—grateful for the protection you have provided for me and my family and my fellow countrymen—I thank you, and I wish you Godspeed. Thank you all, and God bless the United States of America. Thank you very much.

Note: The President spoke at 12:29 p.m. at the West Front of the Capitol. In his opening remarks, he referred to Suzy Sawyer, executive director of the Fraternal Order of Police Ladies Auxiliary; Dewey Stokes, national president of the Fraternal Order of Police; and Craig Floyd, president of the National Law Enforcement Officers Memorial Fund.

White House Fact Sheet on Combating Violent Crime
May 15, 1989

The President outlined today a comprehensive program to combat violent crime. The program is designed to strengthen the Nation's criminal justice system and the Federal, State, and local law enforcement partnership. The program is grounded in the President's belief that greater certainty of apprehension, prosecution, and punishment will help deter crimes of violence. It includes proposals to strengthen current Federal, State, and local laws, to step up enforcement and to hold perpetrators of crimes fully accountable for their actions.

The President is proposing a commonsense approach to crime with initiatives to limit access to weapons by criminals, to reform the criminal justice system, to enhance enforcement and prosecution, and to expand prison capacity to ensure both the certainty and severity of punishment.

Fundamental Principles

Four principles underlie the goals of our criminal justice system and the means for accomplishing them.

- A primary purpose of government is to protect citizens and their property. Americans deserve to live in a society in which they are safe and feel secure.
- Those who commit violent criminal offenses should, and must, be held accountable for their actions.
- Our criminal justice system must have as its objective the swift and certain apprehension, prosecution, and incarceration of those who break the law.
- Success in accomplishing our criminal justice system goals requires a sustained, cooperative effort by Federal, State, and local law enforcement authorities.

The President today proposed a comprehensive four-part program to strengthen current laws, enhance enforcement and apprehension of criminals, facilitate prosecutions, and expand Federal prison capacity.

Comprehensive Crime Control Act of 1989

I. STRENGTHENING CURRENT LAWS

To ensure that those who commit violent criminal offenses are held fully accountable for their actions, it is essential to eliminate certain gaps in existing law and to strengthen some existing statutes.

A. Enhanced Penalties for Firearms Violations

The President proposed seven changes in Federal firearms laws which would:

1. double the mandatory penalty from 5 to 10 years under 18 U.S.C. 924(c) for the use of a semiautomatic firearm during the commission of a violent crime or drug felony;
2. amend the Armed Career Criminal statute to count as predicate offenses acts of juvenile delinquency which if

committed by an adult would constitute a serious drug offense; many youthful repeat offenders now escape the enhanced career criminal penalties because most of their prior offenses were charged as juvenile delinquency;
3. allow for pretrial preventive detention of defendants in cases involving certain serious Federal firearms and explosive offenses;
4. authorize criminal penalties and mandatory minimum sentences for theft of a firearm;
5. enhance penalties for smuggling firearms into the United States while engaged in, or in the furtherance of, drug trafficking;
6. require mandatory revocation of Federal supervised release for those possessing a firearm anytime before the term of their supervised release expires;
7. double the current penalty for a knowing and materially false statement on ATF Form 4473 to a maximum sentence of 10 years imprisonment.

The President also urged all States to adopt model legislation providing mandatory minimum sentences for criminal offenses involving firearms to parallel Federal mandatory minimum provisions.

He directed the Attorney General to provide the States with related technical assistance through the Law Enforcement Coordinating Committees (LECC's). At present, 30 States have some provision for mandatory terms of imprisonment for use of firearms in the commission of a crime.

The President proposed providing a 5-percent bonus to the formula portion of drug law enforcement grants for those States which adopt this model legislation.

B. Restricting Plea Bargaining

If our criminal justice system is to achieve its objective of ensuring that those who commit violent firearms offenses are held fully accountable for their actions, plea bargaining practices nationwide must be reformed. Too often, serious felons walk away from court after pleading guilty to minor offenses and misdemeanors because overburdened prosecutors have accepted plea agreements rather than going to trial. The lesser charges result in lesser sentences or probation, and repeat offenders continue to beat the system. To speed an end to such plea bargaining:

1. The President directed the Attorney General to issue and fully implement guidelines for Federal prosecutors regarding plea bargaining under the Sentencing Reform Act to ensure that Federal charges always reflect both the seriousness of the defendant's conduct and the Department's commitment to statutory sentencing goals and procedures. This will ensure that Federal prosecutors seek minimum mandatory penalties for all violent firearms offenses.

2. The President urged State and local governments to reform their plea bargaining and sentencing practices along similar lines and to devote increased resources to prosecutions.

C. Enacting Death Penalty Procedures

The criminal justice system must accord paramount importance to the protection of innocent life. The murderous assault-weapon-armed gang member, the terrorist, the traitor, and the assassin, who threaten American lives and the Nation's security, must know that they will face the death penalty for their crimes.

The President proposed to restore an enforceable death penalty for the most aggravated Federal crimes. His proposal includes adequate standards and constitutionally sound procedures for applying the Federal death penalty provisions that now appear in Federal statutes for homicide, espionage, and treason. It would also authorize the death penalty for a number of new offenses, such as murder for hire. In direct response to the increase in firearms-related violence, the proposal specifies that the use of a firearm in committing the offense or a previous conviction of a violent felony involving a firearm constitute aggravating factors justifying capital punishment.

D. Restricting Imported Weapons

When the study of imported weapons by the Bureau of Alcohol, Tobacco and Firearms is completed, the administration will make permanent the temporary suspension on the imported weapons, if any, that fail to meet the criteria specified in the Gun Control Act of 1968 (18 U.S.C. 925).

E. Preventing Circumvention of Import Laws

The administration will propose an amendment to ensure that actions taken under the provisions of the Gun Control Act of 1968 shall not be circumvented by domestic assembly of such weapons or any combination of domestic and foreign assembly of such weapons.

F. Restricting Gun Clips and Magazines

The administration will propose legislation prohibiting the importation, manufacture, transfer, or sale of gun magazines of over 15 rounds for use by private citizens.

G. Limiting Access to Weapons by Criminals

In addition to greater penalties for misusing firearms, it is also important to limit access to weapons by criminals. This can be facilitated in three ways:

1. Strengthening and Expanding Prohibitions on Access to Weapons by Criminals.

a. The President proposed to bar the sale of firearms to, or possession of firearms by, persons convicted of any violent offense, expanding the existing prohibition to cover individuals convicted of violent misdemeanor offenses.

b. The President also proposed to bar the sale of firearms to, or possession of firearms by, persons who are convicted of any serious drug offense.

2. Improving Mechanisms for Identifying Criminals Who Attempt to Purchase Firearms. The Anti-Drug Abuse Act of 1988 requires the Attorney General to develop a system for the immediate and accurate identification of felons and others who attempt to purchase firearms, but are barred by Federal law [18 U.S.C. 922(g)(1)] from buying or possessing firearms. The initial stage of the study must be completed by November 18, 1989.

a. The President directed the Attorney General to expand the National Criminal Records Identification System Implementation study to include a review and evaluation of State and local procedures which have effectively limited criminal access to firearms and, based on that review and in consultation with the Bureau of Alcohol, Tobacco and Firearms, to develop recommendations for model State legislation and procedures to complement and enhance efforts to reduce felons' access to firearms.

Model State legislation or procedures might include a reasonably structured waiting period or use other devices to facilitate accuracy in determining whether an individual seeking to purchase a weapon from a licensed gun dealer is ineligible by reason of Federal law. At present, more than 20 States have waiting periods, identification requirements, or other procedures which effectively limit criminal access to weapons.

b. The President urged States to transfer criminal history conviction, sentencing, and other case disposition records to the proper Federal authorities. He also directed the Attorney General to recommend additional improvements in the criminal records data system. The quality of criminal history data is a critical factor in crime control and prevention. At present, the only criminal history records consistently reported by States and localities are arrest records.

Timely and accurate reporting of conviction, sentencing, and other case disposition records is essential to the effective operation of the Nation's criminal justice system.

To improve the national data base, States should make such criminal record reporting mandatory and take steps to ensure that centralized State criminal history repositories are adequately funded and managed. In addition, States should maintain records and report on all serious crimes committed by juveniles, who frequently continue their criminal careers into adulthood but often escape early identification as repeat offenders and recidivists because their juvenile records are not reported.

3. Eliminating Loopholes and Clarifying Existing Offenses. The President also proposed to eliminate loopholes and clarify existing offenses related to the sale or transfer of firearms, in order to:

a. facilitate the prosecution of unlicensed gun dealers engaged in illegal weapons transfers to aliens or transients;

b. expand Federal jurisdiction to permit

prosecution of transactions in stolen firearms and weapons lacking serial numbers in cases where the firearms have previously moved in interstate or foreign commerce (present law requires the firearms be moving in interstate commerce at the time of the offense);

c. provide a uniform standard to determine whether a person is under Federal firearms disabilities based upon State convictions;

d. require that persons convicted under State law of a serious drug offense or violent felony apply to Federal authorities in order to have their firearms rights restored;

e. amend provisions regarding the disposal of forfeited firearms; and

f. clarify the definition of burglary in the Armed Career Criminal Act to eliminate loopholes caused by differing State laws.

H. Making Drug Testing a Condition of Release

The President also proposed to authorize and fund nationwide implementation in 1990 of drug testing as a mandatory condition of Federal probation, parole, or supervised release. It is estimated that 81,500 people will be on some form of Federal supervised release in 1990. The Justice Department and the Federal Judiciary will coordinate implementation of this program.

The President urged States to adopt similar mandatory drug testing programs as a condition of parole.

II. AUGMENTING ENFORCEMENT

A primary purpose of government is to protect citizens and their property. This requires the sustained cooperative commitment of Federal, State, and local law enforcement officials. Apprehending violent offenders requires increased enforcement personnel, improved cooperation among law enforcement authorities, and not permitting the exclusion of evidence on legal technicalities.

A. Additional ATF Special Agents

The President proposed to increase funds for the Bureau of Alcohol, Tobacco and Firearms to provide for the hiring, training, and equipping of 375 ATF special agents, inspectors, and support personnel to investigate assault weapon and other firearms violations by armed career criminal and repeat offenders.

B. Additional U.S. Marshals

The President proposed to increase funds for the U.S. Marshals to provide for about 150 additional positions for the Marshals Fugitive Investigations and Court Orders Program. This would direct greater Federal efforts to capturing fugitives and career criminals.

C. Additional FBI Agents

The President proposed to increase funds for the FBI to provide for about 300 additional positions for the Bureau's Violent Crime and Major Offenders Program and Organized Crime Program and to assist States and localities to improve their efforts in fighting violent crime through greater Federal/State cooperation.

D. Coordinated Task Forces

The President directed the Attorney General and Secretary of the Treasury to develop a coordinated strategy for the deployment of the additional U.S. Marshals, ATF and FBI agents. Their deployment will emphasize working closely with State and local authorities in task forces to target and investigate career criminals who are subject to prosecution as repeat offenders under Federal firearms laws and related statutes.

E. State and Local Resources

The President urged State and local authorities to increase their law enforcement resources devoted to identifying and apprehending violent criminal offenders.

F. Exclusionary Rule Reform

The President proposed to establish a general "good faith" exception to the exclusionary rule which would permit evidence to be admitted if the officers carrying out a search or seizure acted with an objectively reasonable belief that their conduct was in conformity with fourth amendment requirements. The reform legislation would clarify that, in the absence of explicit statutory authority for doing so, Federal courts may only exclude evidence on the basis of constitutional violations.

III. Enhancing Prosecution

In order to assure that criminals are held accountable for their offenses, certainty of prosecution must accompany severity of punishment. Federal, State, and local authorities must expand and coordinate their prosecutorial efforts.

A. Additional Assistant U.S. Attorneys

The President proposed to increase funds for the U.S. Attorneys Offices to support 1,600 additional positions to handle the increased number of Federal defendants and to prosecute more drug cases, weapons offenses, and other priority matters.

B. Additional Criminal Division Attorneys

The President proposed to increase funds for the Justice Department Criminal Division to support 168 additional positions to focus on drug cases, weapons offenses, and other priority matters, including activities to foster State and local cooperation and coordinated law enforcement strategies.

C. Additional Housing for Unsentenced Prisoners

The President proposed additional funds for the U.S. Marshals Service to provide transportation and 300,000 added jail days for unsentenced prisoners and pretrial detainees.

D. Additional Judicial Branch Resources

The President proposed increasing the administration's budget request for the Judiciary by $40 million for FY 1990 to cover costs associated with processing increased numbers of criminal defendants and for additional Federal criminal prosecutions.

E. Habeas Corpus Reform

The President proposed immediate enactment of habeas corpus reform to establish a general 1-year time limit on Federal applications by State prisoners and to require deference in Federal proceedings to the results of fair and reasonable State court determinations. This will correct the existing system of review, under which over 10,000 cases are annually filed in Federal court.

IV. Expanding Prison Capacity

Prison overcrowding remains a national problem. The most acute problem is at the Federal level. At both the Federal and State level prison overcrowding is a factor in sentencing. At the State and local levels it is often responsible for the early release of convicted criminals.

A. Expanding Federal Prison Construction

The President proposed an additional $1 billion for Federal prison construction, bringing the total 1990 budget to over $1.5 billion. This will increase prison capacity by about 77 percent, adding over 24,000 new Federal prison beds. The present rated Federal prison capacity is 30,951 beds; the present Federal prison population is approximately 48,000.

B. Converting Unused Federal Properties

The President directed the Secretary of Defense, the Secretary of Education, and the Administrator of the General Services Administration to work with the Attorney General to identify expeditiously properties and facilities suitable for conversion for use as Federal prisons or jails.

C. Deporting Criminal Aliens

The President proposed to provide the Attorney General with $14 million for the Immigration and Naturalization Service (INS) and the Executive Office for Immigration Review in order to expedite the deportation of convicted criminal aliens.

Crimes committed by aliens are rising disproportionately in relation to the general population and entailing more violent and drug-related crime.

The Federal Bureau of Prisons has identified 9,254 aliens in its facilities, 20.6 percent of its total inmate population.

D. Encouraging State Prison Construction

The President commended and encouraged State prison construction efforts. States currently have construction of 63,452 new bedspaces underway. An additional 78,094 bedspaces are planned, and funding has been secured for their construction. Moreover, States have requested construction of 72,190 additional bedspaces.

E. Review of Court-Ordered Prison Caps

The President directed the Attorney General to conduct a review of the role of court orders and consent decrees in prison crowding situations, including an assessment of the scope of judicial authority in formulating and issuing such orders, the impact of such orders on the operation of prison systems and public security, and nonjudicial means of addressing prison crowding. The Attorney General will report his findings to the President and recommend any necessary remedial actions.

Legislation to implement elements of this initiative will be transmitted shortly by the Attorney General.

FUNDING SUMMARY

Enforcement:	
BATF	$18.8 million
U.S. Marshals	$12.0 million
FBI	$19.5 million
Prosecution:	
U.S. Attorneys	$49.6 million
Criminal Division	$5.4 million

FUNDING SUMMARY—Continued

Unsentenced Prisoner Support	$13.0 million
Courts	$40.0 million
Drug Testing:	
Mandatory Testing	$10.7 million
Criminal Alien Deportation:	
INS	$12.5 million
EOIR (Executive Office for Immigration Review)	$1.6 million
State Grant Bonus:	
Office of Justice Programs (Bonus)	$6.0 million
Subtotal (nonprison)	$189.1 million
Prisons:	
Federal Prison Construction	$1.0 billion

This will bring the total 1990 prison construction budget to over $1.5 billion, which includes $115 million available from the Special Forfeiture Fund available to the Office of National Drug Control Policy, and $401 million in the original Bush Budget.

Total Increase .... [1] $1,189.1 billion

[1] This total can be accommodated within the overall domestic discretionary spending cap set in the Bipartisan Budget Agreement.

White House Statement on the President's Meeting With Cornelio Sommaruga of the International Committee of the Red Cross

May 15, 1989

The President met today with Cornelio Sommaruga, president of the International Committee of the Red Cross (ICRC). The visit provided an opportunity for President Bush to express American appreciation for the impressive humanitarian and human rights work of the ICRC around the world. ICRC efforts on behalf of refugees, the hungry, the displaced, political prisoners, and prisoners of war are well-known and well-respected.

The President and Mr. Sommaruga specifically discussed ICRC activities in Afghanistan and Sudan, and Mr. Sommaruga thanked President Bush for the recent special contribution of $10 million as a humanitarian gesture for ICRC activities in these countries.

Remarks to the Crewmembers of the Space Shuttle *Atlantis* and the Winners of the Orbiter-Naming Competition
May 16, 1989

I'd say please be seated, but I don't—well, you all, please be seated. And to our Senators and Congressmen here, a special warm welcome. And Admiral Truly, I'm very delighted to see you, sir. And of course, to Captain David Walker and Ron and Mary and Mark and Norm, let me say this: that Commander Walker and crew, friends and families of the shuttle *Atlantis*, distinguished members, we are just pleased that you all are here and sorry that the weather did not cooperate.

You know, the late Jackie Gleason immortalized the words, "And away we go." Well, it's a pleasure to be here with Americans who, by exploring the horizons of outer space, have made those words reality. And so, we gather here today to celebrate the continuity of our space program and really of our country itself, of America herself. In a sense, today's setting reflects the continuity. You are pioneers pushing back the boundaries of our technological future. And this house embodies the greatness of America's present and past.

And the two space programs that we celebrate—they, too, reflect America's continuity. For in *Atlantis*' deployment of *Magellan*, we salute achievement which has come to pass; and in *Endeavor*, the glory which still lies ahead. Some of you may recall that Winston Churchill said, "The farther backward you can look, the farther forward you are likely to see."

Well, *Magellan* was named after the seafaring explorer of the 16th century. And as the first U.S. planetary mission since 1978, it marks the rebirth of America's planetary program. From *Magellan*, we're going to learn more about Venus and, thus, ourselves. For Venus, I am told, is the planet most like Earth.

To Commander Walker and his outstanding *Atlantis* crew, and to the entire NASA organization, my heartfelt congratulations. Every time I talk to one of these astronauts, they always point out the support they get from a magnificent team that for a fleeting moment they leave behind on Earth. So, my salute goes to everybody involved in this important work. We salute the courage and enterprise of this crew especially, but also all who are on this team. You've reaffirmed your nation's genius in science and technology; and yet, I think we would all agree, it really is only just a beginning: 4 more solar system missions through the mid-1990's, 13 more shuttle flights in 1989 and '90. These flights will chart new frontiers in science and exploration. And we'll explore those frontiers through the leaders of tomorrow.

And so, we see some of those leaders in the students we have here today from Mississippi and from Georgia. For in a nationwide orbiter-naming competition, involving over 71,000 students and 6,100 entries from elementary and secondary schools, you showed how the possibilities of tomorrow point us onward and upward.

My friends, you know, choosing a name can be a thankless task. Consider the new father who was once reproached by Sam Goldwyn. "You're going to call your son William?" he said. "What kind of a name is that? Every Tom, Dick, and Harry is called William." [*Laughter*]

Well, somehow you all fared much better than that. Both of your schools chose the name *Endeavor*, which Webster's defines as "to make an effort, strive; to try to reach or achieve." And each of your schools has lived that definition. In the division 1 category, kindergarten through grade 6, the national winner is a team of 9 fifth-graders from Senatobia Middle School, in Senatobia, Mississippi. And through your team, younger elementary students learned about space up close and personal, like simulating a space camp's wireless communications or trying on a team-made spacesuit. And then in division 2, grades 7 through 12, the winning team came from a nearby State: Tallulah Falls Schools, Inc., in Tallulah Falls, Georgia. Here students developed a math magazine, "Math Exploration With James Cook," and then created a play comparing Cook's 18th-century sea exploration to *Endeavor's* 20th-century space exploration.

The orbiter-naming contest was, and is, a partnership between NASA and the Council of Chief State School Officers. The CCSSO played a key role in organizing this tremendous contest. And I'd like to thank its members and also my good friend, Congressman Tom Lewis, whose legislation created the event. But most of all, I want to thank you, Commander Walker; the crew; and the students. For you've acted not for us alone but for generations to come. And in so doing, you're making possible, now and tomorrow, that picture of the orbiter lifting off, its rise a swirl of magic, and of Americans cheering its safety and success and dreaming of the new worlds and faraway heavens which form America's destiny. And that is the continuity of America and of our space shuttle program, which points us toward the stars.

And so, thank you; my heartfelt congratulations. God bless you all, and God bless the United States of America. Thank you very, very much.

Note: The President spoke at 1:17 p.m. in Room 450 of the Old Executive Office Building. In his opening remarks, he referred to Adm. Richard H. Truly, Administrator of the National Aeronautics and Space Administration. The crew of the "Atlantis" included: Capt. David M. Walker, USN, commanding officer; Lt. Col. Ronald J. Grabe, USAF, pilot; Mary L. Cleave, mission specialist; Maj. Mark C. Lee, USAF, mission specialist; and Norman E. Thagard, mission specialist.

Message to the Congress Transmitting the Annual Report of the National Science Foundation
May 16, 1989

To the Congress of the United States:

I am pleased to transmit the annual report of the National Science Foundation for Fiscal Year 1988. This report describes research supported by the Foundation in the mathematical, physical, biological, social, behavioral, and computer sciences; engineering; and education in those fields.

Achievements such as the ones described here are the basis for much of our Nation's strength—its economic growth, national security, and the overall well-being of our people.

Federal investments in research and development should be increased even beyond the current strong levels. Such investments should focus on basic research.

As we move into the 1990's, the Foundation will continue its efforts to expand our Nation's research achievements, our productivity, and our ability to remain competitive in world markets through innovation and discoveries.

I commend the Foundation's work to you.

GEORGE BUSH

The White House,
May 16, 1989.

Nomination of Robert D. Orr To Be United States Ambassador to Singapore
May 16, 1989

The President today announced his intention to nominate Robert D. Orr to be Ambassador Extraordinary and Plenipotentiary of the United States of America to the Republic of Singapore. He would succeed Daryl Arnold.

In 1980 Governor Orr was elected Governor of Indiana, and reelected in 1984. Prior to this he was elected Lieutenant Governor of Indiana in 1972. He has also served as a member of the Indiana State Senate, 1968–1972. Governor Orr is the former chairman of the Republican Governors' Association and has served on the National Governors' Association executive committee.

Governor Orr graduated from Yale University (A.B., 1940). He was born November 17, 1917, in Evansville, IN. He served in the U.S. Army during World War II and was awarded the Legion of Merit. He is married and has three children.

Remarks to Members of the American Retail Federation
May 17, 1989

Thank you so much for that warm welcome. And let me just say to Don Seibert and Joe O'Neill that I'm delighted to be here. It gives me a chance to express to all of you my appreciation for the support that this organization has given us already and the support that you gave to the previous administration, of which I was very proud to have been a part. I heard John Sununu [Chief of Staff to the President] refer to the minimum wage, and that's what I wanted to talk to you about and solicit your support on today.

We're moving, as you know, toward a very different business climate in this country, and our view of what it takes to compete must change. You know, I think we've heard enough about the shop-worn liberal agenda of more government: mandated government, more broad attempts to run the businesses, and intrusive campaigns to legislate competitiveness. That tired agenda doesn't work. The notion that the Government should control business decisions has never made much sense, and it makes very little sense to me today. So, it is time to move on to the real issue: building a better, more competitive United States—and not through the intrusion of government but through the energy and the will of the American people. And I still believe that free markets work. I know that there is no such thing as pure free trade in the world today, but we believe in free trade, and obviously in fair trade as well.

What the world has learned over the last 40 years is that government intervention cripples economies, creates barriers for business, kills innovation; and in the final analysis, it costs jobs. And yet, even as the world is beginning now to recognize this truth and you see the changes going on, even in many of the Socialist economies, there are those who are still trying to keep the agenda of government intervention alive and active here at home. And many are well-intentioned, but you know what they say about good intentions. Let me assure you, we are not going down that road.

And we've already made progress in limiting excessive paperwork and regulations, and that work has got to continue—can't begin to tell you I think it's finished. I'd be thrown out of here by you people that have to wrestle with some of these forms. Drawing on the creative energy of the private sector, I believe we can reach a regulatory balance that is flexible and responsive at the lowest possible cost to business.

And so, thanks to American enterprise and a government that got out of the way, we've created almost 20 million new jobs since the recovery began in 1982. And employment, as you all know, is at record levels. This brings its own challenges. With labor markets getting tighter, opportunities for jobs abound. Many businesses are scrambling for people, with labor shortages driving up wages. Entry-level jobs in some regions of the country with low unemployment start at $5.00 an hour. And this is a case where the market alone is doing more than the Government could do or should do.

Across America, the skills gap is eclipsing

the wage gap, and that's the real problem. And that's a problem where I think the Government does have a role. Caught up in the politics of the minimum wage, it's too easy to forget who it is we're trying to help, and how. The issue is not minimum wage: it's a question of minimum skills. And we're entering a new era of opportunity. Impending labor shortages offer the promise of a job for everyone who is serious about wanting a job—if they're prepared. My difference with the majority in Congress is not about 30 cents an hour on the minimum-wage legislation: it's about hundreds of thousands of people—largely young people, largely unskilled people—who won't have a job to go to if the minimum wage legislation before the Congress now becomes law.

Artificial wage hikes simply mean the entry-level jobs are cut back on. The first to go are the young and the disadvantaged who are just beginning to develop workplace skills. It is haunting how thousands of young Americans in the inner cities believe that they have no stake in our system, no future, no hope. Believing they have nothing to lose, they act as if they have absolutely nothing to gain. And we can't allow this to continue, and it won't if we make sure that more of them can find jobs. I am absolutely, firmly convinced that the best poverty program is a job with dignity in the private sector. And the vast majority of minimum-wage workers are young secondary earners from families with incomes well above the poverty line, if you look at the statistics. And the fact is, fewer than 1 in 10 minimum-wage earners are heads of households and in poverty. They deserve our help, and raising the minimum wage may help some of them. But the cost will be measured in lost jobs, losses that will weigh hardest on the minimum-wage earners who are young and disadvantaged. And most need the experience that those entry-level jobs can provide.

So, I say to Congress: If you want to help the poor, don't take away their jobs. And there are other better strategies to help the working poor that won't cost them their jobs. And I've proposed an effective training wage—we've had a long battle about that. Minimum-wage differential, it used to be called; now we call it a training wage that would preserve jobs, promote skills development, and give more Americans access to work experience.

We've proposed, also, a new child-care tax credit to enhance the incomes of poorer working families with young children, and enable them to take, or train for, a real job. And I might say that, in the process, we have preserved the concept of parental choice, which I think strengthens the family, as opposed to the legislation on child care being proposed by others up there, which mandates standards from Washington, DC and restricts parental choice.

The jobs we're creating demand higher levels of skills than ever before, so we've set up a package of educational reforms to promote parental choice and encourage excellence and to make our educational system more accountable. We've proposed alternative certification for teachers and principals so that interested, capable people from business or science or engineering and other professions can go ahead and help teach in the public schools. It's a shame when somebody wants to take a sabbatical out of business or elsewhere, is prohibited by almost meaningless regulations that have been promulgated over the year by the education establishment. So, we're trying to move forward in terms of alternative certification, and I would enlist the support of all of you for this worthy goal.

We're proposing significant improvements in the Job Training Partnership Act, already so effective at linking public and private efforts to help those young people that are most at risk get the training that they need for productive lives.

But the best way to make disadvantaged youth and the working poor part of a competitive, opportunity-based economy is to continue to create jobs and prepare people to fill them. And we must limit any increase in the minimum wage so that it won't extract an excessive cost in lost jobs and that it won't increase inflation in the United States. And then we have to have that effective training wage to preserve opportunity for those who need it the most.

And I have a choice to make. I can sign the legislation pending in Congress and go back to the tired agenda of government intervention that so often hurts the very people that it attempts to help, or we can step forward to keep America on the path to a competitive future, a future that is bright with opportunity. And for me, the choice is very clear: If the majority in the Congress rejects my offer of a reasonable compromise—and we have made such a proposal—a veto is going to be inevitable. And one thing I will not compromise: I will not compromise the future of the working poor, and that is what's at stake in this legislation before Congress today. And I'm not going to compromise either a generation of young people. They deserve more than the false promises and failed ideas that hurt their chances to have a job. They deserve a job in a growing, noninflationary economy, and I'm going to do my level best to see that everybody has that opportunity.

I thank you, and I refuse to leave here without soliciting your help in sustaining my veto, if that is required. And I would also solicit your help for my parental choice child-care initiative that I think many would find far superior to the legislation that's being created on the Hill that would have the Government mandate to local communities, to churches, to whatever, all the standards. We cannot go that route in this country if we're to preserve the strength of the family and of the community in our social structure. So, I solicit your support for that. And again, looking over my shoulder, I thank you for all the support you've already given us. Thank you all very, very much.

Note: The President spoke at 10:03 a.m. in Room 450 of the Old Executive Office Building. In his opening remarks, he referred to Donald Seibert and Joseph P. O'Neill, chairman of the board and president of the federation, respectively.

Continuation of Roland R. Vautour as an Under Secretary of Agriculture
May 17, 1989

The President today announced that Roland R. Vautour will continue to serve as Under Secretary of Agriculture for Small Community and Rural Development.

Since September 1987, Mr. Vautour has served as Under Secretary for Small Community and Rural Development at the Department of Agriculture in Washington, DC. Prior to this, he served as the Farmers Home Administration State Director for Vermont, New Hampshire, and the U.S. Virgin Islands, 1981–1987. He was owner and principal broker for Sterling Realty, 1969–1981, and vice president and general manager of the Madonna Mountain Corp., 1964–1969.

Mr. Vautour received a bachelor of science degree in business administration from the University of New Hampshire. He is married and has four children.

Continuation of Charles E.M. Kolb as a Deputy Under Secretary of Education
May 17, 1989

The President today announced that Charles E.M. Kolb will continue to serve as Deputy Under Secretary of Education for Planning, Budget, and Evaluation.

Since September 1988, Mr. Kolb has served as Acting Deputy Under Secretary in the Office of Planning, Budget, and Evaluation at the Department of Education in

Washington, DC. Prior to this, he served as the Deputy General Counsel for Regulations and Legislation at the Department of Education, 1986–1988, and Assistant General Counsel for the Office of Management and Budget, 1983–1986. He was an associate with Foreman and Dyess in Washington, DC, 1982–1983, and an associate with Covington and Burling in Washington, DC, 1979–1982. He also served as a law clerk to the Honorable Joseph H. Young, United States District Judge in the U.S. Court House in Baltimore, MD, and as an associate with Cahill, Gordon, and Reindel in New York, NY.

Mr. Kolb graduated from Princeton University (A.B., 1973); Balliol College, Oxford University (B.A., 1975; M.A., 1980); and the University of Virginia (J.D., 1978). He was born in Salisbury, MD, on November 6, 1950. He resides in Alexandria, VA.

Nomination of Antonio Lopez To Be an Associate Director of the Federal Emergency Management Agency

May 17, 1989

The President today announced his intention to nominate Antonio Lopez to be an Associate Director of the Federal Emergency Management Agency (National Preparedness Directorate). He would succeed George Woloshyn.

Mr. Lopez most recently served as Special Assistant to the President and Director of the White House Military Office in Washington, DC. Prior to this he served on the George Bush for President and Bush-Quayle 1988 campaigns. From 1985 to 1987, Mr. Lopez was self-employed in Covington, TN, as an international business development consultant. He served as manager for business development, Latin America, for the Vollrath Co. in Sheboygan, WI, 1982–1985.

Mr. Lopez received a bachelor of science degree in mechanical engineering from the University of Colorado at Boulder, and a master of science degree in systems management from the University of Southern California at Los Angeles. He served in the U.S. Air Force from 1955 to 1982, retiring as a colonel. Among his many military decorations, Mr. Lopez was awarded the Defense Superior Service Medal, the Distinguished Flying Cross, and 12 air medals. He is a Vietnam war veteran and flew 389 combat missions. He was born in Los Angeles, CA. Mr. Lopez is married to the former Ruth B. Fryer. They have four children and four grandchildren.

White House Statement on the Proposed Foreign Acquisition of the ABB-Westinghouse Joint Venture

May 17, 1989

The President today decided against intervening in the possible acquisition by ASEA Brown Boveri Ltd. (ABB), a Swiss/Swedish firm, of Westinghouse Electric Corporation's interest in an ABB-Westinghouse joint venture for the manufacture, distribution, sale, and servicing of electrical transmission and distribution equipment in the United States.

The President based his decision on the results of the investigation by the Committee on Foreign Investment in the United States (CFIUS), chaired by Treasury Secretary Nicholas F. Brady. CFIUS conducted a thorough investigation of various issues relating to the manufacturing and maintenance of extra-high voltage (EVH) transformers. During the investigation, ABB reconfirmed its intention to continue the manufacture, servicing, repair, research, and design in the United States of these high voltage transformers.

The ABB-Westinghouse investigation was conducted pursuant to section 5021 of the Omnibus Trade and Competitiveness Act of 1988. That provision, known as the Exon-Florio provision, authorizes the President to investigate and, if necessary, to suspend or prohibit a proposed foreign acquisition of a U.S. business engaged in U.S. interstate commerce. The criteria to suspend or prohibit a transaction are that the President must find:

—credible evidence to believe that the foreign investor might take actions that threaten to impair the national security;

—that existing laws, other than the International Emergency Economic Powers Act and the Exon-Florio provision itself, are inadequate and inappropriate to deal with the national security threat.

Remarks on Signing the Martin Luther King, Jr., Federal Holiday Commission Extension Act

May 17, 1989

Mrs. King. President Bush, Vice President Quayle, Members of the Cabinet and the Congress, and to all of my friends and supporters, ladies and gentlemen, this is a great occasion for those of us who have struggled to make a reality the dream of Martin Luther King, Jr., and this is a continuing effort in that direction to institutionalize his teachings and his great legacy. It is a great honor to join with you on this historic occasion in this ceremony today.

First, I want to thank Congressman John Conyers on the House side and Senator Sam Nunn on the Senate side for all of their outstanding leadership as sponsors of the Martin Luther King, Jr., Federal Holiday Legislation Extension Act, and all of the congressional cosponsors from both sides of the aisle who helped to pass this legislation extending the Martin Luther King Federal Holiday Commission. I can say that it was genuinely a great bipartisan victory in the spirit of President Bush's Inaugural Address, and I want to thank all of the Members who have cooperated so beautifully. With pride and the highest hopes for the future, it gives me greatest pleasure to thank our President for his outstanding leadership in helping to make our newest national holiday all that it should be, all that it must be if we are to fulfill the promise of democracy.

The observance of this holiday is both an important learning experience and a call to action to address injustice anywhere. Through the holiday, we can learn about the values and responsibilities of our democracy. We can learn about how a great vision and a great nation began to confront and nonviolently challenge institutional racism. We can honor our obligation to protest evil and injustice as one of the highest traditions of our American heritage. We can learn about the values of tolerance and compassion and develop a greater sense of responsibility to the poor and suffering, and even to each other. We can learn about the values of brotherhood and sisterhood, love, peace, reconciliation, community service, honesty, courage, freedom, and self-discipline. These values transcend politics, ideology, and national boundaries; for they speak to the essence of the human soul in a way that can only be universally uplifting and challenging.

May the Almighty God bless this occasion and all that it represents. May He enable us to apply the gifts and talents He has given us in the service to others. May His grace strengthen us to work with order and patience, with forgiveness, gratitude, and joy, as we seek to make this a better nation and world so that generations yet unborn will continue to sing with pride: America, God shed His grace on thee, and crown thy good with brotherhood and sisterhood from sea to shining sea.

The President. Coretta, thank you for those inspiring words. I know I speak for everybody in paying tribute to you for your steadfast support of this most worthwhile Commission. I planned on welcoming you all to the tropical rain forest—[*laughter*]—that we call the Rose Garden. But the East Room has an advantage: leakproof—if anything in the White House can be leakproof. [*Laughter*] At least it's dry. And we're delighted that Coretta Scott King and Dexter and so many others are here.

I want to welcome the members of the Commission, the King Federal Holiday Commission; the Members of Congress that are here, the leadership in the Senate and in the House. And I'm just delighted that you all are here, and thank you for your important role in all of this. I salute the party leaders that are here. I see Lee and others—Lee Atwater—and everybody joining in a tribute to Dr. Martin Luther King, Jr., and his ideals.

The bill that I'll be signing shortly underscores the importance of honoring the memory and the shining ideals of a great American hero, Martin Luther King, Jr. And all of us know his creed of faith, centered firmly in the great heritage of American ideals. On the steps of the Lincoln Memorial, Dr. King issued his challenge in the words of Thomas Jefferson: "We hold these truths to be self-evident, that all men are created equal." And he was a reformer and a crusader. His mission was to move America closer to the ideal, to bring the promise of equality and liberty and justice for all within the reach of all.

The Martin Luther King, Jr., Federal Holiday Commission plays a central role in preserving a great national treasure. And over the past 5 years, the Commission's done a great deal to make observance of the King holiday a national and international event. And our agenda for the next 5 years must be to build on that beginning, to see to it that the third Monday of every January becomes a day of hope, renewal, and rededication to the ideals of Dr. King, those that he upheld—a day dedicated to the memory, if you will, of a man who campaigned for peaceful change; of a man who stood for human dignity and certainly the fulfillment of individual excellence; of a man determined, committed, mind and heart, to march, to live, and to die for those—America's ideals.

So, Reverend King once wrote: "Injustice anywhere is a threat to justice everywhere." And simple words expressing a great truth: Justice is indivisible. And all of us must draw on the best in ourselves to make justice for all our cause. We've made great progress. But the memory of all that Dr. King stood for reminds us that our work is not done. So, let's continue his work towards a society that treats all men and women, whatever their origin, whatever the color of their skin, with dignity and respect. Let's ensure that our communities, where our children can learn, live, and grow, are free from the fear of violence and, yes, the lure of drugs. And let's work together towards a society that extends great opportunities and awakens hope to build a better America for all of us. And let's pass the King legacy on to our children, whose ideals and attitudes will shape our society into the next century.

I want to share with you a few words from the prizewinning essay on Martin Luther King, written by a young man—in this case, a fifth-grader—in Seattle. He writes: "I am only 11 years old, so I cannot really stop the racism. But I can control what happens in my heart and what I do with my life." That kid may only be 11, but there's wisdom in those words for all of us: A truly free society is within reach if, in our hearts, we abolish bias and bigotry and discrimination. And so, let's make that society, one with freedom and equality for all, our living memorial to a great man and a great American.

And now, Coretta, Mrs. King, if you will join me, I will sign this bill formally reauthorizing the Martin Luther King, Jr., Federal Holiday Commission.

Note: The President spoke at 1:31 p.m. in the East Room at the White House. In his remarks, he referred to Dexter King, son of Martin Luther King, Jr., and president of the King Center in Atlanta, GA, and H. Lee Atwater, chairman of the Republican National Committee. H.R. 1385, approved May 17, was assigned Public Law No. 101–30.

Discussion With Teachers at the Wilson Magnet High School in Rochester, New York
May 18, 1989

Ms. Johnston. You've already been somewhat introduced. I'm especially pleased that you asked for an opportunity to meet with the teachers of Wilson, really for a couple of reasons. Primary in the whole development of Wilson is very much akin to your message of accountability. It was a real driving force in our development. And the other reason is that, really, from my perspective, in terms of school reform, in school improvement, the real critical key role is the teacher role. It's creative and loving talent of teachers that really make a difference between a school that is just adequate and a school that really stretches for excellence for all kids.

This is a wonderful group of people, and I think that you're going to be able to have an opportunity to hear a lot of different perspective. I'd like to start with Mr. Hathaway, who's on your left. Eddie's with us since about 1980.

Teacher. Right, 10 years. [*Laughter*]

Ms. Johnston. Ten of your best, right, Eddie? Mr. Hathaway, I think, can give you a little overview of the building.

The President. Yeah. I'd love to know about the change and all that, too.

Teacher. Well, Mr. President, Wilson is one building that's made up of three houses, three programs, if you will, but with one common goal. You know the building, of course, is Wilson Magnet, but the three houses that we have in here—the Academy of Excellence, which meets the needs of the humanities and languages—is our draw. We have a house known as Transition Tech, which meets the special needs of students in special need, and we also have the School of Science and Technology. I'm a part of that program. And in that program, we teach and emphasize computers and science. Our goal though, of course, is total commitment to the students. We've been fortunate here in the Rochester community because we have a total commitment from everybody. And we're trying to meet the needs of society by using the whole community as a team: industry, the outside forces right here in the community, higher education, and of course, the hard-working staff here at Wilson. That's Wilson in a nutshell.

The President. Well, it's important, and it's impressive.

Teacher. We've been successful for many reasons. Gary, do you want to mention——

Teacher. Well, we're a small school and——

The President. Like numbers?

Teacher. Well, under a thousand. That makes a successful school. Teachers care, and that's what kids like. I've read papers by kids—I teach English—and some of the papers that the seniors are writing this year—they're talking about—the Wilson teachers care about kids. And kids like to know that there's somebody there that cares about them.

Teacher. Another part of Wilson that really helps make it such a success is our home aids guidance program. We take on a group of youngsters, about 20, from the time they enter the building until the time they graduate; and we become almost parents, surrogate parents. You could talk to anyone on this staff, and they would have stories for you, a lot of the different, wonderful things that are done for our kids, with our kids.

The President. Do you ever run into any parental resentment? You get 20 kids, and you find somebody that maybe needs some love and attention and caring, as Gary said. But do you ever run into some parent that doesn't want that kind of involvement?

Teacher. I never have. As a matter of fact, a particular situation that I'm involved in right now—I have nothing but parents who are very supportive of everything that we're doing.

The President. I think they all would be. I just wondered if some felt that intrusion—don't worry, we'll take care of our kids at home; you look after them at school—because the program goes into the homes, too, or not?

Teacher. Yes, definitely. Mr. Geraci will tell you, we've worked a number of times with students that we've had difficulties with at home. And one of the emphases here at Wilson is the team approach, again. If I have a difficult student—well, go ahead, Bill.

Teacher. Back to your point on the parents, do they resent teachers getting involved? I think parents for so long have been divorced, so to speak, from the process that their kids go through during the day. And finally, somebody is coming to them and asking for their input. And it is a refreshing thing for them to finally have the teachers want their involvement. And that's a big reason why this school has been successful. The community around the school has put a commitment in. The teachers have put a commitment in. The school district has put the commitment in. And really, what we've done here is we've put together commitments from seven or eight different areas—business, college, parents, teachers, kids—put them all together. And over the course of the last 8 or 9 years, during the transition of this building, we've seen quite a bit of success here.

Teacher. We've been lucky, Mr. President, in that the staff works very hard here; just about everybody is willing to go out to the homes and meet with the families, regardless of what the family situation can be. And it can be difficult at times.

The President. A kid doesn't show or is a dropout factor and all that?

Teacher. Every day we can run into that, but we're always there to help the kids.

Teacher. I think part of the commitment idea is being helped with this school-based plan that's been instituted by the school district. This involves a team of people—parents, students, administrators, and teachers together—working for what's best for the school. And we have an outstanding team of 21 individuals, which myself and Eddie are a member of.

The President. Wait a minute! That's a faculty committee?

Teacher. It's a combination committee of parents, students—there are two student members, three parent members, some administrative members, and teaching members. And we are a team that has this commitment, and we realize that for a school to be successful you need all three groups working together—the parents and community, the students, and the faculty and staff. And that is something we've instituted this year through the auspices of the school district. But it's something that I think is going to fit our school very well. And we've had some successes now, and we're starting to move forward with our team.

Teacher. To get back to your original question about parents: Every day we have to make some parental contacts, but most of the time, just about every time, it's been with success. They say thanks for calling, thanks for calling, which could have been rare in other instances, until we instituted some of these programs out here.

Teacher. As a writing assignment, I asked the seniors to write their parents a letter and tell them how much they appreciated things that they've done for them over the years. And I've gotten calls, a couple of calls already. And one father said, "I'm not an emotional man, but this really touched me." He said that it really did.

Teacher. Similar to that, I'm a senior class adviser this year, and in the last will and testament, which usually ends up being kind of a real funny kind of thing, most of the kids are leaving love and thank you to teachers——

The President. That helped them and stuff?

Teacher. ——throughout the building.

The President. That's fantastic.

Teacher. It's been mentioned, I think a couple of times, about industry getting involved. And we have a program called PRISM, Program for Rochester Students in Science and Math. And we take students who are not motivated in those areas, and even though I don't have a home base, I work with the parents through that particular program. And that's been very helpful in getting some of the students to raise their levels of self-esteem. Some of them come in with low self-esteem or low self-expectations for themselves. So, we bring in role models. And they go to industry, and they can see certain areas that they could get into. And it's been a real help as far as trying to motivate some of the students to raise their levels of expectations and working with the parents to give them that idea that, yes, they can achieve this particular goal.

The President. Has this obvious commitment—you can't sit here, but feel that from the beginning—but has this resulted in lower incidence of vandalism or drugs and this kind of thing in the school than in some other schools, would you say? I know everywhere there are problems, everywhere, in all levels of society. But I just can't help but feel that with what you're describing——

Teacher. Mr. President, undoubtedly, it does in the sense that when you lay the districtwide demographics of suspensions or attendance or any of the incidences that is implied in the question against this school, the culture of caring here works against that kind of behavior, and it shows up in the districtwide statistics.

Your first question about the history—10 years ago this was a school where to show up here was to fail. The politics of the community were so negative about coming here that if you were a child whose parents had any power, they had you somewhere else. I mean before. And the 10 years involvement, including tremendous Federal magnet support, gave authority and cooperation opportunities under strong leadership, massive community participation, outstanding involvement by staff people. And they have grown a culture here where there are now waiting lists, and to come here is to assume I will succeed. And then you are picked up and literally carried—pushed—through the system.

The President. How wide is your first strike-zone orbit to come here? What is it, Monroe County that——

Teacher. It's a city magnet school.

The President. So, it's citywide then?

Teacher. Yes.

The President. A magnet attracts people from——

Teacher. Well, we've gone to schools of choice since systemwide—the whole 912 programs—there are no neighborhood schools. But this is one of the models of why to do that. I mean one of the questions I constantly run into with the staff is that the greatest strength of being here is that the students have chosen, the parents have chosen, to come here. That's a piece of the relationship that's very powerful as you start a relationship.

Teacher. Mr. President, we don't skim; we don't take the top 10 percent. We don't get the cream of the crop all the time. We want to pull in different—an A person, not always an A student, somebody who says, I'm interested in this program; I want to go to this magnet, even though——

The President. Who decides that? Who decides who gets in? If you have more applications than you have spaces, is there a board that decides that, or is there——

Teacher. In the early days of recruitment, we really had to go recruit—an application got you here. Since then, as the applications have come up, there's been a constant revision in terms of what role the school plays in the acceptance and what role the central system plays. What we end up doing now is monitoring the distribution of race and sex and previous achievement. And you're absolutely right: This school takes pretty much a cross-section and yet has been able to maintain both the support and the excellence.

The President. A cross section of the economic base.

Teacher. Because the teachers take on the ownership—[*inaudible*].

Teacher. I teach special education. I meet the needs of learning-disabled and disturbed students. And what that means to me is that I can offer them the least restrictive environment. And because of the teachers here—the staff has been so supportive in meeting my needs and my students' needs, in terms of physics or biology, something I couldn't offer to them in the classroom. So, the teachers here offer a cognitive as well as affective education for the students. It's just not academics, and that's where you really get the support of also Wilson Magnet High School.

Teacher. Mr. President, the commitment you're seeing in this community is that the community is trying to make the commitment to raise the level of all students. Wilson Magnet is a leadership school in that process, but it's one school among many where we're trying to raise the level for every kid, including the special-ed kids, the kids in this school, and the kids in the rest of the system. And that's one of the things that makes Rochester unique, because it's such a broad-based effort to do it—total, systemwide—that's got the support of the business community, the social agencies, working with a very responsive school system.

The President. I got a touching letter when I was in New Jersey, to a school of excellence, a really good-achieving high school. I got a letter from this girl who had been standing out on the—she said: "Well, don't forget those of us that"—I forget how she phrased it—"aren't bright, but try harder." And we were saluting, in this instance, excellence, and listening carefully and hoping to use what we learned there to make a national example, as we'd like to do, from this experience. But it was a very moving and touching letter because, you know, what she was saying is, well, we're not the brightest, but we try harder, and we're going to work hard. This was one who was not a high achiever, but was disadvantaged.

Teacher. The skimming concept was a discussion we had before you came in saying—[*laughter*]—saying we as a community are not interested, I don't believe, in a skimming system, but in a system that raises everybody.

The President. Yes, well, that's what I thought of what Ed said.

Teacher. I've just been given a signal that indicates that there are I think about 350 wonderful Wilson students that are most anxious to meet you, Mr. President, so I have to——

The President. Well, let's do it. I'm sure glad our Congressmen—both Congressman LaFalce and Congressman Horton came up with us on Air Force One. And I don't dare speak for Congressmen, but in this instance we were talking about how much we were looking forward to it, and they telling me how much I would enjoy it. And they're right. So, I'm glad they're with us here today.

Teacher. And we're glad, too. Thank you.

Teacher. Thank you, Mr. President.

The President. Thank you all very much. Well, I'm just sorry Barbara's not here because she loves—and she really is trying hard to help on this whole volunteer sector thing. Her main focus has been literacy, but she's—you know, everything ties into literacy. So, she's really working hard at it. But today, I was telling Sue, we're having the President of the French Republic come to our house. So, first she bawled me out about that. And secondly, because the house has been closed all winter—it's up on the seashore—so she's up trying to get everything ready.

Teacher. You just brought up a good point: literacy. We've got to be working as a team always, always.

The President. Yes. It gets through everything—work force and to our competitiveness and being able to compete abroad and to retraining when industries—you know, one's a loser and another's a winner—the whole retraining. It's almost—and you know far better than I—some of the examples are so tragic: people that fight it and hide it and because of pride and not wanting their kids to know. It's just—but anyway, I'll fill my wife in on all of this.

Teacher. And please bring her.

The President. She'd love to. I know she'd love to come sometime.

Teacher. We'd love it.

The President. We'll try, we'll try. I've often thought what it would be like to live in times where you didn't have any budget problems in the Federal Government because there are so many worthwhile things. Thank you all very much—nice to see you.

Note: The President spoke at 10:48 a.m. in the school library. Suzanne Johnston was the principal of the school, and William Geraci, Joseph Baldino, Darlene Sauerhafer, Edward Hathaway, Reggie Simmons, and Barbara Drmacichi were teachers who participated in the discussion. Gary Simon was a school administrator.

Remarks to Students at the Wilson Magnet High School in Rochester, New York

May 18, 1989

Thank you all very much. That is the best educated, brightest Wildcat I've ever seen in my entire life, and I've seen a lot of Wildcats. First, Suzanne Johnston, your able leader, has told me that, in addition to this enthusiastic gathering—and we're plugged in by overflow TV, and so what I want to do is, at the outset, thank those kids and teachers and others who are watching this gala performance from some other room. And I'm sorry that we will miss the personal connection, but I just wanted you to know—I can tell them in here eyeball-to-eyeball, but I wanted the rest of you to know how pleased I am to be here in this great school. And thank you all for this warm welcome. And if ever we need a cheerleader for a serious proposal to go to the Congress, I'm going to call up Walter Jahnke and get him down there and he can—no wonder the guy's staying so fit—anybody going through all those gyrations. [*Laughter*] And then, as for this cheerleading, I commend you on your timing. Had it been off, you would have taken the head off of the guy next to you. [*Laughter*] So, I saw that, and I use this cheering squad here to simply say I am pleased to be here. I'm sorry Barbara is not with me because her interest in this Excellence in Education is really good, and she's really fascinated with this concept and hopes to be able to help this concept of magnet schools. And so, I salute you all.

You know, when I was in school a thousand years ago, they kept telling—you know, study hard, do my work every day, and that way I'd be prepared to choose a field to go into. The only problem is, the teachers were talking about a field of endeavor, politics or law or something, and I was talking about a field—right field, left field, center field, or something of that nature. But then it became clear that sports are important, but it's even more important to make a strong commitment to education—your education—to the future—to your future. And that is why I wanted to come here today.

I've done a little homework, and I know of the reputation of this school in the Rochester area, and indeed nationwide. And I think that if this visit does nothing else but to encourage others to use this model to achieve excellence it will have been well worth it. And so, I'm delighted to be here. And I've just met with some of the teachers—and an impressive group of people. And I don't expect every kid here to get up and give a testimony about how great the teachers are, but I can speak to it because they are sensational. And when you just were in there and listened to that, commitment was the word that kept coming through. And not only do they have it but they were telling us that you all have it, and I salute you—I wish you well.

And I can tell you, I hope that this visit, Sue, hasn't been a terrible drain on the facilities here and on all these advance people and security people and telephone people. But I promised her I would leave on time so you can get back to normal. But I won't forget this visit, because what you're doing is an example for the entire country. And I'm going to do my level best as President—leave aside the politics—as the President of the United States to get this message of excellence and commitment and magnet schools way even beyond the confines of New York, all the way to the West Coast and up to Alaska. You're the future. And I congratulate you, and I thank you very, very much.

Note: The President spoke at 11:16 a.m. in the school gymnasium. In his opening remarks, he referred to Suzanne Johnston, principal of the school, and Walter Jahnke, a math teacher who led the students in cheering. Prior to his remarks, the President attended robotics arm and computer demonstrations by the students.

Remarks to Supporters of the Brainpower Coalition in Rochester, New York
May 18, 1989

President Whitmore, thank you for that warm Rochester welcome. And to President Whitmore and Congressman LaFalce, Congressman for this district, Frank Horton, my friend of long time, I'm just delighted to be here. I want to especially thank the Governor of the State for the courtesy that he shows me, and I thank all of you for coming here today. And I appreciate his taking the time to come and join hands as we salute not just the program that Kodak has, the program of participation, partnership, but the program that we saw just a few minutes ago at the Wilson Magnet School. And I want to take this opportunity to thank all of them, too, for this welcome.

You know, some of you may remember, [former Senator] Barry Goldwater was a talented amateur photographer. And one day he took a picture of President John F. Kennedy and sent it to him, requesting an inscription. And back it came, dutifully inscribed: "For Barry Goldwater, whom I urge to follow the career for which he has shown so much talent—photography." [*Laughter*] "From his friend, John Kennedy." Well, Barry didn't take his friend's advice. He fashioned a brilliant career in politics, not photography.

But today I am really delighted to be back in a city—Rochester—and at a company—Eastman Kodak—which has become synonymous with the career that President Kennedy alluded to. And it is a pleasure to join you. And I came here because Rochester and Kodak embody the notion that helping others through cooperation—partnership agreements between all levels of government, private enterprise, voluntary organizations—is America at her best. And locally, this kind of cooperation has made possible such landmarks as the Eastman Theatre and the Al Sigal Center and helped Rochester become a bastion of commerce and make the Flower City among America's highest cities in terms of corporate participation and corporate giving.

And your story, of course, is well-known locally. But I want this message to get out to the entire Nation. For in being here today, I honor the countless individuals and companies across America who are following your example. And I was telling Kay coming over here—Mr. Whitmore, in the car—that I hope that this visit will symbolize the importance that we place on these partnerships and that the message will be received across our entire country. For those not yet involved, I challenge you to get involved. And for America's public and private sectors, they can exceed the sum of their parts.

In a sense, this is what George Eastman had in mind when he founded Eastman Kodak in 1880. For he knew that cooperation begets productivity and that productivity would enrich America's standard of living and her standard in the world. As President, I intend to spur the partnerships which nurture that productivity. And that is why recently I unveiled a bipartisan partnership with Congress that will cut the Federal deficit by $65 billion over the coming fiscal year. Productivity is the reason, too, that I favor the creation of urban enterprise zones, a partnership with business.

And each of these partnerships will help productivity propel America, and so will an even nobler partnership—and I'm talking here about the one you're involved in—education, a partnership with the future. For ultimately the greatest productivity stems from a creative mind.

Here at Eastman Kodak, you celebrate that fact. For you know what George Eastman said in 1924 is even truer today: "The progress of the world depends almost entirely on education." Kay Whitmore is even more succinct in talking about your own company. "Kodak's future depends on its work force," he said. And he's absolutely correct about that.

And some of you may recall the television series, "Dragnet," and how Sergeant Friday—remember him—was fond of saying, "Just the facts, ma'am." [*Laughter*]

Well, the fact is that Rochester's education challenges parallel the Nation's. The challenges that you face in these school—very much the same in many parts of the country. And the fact is that unless we act our children will be ill-equipped to read, to write, or understand new technologies—to compete in the workplace. And the fact is that education partnerships can help us act boldly and urgently to keep America number one.

Let me share a story with you, a story about two ways to look at education. The master of the house was planning his garden and told his gardener to plant a certain kind of tree. And the gardener objected, explaining that the tree was slow growing and would take a hundred years to reach its full growth. The master's response—that I found interesting—he says, "In that case, there's no time to lose. Plant it this afternoon." [*Laughter*]

And that's the way that Rochester and Eastman Kodak look at education. And that explains why a few years back your business and community and education leaders sat down, faced their problems head-on, and decided to act. And looking at your city's public schools, they didn't like what they saw: a dropout rate of—I was told it was 30 percent; a third of all the ninth-graders dropped out before graduation from high school; and nearly two-thirds of all ninth-graders tested 1 to 2 years below the grade levels.

And these problems demanded the solutions that only partnerships can achieve. So, in 1986 a community task force, headed in this case by the Urban League, issued its report. It was called, "A Call To Action"—to uplift the quality of the public schools. And to make that dream a reality, you came up with a great idea: a new partnership called the Rochester Brainpower Coalition, a partnership anchored by Eastman Kodak which understood that the private sector has the resources and responsibility to help make education better, to help education help America.

And earlier today, as I mentioned, and as Kay said, we were over at the Wilson Magnet High School, where I saw just how much progress has been made. It's hard to choke back a tear or two when you see the commitment of those children and the spirit of the teachers over there. Ten years ago, that school was beset by crime and plunging grades and urban flight. But today, helped by Rochester Brainpower, Wilson is the ninth-ranked school in the State of New York by the Department of Education.

And what made such progress possible? Teamwork between students, parents, and teachers to raise standards and increase accountability, and Rochester's Brainpower support—creative and monetary—of your school district's pioneering plan, which U.S. News terms "a model for educational reform." And some of you—I had a chance to talk to some of your colleagues that are over there helping these kids. And that was inspiring as it could be.

You know, in 1988 Rochester Brainpower received the President's Citation for Private Sector Initiatives. Well, seeing Wilson firsthand today, it is easy to understand why that happened. For it, like other schools, has benefited from the coalition's programs which blend creativity and just plain common sense. One program, for instance, says to the kids: "If you excel now in school, we'll give you a job when you graduate from school." And another program vows: "If you hit the books, local companies will offer college scholarship aid." A third program helps the teachers—God bless the teachers—and helps them hone their skills. And through another, business provides management help to local schools. And a huge media campaign perhaps says it best, as two billboards urge: "Stay In School. You're Too Good To Lose," and "Help A Teacher Help A Child." What marvelous sentiment is reflected on those two billboards. I hope that we see those springing up all across the United States.

And, yes, already Rochester Brainpower has united the community. In the future, its impact will lift the community. And its heart will be Eastman Kodak, not only in 1989 but well into the 21st century—you know, not only in this community but in communities across the country, if they learn the Kodak partnership message and then execute.

Like the wise man planting a tree for

future generations, Kodak is planting its own seeds. For it is you who are lending people and equipment, at company expense, to teach kids engineering and robotics, and providing other long-term financial aid to help at-risk youth discover the meaning of an education. It's Kodak which has given some $125 million to more than 1,000 colleges and universities and which is now more involved than ever at the precollege level, enhancing the academic excellence so central to America.

My administration supports that goal. And accordingly, last month I sent a major new education package to the Congress which demands excellence. We will achieve excellence through greater accountability—and I heard that today from the teachers at Wilson—and by spurring local flexibility and parental choice. And I saw that today at Wilson—the concept of choice in action. And above all, our program, like yours, says that if excellence breeds achievement, then excellence should be rewarded.

We're asking the Congress, for instance, to create a program to recognize and reward the schools that have demonstrated substantial educational improvements and a new Magnet Schools of Excellence program to encourage more schools like Wilson. We're proposing to create urban emergency grants to help school systems hit hardest by drug abuse and trafficking. And through scholarships, we want to give America's youth a special incentive to excel—science, math, and engineering.

No, our program isn't a be-all and an end-all. We're living in times of complicated resource allocation. But it is a commitment, a commitment to help business and academia make America much more productive, a commitment to partnerships, a commitment which you obviously share. And for that, I thank you. And I'd like to think that George Eastman is proud of you, too, looking down, no doubt, through the latest telephoto lens from wherever he may be. [*Laughter*] For he knew that giving—he exemplified this in his life—he knew that giving was a two-way street.

One day in 1924—year that I was born—George Eastman gave away $30 million to the University of Rochester, M.I.T., Hampton, and Tuskegee—a rather amazing gift, I'd say. That was when $30 million was $30 million—[*laughter*]—but all in 1 day. But he began giving to nonprofit institutions—this is the key point—when his salary was $60 a week. Even then he knew that profit and philanthropy were not mutually exclusive.

And I've said repeatedly that from now on in America, any definition of a successful life must include serving others. For while few of us can give away $30 million, all of us can help—can take pride in helping—an inner-city child overcome, perhaps, poverty, to become a productive citizen. Giving means more than money: It means making a commitment to someone else's life. And that is how George Eastman defined success. And that is why when he died the New York Times proclaimed, "George Eastman was a stupendous factor in the education of the modern world." And he showed that productivity could nurture generosity and that generosity could help us all. And then, through the promise of partnerships, let us, too, increase America's productivity so that America's generosity can enrich not merely our age but generations to come.

I salute Kodak for your looking into the future. I salute Wilson for coping with the problems of the present so those kids will have a great future. I salute the farsighted school board that encourages this kind of new thinking. I salute the Members of Congress who have been helpful in pushing forward these objectives. It's a great pleasure for me to be here, and I thank you for inviting me and for this wonderful occasion. I won't forget it. God bless you all. God bless the United States of America. Thank you very much.

Note: The President spoke at 12:01 p.m. in Building One of the Elmgrove Eastman Kodak facility. He was introduced by Kay Whitmore, president of the coalition. In his remarks, the President referred to Gov. Mario Cuomo. Following his remarks, the President attended a luncheon in the facility's lunchroom and then traveled to Kennebunkport, ME.

Statement by Press Secretary Fitzwater on the Savings and Loan Crisis Financing Plan
May 18, 1989

The Ways and Means Committee vote would put the S&L financing plan nominally on-budget, but would waive the entire amount from Gramm-Rudman-Hollings. This amounts to a direct assault on Gramm-Rudman-Hollings budget discipline. It creates an artificial accounting approach that is called on-budget, but is in effect off-budget in terms of the way the spending is counted.

Finally, the committee action creates a contentious issue for the House floor and the conference with the Senate. That means delay, and every day we wait costs at least $10 million. The Senate completed its action a month ago. The House must act and act quickly.

Statement by Press Secretary Fitzwater on the Student Demonstrations in China
May 20, 1989

President Bush this morning received his daily intelligence briefing, including an update on the status of events in China. The situation remains uncertain. Both sides have exercised restraint, and we urge that restraint to continue. The United States stands for freedom of speech and freedom of assembly, and President Bush commented yesterday on the inexorable march of democracy in China. The demonstrations of the last few days indicate that the hunger for change remains strong. We remain hopeful that a dialog between the Government and the students is possible.

Remarks at the Boston University Commencement Ceremony in Massachusetts
May 21, 1989

Thank you, President Silber. And President and Madame Mitterrand, it's a great honor to have you here today. And to Governor Dukakis, my respects—the chief executive of this great State and my friend as well, to Mayor Flynn, His Eminence Cardinal Law, and Dr. Metcalf, Dr. Wiesel, and, yes, Kimberly, to you for that wonderful speech earlier on, and to Nancy Joaquim, who rendered both "The Marseillaise" and "The Star-Spangled Banner" in such fine way.

It's a pleasure to be back in Boston, back in one of my home States—[*laughter*]—and I am delighted and honored to receive a doctor of laws from Boston University along with President Mitterrand. Doctor of laws—does this now make us a couple of Boston lawyers, my friend, Mr. Mitterrand? [*Laughter*] Who knows? I also would like to salute another most distinguished visitor: Prime Minister Mahathir of Malaysia, a friend to the United States, whose son is graduating today. We're honored to have him here. And I want to congratulate Barbara on a BU degree of her very own. [*Laughter*] And now that you're an alumna, take note: this kinder and gentler America that I'm speaking of does not always include the Terriers. [*Laughter*]

My sincerest congratulations go to every Boston University graduate and to all you proud parents cooking out along the 50-yard line there. [*Laughter*] And as Boston University graduates, you take with you a degree from a great institution, and something more: knowledge of the past and responsibility for the future. And take a look at our world today. Nations are undergoing changes so radical that the international system you know and will know in the future will be as different from today's as today's world is from the time of Woodrow Wilson. How will America prepare, then, for the challenges ahead?

It's with your future in mind that, after deliberation and a review, we are adapting our foreign policies to meet this challenge. I've outlined how we're going to try to promote reform in Eastern Europe and how we're going to work with our friends in Latin America. In Texas, I spoke to another group of graduates of our new approach to the Soviet Union, one of moving beyond containment, to seek to integrate the Soviets into the community of nations, to help them share the rewards of international cooperation.

But today I want to discuss the future of Europe, that mother of nations and ideas that is so much a part of America. And it is fitting that I share this forum with a very special friend of the United States. President Mitterrand, you have the warm affection and high regard of the American people. And I remember well about 8 years ago when you joined us in Yorktown in 1981 to celebrate the bicentennial of that first Franco-American fight for freedom. And soon I will join you in Paris, sir, to observe the 200th anniversary of the French struggle for liberty and equality. And this is just one example of the special bond between two continents.

But consider this city—from the Old North Church to Paul Revere's home nestled in the warm heart of the Italian North End, to your famous song-filled Irish pubs, the Old and New Worlds are inseparable in this city—but as we look back to Old World tradition, we must look ahead to a new Europe. Historic changes will shape your careers and your very lives.

The changes that are occurring in Western Europe are less dramatic than those taking place in the East, but they are no less fundamental. The postwar order that began in 1945 is transforming into something very different. And yet certain essentials remain, because our alliance with Western Europe is utterly unlike the cynical power alliances of the past. It is based on far more than the perception of a common enemy; it is a tie of culture and kinship and shared values. And as we look toward the 21st century, Americans and Europeans alike should remember the words of Raymond Aron, who called the alliance a moral and spiritual community. Our ideals are those of the American Bill of Rights and the French Declaration of the Rights of Man. And it is precisely because the ideals of this community are universal that the world is in ferment today.

Now a new century holds the promise of a united Europe. And as you know, the nations of Western Europe are already moving toward greater economic integration, with the ambitious goal of a single European market in 1992. The United States has often declared it seeks a healing of old enmities, an integration of Europe. And at the same time, there has been an historical ambivalence on the part of some Americans toward a more united Europe. To this ambivalence has been added apprehension at the prospect of 1992. But whatever others may think, this administration is of one mind. We believe a strong, united Europe means a strong America.

Western Europe has a gross domestic product that is roughly equal to our own and a population that exceeds ours. European science leads the world in many fields, and European workers are highly educated and highly skilled. We are ready to develop with the European Community and its member states new mechanisms of consultation and cooperation on political and global issues, from strengthening the forces of democracy in the Third World to managing regional tensions to putting an end to the division of Europe.

A resurgent Western Europe is an economic magnet, drawing Eastern Europe closer toward the commonwealth of free nations. A more mature partnership with

Western Europe will pose new challenges. There are certain to be clashes and controversies over economic issues. America will, of course, defend its interests. But it is important to distinguish adversaries from allies, and allies from adversaries. What a tragedy, what an absurdity it would be if future historians attribute the demise of the Western alliance to disputes over beef hormones and wars over pasta. We must all work hard to ensure that the Europe of 1992 will adopt the lower barriers of the modern international economy, not the high walls and the moats of medieval commerce.

But our hopes for the future rest ultimately on keeping the peace in Europe. Forty-two years ago, just across the Charles River, Secretary of State George Marshall gave a commencement address that outlined a plan to help Europe recover. Western Europe responded heroically and later joined with us in a partnership for the common defense: a shield we call NATO. And this alliance has always been driven by a spirited debate over the best way to achieve peaceful change. But the deeper truth is that the alliance has achieved an historic peace because it is united by a fundamental purpose. Behind the NATO shield, Europe has now enjoyed 40 years free of conflict, the longest period of peace the Continent has ever known. Behind this shield, the nations of Western Europe have risen from privation to prosperity, all because of the strength and resolve of free peoples.

With a Western Europe that is now coming together, we recognize that new forms of cooperation must be developed. We applaud the defense cooperation developing in the revitalized Western European Union, whose members worked with us to keep open the sealanes of the Persian Gulf. And we applaud the growing military cooperation between West Germany and France. And we welcome British and French programs to modernize their deterrent capability and their moves toward cooperation in this area. It is perfectly right and proper that Europeans increasingly see their defense cooperation as an investment in a secure future. But we do have a major concern of a different order: There's a growing complacency throughout the West.

And, of course, your generation can hardly be expected to share the grip of past anxieties. With such a long peace, it is hard to imagine how it could be otherwise. But our expectations, in this rapidly changing world, cannot race so far ahead that we forget what is at stake. There's a great irony here.

While an ideological earthquake is shaking asunder the very Communist foundation, the West is being tested by complacency. We must never forget that twice in this century American blood has been shed over conflicts that began in Europe. And we share the fervent desire of Europeans to relegate war forever to the province of distant memory. But that is why the Atlantic alliance is so central to our foreign policy. And that's why America remains committed to the alliance and the strategy which has preserved freedom in Europe. We must never forget that to keep the peace in Europe is to keep the peace for America.

NATO's policy of flexible response keeps the United States linked to Europe and lets any would-be aggressors know that they will be met with any level of force needed to repel their attack and frustrate their designs. And our short-range deterrent forces, based in Europe and kept up to date, demonstrate that America's vital interests are bound inextricably to Western Europe and that an attacker can never gamble on a test of strength with just our conventional forces. Though hope is now running high for a more peaceful continent, the history of this century teaches Americans and Europeans to remain prepared.

As we search for a peace that is enduring, I'm grateful for the steps that Mr. Gorbachev is taking. If the Soviets advance solid and constructive plans for peace, then we should give credit where credit is due. And we're seeing sweeping changes in the Soviet Union that show promise of enduring, of becoming ingrained. At the same time, in an era of extraordinary change, we have an obligation to temper optimism—and I am optimistic—with prudence.

For example, the Soviet Foreign Minister informed the world last week that his nation's commitment to destroy SS–23 missiles under the recently enacted INF treaty may be reversible. And the Soviets must surely know the results of failure to comply with this solemn agreement. Perhaps their purpose was to divide the West on other issues that you're reading about in the papers today. But regardless, it is clear that Soviet "new thinking" has not yet totally overcome the old.

I believe in a deliberate step-by-step approach to East-West relations because recurring signs show that while change in the Soviet Union is dramatic, it's not yet complete. The Warsaw Pact retains a nearly 12-to-1 advantage over the Atlantic alliance in short-range missiles and rocket launchers capable of delivering nuclear weapons and more than a 2-to-1 advantage in battle tanks. And for that reason, we will also maintain, in cooperation with our allies, ground and air forces in Europe as long as they are wanted and needed to preserve the peace in Europe. At the same time, my administration will place a high and continuing priority on negotiating a less militarized Europe, one with a secure conventional force balance at lower levels of forces. Our aspiration is a real peace, a peace of shared optimism, not a peace of armed camps.

Nineteen ninety-two is the 500th anniversary of the discovery of the New World, so we have five centuries to celebrate nothing less than our very civilization—the American Bill of Rights and the French Rights of Man, the ancient and unwritten constitution of Great Britain, and the democratic visions of Konrad Adenauer and Alcide de Gasperi. And in all our celebrations, we observe one fact: This truly is a moral and spiritual community. It is our inheritance, and so, let us protect it. Let us promote it. Let us treasure it for our children, for Americans and Europeans yet unborn. We stand with France as part of a solid alliance. And once again, let me say how proud I am to have received this degree from this noble institution, and to have shared this platform with the President of the French Republic, François Mitterrand.

Thank you very, very much. *Vive la France* and long live the United States of America! Thank you very much.

Note: The President spoke at 12:33 p.m. at Dickerson Field on the campus of the university. In his opening remarks, he referred to John Silber, president of Boston University; Bernard Cardinal Law, Archbishop of Boston; Arthur G.B. Metcalf, chairman of the university's board of trustees; Elie Wiesel, Andrew Mellon Professor in the Humanities; and Kimberly Sudnick, a graduating student and commencement speaker.

The President's News Conference With President Mitterrand of France

May 21, 1989

President Mitterrand. Ladies and gentlemen, the French guests here and myself—we're coming to the end of our stay in the United States; and this meeting with the press is, more or less, the last event. And the journalists who have been good enough to follow us during the last 24 hours will have appreciated, I think, that we've had a very full day. But you will, of course, be able in a moment to ask the questions which you feel most suited to the requirements of the day. And President Bush and myself will be at your disposal to reply to them.

But personally, and also on behalf of my country, I would like to say how very deeply sensitive we are to the way in which Mrs. Bush and President Bush have received us, my wife and myself. They received us in a very warm, homely family, and restful atmosphere; but at the same time, we were able to have some intensive, political, serious conversations which were given, as it were, more life—thanks to the forest air and the sea breeze that we were able to breathe.

Now President Bush will be saying a few words, and then we'll be open to questions. But I'd like to personally thank all those who have been good enough to accompany us during our stay and comment on what we have done.

President Bush. Thank you, Mr. President. Well, first, let me just say what a pleasure it was having President Mitterrand and Madame Mitterrand as our guests in Maine. We've just come from the commencement of Boston University. And nothing better symbolizes the strength of the friendship and the common values which we share—which our two nations share—and which really the President celebrated with us 8 years ago, when he came to Yorktown, celebrating the 200th anniversary of that battle.

So, the weekend was not all work and no play; it provided a good opportunity for us to discuss many of the main issues on the international agenda. And by the end of this week, both of us will be traveling to Brussels for the NATO summit. We agreed on the central role the Atlantic alliance has played in keeping the peace for the past four decades, the enduring value of this partnership in the common defense in the years ahead. And we also agreed on the critical contribution the nuclear deterrent has made in keeping us free and secure and at peace.

We also talked about the opportunities that lie before us in the light of the changes now taking place in the Soviet Union and in Eastern Europe. And both of us will watch developments in the Soviet Union, seeking signs of lasting change. Of course, we discussed the dramatic events now taking place in Beijing, in China. The President, I believe, shares my view—I'll let him speak for himself—that our goal should be a bold one, to move beyond containment, towards the integration of the Soviet Union into the community of nations. And of course, we discussed how the United States will relate to France and the rest of Western Europe in the years ahead.

I sensed an excitement on his part about the future. We exchanged views about the themes that I touched on in my earlier remarks here at BU: America's readiness for a more mature transatlantic partnership, the vision of a commonwealth of free nations as a bridge to overcome the divisions of Europe. And we also discussed the potential for improved cooperation with the EC [Commission of the European Communities] as we approach 1992 and the single European market, as well as the prospects for greater Western European cooperation in addressing the political and global issues around the world. And I heard his clarion's call for cooperative action on the environment, and I salute him for that.

Beyond the NATO summit and East-West relations, we exchanged views on so many subjects, many of which will be on the agenda at the Paris economic summit. We agreed that more needs to be done in practical, realistic ways to deal with the environment and to deal with the problems of global warming. And we also reviewed ways of advancing the peace process in the Middle East, the urgent need to try to find, or be helpful in finding, a solution to the situation in Lebanon.

On the question of peace and democracy in this hemisphere, in Central America, we share the view that democracy must be restored in Panama and that the commitments undertaken at Esquipulas are the key to peace and democracy in the region.

Now we'd be glad to take questions.

Student Demonstrations in China

Q. Mr. President, the students in China have been told to leave Tiananmen Square or face military attack. What's your reaction to that, and do you have any message for the students, other than that the United States supports freedom of speech and freedom of assembly?

President Bush. We do support freedom of speech, freedom of assembly, freedom of the press; and clearly, we support democracy. I don't want to be gratuitous in giving advice, but I would encourage restraint. I do not want to see bloodshed. We revere the model of Martin Luther King in this country for his peaceful protest; and so, I might suggest a familiarization with that for the people in China. And I would urge the Government to be as forthcoming as possible in order to see more democratization and to see a peaceful resolution of this matter.

Short-Range Nuclear Forces in Europe

Q. President Mitterrand, do you think that progress has been made in bringing French and American views—well, in hoping to bring German and American views closer together on the question of modernization of nuclear short-term weapons in Europe? And do you think that you are there to act as an intermediary, a conciliator?

President Mitterrand. The only role I play is the role that is my natural role as a member of the alliance. But I am not particularly there to act as a mediator. Obviously, I'm happy if views can be reconciled and believe, I think, that they can be reconciled. I think that we have now the elements of ideas that could form a decision that will be taken just in a week's time. And I think that the decision that will be taken will be found positive from the point of view of all members of the alliance. You know what my suggestions on the subject are because I made them clear in Paris.

Q. Mr. President, on that point, the indication out of Bonn today was that the West Germans have not accepted the explicit conditions that were handed to Mr. Stoltenberg [West German Finance Minister] on Friday for talks on SNF. A West German spokesman said that those conditions were merely—I think he said—a basis for further dialog. Is the U.S. position negotiable at this point, and how do you sum up the likelihood of resolving this before the NATO summit?

President Bush. I think great progress has been made. One way to guarantee there will not be progress is to lock each other in, in public statements, so I do not intend to comment on the specifics. The report I saw from Bonn was somewhat more encouraging than the way you phrased this one, in terms of being very, very close together with the Germans. This is an alliance that contains many countries, and we are in active consultation with the Germans and others. And of course, I had the benefit over this weekend of hearing directly from President Mitterrand on his views, but I think that we could well have this resolved before the summit.

U.S. Immigration Laws

Q. You spoke about the common bond between the United States and France and the economic changes that will be coming about in 1992 and, of course, the obvious benefit to the United States. Yet we have an immigration law at the present that disfavors Europeans. Do you see this matter being resolved so that Europeans can continue to contribute to the United States?

President Bush. I want to see the immigration matter resolved, and yes, I do foresee it being resolved.

Student Demonstrations in China

Q. Mr. Bush, you have a personal interest in China and the Chinese people, yet your statements have seemed to be very cautious and diplomatic. Have you made any private representation to the Chinese leadership or given any suggestions to them on how to resolve—or what you might help with in the democracy movement in China?

President Bush. We have been in touch with our Ambassador on this very key question. I think this perhaps is a time for caution because we aspire to see the Chinese people have democracy, but we do not exhort in a way that is going to stir up a military confrontation. We do not want to have a situation like happened in Burma or some other place. And so, as we counsel restraint and as we counsel peaceful means of effecting change—that is sound advice. And I think to go beyond that and encourage steps that could lead to bloodshed would be inappropriate.

For President Mitterrand—his next question, unless you've exhausted them all. I'll take a couple of——

Short-Range Nuclear Forces in Europe

Q. It's really primarily for President Bush, but of course, if President Mitterrand wishes to add on—[*laughter*]. Mr. President, you said we could well have agreement on SNF before the summit. I gather you're talking about the West Germans, because we're getting reports out of London that Mrs. Thatcher is not, as the English say, best pleased about this. And this is confusing, because we also understand that you took Mrs. Thatcher's wishes into account when you were formulating your counterproposal and that, in fact, you were in rather close touch with the British. Do you think we could go to Brussels with the British not having signed on to this, and yet you would have agreement with the West Germans?

President Bush. Mr. President Mitterrand?

President Mitterrand. Well, I can appreciate exactly what kind of a dialog you were hoping to achieve, but the rules of the game are that it's my turn to answer. Well, you may be asking for an opinion, but I would say this: that within the Atlantic alliance, there is full equality among all partners. And on this problem, like on other problems, at the outset, people have diverging views, different opinions. But the important thing is to come to a meeting of the minds and to achieve a common answer, and this has always been the case in the alliance. A particular view will only carry more weight if it carries more wisdom and more common sense. So, I'm not going to sit here and award prizes to this view or that view. There's no particular view which would prevail. The important thing is that the general interest of the alliance should prevail, and it will.

Student Demonstrations in China

Q. Mr. President, you called for restraint in China, and you said that the lessons of Martin Luther King could well be heeded here. Do you believe the protesters should go home? Do you think there is a revolution underway in China now?

President Bush. I don't think that it would be appropriate for the President of the United States to say to the demonstrators and the students in Beijing exactly what their course of action should be. That is for them to determine. They know the United States commitment to democracy, to the commitment to freedom, to the aspiration we have that all people will live in democratic societies. But I'm not about to suggest what I think they ought to do, except to spell out peaceful and continue to fight for what you believe in, stand up for what you believe in, but beyond that, I cannot go.

No, go ahead. Follow-on?

Q. How unstable is the situation?

President Bush. Well, I don't know. I think we have to wait and see. There's certainly an enormous expression on the part of many people—students and others—for change, toward movement toward democracy. I lived there; I saw a society totally different than the one that exists in China today. China has moved, in some areas, towards democracy. Now, the quest is—and the appeal from these kids is—to move further. And so, I am one who feels that the quest for democracy is very powerful, but I am not going to dictate or try to say from the United States how this matter should be resolved by these students. I'm not going to do it.

As for John's [John Cochran, NBC News] question, we have been in very close touch with Mrs. Thatcher. And I listened attentively and with great interest to what President Mitterrand said, and I agree with him: that we can get together on this vexing question. There are strong-willed people from strong countries, and they each have an opinion. But my role has been to try, behind the scenes, to be helpful for working this problem out. And I should salute the President of France, as he has tried to be extraordinarily helpful in working this problem out. Now, your job is to know every step of the way the nuances of difference that exist between the parties, and mine is to see if we can't iron out those differences. And that's exactly what I'm doing, what Secretary [of State] Baker is doing, and what others are doing.

East-West Relations

Q. Mr. President, you were talking about the attitude we should have towards the Soviet Union, particularly on the part of the allies. Do you think that the Cold War has come to an end, and if so, has it come to an end once and for all?

President Mitterrand. People seem to want us to play the role of crystal-gazers, which we are not. It's like a revolution, you only know afterwards if a thing turned out to be a revolution. As far as the Cold War is concerned, one thing is clear, and that is that we are moving out of the Cold War. And the chances are that this will be true for a very long time. There will be moments when things will be more difficult, doubtless, but I don't see us slipping right back into the Cold War. Of course, anything is possible—a lot will depend on the trend of developments within the Soviet Union.

Q. Mr. President, you said in your speech today that you're grateful for some of these proposals with Secretary Gorbachev, yet some in your administration have made no secret of their disdain for some of these proposals. In talking about "beyond containment," did the recent proposals of Secretary Gorbachev on conventional and nuclear weapons meet any of your tests for going beyond containment?

President Bush. Yes. I not only encourage him to continue to make proposals but I'd encourage him to unilaterally implement the proposals. Many of them address themselves to conventional forces where they have an extraordinary, preponderant imbalance—where they have the weight on their side. And so, I'd like to see that, but I don't think anybody is criticizing the specific proposals. All we want to see is real progress. And when you have the historic imbalance that exists on conventional forces, yes, I welcome the proposals and like to see them implemented. And it's in that area that we're looking for reality versus rhetoric. And I know that some are quite restless about the pace that I have set in dealing with the Soviet Union, but I think it's the proper pace. And I will be prepared when Jim Baker goes back to talk some more. I'm most anxious to be sure that the alliance is together on these questions.

And so, we have time, and in the meantime, I welcome not only the change of openness and the change of reform but I want to see it continue. And I welcome the proposals, but I would like to see them implemented. And that would still leave a large imbalance in favor of the Soviets on many of these proposals—not all of them. Some of them talk to get where we need to be engaged, because they talked to getting down to equal numbers. But no, I salute the man, as I said, for certain kinds of steps that he has taken. But I hope I'll be forgiven for being cautious and for being prudent and not for being stampeded into something that might prove to be no good for the alliance or not good for the United States.

Soviet President Gorbachev of the Soviet Union

Q. For President Mitterrand and also for President Bush. Mr. Gorbachev has been described by the President's spokesman as a "drugstore cowboy." Do you agree with this description?—a question for both Presidents.

President Mitterrand. I think that one must be wary of caricatures. Mr. Gorbachev is worth very much more than that.

President Bush. So much for Marlin. In fairness to the man——

Mr. Fitzwater. No, don't defend me.

President Bush. No, don't defend you? Which I would be perfectly prepared to do.

Boston Harbor Cleanup

Q. Mr. President, being back in Boston, does it encourage you to do anything about restoring the money for the Boston Harbor that the Congress——

President Bush. Hey, I'm pleased that the cleanup seems to be going forward. How's that for an answer?

U.S. International Influence

Q. This is a question, I guess—it's a question for both people. Do you believe that the American public is aware of the limits of American power and of your ability to really influence political events like those in China, Panama, and Europe?

President Mitterrand. Well, I think on these questions of influence—influence can be of a material kind and military or peaceful. But it can also be of a moral kind and psychological. There's a whole rainbow, a whole range, of possibilities. Of course, the first problem that you're always up against is the problem of noninterference in other people's affairs. That being said—but it's a question of human rights. One mustn't stop at that, and I think one must give priority to the public assertion of the basic principles of human rights, and that is what must be prevailed.

So, I think that, with reference to the countries you are mentioning, these principles should be recalled to the countries concerned. But recourse to arms is probably not the kind of method that is fully in tune with the requirements of our day. And to think that you can win whole populations over to your way of thinking by threatening them with guns or tanks is obviously wrong.

What is also very important, and more important, is to win over international public opinion, to mobilize public opinion, both within and without the country, so that those governments which fail in the respect of human rights will be, both within and without, with their backs to the wall on the subject. That being said, I know of no miracle cure in these matters, no unfailing method that always works. And if I were able to come here to Boston and someone could give me the golden key that would open all these doors, well, I'd be very happy and perhaps somewhat surprised.

American Hostages in Lebanon

Q. Mr. President, in your discussions this weekend concerning Lebanon, did you discuss the situation concerning the hostages, and have you any news concerning avenues that could be pursued towards their eventual release?

President Bush. On the hostages—any avenues to pursue on that?

Q. Did you discuss it this weekend?

President Bush. Well, it was just touched on because—but we discussed Lebanon in depth. And the hostage situation obviously continues to be on our mind, and President Mitterrand was most sympathetic—the French people held various times against their will. And so, that underlies the concerns that I feel. But Lebanon transcends just our own keen interest in the hostage question: to see a once-peaceful country, where various factions could live together, now ripped asunder by war and by outside pressures, demands world action. And yet again, when you look at the alternatives, they aren't that clear. And we have called for the cease-fire, supporting the Arab League posture: getting foreign troops out of Lebanon and trying to have the election process go forward so you can have an elected president that fulfills the will of the people.

President Mitterrand was very helpful because he has a unique view of Lebanon, with France's history there. And yet I don't think either of us came up with a simple answer. I saluted what he tried to do when he encouraged the Secretary-General of the United Nations to go there. But for various reasons, that did not work out. So, we did talk about a couple of other specific approaches that we might take, which I think should remain confidential. But it was discussed in detail. It is a matter of enormous urgency. And in the United States, of course, you heard Cardinal Law [Archbishop of Boston] today appropriately singling out Lebanon because of the religious divisions there. And I wish there was an easy answer to it, and the United States stands ready to help, if we can.

We're off. Thank you.

President Mitterrand. Thank you.

Note: President Bush's 12th news conference began at 1:28 p.m. on Dickerson Field at Boston University. President Mitterrand spoke in French, and his remarks were translated by an interpreter. Marlin Fitzwater was President Bush's Press Secretary. Following the news conference, President Bush returned to Washington, DC.

Remarks on the Observance of Cuban Independence Day

May 22, 1989

What a great pleasure, and thank you for that warm welcome. It's I who should be welcoming you to celebrate this wonderful occasion, the 87th anniversary of Cuban independence, and, you know, a special day. But you know, I would be delighted to be here on any day, for we Americans owe a debt of gratitude to the Cuban people. And that debt goes back to 1776, when George Washington's troops were short of food and supply.

Some of you may remember how the

women of Havana banded together and raised 1.2 million livres for the cause of American freedom. And 126 years later, another people fought bravely for the cause of freedom. For it was on May 20th, 1902, after a long and brutal struggle, that the Cuban Republic was born. And we gather here to remember that victory and the fact that freedom knows no boundaries. Perhaps it was Cuba's George Washington, that great President, José Martí, who said it best: "To beautify life is to give it an object."

My friends, our object is human liberty and a free, united, and democratic Cuba. And as President I am unalterably committed to a free, united, democratic Cuba; and I'm not going to ever falter in that support. I know that you all are with me in that, and so is our country, for we oppose those who mock the very rights that we treasure: freedom of speech, religion, assembly, economic freedom. And in response, our demand is plain and simple: democracy and respect for human rights—not sometime, not someday, but now.

And this afternoon I call on Fidel Castro to free all political prisoners and to conform to accepted international standards regarding human rights. And I challenge him to allow unrestricted access to the United Nations and other organizations monitoring their compliance, and a policy of nonintervention in the internal affairs of other states. And on this celebration of Cuban Independence Day I challenge him, Fidel Castro, to take concrete and specific steps leading to free and fair elections and full democracy.

A useful first step would be to accept a proposed plebiscite in Cuba. I also strongly believe that Cubans who wish to leave Cuba should be allowed to do so—a fundamental human right guaranteed by free nations. And I challenge Castro—[*applause*]—and I challenge him to show that Cuba is truly independent by sharply reducing the Soviet military presence there. And this I pledge: Unless Fidel Castro is willing to change his policies and behavior, we will maintain our present policy toward Cuba. Knock off this wild speculation as just that—some suggesting that our administration is going to unilaterally shift things with Fidel Castro. I am not going to do that, and I'm glad you're here to hear it directly from me.

And until we see some of these changes I'm talking about, we will continue to oppose Cuba's reentry to the Organization of American States. And this too I promise: To help break down the monopoly on information that Castro has maintained for 30 years, we will continue Radio Martí, and we will push forward our proposal on TV Martí. It is important that the people of Cuba know the truth, and we will see that the people of Cuba do know the truth about their dictator and about the world.

And the thirst for democracy is unquenchable. And totalitarian systems everywhere are feeling new pressures from the people. You see it today on the television sets, coming out of China. We've seen those beginnings of it in the Soviet Union and many, many other countries around the world. And so, don't tell me that Cubans don't want freedom and democracy; they do. And I challenge Fidel Castro to let the will of the people prevail.

In short, what we want to do is to advance that day when Cuban Independence Day achieves a new and a richer meaning: freedom from the evil of tyranny and oppression; freedom from the economic misery wrought by the Communist misrule—the freedom that can liberate lives and lift the human heart—and, yes, the freedom of democracy.

To achieve that freedom, heroes must lead the way. In a sense, they already have, and are. For Cuba can claim many, many heroes—those who struggled valiantly almost 90 years ago and those who struggle today—unsung heroes, for example, like longtime political prisoner Alfredo Mustelier Nuevo, who refuses to give up; heroes like Dr. Claudio Benedi, here on stage, who has condemned eloquently—repeatedly—Castro's violation of human rights; or another great patriot of the Western Hemisphere, a hero of mine, a hero of our times, and I'm referring, of course, to Armando Valladares. Let the American people see him now—22 years in Castro's prisons. And he wrote a book about that ordeal. It meant a lot to the entire Bush family and has certainly been an inspiration to me. You've all read it, I hope. And if not, why, we can boost the sales by recommending it. [*Laughter*] It's called "Against All Hope," and it describes how he, how Armando, survived beatings and starvations and unspeakable horror. And I'm sure many of you have read it, but it's a tribute to the arching human spirit, to that will to live, which helped endure the cruelest of regimes; a tribute, also, to the courage of the Cuban people, resolute and unafraid.

I had a discussion—I told Armando, I think, this—with one of the great leaders in this hemisphere. And he wondered why we were doing what we were doing in Central America. And I said, "Well, I'll tell you why. It's a book called 'Against All Hope.' That book relates to the deprivation of human rights in Cuba." And he said, "Well, what does that have to do with Central America?" I said, "Read the book, and you'll see. Read the book, because you'll understand that a deprivation of human rights in a Cuban prison is no different than the deprivation of human rights in a prison in Nicaragua." And he did, and I hope it's made a difference in that country's approach to foreign policy. But whether it did or not, the respect I have for Armando and the courage he has shown really knows no bounds. It is absolutely without limits, and the fact that he headed our delegation fighting for human rights, I think, said an awful lot about our commitment, the commitment of every American to human rights and to freedom.

And so, the courage that is demonstrated by these—and I risk offending by failing to mention others right here in this room—but that courage has helped you and your families endure. And one day it will, I am convinced—I really believe this—unite a million free Cuban Americans with their long-suffering Cuban brothers. And if hope can stay alive in the heart of Armando Valladares, surely we will see Cuba free again.

Thank you for coming. God bless you, and God bless America. Thank you very, very much.

Note: The President spoke at 2:34 p.m. during a briefing in Room 450 at the Old Executive Office Building.

Nomination of Thomas Joseph Murrin To Be Deputy Secretary of Commerce

May 22, 1989

The President today announced his intention to nominate Thomas Joseph Murrin to be Deputy Secretary of Commerce. He would succeed Donna F. Tuttle.

Mr. Murrin was president of Westinghouse Energy and Advance Technology Group, 1983–1987. From 1952 until 1987, he served in various capacities for Westinghouse Electric Corp., including president of the Public Systems Co., 1974; senior vice president of the Public Systems Group, 1974; executive vice president of the Defense and Public Systems Group, 1971; group vice president of defense, 1967; and corporate vice president of manufacturing, 1965. In 1959 he was appointed European manufacturing representative, based in Geneva, Switzerland, and was superintendent of factory planning for the new distribution transformer plant in Athens, GA, in 1955. He joined the Carnegie Mellon University as distinguished service professor in technology and management.

Mr. Murrin graduated from Fordham University (B.S., 1951). He is married, has eight children, and resides in Pittsburgh, PA.

Remarks at a White House Dinner Honoring the Nation's Governors
May 22, 1989

Good evening, everybody. Fellow public servants, politicians, stemwinding orators—[*laughter*]—it's a tough group to speak with, but look, it's an honor to welcome you to what Franklin Roosevelt called the house owned by all the people and which Harry Truman termed the finest prison in the world. [*Laughter*] Incidentally, Barbara and I don't feel that way about this magnificent place. We love it, and please, don't any one of you attempt to do anything about that. [*Laughter*]

I want to commend Governor Baliles for his leadership of the NGA [National Governors' Association], and let me pass our best wishes to Terry Branstad, who's coming in. As you know, Henry Bellmon—I didn't see Henry tonight, but he'll like this one—his fellow Oklahoman Will Rogers once said, "Politics isn't worrying this country one-tenth as much as parking space." [*Laughter*] What he meant was that often Washington loses perspective and we forget what matters: people and their concerns. I concluded long ago that as Governors you are where the action is. And there's always a budget to be balanced or a school to be built, or you've got to find what works. And I, too, like what works. And I try to understand your problems; and if I didn't, I have a hunch that one of your own, John Sununu, my able Chief of Staff, would help me out on that.

But as we gather here tonight beneath a painting which forms a study in how problems can be met and overcome—and I'm talking of course about Healy's magnificent painting of Abraham Lincoln about the end of the War Between the States—it makes a profound impression on me. Incidentally, there's another variety of this painting upstairs that some of you have seen, and it's the exact same pose. But in the one upstairs, he's conferring with his three generals, but in exactly the same pose as this one, except there's a rainbow, which signifies the end of this war that divided us and symbolizes hope for the future.

But Lincoln, as I'm sure for others of you, is one of my favorite Presidents, and I know most Americans feel that way. But I'm reminded daily of him, for so often we pass the room which served as his office upstairs. As he abolished slavery, he saved the Union, and he preserved for future generations the canons of democracy. And in this painting you get a feeling, I think, of his agony and his greatness. In fact, all around it, you feel a sweep of history when you're in this marvelous building, and of the men and women who acted boldly, courageously to write the pages of our history. I believe that our pages, too, can be extraordinary, pages that you all are writing—Barbara and I in some way might be writing.

You look around at the world today—and we were chatting about this here—the fascinating changes that are taking place—obviously in the Soviet Union, but clearly today in China. Bar and I lived there in 1974 and 1975, and if anybody had predicted that the force of democracy was such that you'd see a million kids in Tiananmen Square—and nobody would have believed it back then, and here they are. You look at the changes inside the Soviet Union. You look at the accord in Angola. You look at Panama, where really almost for the first time you've seen this tremendous expression of the democratic will of the people, and then see that aborted by a totalitarian—and then see the countries in Central America unite in a resolution at the OAS [Organization of American States], condemning this kind of behavior, because they themselves sense this inexorable move to democracy. And we are living in very, very exciting times.

And around the globe, leaders are learning what you already know: To survive, government must be responsive and responsible, for if not, the people are gonna find leaders who are. And that's why we have the marvelous device called a free election. And it's not easy, of course.

But sometimes you, I know, must feel as Lincoln did. One night, a stranger found him in the street with two of his sons, both of whom were sobbing uncontrollably.

"Whatever is the matter with the boys, Mr. Lincoln?" a stranger asked. He sighed and observed, "Just what's the matter with the whole world. I've got three walnuts, and each wants two." Well, that's the way our business is. That's the way it is for Governors, and that's the way it is with the President of the United States. We're pulled in countless directions, but we treasure these American lessons. Democracy works; our system works. It works in Dover or in Des Moines; it works in Portland, Richmond—Portland, Oregon; Portland, Maine. And it works because when it comes to problem-solving Washington does not know best; the people do.

Jefferson wrote: "The God who gave us life, gave us liberty at the same time." Let us use that liberty to find solutions, to find what works, enrich our lives. And in that spirit, I ask all of you to raise your glasses to the American people and to you, the Governors, their trustees, and to the American system that remains after 200 years the greatest in the history of the world, the model for nations struggling to be free this very day.

Thank you all for being with us. Jerry, and to you, sir, and all the Governors, Barbara and I salute you and extend to you our most profound respects.

Note: The President spoke at 9:40 p.m. in the State Dining Room at the White House. In his remarks, he referred to Governors Gerald L. Baliles of Virginia and Terry Branstad of Iowa, chairman and vice chairman of the National Governors' Association, respectively, and Gov. Henry Bellmon of Oklahoma.

Letter to Congressional Leaders on Savings and Loan Financing Legislation

May 22, 1989

Dear _________:

I am writing to secure the assistance of the House leadership in resolving the current crisis in the savings and loan industry. At present, several hundred insolvent savings and loans cannot be permanently restructured or closed without passage of new legislation. As Secretary Brady has indicated, each day's delay adds more than $10 million to the cost of this enormous problem. Delay also jeopardizes the confidence in our financial system that expeditious enactment of this legislation was intended to sustain.

On February 6, I asked the Congress "to join me in a determined effort to resolve this threat to the American financial system permanently, and to do so without delay." During my address to a Joint Session of Congress on February 9, I asked that this vital legislation be enacted within 45 days. Shortly thereafter my Administration forwarded comprehensive legislation to Congress to implement this program.

The Senate moved rapidly and, on April 19, 1989, passed legislation very similar to our proposal. In the House, the legislation has been thoroughly debated in the full Banking Committee, the Financial Institutions Subcommittee, and the Ways and Means Committee. Now is the time for the House to act, yet this vital measure still has not been scheduled for floor consideration. At the estimated rate of ongoing losses, more than $330 million in additional taxpayer costs have been incurred since Senate passage.

I ask your cooperation to secure the following actions:

First, the legislation should be reported promptly to the House floor under a rule that expedites passage. Further delay in final House passage of this bill would be both costly and unnecessary.

Second, I ask the leadership of the House to hold absolutely firm against any attempt to weaken those vital elements of the legislation which protect the American taxpayer from additional costs. Such elements include higher capital requirements, sound accounting principles, and strengthened civil and criminal penalties against wrongdoing in insured institutions.

Third, I ask that the interests of American savers and taxpayers be held paramount. Special interest amendments that could weaken the safety and soundness of our financial system, or provisions that impose additional costs for otherwise worthy purposes such as housing subsidies, do not belong in this bill and should be deleted.

Finally, I urge Congress to resist efforts to reformulate the financing program adopted by both the House and Senate Banking Committees. Such efforts can only delay final passage of the legislation and could have undesirable economic consequences. This urgently needed legislation should not become the vehicle for undermining the spending discipline established by the Gramm-Rudman-Hollings law, which proved beneficial in the recent successful budget discussions between Congress and my Administration. This discipline will be essential to achieving our mutual budget deficit reduction goals in the future.

To date, Congress and the Executive Branch have worked cooperatively to protect our financial markets from instability and to avoid unnecessary costs. Indeed, bipartisan majorities in both the Senate and House have defeated determined special interest lobbying against the tough capital standards needed to protect American taxpayers from a repeat of this tragedy. I look forward to working with Congress in passing responsible legislation to resolve the current savings and loan crisis and to insure that this situation will not be repeated.

Sincerely,

GEORGE BUSH

Note: Identical letters were sent to Jim Wright, Speaker of the House of Representatives; Thomas Foley and Robert H. Michel, majority and minority leaders of the House of Representatives, respectively; and Tony Coelho and Newt Gingrich, majority and minority whips of the House of Representatives, respectively. The letter was released by the Office of the Press Secretary on May 23.

Statement by Press Secretary Fitzwater on the President's Meeting With Chairman Wan Li of China

May 23, 1989

The President today met with Wan Li, Chairman of the Standing Committee of the National People's Congress, from 2:30 p.m. to 3:30 p.m. Following the plenary meeting, Wan Li visited the Residence to greet Mrs. Bush.

The Chinese leader briefed the President on the outcome of the recent Sino-Soviet summit and on the student demonstrations in China. "We are strongly committed to democracy around the world," the President said. "It is the underpinning of our being as a nation. I urge nonviolence and restraint in your present situation. I urge that Voice of America not be jammed and that reporters be given open access."

The President told Chairman Wan that he remains personally committed to expanding the normal and constructive relations the United States enjoys with China. The world has a stake in China's economic progress, national security, and political vitality. The United States hopes to see the continuing implementation of economic and political reforms, which undoubtedly will also help advance these goals.

Nomination of Mark L. Edelman To Be Deputy Administrator of the Agency for International Development
May 23, 1989

The President today announced his intention to nominate Mark L. Edelman to be Deputy Administrator of the Agency for International Development, U.S. International Development Cooperation Agency. He would succeed Jay F. Morris.

Since 1987 Mr. Edelman has served as Ambassador to the Republic of Cameroon. Prior to this, he was Assistant Administrator for Africa at the Agency for International Development, 1984–1987, and senior adviser to the Administrator, and Executive Secretary, 1983–1984. He was Deputy Assistant Secretary for the Bureau of International Organization Affairs at the Department of State, 1981–1983, and a program analyst for the Agency for International Development, 1981. He was a legislative assistant to Senator John C. Danforth in Washington, DC, 1977–1981. Mr. Edelman has served as State budget director in Jefferson City, MO, 1973–1976; budget examiner for the Bureau of the Budget in the Office of Management and Budget, 1968–1972; and a management intern and Africa budget analyst for the U.S. Information Agency, 1965–1967.

Mr. Edelman graduated from Oberlin College (A.B., 1965). He was born June 27, 1943, in St. Louis, MO. He is married to the former Nancy M. Wasell.

Message to the Congress Reporting on the National Emergency With Respect to Iran
May 23, 1989

To the Congress of the United States:

I hereby report to the Congress on developments since the last report of November 15, 1988, concerning the national emergency with respect to Iran that was declared in Executive Order No. 12170 of November 14, 1979, and matters relating to Executive Order No. 12613 of October 29, 1987. This report is submitted pursuant to section 204(c) of the International Emergency Economic Powers Act, 50 U.S.C. 1703(c), and section 505(c) of the International Security and Development Cooperation Act of 1985, 22 U.S.C. 2349aa–9. This report covers events through March 28, 1989, including those that occurred since the last report under Executive Order No. 12170 dated November 15, 1988. That report covered events through October 1, 1988.

1. Since the last report, there have been no amendments to the Iranian Assets Control Regulations, 31 C.F.R. Part 535 (the "IACRs"), or the Iranian Transactions Regulations, 31 C.F.R. Part 560 (the "ITRs"), administered by the Office of Foreign Assets Control ("FAC"). The major focus of licensing activity under the ITRs remains the importation of certain non-fungible Iranian-origin goods, principally carpets, which were located outside Iran before the embargo was imposed, and where no payment or benefit accrued to Iran after the effective date of the embargo. Since October 1, 1988, FAC has made 583 licensing determinations under the ITRs.

Numerous Customs Service detentions and seizures of Iranian-origin goods (including carpets, caviar, dates, pistachios, and gold) have taken place, and a number of FAC and Customs investigations into potential violations of the ITRs are pending. Several of the seizures have led to forfeiture actions and imposition of civil monetary penalties. An indictment has been issued in the case of *United States* v. *Benham Tahriri*, which is now pending in the United States District Court for the District of Vermont.

2. The Iran-United States Claims Tribunal (the "Tribunal"), established at The Hague

pursuant to the Claims Settlement Agreement of January 19, 1981 (the "Algiers Accords"), continues to make progress in arbitrating the claims before it. Since the last report, the Tribunal has rendered 22 awards, for a total of 418 awards. Of that total, 308 have been awards in favor of American claimants: 193 of these were awards on agreed terms, authorizing and approving payment of settlements negotiated by the parties, and 115 were decisions adjudicated on the merits. The Tribunal has dismissed a total of 25 other claims on the merits and 56 for jurisdictional reasons. Of the 29 remaining awards, two represent withdrawals and 27 were in favor of Iranian claimants. As of March 28, 1989, awards to successful American claimants from the Security Account held by the NV Settlement Bank stood at $1,136,444,726.00.

As of March 28, 1989, the Security Account has fallen below the required balance of $500 million 25 times. Each time, Iran has replenished the account, as required by the Algiers Accords, by transferring funds from the separate account held by the NV Settlement Bank in which interest on the Security Account is deposited. Iran has also replenished the account once when it was not required by the Accords, for a total of 26 replenishments. The most recent replenishment as of March 28, 1989, occurred on March 22, 1989, in the amount of $100,000, bringing the total in the Security Account to $500,011,034.15. The aggregate amount that has been transferred from the interest account to the Security Account is $624,698,999.39. The amount in the interest account as of March 28, 1989, was $128,220,636.82.

Iranian and U.S. arbitrators agreed on two neutral arbitrators to replace Professor Karl-Heinz Bockstiegel and Professor Michel Andre Virally, who had submitted letters of resignation. On December 16, 1988, Professor Bengt Broms of Finland replaced Professor Bockstiegel as Chairman of Chamber One, and on January 1, 1989, Professor Gaetano Arangio-Ruiz of Italy replaced Professor Virally as Chairman of Chamber Three. Professor Bockstiegel had also served as President of the Tribunal. After Iran and the United States were unable to agree on a new President of the Tribunal, former Netherlands Supreme Court Chief Judge Charles M.J.A. Moons, the appointing authority for the Tribunal, appointed Professor Robert Briner to the position on February 2, 1989. Professor Briner, who has been a member of the Tribunal since 1985, will continue to serve as Chairman of Chamber Two.

3. The Tribunal continues to make progress in the arbitration of claims of U.S. nationals for $250,000 or more. Over 68 percent of the nonbank claims have now been disposed of through adjudication, settlement, or voluntary withdrawal, leaving 169 such claims on the docket. The largest of the large claims, the progress of which has been slowed by their complexity, are finally being decided, sometimes with sizable damage awards to the U.S. claimant. Since the last report, nine large claims have been decided. One U.S. company received an award on agreed terms of $10,800,000.

4. The Tribunal continues to process claims of U.S. nationals against Iran of less than $250,000 each. As of March 28, 1989, a total of 362 small claims have been resolved, 82 of them since the last report, as a result of decisions on the merits, awards on agreed terms, or Tribunal orders. One contested claim has been decided since the last report, raising the total number of contested claims decided to 24, 15 of which favored the American claimant. These decisions will help in establishing guidelines for the adjudication or settlement of similar claims. To date, American claimants have also received 56 awards on agreed terms reflecting settlements of claims under $250,000.

The Tribunal's current small claims docket includes approximately 185 active cases. It is anticipated that the Tribunal will issue new scheduling orders later this spring to bring its active docket to approximately 225 active cases.

5. In coordination with concerned government agencies, the Department of State continues to present United States Government claims against Iran, as well as responses by the United States Government to claims brought against it by Iran. Since the last report, the Department has filed pleadings in eight government-to-govern-

ment claims, and presented one claim at a hearing before the Tribunal. In addition, two claims have been settled.

6. Since the last report, nine bank syndicates have completed negotiations with Bank Markazi Jomhouri Islami Iran ("Bank Markazi," Iran's central bank) and have been paid a total of $11,235,741.87 for interest accruing for the period January 1–18, 1981 ("January Interest"). These payments were made from Dollar Account No. 1 at the Federal Reserve Bank of New York, ("FRBNY"). Moreover, under the April 13, 1988, agreement between the FRBNY and Bank Markazi, the FRBNY returned $7,295,823.58 of Iranian funds to Bank Markazi. That transfer represents the excess of amounts reserved in Dollar Account No. 1 to pay off each bank syndicate with a claim for January Interest against Bank Markazi.

7. The situation reviewed above continues to implicate important diplomatic, financial, and legal interests of the United States and its nationals and presents an unusual challenge to the national security and foreign policy of the United States. The Iranian Assets Control Regulations issued pursuant to Executive Order No. 12170 continue to play an important role in structuring our relationship with Iran and in enabling the United States properly to implement the Algiers Accords. Similarly, the Iranian Transactions Regulations issued pursuant to Executive Order No. 12613 continue to advance important objectives in combatting international terrorism. I shall continue to exercise the powers at my disposal to deal with these problems and will continue to report periodically to the Congress on significant developments.

GEORGE BUSH

The White House,
May 23, 1989.

Remarks at the Annual White House News Photographers Association Dinner
May 23, 1989

Marlin says it's okay to talk; this will be a modified photo op. [*Laughter*] Actually, I dropped in to see if my prints were ready. [*Laughter*] It's no secret that I'm a great fan of the White House photographers. After all, the first 100 days were saved by those puppy pictures. [*Laughter*] An animal lover like me doesn't lightly bestow a fond nickname like "photo dogs." I know that your space is cramped there in the West Wing. Some of the photographers, as a matter of fact, asked if they could set up a darkroom someplace where nothing much is happening. I was all for it until they suggested the Oval Office. [*Laughter*]

And you know, Larry asked me to help hand out the awards a little later on here. And I saw the list, and, yes, it's an impressive group, but some key categories got overlooked. And so, I talked it over with the photo general of the United States, David Valdez, and tonight I'm proud to announce the first annual Presidential Photographers Awards—very serious business here. With Oscars, you get a gold statuette; Grammys, a record player; and Golden Globes. And here it is, this 9-inch step ladder—[*laughter*]—highly coveted. This is the highly coveted Golden Step Ladder Award. [*Laughter*]

We start with the photo dog fashion awards. I asked Director of the CIA Bill Webster why Air Force One never gets taken over by terrorists. And he said, "The bad guys take one look at the way the photographers are dressed and figure that the plane's already been hijacked." [*Laughter*]

There are some exceptions. The first runner-up for this coveted award for the best dressed photographer goes to Time's Diana Walker, affectionately known as Lady Di. She has that "12 days on safari in Botswana" look that you're all striving for. [*Laughter*] She's the one that did that photo essay last week called "Twelve Hours With George Bush." She claimed it felt like the first 100 days.

But anyway, the winner of this coveted award—she only was runner-up—goes to one of Diana's colleagues, Dirck Halstead. [*Laughter*] Now, Dirck has never been suspected of being a terrorist because the Secret Service says that, while terrorists do at times wear Guccis, rarely if ever are their blue jeans starched and pressed. [*Laughter*]

Now, there's a corollary of Murphy's Law, which White House photographers have a knack for proving: Under any conditions, anywhere, whatever you are doing, there is some ordinance under which you can be booked. And so, the 1989 First Amendment Award, coveted award for freedom of expression, goes to the CNN [Cable News Network] cameraman arrested on a pool stakeout this month outside a high security installation—Joe & Mo's. [*Laughter*] And let's hear it for Albert Certo of CNN. [*Applause*] Can someone please remove his handcuffs, because we want him ready for the picture.

Those looking for proof of a kinder and gentler America need only look around the White House press room at the number of people napping. [*Laughter*] And I stopped speaking at photo ops because I was afraid I'd wake up the dozing cameramen. But we call the next award the Rip Van Winkle Award, coveted award given each year to the photographer who earns the most overtime while asleep. [*Laughter*] The competition in this category was tough. [*Laughter*] And the final rankings—and this was scientifically done—are John Bullard of ABC—[*laughter*]—Percy Arrington of NBC, and CNN's Hank Disselkamp. Win, place, and show—a photo finish if there ever was one. Sleep on, out there.

Now, that's not an easy job. Two months ago, a U.S. News and World Report photographer took a fall off the East Room press platform. He said he was okay until I said, "Scratch one newsman." But then he bounced back and carries more equipment than any other three photographers combined. Or from U.S. News and World Report, the winner of this year's Arnold Schwarzenegger Award—[*laughter*]—Darryl Heikes.

The competition is intense among the news magazines. It was Darryl himself who suggested that U.S. News come out with its first annual swimsuit issue. [*Laughter*] Can't quite see Mort Zuckerman in thongs, but—[*laughter*].

And I'm constantly impressed by the ingenuity of this White House press corps. Take the runner-up for our last award, lighting man Marvin Purbaugh of NBC. Marvin recently became the first American to actually produce a Thousand Points of Light. [*Laughter*] He lit the Roosevelt Room by bouncing the kleigs off Marlin's head. [*Laughter*]

And our final award is named for the well-known Milo Minderbinder, the irrepressible entrepreneur on "Catch-22." The winner—you guessed it—has sold keychains to tourists—[*laughter*]—luggage tags to local reporters, press passes to foreign media. [*Laughter*] And so, give me a hand for this unanimous winner of the 1989 Milo Award, Mr. Opportunity Society himself, the guy that's giving entrepreneurship a bad name—[*laughter*]—Newsweek's own Larry Downing, the only guy who gets his trips on Air Force One counted as frequent flyer miles. [*Laughter*] No, one of the things I do like about Larry, though, is his loyalty. In Beijing, the microphones picked up his patriotic challenge to some Chinese security guards: "Stop pushing me," he said. "Our President may sound like an idiot, but he's our President, and we're going to take pictures of him." [*Laughter*] Thanks a lot, Larry. [*Laughter*]

Marlin will see that you receive these coveted awards. But right now, I'd like all these lucky winners to stand up. Diana and Dirck, Albert, John, Percy, Hank, Darryl, Marvin, and Larry. Bad sports—only two of them stood up.

No, but as these awards suggest, the various characters—and I use the word advisedly—assembled in this room probably make up about as diverse a collection of personalities as ever found in a single profession. But over the years, I've observed certain qualities that you do have in common: the determination as well as the ability to work hard; take an elbow, give one in return, Cynthia; a willingness to go the extra mile, even on the slimmest chance that it will produce a memorable shot; grace under pressure—and I mean it—and a total belief in your work. And more importantly, more personally, the very name that I've bestowed, "photo dogs"—and you've adopted—say a lot about the good-natured relationship that we enjoy and the good will that's shared on both sides.

And I will say this from the bottom of a grateful heart: Knowing the Bush family as you do now, I have always appreciated the thoughtfulness and the consideration and the kindness that you have shown to our family and, indeed, the kindness and consideration that you have shown in our quest for privacy from time to time. And that means a great deal. So, thank you all. It's time to declare a lid. And any followup questions can go to Rich Little—and I'm scared to death. [*Laughter*] Thank you all. And lights, please.

Note: The President spoke at 9:20 p.m. in the International Ballroom at the Washington Hilton Hotel. In his remarks, he referred to Marlin Fitzwater, the President's Press Secretary; Larry A. Rubenstein, chairman of the awards dinner and assistant picture editor at Reuters; David Valdez, the President's photographer; Cynthia Johnson and Dirck Halstead, photographers for Time magazine; and entertainer Rich Little.

Statement by Press Secretary Fitzwater on the President's Meeting With Defense Minister Yitzhak Rabin of Israel

May 24, 1989

The President just completed a productive half-hour meeting with Israeli Defense Minister Yitzhak Rabin. President Bush reaffirmed the U.S. commitment to a close relationship with our long-term friend and strategic partner Israel. Toward this end, the President made clear his determination to provide Israel with the resources necessary for its security.

The two leaders also discussed the situation in the West Bank and Gaza. The President told Defense Minister Rabin that the recent elections proposal put forward by the Government of Israel constitutes an important contribution to a process that has the potential to bring about negotiations leading to a comprehensive settlement consistent with Israeli security and Palestinian political rights. The President noted that the Israeli elections proposal gives us something to work with, and we are now looking for a constructive Arab response to it. The President also voiced his deep concern over the escalating violence in the occupied territories and expressed the strong hope that all parties would exercise maximum restraint.

Remarks at the United States Coast Guard Academy Commencement Ceremony in New London, Connecticut

May 24, 1989

Thank you all very much. And Mr. Superintendent, my friend, Rick, thank you for inviting me here. Thank all of the—particularly those in the white uniforms who are fixing to move on—for that warm welcome. To Admiral Yost, the Commandant, and Secretary [of Transportation] Skinner, Dr. Alex Haley, and all the distinguished, broke, but happy parents sitting over here—[*laughter*]—this is a special day. I want to single out Admiral Cueroni, who will be leaving the service that he has served so well. And it was my pleasure as Vice President of the United States to work directly with him when he headed the south Florida effort fighting narcotics. And he showed us a lot of class then, and he showed the country a lot of class for his many years in service to the Coast Guard.

I want to congratulate each member of this year's class on receiving your commission into such a proud service. You mention the Coast Guard, and most people think about lives saved at sea, daring rescue operations; but those daily acts of heroism are just one part of the vital work that this Coast Guard performs. Right now, in Prince William Sound, the Coast Guard continues to work around the clock in a major environmental cleanup. And let me at this point, on behalf of a grateful nation, commend Admiral Yost. Through his personal commitment, his involvement, and the leadership that he has shown, he has served his country in the finest tradition of the United States Coast Guard. And those of us who care about the environment—and that is 250 million Americans at a minimum—he's showing us the way. And your service—backing him up in every way. And I am very proud of what Paul Yost has done.

Right now, off the Florida coast, Coast Guard patrols are chasing down drug smugglers, helping to keep the drugs off the streets. And that may be all in a day's work for the Coast Guard, but it is absolutely vital to our national health, our well-being, and our security.

I'm sure on that long first day of Swab Summer that you never thought 4 years could pass so quickly, but they have; and you've worked hard. Billet Night has come and gone—[*laughter*]—and you're ready—Semper Paratus, in the words of your motto—ready to enter the Coast Guard service, enter the world. And the truth is, that's what commencement is all about. The world is yours, and today's ceremony is really part of the change of command from one generation to the next.

Today our world—your world—is changing, East and West. And today I want to speak to you about the world we want to see and what we can do to bring that new world into clear focus.

We live in a time when we are witnessing the end of an idea: the final chapter of the Communist experiment. Communism is now recognized, even by many within the Communist world itself, as a failed system, one that promised economic prosperity but failed to deliver the goods, a system that built a wall between the people and their political aspirations. But the eclipse of communism is only one half of the story of our time. The other is the ascendancy of the democratic idea. Never before has the idea of freedom so captured the imaginations of men and women the world over, and never before has the hope of freedom beckoned so many—trade unionists in Warsaw, the people of Panama, rulers consulting the ruled in the Soviet Union. And even as we speak today, the world is transfixed by the dramatic events in Tiananmen Square. Everywhere, those voices are speaking the language of democracy and freedom. And we hear them, and the world hears them. And America will do all it can to encourage them.

So, today I want to speak about our security strategy for the 1990's, one that advances American ideals and upholds American aims. Amidst the many challenges we'll face, there will be risks. But let me assure you, we'll find more than our share of opportunities. We and our allies are strong, stronger really than at any point in the postwar period, and more capable than ever of supporting the cause of freedom. There's an opportunity before us to shape a new world.

What is it that we want to see? It is a growing community of democracies anchoring international peace and stability, and a dynamic free-market system generating prosperity and progress on a global scale. The economic foundation of this new era is the proven success of the free market, and nurturing that foundation are the values rooted in freedom and democracy. Our country, America, was founded on these values, and they gave us the confidence that flows from strength. So, let's be clear about one thing: America looks forward to the challenge of an emerging global market. But these values are not ours alone; they are now shared by our friends and allies around the globe.

The economic rise of Europe and the nations of the Pacific Rim is the growing success of our postwar policy. This time is a time of tremendous opportunity, and destiny is in our own hands. To reach the world we want to see, we've got to work, and work hard. There's a lot of work ahead of us. We must resolve international trade problems that threaten to pit friends and allies against one another. We must combat misguided notions of economic nationalism that will tell us to close off our economies to foreign competition, just when the global marketplace has become a fact of life. We must open the door to the nations of Eastern Europe and other Socialist countries that embrace free-market reforms. And finally, for developing nations heavily burdened with debt, we must provide assistance and encourage the market reforms that will set those nations on a path towards growth.

If we succeed, the next decade and the century beyond will be an era of unparalleled growth, an era which sees the flourishing of freedom, peace, and prosperity around the world. But this new era cannot unfold in a climate where conflict and turmoil exist. And therefore, our goals must also include security and stability: security for ourselves and our allies and our friends, stability in the international arena, and an end to regional conflicts.

Such goals are constant, but the strategy we employ to reach them can and must change as the world changes.

Today the need for a dynamic and adaptable strategy is imperative. We must be strong—economically, diplomatically, and, as you know, militarily—to take advantage of the opportunities open to us in a world of rapid change. And nowhere will the ultimate consequences of change have more significance for world security than within the Soviet Union itself.

What we're seeing now in the Soviet Union is indeed dramatic. The process is still ongoing, unfinished. But make no mistake: Our policy is to seize every—and I mean every—opportunity to build a better, more stable relationship with the Soviet Union, just as it is our policy to defend American interests in light of the enduring reality of Soviet military power. We want to see *perestroika* succeed. And we want to see the policies of *glasnost* and *perestroika*—so far, a revolution imposed from top down—institutionalized within the Soviet Union. And we want to see *perestroika* extended as well. We want to see a Soviet Union that restructures its relationship toward the rest of the world—a Soviet Union that is a force for constructive solutions to the world's problems.

The grand strategy of the West during the postwar period has been based on the concept of containment: checking the Soviet Union's expansionist aims, in the hope that the Soviet system itself would one day be forced to confront its internal contradictions. The ferment in the Soviet Union today affirms the wisdom of this strategy. And now we have a precious opportunity to move beyond containment. You're graduating into an exciting world, where the opportunity for world peace, lasting peace, has never been better. Our goal, integrating the Soviet Union into the community of nations, is every bit as ambitious as containment was at its time. And it holds tremendous promise for international stability.

Coping with a changing Soviet Union will be a challenge of the highest order. But the security challenges we face today do not come from the East alone. The emergence of regional powers is rapidly changing the strategic landscape. In the Middle East, in south Asia, in our own hemisphere, a growing number of nations are acquiring advanced and highly destructive capabilities—in some cases, weapons of mass destruction and the means to deliver them. And it is an unfortunate fact that the world faces increasing threat from armed insurgencies, terrorists, and, as you in the Coast Guard are well aware, narcotics traffickers—and in some regions, an unholy alliance of all three.

Our task is clear: We must curb the proliferation of advanced weaponry. We must check the aggressive ambitions of renegade regimes, and we must enhance the ability of our friends to defend themselves. We have not yet mastered the complex challenge. We and our allies must construct a common strategy for stability in the developing world.

How we and our allies deal with these

diverse challenges depends on how well we understand the key elements of defense strategy. And so, let me just mention today two points in particular: first, the need for an effective deterrent, one that demonstrates to our allies and adversaries alike American strength, American resolve; and second, the need to maintain an approach to arms reduction that promotes stability at the lowest feasible level of armaments.

Deterrence is central to our defense strategy. The key to keeping the peace is convincing our adversaries that the cost of aggression against us or our allies is simply unacceptable. In today's world, nuclear forces are essential to deterrence. Our challenge is to protect those deterrent systems from attack. And that's why we'll move Peacekeeper ICBM's out of fixed and vulnerable silos, making them mobile and thus harder to target. Looking to the longer term, we will also develop and deploy a new highly mobile single-warhead missile, the Midgetman. With only minutes of warnings, these new missiles can relocate out of harm's way. Any attack against systems like this will fail. We are also researching—and we are committed to deploy when ready—a more comprehensive defensive system, known as SDI. Our premise is straightforward: Defense against incoming missiles endangers no person, endangers no country.

We're also working to reduce the threat we face, both nuclear and conventional. The INF treaty demonstrates that willingness. In addition, in the past decade, NATO has unilaterally removed 2400 shorter range theater warheads. But theater nuclear forces contribute to stability, no less than strategic forces, and thus it would be irresponsible to depend solely on strategic nuclear forces to deter conflict in Europe. The conventional balance in Europe is just as important and is linked to the nuclear balance. For more than 40 years—and look at your history books to see how pronounced this accomplishment is—for more than 40 years the Warsaw Pact's massive advantage in conventional forces has cast a shadow over Europe.

The unilateral reductions that President Gorbachev has promised give us hope that we can now redress that imbalance. We welcome those steps because, if implemented, they will help reduce the threat of surprise attack. And they confirm what we've said all along: that Soviet military power far exceeds the levels needed to defend the legitimate security interests of the U.S.S.R. And we must keep in mind that these reductions alone, even if implemented, are not enough to eliminate the significant numerical superiority that the Soviet Union enjoys right now.

Through negotiation, we can now transform the military landscape of Europe. The issues are complex, stakes are very high. But the Soviets are now being forthcoming, and we hope to achieve the reductions that we seek. Let me emphasize: Our aim is nothing less than removing war as an option in Europe.

The U.S.S.R. has said that it is willing to abandon its age-old reliance on offensive strategy. It's time to begin. This should mean a smaller force, one less reliant on tanks and artillery and personnel carriers that provide the Soviets' offensive striking power. A restructured Warsaw Pact, one that mirrors the defensive posture of NATO, would make Europe and the world more secure.

Peace can also be enhanced by movement towards more openness in military activities. And 2 weeks ago, I proposed an "open skies" initiative to extend the concept of openness. That plan for territorial overflights would increase our mutual security against sudden and threatening military activities. In the same spirit, let us extend this openness to military expenditures as well. I call on the Soviets to do as we have always done. Let's open the ledgers: publish an accurate defense budget. But as we move forward we must be realistic. Transformations of this magnitude will not happen overnight. If we are to reach our goals, a great deal is required of us, our allies, and of the Soviet Union. But we can succeed.

I began today by speaking about the triumph of a particular, peculiar, very special American ideal: freedom. And I know there are those who may think there's something presumptuous about that claim, those who will think it's boastful. But it is not, for one simple reason: Democracy isn't our creation; it is our inheritance. And we can't take credit for democracy, but we can take that precious gift of freedom, preserve it, and pass it on, as my generation does to you, and you, too, will do one day. And perhaps, provided we seize the opportunities open to us, we can help others attain the freedom that we cherish.

As I said on the Capitol steps the day I took this office as President of the United States: "There is but one just use of power, and it is to serve people." As your Commander in Chief, let me call on this Coast Guard class to reaffirm with me that American power will continue in its service to the enduring ideals of democracy and freedom. Congratulations to each and every one of you. Thank you, and God bless the United States of America. Thank you all very much.

Note: The President spoke at 12:13 p.m. on Nitchman Field at the Academy. He was introduced by Rear Adm. Richard P. Cueroni, Superintendent of the U.S. Coast Guard Academy. In his opening remarks, the President referred to Adm. Paul A. Yost, Jr., Commandant, U.S. Coast Guard; Secretary of Transportation Samuel K. Skinner; and author Alex P. Haley, who received an honorary doctor of humane letters degree from the Academy. Following his remarks, the President returned to Washington, DC.

Nomination of C. Austin Fitts To Be an Assistant Secretary of Housing and Urban Development

May 25, 1989

The President today announced his intention to nominate C. Austin Fitts to be an Assistant Secretary of Housing and Urban Development (Federal Housing Commissioner). He would succeed Thomas T. Demery.

Since 1978 Mr. Fitts has served in several capacities with Dillon, Read & Co., Inc., in New York City, including managing director, 1986 to present; senior vice president, 1984–1986; vice president, 1982–1984; and an associate, 1978–1982.

Mr. Fitts graduated from Bennett College (A.A., 1970), the University of Pennsylvania (B.A., 1974), and the Wharton School of Business (M.B.A., 1978). He was born in 1950 in Philadelphia, PA, and resides in New York City.

Appointment of Barbara Hackman Franklin as a Member of the Advisory Committee for Trade Policy and Negotiations

May 25, 1989

The President today announced his intention to appoint Barbara Hackman Franklin to be a member of the Advisory Committee for Trade Policy and Negotiations for a term of 2 years. She would succeed Lawrence A. Bossidy.

Ms. Franklin is currently president and chief executive officer of Franklin Associates, a Washington-based management consulting firm, which she founded in 1984. Since 1979, she has been senior fellow of the Wharton School of Business of the University of Pennsylvania; and for 8 years she served as director of the Wharton government and business program. Ms. Franklin has served two terms on the Advisory Committee for Trade Negotiations, 1982–1986, and has chaired its Task Force on Tax Reform. In addition, Ms. Franklin serves in various capacities, including member of the Services Policy Advisory Committee; adviser to the Comptroller General of the

United States; and a member of the board of visitors of the Defense Systems Management College. In 1973, Ms. Franklin served as one of the first Commissioners of the U.S. Consumer Product Safety Commission.

Ms. Franklin graduated from Pennsylvania State University (B.A., 1962) and Harvard Graduate School of Business Administration (M.B.A., 1964). She was born in Lancaster, PA. She is married to Wallace Barnes, and the couple resides in Washington, DC.

Designation of Linda Arey Skladany as Acting Chairman of the Occupational Safety and Health Review Commission

May 25, 1989

The President today designated Linda Arey Skladany to be Acting Chairman of the Occupational Safety and Health Review Commission. She would succeed Elliot Ross Buckley.

Since 1988 Mrs. Skladany has served as Commissioner for the Occupational Safety and Health Review Commission. She has served as the Republican candidate for Congress for the Fifth District of Virginia, 1987–1988. She has served on the Advisory Committee for Trade Negotiations, 1988–1989, and as Special Assistant to the President and Deputy Director for Public Liaison at the White House, 1985–1987. She was Director of the Executive Secretariat at the Department of Transportation, 1984–1985; Special Assistant to the Deputy Secretary at the Department of Transportation, 1983–1984; Special Assistant at the Department of Justice, 1982–1983; and Special Assistant to the Executive Secretary at the Department of Education, 1981–1982.

Mrs. Skladany graduated from the College of William and Mary (B.A., 1966); Wake Forest University (M.A., 1975); and the University of Richmond School of Law (J.D., 1977). She was born November 25, 1944. She is married and resides in Alexandria, VA.

Nomination of Fred T. Goldberg, Jr., To Be Commissioner of Internal Revenue

May 25, 1989

The President today announced his intention to nominate Fred T. Goldberg, Jr., to be Commissioner of Internal Revenue at the Department of the Treasury. He would succeed Lawrence B. Gibbs.

Since 1984 Mr. Goldberg has served as Chief Counsel for the Internal Revenue Service. He served as a partner with Latham, Watkins, and Hills in Washington, DC., 1982–1984. He served as Assistant to the Commissioner of the Internal Revenue Service, 1981–1982; Acting Director of the Legislation and Regulations Division, Office of the Chief Counsel, Internal Revenue Service, 1982; and partner with Latham, Watkins and Hills in Washington, DC., 1981. He has also served as an associate with Latham, Watkins and Hills, 1973–1981; as an instructor in political science and economics at Yale College, 1971–1973; as assistant dean, Calhoun College, Yale University, 1971–1973; and as special assistant to the Assistant Director for Programs Planning and Evaluation of the Office of Economic Opportunity, 1970.

He graduated from Yale University (B.A., 1969; J.D., 1973). Mr. Goldberg was born on October 15, 1947. He is married, has four children, and resides in Bethesda, MD.

Nomination of Edward Joseph Perkins To Be Director General of the Foreign Service
May 25, 1989

The President today announced his intention to nominate Edward Joseph Perkins, a career member of the Senior Foreign Service, Class of Career Minister, to be Director General of the Foreign Service at the Department of State. He would succeed George Southall Vest.

Since 1986 Ambassador Perkins has served as Ambassador to the Republic of South Africa. Prior to this he served as Ambassador to the Republic of Liberia, 1985–1986. He was Director of the Office of West African Affairs in the Bureau of African Affairs at the Department of State, 1983–1985; deputy chief of mission for the U.S. Embassy in Monrovia, Liberia, 1981–1983; counselor for political affairs in Accra, Ghana, 1978–1981; and management analysis officer for the Office of Management Operations at the Department of State, 1975–1978. He was administrative officer for the Bureau of Near Eastern and South Asian Affairs, 1974–1975; personnel officer in the Office of the Director General, 1972–1974; and deputy assistant director for management of the U.S. Operations Mission in Thailand, 1970–1972.

Ambassador Perkins served in the U.S. Army for 3 years and the U.S. Marine Corps for 4 years. He graduated from the University of Maryland (B.A., 1967) and the University of Southern California (M.P.A., 1972; D.P.A., 1978). He is married and has two children.

Remarks Upon Departure for Europe
May 26, 1989

Well, I depart for Europe this morning to meet with all our North Atlantic allies and also to pay visits to Italy, Germany, and the United Kingdom for discussions with leaders of those alliance nations on issues of common interest. I'm especially pleased that my first visit to Europe as President is to celebrate the 40th anniversary of NATO. America is a proud partner in the Atlantic alliance, and American interests have been well served by the alliance.

Twice in the first half of this century Europe was the scene of world war, and twice Americans fought in Europe for the sake of peace and freedom. Today Europe is enjoying a period of unparalleled prosperity and uninterrupted peace, longer than it has known in the modern age, and NATO has made the difference. And the alliance will prove every bit as important to American and European security in the decade ahead. The importance of the alliance and its democratic underpinnings is the message I now take to Europe. NATO has been a success by any measure, but success breeds its own challenges. Today dramatic changes are taking place in Europe, both East and West. For us, those changes bring new challenges and unparalleled opportunities.

For too long, unnatural and inhuman barriers have divided the East from the West. And we hope to overcome that division, to see a Europe that is truly free, united, and at peace. We are ready to work with a united Europe, to extend the peace and prosperity we enjoy to other parts of the world. And we hope to move beyond containment: to integrate the Soviet Union into the community of nations. We welcome the political and economic liberalization that has taken place so far in the Soviet Union and in some countries of Eastern Europe. We will encourage more changes to follow.

Many common concerns confront us. Beyond the traditional economic and security spheres, we and our partners in the alliance are working hard on a growing international agenda, from a common approach to environmental protection to cooperation against drug trafficking and against terrorism. We also welcome Europe's progress towards a truly common market and a growing European cooperation on security issues as the basis of an even more dynamic transatlantic partnership. As we approach 1992, it is essential that we work with our European partners to ensure an open and expanding world trading system, and that we take strong steps to prevent trade disputes from obscuring our common political and security concerns. NATO is based on the many bonds between us: our shared heritage, history, and culture; our shared commitment to freedom, democracy, and the rights of the individual. Barbara and I are looking forward to visiting Europe.

Thank you all very much.

Note: The President spoke at 7:07 a.m. on the tarmac at Andrews Air Force Base in Camp Springs, MD.

Statement on United States Action Against Foreign Trade Barriers
May 26, 1989

Today the United States Trade Representative [Carla A. Hills] will submit to the Congress a report concerning actions to be taken under the so-called Super 301 provisions of the Omnibus Trade and Competitiveness Act of 1988. Those provisions provide that priority practices and countries shall be identified for the self-initiation of investigations under section 301.

I have discussed this matter extensively with Ambassador Hills and the other members of the Economic Policy Council. We agreed that the Super 301 provisions should be used (1) as a tool to open foreign markets and (2) in support of the objectives of the United States in the ongoing Uruguay round of trade negotiations of the General Agreement on Tariffs and Trade. This approach is designed to be consistent with the intent of Congress in drafting the legislation.

The list below indicates the specific priority practices and countries that can most effectively be the subjects of investigations under section 301. The priority practices are grouped under headings that correspond to major types of trade barriers and distortions the United States is working to eliminate in the Uruguay round. The priority countries have been selected on the basis of the number and pervasiveness of significant barriers to U.S. exports.

SUPER 301 PRIORITY PRACTICES AND COUNTRIES

Quantitative restrictions/import licensing

1. Licensing of agricultural and manufactured products............... Brazil

Government procurement

2. Satellites.................................... Japan
3. Supercomputers........................ Japan

Standards

4. Forest products......................... Japan

Services

5. Insurance.................................. India

Investment

6. Investment restrictions............ India

A satisfactory resolution of the above issues will significantly advance the objectives of U.S. trade policy. Our goal is to open markets and to eliminate trade barriers. We oppose protectionism in any and all forms. Therefore, I urge the Governments of Japan, India, and Brazil to work constructively with us to resolve these issues expeditiously. The process of investigating and negotiating with priority countries on each of the priority practices will begin by June 16.

We also considered carefully a large

number of practices that are not listed. In several cases, we decided that we could best pursue remedying these practices multilaterally in the GATT or in the Uruguay round of trade negotiations. Two examples are EC airbus subsidies and Japanese rice quotas.

The Uruguay round of the GATT continues to be the centerpiece of our trade strategy. While the lack of effective multilateral rules and enforcement mechanisms has forced us to resort to section 301, we look forward to the day when such actions will be unnecessary.

Finally, I want to announce today a separate administration initiative with Japan. I have directed the Secretaries of State and Treasury and the U.S. Trade Representative to form a high-level committee to include Commerce, Labor, and other interested agencies to propose negotiations with Japan on structural adjustment matters. Such matters include structural impediments to trade, balance-of-payments adjustment, and such issues as bid-rigging, market allocation, and group boycotts. These negotiations would initially focus on major structural barriers to imports, such as rigidity in the distribution system and pricing mechanisms. The negotiations sought by the United States in this Structural Impediments Initiative will address broader issues and will take place outside section 301, which appropriately deals with the investigation and resolution of particular unfair trade practices.

Remarks at the Welcoming Ceremony in Rome
May 26, 1989

Well, let me begin by thanking all of you and my personal friend, my good friend, Prime Minister De Mita, for welcoming us to Italy at this late hour. Since ancient times, the saying goes, "All roads lead to Rome," and that's still true. And it is very fitting that here I begin my first step on this first trip to Europe as President of the United States. Italy has long been a wellspring of Western culture and Western values, fostering the alliance and a more unified Europe. I hope that our visit to Rome will demonstrate just how strongly the United States respects and appreciates Italy's role as a staunch ally and as a constant friend.

When our common security has been threatened, you have been ready to strengthen the alliance. And when Europe appeared ready to loosen the ties that sustained it, you kept these important transatlantic ties alive and strong. And when conflict has threatened, you have been in the front ranks of those searching for solutions. The bond between the United States and Italy runs deep. It's a bond of family, of culture, of shared interests and common vision. The world around us is changing, but we can be sure that our friendship will endure.

Mr. Prime Minister, when we last met, we talked of new developments around the world: of change in the East, of new opportunities for arms reduction, of the growing unity of Europe. And in recent weeks, I've spoken of America's vision for world peace. I have said that we are prepared to move beyond containment, toward policy that works to bring the Soviet Union into the community of nations. We will be actively engaged in Eastern Europe, promoting measures to encourage political and economic liberalization in Poland. The United States welcomes a stronger and more united Europe. We believe, as I know you do, that European unity and the transatlantic partnership reinforce each other.

Over the next 2 days, we'll have the opportunity to engage in renewed dialog, as partners, certainly as friends. And I hope that our conversations are shaped by our shared expectations for the future and by our determination to see our future succeed. I am delighted to be back in Rome. Thank you again for this warm welcome.

Note: The President spoke at 10:27 p.m. on the tarmac at Ciampino Airport.

Remarks Following an Audience With Pope John Paul II in Vatican City
May 27, 1989

His Holiness. Mr. President, your visit this evening represents the latest of many contacts between the United States of America and the Holy See. A number of your predecessors and many other illustrious Americans have been welcomed here before you. Our meeting offers me the opportunity to reciprocate the much-appreciated hospitality that I received in your country and to recall the kind, personal attention that as Vice President you showed me as I left Detroit in September 1987, the year of the bicentennial of your Constitution.

Our encounter this time has also a special historical context, coming as it does in a year that now commemorates the 200th anniversary of your first Congress under the Constitution and, likewise, the 200th anniversary of the establishment at Baltimore of the first Catholic diocese in your land. For the Holy See, this is an occasion to express again its esteem for all the American people and for two centuries of that ethnic and fraternal experience in history called the United States of America.

Thirteen years ago, your country celebrated another historical bicentennial connected with your Declaration of Independence. It was then that my predecessor, Paul VI, spoke words that are applicable once again and that merit new attention. "At every turn," he said, "your bicentennial speaks to you of moral principles, religious convictions, unalienable rights given by the Creator." We honestly hope that this commemoration of your bicentennial will constitute a rededication to those sound moral principles formulated by your Founding Fathers and enshrined forever in your history.

It is America's dedication to the great heritage that is hers, to those values of the spirit, a number of which you alluded to earlier this year in your Inaugural Address, that offers hope and confidence to those who look to her with friendship and esteem. In that inaugural address, Mr. President, you made reference to power as existing to help people, to serve people. This is true at different levels, including power at the political and economic level. We see this, too, at the level of each community, with its power of fraternal love and concern. In all these areas, an immense challenge opens up before the United States in this third century of her nationhood. Her mission as a people engaged in good works and committed to serving others has horizons the length of your nation and far beyond—as far as humanity extends.

Today the interdependence of humanity is being reaffirmed and recognized through world events. The moral and social attitudes that must constitute a response to this interdependence is found in worldwide solidarity. In treating this question in a recent encyclical, I have stated that solidarity is not a feeling of vague compassion or shallow distress at the misfortunes of so many people both near and far. On the contrary, it is a firm and persevering determination to commit oneself to the common good; that is to say, to the good of all and of each individual, because we are all really responsible for all. Truly, the hour of international interdependence has struck. What is at stake is the common good of humanity.

Mr. President, I know how deeply committed you are to the efforts being made to liberate the youth of America from the destructive forces of drug abuse and to alleviate poverty at home and abroad. Material poverty and drug abuse, however, are only symptoms of a deeper moral crisis eating away at the very texture of society in almost every part of the world. All men and women of good will are called to take up the challenge and assume their responsibilities before the human family to address this crisis and to counteract the spiritual poverty that lies at the base of so much of human suffering.

By reason of her history, her resources, her creativity, but above all by reason of the moral principles and spiritual values espoused by her Founding Fathers and institutionally bequeathed to all her citizens, America truly has the possibility of an effective response to the challenges of the present hour: justice for all her citizens; peaceful relations beyond her borders; international solidarity; and in particular, a worldwide solidarity in the course of life, in the course of every human person.

Leaving Detroit and in saying goodbye to America in 1987, I expressed these thoughts: Every human person, no matter how vulnerable or helpless, no matter how useful or productive for society, is a being of inestimable worth, created in the image and likeness of God. This is the dignity of America, the reason she exists, the condition for her survival; yes, the ultimate test of her greatness: to respect every human person, especially the weakest and most defenseless ones, those as yet unborn.

Mr. President, may God bless America and make her strong in her defense of human dignity and in her service to the Almighty.

The President. Your Holiness, Mrs. Bush and I are deeply honored to meet with you once again. Late in 1987—as you said, it was in Detroit, at the close of your second pastoral visit to our country, I had the honor, the privilege, of thanking you on behalf of my fellow citizens for the insightful message that you brought to our shores. And you inspired us, and you challenged us. And this evening, during our private discussion, I've benefited once again from your wise counsel.

When I became President, I did say in my inaugural speech that a new breeze is blowing. And there is no doubt we are witness to dynamic changes in much of the world, changes that move toward greater freedom and basic human rights. In your New Year's greeting to the Vatican diplomatic corps, representing over 100 nations, you stressed the fundamental importance of religious freedom. And when people are free to worship God, they prepare a ground in which a commitment to all human rights can grow strong. Religious freedom is a right that governments must protect, not threaten.

The United States also shares the Holy See's concern for world peace. While we're still far from realizing the biblical injunction to turn our swords into plowshares, we've made progress in reducing armaments and in decreasing the threat of war. And that progress must continue, and it will continue. Fortunately, in Europe our efforts to maintain peace have been successful. And as we look around the world, we're pleased to see that tensions have been reduced in parts of southern Africa and Asia. We're working hard to help bring peace and greater freedom to Central America.

We've heard your eloquent appeals for an end to the violence in Lebanon. And my heart, too, aches for the people of that once peaceful land. And I can assure you that we will continue to do everything we can to help bring peace and to help restore Lebanon's unity, sovereignty, and territorial integrity, with the disbanding of militias and the withdrawal of all foreign forces.

Your Holiness has said several times that peace is more than an absence of war, and we agree. History teaches us that there is no true, lasting peace until human rights are recognized and people are free to develop their full potential. Your Holiness, this spring, in the land of your birth, a historic roundtable agreement was reached which opened the paths to greater freedom and opportunity. That accord is a tribute to the spirit of the Polish people, as well as to the determination of the Polish Church and, indeed, the Holy See. And just this month, due in large part to your leadership, the Church was legalized in Poland. This triumph represents the first full normalization of church-state relations in any Communist state, and it is a tribute to your enduring commitment to freedom.

As you know, I recently announced a package of financial measures that signal our active engagement in encouraging economic and political reform in Poland and elsewhere in Eastern Europe. We hope these programs will help the Polish people achieve the economic recovery and political participation they so rightly deserve.

Your Holiness, I am grateful for this opportunity to visit with you, to share in your wisdom. And I assure you of our intent to work ever more fervently for peace, justice, and freedom throughout the world. On behalf of all of us, thank you very much.

Note: His Holiness Pope John Paul II spoke at 7:10 p.m. in the Papal Library.

Remarks to Students at the American Seminary in Vatican City
May 27, 1989

What a neat welcome, thank you. [*Applause*] I've got to go to supper, come on here. [*Applause*] What a wonderful welcome. You remember the old American expression, often said of a group or an individual, "He hasn't got a prayer." Well—[*laughter*]—I am delighted to meet an audience about whom that will never be said. [*Laughter*] What a wonderful, wonderful welcome!

I'll just say a couple of things. Barbara and I want to thank you for this warm welcome, this touch of America to our European tour—and we're touched. When I heard from my friend, Frank Shakespeare, our Ambassador, how many would be here, I was surprised and touched.

As you know, I've just had an audience with His Holiness Pope John Paul II. He was so generous with his time and so generous with his thinking and imparted to me once again his views on world peace and his views on how perhaps we can all work together to help in that regard. He has devoted his whole life to serving God, and the things that we focused on in this meeting were broad questions of peace and freedom and justice as they apply, or might be applied, all around the world. So, it's a talk that I'll long remember. I leave once again inspired by his moral and spiritual leadership, and I know that that same leadership inspires everyone here—all of you, certainly—as well as has your faith, I might say, in an Almighty through whom all things are possible.

I wish you well. I'd like—lest you don't recognize him—to introduce not all of my colleagues but our distinguished Secretary of State, my friend Jim Baker over here. Next to him is my Chief of Staff, Governor John Sununu. And then next to him is General Brent Scowcroft, my national security adviser. I'm sure most of you recognize our Ambassador to the Vatican, Frank Shakespeare, and his daughter with him.

Bless you all. Thank you for this warm, warm welcome.

[*At this point, the seminarians spontaneously sang "God Bless America."*]

Bless you all, thank you for this warm, warm welcome. And it makes me determined to leave here, inspired as I am, redouble our efforts in every way possible for world peace, for strength, for the family, for freedom of religion, and all the things that everybody here believes in. Thank you for such a warm, cordial welcome. I can't tell you how good it makes me feel.

Note: The President spoke at 7:18 p.m. in the Sala Clementina at the Vatican.

Toast at a Dinner Hosted by Prime Minister Ciriaco De Mita in Rome
May 27, 1989

Mr. Prime Minister and leaders of the legislative branch, distinguished guests, it's a very great honor for me to be welcomed in such a warm and generous way by the

Italian people and their government. You know, Barbara and I have been to this marvelous country, this beautiful country, many times; and as always, we've been received with kindness and generosity. This trip is my first visit to Europe as President of the United States. And I think of no place that is better to begin than right here in Italy and to be right here in Rome.

Mr. Prime Minister, it is traditional when visiting Italy for American leaders to note the millions of our citizens who claim an Italian background, so I will brag—now 12 million and rising. And among the many Italian-Americans, there are Fiorello La Guardia—some old enough to remember—Joe DiMaggio in sports; Tony Fauci, now at the National Institutes of Health; and of course, our Supreme Court Justice Antonin Scalia. And Italian-Americans are one link that binds the United States and Italy—but only one. For we are united by our belief in individual liberty, human dignity, and the rule of law, and by the shared values of family, faith, and work.

We also admire your country's record of success in combating terrorism and organized crime. And I'm especially grateful for your help in stopping the scourge of narcotics, which torments both our nations. We're going to continue our intense cooperative efforts to fight terrorism and narcotics and to protect air travelers. And just as this cooperative effort brings our peoples even closer together and helps to strengthen our already excellent bilateral relations, so, too, will the action that I'm pleased to announce tonight.

After studying ways to relax U.S. visa requirements, we will soon begin a pilot program to end these requirements for your citizens. In the future, Italians who wish to visit our country, whether as tourists or on business, will no longer need to apply for visas; and we look forward to that day.

But along with our domestic initiatives, I think, too, of the strong military ties between our two countries and within the Atlantic alliance, the most enduring alliance in the history of man. And to protect that alliance and the shared commitment to freedom which underlies it is our continuing mission not merely as Americans or Italians but as believers in democracy. Of this, I am certain: We will do our part, and I know Italy will do its part.

For when our common security has been in danger, you have stood ready to defend the alliance. And when the need arose for NATO to relocate that 401st Tactical Fighter Wing within southern Europe, Italy welcomed it. And when strategic interests were at risk in the Persian Gulf and in Lebanon, Italy sent ships and peacekeeping forces. And when NATO confronted widespread Soviet deployment of these multiple-warhead SS–20 missiles, Italy stood tall in response. And at times when Europe seemed ready to turn inward, you have reinforced our transatlantic ties. And for that, Mr. Prime Minister, Italy has our gratitude and our profound respect. So, together, let us reaffirm the ties that bind us, and let's continue to build peace and the commonwealth of free nations not for ourselves but also for our children—the kind of peace and freedom which lasts.

And in that spirit, Mr. Prime Minister, I ask all of our guests tonight to rise and raise their glasses. To Italian-American friendship, our transatlantic heritage, and to the Western alliance and the shared values of freedom and democracy that have made that alliance strong, and to your health, Mr. Prime Minister, and the peace and prosperity of your great country.

Note: The President spoke at 9:20 p.m. in the dining room at Villa Madama.

White House Fact Sheet on the Nonimmigrant Visa Waiver Pilot Program

May 27, 1989

The Nonimmigrant Visa Waiver Pilot Program (NVWPP) is a 3-year test program mandated by law (section 313 of the Immigration Reform and Control Act of 1986) to waive, under certain conditions, temporary visitor visas. The administration must report back to Congress on the pilot program in the summer of 1990.

The countries are selected by the Secretary of State and the Attorney General. They are countries with the highest volume of nonimmigrant visa issuance and which offer reciprocal treatment of American citizen travelers. The purpose of the program is to promote tourism and reduce visa processing costs.

The program was instituted in the United Kingdom and Japan in 1988. Italy is the third country to qualify for the program. Under the program, nationals of these countries, during the duration of the pilot program, will not be required to obtain visas to visit the United States for up to 90 days for tourism and business.

We will work with the countries that participate in the program to ensure the safety of air travelers and to thwart terrorism and drug trafficking.

Remarks at a Memorial Day Ceremony in Nettuno, Italy

May 28, 1989

Mr. Prime Minister, thank you for honoring us today at this service. We gather today to mark Memorial Day in America, to honor the thousands of young men and women buried here and elsewhere who put themselves in harm's way so that others might live in freedom.

As we gather, it's dawn in America, Memorial Day weekend, the first days of summer. And soon, the screen doors will slam; parks are going to sound with the crack of the baseball bat; children's voices will rise in the summer breeze pungent with the scent of barbecue smoke. And the rites of summer are marked by American tradition. As morning comes to Indianapolis, the smells of coffee and gasoline will mingle in the heat rising off that sun-baked raceway. And further west, there's going to be another race, as the blast of a ship's whistle sends the riverboats *Huck Finn* and *Tom Sawyer* steaming down the Mississippi off the docks of St. Louis.

Memorial Day weekend—by the time today's ceremony concludes, the first rays of sunlight will streak across the Potomac, flashing first atop the monument to the founder of our Republic, then reaching down to touch the silent rows of white markers on the green Virginia hillside that is Arlington Cemetery. And soon the gathering light will reveal a lone figure, a man in uniform, standing guard at the Tomb of the Unknown Soldier, a round-the-clock vigil unbroken in more than 50 years. Another moment and the dawn will flood the park that lays beneath the gaze of Lincoln, embracing the candles that flicker each night along the walls of the Vietnam Memorial. And soon the plaintive sound of taps will rise in the wind in cities and hamlets all across America, heard by veterans of four wars as they gather to salute the fallen. In town after town, the ritual at sunrise will be the same, as first the flag is raised, then slowly lowered to half-mast.

The thoughts of some will turn eastward toward the Sun, across the ocean, across four decades, to this grassy plain above the shores of the Mediterranean, where 45 years ago, the U.S. 3d Infantry Division, among the most decorated in World War II, led the bloody advance toward the liberation of Rome. And on that Memorial Day weekend, 1944, I wasn't yet 20 years old, flying torpedo bombers off the U.S.S. *San Jacinto* on the other side of the world, as she headed from Wake Island to Saipan. But like Americans everywhere, the men aboard our ship had eagerly followed the news of the Italian campaign.

And during 4 long months of 1944, the combatants of World War II were locked near Nettuno in a deadly embrace. But before the week was out, the face of the world's greatest conflict would be changed and the fate of the enemy sealed. On June 4th, American troops entered Rome, the streets lined by cheering Italians, and by midnight General Mark Clark's 5th Army stood on the banks of the Tiber. And the word went out to a waiting America: For the first time since the landings at Salerno in September of 1943, the enemy was in full retreat. It was the beginning of the end. And 2 days later a new front opened with D-day, the Normandy landing.

The fight to liberate Italy was as fierce and heroic as any seen in the war. The dangers to each adversary—the danger was such that the outcome of the war itself seemed to hang at that moment on the valor and vigor of each man who struggled near the water's edge. One such soldier was Sergeant Sylvester Antolak, an Ohio farmboy, the youngest son of Polish immigrants. On a drizzly morning some 45 years ago this week, he led Sergeant Audie Murphy and others in a bold charge through the rain and the ruin near Cisterna, one man against a machinegun nest that blocked the road to Rome. And three times he was cut down by fire; three times he got back up, tucking his gun under his shattered arm. And by the time he disabled the gunners, 10 enemy soldiers surrendered to this man whom their bullets could not stop.

Sergeant Antolak fell near Cisterna that same day. He rests here beneath the pines of Nettuno with nearly 8,000 soldiers, his grave one of two marked with our Congressional Medal of Honor. Joined by the names of another 3,000 missing etched in the white marble of the chapel, they come from every American State from Texas to Maine, Alaska to Florida, New York to California. And these white crosses and Stars of David ring the world—across the battlefields of Europe and the jungles of Asia, the deserts of North Africa and the hillsides of our homeland—in silent tribute to America's battles for freedom in this century.

It was with the memory of the sacrifices of the American, British, and French soldiers who fell during the campaign to liberate Italy and the sacrifices of millions of other Europeans and Americans in the cause of freedom fresh in mind that NATO was created after the war.

As I reflect on this scene and anticipate the dynamic and forward-looking Europe of the 1990's, I think of generations of young people on both sides of the Atlantic who have grown up in peace and prosperity. With no experience in the horror and destruction of war, it might be difficult for them to understand why we need to keep a strong military deterrent to prevent war, and to preserve freedom and democracy. The answer is here, among the quiet of the graves.

The cost of maintaining freedom is brought home to us all when tragedy strikes, as it did last month aboard the U.S.S. *Iowa*. The loss of those fine sailors, the tears of their families and the loved ones, remind all of us of the risk and sacrifice in human terms that security sometimes demands. And let me add how impressive were the many expressions of sympathy that I received from leaders around the world, and particularly by the eloquent words of Italy's distinguished President, President Cossiga, as he shared the sorrow of our loss.

Sergeant Antolak also understood the cost of freedom. Today in his hometown of St. Clairsville, Ohio, population 6,000, the townspeople will gather by the local courthouse to dedicate a white granite memorial to the county's Medal of Honor winners. George and Stanley Antolak will be there to remember their brother—their hero and ours. It's the kind of scene that will be repeated today and tomorrow in parks and churchyards all across America.

A bit north of Mark Twain's Hannibal, just up the Mississippi from that steamboat race I mentioned, lies the town of Quincy, Illinois. When World War II came, Quincy offered up her sons in service. Three brothers: Donald, Preston, and William Kaspervik joined the Army Air Corps. And their story is a common one, and yet uncommon in the way of all those who answered the call to serve.

The first brother, Donald, was killed when the two bombers collided on maneuvers in New Mexico, and their mother grieved. Preston, the second brother, died just south of here in Sicily shortly after Patton's successful invasion. And their mother was overcome once again. And 10 days later, the third brother, William, went down during a dangerous bombing mission over the mountains of central Italy. On the day of his death, his mother received a letter from him urging her not to worry. When the third telegram came, she couldn't bring herself to go to the door. William and Preston Kaspervik are buried here in soil that they helped free. Brothers in life, brothers in arms, brothers in eternity.

Their mother died 20 years ago, but back home in Quincy, the extraordinary sacrifice of this ordinary American family is still remembered. And today, as they do every year, the VFW and the American Legion will honor Quincy's fallen natives with a hometown parade down Main Street, high above the banks of the Mississippi.

As we gather today, it is dawn in America, Memorial Day weekend. And as the Sun rises and the summer begins, the images both here and at home are of countries that are prosperous and secure, countries confident of their place in the world and aware of the responsibility that comes with that place. Soon that lone soldier at Arlington will resume his paces, 21 steps in each direction, the changing of the guard precisely on the half hour. And at Gettysburg, the schoolchildren will scatter flowers on other unknown graves, blue and gray, side-by-side, Americans.

On Memorial Day, we give thanks for the blessings of freedom and peace and for the generations of Americans who have won them for us. We also pray for the same strength and moral reserve demonstrated by these veterans, as well as for the true and lasting peace found in a world where liberty and justice prevail.

And with that prayer, I ask that you join in your own silent prayers as we place a wreath to commemorate the sacrifice of those buried here at Nettuno and the sacrifice of all men and women who have given their lives for freedom. Thank you very much.

Note: The President spoke at 10:41 a.m. at the Sicily-Rome American Cemetery.

Remarks to the American Embassy Employees and Their Families in Rome

May 28, 1989

Thank you, Mr. Secretary, and thank all of you for that warm Memorial Day weekend welcome. First, to Ambassador Rabb and Ruth, let me simply add our profound thanks for a job well done. I'll tell you, you stay around Max for about 24 hours, and that exhausting energy level is something. And it all has been steered into improving relations—this energy of his—improving relations between Italy and the United States.

And yesterday, when I met with the Italian leaders, I told them I don't believe this bilateral relationship has ever been stronger. And I think a large bit of the credit for that goes to our able Ambassador and his wife. And then I'd have to add to every single one of you that works here in the United States Embassy: Thank you for a job superbly done!

I will say just a word about our new Ambassador, Pete Secchia, a good friend of both the Secretary's and mine. He'll do a good job—energetic. He knows what he doesn't know. He knows he's going to have to learn a lot from the staff here, but you're going to like him, and I'm convinced the

Italians will, as well. I believe the Senate will act promptly on that nomination. And he and his Joan—that Jim Baker and I know very well—will be along; but what remarkably big shoes they have to fill.

Thanks, in large measure, to your efforts—I agree with Max—this visit has gone well. I saw Barbara Watson, who is the admin officer of the United States Embassy. And I looked at her very carefully before I went over and shook hands. And I wanted to see if she looked in a high state of irritation—[*laughter*]—or if she looked perfectly normal. And I would say this—I saw her—it wasn't that she looked on edge at all. [*Laughter*] But I told her that we would leave on time, and she smiled from ear to ear and was very gracious. [*Laughter*] And I say all that because I have been on the receiving end—when I served in China—the receiving end of a visit from a President of the United States, and I know what it's like: a pluperfect pain. [*Laughter*]

No, she was very pleasant about it. And it gives me the occasion to thank all of you—the admin and the security and the political side of the Embassy and commercial or military, whatever—for the superb cooperation. Our people tell me they've never seen a more cooperative effort, and I think it has shown through in the way this visit has gone. And I might say, parenthetically, my thanks to the members of the U.S. Navy for providing us that wonderful music here on this very celebratory day.

Now, we've had good talks here—substantive talks with President Cossiga and then, of course, with the Prime Minister, the Foreign Minister. We had a gala evening last night and then—I agree with the objective side of what Max said about the ceremony at Nettuno. Oh, I'm sure most of you all have been there. And if you haven't, you've got to see it. You've got to see that tribute to those who gave their lives fighting for our country, fighting for freedom. It was very, very moving for Barbara and me. And I expect any American who goes and takes a look at that beautiful cemetery will have that with them for the rest of their lives. And so, I want to thank those who handle that end of our visit, those who serve to keep up that beautiful memorial to our fallen brothers.

I know, as I say, that this has been a complicated event. And now, as you know, we go on from here to NATO, to the meeting there that is very, very important for the alliance. I happen to believe this alliance has never been stronger. And I salute my immediate predecessor, President Reagan, for his role in guaranteeing the strength of the alliance.

So, we go there in a time of great optimism, a time when our values, worldwide, are winning—the values of freedom and democracy and all the things that we believe in and things these kids learn about in school every single day and get from their families. So, it's an optimistic time for the alliance. And it's a great time for the United States of America.

I look forward to that part of it. But there was something more than symbolic about Italy being my first stop, because I think it signals to the Italian people how important we view not only their participation in NATO and their willingness to undertake complicated NATO assignments but the strength of our bilateral relationship that so many of you have worked many years to encourage and to strengthen. So, I'm grateful again for that. And please make no mistake: When we chose Italy, we did it very, very carefully. And we came here to symbolize exactly this: the strength of the friendship between our two peoples.

Now, thank you all very much. What I really want to do—and I don't know that we can talk these kids into it—but what I really want to do is see if we can get the kids—and to be a kid, you've got to be—[*laughter*]—you guys are out—you've got to be, what, about 15, to come so we can have a group picture taken up here. And if anybody feels offended, we've got to do that. But in the meantime, let me end this way—because this is a marvelous Memorial Day weekend—and let me simply say thank you, and God bless the United States of America. Thank you all very, very much.

Note: The President spoke at 2:30 p.m. at the U.S. Ambassador's residence. He was introduced by Secretary of State James A. Baker III. In his opening remarks, the President referred to Ambassador Maxwell M.

Rabb, Mrs. Ruth Rabb, and Ambassador-designate Peter F. Secchia. Following his remarks, the President traveled to Brussels.

Remarks Upon Arrival at the North Atlantic Treaty Organization Summit Meeting in Brussels
May 28, 1989

Mr. Prime Minister, it is really a pleasure to be back once again in Brussels. And I'm especially pleased that my first visit as President of the United States comes as the nations of NATO celebrate 40 years of alliance and the longest period of peace and freedom that Europe has known in the modern age.

Americans and Belgians share the memories of war and hard-won peace in this century. Flanders, the battle of Ardennes, Bastogne—those names are part of our history as well as your own, part of our shared heritage of freedom and the sacrifices it requires. Belgium, no stranger to conquest and division, recognized from the first the importance of alliance in the postwar world. And today, as permanent home to NATO and the European Community, Brussels stands at the center of a Europe free, at peace, and prosperous as never before, a Europe that is steadily moving toward the single market and unprecedented political and economic opportunities. In Brussels, the signs of this European renaissance are everywhere.

Belgium has been a good friend and a valued ally, one that has always acted with alliance interests in mind. Early in this decade, Belgium was one of five NATO nations that made the difficult decision to base INF systems on its own soil. And those deployments gave us the leverage that we needed to negotiate the first-ever nuclear arms reduction treaty; indeed, one that banned an entire generation of nuclear weapons. That's the kind of courageous and realistic approach that explains NATO's success. NATO is at once ready to ensure the common defense and to reduce arms and seek to diminish tensions with the East.

As I've said a number of times, we seek to move to a policy beyond containment. We want to see an end to the division of Europe, and we want to see it ended on the basis of Western values. We will join Western European nations in encouraging the process of change in the Soviet Union, pointing to the day when the Soviet Union will be welcomed as a constructive participant in the community of free nations.

I'm looking forward to important discussions with the King of the Belgians, King Baudouin, and the NATO heads of government. I look forward, as well, to my meeting with Prime Minister Martens, my friend, my discussions also with Mr. Delors of the European Community, and Secretary-General Woerner at NATO.

The future of NATO depends on the alliance's ability to deal with our enduring security concerns and our evolving economic relationship. We look to Belgium to continue to play its important role in our close and cooperative transatlantic partnership. I am delighted to be back, and thank you, Mr. Prime Minister, for this warm welcome.

Note: The President spoke at 6:07 p.m. on the tarmac at Brussels International Airport. In his remarks, he referred to Jacques Delors, President of the European Communities Commission.

Remarks Announcing a Conventional Arms Control Initiative and a Question-and-Answer Session With Reporters in Brussels
May 29, 1989

The President. I'll have a brief statement before taking some questions. This morning I met with the other NATO leaders and shared with them my views on the role of the North Atlantic alliance in a changing Europe. NATO, we all agree, is one of the great success stories, and it's guaranteed the peace in Europe, provided a shield for 40 years for freedom and prosperity. And now our alliance faces new challenges at a time of historic transition as we seek to overcome the division of Europe.

I call it "beyond containment," and today I'm proposing a major initiative to help move us toward that momentous objective. If it were accepted, it would be a revolutionary conventional arms control agreement. I believe the alliance should act decisively now to take advantage of this extraordinary opportunity, and I urge that NATO adopt a 4-point proposal to bring the Vienna negotiations to a speedy conclusion.

First, lock in Eastern acceptance of the proposed Western ceilings on each side's holdings of tanks and armored troop carriers. Additionally, we would seek agreement on a similar ceiling for artillery, provided there's some definitional questions that have to be resolved there. But all of the equipment reduced would be destroyed.

We would then, number two, expand our current NATO proposal so that each side would reduce to 15 percent below current NATO levels in two additional categories: Attack and assault, or transport helicopters and all land-based combat aircraft. All of the equipment reduced would be destroyed.

And third, propose a 20-percent cut in combat manpower in United States-stationed forces and a resulting ceiling in U.S. and Soviet ground and air forces stationed outside of national territory in the Atlantic-to-the-Urals zone at approximately 275,000 each. This manpower ceiling will require the Soviets to reduce their forces in Eastern Europe by about 325,000 people. Withdrawn soldiers and airmen on both sides would be demobilized.

And then, fourthly, accelerate the timetable for reaching a CFE [conventional armed forces in Europe] agreement along these lines and implementing the required reductions. I believe that it should be possible to reach such agreement in 6 months or maybe a year and to accomplish the reductions by 1992 or 1993.

Now, if the Soviet Union accepts this fair offer, the results would dramatically increase stability on the Continent and transform the military map of Europe. We can and must begin now to set out a new vision for Europe at the end of this century. This is a noble mission that I believe the alliance should be ready to undertake. And I have no doubt that we are up to the task.

And incidentally, in addition to these arms control proposals, I mentioned in there that we are prepared to change our no-exceptions policy on trade. And I called again for a ban on chemical weapons. And I would reiterate my support for our open-skies proposal, and in the meeting it was discussed by the Prime Minister of Canada.

Helen [Helen Thomas, United Press International]?

Q. Mr. President, does this revolutionary plan signal the end of the Cold War?

The President. Well, I don't know what it signals, except it signals a willingness on our part to really put Mr. Gorbachev to the test now. And so, I don't like to dwell in antiquated history. But I do like to get the idea that we are out front as an alliance—because this has broad alliance support—in challenging Mr. Gorbachev to move forward now more quickly on the most destabilizing part of the military balance, and that is on conventional forces.

Q. Well, were you pressured by him and the allies?

The President. No, I think I said when I first came in we were going to take our time and we were going to study and we're going to think it out, and we did exactly that. And you know and I know that some voices were raised in Congress that we were going too slow. But we knew exactly what we were doing all along, and we've now said: "This is what we suggest, and this is the way we plan to lead the alliance and lead the free world."

Q. Mr. President, why is it possible to make such drastic cuts in conventional weapons and not move on nuclear aircraft—nuclear ground-based short-range missiles, which seems to disturb the Germans and really a majority of the alliance?

The President. Because the conventional forces, the existing imbalance, is so great that that is the most urgent problem and the most destabilizing.

Q. Following up on that question: If the Soviets accept this proposal, would that enable us to talk about reducing or eliminating short-range forces?

The President. After agreement was reached and after there was some implementation, yes. We are not unwilling to negotiate on SNF.

Q. What was the reaction of the NATO leaders this morning when you told them? Did you consult with all the allies before you put it on the table?

The President. We had widespread—and I would think everyone was consulted. I know we had widespread consultation and——

Secretary Baker. The answer is yes.

The President. The answer is yes to all NATO members, and—it's been done over the last few days.

Q. What did they tell you about it? Why did they find it appealing?

The President. Well, I'll leave it to them to wax euphoric. But I'll tell you, I was very, very pleased with the response in the meeting just concluded.

Q. Mr. President, can you ever see a time when you might not have nuclear forces in Europe?

The President. No.

Q. Never?

Q. Mr. President, is there any indication——

The President. We need the concept of flexible response, and I can't in the foreseeable future see us getting away from that.

Q. Is there any indication that this disagreement with the West Germans over the SNF issue will be resolved here at the NATO summit?

The President. Well, I'm not really at liberty to go into too much on that, because right now we put together a working group to try to work out some resolution. But you see, this bold proposal—in terms of conventional forces—should give those who have had difficulty with our position on SNF a chance to regroup and rethink and give them a little leeway that they haven't had heretofore.

Q. Do you expect early negotiation by the Secretary of State with Mr. Shevardnadze or Mr. Gorbachev on this proposal, Mr. President?

The President. The sooner the better.

Q. There's been some criticism in Congress, as you mentioned, about that you have been too cautious in approaching the Soviet Union. Was that sentiment expressed today by anyone, and how did they—was there any mention of how the West should respond to Gorbachev?

The President. No, it wasn't mentioned by anyone in there. And generally, when it was—your question about how to respond to Gorbachev—without putting words into the mouths of various participants, there was enthusiastic endorsement. Now, I can't speak for everybody, but for those who have intervened so far.

Q. Mr. Bush, have you "costed out" this proposal? And did the budgetary constraints play any part in your decision to try to——

The President. No, the budgetary constraints didn't, and I haven't seen a full cost analysis. Some of this would be quite expensive for us, short-run—the pulling people out. But we did check militarily; I did not want to propose something that was militarily unsound. And our top military people are for this. Our SACEUR Commander [General John Galvin, Supreme Allied Commander, Europe], who wears many hats, who represents many countries, obviously, is for this. And so, we checked it in that sense.

Q. Mr. President, in some of your early policy speeches, you expressed deep skepticism about what was going on in the Soviet Union. You said this new relationship cannot be bestowed; it must be earned.

Your Secretary of Defense [Cheney] said he felt Gorbachev would fail. What prompted change in your thinking to make a proposal like this?

The President. This is to put it to the test. This is to say: Here we go, we're out there now with a proposal that the United States puts forward and that has widespread alliance support. Now test it. How serious are you? Are you—really want to reduce the imbalances that exist in all these categories, or do we want rhetoric? And so, what we're saying—we're not changing; I'm not changing my mind. I've said I want to see *perestroika* succeed. I said I want to see us move forward in arms reductions. Indeed, we've set a date for the resumption of the START [strategic arms reduction] talks—but eyes wide open. And here we go now, on the offense with a proposal that is bold and tests whether the Soviet Union will move towards balance, or whether they insist on retaining an unacceptable conventional force imbalance.

I've got time for—is this a followup?

Soviet Political and Economic Reforms

Q. This is a followup. On the subject of Mr. Gorbachev, do you believe he will fail?

The President. I want to see him succeed—and I've said that, and I'll repeat it here. I'm not making predictions as to what's going to happen inside the Soviet Union. Those are hard tea leaves to read. But I would like to see him succeed. He seems stronger now than he has been earlier on; but he faces enormous problems. And I hope he looks at this proposal as a way to help solve some of those enormous problems. It gets to the question of finance to maintain this number of troops outside of his country.

Conventional Arms Control Initiative

Q. Mr. President, does this four-point proposal represent your conditions that the Soviets must accept before you will open talks on the short-range missiles?

The President. Well, as I said earlier, we've got to have a reduction in conventional forces and then some implementation of that proposal.

Q. Mr. President, you described this as a proposal to the other allies. Do you expect it's going to be adopted as a formal alliance position at the end of this meeting, and then will you put it on the table at CFE very soon?

The President. I can't answer procedurally. I'd like to see it adopted, but I don't know that the people have had enough time to really—do you know what's planned on that, Al [Alton G. Keel, Jr., Ambassador to NATO]?

Ambassador Keel. I think, clearly, the alliance will adopt it, Mr. President, in terms of the concept, but then will assign it to the proper mechanism here at NATO to finish the details on it.

Q. Why actually destroy the equipment and demobilize the troops?

The President. Well, because then we get verified—we hope—verified reductions that last. You can't just juggle around the players on the chessboard.

Q. Mr. President, following Helen's earlier question, there's been a lot of talk at the White House recently about public relations gambits. Do you believe that this initiative by the United States puts Mr. Gorbachev on the defensive, and does it in any way put the United States back on the top of any public relations war that might be going on?

The President. Well, one, we've eschewed getting involved in a public relations battle. This is too serious a business. Alliance security is too serious; the safety and security of American forces, for which I have direct responsibility as Commander in Chief, is too serious to be jeopardized by feeling we always have to be out front on some public relations gambit. And I think we all know that in certain quarters in the United States, my administration has taken a little bit of a hammering for not engaging in the public relations battle.

But what we've been doing is formulating what I think is a very prudent plan, and now that plan is out there on the table. So, I really can't comment on the public relations aspect. What I'm interested in is the security aspect and the strength of the alliance and then the future—the ability of the alliance to move beyond containment.

Q. A long-term benefit of this proposal would obviously be a decrease in defense spending. Now, how much of this proposal was driven by budget considerations?

The President. Well, I thought I answered that, but let me try again to be clearer: None. What drove the proposal was the military and alliance considerations. And I would agree that if this proposal is fully implemented—longer-run, as you put it—it would result in less spending, particularly if these troops and weapons are demobilized, as we say.

I've got time for one more and then I've got to go to a luncheon.

Q. Mr. President, just to be clear on one point, what you're proposing is an agreement with the Warsaw Pact, not anything that you will do unilaterally; that you won't take any of these steps yourselves outside an overall agreement with the——

The President. This is a NATO proposal, and it would be negotiated with the Pact. But it means that—obviously, when you're dealing with the Pact—that the Soviet Union is going to have to be the key player. And this part of the proposal, as it relates to U.S. troops, clearly is one where both the Soviet General Secretary and I have to have agreement; but I want to keep the negotiations and the initiatives inside of the alliance.

We came over here to say the alliance has worked. It's kept the peace for 40 years, and we want to continue to keep it strong. And that's one reason I am very pleased with the alliance response to our proposal. They don't see it as soloing off there, taking care of U.S. interest; they see it as in the interest of the alliance. And again, I believe I speak—I believe—well, I know most of the people there feel that way, and I hope all of them.

This is the last one, and then I'm going in peace.

Q. A tick-tock question: When did you make the final decision to accept this idea? How did it evolve?

The President. Twelve days ago.

Summit With President Gorbachev

Q. One last one, sir. Do you have any interest in discussing this with Mr. Gorbachev at a summit meeting? Do you have any interest or intention of discussing this proposal or other arms proposals with Mr. Gorbachev at a summit meeting?

The President. When I have a summit meeting with Mr. Gorbachev, I expect we'll discuss a wide array of subjects.

Q. Do you anticipate that this year?

The President. When that happens, I will have wide, far-flung discussions; and no date has been set for that.

Q. Why 12 days ago?

Q. Is it likely to be speeded up, though, Mr. President, because of this proposal?

The President. Hadn't thought of it, Jack [Jack Nelson, Los Angeles Times], in this connection, but I would not rule that out. But we'll see how it's digested there in Moscow—I hope favorably.

Q. Isn't it time for a summit now, sir, now that you've laid this out?

The President. Baker's got some more work to do.

Note: The President spoke at 12:24 p.m. in the United States Mission Annex at NATO Headquarters.

Declaration of the Heads of State and Government Participating in the Meeting of the North Atlantic Council in Brussels
May 30, 1989

I

NATO's 40 Years of Success

1. As our Alliance celebrates its 40th Anniversary, we measure its achievements with pride. Founded in troubled times to safeguard our security, it has withstood the test of four decades, and has allowed our countries to enjoy in freedom one of the longest periods of peace and prosperity in their history. The Alliance has been a fun-

damental element of stability and cooperation. These are the fruits of a partnership based on enduring common values and interests, and on unity of purpose.

2. Our meeting takes place at a juncture of unprecedented change and opportunities. This is a time to look ahead, to chart the course of our Alliance and to set our agenda for the future.

A Time of Change

3. In our rapidly changing world, where ideas transcend borders ever more easily, the strength and accomplishments of democracy and freedom are increasingly apparent. The inherent inability of oppressive systems to fulfill the aspirations of their citizens has become equally evident.

4. In the Soviet Union, important changes are underway. We welcome the current reforms that have already led to greater openness, improved respect for human rights, active participation of the individual, and new attitudes in foreign policy. But much remains to be done. We still look forward to the full implementation of the announced change in priorities in the allocation of economic resources from the military to the civilian sector. If sustained, the reforms will strengthen prospects for fundamental improvements in East-West relations.

5. We also welcome the marked progress in some countries of Eastern Europe towards establishing more democratic institutions, freer elections and greater political pluralism and economic choice. However, we deplore the fact that certain Eastern European governments have chosen to ignore this reforming trend and continue all too frequently to violate human rights and basic freedoms.

Shaping the Future

6. Our vision of a just, humane and democratic world has always underpinned the policies of this Alliance. The changes that are now taking place are bringing us closer to the realization of this vision.

7. We want to overcome the painful division of Europe, which we have never accepted. We want to move beyond the postwar period. Based on today's momentum of increased cooperation and tomorrow's common challenges, we seek to shape a new political order of peace in Europe. We will work as Allies to seize all opportunities to achieve this goal. But ultimate success does not depend on us alone.

Our guiding principles in the pursuit of this course will be the policies of the Harmel Report in their two complementary and mutually reinforcing approaches: adequate military strength and political solidarity and, on that basis, the search for constructive dialogue and cooperation, including arms control, as a means of bringing about a just and lasting peaceful order in Europe.

8. The Alliance's long-term objectives are:

—to ensure that wars and intimidation of any kind in Europe and North America are prevented, and that military aggression is an option which no government could rationally contemplate or hope successfully to undertake, and by doing so to lay the foundations for a world where military forces exist solely to preserve the independence and territorial integrity of their countries, as has always been the case for the Allies;

—to establish a new pattern of relations between the countries of East and West, in which ideological and military antagonism will be replaced with cooperation, trust and peaceful competition; and in which human rights and political freedoms will be fully guaranteed and enjoyed by all individuals.

9. Within our larger responsibilities as Heads of State or Government, we are also committed

—to strive for an international community founded on the rule of law, where all nations join together to reduce world tensions, settle disputes peacefully, and search for solutions to those issues of universal concern, including poverty, social injustice and the environment, on which our common fate depends.

II

Maintaining our Defence

10. Peace must be worked for; it can never be taken for granted. The greatly improved East-West political climate offers

prospects for a stable and lasting peace, but experience teaches us that we must remain prepared. We can overlook neither the capabilities of the Warsaw Treaty countries for offensive military action, nor the potential hazards resulting from severe political strain and crisis.

11. A strong and united Alliance will remain fundamental not only for the security of our countries but also for our policy of supporting political change. It is the basis for further successful negotiations on arms control and on measures to strengthen mutual confidence through improved transparency and predictability. Military security and policies aimed at reducing tensions as well as resolving underlying political differences are not contradictory but complementary. Credible defence based on the principle of the indivisibility of security for all member countries will thus continue to be essential to our common endeavour.

12. For the foreseeable future, there is no alternative to the Alliance strategy for the prevention of war. This is a strategy of deterrence based upon an appropriate mix of adequate and effective nuclear and conventional forces which will continue to be kept up-to-date where necessary. We shall ensure the viability and credibility of these forces, while maintaining them at the lowest possible level consistent with our security requirements.

13. The presence of North American conventional and nuclear forces in Europe remains vital to the security of Europe just as Europe's security is vital to that of North America. Maintenance of this relationship requires that the Allies fulfill their essential commitments in support of the common defence. Each of our countries will accordingly assume its fair share of the risks, roles and responsibilities of the Atlantic partnership. Growing European political unity can lead to a reinforced European component of our common security effort and its efficiency. It will be essential to the success of these efforts to make the most effective use of resources made available for our security. To this end, we will seek to maximize the efficiency of our defence programmes and pursue solutions to issues in the area of economic and trade policies as they affect our defence. We will also continue to protect our technological capabilities by effective export controls on essential strategic goods.

Initiatives on Arms Control

14. Arms Control has always been an integral part of the Alliance's security policy and of its overall approach to East-West relations, firmly embedded in the broader political context in which we seek the improvement of those relations.

15. The Allies have consistently taken the lead in developing the conceptual foundations for arms control, identifying areas in which the negotiating partners share an interest in achieving a mutually satisfactory result while safeguarding the legitimate security interests of all.

16. Historic progress has been made in recent years, and we now see prospects for further substantial advances. In our determined effort to reduce the excessive weight of the military factor in the East-West relationship and increasingly to replace confrontation by co-operation, we can now exploit fully the potential of arms control as an agent of change.

17. We challenge the members of the Warsaw Treaty Organization to join us in accelerating efforts to sign and implement an agreement which will enhance security and stability in Europe by reducing conventional armed forces. To seize the unique opportunity at hand, we intend to present a proposal that will amplify and expand on the position we tabled at the opening of the CFE negotiations on 9th March. [France takes this opportunity to recall that, since the mandate for the Vienna negotiations excludes nuclear weapons, it retains complete freedom of judgment and decision regarding the resources contributing to the implementation of its independent nuclear deterrent strategy.] We will

—register agreement, based on the ceilings already proposed in Vienna, on tanks, armoured troop carriers and artillery pieces held by members of the two Alliances in Europe, with all of the withdrawn equipment to be destroyed. Ceilings on tanks and armoured troop carriers will be based on proposals already tabled in Vienna; definitional questions on artillery pieces remain to be resolved;

—expand our current proposal to include reductions by each side to equal ceilings at the level 15 per cent below current Alliance holdings of helicopters and of all land-based combat aircraft in the Atlantic-to-the-Urals zone, with all the withdrawn equipment to be destroyed;

—propose a 20 per cent cut in combat manpower in US stationed forces, and a resulting ceiling on US and Soviet ground and air force personnel stationed outside of national territory in the Atlantic-to-the-Urals zone at approximately 275,000. This ceiling would require the Soviet Union to reduce its forces in Eastern Europe by some 325,000. United States and Soviet forces withdrawn will be demobilized;

—seek such an agreement within six months to a year and accomplish the reductions by 1992 or 1993. Accordingly, we have directed the Alliance's High Level Task Force on conventional arms control to complete the further elaboration of this proposal, including its verification elements, so that it may be tabled at the beginning of the third round of the CFE negotiations, which opens on 7th September 1989.

18. We consider as an important initiative President Bush's call for an "open skies" regime intended to improve confidence among States through reconnaissance flights, and to contribute to the transparency of military activity, to arms control and to public awareness. It will be the subject of careful study and wide-ranging consultations.

19. Consistent with the principles and objectives set out in our Comprehensive Concept of Arms Control and Disarmament which we have adopted at this meeting, we will continue to use arms control as a means to enhance security and stability at the lowest possible level of armed forces, and to strengthen confidence by further appropriate measures. We have already demonstrated our commitment to these objectives: both by negotiations and by unilateral action, resulting since 1979 in reductions of over one-third of the nuclear holdings assigned to SACEUR in Europe.

Towards an Enhanced Partnership

20. As the Alliance enters its fifth decade we will meet the challenge of shaping our relationship in a way which corresponds to the new political and economic realities of the 1990s. As we do so, we recognize that the basis of our security and prosperity—and of our hopes for better East-West relations—is and will continue to be the close cohesion between the countries of Europe and of North America, bound together by their common values and democratic institutions as much as by their shared security interests.

21. Ours is a living and developing partnership. The strength and stability derived from our transatlantic bond provide a firm foundation for the achievement of our long-term vision, as well as of our goals for the immediate future. We recognize that our common tasks transcend the resources of either Europe or North America alone.

22. We welcome in this regard the evolution of an increasingly strong and coherent European identity, including in the security area. The process we are witnessing today provides an example of progressive integration, leaving centuries-old conflicts far behind. It opens the way to a more mature and balanced transatlantic partnership and constitutes one of the foundations of Europe's future structure.

23. To ensure the continuing success of our efforts we have agreed to

—strengthen our process of political consultation and, where appropriate, co-ordination, and have instructed the Council in Permanent Session to consider methods for its further improvement;

—expand the scope and intensity of our effort to ensure that our respective approaches to problems affecting our common security are complementary and mutually supportive;

—renew our support for our economically less-favoured partners and to reaffirm our goal of improving the present level of co-operation and assistance;

—continue to work in the appropriate fora for more commercial, monetary and technological co-operation, and to see to it that no obstacles impede such co-operation.

Overcoming the Division of Europe

24. Now, more than ever, our efforts to overcome the division of Europe must address its underlying political causes. Therefore all of us will continue to pursue a comprehensive approach encompassing the many dimensions of the East-West agenda. In keeping with our values, we place primary emphasis on basic freedoms for the people in Eastern Europe. These are also key elements for strengthening the stability and security of all states and for guaranteeing lasting peace on the continent.

25. The CSCE process encompasses our vision of a peaceful and more constructive relationship among all participating states. We intend to develop it further, in all its dimensions, and to make the fullest use of it.

We recognize progress in the implementation of CSCE commitments by some Eastern countries. But we call upon all of them to recognize and implement fully the commitments which all CSCE states have accepted. We will invoke the CSCE mechanisms—as most recently adopted in the Vienna Concluding Document—and the provisions of other international agreements, to bring all Eastern countries to:

—enshrine in law and practice the human rights and freedoms agreed in international covenants and in the CSCE documents, thus fostering progress towards the rule of law;

—tear down the walls that separate us physically and politically, simplify the crossing of borders, increase the number of crossing points and allow the free exchange of persons, information and ideas;

—ensure that people are not prevented by armed force from crossing the frontiers and boundaries which we share with Eastern countries, in exercise of their right to leave any country, including their own;

—respect in law and practice the right of all the people in each country to determine freely and periodically the nature of the government they wish to have;

—see to it that their peoples can decide through their elected authorities what form of relations they wish to have with other countries;

—grant the genuine economic freedoms that are linked inherently to the rights of the individual;

—develop transparency, especially in military matters, in pursuit of greater mutual understanding and reassurance.

26. The situation in and around Berlin is an essential element in East-West relations. The Alliance declares its commitment to a free and prosperous Berlin and to achieving improvements for the city especially through the Allied Berlin Initiative. The Wall dividing the city is an unacceptable symbol of the division of Europe. We seek a state of peace in Europe in which the German people regains its unity through free self-determination.

Our Design for Co-operation

27. We, for our part, have today reaffirmed that the Alliance must and will reintensify its own efforts to overcome the division of Europe and to explore all available avenues of co-operation and dialogue. We support the opening of Eastern societies and encourage reforms that aim at positive political, economic and human rights developments. Tangible steps towards genuine political and economic reform improve possibilities for broad co-operation, while a continuing denial of basic freedoms cannot but have a negative effect. Our approach recognizes that each country is unique and must be treated on its own merits. We also recognize that it is essentially incumbent upon the countries of the East to solve their problems by reforms from within. But we can also play a constructive role within the framework of our Alliance as well as in our respective bilateral relations and in international organizations, as appropriate.

28. To that end, we have agreed the following joint agenda for the future:

—as opportunities develop, we will expand the scope of our contacts and co-operation to cover a broad range of issues which are important to both East and West. Our goal is a sustained effort geared to specific tasks which will help deepen openness and promote democracy within Eastern countries and thus contribute to the establishment of a more stable peace in Europe;

—we will pursue in particular expanded contacts beyond the realm of government among individuals in East and West. These contacts should include all segments of our societies, but in particular young people, who will carry the responsibility for continuing our common endeavour;

—we will seek expanded economic and trade relations with the Eastern countries on the basis of commercially sound terms, mutual interest and reciprocity. Such relations should also serve as incentives for real economic reform and thus ease the way for increased integration of Eastern countries into the international trading system;

—we intend to demonstrate through increased co-operation that democratic institutions and economic choice create the best possible conditions for economic and social progress. The development of such open systems will facilitate co-operation and, consequently, make its benefits more available;

—an important task of our co-operation will be to explore means to extend Western experience and know-how to Eastern countries in a manner which responds to and promotes positive change. Exchanges in technical and managerial fields, establishment of co-operative training programmes, expansion of educational, scientific and cultural exchanges all offer possibilities which have not yet been exhausted;

—equally important will be to integrate Eastern European countries more fully into efforts to meet the social, environmental and technological challenges of the modern world, where common interests should prevail. In accordance with our concern for global challenges, we will seek to engage Eastern countries in co-operative strategies in areas such as the environment, terrorism, and drugs. Eastern willingness to participate constructively in dealing with such challenges will help further co-operation in other areas as well;

—East-West understanding can be expanded only if our respective societies gain increased knowledge about one another and communicate effectively. To encourage an increase of Soviet and Eastern studies in universities of our countries and of corresponding studies in Eastern countries, we are prepared to establish a Fellowship/Scholarship programme to promote the study of our democratic institutions, with candidates being invited from Eastern as well as Western Europe and North America.

Global Challenges

29. Worldwide developments which affect our security interests are legitimate matters for consultation and, where appropriate, co-ordination among us. Our security is to be seen in a context broader than the protection from war alone.

30. Regional conflicts continue to be of major concern. The co-ordinated approach of Alliance members recently has helped toward settling some of the world's most dangerous and long-standing disputes. We hope that the Soviet Union will increasingly work with us in positive and practical steps towards diplomatic solutions to those conflicts that continue to preoccupy the international community.

31. We will seek to contain the newly emerging security threats and destabilizing consequences resulting from the uncontrolled spread and application of modern military technologies.

32. In the spirit of Article 2 of the Washington Treaty, we will increasingly need to address worldwide problems which have a bearing on our security, particularly environmental degradation, resource conflicts and grave economic disparities. We will seek to do so in the appropriate multilateral fora, in the widest possible co-operation with other States.

33. We will each further develop our close co-operation with the other industrial democracies akin to us in their objectives and policies.

34. We will redouble our efforts in a reinvigorated United Nations, strengthening its role in conflict settlement and peacekeeping, and in its larger endeavours for world peace.

Our "Third Dimension"

35. Convinced of the vital need for international co-operation in science and technology, and of its beneficial effect on global security, we have for several decades maintained Alliance programmes of scientific co-operation. Recognizing the importance of safeguarding the environment we have also co-operated, in the Committee on the Challenges of Modern Society, on environmental matters. These activities have demonstrated the broad range of our common pursuits. We intend to give more impact to our programmes with new initiatives in these areas.

The Future of the Alliance

36. We, the leaders of 16 free and democratic countries, have dedicated ourselves to the goals of the Alliance and are committed to work in unison for their continued fulfillment.

37. At this time of unprecedented promise in international affairs, we will respond to the hopes that it offers. The Alliance will continue to serve as the cornerstone of our security, peace and freedom. Secure on this foundation, we will reach out to those who are willing to join us in shaping a more stable and peaceful international environment in the service of our societies.

Note: The communique was not issued as a White House press release.

North Atlantic Treaty Organization Communique: A Comprehensive Concept of Arms Control and Disarmament
May 30, 1989

1. At Reykjavik in June 1987, Ministers stated that the arms control problems facing the Alliance raised complex and interrelated issues that needed to be evaluated together, bearing in mind overall progress in arms control negotiations as well as the requirements of Alliance security and of its strategy of deterrence. They therefore directed the Council in Permanent Session, working in conjunction with the appropriate military authorities, to "consider the further development of a comprehensive concept of arms control and disarmament".

2. The attached report, prepared by the Council in response to that mandate, was adopted by Heads of State and Government at the meeting of the North Atlantic Council in Brussels on 29th and 30th May 1989.

A Report Adopted by Heads of State and Government at the Meeting of the North Atlantic Council in Brussels on 29th and 30th May 1989

I. Introduction

1. The overriding objective of the Alliance is to preserve peace in freedom, to prevent war, and to establish a just and lasting peaceful order in Europe. The Allies' policy to this end was set forth in the Harmel Report of 1967. It remains valid. According to the Report, the North Atlantic Alliance's "first function is to maintain adequate military strength and political solidarity to deter aggression and other forms of pressure and to defend the territory of member countries if aggression should occur". On that basis, the Alliance can carry out "its second function, to pursue the search for progress towards a more stable relationship in which the underlying political issues can be solved". As the Report observed, military security and a policy aimed at reducing tensions are "not contradictory, but complementary". Consistent with these principles, Allied Heads of State and Government have agreed that arms control is an integral part of the Alliance's security policy.

2. The possibilities for fruitful East-West dialogue have significantly improved in recent years. More favourable conditions now exist for progress towards the achievement of the Alliance's objectives. The Allies

are resolved to grasp this opportunity. They will continue to address both the symptoms and the causes of political tension in a manner that respects the legitimate security interests of all states concerned.

3. The achievement of the lasting peaceful order which the Allies seek will require that the unnatural division of Europe, and particularly of Germany, be overcome, and that, as stated in the Helsinki Final Act, the sovereignty and territorial integrity of all states and the right of peoples to self-determination be respected and that the rights of all individuals, including their right of political choice, be protected. The members of the Alliance accordingly attach central importance to further progress in the Conference on Security and Cooperation in Europe (CSCE) process, which serves as a framework for the promotion of peaceful evolution in Europe.

4. The CSCE process provides a means to encourage stable and constructive East-West relations by increasing contacts between people, by seeking to ensure that basic rights and freedoms are respected in law and practice, by furthering political exchanges and mutually beneficial cooperation across a broad range of endeavours, and by enhancing security and openness in the military sphere. The Allies will continue to demand full implementation of all the principles and provisions of the Helsinki Final Act, the Madrid Concluding Document, the Stockholm Document, and the Concluding Document of the Vienna Meeting. The latter document marks a major advance in the CSCE process and should stimulate further beneficial changes in Europe.

5. The basic goal of the Alliance's arms control policy is to enhance security and stability at the lowest balanced level of forces and armaments consistent with the requirements of the strategy of deterrence. The Allies are committed to achieving continuing progress towards all their arms control objectives. The further development of the Comprehensive Concept is designed to assist this by ensuring an integrated approach covering both defence policy and arms control policy: these are complementary and interactive. This work also requires full consideration of the interrelationship between arms control objectives and defence requirements and how various arms control measures, separately and in conjunction with each other, can strengthen Alliance security. The guiding principles and basic objectives which have so far governed the arms control policy of the Alliance remain valid. Progress in achieving these objectives is, of course, affected by a number of factors. These include the overall state of East-West relations, the military requirements of the Allies, the progress of existing and future arms control negotiations, and developments in the CSCE process. The further development and implementation of a comprehensive concept of arms control and disarmament will take place against this background.

II. East-West Relations and Arms Control

6. The Alliance continues to seek a just and stable peace in Europe in which all states can enjoy undiminished security at the minimum necessary levels of forces and armaments and all individuals can exercise their basic rights and freedoms. Arms control alone cannot resolve longstanding political differences between East and West nor guarantee a stable peace. Nonetheless, achievement of the Alliance's goal will require substantial advances in arms control, as well as more fundamental changes in political relations. Success in arms control, in addition to enhancing military security, can encourage improvements in the East-West political dialogue and thereby contribute to the achievement of broader Alliance objectives.

7. To increase security and stability in Europe, the Alliance has consistently pursued every opportunity for effective arms control. The Allies are committed to this policy, independent of any changes that may occur in the climate of East-West relations. Success in arms control, however, continues to depend not on our own efforts alone, but also on Eastern and particularly Soviet readiness to work constructively towards mutually beneficial results.

8. The immediate past has witnessed unprecedented progress in the field of arms control. In 1986 the Stockholm Conference on Disarmament in Europe (CDE) agree-

ment created an innovative system of confidence and security-building measures, designed to promote military transparency and predictability. To date, these have been satisfactorily implemented. The 1987 INF Treaty marked another major step forward because it eliminated a whole class of weapons, it established the principle of asymmetrical reductions, and provided for a stringent verification regime. Other achievements include the establishment in the United States and the Soviet Union of nuclear risk reduction centres, the US/Soviet agreement on prior notification of ballistic missile launches, and the conduct of the Joint Verification Experiment in connection with continued US/Soviet negotiations on nuclear testing.

9. In addition to agreements already reached, there has been substantial progress in the START negotiations which are intended to reduce radically strategic nuclear arsenals and eliminate destabilising offensive capabilities. The Paris Conference on the Prohibition of Chemical Weapons has reaffirmed the authority of the 1925 Geneva Protocol and given powerful political impetus to the negotiations in Geneva for a global, comprehensive and effectively verifiable ban on chemical weapons. New distinct negotiations within the framework of the CSCE process have now begun in Vienna: one on conventional armed forces in Europe between the 23 members of NATO and the Warsaw Treaty Organization (WTO) and one on confidence- and security-building measures (CSBMs) among all 35 signatories of the Helsinki Final Act.

10. There has also been substantial progress on other matters important to the West. Soviet troops have left Afghanistan. There has been movement toward the resolution of some, although not all, of the remaining regional conflicts in which the Soviet Union is involved. The observance of human rights in the Soviet Union and in some of the other WTO countries has significantly improved, even if serious deficiencies remain. The recent Vienna CSCE Follow-up meeting succeeded in setting new, higher standards of conduct for participating states and should stimulate further progress in the CSCE process. A new intensity of dialogue, particularly at high-level, between East and West opens new opportunities and testifies to the Allies' commitment to resolve the fundamental problems that remain.

11. The Alliance does not claim exclusive responsibility for this favourable evolution in East-West relations. In recent years, the East has become more responsive and flexible. Nonetheless, the Alliance contribution has clearly been fundamental. Most of the achievements to date, which have been described above, were inspired by initiatives by the Alliance or its members. The Allies' political solidarity, commitment to defence, patience and creativity in negotiations overcame initial obstacles and brought its efforts to fruition. It was the Alliance that drew up the basic blueprints for East-West progress and has since pushed them forward towards realisation. In particular, the concepts of stability, reasonable sufficiency, asymmetrical, reductions, concentration on the most offensive equipment, rigorous verification, transparency, a single zone from the Atlantic to the Urals, and the balanced and comprehensive nature of the CSCE process, are Western-inspired.

12. Prospects are now brighter than ever before for lasting, qualitative improvements in the East-West relationship. There continue to be clear signs of change in the internal and external policies of the Soviet Union and of some of its Allies. The Soviet leadership has stated that ideological competition should play no part in inter-state relations. Soviet acknowledgement of serious shortcomings in its past approaches to international as well as domestic issues creates opportunities for progress on fundamental political problems.

13. At the same time, serious concerns remain. The ambitious Soviet reform programme, which the Allies welcome, will take many years to complete. Its success cannot be taken for granted given the magnitude of the problems it faces and the resistance generated. In Eastern Europe, progress in constructive reform is still uneven and the extent of these reforms remains to be determined. Basic human rights still need to be firmly anchored in law and practice, though in some Warsaw Pact countries improvements are underway. Al-

though the WTO has recently announced and begun unilateral reductions in some of its forces, the Soviet Union continues to deploy military forces and to maintain a pace of military production in excess of legitimate defensive requirements. Moreover, the geo-strategic realities favour the geographically contiguous Soviet-dominated WTO as against the geographically separated democracies of the North Atlantic Alliance. It has long been an objective of the Soviet Union to weaken the links between the European and North American members of the Alliance.

14. We face an immediate future that is promising but still uncertain. The Allies and the East face both a challenge and an opportunity to capitalise on present conditions in order to increase mutual security. The progress recently made in East-West relations has given new impetus to the arms control process and has enhanced the possibilities of achieving the Alliance's arms control objectives, which complement the other elements of the Alliance's security policy.

III. Principles of Alliance Security

15. Alliance security policy aims to preserve peace in freedom by both political means and the maintenance of a military capability sufficient to prevent war and to provide for effective defence. The fact that the Alliance has for forty years safeguarded peace in Europe bears witness to the success of this policy.

16. Improved political relations and the progressive development of cooperative structures between Eastern and Western countries are important components of Alliance policy. They can enhance mutual confidence, reduce the risk of misunderstanding, ensure that there are in place reliable arrangements for crisis management so that tensions can be defused, render the situation in Europe more open and predictable, and encourage the development of wider cooperation in all fields.

17. In underlining the importance of these facts for the formulation of Alliance policy, the Allies reaffirm that, as stated in the Harmel Report, the search for constructive dialogue and cooperation with the countries of the East, including arms control and disarmament, is based on political solidarity and adequate military strength.

18. Solidarity among the Alliance countries is a fundamental principle of their security policy. It reflects the indivisible nature of their security. It is expressed by the willingness of each country to share fairly the risks, burdens and responsibilities of the common effort as well as its benefits. In particular, the presence in Europe of the United States' conventional and nuclear forces and of Canadian forces demonstrates that North American and European security interests are inseparably bound together.

19. From its inception the Alliance of Western democracies has been defensive in purpose. This will remain so. None of our weapons will ever be used except in self-defence. The Alliance does not seek military superiority nor will it ever do so. Its aim has always been to prevent war and any form of coercion and intimidation.

20. Consistent with the Alliance's defensive character, its strategy is one of deterrence. Its objective is to convince a potential aggressor before he acts that he is confronted with a risk that outweighs any gain—however great—he might hope to secure from his aggression. The purpose of this strategy defines the means needed for its implementation.

21. In order to fulfill its strategy, the Alliance must be capable of responding appropriately to any aggression and of meeting its commitment to the defence of the frontiers of its members' territory. For the foreseeable future, deterrence requires an appropriate mix of adequate and effective nuclear and conventional forces which will continue to be kept up to date where necessary; for it is only by their evident and perceived capability for effective use that such forces and weapons deter.

22. Conventional forces make an essential contribution to deterrence. The elimination of asymmetries between the conventional forces of East and West in Europe would be a major breakthrough, bringing significant benefits for stability and security. Conventional defence alone cannot, however, ensure deterrence. Only the nuclear element can confront an aggressor with an unacceptable risk and thus plays an indispen-

sable role in our current strategy of war prevention.

23. The fundamental purpose of nuclear forces—both strategic and sub-strategic—is political: to preserve the peace and to prevent any kind of war. Such forces contribute to deterrence by demonstrating that the Allies have the military capability and the political will to use them, if necessary, in response to aggression. Should aggression occur, the aim would be to restore deterrence by inducing the aggressor to reconsider his decision, to terminate his attack and to withdraw and thereby to restore the territorial integrity of the Alliance.

24. Conventional and nuclear forces, therefore, perform different but complementary and mutually reinforcing roles. Any perceived inadequacy in either of these two elements, or the impression that conventional forces could be separated from nuclear, or sub-strategic from strategic nuclear forces, might lead a potential adversary to conclude that the risks of launching aggression might be calculable and acceptable. No single element can, therefore, be regarded as a substitute compensating for deficiencies in any other.

25. For the foreseeable future, there is no alternative strategy for the prevention of war. The implementation of this strategy will continue to ensure that the security interests of all Alliance members are fully safeguarded. The principles underlying the strategy of deterrence are of enduring validity. Their practical expression in terms of the size, structure and deployment of forces is bound to change. As in the past, these elements will continue to evolve in response to changing international circumstances, technological progress and developments in the scale of the threat—in particular, in the posture and capabilities of the forces of the Warsaw Pact.

26. Within this overall framework, strategic nuclear forces provide the ultimate guarantee of deterrence for the Allies. They must be capable of inflicting unacceptable damage on an aggressor state even after it has carried out a first strike. Their number, range, survivability and penetration capability need to ensure that a potential aggressor cannot count on limiting the conflict or regarding his own territory as a sanctuary. The strategic nuclear forces of the United States provide the cornerstone of deterrence for the Alliance as a whole. The independent nuclear forces of the United Kingdom and France fulfill a deterrent role of their own and contribute to the overall deterrence strategy of the Alliance by complicating the planning and risk assessment of a potential aggressor.

27. Nuclear forces below the strategic level provide an essential political and military linkage between conventional and strategic forces and, together with the presence of Canadian and the United States forces in Europe, between the European and North American members of the Alliance. The Allies' sub-strategic nuclear forces are not designed to compensate for conventional imbalances. The levels of such forces in the integrated military structure nevertheless must take into account the threat—both conventional and nuclear—with which the Alliance is faced. Their role is to ensure that there are no circumstances in which a potential aggressor might discount the prospect of nuclear retaliation in response to military action. Nuclear forces below the strategic level thus make an essential contribution to deterrence.

28. The wide deployment of such forces among countries participating in the integrated military structure of the Alliance, as well as the arrangements for consultation in the nuclear area among the Allies concerned, demonstrates solidarity and willingness to share nuclear roles and responsibilities. It thereby helps to reinforce deterrence.

29. Conventional forces contribute to deterrence by demonstrating the Allies' will to defend themselves and by minimising the risk that a potential aggressor could anticipate a quick and easy victory or limited territorial gain achieved solely by conventional means.

30. They must thus be able to respond appropriately and to confront the aggressor immediately and as far forward as possible with the necessary resistance to compel him to end the conflict and to withdraw or face possible recourse to the use of nuclear weapons by the Allies. The forces of the Allies must be deployed and equipped so as

to enable them to fulfill this role at all times. Moreover, since the Alliance depends on reinforcements from the North American continent, it must be able to keep open sea and air lines of communication between North America and Europe.

31. All member countries of the Alliance strongly favour a comprehensive, effectively verifiable, global ban on the development, production, stockpiling and use of chemical weapons. Chemical weapons represent a particular case, since the Alliance's overall strategy of war prevention, as noted earlier, depends on an appropriate mix of nuclear and conventional weapons. Pending the achievement of a global ban on chemical weapons, the Alliance recognises the need to implement passive defence measures. A retaliatory capability on a limited scale is retained in view of the Soviet Union's overwhelming chemical weapons capability.

32. The Allies are committed to maintaining only the minimum level of forces necessary for their strategy of deterrence, taking into account the threat. There is, however, a level of forces, both nuclear and conventional, below which the credibility of deterrence cannot be maintained. In particular, the Allies have always recognised that the removal of all nuclear weapons from Europe would critically undermine deterrence strategy and impair the security of the Alliance.

33. The Alliance's defence policy and its policy of arms control and disarmament are complementary and have the same goal: to maintain security at the lowest possible level of forces. There is no contradiction between defence policy and arms control policy. It is on the basis of this fundamental consistency of principles and objectives that the comprehensive concept of arms control and disarmament should be further developed and the appropriate conclusions drawn in each of the areas of arms control.

IV. Arms Control and Disarmament: Principles and Objectives

34. Our vision for Europe is that of an undivided continent where military forces only exist to prevent war and to ensure self-defence, as has always been the case for the Allies, not for the purpose of initiating aggression or for political or military intimidation. Arms control can contribute to the realisation of that vision as an integral part of the Alliance's security policy and of our overall approach to East-West relations.

35. The goal of Alliance arms control policy is to enhance security and stability. To this end, the Allies' arms control initiatives seek a balance at a lower level of forces and armaments through negotiated agreements and, as appropriate, unilateral actions, recognising that arms control agreements are only possible where the negotiating partners share an interest in achieving a mutually satisfactory result. The Allies' arms control policy seeks to remove destabilising asymmetries in forces or equipment. It also pursues measures designed to build mutual confidence and to reduce the risk of conflict by promoting greater transparency and predictability in military matters.

36. In enhancing security and stability, arms control can also bring important additional benefits for the Alliance. Given the dynamic aspects of the arms control process, the principles and results embodied in one agreement may facilitate other arms control steps. In this way arms control can also make possible further reductions in the level of Alliance forces and armaments, consistent with the Alliance's strategy of war prevention. Furthermore, as noted in Chapter II, arms control can make a significant contribution to the development of more constructive East-West relations and of a framework for further cooperation within a more stable and predictable international environment. Progress in arms control can also enhance public confidence in and promote support for our overall security policy.

Guiding Principles for Arms Control

37. The members of the Alliance will be guided by the following principles:

—*Security:* Arms control should enhance the security of all Allies. Both during the implementation period and following implementation, the Allies' strategy of deterrence and their ability to defend themselves, must remain credible and effective. Arms control measures should maintain the strategic unity and political cohesion of the Alliance, and should safeguard the principle of the indivisibility of Alliance security by avoiding the creation of areas of unequal security. Arms control measures should respect the legitimate security interests of all states and should not facilitate the transfer or intensification of threats to third party states or regions.

—*Stability:* Arms control measures should yield militarily significant results that enhance stability. To promote stability, arms control measures should reduce or eliminate those capabilities which are most threatening to the Alliance. Stability can also be enhanced by steps that promote greater transparency and predictability in military matters. Military stability requires the elimination of options for surprise attack and for large-scale offensive action. Crisis stability requires that no state have forces of a size and configuration which, when compared with those of others, could enable it to calculate that it might gain a decisive advantage by being the first to resort to arms. Stability also requires measures which discourage destabilising attempts to re-establish military advantage through the transfer of resources to other types of armament. Agreements must lead to final results that are both balanced and ensure equality of rights with respect to security.

—*Verifiability:* Effective and reliable verification is a fundamental requirement for arms control agreements. If arms control is to be effective and to build confidence, the verifiability of proposed arms control measures must, therefore, be of central concern for the Alliance. Progress in arms control should be measured against the record of compliance with existing agreements. Agreed arms control measures should exclude opportunities for circumvention.

Alliance Arms Control Objectives

38. In accordance with the above principles, the Allies are pursuing an ambitious arms control agenda for the coming years in the nuclear, conventional and chemical fields.

Nuclear Forces

39. The INF Agreement represents a milestone in the Allies' efforts to achieve a more secure peace at lower levels of arms. By 1991, it will lead to the total elimination of all United States and Soviet intermediate range land-based missiles, thereby removing the threat which such Soviet systems presented to the Alliance. Implementation of the agreement, however, will affect only a small proportion of the Soviet nuclear armoury, and the Alliance continues to face a substantial array of modern and effective Soviet systems of all ranges. The full realisation of the Alliance agenda thus requires that further steps be taken.

Strategic Nuclear Forces

40. Soviet strategic systems continue to pose a major threat to the whole of the Alliance. Deep cuts in such systems are in the direct interests of the entire Western Alliance, and therefore their achievement constitutes a priority for the Alliance in the nuclear field.

41. The Allies thus fully support the US objectives of achieving, within the context of the Strategic Arms Reduction Talks, fifty percent reductions in US and Soviet strategic nuclear arms. US proposals seek to enhance stability by placing specific restrictions on the most destabilising elements of the threat—fast flying ballistic missiles, throw-weight and, in particular, Soviet heavy ICBMs. The proposals are based on the need to maintain the deterrent credibility of the remaining US strategic forces which would continue to provide the ultimate guarantee of security for the Alliance as a whole; and therefore on the necessity to keep such forces effective. Furthermore, the United States is holding talks with the Soviet Union on defence and space matters in order to ensure that strategic stability is enhanced.

Sub-Strategic Nuclear Forces

42. The Allies are committed to maintaining only the minimum number of nuclear weapons necessary to support their strategy of deterrence. In line with this commitment, the members of the integrated military structure have already made major uni-

lateral cuts in their sub-strategic nuclear armoury. The number of land-based warheads in Western Europe has been reduced by over one-third since 1979 to its lowest level in over 20 years. Updating where necessary of their sub-strategic systems would result in further reductions.

43. The Allies continue to face the direct threat posed to Europe by the large numbers of shorter-range nuclear missiles deployed on Warsaw Pact territory and which have been substantially upgraded in recent years. Major reductions in Warsaw Pact systems would be of overall value to Alliance security. One of the ways to achieve this aim would be by tangible and verifiable reductions of American and Soviet land-based nuclear missile systems of shorter range leading to equal ceilings at lower levels.

44. But the sub-strategic nuclear forces deployed by member countries of the Alliance are not principally a counter to similar systems operated by members of the WTO. As is explained in Chapter III, sub-strategic nuclear forces fulfill an essential role in overall Alliance deterrence strategy by ensuring that there are no circumstances in which a potential aggressor might discount nuclear retaliation in response to his military action.

45. The Alliance reaffirms its position that for the foreseeable future there is no alternative to the Alliance's strategy for the prevention of war, which is a strategy of deterrence based upon an appropriate mix of adequate and effective nuclear and conventional forces which will continue to be kept up to date where necessary. Where nuclear forces are concerned, land-, sea-, and air-based systems, including ground-based missiles, in the present circumstances and as far as can be foreseen will be needed in Europe.

46. In view of the huge superiority of the Warsaw Pact in terms of short-range nuclear missiles, the Alliance calls upon the Soviet Union to reduce unilaterally its short-range missile systems to the current levels within the integrated military structure.

47. The Alliance reaffirms that at the negotiations on conventional stability it pursues the objectives of:

—the establishment of a secure and stable balance of conventional forces at lower levels;

—the elimination of disparities prejudicial to stability and security; and

—the elimination as a matter of high priority of the capability for launching surprise attack and for initiating large-scale offensive action.

48. In keeping with its arms control objectives formulated in Reykjavik in 1987 and reaffirmed in Brussels in 1988, the Alliance states that one of its highest priorities in negotiations with the East is reaching an agreement on conventional force reductions which would achieve the objectives above. In this spirit, the Allies will make every effort, as evidenced by the outcome of the May 1989 Summit, to bring these conventional negotiations to an early and satisfactory conclusion. The United States has expressed the hope that this could be achieved within six to twelve months. Once implementation of such an agreement is underway, the United States, in consultation with the Allies concerned, is prepared to enter into negotiations to achieve a *partial* reduction of American and Soviet land-based nuclear missile forces of shorter range to equal and verifiable levels. With special reference to the Western proposals on CFE tabled in Vienna, enhanced by the proposals by the United States at the May 1989 Summit, the Allies concerned proceed on the understanding that negotiated reductions leading to a level below the existing level of their SNF missiles will not be carried out until the results of these negotiations have been implemented. Reductions of Warsaw Pact SNF systems should be carried out before that date.

49. As regards the substrategic nuclear forces of the members of the integrated military structure, their level and characteristics must be such that they can perform their deterrent role in a credible way across the required spectrum of ranges, taking into account the threat—both conventional and nuclear—with which the Alliance is faced. The question concerning the introduction and deployment of a follow-on system for the Lance will be dealt with in 1992 in the light of overall security developments. While a decision for national authorities, the Allies concerned recognize the

value of the continued funding by the United States of research and development of a follow-on for the existing Lance short-range missile, in order to preserve their options in this respect.

Conventional forces

50. As set out in the March 1988 Summit statement and in the Alliance's November 1988 data initiative, the Soviet Union's military presence in Europe, at a level far in excess of its needs for self-defense, directly challenges our security as well as our aspirations for a peaceful order in Europe. Such excessive force levels create the risk of political intimidation or threatened aggression. As long as they exist, they present an obstacle to better political relations between all states of Europe. The challenge to security is, moreover, not only a matter of the numerical superiority of WTO forces. WTO tanks, artillery and armoured troop carriers are concentrated in large formations and deployed in such a way as to give the WTO a capability for surprise attack and large-scale offensive action. Despite the recent welcome publication by the WTO of its assessment of the military balance in Europe, there is still considerable secrecy and uncertainty about its actual capabilities and intentions.

51. In addressing these concerns, the Allies' primary objectives are to establish a secure and stable balance of conventional forces in Europe at lower levels, while at the same time creating greater openness about military organization and activities in Europe.

52. In the Conventional Forces in Europe (CFE) talks between the 23 members of the two alliances, the Allies are proposing:

—reductions to an overall limit on the total holdings of armaments in Europe, concentrating on the most threatening systems, i.e. those capable of seizing and holding territory;

—a limit on the proportion of these total holdings belonging to any one country in Europe (since the security and stability of Europe require that no state exceed its legitimate needs for self-defence);

—a limit on stationed forces (thus restricting the forward deployment and concentration of Soviet forces in Eastern Europe); and,

—appropriate numerical sub-limits on forces which will apply simultaneously throughout the Atlantic to the Urals area.

These measures, taken together, will necessitate deep cuts in the WTO conventional forces which most threaten the Alliance. The resulting reductions will have to take place in such a way as to prevent circumvention, e.g. by ensuring that the armaments reduced are destroyed or otherwise disposed of. Verification measures will be required to ensure that all states have confidence that entitlements are not exceeded.

53. These measures alone, however, will not guarantee stability. The regime of reductions will have to be backed up by additional measures which should include measures of transparency, notification and constraint applied to the deployment, storage, movement and levels of readiness and availability of conventional forces.

54. In the CSBM negotiations, the Allies aim to maintain the momentum created by the successful implementation of the Stockholm Document by proposing a comprehensive package of measures to improve:

—transparency about military organization,

—transparency and predictability of military activities,

—contacts and communication,

and have also proposed an exchange of views on military doctrine in a seminar setting.

55. The implementation of the Allies' proposals in the CFE negotiations and of their proposals for further confidence and security-building measures would achieve a quantum improvement in European security. This would have important and positive consequences for Alliance policy both in the field of defence and arms control. The outcome of the CFE negotiations would provide a framework for determining the future Alliance force structure required to perform its fundamental task of preserving peace in freedom. In addition, the Allies would be willing to contemplate further steps to enhance stability and security if the immediate CFE objectives are achieved—

for example, further reductions or limitations of conventional armaments and equipment, or the restructuring of armed forces to enhance defensive capabilities and further reduce offensive capabilities.

56. The Allies welcome the declared readiness of the Soviet Union and other WTO members to reduce their forces and adjust them towards a defensive posture and await implementation of these measures. This would be a step in the direction of redressing the imbalance in force levels existing in Europe and towards reducing the Warsaw Pact capability for surprise attack. The announced reductions demonstrate the recognition by the Soviet Union and other WTO members of the conventional imbalance, long highlighted by the Allies as a key problem of European security.

Chemical Weapons

57. The Soviet Union's chemical weapons stockpile poses a massive threat. The Allies are committed to conclude, at the earliest date, a worldwide, comprehensive and effectively verifiable ban on all chemical weapons.

58. All Alliance states subscribe to the prohibitions contained in the Geneva Protocol for the Use in War of Asphyxiating, Poisonous or Other Gases, and of Bacteriological Methods of Warfare. The Paris Conference on the Prohibition of Chemical Weapons reaffirmed the importance of the commitments made under the Geneva Protocol and expressed the unanimous will of the international community to eliminate chemical weapons completely at an early date and thereby to prevent any recourse to their use.

59. The Allies wish to prohibit not only the use of these abhorrent weapons, but also their development, production, stockpiling and transfer, and to achieve the destruction of existing chemical weapons and production facilities in such a way as to ensure the undiminished security of all participants at each stage in the process. Those objectives are being pursued in the Geneva Conference on Disarmament. Pending agreement on a global ban, the Allies will enforce stringent controls on the export of commodities related to chemical weapons production. They will also attempt to stimulate more openness among states about chemical weapons capabilities in order to promote greater confidence in the effectiveness of a global ban.

V. CONCLUSIONS:

Arms Control and Defence Interrelationships

60. The Alliance is committed to pursuing a comprehensive approach to security, embracing both arms control and disarmament, and defence. It is important, therefore, to ensure that interrelationships between arms control issues and defence requirements and amongst the various arms control areas are fully considered. Proposals in any one area of arms control must take account of the implications for Alliance interests in general and for other negotiations. This is a continuing process.

61. It is essential that defence and arms control objectives remain in harmony in order to ensure their complementary contribution to the goal of maintaining security at the lowest balanced level of forces consistent with the requirements of the Alliance strategy of war prevention, acknowledging that changes in the threat, new technologies, and new political opportunities affect options in both fields. Decisions on arms control matters must fully reflect the requirements of the Allies' strategy of deterrence. Equally, progress in arms control is relevant to military plans, which will have to be developed in the full knowledge of the objectives pursued in arms control negotiations and to reflect, as necessary, the results achieved therein.

62. In each area of arms control, the Alliance seeks to enhance stability and security. The current negotiations concerning strategic nuclear systems, conventional forces and chemical weapons are, however, independent of one another: the outcome of any one of these negotiations is not contingent on progress in others. However, they can influence one another: criteria established and agreements achieved in one area of arms control may be relevant in other areas and hence facilitate overall progress. These could affect both arms control possibilities and the forces needed to fulfill Alliance

strategy, as well as help to contribute generally to a more predictable military environment.

63. The Allies seek to manage the interaction among different arms control elements by ensuring that the development, pursuit and realisation of their arms control objectives in individual areas are fully consistent both with each other and with the Alliance's guiding principles for effective arms control. For example, the way in which START limits and sub-limits are applied in detail could affect the future flexibility of the sub-strategic nuclear forces of members of the integrated military structure. A CFE agreement would by itself make a major contribution to stability. This would be significantly further enhanced by the achievement of a global chemical weapons ban. The development of Confidence- and Security-Building Measures could influence the stabilising measures being considered in connection with the Conventional Forces in Europe negotiations and vice versa. The removal of the imbalance in conventional forces would provide scope for further reductions in the sub-strategic nuclear forces of members of the integrated military structure, though it would not obviate the need for such forces. Similarly, this might make possible further arms control steps in the conventional field.

64. This report establishes the overall conceptual framework within which the Allies will be seeking progress in each area of arms control. In so doing, their fundamental aim will be enhanced security at lower levels of forces and armaments. Taken as a whole, the Allies' arms control agenda constitutes a coherent and comprehensive approach to the enhancement of security and stability. It is ambitious, but we are confident that—with a constructive response from the WTO states—it can be fully achieved in the coming years. In pursuing this goal, the Alliance recognises that it cannot afford to build its security upon arms control results expected in the future. The Allies will be prepared, however, to draw appropriate consequences for their own military posture as they make concrete progress through arms control towards a significant reduction in the scale and quality of the military threat they face. Accomplishment of the Allies' arms control agenda would not only bring great benefits in itself, but could also lead to the expansion of cooperation with the East in other areas. The arms control process itself is, moreover, dynamic; as and when the Alliance reaches agreement in each of the areas set out above, so further prospects for arms control may be opened up and further progress made possible.

65. As noted earlier, the Allies' vision for Europe is that of an undivided continent where military forces only exist to prevent war and to ensure self-defence; a continent which no longer lives in the shadow of overwhelming military forces and from which the threat of war has been removed; a continent where the sovereignty and territorial integrity of all states are respected and the rights of all individuals, including their right of political choice, are protected. This goal can only be reached by stages: it will require patient and creative endeavour. The Allies are resolved to continue working towards its attainment. The achievement of the Alliance's arms control objectives would be a major contribution towards the realisation of its vision.

Note: The communique was not issued as a White House press release.

Statement on the Death of Representative Claude Pepper
May 30, 1989

Claude Pepper gave definition and meaning to the concept of public service. He fought for the poor and the elderly in his own determined way. Those who agreed with him were proud to follow his banner. Those who disagreed with him always respected him. Claude Pepper was a gentleman, a noble human being. America will miss him. Barbara and I will miss him, too.

The President's News Conference Following the North Atlantic Treaty Organization Summit Meeting in Brussels
May 30, 1989

The President. Good afternoon. First, I want to pay my respects to Manfred Woerner and thank him for the way in which this meeting has been conducted, for his thorough staff work, and for his able leadership in the hall. And I think that the successful results at this summit have given us a double hit—both conventional forces and short-range nuclear forces. And taken in tandem, it demonstrates the alliance's ability to manage change to our advantage, to move beyond the era of containment.

Our overall aim is to overcome the division of Europe and to forge a unity based on Western values. The starting point, of course, is to maintain our security while seeking to lessen tensions and adapt to changing circumstances. Our conventional parity initiative seeks to capitalize on the opportunity we have and to do so without delay. We want to finally free Europe from the constant threat of surprise attack. We want to free Europe from the political shadow of Soviet military power. And we want to free Europe to become the center of cooperation, not confrontation. We want to open up opportunities for greater U.S.-European cooperation on the other great issues of our day—for example, on environment and regional conflicts. A reduced military presence, when combined with a less threatening Soviet presence in Europe, can create a stronger basis for engagement in Europe over the long haul.

America is and will remain a European power. Similarly, our SNF [short-range nuclear forces] agreement demonstrates our ability to adapt to change while remaining true to our core security principles. We've agreed to future negotiations after the implementation of a conventional forces agreement—after the implementation of the agreement is underway for the conventional force agreement. Any negotiated SNF reductions will not be carried out until the CFE [conventional armed forces in Europe] agreement is implemented. And we've underscored that our objective in negotiations is to achieve partial reductions, clearly leaving an SNF deterrent at lower, equal, and verifiable levels. Partial means partial.

We also stress that our strategy of deterrence requires land-, sea-, and air-based nuclear systems, including ground-based missiles, for as far as we can foresee. And while we will not take the modernization decision until 1992, the allies recognize the value of continued U.S. funding for the research and development of the follow-on to the Lance system.

And lastly, we are placing great emphasis on a rapid negotiated reduction of the conventional asymmetries that threaten Europe. Based on results in that area, we can negotiate SNF reductions, as well, while ensuring the continued presence of the nuclear deterrent.

And now I would be glad to take some questions. Excuse me, we've got to start with our U.S. protocol. Those of you from the non-U.S. press, excuse me if I go first to the UP [United Press International] and then to the AP [Associated Press].

Short-Range Nuclear Forces in Europe

Q. Mr. President, the communique says that chemical weapons are abhorrent, and you called for total elimination. Most people think nuclear weapons are totally abhorrent. Why not totally eliminate them, as your predecessor had called for?

The President. Well, the communique addresses itself to where nuclear forces are concerned—blah, blah, land, sea, air-based systems, including ground-based missiles. In the present circumstances, as far as can be foreseen, they'll be needed in Europe. And I would just stand by that. This is a decision that has been thoroughly consulted with the military and that's the way it is.

Q. Mr. President, your spokesman said today that the formula for negotiations on short-range nuclear missiles was a very strong victory for the United States and the NATO alliance. How can it be a victory for the United States without being a defeat for Chancellor Kohl and Mr. Genscher [West German Foreign Minister], given that the United States and Germany were on such opposing sides of this issue?

The President. Well, they strongly supported it, it's my understanding. And I don't view it as a victory for the United States; I view it as a victory for the alliance. So, they can speak for themselves, but I'm very pleased that it worked out and that there was alliance harmony on this very important question.

Q. Did both sides make concessions, sir?

The President. Well, I can only speak for the United States, and we had certain broad parameters that—I've addressed part one of them, and that was this question of partial reduction, no third-zero question. The other one was to agree to begin the negotiations on SNF following tangible implementation. That was one of our strong conditions, or strong negotiating points, if you will. And then no implementation of agreed reduction on SNF forces before completion of these reductions. So, I'm very happy.

But I want to—put it this way, we're here as part of an alliance, and I don't think we ought to have winners and losers out of a summit that everybody concedes has been very, very unified. And so, it's an alliance victory or an alliance decision, and I'm proud to have had a part in that.

West Germany and the Alliance

Q. Mr. President, all politics may be local, but hasn't the continued insistence of the Germans been damaging to the alliance?

The President. Talk to the people that have been around here for a long time, and they'll tell you that they've never seen more unity and more upbeat feeling after a meeting.

Q. Do you think the Foreign Ministers who missed dinner last night would agree with you on that? [*Laughter*]

The President. No, they probably would dissent, but they went along today, kept their eyes open.

Short-Range Nuclear Forces in Europe

Q. Mr. President, is it possible that you could start negotiations on SNF missiles before the modernization decision has been made? And do you think that's a good way to go into negotiations without a commitment to upgrade these—the Soviets say, okay, if we don't have a commitment, we'll get rid of all of them—and where's your position?

The President. Well, the modernization decision doesn't need to be taken until '92. And we have spelled out the procedures for negotiating on SNF, and that will come after the agreement on the conventional forces.

And that is the important point. I don't believe the layman—I know we've got a lot of experts on this side, and I don't want to restrict my questions to those of us like myself who are not longtime arms control expert—but I can tell you that most people in our country don't realize the imbalance that exists on these conventional forces, and it is destabilizing. And the question is SNF, short-range nuclear forces, where they've got, in terms of launchers, what, 1,200 or something of that nature to our 88. Why don't they just negotiate—just unilaterally reduce to equal numbers? Now, there would be a good challenge.

So, we've got this order set up as to how we're going to go about it. The alliance has taken a firm position, and so I'm not going to go into a hypothetical question of that nature.

Q. On this question——

The President. Oh, sorry, Brit [Brit Hume, ABC News]. Go ahead, Carl [Carl Leubsdorff, Dallas Morning News], and then Brit.

Q. On this question of partial, the word is underlined for emphasis in the document. Was that done at our behest, or Mrs. Thatcher's [Prime Minister of the United Kingdom] behest, or whose behest?

The President. If we can wake up [Secretary of State] Jim Baker, you'll have to ask him. But I would simply say there was total agreement on it, and it speaks for itself. Partial is partial, and to try to interpret it some other way misses the boat.

Conventional Arms Control

Q. Mr. President, in light of the fact that you have added several new weapons categories to the NATO bargaining position and to the conventional arms talks, is it realistic to suppose that these talks can be carried out successfully in the brief period of time that you have now asked for?

The President. Well, yes, we can meet that timetable. We've challenged the Soviets to meet us, you might say—the alliance. NATO is tasked to be back on September 7th with our internals to be farther along. And so, I would certainly say yes, let's do that. We all remember September 7th, don't we? [*Laughter*]

Short-Range Nuclear Forces in Europe

Q. Mr. President, you've said that the modernization decision has been put off until 1992, but you have a commitment to keep the weapons systems up to date. When are changes to be made?

The President. Not before 1992.

Public Opinion

Q. Mr. President, you've said that your efforts here are not a public relations battle with Soviet leader Mikhail Gorbachev, but if this were a battle, who's winning, yourself or Mr. Gorbachev?

The President. Too hypothetical, Ellen [Ellen Warren, Knight-Ridder]—too hypothetical. I've read who some think is winning, but that was yesterday.

Q. Well, do you expect the hammering about your alleged lack of leadership in the United States to quiet down now as a result of your performance here?

The President. I haven't felt under siege in the United States because I've known exactly what we wanted to do. And I made statements to that effect earlier on: that we were going to have a review and then have proposals. And we did exactly that. So, I will concede I've read such reports, but they haven't troubled me any.

Soviet Defense Budget

Q. Mr. Gorbachev has apparently for the first time revealed specific defense budget figures in Moscow today. And he also says he is proposing to cut defense spending by 14 percent over 1990 and '91—that's equal to about $17.3 billion. Is that a lot? Is that meaningful? What do you think about it?

The President. Well, this will help him—this proposal. If he hits our bid, that should save him a lot of money in the long run, because he has a disproportionate number of conventional forces. And therein, as you know, that's where a lot of the expense for defense comes from. So, I don't know, but it sounds like a substantial number to me—but again, I hadn't seen that. I will say this for those who may wonder what the Soviet reaction has been—and it's very preliminary—but the initial contact with our Embassy in Moscow was—I would put fairly positive. Brent [Assistant to the President for National Security Affairs], is that about right?

General Scowcroft. Cautious.

The President. Cautious, but we're leading on the side of saying it's positive. In other words, they didn't really slam the door and come in on a negative vein.

Summit With President Gorbachev

Q. On that point, Mr. President, wouldn't it seem that if you want to strike this agreement even as early as 6 months, that there would be a summit meeting with Mr. Gorbachev before the end of the year?

The President. Well, again, if there was something constructive to come out of such a meeting, I would certainly be prepared to meet, and I believe that Secretary Baker has conveyed that to [Foreign] Minister Shevardnadze.

Q. Has Mr. Gorbachev responded to your letter of Sunday?

The President. No, sir.

NATO Summit

Q. Mr. Bush, you used some strong language yesterday about leading the alliance and leading the free world—that wasn't your term, but did you feel it was important—if not for yourself, then for the alliance, for the United States—to assert yourself in a strong way at this particular summit—this time?

The President. Yes, I think it is highly important that the United States—to be seen as fully engaged, trying to come up with creative proposals, and fulfilling its historic leadership responsibilities. I would like to put it in terms of alliance unity, though, and what—all these decisions. There's plenty of room for credit out there, and I would insist that it's to the degree we got unanimity—an alliance victory.

Short-Range Nuclear Forces in Europe

Q. Mr. President, the stress you put on the speed of negotiations—6 months to a year—and the decision to wait until '92, modernization, are there some progress points if there are no negotiations or progress in the negotiations within a year to reexamine the 1992 deadline?

The President. To be honest with you, I don't know the answer to that question. I expect——

Q. Do I get another one?

The President. No, you don't get another one, either. [*Laughter*] That was too hard. But my own personal view would be that if there were some dramatic change somewhere that changed the theses that underlined this agreement that we'd want to review things; but I'm not predicting that. I want to see it go forward.

Q. To follow up, Mr. President——

The President. Follow up?

Q. Yes, sir, it is a followup.

The President. Is it directly related?

Q. Directly. Following tangible implementation—that's being read as obviously not complete implementation. Can you tell us how far tangible is?

The President. No, I can't tell you how far it is, but it has to be so that you and I would look at it and we'd both agree that there had been sincere implementation.

Q. Mr. President, in the Comprehensive Concept it states that ground-based missiles will be needed as far as can be foreseen. Now, even though the modernization decision has been put off, is there any alternative to modernizing those missiles?

The President. Is there any alternative to modernizing it? We will cross that bridge in 1992.

Conventional Arms Control

Q. As you know, Mr. Gorbachev is coming to Bonn soon, and his operative style has been to try to up the ante when the U.S. makes a proposal. On your conventional arms proposal, do you think you've gone down as far as the West can safely go in reducing conventional forces, and can you go no further than what you've proposed yesterday?

The President. I see no reason talking about further cuts and further reductions when we have just tabled a sound proposal that addresses ourselves to this enormous imbalance, so I just would defer on that.

Q. Mr. President, you were criticized early on for a slow start. Now this proposal is being described as bold; you yourself said revolutionary. I wonder if there is any element of I-told-you-so in your attitude now to reaction to these proposals?

The President. Not really. [*Laughter*] Not really. No, listen, I'm not going to get into that game with Congress or anyone else. [*Laughter*]

Q. Mr. President, looking ahead, what impact do you think your proposals will have on U.S.-Soviet relations, and specifically on strategic arms talks?

The President. I hope that these proposals have an ameliorating effect, that things will get only better. I think it's a serious proposal. I think they see a solid, united alliance, and that is important in this. And so, I would hope that it would have a good effect on whatever follows on, and strategic arms reduction talks follow on. I have never questioned whether Gorbachev knew that we were serious and wanted to move forward with him. I've read speculation on this, but I have reason to believe that he knows that we have been serious, taking our time to formulate proposals. I do think that this one will be tangible evidence of this. And so, I hope it would lead to—if a conventional forces talks can be catalytic for strategic talks, so be it. But I hope that the seriousness of all of this and the unity of the alliance will be persuasive to him, to make him know that we do want to go forward.

Q. Mr. President, as you know, the United States has strongly opposed—and so has NATO—including aircraft in these negotiations up to now. Could you tell us what your thinking was in deciding to reverse that position and to propose the 15-percent cut?

The President. Trying to correct disparity—and it was really that simple. And I realize there have been some concerns of—we are very understanding of the French reservation in this regard—I might say very diplomatically and beautifully expressed by President [François] Mitterrand. But it is simply that: disparity.

East-West Relations

Q. Mr. President, Secretary-General Woerner spoke about the future being as important or more important than the past for the alliance. He spoke about NATO vision. Does NATO's vision include East-West alliance?

The President. I don't see an East-West alliance, but I see a Europe much more free, and one whose innate desire to have more democracy comes to the surface. But I don't see it as an East and West joining in some formal alliance, if that was what the question was.

Q. I believe the game is called a followup question——

The President. You learn fast. [*Laughter*]

Q. NATO exists because of the perceived threat that the Soviet Union provided. Now the Soviet Union isn't perceived as a threat anymore. Surely, an East-West alliance would then exist for a perceived threat from elsewhere——

The President. Well, I've answered my question on—you asked me whether I felt there would be some formal alliance between Pact countries—I guess you meant between Warsaw Pact and NATO. And I don't think it would require a formal alliance in order to have much, much better relationships that include security considerations; but we're a long way from there. We're just beginning to see the differentiation in Europe, and our whole policy for the United States—let me set aside NATO for a minute—will be to watch for those changes and try to facilitate them and work with those who are willing to move towards freedom and democracy.

Indeed, we've made some proposals on Poland. I will be going to both Poland and Hungary, and I will make clear that if they move toward these Western values that have served the alliance so well for a long time that, speaking for the United States, we will be ready to have much better relations.

Arms Reduction

Q. Mr. President, can you say this morning that there will be no third zero? And if you can say it, why cannot the Comprehensive Concept say it?

The President. I thought I already did say it.

Q. I didn't think so.

The President. There will be no third zero. There will be no third zero. [*Laughter*] Partial means partial.

Eastern European Reforms

Q. Mr. President, Vice President Quayle, in an interview with a reporter the other day, said that if some of these Eastern European countries move too far toward Western values that the Soviets might intervene militarily and that we have not planned how we might respond to that. He said we ought to do that. Do you agree that that's a—he called it a big risk. Do you agree it's a big risk, and do you think that we ought to be deciding what to do if the Soviets should——

The President. I'm old enough to remember Hungary in 1956, and I would want to do nothing in terms of statement or exhortation that would encourage a repeat of that. And so, I would leave it right there. I'd like to think that the situation will move in the opposite direction. But who would have predicted the kind of public, up until now peaceful demonstration in Tiananmen Square? Who would have predicted the kind of move inside the Soviet Union on *perestroika* and, indeed, *glasnost*? So, when you're dealing with things as complex as relations between countries, I think prudence is the order of the day, and I've said that all along. But back to your question, I don't think anyone knows the answer to that. I mean, we're not certainly predicting that.

Q. Well, then, do you disagree with the

Vice President?

The President. I don't even know what he said. And, Jack [Jack Nelson, Los Angeles Times], I learned long ago not to comment on things that I haven't read personally when we're trying to get one member of an administration to be juxtaposed against another. It's bad business, and I'm not going to do that. But I have great confidence in the Vice President, I might add, and I think his pronouncements on foreign policy have been very sound.

Conventional Arms Control

Q. Mr. President, notwithstanding the obvious fact that they all work for you anyway, how much of a problem, if any, did you have getting the Pentagon on board on these proposals?

The President. The Pentagon did what it should have done. And they looked at various options from the military standpoint, and they analyzed it. And the Joint Chiefs were fully engaged in the process, and my contacts were principally, but not exclusively, with Bill Crowe [Chairman of the Joint Chiefs of Staff]. One of the things I wanted to do in talking to our alliance partners was assure them that our military was behind the final proposal. Indeed, I was very pleased in talking to General Galvin [Supreme Allied Commander, Europe] before this proposal was tabled to have his assurances that what we have proposed here is sound militarily. And that made it a much better position to present to the alliance.

Q. Do you expect any foot-dragging or grumbling or maybe even a little leaking along the way as you go forward?

The President. In our own leak-proof bureaucracy? No, I don't expect that. [*Laughter*] And I would discourage it. But is it apt to happen? I would hope not.

Last one. Charles [Charles Bierbauer, CNN]?

Q. Mr. President, were you, at any point, unhappy with the pace and the projections of that slow and lengthy policy review to the extent—as you described, you had a 12-day sort of crash course in some of these new proposals. Can you give us some of your personal sense of how you got to this point?

The President. Well, first we undertook these reviews. I'm not sure everyone here understands that. And I said that I needed some time when I became President—new President, January 20th—to review not only this subject, the NATO-related subjects, but a wide array of subjects. We're almost through all of the reviews. And during what Mr. Bierbauer is referring to, during this time, I came under some fire for being recalcitrant, reluctant to move forward. Indeed, when Mr. Gorbachev would make one of his many proposals, they would be coming to me and saying, "Well, don't you think you have to do something?" And I would say, "No, we want to take our time and act in a prudent manner."

I had in my mind that what we wanted to do was to be sure that the alliance was together on any—or would come together on any proposal we made to the alliance. But I think there was some feeling in Congress, some criticism of my speed, or lack of it, in the United States Congress; but I'm so immune to political criticism that I just kind of write it off. I was elected to do what I think is right. And I think we've come up with a good proposal here.

And I will end, this being the last question, not with a filibuster but simply to say I have been told by others here that the alliance really has never had a meeting that's more upbeat and where we've taken rather significant steps in unity. And so, whatever the wait, whatever the political arrows might have been fired my way, it's all been worth it, because I think we have something sound and solid to build on now.

And again, I end by thanking my colleagues, the other heads of government, chiefs of state that were here, for the total cooperation and the spirit in which these proposals were received and discussed and the way in which NATO adopted its final position. I think it's a good thing: it's good for NATO; I really happen to believe that it's good for the entire free world.

Thank you all very much.

Note: The President's 13th news conference began at 12:49 p.m. in the Luns Press Theatre at the North Atlantic Treaty Organization Headquarters. In his opening remarks, he referred to Manfred Woerner, Secretary-General of NATO.

Remarks at the American School in Brussels
May 30, 1989

Thank you all very much. I love this enthusiasm—anything to get out of school. [*Laughter*] And here we are. [*Laughter*] But speaking of which, first, let me thank Dr. Beckwith, Jennifer Beckwith, for extending us this hospitality: a large one-room schoolhouse and the great American tradition of basketball. But I also want to pay my respects to, and recognize, Ambassador Glitman over here. You all know every one of these three, but I am so grateful to each one of them for the leadership they've given the various embassies—Mike Glitman; Al Keel, whom we've been living with for 48 hours; and of course, my old friend, Al Kingon. So, I want to say to them that I am deeply grateful to each of them for the job he is doing.

And I hope that this result of this NATO meeting today will make your lives here much better, because I do think that the alliance, having come together in this meeting, sent a strong signal. And many of you in this room, although you might be in Brussels, or you might be in Al Kingon's office, helped work on this whole NATO initiative and helped spend your time working at NATO. So, I'm grateful to those who have been a part of all of this—but in a way, you all are, because under [Secretary of State] Jim Baker, we have an outstanding team.

Let me say, I have great respect for those of you in the Foreign Service. And you're talking to one who was supported so strongly when I first went up to the United Nations as Ambassador—didn't really know what I was walking into, and here was this fantastic, dedicated service ready to carry out the instructions of the Secretary of State and help this new Ambassador. And it made a profound impression on me. And then I saw it again when I was in China as the head of the liaison office there. So, I have respect for the Foreign Service. I have respect for those of you who are attached to the embassies, be it as career people, from Commerce, and certainly our military, USIA [U.S. Information Agency], and many other organizations. Public service is a noble calling, and you who serve overseas exemplify its very best. So, thank you all very much for what you do all the time.

I didn't quite know how to receive the welcome that I received when I went in here to one of Jennifer's offices, right there outside the girls' locker room. [*Laughter*] This one caught my eye: "Yo, President Bush!" [*Laughter*] I think that's what it said. [*Laughter*] "I think you're really cool." I want the press to listen to this one. "You make all the right decisions," and "I'm glad you're coming to school," and "I love your hair." [*Laughter*] I wonder—that might have been for Barbara—that might have been yours. Maybe that was for the Silver Fox—who knows? Anyway, it was signed "Kohl K.," and both Bushes appreciate it.

And this one caught my eye out there—I didn't have long to digest these: "Dear President Bush, remember me?" [*Laughter*] Funny thing is, I do. "I am Margaret Hogg. I have come to the last three Christmas parties when you were Vice President." And yes, she did, her dad being a distinguished naval officer. "The first one we came to, my brothers and I ate all the strawberries." [*Laughter*] "The second time, we took five big candy bars—five each when we were only supposed to take two." It really would—but nice to see you. "We're waiting for you across the road. We'll be waving," she said. Well, what better welcome can a President have? [*Laughter*]

But we are heading on to Bonn in just a minute, but I really wanted to just pop in here and tell you that you are not forgotten—you are loved; you are respected. And thank you all very much. And to you, Jennifer, thank you for taking the lead in this trilingual—I thought I heard—maybe it was only two—but nevertheless—[*laughter*]—teaching these kids. And I tell you, one of the things that has been marvelous about this summit is the understanding that our values, the alliance's values—but our values are winning the battle around the world. There's no longer a question of whether we've been on the right side on democracy and freedom and those things; we are. And now the beautiful thing about it is, I think, as we look at Eastern Europe and we look in other places in the world, we see that it's the American values that are prevailing. And I think that right here in this wonderful school, the kids—in addition to their families, they get it right here in this school, inculcating in them the values that are carrying the day worldwide for the great United States of America.

Thank you all, and God bless you.

Note: The President spoke at 2:40 p.m. in the school gymnasium. In his opening remarks, he referred to Dr. Jennifer Beckwith, principal of the school; Maynard W. Glitman, U.S. Ambassador to Belgium; Alton G. Keel, Jr., U.S. Ambassador to NATO; and Alfred Kingon, U.S. Ambassador to the Commission of the European Communities.

Remarks and a Question-and-Answer Session With Reporters Following Discussions With Chancellor Helmut Kohl in Bonn, Federal Republic of Germany
May 30, 1989

The Chancellor. Mr. President, ladies and gentlemen: allow me to welcome you, Mr. President, very cordially here to the Federal Republic of Germany. This is a good day for us. A few days ago we celebrated the 40th anniversary of the Federal Republic of Germany, and these 40 years were also 40 years of friendship and partnership with the United States. Over these four decades, American soldiers defended, together with our troops, freedom and peace in our country. And a lot of what was decisive for the early history of our country was initiated by the United States, and we always received support by the United States.

I would like to welcome you very cordially as a proven friend of our country, as a personal friend who has always stood ready to help me in difficult times. And yesterday and today we met in order to celebrate the 40th anniversary of NATO. We jointly discussed in the spirit of friendship difficult questions which are now important for our future. Your initiative, your new proposal for disarmament, is an enormous step into the future, and it shows the inspiration emanating from the leadership role of the United States. Mr. President, that was a wise, a right decision at a very important point in time. And now it's up to the other side to actually take that hand which has been extended to it, and then that will be a great work of peace.

We have taken up already our talks. I would just like to mention two points on our agenda. First of all, we talked about the foundation of the European Community and then about the completion of the internal market of the European Community by the 31st of December, 1992. This will lend a new quality to European policy, and you know the Federal Republic of Germany has been a motor, an engine, behind this development.

But we are also a motor for open world trade. And if from time to time I hear reports and read reports from the United States that people are afraid and we would isolate ourselves against the rest of the world, drawing up barriers to trade, I say to people: This will not happen in any case, and certainly not receive the support of the Federal Republic of Germany. On the contrary, I firmly believe that in the next years to come, the European Community and the United States of America will enjoy deepened relations—political relations and economic relations.

For us, the relationship with the United States is of existential importance. And therefore, we also discussed another very important point which goes beyond day-to-day politics, that is to say, the fact that we want to intensify the exchange of pupils and students. We want as many young Germans as possible to go to the United States and to get to know the country. And we also would like to see as many young Americans as possible come over here to our country. And to use an image that's out of this planting of young trees: A forest may grow which stands as a symbol of the solid friendship between our two countries. To put it quite simply, Mr. President, we're glad you're here. You are a friend among friends.

The President. Let me just be very brief and first thank Chancellor Kohl for this warm reception. I told him that I don't believe German-American relations have ever been better. And secondly, I am very pleased with the reaction to the NATO decision that was taken. I think it shows NATO to be together; it shows NATO to be strong. And indeed, I think in challenging Mr. Gorbachev to come forward now, we have moved in the right direction in unity. It is in the interest of NATO; it is clearly in the interest of the United States and all the members in NATO—the Federal Republic. And I happen to believe that what we've proposed is in the interest of the Soviet Union.

So, we will see what the reaction is, but this was a wonderful celebration of the 40th anniversary of NATO. And, Chancellor Kohl, once again my sincere thanks to you, sir, for your hospitality and for the total cooperation between the United States and the Federal Republic.

Short-Range Nuclear Forces in Europe

Q. Mr. Chancellor, sir, do you consider yourself a winner? Do you consider yourself a winner or a loser on the short-range missiles? Did you get what you wanted, or is it a real compromise?

The Chancellor. I think we were all just winners in Brussels. I think that the alliance has given itself the best kind of birthday present it could have given. After difficult discussions, we came to a joint decision, and this decision is what applies. I think we've—all of us—had the personal experience of having to make compromises, and I think that this is a good thing. And we also came to a compromise here. And just as one concrete answer to your question, there are only winners; and actually that's a very rare experience for a politician, and I relish that.

Q. Is this compromise enough for you to win the election next year? [*Laughter*]

The Chancellor. I am completely certain as to the result of the elections in 1990. And as a very concrete answer to your question, I think it is very helpful with regard to the majority of the German people that we have here a government and a head of government who has proved his friendship with the United States over the course of the years. So, insofar, yesterday and today will indeed be helpful.

Q. Mr. President, when will you go to Berlin?

The President. The answer is, I don't know; and you can have another question. [*Laughter*]

Q. Would you expand the Berlin initiative of your predecessor?

The President. Defend it?

Q. No, expand it, enlarge it?

The President. We might well; we might well. We might have something to say about that tomorrow in Mainz.

Thank you very much.

Note: The Chancellor spoke at 6:21 p.m. in the Chancellery. He spoke in German, and his remarks were translated by an interpreter. Prior to their remarks, the President and the Chancellor participated in a bilateral meeting with U.S. and West German officials.

Toast at a Dinner Hosted by Chancellor Helmut Kohl in Bonn, Federal Republic of Germany

May 30, 1989

Mr. Chancellor, and ladies and gentlemen, it is a very great honor for us to be in this magnificent room and to be received so warmly by the Chancellor of the Federal

Republic of Germany and by all of you. I would have enjoyed my first visit here as President regardless of its timing, for I have often visited this wonderful country. And always, Barbara and I have marveled at the kindness of your people.

But there is a special significance to this visit, for it coincides with two dates of great importance to both our countries: the 40th anniversary of the founding of the Federal Republic of Germany and the Atlantic alliance. For four decades, each event has enriched the other. And today it is hard to imagine a NATO without a democratic Germany, for yours has been, and remains, a success story almost without parallel. It is also hard to envision Germany without NATO, for this alliance has been, and remains, a citadel of freedom at the center of American foreign policy.

The history of postwar U.S.-German relations is of allies resolute and strong, united by the values of family, faith, human rights, and democracy, and ties—economic, cultural, military—that bind our democracies; a common dedication to the cause of peace—that, too, unites us—and the knowledge that Western unity is central to that cause. In 1989 we are nearer our goals of peace and European reconciliation than at any time since the founding of NATO and the Federal Republic, but we will achieve them only if we uphold the principles which have guided our friendship and the Atlantic alliance for 40 years.

Winds of change are blowing in Eastern Europe, including in the Soviet Union. And it's happening, in part, because Mr. Gorbachev has seen that our society works and that his does not. And we welcome these changes and are prepared to move beyond containment to a policy that seeks to integrate the Soviet Union into the community of nations. And we're encouraged by changes in Eastern Europe, particularly in Poland and in Hungary. To encourage fundamental economic and political reform, we will respond with a more active engagement of Eastern European governments and peoples.

And if hope exists for ending the division of Europe, it is because we have for 40 years been willing to defend our own freedom. In the future, let us learn from the past, and that past tells us that preserving a strong defense offers the greatest hope of easing Europe's division and ensuring Europe's freedom. For peace through strength will give the Soviet Union continued incentive to seek its security through democratization, economic reform.

The United States and its allies share a vision of a less militarized Europe, where great armies no longer face each other across barbed wire and concrete walls. And that is why I put forward my conventional arms control initiative yesterday at the NATO summit. We seek a Europe without barriers, united by free markets, united by democracy.

And tonight I'm pleased to make a modest announcement. Beginning shortly, holders of passports of the Federal Republic of Germany visiting the United States as tourists or on business will no longer be required to obtain U.S. visas. I hope this is a modest demonstration of the ever closer relationship between our two countries.

Forty years ago, the world marveled at perhaps Germany's finest profile in courage. Some have termed it "the cradle of the American-German friendship." And I refer, of course, to the Berlin airlift. And together, we stood as allies against the forces of tyranny. And today we must stand again, and will. Apart, we cannot succeed. Together, we cannot fail. And in that spirit, I ask you all to rise and raise your glasses: To the Federal Republic of Germany on its 40th anniversary, to German-American friendship; to the most enduring alliance in the history of man; and to the health of my dear friend and colleague, the Chancellor of the Federal Republic.

Note: The President spoke at 8:51 p.m. in the dining room at Redoute Castle.

Message to the Congress on Trade With Hungary and China

May 31, 1989

To the Congress of the United States:

I hereby transmit the documents referred to in Subsection 402(d)(5) of the Trade Act of 1974 with respect to a further 12-month extension of the authority to waive Subsections (a) and (b) of Section 402 of the Act. These documents constitute my decision to continue in effect this waiver authority for a further 12-month period.

I include as part of these documents my determination that further extension of the waiver authority will substantially promote the objectives of Section 402. I also include my determination that continuation of the waivers applicable to the Hungarian People's Republic and the People's Republic of China will substantially promote the objectives of Section 402. The attached documents also include my reasons for extension of the waiver authority, and for my determination that continuation of the waivers currently in effect for the Hungarian People's Republic and the People's Republic of China will substantially promote the objectives of Section 402.

GEORGE BUSH

The White House,
May 31, 1989.

Presidential Determination No. 89–14—Memorandum on Trade With Hungary and China

May 31, 1989

Memorandum for the Secretary of State

Subject: Determination Under Section 402(d)(5) of the Trade Act of 1974—Continuation of Waiver Authority

Pursuant to the authority vested in me under the Trade Act of 1974 (Public Law 93–618), January 3, 1985 (88 Stat. 1978) (hereinafter "the Act"), I determine, pursuant to Subsection 402(d)(5) of the Act, that the further extension of the waiver authority granted by Subsection 402(c) of the Act will substantially promote the objectives of Section 402 of the Act. I further determine that the continuation of the waivers applicable to the Hungarian People's Republic and the People's Republic of China will substantially promote the objectives of Section 402 of the Act.

This determination shall be published in the *Federal Register.*

GEORGE BUSH

[*Filed with the Office of the Federal Register, 4:39 p.m., June 23, 1989*]

Note: The determination was printed in the "Federal Register" of June 27.

Statement on the Resignation of Speaker of the House of Representatives Jim Wright

May 31, 1989

The Speaker and I are both from Texas. We have been friends for many years. In spite of the present situation, I believe the Wright tenure was one of effectiveness and dedication to the Congress of the United States, and I recognize his distinguished service to the people of his congressional district. Barbara and I wish Jim and Betty well in whatever lies ahead.

Remarks to American Embassy Employees and Their Families in Bonn, Federal Republic of Germany
May 31, 1989

The President. Thank you, Mr. Secretary, and let me just say a word about our Ambassador here in Bonn. We Bushes have known Dick Walters for many years. And I really can't think of any public servant who has served his country in so many diverse assignments, always with excellence, and in whom I have more confidence than Dick Walters. And he is a great Ambassador, a great advocate for the United States; and he can advocate the United States in about 11 different foreign languages, including in German, and I think that's a wonderful thing. And, Dick, thank you for your hospitality and for your leadership in this country that is so vitally important to the United States.

I see a sign up here from Bonn Elementary. And it says—show me what the sign—it says, "We are the world." And you know, they're right—they are absolutely right about that. And the youth are the world. And what happened in NATO a couple of days ago I hope guarantees a more peaceful future for those that are the world—for you young people here. And for that action, I give great credit to the United States authorities that were involved: our Secretary of Defense [Cheney]; our Secretary of State [Baker] stayed up till all hours of the night achieving what now is seen as a wonderful arrangement; my National Security Adviser, who—some of you would recognize his name—is with me here today, Brent Scowcroft, General Scowcroft; our Chief of Staff [Sununu]; and on and on it goes, because this U.S. position was a cooperative position—we worked it out through the entire bureaucracy. And it seems to have captured the imagination certainly of the free world and I hope, eventually, of the Soviet Union.

And so, we came to Bonn in the wake of a very successful NATO meeting. But it isn't a victory for the United States. Ours was a team effort in going to NATO, and the result was a team victory. The victory was for NATO in coming together in unified fashion, demonstrating its solidarity after 40 years of keeping the peace in Europe.

To each of you in the Embassy, whether you be Foreign Service or attached to the Embassy with one of the other services—Commerce, whatever else—USIA [U.S. Information Agency]—so many others, and certainly to our military, let me pay my respects. I normally try to single out the admin officer. And because we've been rushing around, I don't know who that poor embattled soul is in Embassy Bonn——

Q. Harry Geisel.

The President. Harry? There he is, he's still smiling. [*Laughter*] And some of that is because we told Harry we were leaving on schedule and getting out of his way. [*Laughter*] And now he's giving three cheers for that. But I cite him because I was on the receiving end of some of these visits when I lived halfway around the world in China, and I know that they can be a pluperfect pain. And so, I would only think, Harry, and then everybody else in the political and the economic and every section—communications—every section of this tremendous and effective Embassy that has been involved in this visit, Barbara and I are very grateful to each and every one of you. And this hospitality, even though we enjoyed it for such a short time, really rang through loud and clear from the very moment we got here.

I can tell you that we've just finished talks with the Chancellor, and Jim with the Foreign Minister. And I can say that a lot because of your work, your professionalism and—in the military sense, your dedication to duty—the relationship between the Federal Republic and the United States has never been better. And for that same conviction on the part of many of you here, the relationship and the strength of NATO has never been stronger.

So we really dropped by to say hail and farewell and thank you from the grateful heart of this President of the United States. Many, many thanks, and God bless the United States of America. Thank you all very much.

Note: The President spoke at 11:20 a.m. at the residence of Rita Suessmuth, President of the Bundestag, the West German Parliament. In his opening remarks, he referred to Vernon A. Walters, U.S. Ambassador to West Germany. In his closing remarks, the President referred to Harold W. Geisel, administrative officer at the U.S. Embassy in Bonn; Secretary of State James A. Baker III; and West German Foreign Minister Hans-Dietrich Genscher.

Remarks to the Citizens of Mainz, Federal Republic of Germany
May 31, 1989

Thank you, Chancellor Kohl. At the outset, let me tell you that—lest you think that he has forgotten his home State because he is the Chancellor of the Federal Republic—I will only tell you that in the last 24 hours Chancellor Kohl has been convincing me that when I came to this State and to Mainz, I would be coming to heaven. [*Laughter*] And having gotten here, I think he may just about be right, I'll tell you. Thank you all very much.

Dr. Wagner and Lord Mayor, distinguished hosts, I want to also thank these two bands, West German and American, for that stirring music. And Chancellor Kohl, I especially want to thank you again for inviting me to this beautiful and ancient city on my first Presidential trip to the Republic of Germany—the Federal Republic. And Herr Kohl and I have concluded now our deliberations at the NATO summit in Brussels, an excellent start to our working partnership as Chancellor and President.

And here in Mainz, by the banks of the Rhine, it's often said that this heartland of mountain vineyards and villages embodies the very soul of Germany. So, Mainz provides a fitting forum for an American President to address the German people. Today I come to speak not just of our mutual defense but of our shared values. I come to speak not just of the matters of the mind but of the deeper aspirations of the heart.

Just this morning, Barbara and I were charmed with the experiences we had. I met with a small group of German students, bright young men and women who studied in the United States. Their knowledge of our country and the world was impressive, to say the least. But sadly, too many in the West, Americans and Europeans alike, seem to have forgotten the lessons of our common heritage and how the world we know came to be. And that should not be, and that cannot be.

We must recall that the generation coming into its own in America and Western Europe is heir to gifts greater than those bestowed to any generation in history: peace, freedom, and prosperity. This inheritance is possible because 40 years ago the nations of the West joined in that noble, common cause called NATO. And first, there was the vision, the concept of free peoples in North America and Europe working to protect their values. And second, there was the practical sharing of risks and burdens, and a realistic recognition of Soviet expansionism. And finally, there was the determination to look beyond old animosities. The NATO alliance did nothing less than provide a way for Western Europe to heal centuries-old rivalries, to begin an era of reconciliation and restoration. It has been, in fact, a second Renaissance of Europe.

As you know best, this is not just the 40th birthday of the alliance, it's also the 40th birthday of the Federal Republic: a republic born in hope, tempered by challenge. And at the height of the Berlin crisis in 1948, Ernst Reuter called on Germans to stand firm and confident, and you did—courageously, magnificently.

And the historic genius of the German people has flourished in this age of peace, and your nation has become a leader in technology and the fourth largest economy on Earth. But more important, you have inspired the world by forcefully promoting the principles of human rights, democracy, and freedom. The United States and the Federal Republic have always been firm friends and allies, but today we share an added role: partners in leadership.

Of course, leadership has a constant companion: responsibility. And our responsibility is to look ahead and grasp the promise of the future. I said recently that we're at the end of one era and at the beginning of another. And I noted that in regard to the Soviet Union, our policy is to move beyond containment. For 40 years, the seeds of democracy in Eastern Europe lay dormant, buried under the frozen tundra of the Cold War. And for 40 years, the world has waited for the Cold War to end. And decade after decade, time after time, the flowering human spirit withered from the chill of conflict and oppression; and again, the world waited. But the passion for freedom cannot be denied forever. The world has waited long enough. The time is right. Let Europe be whole and free.

To the founders of the alliance, this aspiration was a distant dream, and now it's the new mission of NATO. If ancient rivals like Britain and France, or France and Germany, can reconcile, then why not the nations of the East and West? In the East, brave men and women are showing us the way. Look at Poland, where Solidarity, *Solidarność*, and the Catholic Church have won legal status. The forces of freedom are putting the Soviet status quo on the defensive. And in the West, we have succeeded because we've been faithful to our values and our vision. And on the other side of the rusting Iron Curtain, their vision failed.

The Cold War began with the division of Europe. It can only end when Europe is whole. Today it is this very concept of a divided Europe that is under siege. And that's why our hopes run especially high, because the division of Europe is under siege not by armies but by the spread of ideas that began here, right here. It was a son of Mainz, Johannes Gutenberg, who liberated the mind of man through the power of the printed word. And that same liberating power is unleashed today in a hundred new forms. The Voice of America, Deutsche Welle, allow us to enlighten millions deep within Eastern Europe and throughout the world. Television satellites allow us to bear witness from the shipyards of Gdansk to Tiananmen Square. But the momentum for freedom does not just come from the printed word or the transistor or the television screen; it comes from a single powerful idea: democracy.

This one idea is sweeping across Eurasia. This one idea is why the Communist world, from Budapest to Beijing, is in ferment. Of course, for the leaders of the East, it's not just freedom for freedom's sake. But whatever their motivation, they are unleashing a force they will find difficult to channel or control: the hunger for liberty of oppressed peoples who've tasted freedom.

Nowhere is this more apparent than in Eastern Europe, the birthplace of the Cold War. In Poland, at the end of World War II, the Soviet Army prevented the free elections promised by Stalin at Yalta. And today Poles are taking the first steps toward real election, so long promised, so long deferred. And in Hungary, at last we see a chance for multiparty competition at the ballot box.

As President, I will continue to do all I can to help open the closed societies of the East. We seek self-determination for all of Germany and all of Eastern Europe. And we will not relax, and we must not waver. Again, the world has waited long enough.

But democracy's journey East is not easy. Intellectuals like the great Czech playwright Vaclav Havel still work under the shadow of coercion. And repression still menaces too many peoples of Eastern Europe. Barriers and barbed wire still fence in nations. So, when I visit Poland and Hungary this summer, I will deliver this message: There cannot be a common European home until all within it are free to move from room to room. And I'll take another message: The path of freedom leads to a larger home, a home where West meets East, a democratic home, the commonwealth of free nations.

And I said that positive steps by the Soviets would be met by steps of our own. And this is why I announced on May 12th a readiness to consider granting to the Soviets temporary waiver of the Jackson-Vanik trade restrictions if they liberalize emigration. And this is also why I announced on Monday that the United States is prepared to drop the "no exceptions" standard that has guided our approach to controlling the export of technology to the Soviet Union, lifting a sanction enacted in response to their invasion of Afghanistan.

And in this same spirit, I set forth four proposals to heal Europe's tragic division, to help Europe become whole and free.

First, I propose we strengthen and broaden the Helsinki process to promote free elections and political pluralism in Eastern Europe. As the forces of freedom and democracy rise in the East, so should our expectations. And weaving together the slender threads of freedom in the East will require much from the Western democracies.

In particular, the great political parties of the West must assume an historic responsibility to lend counsel and support to those brave men and women who are trying to form the first truly representative political parties in the East, to advance freedom and democracy, to part the Iron Curtain.

In fact, it's already begun to part. The frontier of barbed wire and minefields between Hungary and Austria is being removed, foot by foot, mile by mile. Just as the barriers are coming down in Hungary, so must they fall throughout all of Eastern Europe. Let Berlin be next—let Berlin be next! Nowhere is the division between East and West seen more clearly than in Berlin. And there this brutal wall cuts neighbor from neighbor, brother from brother. And that wall stands as a monument to the failure of communism. It must come down.

Now, *glasnost* may be a Russian word, but "openness" is a Western concept. West Berlin has always enjoyed the openness of a free city, and our proposal would make all Berlin a center of commerce between East and West—a place of cooperation, not a point of confrontation. And we rededicate ourselves to the 1987 allied initiative to strengthen freedom and security in that divided city. And this, then, is my second proposal: Bring *glasnost* to East Berlin.

My generation remembers a Europe ravaged by war. And of course, Europe has long since rebuilt its proud cities and restored its majestic cathedrals. But what a tragedy it would be if your continent was again spoiled, this time by a more subtle and insidious danger—Chancellor referred to—that of poisoned rivers and acid rain. America's faced an environmental tragedy in Alaska. Countries from France to Finland suffered after Chernobyl. West Germany is struggling to save the Black Forest today. And throughout, we have all learned a terrible lesson: Environmental destruction respects no borders.

So, my third proposal is to work together on these environmental problems, with the United States and Western Europe extending a hand to the East. Since much remains to be done in both East and West, we ask Eastern Europe to join us in this common struggle. We can offer technical training, and assistance in drafting laws and regulations, and new technologies for tackling these awesome problems. And I invite the environmentalists and engineers of the East to visit the West, to share knowledge so we can succeed in this great cause.

My fourth proposal, actually a set of proposals, concerns a less militarized Europe, the most heavily armed continent in the world. Nowhere is this more important than in the two Germanys. And that's why our quest to safely reduce armament has a special significance for the German people.

To those who are impatient with our measured pace in arms reductions, I respectfully suggest that history teaches us a lesson: that unity and strength are the catalyst and prerequisite to arms control. We've always believed that a strong Western defense is the best road to peace. Forty years of experience have proven us right. But we've done more than just keep the peace. By standing together, we have convinced the Soviets that their arms buildup has been costly and pointless. Let us not give them incentives to return to the policies of the past. Let us give them every reason to abandon the arms race for the sake of the human race.

In this era of both negotiation and armed camps, America understands that West Germany bears a special burden. Of course, in this nuclear age, every nation is on the front line, but not all free nations are called to endure the tension of regular military activity or the constant presence of foreign military forces. We are sensitive to these special conditions that this needed presence imposes.

To significantly ease the burden of armed camps in Europe, we must be aggressive in our pursuit of solid, verifiable agreements between NATO and the Warsaw Pact. On Monday, with my NATO colleagues in Brussels, I shared my great hope for the future of conventional arms negotiations in Europe. I shared with them a proposal for achieving significant reductions in the near future.

And as you know, the Warsaw Pact has now accepted major elements of our Western approach to the new conventional arms negotiations in Vienna. The Eastern bloc acknowledges that a substantial imbalance exists between the conventional forces of the two alliances, and they've moved closer to NATO's position by accepting most elements of our initial conventional arms proposal. These encouraging steps have produced the opportunity for creative and decisive action, and we shall not let that opportunity pass.

Our proposal has several key initiatives. I propose that we lock in the Eastern agreement to Western-proposed ceilings on tanks and armored troop carriers. We should also seek an agreement on common numerical ceiling for artillery in the range between NATO's and that of the Warsaw Pact, provided these definitional problems can be solved. And the weapons we remove must be destroyed.

We should expand our current offer to include all land-based combat aircraft and helicopters by proposing that both sides reduce in these categories to a level 15 percent below the current NATO totals. Given the Warsaw Pact's advantage in numbers, the Pact would have to make far deeper reductions than NATO to establish parity at those lower levels. Again, the weapons we remove must be destroyed.

I propose a 20-percent cut in combat manpower in U.S.-stationed forces and a resulting ceiling on U.S. and Soviet ground and air forces stationed outside of national territory in the Atlantic-to-the-Urals zone at approximately 275,000 each. This reduction to parity, a fair and balanced level of strength, would compel the Soviets to reduce their 600,000-strong Red Army in Eastern Europe by 325,000. And these withdrawn forces must be demobilized.

And finally, I call on President Gorbachev to accelerate the timetable for reaching these agreements. There is no reason why the 5-to-6-year timetable as suggested by Moscow is necessary. I propose a much more ambitious schedule. And we should aim to reach an agreement within 6 months to a year and accomplish reductions by 1992, or 1993 at the latest.

In addition to my conventional arms proposals, I believe that we ought to strive to improve the openness with which we and the Soviets conduct our military activities. And therefore, I want to reiterate my support for greater transparency. I renew my proposal that the Soviet Union and its allies open their skies to reciprocal, unarmed aerial surveillance flights, conducted on short notice, to watch military activities. Satellites are a very important way to verify arms control agreements, but they do not provide constant coverage of the Soviet Union. An open skies policy would move both sides closer to a total continuity of coverage while symbolizing greater openness between East and West.

These are my proposals to achieve a less militarized Europe. A short time ago, they would have been too revolutionary to consider, and yet today we may well be on the verge of a more ambitious agreement in Europe than anyone considered possible.

But we're also challenged by developments outside of NATO's traditional areas of concern. Every Western nation still faces the global proliferation of lethal technologies, including ballistic missiles and chemical weapons. We must collectively control the spread of these growing threats. So, we should begin as soon as possible with a worldwide ban on chemical weapons.

Growing political freedom in the East, a Berlin without barriers, a cleaner environment, a less militarized Europe—each is a noble goal, and taken together they are the foundation of our larger vision: a Europe that is free and at peace with itself. And so, let the Soviets know that our goal is not to undermine their legitimate security interests. Our goal is to convince them, step-by-step, that their definition of security is obsolete, that their deepest fears are unfounded.

When Western Europe takes its giant step in 1992, it will institutionalize what's been true for years: borders open to people, commerce, and ideas. No shadow of suspicion, no sinister fear is cast between you. The very prospect of war within the West is unthinkable to our citizens. But such a peaceful integration of nations into a world community does not mean that any nation must relinquish its culture, much less its sovereignty.

This process of integration, a subtle weaving of shared interests, which is so nearly complete in Western Europe, has now finally begun in the East. We want to help the nations of Eastern Europe realize what we, the nations of Western Europe, learned long ago: The foundation of lasting security comes not from tanks, troops, or barbed wire; it is built on shared values and agreements that link free peoples. The nations of Eastern Europe are rediscovering the glories of their national heritage. So, let the colors and hues of national culture return to these gray societies of the East. Let Europe forgo a peace of tension for a peace of trust, one in which the peoples of the East and West can rejoice—a continent that is diverse yet whole.

Forty years of Cold War have tested Western resolve and the strength of our values. NATO's first mission is now nearly complete. But if we are to fulfill our vision—our European vision—the challenges of the next 40 years will ask no less of us. Together, we shall answer the call. The world has waited long enough.

Thank you for inviting me to Mainz. May God bless you all. Long live the friendship between Germany and the United States. Thank you, and God bless you.

Note: The President spoke at 1:16 p.m. in the Rheingoldhalle, an auditorium in Mainz. In his opening remarks, he referred to Dr. Carl-Ludwig Wagner, Minister-President of Rheinland-Pfalz, and Lord-Mayor Herman-Harmut Weyel.

Remarks to Military Personnel and Their Families in Frankfurt, Federal Republic of Germany

May 31, 1989

Thank you very much for that welcome back. Some of you may have all been around here a couple years ago, and my only regret is, I won't get to go running on the track here this time. [*Laughter*] But I was here about 3 years ago as Vice President, and things have changed since then. Now, there's a new number one: the Rhein-Main Rockets. [*Applause*] But Secretary [of State] Baker and I and General Scowcroft [Assistant to the President for National Security Affairs] and our Chief of Staff, John Sununu, and Barbara and all the rest of our traveling squad are just delighted to be here, heading off to London right now and then—eat your hearts out—the good old U.S. of A. on Friday afternoon.

But let me be serious for just a minute and say that it is an honor to stand before an audience of men and women who serve the Armed Forces of the greatest country on the face of the Earth. And for over four decades now—NATO having celebrated its 40th anniversary just 2 or 3 days ago—people like you have left home, often family and loved ones, and you've served as guardians to this gateway to freedom. And your presence here inspires a deep admiration and gratitude—certainly from me personally, that is—we saw at that NATO meeting from people all around the world. And so, thank you for all you're doing to keep freedom secure. You've been directly responsible, each in his own way, for the longest peace that Europe has known in centuries—over 40 years of peace. And that's an achievement that the world now applauds and that history will honor.

You know, people talk often about the "right stuff," but the heroism and the humanity of American soldiers at Rhein-Main and other bases are the stuff of legend. Your dedication, I believe, is constant and enduring, day after day. And I've been told about some instances where your own humanity touches the lives of so many.

This is a special place, a place whose spirit of service reaches back to the tense days 40 years ago of the Berlin airlift, when a pilot named Gail Halverson, during his repeated runs, parachuted bags of candy to the children of Berlin. They called him Uncle Wiggley-Wings or the Chocolate Bomber, and he was a man who brought kindness to the cruelest of times.

And standing among you today is his son, Major Brad Halverson, who organized the Armenian airlift—children injured in that devastating earthquake. And I was told by a high-ranking Soviet official that that outreach to the people of Armenia said as much to the Soviet Union as any message that any President could possibly send. And there's Captain Dawn Oerichbauer, the medical crew director, who said, "The whole mission was worth it when I saw the hope and the hurt in the faces of the children."

And I know that also with us today is Major Bob Anderson, chief of the mental health clinic, a quiet hero who in his own way has helped so many on this base deal with the aftermath of terrorist threats. He's put lives back together, warded off the chill of fear.

And I single out a few because they represent the many. Here at Rhein-Main, with lifesaving medical evacuation missions, triumphant hostage returns, the normal day-to-day mission of flying in the crowded skies of Europe—for you, heroism with a human touch is really the meaning of this mission. And you've seen the tears of those devastated by tragedy, and you've seen the tears of joy stream down the faces of those returning to freedom and of those who love them. And you've performed that everyday acts of vigilance that make preparedness possible. I think of all the security people—some guy out guarding a C–5 all night, supply clerk makes calls all day to find a part that's needed, flight-line attendant deicing planes at 4 a.m. on days something unlike this one.

And just this year, as NATO celebrates its 40th anniversary, we begin to sense new opportunities for coexistence. We may be seeing the dawning of a new age, but the reasons why you are here have not changed. There've been signs of progress from the Soviet Union; and though we hope for more, the nations of the alliance still face a Soviet Union with preponderant and awesome military power. And your presence in West Germany, your contribution to the security of Western Europe, is absolutely essential.

And I might add that I left Germany today feeling that the relations with the Federal Republic and the United States, our bilateral relations, have never been better. And I want to thank each one of you for the way you interact with our German friends. It does show the best side of America to the people in the Federal Republic of Germany. And I know that it's not easy serving away from home, but because of you and the sacrifices, our world is indeed safer and more secure.

You know, in a letter to John Adams, Thomas Jefferson once wrote: "I've seen enough of one war never to wish to see another." And out there today, I know, are a number of children, some of them third generation of Americans stationed here at Rhein-Main, who have never seen war, and I hope they never do. The power to wage war is the power to prevent it, and that's our mission here. And we must remain prepared for war even as we work hard for peace. And believe me, we will strive hard to achieve the lasting peace.

So, carry on. Thank you all. God bless you, and God bless the United States of America. Thank you all very, very much.

Note: The President spoke at 5:43 p.m. on the tarmac at Rhein-Main Air Force Base. Following his remarks, the President traveled to London.

Remarks and a Question-and-Answer Session Following Discussions With Prime Minister Margaret Thatcher in London
June 1, 1989

The President. Let me just thank the Prime Minister on behalf of our entire traveling squad. She and I talked in detail about a wide array of issues. I want to thank her, and I want to assert here that the special relationship that has existed between the United Kingdom and the United States is continuing and will continue. And once again, Madam Prime Minister, my sincere thanks to you for a very encouraging and frank exchange that we had. It's only with friends that you can take off the gloves and talk from the heart. And I felt that I was with a friend today, and I can assure the people in the United Kingdom that, from our side of the Atlantic, this relationship is strong and will continue to be.

The Prime Minister. Thank you very much, Mr. President. Ladies and gentlemen, the President comes here after a very, very successful NATO summit due to the leadership of the United States under the Presidency of George Bush. We talked about the followup to these matters. We talked also about the very difficult situation in the Middle East. We talked about the situation in China. We talked about matters in South Africa. And we have talked about matters in the Argentine and in Central America.

And so, I think you'll agree we have covered an extremely wide range of subjects, and yet the morning has been too short. We spoke together for about an hour and three-quarters and then joined our foreign ministers and Mr. Scowcroft [Assistant to the President for National Security Affairs]. And they, too, had considered some of these matters and others. We then also talked about the problems in Cambodia and the problems with the Vietnamese boat people still going to Hong Kong.

So, you can see that we have compressed a great deal into the time. We think very much the same way, which isn't surprising. And we're absolutely delighted that we have in President Bush a President of the United States who is staunch and steadfast on everything which is of fundamental value to democracy, freedom, and justice—necessary to keep our country secure, and yet forever stretching out the hand of friendship with other nations across the European divide, trying to extend to the world some of the benefits which we enjoy but take for granted.

We are in a period when—as the President has said in some of his most excellent speeches—it's the end of containment. It's freedom on the offensive—a peaceful offensive—throughout the world. I think they have been some of the most valuable and happy talks I've had for a very long time, and we thank and congratulate the President.

Q. Mrs. Thatcher——

Q. Mrs. Prime Minister——

The Prime Minister. No, no, now, one at a time.

Q. All right, Mrs. Thatcher, can I ask, first of all——

The Prime Minister. One moment. You question me frequently. What about the President?

European-U.S. Relations

Q. Well, perhaps I can ask both of you: Is Britain America's most important ally in Europe?

The Prime Minister. I think you might put it more tactfully. [*Laughter*] America has allies throughout Europe and throughout the free world. I would like to think that we pride ourselves of being among the foremost of United States friends, and we will always be. I think it's quite wrong that because you have one friend you should exclude the possibility of other friendships as well. And I'm sure the President doesn't, and I don't. We both have many friends in Europe.

The President. Very good answer.

Q. Mr. Bush, can I ask you: Do you think that West Germany and France will increasingly share the spotlight in the so-called special relationship you have with Mrs. Thatcher?

The President. I think that the special relationship that I referred to in my opening remarks speaks for itself. And I think the remarks that the Prime Minister just made about U.K.'s propensity for friendship with other nations and the United States' friendship with other nations—those remarks speak for themselves. And so, I would simply say I expect this relationship to continue on the steady keel because it is so fundamentally based on common values. And the NATO alliance, for example, is not going to divide up into inside cliques of who is the closest friend to whom.

But the point I want to make here is that I value the judgment, the conviction, the principled stance of Prime Minister Thatcher. I've been privileged to know her and work with her in a—for me, a lesser capacity, for 8 years. And this visit alone—as we crossed many, many borders and discussed the problems—reassures me and just reaffirms what I've always felt: that we have a very, very special relationship. But it needn't be at the expense of our friendship with other countries.

The Prime Minister. Just one more. That's the other television channel. One more.

Eastern Europe

Q. Mr. Bush, what exactly can Britain do to bring about this further freedom in Eastern Europe that you said you want to see?

The President. Well, they've already done one step, and that is to help NATO come out with a very sound proposal. I can tell you that the Prime Minister and her able Foreign Minister [Sir Geoffrey Howe] helped shape this whole NATO proposal, which both of us think is a very forward-looking document, adhering to principles. So, it's not a question of the future; they've already performed, since I've been here in the last few days, a very useful role. And there are many other areas where, just on bilateral basis, that I'm sure the United Kingdom can influence and encourage this trend to democracy that the Prime Minister referred to—many other areas. The U.K. is widely respected in Eastern Europe.

The Prime Minister. Thank you. I think Mrs. Bush awaits. No, that was the last question. Thank you for coming.

Note: The President spoke at 12:40 p.m. at 10 Downing Street, the Prime Minister's residence. Prior to their remarks, the President and the Prime Minister participated in a bilateral meeting with U.S. and British officials.

Remarks to American Embassy Employees and Their Families in London
June 1, 1989

The President. Thank you so much for that warm welcome back. Thank you, Mr. Secretary. I'd like you to meet some that have been traveling with us to NATO and Italy, and then to Germany. I see General Scowcroft standing over here, who I know most of you feel you know because of his many years of public service—Brent Scowcroft. In that far corner over there is a household word for those who plug into CNN: Marlin Fitzwater, my esteemed—standing right over there. I don't see our Chief of Staff, John Sununu, but maybe he branched off. [*Laughter*] But in any event, I owe them a tremendous vote of thanks, to say nothing of our able Secretary of State, for the job that they did as a team representing our interests—the United States interest and, I think, the interest of the free world—at NATO. Their support was absolutely superb—their imagination, their creativity. Jim Baker, who gets tired when he drives to work in the morning—[*laughter*]—stayed up until about 1:30 hammering out in the darnedest way an agreement that has received strong support around the world. And I am grateful to him and, as I say, Brent and all those who are part of our team, to say nothing of the support of Bob Blackwill and others who are with us who did an awful lot of heavy lifting.

So, we come in here today feeling encouraged, not overconfident. But I think the alliance is strong; I think it's together. And I think now we have to follow up and do those things that our joint communique committed us to do. And of course, we will be needing the support of the able Foreign Service offices in every post to get this job done.

I have standing next to me—or I did before I came to this podium—our mystery guest. [*Laughter*] And I know that all of you—it doesn't matter what your religious convictions are—have the same respect and love for Billy that Barbara and I have—Billy Graham, Dr. Graham, who is here once again doing the Lord's work. And I ran into him downstairs, not just by accident, because if he hadn't come to see me, we'd have darn sure gone to see him. And so, I just wanted to welcome the great son of North Carolina.

I want to thank everybody in this Embassy. We're now shifting to bilaterals, as we say, because I have been on the receiving end of Presidential visits. And they can be a pluperfect pain. [*Laughter*] What is your admin officer?

Audience member. Larry Russell.

The President. Larry Russell. Is Larry still speaking to me? Where is he? [*Laughter*] But I want to thank him, wherever he is, because these admin officers bear a disproportionate share of the load. I don't want to single him out, because I know there is political; I know the military play a part in all of this; security plays a part on it; communicators are overworked. And the only thing I can say is, you can breathe easy tomorrow about 10, because I promise to leave on schedule. [*Laughter*] But thank you, in the meantime, for the fantastic support of this, one of the greatest embassies that the United States has anywhere in the world.

I meant what I said about the Foreign Service. I think you have had an outstanding DCM [deputy chief of mission] here, and the fact that he will be assuming very, very high-level responsibilities back in Washington is of enormous comfort to me. And Ray is going to do a superb job back there, taking on the breadth of responsibilities that not many have in that department. And I personally look forward to working with him, and I know I can learn an awful lot from what you taught him right here in this Embassy. [*Laughter*]

I want to mention the Marines—sometimes we forget them, but I don't. And I have great respect for them, and I want to thank them for the job they do. And let me also mention the citizens of the U.K., with whom we all work in the Embassy. And I expect some are here, but you can't tell them from us. [*Laughter*] And that's one of the great things about it. [*Laughter*]

But really, I am indebted to each of you, because I know you never lose your allegiance to your own country—you never should. But the contribution you make to an embassy of this nature is simply incalculable, and I am grateful to all of you. And I hear from the Ambassador and from all of those with whom I have contact back home of the great job that the Brits do who are part of our Embassy. And I hope you feel loved and wanted, because that's the way we feel about you. So, thank you for your contribution to the American foreign policy and to the success of this Embassy.

I, too, want to mention what Jimmy said about—Secretary Baker, I mean, said about—[*laughter*]—Marie Burke. We can't dwell on it, but she was a valued member of the Foreign Service, and I was told that—serving since 1971 in a number of posts. And all I can do is express my condolences to her friends and, obviously, her family, and my sympathy. And I would like to think that someday the culprit can be found and all of that. But the main thing is, I know you all miss her, and I want you to know that I respect that concept of service that she epitomized.

This Embassy has got a new Ambassador, and I have known Henry Catto and his wife, Jessica, for a long time. And he will be an outstanding Ambassador to the United Kingdom. It is one of the very most important posts we have. And the fact that I asked him to come here and that he accepted I hope sends a signal to our British friends that in him they have somebody who is very, very close to this President and who has my full confidence. And I hope that's something that brings joy to you, because I think an Ambassador often is seen as the President's personal representative in these countries. That's the way the law has it, and that's the way it is. And Henry has my full confidence, and as you come to know him, get used to his eccentricities. [*Laughter*] I don't know who to blame for the cow on the front yard at Winfield House, but nevertheless—Jessica? [*Laughter*] No, Jessica and Henry are going to do a first-class job here, and I just wanted you to know from me that I have full confidence in them.

We came here just a few days ago, it seems. We went to Italy, and there we not only had a marvelous bilateral visit, but I had the opportunity to go to Nettuno and there honor our war dead, those who fell at Anzio beachhead. And the spirit of the Italian people—not just at Anzio but in Rome itself—for the American flag as it went by was really wonderful; and I think our relations are good there. And in Belgium, of course, the emphasis was multilateral, although again, we have good relations with Belgium. The emphasis was on trying to bring NATO together and project ourselves out into an optimistic future with strength. And as I say, I think that was accomplished.

We have a big job to follow up on all that now. And again, the political section here, I know, will be asked to present accurately and fully, as will our military here, our position to our friends in the United Kingdom. We've got to stay on the same wavelength with them, and we will. We've been strong, Margaret Thatcher being extraordinarily gracious in her comments about this U.S. initiative and this NATO collective decision. So, that went well.

Yesterday in Germany—I wish all of you could have been with us, not just for the trip that Barbara and I had down the Rhine on a beautiful sunny day, getting to—excuse me, Billy—kiss the wine princess and things like that. [*Laughter*] But again, you'd have been proud, because all along the way, and these castles and tourist hotels, where the American flags were out for about 2 hours—going down the Rhine River on this marvelous cruise boat not only with the Chancellor of the Federal Republic and the Foreign Minister but many of the leaders of Germany.

And so, I can report to you—and I think I can sort through cosmetics and reality—that it's real. The job that many of you have done when posted on the Continent itself is paying off, because the bilateral relationship with Germany is strong. And then today our meetings with Margaret Thatcher went very well, indeed. And of course, we just were honored to be received by Her Majesty the Queen. And we had a delightful luncheon at which the Queen presented Barbara with a picture of the Queen and one of our puppies that she just saw down in Kentucky. [*Laughter*]

So, it's been a wonderful day, and I will simply end where I began by thanking you—all of you—whatever end of this complex Embassy you're in, for your service to the greatest, freest, most wonderful country on the face of the Earth. Thank you, and God bless all of you.

Note: The President spoke at 3:15 p.m. at the U.S. Ambassador's residence in London. He was introduced by Secretary of State James A. Baker III. In his remarks, the President referred to Brent Scowcroft, Assistant to the President for National Security Affairs; Marlin Fitzwater, Press Secretary to the President; Robert D. Blackwill, Special Assistant to the President for National Security Affairs; evangelist Billy Graham; Raymond Seitz, Assistant Secretary of State-designate for European Affairs; and Marie Burke, a Foreign Service officer murdered while serving in the U.S. Embassy in London.

White House Statement on the Anniversary of the Signing of the Intermediate-Range Nuclear Forces Treaty With the Soviet Union
June 1, 1989

One year ago today, on June 1, 1988, the President of the United States and the President of the Soviet Union exchanged the instruments of ratification bringing into force the intermediate-range nuclear forces (INF) treaty, the first in history to bring about actual reductions in nuclear arsenals.

The goal of the INF treaty—the complete elimination of INF missile systems under conditions of strict verification—is being accomplished. Since the summer of 1988, when eliminations began with the destruction of a Soviet SS–20 at Kapustin Yar and an American Pershing II at Longhorn, Texas, both sides have continued to eliminate INF missiles, launchers, and support equipment in the presence of inspectors from the other side.

The achievement of the INF treaty was a signal victory for NATO solidarity and political resolve and a contribution to greater security for our allies. It established the long-held alliance principles of asymmetrical reductions to reach equality of forces and effective verification as essential components of arms control agreements. These principles remain keystones of our approach to arms control.

The agenda ahead is even more challenging as we move forward with NATO's conventional force proposals and the President's initiative this week for added reductions. Further, we seek stabilizing reductions in strategic arsenals and increased reliance on strategic defenses, and a truly global and effective verifiable ban on chemical weapons. We will spare no effort to achieve agreements that will reduce the risk of war and strengthen the foundations for peace.

Statement by Press Secretary Fitzwater on Landsat Satellite Program Funding
June 1, 1989

The President today announced he had approved funding for continued operations of Landsat satellites 4 and 5 and for the completion and launch of Landsat 6. The President's action endorsed a recommendation from the National Space Council, chaired by Vice President Dan Quayle. The President also directed the National Space Council and the Office of Management and Budget to review options with the intention of continuing Landsat-type data collections after Landsat 6.

Landsat, which takes detailed photographs of the Earth, is the U.S. Government's civil, space-based, land-remote sensing program. Landsat-type imagery data is important for such applications as global change research, environmental monitoring, law enforcement, natural resource estimates, national security, and a variety of private sector uses. In addition, Landsat provides a visible symbol of the U.S. commitment to, and leadership in, the use of space for the common good.

Over recent years, it has become increasingly evident that commercializing the entire Landsat program would not be feasible until at least the end of the century. Since earlier government planning was based on commercializing the entire program, the absence of near-term commercial viability threatened continuity of Landsat and jeopardized continuity of Landsat data. The National Space Council, at its first meeting on May 12, recommended the action endorsed by President Bush today.

Continued operation of Landsat 4 and 5 will require an additional $5 million in FY

89 and $19 million in FY 90. Cost of completion and launch of Landsat 6 by 1991 has already been included in the Commerce Department budget.

Nomination of Timothy B. Atkeson To Be an Assistant Administrator of the Environmental Protection Agency

June 1, 1989

The President today announced his intention to nominate Timothy B. Atkeson to be Assistant Administrator of the Environmental Protection Agency (International Activities). He would succeed Jennifer Joy Manson.

Mr. Atkeson is currently a partner with Steptoe and Johnson in Washington, DC. From 1975 to the present, he has been in private practice. Mr. Atkeson served as General Counsel for the Council on Environmental Quality in the Executive Office of the President, 1970 to 1973, and General Counsel to the Office of Technology Assessment, United States Congress, 1974.

Mr. Atkeson graduated from Harvard College (B.A., 1947); Oxford University (B.A., 1949; M.A., 1954); and Yale Law School (LL.B., 1952; J.D., 1951). He was born April 18, 1927, and resides in Washington, DC.

Nomination of Shirley Temple Black To Be United States Ambassador to Czechoslovakia

June 1, 1989

The President today announced his intention to nominate Shirley Temple Black to be Ambassador Extraordinary and Plenipotentiary of the United States of America to the Czechoslovak Socialist Republic. She would succeed Julian Martin Niemczyk.

Ambassador Black has served as a Representative to the 24th General Assembly of the United Nations, 1969–1970. She has also served as United States Ambassador to Ghana, 1974–1976; and as Chief of Protocol at the White House, 1976–1977. She was a Member of the U.S. Delegation on African Refugee Problems in Geneva, 1981; and a Member of the Public Advisory Commission, United Nations Conference on Law of the Sea. She was Deputy Chairman, U.S. Delegation, United Nations Conference on Human Environment in Stockholm, 1970–1972. Ambassador Black has also served as Special Assistant to the Chairman of the President's Council on Environmental Quality, 1972–1974.

Ambassador Black was born April 23, 1928, in Santa Monica, CA. She is married to Charles A. Black.

Continuation of Michael Ussery as United States Ambassador to Morocco

June 1, 1989

The President today announced that Michael Ussery would continue to serve as Ambassador Extraordinary and Plenipotentiary of the United States of America to the

Kingdom of Morocco.

Since 1988 Mr. Ussery has served as Ambassador Extraordinary and Plenipotentiary of the United States of America to the Kingdom of Morocco. Prior to this, he served as Deputy Assistant Secretary for Near Eastern and South Asian Affairs, Department of State, 1985–1988; Special Assistant for White House Liaison, 1983–1985; Special Assistant in the Bureau of International Organization Affairs, Department of State, 1981–1983; and administrative assistant for Congressman Carroll Campbell, 1979–1981. In addition, he has served as planner for the South Carolina Disaster Preparedness Agency, 1975–1976; and as a legislative aide in the Georgia House of Representatives, 1973–1975.

Mr. Ussery graduated from Newberry College (B.A., 1973). He was born January 20, 1951, in Columbia, SC. He is married and resides in Alexandria, VA.

Nomination of C. Howard Wilkins, Jr. To Be United States Ambassador to The Netherlands

June 1, 1989

The President today announced his intention to nominate C. Howard Wilkins, Jr., to be Ambassador Extraordinary and Plenipotentiary of the United States of America to the Kingdom of The Netherlands. He would succeed John Shad.

Mr. Wilkins is the founder of Maverick Development Corp. and has served as the president since 1975. He has also served as chairman of the board for Maverick Restaurant Corp. since 1981. Mr. Wilkins was vice chairman of the board, Pizza Hut, Inc., 1974 to 1975; founder of Pizza Hut Corp. of America and president and chairman of the board, 1970 to 1974; and franchise director, then vice president of Pizza Hut, Inc., 1968 to 1970.

Mr. Wilkins graduated from Yale University (B.A., 1960). He was born in 1938 in Wichita, KS. Mr. Wilkins is married, has five children, and currently resides in Wichita, KS.

Continuation of Richard Wood Boehm as United States Ambassador to Oman

June 1, 1989

The President today announced that Richard Wood Boehm would continue to serve as Ambassador Extraordinary and Plenipotentiary of the United States of America to the Sultanate of Oman.

Mr. Boehm has served as Ambassador Extraordinary and Plenipotentiary of the United States of America to the Sultanate of Oman since 1988. Prior to this, he served as diplomat-in-residence and visiting professor at Howard University in Washington, DC, 1987–1988; United States Ambassador to Cyprus, 1984–1987; Deputy Examiner in the Bureau of Examiners for Foreign Service, Department of State, 1984; Adviser to the United States Delegation to the United Nations General Assembly in New York, 1983; and was appointed career member of the Senior Foreign Service, 1981. In addition, he has served as Public Affairs Adviser at the Bureau of Economic Affairs, Department of State, 1969–1971.

Mr. Boehm graduated from Adelphi University (A.B., 1959) and George Washington University (M.A., 1969). He was born June 25, 1926, in New York, NY. He has two children.

Nomination of Morris Dempson Busby for the Rank of Ambassador While Serving as Coordinator for Counterterrorism

June 1, 1989

The President today announced his intention to nominate Morris Dempson Busby to be accorded the rank of Ambassador during his tenure as Coordinator for Counterterrorism.

Since 1987 Ambassador Busby has served as Roving Ambassador and Special Envoy for Central America. He has also served as Principal Deputy Assistant Secretary for Inter-American Affairs, 1987–1988, and headed a special State Department office to oversee the assistance program to the Nicaraguan resistance, 1987. From 1984 to 1987 he served as Deputy Chief of Mission in Mexico City. Ambassador Busby joined the Department of State in 1973, serving in various capacities, including Director of the Office of Oceans and Polar Affairs, Deputy Assistant Secretary for Oceans Affairs, and Ambassador of the United States for Oceans and Fisheries Affairs. From 1981 to 1983 he was Alternate Representative to the Conference on Disarmament in Geneva, Switzerland.

Ambassador Busby graduated from Marshall University and received a master's degree from George Washington University. He was a naval officer for 15 years. He attended the U.S. Naval Destroyer School, the Defense Intelligence School, and the Naval War College. He has been awarded the Meritorious Service Award, the Navy Commendation Medal, and the Bronze Star. He is a native of Huntington, WV. Ambassador Busby is married and has two children.

Designation of Roger B. Porter as Acting Chairman of the President's Commission on White House Fellowships

June 1, 1989

The President has designated Roger B. Porter to be Acting Chairman of the President's Commission on White House Fellowships.

Currently Mr. Porter is Assistant to the President for Economic and Domestic Policy. Prior to this, Mr. Porter served as IBM professor of government and business at Harvard University and faculty chairman of the program for senior managers in government; Deputy Assistant to the President and Director of the White House Office of Policy Development; Executive Secretary of the Economic Policy Council, 1974–1977; and as Counselor to the Secretary of the Treasury. In addition, he has served as Executive Secretary of the Cabinet Council on Economic Affairs, 1981–1985; assistant dean and tutor in politics at the Queen's College, Oxford, 1971–1972; and associate director of the Utah local government modernization study, 1972.

Mr. Porter received his B.A. degree from Brigham Young University, B.Phil. from Oxford University, and his M.A. and Ph.D. from Harvard University. He is married, has three children, and resides in Washington, DC.

Toast at a Dinner Hosted by Prime Minister Margaret Thatcher in London
June 1, 1989

Well, Prime Minister and Mr. Thatcher and distinguished ladies and gentlemen, Barbara and I and all of our traveling squad are just delighted to be here. And let me start by thanking you, Madam Prime Minister, for your thoughtful and gracious comments. And I also want to thank you for inviting us here and especially for the marvelous chat that we had today and for the extraordinary hospitality of this evening. And I'll speak for Barbara, which I normally don't do—[*laughter*]—thank you for your kind words about Barbara, and she is doing very well indeed at home, thank you. And I am not in the least bit jealous. I wonder when we finish a press conference and Helen Thomas of the UPI says, to end it, "Thank you, Barbara's husband." [*Laughter*] But nevertheless, thank you for your warm words about her, and we're very proud of her.

This is a most distinguished gathering, and if I start singling out the excitement that Barbara and I felt about meeting the various individuals around here, I'd get into serious trouble. I love politics, and we've got some good, competitive politics around this table. Neil [Neil Kinnock, British Labor Party leader], nice to see you, sir, and the associates on the other side. I love sports, and I could learn about that stiff left arm and looking at the pin and not getting nervous on putting from one distinguished guest here, or bending my knees and volleying properly from another. And so, you have adequately accommodated my insatiable quest for being the name-dropper of the year by the distinguished guests here. [*Laughter*]

But I want to single out one. In 1971 or 1972, I was the Ambassador at the United Nations, and a distinguished former Prime Minister was the Foreign Minister of the United Kingdom. And he was in New York for a very high-level meeting. And I was the new boy on the block at that time, just out of Congress, representing our country at the U.N. And Sir Alec had solved some terribly important business at the moment, but it was a Sunday in New York. And Barbara and I were sitting in our luxurious Embassy high atop the Waldorf, and I said to her, "I wonder what Sir Alec Douglas-Home is doing this morning?" She said, "Don't you dare." And I said, "No, I'm going to call him up." And we had only shook hands with him in a long line of other worshipers.

And darned if he didn't say, "Yes, I'd love to go out to Greenwich and see the birds and the sanctuary." And that marvelous gesture on his part of accepting the hospitality of a lowly Ambassador, and certainly a new one in foreign affairs—we've never forgotten it. And I don't know whether his wife has forgotten my boosting her across the fence into the bird sanctuary. But nevertheless, I saw an intimacy there—the affection that the people—I saw why the people of the United Kingdom have this enormous affection for Sir Alec. So, I will single him out and say how pleased we are to see him again. I expect I could still have an awful lot to learn from him.

Margaret, the talks that we held today I found, not in a diplomatic sense but just in a personal sense and an important sense, extraordinarily useful—not just because we're colleagues but we do represent two great nations. This visit—if you're interested in trivial pursuits, a little historic trivia—represents, I think, your and my, at least, 10th meeting—maybe more—six in London alone, I'm sure. And every time I meet with you all's distinguished Prime Minister, I'm reminded of something that Disraeli once said: "There is no wisdom like frankness." And your Prime Minister's honesty, her candor, is an enormous resource not just for the United Kingdom but for the West. And I'm sure it's a reason for this success that she's had as Prime Minister.

Mrs. Thatcher is a seasoned leader, with 10 years of demonstrable success in office, and I do value her judgment and her insight. Americans look to you, Madam Prime

Minister, with great admiration for all you have done for Britain and all that you have done for the alliance and all you have done for those who value freedom, wherever they may be in the world.

As Sir Antony Acland knows, we lived for 8 years as Vice President right next door to the British Embassy. I say he knows it because he's been extraordinarily tolerant when our helicopter would come in at 12 a.m. or 1 a.m. or 2 a.m. from some campaign trip. He never filed a protest—[*laughter*]—and Jenny, indeed, was very tolerant also. And I'm just delighted that they are in Washington. You're being so ably represented there, and I only regret we don't live next door anymore. But nevertheless, every morning and every night, I'd pass your Embassy grounds with this life-sized, marvelous statue of Winston Churchill, cast of rugged iron to withstand our rains and the cold, and the figure is really beautiful, as stoic as the man was in real life.

And Winston Churchill was America's first such partner in leadership really, when we were challenged together by war. And true, the challenge of today is a different one than Churchill and Roosevelt felt at the time, but it is one that really asks no less of us. I do believe that this profound change that's sweeping the nations of the East offers enormous potential. And we in the West support these forces of change. We want them to succeed; we want these changes to endure. And if progress continues, we will work together to move beyond containment of the Soviet Union, to draw the peoples of the East into the commonwealth of free nations.

It was in this very city that, a little more than a century ago, Karl Marx died, leaving behind ideas that were to bear his name. It was in this city, and indeed in some of these same rooms, that a succession of British Prime Ministers worked with my predecessors to stem Marxism at full-tide. But today we can explore possibilities for peace that would have seemed wildly unrealistic just a handful of years ago. With NATO's new conventional arms control initiative—and it is NATO's, and there is no quest for credit—we are an alliance. We are a partnership; we are together. We seek to free Western Europe from the shadow of Soviet military power. And similarly, with our agreement in NATO on short-range nuclear forces, we demonstrated that we can manage change while doing what your Prime Minister has urged on all of us: remaining true to our strategy of deterrence, true to our principles. The recent summit showed NATO at its unified best, a triumph for all who yearned to move beyond a divided Europe—a Europe of armed camps—to a Europe that is whole, a Europe that is free.

And in this quest, I will be looking for our part to our friends in London. Ladies and gentlemen, I ask you to rise and raise our glasses to a British Prime Minister who holds the reins of history, to a friend, a dear friend of the United States of America, our respected friend, the Prime Minister, Margaret Thatcher: to your health and our relationship.

Note: The President spoke at 10:13 p.m. at 10 Downing Street, the Prime Minister's residence.

Informal Exchange With Reporters
June 2, 1989

The President. Thank you all. Great trip; enjoyed it.

Q. How do you feel, Mr. President?

The President. Feel pretty good, feel pretty good—can't wait to take a day off, but——

Q. We're hearing about some more bold new moves, such as the one you made—[*laughter*].

The President. Hey, listen, I'll let you know in the same fashion we let you know on the first one.

Q. ——of your political career?

Strategic Arms Reduction Talks

Q. START talks——

The President. What, Anne?

Q. START talks. Do you think the START talks will now move faster?

The President. Well, I don't know. We haven't really begun them. But I'm determined to get our proposals in shape and go there in a constructive spirit. I don't know that I see a connection at all, although I'm still pleased with what we're hearing from the Soviets. So, maybe there's some linkage.

Excuse me, Helen [Helen Thomas, United Press International]?

NATO Summit Meeting

Q. First, have you heard from Gorbachev? And do you think this is the biggest political success of your long career?

The President. No. [*Laughter*]

Q. Well, when you're the President——

The President. Now we're talking, now we're talking. [*Laughter*]

Q. Have you heard from Gorbachev?

The President. No, not directly. See Brent [Scowcroft, Assistant to the President for National Security Affairs] on here, but I don't think we have, no. It will be a while. I mean, it's normal. You don't expect an instant answer. We hear from him on things, and we don't feel compelled to respond within 24 hours. But I'm confident we will, and I hope it's positive.

Q. Do you think you have a little more respect at home after this trip?

The President. I never felt kind of—you mean, along like Rodney Dangerfield kind of thing? [*Laughter*] I've not suffered from lack of respect. These fellows have all been very pleasant. [*Laughter*] Haven't you guys? Thank you very much.

Summit Meeting With President Gorbachev

Q. You and Gorbachev will both be in Europe at the same time this summer. Any chance——

The President. Well, it might make a case for closer—but I don't have any plans to cross paths in the summer when he's, like, on his way to Paris or we are. There are no plans. We'll just be——

Q. Sound like a good idea?

The President. No. I mean, I don't feel it sounds like a better idea than it was before the NATO meeting. But I've always felt that we eventually will get together, and should.

President's Trip to Poland

Q. What about your trip to Poland? Do you think this is a really crucial time for a trip going to Poland?

The President. Yes. I think my being in Poland is very, very important—just being there, to say nothing of the substance that I hope to talk to the leadership about. The substance is important, and being there. The American President going to Poland by itself is important, given my feelings about the changes in Europe as a whole, and aspirations for a Europe that will be freer and more democratic and with which we will have better relations. So, it is important, but that visit is not going to solve all the economic problems that are afflicting that nation—by a long shot.

House of Representatives

Q. There's a scent of a war going on on the Hill right now in the House. How do you feel about that? Is that good for the——

The President. I don't like it.

Q. What do you think they ought to do, or do you have any suggestions or ideas?

The President. I think the last thing they need is advice from the executive branch as to how to proceed. I have made some broad suggestions, but on these recent events, I said what I wanted to say about Jim Wright, which is saluting his service, and leaving it at that. Do I like it? No, I don't.

Q. Have you talked to him?

The President. No, I have not.

NATO Proposals

Q. You seemed to be hinting in the Washington Post interview you had—[*inaudible*]—proposals up your sleeve.

The President. Not very far—I mean, not very far along.

Q. [*Inaudible*]

The President. Helen, here's the basic problem with answering your question as frankly as I normally would. The process requires consultation with so many people that it is impossible to divulge ahead of time what we might or might not do, because the idea—including this last one—might well get gunned down before you have a chance to really flesh out the proposal. But I don't mean to be mysterious, there's no grand design out there right now. We just want to move forward.

I think the first priority is to follow through on the collective decision that NATO has taken and try to meet these very ambitious time sequences—September 7th—and then moving forward and then, of course, vigorous negotiations. So, we've got some work to do to make this NATO decision into a reality. But I'm determined to kick our bureaucracy and the NATO bureaucracy as best I can, push it forward.

Q. A lot of people seem to think—[*inaudible*].

The President. Well, they're entitled to their opinion. I'm a little more optimistic than their pessimistic assessment. Thank you all.

Weekend Plans

Q. What are you going to do for the rest of the day?

The President. Got to take a look at the ocean, and I could tell you. Just a minute. It's clear enough, I expect I'll be out on *Fidelity* in about 2 hours.

Q. Do you want company?

Q. Are you going out to dinner tonight?

The President. No, we're not going out to dinner tonight. That's a promise. [*Laughter*]

Q. You're not going to Florida, are you? Not going to Florida——

The President. Oh, no. For the funeral? No.

Note: The exchange took place aboard Air Force One en route from London to Pease Air Force Base, ME. In his remarks, the President referred to his boat, "Fidelity." He also referred to the funeral of Representative Claude Pepper of Florida.

Remarks on Arrival in Portsmouth, New Hampshire

June 2, 1989

Well, thank you very, very much. What a surprise and wonderful welcome back; I am delighted and overwhelmed. Thank you so very much.

In the last week, Barbara and I have been to Rome and the Vatican, Brussels, Bonn, and London; and working with our allies in Europe, we set a course for the future. And we must move to fulfill that promise, moving beyond containment, moving beyond the era of conflict and cold war that the world has known for more than 40 years, because keeping the peace in Europe means keeping the peace for America.

Our alliance seeks a less militarized Europe, a safer world for all of us. And I'm now returning from Europe with a message for the American people, a message of hope. We have a great and historic opportunity to shape the changes that are transforming Europe. This chance has been delivered not just because of our strength and resolve but also because of our power of ideas, especially one idea which is sweeping the Communist world: democracy.

For the last 6 weeks, I've presented, in a series of speeches, ways to deal with these changes to make the most of this opportunity. And let me summarize: In Michigan, I stressed that the United States will actively encourage peaceful reform led by the forces of freedom in Eastern Europe. The Texas speech explains America's commitment to a balanced approach in our relationship with the Soviet Union: that we must remain strong and realistic—judge their performance, not their rhetoric—all the while seeking a friendship with the Soviets that knows no season of suspicion. And at Boston University the focus was our partnership with a more united Western Europe, of how a strong Europe means a strong America. And then at the Coast Guard Academy, I said that America is ready to seize every—and I do mean every—opportunity to bring the Soviet

Union into the community of nations.

And then, with my colleagues in Brussels, on the 40th anniversary of the founding of the North Atlantic alliance, we celebrated NATO's 40 years of success in preserving the peace in Europe, the longest period without war in all the recorded history of that continent. And we were reminded that once again the future of so many nations depends on NATO's unity and resolve. We were reminded that NATO must remain strong and together, and we were challenged to seize this new opportunity for progress while staying true to the principles that got us here.

Well, we met that challenge. We agreed to strive, to hope for a Europe that is whole and free. At the Rheingoldhalle in Mainz, in the heart of Germany, I said that the Cold War began with the division of Europe and it must end with a reconciliation based on shared values, where East joins West in a commonwealth of free nations.

And that is my vision for the future, and here is how we get there. The Warsaw Pact has a lot more planes, a lot more arms, a lot more troops in Europe than the NATO alliance; and we challenge the Soviets, if they are serious, to reduce to equal numbers. Our proposal is bold but fundamentally fair, and every single one of our allies agreed with our proposal. We proposed a new initiative for more comprehensive and faster negotiated cuts in conventional arms to lift the West at last from the shadow cast over Europe since 1945 by massive Soviet ground and air forces, and our allies agreed. And we proposed that Berlin, East and West, become a center of cooperation, not confrontation; and our allies agreed. And we proposed that we strengthen the Helsinki process to support free elections in Eastern Europe, and our allies agreed.

Because the threat of environmental destruction knows no borders, we proposed that the West enlist the countries of Eastern Europe in one of the great causes of our time: the common struggle to save our natural heritage.

And with our agreement in NATO on our short-range nuclear forces in Europe, we demonstrated as an alliance that we can manage change while remaining true to the strategy of deterrence which has kept the peace.

In short, this week's NATO summit in Brussels showed that we are ready to help shape a new world. In this period of historic change, the NATO alliance has never been more united, never been stronger; and we issued a summit declaration detailing our vision for the future and plan of action. And ours is not an arrogant challenge to Mr. Gorbachev, it's an appeal in good faith. The summit was a triumph for the alliance, a triumph of ideas, and most of all it was a triumph of hope.

And let me say it is truly gratifying that all of this was understood so well at home and abroad. While keeping our defenses up and our eyes wide open, we must go forward. We must stay on the offensive. We must get to work now to end the Cold War. The world has waited long enough. And if we succeed, the world your children will know, the world of the 21st century, will be all the better.

We are delighted to be here. I salute the men and women of Pease Air Force Base, who help keep the peace. I thank my friends and neighbors from New Hampshire, and I even spot a few from Kennebunkport, Maine, here. I thank the two Governors and the Members of the United States Congress that came out to greet us. And I particularly thank a former Governor of the State of New Hampshire standing over here, my able Chief of Staff, John Sununu; our Secretary of Defense, Dick Cheney; our Secretary of State, Jim Baker; and my very able friend and adviser, the head of the National Security Council, General Brent Scowcroft.

Listen, Barbara and I are overwhelmed by this welcome home. Thank you all. God bless you, and God bless the United States of America. Thank you very much.

Note: The President spoke at 12:15 p.m. at Pease Air Force Base.

Statement on the Chinese Government's Suppression of Student Demonstrations

June 3, 1989

It is clear that the Chinese Government has chosen to use force against Chinese citizens who were making a peaceful statement in favor of democracy. I deeply deplore the decision to use force against peaceful demonstrators and the consequent loss of life. We have been urging—and continue to urge—nonviolence, restraint, and dialog. Tragically, another course has been chosen. Again, I urge a return to nonviolent means for dealing with the current situation.

The United States and People's Republic of China over the past two decades have built up through great efforts by both sides a constructive relationship beneficial to both countries. I hope that China will rapidly return to the path of political and economic reform and conditions of stability so that this relationship, so important to both our peoples, can continue its growth.

White House Statement on the Death of the Ayatollah Khomeini

June 4, 1989

The official Iranian news agency has confirmed the death of the Ayatollah Khomeini. With his passing, we hope Iran will now move toward assuming a responsible role in the international community.

The President's News Conference

June 5, 1989

The President. During the past few days, elements of the Chinese Army have been brutally suppressing popular and peaceful demonstrations in China. There has been widespread and continuing violence, many casualties, and many deaths. And we deplore the decision to use force, and I now call on the Chinese leadership publicly, as I have in private channels, to avoid violence and to return to their previous policy of restraint.

The demonstrators in Tiananmen Square were advocating basic human rights, including the freedom of expression, freedom of the press, freedom of association. These are goals we support around the world. These are freedoms that are enshrined in both the U.S. Constitution and the Chinese Constitution. Throughout the world we stand with those who seek greater freedom and democracy. This is the strongly felt view of my administration, of our Congress, and most important, of the American people.

In recent weeks, we've urged mutual restraint, nonviolence, and dialog. Instead, there has been a violent and bloody attack on the demonstrators. The United States cannot condone the violent attacks and cannot ignore the consequences for our relationship with China, which has been built on a foundation of broad support by the American people. This is not the time for an emotional response, but for a reasoned, careful action that takes into account both our long-term interests and recognition of a complex internal situation in China.

There clearly is turmoil within the ranks of the political leadership, as well as the People's Liberation Army. And now is the time to look beyond the moment to important and enduring aspects of this vital relationship for the United States. Indeed, the budding of democracy which we have seen in recent weeks owes much to the relationship we have developed since 1972. And it's important at this time to act in a way that will encourage the further development and deepening of the positive elements of that relationship and the process of democratization. It would be a tragedy for all if China were to pull back to its pre-1972 era of isolation and repression.

Mindful of these complexities, and yet of the necessity to strongly and clearly express our condemnation of the events of recent days, I am ordering the following actions: suspension of all government-to-government sales and commercial exports of weapons, suspension of visits between U.S. and Chinese military leaders, sympathetic review of requests by Chinese students in the United States to extend their stay, and the offer of humanitarian and medical assistance through the Red Cross to those injured during the assault, and review of other aspects of our bilateral relationship as events in China continue to unfold.

The process of democratization of Communist societies will not be a smooth one, and we must react to setbacks in a way which stimulates rather than stifles progress toward open and representative systems.

And I'd be glad to take a few questions before our Cabinet meeting, which starts in a few minutes.

Student Demonstrations in China

Q. Yes, Mr. President. You have said the genie of democracy cannot be put back in the bottle in China. You said that, however, before the actions of the past weekend. Do you still believe that? And are there further steps that the United States could take, such as economic sanctions, to further democracy in China?

The President. Yes, I still believe that. I believe the forces of democracy are so powerful, and when you see them as recently as this morning—a single student standing in front of a tank, and then, I might add, seeing the tank driver exercise restraint—I am convinced that the forces of democracy are going to overcome these unfortunate events in Tiananmen Square.

On the commercial side, I don't want to hurt the Chinese people. I happen to believe that the commercial contacts have led, in essence, to this quest for more freedom. I think as people have commercial incentive, whether it's in China or in other totalitarian systems, the move to democracy becomes more inexorable. So, what we've done is suspended certain things on the military side, and my concern is with those in the military who are using force. And yet when I see some exercising restraint and see the big divisions that exist inside the PLA, I think we need to move along the lines I've outlined here. I think that it's important to keep saying to those elements in the Chinese military: Restraint—continue to show the restraint that many of you have shown. And I understand there are deep divisions inside the army. So this is, we're putting the emphasis on that side of it.

Q. Have you had any personal contact with the Chinese leadership? Why do you think they moved in the way they did? And why did you wait so long?

The President. Well, I don't think we've waited so long, Helen [Helen Thomas, United Press International]. I made very clear, in a personal communication to Deng Xiaoping [Chairman of China's Central Military Commission], my views on this. I talked to the Ambassador last night, Jim Lilley. He's been in touch constantly with the Chinese officials, and so, I don't feel that we've waited long, when you have a force of this nature and you have events of this nature unfolding. We are the United States and they are China; and what I want to do is continue to urge freedom, democracy, respect, nonviolence, and with great admiration in my heart for the students. So, I don't think we've waited long.

What was the other part of your question?

Q. What impelled the Chinese Government? They did wait a long time, more than we expected really, and——

The President. Yes, they did.

Q. ——then they finally moved in. What do you think is the impetus?

The President. I'm glad you raised that point. We were, and have been, and will continue to urge restraint, and they did.

The army did show restraint. When Wan Li was here, he told me—and this is very Chinese, the way he expressed it—the army loves the Chinese people. And they showed restraint for a long time, and I can't begin to fathom for you exactly what led to the order to use force, because even as recently as a couple of days ago, there was evidence that the military were under orders not to use force. So I think we have to wait now until that unfolds.

Q. Mr. President, could you give us your current best assessment of the political situation there, which leaders are up, which are down, who apparently has prevailed here, and who apparently has lost?

The President. It's too obscure, it's too beclouded to say; and I would remind you of the history. In the Cultural Revolution days, Deng Xiaoping—at Mao Zedong's right hand—was put out. He came back in 1976. He was put out again in the last days of Mao Zedong and the days of the Gang of Four. Then he came back in, and to his credit, he moved China towards openness, towards democracy, towards reform. And suddenly we see a reversal, and I don't think there's anybody in this country that can answer your question with authority at this point. It doesn't work that way in dealing with China.

Q. But Mr. President, there have been reports that Deng was behind the move to order the troops, and other reports that he's ailing and in a hospital. What do you know about that, sir?

The President. Don't know for sure on either, and I've talked to our Ambassador on that, as I say, last night, and we just can't confirm one way or another—on the other.

Q. Mr. President, you spoke of the need for the U.S. to maintain relations with China; but given the brutality of the attacks over the last couple of days, can the U.S. ever return to business as usual with the current regime?

The President. I don't want to see a total break in this relationship, and I will not encourage a total break in the relationship. When you see these kids struggling for democracy and freedom, this would be a bad time for the United States to withdraw and pull back and leave them to the devices of a leadership that might decide to crackdown further. Some have suggested I take the Ambassador out. In my view, that would be 180 degrees wrong. Our Ambassador provides one of the best listening posts we have in China; he is thoroughly experienced. And so, let others make proposals that in my view don't make much sense. I want to see us stay involved and continue to work for restraint and for human rights and for democracy. And then down the road, we have enormous commonality of interests with China, but it will not be the same under a brutal and repressive regime. So, I stop short of suggesting that what we ought to do is break relations with China, and I would like to encourage them to continue their change.

Q. Mr. Bush, you're sending a message to the military and to the Government. A couple of weeks ago, you told the students to continue to stand by their beliefs. What message do you want the students to hear from what you're saying right now?

The President. That we support their quest for democracy, for reform, and for freedom—and there should be no doubt about that. And then, in sending this message to the military, I would encourage them to go back to the posture of a few days ago that did show restraint, and that did recognize the rights of the people, and that did epitomize what that Chinese leader told me, that the army loves the people. There are still vivid examples of that.

Q. Should the students go home? Should the students stop trying to fight the army?

The President. I can't dictate to the students what they should do from halfway around the world; but we support the quest for democracy and reform, and I'd just have to repeat that.

Iran

Q. Mr. President, I'd like to ask you about the other development in Iran. What is your assessment of who is in charge, and what opportunities the changes in Iran create for the U.S.?

The President. We're not sure yet. Khamenei [President Hojatolislam Ali] appears to be the anointed successor, the will having been read by Khomeini's son. But, again, in a society of that nature, it's hard to predict. I would simply repeat what I said on January 20th, that there is a way for a relationship with the United States to improve, and that is for a release of the American hostages. But, Charles [Charles Bierbauer, CNN], I can't give you an answer on that one. No experts here can yet, either.

Q. Well, do you plan any overture?

The President. I just made it.

Q. Do you plan any overtures or any other kind of opening toward Iran, towards the new government?

The President. No, absolutely not, they know what they need to do. They have been a terrorist state. And as soon as we see some move away from oppression and extremism of that nature, we will review our relationship.

Student Demonstrations in China

Q. Would you elaborate, Mr. President, on the question of economic sanctions—back to China. Did you consider economic sanctions for this morning's announcement, and what will you do if the violence escalates?

The President. I reserve the right to take a whole new look at things if the violence escalates, but I've indicated to you why I think the suspension of certain military relationships is better than moving against—on the economic side.

Q. Mr. President, do you feel that the Chinese leadership cares what the United States does or thinks right now?

The President. I think they are in the sense of contradiction themselves right now. China has historically been less than totally interested in what other countries think of their performance. You have to just look back to the Middle Kingdom syndrome. And you look back in history when outsiders, including the United States, were viewed as barbarians. So historically, China, with its immense pride and its cultural background and its enormous history of conflict—internal and external—has been fairly independent in setting its course.

I have had the feeling that China wants to be a more acceptable—acceptable in the family of nations. And I think any observer would agree that indeed, until very recent events, they've moved in that direction. So, what I would like to do is encourage them to move further in that direction by recognizing the rights of these young people and by rebuking any use of force.

Q. Mr. President, more than most Americans, you understand the Chinese. How do you account for the excessive violence of this response? Once the army decided to act, that they would drive armored personnel carriers into walls of people, how can you explain that?

The President. I really can't. It is very hard to explain, because there was that restraint that was properly being showed for a while on the part of the military, challenged to come in and restore—what I'm sure they'd been told—order to a situation, which I expect they had been told was anarchic. And so I can't explain it. I can't explain it, unless they were under orders, and then you get into the argument about, well, what orders do you follow? And so I condemn it; I don't try to explain it.

Let me take these next two rows, and then I'll go peacefully. Sorry about you guys back there.

Q. Will you, Mr. President, be able to accommodate the calls from Congress for tougher sanctions? Many lawmakers felt you were slow to condemn or criticize the violence in China before now, and many are pushing for much tougher action on the part of this country.

The President. I've told you what I'm going to do. I'm the President; I set the foreign policy objectives and actions taken by the executive branch. I think they know, most of them in Congress, that I have not only a keen personal interest in China, but that I understand it reasonably well. I will just reiterate to the leaders this afternoon my conviction that this is not a time for anything other than a prudent, reasoned response. And it is a time to assert over and over again our commitment to democracy, emphasize the strength that we give to democracy in situations of this nature.

And I come back to the front line question here: I do think this change is inexorable. It may go a couple of steps forward and then take a step back, but it is on the move. The genie will not be put back in the bottle. And so, I am trying to take steps that will encourage a peaceful change, and yet recognize the fact that China does have great pride in its own history. And my recommendations are based on my knowledge of Chinese history.

So, I would argue with those who want to do something more flamboyant, because I happen to feel that this relationship is vital to the United States of America, and so is our adherence to democracy and our encouragement for those who are willing to hold high the banner of democracy. So we found, I think, a prudent path here.

Q. Do you think that the events in China can have a chilling effect on democratic reforms occurring in other Communist countries, particularly in the Soviet Union and Eastern Europe, when they look at the kind of uprising that was sparked in China?

The President. No. I think the moves that we're seeing in Eastern Europe today, and indeed, in the Soviet Union, are going to go forward. And I think people are watching, more with horror, and saying: How, given this movement towards democracy, can the Chinese leadership react in the way they have? And so, I think this may be a sign to others around the world that people are heroic when it comes to their commitment to democratic change. And I would just urge the Chinese leaders to recognize that.

Q. Mr. President, there are reports that the Chinese military is badly divided and that, with this crackdown, the authorities brought in some troops from the Tibet conflict. If that's the case, how does suspending these military relationships encourage any kind of change? I mean, could you explain what the point of doing that is——

The President. I already did, David [David Hoffman, Washington Post]. You missed it. I explained it because I want to keep it on the military side. I've expressed here, rhetorically, the indignation we feel. I've recognized the history of China moving into its own Middle Kingdom syndrome, as it's done in various times in its past, and I want to encourage the things that have helped the Chinese people. And I think now the suspension is going to send a strong signal. I'm not saying it's going to cure the short-range problem in China. I'm not sure any outside country can cure the short range, the today-in-Tiananmen-Square problem. But I think it is very important the Chinese leaders know it's not going to be business as usual, and I think it's important that the army know that we want to see restraint. And this is the best way to signal that.

Q. Would you fear conflict? You talked about the divisions within the Chinese Army. Do you or your advisers fear that there could actually be a civil conflict between army commanders?

The President. Well, I don't want to speculate on that, but there are differences, clearly, within the army in terms of use of force. Otherwise, they wouldn't be doing what David Hoffman properly pointed out is happening: units coming in from outside.

And it is not, incidentally, just in Tiananmen Square that this problem exists. It is in Shanghai, it's in Chengdu today; it's in Guangzhou, I'm told, in a much smaller scale. But they brought the troops in from outside because the Beijing troops apparently demonstrated a great sensitivity to the cause of the young people and disciplined though they were, they opted for the side of democracy and change in the young people. So, those others came in. But I certainly don't want to speculate on something that I don't have—I can't reach that conclusion, put it that way.

Q. There were some news reports that some of the soldiers' units had burned their own trucks in—have you received the same type of intelligence reports?

The President. I just saw speculation. I haven't got it on any—I don't believe the intelligence said that. But there are reports that it is very difficult for some of the military, who are much more sympathetic to the openness, to the demonstrators. And I, again, go back to the original question here that Tom asked. I think, with the change that's taken place so far, we're beyond kind of a Cultural Revolution response. I think the depth of the feeling towards democracy is so great that you can't put the genie back in the bottle and return to total repression. And I think what we're seeing is a manifestation of that in the divisions within the PLA. But I certainly want to stop short of predicting a civil war between units of the People's Liberation Army.

Thank you all very much. I have a Cabinet meeting at 10 a.m.

Elections in Poland

Q. What about Poland? What do you think of the elections?

The President. Well, to make a profound statement, I think they were very interesting. We haven't seen the final results, but Communist bureaucrats beware in Poland. It looks to me like there's quite a move, moving towards the freedom and democracy.

Note: The President's 14th news conference began at 9:40 a.m. in the Briefing Room at the White House.

Letter to the Speaker of the House of Representatives and the Chairman of the Senate Foreign Relations Committee Reporting on the Cyprus Conflict
June 5, 1989

Dear Mr. Speaker: (Dear Mr. Chairman:)

In accordance with Public Law 95–384, I am submitting to you this bimonthly report on progress toward a negotiated settlement of the Cyprus question.

During the past 2 months the two Cypriot parties have continued their efforts, under the auspices of the United Nations Secretary General, to assemble the basic elements of a settlement in Cyprus. Following numerous meetings between the two leaders in Nicosia, they met with the Secretary General in New York, April 5–7, to review progress. On April 6, the United Nations issued a communique that noted that the Secretary General and the two leaders "reviewed the second round of talks whose objective was to develop a common understanding of the issues and to explore a range of possible options. They shared the Secretary General's view that the efforts made so far have been useful. They agreed to continue the talks with the objective of achieving results by June 1989."

The communique also noted that the objective in the coming weeks would be to prepare "a draft outline of an overall agreement in which the goals to be achieved for each of the elements of the outline would be described. . . . The two leaders accepted the Secretary General's invitation to meet with him again in June, if necessary, to complete the draft outline, to consider its status, and to decide how to proceed."

The United States Permanent Representative to the United Nations, Ambassador Thomas Pickering, met with both leaders during their visit to New York. They reiterated to Ambassador Pickering their confidence in the Secretary General, their appreciation of his commitment to solving the Cyprus problem, and their intention to continue working with the Secretary General and his representatives toward a negotiated solution.

We continue vigorous efforts to consult with and offer advice and assistance to key interested parties to the Cyprus dispute. I met with Prime Minister Ozal in Tokyo in February, as did Secretary of State Baker. Secretary Baker also has held meetings with the Prime Ministers and Foreign Ministers of Greece and Turkey and with the Foreign Minister of the Republic of Cyprus. The Department of State Special Cyprus Coordinator, M. James Wilkinson, traveled to Cyprus, Greece, and Turkey March 23–April 4 and is consulting regularly with concerned European allies.

In my previous report to the Congress, I noted that the United Nations was working with the two parties to adjust the military positions in Nicosia of Greek and Turkish Cypriot soldiers. I am pleased to report that the U.N.'s deconfrontation plan went into effect on May 17, greatly alleviating the probability of incidents posed by the dangerously close proximity of the two sides' military units in the Nicosia area. The United States worked hard in support of this U.N. effort. Congratulations are due to the Secretary General's political and military representatives on the island and to the parties themselves. We are hopeful that this achievement will prove the prelude to further progress, in terms both of immediate steps and the difficult questions underlying the Cyprus problem.

Finally, I would like to note that Major General Clive Milner of Canada became the new commander of the U.N. Peacekeeping Force in Cyprus (UNFICYP) on April 10, 1989, replacing Major General Guenther Greindl of Austria, UNFICYP's commander since 1981. I welcome the choice of General Milner for this important position and commend General Greindl whose performance under difficult and frustrating conditions was exemplary. He deserves the gratitude and appreciation of all those countries, groups, and individuals who benefited from his outstanding leadership.

Sincerely,

GEORGE BUSH

Note: Identical letters were sent to Jim Wright, Speaker of the House of Representatives, and Claiborne Pell, chairman of the Senate Foreign Relations Committee.

Nomination of Edward C. Stringer To Be General Counsel of the Department of Education

June 5, 1989

The President today announced his intention to nominate Edward C. Stringer to be General Counsel at the Department of Education. He would succeed Wendell L. Willkie, II.

Since 1980 Mr. Stringer has served in various capacities at the Pillsbury Company, including senior vice president and general counsel, 1980–1982; executive vice president and general counsel, 1982–1983; and executive vice president, general counsel, and chief administrative officer, 1983–1989. Prior to this, Mr. Stringer served as a partner with the law firm of Briggs and Morgan in Minneapolis, MN, 1969–1980; and as an associate and partner with Stringer, Donnelly, and Sharood, in Minneapolis, MN, 1960–1969.

Mr. Stringer graduated from Amherst College (B.A., 1957) and the University of Minnesota Law School (LL.B., 1960). Mr. Stringer resides in Minneapolis, MN.

Nomination of Constance Bastine Harriman To Be an Assistant Secretary at the Department of the Interior

June 5, 1989

The President today announced his intention to nominate Constance Bastine Harriman to be Assistant Secretary for Fish and Wildlife at the Department of the Interior. She would succeed Becky Norton Dunlop.

Since 1987 Ms. Harriman has served as an associate with the law firm of Steptoe and Johnson in Washington, DC. Prior to this, she served in various positions, including Associate Solicitor for Energy and Resources at the Department of the Interior, 1986–1987; Special Assistant to the Solicitor, 1985–1986; associate with Sheppard, Mullin, Richter and Hampton, 1980–1985; and attorney adviser in the Office of Legal Policy at the Department of Justice, 1982.

Ms. Harriman graduated from Stanford University (B.A., 1970; M.A., 1973) and the University of California (J.D., 1980). She resides in Bethesda, MD.

Appointment of Everett Ellis Briggs as Special Assistant to the President for National Security Affairs
June 5, 1989

The President today announced the appointment of Everett Ellis Briggs as Special Assistant to the President for National Security Affairs at the White House. Ambassador Briggs will be Senior Director for Latin America and the Caribbean at the National Security Council.

Since 1986 Ambassador Briggs has served as Ambassador to Honduras. Prior to this he was selected to be the Vice President of the National Defense University in Washington, DC. He served as United States Ambassador to Panama, 1982–1986; Deputy Assistant Secretary for Inter-American Affairs, 1981–1982; and Deputy Coordinator and Country Director for Mexican Affairs at the Department of State, 1979–1981. He served as deputy chief of mission in Asunción, Paraguay, 1974–1978; deputy chief of mission in Bogota, Colombia, 1978–1979; and Consul General in Luanda, Angola, 1972–1974. Ambassador Briggs has served in the State Department in the Inter-American, European, and International Organizations bureaus.

Ambassador Briggs was born in Cuba. He graduated from Dartmouth College and George Washington University. He is married, has five children, and resides in New Hampshire.

Appointment of Deane E. Hoffman as Special Assistant to the President for National Security Affairs
June 5, 1989

The President today announced the appointment of Deane E. Hoffman as Special Assistant to the President for National Security Affairs and Senior Director for International Economic Affairs at the National Security Council.

Mr. Hoffman served as National Intelligence Officer for Economics at the National Intelligence Council in Washington, DC. Mr. Hoffman is a career intelligence officer who has served in several positions within the Intelligence Directorate of the Central Intelligence Agency.

Mr. Hoffman was born in Norwood, MA, in 1942. He graduated from Babson College (B.A., 1966) and the University of Maine (M.A., 1978). He is married to the former Janet MacQuilken of Boston, MA, and has one daughter.

Appointment of Arnold Kanter as Special Assistant to the President for National Security Affairs
June 5, 1989

The President today announced the appointment of Dr. Arnold Kanter as Special Assistant to the President for National Security Affairs and Senior Director for Defense Policy and Arms Control at the National Security Council.

Since 1985 Dr. Kanter was a senior staff member at the RAND Corp. in Santa Monica, CA. Prior to this, he served for 8 years in the Department of State, most recently as Deputy Assistant Secretary of State for Politico-Military Affairs, and as

Deputy to the Under Secretary of State for Political Affairs. Dr. Kanter was a member of the faculty of Ohio State University, 1971–1972, and the University of Michigan, 1972–1977. He is a member of the Council on Foreign Relations and the International Institute of Strategic Studies.

Dr. Kanter graduated from the University of Michigan and Yale University with a M.Phil. and Ph.D. in political science. He was born in Chicago, IL. Dr. Kanter is married to the former Anne Elizabeth Strassman, and they have two children.

Statement on the Observance of World Environment Day
June 5, 1989

Over the last several years, people all over the world have become more and more concerned about the global environment, the warming of the world's climate, the depletion of the ozone layer, the loss of plant and animal species, our mounting waste disposal problems, and the pollution of the oceans. These are enormous challenges which cannot and should not be minimized.

But at the same time, on this anniversary of World Environment Day, I am optimistic about the future. Here in the United States we have made remarkable progress in cleaning up our air and water. We have shown what we can do when the will is there and we work together. I believe that the world community of nations can, and indeed must, make that same kind of progress on a global scale. We may speak different languages and worship God in different ways, but we all share the same Earth. If we can probe the depths of space and engineer the genetic building blocks of life, we can surely protect the quality of our environment. We just need the will to do it.

I would like to take this occasion to announce that the United States intends to ban the importation of elephant ivory from all countries. We do this out of mounting concern for the rapid decline of the wild elephant, one of nature's most majestic creatures. If their populations continue to diminish at current rates, the wild elephant will soon be lost from this Earth. We urge the nations of the world to join us in this ban. We further urge the countries responsible for the elephant to practice sound stewardship of these precious creatures so they will not be lost to future generations.

Accordance of the Personal Rank of Ambassador to Peter Tomsen While Serving as Special Envoy to the Afghan Resistance
June 5, 1989

The President today accorded the personal rank of Ambassador to Peter Tomsen, of California, a career member of the Senior Foreign Service, Class of Minister-Counselor, in his capacity as Special Envoy to the Afghan Resistance.

Mr. Tomsen entered the Foreign Service in 1967. He has most recently completed an assignment as the deputy chief of mission of the U.S. Embassy in Beijing. He served in the political-military office of the U.S. Embassy in Bangkok, 1967–1968. After a year of Vietnamese language training in Washington in early 1969, he was assigned to the U.S. Civilian-Military Advisory Organization in Vietnam, 1969–1970. He was a political officer of the U.S. Embassy in New Delhi, 1971–1975; a political officer of the U.S. Embassy in Moscow, 1977–1978; and a political officer of the U.S. Embassy in Beijing, 1981–1983. From 1984 to 1987, he served in the Department of State as office director of India, Nepal, Sri Lanka, Bhutan, and the Maldives.

Mr. Tomsen was born November 19, 1940 in Cleveland, OH. He graduated from Wittenberg University (B.A., 1962) and received a master's degree from the University of Pittsburgh in 1964. He served in the Peace Corps in Nepal, 1964–1966. Mr. Tomsen is married and has two children.

Continuation of Peter W. Rodman as Special Assistant to the President for National Security Affairs
June 5, 1989

The President today announced the reappointment of Peter W. Rodman as Special Assistant to the President for National Security Affairs and National Security Council Counselor.

Since March 1986, Mr. Rodman served in several capacities on the National Security Council at the White House: N.S.C. Counselor and Special Assistant for National Security Affairs, 1987, and Assistant to the President for National Security Affairs (Foreign Policy), 1986–1987. Prior to this Mr. Rodman served as Director of the Policy Planning Staff at the Department of State, 1984–1986. He was a fellow in diplomatic studies and a principal research assistant to Dr. Kissinger at the Center for Strategic and International Studies at Georgetown University, 1977–1983. Mr. Rodman was a member of the National Security Council staff and special assistant to Dr. Kissinger and special assistant to General Brent Scowcroft, 1969–1977.

Mr. Rodman was born November 24, 1943, in Boston, MA. He graduated from Harvard College (A.B., 1964), Oxford University (B.A., M.A., 1966), and Harvard Law School (J.D., 1969). He is married, has two children, and resides in Washington, DC.

Remarks at the Annual Meeting of the Business Roundtable
June 5, 1989

Thank you very much, Ed. Thank you so much. Barbara and I are delighted to be here. And, Ed, to you, my sincere thanks not just for the invitation and the introduction but for all you do for education. My respects to John Akers, who is the chairman of your human resources task force. My respects to the Members of the Senate and the House that are here tonight and to members of my Cabinet. I see our Secretary of Education here, Larry Cavazos, who is doing an outstanding job—Larry, delighted to see you. And one of your own, or one from industry, Bruce Gelb, I see sitting here, who's now heading the U.S. Information Agency, taking on a very important job. So, I'm going to stop right there before I get in trouble. [*Laughter*]

But I spent some time today just thinking about the trip that was just completed and then how I would tie that in to what I'd be saying here tonight. But let me just say a word on the European trip. I am convinced that the alliance that is so vital to American interests—and, I think, to interests of every Western European country—are in good shape. I think the alliance itself is together, perhaps stronger, and more united than it's ever been. The spirit of Brussels was one of change and opportunity and the challenge we face in moving towards a future of freedom, prosperity, and peace; and I've labeled it "beyond containment."

And many of you people in this room know very well what I'm talking about when I talk about a relationship with the

Soviet Union that goes beyond containment. And admittedly, a lot has to be done in terms of performance. But I think, with the alliance together—the challenge now to Mr. Gorbachev to come forward and make these serious reductions to parity in U.S. and Soviet forces—I think we're on the move; I think we're on the offense. And I must say I was very, very pleased by the firm and united reaction from our European allies.

But even as we talked about the matter of arms control and arms reductions, the subject that joins us here tonight, the subject of education, came up—everybody recognizing that we're moving into a much more competitive age. And education is a means of equipping ourselves to excel in an increasingly competitive global marketplace. That is one of the things we're facing. Education can be the root of mutual understanding and can make an enormous step towards peace in the world.

And so, before I mention a subject which I told Ed I'm a little reluctant to talk about with Larry Cavazos here and with many of you already involved in it, let me just say a word about another subject, the one that has dominated the news for the last 48 hours, and before, as well. I'm talking about the tragic, deplorable events taking place in China. I have a special affection for the Chinese people. I've kept up my knowledge of China and my relationship with various leaders there. I've been back to China five times since Barbara and I left in 1975. And she's been back six times. And it is with a saddened heart that I, joining many of you, watched the proceedings in Tiananmen Square.

I was so moved today by the bravery of that individual that stood alone in front of the tanks rolling down the main avenue there. And I heard some speculation on the television on what is it that gives a young man the strength, gives him the courage, to stand up in front of a column of tanks right there in front of the world. And I'll tell you, it was very moving, because all of us have seen the bravery and the determination of the students and the workers, seen their commitment to peaceful protest. And that image, I think, is going to be with us for a long time. And all I can say to him, wherever he might be, or to people around the world is: We are and we must stand with him. And that's the way it is, and that's the way it's going to be.

I know that many in this room do what we have encouraged you to do—do business with the People's Republic of China. And I don't want to disturb that. I don't want to hurt the very business community in China and here that has moved things forward toward democracy. I did take some steps that some of you may have seen in the military side today. I am convinced that there are many in the People's Liberation Army who are sympathetic to the demonstrators. But I think the way to move, to take action, and to express the outrage we feel is on that military supply side. And I'm very hopeful that this message we sent today will be strong enough to convince the leaders of the Chinese military to go back to the policy of restraint and negotiation and peace, as opposed to this crushing of the human spirit in Tiananmen Square.

Tonight, I want to focus on the partnership that we can build to create the world-class education system that this country needs. A gathering like this is a very, very good sign—all of you busy. And you've got the Business Roundtable; the chamber; the NAM, National Association of Manufacturers; the American Business Conference coming together on this matter of urgent concern to our great country. And our schools are in trouble; they're in real trouble. And that means our kids are in trouble, too. So, what are we going to do about it?

Well, together we can lead a nationwide crusade for excellence in education. You won't find too many times when the subject is education that I'll come out against studying, but this is one of them. We've spent plenty of time studying the problem, hundreds of studies in the past few years alone, showing that our schools simply do not measure up. And we've all heard the stories about the kids who can't find the U.S. on a map, and we've seen the low test scores. And so, I really believe that the time for study is past, and it's time to take action.

Improving our schools is going to take a national effort, one that involves all levels of government, parents, local communities, the private sector as well. And it's going to take an honest effort. And if we're serious about excellence in education, we've got to put the politics on the back burner. And Ed was telling me about the magnificent program you had here today with people from all elements in the educational community, and I think that's a very, very good thing.

I've heard plenty of complaints that we're not spending enough. The typical Washington reaction says, well, if you've got a problem, double the spending, and that'll take care of it. The fact is that we spend more per capita than many of our toughest competitors. And as a nation, we devote more than $300 billion a year to educating our children. And that's not stingy; it's staggering. And the resources are there, and it's how we put those resources to work that counts.

And there's something more that we need to recognize: We can multiply success. There's no monopoly on ideas, no one right answer when it comes to improving our schools. We can learn from each other. Look at the States, today's entrepreneurs of education policy, if you will. We're witnessing the emergence of 50 laboratories of reform—50 States, 50 laboratories of reform. And, yes, Federal leadership is crucial; and as you know, we've introduced a package of education initiatives designed to reward excellence, improve accountability, and promote quality schools through choice. I expect our ideas to get full and fair hearings when Congress begins working on our bill next week.

And right now, I want to highlight an idea that's proved its value in the business world, an idea that can play a central role in education as well—and I'm talking about competition. The business world knows that competition brings out the best in individuals and institutions. And the same is true for our schools; proof already exists. America's postsecondary education system is widely recognized as the strongest and most successful system in the world, and it's also extremely competitive. Schools compete to attract the best students and first-rate faculties, and the plain fact is that this competition is good. Superior schools inspire others to reach for excellence. And our elementary and secondary schools are the weak links in our system. Competition and choice can help us make them stronger.

But what government can do is only part of the story. In the private sector and in this business community, hundreds of companies, thousands of employees are going into the classrooms to help children learn. And you didn't wait for a signal from Washington; you saw an opportunity, and you got involved. And the numbers are impressive: 186 corporations from the Business Roundtable alone and hundreds of others as well. And that tells me that the great American tradition of serving others is alive and thriving in corporate America.

Improving our schools is a national problem, but the search for solutions must take place on the local level, in our communities. Local solutions work. Last month, just before I went abroad, I was up in Rochester to visit the Wilson Magnet School, a school that just turned itself around. And 10 years ago, Wilson was plagued by crime and plunging grades and, indeed, urban flight. And today that Wilson Magnet School is one of the top-ranked high schools in the State of New York, a night-and-day change. And you might say, well, how did it happen? Over and over, everyone that I asked there said, I have one answer, and that answer: commitment. They used that word over and over again—commitment on the part of parents, teachers, students, and commitment on the part of the corporation that calls that community home. Eastman Kodak contributed the equipment and the expertise that helped bring learning alive for the kids at Wilson.

And I saw those Kodak employees sitting side by side with the students at the computers, pitching in, doing a whale of a job. And today Wilson has many more applicants than it has space for students. And it's a success story that I'd like to see repeated all across this country. And business, it was you; it was business that played this key role. Efforts like the one at Wilson, like the ones that many of your companies are now engaged in, are producing real, lasting results—one school at a time, one student at a time. And all of us know the magnitude of the challenge, and all of us can do our part to strengthen our schools.

And that's why I'm announcing tonight the creation of an advisory committee, my first as President, to focus on education: the President's Education Policy Advisory Committee. And I'll call on this Committee to bring me innovative ideas, to bring together leaders from business and labor, educators at every level, State and local government officials, and the media in a partnership to improve our schools.

The students who need our help can't wait. It's early June; school's about to end for this year. And on graduation day, how many kids won't be walking across that stage to get their diploma? How many kids who walk out of that classroom a few weeks from now won't be back in September? How many will get that degree and go out into the world, come to work in your companies without the skills they need? Even a single young man or woman is one too many, and yet there are millions.

Everyone in this room, I know, shares my concern. And tonight I want to issue a challenge, a corporate call to action, if you will: four ways that you can make a real difference. Start by raising the literacy levels. Someone once asked Ben Franklin who he thought was the most pitiful man in the world, and he said, "A lonesome man on a rainy day who does not know how to read." And Franklin understood that literacy is an open door to opportunity and self-knowledge, to history, culture, and a world of experience. But make no mistake, reading isn't just a rainy day diversion: It's a survival skill. And how can young people do the job if they can't read the job application?

Some of you have spoken to me about this problem. I know many of you have been engaged with Barbara in her effort to help make this country more literate. And tonight, I ask all of you to start at home and your offices, on the shop floor; make it your business to help every employee who can't read but wants desperately to learn.

And second, let's raise our sights and our standards. All of you know the kind of new employees that you're looking for, and that's why it makes sense to work with the schools to create programs that develop skills for the real world, for the millions of new jobs that our economy is creating each year. And all of you know how difficult it is for your companies to keep pace in a world where change is measured in milliseconds. And we must do all we can to equip our children, our future work force, with the thinking skills they'll need to make careers in the information age.

You can't start too early. IBM is working in partnership with Head Start in Baltimore, teaching 4-year-olds how to use computers. And listen to what one mother says: "The computer will be just like the telephone; everyone will have one. My kids have to learn this, and so do I." That may be a good sales program for John Akers, but it's also a whale of a good education program, I'll tell you. [*Laughter*]

We have to understand, and we have to be involved. And many of us grew up in a time when a worker would spend an entire career in the same job, and those days are ending. Workers entering the economy today can expect to train and retrain several times to keep pace with changed working conditions. And it's up to our corporations to create a working environment where employee education and retraining and training never stops. From now on, in America, learning must be a lifelong occupation.

And third, I challenge every CEO in this room to get involved—personally involved—with the schools in your own community. Walk into the classroom not as a CEO but as a concerned parent, as a good citizen, right there in the community. And I know you and your companies are doing a great deal now to improve our schools, but it's got to be personal. Be a catalyst for change.

Let me tell you about a businessman I know in New Orleans who did exactly that—Patrick Taylor. He walked into one of the worst schools in New Orleans and made a promise to the entire eighth grade class, over 200 kids. And he told them if they kept up a B average and graduated he'd guarantee that they go to college. And here's how he looks at it: You don't always get from individuals what you expect. But if you expect nothing, you're going to get nothing. And Pat Taylor is telling those kids that they've got a future, and he's ready to help them get there.

And now the last challenge: Everyone in this room is here because you know how much education matters. And I want you to take a message to the companies who aren't here tonight. Reach out, bring others in this business community on board. I want to see all of America's corporations involved in a truly common effort.

And I know that you've got the energy and the ingenuity to meet these challenges. Start now! I want to hear from you by next Labor Day—see the report card, if you will, your action plan for excellence in education. And if I don't hear from you, I'll get Barbara Bush on your case. [*Laughter*] She's told me over and over again about many of you, of your personal and your company's interest in literacy and in education in general. And she has been inspired by what so many of you have already done. She's your cheerleader—for those who are already constructively involved. You've taken your skills and resources into our classrooms because you know the bottom line: We can't have a world-class economy with second-class schools.

So, take the challenges to heart, build on the fine work that's already started and that's already going on in a big way. And thank you for all you are doing, and thank you for what I'm confident all of you will be doing in the future. Thank you all very, very much.

Note: The President spoke at 7:12 p.m. in the Capitol Ballroom of the J.W. Marriott Hotel. In his opening remarks, he referred to Edmund T. Pratt, Jr., chairman of the Business Roundtable.

Remarks at the Welcoming Ceremony for Prime Minister Benazir Bhutto of Pakistan

June 6, 1989

The President. Prime Minister Bhutto, Mr. Zardari, and distinguished guests, Franklin Roosevelt once called this the house owned by all the American people. Well, on behalf of all the American people, Barbara and I are honored to welcome you to the White House.

Your visit marks an occasion for both of us to celebrate and renew the ties of friendship between democratic Pakistan and the United States and to chart new ways to strengthen old bonds in the many years to come. These bonds are formal, but they are also personal, for you are no stranger to America nor to Americans themselves. We remember you as a college student, eager to learn, eager to teach us about your homeland. And I remember first meeting you at your father's side at the United Nations, as he pleaded the cause of Pakistan with such eloquence. And we remember your visits as a courageous opposition leader, tireless in your zeal to foster democratic change. And now we are proud to greet you as Prime Minister and leader of a great nation.

Woodrow Wilson once said: "I believe in democracy because it releases the energies of every human being." And Madam Prime Minister, the people of Pakistan have chosen you to help democracy flourish in Pakistan. This return to democracy under your leadership deserves and has won America's profound admiration. It has strengthened America's already firm resolve to work closely with Pakistan. And I congratulate you and the people of Pakistan, and I salute those in your country, civil and military, whose adherence to the constitutional process was so important in bringing about democracy in Pakistan.

Madam Prime Minister, your visit is a time to reaffirm an historic relationship, newly forged on the anvil of democracy; but it is also a time to look ahead, to reaffirm liberty and freedom. And both our governments are in their first year, and let us use that to our advantage by building on the fundamental strength of our friendship. Let us craft new ideas, new initiatives to meet the challenges of our changing world.

I have looked forward to this meeting very much. And you will find us frank and open, as befits old friends, and attentive listeners who value your judgment. To America, you are a woman of great personal courage and faith. To America, you are a wise leader who embodies the very spirit of her people. And to all of us, you are a living symbol of those who risk all and sacrifice much so that others might know democracy and freedom.

Madam Prime Minister, welcome to the United States of America.

The Prime Minister. Mr. President, Mrs. Bush, and distinguished guests, I'm delighted to be in Washington, the capital of freedom, as the guest of a President who knows Pakistan well and has been its friend. I recall our first meeting in 1971 at the United Nations, at a crucial turn in Pakistan's history. The U.S.-Pakistan friendship has grown in strength; we are friends and partners.

Standing here on this beautiful lawn, one sees the monuments which recall America's odyssey of freedom. As I look at these monuments, I think of Pakistan, which too has traveled a long and difficult way along the path of freedom. It was not so long ago that Pakistan was a dictatorship and I was in prison. But as you said, Mr. President, giving heart to all those living under tyranny, the day of the dictator is over.

Today I am privileged to stand here as the elected Prime Minister of the Islamic Republic of Pakistan, a woman Prime Minister of a Muslim country, whose people have given a verdict against tyranny and for freedom, progress, and human dignity, for justice and for the rule of law. Our two nations are united in a partnership inspired by common goals and shared interests, a partnership now bound by democracy.

The United States and the people of Pakistan have also stood together as partners over the last difficult decade, helping restore freedom and independence to Afghanistan. Our countries have developed a vital security relationship and a major program of economic cooperation. This has enabled Pakistan to work with confidence for peace in our region. And today, Mr. President, we begin our discussions of a new partnership. We are here today with new priorities to talk to the world's greatest democracy. New challenges confront us in the closing but complex phase of the Afghan war and as we focus on the economic, social, and educational needs of our people. We come to talk about how we, together, as partners, may take our relationship and our people into the 21st century.

And as we begin on this auspicious day in this magnificent country of freedom, achievement, and opportunity, I offer a simple prayer: May God bless all countries of the world with the enduring values of freedom, achievement, and opportunity that we see in this great country of yours. I thank you, Mr. President.

The President. Thank you very much.

Note: The President spoke at 10:11 a.m. at the South Portico of the White House, where Prime Minister Bhutto was accorded a formal welcome with full military honors. Following the ceremony, the President and the Prime Minister met in the Oval Office.

Remarks Following Discussions With Prime Minister Benazir Bhutto of Pakistan
June 6, 1989

The President. Well, it was a special pleasure for Barbara and me to welcome Prime Minister Bhutto to the White House this morning. In fact, our relationship goes back to 1971, when she attended Harvard and came with her dad to the United Nations. And I have often remarked that her father's 1971 appeal was literally one of the most moving speeches that I ever heard at the United Nations. And more recently, we met in Tokyo last February, where I believe that we were the most newly elected heads of government.

Pakistan and the United States have enjoyed a long history of good relations—friends since the time that Pakistan became an independent nation. And I welcome this opportunity to reaffirm those ties and to reassure the Prime Minister of our continued commitment to assist in Pakistan's security and its economic and cultural development.

The Prime Minister knows our country well, and she has many friends here. And on behalf of the American people, I congratulated her on Pakistan's historic return to democracy last year, a development of which the people of Pakistan can be truly proud. We discussed how important it is for all elements of Pakistan society to ensure that democracy isn't just an abstract concept, but that it works.

And the Prime Minister and I reviewed the situation in Afghanistan. For the last decade, the U.S. and Pakistan cooperated in supporting the Afghan resistance in its fight against foreign occupation. And Pakistan deserves great credit and admiration for its extraordinary, extraordinary humanitarian efforts in support of the millions of Afghan refugees during this period. The effectiveness of our mutual policy was proven last February, when the last Soviet troops withdrew from Afghanistan. And we agreed, however, that the job is not done. The *Mujahidin* continues, and their struggle for self-determination goes on, a goal that both the United States and Pakistan continue to support. Prime Minister Bhutto and I discussed ways to encourage a political solution in Afghanistan that will lead to a nonaligned, representative government, willing to live in peace with its neighbors, to replace the illegitimate regime in Kabul. The United States and Pakistan will continue to explore any serious avenue towards this end.

The Prime Minister and I also reviewed our efforts to enhance stability in south Asia, an important objective of both governments. And I expressed our strong support for Pakistan's efforts, and India's as well, to improve relations, and stressed the critical importance of avoiding a regional nuclear arms race in the subcontinent. And she assured me that Pakistan's nuclear program is committed to peaceful purposes. I underlined my administration's commitment to discourage proliferation of nuclear and chemical weapons, ballistic missiles, in the south Asia region and around the world.

We also shared our concern about the scourge of drug production and trafficking. Not much detail yet on that, but we're going to go into that one in much more detail later on. It's a matter of grave concern to the United States. I applauded her tough stance on eradicating the opium cultivation and expressed our appreciation for the extradition of alleged drug trafficker Saleem. To effectively combat this menace, we've got to undertake a vigorous enforcement campaign, offering U.S. assistance wherever possible.

And let me say that, as far as I'm concerned, these discussions have been productive. And let me note, too, that that ceremony outside today, the first since I've been President, was a wonderful way to welcome the Prime Minister. And we just walked by the Rose Garden, which also is a lovely setting, and as the Prime Minister has observed, roses have a very special meaning in her life. And when she was younger, her father would bring back roses every time he traveled abroad, and in time, her family's gardens became filled with varieties of color. And during her own detention, she struggled bravely to keep the gardens alive, for as she has written, "I could not bear to watch the flowers wither, especially my father's roses."

And so, Madam Prime Minister, you've described your time among the roses and the cool shade of the gardens as "the happiest hours of my life." And now, as a gesture of friendship between our people and to continue your father's tradition, it is my privilege to present you with this American rosebush. May it—and you—prosper in the years to come. And welcome again.

The Prime Minister. I'm very grateful to President Bush for the kind invitation to pay an official visit to the United States, and I'd like to thank the President for his consideration in giving me one of the rosebushes from the White House. It shall always remind me of this very useful, productive, and helpful visit—supportive visit—of mine to the United States.

My presence here underlies the great importance that Pakistan attaches to our relations with your country. This is not only because geopolitical realities require a close relationship but, more importantly, because of the ideals and the objectives that we share. As you know, this is not my first visit to Washington or, indeed, to the United States. I have pleasant memories of my student days at Radcliffe, past visits to Washington, one of the great citadels of democracy. But it is a special privilege and honor to be here as the democratically elected leader of a country which has traditionally enjoyed close, friendly ties with your country.

Over the last 10 years, Pakistan has been in the forefront of two great struggles. We have actively supported the cause of the Afghan people and their brave fight against foreign military intervention, and at the same time, at home in Pakistan, we've struggled against military dictatorship to establish a system based upon democratic values and the respect for human rights. In both these epic struggles, we received from the United States unwavering support, and material as well as moral encouragement. It has, therefore, been a special pleasure and privilege to come to Washington and to thank President Bush and the Government and the people of the United States for their friendship and their generosity.

The President and I have had wide-ranging discussions on a number of issues, and I am convinced that this exchange will be of immense benefit to the bilateral relations that exist between us and also to the cause of world peace. President Bush has just returned to Washington from a spectacularly successful visit to Europe, and where he has launched a series of initiatives which could open an entirely new era in international relations, with the exciting prospect of a genuine and durable peace. Pakistan, which is situated in one of the more sensitive geopolitical regions of the world, will contribute towards these objectives and efforts.

While the withdrawal of Soviet forces has brought a welcome change in Afghanistan, the continued fighting and prolonged presence of over 3½ million Afghan refugees pose serious threats to the peace and stability of the region. The President and I have reviewed the situation in the light of the prevailing circumstances, and we are in complete accord, both in terms of our analyses as well as the future policies that need to be evolved. Pakistan remains committed to a political solution of the Afghan problem, whereby the brave people of Afghanistan will have the right to freely choose their own government without interference from outside. Pakistan's commitment to peace and democracy are fundamental.

In thanking President Bush for the valuable support that the United States has rendered to us in the pursuit of these objectives, I have assured him of our continuing efforts towards maintaining peace in the south Asian region and of our determination to strengthen the process of nuclear nonproliferation by seeking accords, both bilateral and international, within the regional context.

The President and I discussed measures to increase our cooperation in the fight against drugs. We have already achieved some success in this direction in Pakistan, but much remains to be done.

In conclusion, I would once more wish to thank President Bush for the generous hospitality, for the warmth and the friendship with which we have been received. I go home greatly encouraged by our constructive and fruitful discussions. I look forward to the opportunity of reciprocating in Pakistan some of the warmth, kindness, and hospitality that my husband and I have been privileged to receive from the President and Mrs. Bush in Washington. Thank you very much.

Note: The President spoke at 11:33 a.m. in the East Room of the White House.

Nomination of Michael J. Astrue To Be General Counsel of the Department of Health and Human Services

June 6, 1989

The President today announced his intention to nominate Michael J. Astrue to be General Counsel of the Department of Health and Human Services. He would succeed Malcolm M.B. Sterrett.

Since 1988 Mr. Astrue has been Associate Counsel to the President in the Executive Office of the President in Washington, DC. Prior to this he was Counselor to the Commissioner for the Social Security Administration, Department of Health and Human Services, 1986–1988; and Acting Deputy Assistant Secretary for Human Service Legislation, 1985–1986. He was an associate with Ropes & Gray, 1984–1985; and a law clerk with the Honorable Walter J. Skinner, 1983–1984.

Mr. Astrue graduated from Yale University (B.A., 1978) and Harvard Law School (J.D., 1983). He resides in Belmont, MA.

Statement on the 45th Anniversary of D-Day

June 6, 1989

Today we remember those who fought for freedom 45 years ago at Normandy in the Allied invasion that hastened the liberation of Europe. In so doing, we remember all Americans who have fought to keep us free, and the young men and women who today act as guardians of the peace and freedom that America's veterans achieved through courage and sacrifice.

The alliance of Americans, Canadians, British and French, and others who fought together that misty morning was forged in the fire of battle. Last week in Europe, that alliance, now greatly broadened, was further cemented by an extraordinarily successful NATO summit. The mutual agreement of the allies on a future course for Europe has the potential to brighten the prospects for peace—real peace—and freedom.

From the vantage point of 1989, after four decades of peace in Europe, it is difficult to remember that on the morning of June 6, 1944, General Eisenhower carried in his pocket a draft message declaring the invasion to have been a failure and taking personal responsibility for that failure. He never needed to use that draft, of course, because all the years of painstaking preparations bore the fruit of victory. The turmoil and confusion of battle that day belied the calm purposefulness with which freedom confronts tyranny. In recent days, the face of the world has again been marked by dramatic occurrences—winds of change—that signify the determination with which freedom confounds its adversaries. As with General Eisenhower then, we cannot know with certainty today whether the forces of freedom will prevail soon or in every instance. Yet the ultimate victory of freedom and democracy is inevitable. The new breeze of democratic change will bring mankind to better, more tranquil times.

Last week's success of allied unity; the first free elections in Poland in more than 50 years; and even the momentous, tragic events in China give us reason to redouble our efforts to continue the spread of freedom and democracy around the globe, to end the division of Europe, to broaden the community of free nations, and to reaffirm the rights of man.

In light of the striking events in the world of the past week, and in remembrance of those brave Americans who fought at Normandy on this date 45 years ago, several lines often quoted by Winston Churchill in the darkest days of World War II seem especially apt today:

For while the tired waves, vainly breaking,

Seem here no painful inch to gain,
Far back, through creeks and inlets making,
Comes silent, flooding in, the main.
And not by eastern windows only,
When daylight comes, comes in the light,
In front, the sun climbs slow, how slowly,
But westward, look, the land is bright.

Letter to the Speaker of the House of Representatives and the President of the Senate Transmitting a Report on the Export-Import Bank of the United States

June 6, 1989

Dear Mr. Speaker: (Dear Mr. President:)

This report is being transmitted pursuant to Section 7(a)(2) of the Export-Import Bank Act of 1945, as amended (12 U.S.C. 635e(a)(2)).

Based on the information supplied by the Export-Import Bank, I have determined that for fiscal year 1989 (i) the amount of direct loan authority available to the Bank is sufficient and (ii) the amount of guarantee authority available to the Bank may be greater than needed.

Although there could be substantial excess guarantee authority, I believe that its continued availability will be advantageous. Guarantees represent an important means of support for U.S. exports and involve only a limited subsidy. Moreover, a portion of any unused 1989 authority will be carried over into 1990 when demand may be higher.

Therefore, I do not seek legislation to rescind any authority of the Bank. I have concluded that the statutory fiscal year 1989 limits for the Export-Import Bank authority should remain unchanged.

Sincerely,

GEORGE BUSH

Note: Identical letters were sent to Thomas S. Foley, Speaker of the House of Representatives, and Dan Quayle, President of the Senate.

Statement on the Elections in Poland

June 6, 1989

Sunday's elections in Poland marked an important step toward freedom and democracy. I am encouraged by the responses of both the Polish Government and members of the opposition to the election results. I hope the movement toward political pluralism will continue to follow the responsible, constructive path it has taken since the historic roundtable agreements in April.

As I said in my speech in Hamtramck, Michigan, April 17, the Polish people are now taking steps that deserve our active support. We will work in concert with our allies to help Polish democracy take root anew and sustain itself. The Polish people face a difficult task ahead, but their first steps have been firmly in the right direction.

Nomination of Sherrie Sandy Rollins To Be an Assistant Secretary of Housing and Urban Development

June 6, 1989

The President today announced his intention to nominate Sherrie Sandy Rollins to be an Assistant Secretary of Housing and Urban Development (Public Affairs). She would succeed Harry K. Schwartz.

Since 1985 Ms. Rollins has been vice president of communications for the Oliver Carr Co. in Washington, DC. She served as director of network support for the 1988 Republican National Convention. She was assistant press secretary and media liaison for the Presidential Inaugural Committee, 1984–1985; state press coordinator and media liaison for the Reagan-Bush 1984 Campaign, 1984; executive director for the Business and Professional Association of Georgetown, 1981–1984; and an account executive for the public relations firm of Gleason and Thomasson, 1980–1981.

Ms. Rollins graduated from the University of Virginia (B.A., 1980). She is married and resides in Alexandria, VA.

Nomination of Roy M. Goodman To Be a Member of the National Council on the Arts

June 6, 1989

The President today announced his intention to nominate Roy M. Goodman to be a member of the National Council on the Arts, National Foundation on the Arts and the Humanities, for a term expiring September 3, 1994. He would succeed C. Douglas Dillon.

Currently State Senator Goodman is serving his 10th term in the New York Legislature, representing the 26th District. He also served as chairman of the senate committee on investigations, taxation, and government operations, 1978 to present. From 1969 to 1978, he was chairman of the senate committee on housing and urban development. Mr. Goodman was chairman of the New York State Charter Revision Commission for New York City, 1972–1975, and finance commissioner and treasurer of the City of New York, 1966–1968. In addition, Mr. Goodman was appointed by President Reagan to be a Commissioner of the National Commission of Fine Arts, 1985.

Mr. Goodman was born March 5, 1930, in New York City. He graduated from Harvard College (A.B., 1951) and Harvard Graduate School of Business Administration (M.A., 1953). He served in the U.S. Navy, 1953–1956. He is married, has three children, and resides in Manhattan, NY.

Toasts at the State Dinner for Prime Minister Benazir Bhutto of Pakistan

June 6, 1989

The President. Prime Minister Bhutto, Mr. Zardari, it's a great pleasure and an honor for Barbara and me to welcome you to the United States and to the White House. I also want to welcome a third honored guest not here tonight, the master, Bilawal Zardari. [*Laughter*] He's 9 months old. He had to go to bed early, so he couldn't come to the White House. And we're all heartbroken, but I hope he's having a good time in the United States.

Madam Prime Minister, I've had many years of dealings with the Pakistani people, and always I've marveled at that blend of warmth and kindness best embodied in your phrase, *Zindabad*—"Long live the friendship." And this evening it is my great pleasure to return that friendship and to say what a privilege it is to salute a woman whose reputation for eloquence and intelligence and courage is all here—we'll see in a moment—is eminently well-deserved. And in that context, I should note how one observer said that it was an asset to today's talks that the leaders of both our countries are fluent in the same tongue. [*Laughter*] That was very nice. Fluency in English is something that I'm often not accused of. [*Laughter*]

But we've just concluded a round of very frank discussions—meaningful. And I don't mean it in the diplomatic sense, the U.N. sense, that we used to talk about, but meaningful discussions on a matter of traditional importance. And I think it's a fair characterization to say that the Prime Minister has flatly refused my latest offer: She's not going double or nothing on this year's Harvard-Yale game. [*Laughter*]

What we did, though, agree to was the steadfast conviction that the cooperation between our countries will grow stronger by the year and to address regional and international issues in the spirit of our shared commitment to liberty, individuality, and democratic ideals. And as you know, I have just returned from Europe, where those ideals strengthen the already close ties between America and her European allies. And that same commitment to democracy joins Pakistan and America as we move towards a more stable and prosperous Asia.

We also talked at length about the plague of drug abuse which afflicts both America and Pakistan. And neither country can afford to allow the scourge of drugs to continue. And throughout our talks we reaffirmed the values which bind us, bind the United States and Pakistan—values of faith and family and the dignity of work. And we pledge to continue our work together to bring peace and freedom to Afghanistan, stability to all of south Asia.

Madam Prime Minister, our goals are great goals, worthy goals. And together our countries have already done much. And in particular, let me simply salute your role in Pakistan's return to democracy. It was the great Pakistani poet-philosopher Muhammad Iqbal who once observed, simply, "Love is freedom and honor." And, Madam Prime Minister, your entire life shows the meaning of those words. And in that spirit, I ask all of us here tonight, all our guests, to rise and raise their glasses to Pakistan-American friendship; to a safer world for your son and for all children; and to your health and what you symbolize, both for Pakistan and for the rest of the world. God bless you, and good luck.

The Prime Minister. Thank you. I thank you, Mr. President, for the warm and gracious words that you have spoken about Pakistan and about me, personally. We hold you in high esteem because of your exceptional experience in world affairs, the moderation of your approach to the problems facing mankind, and the wisdom and moral quality of your statesmanship.

It is an honor for me to be in this world capital of freedom, in this historic room as the elected leader of the Islamic Republic of Pakistan. Yet standing here before you, I cannot help but remember the darker days, the days of dictatorship. I feel gratified that our faith, our determination, and our commitment to the universal principles of human dignity and freedom sustained us to this glorious evening, to this glorious day.

Mr. President, I stand with the leader of the world's greatest democracy. I look forward to a new partnership between your country and mine, with democracy giving a fresh dimension to our relationship. Pakistan and the United States have been friends of longstanding. With the triumph of democracy, the relationship is now at the threshold of a new vitality.

This springs from the reservoir of good will that has been nourished by our sustained joint endeavor in support of a worthy cause in Afghanistan: the cause of freedom. We look forward to the day when real peace and stability will return to Afghanistan, when power is transferred to a genuinely representative government. This will allow millions of refugees who have sought sanctuary in Pakistan to return to their homes in honor and dignity.

We now need to look at broader horizons. The people of Pakistan seek peace and stability in their region and a world free of tensions. We would like to see mankind progress and prosper. Pakistan would like to strengthen its friendship with the United States, which shares these objectives.

We have come here with new priorities, Mr. President, new priorities to take our nation and our people into the 21st century. We have come to enrich our friendship and strengthen the partnership between our two nations. Mr. President, I wonder whether you know—I didn't until very recently—that we have something in common. We are born, apparently, under the same star. And when I was in Pakistan and the government had just been formed, we weren't allowed much of a political honeymoon by the press. I believe you weren't allowed much of a political honeymoon, either. But I'm glad to know that your trip to Europe in connection with NATO was a big success, because if you've had a successful trip, I must have one, too.

Ladies and gentlemen, I studied at Harvard, and believe me, I didn't know until tonight that Yale ever produced charming men. I'm glad I met the only one. [*Laughter*]

May I now request you to join me in a toast to the health of the President of the United States and Mrs. Bush, to the strength and prosperity of America and friendship between our people.

Note: The President spoke at 10:16 p.m. in the State Dining Room at the White House.

Message on the Observance of National Fishing Week, June 5–11, 1989

June 7, 1989

America is a land blessed by bountiful natural resources. Enjoying our outdoor treasures has always been an indelible part of the spirit of our people. That is why it gives me great pleasure to pay tribute to one of our most popular outdoor leisure activities—recreational fishing—during National Fishing Week. For some, fishing is a full-time occupation. But for most of the 60 million Americans who fish, it is a means of renewing our bonds with nature and sharing special moments with family and friends.

Fishing is an especially valuable experience for our younger generation. Today, more than ever, it is important to instill in our children a sense of appreciation and responsibility for stewardship of our lands and waters. One brisk morning spent fishing on a misty lake can bring home to a child the beauty, drama, and fragility of our natural heritage in a way a thousand classroom presentations never could.

Our nation's public investment in fishery conservation, restoration, and enhancement is, in great part, paid for by fishermen through taxes on fishing equipment. Last year, government agencies working with many private organizations successfully completed a National Recreational Fisheries Policy. This effort was an important first step in focusing attention on the social and economic importance of sport fishing.

By continuing to work together, we can ensure that generations to come will have the opportunity to experience the pleasures found in fishing. As an avid fisherman, I'm happy to send a special salute to all my fellow "anglers" during National Fishing Week.

GEORGE BUSH

Nomination of Michael R. Deland To Be a Member of the Council on Environmental Quality, and Designation as Chairman
June 7, 1989

The President today announced his intention to nominate Michael R. Deland to be a member of the Council on Environmental Quality. He would succeed A. Alan Hill. Upon confirmation he will be designated Chairman.

Since 1983 Mr. Deland has been Regional Administrator for Region I of the Environmental Protection Agency in New England. Prior to this he was an environmental counsel and consultant with Environmental Research and Technology, Inc., 1976–1983. From 1971 to 1976, he served in several capacities for the Environmental Protection Agency in New England, including chief of the enforcement branch for Region I, 1973–1976; chief for the legal review section, 1972–1973; and as an attorney, 1971–1972. Mr. Deland has also served as a staff assistant and legal counsel to the president of the University of Massachusetts, 1971.

Mr. Deland graduated from Harvard College (A.B., 1963) and Boston College Law School (J.D., 1969). He served in the U.S. Navy, 1963–1965. He is married, has two children, and resides in Boston, MA.

Remarks to Members of Ducks Unlimited
June 8, 1989

Thank you, Harry, very, very much, and all of you for that warm welcome. Every member of Ducks Unlimited can eat his heart out—or hers—and I say that because you should be very jealous of me. You ought to see the beautiful carvings that you all gave to me carved by Bill Veasey—two ducks—one of the most spectacular pieces of duck artwork that I believe I've ever seen. And so, I'm grateful to all of you for that presentation that Harry made.

I want to salute the Members of Congress that are here. I want to pay my respects to the head of the EPA, Bill Reilly. We are very fortunate to have him leading our Environmental Protection Agency. I want to pay my respects to our Secretary, Manuel Lujan, who is going to do a fantastic job for us. I served with him in the Congress, and he rates and merits your confidence. Mike Deland was supposed to be here, and he—showing the fact that he's human—he is caught up at the airport in Washington right now—[*laughter*]—so I expect we'll see him in a while. But most of you know him. And I would simply say that the Members of Congress and friends—it's a real pleasure to be here.

One of my greatest pleasures is going fishing with my grandchildren and seeing the Grand Tetons through the eyes of a 10-year-old grandson or teaching our 6-year-old twin granddaughters—now Texans again—the wonders of the ocean—makes life really sing for me. And when I am out in the great outdoors with my own kids or grandkids, I realize how true it is that our children will inherit the Earth. And so, any vision of a kinder, gentler America—any nation concerned about its quality of life, now and forever, must be concerned about conservation. It will not be enough to merely halt the damage we've done; our natural heritage must be recovered and restored. And we saw it at Mount St. Helens, and we see it now at Yellowstone Park and in the growth of spring: nature healing its wounds, coming back to life. We can and should be nature's advocate. And that means an active stewardship of the natural world. And it's time to renew the environmental ethic in America and to renew U.S. leadership on environmental issues around the world. Renewal is the way of nature, and it must now become the way of man.

And that's why I so readily accepted

when Harry invited me, and that's why I wanted to talk to you today. When this organization was founded over 50 years ago, in the Dust Bowl days, there was just a handful of you committed to preserving and restoring our wetlands. And just about that time, a few hunters got together and formed a little group called Ducks Unlimited; and thank goodness they did. And since then, you've set aside, I am told, over 5 million acres as habitat, raised nearly half a billion dollars, started wetlands projects in each of the 50 States, for a simple reason: 75 percent of the remaining wetlands in the continental U.S. are privately owned. We can't do it without your help. The partnerships you've set up with State and Federal agencies and with conservation groups like the Nature Conservancy and the Wildlife Foundation have been outstanding.

And that's good news for ducks. Remember, though, what Dick Darman [Director of the Office of Management and Budget] said about taxes. Anything that looks like a duck or walks like a duck or quacks like a duck is going to hear from him. [*Laughter*] The poor guy; the very thought of Ducks Unlimited keeps him up at night. [*Laughter*] But your work is even better news for America, for what you're doing represents just the kind of local, on-site private sector initiative that we must bring to every environmental challenge.

As you know too well, our wetlands are being lost at a rate of nearly half a million acres a year. So, every year, fewer mallards and pintails make it to the pothole country. You may remember my pledge, that our national goal would be no net loss of wetlands. And together, we are going to deliver on the promise of renewal, and I plan to keep that pledge. I've set up an interagency task force, under our Domestic Policy Council, to work with you, with governments at all levels, with the private sector, to stop the destruction of those precious habitats. Their first task is to develop a united Federal policy for the North American Waterfowl Management Plan here, and in Canada as well—and Canada has lost over 40 percent of her wetlands. And the time has come to simply say, "Stop!"

And to support the plan, this week Secretary Lujan proposed a new trust fund, using interest from the Pittman-Robertson Fund, that would contribute about $10 million. And our goal is to restore a fall flight of more than 100 million birds. And we're looking at legislation from Senators Mitchell and Chafee, Congressmen Dingell and Conte, and there are a few details to be worked out, but the basic thrust of the legislation is sound. I look forward to signing a bill to conserve North American wetlands this year. And we've asked for nearly $200 million in new funding for acquisitions under the Land and Water Conservation Fund. We've also increased funding for coordinated water quality programs to protect the wetlands we already have, and for the first time in 7 years, some of those dollars will go towards acquiring wetlands.

But we're looking far beyond the Federal role. We want to improve the management of federally owned wetlands by leasing them to concerned groups like yours. And you know, the local momentum is picking up. Just last month, Maryland's Governor Schaefer approved the Nation's first State nontidal wetlands law, and it's an outstanding piece of work. Bill Reilly emerged as a key supporter for that bill, and I certainly would encourage him to do more; but in his case, he's the one that's encouraging me to do more all the time. And again, I'm grateful for his leadership.

We're working with American farmers through the farm bill program to provide technical assistance for wetland conservation. Wherever wetlands must give way to farming or development, they will be replaced or expanded elsewhere. It's time to stand the history of wetlands destruction on its head. From this year forward, anyone who tries to drain the swamp is going to be up to his ears in alligators. [*Laughter*]

Let me just spend a few minutes outlining our environmental philosophy. Our approach to wetlands conservation is driven by a new kind of environmentalism, a set of principles that apply to all of the environmental challenges that we face. We believe that pollution is not the inevitable byproduct of progress. So, the first principle is that sound ecology and a strong economy can coexist. But let's remember: The burden of proof is on man, not nature. And the fact is, our ecology and the economy are interdependent. Environmentalists and entrepreneurs must see how much their interests are held in common. It's time to harness the power of the marketplace in the service of the environment.

The second principle is that a true commitment to restoring the Nation's environment requires more than just a Federal commitment. The tradition of purely Federal, "top-down" directives will never again be enough. So, we're working to promote more creative State and local initiatives, drawing on the energy of local communities and the private sector into the cause—pulling them into the cause of conservation. All of you in this room have made that commitment, and now it must be made an all-American commitment.

And our third principle is obvious, but too rarely acted on: that preventing pollution is a far more efficient strategy than struggling to deal with problems once they've occurred. For too long, we've focused on cleanup and penalties after the damage is done. It's time to reorient ourselves, using technologies and processes that reduce or prevent pollution—to stop it before it starts. In the 1990's, pollution prevention will go right to the source.

Technology has given us tremendous, awesome power to alter the face of the Earth. We must use it to do good. Environmental soundness, industrial design must be partners. Industry is making—and must continue to make—environmental soundness an essential fact of American industrial life.

We've already taken several steps in that direction. And as you know, I've called for the elimination of CFC's [chlorofluorocarbons] by the year 2000. And we've also reviewed the Corporate Average Fuel Economy, those CAFE standards. We've tightened the standard, as the law originally intended. More efficient cars are good for our environment and good for our energy security. We're going to promote the use of alternative "neat" fuel technology. And I've proposed full funding to develop clean coal technology.

The fourth principle is a recognition that environmental problems respect no borders. I'm delighted to see the Ambassador from Canada here. So, we're working with nations around the world to provide leadership in finding cooperative international solutions. From Japan to Brazil, we're discussing ways to reverse rainforest devastation. And we've recommended a ban on international shipment of hazardous waste unless an agreement is signed that makes sure waste is disposed of safely. In Germany 2 weeks ago, I announced our intention to provide technical assistance and new technologies to the nations of Eastern Europe to help them handle pollution problems. And some of the rivers in those countries are now so polluted they can't even be used for industrial cooling because they're too corrosive. And even our recommendation to ban the importation of elephant ivory underscores this new international emphasis.

The fifth and final principle is that existing environmental laws will be vigorously and firmly enforced. And I've requested funds to hire more environmental prosecutors at the Justice Department. And next week, Bill Reilly will deliver to Congress a report on overhauling the Superfund program for hazardous waste. Our message about environmental law is simple: Polluters will pay.

And finally, on Monday, I will unveil the most sweeping changes to the Clean Air Act since it was last amended 12 years ago. And it will allow us to recover and restore precious forests, lakes, and streams. And whether Americans live near factories or in cities or in high woodland country, it'll significantly improve every North American's quality of life.

So, those are our five principles: harnessing the power of the marketplace, State and local initiative, promoting prevention, international cooperation, and strict enforcement.

But behind all of the studies, the figures, and the debates, the environment is a moral issue. For it is wrong to pass on to future generations a world tainted by present thoughtlessness. It is unjust to allow the natural splendor bestowed to us to be compromised. It is imperative that we preserve the Earth and all its blessings—to meet the challenge of renewal.

Some 40 years ago, a man named Aldo

Leopold wrote a book that some of you may have heard of. It was called "A Sand County Almanac." And in it, he talked about values, values that you and I share. "That land is to be loved and respected," Leopold wrote—let me start—"That land is to be loved and respected is an extension of ethics." That was 40 years ago. And since then, millions of acres of wetlands, habitat for so many plants and animals, have disappeared. And they continue to vanish at an alarming rate, some one-half million acres a year.

And I want to ask you today what the generations to follow will say of us 40 years from now. It could be they'll report the loss of many million acres more, the extinction of species, the disappearance of wilderness and wildlife; or they could report something else. They could report that sometime around 1989 things began to change and that we began to hold on to our parks and refuges and that we protected our species and that in that year the seeds of a new policy about our valuable wetlands were sown, a policy summed up in three simple words: "No net loss." And I prefer the second vision of America's environmental future.

A man I greatly admire, Theodore Roosevelt, was the first President to act on that ideal. And when he set aside the Grand Canyon as a national monument of nature, his words of warning were driven by great personal conviction. "Leave it as it is," he said. "You cannot improve on it. The ages have been at work on it, and man can only mar it. What you can do is keep it for your children and your children's children."

Recovery, restoration, and renewal—that is our moral imperative. And from today forward, it is the ethical legacy we must inspire in every American.

To one of the great private sector organizations in America, I thank you. God bless you, and God bless the United States of America. Thank you very, very much.

Note: The President spoke at the Sixth International Waterfowl Symposium at 1:10 p.m. in the Arlington Ballroom at the Crystal Gateway Marriott in Arlington, VA. In his opening remarks, he referred to Harry D. Knight, president of Ducks Unlimited, and Michael R. Deland, member-designate of the Council on Environmental Quality.

Nomination of Debra Russell Bowland To Be Administrator of the Wage and Hour Division at the Department of Labor

June 8, 1989

The President today announced his intention to nominate Debra Russell Bowland to be Administrator of the Wage and Hour Division at the Department of Labor. She would succeed Paula V. Smith.

Mrs. Bowland is currently Deputy Director of the Women's Bureau at the Department of Labor. From 1985 to 1988, she was a Special Assistant to the Assistant Secretary of Policy, Department of Labor; the Deputy Under Secretary for Employment Standards, Department of Labor; the Assistant Secretary for Vocational and Adult Education, Department of Education; and a member of the Federal Labor Relations Authority. Mrs. Bowland was director of the department of citizens' service in Baton Rouge, LA, 1985; executive director in Louisiana for Reagan-Bush '84, 1984; owner of Debra Bowland and Associates, 1982–1984; and the secretary of labor for Louisiana, 1980–1982.

Mrs. Bowland attended the University of Wyoming, 1963–1965, and Louisiana State University, 1975–1976. She was born January 24, 1944, in Dayton, OH. Mrs. Bowland is married, has three children, and resides in Fairfax, VA.

Nomination of William C. Brooks To Be an Assistant Secretary of Labor

June 8, 1989

The President today announced his intention to nominate William C. Brooks to be an Assistant Secretary of Labor (Employment Standards Administration). He would succeed Fred William Alvarez.

Since 1973 Mr. Brooks has served in several capacities for the General Motors Corp., including executive director of personnel administration, since January 1989; manager of executive recruiting; director of education systems and program services; director of personnel planning, industrial relations staff; director of personnel, Fisher Body Division engineering center; general director of personnel and public relations, Delco Moraine division; general director of personnel administration; and executive director of the personnel analysis group. Prior to this, Mr. Brooks held several positions in the Federal Government: in the Office of Management and Budget in the Executive Office of the President, the Department of Defense, the Department of Labor, and the Department of the Air Force.

Mr. Brooks received a bachelor of arts degree from Long Island University in Brooklyn, NY, and a master's degree in business administration from the University of Oklahoma, Norman, OK. He is also a graduate of Harvard Business School's advanced management program and has received an honorary doctor of humane letters degree from Florida A&M University. Mr. Brooks was born in Ste. Genevieve, MO. He is married, has three children, and currently resides in Detroit, MI.

The President's News Conference

June 8, 1989

The President. Welcome to the East Room. Please be seated, and we shall proceed.

Helen [Helen Thomas, United Press International]?

China-U.S. Relations

Q. Mr. President, cutting off military sales to China does not seem to have made an impression on the rulers there, and they've become more repressive. What else are you going to do to express this nation's outrage? And do you have any other plans?

The President. Helen, I think that the position we took, aiming not at the Chinese people but at the military arrangements, was well received around the world and was followed by many countries. Right after we did that, many of the European countries followed suit. The events in China are such that we, obviously, deplore the violence and the loss of life, urge restoration of order with recognition of the rights of the people. And I'm still hopeful that China will come together, respecting the urge for democracy on the part of the people. And what we will do in the future, I will announce at appropriate times; but right now, we are engaged in diplomatic efforts, and other countries are doing the same thing. And let's hope that it does have an ameliorating effect on this situation.

Q. Does your support of human rights and democracy extend to other places in the world, like South Africa, the West Bank, where they've been fighting a lot longer than in China against repression?

The President. Yes, it does; it certainly does. Concern is universal. And that's what I want the Chinese leaders to understand. You see, we've taken this action. I am one who lived in China; I understand the importance of the relationship with the Chinese people and with the Government. It is in the interest of the United States to have good relations, but because of the question that you properly raised, we have to speak out in favor of human rights. And we aren't going to remake the world, but we should stand for something. And there's no question in the minds of these students that the United States is standing in their corners.

I'll tell you a little anecdote: When our cars went out to the university to pick up some of the students and bring them out, they were met by universal applause. And then the students in this country have been quite supportive of the steps that I have taken. We had a few into the Oval Office the other day, and I must say my heart goes out to them. They cannot talk to their families, and it's very difficult.

But, yes, the United States must stand wherever, in whatever country, universally for human rights. And let me say, you mentioned South Africa? Absolutely appalling. Apartheid must end.

Yes, Terry [Terence Hunt, Associated Press].

Q. Mr. President, can the United States ever have normal relations with China as long as the hardliners believed responsible for the massacre, such as Deng Xiaoping [Chairman of the Central Military Committee] and Premier Li Peng, remain in power? In other words, what will it take to get U.S.-Chinese relations back to normal?

The President. It will take a recognition of the rights of individuals and respect for the rights of those who disagree. And you have cited two leaders, one of whom I might tell you is—you mentioned Deng Xiaoping. I'm not sure the American people know this: He was thrown out by the Cultural Revolution crowd back in the late sixties; came back in; 1976, was put out again because he was seen as too forward looking. And all I'm saying from that experience is: Let's not jump at conclusions as to how individual leaders in China feel when we aren't sure of that.

But the broad question that you ask—we can't have totally normal relations unless there's a recognition of the validity of the students' aspirations. And I think that that will happen. We had a visit right here, upstairs in the White House, with Mr. Wan Li [Chairman of the Standing Committee of the National People's Congress]. Now, I don't know whether he's in or out, but he said something to me that I think the American people would be interested in. He said, "The army loves the people." And then you've seen soldiers from the 27th Army coming in from outside of Beijing and clearly shooting people. But having said that, I don't think we ought to judge the whole People's Liberation Army of China by that terrible incident.

What I want to do is preserve this relationship as best I can, and I hope the conditions that lie ahead will permit me to preserve this relationship. I don't want to pass judgment on individual leaders, but I want to make very clear to those leaders and to the rest of the world that the United States denounces the kind of brutality that all of us have seen on our television.

Right here, Brit [Brit Hume, ABC News].

House Speaker Foley

Q. Mr. President, I want to ask you about the now infamous memorandum the Republican National Committee distributed concerning Speaker Foley. First, do you think it's credible that this memorandum, which you called disgusting, was not known about by anybody above the level of the staffer who wrote it? And second, do you think it's enough, sir, for this staffer to resign and for everyone then to simply say that the matter is closed?

The President. Well, in the first place, I have great respect for Tom Foley. And he's the one that says the matter should be closed, and he's right. And let me just repeat: It was disgusting. It's against everything that I have tried to stand for in political life. But I discussed that matter with Lee Atwater [Republican National Committee Chairman]. He looked me right in the eye and said he did not know about it. He moved promptly to remove the person that did know about it. And so, I accept that.

But I think that Speaker Foley, a most honorable man, who obviously was done a terrible ill service to by this, is correct when he says, "Let's get it behind us." And I'd like to shift the gears and move into ethics legislation, all the time being sure we try to avoid this kind of ugliness on either side.

Is this a followup question?

Negative Politics

Q. Speaker Foley has indicated that he'd like to change the atmosphere, which has been somewhat poisonous on Capitol Hill this year. Some Democrats have said that you as the leader of your party here in town should do something to try to get the Republicans to join in that effort. What do you say to that call, sir?

The President. I don't think the atmosphere is caused by one part or another. I expressed the same kind of outrage—that I've just expressed about Speaker Foley—about John Tower. I think any fairminded person, no matter how the situation worked out—but you know and I know that he was vilified by rumor and innuendo—vilified. And I don't like it there, and I didn't like what happened to Mr. Foley. And, yes, Brit, I hope I can find a way to elevate it and keep it on the issues.

You know, I'm a realist; I've been around this track for a long time. But we've got to do better. This ugliness of this climate is bad, and I don't like it. And I'd like to think that I could help—maybe this itself will help.

China-U.S. Relations

Q. Mr. President, I'd like to return to China for a moment. You mentioned that your goal is to preserve our relationship with the Chinese Government. But what do you say to the American people who might wonder why we are not more forceful in being the world's leading advocate of democracy? And are we not living up to that responsibility in this situation?

The President. Well, some have suggested, for example, to show our forcefulness, that I bring the American Ambassador back. I disagree with that 180 degrees. And we've seen, in the last few days, a very good reason to have him there. In fact, one of your colleagues, Richard Roth of CBS, was released partially because of the work of our Embassy, of Jim Lilley, our very able Ambassador.

Some have suggested, well, you've got to go full sanctions on economic side. I don't want to cut off grain, and we've just sold grain to the People's Republic of China. I think that would be counterproductive and would hurt the people.

What I do want to do is take whatever steps are most likely to demonstrate the concern that America feels. And I think I've done that, and I'll be looking for other ways to do it if we possibly can.

Asylum for Chinese Dissident

Q. Mr. President, Chinese dissident Fang Lizhi has taken refuge in the U.S. Embassy, apparently fearing for his own safety. The Chinese Government has called that a wanton interference in internal affairs and a violation of international law. What is your reaction to that? And will the United States grant Fang political asylum in the United States?

The President. First, let me remind the audience here that we do not discuss asylum. It's almost like a public discussion of intelligence matters. But in terms of your question, we have acted in compliance with the international law as an extraordinary measure for humanitarian reasons. His personal safety was involved here, he felt. And then we try, historically, to work these things out in consultation with the sovereign state. So, we are not violating international law, in the opinion of our attorneys. And it is awful hard for the United States, when a man presents himself—a person who is a dissident—and says that his life is threatened, to turn him back. And that isn't one of the premises upon which the United States was founded. So, we have a difference with them on that, you're right, but I hope it can be resolved.

Fair Employment Standards

Q. Mr. President, this week the Supreme Court reversed an 18-year standard for fair employment decisions. Now, under the old standard, employers had to justify as legitimate practices that excluded women and minorities. The Court's decision now puts the burden of proof on the plaintiffs to show that the practices they're challenging are not legitimate. Civil rights advocates say that the decision makes it much more difficult for women and minorities to challenge practices that exclude them. Do you support efforts to restore the old standard?

The President. I have not yet received the

memo from the General Counsel on this decision, and thus I really have to defer. I wish I could tell you; but I am one who, when the Supreme Court makes a ruling, figures that the President of the United States must adhere by the law as determined. But we're getting that analyzed. And then sometimes you can take remedy in suggested legislation.

Iran-U.S. Relations

Q. Mr. President, the Iranian government, of course, has changed. And the question to you is: Is there hope that there might be restored some kind of relations with that country? As you know, today the Iranians set forth, informally, an offer for some kind of a deal: that if the Americans would help free some Iranians held by the Phalangists that they might help us free some of our prisoners as well—or our hostages. Is there any hope for any change in the near future?

The President. For a change in relationship? I stated the other day what it would take to have improved relationships, and that would be a renunciation of terror. We can't have normalized relations with a state that's branded a terrorist state. And secondly, they must facilitate the release of American hostages. And so, that is what it would take. And there was a case a while back where Iran asked for information regarding their hostages—never accused us, properly so, of holding people hostage or in any way condoning that—we condemn it. And we've supplied them information. But it's going to take a change in behavior. We don't mind name calling. They keep calling us the Great Satan—that doesn't bother us. Sticks and stones—remember the old adage—will hurt your bones. The names don't hurt you; but performance is what we're looking for. And I don't see so far any sign of change.

I held out the olive branch at my inauguration speech, and I said, look, we want better relations with Iran. I remember when we had good relations. We like the Iranian people; we have a lot of Iranians living in this country. And I said, look, you want better relations, do what's right, do what's right by people that are held against their will. And we've seen no movement. I would repeat that offer tonight.

China-U.S. Relations

Q. Mr. President, the other day you picked up the phone and talked to Richard Nixon about China. I'm wondering, since you know some of the Chinese leaders personally, why you don't pick up the phone and talk to them.

The President. I tried today. Isn't that a coincidence that you'd ask that question? [*Laughter*]

Q. And what did you learn?

The President. The line was busy. [*Laughter*] I couldn't get through.

Q. And Mr. President——

The President. Oh, yes, you've got a followup. Go ahead.

Q. Well, I'm wondering if you learned anything from those phone calls about who's really running China?

The President. I said I couldn't get through. And I talked to our Ambassador, knowing that we'd understandably get questions on China tonight, and the situation is still very, very murky. And that's the way it's been.

I remember, Johanna [Johanna Newman, USA Today], I remember being in China when the way we'd tell who was winning and who was losing, who was up and who was down—we'd send people out around town to count the red-flag limousines. And then they'd say, "Oh, there's 30 of them gathered here; there must be an important meeting." And everybody would hover around trying to see who emerged or who stood next to somebody on a parade on festival day. And it's opened up much more than that. There have been dramatic changes since then.

But in terms of our trying to figure out their internal order, it is extraordinarily difficult. And I did try to contact a Chinese leader today, and it didn't work; but I'm going to keep on trying. I want them to know that I view this relationship as important, and yet I view the life of every single student as important.

Defense Spending

Q. Mr. President, during the 1988 campaign, the Republicans ran ads featuring Chuck Yeager [former test pilot] saying that thousands of defense jobs would be lost with the election of Michael Dukakis. Yet your defense budget would cut several thousand jobs in your home State of Texas, including the elimination of the V–22 *Osprey.* Is there an inconsistency or conflict with your defense——

The President. None whatsoever, none whatsoever. Do you want to follow up? Go ahead.

Q. Is there any hope for revitalizing those programs that are going to be cut?

The President. Well, not programs that the Secretary of Defense [Richard B. Cheney], in consultation with the White House—that felt were less than priority. And you know, when you go to assign priorities, it isn't easy. And we had a program on to facilitate a way to close bases. And lo and behold, everybody in whose district there was no base thought it was a wonderful idea. And everybody in whose district there was a base, or whose State—felt, well, we ought to fine-tune this one; they don't seem to understand.

It is hard to do this, Dave [David Montgomery, Fort Worth Star-Telegram]. And I know there's some people who are thrown out of work. But our defense budget is, in my view, ample for the national security needs of this country. But the Defense Secretary has had to make certain tough calls on systems. And, yes, some people have been thrown out of work. But if this economy keeps moving, I expect they'll find work, because we do have a strong level of defense spending.

Chinese Politics

Q. Earlier, sir, you made reference to Deng Xiaoping, suggesting that he may, if I read you right, not necessarily have been responsible for the actions. You said that he was a reformer, twice out, back in. What were you trying to say? Do you have information that he is not——

The President. I was trying to say that I don't know. And I'm trying to say you don't know, and he doesn't know, and she doesn't know. And nobody knows—outside. And that's the way the Chinese system works. So, for us to read every day some new name out there—it just isn't right. And I don't want to misrepresent this to the American people, but what I do know is that there's events over there that—it doesn't matter who's in charge—we condemn. And there's a relationship over there that is fundamentally important to the United States that I want to see preserved. And so, I'm trying to find a proper, prudent balance, not listening to the extremes that say, take your Ambassador out; cut off all food to the Chinese people so you show your concern. And I think we found a proper avenue there, but I cannot—and you ask a good question—I simply cannot tell you with authority who is calling the shots there today.

Q. Let me follow by asking you this, then: When you were in China earlier in the year, you met with Li Peng, and I believe you told him that China was exempted from your policy review because you knew China, you understood China. Have you been let down personally? Have you been misled in any way?

The President. I feel a certain sense of personal disappointment. But they weren't exempt from the norms of behavior that are accepted internationally in terms of armed people don't shoot down unarmed students. Nobody suggested that.

There was an interesting point in there—and I don't want to delve into the detail of private conversations—but one of the Chinese leaders, a very prominent name, told me, "We want change, but people have to understand it's very complicated here, how fast we move on these reforms. We've come a long way." And indeed, they did move dramatically faster on economic reforms than I think any of us in this room would have thought possible.

But what hasn't caught up is the political reforms and reforms in terms of freedom of expression. The freedom of press caught up a little bit; but it hadn't gone, obviously, near far enough, and now there's martial law and censorship. But we were cautioned on that visit about how fast China could move. Some of it was economic, and clearly, some of the message had to do with how fast they could move politically.

AIDS Testing

Q. Mr. President, turning your attention to a matter that's devastating here at home and all over the world, the question of AIDS. Respected experts are now starting to suggest that instead of the anonymous testing that has existed in the past, there should be mandatory reporting of new cases by name and numerous followups on sexual partners and needle-sharing partners. Do you favor such an approach, sir?

The President. I've spoken at an international AIDS conference, at which I was roundly booed, 2 years ago or so, advocating certain kinds of testing. And I don't want to have—you said mandatory for everybody?

Q. Yes, or at least an end to the anonymity of it?

The President. No, I don't favor that. I think there is a certain right to privacy that we should respect. And so, in terms of anonymity, I would like to suggest that records of that nature should be kept private. There's a lot of suffering for AIDS victims. There's a lot of human tragedy that we haven't really focused on too much. And I think something less than very discreet handling of that information would not be helpful. But do I encourage people to come forward and talk to their doctors and all about partners that may affect others? Yes, I do think you need that kind of frankness, and I do favor certain kinds of testing.

Lesley [Lesley Stahl, CBS News]?

China-U.S. Relations

Q. Mr. President, back to China. There are reports tonight that the Government there has begun rounding up the student leaders, who face at the very least, persecution; at the most, possibly charges of treason and whatever punishment that will bring. You have talked tonight about your strong desire to keep this relationship going and to keep the dialog and all our business as usual moving forward. If the——

The President. Not all of them. Excuse the interruption——

Q. Well, except for the military——

The President. Yes.

Q. Except for the military, sir. If we find out that the people who perpetrated the killings in Tiananmen Square and who were rounding up these students are running the Government, can the United States maintain fairly normal relationships with them, given our aim to foster human rights and promote democracy?

The President. It would make it extraordinarily difficult; but the question is so hypothetical that I'm going to avoid answering it directly. But anything that codifies the acceptance of brutality or lack of respect for human rights will make things much more difficult—there's no question about that.

Visa Extensions for Chinese Students

Q. I have one followup. There are 20,000 Chinese students in the United States.

The President. Yes.

Q. Many of them have spoken out. Are you prepared to grant them political asylum in this country, should these——

The President. They're not seeking asylum. I'll tell you why I answer the question that way. They're not seeking asylum. We had four of them in the other day. And the first thing that one of them—Jia Hao said, "I love my country." And he wants to go back to his country. But what I have done is extend the visas so that people are not compelled to go back to our country. He's not seeking asylum. This man is not going to turn his back on his own country. He wants to change things; but he also wants to know that he is going to be safe, and I don't blame him for that. So, it's not a question of all these people—asylum is a legal status, and that's not what they're looking for.

Q. ——in light of the student roundups. I mean, if they face——

The President. I think it's appalling, and so I would simply say that what we've already done would say to these people, you don't have to go back. But I'm not going to ask them to turn down the flag that they love and turn their back on China. These are patriotic young people who fear because of seeing their own brothers and sisters gunned down, but they're not seeking asylum. They don't want to flee China; they want to help change China.

Soviet Union

Q. Mr. President, we can discuss another Communist country for a while. Your attitude towards the Soviet Union seems to have shifted a bit since you became President, from deep skepticism to seeming acceptance of their intentions. Do you now accept Mr. Gorbachev's sincerity in regard to his pledge of new thinking? And can you tell us a little bit about why you've changed——

The President. I don't think it's shifted as much as you think, Michael [Michael Gelb, Reuters]. I don't think it's shifted as much. What I did was to say, we need a time to make some prudent investigation and discovery and then to go forward with a proposal. And we've done exactly that. The proposal we made at NATO has unified the alliance, and some of the leaders told me that it's more unified than it's been in history. We've made a good proposal now, and I hope the Soviets will take it on good faith, and I am encouraged by the response so far.

Having said that, in dealing with the Soviet Union, I am going to continue to keep my eyes wide open. I will also say I want to see *perestroika* succeed. I want to see it succeed, not fail; And I told Mr. Gorbachev that one-on-one last fall at Governors Island. So, I don't think he believes that I view this as some kind of a Cold War relationship, or that I want to see *perestroika* fail. He did say that he felt there were some elements in this country that did, but I hope that now he knows that I don't look at it that way.

Q. Well, let me just follow up. Do you accept that he is sincere in terms of—are you operating on the assumption that he is sincere when he says he's interested in new thinking in international affairs?

The President. He's already demonstrated that he's interested in new thinking. Who would have thought that we would sit here and, on television, see a relatively lively debate? It's nothing like our Congress, but it had some similar aspects to it. And so, I think he has already demonstrated his commitment to change and to reform.

But there's ways now to solidify these changes. They have 600,000 troops, and we have 305,000. And I made an offer to him. I said the best way to guarantee stability and less warlike attitude is to go to equal numbers. And they are being asked to take out many, many more troops than we are. But I've said, "What's wrong with being equal? The United States will have 275,000 troops deployed, and you, sir, will have 275,000." So, here's a test now. Nobody can argue the inequity of that, particularly since we've put aircraft and helicopters and these other categories on the table.

And I am inclined to think that if I do my work properly and we keep NATO moving forward on this quick timetable, that we can succeed. And if we do, he will once again have demonstrated his desire for change.

First Lady

Q. Mr. President, first, at the great risk of appearing to be trying to make points, please convey birthday wishes to Mrs. Bush.

The President. You've made them. She asked not be reminded of her birthday, but she's doing very well, and thank you.

And if I could editorialize here one minute, there have been a lot of expressions, unrelated to her birthday, about her health. And may I say that we have been very moved by that and that she is doing just fine. And I think her doctors would say the same thing. She's got this Grave's disease under control. Please, excuse the personal interruption there.

Panama Situation

Q. Mr. President, some of your critics say that, despite your rhetoric, General Noriega can sit in Panama for as long as he wishes, in effect laughing at you, sir, laughing at the United States. Can you do anything about it? Should you?

The President. You know, as you look around the world and you see change, respect for the election process, I would simply say Panama is not immune. We're all traumatized—and properly—by the terrible excesses in Tiananmen Square. But I haven't forgotten the brutal beating of Guillermo Ford in Panama [opposition Vice Presidential candidate], and the world hasn't forgotten it. And European public opinion has changed dramatically as they look at Mr. Noriega now. And it is my fervent hope that the Organization of American States will stay with their mission and will keep working on their mandate until

Mr. Noriega leaves.

And let me repeat an important point here. I think there is some feeling in Panama that we are against the PDF, the Panama Defense Forces. We have no argument with the PDF. Many of their people have trained in the United States. We respect the Panamanian people. And so, the problem is Noriega. And if he gets out and they recognize the results of a freely held election—and certifiably freely held, I will say—they would have instant improved relations with the United States.

So, I am not going to give up on this. I think we're proper to use multilateral diplomacy in this instance, as well as doing what we can bilaterally; and I intend to protect our treaty rights, for example, and certainly the best I can to guarantee the safety of Americans.

Trude [Trude Feldman, Trans-Features]?

Short-Range Nuclear Forces in Europe

Q. Mr. President, turning to NATO——

The President. Can't hear you, Trude.

Q. The agreement between Bonn and Washington on the nuclear issue only temporarily bridges the differences. At what point do you visualize the Lance missile going into Germany, and can any German Government accept it?

The President. Well, that matter has been properly deferred under the agreement at NATO. Research can go forward, but the deployment matter has been properly deferred, and let us just go forward on the NATO arrangements that were announced in Brussels. And, yes, there are differences—you're absolutely right. There are differences in Germany on this whole question, not just of the Lance follow-on but a whole difference there on the question of SNF, short-range nuclear forces. And it is in our interest to quickly move forward, because if we can get implemented, within our timeframe, the agreement on conventional forces, that will take a tremendous amount of pressure off the Germans on short-range forces.

Q. Thank you.

The President. Time flies when you're having fun.

Q. Could I just follow that up?

The President. All right, this is the followup, and then if it's 30 minutes——

Q. Poland—there was no question about Poland. I'm a Polish reporter. Maybe you would answer a question about—what are you expecting from your visit to Poland?

The President. She's got a followup. You've misunderstood; she's got a followup question.

Q. NATO was regarded as your success because of your initiatives there and—but isn't the West German challenge just the first of many, now that the Soviet threat is diminishing in Western Europe?

The President. Well, but let me use this question to reply to the question about Poland, too. There will be new challenges for NATO, as the level of concern about armed conflict reduces. I will keep reminding our friends, and they will keep reminding me, that we must keep whatever force is required to deter war. But part of what's happening—and I'm glad the gentleman raised Poland—is this quest for democracy in Poland. And if that goes forward, I can see a much better relationship for the United States with Poland, in one that will, in Poland itself, convince the people that they have less of a stake in military confrontation or in a East bloc confrontation with the West.

So, it is fascinating—the change that is going on there—it is absolutely fascinating. And we should be positioned. And I'm going there to tell this to the leaders: We want to work with you. You've got to reform your economy. We don't feel that you have any bad intentions toward the United States, but we want to see this policy of differentiation continue. When a country moves like Poland did, down democracy's path, the United States should respond as best it could.

Helen [Helen Thomas, United Press International], thank you very much.

Note: The President's 15th news conference began at 8 p.m. in the East Room at the White House. It was broadcast live on nationwide radio and television.

Appointment of the 1989–1990 White House Fellows
June 9, 1989

The President today announced the appointments of the 1989–1990 White House fellows. This is the 25th class of fellows since the program was established in 1964. Fourteen fellows were chosen from nearly 1,000 applicants who were screened by 11 regional panels. The President's Commission on White House Fellowships, chaired by Roger B. Porter, interviewed the 33 national finalists prior to recommending the 14 persons to the President. Their year of government service will begin September 1, 1989.

Fellows serve for 1 year as Special Assistants to the President's principal staff, the Vice President, and members of the Cabinet. In addition to the work assignments, the fellowship includes an education program that parallels and broadens the unique experience of working at the highest levels of the Federal Government. The program is open to U.S. citizens in the early stages of their careers and from all occupations and professions. Federal Government employees are not eligible, with the exception of career Armed Forces personnel. Leadership, character, intellectual and professional ability, and commitment to community and national service are the principal criteria employed in the selection of fellows.

Applications for the 1990–91 program are available from the President's Commission on White House Fellowships, 712 Jackson Place, NW., Washington, DC, 20503.

The 1989–1990 White House fellows are:

Antonio M. Angotti, of New York. Mr. Angotti is the head of sovereign debt for Security Pacific National Bank, concentrating primarily on the third world debt problem. He has also adapted the debt-for-equity conversion concept to the needs of private nonprofit organizations. Mr. Angotti graduated from the University of California at Berkeley (B.A., 1981) and later undertook graduate studies in foreign policy at Cambridge University and the Johns Hopkins School of Advanced International Studies (SAIS). He was born January 15, 1958 in Whittier, CA.

Thomas P. Bostick, of Fort Leavenworth, Kansas. Major Bostick is presently a student in the U.S. Army Command and General Staff College (CGSC) at Fort Leavenworth, KS, and has been an instructor at the U.S. Military Academy. He graduated from the United States Military Academy in 1978 and earned an M.S. degree in both mechanical and civil engineering at Stanford University in 1985. Major Bostick was born September 23, 1956 in Fukuoka, Japan.

John W. Danaher, of California. Dr. Danaher is a senior medical resident at Stanford University Hospital and has been selected to be chief medical resident in 1990–91. He graduated from Trinity College (B.S., 1980) and the Dartmouth Medical School (M.D., 1986). Dartmouth Medical School awarded him the Julian and Melba Jarrett Memorial Award for humanitarian achievement. Dr. Danaher was born September 1, 1958 in Torrington, CT.

Wade T. Dyke, of Ohio. Mr. Dyke is an assistant professor of public administration, school of public administration, at the Ohio State University. He graduated from the University of Wisconsin (bachelor of business administration, 1980), and received a Rhodes scholarship to study at the University of Oxford, where he received an M.A. in politics and economics and a doctorate in politics. Mr. Dyke was born October 11, 1957 in Madison, WI.

Gregory P. Hess, of Florida. Dr. Hess is president and CEO of Emergency Medicine Physicians in Longwood, FL. He graduated from Skidmore College (B.A., 1978) and Albany Medical College (M.D., 1984). Dr. Hess recently took a sabbatical from his emergency practice to complete a fellowship in the field of sports medicine. He is also consulting in practice management and medicolegal issues. Dr. Hess was born October 24, 1956 in Troy, NY.

Michael D. Klausner, of Washington, DC. Mr. Klausner is an attorney with the Washington, DC, office of Gibson, Dunn & Crutcher. Following his graduation from law school, he served as a law clerk to Justice William Brennan of the United States Supreme Court. He was one of the first Americans to teach law in the People's Republic of China. He graduated from the University of Pennsylvania (B.A., 1976) and Yale University (J.D. and M.A., 1981). Mr. Klausner was born December 12, 1954 in Philadelphia, PA.

Robert G. Marbut, Jr., of Texas. Mr. Marbut is president, XIII AAU Junior Olympic Games

Committee, San Antonio, TX. Prior to his association with the Games committee, he was the top staff person to the mayor of San Antonio. Robert was a CORO fellow and is very active with dyslexia and learning disorder organizations. He graduated from Claremont Men's College (B.A., 1983) and Claremont Graduate School (M.A., 1985). He was born May 5, 1960 in Savannah, GA.

Barry R. McBee, of Texas. Mr. McBee is deputy general counsel to Governor William P. Clements, Jr., Austin, TX. He graduated from the University of Oklahoma (B.A., 1978) and Southern Methodist University School of Law (J.D., 1981), where he was editor-in-chief of the law review and Order of the Coif. Mr. McBee was born July 28, 1956 in McAlester, OK.

John McKay, of Washington. Mr. McKay is an attorney with Lane, Powell, Moss & Miller in Seattle, WA. He has served as legal counsel and consultant to numerous political campaigns and currently is the president of the Washington Young Lawyers division. He is the founder and director of the Northwest Minority Job Fair. He graduated from the University of Washington (B.A., 1978) and Creighton University (J.D., 1982). Mr. McKay was born June 19, 1956 in Seattle, WA.

John W. Orrison, of Florida. Mr. Orrison is special assistant to the president, CSX Transportation, in Ponte Verde Beach, FL. He is a scoutmaster and district commissioner for the Boy Scouts, as well as national chairman for the committee on continuing education of the American Railway Engineering Association. He graduated from Auburn University (B.S., 1980) and Harvard University (M.B.A., 1985). Mr. Orrison was born January 15, 1957, in Oak Ridge, TN.

Daniel P. Poneman, of Virginia. Mr. Poneman is an attorney with Covington & Burling in Washington, DC. He is the author of "Nuclear Power in the Developing World," his first book, and "Argentina: Democracy on Trial," which he wrote following a year of study in that country. He has also written articles which have appeared in numerous books, journals, and newspapers. He graduated from Harvard College (A.B., 1978), Oxford University (M. Litt., Politics, 1980), and Harvard Law School (J.D., 1984). Mr. Poneman was born March 12, 1956 in Toledo, OH.

Joyce J. Rayzer, of Kentucky. Ms. Rayzer is deputy director, office of human services, Louisville, KY. She has been an active participant in Teenage Life Choices, an organization established to provide social guidance to adolescents. She graduated from the University of Louisville (B.A., 1974) and the University of Cincinnati School of Planning & Design (B.S., 1986). Ms. Rayzer was born December 30, 1950 in Clarksville, TN.

Wayne Tuan, of New Jersey. Mr. Tuan is vice president, Capital Markets Group, Goldman, Sachs & Company, Jersey City, NJ. During his career, he has worked as an economic consultant for CARE and has assisted in developing programs more directly focused on economic development as compared to economic relief. He graduated from the University of Chicago (A.B., 1981; M.B.A., 1982). Mr. Tuan was born January 19, 1961 in Belleville, NJ.

Leigh Warner, of Connecticut. Ms. Warner is manager, corporate planning, General Foods Corp., White Plains, NY. While managing the Post Natural Raisin Bran business, she established the National Park Enhancement Fund, the first public/private partnership focused on contributing to the entire National Park System. She graduated from Cornell University (B.A., 1976; M.B.A., 1978). Ms. Warner was born October 20, 1955 in Camden, NJ.

Nomination of Thomas Patrick Melady To Be United States Ambassador to the Holy See
June 9, 1989

The President today announced his intention to nominate Thomas Patrick Melady to be Ambassador Extraordinary and Plenipotentiary of the United States of America to the Holy See. He would succeed Frank Shakespeare.

Since 1986 Dr. Melady has been president of the Connecticut Public Expenditure Council in Hartford, CT. He was president of Sacred Heart University, 1976–1986. Dr. Melady has also served as a consultant to the U.S. Secretary of Education, 1982–1984, and an Assistant Secretary for Post-secondary Education, 1981–1982. He was Ambassador to the Republic of Burundi, 1969–1972, and Ambassador to the Republic of Uganda, 1972–1973. Dr. Melady was a professor at Seton Hall University, 1973–1974; a consultant for the National Urban League in New York, 1968–1969; and chairman of Seton Hall University, 1967–1969. He was an adjunct professor at Fordham University, 1966–1969; an adjunct professor at St. John's University; and president of the Africa Service Institute in New York, 1959–1967.

Dr. Melady graduated from Duquesne University (B.A., 1950) and Catholic University of America (M.A., Ph.D., 1954). He was born March 4, 1927, in Norwich, CT. He served in the U.S. Army, 1945–1947. Dr. Melady is married and has two children.

Statement by Press Secretary Fitzwater on President Bush's Meeting With President Soeharto of Indonesia

June 9, 1989

The President met with President Soeharto of Indonesia for a half hour this afternoon in the Oval Office. President Bush expressed his appreciation for the hospitality extended by President Soeharto and the Indonesian Government during the Vice President's trip to Jakarta in April.

The two Presidents discussed the situation in Cambodia. President Bush reaffirmed the need for a comprehensive settlement, including verified withdrawal of all Vietnamese troops, prevention of Khmer Rouge return to power, and self-determination for the Cambodian people. The President reiterated the U.S. economic and military role in the development of Southeast Asia. President Bush stated that he looks forward to greater two-way trade and investment and praised Indonesia's debt management as an example of the Government's sound economic policies.

Statement by Press Secretary Fitzwater on the Murder of José Antonio Rodriguez Porth of El Salvador

June 9, 1989

The President strongly condemns the vicious murder of Salvadoran President Cristiani's newly appointed Salvadoran Minister of the Presidency, José Antonio Rodriguez Porth. Mr. Rodriguez died of wounds suffered earlier today when assailants machine-gunned him and his party as they were traveling through a residential neighborhood in San Salvador.

The President noted a pattern of violence against government officials in El Salvador by those who seek to destroy the democratic gains made in that country. This brutal assassination follows the recent killing of President Duarte's Attorney General, Roberto Garcia Alvarado, and attacks on the homes of other government and military officials.

We hope the Salvadoran police forces will find those responsible for this despicable act. We note that the security forces uncovered on May 30 the largest cache of Soviet-bloc weapons ever captured in El Salvador, including almost 250 AK–47 assault rifles.

The President again calls on extremist groups to put an end to the violence in El Salvador, noting that only through the renunciation of terrorism and war, and the acceptance of democracy, will there be peace.

Vice President Quayle will personally deliver the President's condolences to the Rodriguez Porth family and to President Cristiani when he arrives in San Salvador next week.

Remarks Announcing Proposed Legislation To Amend the Clean Air Act
June 12, 1989

Well, in this room are Republicans and Democrats, leaders from both sides of the aisle in Congress, Governors, executives from some of the most important companies and business organizations in America, leading conservationists, and people who have devoted their lives to creating a cleaner and safer environment. And I've invited you here today to make a point. With the leadership assembled in this room, we can break the stalemate that has hindered progress on clean air for the past decade; and with the minds, the energy, the talent assembled here, we can find a solution.

So, let me tell you the purposes of this morning's gathering. First, I'd like to lay on the table my proposals to curb acid rain and cut urban smog and clean up air toxics. And second, I want to call upon all of you to join me in enacting into law a new Clean Air Act this year. But first, we should remember how far we've come and recognize what works.

The 1970 Clean Air Act got us moving in the right direction with national air quality standards that were strengthened by amendments in 1977. Since 1970, even though we have 55 percent more cars going 50 percent farther, in spite of more utility output and more industrial production, we've still made progress. Lead concentrations in the air we breathe are down 98 percent. Sulfur dioxide and carbon monoxide cut by over a third. Particulate matter cut 21 percent; even ozone-causing emissions have been cut by 17 percent. And still, over the last decade, we have not come far enough.

Too many Americans continue to breathe dirty air. And political paralysis has plagued further progress against air pollution. We have to break this logjam by applying more than just Federal leverage. We must take advantage of the innovation, energy, and ingenuity of every American.

The environmental movement has a long history here in this country. It's been a force for good, for a safer, healthier America. And as a people, we want and need that economic growth, but now we must also expect environmental responsibility and respect the natural world. And this will demand a national sense of commitment, a new ethic of conservation. And I reject the notion that sound ecology and a strong economy are mutually exclusive. So, last week I outlined five points of a new environmental philosophy: one, to harness the power of the marketplace; two, to encourage local initiative; three, to emphasize prevention instead of just cleanup; four, to foster international cooperation; and five, to ensure strict enforcement—polluters will pay.

We know more now than we did just a few years ago. New solutions are close at hand. It's time to put our best minds to work; to turn technology and the power of the marketplace to the advantage of the environment; to create; to innovate; to tip the scales in favor of recovery, restoration, and renewal. Every American expects and deserves to breathe clean air, and as President, it is my mission to guarantee it—for this generation and for the generations to come. If we take this commitment seriously, if we believe that every American expects and deserves clean air, and then we act on that belief, then we will set an example for the rest of the world to follow.

Today I am proposing to Congress a new Clean Air Act and offering a new opportunity. We've seen enough of this stalemate; it's time to clear the air. And you know, I think we will. We touched a lot of bases as we prepared this bill, and we've had the benefit of some good thinking on the Hill. And we've met with business leaders who see environmental protection as essential to long-term economic growth, and we've talked with environmentalists who know that cost-effective solutions help build public support for conservation. And we've worked with academics and innovative thinkers from every quarter who have laid the groundwork for this approach. And just this morning I spoke by phone with Prime Minister Mulroney of Canada. I believe he's excited about the prospect, too. I have no pride of authorship. Let me commend Project 88 and groups like the Environmental Defense Fund for bringing creative solutions to longstanding problems, for not only breaking the mold but helping to build a new one.

And we've had to make some tough choices. And some may think we've gone too far, and others not far enough; but we all care about clean air. To the millions of Americans who still breathe unhealthy air, let me tell you, I'm concerned—I'm concerned about vulnerable groups like the elderly and asthmatics and children, concerned about every American's quality of life; and I'm committed to see that coming generations receive the natural legacy they deserve.

We seek reforms that make major pollution reductions where we most need them. First, our approach is reasonable deadlines for those who must comply. It has compelling sanctions for those who don't. It accounts for continued economic growth and expansion; offers incentives, choice, and flexibility for industry to find the best solutions; and taps the power of the marketplace and local initiative better than any previous piece of environmental legislation.

This legislation will be comprehensive. It will be cost-effective; but above all, it will work. We will make the 1990's the era for clean air. And we have three clear goals and three clear deadlines. First, we will cut the sulfur dioxide emissions that cause acid rain by almost half, by 10 million tons, and we will cut nitrogen oxide emissions by 2 million tons, both by the year 2000. We have set absolute goals for reductions and have emphasized early gains. And that means 5 million tons will be cut by 1995, and the degradation caused by acid rain will stop by the end of this century. To make sure that coal continues to play a vital role in our energy future, we've provided an extension of 3 years and regulatory incentives for the use of innovative, clean-coal technology. We've set an ambitious reduction target, and applying market forces will be the fastest, most cost-effective way to achieve it. So, we're allowing utilities to trade credits among themselves for reductions they make, to let them decide how to bring aggregate emissions down as cost-effectively as possible. Cleaner fuels, better technologies, energy conservation, improved efficiency—in any combination, just as long as it works.

There's a wisdom to handing work to those most qualified to do it. Four hundred years ago Montaigne wrote: "Let us permit nature to have her way. She understands her business better than we do." Well, it's true. Acid rain must be stopped, and that's what we all care about. But it's also true that business understands its business better than we do. So, we're going to put that understanding to work on behalf of clean air and a sound environment. We've provided the goals, but we won't try to micromanage them. We will allow flexibility in how industry achieves these goals, but we stand firm on what must be achieved.

Second, this Federal proposal will cut the emissions that cause urban ozone, smog, virtually in half. This will put the States well on the road to meeting the standard. Twenty years ago, we started on the job. And if Congress will act on the clean air reforms that I'm offering today, 20 years from now, every American in every city in America will breathe clean air. Today 81 cities don't meet Federal air quality standards. This legislation will bring clean air to all but about 20 cities by 1995, and within 20 years, even Los Angeles and Houston and New York will be expected to make it.

In the nine urban areas with the greatest smog problems, we propose bold new initiatives to reconcile the automobile to the environment, ensuring continued economic growth without disruptive driving controls. We'll accomplish this through alternative fuels and clean-fueled vehicles. We propose to put up to a million clean-fueled vehicles a year on the road by 1997. But we're also proposing flexibility on the means, even as we remain firm on the goals. A city can either request inclusion in the program or, if they show they can achieve these ambitious reductions through other measures, we will scale back the clean-fuel vehicle requirements accordingly. Also, we're sensitive to the problems of smaller cities, whose own ozone problems are due largely to pollutants that are generated in other areas, other regions, other cities. They will not be penalized for pollution problems outside their control.

Our program incorporates a mix of cost-effective measures to cut emissions from cars, fuels, factories, and other sources. But I'm asking the EPA to develop rules like those we're employing on acid rain to allow auto and fuel companies to trade required reductions in order to meet the standard in the most cost-effective way. Our challenge is to develop an emissions trading plan; their challenge is to meet the standards.

The third leg of our proposal is designed to cut all categories of airborne toxic chemicals by three-quarters within this decade. Our best minds will apply the most advanced industrial technology available to control these airborne poisons. The very best control technology we have will determine the standard we set for those plants. And until now, because of an unworkable law, the EPA has been able to regulate only 7 of the 280 known air toxics. The bill I am proposing today will set a schedule for regulating sources of air toxics by dates certain. In addition, it will give the dedicated people of the EPA the right tools for the job, and it will make state-of-the-art technology an everyday fact of doing business. And that's the way it should be.

In its first phase, this initiative should eliminate about three-quarters of the needless deaths from cancer that have been caused by toxic industrial air emissions. And we plan a second phase to go after any remaining unreasonable risk. People who live near industrial facilities should not have to fear for their health.

And for 10 years, we've struggled to engage a united effort on behalf of clean air, and we're now on the edge of real change. Nineteen eighty-nine could be recorded as the year when business leaders and environmental advocates began to work together, when environmental issues moved out of the courts, beyond conflict, into a new era of cooperation. And this can be known as the year we mobilized leadership, both public and private, to make environmental protection a growth industry and keep our ecology safe for diversity. The wounded winds of north, south, east, and west can be purified and cleansed, and the integrity of nature can be made whole again. Ours is a rare opportunity to reverse the errors of this generation in the service of the next; and we cannot, we must not, fail. We must prevail. I ask for your support. We need your support to make all of this into a reality.

Thank you all, and God bless you, and thank you very much for coming.

Note: The President spoke at 11:15 a.m. in the East Room of the White House.

White House Fact Sheet on the President's Clean Air Plan
June 12, 1989

Fulfilling a major campaign commitment, President Bush today proposed a comprehensive program to provide clean air for all Americans. The President's plan calls for the first sweeping revisions to the Clean Air Act since 1977 and represents the first time an administration has put forward a proposal since that time. The President's plan is designed to curb three major threats to the Nation's environment and to the health of millions of Americans: acid rain, urban air pollution, and toxic air emissions.

While emissions of some pollutants—such as sulfur dioxide, urban ozone, and carbon monoxide—have been reduced since passage of the 1970 law, progress has not come quickly enough. The President's plan will dramatically accelerate the pace of pollution reduction and put America on the path toward markedly cleaner air by the end of the century.

The President's plan will:

• Cut sulfur dioxide emissions virtually in half by the year 2000. The plan calls for a 10-million-ton reduction in SO_2 and a 2-million-ton cut in nitrogen oxide (NO_x) emissions, for a total reduction of 12 million tons in acid-rain-causing emissions.

• Bring all cities currently not meeting the health standards for ozone and carbon monoxide into attainment. Most cities will attain the standard by 1995, and the plan is designed to ensure attainment in all but the most severely impacted cities by the year 2000.

• Require factories and plants emitting toxic compounds into the air to employ the best technology currently available in order to achieve in the near term a cut estimated at 75 to 90 percent in pollutants suspected of causing cancer. Taken together with efforts to reduce cancer-causing emissions from cars and trucks, it is estimated that the plan will eliminate in its first phase over three-fourths of the annual cancer deaths that air toxics are suspected of causing.

Fundamental Principles

Five goals underlie the President's clean air proposals and the means for accomplishing them:

• *Protecting the Public's Health.* The goal of the legislation is to prevent public exposure to cancer-causing agents and to protect those citizens, especially vulnerable populations—such as the elderly, asthmatics, and children—who live in cities with dirty air that does not conform to national health standards.

• *Improving the Quality of Life.* The proposal will improve the quality of life for all Americans by exercising responsible stewardship over the environment for future generations.

• *Achieving Early Reductions and Steady Progress.* The proposal establishes realistic timetables to meet air quality standards, but contains provisions to cut substantial amounts of air pollution in the near term while requiring steady progress toward reducing emissions that are harder to control.

• *Harnessing the Power of the Marketplace.* The proposal calls for the use of marketable permits to achieve acid-rain reductions and emissions trading to achieve reductions from the automobile pollution, so as to clean the air to a definite standard while minimizing the burden on the American economy.

• *Employing Innovative Technologies.* The proposal encourages development of clean coal technology, alternative fuel systems for automobiles, and other cost-effective means of using new technology to cut pollution.

The President's plan allows for both environmental protection and economic growth, two longstanding concerns often considered at odds with each other. By incorporating both concerns in his proposal, the President seeks to break the gridlock which has characterized the debate on clean air for the past several years.

ACID RAIN

Highlights

- Requires sulfur dioxide reductions of 10 million tons and nitrogen oxide reductions of 2 million tons.
- Calls for 5 million tons of reductions in the first phase by the end of 1995.
- Establishes a system of marketable permits to allow maximum flexibility for utilities to achieve required reductions in the most efficient and least costly manner.

Background

Acid rain occurs when sulfur dioxide (SO_2) and nitrogen oxide (NO_x) emissions undergo a chemical change in the atmosphere and return to the Earth in rain, fog, or snow.

Approximately 20 million tons of SO_2 are emitted annually in the United States, three quarters from the burning of fossil fuels by electric utilities; 20 percent from other, more widely dispersed industrial sources; and 5 percent from transportation sources.

The source of most SO_2 emissions causing acid rain are old (pre-1971) electric powerplants, not subject to the existing Clean Air Act's strict emissions requirements on newer plants. Fifty power plants are responsible for about half of all SO_2 emissions.

Acid rain causes damage to lakes, forests, and buildings; contributes to reduced visibility; and is suspected of causing damage to human health.

Since 1970 the United States has spent $225 billion to control air pollution. American industry spends about $33 billion a year on air pollution controls ($10 billion by the electric utility industry). One result of this expenditure is that SO_2 emissions have been reduced by almost 20 percent since 1977, despite a substantial increase in coal consumption during the period since then.

Any acid rain control program will increase electricity rates for affected utilities. Generally speaking, however, proposals with greater flexibility will result in smaller rate increases. Thus, the President's proposal to allow trading among utility companies will ensure that protection from acid rain is achieved in a less costly fashion than many of the more traditional "command and control" proposals that have been advanced.

The President's plan represents a major new innovation in harnessing the power of the marketplace to protect the environment.

The President's proposal calls for:

• A reduction of 10 million tons of sulfur dioxide by the year 2000, using a baseline year of 1980 for tons of SO_2 emitted, primarily from coal-fired powerplants.

• A two-phase program in order to ensure early reductions. A reduction of 5 million tons is required during the first phase, by the end of 1995. All dates assume enactment of this legislation by December 31, 1989.

• A 2-million-ton reduction of NO_x in Phase II. The plan would allow utilities to trade reductions of NO_x for reductions of SO_2 or vice versa, and thus represents a call for a total reduction of 12 million tons in acid rain-causing pollutants.

• A 3-year extension of the Phase II deadline for plants adopting clean coal-repowering technologies, combined with regulatory incentives designed to smooth their transition into the marketplace. This will allow the United States to make good on the major investment the President has called for in clean coal and will ensure that coal continues to play an important role in America's energy future.

• Freedom of choice in cutting pollution. The plan requires all plants above a certain size in affected States to meet the same emissions standard, but does not dictate to plant managers how the standard should be met. The plan requires the largest polluting plants to make the greatest cuts in pollution. The emissions standard would be set at the rate necessary to achieve 5 million tons in the first phase. The plan envisions a standard of 2.5 lbs. per million BTU, which would affect 107 plants in 18 States. The standard would then be tightened to approximately 1.2 lbs. per million BTU's so as to achieve a 10-million-ton reduction in Phase II.

• Maximum flexibility in obtaining reductions. The plan would allow utilities to trade required reductions so that they will be achieved in the least costly fashion. In the first phase, trading would be allowed among electric plants within a State or within a utility system. In addition, full interstate trading would be allowed in Phase II.

• The estimated cost of the President's proposal would be $3.8 billion annually in the second phase and approximately $700 million per year in the first phase. While this represents an increase of over 2 percent by the year 2000 in the Nation's $160-billion-a-year electricity bill, the flexibility built into the President's plan reduces by up to half the cost of various competing proposals mandating the use of specific technologies.

Urban Air Quality

Highlights

- Employs a mix of Federal measures and State initiatives to cut sharply air pollution in our nation's cities. The Federal measures alone will cut emissions that cause urban ozone, the primary contributor to urban air pollution, nearly in half and help bring all cities into compliance with air quality standards.

- Sets realistic timetables for attaining the standards but is designed to ensure steady progress toward meeting that goal.
- Contains new initiatives to promote alternative fuels to reduce pollution from cars, buses, trucks, and motor fuels, and to harness the power of the marketplace to ensure cost-effective reductions.

OZONE

Background

Based on data measured during the summers of 1985 to 1987, over 100 million people live in 81 urban areas across the country that exceed the health standard for ozone. In some cities, such as Los Angeles, the situation is persistent and severe (176 days in violation of the health standard in 1988); in other cities the problem is marginal (Lancaster, PA, is listed as a nonattainment area, but in fact has exceeded the Federal standard for only a few hours in the last 3 years).

The President's plan is designed to ensure that over two-thirds of the cities now out of attainment—all but about 25 cities—come into attainment by 1995. All but the 3 most seriously polluted areas—Los Angeles, Houston, and New York—will come into attainment by the year 2000; and these special cases will be given until 2010, contingent upon a requirement in the President's plan that they show significant annual progress toward cleaning the air and meeting the health standard.

Ozone is formed when volatile organic compounds (VOC's) are mixed with nitrogen oxides (NO_x) in the presence of sunlight. Heat speeds up the reaction, and therefore, concentrations are usually higher in the summer months. Excesses above the ozone standard (.12 parts per million) grew sharply during the especially hot summer of 1988. If a city exceeds the standard for at least 1 hour on 4 or more days during a 3 year period, it is judged to be "out of attainment" with the standard.

Exposure to ozone causes short term effects, such as shortness of breath, coughing, and chest pains, that are particularly acute for asthmatics, children, and senior citizens. Moreover, ozone is suspected of playing a role in the long-term development of chronic lung diseases and permanent lung structure damage. In addition to health effects, ozone has effects on vegetation, including crops such as soybeans, wheat, and corn; is damaging forests in California; and is suspected as a contributing agent in damage to forests in the southeastern United States.

The major sources of VOC's, the most important ozone precursor, are motor vehicles (40 percent); small area sources, e.g., bakeries, dry cleaners, and consumer solvents (40 percent); large point sources, e.g., petroleum refineries (15 percent); and gasoline refueling (5 percent). Many large point sources have already been required to reduce emissions by roughly 80 percent from uncontrolled levels under the Clean Air Act, and tailpipe emissions from new vehicles have been reduced by 96 percent. The smaller area sources are largely uncontrolled.

VOC and NO_x emissions have decreased nationally since 1978—VOC's by 17 percent and NO_x by 8 percent—despite growth in population, travel, and industrial activity. As a consequence, the trend in ambient ozone concentrations declined by 9 percent from 1979 to 1987. Increases occurred again, however, in the hot summers of 1987 and 1988.

The deadline for meeting urban ozone standards set back in 1977 under the existing Clean Air Act has already expired. Despite this progress in reducing ozone, the health standards have not been met within the deadlines. Without new legislation, the Environmental Protection Agency (EPA) will be required by law to impose Federal Implementation Plans (FIP's) on several major American cities. Courts are, for example, already preparing to impose such requirements on Chicago and Los Angeles. These FIP's could involve extraordinary controls that would sharply curb economic growth and dramatically alter the lifestyles of local residents.

Over the next decade, both EPA and the

Federal Highway Administration estimate that growth in automobile use will begin to outstrip reductions occurring from fleet turnover, so that VOC emissions will increase after 2000.

Thus, additional measures to reduce ozone-causing emissions are needed if Americans are to have air that is clean enough to meet the health standard. The President's plan sets forth these additional clean air measures.

Some measures required under current law will help reduce VOC's. These include:

- The effect of tightened automobile-and truck-tailpipe emission standards, which will continue to cut emissions as older cars are replaced with new ones;
- The implementation of required inspection and maintenance programs for motor vehicles by State and local governments;
- Volatility controls on gasoline. Earlier this year, the Bush administration required a reduction of gasoline volatility to a standard of 10.5 pounds per square inch;
- Selected stationary source controls on refineries and other factories.

It is estimated that these measures will reduce VOC emissions from baseline levels by 18 percent by 2005. They will bring 23 cities into attainment by 1995; but without additional controls, increased automobile use would cause many of these to slip back out of attainment, leaving 72 cities out of attainment by 2005.

Additional Federal Measures Under the President's Proposal

In an ambitious effort to bring all cities into attainment, the President's proposals call for:

- Further tightening the volatility requirements for gasoline nationwide during the summer months to reduce evaporative emissions which cause ozone formation. This will reduce VOC emissions by an estimated 8 percent.
- Reductions in vehicle evaporative emissions caused by automobile running losses, which will cut VOC emissions by an estimated 4.2 percent.
- Federal regulations to control emissions from treatment, storage, and disposal of hazardous wastes, which will cut VOC emissions by 3.2 percent.
- Providing EPA with the authority to regulate VOC emissions from small sources and consumer products, such as consumer solvents and paints, which EPA estimates will cut VOC emissions by 2.5 percent.
- Tightening hydrocarbon emission tailpipe standards for automobiles by almost 40 percent. The current standard will be tightened to the level soon to be required on all California vehicles (from .41 to .25 grams per mile). This will cut VOC emissions by 0.4 percent.
- A first-time requirement for light-duty trucks to meet the same tailpipe standard now required of automobiles (.41 gpm). This will cut VOC emissions by 0.2 percent.
- Expanded vehicle inspection and maintenance programs in serious nonattainment areas, which will cut VOC emissions by 1.2 percent.
- Controls to reduce evaporative emissions which occur during refueling of motor vehicles. These stage II controls would require refueling stations to install special nozzles on gasoline pumps in nonattainment areas and are expected to reduce VOC's by up to 2 percent in such areas.
- Provide EPA new authority to issue control technology guidelines (CTG's) to major stationary source emitters (factories and plants). The most cost-effective control guidelines will be issued first. These guidelines are expected to result in a 3.5-percent reduction in VOC emissions.
- Provide for the use of alternative fuels—such as clean-burning methanol, natural gas, and ethanol—in the most serious nonattainment areas. The President's plan is designed to ensure that 1 million clean-fueled vehicles per year are introduced into America's most polluted cities by the year 1997. The program will not only reduce VOC emissions by an additional 2 to 5 percent, it will dramatically reduce toxic air emissions, such as benzene, toluene, and xylene.
- It is estimated that these new Federal measures to curb ozone pollution will add $3 to $4 billion in annual costs to the economy when fully implemented.

The Long-Term Clean Fuels Program

The clean fuels program proposed by the President is perhaps the most innovative and far-reaching component of his proposal. It is designed to provide a long-term reconciliation of the environment and the automobile so that Americans can continue to enjoy economic growth, freedom in using their motor vehicles, and clean air.

The administration proposes to replace a portion of the motor vehicle fleet in certain cities with new vehicles that operate on clean-burning fuels. In the 9 major urban areas where current data shows the greatest concentration of ozone, the administration's plan calls for a 10-year program for the phased-in introduction of alternative fuels and clean-fueled vehicle sales according to the following schedule:

—500,000 vehicles in 1995
—750,000 vehicles in 1996
—1,000,000 vehicles each year from 1997 through 2004

The major metropolitan areas affected by the plan are Los Angeles, Houston, New York City, Milwaukee, Baltimore, Philadelphia, greater Connecticut, San Diego, and Chicago. If these areas are able to demonstrate that they can achieve analogous reductions in VOC's and toxic air chemicals through other measures, the plan would allow them to opt out of the clean-fueled vehicle and alternative fuels program, in which case the vehicle target numbers would be scaled down proportionately. The plan would also allow other cities to be included in the program at their request.

The President's alternative fuels program, combined with other motor vehicle and fuel measures in the plan, will shrink the contribution of vehicles to the ozone problem from the current 40 percent to 10 percent. This represents not only an alternative to some of the more disruptive driving controls currently being considered by some States but also a bold and innovative means of reconciling continued use of the automobile by a growing society with the need for cleaner air.

Effect of the Federal Measures Proposed by the President

Taken together, the Federal measures proposed by the President, combined with the effect of measures being pursued under current law, will cut ozone-causing VOC emissions nearly in half. EPA estimates the program will reduce annual emissions by 45 percent by the year 2005. In and of themselves, these measures will bring all but about 20 cities into attainment of the ozone standard.

Because of the President's commitment to ensuring clean air in *all* American cities, however, his plan calls for additional measures to be undertaken by the States in order to meet the standard for healthy air.

State Measures Under the President's Proposal

Under the President's proposal, the roughly 20 cities with the most serious ozone pollution problems would be required to take steps to cut ozone-causing emissions by 3 percent per year beginning with enactment of the legislation.

This will guarantee that, even as more realistic deadlines for meeting the standard are set, those cities with the most significant air pollution problems will be on a steady path toward cleaner air.

Because of ozone transport, some areas may be unable to attain the standard in spite of adequate efforts to control their own pollution. Cities under 200,000 in population, which are not part of regional airsheds, but whose attainment is prevented as a result of ozone pollution transported from other cities or regions, will not be subject to sanctions under these circumstances.

Emissions Trading: Harnessing the Power of the Marketplace to Protect the Environment

The President has also directed the EPA to develop rules and regulations which will provide companies with the maximum flexibility in achieving the pollution reductions called for in his plan. Specifically, the President's plan would require the Administrator to issue regulations within 18 months to allow automobile manufacturers to engage in emissions trading and refiners to engage in fuel pooling to the maximum extent feasible. Such regulations shall establish performance standards for vehicles and transportation fuels marketed in the most serious and severe nonattainment areas. Companies would then be able to choose to engage in emissions trading and fuel pooling, so long as they can demonstrate to EPA that the combination of measures they select will allow them to achieve the same emissions reductions as the control measures outlined in the President's program.

This emissions trading concept is already being considered by the State of California. It represents a market-based means of reducing both VOC's and reactive aromatics in the most cost-effective way. The EPA would publish these regulations at the same time as it publishes regulations implementing the other control measures in the President's plan. If companies cannot demonstrate alternative means of achieving the same amount of pollution reduction, they would be required to implement the control measures outlined above.

CARBON MONOXIDE

Background

Carbon monoxide (CO) is a colorless, odorless gas that tends to reduce the oxygen carrying capacity of the blood. It is a particularly serious health threat to individuals who suffer from cardiovascular disease, especially those with angina or heart disease. Unlike ozone, carbon monoxide problems are worse in cold weather.

Two-thirds of CO emissions come from motor vehicles. Emissions of carbon monoxide decreased 25 percent from 1978 to 1987, despite a 24-percent increase in vehicle miles traveled during that period, largely because of controls already in place on emissions from cars, buses, and trucks. Some improvement from these controls will continue, as older, more heavily polluting cars are gradually replaced on America's roads by newer, cleaner vehicles. Currently, cars purchased before 1981 amount to only 38 percent of the vehicle miles traveled (VMT), but they account for over 86 percent of CO emissions.

As use of the automobile continues to grow, however, it is expected that many American cities will not attain the health-based carbon monoxide standard. That standard is 9 parts per million (ppm), measured over an 8-hour period. If a representative reading of monitors in an area shows that it exceeds the standard for 2 or more 8-hour periods, it is classified in nonattainment.

There are currently about 50 American cities not meeting the standard. As with ozone, in some cases, cities exceed the standard only moderately. About six urban areas, however, have a carbon monoxide problem classified by EPA as serious.

EPA estimates that even as vehicle miles traveled (VMT) grow, the effect of fleet turnover will bring almost half of those cities currently violating the standard into attainment. Several of the measures in the President's proposal designed to curb ozone-causing emissions will also help reduce carbon monoxide. These include the measures described above to tighten tailpipe standards for light-duty trucks and to improve State and local inspection and maintenance programs.

Even with these measures, however, several American cities will continue to have a carbon monoxide problem. To bring these cities into compliance with the health-based standard, the President's proposal contains several important measures designed to cut carbon monoxide emissions. Specifically, the President's plan calls for:

• A major new program to promote the use of clean-burning oxygenated fuels, which emit dramatically less carbon monoxide. The plan would require those cities with the most serious carbon monoxide problems to use gasoline blended with oxygenated fuels during the winter months. Oxygenated fuels include ethanol, methanol, ETBE, and MTBE. Blending oxygenates into fuel will not only reduce carbon monoxide; it will also sharply reduce toxic air emissions caused by aromatics in conventional gasoline.

• Ethanol and ETBE are generally produced in the United States from corn, wheat, and potato crops. They offer the opportunity both to clean the air and to provide expanded markets for America's farmers. The President's plan would allow cities to opt out of the oxygenated fuels requirements if they could demonstrate to EPA that they would come into attainment of the carbon monoxide standard using other measures. EPA estimates that requiring oxygenated fuels in areas with serious carbon monoxide problems will reduce carbon monoxide emissions by an additional 18 percent in these areas.

- Giving EPA the authority to issue regulations for a carbon monoxide cold temperature standard. Carbon monoxide problems are exaggerated when motor vehicles start in exceptionally cold weather. This standard has the potential to reduce carbon monoxide emissions by 7 to 12 percent.

The President's plan will bring the vast majority of cities into attainment with the carbon monoxide standard by 1995, and will bring *all* American cities into attainment by the year 2000.

Particulate Matter

Background

Particulate matter (PM10) includes acid sulfates, toxic organics and metals, and insoluble dusts that come from traditional stack emissions, as well as area sources such as wood stoves and open burning. Construction, roadways, and mobile sources also contribute to the problem. PM10 can cause premature death in elderly and ill persons, aggravation of existing respiratory disease, increased respiratory illness, and other effects. Particulate matter (PM10) standards were revised in 1987 to address smaller particulate matter particles most likely to penetrate the lungs.

The President's program will:

- Require reasonably available control measures to meet the standard.
- Ensure that the majority of cities meet the standard by 1994, and that *all* cities meet PM10 standards by 2001.

Toxic Air Pollutants

Highlights

- Dramatically accelerates progress in controlling major toxic air pollutants.
- Uses best technology available to cut air toxics.
- Promises certifiable progress in regulating sources of toxic air emissions on a set schedule.

Background

The emission of toxic chemicals into the air is believed to cause cancer and other health effects in humans. Since 1974 EPA has been required to regulate such emissions in order to provide an ample margin of safety to the public. Because this margin has been difficult to define and has been the subject of continued litigation, EPA has had difficulty proceeding with regulation under the law. Since passage of the statute, it has published regulations for only seven toxic air pollutants. Because the statute has proven unworkable, the President has proposed a major revision of the law in order to guarantee greatly accelerated progress in reducing the damaging effects of toxic air pollution.

Data recently released by the EPA indicate that 2.7 billion pounds of toxic chemicals are emitted into the air each year. EPA estimates that these emissions contribute to approximately 1,500–3,000 fatal cancers annually. Toxic chemical emissions are associated also with respiratory disease and birth defects. Motor vehicles and stationary sources each account for approximately half of air toxic emissions. The measures in the President's plan designed to curb VOC emissions and promote alternative fuels will sharply reduce emissions from motor vehicles.

The President's plan also includes a major new initiative to reduce air toxic emissions from stationary sources (factories, plants, and other such sources). A majority of identified carcinogens are emitted by about 30 industrial categories, including steel mills (coke ovens), rubber, pulp and paper, chromium electroplating, and solvent users. The President's plan is designed to reduce quickly emissions from these sources.

The President's program will:

- Establish a set schedule for regulating major sources of toxic air pollution. Under the plan, EPA will publish regulations for controlling 10 source categories within 2 years, 25 percent of source categories within 4 years, 50 percent of source categories within 7 years, and all necessary additional categories of air toxics within 10 years.

- Require emitters of toxic air pollution to use the Maximum Available Control Technology (MACT) to sharply cut pollution. This means that EPA would set a standard based on the best technology currently available. Plants would then be required to meet that standard, with some exceptions to add flexibility for those who have already reduced most air toxics and for very small plants.
- Encourage voluntary reductions early, before standards are even published, by providing credit for those reductions against the MACT requirement.
- After Phase I is implemented, the EPA Administrator shall assess any remaining risk after reductions from state-of-the-art technology and determine if there is a need for further controls. Based on his assessment, the EPA Administrator would set additional standards to prevent the public from being exposed to unreasonable risk, which would allow considerations of cost and technical feasibility as well as health-based risks.

It is estimated that the President's air toxics initiative will eliminate in the first phase about three-quarters of the cancer deaths caused by toxic air emissions from factories and plants. The annual costs of the program are difficult to estimate until actual standards are published, but current EPA estimates center at about $2 billion per year.

Designation of Kenneth M. Carr as Chairman of the Nuclear Regulatory Commission

June 12, 1989

The President has designated Kenneth M. Carr as Chairman of the Nuclear Regulatory Commission, effective July 1, 1989. He would succeed Lando W. Zech, Jr.

Since 1986 Commissioner Carr has served as a member of the Nuclear Regulatory Commission. Prior to this, he served in the U.S. Navy as Deputy and Chief of Staff to the Commander in Chief, Atlantic Command, and the Commander in Chief of the U.S. Atlantic Fleet, retiring as a vice admiral in 1985. From 1977 to 1980, he commanded the submarine force of the Atlantic Fleet and served as Vice Director of Strategic Target Planning at Offutt Air Force Base, NE. In 1972 he was assigned as chief of staff to the commander of the submarine force of the Atlantic Fleet, and in 1973, assumed duties of Military Assistant to the Deputy Secretary of Defense. Commissioner Carr enlisted in the Navy in 1943.

Commissioner Carr graduated from the U.S. Naval Academy in 1949. He has received the Distinguished Service Medal, the Legion of Merit, the Presidential Unit Commendation, and the Defense Distinguished Service and Meritorious Service Medals. He was born March 17, 1925, in Mayfield, KY. He is married to Molly Pace of Burkesville, KY.

Remarks to Students at the Teton Science School in Grand Teton National Park, Wyoming

June 13, 1989

Sorry, Manuel mentioned my birthday—it's so nice to be in Wyoming. Nobody, not one person—your Governor, the Senators, our new Congressman—no one has said,

And now you can ride the subway in Jackson Hole for half-fare. [*Laughter*] I'm delighted, and thank you for your tolerance. But, Manuel, thank you for that warm introduction. Secretary Lujan and I served in Congress. And I liked very much what Lorraine said about him, and I know he'll do a first-rate job with all the responsibilities that the Secretary of the Interior has. I want to thank all of you for one of the best birthday presents a person could possibly have, and that was going fishing yesterday on Lake Jackson with my grandson. The score: caught six, ate two—not bad for 45 minutes worth of work out there.

And I am really thrilled to be here. I'm just sorry that the Silver Fox is not here. That's my wife, Barbara. But some have inquired about her health, and she's doing very well, thank you. And she's off doing the good works for literacy in New York City, I think it is, this evening. I wish she were here. She was with me last time, and she'll never forget your hospitality, either.

I want to thank Governor Sullivan, who showed us the extraordinary courtesy of coming over across the line into Montana to greet us yesterday and—[*laughter*]—was with us here and then had his beautiful daughter come out—and we could see a little more of that wonderful Sullivan family. I'm glad that Senator Malcolm Wallop, a friend of longstanding, is with us. Our new Congressman who's going to do a great job for this State, Craig Thomas, is here. And then I had to put up with [Senator] Al Simpson. [*Laughter*] You see, every January or so, he and I go fishing, but not in Wyoming. And we have to listen for two straight nights to him lying about Wyoming fishing to those of us fishing in Florida. [*Laughter*] But nevertheless, I'm glad he's here. And I also want to just single out another friend, a friend of my dad's, a friend of mine, who I'm told is here. And I didn't actually see, but Al tells me that Cliff Hansen is here. He and Martha—one of the great Wyoming Senators—Governor, everything else. There he is—right over there—looking younger than a spring colt.

Yesterday I announced our proposals for the Clean Air Act—how to improve it, but protecting the environment requires good people as well as good laws. And I'm especially pleased today to announce that my nominee for the Director of the U.S. Fish and Wildlife Service is one of Wyoming's own. His Triangle X Ranch I passed just a minute ago up the road. He's president of the State senate. He's here with us today, your own, my friend, Senator John Turner, who's going to take on this very important responsibility. And, Jack, I want to thank you and Lorraine and all the other troopers out there and the Park Service people, who do such a superb job for the entire country.

I want to just visit with you today on some concepts of the environment. It's well-known that Wyoming's first tourist was a trapper named John Colter, a veteran of the Lewis and Clark expedition. In 1808 Colter was captured by the locals, stripped naked, and hotly pursued—given a chance to run for his life. Seven days later he arrived at a Spanish fort, sore feet and a sunburned back. And today George P. and I, my grandson and I, are awful glad that Wyoming's attitude towards visitors—[*laughter*]—is, what's the phrase?—kinder and gentler. [*Laughter*]

We meet in the heart of an environmental success story, part of a tradition that began when Abraham Lincoln granted Yosemite Valley to California, set aside as a preserve, and continued through Teddy Roosevelt and others who found inspiration in these majestic American peaks. And creating national parks was an American idea, an idea imitated all around the world. And it was one of our very best ideas. Five generations of Americans have since enjoyed Yellowstone and the Tetons, the largest intact natural area in the temperate zones of the Earth. And yesterday afternoon I toured the fire areas north of here, saw how Yellowstone is coming back, and marveled at nature's regenerative power.

But whether restoring a forest or the air that flows above it, nature needs our help. And yesterday I stood in the majestic East Room at the White House to announce the proposal designed to ensure that we do our part to improve and preserve our natural heritage, the very air we breathe, from coast to coast and beyond, for another five generations and beyond. And today, with our backs to the Pacific and the jewels of the American Rockies, I look east across this fertile and productive land and call on the American people and on the Congress to join me in this new initiative for clean air.

I've said it before, when talking about issues like drug abuse, crime, and national security, the most fundamental obligation of the Government is to protect the people—the people's health, the people's safety, and ultimately our values and our traditions. And nowhere are these traditions more real, more alive, than here in the western reaches of Wyoming. It is a land of legend, campfire tales of brave Sioux warriors, of Butch Cassidy and the Union Pacific Railroad, or range wars between cattlemen and the ranchers.

And just over that ridge to the east lies the headwaters of the Wind River, one of the settings—the epic western "Lonesome Dove." And the book, by McMurtry, begins with the famous passage from T.K. Whipple: "All America lies at the end of the wilderness road, and our past is not a dead past, but still lives in us. Our forefathers had civilization inside themselves and the wild outside. We live in the civilization they created, but within us the wilderness still lingers. And what they dreamed, we live, and what they lived, we dream."

Frontier legends have filled America's movie screens and our imagination for most of this century, but the frontier is not the end of the road. It is quite simply our inspiration. The frontiers we face in the final decade leading to the year 2000 are different from those that our forefathers faced in the mountains and meadows of the American Rockies. What we face are the frontiers of the mind—scientific, geographic, cultural—that remain to be crossed. And so, let's cross them.

Last summer I called 1988 the year the Earth spoke back. Time dubbed "Spaceship Earth" the planet of the year. And although, ultimately, medical waste on beaches or that wandering garbage barge may not present as grave a danger as the ozone holes that we cannot see, touch, or smell, they helped provide the jolt that we needed as a nation.

And some say we're running out of time—wrong! The only thing we are running out of is imagination and the will to bring what we can imagine to life. And, yes, there is a new breeze blowing. And borne upon that wind is a new breed of environmentalism. Our mission is not just to defend what's left but to take the offense, to improve our environment across the board.

But it cannot be an American effort alone. As I said in Europe last month, environmental destruction knows no borders. And as the mistrust of the Cold War begins to give way to a new recognition of our common interests, international environmental challenges offer model opportunities for cooperation. I talked about this at the NATO summit to François Mitterrand, to Margaret Thatcher and Helmut Kohl. And it is universal—the concern, international concern—about the environment. Last fall two whales were saved off American shores by a Soviet icebreaker, a Japanese-built tractor, and a group of determined American Eskimos with saws and boathooks. And, yes, there is a new breeze blowing. And as we speak it is carrying a 156-foot schooner from the Statue of Liberty to Leningrad, an East-West voyage for the environment. And a week ago the airwaves rocked with a 5-hour benefit concert—I confess I didn't listen to all of it—broadcast around the world from New York, London, and Brazil—for environmental challenges and our common future.

And many such international events are symbolic, but here at home the substance awaits. It's in my new proposals to Congress, proposals for cleaner air, for an end to acid rain, urban smog, and other toxic emissions. Congress has been deadlocked on clean air for a long time, and when these proposals pass, it will mark the first improvement in the act in 12 years. And other attempts have failed; competing interests have jammed the avenue to action, and there's been a gridlock.

And I understand the traffic jam—before deciding on these proposals, I met with representatives of business and energy, and mining and chemical groups, and Members of Congress. And I met with people like you who share my passion for the great outdoors. And just last Thursday I sat down with the leaders of every major environmental group in the United States. And I've listened to these competing voices—sometimes strident, sometimes thoughtful, always well-intentioned.

And now, no group is going to get everything it wants. Some say we're asking too much, too fast. And others say: Not enough, too slow. But today there's some important common ground, because there is one thing everyone agrees on: We need action, and we need it now. Every American deserves to breathe clean air, and you shouldn't have to drive 2,000 miles to come out here to do it. Environmental gridlock must end!

And now, this isn't the first time Congress has had to struggle with questions about the kind of America we're going to bequeath to our children. And it's not even the first time the debate was carried right into the Tetons. More than 100 years ago, in the summer of 1883, a storm was brewing in Congress over the future of the park. And President Chester Arthur boarded a train headed west. In Chicago, they warned that any reporters who followed would be dropped off the next railroad bridge. Marlin Fitzwater—very interesting. [*Laughter*]

On August 5th that train stopped about 100 miles south of here, at the banks of the Green River. And they embarked by mule wagon for the Wind River Valley, and there the roads ended. And there began a 350-mile odyssey by horseback, as the President traversed the Tetons and Yellowstone. And winding through Jackson Hole, he was followed by nearly 200 pack animals and 75 cavalry troops. So, I hope you'll excuse me—a little parade that came in here—we were very considerate. [*Laughter*] President Arthur emerged from the Tetons and returned to Washington with a new vision of the West, and unlike me, 105 pounds of trout. And you know how the story ended. You're looking at it: a scene so unspoiled that it is little different from the view that John Colter first saw in 1808.

And yet today even the Tetons cannot escape the threat of pollution. It comes not from steam engines and logging saws but from the very west wind that shaped those peaks, bearing the often invisible poisons that gust in from the Sun-baked smog of our cities. And it's ironic that, as I've visited with people in these mountains, again and again people say how nice it is to get away from urban air pollution. Well, the bad news is, it can follow you here. But the good news is, we are not going to put up with it any longer—not here, not at home where you summer visitors live most of your lives. We are not. And the clean air initiatives that we launched yesterday at the White House mark a new chapter in the tradition of protecting our people and our parks. And our aim is to reduce the "big three" in air pollution: acid rain, urban smog, toxic emissions.

And to stop acid rain, we will cut sulfur dioxide emissions nearly in half—10 million tons—and cut nitrogen oxide by 2 million tons before the century is out. And to reduce the emissions that cause smog, we've set an ambitious reduction goal. Our plan will cut emissions from cars and factories. It will promote alternative fuels. And it will launch us towards the goal of clean air in every American city—and that goal will be reached. And on toxics, our plan is designed to cut all categories of airborne toxic chemicals by as much as the best technology we know of will allow, which should be over three-fourths—again, before the century is out. Wherever the next generation may find your children, our goal is nothing less than an America where all air breathes as clean as morning in the Rockies.

June marks the beginning of summer, a family time, a time of remembrance and tradition. An estimated 290 million visitors will come to America's national parks this year. And, yes, I know it sometimes seems like most of them are camped out at your campsite. [*Laughter*] And with each new day, American families clamor across the craggy trails above us, around Jenny Lake, Paintbrush Canyon, and the aptly named Rock of Ages. And people return from these spaces rejuvenated, confident, somehow younger.

America's national parks are also living laboratories, where our boundless curiosity is challenged by nature's unbridled forces. Robin Winks, a professor at one of those eastern Ivy League schools with which I am familiar, Yale University, has said: "Our parks are universities." They are a whole world of wonder, where family and friends can watch nature at work. And yesterday, as we stopped on the helicopters, as we landed at one of the burned-out areas between here and West Yellowstone, leaned down to look at that charred soil, and you could see—coming out of that black, charred soil little tiny green shoots—nature at work, the power of nature.

Our stewardship of the Earth is brief. We owe it to those who follow to keep that in perspective, to be responsible passengers along the way. They have a saying in the Himalayas: "To a flea, alive for 80 days, a man is immortal. And to a man, alive for 80 years, a mountain is immortal. Both are wrong."

And we stand in the shadow of the Tetons, still an unspoiled frontier thanks to the vision of leaders no longer alive. But it's not the last frontier. After the Sun went down last night, we got a glimpse of the frontier beyond. It was up there beyond the peaks, past the clear mountain air that we want to preserve for all Americans, up there in the stars. And as we closed our eyes to rest, we saw the frontier beyond the stars, the frontier within ourselves. In the frontiers ahead, there are no boundaries. We must pioneer new technology, find new solutions, dream new dreams. So, look upon these American peaks and at the American people around you and remember: We've hardly scratched the surface of what God put on Earth and what God put in man.

Thank you all for what you do every single day to preserve the environment for all mankind. Thank you, and God bless you. Thank you very much.

Note: The President spoke at 9:10 a.m. outside of the school. In his remarks, he referred to Lorraine Mintzmeyer, Director of the Rocky Mountain Region of the National Park Service; Prime Minister Margaret Thatcher of the United Kingdom; President François Mitterrand of France; and Chancellor Helmut Kohl of West Germany. Following his remarks, the President traveled to Lincoln, NE.

Nomination of John F. Turner To Be Director of the United States Fish and Wildlife Service

June 13, 1989

The President today announced his intention to nominate John F. Turner to be Director of the United States Fish and Wildlife Service, Department of the Interior. He would succeed Frank H. Dunkle.

Mr. Turner is currently a partner with Triangle X Ranch, a third-generation family business in Jackson Hole, WY. He has served in various advisory capacities, including as a member of the National Wetlands Policy Forum, 1987–1988, and as a member, then vice chairman of the board for the National Wetlands System Advisory Board, 1983–1987. He has also served in the Wyoming State Senate as president, 1987–1989; senate majority floor leader, 1985–1987; and vice president, 1983–1985. He was assistant director for the University of Notre Dame foreign studies program in Innsbruck, Austria, 1964–1965.

Mr. Turner graduated from the University of Notre Dame (B.S., 1964) and the University of Michigan at Ann Arbor (M.S., 1970). He was born March 3, 1942. Mr. Turner is married, has three children, and resides in Moose, WY.

Nomination of Stella Garcia Guerra To Be an Assistant Secretary of the Interior
June 13, 1989

The President today announced his intention to nominate Stella Garcia Guerra to be an Assistant Secretary of the Interior (Territorial and International Affairs). She would succeed Janet J. McCoy.

Since 1985 Ms. Guerra has served as a member of the board of directors of the Mexican-American Cultural Center. In addition, Ms. Guerra has served as a member of the advisory board for Friends of the Philippine General Hospitals, 1986 to present; member of the Presidential Task Force for Women for the Minorities and the Disabled in Science and Technology, 1987 to present; and member of Federally Employed Women, 1983 to present. She also serves as a member of the National Association of Elected and Appointed Officials, 1982 to present, and as a member of the National Federation of Republican Women, 1982 to present.

Ms. Guerra graduated from Del Mar College (A.A., 1965), the University of Texas A&I (B.S., 1967), Our Lady of the Lake (M.A., 1973), and the Federal Executive Institute, 1984. She was born January 31, 1945, and resides in Texas.

Remarks at the University of Nebraska in Lincoln
June 13, 1989

Thank all of you—Governor Orr, distinguished leader of this State, for those kind words, that warm introduction. My thanks also to Dr. Roskens, Chancellor Massengale, Chairperson Hoke, and all the other officials at this wonderful institution. And I also want to thank Dr. Peter Jenkins, my tour guide, who runs the Center for Engine Technology here at the University of Nebraska. And also my special thanks to three members of my Cabinet—Secretary Watkins, Secretary Lujan, and Secretary Clayton Yeutter—for joining me here today.

I hope that this symbolizes to all of you the importance that we place not just on the research that's going on here at the university, at this wonderful university, but the importance of agriculture and Nebraska—the two go together. And we're here to salute you. And Secretary Yeutter, as we've heard, is a graduate of this fine school, and let me put it this way: I'm delighted to have a Cornhusker in my Cabinet. And we have several Members of Congress traveling with me today. Your own Doug Bereuter is here, Congressman from Nebraska—someplace over here—and then three Wyoming officials, Senator Wallop, Senator Alan Simpson, and Congressman Craig Thomas over here—maybe they'd stand up. And lastly, I'd like to thank the Air Force Band from Offutt—first-class music. Anybody who can keep you all awake for 2 hours must have something going for them. So, thank you, sir, thank you very much. Thank you so much for being with us.

I would have made it here a few minutes earlier, but we've been driving around looking for a parking place. [*Laughter*] Actually, I've come from Dr. Jenkins' lab, where I got a short seminar on engine testing and alternative fuels—fascinating, trailblazing work. You can't help but see it to realize that we have a window to the future. And I'm a believer in alternative fuels and conservation. This winter I'm putting windmills in Washington. [*Laughter*] Henceforth, hot air is going to heat the entire city.

Let me tell you a bit about the pathbreaking work that I've just seen in this engine lab. They've got two cars hooked up to emissions monitors, one running on gasoline, the other on new ethanol blend that they're working on; and the results are impressive. The proof is right there before you in the readout: the car runs cleaner on the ethanol mix. And they're confident down there. I asked about performance, and they told me to take a car out on a test drive. I don't do a lot of driving these days, so I'm not sure that I'm the best judge, but I enjoyed the ride. And it had a lot of pickup—certainly got more pickup than the 14,000-pound limousine sitting outside this place. [*Laughter*]

Many of you know that yesterday I announced some sweeping changes to the Clean Air Act—the first amendments to that landmark legislation in more than a decade. And whether you live in the city or in the country or on a farm or near a factory, the changes that we're calling for are going to improve the quality of the air we breathe and, therefore, the quality of life for all Americans.

This is a nation rich in the majesty of nature. In the past 24 hours, I've seen some of the magnificent sights that this great land has to offer: nature renewing itself in Yellowstone after those devastating fires; the Tetons rising up, postcard-perfect, from the Wyoming plateau. Sights like those make me all the more determined that this nation dedicate itself to the restoration and renewal of our natural heritage.

My approach is driven by a new kind of environmentalism, built on five principles: harnessing the power of technology and the marketplace, promoting State and local environmental initiatives, encouraging a common international effort, concentrating on pollution prevention, and strict enforcement of environmental standards. Today I want to focus on the first of these five, on ways that we can harness the power of technology in service to our environment.

The work you're doing here puts Lincoln on the leading edge of that effort. Alternative fuel is going to help us reconcile the automobile to our environment. And right now, 81 American cities exceed Federal clean air standards. Expanded use of alternative fuels is a key element in my plan to guarantee that 20 years from now every American, in every city across this country, will breathe clean air. Alternative fuels are going to help us get there. In the nine urban areas with the worst ozone pollution, we're requiring a million clean-fuel vehicles on the street by the year 1997—a million a year by the year 1997. Our clean air plan also calls for cities with the worst carbon monoxide problems to use oxygenated fuels to cut emissions during peak winter months.

And our plan preserves flexibility. The urban areas targeted for cleanup can opt out of requirements, provided they find other ways to make equivalent cuts in pollution levels. And although we're proposing some tough pollution control measures, we're going to develop ways to allow automobile manufacturers and fuel companies to trade emissions reductions credits among themselves, so long as the overall emissions standard is met. And our goal—clean air. And we're going to achieve it in the most efficient way possible, but make no mistake about it: we are going to achieve our goal.

I came out to the University of Nebraska to get a firsthand look at one of the clean air technologies of tomorrow: an alternative fuel called ETBE, made from ethanol and Nebraska corn. I thought I left all those acronyms behind me in Washington. Incidentally, ETBE is short for ethyl tertiary-butyl ether—maybe the acronym isn't so bad after all. [*Laughter*] But ETBE isn't quite a household word, but it may just become one, based on what I've seen today. Right now, ethanol-blend fuels account for only a fraction of America's overall gasoline consumption—about 8 percent. And that's going to change in the years ahead. Gasohol, ETBE, natural gas-based fuels like methanol, CNG, and MTBE—all are going to play a role in a transition to cleaner, more efficient engines.

Cutting auto exhaust is an effective avenue to cleaner air. Motor vehicles produce about two-thirds of all the carbon monoxide emissions and about 40 percent of all ozone pollution—chemical threats to our environment that we have all had to live with. And we're learning every day that pollution respects no borders. There's no safe haven from the damaging long-term effect of chronic environmental abuse. Exhaust pollution isn't just a big-city problem anymore. We know it's time to cut exhausts, and the question then is: How?

In this great country of ours, we shouldn't have to choose between clean air and continued progress, between sound ecology and sustained economic growth. The answer isn't to shut off our engines and throw away our keys. That's a horse-and-buggy solution to a 21st-century problem, and we can do better than that. We've got to follow your lead, push forward technologies that promise cleaner fuels for the future. And there is more the automobile industry can, and will, do; but it's time now to produce cleaner fuels our cars will burn in the future.

Let me tell you just a little of what I learned in your lab. Results so far show that gas blended with ETBE additive lowers environmentally harmful emissions and increases engine performance. That's a promising combination. Think about what that means: ETBE and other alternative fuels can help us meet more stringent air quality standards and strengthen our domestic energy industry at the same time.

And America must work towards energy independence. You know, last year 37 percent of the oil that America consumed was imported, and so far this year, that figure's up to almost 40 percent. And that trend means trouble. We worked hard to cut our consumption of foreign oil, and I will not stand by and watch our country slip back into a dangerous state of dependency, wide open to the next oil shock from some country halfway around the world. We're not going to do that in this country. We've got to plan for the future now. We need secure, reliable sources of energy right here at home. Alternative fuels are an American answer.

And take a look at ETBE. It's made from ethanol, which I've long supported. And ethanol's made from corn and other grains we grow in abundance. And that's good for American farmers, and it's good for all American taxpayers who are now paying more than $5 billion a year in corn price supports. Ethanol is a homegrown energy alternative. And that's good for national security, and that's good for our trade deficit. And ethanol produces a fuel that burns cleaner. And that's good for our environment—just plain and simple, good for our environment. A source of energy that's clean, abundant, and made right here in the United States—three good reasons why ethanol and ETBE are fuels of the future.

I've got great faith in farm country. Some folks might be surprised to see the kind of work going on here, to see Nebraska leading the way on alternative fuels; but we all know the heartland's been high tech for a long time. The American farmer has long been the most productive and efficient in the world. You've put food on America's table, and now you're going to help America fill up its tank. The modern farmer is as comfortable talking about gene splicing and biotechnology as he is taking the wheel off a tractor—you've been pioneering in agriculture for years. And I'm not surprised to see you moving from agriculture to energy—and a car that runs on corn.

And Nebraska's going to make it work. These alternative fuels are going to take the market by storm—kind of like the Big Red [University of Nebraska football team] rolling into Norman, Oklahoma. You know, what you're doing here will mean cleaner air in Los Angeles and New York and dozens of cities in between now plagued by smog and air pollution. And that's the kind of environmental impact that can improve the quality of life across America and around the world.

And we won't stop with alternative fuels. In the future, we're going to be using other technological alternatives, like biodegradables in the battle against litter and waste disposal, to ease the threats to our environment. Out here there's always been a strong environmental ethic. In this part of the country, taking care of the land is a way of life—it's natural. And that's why I know when I call on all Americans to make renewal and restoration our new environmental watchwords, I can count on you.

So, let me say to all of you here today in this magnificent auditorium, stadium, area of combat—[*laughter*]—all Nebraskans should be proud of the pioneer work being done here at this great university. It's been a privilege for me as President of the United States to visit this great State, to listen, to learn, to catch a glimpse of progress in the making.

And for those of you in the overflow

room and those along the streets from the airport into the city, let me thank you for that warm Nebraska welcome—I'll never forget it. God bless you, and God bless the United States of America. Thank you very much.

Note: The President spoke at 3:25 p.m. in the Bob Devaney Sports Center on the campus of the university. In his opening remarks, he referred to Ron Roskens, Martin Massengale, and Nancy Hoke, president, chancellor, and chairperson of the board of regents of the university, respectively; Secretary of Energy James D. Watkins; Secretary of the Interior Manuel Lujan, Jr.; and Secretary of Agriculture Clayton Yeutter. Prior to his remarks, the President toured university facilities. Following his remarks, he returned to Washington, DC.

Message to the House of Representatives Returning Without Approval the Fair Labor Standards Amendments of 1989
June 13, 1989

To the House of Representatives:

I am returning herewith without my approval H.R. 2, the "Fair Labor Standards Amendments of 1989."

This bill would increase the minimum wage by an excessive amount and thus stifle the creation of new job opportunities. It would damage the employment prospects of our young people and least advantaged citizens. It would accelerate inflation. It would not help those in poverty. And thus it would fail to properly reflect the thought behind this measure: to help our lowest paid workers.

H.R. 2 would increase the minimum wage to $4.55 an hour and would provide a training wage only for 60 days and only for a temporary period. Economists universally agree that such an increase in the minimum wage will result in the loss of job opportunities. This is because, as the minimum wage rises, employers in today's highly competitive marketplace must respond. Some close their doors. Some automate. Others reduce their work force or cut the services they provide to their customers.

That is why I made it clear that I could accept an increase only if it were a modest one, and only if it were accompanied by a meaningful training wage for new employees of a firm, to help offset the job loss. As I have said many times, I could sign into law an increase in the hourly minimum wage to $4.25, phased in over 3 years, which preserves job opportunities through a 6-month training wage for all new hires. The bill the Congress has sent to me fails to meet these standards.

The increase in the minimum wage I said I could accept amounts to 27 percent—totalling 90 cents an hour in three equal annual increments of 30 cents. The increase in H.R. 2 exceeds that amount by a full one-third. In the interest of preserving job opportunity, I cannot approve this legislation.

I wish to be clear about this. My difference with the Congress is not just about 30 cents an hour. It is about hundreds of thousands of jobs that would be preserved by my Administration's approach, as opposed to those that would be sacrificed under the excessive increase included in this legislation.

The "training wage" included in H.R. 2 is ineffective. Its 60-day limitation is too short and unrealistically restrictive. The principal justification for a training wage is preservation of opportunity—for jobs and for training. This can be accomplished only through a permanent trainee differential. H.R. 2 provides only temporary training wage authority that would expire in 3 years. This means that within 4 years the minimum wage for trainees would rise to the regular minimum wage. That defeats the job-saving purpose of the training wage. This provision of H.R. 2 would do little to save jobs. I cannot support it.

Minimum wage jobs are for the most part entry-level jobs—those jobs that give our workers the valuable work experience and basic training they will need for advancement to future opportunities. When those jobs are lost, the losers are the young and disadvantaged, grasping for the first rung on the ladder of economic opportunity.

I am also deeply concerned that an excessive increase in the minimum wage will increase inflation, which has rightly been called the cruelest tax. Inflation is hardest on those living on fixed incomes, many of whom are poor and elderly. As the minimum wage increases, employers' costs rise, and they must charge the consumer more for goods and services just to break even.

The Federal budget deficit also would increase. The jobs lost due to a large minimum wage increase would have generated tax revenues for the Federal Government. Certain Government programs are tied directly to the minimum wage; other Government expenditures are indexed to inflation. As the minimum wage and inflation increase, those expenditures will increase, and so will the budget deficit.

H.R. 2 provides for a Minimum Wage Review Board, which threatens to compound the bill's inflationary effect. The Board would be permanent; it would be required to make annual recommendations to the Congress for increasing the minimum wage in light of increases in wages and prices since any previous minimum wage adjustment. This has been termed, accurately, a "back-door" indexing provision. It is unacceptable.

Contrary to what proponents of H.R. 2 have been saying, increasing the minimum wage is not an effective way to help the poor. The poverty population and the minimum wage earners are, by and large, different people. Most minimum wage earners are young, they are single, they live in households with other workers, and most importantly, they are not poor.

We must never forget that a healthy and growing private economy is essential to remedying poverty. We are now in the 78th month of an unprecedented economic expansion. Over the last few months, the unemployment rate has been lower than at any time since 1974. Since the beginning of this economic expansion at the end of 1982, our economy has created nearly 20 million new jobs. Since 1981 the number of workers earning no more than the Federal minimum wage has been cut in half—from 7.8 million to 3.9 million last year. Now is not the time to turn back or halt the progress we have made.

In the contemporary American market, wages rise—not because of mandated increases, but because of market forces and the changing nature of America's workplace, which demand higher skills and offer better pay to the workers who possess them. An excessive increase in the minimum wage would reduce any chance for hundreds of thousands of less skilled workers to get entry-level employment and experience the on-the-job training and advancement opportunities that go with it.

Most, though not all, of those denied the opportunity would be young people. I remain, as I have said before, haunted by the fact that by the thousands, young Americans in inner cities believe they have no stake in our system, no future, no hope. Believing they have nothing to lose, they act as if they have nothing to gain. We cannot let this continue. Work can give them something to gain—and we cannot sit by, destroying opportunity with well-intentioned but misguided policies—jinxing another generation—and live easily with ourselves.

It is regrettable that this debate must end with a veto; once the majority in the Congress determined to reject my offer of compromise on minimum wage legislation, however, it also became inevitable.

In the discussions of this issue, my objectives have been and remain twofold: first, to preserve job opportunities for entry-level workers seeking to get their feet on the ladder of economic opportunity; and second, to increase the take-home pay of the heads of low-income households. My proposal was designed to accomplish those twin objectives.

If the Congress remains unwilling to support this job-saving approach, I am prepared to examine with the Congress, within the confines of our fiscal limitations, changes in the Earned Income Tax Credit, which could better help the heads of low-income households.

I renew my invitation to the Congress to work with the Administration, in a cooperative and bipartisan way, on what I believe is the compelling work force challenge. We need to improve American education so Americans of all ages can prepare for the more demanding jobs that this economy is creating. Growth offers opportunity for those prepared to seize it. For those not now prepared and lacking the basic skills of language and literacy, computation skills, and the like, we need to provide or refine our training programs.

I have proposed a package of educational reforms to enhance our Federal approach to elementary and secondary education. We can offer a better quality of education to our children than we do and a wider degree of educational choice to them and their parents.

My Administration has also proposed a package of reforms in vocational education that can improve this system, so vital to training and retraining our Nation's work force. We should move quickly to improve the quality of vocational education, to simplify it, to expand choice, to make the system more accountable, and, importantly, to integrate it better with other job training efforts.

We will be proposing significant improvements in the Job Training Partnership Act. These will include a package of youth initiatives to increase the targeting of critical training resources on those in need of help. These initiatives will also offer improvements in the quality of training made available to "at-risk" youth and incorporate higher standards for achievement and competency after training.

We continue to believe that proposals such as these and our child tax credit are preferable and more effective measures for assisting low-income working families. Unlike a minimum wage increase, they can be much more precisely targeted to help only those who need the help, with none of the job-loss or inflationary effects of raising the minimum wage.

The Congress this year has the opportunity to move these legislative proposals in a concerted way. We need to refine our basic skills training, literacy, and remedial education, not just job training, to prepare youth for a *lifetime* of productive work, not just a job. Let us approach these separate statutes and programs not separately, but as parts of a whole, as components of an integrated Federal policy on real workplace needs.

As I said in my Inaugural Address, I wish to proceed together with both parties in both Houses of Congress. For those of us whose legislative priorities include the real needs of America's work force, there can be no more important items on that agenda than education and skills preparation.

During this year, and this Congress, even with limited budget resources—we can make a difference. Let us get started.

GEORGE BUSH

The White House,
June 13, 1989.

White House Statement on the President's Meeting With Foreign Minister Sa'ud al-Faysal Al Sa'ud of Saudi Arabia

June 14, 1989

The President met today with Prince Sa'ud al-Faysal, Foreign Minister of Saudi Arabia, to discuss the efforts of the Arab League to resolve the Lebanon crisis. The President welcomed the collective efforts of Saudi Arabia, Morocco, and Algeria and expressed U.S. support for their mandate to pursue urgently a political process in Lebanon leading to elections, reforms, and a new national consensus. The President pledged the commitment of the United States to do all it can to promote a political solution that would bring Lebanon's turmoil to an end.

The United States encourages the Arab League's efforts to foster a political dialog among the Lebanese. Such a dialog, in the context of a cease-fire, is the necessary first step toward a solution of Lebanon's suffering, which has gone on too long. The President reaffirmed the commitment of the United States to Lebanon's unity, sovereignty, and territorial integrity, with the withdrawal of all foreign forces and the disbandment of the militias.

The President said that the United States believes that all parties to the conflict in Lebanon must show restraint and flexibility at this crucial point. All concerned must do their part to promote a genuine political process, devoid of threats and coercion. Outside interests must not add to Lebanon's misery.

Message to the Congress Transmitting the Denmark-United States Fishing Agreement
June 14, 1989

To the Congress of the United States:

In accordance with the Magnuson Fishery Conservation and Management Act of 1976 (Public Law 94–265; 16 U.S.C. 1801 *et seq.*), I transmit herewith an agreement effected by exchange of notes at Washington on March 28, 1989, extending for the period of 2 years from July 1, 1989, until July 1, 1991, and amending to conform with current U.S. law, the Governing International Fishery Agreement between the Government of the United States of America of the one part and the Home Government of the Faroe Islands and the Government of Denmark of the other part Concerning Faroese Fishing in Fisheries off the Coasts of the United States, signed at Washington on June 11, 1984. The exchange of notes, together with the present agreement, constitute a governing international fishery agreement within the meaning of section 201(c) of the act.

U.S. fishing industry interests have urged prompt consideration of this agreement and, similarly, I request the Congress give favorable consideration to this agreement at an early date to avoid disruption of cooperative ventures.

Since 60 calendar days of continuous session, as required by the legislation, will not be available before the current agreement is scheduled to expire, I recommend the Congress consider passage of a joint resolution.

GEORGE BUSH

The White House,
June 14, 1989.

Continuation of Richard Schifter as an Assistant Secretary of State
June 14, 1989

The President today announced that Richard Schifter will continue to serve as Assistant Secretary of State for Human Rights and Humanitarian Affairs.

Since 1985 Mr. Schifter has been the Assistant Secretary of State for Human Rights and Humanitarian Affairs. He is a member of the board of directors of the U.S. Institute of Peace and serves as the Department of State representative on the Commission for Security and Cooperation in Europe. He also served as Deputy United States Representative in the Security Council of the United Nations, with the rank of Ambassador, 1984–1985, and as the U.S. member of the United Nations Human Rights Commission, 1983–1986. Prior to this Mr. Schifter was a practicing attorney in Washington, DC.

Mr. Schifter graduated from the College of the City of New York in 1943 and received his LL.B. from Yale Law School in 1951. He served in the U.S. Army, 1943–1946. He was born in Vienna, Austria, in 1923. He is married and has five children and eight grandchildren.

Exchange With Reporters Following Discussions With Foreign Minister Sa'ud al-Faysal Al Sa'ud of Saudi Arabia

June 14, 1989

Q. When is the initiative, Mr. President?

Q. ——prospect for Lebanon, sir?

The President. ——with the Foreign Minister of Saudi Arabia on that. But they are engaged in a mission that comes with the greatest of intentions and met with the strong enthusiastic support of the United States, as they try to be helpful in bringing peace to Lebanon, and that's something we're all very much concerned about.

Note: The President spoke at 10:09 a.m. in the Oval Office at the White House. He referred to the Arab League's efforts to bring peace to Lebanon. A tape was not available for verification of the content of the exchange.

Statement by Press Secretary Fitzwater on President Bush's Meeting With President Jacques Delors of the Commission of the European Communities

June 14, 1989

The President held a working lunch today with Jacques Delors, President of the Commission of the European Communities (EC). President Bush had invited President Delors for the luncheon when they met in Brussels on May 30. The two, who were accompanied by senior advisers, discussed ongoing cooperation between the United States and the EC Commission on issues of mutual interest, including the implications of the EC's 1992 integration program; international trade and the Uruguay round; the efforts toward political and economic reform in Eastern Europe and the Soviet Union; and transnational problems, such as the urgent need to protect the environment.

The President reiterated his support for European integration and the EC's single-market program. He reaffirmed that a stronger Europe means a stronger America. He also noted that there will be new challenges as the EC carries out its single-market program. He stressed the importance of open markets in a more closely integrated Europe and said that the United States would work with the EC Commission and the member states to ensure that U.S. interests are taken fully into account in the 1992 process. The President underlined the need for both the United States and the EC to continue to combat protectionism and to conclude the current round of trade negotiations successfully by the end of 1990.

The President reiterated a key point in his Boston University speech—that the United States and the European Community must strengthen their dialog and cooperation. He stressed the importance of the annual U.S.-EC Ministerial meeting in December as an opportunity for a high-level review of all aspects of the relationship. He also said that other channels, such as the sub-Cabinet consultations held in November

1988, can help to broaden U.S.-EC understanding.

The President said that he looked forward to seeing President Delors again next month at the Paris economic summit.

Remarks Prior to a Meeting With the Congressional Leadership on Savings and Loan Crisis Legislation

June 14, 1989

The President. What I want to do was to first welcome two new members of the congressional leadership team, Dick Gephardt and Bill Gray. And just let me say, I look forward to working with you, arguing with you, working with you—and I do mean that. And I congratulate both of you.

The purpose of the meeting today: I wanted to discuss this savings and loan bill that's going to be on the House floor. And I think that every American citizen has every right in the world to be disturbed and shocked by this situation. Tens of billions of dollars are going to have to be spent to clean up this whole matter of savings and loan, and our estimate is that it's costing about $10 million a day for every day that action is not taken. And now some of the smaller—or the weaker S&L's, I would say, are demanding the right to continue to treat goodwill as capital, even though goodwill has no tangible value. And the result could be that—up to $600 billion in loans without one dollar in real capital for decades to come. And in my view, it is time for the American public and our administration to say that enough is enough, and to earnestly ask for the support of the Congress. We've had good support on the Hill, and now it's getting critical. And I would simply like to ask you as leaders, both Republican and Democrat, for your support.

I wanted you to know how strongly I feel about it. I have a certain sense of obligation to the American people to get legislation through that is going to protect the people against the abuses of the past and to fix it, and fix it for once and for all. So, this is what I wanted to do. But, Mr. Speaker, I want to hear from you on this to start with, and then the leader.

Speaker Foley. Mr. President, we certainly share your view that this is critical legislation. The House will take up the rule and proceed with general debate today, and will finish the bill this week. We intend to work as long as it's required tomorrow and on Friday to see to it that the amendments are all considered and voted upon and the final action on the bill is taken before this week ends. And I can give you that assurance.

There are amendments that the House will have to consider—15 of them in number, down from about 107 that were requested. But I'm satisfied, Mr. President, that when the week comes to an end, there will be a strong bill from the House of Representatives and that, together with the Senate, we can send you at an early date legislation that you'll be proud to sign.

The President. Senator Dole, do you want to add anything?

Minority Leader Dole. Well, there are a lot of experts in the room here—men, in this case, who have dealt with it from day one. But it seems to me it's sort of a time bomb that might go off one of these days unless we have a very strong piece of legislation, stripped of all the special interest amendments, and knock out the goodwill wherever you can. There isn't much good will for S&L's, I find, around. [*Laughter*] Most of the people have been taken for a ride long enough.

So, I think I—first, thank the President for again emphasizing the importance of this and the obligation he has to the American people. It doesn't get a lot of attention. It's only a $200 billion or $300 billion problem. But it's heartening to hear Tom Foley indicate the House is going to be tough and give us a strong bill. I know that Senator Garn and Senator Riegle and others on our side will be working toward that end in conference.

The President. It has gone through the Senate. And I would like to take this opportunity to thank Chairman [Senate Banking, Housing, Urban Affairs Committee] Riegle and Jake Garn, the guys who have raised that, and those around the table here and now—Senator Cranston, Senator Simpson—all. But I'm not singling out the House, but that's where the action is today.

And thank you, Mr. Speaker, for your determination to move this thing.

Note: The President spoke at 1:40 p.m. in the Cabinet Room at the White House. In his remarks, he referred to Representatives Richard A. Gephardt of Missouri and William H. Gray III of Pennsylvania, and Senators Donald W. Riegle, Jr., of Michigan and Jake Garn of Utah.

Remarks at the Unveiling Ceremony for the Design of the Korean War Memorial

June 14, 1989

Thank you all. Thank you, General Davis and General Stilwell; General Goodpaster; our Commandant, General Gray; Secretary Lujan; members of the Commission; winners; second place winners; third place winners; fellow veterans; distinguished guests; leaders of the Congress. It is a pleasure to welcome you to the White House, and I want to thank you for the privilege of sharing this occasion.

Woodrow Wilson once said: "A patriotic American is never so proud of his flag as when it comes to mean for others, as to himself, a symbol of liberty." Well, fittingly, we meet here on Flag Day and the day of the U.S. Army's founding, and as patriotic Americans, to publicly unveil the winning design of a symbol of liberty—the Korean War Veterans Memorial.

And there are, of course, many such symbols in this great Capital of ours, memorials which rightly hail veterans from Bunker Hill to Gettysburg to the rice paddies of Vietnam. And they are a part of our history and of our lore, monuments to the dead and the living. But until recently, the Korean war was not formally remembered, nor were the over 5.7 million American servicemen and women who were directly and indirectly involved. And today we say: No more! It's time to remember, for we are here to pay tribute to America's uniformed sons and daughters who served during the Korean conflict and to recall an American victory that remains too little appreciated and too seldom understood.

We recall that when the war began the forces of totalitarianism seemed ready to overrun all of Asia; but it never happened. For Korea was the first allied effort in history to contain communism by combining strength. Fighting side by side under the flag of the United Nations, the freedom-loving countries of the United States and the Republic of Korea and other allies strove to halt aggression. And we succeeded and built a stable peace that has lasted for more than 35 years. And together, we held the line.

And today we are still holding it—and let me salute those American troops who guard the 38th parallel. And I want to salute our allies, for they, too, have sacrificed on freedom's behalf. And what will happen in much of Asia, we can't be sure; but of this we are certain: In retrospect, the policy of containment so exemplified by the Korean conflict created the conditions for the tide toward democracy now changing and uplifting our globe.

The design we unveil today honors that democracy and the American men and women who took up arms and bore our burden so that freedom could survive. And our nearly 5 million Korean war veterans alive today—we honor them. Our 103,000 wounded in the conflict—we honor them; our more than 8,000 missing or unaccounted for; the 54,246 Americans who gave their lives, who gave, as Lincoln said, "the last full measure of devotion."

This day marks another step toward the memorial that Korea's veterans deserve and will have, a process which began when President Reagan signed legislation authorizing the creation of a Korean War Veterans Memorial in the District. And last September a site was approved for the Washington Mall. The memorial will be built in Ash Woods, a grove of trees near the Lincoln Memorial, across the reflecting pool from the Vietnam Memorial. And its existence will be due to a number of friends. Among them are members of both parties who helped pass this legislation and, of course, the sponsors of this memorial. And in that context, I would like to thank the Battle Monuments Commission—ably chaired by General Goodpaster, who was years ago, right in this building, the Staff Secretary to President Eisenhower—and also the Korean War Veterans Memorial Advisory Board.

And now let me thank the men and women who chose this design. And to Chairman Ray Davis, my special thanks for chairing the committee. I want also to repeat, as General Stilwell has noted, that every dollar of this funding has been privately financed; and to commend, as he did, Max Jamiesson, whose company donated $1 million, and then Abby—"Dear Abby," Abigail Van Buren, whose readers raised, almost unbelievably, $330,000 for the veterans memorial.

General Davis has observed how the design for their—rather, for your memorial was crafted by four professional architects and designers on the faculty of Penn State, the department of agriculture [architecture]. You met them—Dr. Leon, Oberholtzer, and John and Veronica Lucas. And to all of them, my congratulations. Somehow it seems that you might even eclipse Joe Paterno [football coach at the university] and the Nittany Lions as Penn State's most noted team.

But let me add that I look forward to the day when the memorial itself is unveiled, for it will stand as America's lasting tribute to those who fought so valiantly in an unknown land, as liberty's Horatio at the bridge. And as you view it, think of such names as Ridgway and Van Fleet, MacArthur, shell-torn uplands, Pork Chop, Bloody Arrowhead. Remember Panmunjom and, yes, Inchon and the heroism of the soldiers who fought across the rugged, snow-covered hills.

Think of men like James Garner, Neil Armstrong, or the many Members of the United States Congress who served in Korea—Warren Rudman among them, and John Glenn—and John's wingman, Ted Williams—Ballgame Teddy, they called him, greatest hitter who ever lived—or General Al Gray, sitting right here, who volunteered twice to serve on the front line, first as an enlisted marine and later as a commissioned officer, courageously leading an infantry platoon—heroes who showed that ours would not be the land of the free if it were not also the home of the brave.

And, yes, think of them, honor them, remember how they served from Pusan to Pyongyang, heroes like Rosemary McCarthy, a courageous Army nurse; or our good friend—my good friend—Pete McCloskey, who endured superior forces to charge up and take his hill and whose troops so admired him that they named a baseball field in his honor in Korea; or Wally Lukens, who braved enemy fire to replace another platoon leader, then picked up a gravely wounded infantryman and carried him to the rear. His effort to save that life was in vain, but his selfless devotion to his men—his grit and his guts—lives on in the souls of all Americans in uniform today.

To my right sits such an American—stands such an American—he's supposed to be seated—Ray Davis. He was a lieutenant colonel during the war, received the Congressional Medal of Honor. And 37 years ago, in this very place, President Truman, himself a veteran, presented the medal; and then he said, "Colonel, I'd rather have this than be President." Ray Davis won his medal for you and for me and our country, and he's wearing it today.

And it makes us proud, and so will this design of the veterans memorial. It speaks of walking toward freedom and toward home, in the cold that was Korea. Mike McKavitt was a fighter pilot in Korea, and he tells me he couldn't sleep for 3 nights after first seeing this memorial. And now we all are about to see why. So, could we move over and do the honors.

Note: The President spoke at 2:14 p.m. in the Rose Garden at the White House. In his remarks, he referred to Gen. Raymond G. Davis, USMC, Ret.; Gen. Richard G. Stilwell, USA, Ret.; and James D. "Mike" McKavitt, vice chairman, chairman, and member of the Korean War Veterans Memorial Advisory Board, respectively; Gen. Andrew J. Goodpaster, USA, Ret., Chairman of the American Battle Monuments Commission; Gen. A.M. Gray, Jr., Commandant of the Marine Corps; Secretary of the Interior Manuel Lujan, Jr.; Max Jamiesson, executive vice president and chief operating officer of Hyundai Motor America; actor James Garner; astronaut Neil Armstrong; Senators Warren Rudman of New Hampshire and John Glenn of Ohio; Ted Williams, former member of for the Boston Red Sox; and Paul N. "Pete" McCloskey, Jr., former Representative from California.

Nomination of Chas. W. Freeman, Jr., To Be United States Ambassador to Saudi Arabia

June 14, 1989

The President today announced his intention to nominate Chas. W. Freeman, Jr., to be Ambassador Extraordinary and Plenipotentiary of the United States of America to the Kingdom of Saudi Arabia. He would succeed Walter Leon Cutler.

Mr. Freeman joined the Foreign Service of the United States in 1965. After service in Madras, India, and in Taiwan, he was assigned to the mainland China desk at the Department of State. He was the principal American interpreter during President Nixon's visit to the People's Republic of China in February 1972. From 1974 to 1975, he was a visiting fellow at Harvard University's East Asian Legal Research Center. He then served successively as the Department of State's Deputy Director for Republic of China (Taiwan) Affairs, as Director of Public Programs, and as Director of Plans and Management in the Bureau of Public Affairs. In 1978 Mr. Freeman became Director of Program Coordination and Development at the U.S. Information Agency, and in 1979 he was named Deputy U.S. Coordinator for Refugee Affairs. In the summer of 1979, Mr. Freeman became Director for Chinese Affairs. From 1981 to 1986, he was successively deputy chief of the U.S. missions at Beijing, China, and Bangkok, Thailand. In 1986 he was named Principal Deputy Assistant Secretary of State for African Affairs.

Mr. Freeman received a bachelor of arts from Yale University and a juris doctorate from the Harvard Law School. He was born March 2, 1943, in Washington, DC. He is married, has three children, and resides in Washington, DC.

Nomination of Warren A. Lavorel for the Rank of Ambassador While Serving as United States Coordinator for the Multilateral Trade Negotiations

June 14, 1989

The President today announced his intention to nominate Warren A. Lavorel to the rank of Ambassador during his tenure of service as the U.S. Coordinator for Multilateral Trade Negotiations.

Since 1987 Mr. Lavorel has served as the

U.S. Coordinator for Multilateral Trade Negotiations in the Office of the U.S. Trade Representative in Washington, DC. Prior to this, he served as deputy chief of mission in Geneva, Switzerland, for the Office of U.S. Trade Representative, 1981–1987; financial attaché for the U.S. Mission to the European Community, 1980–1981; and U.S. Representative to GATT [General Agreement on Tariffs and Trade] in Geneva, 1978–1980. Mr. Lavorel was a negotiator for the multilateral trade negotiations in Geneva, 1975–1977, and he served as an economic/commercial officer at the U.S. Embassy in Luxembourg, 1973–1975. He served in the Trade Agreements Division at the Department of State, 1970–1973, and as an economic/commercial officer at the U.S. Embassy in Paris, 1967–1969.

Mr. Lavorel graduated from the University of California (B.A., 1961) and Stanford University (M.A., 1970). He was born October 29, 1935, in Oakland, CA. He served in the U.S. Army, 1958–1960. Mr. Lavorel resides in California and has two children.

Nomination of Edward T. Timperlake To Be an Assistant Secretary of Veterans Affairs

June 14, 1989

The President today announced his intention to nominate Edward T. Timperlake to be an Assistant Secretary of Veterans Affairs (Congressional and Public Affairs). This is a new position.

Mr. Timperlake most recently served as director of Veterans for Bush and codirector of the national security task force on the campaign staff of Bush/Quayle '88. Prior to this he was the commanding officer of VMFA 321 from 1985–1987. Mr. Timperlake was the principal director of mobilization, planning, and requirements (SES–2) in the Office of the Secretary of Defense, 1984, and the national director of the Vietnam Veterans Leadership Program, 1981–1983. Mr. Timperlake was also the section manager at the Analytic Sciences Corp., 1978–1981, and a business analyst for Exxon Enterprises, Inc., 1977–1978.

Mr. Timperlake graduated from the U.S. Naval Academy (B.S., 1969), Naval Air Training Command (1971), and Cornell Graduate School of Management (M.B.A., 1977). He was a captain in the U.S. Marine Corps, 1969–1975. Mr. Timperlake was born November 22, 1946, in Perth Amboy, NJ. He is married, has two daughters, and resides in Oakton, VA.

Nomination of Raoul L. Carroll To Be General Counsel of the Department of Veterans Affairs

June 14, 1989

The President today announced his intention to nominate Raoul L. Carroll to be General Counsel of the Department of Veterans Affairs. This is a new position.

Since 1986 Mr. Carroll has been a partner with Bishop, Cook, Purcell and Reynolds in Washington, DC. Prior to this he was a partner with Hart, Carroll and Chavers, 1981–1986. He was an associate member of the U.S. Board of Veterans Appeals, 1980–1981, and an Assistant United States Attorney in the Office of the United States Attorney, 1979–1980. He was an appellate defense attorney for the Defense Appellate Division, U.S. Army Legal Services Agency, 1977–1979.

Mr. Carroll graduated from Morgan State College (B.S., 1972) and St. John's University School of Law (J.D., 1975). He was born March 16, 1950, in Washington, DC. He served in the U.S. Army, 1975–1979. He is married, has two children, and resides in Washington, DC.

Remarks at the Annual Republican Congressional Fundraising Dinner
June 14, 1989

What a spectacular evening. Thank you, Don, and thank all of you. Thank you so very, very much. Barbara and I are delighted to be here. Thank you. Senator Nickles, thank you for that introduction and the great job that you're doing as head of the Senate campaign committee. That is important work, and Don is doing a superb job.

Way down there, Marilyn Quayle—Marilyn, it's a delight to be with you on this evening. And I want to welcome back your husband, Dan, from Central America. And thank you, Mr. Vice President, once again for taking our message of hope and democracy to our important friends and neighbors. Dan Quayle is doing an outstanding job for the United States of America, and I am proud he is at my side in the White House.

And the warrior of all times, David Murdock—thank you for your dedication, not just for this evening, but especially for this evening—making this event possible. What a job you've done—and your cochairmen and their cochairmen—and there's never been a political event like this in the history of the country, and I'm grateful to you from the bottom of my heart. Thank you, sir. And as to our able chairman of the House campaign committee, Guy Vander Jagt, great to see you, and thank you for your work. I want to thank Mary Hart and Willard Scott. Willard, may your future be free of cumulus clouds. [*Laughter*] And may I thank the members of my Cabinet. I am so lucky, as President of this country, to have the support of an outstanding Cabinet—men and women of excellence—total dedication to our country. And believe me, I count my blessings every day for that.

It was at the last President's Dinner that Ronald Reagan, then the 40th President of the United States, stood before us and formally challenged all of us to hold on to the Presidency, no matter how tough the odds. And since then, President Reagan has returned to his beloved California, and you and I have fought shoulder-to-shoulder, battling our way to a 40-State win on election day. And I'm grateful to every one of you for that support.

But none of us here, not one of us, fought the battle we fought—we didn't put ourselves and our families through the turmoil of a campaign simply to win an election. And we fought because we believed in certain ideas and certain ideals. We fought because we believe that together we can build a better America. The American people defined our mission, and in the 5 months since the Inaugural—without fanfare or partisan furor—we have worked together to quietly follow our assigned mission, to achieve what was considered to be outlandishly impossible.

The American people want action on the budget deficit, and we reached an agreement with the Congress to reduce the deficit by a whopping $65 billion. And we aim to achieve this without raising the taxes on the working men and women of this country.

The American people want action on a festering problem—the hemorrhaging of the savings and loan system. And our reform plan will restore stability, eliminate unsafe and extravagant practices, and punish those who abuse the trust of the depositors. The American people will have to pay billions of dollars to clean up this mess. And we must make sure that it never happens again. And the Senate, under the able leadership of Bob Dole and Jake Garn and others, approved our plan 91 to 8. And now I call on the House of Representatives to follow suit.

The American people want action on ethics. And clearly, it is time for an even-handed ethics approach across all branches of government. This is the goal of our ethics proposal that I sent to the Congress in April. We must all—all—be equal before the law.

And as President, I will strive for a constructive working relationship with the new Speaker, Speaker Foley; the leader in the Senate, Senator Mitchell; and the rest of the Democratic leadership. But while we are in competition with each other, we will keep that competition on the issues and fighting for what we believe in. For we Republicans are bound together in a common purpose: to wage a vigorous debate on the important issues that unite us. We are confident that in taking our message of peace and prosperity to the American people in an open, honest, and direct manner we will become the majority party in America.

The American people—Republican, Democrat, young and old—want action on the environment. And yesterday, surrounded by the natural jewels of the Grand Tetons, enjoying that crisp, pristine mountain air, I called on Congress to join me in a quest for cleaner air—an end to acid rain, ozone depletion, and other harmful emissions. You shouldn't have to become a mountain man just to breathe good, clean air.

And, oh, how the American people want action on crime. This administration will not rest until we've lifted the shadow of fear from the homes and the shops and the streets and the neighborhoods of America. And that's why I called last month for tough new laws, more law enforcers and prosecutors to back them up. This administration is going to lead the charge to take back the streets—take them back from the criminals who threaten our neighborhoods and our families—not just in the cities but all across this country. We are going to win the battle against the criminal.

And the American people want action on foreign policy, a sensible, yet bold plan to deal with the changes sweeping through the Communist world. And our bipartisan agreement with Congress on Central America allows the United States to speak with one clear message, one voice. Let freedom ring in Managua. Let freedom ring throughout the Communist world, from Beijing to Budapest to Warsaw. In Brussels, at our historic NATO meeting, I said that we face an historic opportunity to move beyond containment of the Soviet Union. I said that the world has waited long enough, that Europe can be whole and free, that we can move beyond armed camps divided by suspicion and fear. And we asked the Soviets—challenged them—to join us in a peace of trust over a peace of tension. And we offered our vision for a future of peace and freedom, the spirit of Brussels.

But this, the first 5 months of this administration, is just a start. We must work together to protect what is already the longest peacetime expansion in our history, to keep America competitive, at work, on the job. We must fight drug abuse on every front to redeem thousands of children—it's the children that hurt the most—to return promise to their lives.

And we must revitalize our schools so that a solid education is once again the birthright of every American kid. And to make this kind of progress will require more than a government program or another grant initiative. Republicans believe that it will take the active involvement of parents and students and teachers and business and local government and churches, yes, and our schools. And this is what we mean by a Thousand Points of Light. As powerful and resourceful as government is, government alone cannot come close to overcoming these problems.

And next week, I'll announce a major initiative to challenge our young people to serve their communities. From now on, the definition of the good life in America must include service to others. But as you know, achieving our highest goals depends to a large extent—you heard it here tonight—on winning elections in Congress. We must take our case to the American people, precinct by precinct, block by block. And I believe it is no coincidence that our party slipped to minority status in the House as we became a minority in the State legislatures.

Today Democrats now have a redistricting advantage in States that compose about 90 percent of the seats in Congress. And that is why we Republicans must make solid gains at the State level. Critical gubernatorial and legislative races in the eight largest States alone will determine whether Republicans will be treated fairly in the drafting of 209 congressional districts. From Springfield to Sacramento, from Austin to Albany, we must win the fight for fair competition. A majority or even a large minority of Republicans in State legislatures can join with Republican Governors to sustain the veto of outrageous gerrymandering schemes, strengthening our numbers in the U.S. House. Bob Michel, our able leader in the House, is outgunned, outmanned. So, let's help him by picking up more seats in the House of Representatives.

Strong State parties can help us win back the U.S. Senate, one of our most critical goals. And I salute our leader, Bob Dole. What a job he is doing as Republican leader in the Senate, but he needs more troops. He needs some help over there. So, let's win back the Senate. Let us again make it a Republican Senate, and that will be good for the United States of America.

In the next election, we have a good shot at making big gains. And of course, the party that controls the White House is often expected to do poorly in midterm elections, but there are no ironclad rules in politics. After all, if there were, I would never have become the only living member of the Martin Van Buren Society.

With your support and leadership, the leadership of so many great Republicans—I don't want to embarrass him, but in his work tonight and the support he's given me and so many other elected officials in this room, men like Carl Lindner of Ohio, who has done a superb job here—we can again defy the precedents; we can again make history. In order to win, we must work together as a team, not as an association of acronyms—the RNC or the NRCC or the RGA or the NRSC. These are top-notch, well-managed organizations staffed by the best people in politics today, but our Republican Party must be greater than the sum of its parts. We must be inspired by a common purpose. We must bring opportunity to new constituencies and campaign in their neighborhoods, in the inner cities, the barrios once considered to be the exclusive domain of the opposition. And I salute our Secretary of Housing and Urban Development for taking this message right into the inner city—Jack Kemp.

And our party chairman, Lee Atwater, who's doing a great job. And he's been a strong voice and a correct voice, arguing that we Republicans need to reach to minorities and the disadvantaged. And these groups can benefit the most from our philosophy, which simply maximizes opportunity and rewards initiative. And that is a message I believe in, and it's a message that we as a party must be prepared to act upon.

To win, we must also recruit the very best men and women to represent our party as candidates and as officeholders.

And so, these are my strategies for victory, but strategies are useless without a great purpose. And we have such a purpose: to build a better America for today and for the new century ahead. And we've shed a lot of blood, sweat, tears to rebuild the Republican Party since the early seventies. The best way to keep our party growing is to win more elections in 1990, from the courthouse to the statehouse to Capitol Hill. And with your help, let's prove to the Democrats that the successes of the 1980's are not a fluke, that they in fact spell the beginning of the end of Democratic dominance in the United States Congress.

Thank you all, each and every one of you, for your unbelievable contribution to these goals—thank you. Barbara and I send you our best wishes. Good night, and God bless each and every one of you, and God bless the United States of America. Thank you very, very much.

Note: The President spoke at 9:45 p.m. in Hall A at the Washington Convention Center. In his remarks, he referred to weatherman Willard Scott, who led the Pledge of Allegiance, and television host Mary Hart, who sang the national anthem. He also referred to the Republican National Committee (RNC), the National Republican Congressional Caucus (NRCC), the Republican Governors Association (RGA), and the National Republican Senatorial Committee (NRSC).

Letter to the Speaker and the Minority Leader of the House of Representatives on the Financial Institutions Reform, Recovery and Enforcement Act of 1989

June 14, 1989

Dear ________:

Today the House of Representatives begins floor consideration of the Financial Institutions Reform, Recovery and Enforcement Act of 1989 (FIRREA). This legislation will provide vitally needed funds to restructure or close insolvent thrift institutions. The legislation would also overhaul the existing system of thrift regulation. Inadequacies in capital rules, accounting practices and supervisory oversight in the past were fundamental causes of this disaster.

In addition to protecting depositors, passage of this bill will allow us to begin reducing the ongoing losses in the S&L industry. This program will cost the American public tens of billions of dollars to replace deposits of the public lost through speculation, criminality, fraud and irresponsible risk-taking.

I am determined that in the future federally-insured institutions should have to put their own money at risk before that of the insurance fund and the taxpayers. This is an essential element in protecting against any future repetition of this problem.

The capital provisions of the legislation adopted by the Banking Committee recognize the need for a new core capital requirement to protect the public. Thrifts that fail this capital standard would be required to submit a prudent business plan, and they would generally be subjected to closer supervisory oversight and limitations on excessive future growth.

Unfortunately, amendments have been offered that would allow as much as $20 billion of "supervisory goodwill" to be included in the computation of tangible net worth, even though it has no tangible value. Any such amendment could permit a relatively small group of firms to maintain $600 billion in loans without investing one dollar in tangible capital. Under this approach the American public could be required to carry 100% of this risk for decades.

I adamantly oppose each of the proposed amendments that will be debated on the House floor concerning supervisory goodwill. Giving recognition to goodwill as capital or creating procedural changes that could have the same effect is not justifiable. There should be no mistake. This matter goes to the very heart of my determination to clean up the abuses of the past among the savings and loans, about which every voter is entitled to be outraged. Each of the amendments to the tough capital standards proposed by the Banking Committee would render this bill unacceptable to me.

In financing the thrift plan, the Administration's proposal, as adopted by the Senate and the House Banking Committee, preserves the Gramm-Rudman-Hollings (GRH) process. It properly scores on-budget all Treasury payments, while industry contributions to the financing package are kept out of the budget. The alternative proposal by the Ways and Means Committee requires a waiver of $44 billion to GRH, which is our only statutory bulwark for fiscal discipline. Maintaining bipartisan efforts to control our budget process is a critical objective to continuing a positive domestic and international economic climate.

The legislation I submitted also seeks a number of other important provisions to strengthen our supervisory system. These include a substantial increase in civil and criminal penalties for those who have committed wrongdoing in insured institutions. As the legislation moves forward, I ask each Representative to review carefully the specific items outlined in the Administration Statement of Position as well as my letters of May 22 to the House leadership.

As I stated in today's meeting, I am firmly committed to these principles and offer again my support to your efforts to enact responsible legislation. The United States Government must seek to ensure the safety and soundness of the thrift industry once and for all, as well as to protect the trust of insured depositors and the interest of the American public.

Since I sent my proposed legislation to the Congress, more than $1.1 billion in potentially avoidable losses have occurred. The industry had total losses of $3.4 billion in the first quarter alone, on top of more than $13 billion in 1988. This financial hemorrhage continues to mount at a cost of more than $10 million every day. I urge Congress to complete its work and pass an effective and responsible bill that reflects adequately my concerns, and those of the American public.

Sincerely,

GEORGE BUSH

Note: Identical letters were sent to Thomas S. Foley and Robert H. Michel, Speaker and minority leader of the House of Representatives, respectively. The letters were released by the Office of the Press Secretary on June 15.

Message to the Congress Transmitting Proposed Legislation To Combat Violent Crime
June 15, 1989

To the Congress of the United States:

Today I am pleased to transmit proposed legislation entitled the "Comprehensive Violent Crime Control Act of 1989." As the American people are aware, our Nation is experiencing a surge of violent criminal behavior, linked in no small degree to the scourge of illegal drugs currently prevalent in our border areas, our cities, and our neighborhoods.

On May 15, 1989, I outlined a comprehensive program, consisting of both legislative and non-legislative items, to combat violent crime. This program is a logical approach to the violent crime problem that focuses on four major objectives: strengthening current laws; augmenting enforcement; enhancing prosecution; and expanding prison capacity. The seven-title proposal that I am sending you today represents the actions that we believe the Congress should take in each of these areas. Its enactment would help reduce the incidence of violent crime in our society.

Dealing with crime is not a novel problem, nor is it one with which we can ever expect fully to succeed. Nevertheless, assuring the physical safety of our citizens and inhabitants is among the very highest responsibilities of government, and it is a top priority of my Administration.

Traditionally, dealing with violent crime has been, and should properly remain, primarily the function of State and local law enforcement authorities. Yet it is clear that the Federal Government also has an important leadership role to play.

The Federal Government cannot properly discharge its duties in this regard, however, unless the Nation's criminal laws, the essential backbone of the Federal justice system, are modernized and strengthened. A substantial strengthening of our laws would help all elements of the Federal criminal justice system—law enforcement officials, prosecutors, judges, and correctional authorities—to execute their responsibilities with maximum effectiveness.

In recent years, substantial progress has been made toward this goal. Each of the last three Congresses, with the participation of the previous Administration, passed a major bipartisan piece of anti-crime legislation. Together, these enactments have served greatly to assist in the struggle against violent and drug-related crime.

But much remains to be done to create the statutory framework necessary to cope with the still rising incidence of drug-related violent crime. *Now* is the time for this Congress to act—before the end of this year—on the proposed legislation I am transmitting today. Long-range solutions also lie in other directions, such as better education and job opportunities for our citizens. Our immediate task, however, and the one with which the present set of proposals is concerned, is to improve the Federal criminal justice system to render it able to dispense swift, sure, and fair justice. Persons who endanger society through the commission of violent offenses must know that their behavior will not be tolerated.

The present bill would improve the criminal justice system in several important ways.

First, the laws relating to firearms possession and use need to be carefully scrutinized to insure that, while the legitimate rights of firearm owners are protected, illegitimate use and possession of firearms are subject to proper punishment. In this regard, the Congress passed a major firearms statute in 1986, which generally struck a proper balance in this area. But our examination has revealed a number of instances in which the provisions of that law should be strengthened.

For example, I do not think it was the intention of the Congress to permit convicted felons, imprisoned for dangerous crimes, to be able to purchase firearms immediately upon their release from prison, merely because State law generally restores rights of citizenship to persons who have served their sentences. Yet that result may be required under the Federal statute as it is written today. Similarly, persons who use a semiautomatic weapon to commit a violent or drug felony are punished no more severely under present law than if an ordinary handgun had been employed. Existing Federal law also contains no penalty for stealing a firearm and lacks a clear definition of the offense of burglary. These defects and others would be remedied under a package of proposed firearms amendments that is included in the proposed legislation.

Second, building on the work of the 100th Congress, which, for the first time in recent memory, created a limited Federal death penalty for certain drug-related killings, this proposal would establish procedures necessary to institute a capital sanction for murders committed in violation of other Federal statutes, such as those involving murder-for-hire and the murder of a kidnap victim or a Federal prison guard. The proposed provisions are in compliance with all relevant Supreme Court decisions, and their enactment is long overdue. I believe it is absolutely essential to bring Federal law into conformity with the law in the more than three-quarters of the States that have passed statutes to reinstate the death penalty for a limited number of heinous crimes.

Third, the proposal includes provisions designed to impose severe restrictions on ammunition clips and other ammunition feeding devices frequently used to enable so-called "assault weapons" to fire a large number of rounds rapidly and without reloading. Under my Administration's proposal, a magazine or other ammunition feeding device with a capacity of greater than 15 rounds would be subject to strict regulation and generally could no longer be imported, manufactured, received, or possessed. Persons already in possession of such devices would be allowed to retain and use them lawfully. No transfer to another owner would be permitted unless a record was made of that transfer, which would permit tracing in the event of a criminal misuse.

Limited manufacture or importation for purposes of export or for sale to Government agencies would be authorized, but such large-capacity devices, like a firearm today, would be subject to identification by requiring serial numbers. While an ammunition feeding device, like a firearm itself, is not inherently evil, the enhanced potential for danger to law-abiding citizens posed by the unlawful use of weapons equipped with such devices in criminal hands makes it necessary to impose these restrictions in the interest of public safety.

Fourth, My proposal would establish a nationwide program of mandatory drug testing for defendants on post-conviction release, including probation, parole, or supervised release. It is estimated that upwards of 81,000 individuals will be on some form of Federal supervised release in 1990. The known association between criminal behavior and drug abuse is such that drug testing as a condition of release for convicted persons is an essential precaution to help enhance the public safety, while also promoting rehabilitative goals. I have proposed that $10.7 million be appropriated for this activity in fiscal year 1990.

Fifth, the proposal contains provisions to

reform the so-called "exclusionary rule." Under this rule, Federal courts today exclude or suppress probative evidence obtained by searches and seizures conducted in good faith by law enforcement officials. The result is that factually guilty individuals avoid conviction and punishment. Under my proposal, any evidence that is obtained as a result of a search or seizure undertaken in objectively reasonable good faith, as determined by a court, would be admissible at trial, notwithstanding that a magistrate or judge later found that the search did not satisfy constitutional requirements.

Suppression of evidence in criminal trials—which are supposed to represent a search for truth on the issue of a defendant's guilt or innocence—is not an appropriate remedy to redress innocent mistakes. Law enforcement officers must frequently make split-second decisions on matters involving difficult constitutional issues on which even judges may disagree. Enactment of this proposal is necessary in order to make the justice system work effectively.

The exclusionary rule would remain, under my proposal, as a permissible sanction for intentional violations, but no longer would a criminal escape punishment because of a technical mistake in conducting a search or seizure. The House of Representatives last year passed a similar proposal, which unfortunately was deleted in the conference agreement on the Anti-Drug Abuse Act of 1988. The proposal should be enacted this year.

Sixth, the proposed bill would restore an appropriate degree of finality to State and Federal criminal convictions by curtailing abuses of the writ of *habeas corpus.* Under current interpretations of Federal statutes, defendants whose convictions have been affirmed by courts of appeals may nonetheless later seek to relitigate in Federal courts the claims previously raised or waived on direct appeal. Not infrequently, defendants with nothing to lose exercise this novel opportunity, which is afforded by no other civilized society in the world, through several rounds of litigation lasting many years and tying up our already overburdened Federal courts.

With the massive delays in many Federal districts occasioned by an overwhelming caseload, we can no longer afford the luxury of this system of excessive opportunity for review of "final" criminal judgments. An effective justice system requires that final adjudications not be subject to continuous review. No innocent individual should be denied an avenue through which to petition the Federal courts to review his or her conviction. But at the same time, those persons who have been tried and found guilty, and whose legal claims have been rejected after full and fair consideration, should not be allowed to relitigate endlessly in the Federal courts.

Under the proposed amendments, the opportunity for certain kinds of collateral attacks upon a conviction would be limited by a time period of 1 or 2 years, with due exceptions for the assertion of rights newly created or facts newly discovered. Similarly, Federal courts would be admonished to give presumptive validity to any full and fair determination of a factual issue by a State court.

A nearly identical proposal was overwhelmingly passed by the Senate in 1984. Its enactment this year would improve the justice system and relieve the Federal courts, thereby freeing them to hear other cases and to dispense justice to others more promptly.

Seventh, and finally, the proposed bill would authorize appropriations for several activities of the Department of Justice to augment Federal law enforcement personnel, increase prosecutorial efforts, and expand prison capacity. These appropriation authorizations, along with the increased funding I have requested for the Judiciary and the Bureau of Alcohol, Tobacco and Firearms in the Department of the Treasury—a total government-wide increase of about $1.2 billion in 1990—will make possible a tougher, more vigorous and more effective fight against violent crime.

When I stood before the United States Capitol on May 15 and addressed the families of the brave and valiant peace officers who gave lives in the battle to rid America of drugs and crime, I promised them—as I did the American people on the day I assumed this office—that "this scourge will stop." Enactment of the set of proposals that I present to you today, as well as implementation of the other initiatives that I announced last month, will be a major step in keeping that promise. I urge that these important proposals promptly be considered and enacted. We owe the people of our great Nation no less.

GEORGE BUSH

The White House,
June 15, 1989.

Remarks to Law Enforcement Officers at the Federal Training Center in Glynco, Georgia
June 15, 1989

I don't want to do anything less than solemn on an occasion like this, but I'll be darned if I'm going to sweat up here. I'm going to take my coat off, and I hope all you will, too.

Well, thank you all very much. In a sense, there's a little nostalgia in the air, because just 44 and a half years ago, Barbara and I had our honeymoon 14 miles from here, or just a few miles from here. So, I feel like it's coming back in a sense.

And I want to thank Charlie Rinkevich, who has really epitomized what cooperation stands for between law enforcement agencies. And I worked with him, as Nick Brady said, hand-in-hand, as we did battle against narcotics in south Florida. And the South Florida Task Force was a success. And one of the reasons that this place here has been a demonstrable success is that Charlie brought those same skills that he had of getting people working together and has applied them right here at Glynco.

I want to salute our Attorney General [Richard L. Thornburgh], who really is doing a superb job, shaping for me an anticrime package that I want to talk with you a bit about today. I want to salute Secretary Brady—many don't realize that the Secretary of the Treasury has tremendous responsibilities in the field of law enforcement, and Nick's doing an outstanding job.

And then on the political front, I wasn't quite sure that anybody could ever fill the shoes of Bo Ginn, who's over here, your own. And sure enough, [Representative] Lindsay Thomas, who flew down with us on Air Force One, is doing a superb job for Georgia; and he's right here with us today, and I want to say I'm pleased he's here.

And unrelated though it is to battling crime, we brought with us another son of Georgia, and that is the Honorable Paul Coverdell, who had been a member of the State senate here, and is now the Director of the Peace Corps, worldwide—Paul, over here.

And the last thing I would like to do—those of you in the back can't see them—but one of the things this center does is offer training in certain anticrime techniques and self-preservation techniques to Ambassadors. And I see that several of those who I have selected to be United States Ambassadors serving in foreign countries are here with us today, and I'd like to ask them to stand. [*Applause*]

This is such a warm summer day, I think Charlie ought to take you all over to Pam's. [*Laughter*] Sorry about that, Charlie. [*Laughter*]

We've had a lot of talk about the various kinds of training that our law enforcement people from all different agencies go through, and they were telling me about the shooting range. I also hear that a distinguished graduate of one of the courses was a predecessor in the ambassadorial training—Shirley Temple Black was here, soon to be our Ambassador to Czechoslovakia, a tough assignment which she'll do very well. But I'm told that in shooting she had an almost perfect score: four shots right on the target. The target was a picture of a tourist with a camera. [*Laughter*] She's going to do well in Czechoslovakia.

But when you graduate from this center, the Federal Law Enforcement Training

Center, you're going to leave, you graduates, with a knowledge that you've already confronted the hardest questions that any peace officer must face. You will have already been tested under fire. And you will know, from the firearm training center, whether or not you would shoot when you must shoot and if you would hold your fire when the apparent bank robber turns out to be a child with a toy gun. And you will know from "Hogan's Alley" just how fast your reaction time really is. And in short, you will have been tried and tested, all of your reflexes—physical, mental and moral. And when you return to duty—whether your duty is at the Federal courthouse in Atlanta, the mountain hollows of West Virginia, or the city streets of New York—you will take with you a confidence and a self-assurance that can only be earned, never bestowed.

And you might guard a NASA rocket, a witness under the threat of a murder contract, or a visiting Prime Minister. Or you might be a member of the U.S. Customs, the Secret Service, or practically any Federal agency. Or you might be a local or State law enforcer. But wherever you're from, whatever you do, you wear a badge over your heart, a badge of service, a badge of honor. And I came here to salute each and every one of you.

This center is dedicated to a special partnership between every man and woman with a badge. The bulk of law enforcement is provided by one partner: the States and localities, those closest to the streets and homes of America. The other partner, the Federal Government, is best equipped to fight specialized crimes, from interdicting drugs on the high seas to putting prison stripes on high-rolling crooks that are now in pinstripes. And the Federal Government is adept at yet another task: training. And that's why this center is so well suited to this special partnership.

This center is renowned for its high-tech, state-of-the-art facilities and many talented instructors. And it was my pleasure just now to meet several of those talented instructors. But it's more than your ample resources and your excellent faculty that make Glynco one of the most unique law enforcement training facilities in the world. It's also your singular and unwavering commitment to fighting crime. And you teach many agencies, but you are one academy with one purpose: to catch today's criminals with tomorrow's methods and to lift the shadow of fear from our neighborhoods, from our communities—yes, from our entire country.

And here, investigators learn how to track down insurance or telecommunications fraud, money laundering, computer crimes. Glynco's Financial Fraud Institute will allow agencies to keep up with a boom industry, the quiet larcenies of white-collar crime. And let me just say parenthetically: If we are going to be fair about it, the white-collar criminal has got to pay along with the common street criminal.

But right here, State law enforcers work with Federal agents to learn how to crack a drug ring. And here, our U.S. Ambassadors learn to recognize and avoid terrorists. Investigators and regulators—they learn how to work together to track down those who would poison our lakes and our rivers.

And nowhere else do law enforcers from so many agencies train together. You may be a security officer from the State Department or a U.S. Marshal. At this center you learn that there are many agencies that fight crime, but you are all members of one team, the united forces of justice.

The Peace Officers Memorial here at Glynco is a somber reminder of this shared cause and shared sacrifice. Thirty-nine names, thirty-nine slain Federal officers. All were graduates of this Center. Among the names is one that I recognize and knew well: Ariel Rios, a Special Agent of the Bureau of Alcohol, Tobacco and Firearms, graduated from the Center in March 1979 and gunned down, shot to death, while working undercover trying to break up a drug ring in south Florida just 3 years later, in December of 1982. Julie Cross, Special Agent, U.S. Secret Service—her name marks a poignant distinction. When she was killed in Los Angeles in June of 1980 while working a criminal counterfeit investigation, Julie became the first female Secret Service Agent to die in the line of duty. And sadly, these are not the only names of slain officers. Of 161 officers killed in the line of duty last year, 152 were State or local officers. More than 1,500 law enforcement officers have been killed in the past 10 years. And that is almost one death every 2 days. And one death for every 2 days—that is too much.

I'm here today to deliver a message. And I said it in New York, after the murder of Special Agent Everett Hatcher. And I came here to Georgia to lay a wreath and to repeat a warning: Better that you had never been born than to attack one of America's finest. We are going after those who kill or wound our police officers.

And so, I've also come here to send a message to the United States Congress: We can work together to protect those who protect us. And I've come here today to sign a transmittal, an official message to Congress detailing our crime package. Usually, this would entail nothing more than a quick flourish of the pen and then sending an aide on a 10-minute car ride up from Pennsylvania Avenue, 1600, on up to Capitol Hill. But when it comes to fighting crime, you deserve more than business as usual. And that's why I have come almost a thousand miles to this wonderful Center to let you know we intend to back you where it counts—on the streets and in the courtroom.

And first, I call on Congress to do for dangerous firearms what it has wisely done for dangerous drugs. I propose to double the mandatory penalties for the use of semiautomatic weapons in crimes involving violence or drugs. And those who use a semiautomatic weapon in Federal crimes, or so much as have one during the commission of a crime, will do an automatic 10 years in Federal prison—and I mean 10 years—no excuses, no probation, no parole. And let's put the handcuffs on the criminals, not on the criminal justice system.

Secondly—and I know our able Attorney General agrees with this—we can't plea-bargain away the lives of your loved ones, the lives of fellow cops and kids. And I have directed the Attorney General to advise America's Federal prosecutors to end plea-bargaining for violent Federal firearms offenses. Our message: Pack a gun, and we will pack you away. No plea-bargaining for that kind of crime.

And third, when a criminal commits a crime with a gun and someone dies, justice demands something in return: the ultimate penalty, the death penalty. And I call on Governors to match this Federal initiative and propose these same three standards at home—mandatory time, no deals without cooperation, and the death penalty for these kinds of crime.

Fourth, at my direction, the Bureau of Alcohol, Tobacco and Firearms suspended the importation of certain assault weapons. ATF is continuing its examination to determine which, if any, of these weapons are not acceptable under the standards in existing law. And the standard talks about suitability for sporting purposes—and you're hearing this from one who prides himself on being a sportsman, and have been a hunter all my life. And at the conclusion of this study, and after careful consideration, we will permanently ban any imports that don't measure up to these standards. I am going to stand up for the police officers in this country.

And toward this end, I am proposing the prohibition of the importation and manufacture of gun magazines of more than 15 rounds for citizens' use. I just don't believe that sportsmen require these 30-round magazines if the legitimate purpose is sports.

And finally, I am requesting funding for the hiring of 825 new Federal agents and staff: 375 at Alcohol, Tobacco and Firearms; 300 at the FBI; and 150 new deputy U.S. marshals. And these new law enforcers should be matched by 1,600 new prosecutors and staff. And we're asking for an additional $1 billion, over and above $500 million already slated for 1990, for Federal prison construction. This will mean 24,000 new beds to boost Federal prison capacity by nearly 80 percent. In short, I am proposing more law enforcers to catch criminals, more staff to prosecute them, and more prisons to keep them off the streets.

You here at Glynco play a major role in this war on crime. And to say it exists to "foster interagency cooperation" is a forgivable understatement. It creates a bond between you and your roommates, your classmates, your fellow officers of the law. And this is a bond that can be known only by those who put themselves on the line every day in the service of a great cause. In a country where criminals threaten to erode the very liberties that we hold so dear, you here at Glynco are domestic freedom fighters in this war on crime. And for this reason, you have a friend in the majestic Oval Office, and you have the gratitude and the support of the American people.

Thank you. God bless you, and God bless the United States of America. Thank you very, very much.

Note: The President spoke at 11:41 a.m. in the Steed Building. Prior to his remarks, he participated in a wreath-laying ceremony at the Peace Officers Memorial. In his remarks, the President referred to Charles F. Rinkevich, Director of the Center, and Pam's, a local bar. At the conclusion of his remarks, the President returned to Washington, DC.

Nomination of Stephen A. Wakefield To Be General Counsel of the Department of Energy

June 15, 1989

The President today announced his intention to nominate Stephen A. Wakefield to be General Counsel of the Department of Energy. He would succeed Francis S. Ruddy.

Since 1986 Mr. Wakefield has served as a senior partner in the law firm of Baker and Botts in Houston, TX. Prior to this, he served as vice chairman and general counsel of United Energy Resources, Inc., 1985, and in 1985 when United Energy Resources, Inc., merged with the MidCon Corp., he became an executive vice president and member of the board of directors. He served as an attorney with the law firm of Baker and Botts in Houston, 1974–1985; Assistant Administrator for International Affairs at the Department of Energy, 1974; and Assistant Secretary of the Interior for Energy and Minerals, 1973. Prior to this, he served in various positions, including assistant to the General Counsel of the Federal Power Commission and Deputy Assistant Secretary of the Interior, 1970–1973.

Mr. Wakefield graduated from the University of Texas and the Texas School of Law. He was born in Olney, IL. He is married, has six children, and resides in Texas.

Nomination of J. Michael Davis To Be an Assistant Secretary of Energy

June 15, 1989

The President today announced his intention to nominate J. Michael Davis to be an Assistant Secretary of Energy (Conservation and Renewable Energy). He would succeed John R. Berg.

Since 1986 Mr. Davis has served as president of GlowCore Colorado, Inc., in Englewood, CO. Mr. Davis served as vice president of Sunbelt Energy Corp. in Englewood, CO., 1982–1986. Mr. Davis has served in several positions with the Solar Energy Research Institute in Golden, CO, including manager of planning and special programs, 1981–1982; acting associate director for analysis and applications, 1981; and buildings division manager, 1980–1981. Mr. Davis also served as a division manager at the Department of Energy in Washington, DC, 1977–1980.

Mr. Davis graduated from the U.S. Air Force Academy (B.S., 1969) and the University of Illinois (M.S., 1970). He served with the U.S. Air Force, 1969–1977, achieving the rank of captain and receiving the Bronze Star and the Vietnam Honor Medal. Mr. Davis has three children and currently resides in Lakewood, CO.

Nomination of Luigi R. Einaudi To Be Permanent United States Representative to the Organization of American States

June 15, 1989

The President today announced his intention to nominate Luigi R. Einaudi to be the Permanent Representative of the United States of America to the Organization of American States, with the rank of Ambassador. He would succeed Richard Thomas McCormack.

Since 1977 Dr. Einaudi has been Director of the Office of Policy Planning Coordination at the Bureau of Inter-American Affairs at the Department of State, and a member of the Policy Planning Staff, 1974–1977. Dr. Einaudi was visiting professor at the University of California at Los Angeles, 1964–1974. He served as a senior social scientist for the Rand Corp., 1962–1974, and was a teaching fellow and tutor in government at Harvard University, 1960–1961.

Dr. Einaudi graduated from Harvard College (A.B., 1957) and Harvard University (Ph.D., 1966). He was born March 1, 1936, in Cambridge, MA. He served in the U.S. Army, 1957–1959. He is married, has four children, and resides in Bethesda, MD.

Remarks at a Reception for Participants in the Very Special Arts International Festival

June 15, 1989

Thank you, Jean, for that warm introduction; and Barbara and I are just delighted to be here. I'm only sorry that the six puppies are not here. [*Laughter*] We'd have had a heck of a good time with them. But, Jean, thank you for all you do—you and everyone else involved in this Very Special Arts program.

Let me tell you how pleased that Barbara and I are to have front-row seats for a program like this. I'll tell you, I used to be a Kenny Rogers fan—I've got to admit it—and I still am. But I'm also a Phong Sak fan—[*laughter*]—Phong Sak Meunchanai, the son of Thailand—what a magnificent performance! Maybe it's not such a long journey from the streets of Thailand, of Bangkok, to the South Lawn at the White House. It tells us all that there's no limit to how far we can go or what we can achieve. And here at the White House, we're very privileged—every President is—to have the great artists come to this magnificent home, the people's home. And it's a special treat for us to see, Jean, so many talented young people, from across the country and around the world, bring your art, your special abilities, here to Washington. And I only wish that every performer here—and I know there's a lot—could have performed right here on this stage.

You're all well on your way to the kind of life that I want to see for every American: a life of independence and opportunity and productive involvement in our mainstream. And that means a commitment on society's part to end discrimination, to increase access and opportunity in our schools, on the job, and in every aspect of our society. You guys don't let any disabilities stand in your way, and so it's up to us to make sure that discrimination doesn't stop you. And Federal law must protect individuals with disabilities, and I'm going to do my level best to see that it does.

I want to share, in conclusion, just one little story told to me by Jean Kennedy Smith about a blind young man, a sculptor. Jean met him in Ireland several years ago, and she watched as this sightless boy sculpted a face from clay, a marvel of detail, masterful expression. And what Jean said made an impression on me: "Art gave that boy the power to see for the rest of us." And that's true—all art is a vision that comes from within; and each of you has a very special talent to make us see what you see, feel what you feel, hear what you have to say.

And so, share your gift, and it will grow. And you've made this a very, very special afternoon at the White House. Thank you, and God bless each and every one of you. Thank you very much.

Note: The President spoke at 2:43 p.m. on the South Portico at the White House. In his remarks, he referred to Jean Kennedy Smith, founder of the Very Special Arts Foundation, and Phong Sak Meunchanai, a participant in the Festival who sang prior to the President's remarks.

Remarks at a Briefing on Law Enforcement for United States Attorneys
June 16, 1989

Welcome to the White House. Thank you all very much. Thank you, Dick, and thank all of you for that warm welcome here. But let me welcome you to the White House. I'm just delighted to have the U.S. attorneys here.

First, a word about our able Attorney General. I feel very confident about our Justice Department under his able leadership. And the integrity that Dick brings to this job is known nationwide, and I know it's going to enhance the work that you all are involved in every day of your lives, serving this country. So, I want to thank the Attorney General for all he is doing and to salute him in front of you who work closely with the Department and with him.

This is a time where we get around and tell lawyer's jokes. [*Laughter*] I was thinking of having Frank Donaldson come up—Alabama's own—to tell a few—[*laughter*]—but this is a kinder and gentler White House, and I'm not sure we need that. But—[*laughter*].

You know, when I flew out to Wyoming on Monday, I got off Air Force One out there—beautiful—and Richard Stacy was there to shake my hand. And he said, "I'm here to represent rural America." [*Laughter*] Simple, dramatic words. So, my name is George Bush, and I represent the United States. [*Laughter*] And with words like these, you and your assistants begin a Federal criminal trial. And it's a great and rare honor to represent the United States, and I'm honored to share that distinction with you. I share the pride that you feel every time you say that.

Two hundred years ago, a few months after becoming President, George Washington signed the act that gave birth to the offices that you hold. And it's a distinguished tradition. And one of the reasons that I was so delighted when Dick arranged for this little meeting was that I wanted to be able to tell you the respect I feel for the job that you all do. And, in the words of a former Attorney General, you represent "one of the most powerful peacetime forces known to man."

Peacetime? Well, I expect some of you would debate that. The situation in our streets has been aptly compared to a shooting war—and that's why you're here, for an assembly unprecedented in modern times. And I did want you to know how strongly I feel—and I'm grateful to Dick for his comments on this—about violent crime in America, and how firmly I support what you all do every single day.

The problem today is violent crime—some call it blood and thunder—involving these high-powered weapons of a new class of criminals who impose the law of the jungle out of the barrel of a gun. And the fundamental responsibility for protecting America's streets and neighborhoods from violent crime must remain with our cities and States. But there's an increasing and important Federal role in fighting violent crime. And when leadership is called for, we've got to respond, we've got to seize the day.

One month ago, on a really somber, rainy day here, I was standing in front of the Capitol to commemorate the police officers who were slain in the line of duty. And many were agents or officers who had worked with you or the prosecutors that you supervise. And to honor their sacrifice, I called upon the United States Congress to join me in launching a new national strategy, a new partnership with America's cities and States, to take back the streets. And to do that we must raise our voices to correct an insidious tendency—the tendency to blame crime on society rather than on the criminal.

And let me be extra clear on my own beliefs here today. I, like most Americans, believe that we can start building a safer society by first agreeing that society itself doesn't cause the crime—criminals cause the crime. And we are foursquare behind the men and women like you who make sacrifices every day to protect the vulnerable, to safeguard the law-abiding, and to ensure that those who scorn justice are brought to justice. And we must hold people accountable for their actions. And I said it at the Capitol: A commonsense approach to crime means that criminals must know that if they commit a crime, they will be caught; and if caught, they will be prosecuted; and if convicted, they will do time.

A plain-speaking predecessor of mine was Harry Truman. And he said it pretty well 37 years ago when he met with the U.S. attorneys here at the White House. And he summed it up: "We don't want any crooks left out of jail when they do crooked things." And nowhere is this precept more critical than in combating violent crime. The killing must stop, and it must stop now. And I'm here to ask your help—to ask you to take a leadership role in your districts in helping put away our nation's most wanted: the privileged class of violent, repeat, and fugitive offenders hellbent on proving that crime really does pay.

The comprehensive plan that we sent to Congress seeks to take violent criminals off the streets with an attack on four fronts: new laws to punish them, new agents to arrest them, new prosecutors to convict them, and new prisons to hold them. And all four are essential. Your role is essential. A chain is only as strong as its weakest link.

The first link is some tough new laws, and everyone here is familiar with title 18's section 924(c). And, well, we have asked Congress to do for dangerous firearms what it has wisely done for dangerous drugs—double the mandatory penalties. As we've said, the math is simple. Anyone using a semiautomatic for crime, or so much as having one in hand during a crime, will do an automatic 10 extra years in Federal prison—no probation, no parole, no matter which judge they get.

And I'm asking each of you to see that this message is brought to life in the streets and courtrooms of your cities and towns. Because for these laws to be effective, we can't plea-bargain away the lives of our cops and our kids. And I want and expect that when suspects are arrested with serious weapons, that they'll face serious weapons charges. And so, last month, I directed the Attorney General to issue guidelines to ensure that, in all but the most exceptional cases, all firearms offenders are prosecuted to the fullest extent of the law.

And those guidelines are being distributed today, I'm told, and you've been summoned to Washington to hear it from the top. No more loopholes, no conditional surrender, no more rolls of the dice—if a criminal carries a gun, all deals are off. And when a criminal carries a gun and someone dies, I firmly believe that that person should pay with his life.

We're going to up the stakes for those who calculate that our criminal justice system is a crapshoot where the risks are worth the rewards. And when criminals think about reaching for a gun, they're going to know, and they're going to learn, that they will do time—hard time. And yes, this policy may mean more trials. And I understand that firearms cases, like narcotics cases, are not always very popular with some on the bench. But it can be done and, in fact, already is being done—even in districts with these overcrowded dockets like the Southern District of New York, where plea bargains for 924(c) violations have been banned since 1987.

And yes, we recognize that more offenders serving longer sentences obviously means more prison space. And here again we've matched our rhetoric with resources: an unprecedented $1.5 billion building program for federal prisons, boosting present capacity by 80 percent. These are tough budgetary times, as everybody here knows. But $1.5 billion is what I want to see go into this program.

And finally, yes, we also know how understaffed and overworked your offices are. And we've called in the cavalry—Federal reinforcements are on the way. And if Congress will move—and move quickly—in addition to 825 new agents to investigate violent crime, I have asked the Congress to provide funding for 1,600 new prosecutors—new positions for your district—the largest one-time expansion in U.S. history—with increases in both prosecutors and then the support staff. And we're also seeking over 150 new attorneys at this end, adding more muscle to the Department's Criminal Division.

These forces must be marshaled effectively. And the Attorney General is proposing to consolidate the strike forces so that they are led not from distant Washington, but by you—the commanders at the front lines. And of course, new laws and new manpower aren't the only tools at your disposal. Your leadership on the law enforcement coordinating committees has already produced new initiatives to meet the challenge of violent crime. In Chicago, Tony Valukas has led a cooperative effort to rid the community of dangerous offenders by charging gang leaders and other repeat offenders under tough Federal armed-career-criminal laws. And in the last 2 years, working together, we've jammed the revolving door on 20 such criminals—all are now serving life without parole in Federal prisons. And one of Tony's counterparts, the director of the Illinois State Police, responded to the Federal initiative by launching a violent crime task force. Similar partnerships on violent crime are being led by U.S. attorneys like Benito Romano up in New York, Jay Stephens right here in the District, Rob Bonner in L.A., whose promotion to the Federal district court was recently confirmed by the Senate.

And there are other innovations. To attack the profusion of gang and street violence, you may use some of your new slots to recruit seasoned ADA's or others trained in prosecuting gunshot crime. In those States where police are not protected by death penalty provisions, we should make full use of those Federal laws that permit the death penalty for cop-killers. And we should always use our unique Federal resources and expertise to wipe out the kind of violent crime that operates beyond the reach of any one State—like the Rukn street gang whose members were convicted of conspiring with Libya to acquire military weapons for terrorist operations in America.

And in addition to my directive on plea bargaining, there's a second important message that I ask you to bring home to your districts. Your colleagues in State and local law enforcement need the same tools we've proposed for you: mandatory time for weapons offenders, no plea bargaining on guns, the death penalty for heinous crimes, and the kind of increased resources—police, prosecutor, prisons—that ensure these vicious thugs will be pursued, prosecuted, and put away for good.

United States attorneys are a breed apart—invariably bright, committed, tenacious public servants. I really believe the country understands that about all of you. Four former U.S. attorneys hold leadership roles in our administration: Dick Thornburgh of Western Pennsylvania, [Secretary of Transportation] Sam Skinner of Northern Illinois, [Director of Central Intelligence] Bill Webster of Eastern Missouri, and [Director of the Federal Bureau of Investigation] Bill Sessions of Western Texas. And we hope to see yet another—Bob Fiske of New York, joining our ranks here soon.

Your efforts against violent crime are important, but no less important than the other law enforcement priorities that you have so ably addressed. And over the years, America has watched in admiration, and sometimes awe, as the accomplishments of your offices roll across America's television screens. And we're not going to tolerate the corruption of labor by organized crime, as the landmark Teamster settlement proved. And crime is crime, whether committed with a briefcase or a gun. And we will not tolerate greed over honest business, whether the business is defense contracting—Operation Ill Wind; Wall Street—where you're owed congratulations on last week's convictions; banking—Polar Cap was the largest money laundering case in history; savings and loans—where the legislation we've proposed will give you the tools you need to wipe out the financial fraud that has devastated that industry.

Nor will we tolerate civil rights violations, as the recent Klan convictions in Alabama prove. And as the recent indictments against two major drug gangs right here in Washington show, we will not tolerate the corruption of our youth by the poison they call cocaine. This scourge will stop. I said it in my Inaugural Address and I'll repeat here: This scourge will stop.

And it's easy to understand why our people are so grateful to those of you who have sacrificed to serve on the firing line—whether in court or on the streets. And day and night your skypagers and mobile phones are active, as those you command monitor court-authorized intercepts or move undercover into the breach. It is exciting and principled work, an integral link in a system of justice that remains the envy of the world. In today's new effort, and in all your efforts, you have the gratitude, the respect, and the support of the American people—and certainly of me. For your kids, for mine, for America's kids: Take back the streets.

And thank you for coming here today. Godspeed in the challenges ahead. And God bless you, your families, and the Nation that you work so ably to protect. Thank you for coming to the White House.

Note: The President spoke at 10:09 a.m. in the East Room at the White House. In his remarks, he referred to Frank W. Donaldson, U.S. Attorney for the Northern District of Alabama, and Richard A. Stacy, U.S. Attorney for the District of Wyoming.

Remarks Congratulating the Wichita State University Shockers on Winning the NCAA Baseball Championship

June 16, 1989

First, let me salute the two Kansas Senators, Senator Dole, Senator Kassebaum; members of the Kansas congressional delegation; President Armstrong; Coach Stephenson; Shocker players; staff; friends; secret admirers. Welcome to the White House, and heartfelt congratulations on wrapping up and winning the NCAA Baseball Championship. And nothing personal at all in your having kicked the Texas Longhorns out to pasture. [*Laughter*] I'd forgotten that.

But it's a special treat to be here, for as you may have heard, I love the game. In fact, watching Greg Brummett's fastball last weekend reminded me of another one from the olden times—threw that high, hard fast one—the fabled Dizzy Dean, St. Louis Cardinal fame. As a player, he fractured the opponents' bats; but later, as a broadcaster, he fractured the English language. [*Laughter*] And he said once, of a homerun hitter: "He's standing confidentially at the plate." [*Laughter*] And then he delighted listeners with his trademark quote that I'm sure even young guys remember: "That runner slud into third." [*Laughter*]

Well, by winning Wichita State's first-ever national baseball title, you have slud headfirst into the sports hearts of America. And they're calling it Shocker Success or Midwest Magic. And remember how Judy Garland once said of Kansas, "There's no place like home"? Well, with apologies to Senator Dole and Senator Kassebaum, you've proven there's also no place like Omaha and the College World Series.

If you'll excuse a personal reminiscence, I played in 1947 in the first College World Series finals. It started in Kalamazoo, Michigan. I think they played there 2 or 3 years before a move to Omaha. And next year, '48, again our Yale team reached the finals, but there was one problem. We had a good coach—great National League baseball player, Ethan Allen; and we walked the eighth hitter, bases loaded, I think, to get to the ninth hitter. The ninth hitter was their pitcher, Jackie Jensen, who went on to be one of the greatest sluggers the Boston Red Sox ever had. And he hit a ball that's still rolling in Kalamazoo, Michigan. [*Laughter*] So, we lost both times. So, baseball can keep you humble.

But in 1989, you were the ones that kept your opponents humble—58–14 they were—58–14 on the regular season. Five victories in the College World Series, batting, pitching, fielding—all of it right into the history books. Greg Brummett, of course, now famous nationally, led you there: only the seventh pitcher to win three games in a College World Series. Greg, the pickoff move of yours would nab Ricky Henderson [New York Yankees player]. And help came, too, from the Shockers' answer to the question, "How do you spell relief?" Well, Jim Newlin, only the fourth college pitcher to get three saves in a College World Series. And then there's Eric Wedge, your catcher; shortstop Pat Meares, clubbing a homerun in the title game—called NASA this morning, and that ball's still in orbit. And Jim Audley, Todd Dreifort—each of the four, All-Tournament selections.

So, don't worry; I'm not forgetting Mike Wentworth here. One week ago, you started reading the comic that covers a piece of bubble gum, and you came upon this fortune: "Something magical will happen." And hours later, you belted a three-run homer to help beat top-seeded Florida State. And the next day, Gene Stephenson's team completed the magic act, becoming the first NCAA baseball champion in 23 years not located in California, Texas, Arizona, or Florida. And last week, Gene said, "We wanted to prove to people all over the country that somebody outside those States can play baseball." Don't worry, Coach; they got the message.

And in that final game, Bryant Winslow had to leave because of a stress fracture in his right leg—one of four major injuries to hit this ball club. He had, as we all would, tears in our eyes at a difficult situation like that. He didn't want to leave, but he led his teammates from the bench.

And a writer once observed, "The Kansas spirit is the American spirit double-distilled." And my friends, you embody that spirit. And it—and you—have made the Shockers number one.

The Vice President and I are delighted to be here to salute you, along with our distinguished Members of the Congress. Congratulations to a team of champions—well done! Thank you.

Note: The President spoke at 11:03 a.m. in the Rose Garden at the White House. In his remarks, he referred to Warren B. Armstrong, president of the university, and Gene Stephenson, coach of the team.

Nomination of Stephen John Hadley To Be an Assistant Secretary of Defense
June 16, 1989

The President today announced his intention to nominate Stephen John Hadley to be an Assistant Secretary of Defense (International Security Policy). He would succeed Ronald F. Lehman II.

Since 1981 Mr. Hadley has been a partner with Shea and Gardner, Attorneys at Law, in Washington, DC. Prior to this he was an associate with Shea and Gardner, 1977–1981. Mr. Hadley served on the National Security Council staff in the Office of Program Analysis, 1974–1977, and as a member of the analysis group for the Assistant Secretary of Defense (Comptroller), 1972–1974.

Mr. Hadley graduated from Cornell University (B.A., 1969) and Yale Law School (J.D., 1972). He was an active-duty U.S. naval officer, 1972–1975. Mr. Hadley was born February 13, 1947, in Toledo, OH. He is married, has two children, and resides in Washington, DC.

Nomination of Henry S. Rowen To Be an Assistant Secretary of Defense

June 16, 1989

The President today announced his intention to nominate Henry S. Rowen to be an Assistant Secretary of Defense (International Security Affairs). He would succeed Richard Lee Armitage.

Mr. Rowen is currently a professor of public policy studies at Stanford University's Hoover Institution on War, Revolution, and Peace. Mr. Rowen served as Chairman of the National Intelligence Council at the Central Intelligence Agency, 1981–1983. He has served as a member of the Defense Science Board since 1983. Mr. Rowen served as president of the Rand Corp., 1967–1972; Assistant Director of the Bureau of the Budget, 1965–1966; and Deputy Assistant Secretary of Defense for National Security Affairs, 1961–1964. He also served as an economist with the Rand Corp. from 1950 to 1961.

Mr. Rowen received his bachelor of arts degree from the Massachusetts Institute of Technology, 1949, and his master's degree from Oxford University, 1955. He served in the U.S. Navy, 1943–1946, in the Pacific theater of operations. He was born October 11, 1925, in Boston, MA.

Nomination of Andrew Camp Barrett To Be a Member of the Federal Communications Commission

June 16, 1989

The President today announced his intention to nominate Andrew Camp Barrett to be a member of the Federal Communications Commission for the term expiring June 30, 1990. He would succeed Mark S. Fowler.

Since 1980 Mr. Barrett has been commissioner for the Illinois Commerce Commission. Prior to this he was assistant director of the Illinois Department of Commerce and Community Affairs, 1979–1980. He was director of operations for the Illinois Law Enforcement Commission, 1975–1979; executive director for the Chicago branch of the NAACP, 1971–1975; and associate director for the National Conference of Christians and Jews, 1969–1971.

Mr. Barrett graduated from Roosevelt University of Chicago and received his master's degree from Loyola University of Chicago. He currently resides in Chicago, IL.

Nomination of Sherrie P. Marshall To Be a Member of the Federal Communications Commission

June 16, 1989

The President today announced his intention to nominate Sherrie P. Marshall to be a member of the Federal Communications Commission for the remainder of the term expiring June 30, 1992. She would succeed Dennis R. Patrick.

Since 1989 Ms. Marshall has been a partner with Wiley, Rein and Fielding in Washington, DC. Prior to this she was an attorney with the White House Counsel's Office in the office of the President-elect, 1988–1989. She was Director of the Office of Legislative Affairs at the Federal Communications Commission, 1987–1988; an attorney with Wiley, Rein and Fielding, 1986–1987; and Executive Secretary for the Department of Treasury, 1985–1986. She served as Associate Counsel to the President, 1982–1985; Special Assistant to the President for Legislative Affairs, 1981–1982; and executive assistant to the Chairman of the Federal Election Commission, 1979–1981. She has also served as the minority counsel for elections for the Senate Committee on Rules and Administration, 1978–1979; and as an attorney in the Office of the General Counsel for the Federal Election Commission, 1977–1978.

Ms. Marshall graduated from the University of North Carolina (A.B., 1974) and the University of North Carolina School of Law at Chapel Hill (J.D., 1977).

Statement by Press Secretary Fitzwater on Hungarian Political Reforms

June 16, 1989

The United States welcomes the announcement of the Hungarian Government's intention to begin discussions with the opposition as a first step to multiparty elections. On April 17, in Hamtramck, MI, the President pledged support to East European countries which embarked upon the path of fundamental political and economic reform. In view of Hungary's progress, the President will seek legislation to accord Hungary GSP (Generalized System of Preferences) and to permit the Overseas Private Investment Corporation (OPIC) to operate in Hungary.

Continuation of Edward L. Rowny as Special Advisor to the President and Secretary of State for Arms Control Matters

June 16, 1989

The President today announced that Edward L. Rowny will continue to serve as Special Advisor to the President and Secretary of State for Arms Control Matters.

In 1985 Ambassador Rowny was named Special Representative for Arms Control and Disarmament Negotiations at the U.S. Arms Control and Disarmament Agency. From 1981 to 1985, he served in Geneva as chief negotiator and head of the first U.S. delegation for strategic arms reduction negotiations. From 1941 to 1979, he served in the U.S. Army, retiring with the rank of lieutenant general. He commanded units from platoon through corps, serving in Africa and Italy in World War II; in Korea,

1950 to 1952; and in Vietnam, 1962 to 1963. In 1971 he was assigned to Brussels as the Deputy Chairman of the NATO Military Committee, where he set up the mutual balanced force reduction (MBFR) negotiations. From 1973 to 1979, General Rowny was the Joint Chiefs of Staff representative to the Strategic Arms Limitation Talks (SALT) in Geneva.

Ambassador Rowny graduated from Johns Hopkins University (B.S., 1937); the U.S. Military Academy, second lieutenant, Corps of Engineers, 1941; Yale University (M.A. and M.S., 1949); and American University (Ph.D., 1977). From 1980 to 1981, he was a fellow at the Woodrow Wilson Center of the Smithsonian Institution. He was born April 3, 1917, in Baltimore, MD.

Remarks at the Presentation Ceremony for the Drug-Free Schools Awards
June 19, 1989

Thank you, Secretary Cavazos. Mr. Vice President, students, parents, teachers, and friends: Welcome to the White House, the steamy Rose Garden. [*Laughter*] We're delighted you're here. I thought long and hard about what to say today, how to talk about the importance of drug education and prevention, and of how we can save our schools and our children from drugs. And then I read the judges' reports about this year's Drug-Free Schools Award winners, and these reports were simply incredible. So, today I'd like to just tell some American stories, stories about drug-free schools and, really, some American heroes.

Let's start with Spingarn High School, right here in Washington, DC. Spingarn is in one of Washington's worst drug areas—a tough area—and one teacher said: "Five years ago, teachers were afraid to go out in the hall between classes. There's no fear here now." One man, a teacher named Frank Parks, saw the drug dealers in the hallways, the expensive clothes; he smelled the marijuana in the bathrooms and the locker rooms. So, he started Operation SAND—Student Activities, Not Drugs—and recruited popular athletes as peer counselors. And he set up these "rap rooms" for kids to confidentially talk about the drug problems. And he founded a program that worked; he found answers. And he's here today, and despite the fact that his office was bombed a year ago. And I'm told he and his wife are available 24 hours a day for the kids, as they have been for years. And I hope that the students will be lucky enough to have him for years to come. Mr. Parks, thank you, and congratulations.

And next, let me tell you about St. John the Baptist School in Brooklyn, New York. Here's what one of the judges who visited the school wrote: "This school is a total drug-free oasis in a sea of crack dealers. This crusade to be a beacon of hope in a neighborhood of burned-out buildings and frequent killings is taken with serious risk. The school is almost the last liferaft available to families whose neighborhood peace and quiet has been overturned by the violence of alcohol and drugs. And if this school is not a model of a drug-free school, then no such model exists."

But keeping their school drug free was not enough for the St. John's students. They've asked Mayor Koch to deliver the neighborhood a drug-free community—to declare it a drug-free community, telling him about the crack houses and of the horror and despair they see during breaks. Drug dealers recently broke into the office of Sister Mary Jane Raeihle, the principal, ransacking it, breaking into the safe where the school's money is kept. But they left the money on her desk as a warning, as a message to the school to stop its activities, but St. John's has not stopped. And just last week, during graduation practice, the brave nuns stood between the drug dealers and the children to protect them as they marched to the church. Sister Raeihle says: "We're very proud of the children. Even the little ones know what it's all about, which is a shame. We have good will and kids with a lot of hope. It's so hard for them, and they have so much hope." God bless you, Sister, and God bless the children.

Roosevelt Vocational School, from Lake Wales, Florida—local police say this school is "sitting in the middle of a drug supermarket." The students there are "high-risk" for drug use, many with difficult disabilities. And yet some ride 2 and 3 hours to get to Roosevelt. Let me tell you why: Less than 10 years ago, only 10 percent of Roosevelt's graduates got and held jobs. But students soon realized that in order to get the jobs they'd been trained for, they had to be drug free. So, they looked to the Kennedy Space Center which you can see from the school windows, and adopted the motto, "Aiming for the Highest." And they kicked drugs out of the school, stopped feeling sorry for themselves, turned their attention to others who needed help, adopting a local family whose father has Lou Gehrig's disease and raising thousands of dollars to help them make ends meet—and now 75 percent of the students are employed after graduation. And they aimed for the highest and made it, and they're here today, too.

In fact, I heard a story about the principal, Harold Maready, who made a bet with the students during Red Ribbon Week, when students who are drug free wear red ribbons and clothes. He bet them that if at least half the school wore red—that is, were drug free—he'd paint his bald head with the words "Just Say No." Well, 225 out of 295 showed up in red—[*laughter*]—and guess what happened? I wore this red ribbon today and this red tie because I think Mr. Maready had a great idea, and I'm looking for Marlin Fitzwater [the President's Press Secretary] here somewhere. [*Laughter*]

Finally, a story from out West—Live Oak, California, is a small town that started as a railroad stop serving ranchers. The residents fill only five pages of the phone book—one traffic light; no hospital; no jail—just a drugstore, a few restaurants, a post office. A quiet, small town? No, not at all. Drugs arrived over the border, brought by transient workers. This county is now one of California's major producers of methamphetamines and a major contact area for drugs arriving from Mexico. The drugs got into the school and things went downhill fast. And during the last 4 years, however, this school developed a drug-free education program that is gradually influencing the face of the entire community. Students, parents, business leaders, and teachers came together and changed it from what we used to call the three R's to the four R's: respect, responsibility, recognition, and recreation.

And what made the difference was a temporary principal, Mrs. Paulla McIntire, assigned to the school for 4 months in 1985. Temporary—she's still there. [*Laughter*] And one judge called her "the visionary dynamo behind the progress" at one of the most overwhelmed and understaffed schools around. She and a teacher, Michael Dahl, beat the odds by "vision, no-nonsense leadership, compassion, and professional expertise." Mrs. McIntire and Mr. Dahl, thank you for making the trip today, all this way, and thank you for a job so well done.

As I look around here today, I see some of the top commandos in the war on drugs: our teachers, principals, community leaders, parents, and students. You're the ones winning this war because you are the ones looking to tomorrow. You're the ones who know that it takes a clear mind to get a good education and lead a productive life. You understand that students have a right to learn in drug-free schools. And I know that school's out for the summer, but there's one last lesson all America can learn from the courage and commitment and, yes, the downright stubbornness of each of these heroes here today who never gave up: Every school in this country can win; every school in this country can be safe and drug free. Thank you, and God bless you all, and congratulations!

And now I'd like to welcome the students that are here from each school and join the Vice President and Secretary Cavazos in presenting these awards, or at least shaking hands before you get to the main event—the award from our great Secretary of Education. Thank you very much.

Note: The President spoke at 10:04 a.m. in the Rose Garden at the White House.

Message to the Senate Transmitting the United Nations Convention Against Illicit Traffic in Narcotic Drugs and Psychotropic Substances
June 19, 1989

To the Senate of the United States:

With a view to receiving the advice and consent of the Senate to ratification, I transmit herewith the United Nations Convention Against Illicit Traffic in Narcotic Drugs and Psychotropic Substances, done at Vienna on December 20, 1988. I also transmit, for the information of the Senate, the report of the Department of State with respect to the Convention.

The production, trafficking, and consumption of illicit narcotics have become a worldwide menace of unprecedented proportions. Narcotics trafficking and abuse threaten the developing and industrialized nations alike, eroding fragile economies, endangering democratic institutions, and affecting the health and well-being of people everywhere. The profits made from the international drug trade are consolidated in the hands of powerful drug lords who operate with impunity outside the law. The widespread corruption, violence, and human destruction associated with the drug problem imperil all nations and can only be suppressed if all nations cooperate effectively in bringing to justice those who engage in illicit trafficking and abuse.

Patterned after many existing U.S. laws and procedures, the present Convention represents a significant step forward in international efforts to control the illicit traffic in narcotic drugs and psychotropic substances. The Convention obligates states party to the agreement to cooperate in suppressing illicit traffic and to take specific law enforcement measures and enact domestic laws, including those relating to money laundering, confiscation of assets, extradition, mutual legal assistance, and trade in chemicals, materials, and equipment used in the illegal manufacture of controlled substances. These and other provisions seek to establish a comprehensive set of laws and guidelines for a concerted and more effective effort on an international basis to combat illicit trafficking.

Having taken 4 years to complete, work on the Convention began in 1984 under United Nations auspices, and it was adopted at an international conference held in Vienna in November and December 1988. The United States and 43 other nations signed the Convention at that time, and 16 others have signed since then. The Vienna Convention is a tribute to the United Nations and represents the broadest and most far-reaching set of laws and agreements ever adopted in this field. It is strongly indicative of the political will of the states that adopted it and puts those who profit from this evil trade on notice that it will no longer be tolerated. It is clear the Convention has enthusiastic support in the international community, and it is expected that all states will unreservedly endorse this major step to unify and internationalize the fight against drugs and to generate universal action.

I recommend, therefore, that the Senate give early and favorable consideration to this Convention and give its advice and consent to ratification.

GEORGE BUSH

The White House,
June 19, 1989.

Statement on the Resumption of the Soviet-United States Nuclear and Space Arms Negotiations
June 19, 1989

Today marks the opening of round XI of the nuclear and space talks in Geneva. Ambassador Richard Burt, the chief negotiator to the strategic arms reduction talks, heads the U.S. delegation. Ambassador Henry Cooper is our chief negotiator to the defense and space talks. My objective for these negotiations is to achieve verifiable agreements that improve our security while enhancing stability and reducing the risk of war. In the strategic arms reduction talks, our emphasis will be on creating a more stable nuclear balance and strengthening deterrence by reducing and constraining those strategic nuclear forces which pose the greatest threat to security and stability. We will pursue complementary goals in the defense and space talks, seeking an agreement on a cooperative transition to a more stable nuclear balance that relies increasingly on defenses.

After extensive deliberations with my advisers, I have approved instructions for the U.S. START delegation. These instructions reaffirm much of the treaty text negotiated with the Soviets by the previous administration. Modifications will be proposed in some cases. The United States will be prepared to address all the issues on which the two sides have not reached agreement, as the negotiations proceed. In addition, I have reserved the right to introduce new initiatives aimed at further enhancing security and strategic stability.

Of all the outstanding START issues, verification may be the most complex. It will be especially critical in determining whether START enhances U.S. security and strategic stability. As part of our overall negotiating effort, as the talks resume in Geneva, the United States will also propose that the two sides make a special effort to agree on, and to begin implementing as soon as possible, certain verification and stability measures drawn from proposals that both sides have already advanced in START or other contexts. These measures will enhance verification of a START treaty and contribute to strategic stability. Early agreement and implementation of them will speed resolution of outstanding issues and give added momentum to the efforts of our two countries to conclude expeditiously a START agreement.

Our approach to these arms negotiations and to our force modernization programs are complementary and mutually reinforcing. Maintaining credible and effective nuclear deterrent forces is essential both to our security and to our ability to negotiate sound and stabilizing agreements. A successful START treaty will reduce the risk of war, but will not diminish our need to rely on modernized, effective strategic forces for continued deterrence. Indeed, our security would be reduced rather than enhanced if we do not modernize our forces while the Soviets continue to modernize theirs. We must continue to pursue both our force modernization and arms control and not make the mistake of treating one as a substitute for the other.

Our negotiators return to the bargaining table with my firm pledge that we will work vigorously to achieve fair and far-reaching agreements that strengthen peace. Nothing has higher priority. I am heartened by the growing evidence that the Soviet Union is prepared to negotiate seriously about agreements that promise to reduce the risk of war. Much has already been accomplished in the negotiations; much remains to be done. Our commitment is unwavering. We must build on our achievements thus far to reach agreements that fulfill our objectives of reducing the risk of war and enhancing security and stability.

Remarks at the Cheltenham High School Commencement Ceremony in Wyncote, Pennsylvania

June 19, 1989

Thank you, Hang Nguyen, for that introduction and that welcome to this wonderful school. And thank you all for that very generous reception. Mr. Secretary, Dr. Stefanski, Mr. Rodgers, Mr. Bell, members of the board, faculty and administrators, parents—grateful parents—students, I am delighted to be here. And, Jeffrey, I can see why they elected you president. You did a first-class job there representing your class in that word of welcome. Thank you very much. And I'm delighted we have so many distinguished guests. But I want to single out one: my friend of longstanding, the Congressman from this district, Congressman Larry Coughlin, your own, who came here with us tonight from Washington. Larry—delighted he's here.

Last night, under the able leadership, you might say, of John Denver, at the White House—we have a program that goes on four times a year, and it's called "In Performance at the White House," where they had some musical talent. And you'll see what we saw last night live—you'll see it, I think, on July 5th on PBS [Public Broadcasting Service]. But I think they could all take a lesson from the vocal ensemble over here who did a—whoops, they're gone, but they were great.

And so, I'm here from Washington—a privilege to be at the magnificent success that is Cheltenham High School and to say, paraphrasing Mark Twain, that reports of your reputation have not "been greatly exaggerated." You know, as Marine One flies, it's about 120 miles from Washington to Philadelphia. And on the way up here, Secretary Cavazos, my friend and that ardent champion of American education, detailed for me your superb record of achievement in social services and music and the academics and the humanities. And now that I've seen you—a little bit of you—up close and personal, I can say that Mr. Trimble is right: Cheltenham, "you are beautiful."

And I am enjoying my first visit here, and I want you to enjoy today. And it's hot in here! [*Laughter*] And I promise I'll be relatively brief. After all, you've worked and studied and struggled for 4 years, and now comes the hard part: listening to a commencement address.

I'll never forget at Yale University, a graduation speaker, a minister, got up at my old college and said, "And now I will give your commencement address." And he picked Yale—Y is for youth—went on about 25 minutes on youth. [*Laughter*] A is for altruism—took about 18. L is for loyalty—37 minutes on loyalty. [*Laughter*] And of course, E for excellence—finished in 17 minutes. And when he finished, there was one person left praying. [*Laughter*] And he said, "How lovely that you're praying. Were you giving thanks for my words?" He said, "No, I'm just thanking God that you didn't speak at my high school graduation at Cheltenham High School." [*Laughter*]

Let me assure you, I do remember how it feels. For it seems like only yesterday that I, too, was listening to a commencement speech at my graduation. Believe me, I wish it were only yesterday, but nevertheless, in school I loved history and English and major league baseball—not necessarily in that order. But most of all, I loved the possibilities and horizons of the rainbow called tomorrow, a rainbow that, here at this magnificent school, you color blue and gold. And today I'd like to talk about your possibilities as individuals and our horizons as a great nation. I do so believing that you can enrich the world, charitably and courageously, through your choices and your deeds and through a few things that I've learned that I would like to share with you—things about America, things about her people.

And I've learned, for instance, that we are not black and white, rural and urban, the privileged and the poor. We are—as Dr. Stefanski said—we are Americans. And I've learned that any definition of a successful life insists that we help those for whom the American dream seems like an impossible dream. And I have learned that for different generations this help may take different forms, for conditions vary, challenges change. And yet what does not, must not, change is our capacity—responsibility—to assist society at large.

Two centuries ago, for instance, our forefathers banded together to secure independence. Their challenge was to found the Colonies and then push back the wilderness. And 90 years later, the challenge for many of your great-great-great-grandfathers was to preserve the Republic so that, united, we stood. A later generation helped pull us out of the Depression, and still another placed a man on the Moon. And at times, we've been ragged in goods, but we've always been rich in spirit. Even in 1933, with 25 percent of America's work force out of work, President Franklin D. Roosevelt could say, surveying the Republic: "Our troubles concern, thank God, only material things."

FDR knew then, as we know now, that life is measured not by what's in our bank account but by holding ourselves to account for the well-being of our community. And this belief is as timeless as the spirit of 1776. It embodies what President Eisenhower meant when he said: "We must be willing, individually and as a nation, to accept what sacrifices may be required of us."

As Americans, we've made those sacrifices—eagerly, selflessly—for over 200 years. Think of Bunker Hill and Bastogne, where we upheld the tenets of democracy, or the Marshall plan, where we rebuilt postwar Europe, or groups like the Peace Corps, the Salvation Army, or UNICEF.

You know, a student told me a while ago that high school is a great place to learn about personal risktaking. I asked him,"How do you figure?" And he said, "Have you ever tasted cafeteria food?" [*Laughter*]

Well, my friends, I ask you today to take a risk for a cause larger than ourselves. It's the cause of Clara Barton and the Red Cross; Raoul Wallenberg, who helped refugees escape oppression; Mary McLeod Bethune, who made higher learning a bequest. It's the cause of helping others and, thereby, helping America. It's the cause of democratic ideals.

Abroad, this cause insists that we help, by word and by deed, the young people who demand such rights as assembly, religion, press, free speech—the rights our ancestors secured for us and that we too often take for granted in this country. Look to the Soviet Union, where brave people press for religious, intellectual, and political liberty. Look to Poland, where Solidarity's long struggle has borne fruit in the results of free elections. The free election process in Poland makes me count my blessings for the free election process that we take for granted right here in the United States. And, yes, look to China, where students have demanded freedom—a demand that will not, and must not, be stilled.

Who will ever forget the picture of that young Chinese, solitary and vulnerable, facing down an entire column of tanks? That vivid, unforgettable image illustrates how precious is the freedom that underlies everything that we stand for. We don't have to stand in front of tanks in America, thank God, but we do have to summon the same courage to confront the evil that exists in the world. We have to stand in front of the forces of cruelty and violence, and confront the dark powers of poverty and despair. We have to summon the courage to face down the scourge of drugs that stalks and harms our young people. And fortunately, we Americans have an advantage. We have a heritage of bravery, of faith in God, of liberty and human dignity, and the Golden Rule: Do unto others as you would have them do unto you.

In recent weeks, at college commencement speeches, I've spoken of these values and called for the right of peoples everywhere for free expression. Well, those values also guide our challenge at home not merely to ensure free expression—for the most part, that war has already been won—rather to win the struggle not yet decided: the fight for justice, equality, and hope. To win that fight will require you and you and you and others enlisting in our crusade. And it will demand the little-noted deeds that make headlines not in the national magazines but in the local weekly, deeds that once moved Lafayette, in his early twenties, when he led Washington's troops at Yorktown, to write of America: "What most charms me is that all the citizens are brethren."

And we term these deeds voluntarism, or community service, and they're central to our fabric as a nation and as a people. And, no, they aren't as dramatic as the profiles in courage of Warsaw or the gulags or of Tiananmen Square, but they reflect the same sense of sacrifice and of concern—concern for country, decency, and our fellow man. This concern uplifts voluntarism groups and individuals, groups like the Youth at Risk Program; the Boy Scouts; and your United Way Youth Council chapter; individuals like

Anneke Cooper, who assists a neighborhood nursing home; or Keithe Damsker, translating materials into Korean for the American Cancer Society; or two Jennifers, Payes and Lowe, who serve at Moss Rehabilitation Center and Holy Redeemer Hospital.

And the thing is, at Cheltenham that's just a partial reading. The list is endless; their deeds go on. And another thing: Across America we need to expand this roll of volunteers, for they can combat—nationally, as you are doing locally—issues like hunger and health care, drug abuse and homelessness. To achieve that aim, our administration recently created the Office of National Service. And this week we're going to take another step. For by announcing our administration's new YES, or YES to America initiative—Youth Entering Service—we will refute those who speak of the "me generation." Instead, this program can build a cathedral of the spirit and help yours become a global "we generation."

Let me tell you a story about that generation and its spirit. One day a man stepped aboard a train. And as he did, a shoe slipped off and landed on the track. Unable to retrieve it as the train was moving, the man calmly took off his other shoe and threw it back along the track in the direction of the first one, and his fellow passengers were amazed. Smiling, Mahatma Gandhi explained his action: "The poor man who finds the shoe lying on the track will now have a pair that he can use." Gandhi knew, as we must, that the "we generation" rejects a new gilded age of mindless self-gratification. But only we—not me—only we can define a successful life both for the individual and the Nation.

Remember those beliefs and treasure them. And remember, too, two signs which I'm told are posted right here in this gym. One suggests that "Success is a journey, not a destination," often perilous, even cruel, but possessed of the challenges and values linking the students of this high school with the students of the world. And the other sign reads, "If a man never fails, it may be because he never tries." My friends, some of you may try for President. I hope you do—great; but whatever, do something truly inspiring. Become a doctor, like your alumnus, Michael Brown; become a teacher, like Lew Shaten, retiring tomorrow after 32 years, committed to broadening the minds of thousands of young people; an artist, like Edward Hergelroth, who has painted my own house up in Kennebunkport; or writers, like Levinson and Link.

Whatever you decide, whatever, you will act not for yourselves alone but for a larger community, whether in Cheltenham or China. And in that spirit, let me close with another story, a story about the most famous Pennsylvanian of them all. Two hundred and two years ago, Benjamin Franklin looked at the President's chair on the last day of the Constitutional Convention, and addressing a friend, he made a confession. Often, Franklin admitted, he'd wondered during Philadelphia's long, hot summer whether the Sun painted on the chair—remember—was rising or setting. But at last he said he had the pleasure to know that it was a rising, not a setting, Sun.

For America, for this high school, for you as individuals, our Sun is rising too. In coming years, expand America's possibilities; enlarge her horizons as a people. Say yes to liberty and to the dignity of man. And as you do, remember that your inheritance is the future—guard it, cherish it. And together, let us shape tomorrow in the image of our dreams, not merely for this generation but for the generations to come.

Good luck to each and every one of you graduating here this evening. My most heartfelt congratulations. And God bless you, and God bless your parents, and God bless this wonderful school, and God bless the United States of America.

Note: The President spoke at 7:07 p.m. in the school gymnasium. In his remarks, he referred to Hang Nguyen, an honors student; Secretary of Education Lauro F. Cavazos; Charles F. Stefanski and James Bell, superintendent of schools and president of the Cheltenham Township School District, respectively; Joseph W. Rodgers, principal of the school; Jeffrey Schwarzschild, president of the graduating class; and Robert Trimble, teacher and director of external education at the school. Following his remarks, the President returned to Washington, DC.

Remarks Congratulating the Detroit Pistons on Winning the National Basketball Association Championship
June 20, 1989

Well, I see we have the two Senators from Michigan and much of the congressional delegation here, and we want to welcome Senator Levin and Senator Riegle, Congressmen Schuette, Broomfield, and etcetera, etcetera. And I'm just delighted you all are here. Commissioner Stern, welcome, sir. And then I want to welcome the unsung heroes, the heroines, of the Detroit Pistons, the players' wives; and owner Bill Davidson; and then the—I think they all got in in spite of the weather—D.C. Police Boys and Girls Club. Welcome! Who is with that? Right around here? You guys right here. Great. Right there? That guy? Okay. That's wonderful.

And you may have noticed my special greeting from Bill Laimbeer. He and his wife Chris were with him in October, and he told me back in October that he'd see me at the White House in June. Actually, he was sure he'd be here, not so sure about me. [*Laughter*] But sure enough, there they are.

And to all our guests today, I'm just delighted that you've joined me to congratulate the world champions of basketball, the Detroit Pistons.

You guys won it in style—four straight, four straight over the [Los Angeles] Lakers. And I know you had a special incentive to make it a sweep. Just think of Chuck Daly's dry cleaning bill for a seven game series. [*Laughter*] You know, Chuck's known as the Dick Clark of the NBA, 59 going on 29—[*laughter*]—but don't let those youthful looks fool you. He's waited 35 years for this day, for a coach's dream come true.

And he's got a team loaded with talent and determination. No team goes a full 82 games and into the playoffs without a few injuries along the way, and the Pistons were no exception. The difference is that somehow the Pistons managed to keep all the parts in working order. Isaiah Thomas played hurt—played hard—with a broken hand for the past 2 months. And credit a couple of championship-sized assists to your trainer and team physician, Mike Abdenour and Dr. Benjamin Paolucci.

And someone once said basketball is ballet with a backboard. Whoever it was definitely wasn't under the boards with Laimbeer and Mahorn when a shot goes up there. I would not liken that to Swan Lake—[*laughter*]—but your brand of bump-and-run basketball is a winner.

And I know that your aggressive style has given the Pistons something of a reputation. But Commissioner Stern told us also something else about the work that you do in the Detroit community with the Special Olympics, muscular dystrophy—many other worthy causes. And you may be to some the bad boys of basketball, but off the court, people see the kinder, gentler side of the Detroit Pistons. [*Laughter*]

And now, you can have all the talent in the world, but you can't win it all unless you've got that one special ingredient—nicknames. And the Pistons have some league leaders: the Microwave, Vinnie Johnson—he heats up in a hurry—[*laughter*]—the Spider and Worm, John Salley and Dennis Rodman, a couple of superheroes off the bench. And then there's the guy without the nickname, the most valuable player, Joe Dumars, the pride of Lake Charles, Louisiana. Here's a man who keeps quiet and lets the scoring do the talking. Take game three: 21 points in 12 minutes—sounds more like pinball than basketball. [*Laughter*]

But all of you have accomplished the extraordinary. And some of the best players in the NBA go an entire career without winning that ring. And it takes a team to win—talent, drive, and dedication that goes 12 men deep. And that's the secret of success of any kind, and it's the winning formula. You kids watch and learn from all of that—the winning formula that made the Detroit Pistons the world champs.

Thank you for visiting us. I'm glad you are now out of low orbit around the airfield out here. And once again, congratulations to all of you, to the city of Detroit, and to the State of Michigan. I am delighted that you are here at the White House. Thank you very much for coming.

Note: The President spoke at 11:50 a.m. in Room 450 at the Old Executive Office Building.

Remarks at the Presentation Ceremony for the Presidential Scholars Awards
June 20, 1989

Thank you all, and welcome to the White House. Ronna, you're in charge of keeping the rain off. [*Laughter*] Secretary Cavazos and Ronna Romney and members of the Commission, sponsors, guests, distinguished teachers, and Presidential Scholars: Let me officially welcome you to the White House.

You know, that great English leader, Benjamin Disraeli, once said: "Youth of a nation are the trustees of posterity." And the poet James Lowell was moved to write: "If youth be a defect, it is one we outgrow only too soon." Well, as this year's Presidential Scholars, you remain the trustees of our posterity. And I hope you'll accept some counsel from one who is a little long in the tooth, maybe. If youth is a defect, treasure it as many years as you can.

We meet here on the 25th anniversary of the Presidential Scholars program, and to honor some of the best and the brightest students in American education. This marks the highest scholastic honor that a President can bestow, and I am honored to bestow it. For while already you have done much, I know you will do more, and not for yourselves alone but for nation and neighbor—learning, caring, helping education lead the way.

I believe in education. And so do you, for the evidence is your lives. And you come from backgrounds of every race and creed, and from all 50 States, the District of Columbia, U.S. territories, and families living abroad. And you've excelled in the classroom and outside it, through leadership, character and, yes, community service. You know, as I do, how education can unleash your talents. Take Presidential Scholar Eben Hewitt, of Muncie, Indiana—he started a Shakespeare Club at his high school; or another scholar, Clarity Haynes, of Washington, DC's Ellington School of the Arts—she is fluent in Portuguese and Spanish. I'm a little jealous—some say I'm not even fluent in English.

Education can be the great uplifter—individually, and for America. Perhaps Meath Bowen, a Presidential Scholar from Anchorage, Alaska—I think I see her—put it best: "An educated person," she said, "has choices, alternatives, and can exercise freedom of mind in all areas of life."

Now, I know what you're thinking: It won't be easy. And you're right, there'll be roadblocks along the way. And I'm reminded of how once, marking an examination paper written shortly before Christmas, the noted scholar teaching at Yale, William Lyons Phelps, came across this note: "God only knows the answer to this question. Merry Christmas!" [*Laughter*] Phelps returned the paper with the annotation: "God gets an A. You get an F. Happy New Year!" [*Laughter*]

Roadblocks? Sure, you bet. But you can overcome them, and as you do, remember that an educated person also has duties and responsibilities. I've said that in America the definition of a successful life must include serving others. Well, that goes double for America's best. Many have labored to share their knowledge with you, and you can give them no greater gift than to share your knowledge with others.

In that spirit, a number of people have brought you here, and they deserve our thanks—like Ronna Romney sitting right here, Chairman of the White House Commission on Presidential Scholars, and the Commission sponsors. And let me salute the 47 Commission members, whom I just met with, who chose you, 141 honorees, from America's high school graduates. But most of all, I want to thank, and ask you to thank, all of those people who form the fabric of your life. Today and in the years to come, remember that favorite teacher—the history instructor who was a friend and mentor; the biology teacher who did the impossible—helped you dissect a frog. And remember the guidance counselor who cared or the football coach who gave of his time and of himself as well.

And remember those who love you most and point you toward the stars, what scholar Christine Oh, of Bellville, Georgia, has called "the backbone of my success: my family." My friends, this is your day, but it is also their day. So, let me close with a story your family might appreciate about learning and teaching and scholars of all ages. The story goes that physicist James Franck was professor at Gottingen University in Germany when Robert Oppenheimer, then only 23, was being examined for his doctorate. On emerging from the oral exam, Franck remembered—this is the professor—Franck remembered, "I got out of there just in time. He was beginning to ask me questions." [*Laughter*]

Well, in coming years, you'll ask many questions, questions about your faith and future, problems and priorities, about what we can become, why we are here. Education can provide some answers, and so can the people who believe in it and you—your lifelong local minister, the father who trudged his son to Little League, the mother who toiled night and day so that her daughter could go to college. Trust these people; make them proud. Honor them by the lives you lead. And as you do, remember how their values, which are education's values, can make ours a better, richer, most decent world.

To every Presidential Scholar, Barbara and I and our great Secretary, Larry Cavazos, give you our heartfelt congratulations! And to all of you here, thank you for coming to the White House. God bless you, and God bless our great country. Thank you all very, very much.

Note: The President spoke at 2:37 p.m. in the Rose Garden at the White House. In his remarks, he referred to Secretary of Education Lauro F. Cavazos.

Continuation of Frank G. Wisner as United States Ambassador to Egypt
June 20, 1989

The President today announced that Frank G. Wisner will continue to serve as Ambassador Extraordinary and Plenipotentiary of the United States of America to the Arab Republic of Egypt.

Since 1986 Mr. Wisner has served as Ambassador Extraordinary and Plenipotentiary of the United States of America to the Arab Republic of Egypt. Prior to this he served as Senior Deputy Assistant Secretary for African Affairs, 1982–1986, and Ambassador to Zambia, 1979–1982. He was Deputy Executive Secretary of Southern African Affairs, 1977–1979, and Director of the Office of Southern African Affairs, 1976–1977. Mr. Wisner has served as special assistant to the Under Secretary for Political Affairs, 1975–1976, and special assistant and then Deputy Director for the Interagency Task Force on Indochina Refugee Affairs. In addition he served as the Director of the Office of Plans and Management, Bureau of Public Affairs, 1974; chief of the political section in Dacca, Bangladesh, 1973–1974; and chief of the economic/commercial section at the U.S. Embassy in Tunis, 1971–1973.

Mr. Wisner graduated from Princeton University (B.A., 1961). He served in the Foreign Service from 1961 to 1968. Mr. Wisner was born July 2, 1938, in New York. He is married and has four children.

Nomination of S. Anthony McCann To Be an Assistant Secretary of Veterans Affairs

June 20, 1989

The President today announced his intention to nominate S. Anthony McCann to be an Assistant Secretary of Veterans Affairs (Finance and Planning). This is a new position.

Since 1986 Dr. McCann has been Assistant Secretary of Management and Budget at the Department of Health and Human Services in Washington, DC. Prior to this he was senior health analyst and division leader for the Committee on the Budget of the United States Senate, 1985–1986, and a staff member for the Committee on the Budget of the United States Senate, 1981–1985.

Dr. McCann graduated from Lake Forest College (B.A., 1966) and Syracuse University (M.A., 1969; Ph.D., 1972).

Continuation of Henry E. Hockeimer as an Associate Director of the United States Information Agency

June 20, 1989

The President today announced that Henry E. Hockeimer will continue to serve as an Associate Director of the United States Information Agency (Management).

Since 1988 Mr. Hockeimer has served as an Associate Director of the U.S. Information Agency (Management) in Washington, DC. Prior to this he was Assistant Director of the U.S. Information Agency in Washington, DC, 1987–1988, and Deputy Director of the Television and Film Service for USIA, 1986–1987. He also served as president of Ford Aerospace and Communications Corp., 1975–1985.

Mr. Hockeimer graduated from the RCA Institute (1947) and New York University (1949). He was born April 3, 1920, in Winzig, Germany. He served in the U.S. National Guard, 1947–1949. He is married and has two children.

Nomination of Wade F. Horn To Be Chief of the Children's Bureau

June 20, 1989

The President today announced his intention to nominate Wade F. Horn to be Chief of the Children's Bureau, Department of Health and Human Services. He would succeed Dodie Truman Livingston.

Since 1986 Dr. Horn has served as director of outpatient psychological services in the department of psychiatry for Children's Hospital National Medical Center; vice chairman of the department of psychology for Children's Hospital National Medical Center; and an associate professor of psychiatry and behavioral sciences and of child health and development at George Washington University School of Medicine in Washington, DC. Dr. Horn served in several capacities at Michigan State University, including adjunct faculty member in the department of pediatrics, College of Human Medicine, 1983–1986; director of the pediatric psychology specialty clinic, 1984–1986; associate director for the psychological clinic, 1984–1986; and assistant professor in the department of psychology, 1982–1986.

Dr. Horn graduated from American University (B.A., 1975) and Southern Illinois

University (Ph.D., 1981). He was born December 3, 1954, in Coral Gables, FL. He is married, has two children, and resides in Gaithersburg, MD.

Nomination of Susan M. Coughlin To Be a Member of the National Transportation Safety Board

June 20, 1989

The President today announced his intention to nominate Susan M. Coughlin to be a member of the National Transportation Safety Board for the term expiring December 31, 1993. She would succeed Lemoine V. Dickinson, Jr.

Since 1987 Mrs. Coughlin has been Deputy Administrator of the Federal Railroad Administration at the Department of Transportation in Washington, DC. Prior to this she was Acting Vice President for the Export-Import Bank of the United States, Office of Public Affairs and Publications, 1986–1987, and Deputy Vice President, 1983–1986. She was an officer for intergovernmental relations at the Department of Transportation in the Office of the Secretary, 1981–1983.

Mrs. Coughlin graduated from Moravian College (B.A., 1972).

Statement by Press Secretary Fitzwater on United States Sanctions Against the Chinese Government

June 20, 1989

The President today directed that the U.S. Government suspend participation in all high-level exchanges of government officials with the People's Republic of China, in addition to the suspension of military exchanges previously announced. This action is being taken in response to the wave of violence and reprisals by the Chinese authorities against those who have called for democracy. The United States has supported the legitimate democratic aspirations for freedom of peoples throughout the world. The United States will continue to voice its concern and its support for these aspirations.

The United States hopes that the current tragedy in China [can] be brought to a peaceful end and that dialog will replace the atmosphere of suspicion and reprisal. China is an important state with which we hope to continue productive relations.

In addition to the ban on exchanges, the United States will seek to postpone consideration of new international financial institutions' loans to China. The situation in China is of international concern, as witnessed by the variety of voices that have spoken up on the issue. We urge continued international expressions of concern.

Continuation of Stephen M. Duncan as an Assistant Secretary of Defense

June 20, 1989

The President today announced that Stephen M. Duncan will continue to serve as an Assistant Secretary of Defense (Reserve Affairs).

Since 1987 Mr. Duncan has served as Assistant Secretary of Defense for Reserve Affairs. From 1973 to 1987, he was engaged in the private practice of law in Denver, CO, most recently as a partner in the firm of Hopper, Kanouff, Smith, Peryam, Terry and Duncan. He also served as an assistant U.S. attorney, 1972–1973, and as assistant professor of naval science at Dartmouth College, 1967.

Mr. Duncan graduated from the U.S. Naval Academy (B.S., 1963), Dartmouth College (M.A., 1969), and the University of Colorado (J.D., 1971). He was born March 28, 1941, in Oklahoma City, OK. He is married and has two daughters.

Continuation of Robert W. Page, Sr., as an Assistant Secretary of the Army

June 20, 1989

The President today announced that Robert W. Page, Sr., will continue to serve as an Assistant Secretary of the Army (Civil Works).

Since 1987 Mr. Page has served as Assistant Secretary of the Army for Civil Works in Washington, DC. Prior to this, he served in several capacities with Kellogg Rust, Inc., including chairman and chief executive officer, 1982–1987; president and chief executive officer with M.W. Kellogg Co., 1981–1983; and president and chief executive officer for Kellogg Rust, Inc., 1983–1984. From 1976 to 1981, he was president and chief executive officer with the Rust Engineering Co. He was president and chief executive officer for George A. Fuller Co., 1972–1976, and vice president of construction for Rockefeller Family and Associates, 1967–1972. He was assistant general manager for the Bechtel Corp., 1962–1967, and vice president for the Southeast Drilling Co., 1961–1962.

Mr. Page graduated from Texas A&M University (B.S., 1951). He served in the U.S. Navy in the Pacific theater during World War II. He was born January 22, 1927, in Dallas, TX. He is married and has four children.

Remarks Announcing the Youth Engaged in Service to America Initiative

June 21, 1989

You'd better watch that guy, he might be President someday. [*Laughter*] Well, first let me thank Mike Love and Bruce, the Beach Boys, for being with us and providing this marvelous presence and entertainment—Robert Lamb as well. We're privileged they give of themselves to help others, and I'm just delighted that they're here with us today. I also want to thank Carissa and Dale and Michael and Ron. Thanks for sharing those stories with us, those remarkable stories.

You know, this is a wonderful sight. The guy I was sitting next to up here said, "There's a lot of people here." And he's right—a lot of people, but your problems and possibilities are as diverse as the Nation itself. But all of you share a precious inheritance because, as I see it, you are the future of America. But to understand the future, sometimes we need to look to the past. So think back for a moment with me to a small town tradition that America must never forget, a simpler time: a time when if there was trouble or a neighbor needed help every town had a way to send that message out to all the townspeople. Someone raced to the top of the townhall or the church steeple and rang a bell, and when people heard that bell, they didn't stop to ask why it was ringing, they just came—horseback or foot, by buggy or bicycle, honking the horn of a Model T—they just came. Whatever the problem, whoever was in need of help, they were ready to help.

And I've asked you here today, invited you to this marvelous White House lawn, because I need your help, because America needs your help. And the bells have been silent too long; so, let them ring in your hearts and across the land. And I know you're ready, whatever the problem, whoever is in need. We need you now.

And I know that Presidents have called on the young people of this country before. In time of war, our young have rushed to answer the call, to fight and die for our freedoms, if necessary. Today we're fortunate. We live in a time of peace, a time of great and growing prosperity. And there's no need for that kind of call to arms, but it is time for a call to action. It's a time of need for millions of Americans. The storm clouds of war fortunately are not on the horizon, but you and I know that the storm clouds of a different kind are gathering.

A simple fact in America today is that too many people are free-falling through society with no prospect of landing on their feet. No one—young, old, white, brown or black—should be permitted to go through life unclaimed. You must show us how to reclaim these lives. We need you. And so, today I call on you to commit yourselves—listen to the bells—make it your mission to make a difference in somebody else's life.

And I don't have to tell you that youth gets blamed—its share, and more—for society's problems. Pick up the newspaper, turn on the television, and there's another story about youth gone wrong. You don't hear often enough about the good that you can do, the good that you already are doing. And I know better, and you know better. Your commitment can convince yourselves and your nation that you're not the problem; you are the solution.

Take a look at what's happening today, what's happening to kids like you. One-third of all victims of violent crime haven't reached their 20th birthday—one-third. The three leading causes of death for teenagers are accidents—many involving drugs or alcohol—suicide, and murder. On a tragically typical day, almost 1,700 high school students drop out, over 4,000 teenagers run away from home, 2,700 become pregnant, over a dozen will take their own lives. And these aren't simply cold statistics; some of them are kids in your school, kids who live on your street. Some of them are your friends. And some of them may be about you right here today.

You heard Michael Johnson and his Big Brother, Dale. You heard Carissa and Ron. You heard their message, how much it means to know that someone cares, and how much it means to care for someone else. And you can carry that message across this country, from the inner city out to farm country and every community in between. You can let the phrase "one-to-one" symbolize all America's commitment to each other. And regardless of the life that you are living, there is something special about each and every one of you. And your gifts are all different, but you each have a gift that America needs, and I'm asking you to give that gift now.

You know, I've talked to hundreds of kids over the years, and my own kids growing up. And I've asked them: What is it you're looking for? What is it that you want to be? What is it that you want from life? And so many times I hear the same answer. It isn't money—it's how you look, what kind of car you drive. You've all thought about it. You know that's not what it's all about. When it comes right down to it, what you want, what all of us want out of life, are two things: meaning and adventure. Meaning: a sense of purpose in life, to be a part of something that counts, something that matters. And adventure—excitement—matters, too. There are lots of ways to find adventure. Some are self-destructive, and some bring a sense of self-enrichment and satisfaction beyond belief. The choice is up to all of you. And I'm telling you today, you can find what you're looking for in helping others. If you walk this path with me, I can promise you a life full of meaning and adventure.

And that's why I've asked you all here. You represent millions like you, all across this country. That's why I'm asking you to be a part of an initiative that Mike mentioned, called Youth Engaged in Service to America, YES to America. I'm not talking about another government program. Another bureaucracy is the last thing we need—believe me, I understand that. Youth Engaged in Service is a movement, a way of looking at life. And tomorrow I'm going up to New York to announce a nationwide initiative for national service, to encourage volunteers of all ages, all backgrounds, all abilities. But today let me tell you what YES is all about and what it's for, who it's for.

It's for young people of all ages, 5 to 25. Even the youngest of us have gifts to give. Let me ask you today. Don't worry whether it's a lot or a little; do what you can. Get in the habit of helping others, and that's one habit that you'll never ever break. And all of you have something to offer—kids from tough neighborhoods, kids from broken homes, kids who have grown up on food stamps and hand-me-downs—and maybe you think you've got nothing anyone wants. You're wrong. The gifts I'm talking about are more precious: your energy and experience, your time and talents—gifts that come right here, from the heart. And if you've got the will to help, you really have all that you need.

So, first, YES is voluntary, truly voluntary. You don't need to be bribed with incentives and threatened with penalties to get engaged in community service. And that's not what the idea of service is all about anyway—service is its own reward, satisfaction guaranteed. Didn't you feel it when those kids were talking to us a few minutes ago?

And second, serving others shouldn't be a detour on your career path. It's not something you do when you're young and then outgrow when you're a little bit older. It's a way of life, something you start when you're young and stick with it, all life long.

And third, YES means getting involved where you know you can make a difference in your own community. I want service organizations in the cities and towns where you live to open their doors, to make room for people your age to contribute.

And some of you may be saying, "Oh, I know it, I can hear it. Mr. President, I'm ready, I'm willing, I'm able. But what can I do, what should I do?" The fact is, you don't have to go far to find people who need your help. They're right there in your own community. There's an elderly man, facing nothing but empty days and isolation, and he needs you. There's a man who can't read, living behind a locked door of illiteracy—that person needs you. There's a family with no home, no place to sleep—that family needs you. There's a boy or girl less fortunate than you, without family, without a friend, without hope in the future, and they need you. I ask you, what would it be like going through life without one single friend? You can be that friend. There's a woman in a hospital bed, battling hard against her illness—she needs you. Millions of people—people in the cities and towns where you live—just like them—America needs you.

Maybe you've never been asked before. Well, I'm asking you: Say YES to America. Make a commitment: reach out a hand to people in need. Build a better future for yourselves, a better future for America.

So, listen to the sound of those bells, like long ago, ringing in the hearts of Americans across this country—ringing in the inner city, out in farm country, and every community in between. And I ask each of you, all young people in America: Answer the call. From now on, make it your mission to serve others in need.

Thank you. Thank you for coming to the White House. God bless you, and God bless America. Thank you all very, very much.

Note: The President spoke at 11:24 a.m. on the South Lawn at the White House. In his opening remarks, he referred to Ron Brooks, who spoke earlier. He also referred to entertainers Mike Love, Bruce Johnston, and Robert Lamb, and volunteers Carissa Griesinger, Dale Long, and Michael Johnson.

Nomination of John J. Easton, Jr., To Be an Assistant Secretary of Energy
June 21, 1989

The President today announced his intention to nominate John J. Easton, Jr., to be an Assistant Secretary of Energy (International Affairs and Energy Emergencies). He would succeed David B. Waller.

Since 1987 Mr. Easton has been an attorney with Miller, Eggleston and Rosenberg, Ltd., Attorneys at Law, in Burlington, VT. Prior to this he was vice president for SynCronamics, Inc., 1986–1987. He was in the private practice of law in 1985. In 1984 Mr. Easton was the Republican candidate for Governor of Vermont. He was the attorney general for the State of Vermont, 1981–1985; director of the division of rate setting for the agency of human services, 1978–1980; and assistant attorney general for the chief of the consumer protection division, 1975–1978. He was an attorney with Davison and Easton, 1972–1975, and Paterson, Gibson, Noble and Brownell, Attorneys at Law, 1970–1972.

Mr. Easton graduated from the University of Colorado (B.S., 1964) and Georgetown University Law Center (J.D., 1970).

Nomination of Victor Stello, Jr., To Be an Assistant Secretary of Energy
June 21, 1989

The President today announced his intention to nominate Victor Stello, Jr., to be an Assistant Secretary of Energy (Defense Programs). He would succeed Sylvester R. Foley, Jr.

Since 1986 Mr. Stello has been Executive Director for Operations for the Nuclear Regulatory Commission in Washington, DC. He has held several positions with the Nuclear Regulatory Commission, including Deputy Executive Director for Regional Operations and Generic Requirements, 1981–1986; Director of the Office of Inspection and Enforcement, 1979–1981; Director of the Division of Operating Reactors, 1976–1979; Assistant Director for Reactor Safety, 1973–1976; and Chief of the Reactor Systems Branch, 1972–1973.

Mr. Stello received a bachelor of science degree and a master of science degree from Bucknell University. In 1988 he was awarded the Distinguished Rank Award.

Remarks to Members of the Family Motor Coach Association in Richmond, Virginia
June 21, 1989

Thank you all very much. I'd like full credit for having cleared it up here. [*Laughter*] Thank you very, very much for that warm welcome. And Richard, thank you and Karen for your hospitality and for inviting us to come here today. I want to pay my respects to Senator Warner, an outstanding Member of the United States Senate, who you welcomed a minute ago, and my dear friend, the Congressman from this area, Tom Bliley. We've got two good ones with us here today.

You know, at the White House I hear a lot about technological achievements. Scientists tell me about our latest advances in electronics and computers and biogenetics. And that's all very interesting, but I still can't get over the fact that here in America we have houses that can do 55 miles an hour into a headwind. [*Laughter*]

You may remember in "The Wizard of Oz" how Auntie Em's house got lifted up and carried off by a tornado—America's first airborne RV. But she had the advantage of a tailwind. Your mileage may vary. [*Laughter*]

It is wonderful to be visiting with such an outstanding group of Americans on the move. And I might say, I'm very pleased to see Derrick Crandall here, who has been a good friend of mine and who has shown me the wonders of some of our most beautiful parks, borrowing, I am sure, the vehicles to house us from some of you sitting right here. But nevertheless, welcome and thank you, sir, for your leadership in this marvelous recreational outdoors usage.

When this organization was founded by a handful of families in 1963, no one could have predicted that 26 years later you'd be 65,000 strong and still growing. But you're an example of a longstanding tradition in this country, and that began 150 years ago, when Americans set out to explore the lands west of the Mississippi River. And today you continually rediscover the miracle of America's abundance through the romance of the road. And every morning, when a convoy picks up and takes off, you give a happy new meaning to the phrase, "There goes the neighborhood." [*Laughter*]

You've come to know the America that most of us only hear about now and then. You've traded in real estate for wheel estates, traveled to and through towns with names like Dime Box, Texas; Scratch Ankle, Alabama; Truth Or Consequences, New Mexico; Gnawbone, Indiana—and one of my favorites—Nameless, Tennessee. [*Laughter*]

And whether you escape for weekends or migrate for months at a time, all of you have found and fostered a special fellowship in the camaraderie of the road. And I saw it tonight, just as we drove into this park—people out there in front of their homes giving us a friendly welcome, standing neighbor to neighbor.

You know, as those miles roll out beneath you, it seems that your ideals, traditional American ideals, become ever more firmly rooted. And they're the ideals of freedom, self-reliance, the love of nature and of this nation, and above all, the nurturing of family values. Today these fundamental American values must be reaffirmed. We're at a point in our history when there can be no standing still. We must either move forward or risk sliding backward.

And it's time to renew our commitments, both to nature and to our fellow man. The American spirit of exploration must be joined with the new sense of restoration. And the natural world that supports us and the society that sustains us both need our help. The natural beauty that you and I enjoy today is a sacred trust. So, we must do more than simply limit the damage that we've already done. We must work to preserve and restore the integrity and richness of this continent's natural splendor.

You never feel that more fully than when you see the great outdoors through the eyes of a child or of a grandchild. And I had the pleasure of seeing it once again in Lake Jackson through the eyes of our 13-year-old grandson just the other day. Barbara and I had been with him a year or two ago in the same spot. And that's one reason that I believe it's time to renew the environmental ethic in America.

Henry David Thoreau's ideal was that if you borrow an axe, you should return it sharper than when you got it. And President Eisenhower probably had that in mind when he decided to buy some farmland with rundown soil near Gettysburg to let nature's restoration take its course. And he lived to see his experiment working. "There are enough lush fields," he said, "to assure me that I shall leave the place better than I found it." And that must be every American's goal.

And that's why we need to do more for our national parks. The idea of a "national" park is an American original that the rest of the world has come to admire and to imitate, because those parks are wide open, for everybody to enjoy. And it was once said that "The national parks are America's unique contribution to the democratic ideal." And it's true: Our parks are our most open institutions—80 million acres of the most spectacular terrain on the planet, open to the wind, the sky, and the stars—and open to every traveler with the sense and spirit to stay a moment and appreciate nature's beauty.

We need to make that kind of experience available to even more Americans, in more parts of America. So, I've proposed to Congress an increase of nearly $200 million a year for recreational land acquisitions in 27 States through the National Park Service and Fish and Wildlife Service and BLM—the Bureau of Land Management—and the Forest Service. And these funds will go for everything from "Parks for People" in urban areas to valuable habitats as close by as the James River and the Eastern Shore here in Virginia. Some of the other acquisitions range all the way out to Big Hole River in Montana, the Bizz Johnston Trail in California, Pelican Island in Florida, Mount Baker in Washington. And many of you will see those places. Take a few pictures for me, if you will—they don't let me out enough. [*Laughter*]

But I want to preserve our scenic byways, those picturesque roads that offer powerful views of the Nation's natural splendor. These are the roads that Americans love, and such scenic roads can and should be designated for the enjoyment and the convenience of travelers. And we've already designated 43 national forest scenic byways in 25 States. And the Chief of the Forest Service expects to set aside many more. By the end of this week, the Bureau of Land Management expects to identify about 25 new back-country byways nationwide, and we will do more.

As I look around this crowd, I recognize the profile of some that might fit the description of hunters. I'm one—hunted and enjoyed the outdoors all my life, and I'm interested in the wetlands. And to protect our wetlands, we've set up a Federal task force to deliver on my pledge of no net loss of wetlands, no net loss of these precious habitats. And we've asked for nearly $200 million in new funding for acquisitions under the Land and Water Conservation Fund. And I'm looking to Congress to provide a comprehensive wetlands bill that I can sign this year.

Ten days ago, I outlined badly needed reforms to the Clean Air Act. And if Congress will pass that legislation, the degradation to our lakes and streams caused by acid rain, and the damage to our forests caused by windblown urban ozone will stop by the end of this century. All categories of airborne industrial toxic chemicals will be cut by three-quarters by the end of this century. And 20 years from now, every American, in every city in America, will breathe clean air, and that should be a national goal.

And it's good to hear that so many of you are reaffirming the ethic of conservation by getting involved in the Take Pride in America program, promoting the careful stewardship of our public lands and resources. I know that Barbara is delighted to be chairing a panel of judges for that program. And we need to get the word out that our national parks and other Federal land management agencies depend on volunteers. This is just the kind of voluntary local effort that it will take to bring us into a better partnership with nature.

Many of you are already involved with voluntary environmental efforts, so let me pay my respects to a great group of rambling recyclers out there, the San Diego Can Crushers—let's hear it for the San Diego Can Crushers. [*Applause*] Now, we can do better than that. [*Applause*]

But I mentioned a second commitment a few minutes ago—to our fellow man. We must take that commitment to heart as well. For even as we work to restore nature to its balance, we must also restore the fabric of our society, reweaving the threads of lives torn by poverty and despair and alienation. And that means renewing our neighborhoods; restoring shelter to those who have lost it; providing the power of literacy to those who lack it; and offering support and an example to children who need it; and lending a hand to the vulnerable, the infirm, the forgotten.

Many of you have already put your belief in the value of shared strength and strong family life—put it to work, reaching out to help the homeless through the Better Homes Foundation with transitional housing, day care, medical care, counseling, and job training. And out there I know today that there are members of Achievers International, who do outstanding work with the disabled. And other FMCA members have joined forces with the Literacy Volunteers of America—one of Barbara's very special programs that she does so much to help with—that program in a "Roundup of Literacy" campaign is getting your help, provides tutoring through 350 community programs in 38 States. And I'm told that in the past 2 years alone the numbers of students and volunteers grew by 47 percent. One former student said, "I see the world in a totally new way." And another said, "I feel as though a light has been turned on in my life." As good as that student felt, imagine what it felt like for the tutor—there is no greater feeling than to have someone depending on you and to live up to their expectations.

Your involvement makes you part of a constellation of concerned citizens committed to building a better America, both in her natural beauty and in the qualities of her citizens. And so, let me add my voice to those thanking you, and let me encourage you to do even more. It won't be easy, but it will be worth it.

And many of you have probably read the book about life on the road called "Blue Highways." It's written by a man who travels all over America, avoiding the interstates, deliberately taking the older, smaller roads—the blue ones on his map. And there's a lesson there that so many of you have already learned and are living, a lesson that more Americans must heed. More of us must feel ourselves compelled to look beyond the wide and easy path, to follow a less traveled, perhaps older route. And sometimes it's more difficult. It's often more time consuming. But it's always more rewarding.

It's a path where progress is measured by the good we do for others. On that score, many of you are like Vena Hefner, who is with us today, a great lady—76 years old. She served as a driver for Secretary Marshall during World War II, and after suffering a motorcycle accident, she helped found the Paralyzed Veterans Association and has been a key member of the Disabled American Vets. And since her accident, she has found time to drive over 1 million miles, in every State in the lower 48. By her tough, inspirational example, Vena has helped disabled Americans across the country, sharing her strength along the road.

Those who have traveled widely and have seen America's broad expanses know how much we have been given as a people, and their spirits have grown accordingly. The expansive spirit of America has boundless capacity to do good. And so, I'll leave you with a simple request. In whatever effort you make to restore this country's natural beauty or to help other Americans in need, make it a pilgrimage with a purpose—work to make a difference. And I'd ask you that you stop not simply to smell the flowers along the way but to help them grow. We are privileged to live in the greatest, freest, most inspirational country in the entire world. Let's make it all a little better.

Thank you. God bless you, and God bless the United States of America. Thank you all very much.

Note: The President spoke at 5:41 p.m. at the Virginia State fairgrounds. In his remarks, he referred to Richard H. Hammann, president of the Family Motor Coach Association, Inc.; Mr. Hammann's wife, Karen; and Derrick Crandall, president of the American Recreation Association.

Statement on Signing the Puyallup Tribe of Indians Settlement Act of 1989

June 21, 1989

Today I am signing into law H.R. 932, the "Puyallup Tribe of Indians Settlement Act of 1989." This bill resolves long-standing land, fishing, and jurisdictional disputes between the Tribe and the local non-Indian community in the area of Tacoma, Washington. Disagreements over land ownership have resulted in uncertainty for many local landowners and economic development of the region has been hindered.

Negotiations to resolve these disputes were initiated over 4 years ago between the Tribe and local non-Indian parties to the settlement. Resolving the disputes through negotiation rather than litigation was accomplished due to the diligent, good-faith efforts of all parties involved.

While H.R. 932 was pending in the Congress, the Administration expressed concern about the extent of the Federal contribution to the settlement, in light of the marginal risk of Federal liability related to the Puyallup claims. The Federal Government will, nevertheless, commit substantial resources to settle these claims pursuant to H.R. 932. Although the Administration favors negotiated settlements over litigation, careful attention must be paid when Federal taxpayers are asked to contribute substantially more than they might otherwise pay as a result of litigation involving the Federal Government's alleged breach of specific trust responsibilities.

The Administration expects to continue to work toward settlements of legitimate Indian land and water rights claims to which the Federal Government is a party. These efforts will recognize the importance of settling legitimate claims brought by tribes against States, private entities, and the Federal Government. We will also strive to ensure that all responsible parties make appropriate contributions to a settlement. In this regard, H.R. 932 provides for State, local, and private, as well as Federal, contributions to the Puyallup Tribe settlement.

Indian land and water rights settlements involve a complicated blend of law, treaties, court decisions, history, social policies, technology, and practicality. These interrelated factors make it difficult to formulate hard-and-fast rules to determine exact settlement contributions by the various parties involved in a specific claim.

In recognition of these difficulties, this Administration is committed to establishing criteria and procedures to guide future Indian land and water claim settlement negotiations, including provision for Administration participation in such negotiations.

GEORGE BUSH

The White House,
June 21, 1989.

Note: H.R. 932, approved June 21, was assigned Public Law No. 101–41.

Nomination of Claire E. Freeman To Be an Assistant Secretary of Housing and Urban Development

June 21, 1989

The President today announced his intention to nominate Claire E. Freeman to be an Assistant Secretary of Housing and Urban Development (Administration). She would succeed Judith L. Tardy.

Since 1984 Ms. Freeman has been Deputy Assistant Secretary (Civilian Personnel Policy) at the Department of Defense in Washington, DC. Prior to this, she was Deputy Assistant Secretary for Community Planning and Development at the Department of Housing and Urban Development, 1981–1984. She was the housing and community development manager for the California Association of Realtors, 1978–1980, and the human affairs supervisor for the City of Inglewood, California, Housing, Community and Development Division, 1973–1977.

Ms. Freeman graduated from the University of California at Riverside (B.A., 1969) and the University of Southern California (M.S., 1973). She resides in Alexandria, VA.

Nomination of Gerard F. Scannell To Be an Assistant Secretary of Labor

June 21, 1989

The President today announced his intention to nominate Gerard F. Scannell to be an Assistant Secretary of Labor (Occupational Safety and Health). He would succeed John A. Pendergrass.

Since 1979 Mr. Scannell has served as director of corporate safety/fire/environmental affairs, worldwide responsibility, at Johnson and Johnson in New Brunswick, NJ. Prior to this, he served in various positions at the Department of Labor in Washington, DC, including Director of the Office of Federal Agency Safety and Health Programs, 1974–1979; Director of the Office of Standards, OSHA, 1972–1974; and Special Assistant to the Assistant Secretary of Labor for Occupational Safety and Health, 1971–1972. Mr. Scannell also served as the safety director at Rohm and Haas Co. in Bristol, PA, 1965–1971; safety manager at the Thiokol Chemical Corp. in Bristol, PA, 1962–1965; and supervisor of the safety engineering department at Aetna Casualty and Surety Company in Worcester, MA, 1958–1962.

Mr. Scannell graduated from the Massachusetts Maritime Academy (B.S., 1955). He served in the U.S. Navy as a safety officer, 1955–1958. He is married, has five children, and resides in Hampton, NJ.

Nomination of Richard A. Clarke To Be an Assistant Secretary of State

June 21, 1989

The President today announced his intention to nominate Richard A. Clarke to be an Assistant Secretary of State (Politico-Military Affairs). He would succeed H. Allen Holmes.

Since 1985 Mr. Clarke has been Deputy Assistant Secretary of State for Intelligence Analysis. Prior to this, he served in several capacities at the Bureau of Politico-Military Affairs in the Department of State, 1979–1985; as a senior analyst with Pacific Sierra Research Corp., 1978–1979; and in several positions in the Office of the Secretary of Defense, 1973–1977.

Mr. Clarke graduated from the University of Pennsylvania (B.A., 1972) and the Massachusetts Institute of Technology (S.M., 1978).

Remarks at a Republican Party Fundraising Dinner in Richmond, Virginia

June 21, 1989

Thank you all very, very much. Barbara and I are delighted to be here, but inasmuch as we're speaking before the olives and before the celery, I will be mercifully brief.

But first let me pay my respects to various stars here at this head table. I want to single out our congressional delegation—the five Members that are here—my able chairman, Tom Bliley, and Frank Wolf and Stan Parris and Herb Bateman, French Slaughter, and all of them are doing an outstanding job for this State. Of course, I'm delighted that Tom and I were joined—or perhaps you might say led, inasmuch as we came from the Pentagon—by the former Secretary, your great Senator. John Warner flew down with us on Marine One, and I'm very pleased that he is here. And I want to salute, of course, the three gladiators from the primary, all of whom I know and all of whom I respect: Paul Trible, Stan Parris, and Marshall Coleman.

And let me say, it's great to be back in Virginia. You know, on the way down here, I couldn't help—as we looked out of the window of the helicopter—but notice that King's Dominion [a local amusement park] was open for business. [*Laughter*] If I'm not mistaken—although I could have been from the height of a thousand feet—I could swear I saw the entire Virginia Democratic ticket riding Shockwave. [*Laughter*]

Now, we all know that as good Republicans we had to resolve a few differences. When I told Barbara I was hoping to visit some historic battlefield sites in Virginia, she said she didn't know if I was referring to the Civil War or to the Republican gubernatorial primary. [*Laughter*]

But, Marshall, you're our candidate. Certainly you have my full support, and you know Virginia better than I do, but let me give you a little free advice: Don't film your TV ads riding around in a tank. [*Laughter*]

But all kidding aside, with Stan, whom I see and work with in the Congress, with Paul, who served with such distinction in the Senate, and with Marshall Coleman, who's been at my side for a long, long time in my political efforts, in this competition, all three of them, one thing—and I was an outsider at that; I don't believe in getting involved in primaries from the office I now hold—but one thing was certain: with these three outstanding people, Virginia could not lose.

And, yes, I am pleased that Virginia held this primary, our first in 40 years. And, yes, there was a rough-and-tumble competition, and Republicans turned out in huge numbers, but we've proven once again that we are different than the other party. We are united by principles, by a great cause; and that's why, now that the dust is settled, we are all still Republicans. And I am convinced we are going to win the gubernatorial seat in Richmond come fall.

And I do feel, and people have told me—John, coming down here, the others as well—that we were getting into a united frame of mind for this fall. And you can feel it, and I am delighted that we are uniting behind Marshall Coleman. It is absolutely essential, because as you remember, it is every 4 years that this State and one other are in the eyes of the entire Nation. They are going to be on us, looking for little straws in the wind regarding the 1990 nationwide elections. And so, unity behind our candidates here tonight is terribly important.

And let me say, I do believe from the bottom of my heart that Marshall will make a great Governor of the Commonwealth, for he is a Virginian through and through. From his Marine days to his service as a delegate and State senator, he's always been a trailblazer. And he knows best and can meet the challenges that are facing your State. And as I said, I will always be grateful to him for his early support, and I know that he can stand up for what he believes in.

This former attorney general has a tough, hardnosed plan for putting away violent criminals for good. And he has solid proposals dealing with the scourge of drugs, proposals that only a veteran crimefighter could conceive and implement. And what happens in Virginia will be of tremendous help to what happens across this country.

And then for 1990, Virginia is also going to be a battleground between the parties in the 1990's. And the question that comes: Will Virginia be fairly represented? We need a Republican watchdog in Richmond, protecting the fairness of the reapportionment process and vetoing liberal legislation.

And let me just say a word about the ticket that Marshall heads, a strong, impressive Republican ticket. I've known her for a long time—up close and personal, as they say. Not that personal—up close and friendly. [*Laughter*] But I had great respect for Eddy's husband, and I have great respect for her, and so does Barbara. And we know deep in our hearts that Eddy Dalton is going to make a great Lieutenant Governor for this Commonwealth. She's got the experience—as a State senator, led the charge against the drug thugs, demanding mandatory sentencing for those convicted of selling drugs to minors. And her commitment to curbing State spending is so strong that she'll begin with the office of Lieutenant Governor the minute she takes over.

And you also have nominated another excellent candidate in State Senator Joe Benedetti for attorney general of this Commonwealth. You deserve a full-time attorney general who is willing to lead the fight on drugs and crime. And this ticket, with Joe on there for attorney general, offers leadership, great leadership, for Virginia.

But to win, it seems to me the Republicans have got to develop an appeal as diverse as this State. Virginia has changed, no longer simply what some thought of as a rural State. You now have large metropolitan areas growing at both ends of this great State, and your State has changed in other ways, too. We Republicans must do more than recognize the change; we must take our message to every neighborhood and every community. And we will take our Republican message, a message of hope and opportunity, to the black and other minority voters of Virginia. Marshall Coleman and I agree: We will not concede a community, a precinct, or a single voter to the opposition.

And so, it's up to you people in this room—doesn't matter who you were for in the primary—to come together, because we must win. And I'm thinking nationally now. We must win in Virginia, as in New Jersey, to set the stage for 1990, the critical year, the year that my friend and your great Senator, John Warner, will be reelected to his third term; a year that these outstanding Virginia Congressmen will be reelected to the House of Representatives—and as President, I can tell you, I wish we had more like them to deal with every single day up there; a year that will shape the future of American politics well into the next century.

But there are other reasons, some practical and some sentimental, why we want a victory in November. Every American, from Maine to Texas, looks to Virginia as the cradle of democracy. Every American heart quickens at the ideals of the builders of Monticello, Mount Vernon, and Montpelier. From the mountains of the Shenandoah to the rivers of the Tidewater, from the country lanes of Abingdon to the city lights of Alexandria, what Thomas Jefferson said is still true: "Old Dominion is the mother of us all." Let's show what we can do come fall.

Thank you for inviting me to Richmond. God bless you, God bless our ticket, and God bless the United States of America. Thank you all.

Note: The President spoke at 7:32 p.m. in the first floor Exhibition Hall of the Richmond Center. Following his remarks, he returned to Washington, DC.

Nomination of Lou Gallegos To Be an Assistant Secretary of the Interior

June 22, 1989

The President today announced his intention to nominate Lou Gallegos to be an Assistant Secretary of the Interior (Policy, Budget and Administration). He would succeed Henry M. Ventura.

Since 1987 Mr. Gallegos has served as cabinet secretary of the human service department for Gov. Garrey E. Carruthers in the State of New Mexico. He was the Farmers Home Administration State Director for New Mexico at the Department of Agriculture, 1985–1986; executive director for the Republican Party of New Mexico, 1985; a candidate for the United States Congress, 1984; and director of field operations for Senator Pete V. Domenici, 1977–1984.

Mr. Gallegos attended the University of Maryland and New Mexico Highlands University. He currently resides in Sena, NM.

Nomination of Richard Burleson Stewart To Be an Assistant Attorney General
June 22, 1989

The President today announced his intention to nominate Richard Burleson Stewart to be an Assistant Attorney General (Lands and Natural Resources), Department of Justice. He would succeed Roger J. Marzulla.

Mr. Stewart is currently a Byrne professor of administrative law at Harvard Law School and a member of the faculty of the J.F. Kennedy School of Government, Harvard University. He has served as a visiting professor of law at the University of Chicago Law School, and as a visiting fellow at the European University Institute in Florence, Italy. He was a visiting scholar for the Environmental Protection Agency, 1980; visiting professor of law at the University of California at Berkeley, 1979–1980; professor of law at Harvard Law School, 1975–1984; and an assistant professor of law, Harvard Law School, 1971–1975. He was special counsel for the Senate Select Committee on Presidential Campaign Activities, 1973, and an attorney with Covington and Burling in Washington, DC.

Mr. Stewart graduated from Yale University (B.A., 1961); Oxford University (Rhodes scholar, 1963); and Harvard Law School (LL.B., 1966). He is married, has three children, and resides in Cambridge, MA.

Nomination of Thomas E. Collins III To Be an Assistant Secretary of Labor
June 22, 1989

The President today announced his intention to nominate Thomas E. Collins III to be Assistant Secretary of Labor for Veterans' Employment and Training. He would succeed Donald E. Shasteen.

Most recently, in 1988, Mr. Collins was the Republican congressional candidate for Mississippi's Fourth District. Prior to this, he served as the executive director for the Mississippi veterans' farm and home board. Mr. Collins was the president and chief executive officer of Collins Investments, Inc., 1980–1981, and a member of the board of directors for Donnie Collins Properties, Inc., 1986–1987. Since 1973 he has actively pursued various private enterprises.

Mr. Collins graduated from Mississippi State University (B.S., 1959) and the University of Southern Mississippi (M.B.A., 1975). He served in the U.S. Air Force from 1959 to 1980. Mr. Collins was born in 1937. He is married and has two children.

Nomination of John D. Macomber To Be President of the Export-Import Bank of the United States
June 22, 1989

The President today announced his intention to nominate John D. Macomber to be President of the Export-Import Bank of the United States for a term of 4 years expiring January 20, 1993. He would succeed John A. Bohn, Jr.

Mr. Macomber is chairman of J.D. Macomber and Co. In addition, he serves as director of several private and public companies in the United States and Europe. He was chairman of the board and chief executive officer of Celanese Corp. and senior director of McKinsey and Co., Inc., in Paris, France.

Mr. Macomber graduated from Yale University in 1950 and received a master of business administration degree from the Harvard School of Business Administration in 1952. He was born January 13, 1928, in Rochester, NY. Mr. Macomber served in the U.S. Air Force for 2 years.

Nomination of Eugene Kistler Lawson To Be First Vice President of the Export-Import Bank of the United States

June 22, 1989

The President today announced his intention to nominate Eugene Kistler Lawson to be First Vice President of the Export-Import Bank of the United States for a term of 4 years expiring January 20, 1993. He would succeed William F. Ryan.

Since 1988 Dr. Lawson has been Deputy Under Secretary of Labor for International Affairs. Prior to this he was executive director for Russell Reynolds Associates, 1984–1988. He was Deputy Assistant Secretary of Commerce for East Asia and the Pacific, 1982–1984; Deputy Assistant Secretary of Commerce for East-West Trade, 1981–1982; and director of the China advisory group, Government Research Corp./National Journal, 1980–1981. Dr. Lawson has also served as director of the master of science in foreign service program, director of the program for China studies, and professorial lecturer in the school of foreign service at Georgetown University, 1977–1980; and Deputy Director of the Office for Special Bilateral Affairs at the Department of State, 1975–1977.

Dr. Lawson graduated from Princeton University (B.A., 1961) and Columbia University (M.A., 1967; Ph.D., 1982). He served in the U.S. Navy in the Pacific, 1961–1963. He is married, has three children, and resides in Washington, DC.

Continuation of Charles L. Grizzle as an Assistant Administrator of the Environmental Protection Agency

June 22, 1989

The President today announced that Charles L. Grizzle will continue to serve as an Assistant Administrator of the Environmental Protection Agency (Administration and Resource Management).

Since 1988 Mr. Grizzle has served as an Assistant Administrator of the Environmental Protection Agency. Prior to this, Mr. Grizzle served in various capacities at the Department of Agriculture, including Deputy Assistant Secretary for Administration, 1983–1988; Confidential Assistant to the Secretary of Agriculture; and staff assistant to the Director of the Office of Operations and Finance. In addition, Mr. Grizzle served as a banking officer for the First National Bank of Louisville, 1974–1981, and as executive director of the Republican Party of Kentucky.

Mr. Grizzle received his bachelor's degree from the University of Kentucky. He now resides in McLean, VA.

Informal Exchange With Residents of Covenant House in New York, New York
June 22, 1989

Reverend Ritter. Mr. President, may I just say very briefly, thank you again for visiting us. You probably don't know this yet, but the biggest gift you're giving our kids is hope. The fact that you and Mrs. Bush have cared enough to come and talk with them and understand them better and possibly help them means an awful lot to them and to us.

The President. Do you normally have this many cameras around for these guys? [*Laughter*]

Resident. Every day. [*Laughter*]

Resident. Normal occurrence.

Reverend Ritter. I've asked the kids not to talk to me, but to address themselves to you and the First Lady. And a good way of simply beginning the conversation is to pick any kid and ask them——

The President. How did you happen to come here?

Resident. Well, I was having problems, and I didn't really have anywhere to go. I met a friend, and he called Covenant House, and he told me about it.

The President. So, how long do you stay here? How long do you——

Resident. Well, right now I've been here for a month. And so, they find me a place here so I can go to school, and my daughter's here.

Reverend Ritter. How many of the kids here have lived on the streets for more than 3 or 4 years? [*Most hands were raised.*] And you're 18, 19 years old, so you lived on the street when you were 12 and 13 years old.

The President. Just for example, when you were a little guy—a real little, young one, did you just come from New York or did you come from outside somewhere?

Resident. Well, I was born in California and raised in Japan. And my parents got divorced and then got remarried. My stepmom was, like, an alcoholic.

The President. She was drinking?

Resident. Yes. And she liked to sort of, like, call the cops on me and get me into jail, and that's where I've been for the past couple of years, in jail——in and out. And I got thrown out a couple times.

Mrs. Bush. How old are you?

Resident. Eighteen.

Mrs. Bush. You're a great-looking man.

The President. So, now what are your hopes? Have you got any hopes out here?

Resident. Well, I have a job right now in Fort Lauderdale, and I'm just trying to get my life straight—I'm trying to get off of alcohol.

The President. Have you been in the drug scene a little bit?

Resident. I've been in—yeah.

The President. Crack?

Resident. I smoked crack once.

The President. Crack is getting more and more, I gather, around here.

Resident. It sure is.

Reverend Ritter. How many kids here have used crack?

The President. What's the difference? I mean, is it just immediately addictive and you've-got-to-have-more-the-next-day kind of thing?

Resident. Kind of.

Resident. It causes all kinds of problems. It causes problems—at first you get high, and it goes from problems to addiction.

The President. So, you have to get into horrible things to keep the habit up and make the money to do it, and you have to do bad stuff to do it?

Resident. You do what you got to do to get high.

The President. But how do you get the money to get it?

Resident. How?

Reverend Ritter. Rob, steal——

Resident. Some people rob, steal, prostitute, sell it. I used to sell it all the time, and that's how I used to get high.

The President. You have to do that, yes.

Reverend Ritter. Will you tell the President and Mrs. Bush what it's like for a kid to live on the street? And I'm not asking for your personal experiences, because that is personal, and that's private. But what's it like for a kid to live on the street?

Resident. It's rough.

Resident. Scary.

Resident. You live 1 day at a time.

The President. Were you worried—I mean, were you scared of the law getting you, or are you scared of getting beat up?

Resident. Scared of the streets.

Resident. Scared of getting beat up or——

Resident. Scared of the streets, because you're forced to live there. You don't want to be there, but you know that there are other people who are out there, and you don't know where they're from or what they're into or what they can do to you.

The President. Can you ever make friends, or is it you're always worried about doing that, even?

Resident. You can't make friends on the streets.

Resident. Even if you meet someone you like, you can't call them a friend.

Resident. You can't make friends on the streets; you don't know how they are.

Resident. It's like a survival—survive, you've got to learn how to survive.

Resident. You have to use the people you stay with. You practically have to use every means of survival that you have inside of you to try to do what you need to do. And it's scary because you can meet somebody—they might even use you without you knowing it. But at the same time, you get what you need to do and leave and go to another place if you have to.

Resident. It's real hard to trust people.

Resident. Yeah.

The President. Just by example—and again, I'm protecting the real personal stuff—but I mean, say, in your case, how did you decide to come here? Did you just get so down you figured, there's got to be something better than this?

Resident. The thing that happened was—I'm in New Orleans right now—the thing that happened was I was living in a town close to New Orleans, and I was physically abused by my parents and everything. And the thing is I finally decided to leave—they would not let me leave until I turned the age of 18. And so, the thing is that when I left, a neighbor—a really good Christian and everything—she called some places, and Covenant House said they would take me in with no problems. So, I've been in the program for a year and 2 months now, and doing great.

The President. You're doing good?

Resident. Yes.

The President. That's great. How about you?

Resident. Well, when I turned 18, I moved to California because, like, back home I was in a drug scene—and for me, in order to get out of that is to leave. And so, I left for California and went to school up there. And I came to Houston, and I found Covenant House, and they're helping me to finish school, because I'm going to college——

The President. Are you?

Resident. Yes, and I'm studying commercial art, and I graduate in December, thanks to Covenant House. So, without their help, I would have probably ended up back in the streets.

The President. Did you have your hand up when I mentioned the drugs thing? I mean, do you ever get—goes not just for one guy—but I mean the pressure to go back into the drug deal?

Resident. All the time.

Resident. Well, see, when you're in a drug situation, you do it for a reason. Some people do it to feed their family—you know, that's kind of hard. You could go out and work, but it's easier to do that. Or if you have an addiction, you have to sell the drugs to keep yourself high, and you need it—you need it, and you'll do anything for it, until you get to a point where you die, you quit——

Resident. Wind up in jail.

Resident. Or you end up in jail.

Resident. One of three places.

The President. Die or go to jail.

Resident. Not too much choice——

Resident. Lot of kids get on drugs——

The President. Crack? Yes.

Resident. You can be rich—crack will put the rich man to the poorhouse. It's really bad news. You get really skinny—it's like you're just a walking skeleton.

The President. Can you tell a guy—now that you're kind of getting it out and getting it together—can you look around and see somebody, without even knowing them, and say, that person is a crack addict?

Resident. Definitely.

Resident. Yes.

Resident. Definitely.

Resident. I've been sober 6 months now. I came to Covenant House. I was incarcerated. I got out, and I'm going to high school now; I'm working. And sobriety—that's where it's at.

The President. So, you can just spot a guy, though, and——

Resident. Instantly.

Resident. Yes.

Resident. Just look in your eyes.

Resident. Just look at you and tell.

Resident. Their body. But see, it's not always a matter of people who are using the drugs, because I was never one of those people, fortunately, who was living on the streets. I had a lot of problems in the home, and I stayed stuck in the home until I could get out. Then when I finally left the home, I was in a situation where I didn't do drugs, but everyone around me was doing drugs.

Resident. Yes.

Resident. Such as these ladies—and it still hurts you. And that's why I ended up in Covenant House. My boyfriend put me up in his aunt's house, and he got onto crack and messed up the relationship. And since I didn't know anyone, I had no one but myself, and I was living with his family. And there were other people in his family doing drugs badly. And eventually I had a problem with work. And they don't care about so much as you, but they need that money. So, once I no longer—all I needed was a couple of weeks to get back on my feet with a new job and wait for the first check, but it's not a matter of that. So, it's not always people who are on the streets; it can be people in the homes being abused by people who use drugs or people who don't, who just have problems. There are many different problems.

The President. Let me ask you a personal question, and you don't have to take it. In the home, did you get beat up on, abused in your own home?

Resident. No.

The President. Nothing like that.

Resident. Well, all right, there was—I say, no, not beaten up, because I was never struck extensively, but there was a time when—I mean, at a young age, to be tied up and hanging over a staircase, a spiral staircase, just hanging there at a young age, that stays in your mind. But I say not abused that way, because that was nothing compared to other problems that go on for years sometimes, because when you're a child—if you're of that age, you don't know what's going on, and you can be raised with certain problems.

The President. What do you want to say?

Resident. Just that I know there's a lot of kids out there that need help. And Covenant House has helped me a lot, and it has helped a lot of other people, and I would like them to know that there is someplace out there.

Reverend Ritter. When we talked last night, you mentioned something that surprised me and really bothered me: that you met a lot of young kids out there.

Resident. Yes.

Reverend Ritter. Tell the President about that.

The President. Real young?

Resident. Yes, when you go out there, a lot of the people, society itself, will look at somebody who's 12, 13 years old and say, well, they can't possibly be on the streets; they're too little. And I just came back from Fort Lauderdale, and there's a couple of kids down there, 13, 14 years old. In Chicago, my hometown, they're out there—11, 12 years old, no place to go.

The President. Prostituting and stuff?

Resident. Yes. They do anything. When you're on the street, you do anything to get by—steal, prostitute, sell drugs, anything you can do to get money. You need it. And people are ignoring the fact that they're not only 18, 19 years old on the street, there are little bitty kids this tall on the street, too.

The President. And how did they get there to begin with? Just no homes?

Resident. Bad homes, bad homes. I was out of my house when I was 13.

The President. Were you really? Nobody cared about you, or they were just beating you up?

Resident. My old man was an alcoholic;

he beat me up. He told me one day, "Out of the house! I don't want you back." My mom put up no argument, and I haven't been back.

Resident. Sometimes it could even be the parents. Like my dad was there for 3 years when I was living with—my daughter was born, and for 3 years he's been using drugs and crack and stuff. And it's just like—the situation just gets worse. It's like you're living in some type of hell or something, because it just keeps hurting you and hurting you. You don't have no money; you don't have no way to get to school or to take care of yourself or your children. And then he'll get really aggravated because he don't got the money for the drugs, and he'll take it out on me or my sister or anybody.

The President. Physically—sexually abuse you or more beaten up?

Resident. Physically—because he don't have no money to get it. And he says he's going to stop, but it's right there, the drughouse is right there—like three or four of them, where I lived in Brooklyn. And they'll close them down, and the next day they'll be right open again—it seems like they could never stop.

Resident. Three blocks from here, there's a really popular area, 42d Street—everyone knows about 42d Street. On 42d and 8th, there could be up to 20 drug dealers out there on the corner. And the police would call the sweep and get all of them off the street, and their backups will start up again—not even tomorrow—it could be by that evening.

Resident. Yes.

Resident. A couple of hours later.

The President. Do you get so you know them? There goes Joe over there——

Resident. No. I don't——

The President. No, but I mean, somebody——

Resident. ——but people do know them, yes. I have to walk through to get over to Lexington Avenue to work and stuff, and you see the same faces. And you could have just heard that they were arrested the night before.

The President. Are they rich guys now, I mean for selling this stuff?

Resident. Depending on if they do the drug. If they do the drug, they're wasting money.

Resident. They ain't rich. They ain't getting—some guys out here, they ain't getting no money. They think they get money. But a lot of guys come in here, such as myself, which I needed some help, being the simple fact that all I know how to do is sell the drug—that's all I know how to do. I'm 18, going on 19; I never had a job a day in my life, so all I did to get money was to sell drugs.

I see a lot of people that come off the streets, that come to Covenant House and want to stop selling and want to stop getting high, but then they get depressed here. And somebody else will talk them into it, and they go right back on 42d Street and do the same thing. I've seen a lot of guys who come and go, and all they do is go to 42d Street. And the next time I see them they be all——

The President. Well, tell me this. When a guy goes to 42d Street and he gets one of these sellers, and the guy says, "Here's some stuff—you go out and sell it and bring me back the money."

Resident. Yeah, that's just it.

The President. And you get to keep a little?

Resident. It's just that easy.

The President. And then if he doesn't turn the money in, he gets all beat up?

Resident. Killed.

Resident. And it pays more than working.

The President. Beaten or killed.

Resident. My brother got killed.

The President. Your brother got killed?

Resident. Shot in his heart with a .44 magnum.

The President. Because he what? Shortchanged the guy?

Resident. Okay, it was two of my brothers. They went to Ohio. They were selling drugs, and one of them stopped because he met a girl. And all of them came back to New York, and the one that stopped got killed—his whole chest was blown up.

The President. But what——

Resident. Because I guess they shortchanged him. Since they said—well, they'd gone—well, he was with them before, and they said——

Resident. Little 10-year-olds, and everything—they see what everybody else is doing. They say, "Well, my friend has a car. He knows all the ladies, and he has money all the time, and he's always partying. I want to do that."

Resident. Because it pays more.

The President. That's down in—you're talking New Orleans or everyplace?

Resident. That's everywhere.

Resident. The stuff is everywhere.

Resident. When you're on the street, you know everything from all parts of——

The President. The street experience—what I'm getting at is the street experience in New Orleans is just an overlay of Chicago or California or New York.

Resident. It could be done in a different way, but it's——

Resident. It's all the same process.

Resident. ——all the same.

Resident. We all end up in the street. We don't have no place to go.

Resident. A lot of times—like Walter—we were talking last night, and he said one big thing is the only thing he knows how to do is sell drugs—no other skills. Because he's selling the drugs, he had a car and all kinds of things, and that's the way everyone sees it. If you work and you're young, such as our ages, it's hard to get good jobs that pay. Working in McDonald's—minimum wage—you can't get anything from that.

Resident. I'm not working for $1.25 an hour, $1.10—there's no way—for a whole week and sitting over a hot oven flipping hamburgers?

Resident. When you can go out there and sell drugs and get $2,000 in a couple of days.

The President. How old are you?

Resident. I'm 20.

The President. Twenty years old.

Resident. We struggle to work and everything, and you see people out there—all they have to do is work a couple of hours—they get a few thousand dollars. And we over here have to bust ourselves trying to do our best—everything straight—and they always end up poor. That's why so many people selling drugs.

Resident. And come home with $100.

Resident. One hundred dollars a week—that ain't no money. I can make a hundred dollars in 15 minutes.

The President. You can?

Resident. I can make $100 in 15 minutes.

Mrs. Bush. But your three choices, though, are jail, death, and whatever the third one was.

Resident. Doesn't always happen, though.

Reverend Ritter. Mrs. Bush, the kids are bullet-proof.

Mrs. Bush. Oh, I forgot that.

Reverend Ritter. Really. The only problem with being a kid is that you don't really know that you are and you don't really think about consequences. You really have to live for the moment and you have to survive.

Resident. There has to be a down side, or else these people who were doing drug dealing or working for people wouldn't be trying to clean themselves up. They know that it's not the way.

Resident. Jail, too much jail.

Resident. Maybe it's a lot of money, but it's not the way. You can't retire on being a drug dealer.

Resident. You can't.

Reverend Ritter. I'll tell you what, you guys. This is the man, right? You'll never get a chance to talk to the President again, probably. What's really the most important thing you want him to know about street kids? What should he know?

Resident. Jobs are hard to get, and when you get them, sometimes they don't pay enough to stay off the street.

Resident. I would like him to know that there's people out there that help Ethiopia—help outside people, outside the United States—but there's a lot of people in the United States that need the help, people in the street that need somewhere to go. And we don't have nowhere to go but the street, and I think we really need that help.

Resident. We're funding everybody but us.

Resident. Yes.

Resident. We're funding every country that's got problems, except when you look down in the streets, there's all kids like us everywhere. And they're funding everyplace else.

Resident. Last night, Michelle and I took these people on a tour, and they couldn't believe the way we have bums and stuff sleeping outside. They don't have that as much. And we just went half a block from here, just to smoke a cigarette, and there was a lady pulling out her sheets and getting ready to go to bed out on the sidewalk. And they're staring at her, like, wow. And to us, it's, like, oh, that's normal—we're used to it.

And as we're walking, we see over 20 people laying on the street—some coupled together, some have missing limbs, some are all swollen from being unhealthy. And then when you think about all the money and funds that are going to another country—that's wonderful, yes, great, help everybody—but don't forget there are people here who need help.

Reverend Ritter. Let me ask a question a little more specifically. What does the street kid really need—concretely, practically?

Resident. Education.

Resident. I think that the kids need a place to go where they can talk to a person and get help, and I found out that Covenant House can help a person. Like, say, you're 15, 16 years old—the most important thing, I think, is to go to school, and Covenant House will let you do that. Because if you're on the street and you try to go back to school, they won't let you because you're not living with your parents; you ain't got a guardian.

The President. No legal rights.

Resident. No legal rights.

Resident. My mother and father have been dead—my father has been dead since I was 1; my mother died 5½ years ago. And I stopped going to school for a little while for the simple fact I had to put up the money for my brothers and sisters. They went to foster care. Nobody else wanted me—I was rejected. So, I just stayed out on the streets and sold drugs. Then I wanted to stop and go to school. Anytime I went to Louis D. Brandeis, I had to have a parent. I ain't got none—what do you want me to do? Well, you can't go to school.

The President. We can't help you?

Resident. No, they can't help me. So, then that means—I think, "Well, if you don't want to help me, I'm going to be the person that you want me to be: a criminal." So, I came out here and did what I had to do to survive. I got shot; I got cut; I got stabbed; I got beat up—and I did this to other people, too. I'm tired of doing things like that, because I see nothing but a wall waiting, a dead end. Like you said, life on the street is a dead end. And that's just what it is, and I'm just smart enough to open my eyes and see that that is exactly what it is.

The President. What do you want to be now?

Resident. What do I want to be now?

The President. What do you want to do? What do you want to be? Got any hope?

Resident. Yes. See, I want to learn electronics or carpentry, plumbing. I want a good job so I can get a house, a dog, a rabbit, a bird—[*laughter*]—a wife, and a baby. That's all I want. I don't want nothing else but a house, a dog, a rabbit, and a baby, and a house—that's all I want out of life. I've had my fun; the fun time is over. It's time to get into reality.

Resident. Something else, too. They need rehabilitation—rehabs for kids. There's a lot of kids out there that are on drugs—and we need that.

Resident. Yes, but they got rehabs. You go to one, and they want all this money, all this money that you ain't got.

Resident. Right.

Resident. You're sleeping on the streets or you just got out of jail or prison or something, and you don't have the money. I was fortunate enough to find a rehab that they didn't ask for nothing. And they gave me this ring, a sign of my sobriety. They gave me a lot of tools that I use each and every day of my life.

The President. What are you doing now? What are you going to be?

Resident. I want to become a chef, a culinary artist.

The President. Are you?

Resident. Yes. But still it's—you go to one of these places, Fair Oaks Hospital or something, and they want $18,000–$20,000, and you don't even have a quarter in your pocket to make a phone call. Sure, they're going to bill you later. [*Laughter*] We'll bill you—yeah, right.

Resident. One of the most important things for me, for most of the—I speak also for most of the kids in New Orleans—is a certain personal touch that most kids need——

Resident. Yeah.

Resident. ——to give them the self-confidence to get out there and do what they need to do. Because throughout their lives, they've been always told they were no good, they——

Resident. Dirt.

Resident. Losers.

Resident. ——they're not their children. They shouldn't be around them, and everything. And that's what I mainly needed when I went to Covenant House, and that's what I think should be——

The President. How many of your parents were into drugs and made that problem horrible for the home front? Almost everybody. You didn't have it—you escaped that.

Reverend Ritter. Or alcohol.

The President. Substance abuse.

Reverend Ritter. That would be almost everybody.

Resident. Alcohol's a drug.

Reverend Ritter. That would be everybody. There's no mystery, Mr. President, why a kid leaves home.

The President. In other words, there's nothing—I mean, it's just the environment in the home.

Reverend Ritter. It's too painful to stay.

Dr. Lee. Father Ritter, could I just say one thing? I want the President and Mrs. Bush to come away with this: My one thought is that no kid in this room and no kid in Covenant House wants to be here. Not one kid ran to this life; they are running from another life. And the last thing is: Whose children are they? Well, they're Father Ritter's, and I feel they belong to me. And I know what President and Mrs. Bush feel like.

Reverend Ritter. I'm getting all sorts of signals to sort of wrap this up and so forth, but let me just conclude by saying that my kids have a number of things in common. And that's how good they are and how brave they are and how beautiful they are and how much they really want to make it back off the streets. Not many do unless they receive the help that they need.

And the fact that you and the First Lady came here today—you have no idea of how much hope you create in these kids. I can only say that to a street kid, hope is sort of a hand grenade in their heart. It's a very dangerous thing; they've been disappointed so many times.

Resident. All we need is for someone to help us. All we need is unity, because everybody is all for themselves. I think the world would be a much better place to live in if we just help each other out and love one another.

Resident. Be treated like human beings.

Reverend Ritter. I'd like the President and the First Lady to go upstairs for just a moment and meet a couple of our really special kids with AIDS. I know they're very anxious to greet you briefly.

The President. Well, listen, good luck to all of you.

Resident. I'd like to say thank you for taking the time out of your busy schedule.

Resident. Yes.

Resident. Yes.

Resident. Nobody believed us when we called home to tell—[*laughter*]—President Bush is coming to Covenant House in New York. They never believed this. And I really appreciate that you took time.

The President. I just admire Father Ritter and what he's doing, and you guys for fighting——

Resident. We're doing the best we can.

The President. ——and trying to do something. I hope you make it, all of you.

Note: The exchange began at 11:35 a.m. Rev. Bruce Ritter was the executive director of Covenant House. Dr. Burton Lee III was the Physician to the President.

Remarks at a Luncheon Hosted by the New York Partnership and the Association for a Better New York in New York, New York
June 22, 1989

Distinguished guests and ladies and gentlemen, Barbara and I appreciate this wonderful turnout, this generous reception. And let me salute that magnificent film and thank you, Ray, for putting it together. I just stopped choking up coming from Covenant House, and now I had to go through it again here at lunch. But it was a moving call to action.

What a few weeks it's been! Things are moving on a lot of fronts: NATO moving in the right direction, China—we're all very concerned about that. As I say, I just came from Covenant House, so I feel uplifted by that. And yesterday—if I might make a very personal observation before addressing myself to the subject at hand, I want to comment on the Supreme Court decision about our flag. I understand the legal basis for that decision, and I respect the Supreme Court. And as President of the United States, I will see that the law of the land is fully supported. But I have to give you my personal, emotional response. Flag-burning is wrong—dead wrong—and the flag of the United States is very, very special.

It is indeed an honor to address the members and guests of the New York Partnership and also the Association for a Better New York, for already you've enriched fields from business and labor to education and the media. And we meet today to go still further—to join hands and link hearts, as the film said, to light the American sky.

I begin with a single, simple statement: There is no problem in America that is not being solved somewhere. There is no problem in America that is not being solved somewhere—think of that. Today millions of Americans, the quiet Americans, the selfless Americans, are giving of their time and themselves. And they work at day-care centers and inner-city schools, homes for the elderly, anywhere there's a need, anytime they are needed, making a difference in the lives of those for whom the American dream seems an impossible dream.

And already, this involvement—what we term national or community service—has helped countless Americans find self-respect and dignity, but the job is far from complete. Too many Americans still endure a living nightmare of want, a living nightmare of isolation—and that must stop. Ladies and gentlemen, we must bring back those who feel unwelcome. We must reawaken their hope for the future.

We know that government can't rebuild a family or reclaim a sense of neighborhood. We know that during the past two decades we've spent more money on more social programs than at any time in our history, and some problems aren't better—in fact, some are worse. Most Americans understand that the key to constructive change is building relationships, not bureaucracies. And they know that those who say, "It's government's problem," are really part of the problem themselves.

All my life I've believed that government could not substitute for "do unto others." Barbara and I, like I told Lew and David and Jim Robinson—it's like preaching to the choir here today—that Barbara and I, like all of you here, have tried to pitch in, in some way do our small part. Midland, Texas—I'll never forget it—it was starting a YMCA, working with the United Way, coaching a little league ball team, helping to build a community theater—and dating way back to my days in New Haven, raising funds for the United Negro College Fund. And I'm not going to give you equal time, because so many of you have done so much more.

We've all done these things, and as we participated, we fulfilled ourselves, learning that we are not what we drive or where we live or what kind of clothes we wear—rather, learning that America's greatness rests on the goodness of her people. And these beliefs are beyond any individual; they're timeless. Today more than ever, we need community service to help dropouts, pregnant teens, drug abusers, the homeless, AIDS victims, the hungry and illiterate.

Often they are disadvantaged, and as their communities disintegrate around them, they become disconnected from society.

Our challenge, then, is to raise their spirits and their expectations by engaging each citizen, school and business and church, synagogue and service organization and civic group. For this is what I mean when I talked about a Thousand Points of Light: that vast galaxy of people and institutions working together to solve problems in their own backyard.

I am here today to ask that both sectors, private and public, and all branches of all levels of government, join this great movement to extend national service into every corner of America—for it's a movement, bold and unprecedented. This is not a program, not another bureaucracy.

Let me tell you the strategy of this movement: first, to issue a call to action and to claim problems as your own; second, to identify, enlarge, and recreate what is working; and third, to discover and encourage new leaders.

First, our call to action—it is individual, and yet collective, and it begins this afternoon with you. So, today I ask all Americans and all institutions, large and small, to make service central to your life and work. I urge all business leaders to consider community service in hiring, compensation, and promotion decisions. I call upon nonprofit and service groups to open your doors to all those who want to help, irrespective of age, background, or level of experience. And leaders of high schools and colleges, I urge you to uphold the values of community service and to encourage students, faculty, and personnel to serve others. To every corporation, large and small, I say: Begin a literacy program that teaches each employee how to read. And to every member of a body of higher learning: Start a Big Brother or Big Sister program for kids in your neighborhood. Of every church and synagogue, I ask: Become an around-the-clock community center. And of every restaurant and grocery store: Distribute surplus food to soup kitchens and local shelters.

And to the youth of America, I issue a special appeal. Yesterday on the South Lawn of the White House, we held a kickoff rally for a key element of our strategy: the YES Initiative, or Youth Engaged In Service to America. It was attended by thousands of kids, some of those Points of Light I like to talk about. And I challenged every young American to fight against self-absorption and to emulate those leaders who have shown that there is no problem in America that is not being solved somewhere.

Their presence reminded me of the saying, "Life is not a state of time; life is a state of mind." So is our call to community service; it summons the young and the old. I believe Americans will listen to that call. Emerson once said, "The greatest gift is a portion of thyself." Well, today, across our 50 States, groups and individuals are giving of—not to—themselves. Americans like these are missionaries, and they're heroes. And our mission is to achieve nationally what they're doing locally.

To complete it will require a catalyst. And so, that brings me to the second part of our strategy, and I am proud to announce it now: a new effort to identify service programs that work and then carry them to America. We call this catalyst the Points of Light Initiative, a foundation of which I will serve as honorary chairman and that will help make our movement a reality.

I will soon ask Congress for $25 million annually to support this initiative, which in turn will seek matching funds from the private sector. But I will also name an advisory committee to report to me within 45 days of its first meeting on the structure, composition, and legislation needed to achieve the foundation's goals. And I am very pleased and proud to announce today that Governor Tom Kean of New Jersey, one of this nation's most dedicated and caring public servants, has agreed to head this committee. Tom, thank you very much.

But look, a Federal effort alone cannot succeed. And therefore, today we invite each Governor, and through them the mayors of all municipalities, to join our movement by forming State and local Points of Light working groups composed of outstanding leaders. These individuals will become a vehicle to solve problems locally and to help solve problems nationally. The Points of Light Initiative will be a magnet for the best ideas and brightest programs in community service. For while countless service initiatives are already working successfully, they're too often isolated, too often unknown to others. Our foundation will change all that. By bringing success stories to other communities, we will repeat them across the nation.

We will repeat them through a foundation initiative to be called the ServNet Project. Professional firms, corporations, unions, schools, religious, civic, and not-for-profit groups will be asked to donate the services of some of their most important, talented, and promising people for a period of time. These extraordinary individuals will form and lead peer-to-peer working groups—for example, lawyers going to fellow lawyers, teachers to fellow teachers, union members to fellow union members. ServNet will provide training and technical assistance, showing what works and what doesn't.

But we also have to improve current methods of matching people with meaningful service opportunities. Volunteer centers should be directly accessible to all Americans in their neighborhoods. Such contact points may be in a place of worship or union hall or library or fire station, a business building, service group headquarters, neighborhood home—you name it.

Over time, through an initiative called the ServLink Project, the foundation will stimulate the development through private sector resources of technology links between those who wish to serve and those needing service in the inquirer's own community. And in addition, we will ask banks, credit card users, telephone and utility companies to include in statement envelopes information about how people and their institutions can become engaged in serving others.

And like the foundation itself, these efforts can help individuals and institutions provide new hope to America. And so can the third part of our movement's strategy: our initiative to discover and encourage new leaders of every age in every town and city, and to inspire them to devote their talents and energies to national service, and then to honor those who excel.

Through the foundation, the YES Initiative will annually select two college-aged youth from each State as President's National Service Youth Representatives. And they'll spend 1 year traveling through their regions as service ambassadors, urging other young Americans to get involved. And Points of Light will convene youth and regional Presidential Leadership Forums, uniting young people, educators, and community activists.

From such action will come achievement. And such achievement should be rewarded. And so, we'll ask media from small-town weeklies to network television to profile the brightest stars of community service. And our foundation will also recognize successful community initiatives and outstanding leaders through two new Presidential awards: the National Service Youth Leadership Awards, given each year to individuals, and the Build A Community Award, honoring partnerships which work together to strengthen families and decaying neighborhoods in America.

All of this will help fulfill us as Americans by asking us to combat problems like loneliness and poverty and drug abuse and homelessness. We cannot afford to fail, and we won't. For as Americans, we know what is at stake. We know that voluntarism can help those free-falling through society. We know that as citizens and institutions we can use one-to-one caring to truly love thy neighbor. And we know, finally, that from now on any definition of a successful life must include serving others. And we must resolve to carry this belief to every person in the land.

Two centuries ago just last year, Alexander Hamilton sent a letter urging General Washington to seek the Presidency. And he wrote him: "The point of light in which you stand will make an infinite difference." My friends, national service will succeed. It can make an infinite difference in the life of these United States, for a Thousand Points can light the lives of a people and a nation. Remember, there is no problem that is not being solved somewhere in America. You—you in this room who have already done so much—can prove that statement a thousand times over. It is in our hands.

God bless you. We need your help. And God bless our great country. Thank you.

Note: The President spoke at 1:35 p.m. in the Grand Ballroom of the New York Hilton Hotel. In his remarks, he referred to Ray Chambers, chairman of WESRAY Capital Corp.; Lewis Rudin, chairman of the Association for a Better New York; David Rockefeller and James D. Robinson III, founder and chairman of the New York Partnership, respectively. Prior to the President's remarks, a video on voluntarism was shown.

White House Fact Sheet on the Points of Light Initiative
June 22, 1989

CHALLENGE

Though America is at peace and more Americans are enjoying a greater degree of prosperity than ever before in our history, we still have work to do. As long as millions of Americans are illiterates, dropouts, drug abusers, pregnant teens, delinquent or suicidal young people, AIDS victims, and among the homeless and hungry, America has not yet fulfilled its promise. Our challenge is to overcome the disintegration of communities, large and small. While the Government's role is critical, government cannot overcome this challenge alone.

MISSION

The President believes in the readiness and ability of every individual and every institution in America to initiate action as "a point of light." Meaningful one-to-one engagement in the lives of others is now required to overcome our most serious national problems. The growth and magnification of "points of light" must now become an American mission.

STRATEGY

I. CLAIM PROBLEMS AS YOUR OWN

A. The President's Call for Action

The President calls on all Americans and all American institutions, large and small, to make service of central value in our daily life and work. The President calls on the heads of businesses and professional firms to include community service among the factors considered in making hiring, compensation, and promotion decisions. The President calls on newspapers, magazines, radio and television stations, cable systems, and other media institutions to identify service opportunities, spotlight successful service initiatives, and profile outstanding community leaders regularly. The President calls on State and local education boards to uphold the value of service and to encourage students, faculty, and personnel to serve others. The President calls on college and university presidents to recognize the value of community service in considering applicants; to uphold the value of community service; and to encourage students, faculty, and personnel to serve others. The President calls on not-for-profit service organizations to build the capacity to absorb increasing numbers of volunteers in purposeful roles. The President challenges all young people to lead the nation in this movement of community service through the YES (Youth Engaged in Service) to America Initiative. The President will call all young people to help overcome society's challenges by serving others through existing organizations or new initiatives.

He will also challenge:

- leaders from all institutions to engage their organizations in the development of young people;
- community leaders and students to reach out to alienated young people and develop community service opportunities which redirect their lives in a positive way;
- community service organizations to build the capacity to absorb large numbers of young people in purposeful community service.

Through the foundation, the President will:

- select the President's National Service

Youth Representatives, who will lead other young people in community service in their regions, suggest ways that other young people can engage in community service, and assist in developing and implementing local programs;
- initiate the President's National Service Youth Leadership Forums; and
- present the President's National Service Youth Leadership Awards to honor outstanding youth community leaders.

YES to America is not a Federal Government program, but a nationwide service movement. It is:
- a movement that is grassroots and community-based rather than devised in and imposed from Washington;
- a movement that does not compensate people with Federal dollars for what should be an obligation of citizenship;
- a movement that integrates service into young people's normal life and career pattern, developing in them a lifelong commitment to service rather than a temporary, 1- or 2-year involvement.

B. One-to-One Problem Solving

Every individual should "connect" with his or her institution—businesses, professional firms, the media, labor, education, religion, civic groups, associations of all kinds, and not-for-profit service organizations—and engage in the lives of others in need on a one-to-one basis. Examples of the kinds of engagement the President calls for include:
- starting a literacy program to teach every employee or member who wants to learn to read;
- adopting a school, class, or single student, providing tutoring, computers and other learning aids, food, clothing, or shelter for each student who needs them;
- adopting a nursing home, offering comfort and cheer;
- starting a one-to-one mentoring program for needy young people;
- forming a consortium to make decent, affordable housing available to the homeless;
- contributing and distributing surplus food to soup kitchens each day to feed the hungry.

Individuals wishing to help another in any of the above ways independently of an institution are encouraged to establish a one-to-one relationship with an individual in need.

II. IDENTIFY, ENLARGE AND REPLICATE WHAT IS WORKING

The President will serve as Honorary Chairman of a foundation called the Points of Light Initiative. The President will convene an advisory committee to make recommendations (within 45 days of its first meeting) on the structure and composition of the foundation and the legislation most appropriate to accomplish the purpose of the President's national service initiative.

The President will seek a congressional appropriation of $25 million annually for the foundation, which will, in turn, seek to match that amount from private sector contributions.

The President will challenge each Governor to replicate this initiative in each State and encourage State and local leaders to develop Points of Light Working Groups composed of community leaders. These groups will marshal resources within their communities and deploy them to overcome local problems.

The President believes that virtually every problem in America is being solved somewhere. There are already countless service initiatives working successfully throughout America. However, these successful initiatives are too often isolated and unknown to others. These initiatives must be replicated over and over again by individuals and teams until everyone is connected to someone, one to one.

A. Peer-to-Peer Working Groups

Through a foundation initiative to be called the ServNet Project, corporations, professional firms, unions, schools, religious groups, civic groups, and not-for-profit service organizations will be asked to donate the services of some of their most talented and promising people for a period of time. These extraordinary individuals will form and lead peer-to-peer working groups, e.g., lawyers going to fellow lawyers, teachers to fellow teachers, union members to fellow union members, bringing examples of successful initiatives and providing training, technical assistance, and other support to enable other institutions to devise similar initiatives.

B. Linking Servers to Needs

One of the foundation's objectives is to help to improve existing methods of matching would-be volunteers with purposeful service opportunities. Over time, through an initiative called the ServLink Project, the foundation will stimulate the development through private-sector resources of technology links between those who wish to serve and those who need service, e.g., telephone calls, interactive computers, etc.

Volunteer centers should be easily accessible to all Americans in their neighborhoods, matching people with service opportunities. Such contact points may be in a place of worship, union hall, library, fire station, business building, service group headquarters or neighborhood home. In addition, every bank, credit card issuer, telephone and utility company will be asked to include in billing and statement envelopes printed information about how people and their institutions can become engaged in serving others.

C. Recognition and Awards

In order to encourage others to engage in service, every newspaper, magazine, radio and television station will be asked to identify service opportunities, spotlight successful service initiatives and profile outstanding community leaders regularly.

The President's Build a Community Awards will honor those people and institutions who have worked together to rebuild families or to revitalize communities. Through the foundation, the President will recognize and present awards and other forms of commendation to talented community leaders and successful initiatives that are solving the Nation's most critical social problems.

III. DISCOVER AND ENCOURAGE NEW LEADERS

America's community service movement must have the strongest, most creative leadership, nationally and locally. Such leadership must be constantly recruited. The foundation, with the help of existing organizations, will identify the most promising new leaders in all walks of life who are not now engaged in community service and encourage them to devote part of their talent and energy to community service. The foundation will give special attention to young people and to those who have not had the opportunity to fulfill their leadership potential.

IV. CONCLUSION

The President's national service initiative focuses on the most critical domestic challenges facing the Nation today. These problems were long in coming and cannot be solved overnight. But if each American citizen and each American institution responds to the President's call to engage "one to one" in the life of another person in need, this initiative will be the most comprehensive and inclusive movement of our time. This movement can dramatically reverse negative trends on many fronts and ensure the fulfillment of America's promise.

Remarks at a Republican Party Fundraising Dinner in New York, New York

June 22, 1989

I am just delighted. Thank you all for that warm welcome. I look around this room, and I think to myself, okay, I'm President of the United States, but I know how I got here. And I see many, many people in this room to whom I will always feel indebted for that long-ago political action, and then when we all came together in the fall of

1988 for the election.

And so, I'm delighted to be here at this major political event. I want to thank Pat Barrett, my brother John, and Joe Fogg, outgoing chairman—my friend Tony Colavita. And it's always great to be back in New York; it's the first place I've ever come to that they named a dessert for my wife—just look at your program. I don't know what Bombe a la Barbara means—[*laughter*]—but nevertheless, we don't take that as a slight at all. We're pleased that you named it that. [*Laughter*] Maybe she does take it as—no, no. [*Laughter*]

No, it's great to be back in New York. Where else can you find newspapers with headlines like "Picked Pot Packed In Pickled Peppers"—that was out there—or my personal favorite from the New York Daily News, a headline that accompanied before and after pictures of a famous actor that read, "Brando Expando." [*Laughter*]

You're wondering why we're all dressed up. We're off to the Wall Street Journal 100th anniversary here in a few minutes, and the Wall Street Journal maintains a more dignified air with its no-photos policy. If they were ever to run a swimsuit issue, it would be Lee Iacocca in thongs. [*Laughter*]

I am here today to celebrate a new fact in American politics: the emergence of a strong, united New York State Republican Party. And we've had good times and bad, but this is due in no small measure to the leadership of our outgoing chairman, Tony Colavita. I'd like to give some credit, also, to my brother John, who fought the financial side of the equation.

And to the promise of success from your new cofinance chairman, Joe Fogg, an outstanding man who did a marvelous job on this dinner, and of course, to our new able Chairman Pat Barrett. Pat—he's a friend to many here, and Barbara and I consider him a friend. He has everything in the world going for him upstate, and now he's taken on this major job. He's shown the proven ability to reach out and attract new voters to the Republican Party. Pat, you've worked wonders as the county chairman up there in Onondaga County, and we look forward to your work and this Barrett magic all across New York State, and every single one of you ought to help him every way you possibly can.

It is no surprise to me that New Yorkers, in particular minority and ethnic voters, are shifting—they are shifting from automatic loyalty to the other party and voting Republican more and more. And it was, after all, the Republican Party that was the original party of civil rights, equal opportunity. It was the Republican Party that first attracted immigrants and the sons and daughters of immigrants into politics. Think of Mayor Fiorello La Guardia, The Little Flower of Italy.

And now we are proud to have a new generation of Republican leaders, with your great Senator, Alfonse D'Amato, heading our New York Republican delegation for a second term in the United States Senate. And I'm glad that his TV star of a mother is here. No United States Senator works harder, and I've seen them all in action. For 8 years I was President of the Senate; no United States Senator works harder for his constituents than Al D'Amato. And he will be reelected overwhelmingly, I'm sure, come 4 years.

Republicans take great pride in our New York Members of Congress, and you've got a good delegation, now 13 strong. I want to keep that number at 13—because Guy Molinari has decided to leave Congress to run for borough president, and I want him to win that race, and I want all of you to support him. But the Nation's loss is Staten Island's gain. And then with Susan already on the New York Council, the Molinaris will be even more of a powerhouse in the State, and I will always be grateful to Guy.

We are also justly proud of how far we've come as a party, so far that we now have a good chance—and I mean a real good chance—of winning the mayor's office in New York City, the most powerful local office in America. And it's a tremendous opportunity for the Republican Party to show that our commitment to executive leadership extends far beyond the executive branch in Washington, DC—far beyond the White House, to the city streets and the sidewalks of New York, where the action really is. And accordingly, I would like to commend our three mayoral candidates, Rudolph Giuliani—Rudy—[*laughter*]—sorry about that—Ron Lauder, and Herb London—for offering their considerable abilities to the voters.

And my plea, in advance of this September primary, is that we recognize that we can and will win the race if we pull together as a party. And that is my pitch to you tonight, and I hope every one of you will get behind whoever our nominee is.

And as we win the top executive job in America's top city, we will also make big legislative gains in Albany, keeping the State senate, making big strides in the assembly. The State senate has been our Republican watchdog in Albany, you might say, and it must be our first line of defense in the fight for fair representation in the 1990's. As I look around our country with a sense of fairness motivating me, it is absolutely essential that we block the gerrymandering ways of the Democratic Party in all 50 States. They've done it to us in the past, and we cannot let them do it to us again.

So, Pat, under your leadership—a strong, united New York Republican Party with unity and with courage—I know you'll go the distance. And the era of the Democratic dominance will be a story from the past.

So, I just wanted to come up here tonight with Barbara and wish you well; thank and salute your new leadership; thank all of you who have supported this, the most successful fundraiser that a party has had, as Pat said, in the State's history; and say to you, we are lucky to live in the greatest, freest country in the world. And part of all that freedom stems from our participation in politics, so don't think that there's something wrong with it. Roll up your sleeves and go to work, and let's win the mayor's race in the fall, and let's build this party so we pick up seats in the Congress in 1990.

Thank you all. God bless you, and keep up the good work.

Note: The President spoke at 7:16 p.m. in the Grand Ballroom at the New York Hilton Hotel.

Remarks at the Wall Street Journal Anniversary Dinner in New York, New York

June 22, 1989

Well, thank you, Warren, and all of you at Dow Jones, Wall Street Journal for inviting Barbara and me to be with you tonight; and I really am pleased to be here. I'm delighted to see so many friends, including this one right up here—Lionel Hampton. This is a nonpartisan evening, but politically, we've been together for a long, long time.

Your 100th birthday—talk about a big event. This morning, I saw Willard Scott on TV holding up a birthday snapshot of the Wall Street Journal. And speaking of television, Barbara and I have staying with us our grandson, George P.—our oldest grandson, from Florida. And I told him I'd be spending the evening with a lot of famous people in the media, the media elite. He asked me to get an autograph from Morton Downey. [*Laughter*] But seriously, Warren was telling me about this get-together, and this is an impressive audience. And as I look around, if anything catastrophic happened in the Winter Garden, the Fortune 500 would be lucky to keep in the just double digits.

But 100 years ago, what was it like? It wasn't cars but carriages that crowded the New York cobblestones on July 8, 1889. Telephones and electric lights were just catching on. It was the year that the Oklahoma Territory opened and the Johnstown flooded and Mark Twain penned "A Connecticut Yankee." Another year would pass before Sitting Bull would perish in the Sioux uprisings. And as the Sun rose over Manhattan on that hot July Monday, John D. Rockefeller was preparing to celebrate his 50th birthday. And upriver—I saw Eli Jacobs here, and he'll be interested in this—upriver, 10,000 baseball fans filled the new Polo Grounds, with another 5,000 crowding the nearby bluffs, to see New York down

Pittsburgh 7 to 5.

And from a modest office not far from where we stand, the Wall Street Journal was distributed to a few hundred readers for 2 cents a copy. And the first front page contained another historic first—your first typo. [*Laughter*] It was in a story about John L. Sullivan's victory in the bare-knuckle heavyweight championship, won after 75 grueling rounds. It was to be the Nation's last such drawn-out, bare-knuckle fight until they invented leveraged buyouts and Presidential primaries. [*Laughter*]

From those modest beginnings, the Wall Street Journal emerged to become America's ledger sheet, chronicling war and depression and prosperity, as we grew from a frontier society to the frontiers of space—the world's dominant financial power.

Arthur Miller observed that "a good newspaper is a nation talking to itself." Well, in my view, the Journal is like that. In a changing world that offers 64 channels of cable television, the 6 columns of the Wall Street Journal are as familiar as the morning coffee at our breakfast tables. And its pages tell the story of our times. Only once in 100 years did it carry a banner headline. The day after Pearl Harbor, September 7th, 1941—[*laughter*]—make that December 7th, 1941. But after the war, the Journal came to Texas the same year I did, 1948, when it began printing in Dallas. Your chairman, Warren Phillips, had been hired as a copyreader the year before, in time to see the first of the paper's 13 Pulitzers. Not that every article was a Pulitzer Prize winner. In 1967 a front-page story on China predicted the Communist government wouldn't last the year. A decade later, in 1979, the Wall Street Journal became the largest circulation daily in the Nation, but one rival complained that it was only because so many subscribers were at an age where they forgot to cancel. [*Laughter*]

Speaking of age—and literally apropos of absolutely nothing—Bob Hope told this story about aging at the Joe Gibbs charity dinner in Washington this week that Barbara and I attended, and that our guest here Kay Graham's son sponsored. Two men, two old men, sitting on a park bench—and the first one said, "Do you know how old I am?" The second one said, "Stand up, turn around, drop your trousers down. Now pat yourself on the back. Okay, pull up your trousers, sit back down here on this bench." The man said, "Well, how old am I?" He said, "You're 93 years old, 4 months and 3 days." The first guy said, "How did you know that?" He said, "You told me yesterday." [*Laughter*]

Well, anyway, on the day after the 1980 election, the lead editorial—the 1980 election—the lead editorial celebrated Ronald Reagan's mandate. And President Reagan told me, "Well, one day your day will come." And it did. And the day after I was elected President, the headline read—and I kid you not—"Jim Wright's Mandate." [*Laughter*] Go look it up. [*Laughter*]

I told Al Hunt, though, how much I enjoy the Journal. He asked if it's the front page, the conservative editorials, or the news coverage. I said, "No, none of those, none of the above. It's because you don't carry "Doonesbury." [*Laughter*]

All kidding aside, the Wall Street Journal has a proud and enviable tradition. And although you deal in the world's most perishable product—news, polls have repeatedly shown that your paper is one of America's most trusted publications. A reputation like that can only be earned by adherence to your founders' pledge to always have the news "honest, intelligent, and unprejudiced." In modern times, your reporters have carried this pledge beyond business reporting, in coverage of events like the civil rights struggle, the recent tragedy in Beijing—carrying on a proud American tradition of braving intimidation to bring the truth into the light.

And many at the Journal have gone beyond their professional obligations and set examples of another old-fashioned tradition that is very much on my mind today: the tradition of public service. Three years ago, John Fialka wrote a column-one story entitled "Sisters In Need," chronicling the poverty that had befallen the growing ranks of retired clergy in America, and it provoked a swell of readership response. And so, John and others at the Journal founded "SOAR"—"Support Our Aging Religious"—and raised more than $1 million to aid 30 different orders.

A similar public response occurred in 1987 after the publication of "Urban Trauma," Alex Kotlowitz's moving account of 3 months in the life of a kid, Lafayette Wilson—a kid, a 12-year-old boy struggling to survive in a dangerous Chicago project. And Alex stayed in touch with Lafayette. And last summer they passed the hat at the Journal and gave this kid and his brother a season of peace in the woods of a Wisconsin boy's camp.

Personal gestures, profound actions, sometimes life-changing in their effect—these are the works of men and women who know that prosperity without purpose means nothing.

And earlier today, I announced a new initiative calling on all levels of government—both sectors, public and private—to enlist in a new crusade to bring national service into every corner of America. And that crusade begins with a simple truth: From now on, any definition of a successful life must include serving others.

And I may never have as important an audience to carry this message to as you who are gathered in the Winter Garden tonight—the American business community, who has supported conservative policies. We're enjoying prosperous years, but not all Americans are part of that prosperity, and I ask that business do its part. Prosperity cannot be truly enjoyed unless the Points of Light about which I've spoken shine on every American in need. Many of you are CEO's [chief executive officers] with galaxies at your command. And it is my request—and I believe, your obligation—to donate the services of the talented and the enterprising within your ranks. Many of you are setting the pace; many of you are doing this now. Everyone should do this now.

And shortly after the Wall Street Journal was founded, 100 years ago, the Census Bureau declared that the frontier no longer existed in America. But the Wall Street Journal—you've proven them wrong by advancing across ever-new frontiers of technology and geography and innovation. And I said it a week ago, looking eastward across America from the foot of those majestic Grand Tetons: The challenges ahead are in the frontiers of the mind and in the good that hard work and the human imagination can bring to pass.

Not long after bringing home the Journal's first Pulitzer Prize, William Grimes expressed a simple creed. He wrote: "We believe in the individual, in his wisdom and his decency." Now, that's a worthy tenet, one we can all carry forth from tonight's celebration and on to a renewed commitment to service tomorrow. To all at the Journal, I send you my heartfelt congratulations on this landmark, wish you success as your second century begins. And to all here tonight: Thank you, God bless you, and God bless the United States of America. Thank you very, very much.

Note: The President spoke at 8:49 p.m. in the Winter Garden at the World Financial Center. In his remarks, he referred to Warren Phillips, chief executive officer of Dow Jones & Co., Inc.; entertainer Lionel Hampton; television personalities Willard Scott and Morton Downey; Eli S. Jacobs, owner of the Baltimore Orioles; playwright Arthur Miller; Katherine and Donald Graham, chairman of the board and publisher of the Washington Post, respectively; and Albert Hunt, Washington bureau chief of the Wall Street Journal. Following his remarks, the President returned to Washington, DC.

Nomination of Five Members of the Defense Nuclear Facilities Safety Board, and Designation of Chairman and Vice Chairman
June 23, 1989

The President today announced his intention to nominate the following individuals to be members of the Defense Nuclear Facilities Safety Board, for the terms indicated. These are new positions.

Edson G. Case, of Maryland, for a term of 1 year. Since 1975 Mr. Case has been Deputy Director of the Office of Nuclear Reactor Regulation at the Nuclear Regulatory Commission in Washington, DC.

John T. Conway, of New York, for a term of 5 years. Upon confirmation, the President intends to designate Mr. Conway as Chairman. Since 1982 Mr. Conway has been executive vice president for corporate affairs for the Consolidated Edison Co. of New York.

John W. Crawford, Jr., of Maryland, for a term of 2 years. Since 1981 Mr. Crawford has been a consultant in nuclear engineering. Prior to this he was Principal Deputy Assistant Secretary for Nuclear Energy at the Department of Energy, 1979–1981.

A.J. Eggenberger, of Montana, for a term of 4 years. Upon confirmation, the President intends to designate Mr. Eggenberger as Vice Chairman. Since 1984 Mr. Eggenberger has been program director and leader of the Earthquake Hazard Mitigation Program for the National Science Foundation in Washington, DC; and since 1982, an expert consultant in nuclear safety for the International Atomic Energy Agency in Vienna, Austria.

Herbert Kouts, of New York, for a term of 3 years. Since 1976 Dr. Kouts has been with the Brookhaven National Laboratory in Upton, NY, most recently serving as senior physicist in the department of nuclear energy.

Statement on the 25th Anniversary of the Slaying of Civil Rights Activists James Chaney, Andrew Goodman, and Michael Schwerner

June 23, 1989

James Chaney, Andrew Goodman, and Michael Schwerner gave their lives in the struggle to guarantee one of democracy's most basic civil rights—the right to vote—for all Americans. The savage execution of these three brave men rightfully shocked our national conscience. The public outcry galvanized this country's progress on civil rights.

Today, 25 years later, we have not forgotten these three brave young men and their sacrifice. When they saw the promise of democracy unfulfilled in their homeland, they risked all so that others might know the joy of true freedom. We have come far because of James and Andrew and Michael. We can erect no greater monument to their memory than to ensure that the arrogance and bigotry that took their lives never again exists in America. The courageous family members whom I met this morning have embarked on a symbolic journey to commemorate the sacrifice of these American heroes, and I wish them Godspeed.

Message to the Congress Transmitting the Report of the Council on Environmental Quality

June 23, 1989

To the Congress of the United States:

I am pleased to transmit to the Congress the annual report of the Council on Environmental Quality, *Environmental Quality 1987–1988*. This report focuses on the Nation's air, land, and water resources that are particularly affected by the urbanization of our population and by other intensive uses. It presents CEQ's analysis of the historical trends, current status, and outlook for urban air quality, developed water resources, and the growing burden of municipal solid waste on the urban landscape. It also offers an assessment of the Federal lands reserved for our national defense installations, which present special environmental challenges.

Americans built great cities that have facilitated commerce and economic growth and prosperity, and provided homes to millions of new citizens from all over the world. Today nearly three-fourths of our people reside in communities classified as "urban", which make up only about 2 percent of this country's total land acreage. As our Nation has generally prospered by intensively developing these urban areas, expectations for human health and quality of the natural environment have also increased.

Hence, for nearly 2 decades, governments at all levels have increased their efforts to address pollution and environmental degradation. Parallel efforts in the private sector have accompanied government programs to protect the human environment. As a result, we can point proudly to improvements on a number of fronts. Some of these are reviewed in this CEQ report. For example, the Federal motor vehicle control program, which sets emissions standards for all new production vehicles, has brought about a clearly demonstrated improvement in the quality of the air in cities throughout the Nation.

But we can do better. That is why we are committed to cleaner air in the Nation's cities, and why we believe that a fresh approach to the Clean Air Act can help meet the Nation's environmental needs without compromising our record of unprecedented economic growth. It is now clear that different cities have varying climatic conditions, industrial mixes, and automobile use patterns. Cleaner air in our cities will thus require credible commitment, timetables, and strategies for the different regions of the country. Innovative solutions tailored to meet local circumstances will be required. Draconian limits on economic growth and on the use of the automobile should not be necessary in order to give Americans clean air at levels they are willing to pay for, but it will require significant Federal, State, and local leadership and innovative approaches from government and industry.

We must do better. This country must make every effort to stem the rising tide of garbage and industrial waste through a more aggressive use of waste minimization and recycling practices. America as a nation is filling landfills faster than it can establish new ones. The waste problem is not going away, and it can no longer be neglected. Waste minimization must start at home and in the local communities, by reducing household garbage and separating wastes for recycling. In many cases it is in the economic self-interest of industry to recycle its wastes, to minimize waste generation at the source, or to adopt less polluting processes. Innovative techniques that have proven effective in reducing wastes both in industry and in local communities should be widely shared.

We will do better. The development of America's abundant water resources has stimulated economic advancement in nearly all regions of the country and has facilitated growth in interstate commerce generally. Since 1972, a national expenditure of $350 billion for water pollution abatement and control has restored water quality in many places so that today some three-fourths of our rivers, lakes, and estuaries can fully support fishing and swimming. But the pollution that washed ashore on popular beaches last summer has again focused attention on the condition of the Nation's coastal waters. Abuses of the oceans and the Great Lakes must end and will end, and we will work closely with the States to enforce and strengthen the effectiveness of the Ocean Dumping Act and the Clean Water Act. We must also better protect America's wetlands, by working towards a goal of no net loss through a coordinated wetlands policy. We are also committed to protecting the Nation's surface and ground water resources from contamination by fertilizers and pesticides without jeopardizing the economic vitality of U.S. agriculture, and we will work with farmers to adopt environmentally sound production practices, safer chemicals, and biological pest controls.

Doing a better job of cleaning the air will make our cities more healthful. Doing a better job of solid waste management will make our landscapes safer and more attractive. Doing a better job of protecting our water resources will add importantly to the overall opportunities for outdoor recreation within and near our urban communities, closer to where most Americans spend most of their time. Recent studies of outdoor recreation have pointed out the enormous popularity of water-based recreation activities and have stressed the positive relationship between improvements in water quality and the effective use of urban lands available for outdoor recreation.

A better life for all Americans is our great common desire, and I believe that economic growth and a clean environment are both part of what all Americans understand a better life to mean. The protection of the environment and the conservation and wise management of our natural resources must have a high priority on our national agenda. Given sound research, hard work, sufficient public and private funds, and—most important—the necessary political will, we can achieve and maintain an environment that protects the public health and enhances the quality of life for us all.

GEORGE BUSH

The White House,
June 23, 1989.

Remarks at the Annual Meeting of the American Association of University Women
June 26, 1989

Sarah, thank you very much for that introduction—and all of you for that warm welcome—and congratulations to you as you complete your distinguished term as president of AAUW. And welcome to Sharon Schuster, the new president. And may she run the meetings with the same iron hand—[*laughter*]—and put-down of dilatory proceedings, such as free debate—[*laughter*]—that Sharon did. I say all that because she told me coming in here that there was a harmonious meeting, and one that—plenty of substance discussed—that went very, very well indeed. So, congratulations!

There's another AAUW president, a past president, that I'd like to say hello to, from Des Moines, Iowa, and now the head of your educational foundation: Mary Grefe. Is it really Grefe? I didn't want to say grief. [*Laughter*] I pronounced it my way. [*Laughter*]

In America today, there is no greater imperative, moral or practical, than providing equal opportunity to every man, woman, and child. And this means equal opportunity in housing and jobs, and flexibility and parental choice in child care and education. And it means equal protection from hostile elements, whether criminal or environmental, and equal opportunity in service and community action, whether through public, private, or nonprofit organizations.

And today I'd like to talk about two issues in particular: education and public safety. Both are important to this association and to any thinking person who cares about the quality of life and opportunity in America. And both are the subject of major administration proposals now pending before the United States Congress.

And there's a third issue that I know you're familiar with: community action—what I have called a Thousand Points of Light. And last week I traveled up and down the eastern seaboard, issuing a call to action for community service. And we carried the message from Main Street to Wall Street, enlisting young and old, black and white and brown—America's diversity—to join a movement predicated on one simple idea: From now on, any definition of a successful life must include services to others. For over a hundred years, your predecessors, and now you in this room, have built successful lives through community action. You were ahead of the curve, way out ahead of the power curve, by about a century. And often your service has addressed the very issues we're talking about today: education and public safety.

The AAUW foundation that Mary Grefe—[*laughter*]—now directs—what is it about me and Iowa, where I'm always having trouble?—[*laughter*]—began handing out educational fellowships in 1888. And it's a great tradition, at once combining America's values of service and education. And the scholarships you provide are more than just money in the hands of deserving students: They are money in the bank for the future of America. And your association represents 140,000 reasons why America will succeed.

Your contributions are important, and equally important is the recent and renewed commitment to an old-fashioned American idea: partnership between the Government and the community in seeking educational excellence. Government, and especially Federal Government, cannot provide all the answers, but it has an obligation to lead.

And earlier this year, I sent to Congress the Educational Excellence Act of 1989. And it proposes solutions based on some sound and time-tested ideas: rewarding excellence, helping those in need, accountability—and one that's close to the traditions of this organization—parental choice and flexibility. To achieve these goals, my new initiative proposes a seven-point plan: first, cash awards for merit schools; second, merit awards for America's best teachers—[*applause*]—a little dissent on that one—[*laughter*]—third, a new program for high school science scholarships; fourth, $400 million to boost magnet schools; fifth, new money for new teachers, using alternative certification to expand the pool of skilled educators; sixth, emergency grants to help our schools become drug free; and seventh, expanded Federal help to our historically black colleges and universities.

Given the number of experienced educators right here in this room, it will come as no surprise to learn that many of these initiatives were developed from the classroom success stories of teachers like those in your association. And other guidance came from people like Sarah Harder, who I met with in Washington following my election as President. And my administration is grateful for the benefit of your experiences and your views.

And today I'd like to talk briefly about four of these initiatives in particular. Two of the points call for merit awards—cash incentives for our most successful schools and the top teachers in every State. I want the best teachers our educational system can attract, because teachers shape the minds that shape the future of the country.

Last year, at the centennial celebration of the first AAUW educational fellowship, Justice Sandra Day O'Connor received your Achievement Award. And when we talk about merit schools and merit teachers, there could hardly be a better example than this year's winner, the founder of the Westside Preparatory School in Chicago's inner city, Marva Collins. Says Marva, "Any child can learn if they are not taught so thoroughly that they cannot." [*Laughter*] Think about that one, now.

She got results, working with students who have been written off by the public schools. It's said that 98 percent of her students go on to high school and then college. And her students got results. It was reported that one of Marva's 6-year-olds could recite Jesse Jackson's 1988 convention address from memory. [*Laughter*] Hmm. [*Laughter*] Now look, Marva, Jesse is a very gifted speaker, and you're being too tough on those kids. [*Laughter*] Give them my convention speech, and I bet they can do it at age 3. [*Laughter*]

But I've also heard of one young girl who began pounding her lunch box on the desk in the middle of the class. Marva told the girl, "No, darling, no one is going to be handing out good jobs to people who pound their lunch boxes on their desks. President Bush does not pound his lunch box on the desk." [*Laughter*] Obviously, Marva's never been to one of our Cabinet meetings. [*Laughter*]

America needs results, too. So, another part of my education plan calls for a similar kind of new incentive: science scholarships of up to $40,000 for more than 500 of our best high school seniors. And this is an idea that also resonates in your association. Last year you founded the Eleanor Roosevelt Fund—what you call an intergenerational partnership—to address the underrepresentation of women and girls in math and science.

And I know that many of you are familiar with "Workforce 2000," which concludes that almost two-thirds of the new entrants to the labor force in the next 11 years will be women. To stay competitive in a competitive world, we must provide incentives and opportunities for this new generation of women to get the education and training they need to be second to none. And if we cannot compete with other countries in the classroom, we cannot compete with them in the boardroom.

And the last of our education initiatives calls for drug-free schools. And we've asked Congress to finance urban emergency grants to help our hardest hit school districts. And if we want to stop our kids from putting drugs in their bodies, we must first put character in their hearts and common sense in their heads.

Let me just stop here a minute. Barbara and I were up in Covenant House the other day in New York, and Barbara's good at this—she can handle the emotion of the young kids; her husband is not. But if you'd seen it, and I expect some of you had, these kids—the matrix joining the meeting was narcotics use, prostitution, and hopelessness, really—and it was tragic. And it brought home to me, loud and clear, how much we have left to do in terms of offering hope, through education, to the young people afflicted by this scourge of narcotics. We've got to succeed as a nation.

So, as with education, the subject of drugs and crime, as well—especially violent crime—has been on my mind in recent weeks. And last month, I was out standing before the U.S. Capitol on a somber, rainy afternoon to call on Congress to join me in a new partnership with America's cities and States to take back the streets. And at the Federal level, we're going to do our part by taking violent criminals off the streets. And it's an attack on all four fronts: new laws to punish them, new agents to arrest them, new prosecutors to convict them, and new prisons to hold them. And incidentally, I feel just as strongly about the white-collar criminal that traffics in narcotics as I do about the street criminal.

The comprehensive initiative that I'm talking about here is directed at violent crime and, in particular, the explosion of urban gunfire that often accompanies drug trafficking. But all too often, violent crime also means crime against women, and I am angered and disgusted by the crimes against American women and by the archaic and unacceptable attitudes that all too frequently contribute to those crimes. Whether it involves spouse abuse at home or violence in the street, these are evil acts that transcend racial and class lines. This war against women must stop, and I hope we can prove to be a constructive force for ending it.

Our cities and States must step up their efforts to combat violence against women, to treat victims with compassion and respect. And they must follow our Federal example of enacting tougher laws—backed up by more police, prosecutors, and prisons—to put away every violent offender.

Fundamentally, violence against women won't subside unless public attitudes change. We must continue to educate police and prosecutors, judges and juries. And we must engender a climate where the message our children get—from television and films, from schools and parents—is that violence against women is wrong. A kinder and gentler nation must protect all its citizens. And no matter how equal the opportunities in our schools and workplace, women will never have the same opportunities as men if a climate of fear leaves them justifiably concerned about walking to the campus library at night or reluctant to work late hours for fear of getting out of some parking lots safely.

I have a daughter and four daughters-in-law. And when we talk about what kind of schools and the kind of society we are shaping for the next century, I think about my own 11 grandchildren—seven are girls. And it is unthinkable that any opportunity should be available to my pride and joy, our oldest grandson, George P., that isn't also out there for his cousin Jenna Bush.

And one opportunity—and maybe I'm preaching to the choir here—[*laughter*]—that some women in this room should not overlook is rolling up your sleeves and running for public office. I encourage you to do that, and it is challenging and enormously satisfying. This day and age there seems to be more public flak and all of that, but believe me, I still feel strongly that public service is an honorable calling. And we've got to inculcate that into the life of every single child in this country, and you can help by running for office.

Over the years, I have had the privilege of working with many talented leaders like Carla Hills and Elizabeth Dole and Sandra Day O'Connor and Nancy Kassebaum, and their record of public service—like the work of so many in your own association—confirms the long-ago observation of one of the patron saints of community service, Alexis de Tocqueville. He wrote, "If I were asked to what the singular prosperity and growing strength of the American people ought mainly to be attributed, I should reply: to the superiority of their women."

I am pleased to be the first President to address the AAUW and very honored—maybe I'm getting a little out ahead of the power curve here—to be awarded an official membership. [*Laughter*] Wait a minute! So, technically that makes me the first AAUW member to be President of the United States, but I know I won't be the last.

Thank you all, and God bless all of you. Thank you very much.

Note: The President spoke at 11:27 a.m. in the Sheraton Washington Ballroom at the Sheraton Washington Hotel. In his remarks, he referred to Sarah Harder, president of the association; U.S. Trade Representative Carla A. Hills; Secretary of Labor Elizabeth H. Dole; and Senator Nancy Landon Kassebaum of Kansas.

Statement by Press Secretary Fitzwater on the President's Meeting With Foreign Minister Hiroshi Mitsuzuka of Japan

June 26, 1989

The President met with Japanese Foreign Minister Hiroshi Mitsuzuka in the Oval Office for 20 minutes this afternoon. The President congratulated the Foreign Minister on assuming his new post and reaffirmed the importance of the U.S.-Japanese relationship not only for the two nations but for the whole globe. Minister Mitsuzuka stressed the continuity of Japanese diplomacy and that the U.S.-Japan relationship will continue to be the cornerstone of Japan's foreign policy. There was a brief discussion of trade issues, and the President indicated that trade would be a major point of discussion in the upcoming economic summit in Paris. The President and Foreign Minister discussed the situation in China.

The Foreign Minister said Japan was encouraged by the President's experience in the region and hoped our two countries would keep each other informed on our views. The President said that we would continue trying to convince the Chinese leadership that it is in their interest to keep reform moving forward. During the course of the meeting, Foreign Minister Mitsuzuka invited Vice President Quayle to visit Japan in September, and the Vice President accepted in principle.

Remarks to New Members of the Republican Party

June 26, 1989

Thank you very much. And all of you, greetings, welcome to the Rose Garden. To Lee Atwater and Jeannie Austin—delighted that the leaders of our party are here for this important occasion. And of course, to our special friend, Congressman Bill Grant of Florida—a great, great pleasure to see you again and have you here with us. And to State officials, key elected leaders, fellow Republicans all—welcome to the White

House. And welcome officially—you don't need it from me—but welcome to the Republican Party!

It was once said that some men change their principles for their party, while others change their party for their principles. And since the election, scores of elected Democratic officials, men and women, have made the right choice and joined the Republican Party because the values and principles of the Democratic Party were not their values and principles, and I think many more will follow them.

The switch is on to the party in sync with the American principles. The switch is on to the Republican Party. In February—seems like just yesterday—Bill Grant, Congressman, came to the White House to announce his switch from Democrat to Republican. And now he's with the party of opportunity, the party of ideas, the party of the future—because in the future, I honestly believe there will be many more Democrats joining our ranks.

And people say the Republican Party is on the move. Well, when I look around here today, I'd say that's true. We're moving in the right direction. But the Democratic Party is on the move, too: to the left and out of the mainstream. And as the greatest former Democrat of them all, President Reagan, once said: "I didn't leave the Democratic Party. The Democratic Party left me." The Democratic Party is leaving droves of voters behind as it moves over onto the more liberal side, the left side of the political equation. And now many of those stranded voters have made a move on their own—to the Republican Party, our party of family, faith, and the future.

And each of you here has made a courageous decision, sometimes a very tough political decision, to join us—taking considerable political risk in the process. But you've also made a move to be on the winning side in the contest of ideas and issues in America. And when you made that bold choice to join us, we made a choice, too. We will support you; we will back you up in every way we can. You've made a tough decision—the right decision—and we're with you. And when you're out there on the front lines for us, you won't be fighting alone. This party will stand with you shoulder to shoulder.

As former Democrats, you are the most visible sign of the great sea changes that are going on in the American political scene. I'm told that since 1984, the Republican Party in Florida has increased its voter registration by nearly half a million; and in the last 60 days, Republicans have been outregistering Democrats in that State by better than 3 to 1. And that's because mainstream Americans believe in peace through strength, and economic opportunity, traditional family values. And with the Republican Party, they're swimming with the current.

We know which party stands for a strong America and a growing economy, and Americans know that, too. And that's why with the able leadership of Lee Atwater, Jeannie Austin, the party will become the majority party in America. We can do it—I want to help—we will do it because of the courage of you and thousands like you. On behalf of Republicans everywhere, then, thank you, congratulations, welcome to the Republican Party. Thank you all very, very much for coming.

Note: The President spoke at 3:44 p.m. in the Rose Garden of the White House. In his remarks, he referred to H. Lee Atwater and Jeannie Austin, chairman and cochairman of the Republican National Committee.

White House Statement on the Soviet-United States Nuclear Testing Negotiations

June 26, 1989

Today marks the beginning of round IV of the nuclear testing talks (NTT) in Geneva between the United States and the Soviet Union. Ambassador C. Paul Robinson heads the U.S. delegation to the talks.

The U.S. approach to these negotiations complements our efforts to reach agreements that will strengthen our security and enhance stability. A priority for these step-by-step talks is to complete protocols to provide for effective verification of the Threshold Test Ban Treaty of 1974 (TTBT) and the Peaceful Nuclear Explosions Treaty of 1976 (PNET), neither of which has been ratified because they were not verifiable in their original form.

Much has been accomplished in the negotiations, and we will build on the progress that has been made. We have substantially completed the protocol to the PNET, and we will be working to complete the TTBT protocol, which governs nuclear weapons testing. Since the TTBT and PNET are complementary treaties, they and their protocols will be submitted to the Senate as a package for advice and consent to ratification.

Our approach to these negotiations is based on a realistic approach to our security: For the past four decades, a strong nuclear deterrent has been the foundation of our security and freedom. As long as we must rely on nuclear weapons, we must continue to test to ensure their safety, security, reliability, effectiveness, and survivability. We resume these negotiations determined to complete the task of concluding the verification provisions, which are essential to sound and stabilizing agreements.

Statement by Press Secretary Fitzwater on the Persecution of the Turkish Minority in Bulgaria

June 26, 1989

In the last month, over 60,000 people have either fled or been forcibly expelled from Bulgaria to Turkey—many with nothing more than the clothes on their backs—and more are arriving in Turkey every day.

This mass migration is the result of the Bulgarian Government's systematic denial of basic human rights to its Turkish minority. Since 1984 the Bulgarian authorities have been carrying out a campaign of forced assimilation of Bulgaria's ethnic Turkish minority, forcing its members to slavicize their names and denying them the right to speak their language and practice their religion. Members of the minority who have objected have been imprisoned without trial and treated with great brutality.

Over the past month, this campaign against ethnic Turks has taken on a new dimension, as Bulgarian forces have fired on peaceful demonstrators, killing some and wounding others. There are reports that the violence continues. We deplore Bulgaria's blatant violations of the human rights of its citizens, rights which Bulgaria has committed itself to protect as a signatory of the Helsinki accords and other international agreements. We urge the Government of Bulgaria to cease these violations and to allow for the orderly emigration of those ethnic Turks who desire to leave.

Statement by Press Secretary Fitzwater on President Bush's Meeting With President Mário Alberto Soares of Portugal

June 26, 1989

The President met today with Portuguese President Mário Soares. The President expressed his appreciation for Portugal's positive contribution to the North Atlantic alliance. The two leaders discussed the European Community, China, and Central America. Southern Africa was also discussed, particularly the Angola peace process. The meeting lasted 35 minutes. Deputy National Security Adviser Robert Gates and Deputy Secretary of State Lawrence Eagleburger also attended the meeting.

Nomination of Evelyn Irene Hoopes Teegen To Be United States Ambassador to Fiji, Tonga, Tuvalu, and Kiribati

June 26, 1989

The President today announced his intention to nominate Evelyn Irene Hoopes Teegen to be Ambassador Extraordinary and Plenipotentiary of the United States of America to Fiji and to serve concurrently and without additional compensation as Ambassador Extraordinary and Plenipotentiary of the United States of America to the Kingdom of Tonga, Tuvalu, and Kiribati. She would succeed Leonard Rochwarger.

Ms. Teegen is presently the Republican national committeewoman for Minnesota and the executive director of the Minnesota Seat Belt Coalition. Since 1987 Ms. Teegen has also been vice president of Teegen and Associates in Minneapolis. She also served as a member of the U.S. delegation to the 25th anniversary of the independence of Kenya, 1988; as a member of the 15th Air Command/Civilian Distinguished Visitors trip, 1987; as a member of the National Academy of Science for the Study of the Benefits and Costs of the 55 MPH Speed Limit, 1986; as a member of the National Highway Safety Advisory Committee, 1982–1985; and as a member of the Republican National Committee delegation to the People's Republic of China, 1984. Ms. Teegen is a member of the board of directors of Africare and the Minnesota Safety Council, as well as a member of the American Coalition of Traffic Safety and the Minnesota Citizens Council on Crime and Justice.

Ms. Teegen graduated from Iowa State University with a bachelor of science degree, 1953. She was born November 17, 1931, in Muscatine County, IA. Ms. Teegen is married, has two children, and currently resides in Minneapolis, MN.

Nomination of Thomas F. Stroock To Be United States Ambassador to Guatemala

June 26, 1989

The President today announced his intention to nominate Thomas F. Stroock to be Ambassador Extraordinary and Plenipotentiary of the United States of America to the Republic of Guatemala. He would succeed James H. Michel.

Mr. Stroock is currently president of Alpha Exploration, Inc., and the Stroock Leasing Corp., in Casper, WY. In addition, he is a Wyoming State senator and serves as vice president, chairman of the Wyoming Senate Appropriations Committee, and cochairman of the Wyoming Joint Legislative Appropriations Committee. He has also served as director of Key Bank of Wyoming and as director of Key Bancshares of Wyoming. He worked for the National Public Lands Council, 1981–1984; the National Small Business Advisory Council, 1981–1983; and as director of Century Oil and Gas Co., 1976–1982. He has served as a member of the National Petroleum Council, 1970–1977; director of Mid-America/Great Plains Financial Corp., 1967–1973; and director of the Wycom Corp., 1968–1975.

Mr. Stroock graduated from Yale University (B.A., 1948). He was born October 10, 1925, in New York City. He is married, has four children, and resides in Casper, WY. He served in the U.S. Marine Corps, 1943–1946.

Nomination of Alexander Fletcher Watson To Be Deputy United States Representative to the United Nations

June 26, 1989

The President today announced his intention to nominate Alexander Fletcher Watson to be the Deputy Representative of the United States of America to the United Nations, with the rank of Ambassador Extraordinary and Plenipotentiary. He would succeed Herbert Stuart Okun. Mr. Watson is a career member of the Senior Foreign Service, Class of Minister-Counselor.

Ambassador Watson entered the Foreign Service in 1962. He initially served as a consular officer in Santo Domingo, 1962–1964, and Madrid, 1964–1966. Following these assignments he served in the Department of State as an intelligence analyst in the Bureau of Intelligence and Research, 1966–1968. In 1968 he attended graduate school at the University of Wisconsin at Madison. Ambassador Watson was a political officer in the U.S. Embassy in Brazil, 1969–1970; principal officer, American consulate in Salvador de Bahia, Brazil, 1970–1973; and country officer, Office of Brazilian Affairs, Bureau of Inter-American Affairs, Department of State, 1973–1975. In 1975 Ambassador Watson was named Special Assistant for Legislative and Public Affairs to the Assistant Secretary for Economic and Business Affairs. In 1977 Ambassador Watson became Deputy Director, and then Director, of the Bureau's Office of Development Finance. He then served as deputy chief of mission in the U.S. Embassies in Bolivia, 1979–1981; Colombia, 1981–1984; and Brazil, 1984–1986. Since 1986 Ambassador Watson has been serving as Ambassador to the Republic of Peru.

Ambassador Watson graduated from Harvard College (A.B., 1961) and the University of Wisconsin (M.A., 1969). He was born August 8, 1938, in Boston, MA. Ambassador Watson is married and has two children.

Continuation of Michelle Easton as Deputy Under Secretary of Education

June 26, 1989

The President today announced that Michelle Easton will continue to serve as Deputy Under Secretary for Intergovernmental and Interagency Affairs at the Department of Education.

Since 1988 Mrs. Easton has served as Deputy Under Secretary for the Office of Intergovernmental and Interagency Affairs at the Department of Education. Prior to this, she was Director of Intergovernmental Affairs at the Department of Education, 1987–1988, and Director of the Missing Children's Program in the Office of Juvenile Justice and Delinquency Prevention at the Department of Justice, 1985–1987. She was private voluntary organizations liaison officer for the Africa Bureau of the Agency for International Development, 1983–1985; Special Assistant to the General Counsel at the Department of Education, 1981–1983; and an attorney with the Department of Justice in the Office of the U.S. Trustee, 1981.

Mrs. Easton graduated from Briar Cliff College (B.A., 1972) and Washington College of Law, American University (J.D., 1980).

Nomination of Harry M. Snyder To Be Director of the Office of Surface Mining Reclamation and Enforcement
June 26, 1989

The President today announced his intention to nominate Harry M. Snyder to be Director of the Office of Surface Mining Reclamation and Enforcement, Department of the Interior. He would succeed Robert H. Gentile.

Mr. Snyder is resident vice president for State relations for CSX Corp. in Kentucky. He has served as director of finance and legal counsel and then executive director for the Kentucky Council on Higher Education. He has also been a member of the finance staff of the University of Kentucky and served as legal counsel and a professor of commercial and constitutional law at Georgetown College.

Mr. Snyder graduated from Georgetown College (B.S., 1963) and the University of Kentucky College of Law in 1966. He was born in Corbin, KY, in 1941 and grew up in London, KY. He has two daughters and resides in Lexington, KY.

The President's News Conference
June 27, 1989

The President. I have a brief opening statement, and then I'd be glad to take questions.

On Wednesday morning, the Supreme Court issued a decision which held that a person could not be convicted for desecration of our flag, the American flag, because to do so would infringe upon the right to political protest. Now, we've got to be very careful in our society to preserve the right to protest government action. However, I believe that the flag of the United States should never be the object of desecration. Flag-burning is wrong. Protection of the flag, a unique national symbol, will in no way limit the opportunity nor the breadth of protest available in the exercise of free speech rights.

And I have the greatest respect for the Supreme Court and, indeed, for the Justices who interpreted the Constitution, as they saw fit. But I believe the importance of this issue compels me to call for a constitutional amendment. Support for the first amendment need not extend to desecration of the American flag. And we are reviewing proposed language for a constitutional amendment. We are beginning consultation with Members of the United States Congress who hold similar views. And as President, I will uphold our precious right to dissent. But burning the flag goes too far, and I want to see that matter remedied.

China-U.S. Relations

Q. Mr. President, when you were last with us, you said that you had tried to contact the leaders of China, and the line was busy. You were unable to get through. In light of the fact that there's now a new party secretary, have you renewed that try? And also in light of what you just said, do you plan to ask Prime Minister Li Peng to return the Texas cowboy boots with the American flag on them that you gave him in China?

The President. I have no such plans, and I hope he doesn't ask for his bicycles back, either. But in terms of contacts, we are trying, through our Embassy, to have contacts. We have contact. Their Ambassador has access to, and contact with, our officials here; and so, there has been some exchange of views. But I have not, you know, renewed a phone call request, if that was your question.

Q. As a followup, Mr. President, do you intend to go ahead and send a Peace Corps team to China in the fall to teach English, or will you go along with the Chinese request that that be delayed?

The President. Well, you have no choice, Tom [Tom Raum, Associated Press]. If the Chinese say they're not welcome, they can't come in. And it's too bad, because one of the things that moved forward the reforms was contact with Americans. And I don't want to see those contacts cut off, and I'm sorry that the Chinese have made that decision.

I would like to have seen those young volunteers go to China and help teach English to the Chinese, and I like these student exchanges. And I don't want to hurt the Chinese people. Now, I have expressed my concern about what went on in China. I reiterate my concern here today. But I reiterate also my desire not to do damage to the people themselves, because I believe that it was contact with the United States and others in the West that have moved the process of economic reform forward and, hopefully, someday will move the process of political reform forward.

Helen [Helen Thomas, United Press International]?

HUD Contracts

Q. Mr. President, while you were Vice President, millions were siphoned off from HUD through self-confessed influence-peddlers, many of whom were your friends. The homeless grew by the thousands. I have not heard one word of outrage about this from you. You seem to absolve Pierce [former HUD Secretary], who sat on this gold mine, permitted this kind of abuse for so many years, and—not absolved him, but you don't criticize him at all. Who was to blame? Where did the buck stop?

The President. That matter is being looked into by our very able, dedicated Secretary of HUD. And we are going to do everything we can to clean up any cronyism or see that matters of that nature not recur. But you're always looking for winners and losers, and I am not about to prejudge the Secretary himself. I assume that he would accept responsibility for what happened—past tense—in his Department, just as I would have to assume responsibility for something that goes on in my administration, whether I know about it or not. But let's not be trying to find winners and losers. Let's guarantee the American people that we are not going to have cronyism and special favors and giving contracts because of who you know, but keep it on the merits.

Q. But the people were the losers in this.

The President. Yes.

Q. And the Republican leaders—apparently, their influence-peddlers and so forth were the winners. Where were you in 8 years?

The President. I wasn't handling HUD, Helen, in 8 years, and——

Q. I know you weren't handling HUD, but——

The President. ——but look, if this will give you a little relief, if you want to assign blame to the Vice President for what happened over the past 8 years, okay, that's fine. I accept it, but what I want to do as President is see that we don't have any recurrence. And I have total confidence that Jack Kemp is working to see that this not happen again, and I hope that the message has gone out loud and clear to every Cabinet officer that we want the highest possible ethical standards.

Q. Well, were you aware of any atmosphere? That's all I'm asking.

The President. No. Yes, Brit [Brit Hume, ABC News]?

Flag Desecration

Q. Mr. President, in light of your renewed concern about the display of proper reverence for the flag, I wonder if you think it helps the situation, sir, for you and other political figures of both parties to make the flag the kind of instrument of partisan politics that it was in your campaign last fall—with a visit to Flag City and the tour of flag factories and flags at all the conventions and so on?

The President. I don't view that as partisanship. I think respect for the flag transcends political party. And I think what I've said here is American. It isn't Republican or Democrat; it isn't liberal or conservative; and I just feel very, very strongly about it. And perhaps I haven't been quite as emotional as I feel about it, but I want to take this opportunity to say protest should not extend to desecration of the unique symbol of America, and that is our flag.

Followup?

Q. You wouldn't dispute, would you, sir, that your visit to Flag City, U.S.A., and your visit to the flag factory last year were for the purpose of advancing your political campaign?

The President. Everything I did last year was the purpose of advancing my—everything I did politically—advancing my election. And of course, I'm not going to say that, but I didn't put it on the basis that Republicans are for the flag and Democrats are not.

John [John Mashek, Boston Globe]?

Government Ethics

Q. Mr. President, leaving aside the winners and losers question in the HUD scandal, isn't it fair criticism, nevertheless, that the laissez-faire sort of management exhibited by Sam Pierce was, as a matter of fact, encouraged by the President himself and that they really didn't pay attention to what was going on over there?

The President. John, something might be happening in some Department today that I know nothing about. We've got an enormous bureaucracy; we've got a tremendous bureaucracy that extends all around the world. And there might well be some corruption out there that's going on that I would be responsible for, but that I don't know about. But I am not going to try to assign blame; I want to look to the future. And that's the way I'm going to handle that one.

Yes, Lesley [Lesley Stahl, CBS News]?

Affirmative Action

Q. Mr. President, you've spoken out emotionally, obviously, about the Supreme Court's decision on the flag. I wonder if you'd like to take this chance to speak out emotionally on their affirmative action decisions which make it harder for women and minorities to sue for discrimination.

The President. I'm not sure that I agree with the hypothesis of your question. As I said at the last press conference—formal press conference—I was going to ask our Attorney General and our General Counsel to look into this matter. And I am strongly committed to equal opportunity for all Americans, and I am advised that nothing in these decisions jeopardizes that principle or calls into question affirmative action or minority outreach efforts. This is the opinion of the Attorney General, who I understand will be speaking on this at noon today. The Justice Department has told me that the decision reflects interpretation of the civil rights laws by the Court on technical subjects, and we're talking about burdens of proof and statutes of limitations. But that is the advice I am getting, and I will certainly support the Attorney General.

Q. All right. Constitutional scholars say, for instance, that if a minority student faces racial harassment at a private school they are no longer covered. There are some situations where people cannot sue for racial harassment, for instance, and there are other sort of niggling things. But it's really the question of your emotional response, because you jump out of the box on the flag.

The President. I've just given it to you. Affirmative action—you know my position on that. Commitment to equal opportunity—I hope people know my commitment on that, but we're getting into a technicality that neither you or I are competent to discuss. And you're going on the advice of who you call legal scholars, and I'm going on the advice of the Attorney General and a very fine General Counsel. So, I think we have a difference on the interpretation of what this means, and I've seen that some of the civil rights leaders disagree—but I am committed. And if the decisions actually turn out to hamper civil rights enforcement along the lines you're talking about, obviously I would want to take steps to remedy the situation.

Q. But are you saying you won't support legislation——

The President. This is your third question. Come on, Lesley.

Q. I'm sorry.

The President. Go ahead.

Q. Are you saying you won't support legislation that——

The President. I'm saying that my advice from the Attorney General is that legislation isn't necessary.

Abortion

Q. Mr. President, you've expressed your strong feelings again on the Supreme Court decision on the flag-burning; but the Supreme Court is expected to make a decision this week on the abortion issue, which is among the most emotional in the country. And I wonder, going into that decision, if you view your role as a healer after this decision, as simply to enforce the law? What is your view, going into that decision as the President, and this very important emotional issue?

The President. It is an emotional issue, and I am firmly positioned in favor of overturn of *Roe* v. *Wade.* And that's my position, and I'm not going to change that position. But I don't want to see the divisiveness that that whole issue causes split this country. And yet the decision is going to be—I don't know what they're going to decide, but my position on it is very clear.

Owen [Owen Ullman, Knight-Ridder]?

Balanced Budget Amendment

Q. During the campaign, you came out many times for a constitutional amendment to balance the budget. Yet I'm curious why now you've moved so quickly to call for a constitutional amendment concerning flag-burning, which is solely a symbolic issue, and yet you haven't moved at all on balancing the budget, in terms of a constitutional amendment, which is substantive and which a lot of people in this country think would accomplish a lot more for the economy. Can you explain that?

The President. Yes—oh, easily. Let me take this opportunity to make a clarion call for a balanced budget amendment. [*Laughter*] Absolutely—it has to be phased in, but I'd like to see it.

Q. Well, why do you have to be prompted to do that? Why do you give such a high priority——

The President. Because my position is so well-known on it, Owen.

Flag Desecration

Q. Why do you give such a high priority to the issue of flag-burning, and you haven't said anything until now about a balanced budget amendment?

The President. I've said a lot about it all last year. I thought you got tired of hearing it—[*laughter*]—but I will repeat it. But if you want to know—I've got to confess, I do feel viscerally about burning the American flag, and therefore, I express it. And I feel viscerally about fiscal sanity, also. But this decision just came down, and it is one that causes, I think, the American people, and certainly this President, great concern. And I think it can be remedied without doing violence to a person's right to protest.

Economic Assistance for Poland

Q. Mr. President, you're going to Poland in a few weeks, and I wonder—a lot's happened since your Hamtramck speech. We've had the free elections. Solidarity now may have a much bigger role in what happens in Poland. When you go, are you interested in bringing some expanded debt relief, financial aid? Walesa [Chairman, Independent Free Trade Union of Solidarity] has been saying to the world that he really needs help now. Do you think you are in a position to bring it?

The President. Yes, I'm in a position to discuss it; inasmuch as some of what I want to do will require legislation, that will not have been completed. But I called [Senator] Lloyd Bentsen, the chairman of the Finance Committee, to thank him over the weekend for his stance in the Finance Committee in terms of support for Poland. And so, we will have a package that I'm not prepared to discuss now in detail that I hope will help.

I know this will be a subject of great concern, after the visit to Poland, in our economic summit meeting. But the problem is, we would like very much to help Poland. I am very encouraged with what's happened in Poland, but I want to be sure that when we do offer the specifics and the specific plan to help Poland, that Poland itself will have taken the steps necessary to have the money well spent. I don't want to just push money down the drain. So, I think along with what we can offer will have to come from their side some reforms. And that, I want to talk to General Jarulzelski [Chairman, Council of State] about, and obviously Lech Walesa, and we'll see where we go.

President's Visit to Eastern Europe

Q. Let me follow on the Poland question. Both there and in Hungary, you're entering countries that are in a transition and in a very delicate situation, politically and vis-a-vis their own allies. What cautions do you take and do you exercise going in there so as not to be a negative catalyst?

The President. I think being there is the significant thing. It is important that the United States show its interest in these countries that are undergoing change. You don't want to over exhort; you don't want to over promise; you don't want to rally people to levels of political activity that might cause repression. And so, what I want to do is make clear where the United States stands in terms of our respect for freedom; encourage reform as much as possible; and then, back to David's [David Hoffman, Washington Post] question, offer some specifics where we can help on the economy.

My views on differentiation have not changed over the last few years. We will differentiate; we will support those that move towards us—economically, politically, and in terms of human rights. And it's more on those general themes that I will be talking to the Hungarian leaders and the Polish leaders.

Q. If I could follow: Do you send any signal at the same time to the Soviet Union, or have you had any communication to them about the purposes of your visit?

The President. No, but I would not expect them to be uptight about it. Mr. Gorbachev goes to Western Europe and is well received; and I will go to Eastern Europe, and I will be well received. And I think it was a good thing, his trip to Germany. I've talked to Chancellor Kohl about it personally, and I don't get into some state of competition when I see Mr. Gorbachev get a good, warm response in Germany.

The NATO alliance is together. One of the things that came out of the Brussels NATO summit meeting was the fact that there is strong unity there. And so, it's a good thing for him to go to Western Europe, and it's a good thing for the President of the United States to go to Eastern Europe. And I want to see us move beyond containment. I want to see a much more open Europe. So, the importance of this visit is along that line, and it's not going to be we're going to solve the problem of the Hungarian economy or the Polish economy.

John [John Cochran, NBC News]?

Abortion

Q. Let me ask another question about abortion and *Roe* v. *Wade*. We may get that decision this week. As I understand your position, you're for a constitutional amendment regardless of which way the Supreme Court rules. Is that right?

The President. Yes, of course.

Q. Is that right? Now, if the Supreme Court strikes down *Roe* v. *Wade* and sends this back to the States, would it not be less divisive to let the States decide this rather than go through the whole long, tortuous process of constitutional amendment?

The President. John, I hate to not respond to your question. But the Court is probably going to make a decision very soon, and I would prefer to address myself to the question after the Court has decided.

Q. It is still your position, though, sir, that you favor a constitutional amendment regardless?

The President. My position on that abortion question has not changed.

Campaign Finance Reform

Q. Mr. President, you will soon be proposing some campaign finance reforms. What is it about the current system of campaign financing that makes you think some kind of broad reform is required? And if broad reform is important, why not go ahead and go all the way to public financing of campaigns or some kind of a limit on overall spending on congressional campaigns?

The President. I oppose public financing of these campaigns. I think people should be able to attract private support, and I think participation by individuals in the political process through financial support is very, very important. I don't want to see the eroding of participation by Americans in the political process. So, I will oppose, and have opposed, the public financing of all these campaigns. Now, there are proposals that I am not prepared to discuss in detail, though I see others have already started discussing what I might do on Thursday.

I will have specific proposals. And I think they'll be fairly far reaching, because I want to see reform—real reform. And they'll be good proposals. But I'm not prepared to go into what I am going to do now except to say I will not support kicking the citizen out of the political process by saying that citizen cannot financially support the candidate of his or her choice.

Q. Well, if I could follow up: If the broad outlines of what you are going to do as reported are correct, there are going to be some accusations that they help Republicans more than Democrats. How are you going to respond?

The President. Why would anyone make a charge like that against me, when I'm looking at it as objectively as I can? Let's wait until you see what the proposals are. I mean, I would be outraged by a suggestion of that nature.

Soviet-U.S. Relations

Q. You and Mr. Gorbachev are touring each other's backyards in Europe. Now that you've finished your foreign policy reviews with regard to the Soviet Union, have you moved any closer to perhaps meeting with the General Secretary?

The President. I wouldn't say closer. That matter will be discussed again—its having been discussed once by the Secretary [of State James A. Baker III] and Foreign Minister Shevardnadze. So, I guess I'd leave it right there. There will obviously at some point be a meeting, but I still feel I'd like the meeting to be seen as productive rather than just the meeting itself.

But let me say this: I feel comfortable about the wavelength we're on with the Soviet Union now, and I think they feel comfortable in the sense that I think they know we want to move forward with START [strategic arms reduction talks]. They know that we're prepared to move swiftly forward with rectifying the conventional force imbalance. And indeed, I got the feeling from talking to Chancellor Kohl that Mr. Gorbachev was not hung up on the timetable that we set.

So, we're coming closer on some of these broad-scale objectives. And then there are some very nice, smaller things: that Soviet ship helping with the cleanup; and our kids from Brooke's [Institute of Surgical Research, Brooke Army Medical Center] going over to help with the burn—our specialized burn unit, really qualified people, the best in helping with burns—going to the Soviet Union; and then the outreach at the time of Yerevan.

So, there are some atmospherics that I think are very, very important and harmonious that will help when we sit down to hammer out the details on the strategic arms talks or on these other matters.

Q. Could I ask you—to follow up—to perhaps define a little bit more what useful or progress would be, in terms of a meeting? Are you setting a precondition, as President Reagan did, that you need something to sign, or is there——

The President. No, I don't think it should be something to sign, but I would like to think that the governing criterion would be so that the world would see the meeting as having been successful, something good happening out of it. And it doesn't have to be signing, necessarily, although I've been around this track long enough to know that you can always whip out something to sign, a fishing agreement or something of this nature. [*Laughter*]

So, we could have that, but I'm not saying that it should be hung up on a major treaty of some sort before I would sit down with Mr. Gorbachev. Maybe we'll do it like this: say, hey, let's get together. And I'm interested in what he thinks about it. And we've had some communication back and forth, but all I want to say is, I think the relationship is going in the right general direction, albeit we have tremendous differences with the Soviet Union, still. And I still have—guided by a certain sense of caution.

China-U.S. Relations

Q. Mr. President, you made much during the campaign and after your election of your relationship with China's leaders, and yet for the past several weeks you've been unable to contact them. And China appears to have ignored our calls for clemency and for dialog. Sir, do you not think the relationship was oversold?

The President. No, I don't think it was oversold.

Q. Then tell us what benefit we've gained from it.

The President. What we've gained is, China has a much more open economic system than when the Shanghai communique was signed quite a few years ago. What we've gained is 30,000 students right this minute, I think the figure is, studying in the United States—Chinese kids that are going back there with a sense of what freedom and democracy is all about. What we have gained is helping China move out of a period of cultural revolution isolation. And this relationship is important. And I can continue to express my outrage about what happened in Tiananmen Square, and I will. But I am determined to do my level best to keep from injuring the very people that we're trying to help. And I'm talking about the Chinese people generally.

So, we've gained a lot from this relationship, and so have they. And I still think that it is in the strategic interests of the United States. I'm not talking about the old adage of playing the "China card" or something of that nature, playing the "Soviet card." But if you look at the world and you understand the dynamics of the Pacific area, good relationships with China are in the national interest of the United States. Now, it's hard to have them. It's impossible at this moment to have what I would say normalized relations, for very obvious reasons. But I am going to do my level best to find a way to see improvement there that will help the Chinese people.

Q. If I could follow, sir, it's the personal relationship with China's leaders that I'm speaking of. I'm looking for the benefit when you cannot even complete a phone call to Deng Xiaoping. I'm wondering if the personal——

The President. The benefit is, I understand the situation. That's the benefit, and leaders are changing all the time over there—I mean, recently. So, we've got to deal with who is there. We don't dictate to China about their leaders. We express our concerns, as other leaders have.

But let me be very clear: In my view, the United States has been out front. We've been out front on the steps we've taken, and I am very pleased that there has been broad support for the position I've taken.

And I heard it just today from the Prime Minister of Australia [Robert Hawke], one of the most knowledgeable men about China. The Australians, you see, have always had a—they've been a little out front. They've had relations before we did, and they have almost a unique standing in China. They've done a lot of business with China; they've had a lot of exchanges with China. Bob Hawke feels that he knows most of the Chinese leaders, the ones that we had been dealing with. And to be as supportive as he was today was very reassuring to me.

Q. Mr. President, how concerned are you that the political retreat that we've seen in China in recent weeks could be duplicated in the Soviet Union?

The President. Well, I did not predict what would happen in Tiananmen Square, and I don't know of any China expert, scholar or otherwise, who predicted that. And I guess the lesson is: Go forward as best you can. Keep your eyes open. Hold high the banner of values that we believe in—the United States. We have a special responsibility around the world in terms of human rights and democracy, freedom. But keep your eyes open. That's what I've learned from this.

Q. Have you had any communications with Secretary Gorbachev on the situation in China?

The President. Not on China. Maybe others in the administration—not Gorbachev personally, but I followed carefully the statements out of there. And obviously the Soviet Union has tried to—with Gorbachev's visit to China—tried to improve relations, but I think that's on a little bit of a hold, although maybe they're more accommodating than we are right now.

Violent Crime Against Women

Q. Mr. President, women's groups have

been very pleasantly surprised and saluting you for your statements yesterday about violent crimes against women and spousal abuse. And a couple have asked the question whether you will be willing to take that message to men's groups—those macho groups, such as the NRA [National Rifle Association], the American Legion, the Police Chiefs of America—and ask them to get the word out to stop beating their wives and stop beating—the generic "they," not specific.

The President. Hey, listen, I'm a member of the NRA. You're hurting my feelings, as they say in China.

Q. And the question is whether you will take the message to men's groups instead of to the American Association of University Women.

The President. Jessica [Jessica Lee, USA Today], because of the line of work you all are engaged in, I hope that message got to every group. But I don't want to single out or acquiesce in the hypothesis here and say that NRA is against women or—the other groups you singled out? Come on, Jessie.

Q. No, no, no, but you spoke——

The President. Come on, Jessie.

Q. But you talked about it to women who are very well aware of the problem. Your staffers here say they move their cars closer to the White House after dark and have someone walk out with them. So, women know about the problem. My question is whether you will go and take the message to the men's group and ask their help in eradicating the problem.

The President. I'm trying to take the message to the whole country. That's what our whole crime package is about, absolutely—anybody that wants to listen.

Q. Now, you said also that you wanted——

The President. This is the followup. Yes?

Q. Please—that you want to be sure that your seven granddaughters have the same opportunities that your pride and joy, George P., has. George P. is the one whom you take on fishing trips and to the back rooms with the boys and to the research camps at the University of Nebraska and things like that. I wonder if you're planning to take some of the granddaughters on some of these kinds of excursions where you're doing the business of the Nation to prepare them to be President.

The President. Yes. When they get older than about 3—[*laughter*]—I will do that, because, now, I know—now, don't you say it, I'll say it—Jenna and Barbara are about 7. But that's a little young to go fishing at Jackson Hole with their grandfather and put up with Marlin Fitzwater and all these people. [*Laughter*] I mean, I want them prepared for the real world. I'm serious: I want them prepared. And I look forward to the day that those—Noelle, who is just a couple years behind George P., she came up here. We had her with us, and she brought her cousin, and we had a wonderful time. And I want her to come back; indeed, they'll be with us this summer.

But, no, you raise a good point. My affection for our oldest grandson is just that he's there and he's ready and he plays ball and he does stuff. And we're going to the Orioles game tomorrow, I think it is. [*Laughter*] But it is not discriminatory. It is not discriminatory.

Q. The secret's out.

The President. Yes?

Q. Mr. President, if I could ask one last question.

The President. Oh, wasn't I not supposed to say that? [*Laughter*] What, about the ballgame? [*Laughter*] Come on.

HUD Contracts

Q. If I could ask one last question on the HUD scandal.

The President. Yes?

Q. I think that many people would think it's unfair to hold you responsible when you were Vice President for the things that were going on at HUD. But some of the people who have been implicated in this scandal are very close to you. I'm thinking of Frederick Bush, who was your chief fundraiser in the campaign, and Paul Manafort, who was an adviser to your campaign and a partner of Lee Atwater, your campaign manager. Have you made any effort to find out exactly what these people who are close to you were doing with HUD, or to express your views of it to them? Have you made any efforts in those regards?

The President. I'm not singling out any—

you know, going, "Say, look for people that I know that may have done business with HUD in the past." What I'm trying to do is do it generically—say: to the degree there was any breaking of the law, obviously the people should pay whatever the price is. To the degree we can guard against any abuse for the future, I want to go the extra mile to do that.

And one of the first things I did as President, unnoted though it was, was to meet with the Inspectors General in here and encourage them towards independence and thorough investigation. And so, that's the way I'm trying to handle that matter.

Q. And to follow up: Does this affect your relationship with these people—to know that they were involved, apparently, in influence-peddling?

The President. Well, it doesn't improve things. But on the other hand, I want to be fair. I want to be sure that I don't jump at conclusions as to what guilt is and what it isn't, whether the law is broken or were people just out there doing what was permitted. I want to have the standard higher, though; even if it's permitted, I want to have the highest possible standard. But I haven't put it on that kind of a personal basis yet.

Child-Care Legislation

Q. Mr. President, the Senate has just passed a child-care bill that would spend almost $9 billion in Federal funds for child care.

The President. I know it.

Q. Your spokesman says that bill is a candidate for a veto. Do you intend to veto that bill, and what are your objections?

The President. I want to see what comes down here, but if there was one thing that was clear—you've got to be careful of these [hand] gestures, the way Rich Little and these guys—[*laughter*]. But if there was one thing that was clear, it was my position on child care: maximum choice through credits. And the ABC bill does not fit what I think is the proper description for child care. And for me to take the back seat and say I'm less concerned about child care because I'm unenthusiastic about the ABC bill, I don't accept that at all.

So, I remain convinced that what I have proposed is the right way to go about it. I would like to see what comes down here before I make further statements about what action I will take or won't take. I want to know the final piece of legislation that hits this desk.

Q. But you would veto the bill as it stands now.

The President. I've made my position clear on the ABC bill.

HUD Contracts

Q. You say you don't want to prejudge Secretary Pierce, but doesn't the evidence of mismanagement and influence-peddling make it evident to you that there were major problems there at the very top?

The President. Yes, yes.

Q. And what can be done about that?

The President. Well, that's what the Secretary is trying to do right now—is to make guarantees and put out regulations to see that these kinds of abuses—a woman sitting in Maryland ripping off $5 million from the American taxpayers, that's wrong. And I expect that's in the courts, I don't know. That's where it should be, in my view.

Yes, Frank [Frank Sesno, CNN]? Then I've got to go. We've got [Australian Prime Minister] Bob Hawke appearing, about whom I spoke highly because of his support for our policies. [*Laughter*]

Federal Pay Raise

Q. On the rescinding of the pay raise, you said that action was necessary for judges and top Federal officials. It's been some time now. I'd like to ask what you're doing about that and when you plan to propose some action? People are still quitting.

The President. Well, I know it, and I want to see that remedied. I still would like to see the separation of consideration for judges and other key executive branch posts—I'm thinking of some of the researchers in the NIH [National Institutes of Health] and people of this nature. And I want to see it separated out so it doesn't get caught on the question of congressional pay.

Now, whether the Congress is willing to do what I've suggested, I don't know. But I will have suggestions when we make our announcements, I think, Thursday—further announcements along this line—as to what I think needs to be done. And I am not trying to dictate to the legislative branch, but I am going to have to make some recommendations. And maybe I can do that as a former Member of Congress who is concerned about what the legislative branch ought to do. This is a matter of considerable concern.

This is the last, and then one behind you. And then I've got to go, because Bob Hawke is appearing.

Q. Mr. President, are you——

The President. Next time, Sarah [Sarah McClendon, McClendon News]. I'm sorry. I've got two-thirds back there. Yes?

Q. Your suggestions will be specific pay raise proposals, and will they take the form of a proposed legislative bill?

The President. Excuse me?

Q. Will your suggestions, when you mention them on Thursday, be specific as to salary increases, and will they take the form of a bill?

The President. Yes, I think we will have specifics on the—I haven't gone over this with the final recommendations internally, although I'm reading now what I've decided. [*Laughter*] And—very clear. But there will be some specific recommendations with amounts.

Johanna [Johanna Neuman, USA Today]?

Gambling in Baseball

Q. Mr. President, a lot of Americans this summer are talking about Pete Rose [Cincinnati Reds manager]. And I wondered, without prejudging his case, what you think about betting on baseball and whether you think that that should be reviewed by the courts or the commissioner of baseball?

The President. I am not going to get into how that matter should be resolved. Baseball, a national pastime, has sound rules regarding betting on baseball games, and I'm not going to get into that one. This is the last one, Mr. Matthews [Mark Matthews, Baltimore Sun], and then I'm going.

China-U.S. Relations

Q. Mr. President, are you concerned that a deterioration in the U.S. relations with China would disrupt the strategic balance between the U.S. and the Soviet Union? And is that of overriding importance in your reaction to events there?

The President. It is a matter that—as you look at the whole Pacific area, you have to consider that. I have never been one who thinks that the relationship with China ought to be based on playing the "Soviet card," or playing the "China card." I will not overlook fundamental abuse of the human rights because of a strategic concern; but of course, when you look at all your relationships, a President must be concerned about the strategic importance of the relationships. And not only is our relationship with China of strategic importance, it has this whole cultural and educational and art and—hopefully, someday—human rights side of it.

So, you look at it in what is right between China and the United States, but of course, I'm concerned about the strategic implications. And it's not just the strategic implications vis-a-vis the Soviet Union. Take a look at what Deng Xiaoping used to call encirclement, and look at what he means. Just take a look at China on the map, and you'll understand why the Chinese leaders still, as recently as 3 months ago, talked about encirclement. And that gets you into the questions of the ASEAN [Association of South East Asian Nations] countries. It gets you into the question of what's happening in Cambodia today. It gets you into the question of, obviously then, Vietnam, the Korean Peninsula. And there's a lot of strategic interests involved here.

Q. Sir, why don't you do something about it? Why don't you let me have a question, then? [*Laughter*]

The President. A real short one, and I'll go.

Home Health Care

Q. All right. When you went out to see [Representative] Claude Pepper and he was dying, he rose up and said, "Mr. President, when are we going to get home health care?" And you looked at him, and you wanted to cooperate with him. And I'm sure you are anxious to do something about that. Will you tell us if you're going to do something about it?

The President. Regrettably, we can't go

the route that the late Claude Pepper wanted. But I hope we can have more emphasis on care at home, and I think that would be a very good way to approach the health care needs of this country.

Q. Thank you, sir.

The President. But we can't go totally with what Claude was suggesting.

Flag Desecration

Q. You didn't explain why you went the constitutional route instead of legislative on flag-burning.

The President. Because I am told that legislation cannot correct the—in my view—egregious offense: burning the American flag.

Q. How about the death penalty for teenagers and the retarded?

The President. I really do have to go.

Note: The President's 16th news conference began at 9:04 a.m. in the Briefing Room at the White House.

Remarks at the Welcoming Ceremony for Prime Minister Robert Hawke of Australia

June 27, 1989

The President. Prime Minister and Mrs. Hawke, Barbara and I are very pleased to welcome you as old friends to the United States and to the White House. We had the opportunity to enjoy Australia's renowned hospitality in 1982 during Australian-American Friendship Week. And so, Barbara and I are just delighted to try to return that marvelous hospitality.

And there's another reason why it is so fitting for Australia's Prime Minister to be among the first official guests. Our nations share a similar heritage: a pioneer heritage in the taming of two vast continents, a heritage of democratic ideas, and a heritage of common sacrifice in war and common efforts in peace. And in our last visit, Barbara and I joined your countrymen in the commemoration of one of the most costly battles of the Second World War, the Battle of the Coral Sea—a poignant reminder of how much Americans and Australians have sacrificed four times in this century in the defense of freedom.

So, this is not just an alliance between two great powers. It is an intimate partnership between two peoples. And your visit reaffirms the vigor of this partnership, the enduring strength of our alliance.

The giant strides that we've made recently toward many of our common goals—major progress in arms reductions; major progress in resolving conflicts in Afghanistan, Angola, and Cambodia—all were made possible by the resolve of the West. Our countries prize peace, but recognize that peace comes only through Western strength and vigilance. And we must maintain our alliances and stand by our friends if we are to fulfill the promise of a new era of lessened tension and confrontation. And that is why the United States is so grateful for Australian leadership in our common defense.

America also admires Australia's bold leadership in foreign policy, both close to home and far from your shores. From the South Pacific to Africa, Australia is a force for economic growth and a beacon of democracy. And we value your contribution, your good judgment, and your advice.

Mr. Prime Minister, we have much to discuss at an important moment in history. Events in China call for close consultation among the free nations. And the United States and Australia have a longstanding tradition of such consultation on important issues, and I am interested in hearing your assessments of recent world events.

There are many pressing international issues. And, Mr. Prime Minister, your leadership in organizing global efforts to cope with the threat of chemical weapons is one position that is greatly admired by Americans. The United States supports Australia's efforts, and you may be assured of our commitment to the early achievement of an effectively verifiable treaty banning these weapons.

And so, today we shall discuss world events, arms control, trade, Pacific regional cooperation, economic cooperation, other subjects. But, Mr. Prime Minister and Mrs. Hawke—Bob and Hazel, if you will—you have a busy schedule in your very brief time with us, but we hope to make your visit to Washington as pleasant and as memorable as ours was to your great country. Welcome to Washington, sir.

The Prime Minister. Mr. President, Barbara, it's an immense pleasure for me, in these 3 days in Washington, to renew our long friendship. And it is a special pleasure and privilege to join with you as the elected Chief of the greatest democracy in reaffirming the deep, abiding friendship of our two countries. In you, Mr. President, the Western World has an experienced and forward-looking leader. And in you, Australia has a valued and longstanding friend.

Today, as you've said, Mr. President, I look forward with you to continuing the exchange of views on all the issues affecting our countries in the spirit of friendship and of frankness which has always characterized our association and which befits the relationship and, if I may say, the partnership between Australia and the United States. As you say, Mr. President, we are meeting at a time of historic and far-reaching change across the world. There now exists unparalleled new opportunities, challenges, and, may I say, responsibilities for leadership and positive achievement on crucial issues of peace and security, East-West relations, economic progress, world trade, and the protection of the world environment.

You have already demonstrated, Mr. President, your determination to give leadership. Your constructive approach to East-West relations is demonstrated by your creative and bold proposal for the reduction of conventional weapons in Europe. In this and other arms controls endeavors aimed at reducing nuclear armaments and, as you importantly emphasize, banning chemical weapons, you know, Mr. President, that you can count consistently on the support of Australia.

In this new and challenging era, the constancy, the depth, and the vitality of the alliance between Australia and the United States will remain crucially important to the national interests of both our countries. But it has a wider regional and, indeed, global significance. Under ANZUS [Australia, New Zealand, United States security treaty], the joint Australia-United States defense facilities in Australia are significant elements in maintaining the peace and in supporting the effectiveness of arms control and disarmament agreements. Over recent years, our cooperation and consultations at the highest levels have been stronger, broader, and more productive than at any other time since ANZUS was formed.

But, Mr. President, as we both agree, our alliance goes far beyond our defense alliance. It encompasses dynamic economic links and broad and deep human and cultural associations. But above all, it is based on the firmest of foundations: our shared commitment to democracy and to individual liberty within the rule of law.

Mr. President, it is precisely because of the depth and the maturity of our relationship that the differences of views that do exist between us can be faced openly and honestly—as, for example, on some trade matters, particularly aspects of agricultural policy. I am quite confident that today we will be able to focus on ways to minimize, if not entirely resolve, such differences. I look forward to exploring with you means of cooperating in the current Uruguay round of multilateral trade negotiations to achieve some progress toward the goal that we both want: an international trading system based on free and fair competition.

I know that we both understand that moving in the opposite direction toward a world of separate and competing trade blocs would be economically disastrous and quite possibly strategically destabilizing. That is one of the reasons, I might add, why earlier this year I suggested the development of closer regional economic cooperation in the Asia-Pacific region. Implementation of my proposal could, I believe, improve significantly the chances for success in the Uruguay round, as well as acting for a catalyst for further growth in our dynamic region. I'm very keen, Mr. President, to exchange views with you on this proposal.

And may I say, Mr. President, that I indeed welcome Secretary [of State] Baker's support last night for a new mechanism for multilateral cooperation among the nations of the regions as an idea whose time has come. I am delighted that the United States supports my call for a ministerial meeting this year as a first step if, as I hope and expect, there is consensus in the region.

Mr. President, I make this final point. The American presence has been a prime factor in creating and in maintaining the conditions for stability and prosperity in the Asia-Pacific region. America's continuing involvement in our region remains a key to its future progress. As you say, Mr. President, we have before us an imposing dialog that we have to deal with.

What gives this visit and our discussions their real substance, however, and what will make them so mutually beneficial is the sense of common purpose that we bring to these matters, based on our common national and international interests and on our common commitment to peace and to freedom.

Mr. President—George—I thank you again for the warmth of your welcome not merely today but since I have arrived. May I say, not just the warmth—[*laughter*]—we're used to that. And I know you have enormous power, perhaps more than any in the world, but I know there are limits to your power. [*Laughter*] That warmth is a coincidence, but, George, there is no coincidence about the personal warmth that you and Barbara have extended to Hazel and myself. For that, I thank you. And I conclude, George, by saying this: You have visited Australia, as you say, as Vice President; and I look forward to welcoming you to our country as President of the United States and as a true friend of Australia.

Note: The President spoke at 10:10 a.m. at the South Portico of the White House, where Prime Minister Hawke was accorded a formal welcome with full military honors. Following the ceremony, the President and the Prime Minister met in the Oval Office.

Message on the Observance of Independence Day
June 27, 1989

Growing up in Connecticut—"the Constitution State"—the Fourth of July represented the best of holidays. It held the promise of parades, picnics, and fireworks. More important, however, it introduced a small boy to the promise of America.

Everywhere I turned, I would see the red, white, and blue of our flag. As I grew older, I realized that the flag has reminded generations of Americans how fortunate we are to live in a free and democratic Republic. It is a banner respected around the world. The Fourth of July is a day to pause and thank God that men such as Thomas Jefferson and Ben Franklin had the strength, courage, and insight to forge a nation predicated upon the noble ideal, "that all Men are created equal, that they are endowed by their Creator with certain unalienable Rights. . . ."

Today, as we celebrate the 213th birthday of our Nation's founding, let us recall the words spoken by President George Washington during his first Inaugural Address on April 30, 1789: "The preservation of the sacred fire of liberty, and the destiny of the republican model of government, are justly considered as deeply, perhaps as finally staked, on the experiment entrusted to the hands of the American people."

After 213 years, Americans can say that the experiment is a resounding success. The Fourth of July is a time to rejoice in this success, which has inspired all who seek to break the shackles of totalitarian rule and breathe in the life-giving air of liberty.

Experience has shown us that success can exact a heavy price. We must never forget that this experiment in self-government continues to thrive because our Nation is blessed with an abundance of brave men and women who proudly serve in its Armed

Forces. These individuals stand guard on the ramparts of liberty so that all Americans can say with pride and confidence, "I'm free."

To every American citizen, here and abroad, Happy Fourth of July! God bless you and God bless America!

GEORGE BUSH

Toasts at the State Dinner for Prime Minister Robert Hawke of Australia
June 27, 1989

The President. Mr. Prime Minister and Mrs. Hawke—Bob and Hazel to us, to all of you—we are just delighted to have this opportunity to welcome you back to Washington, sir. I would once more reminisce about the fondness with which I remember our visit to Australia a few years ago, and then, of course, your own previous visits to Washington, DC, as Prime Minister. And now we have been delighted with your gracious company during this all-too-brief stay.

And lest you wonder about the Prime Minister's travel plans, it is my understanding that he and Hazel go right to the airport, climb onto an airplane, and will be seen smiling and greeting the Chancellor of the Federal Republic of Germany about 1 p.m. Federal Republic of Germany time. So, we will be brief, and—[*laughter*]. But I think the friendship that we feel towards our distinguished visitor is but a reflection of a deeper closeness.

Wilbur Garrett, the editor of the National Geographic, wrote that, "Both America and Australia exert an enduring fascination on each other, like brothers growing up in different parts of the world." Well, we've borne great sacrifices as brothers in war, and now we share great responsibilities as brothers in peace. And in this century, Australia has risen in stature from a dominion of England to become a nation, a great nation, in culture and in the arts. The world has taken note: Australia, the rising star.

In classic films like "Gallipoli" and "Breaker Morant" and so many others—Patrick White's Nobel Prize for literature—are moving examples of why Australia is emerging as this leading light in world culture. Australia has an even more profound contribution to make to the world: the encouragement and spread of democracy. Australia is the shining light in the Pacific, a lamp of liberty for the oppressed peoples of the East.

And so, Bob, let me just take a moment to acknowledge your own outstanding personal leadership in the region. You've led with ideas to better organize the trading partners of the Pacific Basin, and you've been a champion of freedom's cause. Your nation's magnificent new Parliament building is a fitting monument to democratic principles. Little wonder that so many Americans, including Members of our own Congress, joined you for the inauguration of that building and even contributed to its architecture in a reaffirmation of our kinship. It's a kinship that is more profound than heritage, deeper than a shared language. It is the universal kinship, the brotherhood of democracy.

Recent events in the Asia-Pacific region show that it is not enough to let a man buy what he wants. He must be allowed to say what he believes. He must be allowed a voice in the governing of the society. And economic freedom alone and political freedom, indeed, go hand in hand. They depend one on the other. And therefore, it is very timely for us to meet, consult—and I mean consult in the real spirit of consultation—and once again affirm the solidarity of our U.S.-Australian alliance.

The United States is fully engaged in Asia to support the forces of peace, democracy and, yes, human rights. And our abiding commitment to Australia and our friends and allies in the region is going to remain strong and abiding. And I know that you stand with us, sir, not just in favor of the free flow of goods but one of ideas and ideals of freedom.

So, ladies and gentlemen, let me say that Australia is a strong fellow democracy, a very close ally of the United States of America. This visit, in my view, sir, has been an outstanding success. We are delighted that you have been with us, you and Hazel.

And now I would like to offer a toast to Her Majesty, Queen Elizabeth, Queen of Australia.

The Prime Minister. Mr. President—George and Barbara—and friends, I think the people of this country probably imagine that they have a fair idea of the capabilities of their new President, as well they should. He has been in the public eye for a very many, many years. I may say that Barbara has given me a few insights into some aspects of his character that are probably—[*laughter*]—not so well known; but I want to assure you, my friends, that I've come to learn, just in the last 3 days, that he has a capacity for shrewdness which is almost limitless.

It occurred on the golf course. [*Laughter*] We were lined up there—the President, the Prime Minister [Secretary of State] Jim Baker, and [House Minority Leader] Bob Michel. And I know that my friend, Jim Baker, will take no offense; and I, with my well-known modesty, take no offense in acknowledging that of the three of us, apart from the President, there was not a doubt that Michel is the best player. [*Laughter*] So, with an innocence which was all-belying, the President of the United States said, "We will now work out who plays one with the other." So, I thought that there would be a fairly reasonable process that would be followed. It was very exotic, I can assure you. He gets his ball, and he takes a ball from each of us. He puts his on the ground, and he said, "Now, here they go." He said, "The ball nearest mine will be my partner." And there was no doubt which ball was nearest his; it was Michel's, of course. [*Laughter*] It was never going to be any other way—a very, very shrewd operator. [*Laughter*]

Now, we have shrewdness in sport, too, in our country. George, I might say, I've had the opportunity of sitting next to—here—to Sarah, who shares my passion for racing. And I can tell you a brief, true story about horse racing in Australia, which will give an indication that there is certain shrewdness in sport in our country. It's a true story, I can assure you.

It was a country race meeting out in the bush in Australia, and this event was a three-horse race—literally a three-horse race. This punter went up to the bookmaker and said, "I'll have $5,000 on Blue Vein." And the bookmaker took his $5,000 with a huge grin and shoved it into his bookmaker's bag and said, "Thank you very much. That's my horse." To which the punter replied, "It's going to be a bloody slow race, isn't it? I own the other two." [*Laughter*]

Well, my friend, George, coming to more serious matters, you and I and our two countries are not in a slow race. We're certainly not in a race in which we're not trying. It's an increasingly fast race. It's an increasingly serious race. It's a race which requires all of our commitments and our courage and devotion and best efforts.

George, you and I are both politicians. We've had a long experience in politics. It would be honest enough to say that there are times when you have to talk about persons, even perhaps some times when you have to talk about nations, and where there is no substance in the relationship with the person or the nation with which you're talking, as politicians you have to delve fairly deeply into the wells of rhetoric and platitudes to do justice to the situation.

But we're fortunately in the situation where we have to do nothing of that kind. Between our nations, there is an enormous, immeasurable substance. It's a substance, a relationship, which has been formed on the battlefields. On four occasions in this century, our soldiers have fought next to one another; they have died next to one another in defense of the fundamental beliefs that we share. And in the times of peace, our nations also have been as one in pursuing not only for the people of their own nations but for others the achievement of those ideals of freedom and liberty.

As for us as individuals, George, we have had the pleasure of not merely knowing one another but of being friends for the greater part of this decade, certainly a friendship which I cherish. And may I say to you, my friends, that in getting to know George Bush I've got to know a man whose integrity I admire, whose courage in defending lasting truths I admire, and whose boldness in testing new frontiers of experience I have also increasingly come to admire.

It is the case, George, that you and I, through the responsibilities of leadership in our nations, have the experience now of living at a point in history which I would suggest by almost any definition is at one and the same time the most exciting and challenging of any time in this 20th century—certainly the most challenging and promising, in a sense, than at any time in the nuclear age.

We are entitled—the rest of us in the world—to say of the leadership of the United States in recent times that, by the discharge of your responsibilities, by the preparedness, as I say, to exercise boldness in testing new frontiers, that you have given us cause for a greater degree of optimism about the possibility of living in a world in peace than at any other time in the nuclear age.

When I was here 12 months ago, in speaking to a Joint Session of the Congress, I referred to that thesis which had been gaining some currency: that this was a nation in some sort of relative decline. I said then that that was a thesis that I dispute, a concept that I reject, because all the evidence of recent times, in my analysis, points in the other direction. It is not merely a question of the continuation of your great economic might but, on all the evidence, of leadership that has been—the courage of the previous administration of which you were such a leading part, and which you now, as President, have taken to new frontiers.

It is that courage, that leadership, that boldness which, with a certain responsiveness from the leadership in the Soviet Union, has offered to mankind, to this generation and to our children and to theirs, a greater hope for peace than at any other time in this nuclear age, which so frequently—almost consistently—has been fraught with the ultimate danger of obliteration.

And it takes courage, it takes strength, it takes leadership, it takes boldness to have done those things. And, George, I want to say to you that my country looks with enormous appreciation to what this country has done and what you now as President are doing. We thank you for the strength of our alliance. May I say in the presence of the Ambassador-elect, who I have just recently gotten to know—Mel Sembler and his wife, Betty—I thank you for your decision in choosing them as your representative in our country. We look forward to welcoming them, and I take your selection of Mel Sembler as an indication of the importance that you attach to our relationship.

Our friendship, as I say, the friendship of our two countries, forged in war and advanced in peace, rests on unshakable foundations. It involves a commitment to ensure that the peoples of our own nations, the United States and Australia, shall advance in prosperity and in security. But more importantly even than that, I think the strength of our relationship is in our commitment that we shall do everything in our power to see that those freedoms that we have nurtured and which have given us our strength, our pleasure, our hope for the future shall be freedoms and rights that increasingly, as a result of our efforts, shall be enjoyed by men and women around the globe. That is our great responsibility, it's our great opportunity, and our great challenge.

And may I say, George, for me, that it is an immeasurable pleasure that I have this opportunity at this stage of history of sharing with you the leadership of two great countries so firmly united.

Ladies and gentlemen, may I offer you a toast to the President of the United States and to the abiding friendship and partnership of the United States and Australia.

Note: The President spoke at 9:25 p.m. in the State Dining Room at the White House. In his remarks, the Prime Minister referred to Sarah Farish, a Bush family friend.

Continuation of David S.C. Chu as an Assistant Secretary of Defense
June 28, 1989

The President today announced that David S.C. Chu will continue to serve as an Assistant Secretary of Defense (Program Analysis and Evaluation).

Dr. Chu has served as the Assistant Secretary of Defense (Program Analysis and Evaluation) since July 1988. Prior to this Dr. Chu was the Director of Program Analysis and Evaluation in the Office of the Secretary of Defense, 1981–1988. Dr. Chu also served as assistant director for the national security and international affairs division in the Congressional Budget Office, 1978–1981; as associate head of the economics department at the Rand Corp., 1975–1978; and as a senior economist at the Rand Corp., 1970–1978.

Dr. Chu graduated from Yale University (B.A., 1964; M.A., 1965; M. Phil., 1967; Ph.D., 1972). He served in the U.S. Army from 1968 to 1970. Dr. Chu was born in New York City on May 28, 1944. He currently resides in Washington, DC.

Nomination of Alfred C. Sikes To Be a Member of the Federal Communications Commission, and Designation as Chairman
June 28, 1989

The President today announced his intention to nominate Alfred C. Sikes to be a member of the Federal Communications Commission for a term of 5 years from July 1, 1988. He would succeed Mary Ann Weyforth Dawson. Upon confirmation by the Senate he will be designated Chairman.

Since 1986 Mr. Sikes has served as Assistant Secretary of Commerce and Administrator of the National Telecommunications and Information Administration in Washington, DC. Prior to this he was president of Sikes and Associates, Inc., a broadcast management and media consulting company, 1978–1986. From 1977 to 1978, he served as an officer in a number of companies that owned and operated radio stations in Texas, Louisiana, and New Mexico. He was director of the Missouri Department of Consumer Affairs, Regulation, and Licensing, 1974–1976; director of the Missouri Department of Community Affairs, 1973–1974; director of the Missouri transition government for Governor-elect Bond, 1972–1973; and campaign manager for Christopher Bond for Governor, 1972. He also served as assistant attorney general for the State of Missouri, 1969–1972, and campaign manager for attorney general John C. Danforth, 1970. Mr. Sikes was an associate and junior partner in the law firm of Allen, Woolsey and Fisher, 1964–1968.

Mr. Sikes graduated from Westminster College (B.A., 1961) and the University of Missouri (LL.B., 1964). He was born December 16, 1939, in Cape Girardeau, MO. He is married, has three children, and resides in Bethesda, MD.

Statement by Press Secretary Fitzwater on a Proposed Constitutional Amendment Prohibiting Flag Desecration
June 28, 1989

The White House is working with Members of Congress to develop appropriate language for a constitutional amendment on flag-burning. When these consultations are complete, we hope to join with Members of Congress in supporting a proposal that will receive swift consideration. The language will not be ready today.

Remarks Following Discussions With President Mobutu Sese Seko of Zaire

June 29, 1989

President Bush. Zaire is among America's oldest friends, and its President, President Mobutu, one of our most valued friends— entire continent of Africa. And so, I was honored to invite President Mobutu to be the first African head of state to come to the United States for an official visit during my Presidency.

I first met President Mobutu when I was Ambassador to the United Nations, and in that capacity, I first visited Zaire in 1972. And always, I have been impressed by his insight and his vision.

In our talks, the President and I have had the opportunity to review and renew the excellent bilateral relationship between our countries. And we've noted, to our mutual pleasure, that those ties continue to be beneficial and productive.

One of Africa's most experienced statesmen, President Mobutu has worked with six Presidents. And together, they—and we— have sought to bring to Zaire, and to all of Africa, real economic and social progress and to pursue Africa's true independence, security, stability as the bases for that development.

Over the years, President Mobutu has helped international councils from the United Nations to the OAU [Organization of African Unity] to the nonaligned movement address these issues sensibly—and very effectively, I might add. And invariably, he has personally worked to bring about the peaceful resolution of conflicts. Just last week, he brought together, for the first time, in the presence of 18 African chiefs of state, the leadership of Angola's warring factions, setting the stage for national reconciliation in that country. And thanks to President Mobutu, we are nearer the goal long sought, yet long elusive: peace and opportunity in southwestern Africa.

We discussed that goal in our talks here, and the President and I also examined other important aspects of regional conflicts, especially the southern third of the African continent. And there we share goals of a rapid, peaceful end to apartheid; the full implementation of Security Council Resolution 435, leading to the independence of Namibia; and the total withdrawal of Cuban troops from Angola. Zaire's stake in these results is as enormous as its influence. My advisers and I found President Mobutu's analyses valuable, and we support him as he strives to peacefully resolve problems.

In addition to foreign affairs and regional matters, much of our discussion focused on Zaire's efforts to strengthen its economy. And I want to note that Zaire recently took the constructive step of signing an economic policy reform agreement with the International Monetary Fund. Because we believe that strict adherence to its terms can produce a healthy economy for Zaire, we intend to support that effort.

During the President's visit, we also exchanged the instruments of ratification of a bilateral investment treaty. We hope that this treaty will encourage greater American investment in Zaire leading, in turn, to greater economic development.

In conclusion, we thank President Mobutu for coming to the United States at this critical time, and we thank him for his leadership in central Africa. And we look forward to continued cooperation between our countries. Mr. President, the strong ties of friendship between Zaire and the United States endure and prosper. And we are proud and very, very pleased to have you with us today. Thank you, sir.

President Mobutu. Ladies and gentlemen, it is an honor to state in turn that the friendship between Zaire and the United States is today 29 years old. I am particularly pleased to have been honored by the invitation extended by President Bush to come on an official working visit early on in his term of office. This has made it possible for us to hold talks marked by warmth and friendship. This occasion also gave us the possibility of assessing bilateral cooperation between our two countries and of identifying new goals to pursue together.

Thus, we spoke of disarmament, détente, the Third World debt and, more specifically, the African debt. We also spoke of the situation in southern Africa. In this connection, I informed President Bush of the results obtained following the summit held in Gbadolite on June 22d, which lay the groundwork for national reconciliation in Angola. I have asked President Bush to support this process so as to restore once and for all peace in this country which shares a 2,600-kilometer border with the Republic of Zaire.

I wish to express my satisfaction with the attention and the understanding shown by President Bush in addressing these problems. I also welcome the fact that President Bush, because of his long political and diplomatic experience, takes a special interest in African issues, in which, incidentally, he is thoroughly well-grounded.

Regarding my country, Zaire, I spoke to President Bush about the new agreement that I have just signed with the International Monetary Fund and the World Bank on a 3-year structural adjustment program. President Bush has renewed the support of his government to the Executive Council of Zaire in its effort to implement this program. In support of this, President Bush has committed his administration to promoting and encouraging American investment in the Republic of Zaire. This is the reason for which we proceeded to exchange instruments of ratification of the bilateral investment treaty between the United States and the Republic of Zaire. Furthermore, the President reaffirmed United States support for the program for stability and security in the Republic of Zaire.

Finally, I informed the President of the arrangements and measures of protection which have been set up in Zaire for some years now. These arrangements have made it possible for the United Nations Commission on Human Rights to withdraw Zaire from the list of those countries which it monitors for human rights. Since then, Zaire can be ranked among those countries which observe the rule of law, not to be confused or mistaken with any incidental mishaps that are attributable to an administration or to individuals.

The United Nations Commission on Human Rights and the Republic of Zaire invites all governments and organizations concerned with human rights to support by all means possible the efforts deployed by the Zairian Department of Human Rights and Freedoms of the Citizen for the defense and the protection of human rights in Zaire.

In concluding, we would like to thank President Bush and his advisers for the invitation that he extended to us to be the first African head of state to come on an official working visit since Mr. Bush has come to the White House.

Long live the United States of America. Long live Zaire. Long live friendship and cooperation between our two countries. I thank you.

Note: The President spoke at 1:17 p.m. at the South Portico of the White House. President Mobutu spoke in French, and his remarks were translated by an interpreter.

Statement by Press Secretary Fitzwater on President Bush's Meeting With President Mobutu Sese Seko of Zaire
June 29, 1989

The President met with President Mobutu Sese Seko of Zaire for 2 hours and 15 minutes today, including a private one-on-one meeting in the Oval Office, an expanded plenary meeting in the Cabinet Room, and a luncheon in the Residence.

We attach a great deal of importance to the visit to the United States of President Mobutu. Zaire is one of our oldest and closest friends in Africa. The President wanted to emphasize our excellent relations by inviting President Mobutu to be the first African head of state to come to the United States on an official working visit. President Mobutu recently organized and chaired the successful Gbadolite summit, which led to a cease-fire and the start of negotiations between UNITA [National Union for the Total Independence of Angola] and the MPLA [Popular Movement for the Liberation of Angola] in Angola. This considerable diplomatic feat—along with his noteworthy contributions to regional stability in Chad, Burundi, and elsewhere over the years—underscore his importance as an African leader and statesman.

President Mobutu briefed the President about the summit and the status of proceedings to arrange the talks which we hope will lead to national reconciliation in Angola. In addition to events in Angola, the two Presidents reviewed security issues elsewhere in Africa, U.S. assistance to Zaire, Zaire's recent decision to begin an IMF [International Monetary Fund] economic reform program, and human rights issues.

During his Washington stay, President Mobutu also had meetings with Treasury Secretary Brady, Defense Secretary Cheney, and Secretary of State Baker. Tomorrow, Vice President and Mrs. Quayle will be President and Mrs. Mobutu's hosts for a breakfast meeting. During this visit, President Mobutu has also met with Members of Congress, businessmen, and the media.

Remarks to Congressional and Administrative Interns Announcing Campaign Finance Reform Proposals
June 29, 1989

I can understand that warmth of the welcome. Look at it this way, the longer you are here, the longer you don't have to be there in the office working. [*Laughter*] I expect I speak for all of you when I turn to thank the marines for that warm welcome. They are magnificent—always have been and always will be. Apologies to Mr. Billington, the head of the Library of Congress. I have to admit, I feel a little awkward giving a speech at this particular place after all those years of being told not to speak out loud in the library. [*Laughter*]

But the Library of Congress has indeed been called the diary of the American people. In truth, it's a diary of the human race. And in the million stories of achievement it has to tell, one truth is revealed above all others: that for all its blemishes, government of the people is the greatest achievement of all. And as I look around me, I see what I'm told are the best and the brightest of the new generation, and for you, this summer of independence is just a sweet taste of adulthood, of what lies ahead. And trust me, freedom is not as far off as it seems.

Whatever you do in Washington, page or intern, you are apprentices in what I steadfastly feel is a noble profession: public service. And we exalt public service because we do not exalt the primacy of our government. We keep government close to the people it's meant to serve.

And there's another fundamental concept in our way of governing: reform. Ours is not a perfect government; it's a government constantly perfected. A steadily improving government is the result of our open political system. And in this system, elections are more than the deadlines of democracy; they are the marketplace of ideas. They're not just contests between individuals; they are contests between philosophies. And when this sharp edge of competition is dulled, democracy is the loser.

In April, I proposed comprehensive ethics legislation for all branches of government, and today I call on the United States Congress to pass that package. But I also want to address other problems: how to free our electoral system from the grip of special interests, how to spur the free competition of ideas.

You've often heard me speak of the necessity of bipartisanship. And I do strongly believe that we must work together when dealing with the most difficult challenges facing our country, not as partisans but as Americans. But we will not, and should not, cease to be Republicans and Democrats. True, the Founding Fathers envisioned no role for parties, and yet 200 years of political experiences have shown their value. Political parties clarify and sharpen the debate. And they shape coalitions of like-minded people, giving millions of Americans an effective way to support their beliefs and advance their candidates.

Parties are the indispensable organizers of democracy. And yet times have changed, and today's special interest political action committees [PAC's] and their $160 million war chests overshadow the great parties of Thomas Jefferson and Abraham Lincoln. And as the strength of our parties erodes, so does the strength of our political system. Distinctions between candidates get all mixed up; they become muddled. And congressional debate lacks coherence and lacks discipline. By necessity, Members of Congress engage in time-consuming and often degrading appeals for money outside the party structure. As vigorous competition between candidates and between ideas wanes, the clear winner in the race for PAC dollars is incumbency.

Some believe public or taxpayer financing is the best answer. I do not. If we exclude individuals, you see, if we exclude them from the process, we exclude the public. And this is the ironic result of taxpayer financing: It would force taxpayers to support extremist candidates they abhor. It would be a siphon from the U.S. Treasury, already in deficit, to campaign coffers. Taxpayer financing would do nothing to strengthen the parties. If anything, it would strengthen the status quo, and what the voters really need is more choice.

Spending limits are not the answer either. If we're to encourage individuals to participate in the electoral process, if we are to encourage candidates to bring their message to as many voters as possible, we should not have absolute limits on spending. The answer is reform. We need reforms that curtail the role of special interests, enhance the role of the individual, and strengthen the parties.

So, today I propose just that: a sweeping system of reform for our system. More than 90 percent of all PAC contributions come from PAC's sponsored by corporations, unions, and trade associations. So, the cornerstone of this reform—of our reform—is the elimination of those political action committees. I propose to curtail the proliferation of leadership PAC's by limiting all candidates for Federal office to one fundraising committee. And by also barring transfers between fundraising committees, we will further reduce the influence of special interest money in the electoral process.

I propose to end a practice that's known as bundling, where business and unions encourage or coerce contributions from employees or members and then give these contributions as one single donation. And as these reforms curtail special interest money, we must encourage the role of the parties—encourage it. And I propose to more than double the amount of monies parties may donate to congressional campaigns. Increasing party donations to Federal candidates will allow legislators to spend more time legislating and less time raising money. And it will give challengers the means to compete with incumbents. And it will allow all candidates to avoid having to raise money from special interests.

And still, some PAC's must remain because they are protected under our Constitution by the first amendment. And these independent PAC's account for about 10 percent of all contributions, but even these I would limit by halving their allowable contributions to Federal candidates from $5,000 to $2,500—reduce it from $5,000 to $2,500. And new laws must keep such PAC's unaffiliated and independent, so a business or labor group could not use them as a back-door means of influencing the process.

I also propose to strengthen the Supreme Court's Beck decision, which held that union members can't be forced to have their dues go to political causes or organizations they do not support. No American—no American, not one—should be compelled to give money to a candidate against his or her will.

We must do more to truly clean up the system. The basic strength of today's system is disclosure: being honest with the American people. Yet most money spent in American elections is not disclosed. This little-known area of campaign finance laws called soft money concerns dollars spent on voter turnout and registration efforts. And so, I call on the United States Congress today to join me in mandating full disclosure of all soft money contributions by the political parties, as well as corporations, unions, and trade associations.

Other laws govern, now, independent expenditure groups—you know, which can spend any amount of money to elect or defeat a candidate so long as their activities are not coordinated with those of a particular candidate. Now look, some of these groups perform a public service, but too often they mask the motives of hidden contributors acting as mercenary character assassins. Often they deceive the public into thinking that they are a candidate's campaign. And yet, all independent expenditure groups, the good and the bad alike, are protected by the Constitution. In order to provide more information to the public, I propose that such groups be required to more clearly identify the person or organization behind them. Disclosure—full disclosure—that's the answer here.

The third and final area of reform directly concerns the powers of incumbency. Jefferson envisioned a Congress of citizen politicians who suspended their careers in law, in medicine, in agriculture to serve the Nation. Now, how far we've come from that simple vision: Today incumbents stay in office for decades, amassing huge war chests to scare off strong challenges in election after election. This is not democracy in the spirit of Madison and Jefferson. This is not the spirit of democracy at all. And so, I propose to end the rollover of campaign war chests, requiring any excess campaign funds to be donated to the parties, to a fund to retire the national debt, or to be given back to the contributors. And this would apply to all unspent campaign funds, whether it's a race for Congress or a race for the Presidency.

Under our current law, 190 House Members in office in 1980 can also use that leftover campaign money as a personal retirement fund, pocketing hundreds of thousands—even millions of dollars when they leave office. Senators are allowed to convert these funds for official use. This practice must end. And this same principle should apply to Presidential candidates as well.

Another advantage of incumbency arises from the way in which Members of Congress use the public frank to pay for mass mailings that amount to political advertising. The cost to the taxpayers, literally, runs into hundreds of millions of dollars. And the cost to our democracy is also very, very steep. I propose to prohibit the use of the frank for unsolicited mass mailings.

And yet another area in need of reform is redistricting: the way in which parties in power ignore community boundaries and draw district lines favorable to their candidates. No single factor is more basic to restoring competitive elections than ensuring fair redistricting. I propose a new criteria for redistricting without favor to party. To respect established community boundaries, we must draw district lines that respect the needs of the people, not tailor them to the political needs of either party.

And finally, in the next few days I will

also send up legislation to ban honoraria and to address certain aspects of compensation for Federal officials. This package will include a 25-percent pay increase for judges, which I've previously recommended, and an increase for a limited number of specialized professionals, such as scientists and surgeons, where the executive branch is not competitive. And I'll also work with the Congress on the development of details for increasing the pay of those in the Congress, as well as other senior employees of the executive branch.

This year, as Congress observes its 200th anniversary, 11,000 Americans have served in the House and Senate in the history of our Republic. And I'm proud to have been one of them. And most have served in the great tradition—Russell and Rayburn, Dirksen and Mansfield, Dole and Mitchell, Foley and Michel. And someday, who knows, you may elect, after your experience here this summer, to follow this path, the path to greatness and achievement through public service. And if you do, I hope the laws that govern our campaigns and our Congress, as well as our executive branch, are as just and honest as the majority of those who serve the public. You know, this vast and honest majority in Congress live the words of George Washington, who said, "The noblest title in the world isn't President, Senator, or Congressman but honest man." Whatever you do in life, you can have no higher title than that.

Thank you all for listening. God bless you and God bless the United States of America.

Note: The President spoke at 2:06 p.m. in the auditorium at the Thomas Jefferson Building of the Library of Congress. In his opening remarks, he referred to the Marine Band.

White House Fact Sheet on the President's Campaign Finance Reform Proposals

June 29, 1989

Today the President announced a comprehensive campaign finance proposal designed to lessen the power of special economic interests and restore competition to American congressional elections. The package reflects the President's strong commitment to increasing the roles of individuals and the political parties in the electoral process. It is also designed to reform the system of campaign finance under which in the 1980's House incumbents have a 97.7-percent reelection rate and Senate incumbents an 85-percent reelection rate. The proposals follow general themes first articulated by the President in his April 12 speech to the American Society of Newspaper Editors:

• Eliminating political action committees (PAC's) supported by corporations, unions, or trade associations, and prohibiting such entities from paying for the overhead or administrative costs of any independent PAC.

• Strengthening political parties by increasing the amounts they can spend on behalf of congressional candidates. This source of funds would permit legislators to spend less time fundraising, would ensure that challengers have greater resources with which to challenge incumbents, and would further limit the role of special economic interests in elections.

• Addressing the problem of the "permanent Congress" by reforms designed to reduce the unwarranted advantages of incumbency. Specifically, the proposals would prohibit the personal use of excess campaign funds, drastically reduce congressional mailings under the frank, ban the rollover of campaign funds from one election cycle to the next, and legislate fair neutral criteria for the redistricting of congressional and legislative lines that will follow the 1990 census.

• Fully disclosing all "soft money" spent

by the political parties and all labor unions, corporations, and trade associations to influence a Federal election.

The President's campaign finance reform package is as follows:

1. CONTRIBUTION LIMITS

Curtailing Political Action Committees (PAC's)

• The proposal calls for the elimination of PAC's sponsored by corporations, unions and trade associations. The bulk of PAC contributions come from these corporate, union, or trade association PAC's: They accounted for nearly 90 percent of the approximately $160 million contributed by PAC's in the 1987–1988 election cycle.

• Contribution limits for the remaining PAC's, i.e. those not sponsored by corporations, unions, or trade associations (the so-called nonconnected or independent PAC's), would be reduced from $5,000 to $2,500 per candidate per election. It appears that freedom of association guarantees under the first amendment make it impossible to eliminate these independent PAC's.

• Corporations, unions, and trade associations would also be prohibited from using Treasury funds for nonconnected PAC administrative or overhead costs, including corporate or union subsidies for payroll deductions to fund a PAC.

• PAC contributions to national and State political parties would stay the same ($15,000 per year). The remaining independent PAC's would also be able to continue funding such participatory activities as voter registration and get-out-the-vote programs, which would become fully reportable.

• The proposal would codify the Beck Supreme Court decision, holding that union members cannot be forced to have mandatory union dues go to political causes or organizations they do not support.

• Leadership PAC's, including those associated with Presidential candidacies, would be curtailed by limiting Federal candidates and elected officials to one fundraising committee and by prohibiting transfers between fundraising committees.

• All but political party committees would be prohibited from bundling, the practice where an organization or its officials solicit contributions from its employees or members at a central location, "bundles" them, and sends them to a candidate without affecting the organization's contribution limits.

• Independent expenditures would be subject to additional notice requirements. Any advertisement or other political communication paid for by independent expenditures would have to include additional disclosure throughout, identifying the person or organization funding it and stating that it is not authorized by any candidate.

Strengthening Political Parties

• The proposal increases to $0.05 from $0.02 times the voting age population the coordinated expenditure limits that parties may spend on behalf of Federal candidates (ranges now from $92,000 to about $1.5 million, depending on population, for a Senate race; about $46,000 for a House race). This would allow a larger percentage of contributions to a candidate to come from political parties.

2. REFORMING UNFAIR ADVANTAGES

Limiting the Use of Excess Campaign Funds

• The rollover of excess campaign funds into the next election cycle would be prohibited by requiring that all campaign treasuries be zeroed out by January 31 following the election. All excess campaign funds would have to go to national or State party committees, the National Debt Retirement Account of the United States Treasury, or all campaign contributors as pro-rata refunds.

• Presidential candidates would also be prohibited from using excess campaign funds from previous races to fund their Presidential efforts.

• The proposal bans the conversion of excess campaign funds for personal use. With regard to the Congress, this would apply as follows: House Members who are grandfathered could no longer convert the funds to personal use. Senators would be precluded from supplementing official accounts with their own excess campaign funds.

Limiting the Use of the Frank

• The proposal bans the use of the frank for unsolicited mass mailings.

• Quarterly filings would be required by all Members of Congress regarding the amounts spent on franked mail. The reports would be due within 30 days of the close of the quarter.

Fairness in Redistricting

• The proposal calls for the end of gerrymandering through the promulgation of criteria for fair redistricting in Federal elections. Such criteria will include requiring district lines to adhere to compactness standards and follow established community boundaries.

• The legislation will emphasize the need for congressional and State legislative plans to follow the provisions of the Voting Rights Act.

3. Soft Money Disclosure

• Full disclosure of all "soft money" contributions and expenditures by political party committees would be required under the proposal.

• Labor unions, corporations, and trade associations would have to disclose all money spent to influence a Federal election, including voter registration and get-out-the-vote activities, as well as any communications which advocate the election or defeat of any Federal candidate.

• The proposal also calls for the adoption of realistic allocation guidelines to attribute the costs of party activities proportionately to Federal candidates. This will assure that non-Federal dollars are not used to support Federal candidates.

4. Honoraria Ban

• Separate legislation will be sent to the Congress in the next few days to ban honoraria and to address certain aspects of compensation for Federal officials. This package will include a 25-percent pay increase for judges, which the President previously recommended, and an increase for a limited number of specialized professionals where the executive branch is currently not competitive, such as scientists and surgeons. The President will also work with Congress on the development of details for increasing the pay of Members of the Congress, as well as other senior employees of the executive branch.

Nomination of Joy A. Silverman To Be United States Ambassador to Barbados, Dominica, St. Lucia, and St. Vincent and the Grenadines

June 29, 1989

The President today announced his intention to nominate Joy A. Silverman to be Ambassador Extraordinary and Plenipotentiary of the United States of America to Barbados and to serve concurrently and without additional compensation as Ambassador Extraordinary and Plenipotentiary of the United States of America to the Commonwealth of Dominica, St. Lucia, and to St. Vincent and the Grenadines. She would succeed Paul Russo.

Mrs. Silverman was a full-time, active participant in President Bush's 1988 campaign. From 1987 to 1988 she served as a member, and later as chairman of the Advisory Council to the New York State Commission on the Bicentennial of the United States Constitution. In 1986 Mrs. Silverman became a member of the New York City Mayor's Commission for Protocol. In addition to extensive work for various educational institutions, she has actively served with various charitable organizations in the New York metropolitan area.

Mrs. Silverman attended the University of Maryland. She is married, has two children, and currently resides in Manhattan, NY.

Nomination of Eugene P. Kopp To Be Deputy Director of the United States Information Agency
June 29, 1989

The President today announced his intention to nominate Eugene P. Kopp to be Deputy Director of the United States Information Agency. He would succeed Marvin L. Stone.

Since 1987 Mr. Kopp has been a government affairs consultant in the private sector. He served with the Union Pacific Corp. of New York in various capacities, including vice president of Washington affairs, 1981–1987, and as associate general counsel of Champlin Petroleum Co., a subsidiary, 1977–1981. From 1969 to 1977, Mr. Kopp served with the U.S. Information Agency as Acting Director, 1976–1977, and Deputy Director, 1973–1976. At the end of his previous service at USIA, Mr. Kopp received the highest award, the Distinguished Honor Award, for his contribution in the field of U.S. public diplomacy. He has also been a member of the board of directors at the Institute for Foreign Analysis since 1979.

Mr. Kopp graduated with honors from the University of Notre Dame (B.A., 1957; M.A., 1958) and the College of Law, West Virginia University (J.D., 1961). He was born November 20, 1934, in Charleston, WV. Mr. Kopp is married to the former Katherine Patricia Rogers of Lynchburg, VA. They have one son, Paul, a student at the College of William and Mary. Mr. Kopp and his wife currently reside in Alexandria, VA.

Continuation of Kathleen Day Koch as General Counsel of the Federal Labor Relations Authority
June 29, 1989

The President today announced that Kathleen Day Koch will continue to serve as General Counsel of the Federal Labor Relations Authority for a term of 5 years. She would succeed Dennis M. Devaney.

Since 1988 Ms. Koch has served as General Counsel of the Federal Labor Relations Authority. Prior to this she was Associate Counsel to the President at the White House, 1987–1988. She was senior attorney at the Department of Commerce, 1984–1987. She was an attorney with the United States Merit Systems Protection Board, 1979–1984, and at the Department of Housing and Urban Development, 1977–1979.

Ms. Koch graduated from the University of Missouri at St. Louis (B.S., 1971) and the University of Chicago Law School (J.D., 1977). Ms. Koch, a native of St. Louis, currently resides with her three children in Annandale, VA.

Nomination of Jean McKee To Be a Member of the Federal Labor Relations Authority, and Designation as Chairman
June 29, 1989

The President today announced his intention to nominate Jean McKee as a member of the Federal Labor Relations Authority for a term of 5 years expiring July 1, 1994. Upon confirmation, she is to be designated Chairman. This is a reappointment.

Since 1988 Ms. McKee has served as Acting Chairman of the Federal Labor Relations Authority, and has served as a member of the Authority since 1986. Prior to this she was Executive Director of the Federal Mediation and Conciliation Service, 1983–1986. From 1980 to 1983, Ms. McKee was director of government relations for the General Mills Restaurant Group. From 1979 to 1980, she was a public affairs consultant in New York and Connecticut. In 1979 she was appointed to a 3-year term on the Advisory Commission on Public Diplomacy; and was Deputy Administrator, then Administrator, of the American Revolution Bicentennial Administration in Washington, DC, 1976–1977. Prior to this she served in several capacities for New York Senator Jacob K. Javits, 1967–1975.

Ms. McKee graduated from Vassar College with a political science degree. She resides in Washington, DC.

Statement on the Death of Alan Woods
June 29, 1989

We are saddened by the loss of Alan Woods, a personal and professional friend who served his country with compassion and distinction.

Alan was committed to focusing AID's [Agency for International Development] work on promoting growth in developing countries. He was convinced that without basic economic growth permanent improvements could not be made in the quality of life and the elimination of poverty in those nations. He cared deeply for those people around the world who needed our help.

He served his country loyally and diligently under two Presidents. On a personal level, Alan was a good friend and family man. While he continued his battle against cancer, he also continued to promote the ideas and programs in which he believed.

Barbara and I send our sympathies to Cameron, Alexandra, and Caroline.

Remarks Announcing the Proposed Constitutional Amendment on Desecration of the Flag
June 30, 1989

Senator Dole, thank you, sir, and Senator Dixon, appreciate your coming all this way to join us on such short notice. To Congressmen Michel and Montgomery, my sincere thanks, and all the Members of the Senate and House that are here, Secretary of Defense and other distinguished civilians, the Defense Department, and of course I salute the members of the Joint Chiefs who have joined us here. I might say I'm delighted to see Admiral Crowe back from his very successful visit to the Soviet Union—welcome back to the U.S. of A., Bill. And also our fellow citizens, citizens of this, the freest, most generous nation on God's Earth—thank you for joining us.

And we stand today before a symbol of hope and of triumph. All across America—above farmhouses and statehouses, schools and courts and capitols—our flag is borne on the breeze of freedom. And it reminds Americans how much they've been given and how much they have to give. Our flag represents freedom and the unity of our nation. And our flag flies in peace, thanks to the sacrifices of so many Americans.

A woman in Florida recently shared with me a letter written by her cousin, a young soldier named Wayne Thomas. On December 16, 1966, he wrote: "Every time we go out on patrol, it gets a little scarier. The only thing that gives us a sense of security is when we walk back into camp and our flag is still flying high." She told me that Wayne stepped on a landmine 11 days later and was killed. He was 18 years old. He understood this banner of freedom and ultimately gave his life for the flag to give others the freedom that it represents.

You know, she also pointed out to me, parenthetically, that she was a registered Democrat. And to me that simply states that patriotism is not a partisan issue; it's not a political issue. Our purpose today transcends politics and partisanship.

And we feel in our hearts, and we know from our experience, that the surest way to preserve liberty is to protect the spirit that sustains it. And this flag sustains that spirit, and it's one of our most powerful ideas. And like all powerful ideas, if it is not defended, it is defamed. To the touch, this flag is merely fabric. But to the heart, the flag represents and reflects the fabric of our nation—our dreams, our destiny, our very fiber as a people.

And when we consider the importance of the colors to this nation, we do not question the right of men to speak freely. For it is this very symbol, with its stripes and stars, that has guaranteed and nurtured those precious rights—for those who've championed the cause of civil rights here at home, to those who fought for democracy abroad.

Free speech is a right that is dear and close to all. It is in defense of that right, and the others enshrined in our Constitution, that so many have sacrificed. But before we accept dishonor to our flag, we must ask ourselves how many have died following the order to "Save the Colors!" We must ask how many have fought for the ideals it represents. And we must honor those who have been handed the folded flag from the casket at Arlington.

If the debate here is about liberty, then we cannot turn our backs on those who fought to win it for us. We can't forget the importance of the flag to the ideals of liberty and honor and freedom. To burn the flag, to dishonor it, is simply wrong.

And today we remember one of the most vivid images of our flag—the one you see behind me—Joe Rosenthal's stunning photograph immortalized in bronze. As you view this memorial, think of its flag and of these men and of how they honor the living and the dead. Remember their heroism and their sacrifice, giving of themselves and others of their lives, fighting bravely, daring greatly, so that freedom could survive.

The Battle of Iwo Jima wrote one of the greatest chapters in the story of America. And even now, it humbles us, inspires us, reminds us of how Henry Ward Beecher said, "A thoughtful mind, when it sees a nation's flag, sees not the flag only but the nation itself."

The Nation itself was ennobled by the Battle of Iwo Jima. It was fought in early 1945, fought on 8 square miles of sand, caves, and volcanic rubble. And it cost our Armed Forces almost 7,000 killed and more than 19,000 wounded—almost a third of the landing force. But like Tarawa and Guadalcanal and the Philippines before, it had to be won. For victory at Iwo would be yet another step towards bringing that ghastly war to a close.

These marines wrote a profile in courage, enduring a torrent of shells, pushing their way up that extinct volcano. And they stormed Mount Suribachi. And when they reached the top, the five men behind me raised a piece of pipe upright, and from one end flew a flag. And in the most famous image of World War II, a photograph was taken of these men and that flag. And what that flag embodies is too sacred to be abused.

As Justice Stevens stated so eloquently in his dissenting opinion in the recent Supreme Court case: "The ideas of liberty and equality have been an irresistible force in motivating leaders like Patrick Henry, Susan B. Anthony, Abraham Lincoln; schoolteachers like Nathan Hale and Booker T. Washington; the Philippine Scouts who fought at Bataan; and the soldiers who scaled the bluff at Omaha Beach. If those ideas are worth fighting for—and our history demonstrates that they are—it cannot be true," he says, "that the flag that uniquely symbolizes their power is not itself worthy of protection from unnecessary desecration." The Justice is right.

And today I am grateful to the leaders here and the leaders of the Congress with us in this audience who have proposed a constitutional amendment to protect the flag. Its language is stark, and it's simple and to the point: "The Congress and the States shall have power to prohibit the physical desecration of the flag of the United States." Simple and to the point, this amendment preserves the widest conceivable range of options for free expression. It applies only to the flag, the unique symbol of our nation.

Senator Dole, Senator Dixon, Congressmen Michel and Montgomery, I know that you have already taken the lead, but please take the lead, working with others here today, in moving this bill forward. With the help of you Members of the Senate and House here today, and with the help of the many more of your colleagues who couldn't be with us today, I am confident that we will succeed. I've seen predictions that this will take a long time; it need not. It is simple, to the point, direct; and it addresses itself to only one thing: Our flag will not be desecrated.

Let me close with a letter from a man named Augusto Moreno. Born in Argentina, now a naturalized citizen, he likes to say that he's more proud to be an American than most of those born in this country. I'm not sure he's right about that, but that's what he likes to say, anyway. He's very serious when he states: "I am proud to say that my blood is represented on our flag. I was wounded while fighting for democracy with the United State Marine Corps in Vietnam. I am now a disabled veteran. I am sure that there is not one day that goes by without you seeing the faces of those who were not so fortunate to return as you and I." And he says: "We must continue our struggle to protect the flag now, as when we were in uniform—if not for us, then for those fallen veterans. We've been entrusted by those who have fought for freedom before us to protect our flag. I cannot allow anyone to desecrate the only symbol of freedom in the world." And he ends saying, "Sir, I realize that you're a Navy veteran, but Semper Fi anyway." [*Laughter*] Those darn marines, I'll tell you.

Well, Mr. Moreno, you have our word on it: For the sake of the fallen, for the men behind the guns, for every American, we will defend the flag of the United States of America.

Thank you. God bless this flag, and God bless the United States of America.

Note: The President spoke at 9:23 a.m. in front of the Iwo Jima Memorial in Arlington, VA. In his remarks, he referred to Secretary of Defense Richard B. Cheney and Adm. William J. Crowe, Jr., USN, Chairman of the Joint Chiefs of Staff.

Statement on Meeting With South African Anti-Apartheid Activist Albertina Sisulu

June 30, 1989

I have been pleased today to welcome to the White House Mrs. Albertina Sisulu, of Soweto, South Africa. "Mama Sisulu," as she is known by her legion of admirers, is co-president of the United Democratic Front, a coalition of multiracial South African organizations opposed to apartheid. The UDF is among the organizations banned by the South African Government, and Mrs. Sisulu has been subjected to imprisonment, house arrest, and to government restrictions on her activities. However, she remains a strong advocate of nonviolence and of a nonracial South Africa.

Mrs. Sisulu has lived a life of sacrifice for the betterment of all South Africans. At age 70, she continues to be active in the service of others. Each day she travels more than an hour to reach her job as a nurse in a clinic which cares for the neediest residents of Soweto. She personifies the struggle for human rights and human dignity, and her presence here is an inspiration to us all.

As I told Mrs. Sisulu in our meeting, the United States also believes fundamentally in human rights and human dignity. We believe strongly that apartheid is wrong and that it must end. We want to see the creation of a nonracial and democratic South Africa as a result of negotiations among legitimate representatives of all of South Africa's people. We support the beginning of a process leading to a peaceful transition to democracy.

To achieve our goal, we intend to expand our assistance to black South Africans to help them both economically and politically so they can play their rightful role in determining the future of their country. We will work with the Congress to increase present programs and develop new ones to assist black South Africans in the critical areas of human rights, education, employment, housing, and community development. Such programs should not be misunderstood as our acquiescing in apartheid, but rather viewed as a determined effort to bring it to an end.

We will also work closely with our allies, particularly the British, Japanese, West Germans, and Portuguese, to develop mutually supporting policies and cooperative programs to resolve the political impasse created by apartheid and to assist in the advancement of black South Africans. These nations have important historical, cultural, and economic ties with South Africa, and their wisdom and influence need to be brought to bear on the problems of South Africa and the region.

Again, it has been an honor to be with Mrs. Sisulu here today. Her struggle and that of her husband, Walter, who remains in prison, and her children, remind us of the price of freedom and the hope which her example inspires in all of us.

Nomination of Jane A. Kenny To Be Director of ACTION

June 30, 1989

The President today announced his intention to nominate Jane A. Kenny to be Director of ACTION. She would succeed Donna M. Alvarado.

Ms. Kenny currently serves as Deputy Director of ACTION, the Federal domestic volunteer agency in Washington, DC, and also serves as Acting Associate Director of the Office of Domestic and Antipoverty Operations. In November 1988 she was appointed Deputy Director of the Office of Domestic Operations and administered the ACTION programs, including the Foster Grandparent, Senior Companion, and Retired Senior Volunteer Programs (RSVP); Volunteers In Service to America (VISTA); and ACTION Drug Alliance. Ms. Kenny joined ACTION in July 1986, serving as Director of VISTA. Prior to this, she was Director of the Executive Secretariat at the General Services Administration. She served in the Office of Vice President George Bush for 4 years, most recently serving as Special Assistant to the Vice President. Ms. Kenny has served as a staff assistant at the National Association of Schools of Public Affairs and Administration, and as a management analyst in the Department of Justice in Washington, DC.

Ms. Kenny graduated from the College of New Rochelle (B.A., 1967) and American University (M.P.A., 1977).

Remarks at a White House Ceremony Commemorating the 25th Anniversary of the Civil Rights Act

June 30, 1989

Well, thank you for that warm reception, and welcome to the White House. We're just delighted that you joined us for this important occasion. And of course, I'm very pleased to see several of our Cabinet members here, leaders of the United States Congress here. I'm particularly pleased to see our Attorney General, Dick Thornburgh, and, I might say, Bill Lucas, a friend of mine of longstanding, our nominee at Justice—both of whom, I can tell you, are fully committed to the vigorous enforcement of civil rights.

And I might say I am just delighted that, among others representing the fine work of the Southern Christian Leadership Conference, we have their president, the Reverend Joseph Lowery, with us over here today. I don't know who the man sitting on his right is, but I'll try to—[*laughter*]. Jesse [Jackson], you know the ground rules. [*Laughter*] But let me be very clear: I'm delighted you are here. It's most important that you be here today, too, sir.

We gather today not only to commemorate an anniversary but to celebrate a movement and to rededicate our efforts to the unfinished work of that movement. Some of America's mileposts are easy to date. In 1776, America invented itself, a nation founded upon an idea—the self-evident truth that all men are created equal. And nearly a century later, our nation fought its bloodiest war that the promise of that Revolution might be extended to all people. But for many Americans, another hundred years were to pass before the promise would even begin to become a reality.

Like the first American Revolution, it began with the quiet courage of ordinary citizens. Perhaps it began on December 1, 1955, when Rosa Parks refused to give up her rightful place on a Birmingham bus. Or maybe, maybe it was October 1, 1962, when James Meredith took destiny into his hands and registered at the University of Mississippi. But by the summer of '64, the revolution had a name. It was called the civil rights movement, and that year marked a watershed for many Americans. The previous August had seen 250,000 gathered—just beyond those windows—to hear Martin Luther King, Jr., proclaim a dream that was due every American. And the following year would see the march on Selma, and Watts would burn.

But in 1964, the debate raged. Good people with honorable intentions struggled with issues as old as the Republic and as young as the movement's leadership. The breakthrough came when the Senate finally invoked cloture, ending the longest debate in its history and a 74-day filibuster. And the result was a statutory package—soon to be bolstered by voting rights and open housing legislation—that stands as a landmark in the civil rights movement.

But it wasn't the year's only milepost. That same summer, the brutal murder of three young civil rights workers, so singularly appalling in its savagery, shocked the conscience of this nation and became critical to our country's progress on civil rights. Twenty-five years later, these mileposts are important symbols of how far we've come as a nation and reminders of how far we must still go.

It's appropriate today that we rededicate ourselves to that most American of dreams: a society in which individuals are judged not "by the color of their skin, but by the content of their character." That means vigilant and aggressive enforcement of all civil rights laws. It means the sensitive application of those laws when competing rights of innocent persons are at stake. The law cannot tolerate any discrimination, and my administration will not tolerate abuse of that principle.

And while celebrating our achievements and recommitting ourselves to their preservation, we must recognize that the full promise of the civil rights movement has still not been achieved. The hard lesson of the passing years is that it has not been enough to wage a war against the old forms of bigotry and inequality. The lives of the disadvantaged in this country are affected by economic barriers at least as much as by the remnants of legal discrimination. And for that reason, I continue to support affirmative action and minority outreach programs. And as I've stated before, we must move beyond the protection of rights to the creation of opportunity.

Creating opportunities for all Americans will require both public and private leadership. And it's time to move forward on a broader front. And we will be satisfied with nothing less than equal opportunity for all

Americans and the removal of final barriers to self-reliance. And that's why—that my administration has proposed new initiatives in education, the key to opportunity, to boost programs such as Head Start, merit schools, adult literacy and, of course, historically black colleges and universities. And we've asked Congress for emergency urban grants to help free our youth from a new form of enslavement: the slavery of drug addiction.

On other fronts, we're supporting landmark new legislation to extend the Nation's civil rights guarantees to those more than 36 million Americans with disabilities, bringing them into the mainstream of American society. And last week we added our voice to those calling for passage of the Hate Crimes Act. My administration's comprehensive crime package isn't just about law enforcement. Earlier this week, I spoke about the impediments to providing equal opportunities for women—if a justifiable fear of violent crime leaves them concerned about walking to a campus library at night or reluctant to work late hours for fear of getting out of the parking lot safely.

And new programs in civil rights also means anticipating the future, a future in which more than 80 percent of those entering the work force will come from the ranks of women, minorities, and immigrants. The challenge of the future will not be just finding jobs for our people but, if you look at the demographics, finding people for our jobs.

And the work force of the future can also benefit from the unique abilities of persons with disabilities. The time-tested laws that give civil rights protections can and ought to be extended to persons with disabilities. This will involve, of course, a careful balance between the needs of persons with disabilities and the needs of business to make real progress towards opening the doors of the workplace.

In the 25 years since the summer of '64, we've seen much progress. It is time now to move forward on a broader front, to move forward into the century's final decade with a civil rights mission that fully embraces every deserving American, regardless of race—whether women, children, or the aged; whether the disabled, the unemployed, or the homeless. And for all these reasons, I'm proud today to honor this year's anniversary by calling on Congress, respectfully, to join me in a new partnership to reauthorize the Civil Rights Commission, with the goal of launching a renewed civil rights mission.

Launching a civil rights mission that can keep pace with a fast-changing world and work force will require commitment, cooperation and, yes, creative thinking. And beyond government, and even beyond the private leadership of dedicated representatives such as those here in this room, achieving the long-delayed dream of civil rights for every citizen will require full support from our businesses, our schools, and families.

As President Kennedy proclaimed in a call to conscience when he proposed the landmark legislation in 1963, even the most comprehensive of laws could never meet the challenge of civil rights. The problem, he declared, "must be solved in the homes of every American in every community across our country." And in this, I ask you and every American for a renewed commitment to this just cause.

And I thank you for coming to the White House today and for honoring the history of this movement—a movement in which many of you here in this room today were in the very forefront of leadership for that movement. Thank you for coming. Now we've got some work to do in the 25 years ahead. Thank you all very, very much.

Note: The President spoke at 2:05 p.m. in the East Room at the White House.

Message on the Observance of Independence Day
June 30, 1989

Like most of you, Barbara and I will be celebrating Independence Day with family. Our Fourth of July wish for all Americans is a day of enjoyment, a day spent with family and friends, a day celebrated the traditional way, with picnics, parades, and fireworks.

But as you celebrate, I want to ask you to take a moment sometime before the last of the fireworks light the sky to think about what this day means, to think about how fortunate we Americans are. That first Fourth of July in 1776 was more than the birth of our nation. It was the first day of a new era, an era that changed the world, that proved that men and women could govern themselves in freedom.

Today, 213 years after the signing of the Declaration of Independence, the idea of democracy is stronger than ever in our nation and around the world. The symbols of liberty speak with power to people everywhere. Lady Liberty in New York Harbor, the goddess of democracy in Tiananmen Square, the flag—our banner of freedom—flying over thousands of town halls across America—these symbols tell us, they tell the world, that the most momentous idea in all of human history—freedom—is alive and unconquerable.

I ask all Americans to remember the precious legacy of liberty we enjoy. Thank you. God bless all of you, and God bless the United States of America on this Fourth of July weekend.

Statement on Signing the Dire Emergency Supplemental Appropriations and Transfers, Urgent Supplementals, and Correcting Enrollment Errors Act of 1989
June 30, 1989

Today, I have signed into law H.R. 2402, the Dire Emergency Supplemental Appropriations and Transfers, Urgent Supplementals, and Correcting Enrollment Errors Act of 1989.

The bill provides emergency funding for several mandatory programs, including Veterans Compensation and Pension programs; Food Stamps; Guaranteed Student Loans; Foster Care; and firefighting programs. The bill also provides emergency funding for several discretionary programs, such as Veterans Medical Care; refugee programs; and U.N. Peacekeeping activities.

I am especially pleased that this bill will provide the long overdue additional funding for our Nation's veterans, particularly for the Veterans Medical Care program. The additional funds will be used to provide for more service to veterans at outpatient clinics; to treat more veterans in nursing homes; and to increase purchases of capital equipment, prosthetic appliances, and a variety of medical supplies.

I want to take this opportunity to commend the Congress for keeping the funding levels in this bill within acceptable bounds. The House, the Senate, and the Administration reached a satisfactory compromise that funds "dire emergencies" while also attending to our mutual responsibility to restore fiscal discipline.

GEORGE BUSH

The White House,
June 30, 1989.

Note: H.R. 2402, approved June 30, was assigned Public Law No. 101–45.

Statement on Signing the Bill Extending Title I of the Energy Policy and Conservation Act
June 30, 1989

S. 694, which I signed into law today, extends until April 1, 1990, the authorization for the Nation's Strategic Petroleum Reserve (SPR). The bill also requires the Secretary of Energy to study alternative financing arrangements for expanding the SPR to a level of one billion barrels.

Although I would have preferred a simple 5-year extension of the SPR authority, I believe that this bill represents an acceptable compromise. It provides for the uninterrupted operation of the SPR, which is important to our Nation's energy security. It also allows sufficient time for the Administration to complete an interagency study of the SPR's size. A study of both the SPR size and alternative financing arrangements is necessary if we are to make an informed decision on the Strategic Petroleum Reserve.

GEORGE BUSH

The White House,
June 30, 1989.

Note: S. 694, approved June 30, was assigned Public Law No. 101–46.

Appendix A—Digest of Other White House Announcements

The following list includes the President's public schedule and other items of general interest announced by the Office of the Press Secretary and not included elsewhere in this book.

January 20

Following the Inaugural luncheon at the Capitol, the President and Mrs. Bush traveled by motorcade to the White House, where they viewed the Inaugural parade from the viewing stand. In the evening, the President and Mrs. Bush attended several Inaugural balls in their honor.

January 21

The President commissioned the following members of his White House senior staff:

John H. Sununu, of New Hampshire, as Chief of Staff to the President;

Brent Scowcroft, of Maryland, as Assistant to the President for National Security Affairs;

David Q. Bates, Jr., of Texas, as Assistant to the President and Secretary to the Cabinet;

Richard C. Breeden, of Virginia, as Assistant to the President for Issues Analysis;

Andrew H. Card, Jr., of Massachusetts, as Assistant to the President and Deputy to the Chief of Staff;

James W. Cicconi, of Texas, as Assistant to the President and Deputy to the Chief of Staff;

David F. Demarest, Jr., of New Jersey, as Assistant to the President for Communications;

Max Marlin Fitzwater, of Kansas, as Assistant to the President and Press Secretary;

C. Boyden Gray, of North Carolina, as Counsel to the President;

Frederick D. McClure, of Texas, as Assistant to the President for Legislative Affairs;

J. Bonnie Newman, of New Hampshire, as Assistant to the President for Management and Administration;

Roger B. Porter, of Utah, as Assistant to the President for Economic and Domestic Policy;

Stephen M. Studdert, of Utah, as Assistant to the President for Special Activities and Initiatives;

Charles G. Untermeyer, of Texas, as Assistant to the President and Director of Presidential Personnel;

Joseph W. Hagin II, of Ohio, as Deputy Assistant to the President for Appointments and Scheduling;

Edward M. Rogers, Jr., of Alabama, as Deputy Assistant to the President and Executive Assistant to the Chief of Staff.

January 22

In the morning, the President and Mrs. Bush attended church services at the National Cathedral.

January 23

The President met at the White House with:

—the Vice President; John H. Sununu, Chief of Staff to the President; Brent Scowcroft, Assistant to the President for National Security Affairs; and members of the CIA briefing staff;

—Senior White House staff, for lunch;

—the Vice President;

—the Cabinet, to discuss staff organization, major issues, foreign policy, and the Federal budget;

—John H. Sununu, Chief of Staff to the President.

In an Oval Office ceremony, John H. Sununu was sworn in as Chief of Staff to the President by the Vice President.

January 24

The President met at the White House with:

—the Vice President; John H. Sununu, Chief of Staff to the President; Brent Scowcroft, Assistant to the President for National Security Affairs; and members of the CIA briefing staff;

—the congressional leadership;

—Frank Nebeker, Director of the Office of Government Ethics;

—John H. Sununu, Chief of Staff to the President.

The White House announced that the President will meet with Prime Minister Brian Mulroney of Canada in Ottawa on February 10 for a working visit to discuss bilateral and international issues.

In the evening, the President hosted a dinner in the Residence in honor of United Nations Secretary-General Javier Perez de Cuellar de la Guerra and Mrs. de Cuellar.

January 25

The President met at the White House with:

—the Vice President; John H. Sununu, Chief of Staff to the President; Brent Scowcroft, Assistant to the President for National Security Affairs; and members of the CIA briefing staff;

—administration officials, to discuss the budget;

—Secretary of State-designate James A. Baker III;

—Malcolm R. Wilkey and Griffin B. Bell, Chairman and Vice Chairman, respectively, of the President's Commission on Federal Ethics Law Reform;
—John H. Sununu, Chief of Staff to the President.

In the evening, the President hosted a reception in the Residence for the Congressional Core Group, political supporters of the President.

The President announced the appointment of the following individuals to positions in the Office of Management and Budget:

Robert E. Grady, of New Jersey, to be Associate Director for Natural Resources, Energy, and Science. Mr. Grady has served as senior adviser to President Bush's transition team. Prior to this he was senior adviser for speechwriting and policy to the Bush-Quayle '88 campaign.

Janet Hale, of the District of Columbia, to be Associate Director for Economics and Government. Ms. Hale has served as Assistant Secretary for Budget and Programs at the Department of Transportation from 1986 to the present.

Edwin L. Dale, Jr., of Pennsylvania, to be Counsellor and Director of External Affairs. Since 1987 Mr. Dale has been Counsellor to the Secretary at the Department of Commerce in Washington, DC.

Thomas A. Scully, of Virginia, to be Associate Director for Congressional Affairs. Since 1986 Mr. Scully has been with the law firm of Akin, Gump, Strauss, Hauer & Feld in Washington, DC.

The President appointed the following individuals as members of the President's Commission on Federal Ethics Law Reform:

Malcolm Richard Wilkey, of Texas, as Chairman. Since 1985 Judge Wilkey has served as U.S. Ambassador to Uruguay. Previously he was a circuit judge on the U.S. Court of Appeals for the District of Columbia.

Griffin B. Bell, of Georgia, as Vice Chairman. Judge Bell served as Attorney General of the United States from 1977 to 1979 and was formerly a circuit judge on the U.S. Court of Appeals for the Fifth Circuit. He is currently a senior partner in the Atlanta and Washington, DC, law firm of King & Spalding.

Jan Witold Baran, of Virginia. Mr. Baran is a partner in the Washington, DC, law firm of Wiley, Rein & Fielding. He currently serves as general counsel to the American Bicentennial Presidential Inaugural Committee and to the Republican National Committee. He was also general counsel to the Bush-Quayle '88 organization. He has previously served as Executive Assistant to the Chairman of the Federal Election Commission.

Judith Hippler Bello, of Virginia. Mrs. Bello is the outgoing General Counsel to the U.S. Trade Representative and has served as the agency's designated ethics official. She will be joining the Washington, DC, office of Sidley & Austin as a partner.

Lloyd N. Cutler, of Maryland. Mr. Cutler is a partner in the Washington, DC, law firm of Wilmer, Cutler & Pickering and is Chairman of the Quadrennial Commission on Executive, Legislative, and Judicial Salaries. From 1979 to 1980, he served as Counsel to President Carter.

Fred Fisher Fielding, of Virginia. Mr. Fielding is a senior partner in the Washington, DC, law firm of Wiley, Rein & Fielding. From 1981 to 1986, he served as Counsel to President Reagan.

Harrison H. Schmitt, of New Mexico. Dr. Schmitt was a U.S. Senator from New Mexico from 1977 to 1983 and served as vice chairman of the Senate Select Committee on Ethics from 1977 to 1979. A former Apollo astronaut, Dr. Schmitt is now a private consultant, scientist, and businessman.

R. James Woolsey, of Maryland. Mr. Woolsey is a partner in the Washington, DC, law firm of Shea & Gardner. From 1977 to 1979, he served as Under Secretary of the Navy, and from 1970 to 1973, he was general counsel to the U.S. Senate Committee on Armed Services.

January 26

The President met at the White House with:
—the Vice President; John H. Sununu, Chief of Staff to the President; Brent Scowcroft, Assistant to the President for National Security Affairs; and members of the CIA briefing staff;
—Ambassador Robert B. Oakley;
—the Vice President, for lunch.

In the afternoon, the President attended the swearing-in ceremony for Richard G. Darman as Director of the Office of Management and Budget.

In the evening, the President hosted a reception in the Residence for members of the Republican congressional leadership.

January 27

The President met at the White House with:
—the Vice President; John H. Sununu, Chief of Staff to the President; Brent Scowcroft, Assistant to the President for National Security Affairs; and members of the CIA briefing staff;
—U.S. Inspectors General;
—John H. Sununu, Chief of Staff to the President.

In the morning, the President telephoned South Korean President Roh Tae Woo to accept President Roh's invitation to make an official visit to Seoul on February 26.

January 28

The President met at the White House with:
—the Vice President; John H. Sununu, Chief of Staff to the President; Brent Scowcroft, Assistant to the President for National Security Affairs; and members of the CIA briefing staff;
—former Secretary of State Henry A. Kissinger.

In the evening, the President attended the annual Alfalfa Club dinner at the Capital Hilton Hotel.

January 29

In the morning, the President left the White House for a brief visit to Camp David, MD. He returned to the White House in the afternoon.

January 30

The President met at the White House with:
—the Vice President; John H. Sununu, Chief of Staff to the President; Brent Scowcroft, Assistant to the President for National Security Affairs; and members of the CIA briefing staff;
—members of the Office of the National Service, to discuss an overall plan to involve other elements of the Government in volunteer work;
—John H. Sununu, Chief of Staff to the President.

January 31

The President met at the White House with:
—the Vice President; John H. Sununu, Chief of Staff to the President; Brent Scowcroft, Assistant to the President for National Security Affairs; and members of the CIA briefing staff;
—John H. Sununu, Chief of Staff to the President.

In the evening, the President hosted a reception on the State Floor at the White House for members of the Senate congressional committee leadership.

The President declared that a major disaster exists in Washington County, UT, as a result of flooding caused by a dike failure at the Quail Creek Reservoir on January 1. He directed the Federal Emergency Management Agency to provide funds to supplement State and local recovery efforts.

The President has commissioned the following members of the White House senior staff:

Paul W. Bateman, of California, as Deputy Assistant to the President for Management and Director of the Office of Administration;

Phillip D. Brady, of California, as Deputy Assistant to the President and Director of Cabinet Affairs;

Nicholas E. Calio, of Ohio, as Deputy Assistant to the President for Legislative Affairs;

B. Jay Cooper, of Connecticut, as Deputy Assistant to the President and Deputy Press Secretary;

Everett Boyd Hollingsworth, Jr., of Wyoming, as Deputy Assistant to the President for Legislative Affairs;

Roman Popadiuk, of New York, as Deputy Assistant to the President and Deputy Press Secretary;

Patricia Presock, of Virginia, as Deputy Assistant to the President;

Gary John Andres, of Virginia, as Special Assistant to the President for Legislative Affairs;

Nancy P. Dorn, of Texas, as Special Assistant to the President for Legislative Affairs;

Juanita Donaghey Duggan, of Alabama, as Special Assistant to the President for Cabinet Affairs;

Cooper Evans, of Iowa, as Special Assistant to the President for Agricultural Trade and Food Assistance;

John S. Gardner, of Maryland, as Special Assistant to the President and Assistant Staff Secretary;

Alixe Reed Glen, of Washington, DC, as Special Assistant to the President and Deputy Press Secretary;

Shirley M. Green, of Texas, as Special Assistant to the President for Presidential Messages and Correspondence;

Stephen T. Hart, of Virginia, as Special Assistant to the President and Deputy Press Secretary;

John W. Howard, of New Jersey, as Special Assistant to the President for Legislative Affairs;

Hector F. Irastorza, Jr., of Virginia, as Special Assistant to the President and Deputy Director of the Office of Administration;

Lehmann K. Li, Jr., of Connecticut, as Special Assistant to the President and Executive Secretary to the Economic Policy Council;

Antonio Lopez, of Tennessee, as Special Assistant to the President and Director of the White House Military Office;

Timothy John McBride, of Michigan, as Special Assistant to the President;

Gordon Bissell Wheeler, of New York, as Special Assistant to the President for Legislative Affairs;

Kenneth P. Yale, of Maryland, as Special Assistant to the President and Executive Secretary to the Domestic Policy Council;

Rose M. Zamaria, of Florida, as Special Assistant to the President and Director of White House Operations.

February 1

The President met at the White House with:
—the Vice President; John H. Sununu, Chief of Staff to the President; Brent Scowcroft, Assistant to the President for National Security Affairs; and members of the CIA briefing staff;
—Secretary of State James A. Baker III;
—members of the National Association of Wholesale Distributors;
—John H. Sununu, Chief of Staff to the President.

In the evening, the President and Mrs. Bush hosted a reception in the Residence for the Diplomatic Corps.

February 2

The President met at the White House with:
—the Vice President; John H. Sununu, Chief of Staff to the President; Brent Scowcroft, Assistant to the President for National Security Affairs; and members of the CIA briefing staff;

—representatives of the banking industry;
—leading female athletes;
—John H. Sununu, Chief of Staff to the President.

In the evening, the President and Mrs. Bush hosted a reception on the State Floor of the White House for the House of Representatives committee leadership.

Later in the evening, the President attended the New Jersey State Chamber of Commerce dinner at the Sheraton Washington Hotel.

February 3

The President met at the White House with:
—the Vice President; John H. Sununu, Chief of Staff to the President; Brent Scowcroft, Assistant to the President for National Security Affairs; and members of the CIA briefing staff;
—Penne Korth and Bobby Holt, cochairmen of the American Bicentennial Inauguration Committee;
—John H. Sununu, Chief of Staff to the President.

In the afternoon, the President left the White House for a weekend stay at Camp David, MD.

February 5

In the afternoon, the President returned to the White House from a weekend stay at Camp David, MD.

February 6

The President met at the White House with:
—the Vice President; John H. Sununu, Chief of Staff to the President; Brent Scowcroft, Assistant to the President for National Security Affairs; and members of the CIA briefing staff;
—John H. Sununu, Chief of Staff to the President.

February 7

The President met at the White House with:
—the Vice President; John H. Sununu, Chief of Staff to the President; Brent Scowcroft, Assistant to the President for National Security Affairs; and members of the CIA briefing staff;
—the Economic Policy Council;
—John H. Sununu, Chief of Staff to the President.

In the morning, the President attended the swearing-in ceremony in the Oval Office at the White House for Michael J. Boskin as Chairman of the Council of Economic Advisers.

In the afternoon, the President attended a Senate policy luncheon at the Capitol to discuss the budget and the savings and loan crisis.

In an Oval Office ceremony, the President received diplomatic credentials from Ambassadors Jaime Moncayo of Ecuador, Pierre François Benoit of Haiti, Kjeld Vibe of Norway, Gustavo Petricioli Iturbide of Mexico, Ali Bengelloun of Morocco, Derek H. Burney of Canada, Angus Albert Khan of Trinidad and Tobago, and Edouard Brunner of Switzerland.

In the evening, the President hosted a reception in the Residence for newly elected Members of Congress.

February 8

The President met at the White House with:
—the Vice President; John H. Sununu, Chief of Staff to the President; Brent Scowcroft, Assistant to the President for National Security Affairs; and members of the CIA briefing staff;
—Secretary of Veterans Affairs-designate Edward J. Derwinski, for lunch;
—Secretary of State James A. Baker III;
—John H. Sununu, Chief of Staff to the President.

February 9

The President met at the White House with:
—the Vice President; John H. Sununu, Chief of Staff to the President; Brent Scowcroft, Assistant to the President for National Security Affairs; and members of the CIA briefing staff;
—Catholicos Vazgen I, Supreme Patriarch of the Armenian Church in the Soviet Union;
—Members of Congress;
—the Vice President, for lunch;
—the Cabinet;
—West German Chancellery Minister Wolfgang Schaeuble;
—John H. Sununu, Chief of Staff to the President.

February 13

In the morning, the President and Mrs. Bush returned to the White House from Manchester, NH.

February 14

The President met at the White House with:
—the Vice President; John H. Sununu, Chief of Staff to the President; Brent Scowcroft, Assistant to the President for National Security Affairs; and members of the CIA briefing staff;
—leaders of the Safe Kids Program, a volunteer organization that fostered the prevention of accidental childhood injuries to children;
—members of the senior White House staff;
—Secretary of the Treasury Nicholas F. Brady; Richard G. Darman, Director of the Office of

Management and Budget; and John H. Sununu, Chief of Staff to the President, for lunch and to discuss the budget;
—the Domestic Policy Council, to discuss organizational strategies;
—John H. Sununu, Chief of Staff to the President.

February 15

The President met at the White House with:
—the Vice President; John H. Sununu, Chief of Staff to the President; Brent Scowcroft, Assistant to the President for National Security Affairs; and members of the CIA briefing staff;
—John Clendenin, U.S. Savings Bond chairman;
—John H. Sununu, Chief of Staff to the President.

In the afternoon, in the Roosevelt Room at the White House, the President presented James C. Young, football coach at the U.S. Military Academy, with the Commander In Chief's Trophy, which was awarded to the leading service academy football team.

February 16

The President met at the White House with:
—the Vice President; John H. Sununu, Chief of Staff to the President; Brent Scowcroft, Assistant to the President for National Security Affairs; and members of the CIA briefing staff;
—Joy Hall, the 1989 Easter Seal Poster Child;
—the Vice President, for lunch;
—the Commission on Merchant Marine and Defense;
—President Juan Antonio Samaranch and other members of the International Olympic Committee, to discuss the possibility of hosting the 1996 Olympic games in Atlanta, GA;
—John H. Sununu, Chief of Staff to the President.

February 17

The President met at the White House with the Vice President; John H. Sununu, Chief of Staff to the President; Brent Scowcroft, Assistant to the President for National Security Affairs; and members of the CIA briefing staff.

In the afternoon, the President and Mrs. Bush left the White House for a weekend stay at Camp David, MD.

In the evening, the President and Mrs. Bush hosted a dinner at Camp David, for His Royal Highness the Prince of Wales.

February 20

In the afternoon, the President and Mrs. Bush returned to the White House from a weekend stay at Camp David, MD.

February 21

The President met at the White House with:
—the Vice President; John H. Sununu, Chief of Staff to the President; Brent Scowcroft, Assistant to the President for National Security Affairs; and members of the CIA briefing staff;
—the congressional leadership;
—Secretary of the Treasury Nicholas F. Brady;
—John H. Sununu, Chief of Staff to the President.

The President transmitted the following reports to the Congress:
—the annual report of ACTION for fiscal year 1988;
—the annual report on mine safety and health activities for fiscal year 1987;
—the annual reports of the Department of Transportation for fiscal years 1985, 1986, and 1987;
—the annual report of the National Endowment for Democracy for fiscal year 1988.

February 22

In the morning, the President and Mrs. Bush left the White House for a trip to the Far East.

February 23

In the afternoon, the President and Mrs. Bush arrived at Haneda Airport, Tokyo, Japan, where they were greeted by Japanese and American officials. The President and Mrs. Bush then went to the U.S. Ambassador's residence, where President Bush and senior staff members attended a working luncheon with President François Mitterrand of France. Following the luncheon, President Bush met with Prime Minister Noboru Takeshita of Japan in the Asahi-No-Ma Room at Akasaka Palace and then proceeded to the Hotel Okura, his residence during his stay in Japan.

In the evening, President Bush returned to the U.S. Ambassador's residence and met individually with President Mário Alberto Soares of Portugal, President Mohammed Hosni Mubarak of Egypt, Prime Minister Chatchai Chunhawan of Thailand, King Juan Carlos I of Spain, King Hussein I of Jordan, and President Chaim Herzog of Israel. Following his meetings, President Bush returned to the Hotel Okura for the evening.

February 24

In the morning, the President and Mrs. Bush attended the funeral ceremony for Emperor Hirohito at Shinjuku Gyoen. At the conclusion of the ceremony, the President and Mrs. Bush went to the U.S. Embassy, where the President greeted members of the staff in the auditorium.

In the afternoon, President Bush went to the U.S. Ambassador's residence, where he met individually with President Richard von Weizsäcker of West Germany, Prime Minister Lee Kuan Yew of Singapore, King Baudouin I of Belgium, Prime Minister Turgut Özal of Turkey, Prime Minister Benazir Bhutto of Pakistan, President Mobutu Sese Seko of Zaire and President Francesco Cossiga of Italy. At the conclusion of his meetings, President Bush returned to his hotel.

In the evening, the President and Mrs. Bush attended a reception at Akasaka Palace hosted by Prime Minister Takeshita. President Bush then met with President Corazon C. Aquino of the Philippines. At the conclusion of the meeting, the President and Mrs. Bush returned to their hotel.

The President declared that a major disaster exists in Kentucky as a result of heavy rains and flooding that began on February 13. He directed the Federal Emergency Management Agency to provide funds to supplement State and local recovery efforts.

February 25

In the morning, the President and Mrs. Bush had an audience with Emperor Akihito at the Imperial Palace. They then went to the U.S. Ambassador's residence, where President Bush met individually with President Ibrahim Babangida of Nigeria and with President José Sarney Costa of Brazil.

In the afternoon, the President and Mrs. Bush left Tokyo and flew to Beijing International Airport, where they were greeted by Chinese and American officials. They then went to the Diaoyutai State Guest House, their residence during their stay in China, and exchanged gifts with Premier and Mrs. Li Peng.

In the evening, President Bush participated in a bilateral meeting and a gift exchange in the Great Hall of the People with President Yang Shangkun. The President and Mrs. Bush then attended a banquet in the Western Hall hosted by President Yang. At the conclusion of the banquet, the President and Mrs. Bush returned to the Diaoyutai State Guest House.

February 26

In the morning, the President and Mrs. Bush attended morning prayer services at the Chongmenwen Christian Church. The President then attended meetings at the Great Hall of the People with Premier Li Peng and Chairman (Central Military Commission) Deng Xiaoping.

In the afternoon, the President and Mrs. Bush attended a luncheon in the Big East Hall hosted by Chairman Deng Xiaoping. At the conclusion of the luncheon, they went to the International Club, where the President visited with friends. He and Mrs. Bush then attended a reception at Ambassador Winston Lord's residence. Upon returning to the Diaoyutai State Guest House, President Bush met with President Norodom Sihanouk of Cambodia. President Bush then met with General Secretary Zhao Ziyang at the Great Hall of the People.

In the evening, the President and Mrs. Bush hosted a tea and dinner for Chinese leaders in the Grand Ballroom at the Sheraton Great Wall Hotel. At the conclusion of the dinner, the President and Mrs. Bush returned to the Diaoyutai State Guest House.

February 27

In the morning, the President and Mrs. Bush bid farewell to Vice Premier Wu Xueqian during an informal departure tea at Beijing International Airport.

In the afternoon, upon arriving at K–16 Airport in Seoul, South Korea, the President and Mrs. Bush were welcomed by Prime Minister and Mrs. Kang Yong Hoon and Korean and American officials in a formal arrival ceremony. They then met with President Roh Tae Woo and First Lady Kim Ok Sook at the Blue House, the official residence of the Korean President, and were invited to sign the guest book. Later in the afternoon, President Bush met privately with President Roh in the study at the Blue House. The meeting was then expanded to include Korean and American officials. Afterwards, the two Presidents and the officials attended a luncheon in the Korean Traditional House. Following the luncheon, President Bush addressed the National Assembly and met with the Assembly's leadership. The President and Mrs. Bush then went to the U.S. Ambassador's residence, where they greeted the American community. At the conclusion of the reception, they left Seoul and returned to Washington, DC.

February 28

The President met at the White House with the Vice President; John H. Sununu, Chief of Staff to the President; Brent Scowcroft, Assistant to the President for National Security Affairs; and members of the CIA briefing staff.

The President transmitted to the Congress the national trade policy agenda for calendar year 1989 and an addendum to the 1988 annual report on the Trade Agreements Program that was sent to the Congress on January 3, 1989.

March 1

The President met at the White House with:

—the Vice President; John H. Sununu, Chief of Staff to the President; Brent Scowcroft, Assistant to the President for National Security Affairs; and members of the CIA briefing staff;

—administration officials, to discuss the budget;

—conservative leaders;

—representatives of the Toys for Tots organization;
—Secretary of State James A. Baker III;
—John H. Sununu, Chief of Staff to the President.

March 2

The President met at the White House with:
—the Vice President; John H. Sununu, Chief of Staff to the President; Brent Scowcroft, Assistant to the President for National Security Affairs; and members of the CIA briefing staff;
—Adm. William J. Crowe, Jr., USN, Chairman of the Joint Chiefs of Staff, and Deputy Secretary of Defense William Howard Taft IV;
—President Vinicio Cerezo Arévalo of Guatemala;
—Senator Barry Goldwater;
—John H. Sununu, Chief of Staff to the President.

March 3

The President met at the White House with:
—the Vice President; John H. Sununu, Chief of Staff to the President; Brent Scowcroft, Assistant to the President for National Security Affairs; and members of the CIA briefing staff;
—Ambassador Jack Matlock;
—Secretary of Labor Elizabeth H. Dole and Secretary of Transportation Samuel K. Skinner, to discuss the Eastern Airlines strike;
—Secretary of State James A. Baker III.

In the morning, the President telephoned President Carlos Andrés Pérez, to express support for the Venezuelan Government in light of the recent rioting.

In the afternoon, the President and Mrs. Bush left the White House for a weekend stay at Camp David, MD.

March 5

In the afternoon, the President and Mrs. Bush returned to the White House from a weekend stay at Camp David, MD.

March 6

The President met at the White House with:
—the Vice President; John H. Sununu, Chief of Staff to the President; Brent Scowcroft, Assistant to the President for National Security Affairs; and members of the CIA briefing staff;
—Secretary of Agriculture Clayton Yeutter, for lunch;
—congressional foreign policy leaders, to discuss the President's recent trip to the Far East;
—John H. Sununu, Chief of Staff to the President.

The President commissioned the following members of his White House senior staff:

Ronald Carlin Kaufman, of Massachusetts, as Deputy Assistant to the President for Presidential Personnel;

John G. Keller, Jr., of the District of Columbia, as Deputy Assistant to the President and Director of Presidential Advance;

Bobbie Greene Kilberg, of Virginia, as Deputy Assistant to the President for Public Liaison;

Charles Gregg Petersmeyer, of Colorado, as Deputy Assistant to the President and Director of the Office of National Service;

James P. Pinkerton, of Massachusetts, as Deputy Assistant to the President for Policy Planning;

William L. Roper, of Alabama, as Deputy Assistant to the President for Domestic Policy and Director of the Office of Policy Development;

Susan Porter Rose, of Virginia, as Deputy Assistant to the President and Chief of Staff to the First Lady;

John Patrick Schmitz, of California, as Deputy Counsel to the President;

Sichan Siv, of Texas, as Deputy Assistant to the President for Public Liaison;

Roscoe Burton Starek III, of Illinois, as Deputy Assistant to the President and Deputy Director of Presidential Personnel;

Chriss A. Winston, of Virginia, as Deputy Assistant to the President for Communications;

G. Philip Hughes, of Virginia, as Executive Secretary of the National Security Council;

Robert A. Estrada, of Texas, as Special Assistant to the President and Associate Director of Presidential Personnel;

Martha H. Goodwin, of Virginia, as Special Assistant to the President and Associate Director of Presidential Personnel;

Anne Brooks Gwaltney, of Connecticut, as Special Assistant to the President and Associate Director of Presidential Personnel;

Thomas F. Kranz, of California, as Special Assistant to the President and Associate Director of Presidential Personnel;

Lee S. Liberman, of Virginia, as Associate Counsel to the President;

Nancy Fleetwood Miller, of Virginia, as Special Assistant to the President and Associate Director of Presidential Personnel;

Jeannette Louise Naylor, of Texas, as Special Assistant to the President and Associate Director of Presidential Personnel;

Doug Wead, of Missouri, as Special Assistant to the President for Public Liaison;

Amy L. Schwartz, of New York, as Associate Counsel to the President.

March 7

The President met at the White House with:
—the Vice President; John H. Sununu, Chief of Staff to the President; Brent Scowcroft, Assistant to the President for National Security Affairs; and members of the CIA briefing staff;

—Secretary of State James A. Baker III.

In the evening, the President and Mrs. Bush hosted a reception in the Residence for members of the National Economic Commission.

March 8

The President met at the White House with:

—the Vice President; John H. Sununu, Chief of Staff to the President; Brent Scowcroft, Assistant to the President for National Security Affairs; and members of the CIA briefing staff;

—Secretary of State James A. Baker III;

—John H. Sununu, Chief of Staff to the President.

In the afternoon, the President attended a luncheon in the Roosevelt Room at the White House for former chairmen of the Republican National Committee.

March 9

The President met at the White House with:

—the Vice President; John H. Sununu, Chief of Staff to the President; Brent Scowcroft, Assistant to the President for National Security Affairs; and members of the CIA briefing staff;

—members of the Bush/Quayle Jewish Campaign Committee, National Jewish Coalition;

—representatives of national Jewish organizations;

—Charles Reynolds, president of the International Association of Chiefs of Police;

—the Vice President, for lunch.

March 10

The President met at the White House with:

—the Vice President; John H. Sununu, Chief of Staff to the President; Brent Scowcroft, Assistant to the President for National Security Affairs; and members of the CIA briefing staff;

—Kevin Dobson, chairman of the Salute to Hospitalized Veterans;

—Secretary of State James A. Baker III;

—John H. Sununu, Chief of Staff to the President.

In the afternoon, the President and Mrs. Bush left the White House for a weekend stay at Camp David, MD.

March 12

In the afternoon, the President and Mrs. Bush returned to the White House from a weekend stay at Camp David, MD.

March 13

The President met at the White House with:

—the Vice President; John H. Sununu, Chief of Staff to the President; Brent Scowcroft, Assistant to the President for National Security Affairs; and members of the CIA briefing staff;

—Representatives John Paul Hammerschmidt of Arkansas and G.V. (Sonny) Montgomery of Mississippi, for lunch;

—administration officials, to discuss the budget;

—John H. Sununu, Chief of Staff to the President.

The White House announced that the President and Mrs. Bush upon learning of the death of John J. McCloy, expressed their condolences to his family.

The President transmitted to the Congress requests for additional appropriations for the fiscal year 1989 budget.

March 14

The President met at the White House with:

—the Vice President; John H. Sununu, Chief of Staff to the President; Brent Scowcroft, Assistant to the President for National Security Affairs; and members of the CIA briefing staff;

—members of the Commission on Federal Ethics Law Reform;

—Spanish Foreign Minister Francisco Fernández-Ordóñez;

—the congressional budget committee;

—John H. Sununu, Chief of Staff to the President.

March 15

The President met at the White House with:

—the Vice President; John H. Sununu, Chief of Staff to the President; Brent Scowcroft, Assistant to the President for National Security Affairs; and members of the CIA briefing staff;

—Members of Congress;

—Attorney General Richard L. Thornburgh, for lunch;

—ranking members of the House of Representatives Permanent Select Committee on Intelligence;

—John H. Sununu, Chief of Staff to the President.

The President transmitted to the Congress the annual report on the U.S.-Japan Cooperative Medical Science Program for the period covering July 1987 to July 1988.

The President transmitted a report on foreign governments engaged in intelligence activities that were harmful to U.S. national security to Senate and House committees on foreign relations and intelligence.

March 16

The President met at the White House with the Vice President; John H. Sununu, Chief of Staff to the President; Brent Scowcroft, Assistant to the President for National Security Affairs; and members of the CIA briefing staff.

March 17

The President met at the White House with:
—recipients of the White House News Photographers Association Award;
—Secretary of State James A. Baker III;
—John H. Sununu, Chief of Staff to the President.

The White House announced that the President asked Representative Dan Rostenkowski of Illinois to be his representative to the Poznan International Trade Fair in Poland from June 11 to June 18.

The President announced that the following individuals will travel to El Salvador, March 18–20, as official U.S. observers of the Presidential election. The United States will be represented by a Presidential delegation composed of Members of Congress, State and local government officials, and private citizens. The Chairman of the delegation will be Senator Mitch McConnell (R-KY), and the Vice Chairman will be Gov. Robert Martinez of Florida.

Congressional Delegates:

Senator Mitch McConnell (R-KY)
Congressman Jon Kyl (R-AZ)
Congressman Bill McCollum (R-FL)
Congressman Robert K. Dornan (R-CA)
Congressman Alan B. Mollohan (D-WV)
Congressman Tony Coelho (D-CA)
Congressman John P. Murtha (D-PA)

State and local government officials:

William Bartlett, of New Hampshire, president, New Hampshire State Senate
Miriam Ramirez de Ferrer, of Puerto Rico, president, State Federation of Republican Women, Commonwealth of Puerto Rico
Gene DeFries, of Virginia, president, Maritime Engineers Beneficial Association/NMU
William C. Doherty, of Virginia, executive director of the American Institute for Free Labor Development/AFL–CIO
Peter Flaherty, of Virginia, president, Conservative Campaign Fund
Daryl Gates, of California, chief of police, Los Angeles Police Department
William R. Haynes, of Texas, attorney, Petroleum Industry
Charles House, of California, deputy sheriff, Los Angeles County
Robert Martinez, of Florida, Governor of Florida
Beryl Milburn, of Texas
Maurice Sonnenberg, of New York, consultant
Frank Tejeda, of Texas, Texas State Senator
William G. Walker, of California, U.S. Ambassador to El Salvador

March 20

The President met at the White House with:
—the Vice President; John H. Sununu, Chief of Staff to the President; Brent Scowcroft, Assistant to the President for National Security Affairs; and members of the CIA briefing staff;
—U.S. Ambassador to the Philippines Nicholas Platt and Gov. Guy Hunt of Alabama, to discuss drug abuse and trafficking;
—Cardinal Casaroli of the Vatican;
—Foreign Secretary Fernando Solana of Mexico;
—John H. Sununu, Chief of Staff to the President.

In the evening, the President and Mrs. Bush hosted a reception in the Residence for U.S. Roman Catholic Cardinals.

March 21

The President met at the White House with:
—the Vice President; John H. Sununu, Chief of Staff to the President; Brent Scowcroft, Assistant to the President for National Security Affairs; and members of the CIA briefing staff;
—Archbishop Iakovos of the Greek Orthodox Archdiocese of North and South America, for the observance of Greek Independence Day;
—the Tennessee State University basketball team;
—John H. Sununu, Chief of Staff to the President;
—Secretary of Labor Elizabeth H. Dole, to discuss the minimum wage.

The President announced that Secretary of State James A. Baker III will serve as his personal representative to attend the funeral of John J. McCloy. Accompanying Secretary Baker as official representatives of the President will be:

Mrs. Dean Acheson, widow of former Secretary of State Acheson
Representative E. Thomas Coleman, of Missouri, vice chairman, Congressional Study Group on Germany
Ambassador Martin J. Hillenbrand, former Ambassador to the Federal Republic of Germany
Former Senator Charles McC. Mathias, of Maryland, chairman of the American Council on Germany
Ambassador George C. McGhee, former Ambassador to the Federal Republic of Germany
Ambassador Joseph Verner Reed, Chief of Protocol
Ambassador Vernon A. Walters, Ambassador-designate to the Federal Republic of Germany

March 22

The President met at the White House with John H. Sununu, Chief of Staff to the President.

In the evening, the President and Mrs. Bush hosted a reception in the Residence for the Inaugural Family Housing Group.

March 23

The President met at the White House with:

—the Vice President; John H. Sununu, Chief of Staff to the President; Brent Scowcroft, Assistant to the President for National Security Affairs; and members of the CIA briefing staff;

—children with life-threatening illnesses, as part of the Make a Wish program;

—administration officials, to discuss the budget;

—John H. Sununu, Chief of Staff to the President.

March 24

The President met at the White House with:

—the Vice President; John H. Sununu, Chief of Staff to the President; Brent Scowcroft, Assistant to the President for National Security Affairs; and members of the CIA briefing staff;

—Members of Congress;

—Darryl Waltrip, Daytona 500 winner;

—Secretary of State James A. Baker III, for lunch.

In the morning, the President and Mrs. Bush attended Good Friday services at St. Johns Church at Lafayette Square.

The President sent to the Congress requests for additional appropriations totaling $2.2 billion in budget authority: $892.4 million in appropriations to liquidate contract authority and $144.6 million in transfer authority for fiscal year 1989, and $444.5 million in budget authority and $62.5 million in appropriations to liquidate contract authority for fiscal year 1990. Most of the increases for fiscal year 1989 are required by law for mandatory Federal programs. All outlays resulting from fiscal year 1989 requests for discretionary programs would be offset mainly through a percentage reduction to be applied to a set of programs identified in a report to be transmitted to the Congress with this package. This transmittal also includes fiscal year 1989 and 1990 appropriation requests for the legislative branch and the judiciary.

In the afternoon, the President and Mrs. Bush left the White House to visit President José Napoleón Duarte Fuentes of El Salvador at Walter Reed Army Hospital. Following their visit, the President and Mrs. Bush went to Camp David, MD, for a weekend stay.

March 26

The President and Mrs. Bush returned to the White House from a weekend stay at Camp David, MD.

March 27

The President met at the White House with:

—the Vice President; John H. Sununu, Chief of Staff to the President; Brent Scowcroft, Assistant to the President for National Security Affairs; and members of the CIA briefing staff;

—Catholic supporters, to discuss religious issues;

—John H. Sununu, Chief of Staff to the President.

In the morning, the President attended the swearing-in ceremony for Richard J. Kerr as Deputy Director of Central Intelligence in the Old Indian Treaty Room of the Old Executive Office Building.

Later in the morning, the President participated in the White House Easter Egg Roll on the South Lawn of the White House.

March 28

The President met at the White House with:

—the Vice President; John H. Sununu, Chief of Staff to the President; Brent Scowcroft, Assistant to the President for National Security Affairs; and members of the CIA briefing staff;

—John H. Sununu, Chief of Staff to the President.

The President designated Anne E. Brunsdale as Chairman of the U.S. International Trade Commission for the term expiring June 16, 1990. She would succeed Susan Wittenberg Liebler. Ms. Brunsdale has been serving as Vice Chairman since June 16, 1986, and as a member since December 17, 1985.

The President also designated Ronald A. Cass as Vice Chairman of the U.S. International Trade Commission for the term expiring June 16, 1990. He would succeed Anne E. Brunsdale. Mr. Cass has been serving as a member since January 19, 1988.

March 29

The President met at the White House with:

—the Vice President; John H. Sununu, Chief of Staff to the President; Brent Scowcroft, Assistant to the President for National Security Affairs; and members of the CIA briefing staff;

—members of the National Commission on Public Service, to receive the Commission's report;

—Secretary of State James A. Baker III;

—John H. Sununu, Chief of Staff to the President.

In an Oval Office ceremony, the President presented Steve Allen and Jayne Meadows with the Cancer Courage Award.

March 30

The President met at the White House with:
—the Vice President; John H. Sununu, Chief of Staff to the President; Brent Scowcroft, Assistant to the President for National Security Affairs; and members of the CIA briefing staff;
—Secretary of Transportation Samuel K. Skinner; William K. Reilly, Administrator of the Environmental Protection Agency; and Adm. Paul A. Yost, Commandant of the U.S. Coast Guard, to discuss the Alaskan oil spill cleanup efforts;
—the Vice President, for lunch;
—John H. Sununu, Chief of Staff to the President.

March 31

The President met at the White House with:
—the Vice President; John H. Sununu, Chief of Staff to the President; Brent Scowcroft, Assistant to the President for National Security Affairs; and members of the CIA briefing staff;
—Secretary of State James A. Baker III;
—John H. Sununu, Chief of Staff to the President.

April 1

The President met at the White House with John H. Sununu, Chief of Staff to the President; Brent Scowcroft, Assistant to the President for National Security Affairs; and members of the CIA briefing staff.

In the evening, the President and Mrs. Bush attended the Gridiron dinner at the Capitol Hilton Hotel.

April 3

The President met at the White House with:
—the Vice President; John H. Sununu, Chief of Staff to the President; Brent Scowcroft, Assistant to the President for National Security Affairs; and members of the CIA briefing staff;
—John H. Sununu, Chief of Staff to the President.

In the afternoon, President Bush attended the opening day of the 1989 baseball season at Memorial Stadium in Baltimore, MD. He threw the first pitch of the game between the Baltimore Orioles and the Boston Red Sox and watched five innings before returning to the White House. President Mohammed Hosni Mubarak of Egypt accompanied President Bush.

April 4

The President met at the White House with:
—the Vice President; John H. Sununu, Chief of Staff to the President; Brent Scowcroft, Assistant to the President for National Security Affairs; and members of the CIA briefing staff;
—President Oscar Arias Sánchez of Costa Rica;
—Secretary of Education Lauro F. Cavazos, for lunch;
—John H. Sununu, Chief of Staff to the President.

April 5

The President met at the White House with:
—the Vice President; John H. Sununu, Chief of Staff to the President; Brent Scowcroft, Assistant to the President for National Security Affairs; and members of the CIA briefing staff;
—Hans-Jochen Vogel, chairman of the West German Social Democratic Party;
—the Vice President, for lunch;
—Secretary of State James A. Baker III;
—John H. Sununu, Chief of Staff to the President.

April 6

The President met at the White House with:
—the Vice President; John H. Sununu, Chief of Staff to the President; Brent Scowcroft, Assistant to the President for National Security Affairs; and members of the CIA briefing staff;
—the Republican congressional leadership;
—John H. Sununu, Chief of Staff to the President.

In the afternoon, the President and Prime Minister Yitzhak Shamir of Israel visited the Smithsonian Institution's National Air and Space Museum.

April 7

The President met at the White House with:
—the Vice President; John H. Sununu, Chief of Staff to the President; Brent Scowcroft, Assistant to the President for National Security Affairs; and members of the CIA briefing staff;
—Gov. William P. Clements, Jr., of Texas;
—Secretary of State James A. Baker III.

In an Oval Office ceremony, the Inaugural Medals Committee gave the President and the Vice President medals commemorating the American Bicentennial Presidential Inaugural. Mrs. Bush and Mrs. Quayle received charms.

In the afternoon, the President and Mrs. Bush attended a reception in the Residence for the Folger Library. Following the reception, the President and Mrs. Bush left the White House for a weekend stay at Camp David, MD.

April 9

In the afternoon, the President and Mrs. Bush returned to the White House from a weekend stay at Camp David, MD.

April 10

The President met at the White House with the Vice President; John H. Sununu, Chief of Staff to the President; Brent Scowcroft, Assistant to the President for National Security Affairs; and members of the CIA briefing staff.

In the afternoon, the President and Mrs. Bush hosted a reception in the Residence for the Republican Eagles.

April 11

The President met at the White House with:
—the Vice President; John H. Sununu, Chief of Staff to the President; Brent Scowcroft, Assistant to the President for National Security Affairs; and members of the CIA briefing staff;
—Secretary of Defense Richard B. Cheney;
—Senator Pete Wilson of California;
—Members of the Cabinet;
—French Foreign Minister Roland Dumas;
—John H. Sununu, Chief of Staff to the President.

April 12

The President met at the White House with:
—the Vice President; John H. Sununu, Chief of Staff to the President; Brent Scowcroft, Assistant to the President for National Security Affairs; and members of the CIA briefing staff;
—the Vice President, for lunch;
—Secretary of State James A. Baker III;
—Prime Minister Arthur Napoleon Raymond Robinson of Trinidad and Tobago;
—Secretary-General Manfred Woerner of the North Atlantic Treaty Organization;
—John H. Sununu, Chief of Staff to the President.

In the morning, the President telephoned Chancellor Helmut Kohl of West Germany to discuss preparations for the upcoming North Atlantic Treaty Organization summit.

In an Oval Office ceremony, the President met with crime victims Tillie Black Bear, Ellen Griggin Dunne, Charles D. Gill, Louis and Patricia Herzog, Stephen M. McNanea, and Jack Russell.

April 13

The President met at the White House with:
—the Vice President; John H. Sununu, Chief of Staff to the President; Brent Scowcroft, Assistant to the President for National Security Affairs; and members of the CIA briefing staff;
—John H. Sununu, Chief of Staff to the President.

The White House announced that President Bush has invited President Virgilio Barco Vargas of Colombia for an official working visit to the United States. The two Governments are discussing exact dates and agenda for the visit.

The White House announced that the President will travel to Hamtramck, MI, on April 17, to visit with Polish leaders and give a speech on foreign policy. The President will also travel across the country, April 24–27, to address the American Newspaper Publishers Association in Chicago, IL, and stay overnight in northern California. On April 25, the President will speak in Palo Alto, CA, and stay overnight in Los Angeles, CA. On April 26, the President will visit former President Ronald Reagan and will address the Texas State Legislature in Austin, TX, and stay overnight in Miami, FL. On April 27, the President will participate in an event with the U.S. Coast Guard, the U.S. Customs Service, and the Drug Enforcement Conference in Miami, FL. On April 30, the President will travel to New York City to attend church services and participate in an event marking the bicentennial of the American Presidents. At the conclusion of the event, the President will return to the White House.

The White House announced that retail sales increased 0.1 percent in March, stating that the reduced growth of retail sales in March as well as the downward revision for February, a 0.6 percent decline, provide further evidence of a pattern of slower consumer spending in recent months, and there is a continued belief that the economy is sound, showing steady growth with low inflation.

The White House also announced that the President will deliver five commencement addresses this year. They include: Texas A&M, College Station, TX, on May 12; Alcorn State University, Lorman, MS, on May 13; Mississippi State University, Starkville, MS, on May 13; Boston University, Boston, MA, on May 21; and the U.S. Coast Guard Academy, New London, CT, on May 24.

April 14

The President met at the White House with:
—the Vice President; John H. Sununu, Chief of Staff to the President; Brent Scowcroft, Assistant to the President for National Security Affairs; and members of the CIA briefing staff;

—Members of Congress, to discuss the Federal budget;
—John H. Sununu, Chief of Staff to the President, for lunch;
—Secretary of State James A. Baker III.

The President declared that a major disaster exists in the State of Washington because of flooding and mudslides that occurred March 8–17. He directed the Federal Emergency Management Agency to provide assistance to supplement State and local recovery efforts.

April 15

In the morning, the President and Mrs. Bush left the White House for a weekend stay at Camp David, MD.

April 16

In the evening, the President and Mrs. Bush returned to the White House from a weekend stay at Camp David, MD.

April 17

The President met at the White House with:
—the Vice President; John H. Sununu, Chief of Staff to the President; Brent Scowcroft, Assistant to the President for National Security Affairs; and members of the CIA briefing staff;
—Foreign Secretary Sir Geoffrey Howe of the United Kingdom;
—John H. Sununu, Chief of Staff to the President;
—Republican members of the House Appropriations Committee.

April 18

The President met at the White House with:
—the Vice President; John H. Sununu, Chief of Staff to the President; Brent Scowcroft, Assistant to the President for National Security Affairs; and members of the CIA briefing staff;
—religious leaders;
—Secretary of Health and Human Services Louis W. Sullivan, to discuss proposed legislation that would provide assistance to infants, children, and pregnant women;
—John H. Sununu, Chief of Staff to the President.

The President transmitted to the Congress the annual report of the Commodity Credit Corporation for fiscal year 1987.

April 19

The President met at the White House with:
—the Vice President; John H. Sununu, Chief of Staff to the President; Brent Scowcroft, Assistant to the President for National Security Affairs; and members of the CIA briefing staff;
—Secretary of State James A. Baker III;
—Walter Momper, mayor of West Berlin;
—the congressional leadership;
—John H. Sununu, Chief of Staff to the President.

April 20

The President met at the White House with:
—the Vice President; John H. Sununu, Chief of Staff to the President; Brent Scowcroft, Assistant to the President for National Security Affairs; and members of the CIA briefing staff;
—the Vice President, for lunch;
—Secretary of Transportation Samuel K. Skinner;
—Prime Minister Manuel A. Esquivel of Belize;
—John H. Sununu, Chief of Staff to the President.

April 21

The President met at the White House with:
—the Vice President; John H. Sununu, Chief of Staff to the President; Brent Scowcroft, Assistant to the President for National Security Affairs; and members of the CIA briefing staff;
—William Croaker, advocate for early cancer detection;
—leaders of the Minimum Wage Veto Coalition;
—Secretary of State James A. Baker III;
—President Aristides Pereira of Cape Verde, to discuss the Namibia-Angola peace settlement;
—President's Dinner fundraisers;
—John H. Sununu, Chief of Staff to the President.

In the afternoon, the President and Mrs. Bush left the White House for a weekend stay at Camp David, MD.

April 23

In the afternoon, the President and Mrs. Bush returned to the White House from a weekend stay at Camp David, MD.

April 25

The President declared that a major disaster existed in Texas as a result of severe thunderstorms and flooding that occurred March 28–29. He directed the Federal Emergency Management Agency to provide assistance to supplement State and local recovery efforts. In the afternoon, the President attended a baseball game between the California Angels and the Baltimore Orioles at Anaheim Stadium in Anaheim, CA.

April 26

In the morning, the President attended a breakfast reception for major political supporters in the Grand Ballroom at the Four Seasons Hotel in Beverly Hills, CA.

April 28

The President met at the White House with:
—John H. Sununu, Chief of Staff to the President; Brent Scowcroft, Assistant to the President for National Security Affairs; and members of the CIA briefing staff;
—James R. Lilley, U.S. Ambassador to China;
—Mayor James Garner of Homestead, NY;
—Secretary of State James Baker III;
—John H. Sununu, Chief of Staff to the President.

April 29

The President met at the White House with Brent Scowcroft, Assistant to the President for National Security Affairs, and members of the CIA briefing staff.

In the evening, the President and Mrs. Bush attended the White House Correspondents Dinner at the Washington Hilton Hotel.

May 1

The President met at the White House with:
—John H. Sununu, Chief of Staff to the President; Brent Scowcroft, Assistant to the President for National Security Affairs; and members of the CIA briefing staff;
—national Protestant leaders;
—John H. Sununu, Chief of Staff to the President.

In an Oval Office ceremony, Paul Coverdell was sworn in as Director of the Peace Corps.

May 2

The President met at the White House with:
—John H. Sununu, Chief of Staff to the President; Brent Scowcroft, Assistant to the President for National Security Affairs; and members of the CIA briefing staff;
—the Republican congressional leadership;
—the U.S. Holocaust Memorial Council leadership;
—William J. Bennett, Director of National Drug Control Policy;
—members of the House Select Committee on Narcotics;
—John H. Sununu, Chief of Staff to the President.

The President transmitted the following reports to the Congress:
—the first comprehensive triennial report on immigration, 1989;
—the 15th annual report of the Federal Council on the Aging for calendar year 1988;
—the 23d annual report of the National Endowment for the Humanities for fiscal year 1988.

May 3

The President met at the White House with:
—John H. Sununu, Chief of Staff to the President; Brent Scowcroft, Assistant to the President for National Security Affairs; and members of the CIA briefing staff;
—Prime Minister Gro Harlem Brundtland of Norway;
—Republican members of the Senate Steering Committee;
—the National Collegiate Athletic Association swimming champions, from Kenyon College;
—the National Collegiate Athletic Association hockey champions, from Harvard University;
—Secretary of Energy James D. Watkins, for lunch;
—Secretary of State James A. Baker III;
—members of the National Law Enforcement Council;
—administration officials, to discuss the budget;
—John H. Sununu, Chief of Staff to the President.

In the morning, the President received a telephone call from Suzanne Smith, a 17-year-old student at the Arizona School for the Deaf and Blind, who participated in inaugurating the General Services Administration's Telecommunications Relay Service.

In the evening, the President and Mrs. Bush attended a reception for the Dole Foundation at the National Museum for Women in the Arts.

May 4

The President met at the White House with:
—John H. Sununu, Chief of Staff to the President; Brent Scowcroft, Assistant to the President for National Security Affairs; and members of the CIA briefing staff;
—Republican Members of the House of Representatives Whip Organization;
—winners of the National Bicentennial Competition on the Constitution and the Bill of Rights;
—the New Jersey Governor's Club "Committee of One Hundred;"
—John H. Sununu, Chief of Staff to the President.

May 5

The President met at the White House with:
—John H. Sununu, Chief of Staff to the President; Brent Scowcroft, Assistant to the President for National Security Affairs; and members of the CIA briefing staff;
—Chancellor Franz Vranitzky of Austria;

—the Vice President, for lunch;
—Secretary of State James A. Baker III.

The President designated Representative William L. Dickinson of Alabama as his representative to the Paris Air Show to be held June 8–18, 1989.

In the afternoon, the President and Mrs. Bush left the White House for a weekend stay at Camp David, MD.

May 7

The President and Mrs. Bush returned to the White House from a weekend stay at Camp David, MD.

May 8

The President met at the White House with:
—John H. Sununu, Chief of Staff to the President; Brent Scowcroft, Assistant to the President for National Security Affairs; and members of the CIA briefing staff;
—King Olav V of Norway;
—Jacques Chirac, mayor of Paris, France;
—John H. Sununu, Chief of Staff to the President.

In the morning, the President attended the swearing-in ceremony in the Oval Office for Bruce S. Gelb as Director of the U.S. Information Agency.

In the evening, the President and Mrs. Bush hosted a reception in the Residence for members of the Republican Congressional Leadership Conference.

May 9

The President met at the White House with:
—John H. Sununu, Chief of Staff to the President; Brent Scowcroft, Assistant to the President for National Security Affairs; and members of the CIA briefing staff;
—members of the Presidential delegation of observers of the Panamanian Presidential elections, to receive their findings;
—Prime Minister Ruud Lubbers of The Netherlands, to discuss environmental issues, the NATO alliance, and the deployment of short-range nuclear forces in Europe;
—administration officials, to discuss the Federal budget;
—John H. Sununu, Chief of Staff to the President.

The President declared that a major disaster exists in areas of Minnesota and North Dakota as a result of flooding that began on March 29. He directed the Federal Emergency Management Agency to provide assistance to supplement State and local recovery efforts.

May 10

The President met at the White House with John H. Sununu, Chief of Staff to the President; Brent Scowcroft, Assistant to the President for National Security Affairs; and members of the CIA briefing staff.

The President declared that a major disaster exists in areas of Alaska as a result of severe freezing conditions that occurred during the period of January 15–February 15. He directed the Federal Emergency Management Agency to provide assistance to supplement State and local recovery efforts.

The President today transmitted to the Congress amendments to the request for appropriations for the Department of Defense-Military to provide funding for fiscal year 1990 consistent with the $305.5 billion for the national defense budget function contained in the recently signed bipartisan budget agreement. The amendments also adjust the fiscal year 1991 request, as well as the fiscal year 1992–1994 requests for advance appropriations for multiyear procurement programs.

May 11

The President met at the White House with:
—John H. Sununu, Chief of Staff to the President; Brent Scowcroft, Assistant to the President for National Security Affairs; and members of the CIA briefing staff;
—the congressional leadership, to discuss the crisis in Panama;
—members of the Columbus Group, representatives of the European and Latin American business community promoting international cooperation;
—the Vice President, for lunch;
—the Air Force Thunderbirds;
—Rev. Edmond Browning, the presiding bishop of the Episcopal Church in the United States;
—Secretary of Labor Elizabeth H. Dole and participants in the Job Training Partnership program;
—Franciszek Gajowniczek, a Polish nationalist leader;
—John H. Sununu, Chief of Staff to the President.

In an Oval Office ceremony, the President and Mrs. Bush received diplomatic credentials from Ambassadors Octavio Errazuriz Guilisasti of Chile, Gendengiin Nyamdoo of Mongolia, Botsweletse Kingsley Sebele of Botswana, Abderrahmane Bensid of Algeria, Michael J. Cook of Australia, Simon Alberto Consalvi of Venezuela, and Willem Udenhout of Suriname.

The President transmitted to the Congress the annual report of the Corporation for Public Broadcasting for fiscal year 1988.

May 12

The White House announced that the following individuals will comprise the Presidential delegation to the inaugural ceremonies of President-elect Andres Rodriguez of Paraguay:

Delegation Chairman:

Dorothy Bush LeBlond of Maine

Congressional Delegation:

Senator Larry Pressler (R–SD)
Representative John Paul Hammerschmidt (R–AR)

Private Citizens:

Paul Coverdell, Peace Corps Director
Tony Salinas, of Texas
Timothy Towell, U.S. Ambassador to Paraguay
Elsie Vartanian, of New Hampshire

May 14

In the morning, the President returned to the White House from his trip to Texas, Mississippi, and Kentucky.

May 15

The President met at the White House with:
—John H. Sununu, Chief of Staff to the President; Brent Scowcroft, Assistant to the President for National Security Affairs; and members of the CIA briefing staff;
—Albert Kurz, Anthony Ky, Steven McInerney, Alex Morcos, and Lenny Ng, winners of the Mathcounts National Competition;
—President Dawda Kairaba Jawara of The Gambia;
—Jozef Czyrek, Polish Communist Party Secretary;
—John H. Sununu, Chief of Staff to the President.

May 16

The President met at the White House with:
—John H. Sununu, Chief of Staff to the President; Brent Scowcroft, Assistant to the President for National Security Affairs; and members of the CIA briefing staff;
—the congressional leadership, to discuss the Federal budget;
—Bishops Dario Castrillon and Oscar Rodriguez, president and general secretary of the Council of Bishops of Latin America, respectively, and Rev. Robert N. Lynch, general secretary of the National Conference of Catholic Bishops;
—the executive committee of the National Governors' Association;
—members of the Domestic Policy Council;
—John H. Sununu, Chief of Staff to the President.

The President transmitted to the Congress the annual report of the National Endowment for the Arts and the National Council on the Arts for fiscal year 1988.

In the afternoon, the President hosted a reception in the Residence at the White House for the Republican Senatorial Trust.

May 17

The President met at the White House with:
—John H. Sununu, Chief of Staff to the President; Brent Scowcroft, Assistant to the President for National Security Affairs; and members of the CIA briefing staff;
—members of the House Republican Conference;
—the Vice President, for lunch;
—Secretary of State James A. Baker III;
—Gov. Terry Branstad of Iowa;
—members of the Domestic Policy Council;
—John H. Sununu, Chief of Staff to the President.

In the evening, the President hosted a reception in the Residence for members of the Senate and House of Representatives budget committees and the budget staff.

May 18

The President met at the White House with Archbishop Desmond Tutu and the Rev.'s Alan Boesak and Beyers Naude, antiapartheid leaders from South Africa.

The President declared that a major disaster exists in North Carolina as a result of tornadoes that struck on May 5–6. He directed the Federal Emergency Management Agency to provide assistance to supplement State and local recovery efforts.

The President sent to the Congress amended budget requests for fiscal year 1990 totaling $245.9 million. Included in this package were the following:
—$68.6 million for the Department of Health and Human Services (HHS). This request would provide $42.9 million to provide health professional training for minority students and $25.8 million to maintain support for research and training for the National Institute for Occupational Safety and Health. The increased fiscal year 1990 outlays resulting from these proposals would be offset by a reduction in another HHS program.
—$59.3 million for the Department of Agriculture and $124 million for the Department of the Interior to implement the Federal recreational land acquisition initiative that was in-

cluded in the President's February 9, 1989 budget transmittal.

—$44 million for the Department of Housing and Urban Development to implement the President's Low Income Home Ownership program.

—$50 million for the Department of Justice to investigate and prosecute instances of suspected fraud involving financial institutions, that was also included in the President's February 9, 1989 budget transmittal.

This transmittal also contains a change in a proposed shift of functions between the Department of Commerce and the Small Business Administration and a fiscal year 1990 appropriation request of $441,000 for the legislative branch.

May 20

In the morning, the President and Mrs. Bush greeted President and Mrs. Mitterrand of France at Walker's Point, their home in Kennebunkport, ME.

In the afternoon, the two Presidents participated in a working luncheon at Walker's Point.

May 21

In the morning, the President and Mrs. Bush attended church services at the First Congregational Church in Kennebunkport, ME. Following the church service, President Bush and President Mitterrand traveled to Boston, MA, where President Bush met briefly with Gov. Michael Dukakis and then with Prime Minister Mahathir bin Mohamad of Malaysia.

In the afternoon, the President and Mrs. Bush returned to the White House.

May 22

The President met at the White House with:

—John H. Sununu, Chief of Staff to the President; Brent Scowcroft, Assistant to the President for National Security Affairs; and members of the CIA briefing staff;

—members of the National Federation of Republican Women Capitol Regents;

—members of the Delaware Governor's Club;

—John H. Sununu, Chief of Staff to the President.

The President declared that a major disaster exists in Louisiana as a result of severe storms and flooding that began on May 5. He directed the Federal Emergency Management Agency to provide assistance to supplement State and local recovery efforts.

May 23

The President met at the White House with:

—John H. Sununu, Chief of Staff to the President; Brent Scowcroft, Assistant to the President for National Security Affairs; and members of the CIA briefing staff;

—members of the Congressional Black Caucus;

—President Vigdis Finnbogadóttir of Iceland;

—John H. Sununu, Chief of Staff to the President.

May 24

The President met at the White House with:

—John H. Sununu, Chief of Staff to the President; Brent Scowcroft, Assistant to the President for National Security Affairs; and members of the CIA briefing staff;

—John H. Sununu, Chief of Staff to the President.

In the afternoon, the President and Mrs. Bush hosted a reception on the State Floor of the Residence for the Federal Judges Association.

May 25

The President met at the White House with:

—John H. Sununu, Chief of Staff to the President; Brent Scowcroft, Assistant to the President for National Security Affairs; and members of the CIA briefing staff;

—the Vice President, for lunch;

—John H. Sununu, Chief of Staff to the President.

In the afternoon, the President and Mrs. Bush went to Walter Reed Army Medical Center to visit Representative Claude Pepper, who had been hospitalized for a stomach ailment. The President presented the Presidential Medal of Freedom to Representative Pepper in recognition of his long years of public service.

May 26

In the evening, the President and Mrs. Bush arrived at Ciampino Airport, Rome, Italy. Following the welcoming ceremony, they went to Villa Taverna, the home of the U.S. Ambassador and their residence during their stay in Italy.

May 27

In the morning, the President and U.S. Ambassador Maxwell Rabb went to Villa Madama, where they participated in a bilateral meeting with Prime Minister Ciriaco De Mita and U.S. and Italian officials.

In the afternoon, President Bush went to Quirinale Palace, where he participated in a bilateral meeting with President Francesco Cossiga and U.S. and Italian officials. President Bush then attended a luncheon hosted by President Cossiga in the State Dining Room at the palace. Following the luncheon, President Bush returned to Villa Taverna.

Later in the afternoon, the President hosted a reception in his residence. After the reception, the President and Mrs. Bush went to the Vatican for an audience with Pope John Paul II in the Papal Library.

In the evening, the President and Mrs. Bush attended a reception and dinner hosted by Prime Minister De Mita at Villa Madama. At the conclusion of the dinner, the President and Mrs. Bush returned to their residence.

May 28

In the morning, the President and Mrs. Bush attended Mass at the Church of San Francesco. Afterwards, they went to the Sicily-Rome American Cemetery, where they participated in a Memorial Day ceremony with Prime Minister De Mita and U.S. and Italian officials. Following the ceremony, the President and Mrs. Bush made a surprise visit to the helicopter carrier U.S.S. *Guadalcanal*, which was off the coast of Italy.

In the afternoon, the President and Mrs. Bush returned to Villa Taverna, where they hosted a private luncheon for Prime Minister De Mita and U.S. and Italian officials. Later that afternoon, the President and Mrs. Bush left Rome and traveled to Brussels, Belgium, for the North Atlantic Treaty Organization summit.

In the evening, following the welcoming ceremony at Zaventem International Airport in Brussels, the President and Mrs. Bush went to Chateau Stuyvenberg, their residence during their stay in Belgium. At the chateau, the President participated in a bilateral meeting with Prime Minister Wilfried Martens and U.S. and Belgian officials.

May 29

In the morning, the President went to NATO Headquarters, where he met with Secretary-General Manfred Woerner and attended the opening ceremony and first working session of the summit.

In the afternoon, the President attended a luncheon at Brussels Palace hosted by King Baudouin I. Following the luncheon, the President returned to NATO Headquarters for the summit's second working session. At its conclusion, he returned to Chateau Stuyvenberg.

In the evening, the President attended a working dinner for NATO heads of state and government. Following the dinner, the President returned to his residence at Val Duchesse.

May 30

In the morning, the President went to NATO Headquarters, where he participated in the third working session of the summit and then met with members of the military staffs.

In the afternoon, President Bush went to Berlaymont, the European Commission Headquarters, where he met with Jacques Delors, President of the Commission of the European Communities, and other Commission representatives. Later, the President and Mrs. Bush left Brussels and traveled to Bonn, Federal Republic of Germany.

The President and Mrs. Bush arrived at Koln-Bonn Airport and went to Villa Hammerschmidt, the official residence of the West German President, where they participated in a welcoming ceremony and a reception hosted by President Richard von Weizsäcker. Later, the President and Mrs. Bush went to the U.S. Ambassador's residence and then to La Redoute Castle, where they attended a dinner hosted by Chancellor Helmut Kohl. Following the dinner, they returned to the Ambassador's residence, where they stayed overnight.

May 31

In the morning, President Bush attended a private breakfast at Villa Hammerschmidt hosted by President von Weizsäcker and then went to the Chancellery, where he participated in a bilateral meeting with Chancellor Kohl and U.S. and West German officials.

In the afternoon, the President and Mrs. Bush, accompanied by Chancellor and Mrs. Kohl, went on a Rhine River cruise, leaving from Oberwesel and arriving at Koblenz. Later the President and Mrs. Bush participated in a departure ceremony at Rhein-Main Air Force Base and then traveled to London, United Kingdom.

Following a welcoming ceremony at Heathrow Airport, London, the President and Mrs. Bush went to Winfield House, their residence during their stay in the United Kingdom.

June 1

In the afternoon, the President and Mrs. Bush attended a luncheon at Buckingham Palace hosted by Queen Elizabeth II. Later in the afternoon, they returned to Winfield House.

June 2

The President and Mrs. Bush left London and traveled to Kennebunkport, ME.

June 4

In the afternoon, the President and Mrs. Bush returned to the White House from Kennebunkport, ME.

June 5

The President met at the White House with:

—John H. Sununu, Chief of Staff to the President; Brent Scowcroft, Assistant to the President for National Security Affairs; and members of the CIA briefing staff;

—members of the Cabinet;

—Chinese students, to discuss the situation in China;
—members of the Domestic Policy Council;
—members of the congressional leadership, to discuss the recent NATO summit.

June 6

The President met at the White House with:
—John H. Sununu, Chief of Staff to the President; Brent Scowcroft, Assistant to the President for National Security Affairs; and members of the CIA briefing staff;
—Secretary of Transportation Samuel K. Skinner, for lunch;
—members of the congressional leadership, to discuss environmental issues;
—President Richard von Weizsäcker of the Federal Republic of Germany.

In the afternoon, the President met with Soviet Ambassador Yuriy V. Dubinin at the Soviet Embassy to discuss the gas pipeline explosion and train disaster that occurred on June 4 in the Soviet Union.

The President transmitted to the Congress:
—the 10th annual report describing Federal actions with respect to the conservation and use of petroleum and natural gas in Federal facilities, which covers calendar year 1988;
—the 1985, 1986, and 1987 reports of the Federal Prevailing Rate Advisory Committee.

June 7

The President met at the White House with:
—John H. Sununu, Chief of Staff to the President; Brent Scowcroft, Assistant to the President for National Security Affairs; and members of the CIA briefing staff;
—President Kenneth D. Kaunda of Zambia;
—Thomas S. Foley and Robert H. Michel, Speaker and minority leader of the House of Representatives, respectively, for lunch;
—Secretary of State James A. Baker III;
—President Quett K.J. Masire of Botswana;
—John H. Sununu, Chief of Staff to the President.

June 8

The President met at the White House with:
—John H. Sununu, Chief of Staff to the President; Brent Scowcroft, Assistant to the President for National Security Affairs; and members of the CIA briefing staff;
—representatives of the Clean Air Business Group;
—the Vice President, for lunch;
—Citizens for a Sound Economy board members;
—environmentalists;
—John H. Sununu, Chief of Staff to the President.

The President declared that a major disaster exists in the counties of Androscoggin, Cumberland, Franklin, and Oxford in Maine as a result of severe storms and flooding that began on May 5. He directed the Federal Emergency Management Agency to provide assistance to supplement State and local recovery efforts.

June 9

The President met at the White House with:
—John H. Sununu, Chief of Staff to the President; Brent Scowcroft, Assistant to the President for National Security Affairs; and members of the CIA briefing staff;
—Senator Pete V. Domenici of New Mexico;
—chief educational officers of Catholic dioceses, to discuss tuition tax credits;
—the rector of Complutense University in Madrid, Spain, to receive the Complutense Gold Medal in honor of signing an educational agreement with Spain;
—editorial cartoonists, for lunch;
—Secretary of State James A. Baker III;
—John H. Sununu, Chief of Staff to the President;
—President Soeharto of Indonesia.

In the afternoon, the President and Mrs. Bush left the White House for a weekend stay at Camp David, MD.

June 11

In the afternoon, the President and Mrs. Bush returned to the White House from a weekend stay at Camp David, MD.

June 12

The President met at the White House with:
—John H. Sununu, Chief of Staff to the President; Brent Scowcroft, Assistant to the President for National Security Affairs; and members of the CIA briefing staff;
—a group of the Nation's Governors, to discuss the administration's clean air plan;
—congressional staff members, to discuss the administration's clean air plan;
—the congressional leadership, to discuss the administration's clean air plan.

The President declared that major disasters exist in areas located along the Yukon and Kuskokwim Rivers in Alaska as a result of flooding that began on May 1 and in areas of Ohio as a result of heavy rains and flooding that began on May 23. He directed the Federal Emergency Management Agency to provide assistance to supplement State and local recovery efforts.

In the afternoon the President traveled to Yellowstone National Park, WY, where he toured Fountain Flats, an area of the park devastated by forest fires in 1988. He then traveled to the

Grand Teton National Park, WY, where he remained overnight at the Brinkerhoff Guest House.

June 14

The President met at the White House with:

—John H. Sununu, Chief of Staff to the President; Brent Scowcroft, Assistant to the President for National Security Affairs; and members of the CIA briefing staff;

—Secretary of State James A. Baker III;

—John H. Sununu, Chief of Staff to the President.

The President appointed Secretary of the Interior Manuel J. Lujan, Jr., as the Federal member of the Delaware and Susquehanna River Basin Commissions.

In the evening, the President and Mrs. Bush attended the President's Dinner at the Washington Convention Center.

June 15

The President met at the White House with John H. Sununu, Chief of Staff to the President.

In the afternoon, the President and Mrs. Bush hosted a reception for members of the Republican National Committee on the State Floor at the White House.

In the evening, the President and Mrs. Bush attended a performance of "Spirit of America" at the Capital Centre.

June 16

The President met at the White House with:

—the Vice President, for breakfast;

—John H. Sununu, Chief of Staff to the President; Brent Scowcroft, Assistant to the President for National Security Affairs; and members of the CIA briefing staff;

—the heads of Federal law enforcement agencies, for lunch;

—Secretary of State James A. Baker III;

—John H. Sununu, Chief of Staff to the President.

The President transmitted to the Congress fiscal year 1990 budget amendments totaling $1,189.1 million to implement his initiative to combat violent crime that was announced on May 15, 1989. These proposals would provide the following:

—$1,119.6 million for the Department of Justice. Of this amount, $1 billion would be used to expand Federal prison capacity. Additional funds are also requested for legal activities of the Department, the FBI, the Immigration and Naturalization Service, and the Office of Justice Programs.

—$50.7 million for the Federal judiciary, of which $40 million would cover the cost of processing increased numbers of criminal defendants and additional Federal criminal prosecutions. The remaining $10.7 million is included for the drug testing of all Federal prisoners released on probation, parole, or supervised release.

—$18.8 million for the Department of the Treasury to enable the Bureau of Alcohol, Tobacco, and Firearms to provide additional personnel to investigate assault weapon and other firearms violations by armed career criminals and repeat offenders.

The details of the President's initiative are contained in the fact sheet entitled "Combating Violent Crime," issued by the White House Press Office on May 15.

The President declared that a disaster exists in Louisiana as a result of severe storms and tornadoes that struck the southern portion of the State on June 7–8.

In the afternoon, the President and Mrs. Bush left the White House for a weekend stay at Camp David, MD.

June 18

In the afternoon, the President and Mrs. Bush returned to the White House from a weekend stay at Camp David, MD.

June 19

The President met at the White House with:

—John H. Sununu, Chief of Staff to the President; Brent Scowcroft, Assistant to the President for National Security Affairs; and members of the CIA briefing staff;

—President Hugh Desmond Hoyte of Guyana;

—John H. Sununu, Chief of Staff to the President.

The President announced his intention to appoint Secretary of Defense Richard B. Cheney, Secretary of Health and Human Services Louis W. Sullivan, and Secretary of State James A. Baker III to be government representatives on the Board of Governors of the American Red Cross, each for a term of 3 years.

June 20

The President met at the White House with:

—John H. Sununu, Chief of Staff to the President; Brent Scowcroft, Assistant to the President for National Security Affairs; and members of the CIA briefing staff;

—Members of the congressional leadership, to discuss defense issues;

—Paul D. Coverdell, Director of the Peace Corps, for lunch;

—John H. Sununu, Chief of Staff to the President.

June 21

The President met at the White House with:

—John H. Sununu, Chief of Staff to the President; Brent Scowcroft, Assistant to the President for National Security Affairs; and members of the CIA briefing staff;

—Members of Congress, to discuss voluntary steel import restrictions;

—West German Foreign Minister Hans-Dietrich Genscher;

—Secretary of State James A. Baker III;

—John H. Sununu, Chief of Staff to the President.

June 22

The President met at the White House with John H. Sununu, Chief of Staff to the President; Brent Scowcroft, Assistant to the President for National Security Affairs; and members of the CIA briefing staff.

June 23

The President met at the White House with:

—John H. Sununu, Chief of Staff to the President; Brent Scowcroft, Assistant to the President for National Security Affairs; and members of the CIA briefing staff;

—Members of Congress, to discuss the situations in Israel and China;

—family members of James Chaney, Andrew Goodman, and Michael Schwerner, civil rights advocates slain 25 years ago in Mississippi;

—the Vice President, for lunch;

—Secretary of State James A. Baker III;

—John H. Sununu, Chief of Staff to the President.

In the afternoon, the President and Mrs. Bush left the White House for a weekend stay at Camp David, MD.

June 25

In the morning, the President met with Prime Minister Robert Hawke of Australia at Camp David, MD.

In the evening, the President and Mrs. Bush returned to the White House, and Prime Minister Hawke went to the Blair House, where he remained overnight.

June 26

The President met at the White House with:

—John H. Sununu, Chief of Staff to the President; Brent Scowcroft, Assistant to the President for National Security Affairs; and members of the CIA briefing staff;

—John H. Sununu, Chief of Staff to the President.

In the evening, the President and Mrs. Bush attended the Marine Corps evening parade at the Marine Barracks in Washington, DC.

June 27

The President met at the White House with John H. Sununu, Chief of Staff to the President; Brent Scowcroft, Assistant to the President for National Security Affairs; and members of the CIA briefing staff.

June 28

The President met at the White House with:

—John H. Sununu, Chief of Staff to the President; Brent Scowcroft, Assistant to the President for National Security Affairs; and members of the CIA briefing staff;

—Polish-American leaders;

—the Vice President, for lunch;

—Secretary of State James A. Baker III;

—John H. Sununu, Chief of Staff to the President.

In the evening, the President and his grandson, George P. Bush, attended a Baltimore Orioles baseball game.

June 29

The President met at the White House with:

—John H. Sununu, Chief of Staff to the President; Brent Scowcroft, Assistant to the President for National Security Affairs; and members of the CIA briefing staff;

—the Republican congressional leadership;

—John H. Sununu, Chief of Staff to the President.

In the evening, the President and Mrs. Bush hosted a dinner for the Cabinet in the Rose Garden.

June 30

The President met at the White House with:

—John H. Sununu, Chief of Staff to the President; Brent Scowcroft, Assistant to the President for National Security Affairs; and members of the CIA briefing staff;

—Secretary of State James A. Baker III;

—John H. Sununu, Chief of Staff to the President.

In the afternoon, the President and Mrs. Bush left the White House and traveled to Kennebunkport, ME.

Appendix B—Nominations Submitted to the Senate

The following list does not include promotions of members of the Uniformed Services, nominations to the Service Academies, or nominations of Foreign Service officers.

Submitted January 20

James Addison Baker III,
of Texas, to be Secretary of State.

John Goodwin Tower,
of Texas, to be Secretary of Defense.

Manuel Lujan, Jr.,
of New Mexico, to be Secretary of the Interior.

Clayton Yeutter,
of Nebraska, to be Secretary of Agriculture.

Robert Adam Mosbacher,
of Texas, to be Secretary of Commerce.

Elizabeth Hanford Dole,
of Kansas, to be Secretary of Labor.

Louis W. Sullivan,
of Georgia, to be Secretary of Health and Human Services.

Jack Kemp,
of New York, to be Secretary of Housing and Urban Development.

Samuel Knox Skinner,
of Illinois, to be Secretary of Transportation.

Adm. James D. Watkins, USN, Ret.,
of California, to be Secretary of Energy.

Edward J. Derwinski,
of Illinois, to be Secretary of Veterans Affairs.

Edward J. Derwinski,
of Illinois, to be Administrator of Veterans Affairs.

Richard G. Darman,
of Virginia, to be Director of the Office of Management and Budget.

Carla Anderson Hills,
of California, to be U.S. Trade Representative, with the rank of Ambassador Extraordinary and Plenipotentiary.

William J. Bennett,
of North Carolina, to be Director of National Drug Control Policy.

Michael J. Boskin,
of California, to be a member of the Council of Economic Advisers.

Thomas R. Pickering,
of New Jersey, to be the Representative of the United States of America to the United Nations with the rank and status of Ambassador Extraordinary and Plenipotentiary, and the Representative of the United States of America in the Security Council of the United Nations.

William Kane Reilly,
of Virginia, to be Administrator of the Environmental Protection Agency.

Submitted February 1

Edith E. Holiday,
of Georgia, to be General Counsel for the Department of the Treasury, vice Mark Sullivan III, resigned.

William M. Diefenderfer III,
of Virginia, to be Deputy Director of the Office of Management and Budget, vice John F. Cogan, resigned.

Submitted February 8

Robert Michael Kimmitt,
of Virginia, to be Under Secretary of State for Political Affairs, vice Michael Hayden Armacost, resigned.

Margaret DeBardeleben Tutwiler,
of Alabama, to be an Assistant Secretary of State, vice Charles E. Redman, resigned.

Janet Gardner Mullins,
of Kentucky, to be an Assistant Secretary of State, vice J. Edward Fox, resigned.

Robert B. Zoellick,
of the District of Columbia, to be Counselor of the Department of State, vice Max M. Kampelman, resigned.

Submitted February 21

Richard J. Kerr,
of Virginia, to be Deputy Director of Central Intelligence, vice Robert M. Gates, resigned.

Submitted February 28

Ferdinand F. Fernandez,
of California, to be United States Circuit Judge for the Ninth Circuit, vice Warren J. Ferguson, retired.

Pamela Ann Rymer,
of California, to be United States Circuit Judge for the Ninth Circuit, vice Anthony M. Kennedy, elevated.

Robert C. Bonner,
of California, to be United States District Judge for the Central District of California, vice Pamela Ann Rymer, upon elevation.

Melinda Harmon,
of Texas, to be United States District Judge for the Southern District of Texas, vice John V. Singleton, Jr., retired.

Vaughn R. Walker,
of California, to be United States District Judge for the Northern District of California, vice Spencer M. Williams, retired.

Submitted March 1

John D. Negroponte,
of New York, a career member of the Senior Foreign Service, Class of Career Minister, to be Ambassador Extraordinary and Plenipotentiary of the United States of America to Mexico.

Submitted March 3

Lawrence S. Eagleburger,
of Florida, to be Deputy Secretary of State, vice John C. Whitehead, resigned.

Bruce S. Gelb,
of New York, to be Director of the United States Information Agency, vice Charles Z. Wick, resigned.

Submitted March 6

Donald Phinney Gregg,
of Maryland, to be Ambassador Extraordinary and Plenipotentiary of the United States of America to the Republic of Korea.

Anthony Joseph Principi,
of California, to be Deputy Secretary of Veterans Affairs (new position).

William Pelham Barr,
of Virginia, to be an Assistant Attorney General, vice Douglas W. Kmiec, resigned.

Submitted March 7

Joseph Verner Reed,
of Connecticut, for the rank of Ambassador during his tenure of service as Chief of Protocol for the White House.

Submitted March 8

David Campbell Mulford,
of Illinois, to be an Under Secretary of the Treasury (new position).

Charles H. Dallara,
of South Carolina, to be a Deputy Under Secretary of the Treasury, vice David Campbell Mulford.

David W. Mullins, Jr.,
of Massachusetts, to be an Assistant Secretary of the Treasury, vice Charles O. Sethness, resigned.

Submitted March 9

Henry E. Catto,
of Texas, to be Ambassador Extraordinary and Plenipotentiary of the United States of America to the United Kingdom of Great Britain and Northern Ireland.

Vernon A. Walters,
of Florida, to be Ambassador Extraordinary and Plenipotentiary of the United States of America to the Federal Republic of Germany.

Wendell Lewis Willkie II,
of the District of Columbia, to be General Counsel of the Department of Commerce, vice Robert H. Brumley II, resigned.

Submitted March 13

Michael Hayden Armacost,
of Maryland, a career member of the Senior Foreign Service, Class of Career Minister, to be Ambassador Extraordinary and Plenipotentiary of the United States of America to Japan.

Eric I. Garfinkel,
of Maryland, to be an Assistant Secretary of Commerce, vice Jan W. Mares, resigned.

Submitted March 14

Richard B. Cheney,
of Wyoming, to be Secretary of Defense.

Donna R. Fitzpatrick,
of the District of Columbia, to be an Assistant Secretary of Energy (Management and Administration), vice Lawrence F. Davenport, resigned.

Submitted March 17

James Roderick Lilley,
of Maryland, to be Ambassador Extraordinary and Plenipotentiary of the United States of America to the People's Republic of China.

Richard Thomas McCormack,
of Pennsylvania, to be Under Secretary of State for Economic and Agricultural Affairs, vice W. Allen Wallis, resigned.

Donald J. Atwood,
of Massachusetts, to be Deputy Secretary of Defense, vice William H. Taft IV, resigned.

Submitted April 4

John R. Bolton,
of Maryland, to be an Assistant Secretary of State, vice Richard Salisbury Williamson, resigned.

Herman Jay Cohen,
of New York, a career member of the Senior Foreign Service, Class of Career Minister, to be an Assistant Secretary of State, vice Chester A. Crocker, resigned.

Terence A. Todman,
of the Virgin Islands, a career member of the Senior Foreign Service, Class of Career Minister, to be Ambassador Extraordinary and Plenipotentiary of the United States of America to Argentina.

Charles Edgar Redman,
of Florida, a career member of the Senior Foreign Service, Class of Minister-Counselor, to be Ambassador Extraordinary and Plenipotentiary of the United States of America to Sweden.

Richard Reeves Burt,
of Arizona, for the rank of Ambassador during his tenure of service as head of delegation on nuclear and space talks and chief negotiator on strategic nuclear arms (START).

Robert R. Glauber,
of Massachusetts, to be an Under Secretary of the Treasury, vice George D. Gould, resigned.

Hollis S. McLoughlin,
of New Jersey, to be an Assistant Secretary of the Treasury, vice Charles H. Dallara, resigned.

Kenneth Winston Starr,
of Virginia, to be Solicitor General of the United States, vice Charles Fried, resigned.

Susan Carol Schwab,
of Maryland, to be Assistant Secretary of Commerce and Director General of the United States and Foreign Commercial Service, vice Lew W. Cramer, resigned.

Constance Horner,
of the District of Columbia, to be Under Secretary of Health and Human Services, vice Donald M. Newman, resigned.

Mary Sheila Gall,
of Virginia, to be an Assistant Secretary of Health and Human Services, vice Sydney J. Olson, resigned.

Elaine L. Chao,
of California, to be Deputy Secretary of Transportation, vice Mary Ann Weyforth Dawson, resigned.

W. Henson Moore,
of Louisiana, to be Deputy Secretary of Energy, vice Joseph F. Salgado, resigned.

John Chatfield Tuck,
of Virginia, to be Under Secretary of Energy, vice Donna R. Fitzpatrick, resigned.

John Theodore Sanders,
of Illinois, to be Under Secretary of Education, vice Linus D. Wright, resigned.

Frank Quill Nebeker,
of Virginia, to be chief judge of the U.S. Court of Veterans Appeals for the term of 15 years (new position).

William G. Rosenberg,
of Michigan, to be an Assistant Administrator of the Environmental Protection Agency, vice J. Craig Potter, resigned.

Constance Berry Newman,
of Maryland, to be Director of the Office of Personnel Management, vice Constance Horner, resigned.

Paul D. Coverdell,
of Georgia, to be Director of the Peace Corps, vice Loret M. Ruppe, resigned.

Withdrawn April 4

Lew W. Cramer,
of California, to be Assistant Secretary of Commerce and Director General of the United States and Foreign Commercial Service (new position—P.L. 100–418), which was sent to the Senate on January 3, 1989.

Submitted April 6

Reginald Bartholomew,
of Virginia, a career member of the Senior Foreign Service, Class of Career Minister, to be Under Secretary of State for Coordinating Security Assistance Programs, vice Edward J. Derwinski, resigned.

Morris Berthold Abrams,
of New York, to be the Representative of the United States of America to the European Office of the United Nations, with the rank of Ambassador, vice Joseph Carlton Petrone, resigned.

John E. Robson,
of Georgia, to be Deputy Secretary of the Treasury, vice M. Peter McPherson, resigned.

Roger Bolton,
of Virginia, to be an Assistant Secretary of the Treasury, vice Edith E. Holiday, resigned.

Jack Callihan Parnell,
of California, to be Deputy Secretary of Agriculture, vice Peter C. Myers, resigned.

Richard Thomas Crowder,
of Minnesota, to be Under Secretary of Agriculture for International Affairs and Commodity Programs, vice Daniel G. Amstutz, resigned.

Kay Coles James,
of Virginia, to be an Assistant Secretary of Health and Human Services, vice Stephanie Lee-Miller, resigned.

Phillip D. Brady,
of Virginia, to be General Counsel of the Department of Transportation, vice B. Wayne Vance, resigned.

Susan S. Engeleiter,
of Wisconsin, to be Administrator of the Small Business Administration, vice James Abdnor, resigned.

Submitted April 7

Richard Thomas McCormack,
of Pennsylvania, to be United States Alternate Governor of the International Bank for Reconstruction and Development for a term of 5 years, United States Alternate Governor of the Inter-American Development Bank for a term of 5 years, United States Alternate Governor of the African Development Bank for a term of 5 years, United States Alternate Governor of the African Development Fund, and United States Alternate Governor of the Asian Development Bank, vice W. Allen Wallis, resigned.

James O. Mason,
of Georgia, to be an Assistant Secretary of Health and Human Services, vice Robert E. Windom, resigned.

Fred M. Zeder II,
of New York, to be President of the Overseas Private Investment Corporation, vice Craig A. Nalen, resigned.

Submitted April 12

Douglas P. Mulholland,
of Maryland, to be an Assistant Secretary of State, vice Morton I. Abramowitz, resigned.

Diane Kay Morales,
of Texas, to be an Assistant Secretary of Energy (Environment, Safety and Health), vice Ernest C. Baynard III, resigned.

John Cameron Monjo,
of Maryland, a career member of the Senior Foreign Service, Class of Career Minister, to be Ambassador Extraordinary and Plenipotentiary of the United States of America to the Republic of Indonesia.

Ronald Frank Lehman II,
of Virginia, to be Director of the U.S. Arms Control and Disarmament Agency, vice William F. Burns, resigned.

Thomas Jones Collamore,
of the District of Columbia, to be an Assistant Secretary of Commerce, vice Katherine M. Bulow, resigned.

Nancy Mohr Kennedy,
of Maryland, to be Assistant Secretary for Legislation, Department of Education, vice Frances M. Norris, resigned.

Dale Triber Tate,
of the District of Columbia, to be an Assistant Secretary of Labor, vice Jerry D. Blakemore.

Withdrawn April 12

Jerry D. Blakemore,
of Illinois, to be an Assistant Secretary of Labor, vice David F. Demarest, resigned, which was sent to the Senate on January 3, 1989.

Submitted April 13

Ivan Selin,
of the District of Columbia, to be Under Secretary of State for Management, vice Ronald I. Spiers, resigned.

Michael Rucker Darby,
of Texas, to be Under Secretary of Commerce for Economic Affairs, vice Robert Ortner, resigned.

Rufus Hawkins Yerxa,
of the District of Columbia, to be a Deputy United States Trade Representative, with the rank of Ambassador, vice Michael A. Samuels, resigned.

Submitted April 17

Alan Charles Raul,
of New York, to be General Counsel of the Department of Agriculture, vice Christopher Hicks, resigned.

Paul Dundes Wolfowitz,
of the District of Columbia, to be Under Secretary of Defense for Policy, vice Fred Charles Ikle, resigned.

Peter F. Secchia,
of Michigan, to be Ambassador Extraordinary and Plenipotentiary of the United States of America to Italy.

Submitted April 18

Walter J.P. Curley,
of New York, to be Ambassador Extraordinary and Plenipotentiary of the United States of America to France.

David George Ball,
of Connecticut, to be an Assistant Secretary of Labor, vice David M. Walker, resigned.

Richard Thomas Crowder,
of Minnesota, to be a member of the Board of Directors of the Commodity Credit Corporation, vice Daniel G. Amstutz, resigned.

Jack Callihan Parnell,
of California, to be a member of the Board of Directors of the Commodity Credit Corporation, vice Peter C. Myers, resigned.

Submitted April 19

Roderick Allen DeArment,
of Virginia, to be Deputy Secretary of Labor, vice Dennis Eugene Whitfield, resigned.

H. Lawrence Garrett III,
of Virginia, to be Secretary of the Navy, vice William Lockhart Ball III, resigned.

Submitted May 1

Morton I. Abramowitz,
of the District of Columbia, a career member of the Senior Foreign Service, Class of Career Minister, to be Ambassador Extraordinary and Plenipotentiary of the United States of America to Turkey.

Melvyn Levitsky,
of Maryland, to be Assistant Secretary of State for International Narcotics Matters, vice Ann Barbara Wrobleski, resigned.

Kenneth W. Gideon,
of Virginia, to be an Assistant Secretary of the Treasury, vice O. Donaldson Chapoton, resigned.

Shirley D. Peterson,
of Maryland, to be an Assistant Attorney General, vice William S. Rose, Jr., resigned.

William Lucas,
of Michigan, to be an Assistant Attorney General, vice William Bradford Reynolds, resigned.

Michael Philip Skarzynski,
of Illinois, to be an Assistant Secretary of Commerce, vice James P. Moore, Jr., resigned.

Gerald L. Olson,
of Minnesota, to be an Assistant Secretary of Health and Human Services, vice Marty T. Goedde, resigned.

Alfred A. DelliBovi,
of New York, to be Under Secretary of Housing and Urban Development, vice Carl D. Covitz, resigned.

Galen Joseph Reser,
of Virginia, to be an Assistant Secretary of Transportation, vice Edward R. Hamberger, resigned.

Robert Refugio Davila,
of the District of Columbia, to be Assistant Secretary for Special Education and Rehabilitative Services, Department of Education, vice Madeleine C. Will, resigned.

Sidney Linn Williams,
of Virginia, to be a Deputy United States Trade Representative, with the rank of Ambassador, vice Alan F. Holmer, resigned.

E. Patrick Coady,
of Virginia, to be United States Executive Director of the International Bank for Reconstruction and Development for a term of 2 years, vice Robert Brendon Keating, term expired.

John B. Taylor,
of California, to be a member of the Council of Economic Advisers, vice Michael Mussa, resigned.

Submitted May 2

Bernard William Aronson,
of Maryland, to be an Assistant Secretary of State, vice Elliott Abrams, resigned.

Carol T. Crawford,
of Virginia, to be an Assistant Attorney General, vice Thomas M. Boyd, resigned.

David Philip Prosperi,
of the District of Columbia, to be an Assistant Secretary of Transportation, vice Wendy Monson DeMocker, resigned.

Chic Hecht,
of Nevada, to be Ambassador Extraordinary and Plenipotentiary of the United States of America to the Commonwealth of the Bahamas.

Thomas Michael Tolliver Niles,
of the District of Columbia, a career member of the Senior Foreign Service, Class of Career Minister, to be the Representative of the United States of America to the European Communities, with the rank and status of Ambassador Extraordinary and Plenipotentiary.

Joseph Zappala,
of Florida, to be Ambassador Extraordinary and Plenipotentiary of the United States of America to Spain.

Francis Anthony Keating II,
of Oklahoma, to be General Counsel of the Department of Housing and Urban Development, vice J. Michael Dorsey, resigned.

Franklin Eugene Bailey,
of Virginia, to be an Assistant Secretary of Agriculture, vice Wilmer D. Mizell, Sr., resigned.

James E. Cason,
of Virginia, to be an Assistant Secretary of Agriculture, vice George S. Dunlop, resigned.

Charles E. Hess,
of California, to be an Assistant Secretary of Agriculture, vice Orville G. Bentley, resigned.

David J. Gribbin III,
of Maryland, to be an Assistant Secretary of Defense, vice M.D.B. Carlisle, resigned.

Louis A. Williams,
of Wyoming, to be an Assistant Secretary of Defense, vice J. Daniel Howard, resigned.

Submitted May 5

Melvin F. Sembler,
of Florida, to be Ambassador Extraordinary and Plenipotentiary of the United States of America to Australia and to serve concurrently and without additional compensation as Ambassador Extraordinary and Plenipotentiary of the United States of America to the Republic of Nauru.

Richard H. Solomon,
of the District of Columbia, to be an Assistant Secretary of State, vice Gaston Joseph Sigur, Jr., resigned.

Jewel S. Lafontant,
of Illinois, to be United States Coordinator for Refugee Affairs and Ambassador-at-Large while serving in this position, vice Jonathan Moore, resigned.

Jo Ann D. Smith,
of Florida, to be an Assistant Secretary of Agriculture, vice Kenneth A. Gilles, resigned.

Kathleen M. Harrington,
of the District of Columbia, to be an Assistant Secretary of Labor, vice Francis J. Duggan.

Kenneth B. Kramer,
of Colorado, to be an Associate Judge of the United States Court of Veterans Appeals for the term of 15 years (new position—P.L. 100–687).

Withdrawn May 5

Francis J. Duggan,
of Virginia, to be an Assistant Secretary of Labor, vice William John Maroni, which was sent to the Senate on January 3, 1989.

Submitted May 10

Frank Henry Habicht II,
of Virginia, to be Deputy Administrator of the Environmental Protection Agency, vice A. James Barnes, resigned.

Submitted May 11

John Hubert Kelly,
of Georgia, a career member of the Senior Foreign Service, Class of Minister-Counselor, to be an Assistant Secretary of State, vice Richard W. Murphy, resigned.

James Buchanan Busey IV,
of Illinois, to be Administrator of the Federal Aviation Administration, vice T. Allan McArtor, resigned.

Submitted May 12

Edward N. Ney,
of New York, to be Ambassador Extraordinary and Plenipotentiary of the United States of America to Canada.

Donald B. Rice,
of California, to be Secretary of the Air Force, vice Edward C. Aldridge, Jr., resigned.

Sean Charles O'Keefe,
of Virginia, to be Comptroller of the Department of Defense, vice Clyde O. Glaister, resigned.

Frank A. Bracken,
of Indiana, to be Under Secretary of the Interior, vice Earl E. Gjelde, resigned.

Jennifer Lynn Dorn,
of Maryland, to be an Assistant Secretary of Labor, vice Michael E. Baroody, resigned.

Jerry M. Hunter,
of Missouri, to be General Counsel of the National Labor Relations Board for a term of 4 years, vice Rosemary M. Collyer, term expired.

Submitted May 16

James Franklin Rill,
of Maryland, to be an Assistant Attorney General, vice Charles F. Rule, resigned.

E. Bart Daniel,
of South Carolina, to be United States Attorney for the District of South Carolina for the term of 4 years, vice Vinton DeVane Lide, resigned.

John Michael Farren,
of Connecticut, to be Under Secretary of Commerce for International Trade, vice W. Allen Moore, resigned.

Robert P. Davis,
of Virginia, to be Solicitor for the Department of Labor, vice George R. Salem, resigned.

John C. Weicher,
of the District of Columbia, to be an Assistant Secretary of Housing and Urban Development, vice Kenneth J. Beirne, resigned.

Nell Carney,
of Virginia, to be Commissioner of the Rehabilitation Services Administration, vice Susan S. Suter, resigned.

Submitted May 17

Della M. Newman,
of Washington, to be Ambassador Extraordinary and Plenipotentiary of the United States of America to New Zealand and to serve concurrently and without additional compensation as Ambassador Extraordinary and Plenipotentiary of the United States of America to Western Samoa.

Robert D. Orr,
of Indiana, to be Ambassador Extraordinary and Plenipotentiary of the United States of America to the Republic of Singapore.

Bryce L. Harlow,
of Virginia, to be a Deputy Under Secretary of the Treasury, vice John K. Meagher, resigned.

Submitted May 18

Antonio Lopez,
of Tennessee, to be an Associate Director of the Federal Emergency Management Agency, vice George Woloshyn, resigned.

Submitted May 31

Keith Lapham Brown,
of Colorado, to be Ambassador Extraordinary and Plenipotentiary of the United States of America to Denmark, to which position he was appointed during the recess of the Senate from October 22, 1988, to January 3, 1989.

William Andreas Brown,
of New Hampshire, a career member of the Senior Foreign Service, Class of Career Minister, to be Ambassador Extraordinary and Plenipotentiary of the United States of America to Israel, to which position he was appointed during the recess of the Senate from October 22, 1988, to January 3, 1989.

Dee V. Benson,
of Utah, to be United States Attorney for the District of Utah for the term of 4 years, vice Brent D. Ward, resigned.

Thomas Joseph Murrin,
of Pennsylvania, to be Deputy Secretary of Commerce, vice Donna F. Tuttle, resigned.

Quincy Mellon Krosby,
of New York, to be an Assistant Secretary of Commerce, vice G. Philip Hughes, resigned.

C. Austin Fitts,
of New York, to be an Assistant Secretary of Housing and Urban Development, vice Thomas T. Demery, resigned.

Jeffrey Neil Shane,
of the District of Columbia, to be an Assistant Secretary of Transportation, vice Gregory S. Dole.

Charles E.M. Kolb,
of Virginia, to be Deputy Under Secretary for Planning, Budget, and Evaluation, Department of Education, vice Bruce M. Carnes, resigned, to which position he was appointed during the

recess of the Senate from October 22, 1988, to January 3, 1989.

Fred T. Goldberg, Jr.,
of Maryland, to be Commissioner of Internal Revenue, vice Lawrence B. Gibbs, resigned.

Reggie B. Walton,
of the District of Columbia, to be Associate Director for National Drug Control Policy (new position—P.L. 100–690).

Delos Cy Jamison,
of Montana, to be Director of the Bureau of Land Management, vice Robert F. Burford, resigned.

Withdrawn May 31

Keith Lapham Brown,
of Colorado, to be Ambassador Extraordinary and Plenipotentiary of the United States of America to Denmark, which was sent to the Senate on January 3, 1989.

William Andreas Brown,
of New Hampshire, a career member of the Senior Foreign Service, Class of Career Minister, to be Ambassador Extraordinary and Plenipotentiary of the United States of America to Israel, which was sent to the Senate on January 3, 1989.

Gregory S. Dole,
of Massachusetts, to be an Assistant Secretary of Transportation, vice Matthew V. Scocozza, resigned, which was sent to the Senate on January 3, 1989.

Charles E.M. Kolb,
of the District of Columbia, to be Deputy Under Secretary for Planning, Budget, and Evaluation, Department of Education, vice Bruce M. Carnes, resigned, which was sent to the Senate on January 3, 1989.

Submitted June 6

Shirley Temple Black,
of California, to be Ambassador Extraordinary and Plenipotentiary of the United States of America to the Czechoslovak Socialist Republic.

Richard Wood Boehm,
of the District of Columbia, a career member of the Senior Foreign Service, Class of Minister-Counselor, to be Ambassador Extraordinary and Plenipotentiary of the United States of America to the Sultanate of Oman, to which position he was appointed during the recess of the Senate from October 22, 1988, to January 3, 1989.

Morris Dempson Busby,
of Virginia, a career member of the Senior Foreign Service, Class of Minister-Counselor, for the rank of Ambassador in his capacity as Coordinator for Counterterrorism.

Michael Ussery,
of Virginia, to be Ambassador Extraordinary and Plenipotentiary of the United States of America to the Kingdom of Morocco, to which position he was appointed during the recess of the Senate from October 22, 1988, to January 3, 1989.

C. Howard Wilkins, Jr.,
of Kansas, to be Ambassador Extraordinary and Plenipotentiary of the United States of America to the Kingdom of The Netherlands.

Eddie F. Brown,
of Arizona, to be an Assistant Secretary of the Interior, vice Ross O. Swimmer, resigned.

Constance Bastine Harriman,
of Maryland, to be Assistant Secretary for Fish and Wildlife, Department of the Interior, vice Becky Norton Dunlop, resigned.

Rockwell Anthony Schnabel,
of California, to be Under Secretary of Commerce for Travel and Tourism, vice Charles E. Cobb, Jr., resigned.

Thomas D. Larson,
of Pennsylvania, to be Administrator of the Federal Highway Administration, vice Robert Earl Farris, resigned.

Kate Leader Moore,
of the District of Columbia, to be an Assistant Secretary of Transportation, vice Janet Hale, resigned.

Edward C. Stringer,
of Minnesota, to be General Counsel, Department of Education, vice Wendell L. Willkie II, resigned.

D. Allan Bromley,
of Connecticut, to be Director of the Office of Science and Technology Policy, vice William R. Graham, resigned.

Deborah Kaye Owen,
of Maryland, to be a Federal Trade Commissioner for the unexpired term of 7 years from September 26, 1987, vice Margot E. Machol.

Timothy B. Atkeson,
of Pennsylvania, to be an Assistant Administrator of the Environmental Protection Agency, vice Jennifer Joy Manson, resigned.

Withdrawn June 6

Richard Wood Boehm,
of the District of Columbia, a career member of the Senior Foreign Service, Class of Minister-Counselor, to be Ambassador Extraordinary and Plenipotentiary of the United States of America to the Sultanate of Oman, which was sent to the Senate on January 3, 1989.

Michael Ussery,
of South Carolina, to be Ambassador Extraordinary and Plenipotentiary of the United States of America to the Kingdom of Morocco, which was sent to the Senate on January 3, 1989.

Becky Norton Dunlop,
of Virginia, to be Assistant Secretary for Fish and Wildlife, Department of the Interior, vice William P. Horn, resigned, which was sent to the Senate on January 3, 1989.

Margot E. Machol,
of the District of Columbia, to be a Federal Trade Commissioner for the term of 7 years from September 26, 1987, vice Patricia Price Bailey, resigned, which was sent to the Senate January 3, 1989.

Submitted June 7

Janice Obuchowski,
of Virginia, to be Assistant Secretary of Commerce for Communications and Information, vice Alfred C. Sikes, resigned.

Michael J. Astrue,
of Massachusetts, to be General Counsel of the Department of Health and Human Services, vice Malcolm M.B. Sterrett, resigned.

Sherrie Sandy Rollins,
of Virginia, to be an Assistant Secretary of Housing and Urban Development, vice Harry K. Schwartz, resigned.

Richard Harrison Truly,
of Texas, to be Administrator of the National Aeronautics and Space Administration, vice James C. Fletcher, resigned.

Roy M. Goodman,
of New York, to be a member of the National Council on the Arts for a term expiring September 3, 1994, vice C. Douglas Dillon, term expired.

Submitted June 13

Joseph Bernard Gildenhorn,
of the District of Columbia, to be Ambassador Extraordinary and Plenipotentiary of the United States of America to Switzerland.

Martin Lewis Allday,
of Texas, to be Solicitor of the Department of the Interior, vice Ralph W. Tarr, resigned.

John F. Turner,
of Wyoming, to be Director of the United States Fish and Wildlife Service, vice Frank H. Dunkle, resigned.

Deborah Wince-Smith,
of Ohio, to be Assistant Secretary of Commerce for Technology Policy, vice D. Bruce Merrifield, resigned.

Submitted June 15

Frederick Morris Bush,
of Maryland, to be Ambassador Extraordinary and Plenipotentiary of the United States of America to Luxembourg.

Chas. W. Freeman, Jr.,
of Rhode Island, a career member of the Senior Foreign Service, Class of Minister-Counselor, to be Ambassador Extraordinary and Plenipotentiary of the United States of America to the Kingdom of Saudi Arabia.

Stella Garcia Guerra,
of Texas, to be an Assistant Secretary of the Interior, vice Janet J. McCoy, resigned.

Edward T. Timperlake,
of Virginia, to be an Assistant Secretary of Veterans Affairs (Congressional and Public Affairs) (new position).

Raoul Lord Carroll,
of the District of Columbia, to be General Counsel, Department of Veterans Affairs (new position).

Withdrawn June 15

Janet J. McCoy,
of Oregon, to be an Assistant Secretary of the Interior, vice Richard Thomas Montoya, resigned, which was sent to the Senate on January 3, 1989.

Submitted June 19

Andrew Camp Barrett,
of Illinois, to be a member of the Federal Communications Commission for the term expiring June 30, 1990, vice Mark S. Fowler, resigned.

Submitted June 21

S. Anthony McCann,
of Maryland, to be an Assistant Secretary of Veterans Affairs (Finance and Planning) (new position).

Wade F. Horn,
of Maryland, to be Chief of the Children's Bureau, Department of Health and Human Services, vice Dodie Truman Livingston, resigned.

Susan M. Coughlin,
of Pennsylvania, to be a member of the National Transportation Safety Board for the term expiring December 31, 1993, vice Lemoine V. Dickinson, Jr., term expired.

Henry E. Hockeimer,
of Michigan, to be an Associate Director of the United States Information Agency, vice Woodward Kingman, resigned, to which position he was appointed during the recess of the Senate from October 22, 1988, to January 3, 1989.

Withdrawn June 21

Henry E. Hockeimer,
of Michigan, to be an Associate Director of the United States Information Agency, vice Woodward Kingman, resigned, which was sent to the Senate on January 3, 1989.

Submitted June 22

Richard A. Clarke,
of Virginia, to be an Assistant Secretary of State, vice H. Allen Holmes, resigned.

Gerard F. Scannell,
of New Jersey, to be an Assistant Secretary of Labor, vice John A. Pendergrass, resigned.

Claire E. Freeman,
of Virginia, to be an Assistant Secretary of Housing and Urban Development, vice Judith L. Tardy, resigned.

John J. Easton, Jr.,
of Vermont, to be an Assistant Secretary of Energy (International Affairs and Energy Emergencies), vice David B. Waller, resigned.

Submitted June 23

Julia Chang Bloch,
of the District of Columbia, to be Ambassador Extraordinary and Plenipotentiary of the United States of America to the Kingdom of Nepal.

Kyo Ryoon Jhin,
of Maryland, to be Chief Counsel for Advocacy, Small Business Administration, vice Frank S. Swain, resigned.

Appendix C—Checklist of White House Press Releases

The following list contains releases of the Office of the Press Secretary which are not included in this book.

Released January 26

Advance text:
Remarks to members of the Senior Executive Service

Released January 31

Advance text:
Remarks to the crew of the U.S.S. *America* and naval shipyard employees in Norfolk, VA

Released February 2

Transcript:
Press briefing on the President's meeting with Prime Minister Noboru Takeshita of Japan—by Gaston J. Sigur, Assistant Secretary of State for East Asian and Pacific Affairs

Released February 6

Transcript:
Press briefing on the savings and loan crisis—by Secretary of the Treasury Nicholas F. Brady; Richard G. Darman, Director of the Office of Management and Budget; Attorney General Richard Thornburgh; Alan Greenspan, Chairman of the Board of Governors of the Federal Reserve System; M. Danny Wall, Chairman of the Federal Home Loan Bank Board; and L. William Seidman, Chairman of the Federal Deposit Insurance Corporation

Released February 7

Transcript:
Press briefing on the President's upcoming visit to Canada—by Brent Scowcroft, Assistant to the President for National Security Affairs

Released February 8

Fact sheet:
Economic Policy Council and Domestic Policy Council

Released February 9

Advance text:
Address before a joint session of the Congress

Fact sheet:
President's Bush's Agenda: Building a Better America

Transcript:
Press briefing on the fiscal year 1990 budget—by Richard G. Darman, Director of the Office of Management and Budget

Released February 10

Transcript:
Press briefing on the President's meeting with Prime Minister Brian Mulroney in Ottawa, Canada—by Secretary of State James A. Baker III

Released February 13

Advance text:
Remarks to the members of the Business and Industry Association of New Hampshire in Manchester

Released February 15

Advance text:
Remarks to the South Carolina State Legislature in Columbia

Released February 17

Advance text:
Remarks to students at Washington University in St. Louis, MO

Released February 22

Advance text:
Remarks to Armed Forces personnel at Elmendorf Air Force Base, Anchorage, AK

Announcement:
Nomination of Robert C. Bonner to be United States District Judge for the Central District of California

Announcement:
Nomination of Vaughn R. Walker to be United States District Judge for the Northern District of California

Announcement:
Nomination of Ferdinand F. Fernandez to be United States Circuit Judge for the Ninth Circuit

Announcement:
Nomination of Melinda Harmon to be United States District Judge for the Southern District of Texas

Announcement:
Nomination of Pamela Ann Rymer to be United States Circuit Judge for the Ninth Circuit

Released February 23

Transcript:
Press briefing on the President's trip to the Far East—by Secretary of State James A. Baker III

Released February 24

Transcript:
Interview of Secretary of State James A. Baker III by Tom Brokaw of NBC News

Transcript:
Interview of Secretary of State James A. Baker III by Harry Smith of CBS News

Transcript:
Interview of Brent Scowcroft, Assistant to the President for National Security Affairs by Charles Gibson of ABC News

Released February 25

Advance text:
Toast at the welcoming banquet in Beijing, China

Released February 26

Transcript:
Interview of Secretary of State James A. Baker III by Bill Plante of CBS News

Advance text:
Remarks to U.S. and Chinese officials at a banquet hosted by the President in Beijing, China

Transcript:
Interview of John H. Sununu, Chief of Staff to the President, by Frank Sesno and Charles Bierbauer of Cable Network News

Released February 27

Advance text:
Address to the National Assembly in Seoul, South Korea

Released February 28

Transcript:
Press briefing on the Senate's deliberations on the confirmation of John Tower as Secretary of Defense—by Senators Robert Dole and John Warner

Released March 9

Advance text:
Remarks to Drug Enforcement Administration officers in New York, NY

Advance text:
Remarks at the United Negro College Fund dinner in New York, NY

Released March 13

Statement:
Condolences on the death of John J. McCloy

Released March 15

Fact sheet:
Building a Better America: President Bush's Child Care Proposals

Advance text:
Remarks at the Electronic Industries Association's annual Government-Industry Dinner

Released March 16

Advance text:
Remarks at a luncheon hosted by the Forum Club in Houston, TX

Advance text:
Remarks at the Junior Achievement National Business Hall of Fame Dinner in Colorado Springs, CO

Released March 21

Fact sheet:
President's minimum-wage proposal

Released March 22

Advance text:
Remarks to students at Conestoga Valley High School in Lancaster, PA

Advance text:
Remarks to the law enforcement community in Wilmington, DE

Released March 23

Advance text:
Remarks to the National Association of Manufacturers Congress of American Industry

Released March 24

Transcript:
Press briefing on the bipartisan accord on Central America—by Secretary of State James A. Baker III; Jim Wright, Speaker of the House of

Representatives; George Mitchell and Robert Dole, majority and minority leaders of the Senate, respectively; Thomas S. Foley and Robert H. Michel, majority and minority leaders of the House of Representatives, respectively

Released March 29

Announcement:
Nomination of Wayne A. Budd to be United States Attorney for the District of Massachusetts

Released March 30

Transcript:
Press briefing on the oil spill in Prince William Sound, Alaska—by Secretary of Transportation Samuel K. Skinner; William K. Reilly, Administrator of the Environmental Protection Agency; and Adm. Paul A. Yost, Commandant of the U.S. Coast Guard

Advance text
Remarks to members of the American Association of Community and Junior Colleges

Released April 4

Advance text:
Remarks at a White House briefing for members of the American Business Conference

Transcript:
Press briefing on Central America—by President Oscar Arias Sánchez of Costa Rica

Released April 5

Transcript:
Press briefing on the proposed Educational Excellence Act of 1989—by Secretary of Education Lauro F. Cavazos and Under Secretary of Education Charles Kolb

Announcement:
Nomination of Frank Quill Nebeker to be chief judge of the U.S. Court of Veterans Appeals

Released April 6

Transcript:
Press briefing on Federal assistance for the Alaskan oil spill cleanup—by Secretary of Transportation Samuel K. Skinner; Secretary of Defense Richard Cheney; and William K. Reilly, Administrator of the Environmental Protection Agency

Released April 12

Fact sheet:
President's ethics reform proposals

Advance text:
Remarks at the Congressional Fire Services Institute dinner

Advance text:
Remarks to participants in Project Educational Forum in Union, NJ

Released April 14

Transcript:
Press briefing on the budget—by the budget agreement negotiating group

Released April 17

Advance text:
Remarks to citizens in Hamtramck, MI

Fact sheet:
U.S. support for Polish reforms

Released April 18

Fact sheet:
Implementation of the bipartisan accord on Central America

Released April 24

Advance text:
Remarks at the memorial service for crewmembers of the U.S.S. *Iowa* in Norfolk, VA

Advance text:
Remarks at the Associated Press business luncheon in Chicago, IL

Advance text:
Remarks at the dedication ceremony for the Centennial Grove in Bismarck, ND

Released April 25

Advance text:
Remarks to employees of the Ford Aerospace Space Systems Division in Palo Alto, CA

Advance text:
Remarks to members of the law enforcement community at Rancho del Rio in Orange County, CA

Advance text:
Remarks to members of the Spanish-American community in Los Angeles, CA

Released April 26

Advance text:
Remarks to the State legislature in Austin, TX

Released April 27

Advance text:
Remarks at the International Drug Enforcement Conference in Miami, FL

Advance text:
Remarks at the dedication ceremony for the Drug Command Coordination Control and Intelligence Center in Miami, FL

Advance text:
Remarks at the dedication ceremony for the Michael Bilirakis Alzheimer's Center in Palm Harbor, FL

Advance text:
Remarks at the Andrew Mellon dinner in Washington, DC

Released April 28

Fact sheet:
Executive order on historically black colleges and universities

Released May 2

Advance text:
Remarks to the Council of the Americas

Released May 5

Announcement:
Nomination of Kenneth B. Kramer to be an Associate Judge of the United States Court of Veterans Appeals

Released May 11

Transcript:
Press briefing on the crisis in Panama—by Brent Scowcroft, Assistant to the President for National Security Affairs

Released May 12

Advance text:
Remarks at the Texas A&M University commencement ceremony in College Station, TX

Fact sheet:
"Beyond Containment"—the President's Texas A&M University commencement address

Fact sheet:
President's "Open Skies" initiative

Fact sheet:
The Jackson-Vanik amendment

Announcement:
Nomination of E. Bart Daniel to be the United States Attorney for the District of South Carolina

Released May 17

Fact sheet:
Martin Luther King, Jr., Federal Holiday Commission Extension Act

Released May 18

Advance text:
Remarks to supporters of the Brainpower Coalition in Rochester, NY

Released May 20

Transcript:
Press briefing on President Bush's meeting with President Mitterrand of France in Kennebunkport, ME—by Secretary of State James A. Baker III and French Foreign Minister Roland Dumas

Released May 23

Transcript:
Press briefing on the resumption of Strategic Arms Reduction Talks with the Soviet Union and the President's participation in the upcoming NATO summit—by Secretary of State James A. Baker III

Released May 24

Announcement:
Nomination of Dee V. Benson to be United States Attorney for the District of Utah

Released May 25

Statement:
Presidential decision on U.S. action against foreign trade barriers

Released May 26

Advance text:
Remarks upon departure for Europe

Advance text:
Remarks at the arrival ceremony in Rome

Released May 27

Advance text:
Toast at a state dinner hosted by Prime Minister Ciriaco De Mita in Rome

Released May 28

Transcript:
Interview of Brent Scowcroft, Assistant to the President for National Security Affairs, by ABC's "This Week with David Brinkley"

Advance text:
Remarks at a Memorial Day ceremony at the Sicily-Rome American Cemetery in Nettuno, Italy

Transcript:
Interview of John H. Sununu, Chief of Staff to the President, by CNN's "Newsmaker Sunday"

Released May 29

Fact sheet:
President's initiative on conventional arms control

Released May 30

Joint communique:
Statement on the Ministerial Meeting of the North Atlantic Council at Reykjavik

Fact sheet:
NATO summit declaration (two documents)

Transcript:
Interview of Brent Scowcroft, Assistant to the President for National Security Affairs, by Frank Sesno, Cable News Network

Transcript:
Press briefing on the North Atlantic Treaty Organization Summit—by Secretary of State James A. Baker III

Advance text:
Toast at a state dinner hosted by Chancellor Helmut Kohl in Bonn, Federal Republic of Germany

Released May 31

Advance text:
Remarks to citizens in Mainz, Federal Republic of Germany

Advance text:
Remarks to military personnel and their families in Frankfurt, Federal Republic of Germany

Released June 1

Transcript:
Press briefing on the President's meeting with Prime Minister Margaret Thatcher of the United Kingdom and the North Atlantic Treaty Organization summit—by Secretary of State James A. Baker III

Advance text:
Toast at a state dinner hosted by Prime Minister Margaret Thatcher of the United Kingdom in London

Released June 5

Advance text:
Remarks at the annual meeting of the Business Roundtable

Released June 8

Advance text:
Remarks to members of Ducks Unlimited

Released June 9

Announcement:
Nomination of William Braniff to be United States Attorney for the Southern District of California

Released June 12

Transcript:
Press briefings on the President's Clean Air Act amendment proposals—by William K. Reilly, Administrator of the Environmental Protection Agency, and James D. Watkins, Secretary of Energy

Released June 13

Advance text:
Remarks to students at the Teton Science School in Grand Teton National Park, WY

Advance text:
Remarks at the University of Nebraska in Lincoln

Released June 15

Fact sheet:
President's trip to Glynco, GA

Advance text:
Remarks at the Federal Law Enforcement Training Center in Glynco, GA

Announcement:
Nomination of Margaret Person Currin to be United States Attorney for the Eastern District of North Carolina

Released June 16

Announcement:
Distribution by Attorney General Richard L. Thornburgh to U.S. attorneys of guidelines for plea bargaining in cases involving firearms

Released June 19

Advance text:
Remarks at the Cheltenham High School commencement ceremony in Wyncote, PA

Released June 21

Advance text:
Remarks to members of the Family Motor Coach Association in Richmond, VA

Advance text:
Remarks to State Republican leaders at a fundraising dinner in Richmond, VA

Released June 22

Advance text:
Remarks at a luncheon hosted by the New York Partnership and the Association for a Better New York in New York, NY

Advance text:
Remarks at a Republican Party fundraising dinner in New York, NY

Advance text:
Remarks at the Wall Street Journal anniversary dinner in New York, NY

Released June 27

Transcript:
Press briefing on the President's meeting with Prime Minister Hawke of Australia—by William Clark, Acting Assistant Secretary of State for Near Eastern and South Asian Affairs

Released June 29

Transcript:
Press briefing on the economic summit and China—by Secretary of State James A. Baker III

Released June 30

Advance text:
Remarks at a White House ceremony commemorating the 25th anniversary of the Civil Rights Act

Appendix D—Acts Approved by the President

Approved February 7

H.J. Res. 129 / Public Law 101-1
Disapproving the increases in executive, legislative, and judicial salaries recommended by the President under section 225 of the Federal Salary Act of 1967

Approved March 15

H.J. Res. 22 / Public Law 101-2
To designate the week beginning March 6, 1989, as "Federal Employees Recognition Week"

Approved March 21

S.J. Res. 64 / Public Law 101-3
To designate March 25, 1989, as "Greek Independence Day: A National Day of Celebration of Greek and American Democracy"

Approved March 23

H.J. Res. 117 / Public Law 101-4
To proclaim March 20, 1989, as "National Agriculture Day"

H.J. Res. 167 / Public Law 101-5
To designate March 16, 1989, as "Freedom of Information Day"

Approved March 24

H.J. Res. 148 / Public Law 101-6
Designating the month of March in both 1989 and 1990 as "Women's History Month"

Approved March 29

S. 553 / Public Law 101-7
To provide for more balance in the stocks of dairy products purchased by the Commodity Credit Corporation

S.J. Res. 87 / Public Law 101-8
To commend the Governments of Israel and Egypt on the occasion of the tenth anniversary of the Treaty of Peace between Israel and Egypt

Approved March 31

H.R. 1373 / Public Law 101-9
To authorize the Agency for International Development to pay the expenses of an election observer mission for the 1989 presidential elections in Panama

Approved April 2

S.J. Res. 50 / Public Law 101-10
To designate the week beginning April 2, 1989, as "National Child Care Awareness Week"

Approved April 7

H.R. 829 / Public Law 101-11
Wildfire Suppression Assistance Act

Approved April 10

S. 20 / Public Law 101-12
Whistleblower Protection Act of 1989

Approved April 13

S.J. Res. 43 / Public Law 101-13
Designating April 9, 1989, as "National Former Prisoners of War Recognition Day"

Approved April 18

H.R. 1750 / Public Law 101-14
To implement the Bipartisan Accord on Central America of March 24, 1989

H.J. Res. 173 / Public Law 101-15
To designate April 16, 1989, and April 6, 1990, as "Education Day, U.S.A."

Approved April 19

H.J. Res. 102 / Public Law 101-16
To designate April 1989 as "National Recycling Month"

Approved April 20

H.R. 666 / Public Law 101-17
To allow an obsolete Navy drydock to be transferred to the city of Jacksonville, Florida, before the expiration of the otherwise applicable 60-day congressional review period

H.J. Res. 112 / Public Law 101-18
Designating April 23, 1989, through April 29, 1989, and April 23, 1990, through April 29, 1990, as "National Organ and Tissue Donor Awareness Week"

Approved May 1

S.J. Res. 45 / Public Law 101–19
Designating May 1989 as "Older Americans Month"

S.J. Res. 92 / Public Law 101–20
To invite the houses of worship of this Nation to celebrate the bicentennial of the inauguration of George Washington, the first President of the United States, by ringing bells at 12 noon on Sunday, April 30, 1989

Approved May 2

S.J. Res. 60 / Public Law 101–21
To designate the period commencing on May 1, 1989, and ending on May 7, 1989, as "National Drinking Water Week"

S.J. Res. 84 / Public Law 101–22
To designate April 30, 1989, as "National Society of the Sons of the American Revolution Centennial Day"

S.J. Res. 52 / Public Law 101–23
To express gratitude for law enforcement personnel

Approved May 3

H.J. Res. 124 / Public Law 101–24
To recognize the seventy-fifth anniversary of the Smith-Lever Act of May 8, 1914, and its role in establishing our Nation's system of State Cooperative Extension Services

Approved May 5

S.J. Res. 25 / Public Law 101–25
To designate the week of May 7, 1989, through May 14, 1989, as "Jewish Heritage Week"

Approved May 11

H.R. 678 / Public Law 101–26
To make a correction in the Education and Training for a Competitive America Act

S.J. Res. 62 / Public Law 101–27
Designating May 1989 as "National Stroke Awareness Month"

Approved May 15

S. 968 / Public Law 101–28
To delay the effective date of section 27 of the Office of Federal Procurement Policy Act

Approved May 17

S.J. Res. 37 / Public Law 101–29
Designating the week beginning May 14, 1989, and the week beginning May 13, 1990, as "National Osteoporosis Prevention Week"

H.R. 1385 / Public Law 101–30
Martin Luther King, Jr., Federal Holiday Commission Extension Act

Approved May 22

H.J. Res. 135 / Public Law 101–31
To designate the week beginning May 7, 1989, as "National Correctional Officers Week"

S.J. Res. 58 / Public Law 101–32
To designate May 17, 1989, as "High School Reserve Officer Training Corps Recognition Day"

Approved May 23

S.J. Res. 68 / Public Law 101–33
To designate the month of May 1989, as "Trauma Awareness Month"

Approved May 25

H.J. Res. 170 / Public Law 101–34
Designating May 1989, as "National Digestive Disease Awareness Month"

H.J. Res. 247 / Public Law 101–35
Designating May 29, 1989, as the "National Day of Remembrance for the Victims of the USS IOWA"

Approved June 9

S.J. Res. 128 / Public Law 101–36
Authorizing a first strike ceremony at the United States Capitol for the Bicentennial of the Congress Commemorative Coin

Approved June 15

S. 767 / Public Law 101–37
Business Opportunity Development Reform Act Technical Corrections Act

Approved June 19

H.J. Res. 274 / Public Law 101–38
To designate the week beginning June 11, 1989, as "National Scleroderma Awareness Week"

S.J. Res. 63 / Public Law 101–39
Designating June 14, 1989, as "Baltic Freedom Day", and for other purposes

Approved June 20

H.R. 964 / Public Law 101–40
To correct an error in Private Law 100–29 (relat-

ing to certain lands in Lamar County, Alabama) and to make technical corrections in certain other provisions of law

Approved June 21

H.R. 932 / Public Law 101–41
Puyallup Tribe of Indians Settlement Act of 1989

Approved June 28

H.R. 881 / Public Law 101–42
Coquille Restoration Act

H.J. Res. 111 / Public Law 101–43
Designating June 23, 1989, as "United States Coast Guard Auxiliary Day"

Approved June 30

H.R. 2344 / Public Law 101–44
To authorize the transfer to the Republic of the Philippines of two excess naval vessels

H.R. 2402 / Public Law 101–45
Dire Emergency Supplemental Appropriations and Transfers, Urgent Supplementals, and Correcting Enrollment Errors Act of 1989

S. 694 / Public Law 101–46
To extend title I of the Energy Policy and Conservation Act

S. 1077 / Public Law 101–47
To authorize the President to appoint Admiral James B. Busey to the Office of Administrator of the Federal Aviation Administration

S. 1180 / Public Law 101–48
To authorize the President to appoint Rear Admiral Richard Harrison Truly to the Office of Administrator of the National Aeronautics and Space Administration

S. 1184 / Public Law 101–49
To allow the obsolete destroyer United States ship Edson (DD 946) to be transferred to the Intrepid Sea-Air-Space Museum in New York before the expiration of the otherwise applicable sixty-day congressional review period

S.J. Res. 96 / Public Law 101–50
Designating July 2, 1989, as "National Literacy Day"

Appendix E—Proclamations and Executive Orders

NOTE: *The texts of the proclamations and Executive orders are printed in the Federal Register (F.R.) at the citations listed below. The documents are also printed in title 3 of the Code of Federal Regulations and in the Weekly Compilation of Presidential Documents.*

PROCLAMATIONS

Proc. No.	*Date 1989*	*Subject*	*54 F.R. page*
5936	Jan. 20	National Day of Prayer and Thanksgiving, 1989	3575
5937	Feb. 21	American Heart Month, 1989	7751
5938	Feb. 28	American Red Cross Month, 1989	8723
5939	Mar. 1	Save Your Vision Week, 1989	9193
5940	Mar. 2	National Poison Prevention Week, 1989	9195
5941	Mar. 8	Federal Employees Recognition Week, 1989	10261
5942	Mar. 17	National Day of Prayer, 1989	11483
5943	Mar. 18	National Agriculture Day, 1989	11485
5944	Mar. 21	Greek Independence Day: A National Day of Celebration of Greek and American Democracy, 1989	12165
5945	Mar. 24	Women's History Month, 1989 and 1990	12573
5946	Mar. 24	Actors' Fund of America Appreciation Month, 1989	12869
5947	Mar. 27	National Earthquake Awareness Week, 1989	13043
5948	Apr. 2	National Child Care Awareness Week, 1989	13663
5949	Apr. 6	Cancer Control Month, 1989	14329
5950	Apr. 6	National Consumers Week, 1989	14331
5951	Apr. 7	National Former Prisoners of War Recognition Day, 1989	14617
5952	Apr. 10	National Volunteer Week, 1989	14619
5953	Apr. 12	Crime Victims Week, 1989	15157
5954	Apr. 13	Pan American Day and Pan American Week, 1989	15163
5955	Apr. 13	Amending the Generalized System of Preferences	15357
5956	Apr. 14	Education Day, U.S.A., 1989 and 1990	15737
5957	Apr. 19	National Recycling Month, 1989	17687
5958	Apr. 20	National Organ and Tissue Donor Awareness Week, 1989 and 1990	17695
5959	Apr. 21	Law Day, U.S.A., 1989	17697
5960	Apr. 21	Death of American Servicemen on Board the USS Iowa	17699

Proc. No.	*Date 1989*	*Subject*	*54 F.R. page*
5961	Apr. 28	National Arbor Day, 1989	18859
5962	Apr. 28	Loyalty Day, 1989	18861
5963	Apr. 28	Bicentennial Celebration of the Inauguration of George Washington	18863
		(Correction to Proclamation 5963-line 1)	22054
5964	Apr. 28	National Drinking Water Week, 1989	18865
5965	Apr. 28	National Society of the Sons of the American Revolution Centennial Day, 1989	18867
5966	May 1	Jewish Heritage Week, 1989	19153
5967	May 2	National Maritime Day, 1989	19343
5968	May 2	Fire Prevention Week, 1989	19345
5969	May 3	Smith-Lever Act 75th Anniversary, 1989	19537
5970	May 4	Older Americans Month, 1989	19539
5971	May 5	World Trade Week, 1989	19867
5972	May 8	Asian/Pacific American Heritage Week, 1989	20113
5973	May 8	Small Business Week, 1989	20115
5974	May 10	Mother's Day, 1989	20781
5975	May 11	National Stroke Awareness Month, 1989	21043
5976	May 11	National Correctional Officers Week, 1989	21045
5977	May 12	National Farm Safety Week, 1989	21181
5978	May 12	To Implement in Terms of the Harmonized Tariff Schedule of the United States the Nairobi Protocol to the Florence Agreement on the Importation of Educational, Scientific, and Cultural Materials	21187
5979	May 15	Trauma Awareness Month, 1989	21193
5980	May 16	National Defense Transportation Day and National Transportation Week, 1989	21587
5981	May 17	National Osteoporosis Prevention Week, 1989 and 1990	21589
5982	May 17	High School Reserve Officer Training Corps Recognition Day, 1989	21591
5983	May 17	Armed Forces Day	21593
5984	May 22	National Digestive Disease Awareness Month, 1989	22405
5985	May 22	Prayer for Peace, Memorial Day, 1989	22407
5986	May 24	National Day of Remembrance for the Victims of the USS IOWA	22737
5987	May 24	National Safe Boating Week, 1989	22875

Proc. No.	*Date 1989*	*Subject*	*54 F.R. page*
5988	June 7	Flag Day and National Flag Week, 1989	24885
5989	June 9	Father's Day, 1989	25435
5990	June 14	Baltic Freedom Day, 1989	25701
5991	June 15	National Grasslands Week, 1989	25837
5992	June 16	National Scleroderma Awareness Week, 1989	26015
5993	June 19	National Lighthouse Day, 1989	26183
5994	June 23	United States Coast Guard Auxiliary Day, 1989	26941
5995	June 30	National Literacy Day, 1989	28409

EXECUTIVE ORDERS

E.O. No.	*Date 1989*	*Subject*	*54 F.R. page*
12668	Jan. 25	President's Commission on Federal Ethics Law Reform	3979
12669	Feb. 20	Organization of Eastern Caribbean States	7753
12670	Mar. 9	Nuclear Cooperation With EURATOM	10267
12671	Mar. 14	Exclusion of the Customs Office of Enforcement From the Federal Labor-Management Relations Program	11157
12672	Mar. 21	Interagency Committee on Handicapped Employees	12167
12673	Mar. 23	Delegation of Disaster Relief and Emergency Assistance Functions	12571
12674	Apr. 12	Principles of Ethical Conduct for Government Officers and Employees	15159
12675	Apr. 20	Establishing the National Space Council	17691
12676	Apr. 26	Delegating Authority To Provide Assistance for the Nicaraguan Resistance	18639
12677	Apr. 28	Historically Black Colleges and Universities	18869
12678	Apr. 28	Level IV of the Executive Schedule	18872
12679	June 23	Level IV of the Executive Schedule	27149

Subject Index

Name Index

Document Categories List

Statements by the President

Statements Other Than Presidential

Statements Other Than Presidential—Continued